CURRENT LAW
STATUTES
ANNOTATED
1986

VOLUME TWO

EDITOR IN CHIEF

PETER ALLSOP, C.B.E., M.A.
Barrister

GENERAL EDITOR

KEVAN NORRIS, LL.B.
Solicitor

ASSISTANT GENERAL EDITOR

JULIE HARRIS, LL.B.

ADMINISTRATION

GILLIAN BRONZE, LL.B.

LONDON

SWEET & MAXWELL STEVENS & SONS

EDINBURGH

W. GREEN & SON

1987

Published by
SWEET & MAXWELL LIMITED
and STEVENS & SONS LIMITED
of 11 New Fetter Lane, London,
and W. GREEN & SON LIMITED
of St. Giles Street, Edinburgh,
and Printed in Great Britain
by The Eastern Press Ltd.,
London and Reading

ISBN This Volume only : 421 38030 6
As a set : 421 38060 8

CONTENTS

CHRONOLOGICAL TABLE

VOLUME TWO

STATUTES

c.41. Finance Act 1986
42. Appropriation Act 1986
43. Crown Agents (Amendment) Act 1986
44. Gas Act 1986
45. Insolvency Act 1986

INDEX OF SHORT TITLES

VOLUME TWO

References are to chapter numbers of 1986

FINANCE ACT 1986*

(1986 c. 41)

ARRANGEMENT OF SECTIONS

PART I

CUSTOMS AND EXCISE AND VALUE ADDED TAX

CHAPTER I

CUSTOMS AND EXCISE

The rates of duty

Other provisions

CHAPTER II

VALUE ADDED TAX

PART II

INCOME TAX, CORPORATION TAX AND CAPITAL GAINS TAX

CHAPTER I

GENERAL

Tax rates and main reliefs

Employee shareholding

* Annotations by Christopher Cant, M.A., Barrister; Ian Ferrier, M.A., Barrister; David Goy, LL.M., Barrister and John Shock, M.A., F.C.A., Barrister.

Depositary receipts

Clearance services

Reconstructions and acquisitions

Loan capital, letters of allotment etc.

Changes in financial institutions

PART IV

STAMP DUTY RESERVE TAX

Introduction

The principal charge

Other charges

General

An Act to grant certain duties, to alter other duties, and to amend the law relating to the National Debt and the Public Revenue, and to make further provision in connection with Finance. [25th July 1986]

PARLIAMENTARY DEBATES

Hansard: H.C. Vol. 94, col. 628; Vol. 97, cols. 77, 155; Vol. 99, col. 384; Vol. 101, cols. 172, 1198; H.L. Vol. 478, col. 1162, Vol. 479, col. 500.

The Bill was considered by Standing Committee G.

Part I

Customs and Excise and Value Added Tax

Chapter I

Customs and Excise

The rates of duty

Tobacco products

1.—(1) For the Table in Schedule 1 to the Tobacco Products Duty Act 1979 there shall be substituted—

"Table

1. Cigarettes	An amount equal to 21 per cent. of the retail price plus £30·61 per thousand cigarettes.
2. Cigars	£47·05 per kilogram.
3. Hand-rolling tobacco	£49·64 per kilogram.
4. Other smoking tobacco and chewing tobacco	£24·95 per kilogram."

(2) This section shall be deemed to have come into force on 21st March 1986.

General Note

The noteworthy feature is an increase of 13·5 per cent. in the duty on cigarettes. In contrast the duty on cigars is unchanged as is the duty on alcoholic beverages. The treatment of cigarettes is a reflection of concern regarding their effect on health. Despite a decline of nearly a fifth in the consumption of cigarettes since 1980, the tax yield remains buoyant at over £4 billion.

Hydrocarbon oil

2.—(1) In section 6(1) of the Hydrocarbon Oil Duties Act 1979 for "£0·1794" (light oil) and "£0·1515" (heavy oil) there shall be substituted "£0·1938" and "£0·1639" respectively.

(2) In subsection (1) of section 11 of that Act (rebate on heavy oil) for paragraphs (*a*) and (*b*) there shall be substituted—

"(*a*) in the case of fuel oil, of £0·0077 a litre less than the rate at which the duty is for the time being chargeable;

(*b*) in the case of gas oil, of £0·0110 a litre less than the rate at which the duty is for the time being chargeable; and

(*c*) in the case of heavy oil other than fuel oil and gas oil, equal to the rate at which the duty is for the time being chargeable."

(3) For subsection (2) of section 11 of that Act (definition of types of heavy oil), there shall be substituted—

"(2) In this section—

'fuel oil' means heavy oil which contains in solution an amount of asphaltenes of not less than 0·5 per cent. or which contains less than 0·5 per cent. but not less than 0·1 per cent. of asphaltenes and has a closed flash point not exceeding 150°C; and

'gas oil' means heavy oil of which not more than 50 per cent. by volume distils at a temperature not exceeding 240°C and of which more than 50 per cent. by volume distils at a temperature not exceeding 340°C."

(4) This section shall be deemed to have come into force at 6 o'clock in the evening of 18th March 1986.

General Note

The duty on petrol and derv is increased by 8 per cent., rather more than the amount required to compensate for inflation but this is balanced by no general increases in vehicle excise duty (see the Notes to s.3 and Sched. 1). The duty on fuel oil remains unchanged but that on gas oil (mainly avgas for aircraft) is increased by the equivalent of 1·5p a gallon. The duties on aviation turbine fuel (avtur) and on most lubricating oils are abolished.

Vehicles excise duty

3.—(1) The Vehicles (Excise) Act 1971 and the Vehicles (Excise) Act (Northern Ireland) 1972 shall be amended in accordance with this section.

(2) For Part II of Schedule 2 to each of the Acts of 1971 and 1972 (annual rates of duty on hackney carriages) there shall be substituted the provisions set out in Part I of Schedule 1 to this Act.

(3) In Schedule 4 to each of the Acts of 1971 and 1972 (annual rates of duty on goods vehicles)—

(*a*) in Part I, in sub-paragraph (2) of paragraph 6 (farmer's goods vehicle or showman's goods vehicle having a plated gross weight or a plated train weight) in paragraph (*b*) (weight exceeding 7·5 tonnes but not exceeding 12 tonnes) for "£135" (which applies to farmers' goods vehicles only) there shall be substituted "£155"; and

(*b*) in Part II, for Tables A(1), C(1) and D(1) (rates for farmers' goods vehicles having plated weight exceeding 12 tonnes) there shall be substituted the Tables set out in Part II of Schedule 1 to this Act.

(4) In section 16 of the Act of 1971, in subsection (5) (annual rates of duty for trade licences), including that subsection as set out in paragraph 12 of Part I of Schedule 7 to that Act, for "£46" and "£9" there shall be substituted respectively "£70" and "£14".

(5) In section 16 of the Act of 1972, in subsection (6) (annual rates of duty for trade licences), including that subsection as set out in paragraph 12 of Part I of Schedule 9 to that Act, for "£46" and "£9" there shall be substituted respectively "£70" and "£14".

(6) Subsections (2) and (3) above apply in relation to licences taken out after 18th March 1986; and subsections (4) and (5) above apply in relation to licences taken out after 31st December 1986.

(7) The Act of 1971 shall have effect subject to the further amendments in Part I of Schedule 2 to this Act; and the Act of 1972 shall have effect subject to the further amendments in Part II of that Schedule.

(8) The amendments made by paragraphs 4 and 9 of Schedule 2 to this Act shall not come into force until 1st January 1987; and the amendments made by paragraphs 5 and 10 of that Schedule shall not have effect with respect to the surrender of licences taken out before that date.

General Note

The duty on cars and vans remains unchanged. For changes in other rates, see the Note to Sched. 1. The rates for trade licences, which have lagged behind those for vehicles in normal use, are in future to be linked to those for private cars. As a first step, the trade licence rate for cars is increased from £46 to £70, and for motor cycles from £9 to £14. Improvements are being made to the trade licensing scheme: see the Note to Sched. 2.

Other provisions

Beer duty: minor amendments

4.—(1) In subsection (2) of section 46 of the Alcoholic Liquor Duties Act 1979 (remission or repayment of duty on beer which, having been removed from entered premises, has accidentally become spoilt or otherwise unfit for use)—

(*a*) the word "accidentally" shall be omitted; and

(*b*) after the words "subject to" there shall be inserted "subsection (2A) below and to";

and at the end of that subsection there shall be inserted the following subsection—

"(2A) For the purpose of determining the amount of duty to be remitted or repaid under subsection (2) above in respect of any beer, it shall be assumed that, at any material time, the worts of the beer had an original gravity of one degree less than they actually had and that duty on the beer was charged accordingly."

(2) After section 49 of the Alcoholic Liquor Duties Act 1979 there shall be inserted the following section—

"Drawback allowable to brewer for sale

49A.—(1) For the purpose of any claim for drawback by a brewer for sale in respect of duty charged on beer, duty which has been determined in accordance with regulations under section 49(1)(*bb*) above shall be deemed to be duty which has been paid (whether or not it is in fact paid by the time the claim is made).

(2) Subject to such conditions as the Commissioners see fit to impose, drawback allowable to a brewer for sale in respect of beer may be set against any amount to which the brewer is chargeable under section 38 above and, in relation to a brewer for sale, any reference in this Act or the Management Act to drawback payable shall be construed accordingly."

General Note

Two changes are made to the administration of beer duty. Firstly, it will no longer be necessary to show that beer had been accidentally spoilt to claim a refund of duty on spoilt beer which has left the brewer's premises, but to offset this the refund will be calculated on a notionally lower gravity. Secondly, the allowance of drawbacks to brewers will be expedited and widened in scope.

Warehousing regulations

5. Schedule 3 to this Act (which contains amendments about warehousing regulations) shall have effect.

General Note

It was held in *R.* v. *Commissioners of Customs and Excise, ex p. Hedges & Butler Ltd.* [1986] 2 All E.R. 164 that a regulation requiring occupiers or proprietors of excise warehouses to preserve all records relating to their businesses for not less than two years was "a wholly unwarranted arrogation of powers." Sched. 3 clarifies and amends the powers of the Commissioners to make regulations in connection with warehouses. New regulations will be issued after consultations with the trade.

Betting duties and bingo duty in Northern Ireland

6.—(1) The Betting and Gaming Duties Act 1981 (in this section referred to as "the 1981 Act") shall have effect subject to the amendments in Part I of Schedule 4 to this Act, being amendments designed to extend to Northern Ireland—

(*a*) the provisions of the 1981 Act relating to general betting duty and pool betting duty (in place of the provisions of Part III of the Miscellaneous Transferred Excise Duties Act (Northern Ireland) 1972 relating to those duties); and

(*b*) the provisions of the 1981 Act relating to bingo duty.

(2) Part II of Schedule 4 to this Act shall have effect for the purpose of making consequential amendments of certain Northern Ireland

legislation; and Part III of that Schedule shall have effect for the purpose of extending to Northern Ireland certain subordinate legislation made under the 1981 Act.

(3) Schedule 4 to this Act,—

(*a*) so far as it relates to general betting duty or pool betting duty, shall come into force on the betting commencement date, but shall not have effect in relation to duty in respect of bets made before that date; and

(*b*) so far as it relates to bingo duty, shall come into force on the bingo commencement date, but shall not impose any charge to duty in respect of bingo played in Northern Ireland before that date.

(4) Part III of the Miscellaneous Transferred Excise Duties Act (Northern Ireland) 1972 shall cease to have effect on the betting commencement date except in relation to duty in respect of bets made before that date.

(5) In this section and Schedule 4 to this Act—

"the betting commencement date" means 29th September 1986 or, if later, the day appointed for the coming into operation of Part II (betting) of the Betting, Gaming, Lotteries and Amusements (Northern Ireland) Order 1985; and

"the bingo commencement date" means 29th September 1986 or, if later, the day appointed for the coming into operation of Chapter II of Part III (gaming on bingo club premises) of that Order.

General Note

F.A. 1985, s.8 and Sched. 5 began the process of adapting the Betting and Gaming Duties Act 1981 in anticipation of changes in the Northern Ireland social law bringing it into line with the rest of the United Kingdom. This section and Sched. 4 complete the task. Casinos remain illegal in Northern Ireland.

Betting and gaming duties: evidence by certificate, etc.

7. After section 29 of the Betting and Gaming Duties Act 1981 there shall be inserted the following section—

"Evidence by certificate, etc.

29A.—(1) A certificate of the Commissioners—

(*a*) that any notice required by or under this Act to be given to them had or had not been given at any date, or

(*b*) that any permit, licence or authority required by or under this Act had or had not been issued at any date, or

(*c*) that any return required by or under this Act had not been made at any date, or

(*d*) that any duty shown as due in any return or estimate made in pursuance of this Act had not been paid at any date,

shall be sufficient evidence of that fact until the contrary is proved.

(2) A photograph of any document furnished to the Commissioners for the purposes of this Act and certified by them to be such a photograph shall be admissible in any proceedings, whether civil or criminal, to the same extent as the document itself.

(3) Any document purporting to be a certificate under subsection (1) or (2) above shall be deemed to be such a certificate until the contrary is proved."

General Note

This section simplifies the provision of evidence in cases where proceedings are brought in relation to failure to pay betting or gaming duties or to comply with statutory requirements relating to those duties. The facts to be covered by certificates are rarely in dispute.

Licences under the customs and excise Acts

8.—(1) No excise licence duty shall be chargeable on the grant after 18th March 1986 of an excise licence under any provision of the Alcoholic Liquor Duties Act 1979 (licensing of various activities relating to the production of alcoholic liquor) or under section 2 of the Matches and Mechanical Lighters Duties Act 1979 (licensing of manufacture of matches).

(2) The following enactments shall cease to have effect—

(*a*) sections 12(2), 18(3), 47(3), 48(2) and 75(3) of the Alcoholic Liquor Duties Act 1979 and section 2(2) of the Matches and Mechanical Lighters Duties Act 1979 (which provide for certain excise licences, the duty on which is abolished by subsection (1) above, to expire on a specified date in each year); and

(*b*) section 81 of the Alcoholic Liquor Duties Act 1979 (under which a licence is required for the keeping or using of a still by any person otherwise than as a distiller, rectifier or compounder).

(3) The holder of a licence under any of the enactments specified in subsection (5) below may surrender the licence to the Commissioners of Customs and Excise at any time.

(4) The Commissioners of Customs and Excise may at any time revoke a licence granted in respect of any premises under any of the enactments specified in subsection (5) below if it appears to them that the holder of the licence has ceased to carry on at those premises the activity in respect of which the licence was granted.

(5) The enactments referred to in subsections (3) and (4) above are—

(*a*) section 12 of the Alcoholic Liquor Duties Act 1979 (distillers),
(*b*) section 18 of that Act (rectifiers),
(*c*) section 47 of that Act (brewers),
(*d*) section 48 of that Act (persons using premises for adding solutions to beer),
(*e*) section 54 of that Act (wine producers),
(*f*) section 55 of that Act (made-wine producers), and
(*g*) section 2 of the Matches and Mechanical Lighters Duties Act 1979 (match manufacturers).

(6) Schedule 5 to this Act shall have effect for the purpose of supplementing the provisions of this section.

General Note

A number of licences, many of which have existed since last century with unchanged rates, are abolished at a cost to the revenue of only £10,000 a year.

Chapter II

Value Added Tax

Fuel for private use

9.—(1) The provisions of this section apply where, in any prescribed accounting period beginning after 6th April 1987, fuel which is or has previously been supplied to or imported or manufactured by a taxable person in the course of his business—

(*a*) is provided or to be provided by the taxable person to an individual for private use in his own vehicle or a vehicle allocated to him and is so provided by reason of that individual's employment; or

(*b*) where the taxable person is an individual, is appropriated or to be appropriated by him for private use in his own vehicle; or

(*c*) where the taxable person is a partnership, is provided or to be provided to any of the individual partners for private use in his own vehicle.

(2) For the purposes of this section fuel shall not be regarded as provided to any person for his private use if it is supplied at a price which,—

(*a*) in the case of fuel supplied to or imported by the taxable person, is not less than the price at which it was so supplied or imported; and

(*b*) in the case of fuel manufactured by the taxable person, is not less than the aggregate of the cost of the raw material and of manufacturing together with any excise duty thereon.

(3) For the purposes of this section and Schedule 6 to this Act—

(*a*) "fuel for private use" means fuel which, having been supplied to or imported or manufactured by a taxable person in the course of his business, is or is to be provided or appropriated for private use as mentioned in subsection (1) above;

(*b*) any reference to an individual's own vehicle shall be construed as including any vehicle of which for the time being he has the use, other than a vehicle allocated to him;

(*c*) subject to subsection (9) below, a vehicle shall at any time be taken to be allocated to an individual if at that time it is made available (without any transfer of the property in it) either to the individual himself or to any other person, and is so made available by reason of the individual's employment and for private use; and

(*d*) fuel provided by an employer to an employee and fuel provided to any person for private use in a vehicle which, by virtue of paragraph (*c*) above, is for the time being taken to be allocated to the employee shall be taken to be provided to the employee by reason of his employment.

(4) Where under section 29 of the principal Act any bodies corporate are treated as members of a group, any provision of fuel by a member of the group to an individual shall be treated for the purposes of this section as provision by the representative member.

(5) In relation to the taxable person, tax on the supply or importation of fuel for private use shall be treated for the purposes of the principal Act as input tax, notwithstanding that the fuel is not used or to be used for the purposes of a business carried on by the taxable person (and, accordingly, no apportionment of tax shall fall to be made under section 14(4) of that Act by reference to fuel for private use).

(6) At the time at which fuel for private use is put into the fuel tank of an individual's own vehicle or of a vehicle allocated to him, the fuel shall be treated for the purposes of the principal Act as supplied to him by the taxable person in the course or furtherance of his business for a consideration determined in accordance with subsection (7) below (and, accordingly, where the fuel is appropriated by the taxable person to his own private use, he shall be treated as supplying it to himself in his private capacity).

(7) In any prescribed accounting period of the taxable person in which, by virtue of subsection (6) above, he is treated as supplying fuel for private use to an individual, the consideration for all the supplies made to that individual in that period in respect of any one vehicle shall be that which, by virtue of Schedule 6 to this Act, is appropriate to a vehicle of that description, and that consideration shall be taken to be inclusive of tax.

(8) In any case where,—

(*a*) in any prescribed accounting period, fuel for private use is, by virtue of subsection (6) above, treated as supplied to an individual in respect of one vehicle for a part of the period and in respect of another vehicle for another part of the period; and

(*b*) at the end of that period one of those vehicles neither belongs to him nor is allocated to him,

subsection (7) above shall have effect as if the supplies made to the individual during those parts of the period were in respect of only one vehicle.

(9) In any prescribed accounting period a vehicle shall not be regarded as allocated to an individual by reason of his employment if—

(*a*) in that period it was made available to, and actually used by, more than one of the employees of one or more employers and, in the case of each of them, it was made available to him by reason of his employment but was not in that period ordinarily used by any one of them to the exclusion of the others; and

(*b*) in the case of each of the employees, any private use of the vehicle made by him in that period was merely incidental to his other use of it in that period; and

(*c*) it was in that period not normally kept overnight on or in the vicinity of any residential premises where any of the employees was residing, except while being kept overnight on premises occupied by the person making the vehicle available to them.

(10) In this section and Schedule 6 to this Act—

"employment" includes any office; and related expressions shall be construed accordingly;

"the principal Act" means the Value Added Tax Act 1983;

"vehicle" means a mechanically propelled road vehicle other than—

(*a*) a motor cycle as defined in section 190(4) of the Road Traffic Act 1972, or, for Northern Ireland, in Article 37(1)(*f*) of the Road Traffic (Northern Ireland) Order 1981, or

(*b*) an invalid carriage as defined in section 190(5) of that Act or, for Northern Ireland, in Article 37(1)(*g*) of that Order.

(11) This section and Schedule 6 to this Act shall be construed as one with the principal Act.

General Note

Hitherto the assessment of output tax on petrol purchased by businesses and used for private purposes has been negotiated on an individual basis. From April 6, 1987, a scale system identical with that used by the Inland Revenue under F.A. 1976, s.64(A) will apply. The effect will be to reduce the administrative burden and increase revenue by £40m. a year.

Registration of two or more persons as one taxable person

10.—(1) In Schedule 1 to the Value Added Tax Act 1983 (registration) after paragraph 1 there shall be inserted the following paragraph—

"1A.—(1) Without prejudice to paragraph 1 above, if the Commissioners make a direction under this paragraph, the persons named in the direction shall be treated as a single taxable person carrying on the activities of a business described in the direction and that taxable person shall be liable to be registered with effect from the date of the direction or, if the direction so provides, from such later date as may be specified therein.

(2) The Commissioners shall not make a direction under this paragraph naming any person unless they are satisfied—

(*a*) that he is making or has made taxable supplies; and

(*b*) that the activities in the course of which he makes or made those taxable supplies form only part of certain activities which should properly be regarded as those of the business described in the direction, the other activities being carried on concurrently or previously (or both) by one or more other persons; and

(*c*) that, if all the taxable supplies of that business were taken into account, a person carrying on that business would at the time of the direction be liable to be registered by virtue of paragraph 1 above; and

(*d*) that the main reason or one of the main reasons for the person concerned carrying on the activities first referred to in paragraph (*b*) above in the way he does is the avoidance of a liability to be registered (whether that liability would be his, another person's or that of two or more persons jointly).

(3) A direction made under this paragraph shall be served on each of the persons named in it.

(4) Where, after a direction has been given under this paragraph specifying a description of business, it appears to the Commissioners that a person who was not named in that direction is making taxable supplies in the course of activities which should properly be regarded as part of the activities of that business, the Commissioners may make and serve on him a supplementary direction referring to the earlier direction and the description of business specified in it and adding that person's name to those of the persons named in the earlier direction with effect from—

(*a*) the date on which he began to make those taxable supplies, or

(*b*) if it was later, the date with effect from which the single taxable person referred to in the earlier direction became liable to be registered.

(5) If, immediately before a direction (including a supplementary direction) is made under this paragraph, any person named in the direction is registered in respect of the taxable supplies made by him as mentioned in sub-paragraph (2) or sub-paragraph (4) above, he shall cease to be liable to be so registered with effect from whichever is the later of—

(*a*) the date with effect from which the single taxable person concerned became liable to be registered; and

(*b*) the date of the direction.

(6) In relation to a business specified in a direction under this paragraph, the persons named in the direction, together with any person named in a supplementary direction relating to that business (being the persons who together are to be treated as the taxable person), are in sub-paragraphs (7) and (8) below referred to as "the constituent members".

(7) Where a direction is made under this paragraph then, for the purposes of this Act,—

(*a*) the taxable person carrying on the business specified in the direction shall be registerable in such name as the persons named in the direction may jointly nominate by notice in writing given to the Commissioners not later than fourteen days after the date of the direction or, in default of such a nomination, in such name as may be specified in the direction;

(*b*) any supply of goods or services by or to one of the constituent members in the course of the activities of the taxable person shall be treated as a supply by or to that person;

(*c*) each of the constituent members shall be jointly and severally liable for any tax due from the taxable person;

(*d*) without prejudice to paragraph (*c*) above, any failure by the taxable person to comply with any requirement imposed by or under this Act shall be treated as a failure by each of the constituent members severally; and

(*e*) subject to paragraphs (*a*) to (*d*) above, the constituent members shall be treated as a partnership carrying on the business of the taxable person and any question as to the scope of the activities of that business at any time shall be determined accordingly.

(8) If it appears to the Commissioners that any person who is one of the constituent members should no longer be regarded as such for the purposes of paragraphs (*c*) and (*d*) of sub-paragraph (7) above and they give notice to that effect, he shall not have any liability by virtue of those paragraphs for anything done after the date specified in that notice and, accordingly, on that date he shall be treated as having ceased to be a member of the partnership referred to in paragraph (*e*) of that sub-paragraph."

(2) In section 40 of the Value Added Tax Act 1983 (appeals), in subsection (1), after paragraph (*h*) there shall be inserted the following paragraph—

"(*hh*) any direction or supplementary direction made under paragraph 1A of Schedule 1 to this Act".

(3) In the said section 40, for the words from the beginning of subsection (3A) to "paragraph (*m*) above" there shall be substituted—

"(3A) Where there is an appeal against a decision to make such a direction as is mentioned in subsection (1)(*hh*) above, the tribunal shall not allow the appeal unless it considers that the Commissioners could not reasonably have been satisfied as to the matters in paragraphs (*a*) to (*d*) of sub-paragraph (2) of paragraph 1A of Schedule 1 to this Act or, as the case may be, as to the matters in sub-paragraph (4) of that paragraph.

(3B) Where, on an appeal against a decision with respect to any of the matters mentioned in subsection (1)(*m*) above".

General Note

This section is aimed at "disaggregation," *i.e.* the artificial splitting of businesses so as to bring the turnover below the registration level for VAT. The Customs and Excise will be able to direct in such cases that the businesses shall be treated as one. There will be a right of appeal to a VAT Tribunal against such a direction. The closing of this loophole for tax avoidance is estimated to produce £20m. a year.

Long-stay accommodation

11.—(1) In paragraph 9 of Schedule 4 to the Value Added Tax Act 1983 (reduced value provision applicable to supply of accommodation in hotels etc. for periods exceeding four weeks) for the words preceding paragraph (*a*) there shall be substituted—

"(1) This paragraph applies where a supply of services consists in the provision of accommodation falling within paragraph (*a*) of item 1 of Group 1 in Schedule 6 to this Act and—

(*a*) that provision is made to an individual for a period exceeding four weeks; and

(*b*) throughout that period the accommodation is provided for the use of the individual either alone or together with one or more other persons who occupy the accommodation with him otherwise than at their own expense (whether incurred directly or indirectly).

(2) Where this paragraph applies".

(2) This section applies to a supply of services on or after 1st November 1986.

General Note

A relief from VAT is given where accommodation in hotels etc. is occupied for more than 28 days by reducing the charge on the excess period to one fifth of the normal rate. To prevent abuse of the relief through block bookings by trading organisations it is now confined to cases of continuous occupation by individuals.

Conditions for zero-rating of goods exported etc.

12.–(1) In section 16 of the Value Added Tax Act 1983 (zero-rating) at the end of subsection (6) (goods exported or shipped as stores, etc.) there shall be added the words "and, in either case, if such other conditions, if any, as may be specified in regulations or the Commissioners may impose are fulfilled."

(2) In subsection (9) of that section—

(*a*) after the words "zero-rated" there shall be inserted "by virtue of subsection (6) above or";

(*b*) in paragraph (*a*), after the word "exported" there shall be inserted "or shipped"; and

(*c*) in paragraph (*b*), for the word "regulations" there shall be substituted "relevant regulations under subsection (6), (7) or (8) above".

General Note

The amendments to the V.A.T. Act 1983 made by this section provide for the making of regulations governing the zero-rating of goods exported by the supplier. It was held by a tribunal in *Middlesex Textiles Ltd.* v. *Customs and Excise Comrs.* (1979) V.A.T.T.R. 239 that there was no power under the existing law to make such regulations and conditions have been laid down in Public Notices. The change is being made to ensure closer compliance with Article 15 of the Sixth E.E.C. Council Directive.

Transfer of import relief

13. In section 19 of the Value Added Tax Act 1983 (relief from tax on importation of goods to give effect to international agreements etc.) after subsection (1) there shall be inserted the following subsection—

"(1A) In any case where—

(*a*) it is proposed that goods which have been imported by any person (in this subsection referred to as "the original importer") with the benefit of relief under subsection (1) above shall be transferred to another person (in this subsection referred to as "the transferee"), and

(*b*) on an application made by the transferee, the Commissioners direct that this subsection shall apply,

this Act shall have effect as if, on the date of the transfer of the goods (and in place of the transfer), the goods were exported by the original importer and imported by the transferee and, accordingly, where appropriate, provision made under subsection (1) above shall have effect in relation to the tax chargeable on the importation of the goods by the transferee."

General Note

Relief is given by statutory orders made under section 19 of the V.A.T. Act for certain imported goods (S.I. 1984 No. 746 and S.I. 1985 No. 1646). Provision is now made for the transfer of such relief by the original importer.

Penalty for tax evasion: liability of directors etc.

14.—Where it appears to the Commissioners—

(*a*) that a body corporate is liable to a penalty under section 13 of the Finance Act 1985 (civil penalty for value added tax evasion where conduct involves dishonesty), and (*b*) that the conduct giving rise to that penalty is, in whole or in part, attributable to the dishonesty of a person who is, or at the material time was, a director or managing officer of the body corporate (in this section referred to as a "named officer"),

the Commissioners may serve a notice under this section on the body corporate and on the named officer.

(2) A notice under this section shall state—

(*a*) the amount of the penalty referred to in subsection (1)(*a*) above (in this section referred to as "the basic penalty"); and

(*b*) that the Commissioners propose, in accordance with this section, to recover from the named officer such portion (which may be the whole) of the basic penalty as is specified in the notice.

(3) Where a notice is served under this section, the portion of the basic penalty specified in the notice shall be recoverable from the named officer as if he were personally liable under section 13 of the Finance Act 1985 to a penalty which corresponds to that portion; and the amount of that penalty may be assessed and notified to him accordingly under section 21 of that Act.

(4) Where a notice is served under this section,—

(*a*) the amount which, under section 21 of the Finance Act 1985, may be assessed as the amount due by way of penalty from the body corporate shall be only so much (if any) of the basic penalty as is not assessed on and notified to a named officer by virtue of subsection (3) above; and

(*b*) the body corporate shall be treated as discharged from liability for so much of the basic penalty as is so assessed and notified.

(5) No appeal shall lie against a notice under this section as such but,—

(*a*) where a body corporate is assessed as mentioned in subsection (4)(*a*) above, the body corporate may appeal against the Commissioner's decision as to its liability to a penalty and against the amount of the basic penalty as if it were specified in the assessment; and

(*b*) where an assessment is made on a named officer by virtue of subsection (3) above, the named officer may appeal against the Commissioners' decision that the conduct of the body corporate referred to in subsection (1)(*b*) above is, in whole or part, attributable to his dishonesty and against their decision as to the portion of the penalty which the Commissioners propose to recover from him.

(6) For the purposes of the Value Added Tax Act 1983, any appeal brought by virtue of subsection (5) above shall be treated as an appeal under section 40 of that Act; and the reference in subsection (1A) of that section to an amount assessed by way of penalty includes a reference to an amount assessed by virtue of subsection (3) or subsection (4)(*a*) above.

(7) The provisions that may be included in rules under paragraph 9 of Schedule 8 to the Value Added Tax Act 1983 (procedure on appeals to value added tax tribunals) include provision with respect to the joinder of appeals brought by different persons where a notice is served under this section and the appeals relate to, or to different portions of, the basic penalty referred to in the notice.

(8) In this section a "managing officer", in relation to a body corporate, means any manager, secretary or other similar officer of the body corporate or any person purporting to act in any such capacity or as a director; and where the affairs of a body corporate are managed by its

members, this section shall apply in relation to the conduct of a member in connection with his functions of management as if he were a director of the body corporate.

(9) This section does not apply where the conduct of the body corporate giving rise to the penalty took place before the passing of this Act.

GENERAL NOTE

The Keith Committee on Enforcement Powers of the Revenue Departments recommended in its report (Cmnd. 8822, para. 18.4.42) that a provision analogous to that in Customs and Excise Management Act 1979, s.171(4), should be included in the V.A.T. penalties code. Directors and managers of companies are accordingly made personally liable for penalties where their own dishonesty is involved.

Breaches of Treasury orders etc.

15.—In section 17 of the Finance Act 1985 (civil penalties for breaches of regulatory provisions under the Value Added Tax Act 1983) at the end of paragraph (*c*) of subsection (1) there shall be inserted "or

(*d*) any order made by the Treasury under that Act; or

(*e*) any regulations made under the European Communities Act 1972 and relating to value added tax".

(2) At the end of subsection (4)(*b*) of that section (previous failures before the passing of the 1985 Act to be disregarded in determining rate of daily penalty) there shall be added "or, in the case of a requirement falling within paragraph (*d*) or paragraph (*e*) of subsection (1) above, before the passing of the Finance Act 1986".

GENERAL NOTE

The civil penalties regime for non-compliance with V.A.T. regulations is extended to Treasury orders and regulations made under the European Communities Act 1972 relating to V.A.T. There are at present none in the latter category.

PART II

INCOME TAX, CORPORATION TAX AND CAPITAL GAINS TAX

CHAPTER I

GENERAL

Tax rates and main reliefs

Charge of income tax for 1986–87

16.—(1) Income tax for the year 1986–87 shall be charged at the basic rate of 29 per cent.; and in respect of so much of an individual's total income as exceeds the basic rate limit (£17,200) at such higher rates as are specified in the Table below:

TABLE

Higher rate bands	*Higher rate per cent.*
The first £3,000	40
The next £5,200	45
The next £7,900	50
The next £7,900	55
The remainder	60

and paragraphs (*a*) and (*b*) of subsection (1) of section 32 of the Finance Act 1971 (charge of tax at the basic and higher rates) shall have effect accordingly.

(2) Section 24(4) of the Finance Act 1980 (indexation of thresholds) shall not, so far as it relates to the higher rate bands, apply for the year 1986–87.

GENERAL NOTE

The basic rate of income tax is reduced by 1 per cent. for 1986–87. The threshold at which charges to higher rate tax begins is raised by £1,000.

Rate of advance corporation tax

17.—(1) For the financial year 1986 and any subsequent financial year, the rate of advance corporation tax shall be fixed by the fraction—

$$\frac{I}{100-I}$$

where I is the percentage at which income tax at the basic rate is charged for the year of assessment which begins on 6th April in that financial year; and in the following provisions of this section that percentage is referred to, in relation to a particular financial year, as "the basic rate percentage for the appropriate year of assessment".

(2) If, at the beginning of any financial year, the basic rate percentage for the appropriate year of assessment has not been determined (whether under the Provisional Collection of Taxes Act 1968 or otherwise), then, subject to subsection (3) below, advance corporation tax in respect of distributions made in that financial year shall be payable under Schedule 14 to the Finance Act 1972 and may be assessed under that Schedule according to the rate of advance corporation tax fixed for the previous financial year.

(3) Subsection (2) above does not apply with respect to any distribution made in a financial year after—

(*a*) the date on which is determined the basic rate percentage for the appropriate year of assessment; or

(*b*) 5th August in that year,

whichever is the earlier.

(4) If a rate of advance corporation tax for any financial year is not fixed, under subsection (1) above or any other enactment, or if advance corporation tax for any financial year is charged otherwise than as it has been paid or assessed, the necessary adjustment shall be made by discharge or repayment of tax or by a further assessment.

(5) In subsection (2) of section 84 of the Finance Act 1972 (the rate of advance corporation tax) for the words from "for the period" onwards there shall be substituted "for the financial year 1986 and subsequent financial years shall be determined in accordance with section 17 of the Finance Act 1986".

(6) In section 103 of the Finance Act 1972 (charge of advance corporation tax at previous rate until new rate is fixed and change of rate) subsections (1) to (3) shall cease to have effect.

(7) Section 37(2) of the Finance Act 1974 (tax on company in liquidation to be based on Resolution fixing the rate of advance corporation tax) shall cease to have effect.

GENERAL NOTE

The rate of A.C.T. is intended to relate to the basic rate of income tax. In the past the rate has been set on an annual basis. This section does away with this as for the future and enables the rate to be set automatically in line with the basic rate of income tax for the time being in force.

F.A. 1972, s.103 and F.A. 1974, s.37(2) were provisions dealing with the rate of A.C.T. to be applied to distributions made prior to the fixing of the basic rate for the year in question. The terms of subsections (2) to (4) of this section dispense with the need for these provisions.

The A.C.T. rate for distributions made on or after April 6, 1986 is $\frac{29}{71}$ sts.

Corporation tax: small companies

18.—(1) For the financial year 1986 the small companies rate shall be 29 per cent.

(2) For the financial year 1986, the fraction mentioned in section 95(2) of the Finance Act 1972 (marginal relief for small companies) shall be three two-hundredths.

General Note

In line with the reduction in the basic rate of income tax to 29 per cent. the small companies rate of corporation tax is reduced to a like figure.

Personal reliefs: operative date for PAYE

19. For the year 1986–87, in subsection (7) of section 24 of the Finance Act 1980 (which specifies the date from which indexed changes in income tax thresholds and allowances are to be brought into account for the purposes of PAYE) for "5th May" there shall be substituted "18th May".

General Note

Changes in tax thresholds and allowances are only to be brought into account for the purpose of PAYE on and after the 18th of May as opposed to the 5th of May as in the past. This is a purely administrative measure to allow the Revenue more time to implement the changes made by the Act.

Relief for interest

20. For the year 1986–87 the qualifying maximum referred to in paragraphs 5(1) and 24(3) of Schedule 1 to the Finance Act 1974 (limit on relief for interest on certain loans for the purchase or improvement of land) shall be £30,000.

General Note

No change is made to the maximum amount on which mortgage interest relief can be obtained.

Deduction rate for sub-contractors in construction industry

21. Section 69(4) of the Finance (No. 2) Act 1975 (which requires deductions to be made from payments to certain sub-contractors in the construction industry) shall have effect in relation to payments made on or after 6th November 1986 with the substitution for the words "30 per cent." of the words "29 per cent.".

General Note

In line with the reduction in the basic rate of income tax by 1 per cent. the rate at which deductions must be made from payments to sub-contractors in the construction industry is also reduced to 29 per cent.

Employee shareholding

Employee share schemes: shares subject to restrictions

22.—(1) In Schedule 9 to the Finance Act 1978 (approved profit sharing schemes) in paragraph 7 (conditions as to the shares)—

(*a*) in paragraph (*c*) after the word "class" there shall be added the words "or a restriction authorised by sub-paragraph (2) below"; and

(*b*) at the end there shall be added the sub-paragraphs set out in subsection (4) below followed by the additional sub-paragraph set out in subsection (5) below.

(2) In Schedule 10 to the Finance Act 1980 (savings-related share option schemes) in paragraph 17 (conditions as to the scheme shares)—

(*a*) in paragraph (*c*) after the word "class" there shall be added the words "or a restriction authorised by sub-paragraph (2) below"; and

(*b*) at the end there shall be added the sub-paragraphs set out in subsection (4) below.

(3) In Schedule 10 to the Finance Act 1984 (approved share option schemes) in paragraph 9 (conditions as to scheme shares)—

(*a*) in paragraph (*c*) after the word "class" there shall be added the words "or a restriction authorised by sub-paragraph (2) below"; and

(*b*) at the end there shall be added the sub-paragraphs set out in subsection (4) below.

(4) The sub-paragraphs referred to in subsections (1)(*b*), (2)(*b*) and (3)(*b*) above are—

"(2) Except as provided below, the shares may be subject to a restriction imposed by the company's articles of association—

(*a*) requiring all shares held by directors or employees of the company or of any other company of which it has control to be disposed of on ceasing to be so held; and

(*b*) requiring all shares acquired, in pursuance of rights or interests obtained by such directors or employees, by persons who are not (or have ceased to be) such directors or employees to be disposed of when they are acquired.

(3) A restriction is not authorised by sub-paragraph (2) above unless—

(*a*) any disposal required by the restriction will be by way of sale for a consideration in money on terms specified in the articles of association; and

(*b*) the articles also contain general provisions by virtue of which any person disposing of shares of the same class (whether or not held or acquired as mentioned in sub-paragraph (2) above) may be required to sell them on terms which are the same as those mentioned in paragraph (*a*) above."

(5) The additional sub-paragraph referred to in subsection (1)(*b*) above is—

"(4) Except in the case of redeemable shares in a workers' co-operative, nothing in sub-paragraph (2) above authorises a restriction which would require a person, before the release date, to dispose of his beneficial interest in shares the ownership of which has not been transferred to him."

General Note

Companies who have sought to ensure that employees leaving their employment can be called upon to sell their shares have been unable to require this as regards shares used in profit sharing schemes, savings related share option schemes and other share option schemes approved by the Revenue where it was required that the shares concerned should be subject to no different restrictions to those attaching to all shares of the same class. This section now permits a requirement to sell in such circumstances to be placed on shares issued under the schemes. To protect the interests of employees the price to be paid on such sales must be the same as that at which other shares in the company can be required to be sold.

Employee share schemes: general amendments

23.—(1) In this section—

"the 1978 Schedule" means Schedule 9 to the Finance Act 1978 (approved profit sharing schemes);

"the 1980 Schedule" means Schedule 10 to the Finance Act 1980 (savings-related share option schemes); and "the 1984 Schedule" means Schedule 10 to the Finance Act 1984 (approved share option schemes).

(2) In each of the following provisions (which govern the eligibility of shares)—

(*a*) paragraph 8 of the 1978 Schedule,

(*b*) paragraph 19 of the 1980 Schedule,

(*c*) paragraph 11 of the 1984 Schedule,

there shall be made the amendments in subsection (3) below.

(3) After the words "of the same class" there shall be inserted "either must be employee-control shares or" and at the end there shall be added the following sub-paragraph—

"(2) For the purposes of this paragraph, shares of a company are employee-control shares if—

(*a*) the persons holding the shares are, by virtue of their holding, together able to control the company; and

(*b*) those persons are or have been employees or directors of the company or of another company which is under the control of the company."

(4) In the following enactments (which exclude from provisions about restrictions attaching to shares provisions which are derived from a Model Code issued by The Stock Exchange in April 1981), namely—

(*a*) section 41 of the Finance Act 1982 (which relates to the 1980 Schedule and also to Schedule 8 to the Finance Act 1973—share option and share incentive schemes), and

(*b*) paragraph 10(2) of the 1984 Schedule,

"for April 1981" there shall be substituted "November 1984".

(5) For the purpose of bringing the definition of a member of a consortium in the 1978 Schedule and the 1980 Schedule into line with that in the 1984 Schedule—

(*a*) in paragraph 17 of the 1978 Schedule, and

(*b*) in paragraph 26(5) of the 1980 Schedule,

for the words "not more than five" there shall be substituted "a number of".

(6) In each of the 1978 Schedule, the 1980 Schedule and the 1984 Schedule, "recognised stock exchange" has the same meaning as in the Corporation Tax Acts.

General Note

This section makes certain amendments to the rules relating to the approved share schemes referred to in subsection (1). The major amendments are contained in subsections (2) and (3) relating to employee controlled companies. Such companies have been unable to introduce schemes if they have more than one class of shares because of the rule that where there are two classes of issued ordinary shares the majority of shares to be used in the scheme must be held by persons who are not employees of that or associated companies.

Approved profit sharing schemes: workers' co-operatives

24.—(1) In Schedule 9 to the Finance Act 1978 (profit sharing schemes) at the end of Part V (interpretation) there shall be added the following paragraph—

"18. In this Schedule "workers' co-operative" means a registered industrial and provident society, within the meaning of section 340 of the Taxes Act, which is a co-operative society and the rules of which include provisions which secure—

(*a*) that the only persons who may be members of it are those who are employed by, or by a subsidiary of, the society and those who are the trustees of its profit sharing scheme; and

(*b*) that, subject to any provision about qualifications for membership which is from time to time made by the members of the society by reference to age, length of service or other factors of any description, all such persons may be members of the society;

and in this paragraph "co-operative society" has the same meaning as in section 1 of the Industrial and Provident Societies Act 1965 or, as the case may be, the Industrial and Provident Societies Act (Northern Ireland) 1969."

(2) In paragraph 7 of that Schedule (conditions as to shares) for paragraph (*b*) there shall be substituted the following paragraph—

"(*b*) except in the case of shares in a workers' co-operative, not redeemable; and".

(3) In section 54 of the Finance Act 1978 (the period of retention etc.)—

(*a*) at the end of subsection (1)(*d*) there shall be added "or, in the case of redeemable shares in a workers' co-operative, as defined in Schedule 9 to this Act, by redemption"; and

(*b*) at the end of subsection (4) there shall be added "or

(*d*) in a case where the participant's shares are redeemable shares in a workers' co-operative, as defined in Schedule 9 to this Act, the date on which the participant ceases to be employed by, or by a subsidiary of, the co-operative."

(4) Where, for the purpose of securing (and maintaining) approval of its profit sharing scheme in accordance with Part I of Schedule 9 to the Finance Act 1978, the rules of a society which is a workers' co-operative or which is seeking to be registered under the industrial and provident societies legislation as a workers' co-operative contain—

(*a*) provision for membership of the society by the trustees of the scheme,

(*b*) provision denying voting rights to those trustees, or

(*c*) other provisions which appear to the registrar to be reasonably necessary for that purpose,

those provisions shall be disregarded in determining whether the society should be or continue to be registered under the industrial and provident societies legislation as a bona fide co-operative society.

(5) In subsection (4) above "the industrial and provident societies legislation" means—

(*a*) the Industrial and Provident Societies Act 1965, or

(*b*) the Industrial and Provident Societies Act (Northern Ireland) 1969,

and "registrar" has the same meaning as in each of those Acts and "co-operative society" has the same meaning as in section 1 of those Acts.

General Note

While redeemable shares cannot normally be used in an approved profit sharing scheme, this section permits their use in the case of worker co-operatives as defined. In addition subsection (4) secures that rules of a co-operative designed to ensure that approval can be obtained for its profit sharing scheme will not imperil its ability to be registered or continue to be registered under the industrial and provident societies legislation.

Savings-related share option schemes

25.—(1) Schedule 10 to the Finance Act 1980 (savings-related share option schemes) shall be amended in accordance with subsections (2) to (7) below.

(2) Paragraph 2 (schemes may be approved conditionally upon satisfaction as to acquisition price of scheme shares) shall cease to have effect.

(3) In paragraph 8 (provisions as to exercising rights where a person ceases to be eligible to participate in schemes) after the words "may not be exercised at all" there shall be inserted the words "except pursuant to

such a provision of the scheme as is specified in paragraph 10(1)(*e*) below".

(4) At the end of sub-paragraph (1) of paragraph 10 (cases where a scheme may allow options to be exercised after certain events) there shall be added the following paragraph—

"(*e*) if a person ceases to hold an office or employment by virtue of which he is eligible to participate in the scheme by reason only that—

(i) that office or employment is in a company of which the company concerned ceases to have control, or

(ii) that office or employment relates to a business or part of a business which is transferred to a person who is neither an associated company of the company concerned nor a company of which the company concerned has control,

rights under the scheme held by that person may be exercised within six months of his so ceasing".

(5) In paragraph 12 (supplementary provision as to ceasing to be employed) after the words "paragraph 8" there shall be inserted "or paragraph 10(1)(*e*)".

(6) In paragraph 21 (eligibility to participate restricted to current directors and employees) after the words "paragraph 8 above" there shall be inserted "or pursuant to such a provision as is referred to in paragraph 10(1)(*e*) above".

(7) Paragraph 22 (which restricts eligibility to participate in one scheme where, in the same year of assessment, rights have been obtained under another scheme) shall cease to have effect and, accordingly, in paragraph 20 for the words "paragraphs 22 and 23" there shall be substituted "paragraph 23".

(8) Where an existing scheme is altered before 1st August 1988 so as to include such a provision as is specified in paragraph 10(1)(*e*) of Schedule 10 to the Finance Act 1980 (as amended by this section), the scheme as altered may by virtue of this section apply that provision to rights obtained under the scheme before the date on which the alteration takes effect, and where that provision is so applied in relation to such rights,—

(*a*) the scheme may permit a person having such rights to take advantage of the provision, notwithstanding that under the scheme he would otherwise be unable to exercise those rights after he has ceased to hold the office or employment in question; and

(*b*) if, before the date on which the alteration takes effect, a person who held such rights on 18th March 1986 ceases, in either of the circumstances set out in the said paragraph 10(1)(*e*), to hold an office or employment by virtue of which he was eligible to participate in the scheme, then, so far as concerns the rights so held, the scheme may permit him to take advantage of the provision in question as if the alteration had been made immediately before he ceased to hold that office or employment; and

(*c*) the application of the provision shall not itself be regarded as the acquisition of a right for the purposes of the said Schedule 10.

(9) In subsection (8) above "an existing scheme" means a scheme approved under Schedule 10 to the Finance Act 1980 before 1st August 1986; and that subsection has effect subject to paragraph 3(2) of that Schedule (approval of Board required for alteration in scheme).

GENERAL NOTE

Participants in approved savings related share option schemes who have held rights in such schemes for less than three years have previously been unable to exercise such rights on their ceasing to be employed by the company or group concerned unless they left the employment through injury, disability, redundancy or retirement on reaching pensionable age. This section now permits such exercise if the company with whom they are employed leaves the group or if the part of the business of the company in which they work is sold. Such rights can again only be exercised within six months of such events occurring.

The terms of subsection (7) should be noted. This removes the prohibition on a person being eligible to benefit under a scheme if in the same year of assessment that person has obtained rights under another scheme.

Shares and rights to acquire shares obtained by directors and employees

26.—(1) In section 186 of the Taxes Act (directors and employees granted rights to acquire shares), after subsection (5) there shall be inserted the following subsections—

"(5A) In any case where—

(*a*) a person has obtained any such right to acquire shares as is mentioned in subsection (1) above (in this subsection referred to as "the first right"), and

(*b*) as to any of the shares to which the first right relates, he omits or undertakes to omit to exercise the right or grants or undertakes to grant to another a right to acquire the shares or any interest therein, and

(*c*) in consideration for or otherwise in connection with that omission, grant or undertaking, he receives any benefit in money or money's worth,

he shall be treated for the purposes of this section as realising a gain by the assignment or release of the first right, so far as it relates to the shares in question, for a consideration equal to the amount or value of the benefit referred to in paragraph (*c*) above.

(5B) Where subsection (5A) above has had effect on any occasion, nothing in that subsection affects the application of this section in relation to a gain realised on a subsequent occasion, except that on that subsequent occasion so much of the consideration given for the grant of the first right as was deducted on the first occasion shall not be deducted again."

(2) In subsection (11) of that section (notice of certain events relating to right to acquire shares) for the words from "gives any consideration" to "it shall" there shall be substituted "receives written notice of the assignment of such a right or provides any benefit in money or money's worth—

(*a*) for the assignment or for the release in whole or in part of such a right, or

(*b*) for or in connection with an omission or undertaking to omit to exercise such a right, or

(*c*) for or in connection with the grant or undertaking to grant a right to acquire shares or an interest in shares to which such a right relates,

it shall".

(3) In section 79 of the Finance Act 1972 (share incentive schemes) after subsection (5) there shall be inserted the following subsections—

"(5A) Subsection (5B) below applies where—

(*a*) a person has acquired shares or an interest in shares as mentioned in subsection (1) above (and the shares which he acquires or in which he acquires an interest are in the following provisions of this section, other than subsection (6A), referred to as "the original shares"); and

(*b*) the circumstances of his acquisition of the original shares are such that the application of subsection (4) above is not excluded; and

(*c*) by virtue of his holding of the original shares or the interest in them he acquires (whether or not for consideration) additional shares or an interest in additional shares (and the shares which he so acquires or in which he so acquires an interest are in subsection (5B) below referred to as "the additional shares").

(5B) Where this subsection applies—

(*a*) the additional shares or, as the case may be, the interest in them shall be treated as having been acquired as mentioned in subsection (1) above and in circumstances falling within subsection (5A)(*b*) above and, for the purpose of subsection (6)(*a*) below, as having been acquired at the same time as the original shares or the interest in them;

(*b*) for the purposes of subsections (4) and (5) above, the additional shares and the original shares shall be treated as one holding of shares and the market value of the shares comprised in that holding at any time shall be determined accordingly (the market value of the original shares at the time of acquisition being attributed proportionately to all the shares in the holding); and

(*c*) for the purposes of those subsections, any consideration given for the acquisition of the additional shares or the interest in them shall be taken to be an increase falling within subsection (5)(*a*) above in the consideration for the original shares or the interest in them."

(4) In subsection (6)(*c*) of the said section 79 (the period at the end of which a charge to tax arises)—

(*a*) for the words "the shares cease" there shall be substituted "by reason of the shares ceasing"; and

(*b*) at the end there shall be added the words "either of the conditions in subsection (2)(*c*) above would be satisfied in relation to the shares if they had been acquired at that time".

(5) After subsection (6) of the said section 79 there shall be inserted the following subsection—

"(6A) If, on a person ceasing to have a beneficial interest in any shares, he acquires other shares or an interest in other shares and the circumstances are such that, for the purposes of sections 78 to 81 of the Capital Gains Tax Act 1979 (reorganisations etc.) the shares in which he ceases to have a beneficial interest constitute "original shares" and the other shares constitute a "new holding",—

(*a*) section 78 of that Act (which equates the original shares and the new holding) shall apply for the purposes of this section; and

(*b*) if any such consideration is given for the new holding as is mentioned in section 79(1) of that Act, it shall be treated for the purposes of this section as an increase falling within subsection (5)(*a*) above in the consideration for the shares; and

(*c*) if any such consideration is received for the disposal of the original shares as is mentioned in section 79(2) of that Act, the consideration shall be apportioned among the shares comprised in the new holding and the amount which, apart from this paragraph, would at any subsequent time be the market value of any of those shares shall be taken to be increased by the amount of the consideration apportioned to them;

and in paragraphs (*a*) to (*c*) above "the original shares" shall be construed in accordance with the said sections 78 to 81 (and not in accordance with subsection (5A) above)."

(6) In this section—

(*a*) subsections (1) and (2) above have effect where a benefit is received after 18th March 1986;

(*b*) subsection (3) above has effect where the acquisition of additional shares or the interest in shares is after that date;

(*c*) subsection (4) above has effect where the shares cease to be subject to restrictions after that date; and

(*d*) subsection (5) above has effect where the shares which constitute the new holding are acquired after that date.

General Note

This section includes provisions designed to nullify a number of devices used to avoid charges arising under s.186 I.C.T.A. and s.79 F.A. 1972.

Subs. (1)

Charges under s.186 arise on the exercise, assignment or release of a right to acquire shares obtained by a person as an employee. This section deals with two methods by which attempts have been made to avoid the charge, first by persons receiving payment for omitting to exercise rights and secondly by payments being made for the grant of options over the shares to be acquired.

Subss. (3) and (5)

Charges arising under section 79(4) F.A. 1972 arise in respect of the gain made on the shares initially acquired in the circumstances to which the section applies. If the original shares were diluted by a bonus or rights issue or were in some other way affected by a company reorganisation or by a company takeover, the charge did not apply to the new shares acquired. Subsections (3) and (5) deal with the position in this respect by extending the charge to the new shares acquired in such circumstances.

Subs. (4)

The charge under section 79(4) arises on the first to occur of a number of events one of which is the lifting of restrictions from shares. One device to limit any charge to a minimum where the shares issued would not ordinarily be exempt from charge under the provisions of section 79(2)(*c*) was to impose restrictions on the shares but lift them shortly thereafter at a time when no or little gain was inherent in the shares: subsection (4) ensures that this device will no longer be effective. Only if the shares, when free of restrictions, will fall within section 79(2)(*c*) will a charge arise and thus will any further charge be precluded.

Charities

Relief for donations under payroll deduction scheme

27.—(1) This section applies where an individual (the employee) is entitled to receive payments from which income tax falls to be deducted by virtue of section 204 of the Taxes Act and regulations under that section (PAYE), and the person liable to make the payments (the employer) withholds sums from them.

(2) If the conditions mentioned in subsections (3) to (7) below are fulfilled the sums shall, in assessing tax under Schedule E, be allowed to be deducted as expenses incurred in the year of assessment in which they are withheld.

(3) The sums must be withheld in accordance with a scheme which is (or is of a kind) approved by the Board at the time they are withheld and which either contains provisions falling within subsection (4)(*a*) below, or contains provisions falling within subsection (4)(*a*) below and provisions falling within subsection (4)(*b*) below.

(4) The provisions are that—

(*a*) the employer is to pay sums withheld to a person (the agent) who is approved by the Board at the time they are withheld, and the agent is to pay them to a charity or charities;

(*b*) the employer is to pay sums withheld directly to a charity which (or charities each of which) is at the time the sums are withheld approved by the Board as an agent for the purpose of paying sums to other charities.

(5) The sums must be withheld in accordance with a request by the employee that they be paid to a charity or charities in accordance with a scheme approved (or of a kind approved) by the Board.

(6) The sums must constitute gifts by the employee to the charity or charities concerned, must not be paid by the employee under a covenant, and must fulfil any conditions set out in the terms of the scheme concerned.

(7) The sums must not in any year of assessment exceed £100 in the case of any employee (however many offices or employments he holds or has held).

(8) In this section "charity" has the same meaning as in section 360 of the Taxes Act.

(9) This section has effect in relation to sums withheld in the year 1987–88 or any subsequent year of assessment.

General Note

This section is one of a number following which is concerned with charitable giving. As from 1987–88 the section permits payments to charities of up to £100 per annum to be deducted in computing liability to tax under Schedule E and in determining the PAYE deductions. The payments to which the section applies are to be made gross and not net of tax. In order for this relief to be obtained:—

(*a*) the sum must be witheld by the employer from the emoluments paid to the employee;
(*b*) the retentions must be in response to a request by the employee and in accordance with a scheme approved by the Board pursuant to which the employer pays the amounts to an agent (who may itself be a charity) who is to pay them to a charity or charities;
(*c*) the sums must not be paid under covenant and the conditions in the scheme approved by the Board must be met.

Payroll deduction scheme: further provisions

28.—(1) The circumstances in which the Board may for the purposes of section 27 above grant or withdraw approval of schemes (or kinds of scheme) or of agents shall be such as are prescribed by the Treasury by regulations.

(2) The circumstances so prescribed (whether relating to the terms of schemes or the qualifications of agents or otherwise) shall be such as the Treasury think fit.

(3) The Treasury may by regulations make provision—

(*a*) that a participating employer or agent shall comply with any notice which is served on him by the Board and which requires him within a prescribed period to make available for the Board's inspection documents of a prescribed kind or records of a prescribed kind;
(*b*) that a participating employer or agent shall in prescribed circumstances furnish to the Board information of a prescribed kind;
(*c*) for, and with respect to, appeals to the Special Commissioners against the Board's refusal to grant, or their withdrawal of, approval of any scheme (or kind of scheme) or agent;
(*d*) generally for giving effect to section 27 above.

(4) For the purposes of subsection (3) above a person is a participating employer or agent if he is an employer (within the meaning of section 27 above) or agent (within the meaning of that section) who participates, or has at any time participated, in a scheme under that section.

(5) In subsection (3) above "prescribed" means prescribed by the regulations.

(6) The words "Regulations under section 28 of the Finance Act 1986" shall be added at the end of each column in the Table in section 98 of the

Taxes Management Act 1970 (penalties for failure to furnish information etc.).

(7) The power to make regulations under this section shall be exercisable by statutory instrument subject to annulment in pursuance of a resolution of the House of Commons.

General Note

This section provides for the drawing up of regulations to govern schemes intended to fall within section 27.

Donations by companies to charities etc.

29.—(1) On a claim made by a company which is resident in the United Kingdom and is not a close company, a qualifying donation made by the company shall, subject to the provisions of this section, constitute a charge on the income of the company for the purposes of section 248 of the Taxes Act.

(2) Subject to subsection (3) below, a qualifying donation is a payment made by the company to a charity, other than—

(*a*) a covenanted payment to charity, as defined in section 434(2) of the Taxes Act; and

(*b*) a payment which is deductible in computing profits or any description of profits for purposes of corporation tax.

(3) A payment made by a company is not a qualifying donation unless, on the making of it, the company deducts out of it a sum representing the amount of income tax thereon; and in section 55(1) of the Taxes Act (certificates of deduction) after the words "Finance Act 1973" there shall be inserted "or section 29 of the Finance Act 1986".

(4) Where, with a view to securing relief under this section, a company makes a payment subject to such a deduction as is mentioned in subsection (3) above, then, whether or not it proves to be a qualifying donation, the payment—

(*a*) shall be treated as a "relevant payment" for the purposes of Schedule 20 to the Finance Act 1972 (collection of income tax on company payments which are not distributions); and

(*b*) shall in the hands of the recipient (whether a charity or not) be treated for the purposes of the Taxes Act as if it were an annual payment.

(5) In any accounting period of a company, the maximum amount allowable under section 248 of the Taxes Act in accordance with subsection (1) above in respect of qualifying donations made by the company shall be a sum equal to 3 per cent. of the dividends paid on the company's ordinary share capital in that accounting period.

(6) In this section "charity" includes—

(*a*) the Trustees of the British Museum;

(*b*) the Trustees of the British Museum (Natural History);

(*c*) the Trustees of the National Heritage Memorial Fund;

(*d*) the Historic Buildings and Monuments Commission for England; and

(*e*) any Association of a description specified in section 362 of th[e] Taxes Act (scientific research associations);

and, subject to paragraphs (*a*) to (*e*) above, "charity" has the sam[e] meaning as in section 360 of the Taxes Act.

(7) This section applies to payments made on or after 1st April 19[86] and, in the case of a company whose accounting period begins before a[nd] ends on or after that date, the period beginning on that date and end[ing] at the end of that accounting period shall be deemed to be an account[ing] period for the purpose of applying the limit in subsection (5) above.

GENERAL NOTE

A company has in the past generally been able to obtain tax relief in respect of gifts to charities only if these gifts were made pursuant to four year covenants. This section permits single donations to qualify for relief as charges on income if:

(*a*) the company is not a close company;

(*b*) the total payments made do not exceed 3 per cent. of the dividends paid on the company's ordinary share capital; and

(*c*) the payments are made under deduction of tax.

As a corollary to payments being deductible in the hands of the company the payments are treated as annual payments and thus income in the hands of the charity. The charity will be able to recoup the tax deducted so long as it applies the payments for charitable purposes only (*i.e.* satisfies I.C.T.A., s.360(1)(*c*)) and falls outside the provisions of section 31 below.

Certain payments to charities

30.—(1) Any payment which—

(*a*) on or after 12th June 1986 is received by a charity from another charity, and

(*b*) is not made for full consideration in money or money's worth, and

(*c*) is not chargeable to tax apart from this subsection, and

(*d*) is not, apart from this subsection, of a description which (on a claim) would be eligible for relief from tax by virtue of any provision of section 360(1) of the Taxes Act,

shall be chargeable to tax under Case III of Schedule D but shall be eligible for relief from tax under section 360(1)(*c*) of the Taxes Act as if it were an annual payment.

(2) In section 248 of the Taxes Act (allowance of charges on income) after subsection (8) there shall be inserted the following subsection—

"(8A) Notwithstanding anything in any other provision of the Tax Acts, a covenanted donation to charity made by a company after 18th March 1986 shall not be a charge on income for the purposes of this section unless the company—

(*a*) deducts out of it a sum representing the amount of income tax thereon, and

(*b*) accounts for that tax in accordance with Schedule 20 to the Finance Act 1972,

and any such payment from which a deduction is made as mentioned in paragraph (*a*) above shall be treated as a relevant payment for the purposes of the said Schedule 20, whether or not it would otherwise fall to be so treated."

(3) In this section "charity" has the same meaning as in section 360 of the Taxes Act.

GENERAL NOTE

Income and chargeable gains of charities have in the past been exempt from tax broadly so long as the income or gains were applied for charitable purposes. The case of *IRC* v. *Slater (Helen) Charitable Trust Ltd.* [1981] S.T.C. 471 shows that the requirement can be satisfied by an application of money by one charity to another whether or not the recipient itself uses the funds in such a way as would give the donor charity tax exemption if it had applied the funds in that way. Subsection (1) now modifies the position as far as the recipient charity is concerned and makes such grants chargeable to tax under Case III of Schedule D, though eligible for exemption if applied for charitable purposes.

Subsection (2) only allows a payment by a company to a charity to rank as a charge on income if it deducts tax on making the payment. This is so despite the fact that the recipient charity might be within the same group as the payer company and thus otherwise the payments might be made gross under I.C.T.A. s.256. The Tax deducted by the payer company will be refundable so long as the charity satisfies the conditions for exemption.

Charities: restriction of tax exemptions

31.—(1) If in any chargeable period of a charity—

(*a*) its relevant income and gains are not less than £10,000, and

(*b*) its relevant income and gains exceed the amount of its qualifying expenditure, as defined in Part I of Schedule 7 to this Act, and

(*c*) the charity incurs, or is treated by virtue of any of the following provisions of this section as incurring, non-qualifying expenditure, that is to say, expenditure which is not qualifying expediture as defined in the said Part I,

relief under the enactments conferring exemption from tax shall not be available for so much of the excess referred to in paragraph (*b*) above as does not exceed the non-qualifying expenditure incurred in that period.

(2) In relation to a chargeable period of less than twelve months, subsection (1) above shall have effect as if the amount specified in paragraph (*a*) of that subsection were proportionately reduced.

(3) In this section—

(*a*) "charity" has the same meaning as in section 360 of the Taxes Act;

(*b*) "covenanted payment to charity" shall be construed in accordance with section 434(2) of the Taxes Act;

(*c*) "the enactments conferring exemption from tax" means subsection (1) of the said section 360 (income) and section 145 of the Capital Gains Tax Act 1979 (gains); and

(*d*) "relevant income and gains" means—

(i) income which, apart from subsection (1) of the said section 360, would not be exempt from tax, together with any income which is taxable notwithstanding that subsection; and

(ii) gains which, apart from the said section 145, would be chargeable gains, together with any gains which are chargeable gains notwithstanding that section.

(4) If in any chargeable period a charity—

(*a*) invests any of its funds in an investment which is not a qualifying investment, as defined in Part II of Schedule 7 to this Act, or

(*b*) makes a loan (not being an investment) which is not a qualifying loan, as defined in Part III of that Schedule,

then, subject to subsection (5) below, the amount so invested or lent in that period shall be treated for the purposes of this section as being an amount of expenditure incurred by the charity and, accordingly, as being non-qualifying expenditure.

(5) If, in any chargeable period, a charity which has in that period made an investment or loan falling within subsection (4) above,—

(*a*) realises the whole or part of that investment, or

(*b*) is repaid the whole or part of that loan,

any further investment or lending in that period of the sum realised or repaid shall, to the extent that it does not exceed the sum originally invested or lent, be left out of account in determining the amount which, by virtue of subsection (4) above, is treated as non-qualifying expenditure incurred in that period.

(6) If the aggregate of the qualifying and non-qualifying expenditure incurred by a charity in any chargeable period exceeds the relevant income and gains of that period, Part IV of Schedule 7 to this Act shall have effect to treat, in certain cases, some or all of that excess as non-qualifying expenditure incurred in earlier periods.

(7) Where, by virtue of this section, there is an amount of a charity's relevant income and gains for which relief under the enactments conferring exemption from tax is not available, the charity may, by notice in writing to the Board, specify which items of its relevant income and gains are, in whole or in part, to be attributed to that amount and, for this purpose, all covenanted payments to the charity shall be treated as a single item; and if, within thirty days of being required to do so by the Board, a charity does not give notice under this subsection, the items of its relevant income and gains which are to be attributed to the amount in question shall be such as the Board may determine.

(8) Where it appears to the Board that two or more charities acting in concert are engaged in transactions of which the main purpose or one of the main purposes is the avoidance of tax (whether by the charities or any other person), the Board may by notice in writing given to the charities provide that, for such chargeable periods as may be specified in the notice, subsection (1) above shall have effect in relation to them with the omission of paragraph (*a*).

(9) An appeal may be brought against a notice under subsection (8) above as if it were notice of the decision of the Board on a claim made by the charities concerned.

(10) Subsections (1) to (9) above have effect for chargeable periods ending after 11th June 1986; but where a chargeable period of a charity begins before and ends after that date, the charity may by notice in writing given to the Board elect that, for the purposes of subsections (1) to (9) above, that chargeable period shall be treated as two separate chargeable periods, the second of which begins on 12th June 1986 and ends at the end of that chargeable period.

(11) In Schedule 7 to this Act "the principal section" means this section and other expressions have the same meaning as in this section.

General Note

Section 31 and Schedule 7 contain rules designed to curb what has been seen as the misuse of charitable. The reliefs are restricted where funds are used for non charitable expenditure, were payments are made to overseas bodies without reasonable steps being taken to ensure that they are used for charitable purposes, and where loans or investments are made in certain ways which cannot be shown to be for the benefit of the charity and not for the avoidance of tax. These categories of expenditure are described as "non-qualifying expenditure" and are defined in Schedule 7.

The basis rule limiting the reliefs is found in subsection (1) which provides that insofar as the income and gains of a charity in a chargeable period are in excess of what is described as "qualifying expenditure" and there is in that period "non-qualifying expenditure" then there is no relief from tax for the excess to the extent that it does not exceed the "non-qualifying expenditure" in that period. Thus if for example the income and gains of a charity in a chargeable period is 100 with qualifying expenditure of 70 and non-qualifying expenditure of 20 no relief from tax will be available on 20. If the non-qualifying expenditure were to be 40 no tax relief would be available on 30. As regards the excess of 10 this may in certain cases be treated as non-qualifying expenditure in earlier periods (see ss. (6) and Pt. IV of Schedule 7).

Subsection (4) sets out the rule that non-qualifying investments and loans as defined in Schedule 7 rank as non-qualifying expenditure. Insofar as there is any realisation of such investments or repayment of such loans in a chargeable period then any further investment or loans in that period not in excess of the amounts realised or repaid are left out of account in determining the amount of non-qualifying expenditure (see ss. (5)). Any reinvestment in subsequent chargeable periods will not fall to be so disregarded however.

In general terms the rules contained in this section are not appliable if the income and gains of a charity do not exceed £10,000 in a chargeable period (see ss. (1)(*a*)). Such a rule does not apply however where two or more charities acting in concert have been engaged in transactions of which the main purpose or one of the main purposes is the avoidance of tax (see ss. (8)).

Higher rate relief for covenanted payments

32.—(1) In section 457 of the Taxes Act (settlements made on or after 7th April 1965) in subsection (1A) which allows higher rate relief for covenanted payments to charities up to £10,000 in any year of assessment)—

(*a*) at the beginning there shall be inserted the words "Subject to subsection (1B) below"; and

(*b*) the words "and does not exceed £10,000 in any year of assessment" shall be omitted.

(2) After subsection (1A) of that section there shall be inserted the following subsections—

"(1B) If at least £1,000 of an individual's income for any year of assessment consists of covenanted payments to charity which, in the hands of the charities receiving them, constitute income for which, by virtue of section 31 of the Finance Act 1986, relief under section 360(1) above is not available, so much of the individual's income as consists of those payments shall not be excluded from the operation of subsection (1) above by virtue of subsection (1A) above.

(1C) If, for any chargeable period of a charity,—

(*a*) the income of the charity includes two or more covenanted payments to charity, and

(*b*) only a part of the aggregate of those payments constitutes income for which, by virtue of section 31 of the Finance Act 1986, relief under section 360(1) above is not available,

each of the payments which make up the aggregate shall be treated for the purposes of subsection (1B) above as apportioned rateably between the part of the aggregate referred to in paragraph (*b*) above and the remainder."

(3) In Schedule 16 to the Finance Act 1972 (apportionment of income of close companies to participators) in paragraph 5(5A) (effect of covenanted payments to charities) after the words "year of assessment" there shall be inserted "then, except in so far as any such sum is referable to a payment which, if made by the individual, would be treated by virtue of subsection (1) of section 457 of the Taxes Act as the income of the individual for the purposes of excess liability (within the meaning of that subsection)" and for the words from "by whichever is the lesser of" to the end of paragraph (*b*) there shall be substituted "by the amount of that sum or those sums".

(4) This section has effect for the year 1986–87 and subsequent years of assessment.

General Note

As a further incentive to charitable giving this section removes the previous ceiling of £10,000 beyond which relief for covenanted payments would not be available for higher rate tax purposes. Insofar however as payments in excess or £1,000 per year are made to charities who do not obtain tax relief by virture of the provisions of section 31 higher rate tax relief is also unavailable.

Subsection (3) modifies the provisions of F.A. 1972, Sch. 16, regarding the apportionment of income where a close company which makes covenanted payments to charity in line with the removal of the ceiling on the tax relief available on such covenants if made by an individual.

Disclosure of information to Charity Commissioners

33. At the end of section 9 of the Charities Act 1960 (exchange of information between the Commissioners of Inland Revenue and the Charity Commissioners etc.) there shall be added the following subsection—

"(3) Without prejudice to subsection (1) above, no obligation as to secrecy or other restriction upon the disclosure of information shall prevent the Commissioners of Inland Revenue from disclosing to the Commissioners information with respect to any institution which has for any purpose been treated as established for charitable purposes but which appears to the Commissioners of Inland Revenue to be or to have been carrying on activities which are not charitable or to be or to have been applying any of its funds for purposes which are not charitable."

General Note

This section enables the Revenue to give information to the Charity Commissioners on matters relating to the charitable status of a particular body.

Foreign element: expenses

Expenses connected with work abroad

34.—(1) Section 32 of the Finance Act 1977 (expenses in connection with work done abroad) shall be amended in accordance with subsections (2) to (6) below.

(2) In subsection (2) (travel from UK and back) after the words "travelling from" there shall be inserted "any place in" and for the words "returning to" there shall be substituted "travelling to any place in".

(3) In subsection (6) (journeys to or by spouse or child)—

(*a*) for the words "between the United Kingdom and the place of performance of those duties" there shall be substituted "between any place in the United Kingdom and the place of performance of any of those duties outside the United Kingdom",

(*b*) paragraph (*b*), and in paragraph (*c*) the words "or (*b*)", shall be omitted, and

(*c*) for the words "journeys in each direction" there shall be substituted "outward and two return journeys".

(4) After subsection (6) there shall be inserted—

"(6A) Where a person holds an office or employment the duties of which are performed partly outside the United Kingdom, subsection (7) below applies to any journey by him—

(*a*) from any place in the United Kingdom to the place of performance of any of those duties outside the United Kingdom;

(*b*) from the place of performance of any of those duties outside the United Kingdom to any place in the United Kingdom.

(6B) But subsection (7) below does not apply by virtue of subsection (6A) above unless the duties concerned can only be performed outside the United Kingdom and the journey is made wholly and exclusively for the purpose—

(*a*) where the journey falls within subsection (6A)(*a*), of performing the duties concerned; or

(*b*) where the journey falls within subsection (6A)(*b*), of returning after performing the duties concerned.

(6C) Where a person is absent from the United Kingdom for the purpose of performing the duties of one or more offices or employments, subsection (7) below applies to—

(*a*) any journey by him from the place of performance of any of those duties outside the United Kingdom to any place in the United Kingdom;

(*b*) any return journey following a journey of a kind described in paragraph (*a*) above.

(6D) But subsection (7) below does not apply by virtue of subsection (6C) above unless the duties concerned can only be performed outside the United Kingdom and the absence mentioned in subsection (6C) was occasioned wholly and exclusively for the purpose of performing the duties concerned."

(5) In subsection (7)(*a*) for the words "such journey" there shall be substituted "journey to which this subsection applies" and in subsection (7)(*b*) for the words "such office or employment" there shall be substituted "office or employment mentioned in subsection (6), (6A) or (6C) above".

(6) After subsection (7) there shall be inserted—

"(7A) For the purposes of applying subsections (6) to (7) above in a case where the duties of the office or employment or (as the case may be) any of the offices or employments are performed on a vessel, in section 184(3)(*b*) of the Taxes Act the words from "or which" to the end (duties on voyage beginning or ending in UK treated as performed in UK) shall be ignored.

(7B) In such a case as is mentioned in subsection (7A) above, subsection (6B) above shall have effect as if "the duties concerned" in paragraphs (*a*) and (*b*) read "the duties concerned, or those duties and other duties of the office or employment".

(7C) Where, apart from this subsection, a deduction in respect of any cost or expenses is allowable under a provision of this section and a deduction in respect of the same cost or expenses is also allowable under another provision of this section or of any other enactment, a deduction in respect of the cost or expenses may be made under either, but not both, of those provisions."

(7) In section 184(3) of the Taxes Act after the words "subject to" there shall be inserted "section 32(7A) of and".

(8) This section has effect for the year 1984–85 and subsequent years of assessment and all such adjustments (whether by repayment of tax or otherwise) shall be made as are appropriate to give effect to this section.

General Note

Section 32 F.A. 1977 allows certain deductions relating to travel expenses to be made from the emoluments of a U.K. resident working abroad.

Subsection (2) of section 32 allows such a person to deduct the cost of travelling from the U.K. to take up employment and of travelling back to the U.K. on the termination of the employment.

Subsections (6) and (7) of that section extended the deductions in the case of such persons absent from the U.K. for a continuous period of 60 days to cover the costs of the person's spouse and children travelling to visit that person or that person travelling to visit them provided that the employer either paid or reimbursed the employee for such costs. A limit of two journeys in each direction was imposed.

Subsection (2) of this section extended the deductions to cover the cost of the journey to and from the employees home in the United Kingdom and not just that part which involves leaving or arriving in the United Kingdom. For example it covers the cost of the journey to the airport and not just the flight from the United Kingdom.

The same extension is made to the deductions allowed by subsections (6) and (7) of section 32 FA 1977. The employee can make an unlimited number of journeys to visit his or her spouse and children provided that the employee had to go abroad in order to carry out his or her duties.

The deductions will also be permitted if the duties of the office or employment are performed partly abroad and the travel is to and from the place at which they are performed abroad.

Subsection (6) of the section contains special rules for persons working on vessels which start and end their journey in the United Kingdom. It is intended that there will be a deduction available for the reimbursed costs of a seaman travelling to, say, a port in the United Kingdom in order to board a vessel for a voyage abroad. For these purposes the deeming provision contained in s.184(3)(*b*) I.C.T.A. 1970 is disregarded.

These new rules have effect for the tax year 1984/85 and subsequent years.

Expenses connected with foreign trades etc.

35.—(1) This section applies in the case of a trade, profession or vocation carried on wholly outside the United Kingdom by an individual (the taxpayer) who does not satisfy the Board as mentioned in section 122(2)(*a*) of the Taxes Act; and it is immaterial in the case of a trade or profession whether the taxpayer carries it on solely or in partnership.

(2) Expenses of the taxpayer—

(*a*) in travelling from any place in the United Kingdom to any place where the trade, profession or vocation is carried on,

(*b*) in travelling to any place in the United Kingdom from any place where the trade, profession or vocation is carried on, or

(*c*) on board and lodging for the taxpayer at any place where the trade, profession or vocation is carried on,

shall, subject to subsections (3) and (4) below, be treated for the purposes of section 130(*a*) of the Taxes Act (deductions) as having been wholly and exclusively expended for the purposes of the trade, profession or vocation.

(3) Subsection (2) above does not apply unless the taxpayer's absence from the United Kingdom is occasioned wholly and exclusively for the purpose of performing the functions of the trade, profession or vocation or of performing those functions and the functions of any other trade, profession or vocation (whether or not one in the case of which this section applies).

(4) Where subsection (2) above applies and more than one trade, profession or vocation in the case of which this section applies is carried on at the place in question, the expenses shall be apportioned on such basis as is reasonable between those trades, professions or vocations, and the expenses so apportioned to a particular trade, profession or vocation shall be treated for the purposes of section 130(*a*) of the Taxes Act as having been wholly and exclusively expended for the purposes of that trade, profession or vocation.

(5) Where the taxpayer is absent from the United Kingdom for a continuous period of 60 days or more wholly and exclusively for the purpose of performing the functions of one or more trades, professions or vocations in the case of which this section applies, expenses to which subsection (6) below applies shall be treated in accordance with subsection (7) or (8) below (as the case may be).

(6) This subsection applies to the expenses of any journey by the taxpayer's spouse, or any child of his, between any place in the United Kingdom and the place of performance of any of those functions outside the United Kingdom, if the journey—

(*a*) is made in order to accompany him at the beginning of the period of absence or to visit him during that period, or

(*b*) is a return journey following a journey falling within paragraph (*a*) above,

but this subsection does not apply to more than two outward and two return journeys by the same person in any year of assessment.

(7) The expenses shall be treated for the purposes of section 130(*a*) of the Taxes Act as having been wholly and exclusively expended for the purposes of the trade, profession or vocation concerned (if there is only one).

(8) The expenses shall be apportioned on such basis as is reasonable between the trades, professions or vocations concerned (if there is more than one) and the expenses so apportioned to a particular trade, profession or vocation shall be treated for the purposes of section 130(*a*) of the Taxes Act as having been wholly and exclusively expended for the purposes of that trade, profession or vocation.

(9) In subsection (6) above "child" includes a stepchild, an adopted child and an illegitimate child but does not include a person who is aged 18 or over at the beginning of the outward journey.

(10) Nothing in this section shall permit the same sum to be deducted for more than one trade, profession or vocation in respect of expenses in computing profits or gains.

(11) This section applies to expenses incurred after 5th April 1984 and all such adjustments (whether by repayment of tax or otherwise) shall be made as are appropriate to give effect to this section.

General Note

This section relaxes the rules relating to the deduction of expenditure by an individual carrying on a trade profession or vocation wholly outside the United Kingdom. The rules are now similar to those applicable to an employee working abroad. The cost of travelling from and to any place in the United Kingdom is deductible as well as the cost of board and lodging provided that the expenditure is incurred wholly and exclusively for the purposes of the trade, profession or vocation. If the individual is absent continuously for 60 days or more for the purpose of carrying on the trade, profession or vocation then the expenses of two visits to or by his family will be deductible.

In a case where the individual carries on more than one trade or profession or vocation then it will be necessary to have an apportionment (subsection (4)).

These rules apply from April 5, 1984.

Travel between trades etc.

36.—(1) Where a taxpayer, within the meaning of section 35 above, travels between a place where he carries on a trade, profession or vocation in the case of which that section applies and a place outside the United Kingdom where he carries on another trade, profession or vocation (whether or not one in the case of which that section applies) expenses of the taxpayer on such travel shall, subject to subsections (3) to (5) below, be treated for the purposes of section 130(*a*) of the Taxes Act as having been wholly and exclusively expended for the purposes of the trade, profession or vocation mentioned in subsection (2) below.

(2) The trade, profession or vocation is—

(*a*) the one carried on at the place of the taxpayer's destination, or

(*b*) if that trade, profession or vocation is not one in the case of which section 33 above applies, the one carried on at the place of his departure.

(3) This section does not apply unless the journey was made—

(*a*) after performing functions of the trade, profession or vocation carried on at the place of departure, and

(*b*) for the purpose of performing functions of the trade, profession or vocation carried on at the place of destination.

(4) This section does not apply unless the taxpayer's absence from the United Kingdom is occasioned wholly and exclusively for the purpose of performing the functions of both the trades, professions or vocations concerned or of performing those functions and the functions of any other trade, profession or vocation.

(5) Where this section applies and more than one trade, profession or vocation in the case of which section 35 above applies is carried on at the place of the taxpayer's destination or (in a case falling within subsection (2)(*b*) above) at the place of his departure, the expenses shall be apportioned on such basis as is reasonable between those trades, professions or vocations, and the expenses so apportioned to a particular trade, profession or vocation shall be treated for the purposes of section 130(*a*) of the Taxes Act as having been wholly and exclusively expended for the purposes of that trade, profession or vocation.

(6) Nothing in this section shall permit the same sum to be deducted for more than one trade, profession or vocation in respect of expenses in computing profits or gains.

(7) This section applies to expenses incurred after 5th April 1984 and all such adjustments (whether by repayment of tax or otherwise) shall be made as are appropriate to give effect to this section.

General Note

The costs of travelling between two places of work abroad at which different trades are carried on will be a deductible expense if:

(i) the work carried on at the place of departure is in pursuance of a trade or profession carried on wholly abroad

(ii) the individual performed functions of the business at both the place of departure and the place of arrival

(iii) the individual's absence from the U.K. was occasioned wholly and exclusively for the purpose of performing those functions and those of any other trade or profession.

It is not necessary that the trade or profession concerned with the place of arrival should be one which is carried on wholly abroad. If it is not then the expenses of travelling to that place will be deductible from the profits of the trade or profession concerned with the place of departure. If it is then the expenses will be deductible from the expenses of that trade or profession.

If necessary there is provision for apportionment (subsection (5)).

These rules apply to any expenditure incurred after April 5, 1984.

Travelling expenses of employees not domiciled in UK

37.—(1) Subject to subsection (2) below, this section applies in the case of an office or employment in respect of which a person (the employee) who is not domiciled in the United Kingdom is in receipt of emoluments for duties performed in the United Kingdom.

(2) This section does not apply unless subsection (3) below is satisfied in respect of a date on which the employee arrives in the United Kingdom to perform duties of the office or employment; and where subsection (3) is so satisfied, this section applies only for a period of five years beginning with that date.

(3) This subsection is satisfied in respect of a date if the employee—

(*a*) was not resident in the United Kingdom in either of the two years of assessment immediately preceding the year of assessment in which the date falls, or

(*b*) was not in the United Kingdom for any purpose at any time during the period of two years ending with the day immediately preceding the date.

(4) Where subsection (3) above is satisfied (by virtue of paragraph (*a*) of that subsection) in respect of more than one date in any year of assessment, only the first of those dates is relevant for the purposes of this section.

(5) Subsection (7) below applies to any journey by the employee—

(*a*) from his usual place of abode to any place in the United Kingdom in order to perform any duties of the office or employment there, or

(*b*) to his usual place of abode from any place in the United Kingdom after performing such duties there.

(6) Where the employee is in the United Kingdom for a continuous period of 60 days or more for the purpose of performing the duties of one or more offices or employments in the case of which this section applies, subsection (7) below applies to any journey by his spouse, or any child of his, between his usual place of abode and the place of performance of any of those duties in the United Kingdom, if the journey—

(*a*) is made to accompany him at the beginning of that period or to visit him during it, or (*b*) is a return journey following a journey falling within paragraph (*a*) above;

but subsection (7) as it applies by virtue of this subsection does not extend to more than two journeys to the United Kingdom and two return journeys by the same person in any year of assessment.

(7) Subject to subsection (8) below, where—

(*a*) travel facilities are provided for any journey to which this subsection applies and the cost of them is borne by or on behalf of a person who is an employer in respect of any office or employment in the case of which this section applies, or

(*b*) expenses are incurred out of the emoluments of any office or employment in the case of which this section applies on such a journey and those expenses are reimbursed by or on behalf of the employer,

there shall be allowed, in charging tax under Case I or II of Schedule E on the emoluments from the office or employment concerned, a deduction of an amount equal to so much of that cost or, as the case may be, those expenses as falls to be included in those emoluments.

(8) If a journey is partly for a purpose mentioned in subsection (5) or (6) above and partly for another purpose, only so much of the cost or expenses referred to in subsection (7) above as is properly attributable to the former purpose shall be taken into account in calculating any deduction made under subsection (7) as it applies by virtue of subsection (5) or (as the case may be) (6).

(9) For the purposes of this section a person's usual place of abode is the country (outside the United Kingdom) in which he normally lives.

(10) In subsection (6) above "child" includes a stepchild, an adopted child and an illegitimate child but does not include a person who is aged 18 or over at the beginning of the journey to the United Kingdom.

(11) References in the Income Tax Acts to section 189 of the Taxes Act and to deductions allowable under Chapter I of Part VIII of that Act shall be construed as including a reference to subsection (7) above and to deductions allowable under it.

(12) Where, apart from this subsection, a deduction in respect of any cost or expenses is allowable under a provision of this section and a deduction in respect of the same cost or expenses is also allowable under another provision of this section or of any other enactment, a deduction in respect of the cost or expenses may be made under either, but not both, of those provisions.

General Note

This provision enacts extra statutory concession A23. It allows to employees working in the U.K. who are not domiciled here similar reliefs to those given to U.K. residents working abroad.

To qualify the individual must satisfy two conditions as well as not being domiciled in the U.K. These are:

(i) the individual must not have been resident in the U.K. in either of the two years of assessment preceding the year of assessment in which the individual arrived in this country; and

(ii) was not in the U.K. for any purpose during the two years preceding the date of arrival.

In such circumstances the individual will be entitled to relief in respect of the costs of journeys to and from the individual's usual place of abode and if present in the U.K. for a continuous period of 60 days for the purpose of carrying out his or her duties also in respect of the costs of journeys by the individual's spouse or children limited to two journeys each way.

The relief is limited to a period of five years from the date of arrival in the U.K. (subsection (2)).

Section 37: commencement

38.—(1) Section 37 above shall have effect in accordance with subsections (2) to (4) below.

(2) Where the office or employment is under or with any person, body of persons or partnership resident in the United Kingdom, section 37 shall have effect for the year 1984–85 and subsequent years of assessment.

(3) In any other case, section 37 shall have effect for the year 1984–85 and subsequent years of assessment except that subsections (2) to (4) shall have effect only for the year 1986–87 and subsequent years of assessment.

(4) Where by virtue of subsection (3) above any provision of section 37 applies in the case of an employee at any time during the year 1984–85 or 1985–86, that section shall apply in his case for the years 1986–87 to 1990–91 as if the following were substituted for subsections (2) to (4)—

"(2) This section does not apply after 5th April 1991."

(5) All such adjustments (whether by repayment of tax or otherwise) shall be made as are appropriate to give effect to section 37 and this section.

General Note

In the case of an employee within section 37 the rules will apply for the year 1984–85 onwards if the employer is a U.K. resident.

If the employer is not a U.K. resident then although the rules apply from 1984–85 onwards the conditions in subsection (2) to (4) apply only for 1986–87 onwards. This means that the five year limitation is extended in such cases to April 5, 1991 for those employees within the rules in either or both 1984–85 and 1985–86.

Miscellaneous

Personal equity plans

39. Schedule 8 to this Act (which enables the Treasury to make regulations about personal equity plans) shall have effect.

General Note

Schedule 8 empowers the Treasury to make regulations to introduce the new Personal Equity Plan. Individuals will be entitled to invest up to £2,400 in such plans by making payments to authorised managers. These funds will be available to be invested in authorised equities. Provided that shares are held for a minimum period of between one and two years then there will be no tax on any capital gains or reinvested dividend income.

Business expansion scheme

40.—(1) Schedule 5 to the Finance Act 1983 (relief for investment in corporate trades) shall have effect subject to the amendments made by Part I of Schedule 9 to this Act.

(2) In section 26 of the Finance Act 1983 (which, amongst other things, provides for Schedule 5 to that Act to have effect only in relation to shares issued in the year of assessment 1983–84 or in any of the next three years of assessment), for the words "of the next three years" there shall be substituted the words "later year".

(3) The consequential amendments in Part II of Schedule 9 to this Act shall have effect.

General Note

Section 26 F.A. 1983 provided for relief to be given in respect of the issue of shares under the Business Expansion Scheme for 1983–84 and the next three years of assessment. The time limit has now been lifted and the relief will continue unless and until it is withdrawn.

Schedule 9, Part I contains a number of amendments to the relief.

Part II provides for appeals concerning the value of land or interests in land to be heard by the Lands Tribunal.

Enterprise allowance

41.—(1) This section applies to—

(*a*) payments known as enterprise allowance and made by the Manpower Services Commission in pursuance of arrangements under section 2(2)(*d*) of the Employment and Training Act 1973, and

(*b*) corresponding payments made in Northern Ireland by the Department of Economic Development.

(2) Any such payment which would (apart from this section) be charged to tax under Case I or Case II of Schedule D shall be charged to tax under Case VI of that Schedule.

(3) Nothing in subsection (2) above shall prevent such a payment—

(*a*) being treated for the purposes of section 226(9)(*c*) of the Taxes Act (retirement annuities) or section 530(1)(*c*) of that Act (earned income) as immediately derived from the carrying on or exercise of a trade, profession or vocation, or

(*b*) being treated for the purposes of paragraph 8 of Schedule 16 to the Finance Act 1972 (close companies) as trading income.

(4) In consequence of subsection (2) above, the reference in section 9(1) of the Social Security Act 1975 and in section 9(1) of the Social Security (Northern Ireland) Act 1975 (Class 4 contributions) to profits or gains chargeable to income tax under Case I or Case II of Schedule D shall be taken to include a reference to profits or gains consisting of a payment of enterprise allowance chargeable to income tax under Case VI of Schedule D.

(5) This section applies to—

(*a*) any payment made on or after 18th March 1986, and

(*a*) any payment made before that day as part of a distinct series of payments made to the same person, provided one or more of the payments is made on or after that day.

(6) All such adjustments (whether by assessment to tax, repayment of tax or otherwise) shall be made as are appropriate to give effect to this section.

General Note

This section relates to the enterprise allowance (£40 per week) paid to persons for a year who have left the unemployment register to set up in business. It has been taxed under Schedule D Case I as a trade receipt and so is the basis of the individual's liability to income tax for the first three years of the trade due to the opening year rules. This is now changed by taxing the payments as a receipt taxable under Schedule D Case VI. This will also affect the individual's liability to pay Class 4 contributions in that the payments will only be taken into account once. Subsection (4) provides that such payments chargeable under Schedule D Case VI will be subject to the Class 4 levy.

Subsection (3) provides that the payments will form part of the individuals income for the purposes of retirement annuity relief and also part of the individuals earned income. In addition if received by a close company the payments will be part of that company's relevant income for the purposes of determining the amount of income available for apportionment.

Company reconstructions: restriction of relief

42.—(1) Schedule 10 to this Act (which amends sections 252 and 253 of the Taxes Act) shall have effect.

(2) Subject to subsection (3) below, the amendments made by that Schedule have effect where a company ceases to carry on a trade, or part of a trade, after 18th March 1986.

(3) Where section 252(6) applies (successive company reconstructions) and the later event within the meaning of that subsection falls after 18th March 1986 but the earlier event falls on or before that date, those

amendments do not affect the operation of any provision of section 252 or 253 in relation to the earlier event.

GENERAL NOTE

Schedule 10 restricts the loss relief available when a trade is transferred from one company to another in cases where the transferor company is insolvent and the transferee company fails to take over the liabilities of the transferor company.

The provisions of the Schedule apply to the cessation of a trade or part of a trade after March 18, 1986 save that if there have been successive cessations then those occuring on or before that date will be unaffected by the provisions.

Loans to participators

43.—(1) In section 286 of the Taxes Act (loans to participators etc.) in subsection (4) (date when assessed tax is due) after the word "Tax" there shall be inserted "shall be assessable by virtue of this section whether or not the whole or any part of the loan or advance in question has been repaid at the time of the assessment and tax".

(2) In subsection (5) of that section (discharge or repayment of tax on repayment of loan or advance) for the words from the beginning to "loan", in the second place where it occurs, there shall be substituted "Where a close company makes a loan or advance which gives rise to a charge to tax on the company under subsection (1) above and the loan".

(3) The amendments made by this section have effect in relation to any loan or advance made after 18th March 1986 and also in any case where there is a repayment after that date of the whole or any part of a loan or advance made on or before that date.

(4) All such adjustments shall be made, whether by the making of assessments or otherwise, as are required in consequence of the preceding provisions of this section.

(5) This section shall be construed as one with section 286 of the Taxes Act.

GENERAL NOTE

Under section 286 I.C.T.A. 1970 a loan to a participator from a close company will be chargeable to advance corporation tax as if it were a distribution to that participator. Prior to the enactment of this section it has been uncertain what was to happen if the loan was repaid before the assessment was made. If repaid after the assessment relief from the tax is given by discharge or repayment (s.286(5)). With loans repaid before the assessment it was uncertain whether the assessment could then be made and if it was whether it was then possible to obtain relief.

These uncertainties have been removed so that—

(i) notwithstanding the repayment of the loan an assessment is still made in respect of the loan; and

(ii) relief by way of discharge or repayment contained in subsection (5) of section 286 will be available.

This section applies to loans made after March 18, 1986 and repayments after that date no matter when the loan was made.

Entertainers and sportsmen

44. Schedule 11 to this Act (which relates to non-resident entertainers and sportsmen) shall have effect.

GENERAL NOTE

See the Commentary to Schedule 11.

Payments on retirement or removal from office or employment etc.

45.—(1) Schedule 8 to the Taxes Act (relief as respects tax on payments on retirement etc.) shall have effect subject to the following provisions of this section, and in those provisions that Schedule is referred to as "Schedule 8".

(2) On and after 4th June 1986, paragraph 10 of Schedule 8 (aggregation of two or more payments in respect of the same office etc.) shall have effect with the substitution for the words "paragraph 7" of the words "paragraphs 7 and 7A".

(3) Paragraph 12 of Schedule 8 (which provides that any reference in the Schedule to a payment in respect of which tax is chargeable under section 187 of the Taxes Act is a reference to so much of that payment as is chargeable to tax after deduction of relief) shall not apply to any payment which, under subsection (4) of that section, is treated as income received on or after 4th June 1986 and, accordingly, paragraphs 7 and 7A of Schedule 8 shall apply to every such payment without making any deduction therefrom on account of relief under section 188(3) of that Act.

(4) In any case where—

(*a*) tax is chargeable under section 187 of the Taxes Act in respect of two or more payments to or in respect of the same person (whether or not in respect of the same office or employment) and is so chargeable for the same chargeable period, and

(*b*) under subsection (4) of that section at least one of those payments is treated as income received before 4th June 1986 and at least one of them is treated as income received on or after that date,

then, in the application of paragraphs 7 and 7A of Schedule 8 (in accordance with paragraph 10 or paragraph 11 thereof) in relation to any of those payments which is so treated as income received on or after that date, subsection (3) above shall have effect as if any reference therein to 4th June 1986 were a reference to the first day of the chargeable period referred to in paragraph (*a*) above.

General Note

Schedule 8 to the I.C.T.A. 1970 (as amended by s.52 F.A. 1981 and s.43 F.A. 1982) contains rules which provide relief for lump sums paid on retirement or removal from office or employment when exceeding £25,000.

The intention was that the combined effect of paragraphs 7 and 7A of Schedule 8 would be with effect from April 6, 1982 that in respect of such sums

first £25,000	exempt from tax
next £25,000	tax reduced by one half
next £25,000	tax reduced by one quarter
remainder	taxable in full.

However, the Inland Revenue now accepts that the relief operates in the following manner because of paragraph 10

first £25,000	exempt from tax
next £50,000	tax reduced by one half
next £25,000	tax reduced by one quarter
remainder	taxable in full.

The reason for this is that paragraph 12 causes so much of a lump sum payment as is relieved from tax by reason of s.188(3), I.C.T.A. 1970 to be disregarded.

As such deduction of the first £25,000 for the purposes of paragraphs 7 and 7A of Schedule 8 shall be made in respect of any payment treated as income received on or after June 4, 1986. Section 187(4), I.C.T.A. 1970 governs when a payment is so treated—

(i) in the case of payment in commutation of periodic payments it is the date when the commutation is effected; and

(ii) in any other case it is the date of the termination or change in respect of which the payment is made.

Any such payments treated as income received before June 4, 1986 will receive the more favourable treatment and anyone who has paid tax on the basis of the original intention will be able to recover the amount of tax overpaid.

Subsection (2) amends paragraph 10 of Schedule 8 which is concerned with the aggregation of two or more lump sums. As drafted prior to this amendment the lump sums were treated as one payment for the purposes of applying the relief of one half the tax given by paragraph

7 but as separate payments for the purposes of the one quarter relief from tax given by paragraph 7A. From June 4, 1986 (inclusive of that day) the payments will be aggregated for the purposes of the one quarter relief as well.

Pension scheme surpluses

46. Schedule 12 to this Act (which relates to surplus funds in certain pension schemes) shall have effect.

General Note

Schedule 12 sets out provisions dealing with the taxation of surpluses paid out of pension funds.

Building societies

47.—(1) In section 343 of the Taxes Act (building societies), subsection (1A) (which was inserted by the Finance Act 1985 and enables the Board to make regulations requiring societies to account for amounts representing income tax on certain sums) shall have effect and be deemed always to have had effect with the insertion after the words "in accordance with the regulations" of the words "(including sums paid or credited before the beginning of the year but not previously brought into account under subsection (1) above or this subsection)"

(2) In subsection (2) of that section (treatment of building society payments for purposes of corporation tax)—

(*a*) in paragraph (*a*), for the words "the amount" there shall be substituted "any amount"; and

(*b*) in paragraph (*b*), after the words "any such dividends or interest" there shall be inserted "in respect of which the society is required to account for and pay an amount in accordance with the regulations".

(3) At the end of subsection (7) of that section (meaning of "dividend") there shall be added the words "but any sum which is paid by a building society by way of dividend and in respect of which the society is not required to account for and pay an amount in accordance with the regulations shall be treated for the purposes of Schedule D as paid by way of interest".

(4) In consequence of the amendments of the said section 343 effected by section 40 of the Finance Act 1985 (regulations requiring societies to account for amounts representing income tax on certain sums),—

(*a*) in subsection (5) of section 16 of the Finance Act 1973 (amounts paid or credited to trustees of certain trusts) for the word "amounts" there shall be substituted "sums" and for the words from "with which" to "that year" there shall be substituted "being sums in respect of which the society is required to account for and pay an amount in accordance with regulations under section 343(1A) of the Taxes Act"; and

(*b*) in subsection (1) of section 6 of the Finance Act 1975 (amounts paid or credited to exempt pension funds) for the words from "among the sums" to "the Taxes Act" there shall be substituted "sums in respect of which a building society is required to account for and pay an amount in accordance with regulations under subsection (1A) of section 343 of the Taxes Act".

(5) Where a building society investment which is a source of income of any person (the "lender") is not a relevant investment but at any time after 6th April 1986 becomes such an investment, section 121 of the Taxes Act (special rules where source of income ceases) shall apply as if the investment were a source of income which the lender ceased to possess immediately before that time.

(6) Where a building society investment which is a source of income of any person ceases at any time after 6th April 1986 to be a relevant investment, section 120(3) of the Taxes Act shall apply as if the investment were a new source of income acquired by him immediately after that time.

(7) Where a building society investment which was a source of income of any person immediately before 6th April 1986 was not on that date a relevant investment, section 120(3) of the Taxes Act shall apply as if the investment were a new source of income acquired by him on that date.

(8) In subsections (5) to (7) above "building society investment" does not include a quoted Eurobond (as defined in section 35(1) of the Finance Act 1984) but, subject to that, means any shares in, deposit with or loan to a building society (within the meaning of section 343 of the Taxes Act); and for the purposes of those subsections a building society investment is a "relevant investment" if dividends or interest payable in respect of it are sums in respect of which the society is required to account for and pay an amount in accordance with regulations under subsection (1A) of that section.

(9) Subsections (2) to (4) above have effect for the year 1986–87 and subsequent years of assessment.

General Note

This section makes a number of minor amendments to s.343 I.C.T.A. 1970 and other statutory provisions consequent upon the change contained in s.40 F.A. 1985 enabling building societies to pay dividends gross in certain circumstances.

Foreign dividends in recognised clearing system

48.—(1) Paragraph 1 of Schedule C (public revenue dividends payable in UK) shall not apply, in the case of dividends payable out of any public revenue other than the public revenue of the United Kingdom, if the securities in respect of which the dividends are payable are held in a recognised clearing system..

(2) Section 159(2) of the Taxes Act (tax under Section D on foreign dividends entrusted to person in UK for payment in UK) shall not apply if the stocks, funds, shares or securities out of or in respect of which the foreign dividends are payable are held in a recognised clearing system.

(3) In this section "recognised clearing system" means any system for the time being designated as a recognised clearing system under section 35 of the Finance Act 1984 (Eurobonds).

(4) In this section "foreign dividends" has the same meaning as in section 159 of the Taxes Act.

(5) Subsection (1) above has effect in relation to dividends paid after the passing of this Act, and subsection (2) above has effect in relation to foreign dividends paid after the passing of this Act.

General Note

Prior to the enactment of this section an agent acting in the U.K. on the collection or payment of foreign dividends has been required to deduct basic rate tax. This has meant that U.K. agents have been at a considerable disadvantage with respect to work involving clearing systems such as Euroclear in Brussels and CDEL in Luxembourg. Such systems require the amount to be paid out to be the same as the amount received.

As a result of this section such agents will no longer deduct tax on foreign dividends held in a recognised clearing system.

The same change is effected by subsection (1) in respect of dividends payable out of any public revenue other than that of the United Kingdom. Again this is subject to the proviso that the securities are held in a recognised clearing system.

The changes apply to dividends paid after the passing of the Act (July 25, 1986).

Double taxation relief: advance corporation tax

49.—(1) With respect to accounting periods beginning on or after 3rd June 1986, section 100 of the Finance Act 1972 (double taxation relief) shall be amended in accordance with this section.

(2) In subsection (6) (set-off of advance corporation tax against liability to corporation tax on income subject to foreign tax) for paragraphs (*b*) and (*c*) there shall be substituted—

"(*b*) the amount of advance corporation tax which may be set against that liability, so far as it relates to the relevant income, shall not exceed whichever is the lower of the limits specified in subsection (6A) below";

and in the words following paragraph (*c*), the words from "if the limit" to "the relevant income and" shall be omitted.

(3) After subsection (6) there shall be inserted the following subsection—

"(6A) in relation to an amount of income in respect of which the company's liability to corporation tax is taken to be reduced as mentioned in paragraph (*a*) of subsection (6) above, the limits referred to in paragraph (*b*) of that subsection are—

(*a*) the limit which would apply under section 85(2) above if that amount of income were the company's only income for the relevant accounting period; and

(*b*) the amount of corporation tax for which, after taking account of the said reduction, the company is liable in respect of that amount of income."

General Note

This section has been prompted by the decision of Walton J. in *Collard* v. *Mining and Industrial Holdings Limited*. It was held that—

(i) the company could set off any double taxation relief available against its corporation tax liability before set off was given for advance corporation tax. The effect of this is that the changes introduced by the Finance Act 1984 were unnecessary;

(ii) the limit on the amount of advance corporation tax that can be set off in the case of a company with both U.K. and foreign income is determined by reference to the advance corporation tax which would be payable if the whole of that income were applied to the payment of dividends. This means that if the corporation tax on the foreign income is covered by the double taxation relief then the corporation tax on the U.K. income will be matched by the advance corporation tax paid. The intention had been that there should always be a minimum amount of corporation tax payable being the difference between the corporation tax rate and the basic rate of income tax.

To remove the uncertainty subsection (6A) is added to section 100 F.A. 1972 so as to limit the set off of advance corporation tax in respect of U.K. income so that it cannot reduce the minimum mainstream corporation tax payable on it. This is achieved by treating that income as the only income of the company for the purposes of calculating the limit imposed by s.85(2) F.A. 1972.

These changes only apply to accounting periods beginning on or after June 3, 1986. The position prior to this will be governed by the outcome of the appeal by the Inland Revenue from the decision of Walton J.

Offshore funds: conditions of certification

50.—(1) Part II of Schedule 19 to the Finance Act 1984 (offshore funds: modifications of conditions for certification in certain cases) shall have effect subject to the provisions of this section.

(2) In paragraph 11 (which relates to cases of offshore funds with certain wholly-owned subsidiaries) for paragraphs (*a*) and (*b*) of sub-paragraph (1) (which restrict the application of the paragraph to wholly-owned subsidiaries which deal in commodities) there shall be substituted the words "which is a company".

(3) At the beginning of sub-paragraph (2) of paragraph 11 (definition of "wholly-owned subsidiary of an offshore fund") there shall be inserted the words "Subject to sub-paragraph (2A) below".

(4) After sub-paragraph (2) of paragraph 11 there shall be inserted the following sub-paragraph—

"(2A) In the case of a company which has only one class of issued share capital, the reference in sub-paragraph (2) above to the whole of the issued share capital shall be construed as a reference to at least 95 per cent. of that share capital."

(5) In sub-paragraph (3) of paragraph 11 (the modifications applicable in relation to wholly-owned subsidiaries)—

(*a*) at the beginning of paragraph (*a*) there shall be inserted the words "that percentage of"; and

(*b*) in paragraph (*a*) after the word "subsidiary" there shall be inserted "which is equal to the percentage of the issued share capital of the company concerned which is owned as mentioned in sub-paragraph (2) above".

(6) After paragraph 12 there shall be inserted the following paragraph—

"*Disregard of certain investments forming less than 5 per cent. of a fund*

12A.—(1) In any case where—

(*a*) in any account period of an offshore fund, the assets of the fund include a holding of issued share capital (or any class of issued share capital) of a company, and

(*b*) that holding us such that, by virtue of section 95(3)(*c*) of this Act, the fund could not (apart from this paragraph) be certified as a distributing fund in respect of that account period,

then, if the condition in sub-paragraph (3) below is fulfilled, that holding shall be disregarded for the purposes of the said section 95(3)(*c*).

(2) In this paragraph any holding falling within sub-paragraph (1) above is referred to as an "excess holding".

(3) The condition referred to in sub-paragraph (1) above is that at no time in the account period in question does that portion of the fund which consists of—

(*a*) excess holdings, and

(*b*) interests in other off-shore funds which are not qualifying funds,

exceed 5 per cent. by value of all the assets of the fund."

(7) This section has effect with respect to periods which—

(*a*) for the purposes of Chapter VII of Part II of the Finance Act 1984 are account periods of offshore funds; and

(*b*) end after the passing of this Act.

General Note

This section relaxes the rules which have to be satisfied if an offshore fund is to qualify as a distributing fund in accordance with Schedule 19 of the Finance Act 1984. These rules have operated harshly in respect of some funds notwithstanding that those funds have been distributing the greater part of their income.

The reason for this is that the fund's investments include shares which represent more than 10 per cent. of the issued shares of the company.

As a result the rules have been relaxed in two ways.

First the fund can own 95 per cent. or more of the share capital of a subsidiary provided that the fund and the subsidiary on a consolidated basis meet the distribution requirements of Schedule 19.

Second in determining whether or not a fund satisfies the requirements of Schedule 19 any shares or interests in other funds which are not qualifying funds can be disregarded if their aggregate value does not exceed 5 per cent. of the value of the fund's assets.

Pensions paid to victims of National-Socialist persecution

51.—(1) For section 377 of the Taxes Act (under which certain annuities payable by way of compensation for National-Socialist persecution are not regarded as income for any income tax purpose) there shall be substituted the following section—

"377. Annuities and pensions payable under any special provision for victims of National-Socialist persecution which is made by the law of the Federal Republic of Germany or any part of it or of Austria shall not be regarded as income for any income tax purpose."

(2) This section has effect for the year 1986–87 and subsequent years of assessment.

General Note

This section exempts from liability to income tax any pensions payable under the laws of the Federal Republic of Germany or of Austria to victims of Nazi persecution. Certain pensions paid to such victims were already exempt under s.377 I.C.T.A. 1970.

Temporary disregard of increase in certain pensions and allowances

52.—(1) So much of any relevant pension or allowance as is attributable to any general increase taking effect in the year 1986–87 shall be left out of account for all the purposes of income tax charged for that year but not for the purpose of furnishing information relating to any person's income for that year.

(2) For the purposes of this section a pension or allowance is a relevant pension or allowance if it is payable under the Social Security Act 1975, or the Social Security (Northern Ireland) Act 1975, and (in either case) is one of the following—

(*a*) a retirement pension;
(*b*) a widow's allowance;
(*c*) a widowed mother's allowance;
(*d*) a widow's pension;
(*e*) an invalid care allowance;
(*f*) an industrial death benefit by way of widow's or widower's pension.

General Note

The updating of social security benefits is to move from November in each year to April so as to bring it into line with the commencement of the tax year. There is to be a transitional uprating with effect from July 28, 1986. This will cause administrative inconvenience as regards those persons in receipt of any of the benefits within subsection (2) and other income. Consequently any increase in the benefits and allowances within subsection (2) during 1986–87 will be exempt from tax.

Tax treatment of VAT penalties etc. and repayment supplement

53.—(1) Where, under Chapter II of Part I of the Finance Act 1985 (value added tax), a person is liable to make a payment by way of—

(*a*) penalty under any of sections 13 to 17, or
(*b*) interest under section 18, or
(*c*) surcharge under section 19,

the payment shall not be allowed as a deduction in computing any income, profits or losses for any tax purposes.

(2) A sum paid to any person by way of supplement under section 20 of the Finance Act 1985 (repayment supplement in respect of certain delayed value added tax payments) shall be disregarded for all purposes of corporation tax and income tax.

General Note

A person required to pay a penalty, interest or surcharge relating to VAT shall not be entitled to deduct such payment when computing that person's income, profits or loss.

Further any repayment supplement made in respect of delayed value added tax payments will not be taxable as a receipt.

Associated companies; oil and gas industry

54.—(1) At the end of section 19 of the Oil Taxation Act 1975 (definitions relating to the corporation tax provisions of that Act) there shall be added the following subsection—

> "(4) Without prejudice to subsection (3) above, for the purposes of this Part of this Act, two companies are also associated with one another if one has control of the other or both are under the control of the same person or persons; and in this subsection "control" shall be construed in accordance with section 302 of the Taxes Act."

(2) This section has effect in relation to any allowance or distribution made, interest paid or other thing done after 18th March 1986.

General Note

Under the terms of the Oil Taxation Act 1975 a "ring fence" has been placed round the profits arising from exploitation of North Sea oil resources in order to prevent transactions with associated companies eroding those profits.

The definition of associated company contained in section 19(3) of the Oil Taxation Act 1975 has been expanded by the amendment in this section in order to fill a possible gap in the fence.

Chapter II

Capital Allowances

New Code of allowances for capital expenditure on mineral extraction

55.—(1) The provisions of Chapter III of Part I of the Capital Allowances Act 1968 (which relate to allowances for certain capital expenditure incurred in connection with mineral extraction activities and which are in this section referred to as "the old code of allowances") shall cease to have effect on 31st March 1986 except as provided by Schedule 14 to this Act.

(2) The provisions of Parts I to IV of Schedule 13 to this Act have effect to provide for relief in respect of certain new expenditure incurred by persons carrying on a trade of mineral extraction; and the provisions of Schedule 14 to this Act have effect with respect to certain expenditure incurred before 1st April 1987 by persons carrying on such a trade.

(3) Subject to paragraph 2 of Schedule 14 to this Act, for the purposes of the old code of allowances, the following provisions of this section and Schedules 13 and 14 to this Act, as respects any company which on 31st March 1986 was carrying on a trade of mineral extraction, it shall be assumed that, unless the latest accounting period of the company which begins on or before 31st March 1986 in fact ends on that date,—

(*a*) that accounting period ends on that date; and

(*b*) a new one begins on 1st April 1986, the new accounting period to end with the end of the true accounting period.

(4) Subject to paragraph 2 of Schedule 14 to this Act, for the purposes of the provisions referred to in subsection (3) above as they apply to a person who on 31st March 1986 was within the charge to income tax in respect of the profits or gains of a trade of mineral extraction carried on by him, it shall be assumed that, unless the latest basis period of his (determined in accordance with section 72 of the Capital Allowances Act

1968) which begins on or before 31st March 1986 in fact ends on that date,—

(*a*) that basis period ends on that date; and

(*b*) a new basis period begins on 1st April 1986, the new basis period to end with the end of the true basis period.

(5) In any case where—

(*a*) new expenditure is incurred by any person on the provision of machinery or plant for the purposes of mineral exploration and access, as defined in paragraph 1 of Schedule 13 to this Act, and

(*b*) that expenditure is so incurred before the first day on which that person begins to carry on a trade of mineral extraction, and

(*c*) on that first day the machinery or plant belongs to him, and does not fall within paragraph 5(1)(*d*) of Schedule 13 to this Act.

that person shall be treated for the purposes of Chapter I of Part III of the Finance Act 1971 (the normal code applicable to machinery or plant) and section 57 of the Finance Act 1985 (short-life assets) as if he had sold the machinery or plant immediately before that first day and had on that first day incurred capital expenditure on the provision of the machinery or plant wholly and exclusively for the purposes of the trade, being expenditure equal to the expenditure incurred (or, where there has been an actual previous sale and re-acquisition, last incurred) as mentioned in paragraph (*a*) above.

(6) For the purpose of the application of Chapter I of Part III of the Finance Act 1971—

(*a*) in relation to expenditure treated by virtue of subsection (5) above as incurred on the first day on which a person begins to carry on a trade of mineral extraction, and

(*b*) in relation to expenditure actually incurred on or after that day on the provision of machinery or plant for the purposes of mineral exploration and access,

that Chapter shall have effect subject to the amendments in subsection (7) below.

(7) The amendments referred to in subsection (6) above are—

(*a*) in section 50 of the Finance Act 1971 (the interpretation provisions applicable to allowances relating to machinery or plant) in subsection (1), after the definition of "income" there shall be inserted—

" 'mineral exploration and access' and 'trade of mineral extraction' have the same meaning as in Schedule 13 to the Finance Act 1986";

(*b*) after subsection (7) of that section there shall be inserted the following subsection—

"(7A) For the purposes of this Chapter, where a person is carrying on a trade of mineral extraction, expenditure incurred by him in connection with that trade on the provision of machinery or plant for mineral exploration and access shall be taken to be incurred on the provision of the machinery or plant wholly and exclusively for the purposes of that trade";

(*c*) in section 44(5) of that Act (disposal values) at the end of sub-paragraph (ii) of paragraph (*c*) there shall be added the words "or, in the case of machinery or plant which was in use for mineral exploration and access, he abandons the machinery or plant at the site where it was in use for that purpose"; and

(*d*) in paragraph 7 of Schedule 8 to that Act (use after user not attracting capital allowances etc.) sub-paragraph (2) (which relates to machinery or plant used for mineral exploration etc.) shall be omitted.

(8) In this section—

"new expenditure" means, subject to Schedule 14 to this Act, expenditure incurred on or after 1st April 1986;

"old expenditure" means expenditure which is not new expenditure; and

"trade of mineral extraction" has the meaning assigned to it by paragraph 1 of Schedule 13 to this Act.

(9) In consequence of and in connection with the provisions of this section and Parts I to IV of Schedule 13, the amendments in Part V of that Schedule shall have effect.

General Note

The "mines, oil wells, etc." provisions of C.A.A. 1968 (ss.51–66) cease to have effect from March 31, 1986 (or, in certain cases, March 31, 1987—see para. 2 of Sched. 14). The new code is set out in Sched. 13 subject to the transitional provisions in Sched. 14. Expenditure to which the old or the new provisions apply is respectively described as "old expenditure" and "new expenditure" (see subs. (8)).

The new code relates to "mineral extraction activities" (subs. (1)) in place of the old "mines, oil wells, etc." For the meaning of "mineral extraction", see para. 1 of Sched. 13.

Subs. (3) provides for the splitting of accounting periods at March 31, 1986 (or, in certain cases, at March 31, 1987—see above) and subs. (4) contains similar provisions in relation to basis periods.

Where machinery or plant is purchased on or after April 1, 1986 (or, where appropriate, 1987) before trading commences and is still held at the date of commencement of trading, it is treated as though it had, at that date, been sold and reacquired at a cost equal to the expenditure incurred (or last incurred if there had been an actual sale and reacquisition) (subs. (5)). This applies for the purposes of F.A. 1971, Ch. I, Pt. III and F.A. 1985, s.57.

In relation to such a deemed reacquisition and to expenditure incurred after trading commences on machinery or plant provided for the purposes of "mineral exploration and access" (as defined in Sched. 13, para. 1(1)), the normal machinery and plant code in F.A. 1971 applies, as amended by subs. (7) (subs. (6)). Those amendments are as follows:

(*a*) the Sched. 13 definitions of "mineral exploration and access" and of "trade of mineral extraction" are inserted into F.A. 1971, s.50;

(*b*) a new subs. 50(7A) is inserted into F.A. 1971 by which expenditure on machinery or plant for the purposes of mineral exploration and access is deemed to be incurred wholly and exclusively for a trade of mineral extraction which the person incurring it is carrying on;

(*c*) the "disposal values" provisions of F.A. 1971, s.44(5) apply on the abandonment at the site of machinery or plant used for mineral exploration and access; and

(*d*) para. 7(2) of Sched. 8 to F.A. 1971 (use after user not attracting capital allowances) does not apply.

Agricultural land and buildings

56.—(1) With respect to capital expenditure incurred on or after 1st April 1986, other than expenditure under existing contracts, the provisions of Schedule 15 to this Act shall have effect in place of section 68 of the Capital Allowances Act 1968 (allowances for capital expenditure on construction of agricultural buildings and works etc.).

(2) In subsection (1) above "expenditure under existing contracts" means expenditure which—

(*a*) consists of the payment of sums under a contract entered into on or before 13th March 1984 by the person incurring the expenditure; and

(*b*) is incurred before 1st April 1987.

(3) The preceding provisions of this section and Schedule 15 to this Act shall be construed as if they were included in Part I of the Capital Allowances Act 1968.

(4) In section 69 of the Capital Allowances Act 1968—

(*a*) after the words "section 68 above" there shall be inserted "and Schedule 15 to the Finance Act 1986"; and

(*b*) at the end of the definition of "agricultural land" after the word "husbandry" there shall be inserted "(as defined below)"; and

(*c*) at the end of the section there shall be added—

" 'husbandry' includes any method of intensive rearing of livestock or fish on a commercial basis for the production of food for human consumption."

(5) Where an allowance is or has been made under Schedule 15 to this Act in respect of any capital expenditure, none of that expenditure shall be taken into account in determining qualifying expenditure for the purpose of any allowance or charge under section 44 of the Finance Act 1971 (machinery and plant); and where such an allowance or charge is or has been made by reference to an amount of qualifying expenditure which took account of a particular amount of capital expenditure, that capital expenditure shall be left out of account for the purposes of Schedule 15 of this Act.

(6) Any reference to Chapter V of Part I of the Capital Allowances Act 1968 in—

(*a*) section 14 of that Act (exclusion of double allowances), and

(*b*) section 85 of that Act (allowances in respect of contributions to capital expenditure), and

(*c*) paragraph 11 of Schedule 12 to the Finance Act 1982 (capital allowances for dwelling-houses let on assured tenancies),

includes a reference to Schedule 14 to this Act; and the reference to section 68 of the said Act of 1968 in section 75 thereof (writing-down allowances during a period of specified length) includes a reference to that Schedule.

(7) In the following provisions—

(*a*) sections 155(8), 180(7), 227(4), 252(2) and 352(4) of the Taxes Act,

(*b*) the definition of "capital allowance" in section 526(5) of the Taxes Act,

(*c*) section 31(2) of the Capital Gains Tax Act 1979, and

(*d*) the definition of "capital allowance" in subsection (4) of section 34 of the said Act of 1979,

any reference to the Capital Allowances Act 1968 or to Part I thereof includes a reference to Schedule 15 to this Act.

General Note

This section introduces a new system of capital allowances on agricultural and forestry buildings and works. It replaces the provisions of C.A.A. 1968, s.68 by those of Sched. 15 to this Act in relation to expenditure incurred on or after April 1, 1986, with transitional provisions for expenditure incurred up to March 31, 1987, under pre-March 14, 1984, contracts (subss. (1), (2)).

Subs. (3) incorporates these provisions into C.A.A. 1968.

Subs. (4), *inter alia*, gives statutory authority to the extra-statutory concession by which the intensive rearing of livestock and fish on a commercial basis for human consumption was treated as husbandry.

Under subs. (5), allowances under this section and under F.A. 1971, s.44 are made mutually exclusive.

Of particular importance in the changes, provision is now made for a balancing charge or allowance on the disposal, demolition or destruction of the asset (see notes to Sched. 15).

Sched. 23 to this Act repeals F.A. 1985, s.62 and C.A.A. 1968, s.68. Since subs. (6) of the latter section excluded the "basis period" definition of C.A.A. 1968, s.72, that definition now applies.

New expenditure on leased assets etc.

57.—(1) The provisions of subsections (4) to (8) below and Schedule 16 to this Act (which relate to allowances in respect of expenditure on the provision of machinery or plant for leasing and on the provision of certain vehicles) shall have effect with respect to new expenditure, as defined in subsections (2) and (3) below.

(2) In this section and Schedule 16 to this Act, new expenditure means expenditure incurred on or after 1st April 1986, other than—

(*a*) expenditure to which, by virtue of sub-paragraph (2) of paragraph 2 of Schedule 12 to the Finance Act 1984 (expenditure incurred under contracts entered into on or before 13th March 1984), sub-paragraph (1) of that paragraph (progressive withdrawal of first-year allowances) does not apply; and

(*b*) expenditure to which, by virtue of paragraph 4 of that Schedule (transitional relief for regional projects) Part I of that Schedule does not apply; and

(*c*) expenditure falling within paragraph 7 of Schedule 12 to the Finance Act 1980 (television sets, etc); and

(*d*) expenditure excluded by subsection (3) below;

and any expenditure which, by virtue of paragraph 6 of Schedule 12 to the Finance Act 1984 (spreading of expenditure under certain contracts) is deemed for the purposes of Chapter I of Part III of the Finance Act 1971 to be incurred on 1st April 1986 shall also be deemed to be incurred on that date for the purposes of this section and Schedule 16 to this Act.

(3) In any case where–

(*a*) before 1st April 1986 a person (in this subsection referred to as "the original lessor") incurred expenditure on the provision of machinery or plant for leasing, and

(*b*) on or after that date the machinery or plant ceases to belong to the original lessor on being acquired by an associate or successor of his, and

(*c*) by virtue of subsection (9) of section 64 of the Finance Act 1980 (connected persons etc.), the machinery or plant is treated for the purposes of subsection (8) of that section (the requisite period) as continuing to belong to the original lessor so long as it belongs to his associate or successor,

expenditure incurred by his associate or successor on the acquisition of the machinery or plant is excluded from new expenditure; and in this subsection "associate or successor" means a person who, in relation to the original lessor, is of a description specified in paragraph (*a*) or paragraph (*b*) of the said subsection (9).

(4) Subject to subsection (7) below, the separate pooling provisions which are contained in sections 64 to 68 of the Finance Act 1980 and which are applicable to expenditure on machinery or plant which is not used for a qualifying purpose shall not apply to new expenditure but, for the purpose of maintaining a separate pool for expenditure falling within section 70 of the Finance Act 1982 (assets leased outside the United Kingdom) and for excluding from that section certain ships, aircraft and transport containers,—

(*a*) sections 64 to 68 of the Finance Act 1980 shall have effect as amended by Part I of Schedule 16 to this Act;

(*b*) section 70 of, and Schedule 11 to, the Finance Act 1982 shall have effect as amended by Part II of that Schedule; and

(*c*) Part III of that Schedule shall have effect for supplementing the enactments amended by Parts I and II of that Schedule.

(5) In consequence of the preceding provisions of this section, in paragraph 8A of Schedule 8 to the Finance Act 1971 (writing-down allowances for ships) sub-paragraph (9) shall be omitted.

(6) In consequence of the preceding provisions of this section, but subject to subsection (7) below, in subsection (6)(*b*) of section 57 of the Finance Act 1985 (short-life assets: transfer of expenditure on asset beginning to be used otherwise than for a qualifying purpose)—

(*a*) the words "(as it has effect in accordance with section 65 of the Finance Act 1980)" shall be omitted; and

(*b*) for the words from "the separate trade" onwards there shall be substituted "his actual trade".

(7) Notwithstanding anything in the preceding provisions of this section, section 44 of the Finance Act 1971 shall continue to apply separately with respect to expenditure on the provision of any vehicle falling within section 69 of the Finance Act 1980 (writing-down allowances for cars) and, accordingly,—

(*a*) except where such a vehicle is used for the purpose of being leased to such a person as is referred to in paragraphs (*a*) and (*b*) of subsection (1) of section 70 of the Finance Act 1982 and the leasing is not short-term leasing, within the meaning of that section, nothing in Parts I to III of Schedule 16 to this Act applies with respect to any such expenditure; and

(*b*) the amendments made by subsection (6) above do not apply where the asset in question is a vehicle falling within section 69 of the Finance Act 1980.

(8) In consequence of the withdrawal of first-year allowances by section 58 of, and Schedule 12 to, the Finance Act 1984, section 69 of the Finance Act 1980 shall be amended, with respect to new expenditure, in accordance with Part IV of Schedule 16 to this Act.

(9) In section 64 of the Finance Act 1980, as it has effect where—

(*a*) the expenditure on the provision of machinery or plant referred to in subsection (1) of that section is not new expenditure, but

(*b*) the notional purchase of the machinery or plant by the lessee which is referred to in subsection (2)(*a*) of that section would at any time mean the incurring of new expenditure,

after the words "could have been made to the lessee" there shall be inserted "(disregarding for this purpose paragraph 2 of Schedule 12 to the Finance Act 1984)".

(10) In section 56 of the Finance Act 1985 (time when capital expenditure is incurred) at the end of subsection (1) there shall be added "and

(*e*) section 57 of the Finance Act 1986".

General Note

F.A. 1980, ss.64–68, introduced a separate code of capital allowances (including separate pooling) for leased assets not used for a "qualifying purpose". This section makes the amendments necessitated by the abolition of first year allowances. The section relates to "new expenditure" *i.e.*, with the exceptions set out in subss. (2) and (3), expenditure incurred on or after April 1, 1986. The exceptions in subs. (2) are as follows:

(*a*) expenditure under a pre-14 March 1984 contract to which the withdrawal of first-year allowances does not apply;

(*b*) expenditure to which Pt. I of Sched. 12 to F.A. 1984 does not apply; and

(*c*) expenditure on television sets etc.

Subs. (3) excludes certain expenditure where transactions have occurred between persons defined in F.A. 1980, s.64(9)(*a*), (*b*).

Expenditure which, under the "expenditure spreading" provisions of F.A. 1984, Sched. 6, para 12, is deemed to be incurred on 1 April 1986 is deemed to be incurred on that date for the purposes of this section (subs. (2)).

The effect of this section is to end the separate pooling arrangements for machinery and plant leased for a non-qualifying purpose but this does not apply to cars falling within the provisions of F.A. 1980, s.69 (subs. (7)).

Under subs. (4) (subject to certain amendments) assets leased outside the United Kingdom, except for certain ships, aircraft and transport containers, separate pooling continues.

Consequential amendments are made to F.A. 1971, Sched. 8, para. 8A (writing-down allowances for ships) and F.A. 1985, s.57 (short life assets) by subss. (5)–(7). Other consequential amendments are made by subss. (8)–(10).

Chapter III

Capital Gains

Gifts into dual resident trusts

58.—(1) This section applies where there is or has been a disposal of an asset to the trustees of a settlement in such circumstances that, on a claim for relief, section 79 of the Finance Act 1980 (general relief for gifts) applies, or would but for this section apply, so as to reduce the amounts of the chargeable gain and the consideration referred to in subsection (1) of that section.

(2) In this section—

(*a*) "a relevant disposal" means such a disposal as is referred to in subsection (1) above; and

(*b*) "the 1980 provision" means section 79 of the Finance Act 1980.

(3) Relief under the 1980 provision shall not be available on a relevant disposal occurring on or after 18th March 1986 if—

(*a*) at the material time the trustees to whom the disposal is made fall to be treated, under section 52 of the Capital Gains Tax Act 1979, as resident and ordinarily resident in the United Kingdom, although the general administration of the trust is ordinarily carried on outside the United Kingdom; and

(*b*) on a notional disposal of the asset concerned occurring immediately after the material time, the trustees would be regarded for the purposes of any double taxation relief arrangements—

(i) as resident in a territory outside the United Kingdom; and

(ii) as not liable in the United Kingdom to tax on a gain arising on that disposal.

(4) In subsection (3) above—

(*a*) "the material time" means the time of the relevant disposal;

(*b*) a "notional disposal" means a disposal by the trustees of the asset which was the subject of the relevant disposal; and

(*c*) "double taxation relief arrangements" means arrangements having effect by virtue of section 497 of the Taxes Act (as extended to capital gains tax by section 10 of the Capital Gains Tax Act 1979).

(5) In any case where—

(*a*) relief under the 1980 provision has been allowed on a claim relating to a relevant disposal, (whether occurring before, on or after 18th March 1986), and

(*b*) at a time subsequent to that relevant disposal, but not earlier than 18th March 1986, the circumstances become such that paragraphs (*a*) and (*b*) of subsection (3) above would apply if that time were the material time referred to in that subsection, and

(*c*) section 79 of the Finance Act 1981 (which provides for the recovery of relief under the 1980 provision in the event of the emigration of the donee) has not had effect in relation to the relevant disposal before that time and would not (apart from this subsection) have effect at that time, section 79 of the Finance Act 1981 shall have effect as if, at that time, the trustees had become neither resident nor ordinarily resident in the United Kingdom.

General Note

This section is designed to prevent the avoidance of capital gains tax by use of trusts which while resident in the United Kingdom generally for C.G.T. purposes (because of a majority of trustees being resident here) are treated as not resident here for the purpose of a double tax treaty (generally because the general administration of the trust is carried on abroad). Such a trust would not be subject to C.G.T. albeit a transfer of assets to it would ordinarily qualify for the holdover relief conferred by F.A. 1980, s.79. Subsection (3) now precludes the holdover relief from being available where assets are transferred to such a trust. In addition subsection (5) provides for F.A. 1981, s.79 to apply to claw back holdover relief previously obtained where a trust is converted after 18th March 1986 from one resident only in the U.K. to a dual resident trust.

Disposals of options and contracts for gilt-edged securities etc.

59. With respect to disposals occurring on or after 2nd July 1986, for section 67 of the Capital Gains Tax Act 1979 there shall be substituted the following section—

"Exemptions for gilt-edged securities and qualifying corporate bonds etc.

67.—(1) A gain which accrues on the disposal by any person of—

(*a*) gilt-edged securities or qualifying corporate bonds, or

(*b*) any option or contract to acquire or dispose of gilt-edged securities or qualifying corporate bonds,

shall not be a chargeable gain.

(2) In subsection (1) above the reference to the disposal of a contract to acquire or dispose of gilt-edged securities or qualifying corporate bonds is a reference to the disposal of the outstanding obligations under such a contract.

(3) Without prejudice to section 72(3) of the Finance Act 1985 (closing out of certain futures contracts dealt in on a recognised futures exchange), where a person who has entered into any such contract as is referred to in subsection (1)(*b*) above closes out that contract by entering into another contract with obligations which are reciprocal to those of the first-mentioned contract, that transaction shall for the purposes of this section constitute the disposal of an asset, namely, his outstanding obligations under the first-mentioned contract."

General Note

Under the original section 67 disposals of gilt edged securities and qualifying corporate bonds are exempt from C.G.T. on and after July 2, 1986. The new section extends this treatment to future contracts and options in these instruments.

Small part disposals

60.—(1) In section 107 of the Capital Gains Tax Act 1979 (small part disposals) in subsection (1) for the words "is small, as compared with" there shall be substituted "does not exceed one-fifth of".

(2) This section applies to disposals on or after 6th April 1986.

General Note

To avoid the valuation of an entire holding of land on a small part disposal, section 107 of the C.G.T.A. permits a holdover of any gain arising by providing that the disposal is not to be treated as a disposal but treating the consideration received as a deduction from allowable expenditure. This relief only applies if the consideration concerned is less than £20,000 and it is "small" as compared with the market value of the entire holding. The word "small" has in the past been interpreted by the Revenue as not being more than 5 per cent.

This section now provides that the consideration must not exceed 20 per cent. of the total value. The £20,000 limit remains.

Chapter IV

Securities

General Note

The accrued income scheme, introduced under F.A. 1985, ss.73–75 and Sched. 23, came into force on February 6, 1986. Its purpose was to end the practice known as "bond washing" by which income could be converted into capital by the sale of securities "cum div."

The purpose of s.61 and Schedule 17 is to provide for certain circumstances and special cases not envisaged in the 1985 legislation. Schedule 18 takes securities subject to the accrued interest scheme (as defined in F.A. 1985, Sched. 23, para. 1) outside the anti-avoidance provisions in I.C.T.A. ss.469–475, but retains them for other securities, mainly equities and preference shares.

Other amendments are designed to cater for changes resulting from the restructuring of the Stock Exchange in October 1986 ("the Big Bang") and to bring within the ambit of sundry provisions other investment exchanges which will be recognised under the forthcoming Financial Services Act.

Stock lending

61.—(1) Subject to subsection (5) below, this section applies where a person (A) has contracted to sell securities and, to enable him to fulfil the contract, he enters into an arrangement under which—

(*a*) another person (B) is to transfer securities to A or his nominee, and

(*b*) in return securities of the same kind and amount are to be transferred (whether or not by A or his nominee) to B or his nominee.

(2) Subject to subsection (5) below, this section also applies where, to enable B to make the transfer to A or his nominee, B enters into an arrangement under which—

(*a*) another person (C) is to transfer securities to B or his nominee, and

(*b*) in return securities of the same kind and amount are to be transferred (whether or not by B or his nominee) to C or his nominee.

(3) Any transfer made in pursuance of an arrangement mentioned in subsection (1) or (2) above shall not be taken into account for the purposes of the Tax Acts in computing the profits or losses of any trade carried on by the transferor or transferee.

(4) Any disposal and acquisition made in pursuance of an arrangement mentioned in subsection (1) or (2) above shall be disregarded for the purposes of capital gains tax.

(5) The Treasury may provide by regulations that this section, or any provision of it, does not apply unless such conditions as are specified in the regulations are fulfilled; and the conditions may relate to the capacity in which any person involved in any arrangement is acting, the Board's approval of any such person or of the arrangement, the nature of the securities, or otherwise.

(6) This section applies to transfers made after such date as is specified for this purpose by regulations under this section.

(7) In this section "securities" includes stocks and shares.

(8) The power to make regulations under this section shall be exercisable by statutory instrument subject to annulment in pursuance of a resolution of the House of Commons.

General Note

There has long been an extra statutory concession (B15) under which borrowing and lending of securities in order to preserve a fluid market is not treated as a trading transaction or a disposal for capital gains tax purposes. The concession was extended to charges under the accrued income scheme, pending the enactment of this clause, which puts the concession on a statutory basis.

Amendments of Finance Act 1985

62. Schedule 17 to this Act (which contains amendments of provisions of the Finance Act 1985 about securities) shall have effect.

General Note

Schedule 17 deals mainly with various special cases not envisaged when the accrued income scheme was enacted in F.A. 1985. See further the commentary to that Schedule.

Other provisions

63. Schedule 18 to this Act (which contains other provisions about securities) shall have effect.

General Note

The provisions in I.C.T.A. ss.469–475 designed to prevent bond washing are no longer necessary for securities within the accrued income scheme. Schedule 18 accordingly takes them out of the ambit of these sections and makes a number of other changes to the Taxes Acts consequent on the "Big Bang." See further the commentary to Schedule 18.

Part III

Stamp Duty

General Note

The provisions relating to stamp duty in this Finance Act are very extensive and radical in character. There are several reasons for this. The reduction in the rate of duty on share transfers to 0.5 per cent., carried out to keep London competitive with the other leading financial centres, is designed to be fiscally neutral by extending the charge to various instruments hitherto exempt. The reform of the Stock Exchange, operative on October 27, 1986, to so-called "Big Bang", has also necessitated an overhaul of the relevant fiscal legislation.

For the innovation of Stamp Duty Reserve Tax, see the note to Part IV.

Securities

Stock or marketable securities: reduction of rate

64.—(1) In section 55 of the Finance Act 1963 and in section 4 of the Finance Act (Northern Ireland) 1963 (duty on conveyance or transfer on sale) after subsection (1) there shall be inserted—

"(1A) In relation to duty chargeable under or by reference to the heading mentioned in subsection (1) above as it applies to a conveyance or transfer of stock or marketable securities, that subsection shall have effect as if for the words from "following rates" to the end of paragraph (*c*) there were substituted the words "rate of 50p for every £100 or part of £100 of the consideration".

(2) Accordingly—

(*a*) in subsection (1) of each of those sections for the words "(2) and" there shall be substituted the words "(1A) to";

(*b*) in subsection (2) of each of those sections for the words from "under" to "by reference to that heading" there shall be substituted the words "by reference to the heading mentioned in subsection (1) above."

(3) This section applies to any instrument executed in pursuance of a contract made on or after the day on which the rule of The Stock Exchange that prohibits a person from carrying on business as both a broker and a jobber is abolished.

GENERAL NOTE

The rate of stamp duty on share transfers, reduced from 2 per cent. to 1 per cent. by F.A. 1984, s.109, is further reduced to 0.5 per cent. The effective date in subs. (3), the so-called "Big Bang", is October 27, 1986.

Bearers: consequential provisions etc.

65.—(1) In the heading "Bearer Instrument" in Schedule 1 to the Stamp Act 1891, in column (2) (duty on certain overseas bearer instruments twice the transfer duty) for the word "twice" there shall be substituted the words "three times".

(2) The following shall be inserted at the end of section 59(3) of the Finance Act 1963 (meaning of "transfer duty" for purposes of "Bearer Instrument" heading)—

"; and the instrument so postulated shall be taken to transfer the stock on the day of issue or transfer (depending on whether section 60(1) or (2) of this Act applies) and to be executed in pursuance of a contract made on that day."

(3) The following shall be inserted at the end of section 8(3) of the Finance Act (Northern Ireland) 1963 (equivalent provision for Northern Ireland)—

"; and the instrument so postulated shall be taken to transfer the stock on the day of issue or transfer (depending on whether paragraph (*a*) or (*b*) of section 9(1) applies) and to be executed in pursuance of a contract made on that day."

(4) This section applies to any instrument which falls within section 60(1) of the Finance Act 1963 and is issued on or after the day of The Stock Exchange reforms.

(5) This section applies to any instrument which falls within section 60(2) of that Act if the stock constituted by or transferable by means of it is transferred on or after the day of The Stock Exchange reforms.

(6) In this section "the day of The Stock Exchange reforms" means the day on which the rule of The Stock Exchange that prohibits a person from carrying on business as both a broker and a jobber is abolished.

(7) In subsection (4) above the reference to section 60(1) of the Finance Act 1963 includes a reference to section 9(1)(*a*) of the Finance Act (Northern Ireland) 1963 and in subsection (5) above the reference to section 60(2) of the former Act includes a reference to section 9(1)(*b*) of the latter.

GENERAL NOTE

The rate of duty on bearer instruments, currently 3 per cent. on issue if they are inland bearer instruments and 2 per cent. on first transfer in the United Kingdom if they are overseas bearer instruments, is reduced to 1.5 per cent. in both cases, in line with the new charge on depositary receipts (see s.67).

Company's purchase of own shares

66.—(1) This section applies where a company purchases its own shares under section 162 of the Companies Act 1985 or Article 47 of the Companies (Northern Ireland) Order 1982.

(2) The return which relates to the shares purchased and is delivered to the registrar of companies under section 169 of that Act or, as the case may be, Article 53 of that Order shall be charged with stamp duty, and treated for all purposes of the Stamp Act 1891, as if it were an instrument

transferring the shares on sale to the company in pursuance of the contract (or contracts) of purchase concerned.

(3) Subject to subsection (4) below, this section applies to any return under section 169 of the Companies Act 1985, or Article 53 of the Companies (Northern Ireland) Order 1982, which is delivered to the registrar of companies on or after the day of The Stock Exchange reforms.

(4) This section does not apply to any return to the extent that the shares to which it relates were purchased under a contract entered into before the day of The Stock Exchange reforms.

(5) In this section "the day of The Stock Exchange reforms" means the day on which the rule of The Stock Exchange that prohibits a person from carrying on business as both a broker and a jobber is abolished.

General Note

Companies Act 1981, s.46 authorised the purchase under certain conditions of their own shares by companies. Such purchases could be completed by surrender of the shares without liability to stamp duty. These transactions are now brought into charge.

Depositary receipts

Depositary receipts

67.—(1) Subject to subsection (9) below, subsection (2) or (3) below (as the case may be) applies where an instrument transfers relevant securities of a company incorporated in the United Kingdom to a person who at the time of the transfer falls within subsection (6), (7) or (8) below.

(2) If stamp duty is chargeable on the instrument under the heading "Conveyance or Transfer on Sale" in Schedule 1 to the Stamp Act 1891, the rate at which the duty is charged under that heading shall be the rate of £1·50 for every £100 or part of £100 of the amount or value of the consideration for the sale to which the instrument gives effect.

(3) If stamp duty is chargeable on the instrument under the heading "Conveyance or Transfer of any kind not hereinbefore described" in Schedule 1 to the Stamp Act 1891, the rate at which the duty is charged under that heading shall (subject to subsections (4) and (5) below) be the rate of £1·50 for every £100 or part of £100 of the value of the securities at the date the instrument is executed.

(4) Subsection (3) above shall have effect as if "£1·50" read "£1" in a case where—

(*a*) at the time of the transfer the transferor is a qualified dealer in securities of the kind concerned or a nominee of such a qualified dealer,

(*b*) the transfer is made for purposes of the dealer's business,

(*c*) at the time of the transfer the dealer is not a market maker in securities of the kind concerned, and

(*d*) the instrument contains a statement that paragraphs (*a*) to (*c*) above are fulfilled.

(5) In a case where—

(*a*) securities are issued, or securities sold are transferred, and (in either case) they are to be paid for in instalments,

(*b*) the person to whom they are issued or transferred holds them and transfers them to another person when the last instalment is paid,

(*c*) the transfer to the other person is effected by an instrument in the case of which subsection (3) above applies,

(*d*) before the execution of the instrument mentioned in paragraph (*c*) above an instrument is received by a person falling (at the time of the receipt) within subsection (6), (7) or (8) below,

(*e*) the instrument so received evidences all the rights which (by virtue of the terms under which the securities are issued or sold as mentioned in paragraph (*a*) above) subsist in respect of them at the time of the receipt, and

(*f*) the instrument mentioned in paragraph (*c*) above contains a statement that paragraphs (*a*), (*b*) and (*e*) above are fulfilled,

subsection (3) above shall have effect as if the reference to the value there mentioned were to an amount (if any) equal to the total of the instalments payable, less those paid before the transfer to the other person is effected.

(6) A person falls within this subsection if his business is exclusively that of holding relevant securities—

(*a*) as nominee or agent for a person whose business is or includes issuing depositary receipts for relevant securities, and

(*b*) for the purposes of such part of the business mentioned in paragraph (*a*) above as consists of issuing such depositary receipts (in a case where the business does not consist exclusively of that).

(7) A person falls within this subsection if—

(*a*) he is specified for the purposes of this subsection by the Treasury by order made by statutory instrument, and

(*b*) his business is or includes issuing depositary receipts for relevant securities.

(8) A person falls within this subsection if—

(*a*) he is specified for the purposes of this subsection by the Treasury by order made by statutory instrument,

(*b*) he does not fall within subsection (6) above but his business includes holding relevant securities as nominee or agent for a person who falls within subsection (7)(*b*) above at the time of the transfer, and

(*c*) he holds relevant securities as nominee or agent for such a person, for the purposes of such part of that person's business as consists of issuing depositary receipts for relevant securities (in a case where that business does not consist exclusively of that).

(9) Where an instrument transfers relevant securities of a company incorporated in the United Kingdom—

(*a*) to a company which at the time of the transfer falls within subsection (6) above and is resident in the United Kingdom, and

(*b*) from a company which at that time falls within that subsection and is so resident,

subsections (2) to (5) above shall not apply and the maximum stamp duty chargeable on the instrument shall be 50p.

(10) This section applies to any instrument executed on or after the day on which the rule of The Stock Exchange that prohibits a person from carrying on business as both a broker and a jobber is abolished.

General Note

Depositary receipts, usually in the form of American Depositary Receipts ("A.D.R.s"), have become a popular medium for U.S. investors purchasing shares in U.K. companies. A.D.R.'s are issued by financial institutions certifying that they hold the underlying shares and may be traded without charge to stamp duty. To reduce the consequent loss of revenue, a duty of 1·5 per cent., three times the normal rate, is imposed when shares are transferred to holders for the purposes of issuing A.D.R.'s based on them. In the case of a transferor who is a qualified dealer but not a market maker, the rate is reduced to 1 per cent. (subs. (4)) and to a nominal 50p. where the transferor and transferee are both U.K. resident companies (subs. (9)).

Subs. (5) is designed to prevent a double charge in cases involving depositary receipts where payment for shares is made by instalments.

Because the Financial Services Act 1986, regulating the securities markets was passing through Parliament concurrently with the Finance Act, power is given to the Treasury in subss. (7) and (8) to fill *lacunae* in the legislation by statutory instrument in the light of the overall framework.

Depositary receipts: notification

68.—(1) A person whose business is or includes issuing depositary receipts for relevant securities of a company incorporated in the United Kingdom shall notify the Commissioners of that fact before the end of the period of one month beginning with the date on which he first issues such depositary receipts.

(2) A person whose business includes (but does not exclusively consist of) holding relevant securities (being securities of a company incorporated in the United Kingdom)—

(*a*) as nominee or agent for a person whose business is or includes issuing depositary receipts for relevant securities, and

(*b*) for the purposes of such part of the business mentioned in paragraph (*a*) above as consists of issuing such depositary receipts (in a case where the business does not consist exclusively of that),

shall notify the Commissioners of that fact before the end of the period of one month beginning with the date on which he first holds such relevant securities as such a nominee or agent and for such purposes.

(3) A company which is incorporated in the United Kingdom and becomes aware that any shares in the company are held by a person such as is mentioned in subsection (1) or (2) above shall notify the Commissioners of that fact before the end of the period of one month beginning with the date on which the company first becomes aware of that fact.

(4) A person who fails to comply with subsection (1) or (2) above shall be liable to a fine not exceeding £1,000.

(5) A company which fails to comply with subsection (3) above shall be liable to a fine not exceeding £100.

(6) Section 121 of the Stamp Act 1891 (recovery of penalties) shall apply to fines under subsection (4) or (5) above as it applies to fines imposed by that Act.

General Note

A duty is laid upon persons involved in the issue of A.D.R.'s and companies becoming aware that A.D.R.'s are in issue in respect of their shares to notify the Revenue, on pain of a fine of £1,000 and £100 respectively.

Depositary receipts: supplementary

69.—(1) For the purposes of sections 67 and 68 above a depositary receipt for relevant securities is an instrument acknowledging—

(*a*) that a person holds relevant securities or evidence of the right to receive them, and

(*b*) that another person is entitled to rights, whether expressed as units or otherwise, in or in relation to relevant securities of the same kind, including the right to receive such securities (or evidence of the right to receive them) from the person mentioned in paragraph (*a*) above,

except that for those purposes a depositary receipt for relevant securities does not include an instrument acknowledging rights in or in relation to securities if they are issued or sold under terms providing for payment in instalments and for the issue of the instrument as evidence that an instalment has been paid.

(2) The Treasury may by regulations provide that for subsection (1) above (as it has effect for the time being) there shall be substituted a

subsection containing a different definition of a depositary receipt for the purposes of sections 67 and 68 above.

(3) References in this section and sections 67 and 68 above to relevant securities, or to relevant securities of a company, are to shares in or stock or marketable securities of any company (which, unless otherwise stated, need not be incorporated in the United Kingdom).

(4) For the purposes of section 67(3) above the value of securities at the date the instrument is executed shall be taken to be the price they might reasonably be expected to fetch on a sale at that time in the open market.

(5) Where section 67(3) above applies, section 15(2) of the Stamp Act 1891 (stamping of instruments after execution) shall have effect as if the instrument were specified in the first column of the table in paragraph (*d*) and the transferee were specified (opposite the instrument) in the second.

(6) For the purposes of section 67(4) above a person is a qualified dealer in securities of a particular kind if he deals in securities of that kind and—

(*a*) is a member of a recognised stock exchange (within the meaning given by section 535 of the Taxes Act), or

(*b*) is designated a qualified dealer by order made by the Treasury.

(7) For the purposes of section 67(4) above a person is a market maker in securities of a particular kind if he—

(*a*) holds himself out at all normal times in compliance with the rules of The Stock Exchange as willing to buy and sell securities of that kind at a price specified by him, and

(*b*) is recognised as doing so by the Council of The Stock Exchange.

(8) The Treasury may by regulations provide that for subsection (7) above (as it has effect for the time being) there shall be substituted a subsection containing a different definition of a market maker for the purposes of section 67(4) above.

(9) The power to make regulations or an order under this section shall be exercisable by statutory instrument subject to annulment in pursuance of a resolution of the House of Commons.

General Note

Definitions are provided for "depositary receipt" (subs. 1) "qualified dealer" (subs. 6) and "market maker" (subs. 7). In view of the uncertainty in this area, partly resulting from the "Big Bang" and the concurrent passage of the Financial Services Act 1986, the Treasury is given power to supplement or replace these definitions by statutory instrument.

Clearance services

Clearance services

70.—(1) Subject to subsection (9) below, subsection (2) or (3) below (as the case may be) applies where an instrument transfers relevant securities of a company incorporated in the United Kingdom to a person who at the time of the transfer falls within subsection (6), (7) or (8) below.

(2) If stamp duty is chargeable on the instrument under the heading "Conveyance or Transfer on Sale" in Schedule 1 to the Stamp Act 1891, the rate at which the duty is charged under that heading shall be the rate of £1.50 for every £100 or part of £100 of the amount or value of the consideration for the sale to which the instrument gives effect.

(3) If stamp duty is chargeable on the instrument under the heading "Conveyance or Transfer of any kind not hereinbefore described" in Schedule 1 to the Stamp Act 1891, the rate at which the duty is charged under that heading shall (subject to subsections (4) and (5) below) be the

rate of £1.50 for every £100 or part of £100 of the value of the securities at the date the instrument is executed.

(4) Subsection (3) above shall have effect as if "£1.50" read "£1" in a case where—

(*a*) at the time of the transfer the transferor is a qualified dealer in securities of the kind concerned or a nominee of such a qualified dealer,

(*b*) the transfer is made for the purposes of the dealer's business,

(*c*) at the time of the transfer the dealer is not a market maker in securities of the kind concerned, and

(*d*) the instrument contains a statement that paragraphs (*a*) to (*c*) above are fulfilled.

(5) In a case where—

(*a*) securities are issued, or securities sold are transferred, and (in either case) they are to be paid for in instalments,

(*b*) the person to whom they are issued or transferred holds them and transfers them to another person when the last instalment is paid,

(*c*) the transfer to the other person is effected by an instrument in the case of which subsection (3) above applies,

(*d*) before the execution of the instrument mentioned in paragraph (*c*) above an instrument is received by a person falling (at the time of the receipt) within subsection (6), (7) or (8) below,

(*e*) the instrument so received evidences all the rights which (by virtue of the terms under which the securities are issued or sold as mentioned in paragraph (*a*) above) subsist in respect of them at the time of the receipt, and

(*f*) the instrument mentioned in paragraph (*c*) above contains a statement that paragraphs (*a*), (*b*) and (*e*) above are fulfilled,

subsection (3) above shall have effect as if the reference to the value there mentioned were to an amount (if any) equal to the total of the instalments payable, less those paid before the transfer to the other person is effected.

(6) A person falls within this subsection if his business is exclusively that of holding relevant securities—

(*a*) as nominee or agent for a person whose business is or includes the provision of clearance services for the purchase and sale of relevant securities, and

(*b*) for the purposes of such part of the business mentioned in paragraph (*a*) above as consists of the provision of such clearance services (in a case where the business does not consist exclusively of that).

(7) A person falls within this subsection if—

(*a*) he is specified for the purposes of this subsection by the Treasury by order made by statutory instrument, and

(*b*) his business is or includes the provision of clearance services for the purchase and sale of relevant securities.

(8) A person falls within this subsection if—

(*a*) he is specified for the purposes of this subsection by the Treasury by order made by statutory instrument,

(*b*) he does not fall within subsection (6) above but his business includes holding relevant securities as nominee or agent for a person who falls within subsection (7)(*b*) above at the time of the transfer, and

(*c*) he holds relevant securities as nominee or agent for such a person, for the purposes of such part of that person's business as consists of the provision of clearance services for the purchase and sale of relevant securities (in a case where that business does not consist exclusively of that).

(9) Where an instrument transfers relevant securities of a company incorporated in the United Kingdom—

(*a*) to a company which at the time of the transfer falls within subsection (6) above and is resident in the United Kingdom, and

(*b*) from a company which at that time falls within that subsection and is so resident,

subsections (2) to (5) above shall not apply and the maximum stamp duty chargeable on the instrument shall be 50p.

(10) This section applies to any instrument executed on or after the day on which the rule of The Stock Exchange that prohibits a person from carrying on business as both a broker and a jobber is abolished.

General Note

A growing number of share transactions are carried out through settlement systems such as Euroclear. This allows successive dealings without liability to stamp duty. Accordingly provisions similar to those relating to A.D.R.s in s.67 are enacted to charge higher rates of duty when shares are transferred into such systems.

Clearance services: notification

71.—(1) A person whose business is or includes the provision of clearance services for the purchase and sale of relevant securities of a company incorporated in the United Kingdom shall notify the Commissioners of that fact before the end of the period of one month beginning with the date on which he first provides such clearance services.

(2) A person whose business includes (but does not exclusively consist of) holding relevant securities (being securities of a company incorporated in the United Kingdom)—

(*a*) as nominee or agent for a person whose business is or includes the provision of clearance services for the purchase and sale of relevant securities, and

(*b*) for the purposes of such part of the business mentioned in paragraph (*a*) above as consists of the provision of such clearance services (in a case where the business does not consist exclusively of that),

shall notify the Commissioners of that fact before the end of the period of one month beginning with the date on which he first holds such relevant securities as such a nominee or agent and for such purposes.

(3) A company which is incorporated in the United Kingdom and becomes aware that any shares in the company are held by a person such as is mentioned in subsection (1) or (2) above shall notify the Commissioners of that fact before the end of the period of one month beginning with the date on which the company first becomes aware of that fact.

(4) A person who fails to comply with subsection (1) or (2) above shall be liable to a fine not exceeding £1,000.

(5) A company which fails to comply with subsection (3) above shall be liable to a fine not exceeding £100.

(6) Section 121 of the Stamp Act 1891 (recovery of penalties) shall apply to fines under subsection (4) or (5) above as it applies to fines imposed by that Act.

General Note

The providers of clearance services and companies becoming aware that their shares are being held in this way have a similar duty of reporting with similar penalties as in the case of A.D.R.s, (s.68).

Clearance services: supplementary

72.—(1) References in sections 70 and 71 above to relevant securities, or to relevant securities of a company, are to shares in or stock or marketable securities of any company (which, unless otherwise stated, need not be incorporated in the United Kingdom).

(2) For the purposes of section 70(3) above the value of securities at the date the instrument is executed shall be taken to be the price they might reasonably be expected to fetch on a sale at that time in the open market.

(3) Where section 70(3) above applies, section 15(2) of the Stamp Act 1891 (stamping of instruments after execution) shall have effect as if the instrument were specified in the first column of the table in paragraph (*d*) and the transferee were specified (opposite the instrument) in the second.

(4) For the purposes of section 70(4) above "qualified dealer" and "market maker" have at any particular time the same meanings as they have at that time for the purposes of section 67(4) above.

General Note

These general interpretative and consequential provisions may be compared with subs. 69(3) to (7).

Reconstructions and acquisitions

Reconstructions etc: amendments

73.—(1) In section 55 of the Finance Act 1927 and in section 4 of the Finance Act (Northern Ireland) 1928 (reconstructions and amalgamations) in paragraph (B) of subsection (1) for the words "not be chargeable" there shall be substituted the words "be chargeable at the rate mentioned in subsection (9) of this section" and for the words "nor shall any such duty be chargeable" there shall be substituted the word "or".

(2) In consequence, each of those sections shall be further amended as follows—

(*a*) at the beginning of paragraph (B) of subsection (1) there shall be inserted the words "If a claim is made under this section";

(*b*) in paragraph (*a*) of the proviso to subsection (1) the words from "either it" to "liable or" and from "either that" to "duty or" shall be omitted, and in paragraph (*c*) of that proviso the words "for exemption" shall be omitted;

(*c*) in subsection (2) for the words "for exemption under paragraph (B) of subsection (1) of" there shall be substituted the word "under";

(*d*) in subsection (5) the words "for exemption" shall be omitted;

(*e*) in subsection (6), in paragraph (*a*) the words "for exemption from duty" shall be omitted, in paragraph (*c*) for the word "exemption" there shall be substituted the word "claim", and in the words following paragraph (*c*) for the word "exemption" there shall be substituted the word "claim", for the word "remitted" (in the first place where it occurs) there shall be substituted the word "unpaid" and the words from "in the case of duty remitted under paragraph (A)" to "the said subsection" shall be omitted;

(*f*) in subsection (7) for the words "for exemption from duty under subsection (1) of" there shall be substituted the word "under", for the words "such exemption" there shall be substituted the words "such a claim to be allowed" and for the words "have been remitted" there shall be substituted the words "not have been chargeable".

(3) At the end of each of those sections there shall be inserted—

"(9) The rate is the rate of 50p for every £100 or part of £100 of the amount or value of the consideration for the sale to which the instrument gives effect."

(4) In paragraph 12 of Schedule 18 to the Finance Act 1980 (demergers) for sub-paragraph (1) there shall be substituted—

"(1) If a document executed solely for the purpose of effecting an exempt distribution is chargeable with stamp duty under the heading "Conveyance or Transfer on Sale" in Schedule 1 to the Stamp Act 1891, the rate at which the duty is charged under that heading shall be the rate of 50p for every £100 or part of £100 of the amount or value of the consideration for the sale to which the document gives effect.

(1A) If a document executed solely for the purpose of effecting an exempt distribution is chargeable with stamp duty under the heading "Conveyance or Transfer on Sale" in Schedule 1 to the Stamp Act 1891, it shall not be treated as duly stamped unless it is stamped in accordance with section 12 of the Stamp Act 1891 with a particular stamp denoting that it is duly stamped."

(5) In paragraph 12(3) of Schedule 18 to the Finance Act 1980 for the words "this paragraph" there shall be substituted the words "sub-paragraph (2) above".

(6) In section 78 of the Finance Act 1985 (takeovers) the following shall be substituted for subsection (2)—

"(2) If the instrument transferring the shares in company B by way of the exchange is chargeable with stamp duty under the heading "Conveyance or Transfer on Sale" in Schedule 1 to the Stamp Act 1891, the rate at which the duty is charged under that heading shall be the rate of 50p for every £100 or part of £100 of the amount or value of the consideration for the sale to which the instrument gives effect."

(7) In section 79 of the Finance Act 1985 (voluntary winding-up: transfer of shares) the following shall be substituted for subsection (2)—

"(2) If the instrument transferring the shares in company B to company A is chargeable with stamp duty under the heading "Conveyance or Transfer on Sale" in Schedule 1 to the Stamp Act 1891, the rate at which the duty is charged under that heading shall be the rate of 50p for every £100 or part of £100 of the amount or value of the consideration for the sale to which the instrument gives effect."

(8) In section 78 and in section 79 of the Finance Act 1985—

(*a*) in subsection (3) for the word "ignored" there shall be substituted the words "treated as reduced by 50 per cent.";

(*b*) subsection (9) shall be omitted;

(*c*) in subsection (10) for "(3)" there shall be substituted "(2) or (3)".

(9) This section applies to any instrument which is executed after 24th March 1986 unless—

(*a*) it is executed in pursuance of an unconditional contract made on or before 18th March 1986, or

(*b*) it transfers stock or marketable securities and is executed in pursuance of a general offer (for the stock or securities) which became unconditional as to acceptances on or before 18th March 1986.

(10) This section shall be deemed to have come into force on 25th March 1986.

General Note

Three exemptions from stamp duty which were available under F.A. 1927, s.55 for reconstructions and amalgamations, F.A. 1980, Sched. 18, para. 12 for demergers and F.A. 1985, ss.78 and 79 for takeovers and voluntary windings-up are withdrawn by subss. (1)–(3), (4) and (5), and (6)–(8) respectively. Previously exempt instruments will now bear the normal 0.5 per cent. duty.

Reconstructions etc: repeals

74.—(1) The following provisions shall cease to have effect—

(*a*) section 55 of the Finance Act 1927 and section 4 of the Finance Act (Northern Ireland) 1928 (reconstructions and amalgamations);

(*b*) paragraph 12(1) and (1A) of Schedule 18 to the Finance Act 1980 (demergers);

(*c*) sections 78, 79 and 80 of the Finance Act 1985 (takeovers and winding-up).

(2) In paragraph 12(3) of Schedule 18 to the Finance Act 1980 for the words "sub-paragraph (2) above" there shall be substituted the words "this paragraph".

(3) This section applies to any instrument executed in pursuance of a contract made on or after the day on which the rule of The Stock Exchange that prohibits a person from carrying on business as both a broker and a jobber is abolished.

General Note

The legislation affording the three reliefs withdrawn by s.73 is repealed as from the "Big Bang", when the 0.5 per cent. rate will apply generally.

Acquisitions: reliefs

75.—(1) This section applies where a company (the acquiring company) acquires the whole or part of an undertaking of another company (the target company) in pursuance of a scheme for the reconstruction of the target company.

(2) If the first and second conditions (as defined below) are fulfilled, stamp duty under the heading "Conveyance or Transfer on Sale" in Schedule 1 to the Stamp Act 1891 shall not be chargeable on an instrument executed for the purposes of or in connection with the transfer of the undertaking or part.

(3) An instrument on which stamp duty is not chargeable by virtue only of subsection (2) above shall not be taken to be duly stamped unless it is stamped with the duty to which it would be liable but for that subsection or it has, in accordance with section 12 of the Stamp Act 1891, been stamped with a particular stamp denoting that it is not chargeable with any duty.

(4) The first condition is that the registered office of the acquiring company is in the United Kingdom and that the consideration for the acquisition—

(*a*) consists of or includes the issue of shares in the acquiring company to all the shareholders of the target company;

(*b*) includes nothing else (if anything) but the assumption or discharge by the acquiring company of liabilities of the target company.

(5) The second condition is that—

(*a*) the acquisition is effected for bona fide commercial reasons and does not form part of a scheme or arrangement of which the main purpose, or one of the main purposes, is avoidance of liability to stamp duty, income tax, corporation tax or capital gains tax,

(*b*) after the acquisition has been made, each shareholder of each of the companies is a shareholder of the other, and

(*c*) after the acquisition has been made, the proportion of shares of one of the companies held by any shareholder is the same as the proportion of shares of the other company held by that shareholder.

(6) This section applies to any instrument which is executed after 24th March 1986 unless it is executed in pursuance of an unconditional contract made on or before 18th March 1986.

(7) This section shall be deemed to have come into force on 25th March 1986.

General Note

A very limited exemption is retained for schemes of reconstruction where there is no real change of ownership. The consideration must be exclusively the issue of shares or assumption of liabilities (subs. 4), there must be no tax avoidance motive and the shareholdings must remain the same in identity and quantum (subs. 5).

Acquisitions: further provisions about reliefs

76.—(1) This section applies where a company (the acquiring company) acquires the whole or part of an undertaking of another company (the target company).

(2) If the condition mentioned in subsection (3) below is fulfilled, and stamp duty under the heading "Conveyance or Transfer on Sale" in Schedule 1 to the Stamp Act 1891 is chargeable on an instrument executed for the purposes of or in connection with—

(*a*) the transfer of the undertaking or part, or

(*b*) the assignment to the acquiring company by a creditor of the target company of any relevant debts (secured or unsecured) owed by the target company,

the rate at which the duty is charged under that heading shall not exceed that mentioned in subsection (4) below.

(3) The condition is that the registered office of the acquiring company is in the United Kingdom and that the consideration for the acquisition—

(*a*) consists of or includes the issue of shares in the acquiring company to the target company or to all or any of its shareholders;

(*b*) includes nothing else (if anything) but cash not exceeding 10 per cent. of the nominal value of those shares, or the assumption or discharge by the acquiring company of liabilities of the target company, or both.

(4) The rate is the rate of 50p for every £100 or part of £100 of the amount or value of the consideration for the sale to which the instrument gives effect.

(5) An instrument on which, by virtue only of subsection (2) above, the rate at which stamp duty is charged is not to exceed that mentioned in subsection (4) above shall not be taken to be duly stamped unless it is stamped with the duty to which it would be liable but for subsection (2) above or it has, in accordance with section 12 of the Stamp Act 1891, been stamped with a particular stamp denoting that it is duly stamped.

(6) In subsection (2)(*b*) above "relevant debts" means—

(*a*) any debt in the case of which the assignor is a bank or trade creditor, and

(*b*) any other debt incurred not less than two years before the date on which the instrument is executed.

(7) This section applies to any instrument executed on or after the day on which the rule of The Stock Exchange that prohibits a person from carrying on business as both a broker and a jobber is abolished.

General Note

Transfers of property other than shares hitherto exempt from duty under one of the provisions repealed by s.74 will continue to attract the lower 0·5 per cent. rate, provided the conditions set out in subs. (3) are met.

Acquisition of target company's share capital

77.—(1) Stamp duty under the heading "Conveyance or Transfer on Sale" in Schedule 1 to the Stamp Act 1891 shall not be chargeable on an instrument transferring shares in one company (the target company) to another company (the acquiring company) if the conditions mentioned in subsection (3) below are fulfilled.

(2) An instrument on which stamp duty is not chargeable by virtue only of subsection (1) above shall not be taken to be duly stamped unless it is stamped with the duty to which it would be liable but for that subsection or it has, in accordance with section 12 of the Stamp Act 1891, been stamped with a particular stamp denoting that it is not chargeable with any duty.

(3) The conditions are that—

(*a*) the registered office of the acquiring company is in the United Kingdom,

(*b*) the transfer forms part of an arrangement by which the acquiring company acquires the whole of the issued share capital of the target company,

(*c*) the acquisition is effected for bona fide commercial reasons and does not form part of a scheme or arrangement of which the main purpose, or one of the main purposes, is avoidance of liability to stamp duty, stamp duty reserve tax, income tax, corporation tax or capital gains tax,

(*d*) the consideration for the acquisition consists only of the issue of shares in the acquiring company to the shareholders of the target company,

(*e*) after the acquisition has been made, each person who immediately before it was made was a shareholder of the target company is a shareholder of the acquiring company,

(*f*) after the acquisition has been made, the shares in the acquiring company are of the same classes as were the shares in the target company immediately before the acquisition was made,

(*g*) after the acquisition has been made, the number of shares of any particular class in the acquiring company bears to all the shares in that company the same proportion as the number of shares of that class in the target company bore to all the shares in that company immediately before the acquisition was made, and

(*h*) after the acquisition has been made, the proportion of shares of any particular class in the acquiring company held by any particular shareholder is the same as the proportion of shares of that class in the target company held by him immediately before the acquisition was made.

(4) In this section references to shares and to share capital include references to stock.

(5) This section applies to any instrument executed on or after 1st August 1986.

GENERAL NOTE

This section, added at Report Stage on a backbench initiative, enlarges the scope for the relief on corporate reorganisations. Under s.75, relief was only available where the whole or part of an undertaking was transferred from one company to another. S.77 applies where the shares of a company are transferred in pursuance of a reorganisation, for example where a new holding company is put on top of a group. Similar stringent conditions to those in s.75 apply to prevent abuse of the exemption.

Loan capital, letters of allotment, etc.

Loan capital

78.—(1) This section (which reproduces the effect of a resolution having statutory effect under section 50 of the Finance Act 1973 for the period beginning on 25th March 1986 and ending on 6th July 1986) shall be deemed to have had effect during, and only during, that period.

(2) The following provisions shall not apply—

(*a*) in section 62 of the Finance Act 1963, subsections (2) and (6) (commonwealth stock);

(*b*) in section 11 of the Finance Act (Northern Ireland) 1963, subsections (2) and (5) (commonwealth stock);

(*c*) section 29 of the Finance Act 1967 (local authority capital);

(*d*) section 6 of the Finance Act (Northern Ireland) 1967 (local authority capital);

(*e*) section 126 of the Finance Act 1976 (loan capital).

(3) Stamp duty under the heading "Bearer Instrument" in Schedule 1 to the Stamp Act 1891 shall not be chargeable on the issue of an instrument which relates to loan capital or on the transfer of the loan capital constituted by, or transferable by means of, such an instrument.

(4) Stamp duty shall not be chargeable on an instrument which transfers loan capital issued or raised by—

(*a*) the financial support fund of the Organisation for Economic Co-operation and Development,

(*b*) the Inter-American Development Bank, or

(*c*) an organisation which was a designated international organisation at the time of the transfer (whether or not it was such an organisation at the time the loan capital was issued or raised).

(5) Stamp duty shall not be chargeable on an instrument which transfers short-term loan capital.

(6) Where stamp duty under the heading "Conveyance or Transfer on Sale" in Schedule 1 to the Stamp Act 1891 is chargeable on an instrument which transfers loan capital, the rate at which the duty is charged under that heading shall be the rate of 50p for every £100 or part of £100 of the amount or value of the consideration for the sale to which the instrument gives effect.

(7) In this section "loan capital" means—

(*a*) any debenture stock, corporation stock or funded debt, by whatever name known, issued by a body corporate or other body of persons (which here includes a local authority and any body whether formed or established in the United Kingdom or elsewhere);

(*b*) any capital raised by such a body if the capital is borrowed or has the character of borrowed money, and whether it is in the form of stock or any other form;

(*c*) stock or marketable securities issued by the government of any country or territory outside the United Kingdom.

(8) In this section "short-term loan capital" means loan capital the date (or latest date) for the repayment of which is not more than 5 years after the date on which it is issued or raised.

(9) In this section "designated international organisation" means an international organisation designated for the purposes of section 126 of the Finance Act 1984 by an order made under subsection (1) of that section.

(10) In construing sections 80(3) and 81(3) of the Finance Act 1985 (definitions by reference to section 126 of the Finance Act 1976) the effect of this section shall be ignored.

(11) This section applies to any instrument which falls within section 60(1) of the Finance Act 1963 and is issued after 24th March 1986 and before 7th July 1986.

(12) This section applies to any instrument which falls within section 60(2) of that Act if the loan capital constituted by or transferable by means of it is transferred after 24th March 1986 and before 7th July 1986.

(13) This section applies, in the case of instruments not falling within section 60(1) or (2) of that Act, to any instrument which is executed after 24th March 1986 and before 7th July 1986, unless it is executed in pursuance of a contract made on or before 18th March 1986.

(14) In this section references to section 60(1) of the Finance Act 1963 include references to section 9(1)(*a*) of the Finance Act (Northern Ireland) 1963 and references to section 60(2) of the former Act include references to section 9(1)(*b*) of the latter.

General Note

The Chancellor of the Exchequer announced in his Budget speech a charge to stamp duty on loan stocks other than short bonds and gilt edged securities but later decided to drop this proposal. Meanwhile the charge had been brought into force with effect from March 25, 1986, by Budget Resolution No. 36. The charge is annulled as from July 6, 1986, the earliest permissible date under the procedure in F.A. 1973, s.50.

Loan capital: new provisions

79.—(1) The following provisions shall cease to have effect—

(*a*) in section 62 of the Finance Act 1963, subsections (2) and (6) (commonwealth stock);

(*b*) in section 11 of the Finance Act (Northern Ireland) 1963, subsections (2) and (5) (commonwealth stock);

(*c*) section 29 of the Finance Act 1967 (local authority capital);

(*d*) section 6 of the Finance Act (Northern Ireland) 1967 (local authority capital);

(*e*) section 126 of the Finance Act 1976 (loan capital).

(2) Stamp duty under the heading "Bearer Instrument" in Schedule 1 to the Stamp Act 1891 shall not be chargeable on the issue of an instrument which relates to loan capital or on the transfer of the loan capital constituted by, or transferable by means of, such an instrument.

(3) Stamp duty shall not be chargeable on an instrument which transfers loan capital issued or raised by—

(*a*) the financial support fund of the Organisation for Economic Co-operation and Development,

(*b*) the Inter-American Development Bank, or

(*c*) an organisation which was a designated international organisation at the time of the transfer (whether or not it was such an organisation at the time the loan capital was issued or raised).

(4) Subject to subsections (5) and (6) below, stamp duty shall not be chargeable on an instrument which transfers any other loan capital.

(5) Subsection (4) above does not apply to an instrument transferring loan capital which, at the time the instrument is executed, carries a right (exercisable then or later) of conversion into shares or other securities, or to the acquisition of shares or other securities, including loan capital of the same description.

(6) Subject to subsection (7) below, subsection (4) above does not apply to an instrument transferring loan capital which, at the time the instrument is executed or any earlier time, carries or has carried—

(*a*) a right to interest the amount of which exceeds a reasonable commercial return on the nominal amount of the capital,

(*b*) a right to interest the amount of which falls or has fallen to be determined to any extent by reference to the results of, or of any part of, a business or to the value of any property, or

(*c*) a right on repayment to an amount which exceeds the nominal amount of the capital and is not reasonably comparable with what is generally repayable (in respect of a similar nominal amount of capital) under the terms of issue of loan capital listed in the Official List of The Stock Exchange.

(7) Subsection (4) above shall not be prevented from applying to an instrument by virtue of subsection (6)(*a*) or (*c*) above by reason only that the loan capital concerned carries a right to interest, or (as the case may be) to an amount payable on repayment, determined to any extent by reference to an index showing changes in the general level of prices payable in the United Kingdom over a period substantially corresponding to the period between the issue or raising of the loan capital and its repayment.

(8) Where stamp duty under the heading "Conveyance or Transfer on Sale" in Schedule 1 to the Stamp Act 1891 is chargeable on an instrument which transfers loan capital, the rate at which the duty is charged under that heading shall be the rate of 50p for every £100 or part of £100 of the amount or value of the consideration for the sale to which the instrument gives effect.

(9) This section applies to any instrument which falls within section 60(1) of the Finance Act 1963 and is issued after 31st July 1986.

(10) This section applies to any instrument which falls within section 60(2) of that Act if the loan capital constituted by or transferable by means of it is transferred after 31st July 1986.

(11) This section applies, in the case of instruments not falling within section 60(1) or (2) of that Act, to any instrument which is executed after 31st July 1986.

(12) Subsections (7), (9), (10) and (14) of section 78 above shall apply as if references to that section included references to this.

General Note

This section re-enacts, with minor improvements, the pre-Budget position and exemptions in relation to the stocks mentioned. It also provides that for the period between August 1, 1986, and the "Big Bang" loan stocks that are still chargeable to stamp duty—in effect, convertible loan stocks or loan stocks with an equity element—will pay at the 0·5 per cent. rate rather than the 1 per cent. rate and rationalises the charge in the case of certain categories of Commonwealth stock.

Bearer letters of allotment etc.

80.—(1) In Schedule 1 to the Stamp Act 1891, in the heading "Bearer Instrument", paragraph 2 of the exemptions (bearer letter of allotment etc. required to be surrendered not later than six months after issue) shall be omitted.

(2) This section applies to any instrument which falls within section 60(1) of the Finance Act 1963 and is issued after 24th March 1986, unless it is issued by a company in pursuance of a general offer for its shares and the offer became unconditional as to acceptances on or before 18th March 1986.

(3) This section applies to any instrument which falls within section 60(2) of that Act if the stock constituted by or transferable by means of it is transferred after 24th March 1986.

(4) In this section the reference to section 60(1) of the Finance Act 1963 includes a reference to section 9(1)(*a*) of the Finance Act (Northern Ireland) 1963 and the reference to section 60(2) of the former Act includes a reference to section 9(1)(*b*) of the latter.

(5) This section shall be deemed to have come into force on 25th March 1986.

General Note

The exemption for bearer letters of allotment is withdrawn, since this could provide a route for avoidance of the charge on take-overs and in other circumstances.

Changes in financial institutions

Sales to market makers

81.—(1) Stamp duty shall not be chargeable on an instrument transferring stock on sale to a person or his nominee if it is shown to the satisfaction of the Commissioners that the transaction to which the instrument gives effect was carried out by the person in the ordinary course of his business as a market maker in stock of the kind transferred.

(2) An instrument on which stamp duty is not chargeable by virtue only of subsection (1) above shall not be deemed to be duly stamped unless it has been stamped with a stamp denoting that it is not chargeable with any duty; and notwithstanding anything in section 122(1) of the Stamp Act 1891, the stamp may be a stamp of such kind as the Commissioners may prescribe.

(3) For the purposes of this section a person is a market maker in stock of a particular kind if he—

(*a*) holds himself out at all normal times in compliance with the rules of The Stock Exchange as willing to buy and sell stock of that kind at a price specified by him, and

(*b*) is recognised as doing so by the Council of The Stock Exchange.

(4) Subject to subsection (6) below, this section applies to any instrument giving effect to a transaction carried out on or after the day of The Stock Exchange reforms.

(5) The Treasury may by regulations provide that for subsection (3) above (as it has effect for the time being) there shall be substituted a subsection containing a different definition of a market maker for the purposes of this section.

(6) Regulations under subsection (5) above shall apply in relation to any instrument giving effect to a transaction carried out on or after such day, after the day of The Stock Exchange reforms, as is specified in the regulations.

(7) The power to make regulations under subsection (5) above shall be exercisable by statutory instrument subject to annulment in pursuance of a resolution of the House of Commons.

General Note

F.A. 1920, s.42 relieves from *ad valorem* stamp duty transfers of stock to a jobber where the stock acquired is resold within two months. Under the new Stock Exchange rules, member firms will no longer be classified as brokers or jobbers according to their dealing capacity. All firms will in future be known as broker-dealers and any firm will be allowed to apply to the Stock Exchange Council for registration as a market maker in particular stocks. The relief for jobbers is therefore recast and its administration simplified by exempting from stamp duty instruments transferring stock on sale to a market maker or his nominee. Provision is also made for the relief to be extended by statutory instrument to recognised market makers on investment exchanges other than The Stock Exchange.

Borrowing of stock by market makers

82.—(1) This section applies where a person (A) has contracted to sell stock in the ordinary course of his business as a market maker in stock of that kind and, to enable him to fulfil the contract, he enters into an arrangement under which—

(*a*) another person (B), who is not a market maker in stock of the kind concerned or a nominee of such a market maker, is to transfer stock to A or his nominee, and

(*b*) in return stock of the same kind and amount is to be transferred (whether or not by A or his nominee) to B or his nominee.

(2) This section also applies where, to enable B to make the transfer to A or his nominee, B enters into an arrangement under which—

(*a*) another person (C), who is not a market maker in stock of the kind concerned or a nominee of such a market maker, is to transfer stock to B or his nominee, and

(*b*) in return stock of the same kind and amount is to be transferred (whether or not by B or his nominee) to C or his nominee.

(3) The maximum stamp duty chargeable on an instrument effecting a transfer to B or his nominee or C or his nominee in pursuance of an arrangement mentioned in subsection (1) or (2) above shall be 50p.

(4) For the purposes of this section a person is a market maker in stock of a particular kind if he—

(*a*) holds himself out at all normal times in compliance with the rules of The Stock Exchange as willing to buy and sell stock of that kind at a price specified by him, and,

(*b*) is recognised as doing so by the Council of The Stock Exchange.

(5) Subject to subsection (7) below, this section applies to any instrument effecting a transfer in pursuance of an arrangement entered into on or after the day of The Stock Exchange reforms.

(6) The Treasury may by regulations provide that for subsection (3) above (as it has effect for the time being) there shall be substituted a subsection containing a different definition of a market maker for the purposes of this section.

(7) Regulations under subsection (6) above shall apply in relation to any instrument effecting a transfer in pursuance of an arrangement entered into on or after such day, after the day of The Stock Exchange reforms, as is specified in the regulations.

(8) The power to make regulations under subsection (6) above shall be exerciseable by statutory instrument subject to annulment in pursuance of a resolution of the House of Commons.

General Note

F.A. 1961, s.34 provides relief from *ad valorem* stamp duty where a jobber borrows stock to enable him to deliver securities he has sold. A similar relief is now extended to market makers, covering the circumstances where the market maker (labelled A in the section) borrows stock directly from a lender (B) or through an intermediary (C). In all cases, the stock lending arrangement must provide that the borrowed stock is replaced by securities of the same kind and amount. Where the relief applies, maximum stamp duty of 50p is chargeable on transfers back to the lender or the intermediary.

Composition agreements

83.—(1) In section 33(1) of the Finance Act 1970 (composition by stock exchanges in respect of transfer duty)—

(*a*) for the words "any recognised stock exchange" there shall be substituted "any recognised investment exchange or recognised clearing house", and

(*b*) the following shall be substituted for the words from "In this subsection" to the end—

"In this subsection 'recognised investment exchange' and 'recognised clearing house' have the same meanings as in the Financial Services Act 1986."

(2) The words "recognised investment exchange or recognised clearing house" shall be substituted for the words "stock exchange" in section 33(2)(*b*), (*c*) and (*d*), (4) and (5) of the Finance Act 1970.

(3) This section shall come into force on such day as the Commissioners may appoint by order made by statutory instrument.

General Note

F.A. 1970, s.33 enables the Revenue to enter into composition agreements for the payment of stamp duty with The Stock Exchange. Provision is now made for similar arrangements to be made with other clearing houses established under the new regulatory regime being set up by the Financial Services Act 1986.

Miscellaneous exemptions

84.—(1) In section 127(1) of the Finance Act 1976 (no stamp duty on transfer to stock exchange nominee executed for purposes of a stock exchange transaction) the words "which is executed for the purposes of a stock exchange transaction" shall be omitted.

(2) Stamp duty shall not be chargeable on an instrument effecting a transfer of stock if—

(*a*) the transferee is a recognised investment exchange or a nominee of a recognised investment exchange, and

(*b*) an agreement which relates to the stamp duty which would (apart from this subsection) be chargeable on the instrument, and was made between the Commissioners and the investment exchange under section 33 of the Finance Act 1970, is in force at the time of the transfer.

(3) Stamp duty shall not be chargeable on an instrument effecting a transfer of stock if—

(*a*) the transferee is a recognised clearing house or a nominee of a recognised clearing house, and

(*b*) an agreement which relates to the stamp duty which would (apart from this subsection) be chargeable on the instrument, and was made between the Commissioners and the clearing house under section 33 of the Finance Act 1970, is in force at the time of the transfer.

(4) Subsection (1) above applies to any transfer giving effect to a transaction carried out on or after the day of The Stock Exchange reforms.

(5) Subsection (2) above applies to any instrument giving effect to a transaction carried out on or after such day as the Commissioners may appoint by order made by statutory instrument.

(6) Subsection (3) above applies to any instrument giving effect to a transaction carried out on or after such day as the Commissioners may appoint by order made by statutory instrument.

General Note

This section provides an exemption for transfers of shares to a clearing house or an investment exchange similar to that provided by F.A. 1976, s.127 for transfers of stock to the Stock Exchange's nominee holding company under the "Talisman" computerised system for settling bargains.

Supplementary

85.—(1) Section 42(1) of the Finance Act 1920 (reduction of duty in case of certain transfers to jobbers or nominees or qualified dealers) shall have effect, in the case of any transfer giving effect to a transaction carried out on or after the day of The Stock Exchange reforms as if the following were omitted—

(*a*) in that subsection the words "a jobber or his nominee or to" and in the proviso to it the words "jobber or" (in each place);

(*b*) in subsection (3) of that section, paragraph (*d*) of the definition of "qualified dealer" (Stock Exchange brokers).

(2) Section 34 of the Finance Act 1961 and section 4 of the Finance Act (Northern Ireland) 1961 (borrowing of stock by jobbers) shall not apply where stock is transferred in discharge of an undertaking given on or after the day of The Stock Exchange reforms.

(3) Section 42(1) of the Finance Act 1920 shall not apply to any transfer giving effect to a transaction carried out on or after such day as is specified

for this purpose in regulations made under section 81(5) above; and different days may be so specified for different purposes.

(4) Section 127(2) of the Finance Act 1976 (transfer otherwise than on sale from stock exchange nominee to jobber) shall not apply to any transfer giving effect to a transaction carried out on or after the day of The Stock Exchange reforms.

(5) In sections 81, 82 and 84 above and this section—

(*a*) "the day of The Stock Exchange reforms" means the day on which the rule of The Stock Exchange that prohibits a person from carrying on business as both a broker and a jobber is abolished,

(*b*) references to a recognised investment exchange are to a recognised investment exchange within the meaning of the Financial Services Act 1986,

(*c*) references to a recognised clearing house are to a recognised clearing house within the meaning of the Financial Services Act 1986, and

(*d*) "stock" includes marketable security.

General Note

The existing reliefs relating to jobbers and qualified dealers are abolished from the "Big Bang" or when dealers currently entitled to the relief provided by F.A. 1920, s.42 are able to qualify for the exemption provided by s.81.

Subs. (5) provides various definitions for ss.81–84.

Part IV

Stamp Duty Reserve Tax

General Note

The keystone of stamp duty has always been that it is a tax on documents, not on transactions. This new tax, stamp duty reserve tax ("S.D.R.T."), is imposed on transactions themselves, because it applies to agreements to transfer securities, not on the transfer documents. It is designed to underpin stamp duty and extend the charge to transactions which presently escape tax because they are never evidenced in documentary transfers. Where stamp duty is subsequently paid, S.D.R.T. is refundable, but the new tax is the only charge on the transfer of renounceable letters of allotment, where the volume of instruments involved would make the actual stamping an onerous task. The introduction of S.D.R.T. may well foreshadow a change in the basis of the charge on commercial dealings, first introduced in 1694 and last consolidated in the Stamp Act 1891, from a physical tax on documents to a turnover tax on transactions.

Introduction

The tax: introduction

86.—(1) A tax, to be known as stamp duty reserve tax, shall be charged in accordance with this Part of this Act.

(2) The tax shall be under the care and management of the Board.

(3) Section 1 of the Provisional Collection of Taxes Act 1968 shall apply to the tax; and accordingly in subsection (1) of that section after the words "petroleum revenue tax" there shall be inserted the words "stamp duty reserve tax".

General Note

Stamp Duty Reserve Tax ("S.D.R.T.") is introduced and put under the management of the Inland Revenue. Subs. (3) applies Provisional Collection of Taxes Act 1968, s.1 to the charge so that future changes can take immediate effect by Budget resolution.

The principal charge

87.—(1) This section applies where one person (A) agrees with another person (B) to transfer chargeable securities (whether or not to B) for consideration in money or money's worth.

(2) There shall be a charge to stamp duty reserve tax under this section on the expiry of the period of two months beginning with the relevant day, unless the agreement is to transfer the securities to B or his nominee and the first and second conditions mentioned below have been fulfilled by the time that period expires.

(3) In subsection (2) above "the relevant day" means—

(*a*) in a case where the agreement is conditional, the day on which the condition is satisfied, and

(*b*) in any other case, the day on which the agreement is made.

(4) The first condition is that an instrument is (or instruments are) executed in pursuance of the agreement and the instrument transfers (or the instruments between them transfer) to B or, as the case may be, to his nominee all the chargeable securities to which the agreement relates.

(5) The second condition is that the instrument (or each instrument) transferring the chargeable securities to which the agreement relates is duly stamped in accordance with the enactments relating to stamp duty if it is an instrument which, under those enactments, is chargeable with stamp duty or otherwise required to be stamped.

(6) Tax under this section shall be charged at the rate of 50p for every £100 or part of £100 of the amount or value of the consideration mentioned in subsection (1) above.

(7) For the purposes of subsection (6) above the value of any consideration not consisting of money shall be taken to be the price it might reasonably be expected to fetch on a sale in the open market at the time the agreement mentioned in subsection (1) above is made.

(8) In this section "the enactments relating to stamp duty" means the Stamp Act 1891 and any enactment which amends or is required to be construed together with that Act.

(9) This section applies where the agreement to transfer is made on or after the day on which the rule of The Stock Exchange that prohibits a person from carrying on business as both a broker and a jobber is abolished.

(10) This section has effect subject to sections 88 to 90 below.

General Note

Where there is an agreement to transfer securities which are subject to stamp duty and a duly stamped instrument is not generated within two months, S.D.R.T. is chargeable on the consideration at the stamp duty rate (0·5 per cent.). S.D.R.T. is designed to catch transactions closed within the Stock Exchange account, which escape stamp duty. The new tax is effective from the "Big Bang," October 27, 1986. The next three sections contain various exemptions from S.D.R.T.

Section 87: special cases

88.—(1) An instrument on which stamp duty is not chargeable by virtue of—

(*a*) section 127(1) of the Finance Act 1976 (transfer to stock exchange nominee), or

(*b*) section 84(2) and (3) above,

shall be disregarded in construing section 87(4) and (5) above.

(2) Subsection (3) below applies where the chargeable securities mentioned in section 87(1) above are constituted by or transferable by means

of an inland bearer instrument, within the meaning of the heading "Bearer Instrument" in Schedule 1 to the Stamp Act 1891, which—

(*a*) is exempt from stamp duty under that heading by virtue of exemption 3 in that heading, or

(*b*) would be so exempt if it were otherwise chargeable under that heading.

(3) In such a case section 87 above shall have effect as if the following were omitted—

(*a*) in subsection (2) the words from "unless" to the end;

(*b*) subsections (4), (5) and (8).

General Note

Subs. (1) extends to S.D.R.T. the exemption from stamp duty for transfers to stock exchange nominee companies and similar institutions.

Subss. (2) and (3) have the effect of subjecting to S.D.R.T. but not stamp duty, transfers of renounceable letters of allotment. This is designed to end the avoidance scheme known as the "pref-trick," without imposing a necessity to deal physically with large batches of documents at the stamping office.

Section 87: exceptions for market makers etc.

89.—(1) Section 87 above shall not apply as regards an agreement to transfer securities if the agreement is made by B in the ordinary course of his business as a market maker in securities of the kind concerned.

(2) Section 87 above shall not apply as regards an agreement to transfer securities to B or his nominee if—

(*a*) the agreement is made by B as principal in the ordinary course of his business as a broker and dealer in relation to securities of the kind concerned, and

(*b*) before the end of the period of 7 days beginning with the day on which the agreement is made or (in a case where the agreement is conditional) the day on which the condition is satisfied, B enters into an unconditional agreement to sell the securities to another person.

(3) For the purposes of this section, a person is a market maker in securities of a particular kind if he—

(*a*) holds himself out at all normal times in compliance with the rules of The Stock Exchange as willing to buy and sell securities of that kind at a price specified by him, and

(*b*) is recognised as doing so by the Council of The Stock Exchange.

(4) For the purposes of this section, a person is a broker and dealer in relation to securities of a particular kind if he is a member of The Stock Exchange who carries on his business in the United Kingdom and is not a market maker in securities of that kind.

(5) The Treasury may by regulations provide that for subsection (3) above (as it has effect for the time being) there shall be substituted a subsection containing a different definition of a market maker for the purposes of this section.

(6) The Treasury may by regulations provide that for subsection (4) above (as it has effect for the time being) there shall be substituted a subsection containing a different definition of a broker and dealer for the purposes of this section.

(7) For the purposes of subsection (2) above, if the securities which B sells cannot be identified (apart from this subsection) securities shall be taken as follows—

(*a*) securities of the same kind acquired in the period of 7 days ending with the day of the sale (and not taken for the purposes of a previous sale by B) shall be taken before securities of that kind acquired outside that period;

(*b*) securities of that kind acquired earlier in that period (and not taken for the purposes of a previous sale by B) shall be taken before securities of that kind acquired later in that period.

(8) For the purposes of subsection (7) above—

(*a*) securities are acquired when B enters into an agreement for them to be transferred to B or his nominee or (in a case where the agreement is conditional) when the condition is satisfied;

(*b*) B sells securities when he enters into an unconditional agreement to sell them to another person.

(9) The power to make regulations under this section shall be exercisable by statutory instrument subject to annulment in pursuance of a resolution of the House of Commons.

General Note

This section contains an exemption from S.D.R.T. for agreements to transfer securities to market makers or to brokers and dealers, in the latter case where the securities are sold within seven days. Subs. (7) contains rules for identifying such unsold securities.

The Treasury are given powers to amend by statutory instrument the definitions of "market maker" and "broker and dealer" in subss. (3) and (4).

Section 87: other exceptions

90.—(1) Section 87 above shall not apply as regards an agreement to transfer a unit under a unit trust scheme to the managers under the scheme.

(2) Section 87 above shall not apply as regards an agreement to transfer a unit under a unit trust scheme if at the time the agreement is made—

(*a*) all the trustees under the scheme are resident outside the United Kingdom, and

(*b*) the unit is not registered in a register kept in the United Kingdom by or on behalf of the trustees under the scheme.

(3) Section 87 above shall not apply as regards an agreement to transfer securities constituted by or transferable by means of—

(*a*) an overseas bearer instrument, within the meaning of the heading "Bearer Instrument" in Schedule 1 to the Stamp Act 1891;

(*b*) an inland bearer instrument, within the meaning of that heading, which does not fall within exemption 3 in that heading (renounceable letter of allotment etc. where rights are renounceable not later than six months after issue).

(4) Section 87 above shall not apply as regards an agreement which forms part of an arrangement falling within section 93(1) or 96(1) below.

(5) Section 87 above shall not apply as regards an agreement to transfer securities which the Board are satisfied are held, when the agreement is made, by a person whose business is exclusively that of holding chargeable securities—

(*a*) as nominee or agent for a person whose business is or includes the provision of clearance services for the purchase and sale of chargeable securities, and

(*b*) for the purposes of such part of the business mentioned in paragraph (*a*) above as consists of the provision of such clearance services (in a case where the business does not consist exclusively of that).

General Note

Sundry exceptions from S.D.R.T. are dealt with in this section:

subs. (1). Agreements to transfer unit trust units to the managers.

subs. (2). Agreements to transfer offshore unit trust units.

subs. (3). Agreements to transfer inland or overseas bearer instruments. See s.65 for the charge to stamp duty on the transfer of such instruments.

subs. (4). Agreements to transfer securities into A.D.R. form or to clearance services. S.D.R.T. on these is dealt with in ss.93 and 96 respectively.

subs. (5). Agreements to transfer securities by the nominees of approved clearance services.

Liability to tax

91.—(1) Where tax is charged under section 87 above as regards an agreement, B shall be liable for the tax.

(2) But where B is acting as nominee for another person, that other person shall be liable for the tax.

General Note

The liability to pay S.D.R.T. is imposed on the transferee, or where he is acting as a nominee, on his principal.

Repayment or cancellation of tax

92.—(1) If, as regards an agreement to transfer securities to B or his nominee, tax is charged under section 87 above and it is proved to the Board's satisfaction that at a time after the expiry of the period of two months (beginning with the relevant day, as defined in section 87(3)) but before the expiry of the period of six years (so beginning) the conditions mentioned in section 87(4) and (5) have been fulfilled, the following provisions of this section shall apply.

(2) If any of the tax charged has been paid, and a claim for repayment is made within the period of six years mentioned in subsection (1) above, the tax paid shall be repaid; and where the tax paid is not less than £25 it shall be repaid with interest on it at the appropriate rate from the time it was paid.

(3) To the extent that the tax charged has not been paid, the charge shall be cancelled by virtue of this subsection.

(4) In subsection (2) above "the appropriate rate" means 11 per cent. per annum or such other rate as the Treasury may from time to time specify by order.

(5) The power to make an order under this section shall be exercisable by statutory instrument subject to annulment in pursuance of a resolution of the House of Commons.

General Note

Where S.D.R.T. has been paid and subsequently stamp duty is paid on the same transaction, the S.D.R.T. will be repaid with interest on a claim being made within six years.

Other charges

Depositary receipts

93.—(1) Subject to subsection (7) below and section 95 below, there shall be a charge to stamp duty reserve tax under this section where in pursuance of an arrangement—

(*a*) a person falling within subsection (2) below has issued or is to issue a depositary receipt for chargeable securities, and

(*b*) chargeable securities of the same kind and amount are transferred or issued to a person falling within subsection (3) below, or are appropriated by such a person towards the eventual satisfaction of the entitlement of the receipt's holder to receive chargeable securities.

(2) A person falls within this subsection if his business is or includes issuing depositary receipts for chargeable securities.

(3) A person falls within this subsection if his business is or includes holding chargeable securities as nominee or agent for the person who has issued or is to issue the depositary receipt.

(4) Subject to subsections (5) to (7) below, tax under this section shall be charged at the rate of £1.50 for every £100 or part of £100 of the following—

(*a*) in a case where the securities are issued, their price when issued;

(*b*) in a case where the securities are transferred for consideration in money or money's worth, the amount or value of the consideration;

(*c*) in any other case, the value of the securities.

(5) In a case where the securities are transferred and—

(*a*) the transfer is effected by an instrument on which stamp duty under the heading "Conveyance or Transfer of any kind not hereinbefore described" in Schedule 1 to the Stamp Act 1891 is chargeable,

(*b*) at the time of the transfer the transferor is a qualified dealer in securities of the kind concerned or a nominee of such a qualified dealer,

(*c*) the transfer is made for the purposes of the dealer's business,

(*d*) at the time of the transfer the dealer is not a market maker in securities of the kind concerned, and

(*e*) the instrument contains a statement that paragraphs (*b*) to (*d*) above are fulfilled,

subsection (4) above shall have effect as if "£1.50" read "50p" (in a case where the securities are transferred before the day of The Stock Exchange reforms) or "£1" (in any other case).

(6) In a case where—

(*a*) securities are issued, or securities sold are transferred, and (in either case) they are to be paid for in instalments,

(*b*) the person to whom they are issued or transferred holds them and transfers them to another person when the last instalment is paid,

(*c*) subsection (4)(*c*) above applies in the case of the transfer to the other person,

(*d*) before the making of the transfer to the other person an instrument is received by a person falling within subsection (3) above,

(*e*) the instrument so received evidences all the rights which (by virtue of the terms under which the securities are issued or sold as mentioned in paragraph (*a*) above) subsist in respect of them at the time of the receipt, and

(*f*) the transfer to the other person is effected by an instrument containing a statement that paragraphs (*a*), (*b*) and (*e*) above are fulfilled,

subsection (4)(*c*) above shall have effect as if the reference to the value there mentioned were to an amount (if any) equal to the total of the instalments payable, less those paid before the transfer to the other person is effected.

(7) Where tax is (or would apart from this subsection be) charged under this section in respect of a transfer of securities, and ad valorem stamp duty is chargeable on any instrument effecting the transfer, then—

(*a*) if the amount of the duty is less than the amount of tax found by virtue of subsections (4) to (6) above, the tax charged under this section shall be the amount so found less the amount of the duty;

(*b*) in any other case, there shall be no charge to tax under this section in respect of the transfer.

(8) Where tax is charged under the preceding provisions of this section, the person liable for the tax shall (subject to subsection (9) below) be the person who has issued or is to issue the depositary receipt.

(9) Where tax is charged under the preceding provisions of this section in a case where securities are transferred, and at the time of the transfer the person who has issued or is to issue the depositary receipt is not resident in the United Kingdom and has no branch or agency in the United Kingdom, the person liable for the tax shall be the person to whom the securities are transferred.

(10) Where chargeable securities are issued or transferred on sale under terms providing for payment in instalments and for an issue of other chargeable securities, and (apart from this subsection) tax would be charged under this section in respect of that issue, tax shall not be so charged but—

(*a*) if any of the instalments becomes payable by a person falling within subsection (2) or (3) above, there shall be a charge to stamp duty reserve tax under this section when the instalment becomes payable;

(*b*) the charge shall be at the rate of £1.50 for every £100 or part of £100 of the instalment payable;

(*c*) the person liable to pay the instalment shall be liable for the tax.

(11) Subject to subsection (12) below, this section applies where securities are transferred, issued or appropriated after 18th March 1986 (whenever the arrangement was made).

(12) This section does not apply, in the case of securities which are transferred, if the Board are satisfied that they were acquired or appropriated by the transferor on or before 18th March 1986 for or towards the eventual satisfaction of the entitlement of a person to receive securities of the same kind under a depositary receipt (whether issued on or before that date or to be issued after that date).

General Note

This section imposes a charge to S.D.R.T. on the transfer of stock into A.D.R. form comparable to the charge to stamp duty under s.67. The s.67 charge is only applicable from the "Big Bang," October 27, 1986, while the charge under this section is applicable from March 18, 1986, so safeguarding the revenue in the interim.

Depositary receipts: supplementary

94.—(1) For the purposes of section 93 above a depositary receipt for chargeable securities is an instrument acknowledging—

(*a*) that a person holds chargeable securities or evidence of the right to receive them, and

(*b*) that another person is entitled to rights, whether expressed as units or otherwise, in or in relation to chargeable securities of the same kind, including the right to receive such securities (or evidence of the right to receive them) from the person mentioned in paragraph (*a*) above,

except that for those purposes a depositary receipt for chargeable securities does not include an instrument acknowledging rights in or in relation to securities if they are issued or sold under terms providing for payment in instalments and for the issue of the instrument as evidence that an instalment has been paid.

(2) The Treasury may by regulations provide that for subsection (1) above (as it has effect for the time being) there shall be substituted a subsection containing a different definition of a depositary receipt for the purposes of section 93 above.

(3) For the purposes of section 93(4)(*b*) above the value of any consideration not consisting of money shall be taken to be the price it

might reasonably be expected to fetch on a sale in the open market at the time the securities are transferred.

(4) For the purposes of section 93(4)(*c*) above the value of the securities shall be taken to be the price they might reasonably be expected to fetch on a sale in the open market at the time they are transferred or appropriated (as the case may be).

(5) For the purposes of section 93(5) above a person is a qualified dealer in securities of a particular kind if he deals in securities of that kind and—

(*a*) is a member of a recognised stock exchange (within the meaning given by section 535 of the Taxes Act), or

(*b*) is designated a qualified dealer by order made by the Treasury.

(6) For the purposes of section 93(5) above a person is a market maker in securities of a particular kind if he—

(*a*) holds himself out at all normal times in compliance with the rules of The Stock Exchange as willing to buy and sell securities of that kind at a price specified by him, and

(*b*) is recognised as doing so by the Council of The Stock Exchange.

(7) The Treasury may by regulations provide that for subsection (6) above (as it has effect for the time being) there shall be substituted a subsection containing a different definition of a market maker for the purposes of section 93(5) above.

(8) In section 93(5) above "the day of The Stock Exchange reforms" means the day on which the rule of The Stock Exchange that prohibits a person from carrying on business as both a broker and a jobber is abolished.

(9) The power to make regulations or an order under this section shall be exercisable by statutory instrument subject to annulment in pursuance of a resolution of the House of Commons.

General Note

The definitions and other provisions relating to depositary receipts in this section are comparable to those in connection with stamp duty in s.69.

Depositary receipts: exceptions

95.—(1) Where securities are transferred—

(*a*) to a company which at the time of the transfer falls within subsection (6) of section 67 above and is resident in the United Kingdom, and

(*b*) from a company which at that time falls within that subsection and is so resident,

there shall be no charge to tax under section 93 above in respect of the transfer.

(2) There shall be no charge to tax under section 93 above in respect of a transfer, issue or appropriation of an inland bearer instrument, within the meaning of the heading "Bearer Instrument" in Schedule 1 to the Stamp Act 1891, which does not fall within exemption 3 in that heading (renounceable letter of allotment etc. where rights are renounceable not later than six months after issue).

(3) There shall be no charge to tax under section 93 above in respect of an issue by a company (company X) of securities in exchange for shares in another company (company Y) where company X—

(*a*) has control of company Y, or

(*b*) will have such control in consequence of the exchange or of an offer as a result of which the exchange is made.

(4) For the purposes of subsection (3) above company X has control of company Y if company X has power to control company Y's affairs by

virtue of holding shares in, or possessing voting power in relation to, company Y or any other body corporate.

General Note

Exemption from the s.93 charge is provided in the following cases:

subs. (1). Agreements to transfer between nominees.

subs. (2). Agreements to transfer inland bearer instruments. For the charge to stamp duty on the transfer of such instruments see s.65.

subs. (3). Intra-group agreements to transfer.

Clearance services

96.—(1) Subject to subsection (5) below and section 97 below, there shall be a charge to stamp duty reserve tax under this section where—

(*a*) a person (A) whose business is or includes the provision of clearance services for the purchase and sale of chargeable securities has entered into an arrangement to provide such clearance services for another person, and

(*b*) in pursuance of the arrangement, chargeable securities are transferred or issued to A or to a person whose business is or includes holding chargeable securities as nominee for A.

(2) Subject to subsections (3) to (5) below, tax under this section shall be charged at the rate of £1.50 for every £100 or part of £100 of the following—

(*a*) in a case where the securities are issued, their price when issued;

(*b*) in a case where the securities are transferred for consideration in money or money's worth, the amount or value of the consideration;

(*c*) in any other case, the value of the securities.

(3) In a case where the securities are transferred and—

(*a*) the transfer is effected by an instrument on which stamp duty under the heading "Conveyance or Transfer of any kind not hereinbefore described" in Schedule 1 to the Stamp Act 1891 is chargeable,

(*b*) at the time of the transfer the transferor is a qualified dealer in securities of the kind concerned or a nominee of such a qualified dealer,

(*c*) the transfer is made for the purposes of the dealer's business,

(*d*) at the time of the transfer the dealer is not a market maker in securities of the kind concerned, and

(*e*) the instrument contains a statement that paragraphs (*b*) to (*d*) above are fulfilled,

subsection (2) above shall have effect as if "£1.50" read "50p" (in a case where the securities are transferred before the day of The Stock Exchange reforms) or "£1" (in any other case).

(4) In a case where—

(*a*) securities are issued, or securities sold are transferred, and (in either case) they are to be paid for in instalments,

(*b*) the person to whom they are issued or transferred holds them and transfers them to another person when the last instalment is paid,

(*c*) subsection (2)(*c*) above applies in the case of the transfer to the other person,

(*d*) before the making of the transfer to the other person an instrument is received by A or a person whose business is or includes holding chargeable securities as nominee for A,

(*e*) the instrument so received evidences all the rights which (by virtue of the terms under which the securities are issued or sold as mentioned in paragraph (*a*) above) subsist in respect of them at the time of the receipt, and (*f*) the transfer to the other person is effected by an instrument containing a statement that paragraphs (*a*), (*b*) and (*e*) above are fulfilled,

subsection (2)(*c*) above shall have effect as if the reference to the value there mentioned were to an amount (if any) equal to the total of the instalments payable, less those paid before the transfer to the other person is effected.

(5) Where tax is (or would apart from this subsection be) charged under this section in respect of a transfer of securities and ad valorem stamp duty is chargeable on any instrument effecting the transfer, then—

(*a*) if the amount of the duty is less than the amount of tax found by virtue of subsections (2) to (4) above, the tax charged under this section shall be the amount so found less the amount of the duty;

(*b*) in any other case, there shall be no charge to tax under this section in respect of the transfer.

(6) Where tax is charged under the preceding provisions of this section, the person liable for the tax shall (subject to subsection (7) below) be A.

(7) Where tax is charged under the preceding provisions of this section in a case where securities are transferred to a person other than A, and at the time of the transfer A is not resident in the United Kingdom and has no branch or agency in the United Kingdom, the person liable for the tax shall be the person to whom the securities are transferred.

(8) Where chargeable securities are issued or transferred on sale under terms providing for payment in instalments and for an issue of other chargeable securities, and (apart from this subsection) tax would be charged under this section in respect of that issue, tax shall not be so charged but—

(*a*) if any of the instalments becomes payable by A or by a person whose business is or includes holding chargeable securities as nominee for A, there shall be a charge to stamp duty reserve tax under this section when the instalment becomes payable;

(*b*) the charge shall be at the rate of £1.50 for every £100 or part of £100 of the instalment payable;

(*c*) the person liable to pay the instalment shall be liable for the tax.

(9) For the purposes of subsection (2)(*b*) above the value of any consideration not consisting of money shall be taken to be the price it might reasonably be expected to fetch on a sale in the open market at the time the securities are transferred.

(10) For the purposes of subsection (2)(*c*) above the value of securities shall be taken to be the price they might reasonably be expected to fetch on a sale in the open market at the time they are transferred.

(11) For the purposes of subsection (3) above "qualified dealer" and "market maker" have at any particular time the same meanings as they have at that time for the purposes of section 93(5) above.

(12) In subsection (3) above "the day of The Stock Exchange reforms" means the day on which the rule of The Stock Exchange that prohibits a person from carrying on business as both a broker and a jobber is abolished.

(13) Subject to subsection (14) below, this section applies where securities are transferred or issued after 18th March 1986 (whenever the arrangement was made).

(14) This section does not apply, in the case of securities which are transferred, if the Board are satisfied—

(*a*) that on or before 18th March 1986 the transferor (or, where the transferor transfers as agent, the principal) agreed to sell securities of the same kind and amount to the person (other than A) referred to in subsection (1)(*a*) above, and

(*b*) that the transfer is effected in pursuance of that agreement.

General Note

A charge to S.D.R.T. in relation to agreements to transfer securities to clearance services is imposed similar to that in connection with A.D.R.'s in s.93 above. See s.70 for the charge to stamp duty in relation to such transfers.

Clearance services: exceptions

97.—(1) Where securities are transferred—

(*a*) to a company which at the time of the transfer falls within subsection (6) of section 70 above and is resident in the United Kingdom, and

(*b*) from a company which at that time falls within that subsection and is so resident,

there shall be no charge to tax under section 96 above in respect of the transfer.

(2) There shall be no charge to tax under section 96 above in respect of a transfer effected by an instrument on which stamp duty is not chargeable by virtue of—

(*a*) section 127(1) of the Finance Act 1976 (transfer to stock exchange nominee), or

(*b*) section 84(2) or (3) above.

(3) There shall be no charge to tax under section 96 above in respect of a transfer or issue of an inland bearer instrument, within the meaning of the heading "Bearer Instrument" in Schedule 1 to the Stamp Act 1891, which does not fall within exemption 3 in that heading (renounceable letter of allotment etc. where rights are renounceable not later than six months after issue).

(4) There shall be no charge to tax under section 96 above in respect of an issue by a company (company X) of securities in exchange for shares in another company (company Y) where conmpany X—

(*a*) has control of company Y, or

(*b*) will have such control in consequence of the exchange or of an offer as a result of which the exchange is made.

(5) For the purposes of subsection (4) above company X has control of company Y if company X has power to control company Y's affairs by virtue of holding shares in, or possessing voting power in relation to, company Y or any other body corporate.

General Note

Exemption from the charge under s.96 is provided in the same cases as those relative to agreements to transfer securities into A.D.R. form under s.95 above.

General

Administration etc.

98.—(1) The Treasury may make regulations—

(*a*) providing that provisions of the Taxes Management Act 1970 specified in the regulations shall apply in relation to stamp duty reserve tax as they apply in relation to a tax within the meaning of that Act, with such modifications (specified in the regulations) as they think fit;

(*b*) making with regard to stamp duty reserve tax such further provision as they think fit in relation to administration, assessment, collection and recovery.

(2) The power to make regulations under subsection (1) above shall be exercisable by statutory instrument subject to annulment in pursuance of a resolution of the House of Commons.

General Note

Power is given to the Treasury to make regulations by statutory instrument for the administration of S.D.R.T. either through adaptation of the Taxes Management Act 1970 or by special rules.

Interpretation

99.—(1) This section applies for the purposes of this Part of this Act.

(2) "The Board" means the Commissioners of Inland Revenue.

(3) Subject to the following provisions of this section, "chargeable securities" means stocks, shares, loan capital and units under a unit trust scheme.

(4) "Chargeable securities" does not include stocks, shares or loan capital which is (or are) issued or raised by a body corporate not incorporated in the United Kingdom unless the stocks, shares or loan capital is (or are) registered in a register kept in the United Kingdom by or on behalf of the body corporate.

(5) "Chargeable securities" does not include stocks, shares or loan capital the transfer of which is exempt from all stamp duties.

(6) A reference to stocks, shares or loan capital includes a reference to—

(*a*) an interest in, or in dividends or other rights arising out of, stocks, shares or loan capital the transfer of which is not exempt from all stamp duties;

(*b*) a right to an allotment of or to subscribe for, or an option to acquire, stocks, shares or loan capital the transfer of which is is not exempt from all stamp duties,

except that the reference does not include a reference to an interest in a depositary receipt for stocks or shares.

(7) A depositary receipt for stocks or shares is an instrument acknowledging—

(*a*) that a person holds stocks or shares or evidence of the right to receive them, and

(*b*) that another person is entitled to rights, whether expressed as units or otherwise, in or in relation to stocks or shares of the same kind, including the right to receive such stocks or shares (or evidence of the right to receive them) from the person mentioned in paragraph (*a*) above,

except that a depositary receipt for stocks or shares does not include an instrument acknowledging rights in or in relation to stocks or shares if they are issued or sold under terms providing for payment in instalments and for the issue of the instrument as evidence that an instalment has been paid.

(8) The Treasury may by regulations provide that for subsection (7) above (as it has effect for the time being) there shall be substituted a subsection containing a different definition of a depositary receipt; and the power to make regulations under this subsection shall be exercisable by statutory instrument subject to annulment in pursuance of a resolution of the House of Commons.

(9) "Unit" and "unit trust scheme" have the same meanings as in Part VII of the Finance Act 1946.

(10) In interpreting "chargeable securities" in sections 93, 94 and 96 above—

(*a*) the words in subsection (4) above from "unless" to the end shall be ignored, and

(*b*) the effect of paragraph 8 of Schedule 14 to the Companies Act 1985 (share registered overseas) and of section 118 of the Companies Act (Northern Ireland) 1960 and paragraph 7 of Schedule 14 to the Companies (Northern Ireland) Order 1986 (equivalent provision for Northern Ireland) shall be ignored for the purposes of subsection (5) above.

General Note

This is the general definition section applicable to Stamp Duty Reserve Tax.

Part V

Inheritance Tax

General Note

F.A. 1975 (ss.19–52 and Scheds. 4–12) introduced capital transfer tax ("C.T.T.") in replacement of estate duty ("E.D.") which had itself been introduced by F.A. 1894. The provisions of F.A. 1975 and subsequent amendments were codified in the Capital Transfer Tax Act 1984 ("the 1984 Act").

The crucial difference between C.T.T. and E.D. was that C.T.T. imposed a tax on lifetime gifts, while these escaped E.D. altogether provided the donor survived a prescribed period. The general charge on lifetime gifts between individuals is now abolished, thus returning the fiscal system in many respects to the E.D. regime. An important E.D. anti-avoidance provision, denying relief to gifts with a reservation of benefit to the donor, is re-introduced (s.102 and Sched. 20). Gifts made within three years of death will be chargeable in full, with a tapering charge for gifts between three and seven years before death (Sched. 19, para. 2).

The C.T.T. regime for trusts, extensively modified in 1982, and codified in the 1984 Act, Part III, ss.43–93, is largely retained, with a tax charge where appropriate at half the rate on death.

Capital transfer tax to be known as inheritance tax

100.—(1) On and after the passing of this Act, the tax charged under the Capital Transfer Tax Act 1984 (in this Part of this Act referred to as "the 1984 Act") shall be known as inheritance tax and, accordingly, on and after that passing,—

(*a*) the 1984 Act may be cited as the Inheritance Tax Act 1984; and

(*b*) subject to subsection (2) below, any reference to capital transfer tax in the 1984 Act, in any other enactment passed before or in the same Session as this Act or in any document executed, made, served or issued on or before the passing of this Act or at any time thereafter shall have effect as a reference to inheritance tax.

(2) Subsection (1)(*b*) above does not apply where the reference to capital transfer tax relates to a liability to tax arising before the passing of this Act.

(3) In the following provisions of this Part of this Act, any reference to tax except where it is a reference to a named tax is a reference to inheritance tax and, in so far as it occurs in a provision which relates to a time before the passing of this Act, includes a reference to capital transfer tax.

General Note

The tax is re-named inheritance tax ("I.H.T.") and the 1984 Act becomes the Inheritance Tax Act. Strictly, this is a misnomer, since the charge is not on amounts inherited or on inheritors but on amounts given or bequeathed and accordingly primarily on trustees or executors. However, the change of name emphasises a major purpose of the reform, to allow the lifetime transfer of family businesses and family farms without a crippling immediate charge to tax.

Lifetime transfers potentially exempt etc.

101.—(1) The 1984 Act shall have effect subject to the amendments in Part I of Schedule 19 to this Act, being amendments—

(*a*) removing liability for tax on certain transfers of value where the transfer occurs at least seven years before the transferor's death;

(*b*) providing for one Table of rates of tax;

(*c*) abolishing exemptions for mutual transfers;

(*d*) making provision with respect to the amounts of tax to be charged on transfers occurring before the death of the transferor;

(*e*) making provision with respect to the application of relief under Chapter I (business property) and Chapter II (agricultural property) of Part V of the 1984 Act to such transfers; and

(*f*) reducing the period during which the values transferred by chargeable transfers are aggregated from ten years to seven;

and amendments making provisions consequential on or incidental to the matters referred to above and to sections 102 and 103 below.

(2) In consequence of the amendments effected by Part I of Schedule 19 to this Act, section 79 of the Finance Act 1980 (capital gains tax: general relief for gifts) shall be amended as follows—

(*a*) in subsection (5) after the word "is", in the second place where it occurs, there shall be inserted "(or proves to be)" and at the end there shall be added "and, in the case of a disposal which, being a potentially exempt transfer, proves to be a chargeable transfer, all necessary adjustments shall be made, whether by the discharge or repayment of capital gains tax or otherwise"; and

(*b*) in subsection (6)(*a*) for the words "three years" there shall be substituted "seven years".

(3) Part I of Schedule 19 to this Act has effect, subject to Part II of that Schedule, with respect to transfers of value made, and other events occurring, on or after 18th March 1986.

(4) The transitional provisions in Part II of Schedule 19 to this Act shall have effect.

General Note

The section introduces Sched. 19, Part I of which contains necessary amendments to the 1984 Act, while Part II has transitional provisions. The former two Tables of rates are reduced to one, applicable to the charge on death, but charges on trust events will continue to be levied at half the rate on death. The exemption for mutual transfers, contained in ss.148–150 of the 1984 Act, which was little used in practice but was prone to abuse, is abolished. An important feature of C.T.T., the lifetime cumulation of transfers, already reduced to ten years, is further cut to seven years in line with the scheme of the new tax.

Under subs. (2), liabilities for I.H.T. will be allowed as a deductible expenditure in relation to C.G.T. charged on the disposal of a gift, in the same way as liabilities for C.T.T. were allowed.

See further the Commentary to Sched. 19 for detailed discussion of amendments to the 1984 Act.

Gifts with reservation

102.—(1) Subject to subsections (5) and (6) below, this section applies where, on or after 18th March 1986, an individual disposes of any property by way of gift and either—

(*a*) possession and enjoyment of the property is not bona fide assumed by the donee at or before the beginning of the relevant period; or

(*b*) at any time in the relevant period the property is not enjoyed to the entire exclusion, or virtually to the entire exclusion, of the donor and of any benefit to him by contract or otherwise;

and in this section "the relevant period" means a period ending on the date of the donor's death and beginning seven years before that date or, if it is later, on the date of the gift.

(2) If and so long as—

(*a*) possession and enjoyment of any property is not bona fide assumed as mentioned in subsection (1)(*a*) above, or

(*b*) any property is not enjoyed as mentioned in subsection (1)(*b*) above,

the property is referred to (in relation to the gift and the donor) as property subject to a reservation.

(3) If, immediately before the death of the donor, there is any property which, in relation to him, is property subject to a reservation then, to the extent that the property would not, apart from this section, form part of the donor's estate immediately before his death, that property shall be treated for the purposes of the 1984 Act as property to which he was beneficially entitled immediately before his death.

(4) If, at a time before the end of the relevant period, any property ceases to be property subject to a reservation, the donor shall be treated for the purposes of the 1984 Act as having at that time made a disposition of the property by a disposition which is a potentially exempt transfer.

(5) This section does not apply if or, as the case may be, to the extent that the disposal of property by way of gift is an exempt transfer by virtue of any of the following provisions of Part II of the 1984 Act,—

(*a*) section 18 (transfers between spouses);
(*b*) section 20 (small gifts);
(*c*) section 22 (gifts in consideration of marriage);
(*d*) section 23 (gifts to charities);
(*e*) section 24 (gifts to political parties);
(*f*) section 25 (gifts for national purposes, etc.);
(*g*) section 26 (gifts for public benefit);
(*h*) section 27 (maintenance funds for historic buildings); and
(*i*) section 28 (employee trusts).

(6) This section does not apply if the disposal of property by way of gift is made under the terms of a policy issued in respect of an insurance made before 18th March 1986 unless the policy is varied on or after that date so as to increase the benefits secured or to extend the term of the insurance; and, for this purpose, any change in the terms of the policy which is made in pursuance of an option or other power conferred by the policy shall be deemed to be a variation of the policy.

(7) If a policy issued as mentioned in subsection (6) above confers an option or other power under which benefits and premiums may be increased to take account of increases in the retail prices index (as defined in section 8(3) of the 1984 Act) or any similar index specified in the policy, then, to the extent that the right to exercise that option or power would have been lost if it had not been exercised on or before 1st August 1986, the exercise of that option or power before that date shall be disregarded for the purposes of subsection (6) above.

(8) Schedule 20 to this Act has effect for supplementing this section.

General Note

This section and the succeeding one, together with Sched. 20, re-introduce two major anti-avoidance provisions in the E.D. regime. Their absence from C.T.T. made it possible for example for a donor to give his house away and continue living there without any charge on death, provided an equitable interest had not been created. Also, a large tax avoidance industry grew up based on the use of trusts or insurance policies or both. These included arrangements known as PETA (Pure Endowment Term Assurance) schemes, Discounted Gift Schemes and Inheritance Trusts. Their purpose was to allow donors to transfer property so that it passed directly to their beneficiaries while deriving benefit from it during their lifetime. Such schemes, which may in any case be vulnerable under the "associated operations" rule in s.268 of the 1984 Act or the "new approach" of the courts to tax avoidance in the cases of *Ramsay* [1982] A.C. 300 and *Furniss v. Dawson* [1984] A.C. 474, are now to be specifically invalidated.

Section 102 derives its concept and much of its wording from the Customs and Inland Revenue Act 1889, s.11, which amended *ibid.*, 1881, s.38, and was adopted for the purposes of E.D. by F.A. 1894, s.2(1)(c). Where a gift is made with a reservation of interest for the donor, that property will be treated as part of the donor's estate. If the reservation is released at any time, that will be treated as the date of the gift for I.H.T. purposes.

The provision that the property must be enjoyed *virtually* to the entire exclusion of the donor would appear to exclude *de minimis* or purely theoretical benefits from the mischief of the clause. Gifts which are in any case exempt under Part II, Chapter I, of the 1984 Act are also outside the ambit of the clause, except for the annual exemption (section 19 of the 1984 Act).

Subs. (6) provides that the new rules will apply to premiums on pre-Budget insurance policies so long as the policies and their terms are unchanged and subs (7) further excludes the exercise of indexation options during the passage of the Finance Bill.

See further the commentary to Sched. 20 for discussion of detailed provisions supplementing the clause.

Treatment of certain debts and incumbrances

103.—(1) Subject to subsection (2) below, if, in determining the value of a person's estate immediately before his death, account would be taken, apart from this subsection, of a liability consisting of a debt incurred by him or an incumbrance created by a disposition made by him, that liability shall be subject to abatement to an extent proportionate to the value of any of the consideration given for the debt or incumbrance which consisted of—

(*a*) property derived from the deceased; or

(*b*) consideration (not being property derived from the deceased) given by any person who was at any time entitled to, or amongst whose resources there was at any time included, any property derived from the deceased.

(2) If, in a case where the whole or a part of the consideration given for a debt or incumbrance consisted of such consideration as is mentioned in subsection (1)(*b*) above, it is shown that the value of the consideration given, or of that part thereof, as the case may be, exceeded that which could have been rendered available by application of all the property derived from the deceased, other than such (if any) of that property—

(*a*) as is included in the consideration given, or

(*b*) as to which it is shown that the disposition of which it, or the property which it represented, was the subject matter was not made with reference to, or with a view to enabling or facilitating, the giving of the consideration or the recoupment in any manner of the cost thereof,

no abatement shall be made under subsection (1) above in respect of the excess.

(3) In subsections (1) and (2) above "property derived from the deceased" means, subject to subsection (4) below, any property which was the subject matter of a disposition made by the deceased, either by himself alone or in concert or by arrangement with any other person or which represented any of the subject matter of such a disposition, whether directly or indirectly, and whether by virtue of one or more intermediate dispositions.

(4) If the disposition first-mentioned in subsection (3) above was not a transfer of value and it is shown that the disposition was not part of associated operations which included—

(*a*) a disposition by the deceased, either alone or in concert or by arrangement with any other person, otherwise than for full consideration in money or money's worth paid to the deceased for his own use or benefit; or

(*b*) a disposition by any other person operating to reduce the value of the property of the deceased,

that first-mentioned disposition shall be left out of account for the purposes of subsections (1) to (3) above.

(5) If, before a person's death but on or after 18th March 1986, money or money's worth, is paid or applied by him—

(*a*) in or towards the satisfaction or discharge of a debt or incumbrance in the case of which subsection (1) above would have effect on his death if the debt or incumbrance had not been satisfied or discharged, or

(*b*) in reduction of a debt or incumbrance in the case of which that subsection has effect on his death,

the 1984 Act shall have effect as if, at the time of the payment or application, the person concerned had made a transfer of value equal to the money or money's worth and that transfer were a potentially exempt transfer.

(6) Any reference in this section to a debt incurred is a reference to a debt incurred on or after 18th March 1986 and any reference to an incumbrance created by a disposition is a reference to an incumbrance created by a disposition made on or after that date; and in this section "subject matter" includes, in relation to any disposition, any annual or periodical payment made or payable under or by virtue of the disposition.

(7) In determining the value of a person's estate immediately before his death, no account shall be taken (by virtue of section 5 of the 1984 Act) of any liability arising under or in connection with a policy of life insurance issued in respect of an insurance made on or after 1st July 1986 unless the whole of the sums assured under that policy form part of that person's estate immediately before his death.

General Note

The legislative origins of this clause under the E.D. regime can be traced to F.A. 1939, ss.30 and 31. The type of device aimed at in its simplest form is where A gives £X to B and then borrows £X from B. Normally the debt of £X would be deductible from A's estate under s.5(3) of the 1984 Act. Under s.103 the debt would fall to be abated or excluded since it was 'derived from the deceased'.

The section applies to incumbrances created by a disposition as it does to 'debts incurred'. There is no comprehensive definition of 'disposition' in the 1984 Act, but it is a term of very wide meaning—*per* Lord Macnaghten in *Northumberland* v. *Att.-Gen.* [1905] A.C. 406: "The term 'disposition' . . . must have been intended to comprehend and exhaust every conceivable mode by which property can pass, whether by act of parties or by act of the law." It will therefore cover such operations as the creation of a settlement. Section 272 of the 1984 Act provides that 'disposition' includes a disposition by associated operations as defined in section 268.

Subs. (3), derived from F.A. 1939 s.30(3)(*a*), works to the same effect by including in property 'derived from the deceased' property involved in dispositions in concert or by arrangement with other persons and also draws in intermediate dispositions.

Subs. (4), derived from the proviso to F.A. 1943 s.26(2), excludes from the ambit of the clause a disposition which is not a transfer of value if it is not part of associated operations which include a disposition other than for full consideration or operating to reduce the value of the deceased's property.

Subs. (7) excludes as a deduction from a person's estate any liability arising under an insurance policy unless the proceeds of the policy forms part of his estate.

Regulations for avoiding double charges etc.

104.—(1) For the purposes of the 1984 Act the Board may by regulations make such provision as is mentioned in subsection (2) below with respect to transfers of value made, and other events occurring, on or after 18th March 1986 where—

(*a*) a potentially exempt transfer proves to be a chargeable transfer and, immediately before the death of the transferor, his estate includes property acquired by him from the transferee otherwise than for full consideration in money or money's worth;

(*b*) an individual disposes of property by a transfer of value which is or proves to be a chargeable transfer and the circumstances are such that subsection (3) or subsection (4) of section 102 above applies to the property as being or having been property subject to a reservation;

(*c*) in determining the value of a person's estate immediately before his death, a liability of his to any person is abated as mentioned in section 103 above and, before his death, the deceased made a transfer of value by virtue of which the estate of that other person was increased or by virtue of which property becomes comprised in a settlement of which that other person is a trustee; or

(*d*) the circumstances are such as may be specified in the regulations for the purposes of this subsection, being circumstances appearing to the Board to be similar to those referred to in paragraphs (*a*) to (*c*) above.

(2) This provision which may be made by regulations under this section is provision for either or both of the following,—

(*a*) treating the value transferred by a transfer of value as reduced by reference to the value transferred by another transfer of value; and

(*b*) treating the whole or any part of the tax paid or payable on the value transferred by a transfer of value as a credit against the tax payable on the value transferred by another transfer of value.

(3) The power to make regulations under this section shall be exercisable by statutory instrument subject to annulment in pursuance of a resolution of the Commons House of Parliament.

General Note

The abolition of the relief for mutual transfers, contained in ss.148–150 of the 1984 Act, and the introduction of the anti-avoidance provisions relating to gifts with reservation (s.102) and the creation of debts and incumbrances (s.103) could give rise to situations in which property might be charged or chargeable in relation both to an inter vivos disposition and the death of a disponor. Subs. (1) deals with these and similar situations and subs. (2) permits the Revenue to make regulations by statutory instrument for preventing double taxation by setting off transfers of value or tax paid against each other.

For the definition of 'potentially exempt transfer' see Sched. 19, para. 1 and the commentary thereon.

Application of business and agricultural relief where transfer partly exempt

105. With respect to transfers of value made on or after 18th March 1986, after section 39 of the 1984 Act there shall be inserted the following section—

"Operation of sections 38 and 39 in cases of business or agricultural relief

39A.—(1) Where any part of the value transferred by a transfer of value is attributable to—

(*a*) the value of relevant business property, or

(*b*) the agricultural value of agricultural property,

then, for the purpose of attributing the value transferred (as reduced in accordance with section 104 or 116 below), to specific gifts and gifts of residue or shares of residue, sections 38 and 39 above shall have effect subject to the following provisions of this section.

(2) The value of any specific gifts of relevant business property or agricultural property shall be taken to be their value as reduced in accordance with section 104 or 116 below.

(3) The value of any specific gifts not falling within subsection (2) above shall be taken to be the appropriate fraction of their value.

(4) In subsection (3) above "the appropriate fraction" means a fraction of which—

(*a*) the numerator is the difference between the value transferred and the value, reduced as mentioned in subsection (2) above, of any gifts falling within that subsection, and

(*b*) the denominator is the difference between the unreduced value transferred and the value, before the reduction mentioned in subsection (2) above, of any gifts falling within that subsection;

and in paragraph (*b*) above "the unreduced value transferred" means the amount which would be the value transferred by the transfer but for the reduction required by sections 104 and 116 below.

(5) If or to the extent that specific gifts fall within paragraphs (*a*) and (*b*) of subsection (1) of section 38 above, the amount corresponding to the value of the gifts shall be arrived at in accordance with subsections (3) to (5) of that section by reference to their value reduced as mentioned in subsection (2) or, as the case may be, subsection (3) of this section.

(6) For the purposes of this section the value of a specific gift of relevant business property or agricultural property does not include the value of any other gift payable out of that property; and that other gift shall not itself be treated as a specific gift of relevant business property or agricultural property.

(7) In this section—

"agricultural property" and "the agricultural value of agricultural property" have the same meaning as in Chapter II of Part V of this Act; and

"relevant business property" has the same meaning as in Chapter I of that Part."

General Note

This section makes changes to the interaction of two forms of relief under the 1984 Act, namely by way of exemption under ss.18–35 and by way of reduction of value transferred under ss.103–124. The former relates for example to property left to a spouse and the latter to business property or agricultural property, which attract a relief of 30 per cent. or 50 per cent. depending on the circumstances. Under the rules contained in ss.36–42, where a transfer is partly exempt and also includes property qualifying for business or agricultural relief, that relief is given first and then the exempt and chargeable parts of the transfer are ascertained. This can produce anomalous results.

To remedy this, it is provided that where there is a specific gift of property attracting business or agricultural relief, the relief will attach to that property. Otherwise, the relief will be allocated pro rata to the exempt and chargeable parts of the transfer.

Changes in financial institutions: business property

106.—(1) In section 105 of the 1984 Act (relevant business property) the following shall be substituted for subsection (4)(*a*)—

"(*a*) does not apply to any property if the business concerned is wholly that of a market maker or is that of a discount house and (in either case) is carried on in the United Kingdom, and".

(2) At the end of that section there shall be inserted—

"(7) In this section "market maker" means a person who—

(*a*) holds himself out at all normal times in compliance with the rules of The Stock Exchange as willing to buy and sell securities, stocks or shares at a price specified by him, and

(*b*) is recognised as doing so by the Council of The Stock Exchange."

(3) Subsections (1) and (2) above apply in relation to transfers of value made, and other events occurring, on or after the day of The Stock Exchange reforms.

(4) The Board may by regulations provide that section 105(7) of the 1984 Act (as inserted by subsection (2) above) shall have effect—

(*a*) as if the reference to The Stock Exchange in paragraph (*a*) were to any recognised investment exchange (within the meaning of the Financial Services Act 1986) or to any of those exchanges specified in the regulations, and (*b*) as if the reference to the Council of The Stock Exchange in paragraph (*b*) were to the investment exchange concerned.

(5) The Board may by regulations amend section 105 of the 1984 Act so as to secure that section 105(3) does not apply to any property if the business concerned is of such a description as is set out in the regulations; and the regulations may include such incidental and consequential provisions as the Board think fit.

(6) Regulations under subsection (4) or (5) above shall apply in relation to transfers of value made, and other events occurring, on or after such day, after the day of The Stock Exchange reforms, as is specified in the regulations.

(7) The power to make regulations under subsection (4) or (5) above shall be exercisable by statutory instrument subject to annulment in pursuance of a resolution of the Commons House of Parliament.

(8) In this section "the day of The Stock Exchange reforms" means the day on which the rule of The Stock Exhange that prohibits a person from carrying on business as both a broker and a jobber is abolished.

General Note

This is one of a number of provisions in the Finance Act relating to the restructuring of the London financial markets due to take place in October 1986 (known as the "Big Bang"). A Financial Services Act is also currently before Parliament providing for the regulation of these markets after the Big Bang.

Section 105(4)(a) of the 1984 Act exempted jobbers on the Stock Exchange from the general exclusion of dealers in securities from business property relief. After the Big Bang, jobbers will be replaced by 'market makers' and the exemption is extended to them. The Revenue are also given power to extend the exemption by statutory instrument to similar dealers in other investment exchanges.

Changes in financial institutions: interest

107.—(1) In section 234 of the 1984 Act (interest on instalments) the following shall be substituted for subsection (3)(*c*)—

"(*c*) any company whose business is wholly that of a market maker or is that of a discount house and (in either case) is carried on in the United Kingdom."

(2) At the end of that section there shall be inserted—

"(4) In this section "market maker" means a person who—

(*a*) holds himself out at all normal times in compliance with the rules of The Stock Exchange as willing to buy and sell securities, stocks or shares at a price specified by him, and

(*b*) is recognised as doing so by the Council of The Stock Exchange."

(3) Subsections (1) and (2) above apply in relation to chargeable transfers made, and other events occurring, on or after the day of The Stock Exchange reforms.

(4) The Board may by regulations provide that section 234(4) of the 1984 Act (as inserted by subsection (2) above) shall have effect—

(*a*) as if the reference to The Stock Exchange in paragraph (*a*) were to any recognised investment exchange (within the meaning of the Financial Services Act 1986) or to any of those exchanges specified in the regulations, and

(*b*) as if the reference to the Council of The Stock Exchange in paragraph (*b*) were to the investment exchange concerned.

(5) The Board may by regulations amend section 234 of the 1984 Act so as to secure that companies of a description set out in the regulations fall within section 234(3)(*c*); and the regulations may include such incidental and consequential provisions as the Board think fit.

(6) Regulations under subsection (4) or (5) above shall apply in relation to chargeable transfers made, and other events occurring, on or after such day, after the day of The Stock Exchange reforms, as is specified in the regulations.

(7) The power to make regulations under subsection (4) or (5) above shall be exercisable by statutory instrument subject to annulment in pursuance of a resolution of the Commons House of Parliament.

(8) In this section "the day of The Stock Exchange reforms" has the same meaning as in section 106 above.

General Note

Like section 106, this clause results from the Big Bang, and extends a provision in the 1984 Act relating to interest on instalments of tax attributable to shares in jobbing companies to shares in market making companies under the new dispensation. It also allows the Revenue to extend the provision by statutory instrument to the shares of similar companies on other investment exchanges.

Part VI

Oil Taxation

The on-shore/off-shore boundary

108.—(1) For the purposes of the enactments relating to oil taxation, land lying between the landward boundary of the territorial sea and the shoreline of the United Kingdom (as defined below) shall be treated as part of the bed of the territorial sea of the United Kingdom and any reference in those enactments to the territorial sea or the subsoil beneath it shall be construed accordingly.

(2) Any reference to the United Kingdom in the enactments relating to oil taxation, where that reference is a reference to a geographical area, shall be treated as a reference to the United Kingdom exclusive of the land referred to in subsection (1) above and of any waters for the time being covering that land.

(3) In this section—

(*a*) "the landward boundary of the territorial sea" means the line for the time being ordered by Her Majesty in Council to be the baseline from which the breadth of the territorial sea is measured; and

(*b*) "the shoreline of the United Kingdom" means, subject to subsection (4) below, the high-water line along the coast, including the coast of all islands comprised in the United Kingdom.

(4) In the case of waters adjacent to a bay, as defined in the Territorial Waters Order in Council 1964, the shoreline means—

(*a*) if the bay has only one mouth and the distance between the high-water lines of the natural entrance points of the bay does not exceed 5,000 metres, a straight line joining those high-water lines;

(*b*) if, because of the presence of islands, the bay has more than one mouth and the distances between the high-water lines of the natural entrance points of each mouth added together do not exceed 5,000 metres, a series of straight lines across each of the mouths drawn so as to join those high-water lines; and

(*c*) if neither paragraph (*a*) nor paragraph (*b*) above applies, a straight line 5,000 metres in length drawn from high-water line to high-water line within the bay in such a manner as to enclose the maximum area of water that is possible with a line of that length.

(5) If, by virtue of this section, it becomes necessary at any time to establish the high-water line at any place, it shall be taken to be the line which, on the current Admiralty chart showing that place, is depicted as "the coastline"; and for this purpose,—

(*a*) an Admiralty chart means a chart published under the superintendence of the Hydrographer of the Navy;

(*b*) if there are two or more Admiralty charts of different scales showing the place in question and depicting the coastline, account shall be taken only of the largest scale chart; and

(*c*) subject to paragraph (*b*) above, the current Admiralty chart at any time is that most recently published before that time.

(6) In this section "the enactments relating to oil taxation" means Part I of the Oil Taxation Act 1975 and any enactment which is to be construed as one with that Part.

(7) This section shall be deemed to have come into force on 1st April 1986.

General Note

The effective of offshore-onshore dividing line for oil taxation purposes has been where the territorial sea, or three-mile limit, begins. For most of its length this coincides with the low-water mark around the coast, but in certain areas it runs at some distance from the coastline. The section provides for the dividing line henceforth to be the high-water mark, so classifying the largest possible area as offshore and allowing greater tax relief for exploration and appraisal.

Alternative valuation of light gases

109.—(1) Where an election is made under this section and accepted by the Board, the market value for the purposes of the Oil Taxation Acts of any light gases to which the election applies shall be determined, not in accordance with paragraphs 2, 2A and 3 of Schedule 3 to the principal Act (value under a notional contract), but by reference to a price formula specified in the election; and, in relation to any such light gases, any reference to market value in any other provision of the Oil Taxation Acts shall be construed accordingly.

(2) No election may be made under this section in respect of light gases which are "ethane" as defined in subsection (6)(*a*) of section 134 of the Finance Act 1982 (alternative valuation of ethane used for petrochemical purposes) if the principal purpose for which the gases are being or are to be used is that specified in subsection (2)(*b*) of the said section 134 (use for petrochemical purposes).

(3) Subject to subsection (4) below, an election under this section applies only to light gases—

(*a*) which, during the period covered by the election, are either disposed of otherwise than in sales at arm's length or relevantly appropriated; and

(*b*) which are not subject to fractionation between the time at which they are so disposed of or appropriated and the time at which they are applied or used for the purposes specified in the election.

(4) In any case where,—

(*a*) at a time during the period covered by an election, a market value falls to be determined for light gases to which subsection (4)(*b*) or (5)(*d*) of section 2 of the principal Act applies (oil stocks at the end of chargeable periods), and

(*b*) after the expiry of the chargeable period in question, the light gases are disposed of or appropriated as mentioned in subsection (3) above, the market value of those light gases at the time referred to in paragraph (*a*) above shall be determined as if they were gases to which the election applies.

(5) Schedule 18 to the Finance Act 1982 (which applies to elections under section 134 of that Act relating to ethane used or to be used for petrochemical purposes) shall have effect for supplementing this section but subject to the modifications in Schedule 21 to this Act (in which "the 1982 Schedule" means the said Schedule 18).

(6) This section shall be construed as one with Part I of the principal Act and in this section—

(*a*) "light gases" means oil consisting of gas of which the largest component by volume over any chargeable period is methane or ethane or a combination of those gases and which—

(i) results from the fractionation of gas before it is disposed of or appropriated as mentioned in subsection (3)(*a*) above, or

(ii) before being so disposed of or appropriated, is not subjected to initial treatment or is subjected to initial treatment which does not include fractionation;

(*b*) "the principal Act" means the Oil Taxation Act 1975; and

(*c*) "the Oil Taxation Acts" means Part I of the principal Act and any enactment which is to be construed as one with that Part.

(7) In this section "fractionation" means the treatment of gas in order to separate gas of one or more kinds as mentioned in paragraph 2A(3) of Schedule 3 to the principal Act; and for the purposes of subsection (6)(*a*) above,—

(*a*) the proportion of methane, ethane or a combination of the two in any gas shall be determined at a temperature of 15°C and at a pressure of one atmosphere; and

(*b*) any component other than methane, ethane or liquified petroleum gas shall be disregarded.

General Note

When gas or oil is disposed of other than by way of a sale at arms length, for example when it is transferred from the producing company to an associated company, P.R.T. is charged on the market value. The normal valuation rules in para. 2 of Sched. 3 to the Oil Taxation Act 1975 are not satisfactory for ascertaining the market value of light gases such as methane ordinarily sold under long term contracts. The alternative basis now provided will enable P.R.T. valuations to reflect the terms under which comparable gas is actually sold in the open market. See F.A. 1982, s.134 for a similar provision in relation to ethane used for petrochemical purposes.

Attribution of certain receipts and expenditure between oil fields

110.—(1) Section 8 of the Oil Taxation Act 1983 (qualifying assets) shall have effect, and be deemed always to have had effect, subject to the amendments in subsections (2) and (3) below.

(2) In subsection (3) (which determines the oil field to which are attributable tariff receipts or disposal receipts referable to a qualifying asset) after the word "above", both where it occurs in paragraph (*c*) and also in the words following paragraph (*c*), there shall be inserted "and subsection (3A) below".

(3) After subsection (3) there shall be inserted the following subsection—

"(3A) If development decisions were first made in relation to two or more oil fields on the same day, then, for the purposes of subsection (3)(*c*) above, it shall be conclusively presumed that the first of those decisions was made in relation to that one of those fields in connection with which it appeared—

(*a*) at the time of the decision, or

(*b*) if it is later, at the time the asset was acquired or brought into existence by the participator in question for use in connection with an oil field,

that the participator in question would make the most use of the asset."

(4) Paragraph 6 of Schedule 1 to the Oil Taxation Act 1983 (attribution of allowable expenditure) shall have effect and be deemed always to have had effect with the addition of the following sub-paragraph—

"(3) Subsection (3A) of section 8 of this Act applies for the purposes of sub-paragraph (1) above as it applies for the purposes of subsection (3)(*c*) of that section."

General Note

S.8(3)(*c*) of the Oil Taxation Act 1983 provides that where expenditure on assets with shared use such as pipelines has been apportioned between fields in common ownership, tariff and disposal receipts are chargeable on the field which received its development consent first. In order to prevent difficulties in allocating this charge where fields have been given their development consent on the same day, as is usual for cluster developments, a further rule is provided identifying the chargeable field as that in which the participator is likely to make the greatest use of the asset.

Part VII

Miscellaneous and Supplementary

Broadcasting: additional payments by programme contractors

111.—(1) The Broadcasting Act 1981 shall have effect with respect to additional payments payable by programme contractors under that Act subject to the amendments made by Part I of Schedule 22 to this Act.

(2) The transitional provisions made by Part II of that Schedule shall have effect.

(3) This section shall be deemed to have come into force on 1st April 1986.

General Note

See the note to Sched. 22 below.

Limit for local loans

112. In section 4(1) of the National Loans Act 1968 (which provides that the aggregate of any commitments of the Public Works Loan Commissioners in respect of undertakings to grant local loans and any amount outstanding in respect of the principal of such loans shall not exceed £28,000 million or such other sum not exceeding £35,000 million as the Treasury may specify by order) for the words "£28,000 million" and "£35,000 million" there shall be substituted respectively "£42,000 million" and "£50,000 million".

General Note

The potential limit for loans from the Public Works Loan Board to local authorities is raised from £35 bn. to £50 bn. The recent fall in long-term interest rates below 10 per cent. has prompted a sharp increase in this form of borrowing.

"Securities" for purposes of Exchange Equalisation Account Act 1979

113. At the end of section 3 of the Exchange Equalisation Account Act 1979 (investment of the funds of the Exchange Equalisation Account) there shall be added the following subsection—

"(4) Without prejudice to the reference in subsection (1)(*b*) above to special drawing rights, the reference in subsection (3) above to currency of any country includes a reference to units of account defined by reference to more than one currency."

General Note

The funds of the Exchange Equalisation Account may now be invested in securities denominated in units of account comprising more than one currency.

Short title, interpretation, construction and repeals

114.—(1) This Act may be cited as the Finance Act 1986.

(2) In this Act "the Taxes Act" means the Income and Corporation Taxes Act 1970.

(3) Part II of this Act, so far as it relates to income tax, shall be construed as one with the Income Tax Acts, so far as it relates to corporation tax, shall be construed as one with the Corporation Tax Acts and, so far as it relates to capital gains tax, shall be construed as one with the Capital Gains Tax Act 1979.

(4) Part III of this Act shall be construed as one with the Stamp Act 1891.

(5) Part V of this Act, other than section 100, shall be construed as one with the Capital Transfer Tax Act 1984.

(6) The enactments and Orders specified in Schedule 23 to this Act are hereby repealed to the extent specified in the third column of that Schedule, but subject to any provision at the end of any Part of that Schedule.

SCHEDULES

Section 3(2), (3)

SCHEDULE 1

Vehicles Excise Duty: Hackney Carriages and Farmers' Goods Vehicles

Part I

Provision Substituted for Part II of Schedule 2 to the Acts of 1971 and 1972

Description of vehicle	Rate of duty
	£
Hackney carriages	52·50 with an additional £1·05 for each person above 20 (excluding the driver) for which the vehicle has seating capacity.

Part II

Tables Substituted in Part II of Schedule 4 to the Acts of 1971 and 1972

Table A(1)

Rates of Duty on Rigid Goods Vehicles Exceeding 12 Tonnes Plated Gross Weight

Rates for Farmers' Goods Vehicles

Plated gross weight of vehicle		Rate of duty		
1. Exceeding	2. Not exceeding	3. Two axle vehicle	4. Three axle vehicle	5. Four or more axle vehicle
tonnes	tonnes	£	£	£
12	13	210	170	170
13	14	280	175	175
14	15	350	175	175
15	17	475	180	175
17	19	—	240	175
19	21	—	320	180
21	23	—	420	245
23	25	—	720	330
25	27	—	—	465
27	29	—	—	665
29	30·49	—	—	1,090

Table C(1)

Rates of Duty on Tractor Units Exceeding 12 Tonnes Plated Train Weight and Having Only 2 Axles

Rates for Farmers' Goods Vehicles

Plated train weight of tractor unit		Rate of duty		
1. Exceeding	2. Not exceeding	3. For a tractor unit to be used with semi-trailers with any number of axles	4. For a tractor unit to be used only with semi-trailers with not less than two axles	5. For a tractor unit to be used only with semi-trailers with not less than three axles
tonnes	tonnes	£	£	£
12	14	235	215	215
14	16	290	220	220
16	18	330	220	220
18	20	385	220	220
20	22	435	270	220
22	23	465	300	220
23	25	530	365	225
25	26	530	405	265
26	28	530	500	345
28	29	555	555	390
29	31	765	765	495
31	33	1,115	1,115	780
33	34	1,230	1,230	1,150
34	36	1,405	1,405	1,405
36	38	1,580	1,580	1,580

TABLE D(1)

RATES OF DUTY ON TRACTOR UNITS EXCEEDING 12 TONNES PLATED TRAIN WEIGHT AND HAVING THREE OR MORE AXLES

RATES FOR FARMERS' GOODS VEHICLES

Plated train weight of tractor unit		Rate of duty		
1. Exceeding	2. Not exceeding	3. For a tractor unit to be used with semi-trailers with any number of axles	4. For a tractor unit to be used only with semi-trailers with not less than two axles	5. For a tractor unit to be used only with semi-trailers with not less than three axles
tonnes	tonnes	£	£	£
12	14	215	215	215
14	20	220	220	220
20	22	270	220	220
22	23	300	220	220
23	25	365	220	220
25	26	405	225	220
26	28	500	230	225
28	29	555	270	230
29	31	765	325	240
31	33	1,115	495	250
33	34	1,140	725	315
34	36	1,205	1,035	475
36	38	1,390	1,390	710

GENERAL NOTE

The rate for the hackney carriage class, which includes buses, coaches and taxis, is increased by 5 per cent., since these vehicles do not pay their full share of road costs. The increases in the rates for farmers' goods vehicles, which range from around 15 per cent. to 50 per cent., is the second stage in a three year programme to bring the farmers' rates up to a level broadly proportionate to the mileage which farmers' vehicles cover on the roads by comparison with the average lorry.

Section 3(7)

SCHEDULE 2

VEHICLES EXCISE DUTY: MISCELLANEOUS AMENDMENTS

PART I

AMENDMENTS OF VEHICLES (EXCISE) ACT 1971

Additional days to be included in duration of certain licences

1.—(1) In the Vehicles (Excise) Act 1971 (in this Part of this Schedule referred to as "the 1971 Act"), section 2A (power to modify duration of licences and rates of duty) as set out in paragraph 5 of Schedule 7 to that Act (transitional provisions) shall be amended as follows.

(2) In subsection (1) after paragraph (*a*) there shall be inserted the following paragraph—

"(*aa*) in the case of licences taken out on the first registration of vehicles of such description as may be so specified, periods exceeding by such number of days (not exceeding thirty) as may be determined by or under the order the periods for which the licence would otherwise have effect by virtue of section 2(1) above or any provision made under paragraph (*a*) above; or".

(3) In subsection (2), in paragraph (*a*) of the proviso, for the words "other than one of twelve months" there shall be substituted the words "of a fixed number of months other than twelve or for a period of less than a month".

Tower wagons used by street lighting authorities etc.

2. In section 4 of the 1971 Act (exemptions from duty) in subsection (2) for the definition of "tower wagon" there shall be substituted the following—

" 'tower wagon' means a goods vehicle—

(*a*) into which there is built, as part of the vehicle, any expanding or extensible contrivance designed for facilitating the erection, inspection, repair or maintenance of overhead structures or equipment, and

(*b*) which is neither constructed nor adapted for use nor used for the conveyance of any load other than—

(i) such a contrivance and articles used in connection therewith, and

(ii) articles used in connection with the installation or maintenance, by means of such a contrivance, of materials or apparatus for lighting streets, roads or public places".

Visiting forces

3. In section 7 of the 1971 Act (miscellaneous exemptions from duty) after subsection (3) there shall be inserted the following subsection—

"(3A) Regulations under this Act may provide that, in such cases, subject to such conditions and for such period as may be prescribed, a mechanically propelled vehicle shall not be chargeable with any duty under this Act if it has been imported by—

(*a*) a person for the time being appointed to serve with any body, contingent or detachment of the forces of any prescribed country, being a body, contingent or detachment which is for the time being present in the United Kingdom on the invitation of Her Majesty's Government in the United Kingdom, or

(*b*) a member of any country's military forces, except Her Majesty's United Kingdom forces, who is for the time being appointed to serve in the United Kingdom under the orders of any prescribed organisation, or

(*c*) a person for the time being recognised by the Secretary of State as a member of a civilian component of such a force as is mentioned in paragraph (*a*) above or as a civilian member of such an organisation as is mentioned in paragraph (*b*) above, or

(*d*) any prescribed dependant of a person falling within paragraph (*a*), paragraph (*b*) or paragraph (*c*) above."

Trade licences

4.—(1) Section 16 of the 1971 Act (trade licences) shall be amended as follows.

(2) In subsection (1) (issue of trade licences)—

(*a*) at the end of paragraph (iii) (vehicles for which a manufacturer may use a trade licence) there shall be inserted the words "and all vehicles which are from time to time submitted to him by other manufacturers for testing on roads in the course of that business"; and

(*b*) at the beginning of paragraph (*c*) of the proviso (restrictions on use of trade licence) there shall be inserted the words "except in such circumstances as may be prescribed".

(3) After subsection (1) there shall be inserted the following subsection—

"(1A) Subsection (1) above has effect in relation to an application made by a person who satisfies the Secretary of State that he intends to commence business as a motor trader or vehicle tester as it has effect in relation to an application made by a motor trader or vehicle tester."

(4) In subsection (3) (which specifies the cases in which regulations may allow a vehicle to be used under a trade licence to carry a load) after paragraph (*b*) there shall be inserted the following paragraph—

"(*bb*) in the case of a vehicle which is being delivered or collected, a load consisting of another vehicle used or to be used for travel from or to the place of delivery or collection; or".

(5) Subsection (4) (duration of trade licence) shall be amended as follows—

(*a*) for the words "A trade licence", including those words where they appear in the subsection as set out in paragraph 12 of Part I of Schedule 7 to the 1971 Act, there shall be substituted "Subject to subsections (4A) and (4B) below, a trade licence";

(*b*) for paragraph (*b*) there shall be substituted—

"(*b*) for a period of six months"; and

(*c*) in the subsection as set out in paragraph 12 of Part I of Schedule 7 to the Act for the words from "except" to the end there shall be substituted "for a period of six months beginning with the first day of January or of July".

(6) After subsection (4) there shall be inserted the following subsections—

"(4A) A trade licence taken out by a person who is not a motor trader or vehicle tester (having satisfied the Secretary of State as mentioned in subsection (1A) above) shall be for a period of six months only.

(4B) The Secretary of State may require that a trade licence taken out by a motor trader or vehicle tester who does not hold any existing trade licence shall be for a period of six months only."

(7) Subsection (5) (fees) shall be amended as follows—

(*a*) for the words "four months" and "eleven thirtieths" there shall be substituted respectively "six months" and "eleven twentieths"; and

(*b*) in the subsection as set out in paragraph 12 of Part I of Schedule 7 to the Act, for the words "three months" and "eleven fortieths" there shall be substituted respectively "six months" and "eleven twentieths".

(8) In subsection (8), in the definition of "motor trader", for the words from "means" to "this section" there shall be substituted "means—

(*a*) a manufacturer or repairer of, or dealer in, mechanically propelled vehicles, or

(*b*) any person not falling within paragraph (*a*) above who carries on a business of such description as may be prescribed;

and a person shall be treated for the purposes of paragraph (*a*) above".

Surrender of licences

5. In section 17(2) of the 1971 Act (surrender of licences) as set out in paragraph 13 of Part I of Schedule 7 to the Act, paragraph (*a*) and, in paragraph (*b*), the words from the beginning to "class" shall be omitted.

Removal of fee for duplicate registration document

6. Section 23 of the 1971 Act (regulations with respect to the transfer and identification of vehicles) shall be amended as follows—

(*a*) in paragraph (*f*) (replacement documents) the words "and as to the fee payable in prescribed circumstances in respect of any replacement" shall be omitted; and

(*b*) in the section as set out in paragraph 20 of Part I of Schedule 7 to the Act in subsection (1)(*e*) (replacement books) the words "and for the fee to be paid on the issue of a new registration book" shall be omitted.

PART II

AMENDMENTS OF VEHICLES (EXCISE) ACT (NORTHERN IRELAND) 1972

Additional days to be included in duration of certain licences

7.—(1) In the Vehicles (Excise) Act (Northern Ireland) 1972 (in this Part of this Schedule referred to as "the 1972 Act"), section 2A (power to modify duration of licences and rates of duty) as set out in paragraph 5 of Schedule 9 to that Act (transitional provisions) shall be amended as follows.

(2) In subsection (1) for the words from "being" onwards there shall be substituted the following—

"being—

(*a*) periods of a fixed number of months (not exceeding fifteen) running from the beginning of the month in which the licence first has effect;

(*b*) in the case of licences taken out on first registration of vehicles of such description as may be so specified, periods exceeding by such number of days (not exceeding thirty) as may be determined by or under the order the periods for which the licence would otherwise have effect by virtue of section 2(1) or any provision made under paragraph (*a*); or

(*c*) in the case of vehicles of such description, or of such description and used in such circumstances, as may be specified, periods of less than a month."

(3) In subsection (3), for the words "other than one of twelve months" there shall be substituted the words "of a fixed number of months other than twelve or for a period of less than a month".

Tower wagons used by street lighting authorities etc.

8. In section 4 of the 1972 Act (exemptions from duty) in subsection (2) for the definition of "tower wagon" there shall be substituted the following—

" 'tower wagon' means a goods vehicle—

(*a*) into which there is built, as part of the vehicle, any expanding or extensible contrivance designed for facilitating the erection, inspection, repair or maintenance of overhead structures or equipment, and

(*b*) which is neither constructed nor adapted for use nor used for the conveyance of any load other than—

(i) such a contrivance and articles used in connection therewith, and

(ii) articles used in connection with the installation or maintenance, by means of such a contrivance, of materials or apparatus for lighting streets, roads or public places".

Trade licences

9.—(1) Section 16 of the Act (trade licences) shall be amended as follows.

(2) In subsection (1) (issues of trade licences) at the end of paragraph (*c*) (vehicles for which a manufacturer may use a trade licence) there shall be inserted the words "and all vehicles which are from time to time submitted to him by other manufacturers for testing on roads in the course of that business".

(3) In subsection (2), at the beginning of paragraph (*c*) (restrictions on use of trade licence) there shall be inserted the words "except in such circumstances as may be prescribed".

(4) After subsection (2) there shall be inserted the following subsection—

"(2A) Subsections (1) and (2) have effect in relation to an application made by a person who satisfies the Secretary of State that he intends to commence business as a motor trader or vehicle tester as they have effect in relation to an application made by a motor trader or vehicle tester."

(5) In subsection (4) (which specifies the cases in which regulations may allow a vehicle to be used under a trade licence to carry a load after paragraph (*b*) there shall be inserted the following paragraph—

"(*bb*) in the case of a vehicle which is being delivered or collected, a load consisting of another vehicle used or to be used for travel from or to the place of delivery or collection; or".

(6) Subsection (5) (duration of trade licence) shall be amended as follows—

(*a*) for the words "A trade licence", including those words where they appear in the subsection as set out in paragraph 12 of Part I of Schedule 9 to the 1972 Act, there shall be substituted "Subject to subsections (5A) and (5B), a trade licence";

(*b*) for paragraph (*b*) there shall be substituted—

"(*b*) for a period of six months;" and

(*c*) in the subsection as set out in paragraph 12 of Part I of Schedule 9 to the Act for the words from "except" to the end there shall be substituted "for a period of six months beginning with the first day of January or of July".

(7) After subsection (5) there shall be inserted the following subsections—

"(5A) A trade licence taken out by a person who is not a motor trader or vehicle tester (having satisfied the Secretary of State as mentioned in subsection (2A)) shall be for a period of six months only.

(5B) The Secretary of State may require that a trade licence taken out by a motor trader or vehicle tester who does not hold any existing trade licence shall be for a period of six months only."

(8) Subsection (6) (fees) shall be amended as follows—

(*a*) for the words "four months" and "eleven thirtieths" there shall be substituted respectively "six months" and "eleven twentieths"; and

(*b*) in the subsection as set out in paragraph 12 of Part I of Schedule 9 to the Act, for the words "three months" and "eleven fortieths" there shall be substituted respectively "six months" and "eleven twentieths".

(9) In subsection (10), in the definition of "motor trader", for the words from "means" to "this section" there shall be substituted "means—

(*a*) a manufacturer or repairer of, or dealer in, mechanically propelled vehicles, or

(*b*) any person not falling within paragraph (*a*) above who carries on a business of such description as may be prescribed;

and a person shall be treated for the purposes of paragraph (*a*)".

Surrender of licences

10. In section 17(2) of the 1972 Act (surrender of licences) as set out in paragraph 13 of Part I of Schedule 9 to the Act, paragraph (*a*) and, in paragraph (*b*), the words from the beginning to "class" shall be omitted.

Removal of fee for duplicate registration document

11. Section 23 of the 1972 Act (regulations with respect to the transfer and identification of vehicles) shall be amended as follows—

(*a*) in paragraph (*f*) (replacement documents) the words "and as to the fee payable in prescribed circumstances in respect of any replacement" shall be omitted; and

(*b*) in the section as set out in paragraph 20 of Part I of Schedule 9 to the Act in subsection (1)(*e*) (replacement books) the words "and for the fee to be paid on the issue of a new registration book" shall be omitted.

General Note

Various minor amendments are made to the law, including the following.

Para. 1. Previously, vehicle licences were valid only from the first day of a month, expiring exactly 6 months or 12 months later. It will now be possible to license a vehicle for part of a month plus the normal 6 or 12 month period and licences will in future be issued from three additional starting dates in the month.

Para. 2. The purpose of this is to reverse a High Court decision that tower wagons carrying street lighting poles lose the exemption from excise duty.

Para. 3. S.I. 1983 No. 1829, in implementing E.E.C. directive 83/182 of March 28, 1983, had the unintended effect of rescinding an existing relief from duty on the vehicles of members of visiting forces temporarily in Britain. The relief has continued to be applied by way of extra statutory concession, but provision is now made to put it on a statutory basis once more.

Para. 4. The trade licensing system, under which 'trade plates' may be transferred from vehicle to vehicle, is modified and improved. Provision is made for the issue of probationary trade licences to new entrants to the motor business. A wider range of businesses will qualify such as car valet services and accessory fitters. Further new activities can be catered for under the paragraph.

Part II applies the Provisions of Part I where necessary to Northern Ireland.

Section 5

SCHEDULE 3

Warehousing Regulations

1. Section 93 of the Customs and Excise Management Act 1979 (warehousing regulations) shall be amended in accordance with paragraphs 2 to 7 below.

2. There shall be added at the end of subsection (1) (matters which may be regulated) the words "and make provision with respect to goods which are to be warehoused or which have been lawfully permitted to be removed from a warehouse without payment of duty and with

respect to the keeping, preservation and production of records and the furnishing of information."

3. The following shall be inserted after subsection (2)(*e*)—

"(*ee*) providing that goods which are to be warehoused, or which have been lawfully permitted to be removed from a warehouse without payment of duty, are to be treated as if, for all or any prescribed purposes of the customs and excise Acts, they were warehoused;".

4. The following shall be substituted for subsection (2)(*g*) business records)—

"(*g*) imposing or providing for the imposition under the regulations of requirements on the occupier of a warehouse or the proprietor of goods in a warehouse or goods which have been in or are to be deposited in a warehouse to keep and preserve such records as may be prescribed relating to his occupation of the warehouse or proprietorship of the goods;

(*h*) imposing or providing for the imposition under the regulations of requirements on such an occupier or proprietor to preserve all other records kept by him for the purposes of any relevant business or activity, except any records which (or records of a class which) the Commissioners specify as not needing preservation;

(*j*) imposing or providing for the imposition under the regulations of requirements on such an occupier or proprietor to produce or cause to be produced any records which he has been required to preserve by virtue of paragraph (*g*) or (*h*) above to an officer when required to do so for the purpose of allowing the officer to inspect them, to copy or take extracts from them or to remove them at a reasonable time and for a reasonable period;

(*k*) imposing or providing for the imposition under the regulations of requirements on such an occupier or proprietor to furnish the Commissioners with any information relating to any relevant business or activity which they specify as information which they think it is necessary or expedient for them to be given for the protection of the revenue;

(*l*) allowing a requirement to preserve any records which has been imposed by virtue of paragraph (*h*) above to be discharged by the preservation in a form approved by the Commissioners of the information contained in the records."

5. The following shall be inserted at the end of subsection (2)—

"In this subsection 'relevant business or activity' means, in relation to an occupier or proprietor, any business or activity of his which includes occupation of a warehouse or (as the case may be) proprietorship of goods in a warehouse or goods which have been in or are to be deposited in a warehouse, where the goods are of a kind in which the proprietor trades or deals."

6. In subsection (2A) (compensation for lost or damaged documents) for "(2)(*g*)" there shall be substituted "(2)(*j*)".

7. The following shall be substituted for subsection (7) (interpretation)—

"(7) In this section—

(*a*) 'prescribed' means prescribed by warehousing regulations;

(*b*) references to goods which are to be warehoused are references to goods which have been entered for warehousing on importation, which have been removed from a producer's premises for warehousing without payment of duty or which are to be warehoused on drawback."

8. In consequence of the amendments made by the preceding provisions of this Schedule, the following provisions of section 15 of the Alcoholic Liquor Duties Act 1979 (which relate to regulations about distillers' warehouses) shall cease to have effect—

(*a*) subsections (6A) and (6B), and

(*b*) the words "restriction or requirement" in subsection (7) and in subsection (8).

General Note

See the Note to s.5.

Section 6

SCHEDULE 4

Extension to Northern Ireland of Provisions of Betting and Gaming Duties Act 1981

Part I

Amendments of the Betting and Gaming Duties Act 1981

General betting duty and pool betting duty

1.—(1) In section 1 (general betting duty) in subsection (1) for the words "Great Britain" there shall be substituted "the United Kingdom".

(2) In subsection (3) of that section after the words "Act 1963" there shall be inserted the words "or Article 37 of the Betting, Gaming, Lotteries and Amusements (Northern Ireland) Order 1985".

2.—(1) In section 6 (pool betting duty) for the words "Great Britain", wherever they occur, there shall be substituted "the United Kingdom".

(2) In subsection (3)(*b*) of that section—

(*a*) in sub-paragraph (i) after the words "Act 1976" there shall be inserted the words "or, as the case may be, Article 133 or 134 of, or paragraph 6 of Schedule 20 to, the Betting, Gaming, Lotteries and Amusements (Northern Ireland) Order 1985";

(*b*) at the beginning of sub-paragraph (ii) there shall be inserted the words "in Great Britain"; and

(*c*) after that sub-paragraph there shall be added the following sub-paragraph—

"or

(iii) in Northern Ireland, in any society's lottery within the meaning of Article 2(2) of that Order which is not unlawful under that Order.".

3.—(1) In section 9 (prohibitions for protection of revenue) for the words "Great Britain", wherever they occur, there shall be substituted "the United Kingdom".

(2) In subsection (3)(*a*) of that section the words "Northern Ireland or" and "of the Parliament of Northern Ireland or, as the case may be" shall be omitted.

4. In section 12(4) (interpretation of provisions relating to betting duties)—

(*a*) before the definition of "meeting" there shall be inserted the following definitions—

"'betting office licence'—

(*a*) in Great Britain, has the meaning given by section 9(1) of the Betting, Gaming and Lotteries Act 1963, and

(*b*) in Northern Ireland, means a bookmaking office licence as defined in Article 2(2) of the Betting, Gaming, Lotteries and Amusements (Northern Ireland) Order 1985;

'bookmaker'—

(*a*) in Great Britain, has the meaning given by section 55(1) of the said Act of 1963, and

(*b*) in Northern Ireland, has the meaning given by Article 2(2) of the said Order of 1985;

and (in either case) the expression 'bookmaking' shall be construed accordingly;

'bookmaker's permit'—

(*a*) in Great Britain, has the meaning given by section 2(1) of the said Act of 1963, and

(*b*) in Northern Ireland, means a bookmaker's licence as defined in Article 2(2) of the said Order of 1985 ;";

(*b*) after the definition of "promoter" there shall be inserted the following definitions—

"'sponsored pool betting' has the meaning given by section 55(1) of the said Act of 1963;"

'totalisator' has the meaning given by section 55(1) of the said Act of 1963 and Article 2(2) of the said Order of 1985;

'track'—

(*a*) in Great Britain, has the meaning given by section 55(1) of the said Act of 1963, and

(*b*) in Northern Ireland, has the meaning given by Article 2(2) of the said Order of 1985;"; and

(*c*) the words from "and 'betting office licence'" to the end shall be omitted.

Bingo duty

5. In section 17(1) (charge of bingo duty) for the words "Great Britain" there shall be substituted "the United Kingdom".

6. In section 19(2) (bingo played in more than one place)—

(*a*) for the words "Great Britain", in both places where they occur, there shall be substituted "the United Kingdom"; and

(*b*) the words "Northern Ireland or" and the words "the Parliament of Northern Ireland or, as the case may be," shall be omitted.

7. In section 20(2) (interpretation of provisions relating to bingo duty) the definition of "Great Britain" shall be omitted and after the definition of "the promoter" there shall be inserted the following definition—

"'United Kingdom' includes the territorial waters of the United Kingdom;".

General

8. In section 28 (recovery of duty by distress in England and Wales) for subsection (5) there shall be substituted—

"(5) This section extends to England and Wales and Northern Ireland only."

9. In section 29 (recovery of duty by poinding in Scotland) for subsection (5) there shall be substituted—

"(5) This section extends to Scotland only."

10.—(1) In section 35, for subsection (3) (extent) there shall be substituted—

"(3) The following provisions of this Act do not extend to Northern Ireland—

(*a*) sections 13 to 16;
(*b*) sections 29 and 30;
(*c*) Schedule 2;
(*d*) paragraph 15 of Schedule 4;

and sections 27 and 31 do not extend there in their application to the enactments relating to gaming licence duty."

(2) Subsection (4) of that section shall be omitted.

Administration of betting duties

11.—(1) In Schedule 1 (betting duties) in paragraph 7 (production of records) after the words "Act 1963" there shall be inserted the words "or Schedule 8 to the Betting, Gaming and Amusements (Northern Ireland) Order 1985".

(2) In paragraph 15 of that Schedule—

(*a*) in sub-paragraph (2) after the words "England or Wales" there shall be inserted the words "or Northern Ireland";
(*b*) in sub-paragraph (4) after the word "premises" there shall be inserted the words "in England, Wales or Scotland"; and
(*c*) after that sub-paragraph there shall be inserted the following sub-paragraphs—

"(5) Subject to sub-paragraph (6) below, where under sub-paragraph (1) above a court orders that a betting office licence held by a person in respect of premises in Northern Ireland shall be forfeited and cancelled, no court of summary jurisdiction shall entertain an application by that person for the grant (or provisional grant) of a new betting office licence in respect of those premises or any other premises situated in the same petty sessions district as those premises made less than twelve months after that forfeiture and cancellation.

(6) Sub-paragraph (5) above—

(*a*) shall not prejudice the right of such a person as is mentioned in that sub-paragraph to seek the renewal of any betting office licence (other than that which is forfeited) which he holds; and
(*b*) applies notwithstanding anything in Article 12 of the Betting, Gaming, Lotteries and Amusements (Northern Ireland) Order 1985.".

Exemptions from, and administration of, bingo duty

12.—(1) In Schedule 3, in paragraph 2(1) (small-scale bingo) after the words "Act 1968" there shall be inserted the words "or under Chapter II of Part III of the Betting, Gaming, Lotteries and Amusements (Northern Ireland) Order 1985".

(2) In paragraph 5 of that Schedule (small-scale amusements provided commercially) in sub-paragraph (1) after paragraph (*a*) there shall be inserted the following paragraph—

"(*aa*) on any premises in Northern Ireland in respect of which an amusement permit under Article 111 of the Betting, Gaming, Lotteries and Amusements (Northern Ireland) Order 1985 or a pleasure permit under Article 157 of that Order has been granted;".

(3) In paragraph 10(2) of that Schedule (registration of bingo-promoters) after the words "Act 1968" there shall be inserted the words "or under Chapter II of Part III of the Betting, Gaming, Lotteries and Amusements (Northern Ireland) Order 1985".

Part II

Consequential Amendments of Northern Ireland Legislation

13. In section 287(1)(*a*) of the Companies Act (Northern Ireland) 1960 (preferential payments), for head (iv) there be substituted the following head—

"(iv) any amount due from the company at the relevant date by way of general betting duty or bingo duty, or by virtue of section 12(1) of the Betting and Gaming Duties Act 1981, which became due within 12 months next before that date;".

14. In Article 19(*a*) of the Bankruptcy Amendment (Northern Ireland) Order 1980 (preferential payments), for head (v) there shall substituted the following head—

"(v) any amount due from the bankrupt at the relevant date by way of general betting duty or bingo duty, or by virtue of section 12(1) of the Betting and Gaming Duties Act 1981, which became due within 12 months next before that date;".

15.—(1) The Betting, Gaming, Lotteries and Amusements (Northern Ireland) Order 1985 shall be amended as follows.

(2) In Article 7, after paragraph (4), there shall be inserted the following paragraph—

"(4A) In considering the fitness of any applicant to hold a bookmaker's licence, the court shall have regard to—

(*a*) any failure of the applicant or of any other person mentioned in paragraph (3)(*b*); and

(*b*) where the applicant is a body corporate, any failure of any director of the applicant or of any other person mentioned in paragraph (4);

to pay any amount due from him or it by way of general betting duty or pool betting duty.".

(3) In Article 61, after paragraph (4) there shall be inserted the following paragraph—

"(4A) In considering the fitness of any applicant to hold a bingo club licence, a court shall have regard to—

(*a*) any failure of the applicant or of any other person mentioned in paragraph (3)(*b*); and

(*b*) where the applicant is a body corporate, any failure of any director of the applicant or of any other person mentioned in paragraph (4);

to pay any amount due from him or it by way of bingo duty.".

(4) In Article 174 (registration of licences, etc)—

(*a*) in paragraph (2), after head (*g*) there shall be inserted the following head—

"(*gg*) particulars of the forfeiture and cancellation of any bookmaking office licence in consequence of an order made under paragraph 15(1) of Schedule 1 to the Betting and Gaming Duties Act 1981;";

(*b*) in paragraph (4), after head (*b*) there shall be inserted the following—

"or

(*c*) orders the forfeiture and cancellation of a bookmaking office licence under paragraph 15(1) of Schedule 1 to the Betting and Gaming Duties Act 1981;".

(5) In the following provisions, namely—

(*a*) Article 2(16), in so far as it is relevant for the purposes of the provisions mentioned in heads (*b*) and (*c*);

(*b*) Article 185(3) and Schedule 7, in so far as those provisions relate to a bookmaker's licence, a bookmaker office licence or a bingo club licence; and

(*c*) Schedules 1 to 6 and Schedules 9 and 10;

any reference to the sub-divisional commander of the police sub-division shall be construed as including a reference to the Collector of Customs and Excise for the area, and any reference to the police sub-division shall be construed as including a reference to the area for which the Collector is responsible.

Part III

Subordinate Legislation

16.—(1) Any regulations made under Schedule 1 (betting duties) to the Betting and Gaming Duties Act 1981, in so far as they have effect immediately before the betting commencement date, shall have effect on and after that date in relation to Northern Ireland as if—

(*a*) that Act extended to Northern Ireland at the time when the regulations were made, and (*b*) the regulations were made in relation to Northern Ireland as well as to Great Britain.

(2) Any orders or regulations made under Schedule 3 (bingo duty) to that Act, in so far as they have effect immediately before the bingo commencement date, shall have effect on and after that date in relation to Northern Ireland as if—

(*a*) that Act extended to Northern Ireland at the time when the orders or regulations were made, and

(*b*) the orders or regulations were made in relation to Northern Ireland as well as to Great Britain.

GENERAL NOTE

See the note to s.6.

Section 8(6)

SCHEDULE 5

LICENCES UNDER THE CUSTOMS AND EXCISE ACTS

General provisions as to payment of duty on excise licences

1. In section 101 of the Customs and Excise Management Act 1979 (grant of excise licences)—

(*a*) in subsection (1), for the words "the appropriate duty" there shall be substituted "any appropriate duty"; and

(*b*) in subsection (3), for the words "taken out" there shall be substituted "held" and for the words "in any one licence year" there shall be substituted "at any one time".

2. In sections 102(1) and 104(3) of the Customs and Excise Management Act 1979 (payment for and transfer of excise licences), for the words "the duty" there shall be substituted "any duty".

Licences to manufacture spirits

3.—(1) Section 12 of the Alcoholic Liquor Duties Act 1979 (distillers' licences) shall be amended in accordance with this paragraph.

(2) At the end of subsection (4) there shall be added the words "and they may at any time revoke a licence in respect of any premises if, by reason of circumstances arising since the grant of the licence, they could by virtue of this subsection refuse to grant a licence in respect of those premises".

(3) At the end of subsection (5) there shall be added the words "and where the largest still so used on any premises in respect of which a licence is held is of less than that capacity, the Commissioners may revoke the licence or attach to it such conditions as they see fit to impose".

(4) After subsection (6) there shall be inserted the following subsection—

"(6A) If at any time, by reason of circumstances arising since the grant of a distiller's licence in respect of any premises, the Commissioners are not satisfied as mentioned in subsection (6) above, they may revoke the licence unless the distiller gives the undertaking mentioned in that subsection."

(5) In subsection (9), for the words "to whom a licence has been granted upon his giving" there shall be substituted "who, in respect of a licence, has given".

Licences relating to hydrocarbon oil etc.

4. In Schedule 3 to the Hydrocarbon Oil Duties Act 1979 (subjects for regulations under section 21 of that Act), in paragraphs 2, 13 and 18 (which relate to licences for the production etc. of hydrocarbon oil, petrol substitutes and road fuel gas respectively) for the words "Fixing the date of expiration of any such licence" there shall be substituted "Specifying the circumstances in which any such licence may be surrendered or revoked".

Licences to manufacture mechanical lighters

5. In section 7 of the Matches and Mechanical Lighters Duties Act 1979 (regulations about mechanical lighters) in subsection (1) for paragraph (*b*) there shall be substituted—

"(*b*) for enabling licences granted under the regulations to be surrendered or revoked in such circumstances as are specified in the regulations;".

General Note

This contains administrative provisions consequent on the abolition by s.8 of a large number of obsolete licences.

Section 9

SCHEDULE 6

Consideration for Fuel Supplied for Private Use

1. This Schedule has effect to determine the consideration referred to in subsection (7) of section 9 of this Act in respect of any one vehicle; and in this Schedule—

(*a*) "the principal section" means that section;

(*b*) "the prescribed accounting period" means that in respect of supplies in which the consideration is to be determined; and

(*c*) "the individual" means the individual to whom those supplies are treated as made.

2.—(1) Subject to paragraph 3 below, where the prescribed accounting period is a period of three months, the consideration appropriate to any vehicle is that specified in relation to a vehicle of the appropriate description in the second column of Table A below.

(2) Subject to paragraph 3 below, where the prescribed accounting period is a period of one month, the consideration appropriate to any vehicle is that specified in relation to a vehicle of the appropriate description in the third column of Table A below.

Table A

Cylinder capacity of vehicle in cubic centimetres	*3 month period*	*1 month period*
	£	£
1400 or less	120	40
More than 1400 but not more than 2000	150	50
More than 2000	225	75

3.—(1) If in the prescribed accounting period a vehicle is used by the individual referred to in subsection (7) of the principal section for the purposes of business travel to the extent of at least 4500 miles or, if the prescribed accounting period is a period of one month, 1500 miles, then paragraph 2 above shall have effect as if for any reference therein to Table A there were substituted a reference to Table B below.

(2) Where, by virtue of subsection (8) of the principal section, subsection (7) of that section has effect as if, in the prescribed accounting period, supplies of fuel for private use made in respect of two or more vehicles were made in respect of only one vehicle, sub-paragraph (1) above shall have effect as if the reference to a vehicle were a reference to those two or more vehicles taken together.

(3) In this paragraph "business travel" means travelling which an individual is necessarily obliged to do in the performance of the duties of his employment, the partnership or, in the case of the taxable person himself, his business.

Table B

Cylinder capacity of vehicle in cubic centimetres	*3 month period*	*1 month period*
	£	£
1400 or less	60	20
More than 1400 but not more than 2000	75	25
More than 2000	113	38

4. The Treasury may by order taking effect from the beginning of any prescribed accounting period beginning after the order is made substitute a different Table for either of the Tables set out above.

5.—(1) Where, by virtue of subsection (8) of the principal section, subsection (7) of that section has effect as if, in the prescribed accounting period, supplies of fuel for private use made in respect of two or more vehicles were made in respect of only one vehicle, the consideration appropriate shall be determined as follows—

(*a*) if each of the two or more vehicles falls within the same description of cubic capacity specified in Table A or Table B above, the Table in question shall apply as if only one of the vehicles were to be considered throughout the whole period; and

(*b*) if one of those vehicles falls within a description of cubic capacity specified in those Tables which is different from the other or others the consideration shall be the aggregate of the relevant fractions of the consideration appropriate for each description of vehicle under the Table in question.

(2) For the purposes of sub-paragraph (1)(*b*) above, the relevant fraction in relation to any vehicle is that which the part of the prescribed accounting period in which fuel for private use was supplied in respect of that vehicle bears to the whole of that period.

6.—(1) In the case of a vehicle having an internal combustion engine with one or more reciprocating pistons, its cubic capacity for the purposes of Tables A and B above is the capacity of its engine as calculated for the purposes of the Vehicles (Excise) Act 1971 or the Vehicles (Excise) Act (Northern Ireland) 1972.

(2) In the case of a vehicle not falling within sub-paragraph (1) above, its cubic capacity shall be such as may be determined for the purposes of Tables A and B above by order by the Treasury.

General Note

The scales given here will apply from April 6, 1987 for the assessment of output tax on petrol purchased by businesses and deemed to be used for private purposes. Where it can be shown that business mileage exceeds 1,500 a month or 4,500 a quarter the scales in Table B, half of those in Table A, will apply. Provision is made for the tables to be replaced by Treasury order.

Section 31

SCHEDULE 7

Charities: Qualifying Expenditure, Investments and Loans

Part I

Qualifying expenditure

1.—(1) In the principal section "qualifying expenditure", in relation to a chargeable period of a charity, means, subject to sub-paragraph (3) below, expenditure incurred in that period for charitable purposes only.

(2) For the purposes of the principal section (and sub-paragraph (1) above), where expenditure which is not actually incurred in a particular chargeable period properly falls to be charged against the income of that chargeable period as being referable to commitments (whether or not of a contractual nature) which the charity has entered into before or during that period, it shall be treated as incurred in that period.

(3) A payment made (or to be made) to a body situated outside the United Kingdom shall not be qualifying expenditure by virtue of this Part of this Schedule unless the charity concerned has taken such steps as may be reasonable in the circumstances to ensure that the payment will be applied for charitable purposes.

Part II

Qualifying Investments

2. Investments specified in any of the following paragraphs of this Part of this Schedule are qualifying investments for the purposes of the principal section.

3. Any investment falling within Part I, Part II, apart from paragraph 13 (mortgages etc.), or Part III of Schedule 1 to the Trustee Investments Act 1961.

4. Any investment in a common investment fund established under section 22 of the Charities Act 1960 or section 25 of the Charities Act (Northern Ireland) 1964 or in any similar fund established for the exclusive benefit of charities by or under any enactment relating to any particular charities or class of charities.

5. Any interest in land, other than an interest held as security for a debt of any description.

6. Shares in, or securities of, a company which are quoted on a recognised stock exchange (within the meaning of section 535 of the Taxes Act), or which are dealt with in the Unlisted Securities Market.

7.—(1) Units, or other shares of the investments subject to the trusts, of a unit trust scheme within the meaning of the Financial Services Act 1986.

(2) Until the passing of the Financial Services Act 1986, the reference in sub-paragraph (1) above to that Act shall have effect as a reference to the Prevention of Fraud (Investments) Act 1958.

8.—(1) Deposits with a recognised bank or licenced institution (within the meaning of the Banking Act 1979) in respect of which interest is payable at a commercial rate.

(2) A deposit mentioned in sub-paragraph (1) above is not a qualifying investment if it is made as part of an arrangement under which a loan is made by the recognised bank or licensed institution to some other person.

9. Certificates of deposit as defined in section 55(3) of the Finance Act 1968.

10.—(1) Any loan or other investment as to which the Board are satisfied, on a claim made to them in that behalf, that the loan or other investment is made for the benefit of the charity and not for the avoidance of tax (whether by the charity or any other person).

(2) The reference in sub-paragaraph (1) above to a loan includes a loan which is secured by a mortgage or charge of any kind over land.

Part III

Qualifying Loans

11. For the purposes of the principal section, a loan which is not made by way of investment is a qualifying loan if it consists of—

(*a*) a loan made to another charity for charitable purposes only; or

(*b*) a loan to a beneficiary of the charity which is made in the course of carrying out the purposes of the charity; or

(*c*) money placed on a current account with a recognised bank or licensed institution (within the meaning of the Banking Act 1979) otherwise than as part of such an arrangement as is mentioned in paragraph 8(2) above; or

(*d*) any other loan as to which the Board are satisfied, on a claim made to them in that behalf, that the loan is made for the benefit of the charity and not for the avoidance of tax (whether by the charity or any other person).

Part IV

Attribution of Excess Non-Qualifying Expenditure to earlier Chargeable Periods

12. This part of this Schedule applies in the circumstances specified in subsection (6) of the principal section; and in this Part of this Schedule—

(*a*) "the primary period" means the chargeable period of the charity concerned in which there is such an excess as is mentioned in that subsection;

(*b*) "unapplied non-qualifying expenditure" means so much of the excess referred to in that subsection as does not exceed the non-qualifying expenditure of the primary period; and

(*c*) "earlier period", in relation to an amount of unapplied non-qualifying expenditure, means any chargeable period of the charity concerned which ended not more than six years before the end of the primary period.

13.—(1) So much of the unapplied non-qualifying expenditure as is not shown by the charity to be the expenditure of non-taxable sums received by the charity in the primary period shall be treated in accordance with paragraph 14 below as non-qualifying expenditure of earlier periods.

(2) In sub-paragraph (1) above "non-taxable sums" means donations, legacies and other sums of a similar nature which, apart from any provision of the enactments conferring exemption from tax, are not within the charge to tax.

14.—(1) Where, in accordance with paragraph 13 above, an amount of unapplied non-qualifying expenditure (in this paragraph referred to as "the excess expenditure") falls to be treated as non-qualifying expenditure of earlier periods,—

(*a*) it shall be attributed only to those earlier periods (if any) in which, apart from the attribution (but taking account of any previous operation of this paragraph) the relevant income and gains exceed the aggregate of the qualifying and non-qualifying expenditure incurred in that period; and

(*b*) the amount to be attributed to any such earlier period shall not be greater than the excess of that period referred to in paragraph (*a*) above.

(2) Where there is more than one earlier period to which the excess expenditure can be attributed in accordance with sub-paragraph (1) above, it shall be attributed to later periods in priority to earlier periods.

(3) In so far as any of the excess expenditure cannot be attributed to earlier periods in accordance with this paragraph, it shall be disregarded for the purposes of subsection (6) of the principal section (and this Part of this Schedule).

15. All such adjustments shall be made, whether by way of the making of assessments or otherwise, as are required in consequence of the provisions of this Part of this Schedule.

General Note

This Schedule defines the various terms used in section 31 and reference should be made to that section and to the commentary thereto to understand their significance.

Paragraph 1 contains the basic rule as to what is meant by "qualifying expenditure" in a chargeable period. The terms of subparagraph (2) allow expenditure not incurred in a particular period to be treated as incurred in that period if referable to commitments entered into before or during that period. Subparagraph (3) contains the specific rule regarding payments to bodies situated outside the United Kingdom.

While paragraphs 2 to 9 define investments which are qualifying investments it should be noted that any investment can be a qualifying investment so long as it is made for the benefit of the charity and not for avoidance of tax (see para. 10). Loans not made by way of investment are treated as non-qualifying expenditure unless they rank as qualifying loans as defined in para. 11. Again any loan can rank as a qualifying loan so long as made for the benefit of the charity and not for the avoidance of tax.

Paragraphs 12 to 15 contain the detailed rules concerning the carry back of non-qualifying expenditure incurred in a chargeable period to earlier periods. The carryback can only occur when qualifying and non-qualifying expenditure exceeds the income and gains of the charity in the chargeable period and is limited to the excess or such amount of it as does not exceed the non-qualifying expenditure. No carryback can occur however where it can be shown that the non-qualifying expenditure is expenditure of "non-taxable" sums received by the charity in the chargeable period. The attribution can only be made to periods ending not more than six years before the end of the chargeable period concerned and if there is more than one period to which the excess can be attributed it is to be attributed to the later periods in priority to earlier ones.

Section 39

SCHEDULE 8

Personal Equity Plans

1.—(1) The Treasury may make regulations providing that an individual who invests under a plan shall be entitled to relief from income tax and capital gains tax in respect of the investments.

(2) The regulations shall set out the conditions subject to which plans are to operate and the extent to which investors are to be entitled to relief from tax.

(3) In particular, the regulations may—

(*a*) specify the description of individuals who may invest and the kind of investments they may make;

(*b*) specify maximum investment limits and minimum periods for which investments are to be held;

(*c*) provided that investments are to be held by persons (plan managers) on behalf of investors;

(*d*) specify how relief from tax is to be claimed by, and granted to, investors or plan managers on their behalf;

(*e*) provided that plans and plan managers must be such as are approved by the Board;

(*f*) specify the circumstances in which approval may be granted and withdrawn.

2.—(1) The regulations may include provision that in prescribed circumstances—

(*a*) an investor under a plan shall cease to be, and be treated as not having been, entitled to relief from tax in respect of the investments, and

(*b*) he or the plan manager concerned (depending on the terms of the regulations) shall account to the Board for tax from which relief has already been given on the basis that the investor was so entitled.

(2) The regulations may include provision that an investor under a plan or the plan manager concerned (depending on the terms of the regulations) shall account to the Board for tax from which relief has been given in circumstances such that the investor was not entitled to it.

(3) The regulations may include provision adapting, or modifying the effect of, any enactment relating to income tax or to capital gains tax in order to—

(*a*) secure that investors under plans are entitled to relief from tax in respect of investments;

(*b*) secure that investors under plans cease to be, and are treated as not having been, so entitled;

(*c*) secure that investors under plans or plan managers account for tax as mentioned in sub-paragraph (1) or (2) above.

(4) The regulations may provide that a person who is, or has at any time been, either an investor under a plan or a plan manager—

(*a*) shall comply with any notice which is served on him by the Board and which requires him within a prescribed period to make available for the Board's inspection documents (of a prescribed kind) relating to a plan or to investments which are or have been held under it;

(*b*) shall, within a prescribed period of being required to do so by the Board, furnish to the Board information (of a prescribed kind) about a plan or about investments which are or have been held under it.

(5) The regulations may include provision generally for the purpose of bringing plans into existence, and generally for the purpose of the administration of plans and the administration of income tax, corporation tax and capital gains tax in relation to them.

(6) The words "Regulations under Schedule 8 to the Finance Act 1986" shall be added at the end of each column in the Table in section 98 of the Taxes Management Act 1970 (penalties for failure to furnish information etc.).

3.—(1) The power to make regulations under this Schedule shall be exercisable by statutory instrument subject to annulment in pursuance of a resolution of the House of Commons.

(2) In this Schedule "prescribed" means prescribed by the regulations.

General Note

This Schedule empowers the Treasury to pass the necessary regulations to set up the Personal Equity Plan.

Under this scheme individuals resident in the U.K. will be able to invest up to £2,400 p.a. through an authorised manager. Provided the investments are retained for a specified minimum period the dividend income will be free of income tax if reinvested and the gains will be free of capital gains tax.

Section 40

SCHEDULE 9

Business Expansion Scheme

Part I

Amendment of Schedule 5 to Finance Act 1983

1.—(1) Schedule 5 to the Finance Act 1983 shall be amended as follows.

(2) Except where different provision is made by this Schedule, the amendments made by this Schedule have effect in relation to shares issued at any time after 18th March 1986.

Relevant period

2. In paragraph 2(7)(*b*), after "5" there shall be inserted "5A, 5B, 5C".

Research and development companies

3. In paragraph 2A—

(*a*) in sub-paragraph (1)(*a*), for the words from "from" to the end there shall be substituted the words "to be carried on by the company or by any subsidiary of the company and from which it is intended that a qualifying trade (to be so carried on) will be derived; or";

(*b*) in sub-paragraph (2) for the words from "at the time" to "by it; or" there shall be substituted the words "by the company or by any subsidiary of the company on the date on which the shares are issued, or begins so to be carried on immediately thereafter, and from which it is intended that a qualifying trade (to be so carried on) will be derived; or";

(*c*) in sub-paragraph (3), after the word 'company' there shall be inserted the words "or (as the case may be) subsidiary"; and

(*d*) in sub-paragraph (4), the words "and the words 'by the company' shall be omitted" shall be added at the end.

4.—(1) After paragraph 2A there shall be inserted the following paragraph—

"*Modification of paragraph 2 in relation to oil exploration*

2B.—(1) Where eligible shares in a company are issued for the purpose of enabling the company to raise money for oil exploration—

(*a*) to be carried on by the company, or by any subsidiary of the company; and

(*b*) from which it is intended that a qualifying trade (to be so carried on) will be derived;

paragraph 2 above shall apply in relation to the company with the modifications set out in this paragraph.

(2) For paragraph (*b*) of sub-paragraph (1) there shall be substituted the following paragraphs—

'(*b*) those shares are issued to him for the purpose of raising money for oil exploration which—

(i) is being carried on by the company, or by any subsidiary of the company, on the date on which the shares are issued; or

(ii) begins so to be carried on immediately thereafter;

and from which it is intended that a qualifying trade (to be so carried on) will be derived;

(*c*) throughout the period of three years beginning with that date, the company, or any subsidiary of the company, holds an exploration licence which was granted to it, or to another such subsidiary;

(*d*) the exploration is carried out solely within the area to which the licence applies; and

(*e*) on the date on which the shares are issued, neither the company nor any subsidiary of the company holds an appraisal licence or a development licence relating to that area or any part of that area.'

(3) After sub-paragraph (1) there shall be inserted the following sub-paragraph—

'(1A) Where, at any time after the issue of the shares, but before the end of the period mentioned in paragraph (*c*) of sub-paragraph (2) above, the company, or any subsidiary of the company, comes to hold an appraisal licence or development licence which relates to the area, or any part of the area, to which the exploration licence relates, the exploration licence and that other licence shall be treated for the purposes of that paragraph as a single exploration licence.'

(4) For sub-paragraph (4) there shall be substituted the following sub-paragraph—

'(4) The relief shall be given on a claim and shall not be allowed unless and until the company has carried on the exploration for four months'.

(5) In sub-paragraph (5), for the word 'trade' there shall be substituted the word 'exploration'.

(6) In sub-paragraph (7)(*b*), for the words from 'either' to the end there shall be substituted the words 'three years after that date'.

(7) A trade which consists to any substantial extent of oil extraction activities shall, if it would be a qualifying trade were it not for paragraph 6(2)(*d*) below, be treated as a qualifying trade for the purposes of this paragraph (including those of paragraph 2(1)(*b*) as modified)."

(2) This paragraph has effect in relation to shares issued at any time after the passing of this Act.

Individuals qualifying for relief

5.—(1) In paragraph 4, the following sub-paragraph shall be added at the end—

"(5) An individual who is at any time performing duties which are treated by virtue of section 184(3)(*a*) of the Taxes Act (Crown employees serving overseas) as performed in the United Kingdom shall be treated, for the purposes of this paragraph, as resident and ordinarily resident in the United Kingdom at that time."

(2) This paragraph shall have effect in relation to shares issued on or after 6th April 1986.

Qualifying companies

6.—(1) Paragraph 5 shall be amended as follows.

(2) In sub-paragraph (1) the words "Subject to paragraph 5A below" shall be inserted at the beginning.

(3) After sub-paragraph (3) there shall be inserted the following sub-paragraph—

"(3A) Where a company has one or more qualifying subsidiaries, it shall not be a qualifying company if the qualifying trade or trades carried on by the company and its subsidiaries, taken as a whole, are not carried out wholly or mainly in the United Kingdom."

(4) Sub-paragraphs (8) to (11) shall cease to have effect.

7. The following paragraphs shall be inserted after paragraph 5—

"5A.—(1) Subject to paragraph 5C below, a company is not a qualifying company if at any time during the relevant period—

(*a*) the value of the interests in land held by the company at that time; or

(*b*) where lower, the value of the interests in land which were held by the company immediately after the issue of the shares (adjusted in accordance with paragraph 5B below);

is greater than half the value of the company's assets as a whole.

(2) For the purposes of this paragraph, the value of the interests in land held by a company on any date shall be arrived at by first aggregating the market value on that date of each of those interests and then deducting—

(*a*) the amount of any debts of the company which are secured on any of those interests (including any debt secured by a floating charge on property which comprises any of those interests);

(*b*) the amount of any unsecured debts of the company which do not fall due for payment before the expiry of the period of twelve months beginning with that date; and

(*c*) the amount paid up in respect of those shares of the company (if any) which carry a present or future preferential right to the company's assets on its winding up.

(3) For the purposes of this paragraph, the value of a company's assets as a whole shall be arrived at by first aggregating the market value of each of those assets and then deducting the amount of the debts and liabilities of the company.

(4) For the purposes of sub-paragraph (3) above, the amount paid up in respect of those shares of a company (if any) which carry a present or future preferential right to the company's assets on its winding up shall be treated as a debt of the company, but otherwise a company's share capital, share premium account and reserves shall not be treated for those purposes as debts or liabilities of the company.

(5) In this paragraph "interests in land" means any estate or interest in land, any right in or over land or affecting the use or disposition of land, and any right to obtain such an estate, interest or right from another which is conditional on that other's ability to grant the estate, interest or right in question, except that it does not include—

(*a*) the interest of a creditor (other than a creditor in respect of a rentcharge) whose debt is secured by a mortgage, an agreement for a mortgage or a charge of any kind over land; or

(*b*) in Scotland, the interest of a creditor in a charge or security of any kind over land.

(6) In arriving at the value of any interest in land for the purposes of this paragraph—

(*a*) it shall be assumed that there is no source of mineral deposits in the land of a kind which it would be practicable to exploit by extracting them from underground otherwise than by means of opencast mining or quarrying; and

(*b*) any borehole on the land shall be disregarded if it was made in the course of oil exploration.

(7) Where a company is a member of a partnership which holds any interest in land—

(*a*) that interest shall, for the purposes of this paragraph and paragraphs 5B and 5C below, be treated as an interest in land held by the company; but

(*b*) its value at any time shall, for those purposes, be taken to be such fraction of its value (apart from this sub-paragraph) as is equal to the fraction of the assets of the partnership to which the company would be entitled if the partnership were dissolved at that time.

(8) Where a qualifying company has one or more subsidiaries, the company and its subsidiaries ("the group") shall be treated as a single company for the purposes of this

paragraph and paragraphs 5B and 5C below; but any debt owed by, or liability of, one member of the group to another shall be disregarded for those purposes.

(9) The Treasury may by order made by statutory instrument amend sub-paragraph (1) above by substituting a different fraction for the fraction for the time being specified there; and any such order shall be subject to annulment in pursuance of a resolution of the Commons House of Parliament.

(10) Where a company has ceased to be a qualifying company in consequence of the operation of this paragraph, section 62(6) of Chapter II shall apply as if the relief was withdrawn in consequence of an event which occurred at the time when the company so ceased to be a qualifying company.

5B.—(1) For the purposes of paragraph 5A(1)(*b*) above, the value of the interests in land held by a company immediately after the issue of the shares in question ("the original interests") shall be adjusted by—

(*a*) adding—

(i) the cost of any interests in land subsequently acquired by the company ("the later interests"); and

(ii) any expenditure (whenever payable) incurred by the company wholly and exclusively in enhancing the value of any of the original or later interests;

(*b*) deducting any consideration for the disposal by the company of any of the original or later interests or on the grant by the company of any interest in land out of any of those interests; and

(*c*) deducting any consideration otherwise derived by the company from its ownership of any of the original or later interests.

(2) Any sum which is received by a company by way of rent, or which is attributable to the use of any premises by the company, shall be disregarded for the purposes of sub-paragraph (1)(*c*) above.

(3) For the purposes of this paragraph—

(*a*) the cost of an interest in land acquired by a company shall be taken to be the amount or value of the consideration given by the company, or on its behalf, wholly and exclusively for the acquisition of the interest;

(*b*) consideration shall be brought into account without any discount for the postponement of the right to receive any part of it; and

(*c*) the grant of an interest in land out of any of the original interests shall be treated as a disposal of the original interest in question.

(4) Where—

(*a*) the interest of a company as lessee under a lease ("the lease") falls to be valued at any time for the purposes of paragraph 5A above or the cost of acquiring that interest falls to be calculated for the purposes of this paragraph; and

(*b*) the aggregate amount of the rent payable by the lessee under the lease before the end of the relevant period exceeds that which would be so payable under a lease of the premises at a full market rent (but otherwise on the same terms and conditions as the lease);

the value of the company's interest at that time shall be calculated on the assumption that the aggregate amount payable as mentioned in paragraph (*b*) above is a nominal amount and, where the interest was acquired after the issue of the shares in question, it shall be assumed that the company paid the appropriate premium when acquiring the interest.

(5) In determining, for the purposes of this paragraph, the consideration for the disposal or acquisition of an interest in land, no account shall be taken in the first instance of any contingent liability assumed by the company or by any other person.

(6) If it is subsequently shown to the satisfaction of the Board that a contingent liability which was not taken into account in determining the consideration for a disposal or acquisition has become enforceable and is being or has been enforced, such adjustment, whether by way of a further assessment or the discharge or repayment of tax or otherwise, shall be made as is required in consequence.

(7) Where the relief obtainable under sub-paragraph (6) above requires a discharge or repayment of tax, it shall be given on a claim to the Board and such a claim may be made at any time.

5C.—(1) Where a company raises any amount through the issue of eligible shares, paragraph 5A above—

(*a*) shall not have effect to deny relief in relation to those shares if the aggregate of that amount and of all other amounts (if any) so raised within the period of twelve months ending with the date of that issue does not exceed £50,000; and

(*b*) where that aggregate exceeds £50,000, shall have effect to deny relief only in relation to the excess.

(2) Where—

(*a*) at any time within the relevant period, the company in question or any of its subsidiaries carries on any trade or part of a trade in partnership, or as a party to a joint venture, with one or more other persons; and

(*b*) that other person, or at least one of those other persons, is a company;

the reference to £50,000, both in sub-paragraph (1)(*a*) and (1)(*b*) above, shall have effect as if it were a reference to—

$$\frac{£50{,}000}{1 + A}$$

"A" being the total number of companies (apart from the company in question or any of its subsidiaries) which are members of any such partnership or parties to any such joint venture during the relevant period.

(3) Where paragraph 5A, as read with this paragraph, requires a restriction to be placed on the relief given on claims in respect of shares issued to two or more individuals, the available relief shall be divided between them in proportion to the amounts which have been respectively subscribed by them for the shares to which their claims relate and which would, apart from the restriction, be eligible for the relief.

(4) A claimant who is dissatisfied with the manner in which the available relief is divided under this paragraph between him and any other claimant or claimants may apply to the appropriate Commissioners who shall, after giving the other claimant or claimants an opportunity to appear and be heard or to make representations in writing, determine the question for all the claimants in the same way as an appeal.

(5) In this paragraph "the appropriate Commissioners" means—

(*a*) in a case where the same body of General Commissioners has jurisdiction with respect to all the claimants, those Commissioners, unless all the claimants agree that the question should be determined by the Special Commissioners;

(*b*) in a case where different bodies of General Commissioners have jurisdiction with respect to the claimants, such of those bodies as the Board may direct, unless all the claimants agree that the question should be determined by the Special Commissioners; and

(*c*) in any other case, the Special Commissioners.

(6) In calculating the aggregate mentioned in sub-paragraph (1)(*a*) above in respect of any period of twelve months which begins on or before 18th March 1986, any amount raised by the issue of eligible shares on or before that date shall be disregarded.

Qualifying trades

8.—(1) Paragraph 6 shall be amended as follows.

(2) For sub-paragraph (2) there shall be substituted the following sub-paragraph—

"(2) The trade must not at any time in the relevant period consist of one or more of the following activities if that activity amounts, or those activities when taken together amount, to a substantial part of the trade—

(*a*) dealing in commodities, shares, securities, land or futures;

(*b*) dealing in goods otherwise than in the course of an ordinary trade of wholesale or retail distribution;

(*c*) banking, insurance, money-lending, debt-factoring, hire-purchase financing or other financial activities;

(*d*) oil extraction activities;

(*e*) leasing (including letting ships on charter or other assets on hire) or receiving royalties or licence fees;

(*f*) providing legal or accountancy services; or

(*g*) providing services or facilities for any trade carried on by another person which consists to any substantial extent of activities within any of paragraphs (*a*) to (*f*) above and in which a controlling interest is held by a person who also has a controlling interest in the trade carried on by the company."

(3) For sub-paragraph (2B) there shall be substituted the following sub-paragraphs—

"(2B) A trade shall not be treated as failing to comply with this paragraph by reason only of its consisting of letting ships, other than oil rigs or pleasure craft, on charter if—

(*a*) every ship let on charter by the company carrying on the trade is beneficially owned by the company;

(*b*) every ship beneficially owned by the company is registered in the United Kingdom;

(*c*) throughout the relevant period the company is solely responsible for arranging the marketing of the services of its ships; and

(*d*) the conditions mentioned in sub-paragraph (2C) below are satisfied in relation to every letting on charter by the company,

but where any of the requirements mentioned in paragraphs (*a*) to (*d*) above are not satisfied in relation to any lettings of such ships, the trade shall not thereby be treated as failing to comply with this paragraph if those lettings and any other activity of a kind falling within paragraph 6(2) above do not, when taken together, amount to a substantial part of the trade.

(2C) The conditions are that—

(*a*) the letting is for a period not exceeding twelve months and no provision is made at any time (whether in the lease or otherwise) for extending it beyond that period otherwise than at the option of the lessee;

(*b*) during the period of the letting there is no provision in force (whether made in the lease or otherwise) for the grant of a new letting to end, otherwise than at the option of the lessee, more than twelve months after that provision is made;

(*c*) the letting is by way of a bargain made at arm's length between the company and a person who is not connected with it;

(*d*) under the terms of the charter the company is responsible as principal—

(i) for taking, throughout the period of the charter, management decisions in relation to the ship, other than those of a kind generally regarded by persons engaged in trade of the kind in question as matters of husbandry; and

(ii) for defraying all expenses in connection with the ship throughout that period, or substantially all such expenses, other than those directly incidental to a particular voyage or to the employment of the ship during that period; and

(*e*) no arrangements exist by virtue of which a person other than the company may be appointed to be responsible for the matters mentioned in paragraph (*d*) above on behalf of the company;

but this sub-paragraph shall have effect, in relation to any letting between the company in question and its subsidiary, or between it and another company of which it is a subsidiary or between it and a company which is a subsidiary of the same company of which it is a subsidiary, as if paragraph (*c*) were omitted.

(4) For sub-paragraph (4) there shall be substituted the following sub-paragraphs—

"(4) For the purposes of sub-paragraph (2)(b) above—

(*a*) a trade of wholesale distribution is one in which the goods are offered for sale and sold to persons for resale by them, or for processing and resale by them, to members of the general public for their use or consumption;

(*b*) a trade of retail distribution is one in which the goods are offered for sale and sold to members of the general public for their use or consumption;

(*c*) a trade is not an ordinary trade of wholesale or retail distribution if—

(i) it consists to a substantial extent of dealing in goods of a kind which are collected or held as an investment or of that activity and any other activity of a kind falling within paragraph 6(2) above, taken together; and

(ii) a substantial proportion of those goods are held by the company for a period which is significantly longer than the period for which a vendor would reasonably be expected to hold them while endeavouring to dispose of them at their market value;

and, in determining for the purposes of sub-paragraph (2)(*b*) whether a trade is an ordinary trade of wholesale or retail distribution, regard shall be had to the extent to which it has the features mentioned in Schedule 11 to the Finance Act 1981, those in Part I being regarded as indications that the trade is such an ordinary trade and those in Part II being regarded as indications of the contrary.

(5) For the purposes of this paragraph a person has a controlling interest in a trade—

(*a*) in the case of a trade carried on by a company if—

(i) he controls the company;

(ii) the company is a close company for the purposes of the Corporation Tax Acts and he or an associate of his is a director of the company and the beneficial owner of, or able directly or through the medium of other companies or by any other indirect means to control, more than 30 per cent. of the ordinary share capital of the company; or

(iii) not less than half of the trade could, in accordance with section 253(2) of the Taxes Act, be regarded as belonging to him;

(*b*) in any other case, if he is entitled to not less than half of the assets used for, or the income arising from, the trade.

(6) For the purposes of sub-paragraph (5) above there shall be attributed to any person any rights or powers of any person who is an associate of his.

(7) References in this paragraph to a trade shall be construed without regard to so much of the definition of "trade" in section 526(5) of the Taxes Act as relates to adventures or concerns in the nature of trade; but the foregoing provisions do not affect the construction of references in sub-paragraph (2)(*g*) or (5) above to a trade carried on by a person other than the company and those references shall be construed as including references to any business, profession or vocation.

(8) The Treasury may by order made by statutory instrument amend this paragraph in such manner as they consider expedient.

(9) Any order under sub-paragraph (8) above shall be subject to annulment in pursuance of a resolution of the Commons House of Parliament.

(10) In this paragraph—

"film" means an original master negative of a film, an original master film disc or an original master film tape;

"oil rig" means any ship which is an offshore installation for the purposes of the Mineral Workings (Offshore Installations) Act 1971;

"pleasure craft" means any ship of a kind primarily used for sport or recreation; and

"sound recording" means, in relation to a film, its sound track, original master audio disc or, as the case may be, original master audio tape."

(5) Sub-paragraph (2) above, so far as it relates to oil extraction, has effect in relation to shares issued at any time after the passing of this Act.

Disposal of shares

9.—(1) Paragraph 7 shall be amended as follows.

(2) The following sub-paragraph shall be inserted after sub-paragraph (1)—

"(1A) Where an option, the exercise of which would bind the grantor to purchase any shares, is granted to an individual during the relevant period, the individual shall not be entitled to any relief in respect of the shares to which the option relates."

(3) In sub-paragraph (2), for the words "company shall" there shall be substituted the words "company, and any option of the kind mentioned in sub-paragraph (1A) above, shall", and after the word "given", in each place, there shall be inserted the words "(and not withdrawn)".

(4) In sub-paragraph (2A), the words "(and not withdrawn)" shall be inserted after the word "given" and the words "(subject to sub-paragraph (2) above)" shall be inserted after the words "class shall".

(5) The following sub-paragraph shall be substituted for sub-paragraph (4)—

"(4) For the purposes of this paragraph and of Chapter II as applied by this paragraph—

(*a*) references to a disposal of shares include references to the grant of an option the exercise of which would bind the grantor to sell the shares; and

(*b*) shares in a company shall not be treated as being of the same class unless they would be so treated if dealt with on The Stock Exchange."

(6) The amendment made by sub-paragraph (4) above, which is enacted for the avoidance of doubt, shall be deemed to have been incorporated in Schedule 5 to the Finance Act 1983 as originally enacted but otherwise this paragraph has effect in relation to options granted at any time after 18th March 1986.

Value received from company

10.—(1) Paragraph 8 shall be amended as follows.

(2) In sub-paragraph (1), the words "Subject to paragraph 7 above" shall be inserted at the beginning.

(3) For subparagraph (2) there shall be substituted the following sub-paragraph—

"(2) Subject to sub-paragraph (3) below, section 58(2) to (4) and (6) to (9) of Chapter II shall apply but—

(*a*) with the addition, at the end of subsection (2)(*e*), of the words 'which has not been repaid in full before the issue of the shares in respect of which relief is claimed';

(*b*) with the substitution, in subsection (3), of a reference to paragraph 5(5) above for the reference to section 55(5); and

(*c*) with the addition, at the end of subsection (4)(*c*), of the words 'reduced by the amount of any repayment made before the issue of the shares in respect of which relief is claimed',"

(4) The following sub-paragraph shall be added at the end—

"(4) Where relief to which an individual is entitled in respect of eligible shares is reduced by virtue of this paragraph, effect shall be given to the reduction by apportioning it, as between the eligible shares held by him, in such a way as appears to the inspector, or on an appeal to the Commissioners concerned, to be just and reasonable."

(5) The amendment made by sub-paragraph (2) above, which is enacted for the avoidance of doubt, shall be deemed to have been incorporated in Schedule 5 to the Finance Act 1983 as originally enacted.

Value received by persons other than claimants

11.—(1) Paragraph 10 shall be amended as follows.

(2) In sub-paragraph (1)(*b*), after "thereby" there shall be inserted the words "withdrawn or reduced by virtue of paragraph 7 above or".

(3) For sub-paragraph (5A) there shall be substituted the following sub-paragraph—

"(5A) Where relief to which an individual is entitled in respect of eligible shares is reduced by virtue of this paragraph, effect shall given to the reduction by apportioning it as between the eligible shares held by him in such a way as appears to the inspector, or on an appeal to the Commissioners concerned, to be just and reasonable.".

Parallel trades

12. After paragraph 10 there shall be inserted the following paragraph—

"Parallel trades

10A.—(1) An individual is not entitled to relief in respect of any shares in a company where, at the date mentioned in sub-paragraph (2) below—

(*a*) he is one of a group of persons—

(i) who control the company; or

(ii) to whom belongs an interest amounting in the aggregate to more than a half share in the trade carried on by the company;

(*b*) he is also an individual, or one of a group of persons—

(i) controlling another company; or

(ii) to whom belongs an interest amounting in the aggregate to more than a half-share in another trade; and

(*c*) the trade carried on by the company, or a substantial part of it—

(i) is concerned with the same or similar types of property or parts thereof or provides the same or similar services or facilities; and

(ii) serves substantially the same or similar outlets or markets;

as the other trade or (as the case may be) the trade carried on by the other company.

(2) The date mentioned in sub-paragraph (1) above is—

(*a*) the date on which the shares are issued; or

(*b*) if later, the date on which the company begins to carry on the trade.

(3) For the purposes of sub-paragraph (1) above—

(*a*) the persons to whom a trade belongs, and (where a trade belongs to two or more persons) their respective shares in that trade, shall be determined in accordance with subsections (1)(*a*) and (*b*), (2) and (3) of section 253 of the Taxes Act; and (*b*) any interest, rights or powers of a person who is an associate (as defined by section 67(1) of Chapter II) of another person shall be treated as those of that other person.

(4) For the purposes of this paragraph—

(*a*) references to a company's trade include references to the trade of any of its subsidiaries; and

(*b*) "trade", in the expressions "another trade", "other trade" and "trade carried on by the other company", includes any business, profession or vocation."

Claims

13. In paragraph 13, the following sub-paragraph shall be added at the end—

"(10) For the purposes of the provisions of the Taxes Management Act 1970 relating to appeals against decisions on claims, the refusal of the inspector to authorise the issue of a certificate under sub-paragraph (2) above shall be taken to be a decision refusing a claim made by the company."

Assessments for withdrawing relief

14. In paragraph 14(2)(*a*), for the words "or 10(1)" there shall be substituted the words "10(1) or 16A".

Information

15.—(1) After paragraph 15 there shall be inserted the following paragraph—

"15A.—(1) Where—

(*a*) a company has issued a certificate under paragraph 13(2) above in respect of any eligible shares in the company; and

(*b*) it appears to the company, or to any person connected with the company who has knowledge of the matter, that paragraph 5A above may have effect to deny relief in respect of those shares;

the company or (as the case may be) that person or (where it so appears to each of them) both the company and that person shall give notice in writing to the inspector setting out the particulars of the case.

(2) If the inspector has reason to believe that a person has not given a notice which he is required to give under sub-paragraph (1) above, the inspector may by notice in writing require that person to furnish him within such time (not being less than sixty days) as may be specified in the notice with such information relating to the case as the inspector may reasonably require for the purposes of this Part."

Capital gains tax

16.—(1) Paragraph 16 shall be amended as follows.

(2) For sub-paragraph (1) there shall be substituted the following sub-paragraph—

"(1) Where—

(*a*) an individual to whom relief has been given in respect of eligible shares disposes of those shares (withing the meaning of the Capital Gains Tax Act 1979); and

(*b*) the relief is not withdrawn;

any gain or loss which accrues to him on that disposal shall not be a chargeable gain or (as the case may be) allowable loss for the purposes of capital gains tax."

(3) In sub-paragraph (3) after the word "given" in both places, there shall be inserted the words "(and not withdrawn)".

(4) After sub-paragraph (3) there shall be inserted the following sub-paragraphs—

"(3A) Where section 44 of the Act of 1979 (disposals between husband and wife to be on a no gain/no loss basis) has applied to any eligible shares disposed of by an individual to his or her spouse ("the transferee"), sub-paragraph (1) above shall apply in relation to the subsequent disposal of the shares by the transferee to a third party.

(3B) Where section 85 (exchange of securities for those in another company) or 86 (reconstruction or amalgamation involving issue of securities) of the Act of 1979 would, but for this sub-paragraph, apply in relation to eligible shares in respect of which an individual has been given relief, that section shall apply only if the relief is withdrawn."

Reorganisation of share capital

17.—(1) After paragraph 16 there shall be inserted the following paragraph—

"Reorganisation of share capital

16A.—(1) Where shares in respect of which relief has been given and not withdrawn have by virtue of any such allotment, otherwise than for payment, as is mentioned in section 77(2)(*a*) of the Capital Gains Tax Act 1979 fallen to be treated under section 78 of that Act as the same asset as a new holding—

(*a*) a disposal of the whole part or the new holding shall be treated for the purposes of this Schedule as a disposal of the whole or a corresponding part of those shares; and

(*b*) the new holding shall be treated for the purposes of paragraph 7(2) above as shares in respect of which relief has been given and not withdrawn.

(2) Sections 78 to 81 of the Act of 1979 shall not apply in relation to any ordinary shares in respect of which relief has been given if—

(*a*) there is, by virtue of any such allotment for payment as is mentioned in section 77(2)(*a*) of that Act, a reorganisation affecting those shares; and

(*b*) immediately following the reorganisation, the relief has not been withdrawn in respect of those shares or relief has been given in respect of the allotted shares and not withdrawn.

(3) Where—

(*a*) any such reorganisation as is mentioned in sub-paragraph (2) above affects ordinary shares in respect of which relief has been given;

(*b*) immediately before the reorganisation the relief had not been withdrawn; and

(*c*) the amount of relief (or, where the relief has been reduced, the amount remaining) and the market value of the shares immediately before the reorganisation, exceeds their market value immediately after the reorganisation;

the relief shall be reduced by an amount equal to whichever is the smaller of those excesses.

(4) Sub-paragraph (3) above shall also apply where—

(*a*) an individual who has received, or become entitled to receive, in respect of any ordinary shares in a company, a provisional allotment of shares in or debentures of the company disposes of his rights; and

(*b*) sub-paragraph (3) would have applied (apart from his sub-paragraph) had those rights not been disposed of but an allotment of shares or debentures made to him.

(5) Where relief is reduced by virtue of sub-paragraph (3) above—

(*a*) the sums allowable as deductions from the consideration in the computation, for the purposes of capital gains tax, of the gain or loss accruing to an individual on the disposal of any of the allotted shares or debentures shall be taken to include the amount of the reduction, apportioned between the allotted shares or (as the case may be) debentures in such a way as appears to the inspector, or on appeal to the Commissioners concerned, to be just and reasonable; and

(*b*) the sums so allowable on the disposal (in circumstances in which paragraph 16 above does not apply) of any of the shares referred to in sub-paragraph (3)(*a*) above shall be taken to be reduced by the amount mentioned in paragraph (*a*) above, similarly apportioned between those shares.".

(2) Sub-paragraphs (1) to (3) of the inserted paragraph 16A have effect in relation to reorganisations occurring at any time after 18th March 1986 and sub-paragraph (5) of that paragraph has effect in relation to disposals made at any time after that date.

Application to subsidiaries

18. For sub-paragraph (1) of paragraph 17 there shall be substituted the following sub-paragraphs—

"(1) A qualifying company may, in the relevant period, have one or more subsidiaries if—

(*a*) the conditions mentioned in sub-paragraph (1A) below are satisfied in respect of the subsidiary or (as the case may be) each subsidiary and, except as provided in sub-paragraph (1B) below, continue to be so satisfied until the end of the relevant period; and

(*b*) the subsidiary or (as the case may be) each subsidiary exists wholly, or substantially wholly, for the purpose of carrying on one or more qualifying trades or is a property managing, or dormant, subsidiary.

(1A) The conditions are—

(*a*) that the qualifying company, or another of its subsidiaries, possesses not less than 90 per cent. of the issued share capital of, and not less than 90 per cent. of the voting power in, the subsidiary;

(*b*) that the qualifying company, or another of its subsidiaries, would in the event of a winding up of the subsidiary or in any other circumstances be beneficially entitled to receive more than 90 per cent. of the assets of the subsidiary which would then be available for distribution to equity holders of the subsidiary;

(*c*) that the qualifying company or another of its subsidiaries is beneficially entitled to not less than 90 per cent. of any profits of the subsidiary which are available for distribution to equity holders of the subsidiary;

(*d*) that no person other than the qualifying company or another of its subsidiaries has control of the subsidiary within the meaning of section 534 of the Taxes Act; and

(*e*) that no arrangements are in existence by virtue of which the conditions in paragraphs (*a*) to (*d*) above could cease to be satisfied.

(1B) The conditions shall not be regarded as ceasing to be satisfied by reason only of the subsidiary or the qualifying company being wound up, or dissolved without winding up, if—

(*a*) it is shown that the winding up or dissolution is for bona fide commercial reasons and not part of a scheme or arrangement the main purpose, or one of the main purposes, of which is the avoidance of tax; and

(*b*) the net assets (if any) of the subsidiary or, as the case may be, the qualifying company are distributed to its members or dealt with as bona vacantia before the end of the relevant period, or in the case of a winding up, the end (if later) of three years from the commencement of the winding up.

(1C) The conditions shall not be regarded as ceasing to be satisfied by reason only of the disposal by the qualifying company or (as the case may be) by another subsidiary, within the relevant period, of all its interest in the subsidiary if it is shown that the disposal is for bona fide commercial reasons and not part of a scheme or arrangement the main purpose or one of the main purposes of which is the avoidance of tax.

(1D) For the purposes of this paragraph—

(*a*) a subsidiary of a qualifying company is a property managing subsidiary if it exists wholly, or substantially wholly, for the purpose of holding and managing property used by the qualifying company, or by any of its subsidiaries, for the purposes of—

(i) research and development from which it is intended that a qualifying trade to be carried on by the company or any of its subsidiaries will be derived; or

(ii) one or more qualifying trades so carried on;

(*b*) a subsidiary is a dormant subsidiary if it has no profits for the purposes of corporation tax and no part of its business consists in the making of investments; and

(*c*) the persons who are equity holders of a subsidiary and the percentage of the assets of a subsidiary to which an equity holder would be entitled shall be determined in accordance with paragraphs 1 and 3 of Schedule 12 to the Finance Act 1973, taking references in paragraph 3 to the first company as references to an equity holder and references to a winding up as including references to any other circumstances in which assets of the subsidiary are available for distribution to its equity holders."

Miscellaneous

19.—(1) In paragraph 2(9), for the words "to (8A)" there shall be substituted the words "and (8)".

(2) In paragraph 18(4), for the words "section 65(2)(*c*) of Chapter II" there shall be substituted the words "paragraph 17(1A)(*e*) above".

Eligible shares held jointly

20. After paragraph 19 there shall be inserted the following paragraph—

"Eligible shares held jointly

19A. Where eligible shares are held on a bare trust for two or more beneficiaries, this Schedule shall have effect (with the necessary modifications) as if—

(*a*) each beneficiary had subscribed as an individual for all of those shares; and

(*b*) the amount subscribed by each beneficiary was equal to the total amount subscribed on the issue of those shares divided by the number of beneficiaries.".

Interpretation

21.—(1) Paragraph 20 shall be amended as follows.

(2) In sub-paragraph (2) the following definitions shall be inserted at the appropriate places—

"appraisal licence" means an appraisal licence incorporating the model clauses set out in Schedule 4 to the Petroleum (Production) (Landward Areas) Regulations 1984 or a Northern Ireland licence granted for the five year renewal term and includes in either case any modified appraisal licence;

"development licence" means a development licence incorporating the model clauses set out in Schedule 5 to those regulations or a Northern Ireland licence granted for the thirty year renewal term and includes in either case any modified development licence;

"exploration licence" means an exploration licence incorporating the model clauses set out in Schedule 3 to those regulations or a Northern Ireland licence granted for the initial term and includes in either case any modified exploration licence;

"modified appraisal licence", "modified development licence" and "modified exploration licence" mean, respectively, any appraisal licence, development licence or exploration licence in which any of the relevant model clauses have been modified or excluded by the Secretary of State or, in Northern Ireland, by the Department of Economic Development;

"Northern Ireland licence" means a licence granted under the Petroleum (Production) Act (Northern Ireland) 1964 and incorporating the model clauses set out in Schedule 2 to the Petroleum Production (Licences) Regulations (Northern Ireland) 1965, and in relation to such a licence the references above to "the initial term", "the five year renewal term" and "the thirty year renewal term" shall be construed in accordance with Clause 2 of Schedule 2 to those regulations; and

"oil" and "oil extraction activities" have the same meaning as they have by virtue of section 19 of the Oil Taxation Act 1975, in Part II of that Act; and "oil exploration" means searching for oil.

(3) The following sub-paragraphs shall be added at the end—

"(3) For the purposes of this Schedule, the market value at any time of any asset shall be taken to be the price which it might reasonably be expected to fetch on a sale at that time in the open market free from any interest or right which exists by way of security in or over it.

(4) References in this Schedule to relief given to an individual in respect of eligible shares, and to the withdrawal of such relief, include respectively references to relief given to him in respect of those shares at any time after he has disposed of them and references to the withdrawal of such relief at any such time.

(5) Any reference in paragraph 2 above, as modified by paragraph 2B above, to any licence being held by, or granted to, any person shall be read as including a reference to such a licence being held by, or (as the case may be) granted to, that person together with one or more other persons.

(6) The Treasury may by order made by statutory instrument amend any of the definitions set out in sub-paragraph (2) above which relate to licences under the Petroleum (Production) Act 1934 or under the Petroleum (Production) Act (Northern Ireland) 1964.

(7) Any order under sub-paragraph (6) above shall be subject to annulment in pursuance of a resolution of the Commons House of Parliament.".

PART II

CONSEQUENTIAL AMENDMENTS

22. In the Taxes Management Act 1970 the following section shall be inserted after section 47A—

"Special jurisdiction relating to Business Expansion Scheme

47B. If and so far as the question in dispute on any appeal against the refusal of relief under Schedule 5 to the Finance Act 1983 (relief for investment in corporate trades), or against an assessment withdrawing any such relief, is a question of the value of an interest in land (within the meaning of paragraph 5A(5) of that Schedule), it shall be determined—

(*a*) if the land is in England and Wales, on a reference to the Lands Tribunal;
(*b*) if the land is in Scotland, on a reference to the Lands Tribunal for Scotland; and
(*c*) if the land is in Northern Ireland, on a reference to the Lands Tribunal for Northern Ireland".

23. The Table in section 98 of the Act of 1970 (penalties) shall be amended as follows—

(*a*) at the appropriate place in the first column there shall be inserted—
"Paragraph 15A(2) of Schedule 5 to the Finance Act 1983"; and
(*b*) at the appropriate place in the second column there shall be inserted—
"Paragraph 15A(1) of Schedule 5 to the Finance Act 1983".

General Note

This Schedule contains a number of amendments to the rules relating to Business Expansion Schemes contained in Schedule 5 to F.A. 1983. The amendments apply to shares issued after March 18, 1986.

(i) Research and development companies—This extends the rules so that money raised to carry out research and development by a subsidiary as well as the company itself is covered.

(ii) Oil exploration—The relief is extended also to companies carrying on the business of exploring for oil in the U.K. but not to those contracting it. It will also apply to money raised for the purpose of funding oil exploration. A company which uses money under the scheme and as a result of the exploration finds oil which it extracts will not cause the relief to be withdrawn from its BES investors.

To qualify certain conditions have to be satisfied

(i) the company must at the time of the issue of the shares or immediately thereafter be carrying on the activity of oil exploration;
(ii) it must have an exploration licence at that time and for a period of three years thereafter;
(iii) it must carry on the exploration within an area covered by the licence;
(iv) it must not have an appraisal or development licence relating to any part of the whole of the area covered by the exploration licence.

As with research and development the money can be raised for a subsidiary to carry out the exploration.

This provision (paragraph 4) applies to shares issued after July 25, 1986.

(iii) Qualifying individuals—a person carrying out any duties of an office or employment under the Crown of a public nature and whose emoluments are payable out of the public revenue will be treated as resident and ordinarily resident in the U.K. even if not actually so resident and will thereby be eligible for the benefit of the relief. This applies to shares issued after 6th April 1986.

(iv) Qualifying companies—A number of changes are made

(*a*) If a company has one or more subsidiaries then the qualifying trade or trades of the companies must be carried on wholly or mainly in the U.K.
(*b*) The restrictions in para. 5(8)–1(1) of Schedule 5 to F.A. 1981 are removed. These concerned an individual having a controlling interest in the company's trade at any time after April 5, 1983 and also in another similar trade. These restrictions have been replaced by a new set of rules in paragraph 10.
(*c*) Paragraph 6 imposes a new restriction which is intended to prevent the promotion of schemes in which the company has substantial property assets.

The company will not qualify if at any time during the relevant period or at the time of the issue of the shares the value of its interests in land exceeds 50 per cent. of the value of the company's assets as a whole.

There are a number of rules for determining the value of the company's interests in land and its other assets.

In determining the value of the interests in land there is to be deducted

(i) all debts secured on those interests (including by way of floating charge);
(ii) unsecured debts falling due for payment more than twelve months hence;
(iii) the amounts paid up on any preference shares.

When valuing interests in land which have mineral deposits or boreholes certain assumptions are to be made—see para. 5A(6). This is to assist private mining concerns.

In the case of a qualifying company with one or more subsidiaries the group will be treated as one company for the purposes of applying this restriction and inter group indebtedness will be disregarded.

Para. 5B provides for adjustments to the value of a company's interests in land to be made immediately after the issue of the shares.

By virtue of para. 5C the relief will not be lost due to this restriction if the amount raised by the issue of the shares (taken together with amounts raised in the preceding year) does not exceed £50,000. Any amount raised before March 19, 1986 will not be taken into account for these purposes.

When the amount raised exceeds £50,000 it is only the excess which loses the relief.

If the company or any subsidiary is involved in a partnership or joint venture and at least one of the other persons involved is a company then the £50,000 limit will be reduced by the formula provided in 5C(2).

(v) Qualifying trades—There have been important changes in the rules relating to which trades qualify for the benefit of the relief.

The list of activities which are excluded from qualifying have been extended and now includes dealing in goods otherwise than in the cause of an ordinary trade of wholesale or retail distribution. Guidance as to what constitutes such an ordinary trade is given by the new paragraph 6(4) (see paragraph 8(4)). Such exclusion will cover dealings in antiques and wines unless in the latter case they are traded in a normal manner.

Ship chartering is included as a qualifying activity (see paragraph 8(3)) but only if the conditions in the new paragraphs (2B) and (2C) are satisfied. The charters must not be for longer than a year and the ship must be under the management responsibility of the company. It is not sufficient that a managing agent is appointed to have sole responsibility.

(vi) Disposal of shares—The grant of an option relating to shares in a qualifying company will be treated as a disposal of those shares thereby losing the relief in respect of those shares. This applies to options granted after March 18, 1986.

If the grantor owns shares in the company some of which are covered by the relief and some not (whether because they never qualified or because the relief has been withdrawn) then the option will be treated as relating to those covered by the relief first. The same is true of any other disposal of shares. This amendment is retrospective in that it causes shares from which the relief has already been withdrawn to be treated in the same manner as shares which never qualified for the relief.

(vii) Value received from the company—The amendment to paragraph 8 of Schedule 5 prevents any loan repaid before the issue of shares from being treated as value received from the company.

The Inspector is given power (retrospectively) to apportion any reduction in relief amongst the individual's eligible shares in such manner as appears to the inspector just and reasonable with a right of appeal to the Commissioners.

(viii) Parallel trading—The rules in the new paragraph 10A replace those in para. 5(8) of Schedule 5. An individual will not qualify for relief if at the date of the issue of the shares or the commencement of trading (if later)

(i) he either alone or with a group of persons controls the company or is interested in more than a half share in the company's trade; and

(ii) he also alone or with a group of persons controls a company carrying on a parallel trade or is interested in more than a half share in the trade.

(ix) Appeals—The refusal of an inspector to issue a certificate can not be the subject of an appeal.

(x) Information—If it appears to the company or any connected person after the issue of a BES certificate that the relief may be affected by reason of the value of the company's interests in land then it must notify the inspector in writing. Failure to do so may result in a penalty (see paragraph 22).

The inspector has power now to request information and failure to produce it could also result in a penalty.

(xi) Capital gains tax—The disposal of shares covered by the relief will not give rise to a chargeable gain nor to an allowable loss. The same applies if it is the spouse who is disposing of the shares.

(xii) Reorganisation of share capital—Paragraph 17 applies so that any reconstruction involving the BES investor will result in the new shares being covered by the relief provided that no consideration if given. If a consideration is received, for instance if a payment is made or rights disposed of, then the relief will be reduced by the difference in market value of the shares immediately before and after the reconstruction.

(xiii) Subsidiaries—A qualifying company may have one or more subsidiaries provided that the conditions contained in the new paragraph 17(1A) are satisfied.

(xiv) Jointly held shares—if the shares are held on a bare trust for more than one person each individual will be treated separately for the purposes of the relief.

(xv) Lands Tribunal—any appeal relating to the value of land or an interest in it will be heard by the Lands Tribunal (paragraph 22).

Section 42

SCHEDULE 10

COMPANY RECONSTRUCTIONS

1.—(1) Section 252 of the Taxes Act (company reconstructions without change of ownership) shall be amended as follows.

(2) After subsection (3) (successor entitled to carry forward predecessor's loss) there shall be inserted—

"(3A) But where the amount of relevant liabilities exceeds the value of relevant assets, the successor shall be entitled to relief by virtue of subsection (3) above only if, and only to the extent that, the amount of that excess is less than the amount mentioned in that subsection."

(3) In subsection (8) (apportionment of receipts or expenses in case of partial change) for the words from "any", in the second place where it occurs, to the end there shall be substituted "such apportionments of receipts, expenses, assets or liabilities shall be made as may be just."

(4) In subsection (9) (determination of manner of apportionment) for "sum" in each place where it appears there shall be substituted "item".

2. The following shall be inserted at the end of section 253 of the Taxes Act (company reconstructions: supplemental)—

"(5) For the purposes of section 252(3A) above, relevant assets are—

(*a*) assets which were vested in the predecessor immediately before it ceased to carry on the trade, which were not transferred to the successor and which, in the case where the predecessor was the predecessor on a previous application of section 252 above, were not by virtue of section 252(8) above apportioned to a trade carried on by the company which was the successor on that application, and

(*b*) consideration given to the predecessor by the successor in respect of the change of company carrying on the trade;

and for the purposes of paragraph (*b*) above the assumption by the successor of any liabilities of the predecessor shall not be treated as the giving of consideration to the predecessor by the successor.

(6) For the purposes of section 252(3A) above, relevant liabilities are liabilities which were outstanding and vested in the predecessor immediately before it ceased to carry on the trade, which were not transferred to the successor and which, in a case where the predecessor was the predecessor on a previous application of section 252 above, were not by virtue of section 252(8) above apportioned to a trade carried on by the company which was the successor on that application; but a liability representing the predecessor's share capital, share premium account, reserves, or relevant loan stock is not a relevant liability.

(7) For the purposes of section 252(3A) above—

(*a*) the value of assets (other than money) shall be taken to be the price which they might reasonably be expected to have fetched on a sale in the open market immediately before the predecessor ceased to carry on the trade, and

(*b*) the amount of liabilities shall be taken to be their amount at that time.

(8) Where the predecessor transferred a liability to the successor but the creditor concerned agreed to accept settlement of part of the liability as settlement of the whole, the liability shall be treated for the purposes of subsection (6) above as not having been transferred to the successor except as to that part.

(9) A liability representing the predecessor's share capital, share premium account, reserves or relevant loan stock shall, for the purposes of subsection (6) above, be treated as not doing so if, in the period of one year ending with the day on which the predecessor ceased to carry on the trade, the liability arose on a conversion of a liability not representing its share capital, share premium account, reserves or relevant loan stock.

(10) Where a liability of the predecessor representing its relevant loan stock is not a relevant liability for the purposes of section 252(3A) above but is secured on an asset

of the predecessor not transferred to the successor, the value of the asset shall, for the purposes of section 252(3A), be reduced by an amount equal to the amount of the liability.

(11) In this section "relevant loan stock" means any loan stock or similar security (whether secured or unsecured) except any in the case of which subsection (12) below applies.

(12) This subsection applies where, at the time the liability giving rise to the loan stock or other security was incurred, the person who was the creditor was carrying on a trade of lending money."

3. The following shall be inserted after sub-paragraph (5) of paragraph 17 of Schedule 9 to the Finance Act 1981 (restriction of carry forward of unused relief)—

"(5A) Where an amount for which a company is entitled to relief by virtue of section 252(3) of the Taxes Act (company reconstructions: successor's entitlement to carry forward predecessor's loss) is reduced by virtue of section 252(3A) of that Act, the part of the amount in respect of which, by reason of the reduction, there is no relief shall for the purposes of this paragraph be taken to consist—

(*a*) first of capital allowances for accounting periods of the predecessor ending not earlier than 14th November 1980;

(*b*) next of relief under this Part of this Schedule, taking relief in respect of a later period of account before relief in respect of an earlier one;

(*c*) next of losses incurred in the trade in accounting periods of the predecessor ending not earlier than 14th November 1980 (calculated without regard to capital allowances or relief falling within paragraphs (*a*) and (*b*) above) and including any losses treated under section 254(5) of the Taxes Act as incurred in such accounting periods; and

(*d*) lastly of other losses, capital allowances and reliefs.

(5B) In sub-paragraph (5A) above 'the predecessor' has the same meaning as in section 252 of the Taxes Act.".

General Note

Section 252 I.C.T.A. 1970 permits the trade of a company to be taken over by another company and the successor company to claim relief in respect of the losses of the other company if both companies are in common ownership.

This Schedule restricts the availability of the relief to so much of the loss less the amount by which the transferor company's "relevant liabilities" exceed the value of its "relevant assets". The intention is to restrict the loss relief in cases where the transferor company is insolvent and the transferee company does not take over all the liabilities of the transferor company.

Any liability taken over by the transferee company will not be part of the relevant liabilities of the transferor company and will not be part of the consideration received by that company when calculating its relevant assets.

Any liability transferred to the transferee but settled by a part payment shall only be treated as transferred to the transferee to such extent. The remainder will, therefore, be treated as remaining with the transferor company.

Section 44

SCHEDULE 11

Entertainers and Sportsmen

Introduction

1. Where a person who is an entertainer or sportsman of a prescribed description performs an activity of a prescribed description in the United Kingdom (a relevant activity), this Schedule shall apply if he is not resident in the United Kingdom in the year of assessment in which the relevant activity is performed.

Payment of tax

2.—(1) Where a payment is made (to whatever person) and it has a connection of a prescribed kind with the relevant activity, the person by whom it is made shall on making it deduct out of it a sum representing income tax and shall account to the Board for the sum.

(2) The sum mentioned in sub-paragraph (1) above shall be such as is calculated in accordance with prescribed rules but shall in no case exceed the relevant proportion of the

payment concerned; and "relevant proportion" here means a proportion equal to the basic rate of income tax for the year of assessment in which the payment is made.

(3) Where a transfer is made (to whatever person) and it has a connection of a prescribed kind with the relevant activity, the person by whom it is made shall account to the Board for a sum representing income tax.

(4) The sum mentioned in sub-paragraph (3) above shall be such as is calculated in accordance with prescribed rules but shall in no case exceed the relevant proportion of the value of what is transferred; and "relevant proportion" here means a proportion equal to the basic rate of income tax for the year of assessment in which the transfer is made.

(5) References in this paragraph and in the following provisions of this Schedule to a payment include references to a payment by way of loan of money.

(6) References in this paragraph and in the following provisions of this Schedule to a transfer do not include references to a transfer of money but, subject to that, include references to a temporary transfer (as by way of loan) and to a transfer of a right (whether or not a right to receive money).

(7) This paragraph shall not apply to payments or transfers of such a kind as may be prescribed.

3.—(1) Regulations may—

(*a*) make provision enabling the Board to serve notices requiring persons who make payments or transfers to which paragraph 2 above applies to furnish to the Board particulars of a prescribed kind in respect of payments or transfers;

(*b*) make provision requiring persons who make payments or transfers to which paragraph 2 above applies to make, at prescribed times and for prescribed periods, returns to the Board containing prescribed information about payments or transfers and the income tax for which those persons are accountable in respect of them;

(*c*) make provision for the collection and recovery of such income tax, provision for assessments and claims to be made in respect of it, and provision for the payment of interest on it;

(*d*) adapt, or modify the effect of, any enactment relating to income tax for the purpose of making any such provision as is mentioned in paragraphs (*a*) to (*c*) above.

(2) The words "Regulations under paragraph 3 of Schedule 11 to the Finance Act 1986" shall be added at the end of each column in the Table in section 98 of the Taxes Management Act 1970 (penalties for failure to furnish information etc.).

4.—(1) Where in accordance with paragraphs 2 and 3 above a person pays a sum to the Board, they shall treat it as having been paid on account of a liability of another person to income tax or corporation tax; and the liability and the other person shall be such as are found in accordance with prescribed rules.

(2) Where the sum exceeds the liability concerned, the Board shall pay such of the sum as is appropriate to the other person mentioned in sub-paragraph (1) above.

(3) Where no liability is found as mentioned in sub-paragraph (1) above, the Board shall pay the sum to the person to whom the relevant payment or transfer was made; and here "the relevant payment or transfer" means the payment or transfer to which paragraph 2 above applies and which gave rise to the payment of the sum concerned to the Board.

(4) In construing references to a sum in sub-paragraphs (1) to (3) above, anything representing interest shall be ignored.

5. No obligation as to secrecy imposed by statute or otherwise shall preclude the Board or an authorised officer or the Board from disclosing to any person who appears to the Board to have an interest in the matter information which may be relevant to determining whether paragraph 2 above applies to a payment or transfer.

Activity treated as part of trade etc.

6.—(1) Where a payment is made (to whatever person) and it has a connection of the prescribed kind with the relevant activity, the activity shall be treated for the purposes of the Tax Acts as performed in the course of a trade, profession or vocation exercised by the entertainer or sportsman within the United Kingdom, to the extent that (apart from this paragraph) it would not be so treated.

(2) This paragraph shall not apply unless the payment is one to which paragraph 2 above applies.

(3) This paragraph shall not apply where the relevant activity is performed in the course of an office or employment.

(4) References in this paragraph to a payment include references to a transfer.

Income attributed to entertainer or sportsman

7.—(1) Where a payment is made to a person who fulfils a prescribed description but is not the entertainer or sportsman, and the payment has a connection of the prescribed kind with the relevant activity,—

(*a*) the entertainer or sportsman shall be treated for the purposes of the Tax Acts as the person to whom the payment is made, and

(*b*) the payment shall be treated for those purposes as made to him in the course of a trade, profession or vocation exercised by him within the United Kingdom (whether or not he would be treated as exercising such a trade, profession or vocation apart from this paragraph).

(2) Regulations may provide for the deduction, in computing any profits or gains of the entertainer or sportsman arising from the payment, of expenses incurred by other persons in relation to the payment.

(3) Regulations may provide that any liability to tax (whether of the entertainer or sportsman or of another person) which would, apart from this paragraph, arise in relation to the payment shall not arise or shall arise only to a prescribed extent.

(4) This paragraph shall not apply unless the payment is one to which paragraph 2 above applies.

(5) This paragraph shall not apply in such circumstances as may be prescribed.

(6) References in this paragraph to a payment include references to a transfer.

Charge on profits or gains

8.—(1) Where income tax is chargeable under Case I or Case II of Schedule D on the profits or gains arising from payments (made to whatever person) and the payments have a connection of the prescribed kind with relevant activities of the entertainer or sportsman, such tax shall be charged—

(*a*) as if those payments were received in the course of one trade, profession or vocation exercised by the entertainer or sportsman within the United Kingdom separately from any other trade, profession or vocation exercised by him, and

(*b*) for each year of assessment, on the full amount of the profits or gains arising in the year from those payments.

(2) Regulations may—

(*a*) provide for the apportionment of profits or gains between different trades, professions or vocations of the entertainer or sportsman;

(*b*) provide for the apportionment between different years of assessment of the profits or gains arising from relevant activities of the entertainer or sportsman;

(*c*) provide for losses sustained in any trade, profession or vocation of the entertainer or sportsman to be deducted from or set off against the profits or gains of another trade, profession or vocation of the entertainer or sportsman;

(*d*) provide that prescribed provisions of the Tax Acts about losses, or about expenditure, shall not apply (or shall apply with prescribed modifications) in prescribed circumstances relating to the entertainer or sportsman.

(3) References in sub-paragraph (2)(*a*) and (*c*) above to a trade, profession or vocation of the entertainer or sportsman include references to that first mentioned in sub-paragraph (1)(*a*) above as well as to any other exercised by him.

(4) This paragraph shall not apply in the case of a payment unless it is one to which paragraph 2 above applies.

(5) References in this paragraph to a payment include references to a transfer.

Valuation etc.

9.—(1) A payment to which paragraph 2(1) above applies shall be treated for the purposes of the Tax Acts as not diminished by the sum mentioned in paragraph 2(1).

(2) Regulations may provide that for the purposes of the Tax Acts the value of what is transferred by a transfer to which paragraph 2(3) above applies shall be calculated in accordance with prescribed rules.

(3) In particular, the rules may include provision for the calculation of an amount representing the actual worth of what is transferred, for that amount to be treated as a net amount corresponding to a gross amount from which income tax at the basic rate has been deducted, and for the gross amount to be taken to be the value of what is transferred.

General

10. Regulations may make provision generally for giving effect to this Schedule.

11.—(1) In this Schedule "prescribed" means prescribed by regulations.

(2) Regulations under this Schedule may make different provision for different cases or descriptions of case.

(3) The power to make regulations under this Schedule shall be exercisable by the Treasury by statutory instrument subject to annulment in pursuance of a resolution of the Commons House of Parliament.

12. This Schedule shall have effect for the year 1987–88 and subsequent years of assessment.

GENERAL NOTE

This Schedule has been introduced to counter non-payment of tax by visiting foreign entertainers and sportsmen. It provides that persons making payments to such people will be required to deduct and account for tax to the Revenue at a maximum of the basic rate. The Schedule only contains a broad outline of the scheme the details of which will be provided for by statutory instrument. It will come into effect as from April 6, 1987.

Paragraph 1 sets out the circumstances in which the Schedule is to apply. While the term "relevant activity" is not defined the intention is that it will be an appearance in the U.K. of a non-resident entertainer or sportsman. The obligation to deduct tax is contained in paragraph 2 and it should be noted that it is not intended that it will apply only to fees for performances etc. but also to other payments that have a "connection" with the activity. In addition the obligation to account for tax is not limited to cases of such payments but will also apply where transfers of assets are made. It is not intended that there should always be an obligation to deduct tax at the basic rate and the Revenue have said (Inland Revenue Press Statement, 4 June 1986) that regulations will provide for a nil or reduced rate of withholding by agreement with the Revenue and will provide for a threshold, initially of £500, below which deductions need not be made.

Paragraph 4 enables the tax deducted under para. 2 to be set against U.K. liabilities on the payments and allows it to be repaid where appropriate. In this connection the provisions of paragraph 8 are noteworthy in that they provide for charges to tax arising under Case I or II of Schedule D in respect of payments dealt with under the Schedule to be raised on an annual rather than a preceding year basis as is the case normally with Case I and II. This prevents an entertainer claiming that he is not subject to U.K. tax because in the year in which he is amenable he does not work in the U.K.

Paragraph 7 is intended to be an anti-avoidance provision to counter arrangements whereby payments are made to persons other than the entertainer or sportsman concerned (*e.g.* a non-resident company controlled by him). Such payments will be treated as made to him.

Section 46

SCHEDULE 12

PENSION SCHEME SURPLUSES

PART I

PAYMENTS TO EMPLOYERS

1.—(1) This paragraph applies where a payment is made to an employer out of funds which are or have been held for the purposes of a scheme which is or has at any time been an exempt approved scheme.

(2) An amount equal to 40 per cent. of the payment shall be recoverable by the Board from the employer.

(3) This paragraph applies whether or not the payment is made in pursuance of Part II of this Schedule.

(4) Paragraph 4 of Schedule 5 to the Finance Act 1970 (charge to tax on payments to employer) shall not apply to a payment to which this paragraph applies or would apply apart from sub-paragraph (5) or (6) below.

(5) This paragraph does not apply to a payment to the extent that, if this paragraph had not been enacted, the employer would have been exempt, or entitled to claim exemption, from income tax or corporation tax in respect of the payment.

(6) This paragraph does not apply where the employer is a charity; and "charity" here has the same meaning as in section 360 of the Taxes Act.

(7) This paragraph does not apply to any payment of any prescribed description.

(8) This paragraph does not apply to a payment made before the scheme became an exempt approved scheme.

(9) References in this paragraph to a payment include references to a transfer of assets or other transfer of money's worth.

(10) In this paragraph "exempt approved scheme" means an exempt approved scheme within the meaning given by section 21(1) of the Finance Act 1970.

(11) This paragraph applies to a payment made after 18th March 1986 unless made as mentioned in sub-paragraph (12) or (13) below.

(12) This paragraph does not apply to a payment made in pursuance of the winding-up of the scheme where the winding-up commenced on or before 18th March 1986.

(13) This paragraph does not apply to a payment made in pursuance of an application which—

(*a*) was made to the Board on or before 18th March 1986 and was not withdrawn before the making of the payment, and

(*b*) sought the Board's assurance that the payment would not lead to a withdrawal of approval under section 19(3) of the Finance Act 1970.

2.—(1) In relation to an amount recoverable as mentioned in paragraph 1(2) above, regulations may make any of the provisions mentioned in sub-paragraph (2) below; and for this purpose the amount shall be treated as if it were—

(*a*) an amount of income tax chargeable on the employer under Case VI of Schedule D for the year of assessment in which the payment is made, or

(*b*) where the employer is a company, an amount of corporation tax chargeable on the company for the accounting period in which the payment is made.

(2) The provisions are—

(*a*) provision requiring the administrator of the scheme or the employer (or both) to furnish to the Board, in respect of the amount recoverable and of the payment concerned, information of a prescribed kind;

(*b*) provision enabling the Board to serve a notice or notices requiring the administrator or employer (or both) to furnish to the Board, in respect of the amount and payment, particulars of a prescribed kind;

(*c*) provision requiring the administrator to deduct out of the payment the amount recoverable and to account to the Board for it;

(*d*) provision as to circumstances in which the employer may be assessed in respect of the amount recoverable;

(*e*) provision that, in a case where the employer has been assessed in respect of the amount recoverable but has not paid it (or part of it) within a prescribed period, the administrator may be assessed and charged (in the employer's name) in respect of the amount (or part unpaid);

(*f*) provision that, in a case where the amount recoverable (or part of it) has been recovered from the administrator by virtue of an assessment in the employer's name, the administrator is entitled to recover from the employer a sum equal to the amount (or part);

(*g*) provision enabling the employer or administrator (as the case may be) to appeal against an assessment made on him in respect of the amount recoverable;

(*h*) provision as to when any sum in respect of the amount recoverable is payable to the Board by the administrator or employer and provision requiring interest to be paid on any sum so payable;

(*i*) provision that an amount paid to the Board by the administrator shall be treated as paid on account of the employer's liability under paragraph 1(2) above.

(3) For the purpose of giving effect to any provision mentioned in sub-paragraph (2)(*a*) or (*b*) above the words "Regulations under paragraph 2 of Schedule 12 to the Finance Act 1986" shall be added at the end of each column in the Table in section 98 of the Taxes Management Act 1970 (penalties for failure to furnish information etc.).

(4) For the purpose of giving effect to any other provision mentioned in sub-paragraph (2) above, regulations under this paragraph may include provision applying (with or without modifications) provisions of the enactments relating to income tax and corporation tax.

(5) Subject to any provision of regulations under this paragraph—

(*a*) a payment to which paragraph 1 above applies shall not be treated as a profit or gain brought into charge to income tax or corporation tax and shall not be treated as part of the employer's income for any purpose of the Taxes Act, and

(*b*) the amount recoverable shall not be subject to any exemption or reduction (by way of relief, set-off or otherwise) or be available for set-off against other tax.

(6) If the employer is a company and a payment to which paragraph 1 above applies is made at a time not otherwise within an accounting period of the company, an accounting period of the company shall for the purposes of sub-paragraph (1)(*b*) above be treated as beginning immediately before the payment is made.

3.—(1) In this Part of this Schedule "prescribed" means prescribed by regulations.

(2) The power to make regulations under this Part of this Schedule shall be exercisable by the Treasury by statutory instrument subject to annulment in pursuance of a resolution of the House of Commons.

PART II

REDUCTION OF SURPLUSES

4.—(1) The Board may make regulations providing for this Part of this Schedule to apply, as from a prescribed date, in relation to any exempt approved scheme of a prescribed kind.

(2) The Board may make regulations providing for prescribed provisions of this Part of this Schedule to apply, as from a prescribed date, in prescribed circumstances, and subject to any prescribed omissions or modifications, in relation to any exempt approved scheme of another prescribed kind.

(3) In this Part of this Schedule—

(*a*) "exempt approved scheme" has the meaning given by section 21(1) of the Finance Act 1970, and

(*b*) "prescribed" means prescribed by regulations made by the Board.

(4) The power to make regulations under this paragraph shall be exercisable by statutory instrument subject to annulment in pursuance of a resolution of the House of Commons.

5.—(1) The administrator of a scheme in relation to which this Part of this Schedule applies shall, in prescribed circumstances and at a prescribed time, either produce to the Board a written valuation such as is mentioned in sub-paragraph (2) below or give to the Board a certificate such as is mentioned in sub-paragraph (3) below.

(2) The valuation must be a valuation of the assets held for the purposes of the scheme and the liabilities of the scheme, must be determined in accordance with prescribed principles and fulfil prescribed requirements, and must be signed by a person with qualifications of a prescribed kind.

(3) The certificate must state whether or not the value of the assets (as determined in accordance with the prescribed principles) exceeds the value of the liabilities (as so determined) by a percentage which is more than the prescribed maximum, must be in a prescribed form, and must be signed by a person with qualifications of a prescribed kind.

(4) In section 98 of the Taxes Management Act 1970 (penalty for failure to produce documents etc.) the following shall be inserted at the end of the second column of the Table—

"Paragraph 5 of Schedule 12 to the Finance Act 1986".

6.—(1) Subject to paragraph 7(4) below, where a valuation produced under paragraph 5 above shows, or a certificate given under that paragraph states, that the value of the assets exceeds the value of the liabilities by a percentage which is more than the prescribed maximum, the administrator of the scheme shall within a prescribed period submit to the Board for their approval proposals which comply with sub-paragraph (2) below.

(2) The proposals must be for reducing (or, subject to paragraph (*b*) below, eliminating) the excess in a way or ways set out in the proposals and falling within sub-paragraph (3) below; and they must be such as to secure that—

(*a*) by the end of a prescribed period the percentage (if any) by which the value of the assets exceeds the value of the liabilities is no more than the prescribed maximum, and

(*b*) if the way, or one of the ways, set out in the proposals falls within sub-paragraph (3)(*a*) below, there remains an excess which is of a level not less than the prescribed minimum.

(3) Subject to sub-paragraph (4) below, the permitted ways of reducing or eliminating the excess are—

(*a*) making payments to an employer;

(*b*) suspending for a period (of 5 years or less) set out in the proposals an employer's obligation to pay contributions under the scheme or reducing for such a period the amount of an employer's contributions under the scheme;

(*c*) suspending for a period (of 5 years or less) set out in the proposals the obligation of employees to pay contributions under the scheme or reducing for such a period the amount of employees' contributions under the scheme;

(*d*) improving existing benefits provided under the scheme;

(*e*) providing new benefits under the scheme;

(*f*) such other ways as may be prescribed.

(4) In prescribed circumstances sub-paragraph (3) above shall apply subject to such omissions or modifications as may be prescribed.

(5) Subject to paragraph 7(4) below, if the administrator of the scheme fails to submit proposals to the Board within the period mentioned in sub-paragraph (1) above, or if proposals submitted to them within that period are not approved by the Board within a further prescribed period, paragraph 10 below shall apply.

7.—(1) Where a valuation has been produced under paragraph 5 above, the Board may serve on the administrator of the scheme a notice requiring him to furnish the Board, within a prescribed period, with such particulars relating to the valuation as may be specified in the notice.

(2) Where a certificate has been given under paragraph 5 above, the Board may serve on the administrator of the scheme a notice requiring him to produce to the Board, within a prescribed period, a written valuation such as is mentioned in paragraph 5(2) above.

(3) Where a valuation has been produced in compliance with a notice served under sub-paragraph (2) above, the Board may serve on the administrator of the scheme a further notice requiring him to furnish the Board, within a prescribed period, with such particulars relating to the valuation as may be specified in the notice.

(4) Where a notice is served on the administrator of a scheme under sub-paragraph (1) or (2) above, paragraph 6(1) and (5) above shall cease to apply.

(5) In section 98 of the Taxes Management Act 1970 the following shall be inserted at the end of the first column of the Table—

"Paragraph 7 of Schedule 12 to the Finance Act 1986".

8.—(1) Where particulars have been furnished under paragraph 7 above, or a valuation has been produced under that paragraph, the Board shall, within a prescribed period, serve on the administrator of the scheme a notice—

(*a*) stating that they accept the valuation produced under paragraph 5 or, as the case may be, 7 above, or

(*b*) stating that they do not accept the valuation so produced, and specifying their estimate of the value of the liabilities of the scheme at the relevant time and their estimate of the value of the assets held for the purposes of the scheme at that time.

(2) For the purposes of sub-paragraph (1)(*b*) above, the relevant time is the time specified in the valuation produced under paragraph 5 or 7 above as the time by reference to which the values of the assets and liabilities are determined.

(3) Where—

(*a*) in a case falling within sub-paragraph (1)(*a*) above, the valuation shows that the value of the assets exceeds the value of the liabilities by a percentage which is more than the prescribed maximum, or

(*b*) in a case falling within sub-paragraph (1)(*b*) above, the value of the assets as estimated by the Board exceeds the value of the liabilities as so estimated by a percentage which is more than the prescribed maximum,

the administrator of the scheme shall within a prescribed period submit to the Board for their approval proposals which comply with paragraph 6(2) to (4) above.

(4) If the administrator of the scheme fails to submit proposals to the Board within the period mentioned in sub-paragraph (3) above, or if proposals submitted to them within that period are not approved by the Board within a further prescribed period, paragraph 10 below shall apply.

9.—(1) Where proposals are submitted to the Board under paragraph 6(1) or 8(3) above and they approve them within the further prescribed period mentioned in paragraph 6(5) or 8(4) above, the administrator of the scheme shall carry out the proposals within the period mentioned in paragraph 6(2) above.

(2) If the administrator fails to carry out the proposals within that period, paragraph 10 below shall apply.

10.—(1) Where this paragraph applies the Board may specify a percentage equivalent to the fraction—

(*a*) whose numerator represents their estimate of the value of the liabilities of the scheme at the relevant time increased by a prescribed percentage, and

(*b*) whose denominator represents their estimate of the value of the assets held for the purposes of the scheme at that time.

(2) For the purposes of this paragraph, the relevant time is the time specified—

(*a*) in the valuation produced or certificate given under paragraph 5 above, or

(*b*) where a valuation has been produced under paragraph 7 above, in that valuation,

as the time by reference to which the values of the assets and liabilities are determined.

(3) Where a percentage has been so specified—

(*a*) section 21(2) of the Finance Act 1970 (income tax exemption) shall apply only to that percentage of any income derived in the relevant period from the assets held for the purposes of the scheme,

(*b*) section 21(2A) of that Act (further income tax exemption) shall apply only to that percentage of any underwriting commissions applied in the relevant period for the purposes of the scheme,

(*c*) section 21(7) of that Act (capital gains tax exemption) shall apply only to that percentage of any gain accruing on the disposal in the relevant period of any of those assets, and

(*d*) section 26(1) of the Finance Act 1973 (charge to tax on certain profits or gains) shall by virtue of section 26(1)(*a*) not apply only to that percentage of any profits or gains arising to the scheme in the relevant period.

(4) Sub-paragraphs (5) to (8) below shall apply where a percentage has been so specified, securities are transferred in the relevant period, and the transferor or transferee is such that, if he became entitled to any interest on them, exemption could be allowed under section 21(2) of the Finance Act 1970.

(5) Paragraph 32(1) and (2) of Schedule 23 to the Finance Act 1985 (accrued income scheme) shall not apply.

(6) Where, in consequence of sub-paragraph (5) above, section 73(2)(*a*) or (3)(*b*) of the 1985 Act applies, the sum concerned shall be treated as reduced by an amount equal to the specified percentage of itself.

(7) Where, in consequence of sub-paragraph (5) above, section 73(2)(*b*) or (3)(*a*) of the 1985 Act applies, the relief concerned shall be treated as reduced by an amount equal to the specified percentage of itself.

(8) For the purposes of section 74(5) of the 1985 Act, the amount of interest falling to be reduced by the amount of the allowance shall be treated as the amount found after applying section 21(2) of the Finance Act 1970.

(9) In sub-paragraphs (4) to (8) above expressions which also appear in Chapter IV of Part II of the 1985 Act have the same meanings as in that Chapter.

(10) In this paragraph "the relevant period" means the period beginning at the relevant time and ending when it is proved to the satisfaction of the Board that the value of the assets (as determined in accordance with prescribed principles) exceeds the value of the liabilities (as so determined) by a percentage which is no more than the prescribed maximum.

11.—(1) The Board may make regulations providing that an appeal may be brought against a notice under paragraph 8(1)(*b*) above as if it were notice of the decision of the Board on a claim made by the administrator of the scheme concerned.

(2) Regulations under this paragraph may include—

(*a*) provision that bringing an appeal shall suspend the operation of paragraph 8(3) and (4) above;

(*b*) other provisions consequential on the provision that an appeal may be brought (including provisions modifying this Part of this Schedule).

(3) The power to make regulations under this paragraph shall be exercisable by statutory instrument subject to annulment in pursuance of a resolution of the House of Commons.

General Note

This Schedule sets out a framework to be completed by the issue of regulations within which the payment of surpluses from occupational pension schemes can be dealt with.

Part I deals with the taxation of such payments to employers.

It applies to payments out of approved schemes and charges them to tax under Schedule D Case VI at the rate of 40 per cent.

The charge does not apply if

(i) the payment would otherwise be exempt

(ii) the employer is a charity

(iii) it was made before 18th March 1986 or an application had already been made before that date within para. 1(13)

(iv) it was made before the scheme became an exempt approved scheme

(v) it was made pursuant to a winding up order when the winding up commenced on or before 18th March 1986.

The tax shall be paid by the employer but amongst the regulations which the Board may make are regulations requiring the administrator of the scheme to deduct the tax from the payment to the employer. Further regulations may be made allowing an administrator to be assessed and charged.

No other tax shall be charged on the payment to the employer but no other exemption or set off shall apply to it (see paragraph 2(5)).

Part II provides the procedure whereby it will be determined whether or not there is a surplus which requires to be distributed and if there is how it is to be be dealt with.

The skeleton of the procedure is:—

(i) the administrator will periodically produce a valuation or certificate showing the value of the fund's assets and liabilities—para. 5.

Failure to do so may result in a penalty.

(ii) if the value of the assets exceeds the value of the liabilities by more than the prescribed maximum then the administrator must within a prescribed period submit proposals. The possible causes of action open to an administrator are set out in para. 6(3) and include making a payment to the employer.

Failure to do so will cause the fund to lose part of its exemptions in accordance with para.10.

(iii) the Board is empowered to request—

(*a*) particulars relating to any valuation provided

(*b*) a valuation in a case where the adminstrator has supplied a certificate

(*c*) particulars relating to any valuation produced in response to a request by the Board

Any failure to comply with such requests may result in a penalty.

(iv) The Board must state whether or not it accepts any valuation or alternatively state its own valuation within a prescribed period. The adminstrator must then put forward proposals if the assets valuation exceeds the value of the liabilities by the prescribed maximum. Failure to do so will also cause paragraph 10 to operate.

(v) Once the proposals are approved by the Board they must be carried out within the prescribed period and if not paragraph 10 will operate.

(vi) Paragraph 10 takes away from the fund part of its exemption to the extent that its value should have been reduced but it has not been.

Section 55

SCHEDULE 13

Mineral Extraction: The New Code of Reliefs

Part I

Preliminary

Defined terms

1.—(1) In this Schedule—

"development" and "development order" have the meaning assigned to them by the relevant planning enactment;

"mineral asset" means any mineral deposits or land comprising mineral deposits, or any interest in or right over such deposits or land;

"mineral exploration and access" means searching for or discovering and testing the mineral deposits of any source or winning access to any such deposits;

"planning permission" has the meaning assigned to it by the relevant planning enactment;

"pre-trading expenditure on machinery or plant" shall be construed in accordance with paragraph 5 below;

"pre-trading exploration expenditure" shall be construed in accordance with paragraph 6 below;

"qualifying expenditure" shall be construed in accordance with Parts II and IV of this Schedule;

"the relevant planning enactment" means—

(*a*) in relation to land in England and Wales, section 290(1) of the Town and Country Planning Act 1971;

(*b*) in relation to land in Scotland, section 275(1) of the Town and Country Planning (Scotland) Act 1972; and

(*c*) in relation to land in Northern Ireland, Article 2(2) of the Planning (Northern Ireland) Order 1972;

"source of mineral deposits" includes a mine, an oil well and a source of geothermal energy; and "trade of mineral extraction" means a trade which consists of or includes the working of a source of mineral deposits.

(2) Any reference in this Schedule to mineral deposits is a reference to mineral deposits of a wasting nature and, in the case of a mineral asset which consists of or includes an interest in or right over mineral deposits or land, the asset shall not be regarded as situated in the United Kingdom unless the deposits or land are or is so situated.

(3) Any reference in this Schedule to assets representing any expenditure includes, in relation to expenditure on mineral exploration and access, any results obtained from any search, exploration or inquiry upon which the expenditure was incurred.

(4) Any reference in this Schedule to a chargeable period or its basis period is a reference to a chargeable period or, as the case may be, basis period beginning (or treated by virtue of section 55 of this Act as beginning) on or after 1st April 1986.

Application of Capital Allowances Act 1968 etc.

2.—(1) Chapter VI of Part I of the Capital Allowances Act 1968 (miscellaneous and general) applies for the purposes of this Schedule as if it were included in Chapter III of that Part.

(2) In section 77(4) of that Act, any reference to a specific provision of that Act includes a reference to Parts II to IV of this Schedule.

(3) In section 87(1) of that Act, at the end of the definition of "mineral deposits" there shall be added "and, for this purpose, geothermal energy, whether in the form of aquifers, hot dry rocks or otherwise, shall be treated as a natural deposit".

(4) The provisions of this Schedule apply in relation to a share in an asset of any description as, by virtue of the application of section 87(4) of that Act, they apply to a part of an asset; and, for the purposes of those provisions, a share in an asset of any description shall be deemed to be used for the purposes of a trade so long as, and only so long as, the asset is used for those purposes.

(5) In the following provisions—

(*a*) sections 155(8), 180(7), 227(4), 252(2) and 352(4) of the Taxes Act,

(*b*) the definition of "capital allowance" in section 526(5) of the Taxes Act,

(*c*) section 31(2) of the Capital Gains Tax Act 1979, and

(*d*) the definition of "capital allowance" in subsection (4) of section 34 of the said Act of 1979,

any reference to the Capital Allowances Act 1968 or to Part I thereof includes a reference to Part III of this Schedule.

Time when expenditure is incurred

3.—(1) For the purposes of this Schedule, expenditure incurred for the purposes of a trade by a person about to carry it on shall be treated as if it had been incurred by him on the first day on which he does carry it on.

(2) Without prejudice to sub-paragraph (1) above, pre-trading expenditure on machinery or plant and pre-trading exploration expenditure shall be treated for the purposes of Part III of this Schedule as incurred on the first day on which the person who incurred the expenditure carries on a trade of mineral extraction.

Part II

Qualifying Expenditure

General provisions

4.—(1) Subject to sub-paragraphs (2) to (5) below, in relation to a person carrying on a trade of mineral extraction, the following capital expenditure is qualifying expenditure, namely,—

(*a*) expenditure on mineral exploration and access;

(*b*) expenditure on the acquisition of a mineral asset;

(*c*) expenditure on the construction of any works in connection with the working of a source of mineral deposits, being works which, when the source is no longer worked, are likely to be of little or no value to the person working it immediately before that time; and

(*d*) where a source of mineral deposits is worked under a foreign concession, expenditure on the construction of works which, when the concession comes to an end, are likely to become valueless to the person working the source immediately before that time.

(2) Where expenditure falling within sub-paragraph (1)(*a*) above is incurred by any person before he begins to carry on a trade of mineral extraction, it shall not be qualifying expenditure except to the extent that paragraph 5 or paragraph 6 below provides.

(3) Part IV of this Schedule shall have effect to limit in certain cases the amount of expenditure which is qualifying expenditure.

(4) Except as provided by paragraph 5 below, expenditure on the provision of machinery or plant or on any asset which has been treated for any chargeable period as machinery or plant is not qualifying expenditure.

(5) The following expenditure is not qualifying expenditure by virtue of this paragraph—

(*a*) any expenditure on the acquisition of the site of any such works as are referred to in sub-paragraph (1) above, or of rights in or over any such site;

(*b*) any expenditure on works constructed wholly or mainly for subjecting the raw product of a source to any process, except a process designed for preparing the raw product for use as such;

(*c*) any expenditure on buildings or structures provided for occupation by or for the welfare of workers;

(*d*) any expenditure on a building where the whole of the building was constructed for use as an office; and

(*e*) any expenditure on so much of a building or structure as was constructed for use as an office, unless the capital expenditure on the construction of the part of the building or structure constructed for use as an office was not more than one-tenth of the capital expenditure incurred on the construction of the whole building or structure.

(6) Where a person carrying on a trade of mineral extraction incurs expenditure on seeking any planning permission necessary to enable any mineral exploration and access to be undertaken at any place or any mineral deposits to be worked and that permission is not granted, the expenditure shall be treated for the purposes of this Schedule as expenditure on mineral exploration and access; and in this sub-paragraph "seeking", in relation to planning permission, includes not only making any necessary application but also pursuing any appeal against a refusal of permission.

(7) In so far as any provision of this Schedule or of any other enactment is expressed to be about expenditure falling within sub-paragraph (1)(*a*) above or sub-paragraph (1)(*b*) above—

(*a*) expenditure on the acquisition of, or of rights in or over, the site of a source, and

(*b*) expenditure on the acquisition of, or of rights in or over, mineral deposits,

shall be treated as falling within sub-paragraph (1)(*b*) above and not within sub-paragraph (1)(*a*) above.

Pre-trading expenditure on machinery or plant which is sold etc.

5.—(1) This paragraph applies where—

(*a*) capital expenditure is incurred by any person on the provision of machinery or plant; and

(*b*) that expenditure falls within paragraph 4(1)(*a*) above; and

(*c*) that expenditure is so incurred before he begins to carry on a trade of mineral extraction; and

(*d*) before he begins to carry on that trade, the machinery or plant is sold, demolished, destroyed or abandoned.

(2) Where this paragraph applies and there is such an excess of expenditure as is referred to in sub-paragraph (3) below, then, for the purposes of this Schedule the person concerned shall be treated as incurring qualifying expenditure equal to that excess on the first day on which he begins to carry on a trade of mineral extraction; and that qualifying expenditure is in this Schedule referred to as pre-trading expenditure on machinery or plant.

(3) Subject to sub-paragraph (4) below, the excess referred to in sub-paragraph (2) above is the amount by which the capital expenditure referred to in sub-paragraph (1) above exceeds any sale, insurance, salvage or compensation moneys resulting from the event mentioned in paragraph (*d*) of that sub-paragraph.

(4) If, in a case where this paragraph applies, the mineral exploration and access at the source in connection with which the machinery or plant was used ceased before the first day referred to in sub-paragraph (2) above, any capital expenditure which was incurred more than six years before that day shall be left out of account in determining the amount of any excess under sub-paragraph (3) above.

Pre-trading exploration expenditure

6.—(1) This paragraph applies to capital expenditure which—

(*a*) is incurred by any person on mineral exploration and access at any source, and

(*b*) is so incurred before he begins to carry on a trade of mineral extraction, and

(*c*) is not incurred on the provision of machinery or plant.

(2) Where this paragraph applies to any capital expenditure and the mineral exploration and access is continuing at the source in question at the time when the person concerned begins to carry on a trade of mineral extraction, so much of the expenditure as exceeds any relevant capital sum received by him is qualifying expenditure.

(3) Where this paragraph applies to any capital expenditure and the mineral exploration and access has ceased at the source in question before the time when the person concerned begins to carry on a trade of mineral extraction, so much of that expenditure as was incurred within the six years ending at that time and exceeds any relevant capital sum received by him shall be treated as qualifying expenditure incurred on the first day on which he begins to carry on that trade.

(4) In relation to capital expenditure to which this paragraph applies, a relevant capital sum is a capital sum—

(*a*) which is received by the person incurring the expenditure before he begins to carry on a trade of mineral extraction; and

(*b*) which is or, as the case may be, to the extent to which it is reasonably attributable to the incurring of the expenditure at the source in question.

(5) Expenditure which is qualifying expenditure by virtue of sub-paragraph (2) or sub-paragraph (3) above is in this Schedule referred to as pre-trading exploration expenditure.

Contributions by mining concerns to public services etc. outside the United Kingdom

7.—(1) Subject to sub-paragraphs (2) and (3) below, expenditure incurred by a person carrying on a trade of mineral extraction outside the United Kingdom and consisting of contributions of capital sums to the cost of—

(*a*) buildings to be occupied by persons employed at or in connection with the working of a source outside the United Kingdom, or

(*b*) works for the supply of water, gas or electricity wholly or mainly to buildings occupied or to be occupied by persons so employed, or

(*c*) works to be used in providing other services or facilities wholly or mainly for the welfare of persons so employed or their dependants,

is by virtue of this paragraph qualifying expenditure.

(2) Expenditure incurred by any person as mentioned in sub-paragraph (1) above is not qualifying expenditure unless—

(*a*) it is incurred for the purposes of his trade of mineral extraction; and

(*b*) when the source in question is no longer worked, the buildings or works concerned are likely to be of little or no value to the person working the source immediately before that time.

(3) Sub-paragraph (1) above does not apply—

(*a*) to expenditure resulting in the acquisition of an asset by the person incurring the expenditure; nor

(*b*) to expenditure in respect of which an allowance may be made under any provision of the Tax Acts (other than this Schedule, section 61 of the Capital Allowances Act 1968 or any enactment which was re-enacted by that section).

Restoration expenditure

8.—(1) Where a person who has ceased to carry on a trade of mineral extraction incurs expenditure on the restoration of the site of a source to the working of which that trade related and all or any of that expenditure—

(*a*) is incurred within the period of three years immediately following the last day on which he carried on that trade, and

(*b*) has not been deducted for the purposes of corporation tax or income tax in relation to that or any other trade carried on by him, and

(*c*) is expenditure which, if it had been incurred while that trade was being carried on, either would have been qualifying expenditure by virtue of any of the preceding provisions of this Part of this Schedule or would have been allowable as a deduction in computing the profits or gains from that trade,

so much of that expenditure as falls within paragraphs (*a*) to (*c*) above and does not exceed the net cost of the restoration of the site shall be qualifying expenditure by virtue of this paragraph and shall be treated as incurred by him on the last day on which he carried on that trade.

(2) Any reference in this paragraph to the site of a source includes a reference to land used in connection with the working of the source.

(3) In this paragraph "restoration" includes landscaping and—

(*a*) in relation to land in the United Kingdom, the carrying out of any works required by a condition subject to which planning permission for development consisting of the winning and working of minerals was granted; and

(*b*) in relation to land outside the United Kingdom, the carrying out of any works required by any equivalent condition imposed under the law of the territory in which the land is situated.

(4) For the purpose of this paragraph, the net cost to any person of the restoration of the site of a source is the excess, if any, of expenditure falling within paragraphs (*a*) to (*c*) of sub-paragraph (1) above over any receipts which—

(*a*) are attributable to the restoration (whether for spoil or other assets removed from the site or for tipping rights or otherwise); and

(*b*) are received within the period of three years immediately following the last day on which the person concerned carried on a trade of mineral extraction.

(5) As respects the person by whom is incurred any expenditure which is qualifying expenditure by virtue of this paragraph,—

(*a*) expenditure falling within paragraphs (*a*) to (*c*) of sub-paragraph (1) above (not only so much of it as constitutes qualifying expenditure) shall not be deductible in computing his income for any purpose of income tax or corporation tax; and

(*b*) to the extent that any receipts are, under sub-paragraph (4) above, taken into account to determine the net cost of the restoration of the site of a source, those receipts shall not constitute income of his for any purpose of income tax or corporation tax.

(6) All such adjustments shall be made, whether by way of discharge or repayment of tax or otherwise, as may be required in consequence of the preceding provisions of this paragraph.

Part III

Allowances and Charges

Writing-down and balancing allowances

9.—(1) Allowances shall be made in accordance with this paragraph to a person who carries on a trade of mineral extraction in respect of qualifying expenditure incurred by him for the purposes of that trade.

(2) Subject to sub-paragraph (4) below, for the chargeable period related to the incurring of the expenditure, there shall be made to the person incurring it an allowance equal to the appropriate percentage of the excess (if any) of that expenditure over any disposal receipts which he is required to bring into account by reference to that expenditure for that chargeable period.

(3) Subject to sub-paragraph (4) below, for each of the chargeable periods following that related to the incurring of the expenditure, there shall be made to the person incurring it an allowance equal to the appropriate percentage of the excess (if any) of that expenditure over the aggregate of—

(*a*) the allowances made in respect of the expenditure for earlier chargeable periods by virtue of sub-paragraph (2) above and this sub-paragraph; and

(*b*) any disposal receipts which he is or was required to bring into account by reference to that expenditure for the chargeable period in question and any earlier chargeable periods.

(4) For a chargeable period for which, in accordance with paragraph 12 below, a balancing allowance falls to be made to any person in respect of any expenditure, sub-paragraph (2), or, as the case may be, sub-paragraph (3) above shall have effect with the omission of the words "the appropriate percentage of".

(5) Subject to sub-paragraph (6) below, in relation to expenditure which is qualifying expenditure falling within paragraph 4, paragraph 7 or paragraph 8 above, other than expenditure falling within paragraph 4(1)(*b*), the appropriate percentage is 25 and, in relation to all other qualifying expenditure, the appropriate percentage is 10.

(6) If a chargeable period or its basis period is part only of a year or if the period is a year of assessment but the trade has been carried on for part only of it, the percentage appropriate under sub-paragraph (5) above shall be correspondingly reduced.

Disposal receipts

10.—(1) In any case where—

(*a*) qualifying expenditure has been incurred by any person on the provision of any assets (including the construction of any works), and

(*b*) in any chargeable period or its basis period any of those assets is disposed of or otherwise permanently ceases (whether because of the discontinuance of the trade or for any other reason) to be used by him for the purposes of a trade of mineral extraction,

he shall bring into account as a disposal receipt in respect of that expenditure for the chargeable period related to the disposal or, as the case may be, cessation the disposal value of any asset falling within paragraph (*b*) above.

(2) If, at any time after a mineral asset has been acquired by any person, it begins to be used (by him or any other person) in a way which constitutes development but is neither existing permitted development nor development for the purposes of a trade of mineral extraction carried on by him, the asset shall be treated as having permanently ceased, immediately before that time, to be used by him for the purposes of that trade; and for the purposes of this sub-paragraph, "existing permitted development" means—

(*a*) development which, prior to the acquisition, had been or had begun to be lawfully carried out; and

(*b*) any other development for which planning permission is granted by a development order made as a general order and in force at the time of the acquisition;

and sub-paragraph (3) of paragraph 16 below applies for the purposes of this sub-paragraph as it applies for the purposes of sub-paragraph (2) of that paragraph.

(3) Subject to paragraph 18 below, subsections (6) and (7) of section 44 of the Finance Act 1971 (disposal value of machinery or plant) shall apply to determine the disposal value of any asset falling within sub-paragraph (1) above, substituting a reference to that asset for any reference in those subsections to machinery or plant.

(4) In any case where—

(*a*) qualifying expenditure has been incurred by any person, and

(*b*) in any chargeable period or its basis period he receives any capital sum which, in whole or in part, it is reasonable to attribute to that expenditure, and

(*c*) that capital sum does not fall to be brought into account as a disposal receipt by virtue of sub-paragraph (1) above,

he shall bring into account as a disposal receipt in respect of that expenditure for the chargeable period related to the receipt of that capital sum so much of it as is reasonably attributable to the expenditure.

Balancing charges: excess of allowances and disposal receipts over expenditure

11.—(1) If, for any chargeable period for which a person is required to bring into account a disposal receipt in respect of qualifying expenditure incurred by him, the aggregate of—

(*a*) the disposal receipts in respect of that expenditure which he is required to bring into account for that period, and

(*b*) any disposal receipts in respect of that expenditure which he was required to bring into account for earlier chargeable periods, and

(*c*) the net amount of the allowances made to him for earlier chargeable periods under paragraph 9 above in respect of that expenditure,

exceeds the expenditure concerned, there shall be made on him a charge (in this Part of this Schedule referred to as a "balancing charge".)

(2) In relation to any qualifying expenditure, the amount on which a balancing charge is made for a chargeable period shall be whichever is the less of—

(*a*) the amount by which the aggregate referred to in sub-paragraph (1) above exceeds the expenditure; and

(*b*) the net amount of the allowances made as mentioned in paragraph (*c*) of that sub-paragraph.

(3) In relation to any chargeable period, the net amount of the allowances made to any person, for earlier chargeable periods under paragraph 9 above in respect of expenditure incurred by him means the total of those allowances less the total of the amounts on which balancing charges have been made on him for earlier chargeable periods, being charges arising by reason of his bringing into account disposal receipts in respect of that expenditure.

Occasions of balancing allowances

12.—(1) For the chargeable period related to the permanent discontinuance of a trade of mineral extraction, any allowance to which the person carrying on that trade is entitled under paragraph 9 above in respect of qualifying expenditure incurred by him for the purposes of that trade shall be a balancing allowance.

(2) If in any chargeable period or its basis period a person carrying on a trade of mineral extraction permanently ceases to work particular mineral deposits (and sub-paragraph (1) above does not apply in respect of that period) any allowance to which he is entitled for that chargeable period under paragraph 9 above in respect of—

(*a*) expenditure on mineral exploration and access which relates solely to those deposits, or

(*b*) expenditure on the acquisition of a mineral asset which consists of those deposits or any part of them,

shall be a balancing allowance.

(3) Where a person carrying on a trade of mineral extraction is for the time being entitled to two or more mineral assets which at any time were comprised in a single mineral asset or were otherwise derived from a single mineral asset, sub-paragraph (2) above shall not apply until such time as he permanently ceases to work the deposits comprised in all the mineral assets concerned taken together and, for this purpose, where a mineral asset relates to, but does not actually consist of mineral deposits, the deposits to which the asset relates shall be treated as comprised in the asset.

(4) If, in a case where sub-paragraph (1) of paragraph 10 above applies, neither sub-paragraph (1) nor sub-paragraph (2) above has effect in relation to the expenditure referred to in sub-paragraph (1)(*a*) of that paragraph, then for the chargeable period related to the disposal or cessation referred to in sub-paragraph (1)(*b*) of that paragraph, any allowance in respect of that expenditure shall be a balancing allowance.

(5) In relation to pre-trading expenditure on machinery or plant and pre-trading exploration expenditure falling within paragraph 6(3) above, any allowance under paragraph 9 above shall be a balancing allowance.

(6) If in any chargeable period or its basis period a person who has incurred qualifying expenditure on mineral exploration and access (including pre-trading exploration expenditure falling within paragraph 6(2) above) gives up the search, exploration or inquiry to which the expenditure related and does not carry on then or subsequently a trade of mineral extraction which consists of or includes the working of any mineral deposits to which the mineral exploration and access related, any allowance to which he is entitled for that chargeable period under paragraph 9 above in respect of that expenditure shall be a balancing allowance.

(7) In any case where—

(*a*) a person has incurred expenditure consisting of contributions falling within paragraph 7 above to the cost of any buildings or works, and

(*b*) in any chargeable period or its basis period the buildings or works permanently cease to be used for the purposes of, or in connection with, a trade of mineral extraction carried on by him,

then, without prejudice to sub-paragraph (1) above, any allowance to which he is entitled for that chargeable period under paragraph 9 above in respect of that expenditure shall be a balancing allowance.

(8) If in any chargeable period or its basis period any of the following events occurs in relation to assets representing any qualifying expenditure, namely—

(*a*) the person by whom the expenditure was incurred loses possession of the assets in circumstances where it is reasonable to assume that the loss is permanent,

(*b*) the assets cease to exist as such (as a result of destruction, dismantling or otherwise).

(*c*) the assets begin to be used wholly or partly for purposes other than those of the trade of mineral extraction carried on by that person,

any allowance to which that person is entitled for that chargeable period under paragraph 9 above in respect of that expenditure shall be a balancing allowance.

Treatment of qualifying expenditure on mineral exploration and access

13. For the purposes of this Part of this Schedule, where a person is carrying on a trade of mineral extraction, qualifying expenditure incurred by him in connection with that trade (whether before or after the trade began to be carried on) on mineral exploration and access shall be taken to be incurred for the purposes of the trade.

Demolition costs

14.—(1) The net cost to a person of the demolition of an asset representing qualifying expenditure shall, for the purposes of this Part of this Schedule, be added to that qualifying expenditure in determining the amount of any balancing allowance or balancing charge for the chargeable period related to the demolition of the asset.

(2) The cost or net cost to a person of the demolition of any asset shall not, if sub-paragraph (1) applies to it, be treated for the purposes of this Schedule as expenditure incurred in respect of any other asset by which that asset is replaced.

(3) Any reference in this paragraph to the net cost of the demolition of any asset is a reference to the excess (if any) of the cost of the demolition over any moneys received for the remains of the asset.

Manner of making allowances and charges

15. All allowances and charges falling to be made under this Part of this Schedule to or on any person shall be made to or on him in taxing his trade of mineral extraction.

PART IV

LIMITATIONS ON QUALIFYING EXPENDITURE ETC.

Expenditure of the acquisition of land: restriction of qualifying expenditure

16.—(1) In so far as capital expenditure falling within paragraph 4(1)(*b*) above consists of expenditure on the acquisition of an interest in land (whether in the United Kingdom or elsewhere) and that land includes a source of mineral deposits, so much of that expenditure as is equal to the undeveloped market value of the interest shall not constitute qualifying expenditure.

(2) In relation to the acquisition of an interest in land, the undeveloped market value means the consideration which at the time of the acquisition the interest might reasonably be expected to fetch on a sale in the open market on the assumptions—

(*a*) that there is no source of mineral deposits on or in the land; and
(*b*) that it is and will continue to be unlawful to carry out any development of the land other than—
 (i) development which, at the time of the acquisition, has been or has begun to be lawfully carried out; and
 (ii) any other development for which planning permission is granted by a development order which is made as a general order and is in force at that time.

(3) In the application of sub-paragraph (2) above to the acquisition of an interest in land outside the United Kingdom,—

(*a*) any question whether development has been or is being lawfully carried out shall be determined in accordance with the law of the territory in which the land is situated; and
(*b*) any question whether development is of a character for which planning permission is granted by a general development order shall be determined as if the land were situated in England or Wales.

(4) In any case where—

(*a*) the preceding provisions of this paragraph have effect to limit the amount of expenditure falling within paragraph 4(1)(*b*) above which is qualifying expenditure, and
(*b*) the undeveloped market value of the interest in land in question includes the value of any buildings or other structures on the land, and
(*c*) at the time of the acquisition of the interest in land or at any time thereafter, those buildings or structures cease permanently to be used for any purpose.

then at the time referred to in paragraph (*c*) above, the person who incurred the expenditure referred to in paragraph (*a*) above shall be treated as having incurred qualifying expenditure falling within paragraph 4(1)(*b*) above equal to the unrelieved value of the buildings or structures referred to in paragraph (*b*) above.

(5) In sub-paragraph (4) above "the unrelieved value" of buildings or structures falling within paragraph (*b*) thereof means the value of those buildings or structures determined as at the date of the acquisition of the interest in land (and without regard to any value properly attributable to the land on which the buildings or structures stand) less the excess of any allowances over balancing charges which the person treated by sub-paragraph (4) above as incurring expenditure has received in respect of the buildings or structures or assets therein under—

(*a*) the Capital Allowances Act 1968;
(*b*) Chapter I of Part III of the Finance Act 1971 (machinery or plant); and
(*c*) section 55 of this Act.

(6) References in the preceding provisions of this paragraph to the time of the acquisition of an interest in land are not affected by paragraph 3 of this Schedule.

17. In any case where—

(*a*) a person incurs capital expenditure falling within paragraph 4(1)(*b*) above on the acquisition of an asset which is or includes an interest in land, and

(*b*) for chargeable periods previous to the chargeable period for which he first becomes entitled in respect of the expenditure to an allowance under paragraph 9 above, the person incurring the expenditure has been allowed, in respect of that land, any deductions under section 134 of the Taxes Act (deductions where premiums etc. taxable),

the expenditure shall be treated for the purposes of this Schedule as reduced by so much of those deductions as would have been excluded by subsection (5) of the said section 134 if the person concerned had been entitled to an allowance under paragraph 9 above (or, as the case may be, section 60 of the Capital Allowances Act 1968) for the previous chargeable periods referred to in sub-paragraph (*b*) above.

Restriction of disposal receipts

18.—(1) Where a disposal receipt to be brought into account in respect of any expenditure for a chargeable period would, apart from this paragraph, be the disposal value of an interest in land (determined as mentioned in paragraph 10(3) above), only so much of that disposal value as exceeds the undeveloped market value of the interest shall constitute a disposal receipt for the purposes of Part III of this Schedule.

(2) Sub-paragraphs (2) and (3) of paragraph 16 above shall apply to determine the undeveloped market value of an interest for the purposes of this paragraph as they would apply in relation to an acquisition of that interest at the time the disposal value falls to be determined.

Assets formerly owned by traders

19.—(1) Subject to sub-paragraph (2) below, paragraph 20 below applies where a person carrying on a trade of mineral extraction (in this paragraph referred to as "the buyer") incurs capital expenditure in acquiring an asset (in this paragraph referred to as "the purchased asset") from another person in circumstances falling within sub-paragraph (3) below.

(2) This paragraph and paragraph 20 below have effect subject to paragraph 22 below, and neither this paragraph, paragraph 20 nor paragraph 22 below applies if—

(*a*) the purchased asset is a mineral asset situated in the United Kingdom; and

(*b*) the capital expenditure incurred by the buyer consists of the payment of sums under a contract entered into by him before 16th July 1985.

(3) Subject to sub-paragraph (5) below, the circumstances referred to in sub-paragraph (1) above are—

(*a*) that, in connection with a trade of mineral extraction carried on by him, the other person referred to in sub-paragraph (1) above incurred expenditure on the acquisition or bringing into existence of the purchased asset; or

(*b*) that that other person has not incurred expenditure as mentioned in paragraph (*a*) above but, at any time prior to the buyer's acquisition, the purchased asset was owned by a person who, in connection with a trade of mineral extraction carried on by him, had incurred such expenditure as is mentioned in paragraph (*a*) above;

and, in a case where the purchased asset is a mineral asset situated in the United Kingdom, the reference in paragraph (*b*) above to a time prior to the buyer's acquisition does not include any time earlier than 1st April 1986.

(4) In this paragraph "the previous trader" means—

(*a*) where the circumstances are as mentioned in paragraph (*a*) of sub-paragraph (3) above, the person referred to in that paragraph; and

(*b*) where the circumstances are as mentioned in paragraph (*b*) of that sub-paragraph, the last person who, prior to the buyer's acquisition, incurred such expenditure as is mentioned in paragraph (*a*) thereof;

and, subject to sub-paragraphs (5) and (6) below, any reference in paragraph 20 below to the previous trader's qualifying expenditure is a reference to so much of the expenditure incurred by him on the acquisition or bringing into existence of the purchased asset as constituted his qualifying expenditure for the purposes of this Schedule.

(5) Any reference in sub-paragraphs (3) and (4) above to the purchased asset includes a reference—

(a) to two or more assets which together make up the purchased asset; and
(b) to an asset from which or, as the case may be, to two or more assets from the combination of which the purchased asset is derived.

(6) Where the previous trader in fact incurred expenditure on the acquisition or bringing into existence of one or more such assets from which the purchased asset is derived, so much of that expenditure as was qualifying expenditure of his for the purposes of this Schedule and as it is just and reasonable to attribute to the purchased asset shall be taken to be the previous trader's qualifying expenditure.

Limitation of expenditure on asset by reference to previous acquisition

20.—(1) In this paragraph "the buyer's expenditure" means the capital expenditure incurred by him as mentioned in paragraph 19(1) above, less any amount of that expenditure which, by virtue of paragraph 16 above, does not constitute qualifying expenditure.

(2) If the previous trader did not become entitled to an allowance or liable to a balancing charge in respect of his qualifying expenditure, so much of the buyer's expenditure as does not exceed the amount of the previous trader's qualifying expenditure shall be the buyer's qualifying expenditure in respect of the acquisition of the purchased asset.

(3) If the previous trader became entitled to an allowance or liable to a balancing charge in respect of his qualifying expenditure, so much of the buyer's expenditure as does not exceed the residue of the previous trader's qualifying expenditure shall be the buyer's qualifying expenditure in respect of the acquisition of the purchased asset.

(4) In relation to the previous trader's qualifying expenditure, the residue referred to in sub-paragraph (3) above is that expenditure—
(a) less the total of all allowances made to him in respect of that expenditure; and
(b) plus the amount (if any) on which a balancing charge was made in respect of that expenditure.

(5) For the purposes of sub-paragraph (4) above, where the previous trader's qualifying expenditure is an amount attributed to the purchased asset on a just and reasonable basis in accordance with paragraph 19(6) above, any allowances and any balancing charge made by reference to a greater amount of expenditure shall be apportioned on the like basis.

(6) In this paragraph—
"allowance" means an allowance under paragraph 9 above;
"balancing charge" means a balancing charge under paragraph 11 above; and
"the buyer", "the previous trader" and "the purchased asset" have the same meaning as in paragraph 19 above.

Part of expenditure on mineral asset treated as expenditure on mineral exploration and access

21.—(1) This paragraph applies where, in a case falling within sub-paragraph (1) of paragraph 19 above,—
(a) the purchased asset is a mineral asset; and
(b) part of the value of that asset is attributable to expenditure incurred by the previous trader on mineral exploration and access.

(2) Where this paragraph applies—
(a) such part of the buyer's expenditure as it is just and reasonable to attribute to the part of the value referred to in sub-paragraph (1)(b) above (being no greater than the amount of the previous trader's expenditure on mineral exploration and access which is properly attributable to that part of the value) shall be treated for the purposes of Parts II and III of this Schedule as expenditure on mineral exploration and access and the remainder shall be treated for those purposes as expenditure on the acquisition of a mineral asset; and
(b) if, under Part II of the Capital Allowances Act 1968 (scientific research) allowances were made to the previous trader in taxing his trade, the existence of these allowances shall not affect the question whether any of his expenditure on the purchased asset was qualifying expenditure.

(3) In this paragraph "the previous trader" and "the purchased asset" have the same meaning as in paragraphs 19 and 20 above, and "the buyer's expenditure" has the same meaning as in paragraph 20 above.

Oil licences etc.

22.—(1) Where a person carrying on a trade of mineral extraction (in this paragraph referred to as "the buyer") incurs capital expenditure falling within paragraph 4(1)(b) above in acquiring a Petroleum Act licence or any interest in such a licence, only so much of that expenditure as does not exceed the corresponding expenditure of the original licensee shall be the buyer's qualifying expenditure.

(2) In this paragraph a "Petroleum Act licence" means a licence under the Petroleum (Production) Act 1934 or the Petroleum (Production) Act (Northern Ireland) 1964 authorising the winning of oil, as defined in section 1 of the Oil Taxation Act 1975; and in relation to such a licence, "the original licensee" means the person to whom the licence was granted under the enactment in question.

(3) In relation to the acquisition of a Petroleum Act licence "the corresponding expenditure" of the original licensee is the amount of the payment made by him (whether before or after the passing of this Act) to the Secretary of State or, in Northern Ireland, to the Department of Economic Development for the purpose of obtaining the licence, and, in relation to an interest in such a licence, that corresponding expenditure is such portion of the amount of that payment as it is just and reasonable to attribute to that interest.

Transfer of mineral assets within a group

23.—(1) Subject to sub-paragraph (2) below, this paragraph applies where a company (in this paragraph referred to as "the transferee") acquires a mineral asset from another company (in this paragraph referred to as "the transferor") and either—

(*a*) the transferor has control of the transferee or the transferee has control of the transferor, or

(*b*) both the transferor and the transferee are under the control of another person.

(2) This paragraph does not apply—

(*a*) where the acquisition is a sale in respect of which an election is made under paragraph 4 of Schedule 7 to the Capital Allowances Act 1968; nor

(*b*) where the mineral asset in question is, or is an interest in, a Petroleum Act licence as defined in paragraph 22 above;

but, subject to paragraph (*a*) above, this paragraph applies notwithstanding anything in paragraph 2 of the said Schedule 7.

(3) Subject to sub-paragraph (4) below, so much (if any) of the capital expenditure incurred by the transferee on the acquisition of the mineral asset as exceeds the capital expenditure incurred by the transferor on the acquisition of the mineral asset by him shall be left out of account for the purposes of this Schedule (and, accordingly, if the transferee is carrying on a trade of mineral extraction, shall not be qualifying expenditure).

(4) Where the mineral asset acquired by the transferee consists of an interest or right granted by the transferor in a mineral asset acquired by him, the reference in sub-paragraph (3) above to the capital expenditure incurred by the transferor on the acquisition of the mineral asset by him shall be construed as a reference to so much of that expenditure as, on a just apportionment, is referable to the interest or right granted by the transferor.

(5) If the transferee is carrying on a trade of mineral extraction and the expenditure incurred by him on the acquisition of the mineral asset is expenditure falling within paragraph 16 above, any reference in that paragraph to the time of the acquisition of the interest in land is a reference to the time it was acquired by the transferor or, if there is a sequence of two or more acquisitions each of which falls within sub-paragraph (1) above, the time at which the interest was acquired by the company which was the transferor under the earliest of those acquisitions.

(6) If, in a case where sub-paragraph (5) above applies, there is a sequence of two or more acquisitions each of which falls within sub-paragraph (1) above,—

(*a*) any expenditure which one of the companies involved in the sequence is treated as incurring under sub-paragraph (4) of paragraph 16 above shall be treated as incurred by the company which is the transferee from that company and by any subsequent transferee company in the sequence; and

(*b*) the reference in sub-paragraph (5) of that paragraph to the person treated by sub-paragraph (4) thereof as incurring expenditure shall be construed as including a reference to any other company which, under paragraph (*a*) above, is treated as incurring that expenditure.

Assets formerly owned by non-traders

24. Where a person incurs expenditure on mineral exploration and access and, without having carried on a trade of mineral extraction, he sells any assets representing that expenditure, then, if the person who acquires the assests carries on such a trade, only so much of the price paid by him for the assets as does not exceed the amount of the seller's expenditure which is represented by the assets shall be qualifying expenditure for the purposes of this Schedule.

Part V

Amendments of other Enactments

25.—(1) In section 14(1) of the Capital Allowances Act 1968 after the words "of this Act" there shall be inserted "or Schedule 13 to the Finance Act 1986".

(2) In section 93 of that Act (scientific research: prevention of double allowances) at the end of subsection (1) there shall be inserted "and no allowances under Schedule 13 to the Finance Act 1986 shall be made in respect of any expenditure if it is expenditure in respect of which such a deduction may be allowed."

(3) In paragraph 4 of Schedule 7 to that Act (election as to sales where one party has control of the other) at the end of sub-paragraph (2) there shall be added—

"(*d*) in the case of assets representing qualifying expenditure, within the meaning of Schedule 13 to the Finance Act 1986, the excess of that expenditure attributable to those assets over the aggregate of—

(i) any allowances made under that Schedule to the seller in respect of that expenditure before the sale; and

(ii) any disposal receipts which the seller has been required to bring into account by reference to that expenditure by reason of any event occurring before the sale."

26. In section 134 of the Taxes Act (deductions where premiums etc. are taxable) at the end of subsection (5) there shall be added the words "and the reference in this subsection to an allowance under section 60 of the Capital Allowances Act 1968 includes a reference to an allowance under Part III of Schedule 13 to the Finance Act 1986 in respect of expenditure falling within paragraph 4(1)(*b*) of that Schedule".

27. In section 174(8) of the Taxes Act for the words "Chapter III of Part I of the Capital Allowances Act 1968" there shall be substituted "Schedule 13 to the Finance Act 1986" and for the words "that Act" there shall be substituted "the Capital Allowances Act 1968."

28. In section 56 of the Finance Act 1985 (time when capital expenditure is incurred) at the end of subsection (1) and after the amendment made by section 51(10) of this Act there shall be added "and

(*f*) Schedule 13 to the Finance Act 1986."

General Note

This Schedule sets out the new code of capital allowances which replaces C.A.A. 1968, ss.51 to 66. Para. 1 defines the terms used. It should be noted, in particular, that "mineral deposits" must be of a wasting nature and that an interest in, or rights over, mineral deposits or land is or are regarded as situated in the United Kingdom only if the deposits or land are or is so situated (para. 1(2)). In relation to mineral exploration and access, assets representing expenditure include any results obtained from any search, exploration or inquiry on which the expenditure was incurred (para. 1(3)).

A "source of mineral deposits" now includes, as well as a mine or oil-well, a source of geo-thermal energy, *e.g.* aquifers or hot dry rocks. Para. 2 links the new code to the C.A.A. 1968 and para. 3 determines the date on which pre-trading expenditure is deemed to be incurred.

Pt. II of the Schedule defines qualifying expenditure. Subject to the exceptions set out in subparas. 4(2) to (5) and to the limitations in Pt. IV of this Schedule, qualifying expenditure comprises the following:

(*a*) expenditure on mineral exploration and access;

(*b*) expenditure on acquiring a mineral asset;

(*c*) expenditure on the construction of works likely to be of little or no value to the person working a source immediately before that working ceases; and

(*d*) expenditure on the construction of works likely to be of little or no value to the person working the source immediately before the ending of a foreign concession under which it is worked.

As to (*a*) above, see paras. 5 and 6. Expenditure on, or on an asset treated as, machinery or plant is not qualifying expenditure unless it falls within the provisions of para. 5.

Sub-para. 4(5) excludes the following:

(*a*) expenditure on acquiring a site, or rights in or over a site, of works referred to in sub-para. 4(1);

(*b*) expenditure on works wholly or mainly for the subjection of the raw product to any process except one designed to prepare the raw product for use as such;

(*c*) expenditure on buildings or structures provided for occupation by, or the welfare of, workers;

(*d*) expenditure on a building constructed wholly for use as an office; and
(*e*) expenditure on so much of a building or structure as was constructed for use as an office (subject to a one-tenth *de minimis* rule).

The cost of an unsuccessful planning application or an unsuccessful appeal against refusal is qualifying expenditure on mineral exploration and access under sub-para. 4(6).

Under sub-para. 4(7), expenditure on the acquisition of, or of rights in or over, the site of a source or mineral deposits is treated as the acquistion of a mineral asset and not as mineral exploration and access.

Para. 5 deals with pre-trading expenditure on machinery or plant used for mineral exploration and access where that machinery or plant is sold, destroyed, demolished or abandoned before a trade of mineral extraction is commenced. In so far as the cost exceeds any sale, insurance, salvage or compensation monies, that excess is treated as qualifying expenditure. Sub-para. 5(4) excludes, however, any such expenditure incurred more than six years before the commencement of trading if the exploration and access ceases before the trade commences.

Para. 6 makes similar provision in relation to pre-trading expenditure not incurred on the provision of machinery or plant. Referred to as "pre-trading exploration expenditure", this consists of any excess of the expenditure over any "relevant capital sum" as defined in sub-para. 6(4).

Para. 7 includes as qualifying expenditure capital contributions made by a person carrying on a trade of mineral extraction outside the United Kingdom towards the cost of buildings and works listed in sub-para. 7(1)(*a*)(*b*) and (*c*). The expenditure by way of such contributions must be incurred for the purposes of the said trade and the buildings or works must be such as are likely to be of little or no value to the person working the source immediately before that working ceases (sub-para. 7(2)). Sub-para. 7(3) excludes any such expenditure if it results in the acquisition of an asset or if capital allowances are available in respect of it other than under this Schedule or under C.A.A. 1968, s.61.

Para. 8 further extends the meaning of qualifying expenditure to cover the cost of restoring land within three years after the trade of mineral extraction has ceased. It does not cover expenditure which would have been qualifying expenditure if incurred while the trade was being carried on or would have been allowable as a deduction from profits or gains.

The land in question includes any land used in connection with the working of the source (sub-para. 8(2)).

"Restoration" includes landscaping as further defined in sub-para. 8(3). If all the conditions are met, the net cost (as defined in sub-para. 8(4)) is treated as qualifying expenditure incurred on the last day of trading (sub-para. 8(1)).

None of the restoration expenditure (whether or not it is treated as qualifying expenditure) is deductible in computing income for income tax or corporation tax and no receipts taken into account in arriving at the net cost will constitute income (sub-para. 8(5)).

Sub-para. 8(6) provides for the making of any necessary adjustments.

Pt. III of the Schedule details the allowances and changes and the occasions on which they arise. A writing down allowance is made under para. 9(2) or (3) at the percentage set out in sub-para. 9(5). The allowance is made on the excess of qualifying expenditure over the aggregate of disposal receipts and allowances for earlier years, if any.

The appropriate percentage is 25 for expenditure falling within paras. 4, 7 or 8 of this Schedule and 10 for any other qualifying expenditure (sub-para. 9(5)). This rate is reduced under sub-para. 9(6) if the chargeable or basis period is less than a year.

A disposal receipt is, under para. 10, brought into account on the permanent cessation of use of an asset for the purposes of the trade, or where there is deemed to be such cessation of use under sub-para. 10(2).

A disposal receipt is also brought into account under sub-para. 10(4) where a capital receipt can reasonably be attributed to qualifying expenditure incurred.

"Disposal value" is computed on the same basis as for machinery and plant as set out in F.A. 1971, s.44(6), (7) but subject to the restriction in para. 18 of this Schedule (sub-para. 10(3)).

Para. 11 imposes a balancing charge in cases where qualifying expenditure is exceeded by the aggregate of:

(*a*) disposal receipts for the period in question;
(*b*) disposal receipts for earlier periods; and
(*c*) net allowances received.

The amount of the charge is the excess mentioned above but limited to the amount of the net allowances as defined in sub-para. 11(3) (sub-para. 11(2)).

A balancing allowance arises when a mineral extraction trade is permanently discontinued (sub-para.12(1)) or when particular mineral deposits cease to be worked (sub-para. 12(2)).

Where a person is entitled to more than one mineral asset, no balancing allowance is made until both or all of them cease to be worked (sub-para. 12(3)).

Balancing allowances also arise where:

(*a*) a disposal receipt is brought into account under para. 10(1)(*b*) of this Schedule (sub-para. 12(4));

(*b*) an allowance is made under para. 9 in respect of pre-trading expenditure on machinery or plant or exploration under para. 6(3) or on abortive expenditure (including any under para. 6(2)) (sub-paras. 12(5), (6));

(*c*) an allowance is made under para. 9 in respect of a contribution to the cost of buildings or works within para. 7 and they cease permanently to be used for, or in connection with, the trade (sub-para. 12(7));

(*d*) the person incurring the expenditure loses possession of the assets which loss is likely to be permanent;

(*e*) the assets cease to exist; or

(*f*) the assets begin to be used wholly or partly for a trade other than the owner's trade of mineral extraction.

(*d*), (*e*) and (*f*) are set out in sub-para. 12(8).

Expenditure incurred by a person carrying on a trade of mineral extraction is, under para. 13, taken to be incurred for the purposes of that trade if it is incurred in connection with it (before or after it is carried on) on mineral exploration and access.

Para. 14 provides that the net cost (defined in sub-para. (3)) is treated as qualifying expenditure and not as part of the cost of any replacement asset.

Allowances and charges are made in taxing the trade of mineral extraction (para. 15).

Pt. IV of this Schedule imposes limits on the amount of qualifying expenditure and disposal receipts.

Para. 16(1) excludes from qualifying expenditure that part of the cost of an interest in land (in or out of the United Kingdom), including a source of mineral deposits, which is equal to the "undeveloped market value" of the interest. The meaning of that phrase is defined in sub-paras. 16(2) and (3). Relief is given in certain cases where the undeveloped market value includes the value of buildings or other structures on the land. If, at or after the acquisition, those buildings, etc. cease permanently to be used for any purpose, the "unrelieved value" (defined in sub-para. 16(5) is treated as qualifying expenditure under sub-para. 16(4).

Para. 17 provides that the expenditure on the acquisition of a mineral asset is reduced by so much of any deduction under I.C.T.A. 1970, s.134 ("Deductions where premiums etc. taxable") as would have been excluded by subs. 134(5) had an allowance been available under para. 9 of this Schedule or under C.A.A. 1968. s.60 (mineral depletion allowance).

Disposal receipts are limited under para. 18 by a similar exclusion of undeveloped market value.

Paras. 19 and 20 (both subject to para. 22) restrict qualifying expenditure where a purchased asset has, at some previous time belonged to a person carrying on a mineral extraction trade who either bought it or brought it into existence. These provisions do not apply to the purchase of a mineral asset situated in the United Kingdom under a contract entered into before July 16, 1985.

The restriction, in para. 20, depends upon whether or not the previous trader had been entitled to allowances under para. 9 of this Schedule. If he did not become so entitled (or liable to a balancing change) the qualifying expenditure of the later buyer is limited to that of the previous trader (sub-para. 20(2)). In other cases it is limited to the "residue" (as defined in sub-para. 20(4)) of the previous trader's qualifying expenditure (sub-para. 20(3)).

Para. 21 deals with a purchase in the circumstances set out in para. 19(1) of a mineral asset, part of the value of which is attributable to expenditure by the previous trader on mineral exploration and access. In this case, the expenditure is apportioned (on a "just and reasonable" basis) as between expenditure on exploration and access (25 per cent. allowance) and mineral assets (10 per cent. allowance). Any scientific research allowance made to the previous trader is ignored for this purpose (sub-para. 21(2)(*b*).

Under para. 22, the qualifying expenditure of a buyer acquiring a licence or an interest in a licence (defined in sub-para. 22(2)) is limited to the corresponding expenditure of the original licencee.

Para. 23 continues anti-avoidance provisions relating to transfers between companies of which one controls the other or both are under common control. These provisions do not apply where an election has been made under para. 4 of Sched. 7 to C.A.A. 1968 ("sales without change of control") nor to transactions within para. 22 of this Schedule. Where this paragraph does apply, in general terms, expenditure by the transferee is limited to that incurred by the transferor company.

Expenditure by a person carrying on a trade of mineral extraction in the purchase of assets from a vendor who has not carried on such a trade is similarly limited, in computing qualifying expenditure, to expenditure incurred by the vendor, under para. 24.

Section 55

SCHEDULE 14

MINERAL EXTRACTION: OLD EXPENDITURE

Interpretation

1.—(1) In this Schedule—

"mineral asset" and "mineral exploration and access" have the same meaning as in Schedule 13 to this Act;

"new expenditure" and "old expenditure" have the same meaning as in the principal section"

"the new code of allowances" means subsections (5) to (7) of the principal section and Schedule 13 to this Act;

"the old code of allowances" has the same meaning as in the principal section;

"the principal section" means section 55 of this Act;

"the relevant day" means, subject to paragraph 2 below, 1st April 1986;

"trade of mineral extraction" has the same meaning as in Schedule 13 to this Act; and

"the 1968 Act" means the Capital Allowances Act 1968.

(2) In relation to any item of old expenditure "outstanding balance" means, subject to the following provisions of this paragraph,—

(*a*) in the case of old expenditure falling within section 57 of the 1968 Act, so much of that expenditure as, if the old code of allowances had continued in force, would have been the residue of that expenditure in relation to a writing-down allowance under that section to be made for the chargeable period which, or the basis period of which, begins on the relevant day;

(*b*) in the case of old expenditure falling within section 60 of the 1968 Act, the excess referred to in subsection (3) of that section by reference to which, if the old code of allowances had continued in force, a writing-down allowance under that section would fall to be made for the chargeable period referred to in paragraph (*a*) above; and

(*c*) in the case of old expenditure falling within section 61 of the 1968 Act, so much of that expenditure as exceeds any writing-down allowances under that section made in respect of that expenditure for chargeable periods which, or the basis periods of which, ended before the relevant day.

(3) In determining the residue of expenditure mentioned in paragraph (*a*) of sub-paragraph (2) above, it shall be assumed that, in the chargeable period or its basis period referred to in that paragraph, no asset representing expenditure which is qualifying expenditure for the purposes of section 57 of the 1968 Act is sold, demolished or destroyed.

(4) In determining, in relation to the chargeable period referred to in paragraph (*a*) of sub-paragraph (2) above, the excess mentioned in paragraph (*b*) of that sub-paragraph—

(*a*) no account shall be taken of any capital sum accruing in that chargeable period or its basis period to the person to whom a writing-down allowance would fall to be made as mentioned in that paragraph; and

(*b*) it shall be assumed that that person does not cease to work the source in question in that chargeable period or its basis period.

Election to treat certain post March 1986 expenditure as old expenditure

2.—(1) This paragraph applies to expenditure—

(*a*) which is incurred in the year ending 31st March 1987 by a person carrying on a trade of mineral extraction; and

(*b*) which consists of the payment of sums under a contract entered into before 16th July 1985 by the person incurring the expenditure; and

(*c*) in respect of which, but for the provisions of the principal section, an initial allowance would have been made to the person concerned under section 56 of the 1968 Act.

(2) If the person incurring the expenditure so elects, expenditure to which this paragraph applies shall be treated for the purposes of the principal section and Schedule 13 to this Act as not being new expenditure and the old code of allowances shall continue to apply to it until 31st March 1987.

(3) An election under this paragraph—

(*a*) shall be made in writing to the inspector;
(*b*) may not be made more than two years after the end of the chargeable period or its basis period in which the expenditure was incurred; and
(*c*) shall be irrevocable;

and if different parts of the expenditure are incurred at different times, only that part of the expenditure which is first incurred on or after 1st April 1986 shall be taken into account for the purposes of paragraph (*b*) above.

(4) In relation to expenditure to which an election under this paragraph applies—
(*a*) subsections (3) and (4) of the principal section shall have effect as if for any reference to 31st March 1986 or 1st April 1986 there were substituted a reference to 31st March 1987 or 1st April 1987 respectively; and
(*b*) in this Schedule "the relevant day" means 1st April 1987.

Outstanding balances: general rules

3.—(1) If there is an outstanding balance in relation to any item of old expenditure, then, subject to the following provisions of this Schedule, for the purposes of the new code of allowances,—
(*a*) an amount of expenditure equal to that balance shall be treated as expenditure incurred on the relevant day (and, accordingly, as new expenditure); and
(*b*) that amount shall be taken to have been incurred for the same purposes as the item of old expenditure was incurred.

(2) If any item of old expenditure was incurred for more than one purpose, then, so far as may be necessary for the application of the new code of allowances, the outstanding balance of that expenditure shall be apportioned to those different purposes in such manner as may be just and reasonable and sub-paragraph (1) above shall apply separately in relation to the apportioned parts as if they were referable to different items of old expenditure.

Old expenditure with no outstanding balance

4.—(1) This paragraph applies to old expenditure—
(*a*) in respect of which allowances were made under the old code of allowances, and
(*b*) in respect of which there is no outstanding balance on the relevant day.

(2) Where this paragraph applies, the new code of allowances shall have effect as if—
(*a*) the whole of the old expenditure had been incurred on the relevant day; and
(*b*) under the appropriate provisions of the new code of allowances there had been made allowances equal to that expenditure;

and the provisions of the new code about disposal receipts shall have effect accordingly in relation to events happening on or after the relevant day.

Unrelieved expenditure on mineral exploration and access

5.—(1) This paragraph applies to old expenditure incurred on mineral exploration and access.

(2) If, immediately before the relevant day, no allowance had been made in respect of the expenditure under the old code of allowances, and on that day the mineral exploration and access at the source in connection with which the expenditure was incurred has not ceased, and either—
(*a*) the person by whom the expenditure was incurred began to carry on a trade of mineral extraction before the relevant day, or
(*b*) on or after the relevant day and before mineral exploration and access ceases at the source in question, the person by whom the expenditure was incurred begins to carry on a trade of mineral extraction,

then, subject to sub-paragraph (3) below, paragraph 5 or paragraph 6 of Schedule 13 to this Act or, as the case may be, subsection (5) of the principal section shall apply as if the expenditure were new expenditure and, if the expenditure was in fact incurred after the person concerned began to carry on a trade of mineral extraction, as if he had not begun to carry on that trade until the relevant day.

(3) Where sub-paragraph (2) above applies to any item of old expenditure which, apart from this sub-paragraph, would not fall to be treated as incurred on or after the relevant day, it shall (as new expenditure) be treated for the purposes of the new code of allowances as incurred on the relevant day.

Old expenditure on acquisition of mineral asset

6.—(1) This paragraph applies to old expenditure incurred on the acquisition of a mineral asset.

(2) If, immediately before the relevant day, no allowance has been made in respect of the expenditure under the old code of allowances, the expenditure shall be treated for the purposes of the new code of allowances as having been incurred on the relevant day.

(3) Nothing in sub-paragraph (2) above shall affect the time as at which, under paragraph 16 of Schedule 13 to this Act, the undeveloped market value of an interest is to be determined.

(4) If sub-paragraph (2) above does not apply in relation to an item of old expenditure to which this paragraph applies,—

(*a*) paragraph 16 of Schedule 13 to this Act shall not apply in relation to any amount which, by virtue of paragraph 3(1) above, is to be treated as expenditure incurred on the relevant day (and, accordingly, the whole of any such amount shall be qualifying expenditure for the purposes of the new code of allowances); and

(*b*) in determining the amount of any disposal receipt which, by virtue of paragraph 3 or paragraph 4 above, falls to be brought into account in respect of that expenditure under Part III of Schedule 13 to this Act, paragraph 18 of that Schedule shall not apply (so that no deduction shall be made by reference to the undeveloped market value of the land).

Old expenditure on construction of certain works

7.—(1) This paragraph applies to old expenditure which does not fall within paragraph 5 above but which is incurred—

(*a*) on the construction of any works in connection with the working of a source of mineral deposits, being works which, when the source is no longer worked, are likely to be of little or no value to the person working it immediately before that time; or

(*b*) where a source of mineral deposits is worked under a foreign concession, on the construction of works which, when the concession comes to an end, are likely to become valueless to the person working the source immediately before that time.

(2) If, immediately before the relevant day, no allowance has been made in respect of the expenditure under the old code of allowances, the expenditure shall be treated for the purposes of the new code of allowances as having been incurred on the relevant day.

Balancing charges: old allowances to be brought into account

8.—(1) In any case where—

(*a*) by virtue of any of the preceding provisions of this Schedule, the whole or any part of the outstanding balance of an item of old expenditure is treated for the purposes of Schedule 13 to this Act as qualifying expenditure, and

(*b*) a balancing charge falls to be made under paragraph 11 of that Schedule in respect of that expenditure,

then, in determining the amount on which that charge falls to be made, sub-paragraph (2)(*b*) of the said paragraph 11 shall have effect as if it referred not only to allowances made as mentioned in sub-paragraph (1)(*c*) of that paragraph but also, subject to sub-paragraph (2) below, to allowances made in respect of the item of old expenditure under the old code of allowances.

(2) Where the qualifying expenditure in respect of which a balancing charge falls to be made represents part only of the outstanding balance of an item of old expenditure, the reference in sub-paragraph (1) above to allowances made in respect of that item shall be construed as a reference to such part of those allowances as it is just and reasonable to apportion to that part of the balance (having regard to the apportionment of the balance under paragraph 3(2) above).

General Note

This Schedule comprises the transitional provisions consequent on the change from the old to the new system of allowances in relation to mineral extraction.

Para. 1 sets out definitions and particular care is required in connection with sub-para. 1(2) where the meaning of "outstanding balance" depends on whether the "old expenditure" fell within C.A.A. 1968, ss.57, 60 or 61.

Under para. 2 an election may be made to treat expenditure incurred in the year ending March 31, 1987, as "old expenditure" if:

(*a*) it was incurred under a pre-July 16, 1985, contract; and

(*b*) would have qualified for an initial allowance under C.A.A. 1968, s.56.

Where an election is made, the date for application of the new code is April 1, 1987 (see s.55).

Any outstanding balances at "the relevant day" (*i.e.* April 1, 1986, or 1987 as the case may be) are treated as expenditure incurred on that day for the purposes for which the "old expenditure" was incurred (para. 3). If there is no outstanding balance (*i.e.* the whole amount has been covered by allowances), the "disposal receipts" provisions of the new code apply, under para. 4, as though the allowances had been made under the new code.

Paras. 5, 6, and 7 set out provisions for making allowances under the new code where, immediately before the relevant day, no allowance had been made under the old code in respect of (*a*) mineral exploration and access; (*b*) acquisition of a mineral asset; and (*c*) the construction of works likely to be of little or no value to the person working the source on the cessation of that working or of a foreign concession under which the source is worked.

Para. 8 provides for allowances under the old system to be taken into account in relation to a balancing charge under the new system (sub-para. 8(1)) subject to a just and reasonable apportionment of those allowances where the qualifying expenditure in respect of which such a charge is made represents part only of the outstanding balance of the "old expenditure" (sub-para. 8(2)).

Section 56

SCHEDULE 15

Agricultural Land and Buildings

Writing-down allowances

1.—(1) If a person having a major interest in any agricultural or forestry land incurs any capital expenditure on the construction of farmhouses, farm or forestry buildings, cottages, fences or other works, then, during a writing-down period of twenty-five years beginning on the first day of the chargeable period related to the incurring of the expenditure, there shall be made to him, subject to the following provisions of this Schedule, writing-down allowances of an aggregate amount equal to that expenditure.

(2) In any case where—

(*a*) capital expenditure is incurred on the construction of any building, fence or other works, but

(*b*) when the building, fence or other works comes to be used it is not used for the purposes of husbandry or forestry,

the expenditure shall be left out of account for the purposes of this Schedule and, accordingly, any writing-down allowance made in respect of the expenditure under sub-paragraph (1) above shall be withdrawn and all such assessments and adjustments of assessments shall be made as may be necessary to give effect to that withdrawal.

(3) In this Schedule a "major interest" in land means—

(*a*) the fee simple estate in the land or an agreement to acquire that estate;

(*b*) in Scotland, the estate or interest of the proprietor of the *dominium utile* (or, in the case of property other than feudal property, of the owner) and any agreement to acquire such an estate or interest, and

(*c*) a lease.

(4) If an interest in land is conveyed or assigned by way of security and subject to a right of redemption, then, so long as such a right subsists, the interest held by the creditor shall be treated for the purposes of this Schedule as held by the person having that right.

(5) Any reference in the following provisions of this Schedule to a writing-down allowance is a reference to an allowance under sub-paragraph (1) above.

Expenditure qualifying for allowances

2.—(1) No expenditure shall be taken into account for the purposes of this Schedule unless it is incurred for the purposes of husbandry or forestry on the agricultural or forestry land referred to in paragraph 1 above.

(2) Where capital expenditure is incurred on a farmhouse, one-third only of that expenditure shall be taken into account for the purposes of this Schedule or, if the accommodation and amenities of the farmhouse are out of due relation to the nature and extent of the farm, such proportion thereof not greater than one-third as may be just.

(3) Where capital expenditure is incurred on any asset other than a farmhouse and the asset is to serve partly the purposes of husbandry or forestry and partly other purposes, such apportionment of the expenditure shall be made for the purposes of this Schedule as may be just.

Meaning of "the relevant interest"

3.—(1) Subject to the provisions of this paragraph, in this Schedule "the relevant interest" means, in relation to any expenditure falling within paragraph 1(1) above, the major interest in the agricultural or forestry land concerned to which the person who incurred the expenditure was entitled when he incurred it.

(2) Where, when he incurs expenditure falling within paragraph 1(1) above, a person is entitled to two or more major interests in the agricultural or forestry land concerned, and one of those interests is an interest which is in reversion on all the others, that interest is the relevant interest for the purposes of this Schedule.

(3) A major interest shall not cease to be the relevant interest for the purposes of this Schedule by reason of the creation of any lease (or other interest) to which the interest is subject; and where the relevant interest is a lease which is extinguished—

(*a*) by reason of the surrender thereof, or

(*b*) on the person entitled thereto acquiring the interest which is the reversion on the relevant interest,

then, unless a new lease of the land concerned is granted to take effect on the extinguishment of the former lease, the interest into which that lease merges shall thereupon become the relevant interest.

(4) In the application of this paragraph to Scotland "reversion" means the interest of a landlord in property subject to a lease.

Transfers of relevant interest

4.—(1) In any case where—

(*a*) if a person (in this paragraph referred to as "the former owner") continued to be the owner of the relevant interest in any land, he would be entitled to a writing-down allowance in respect of any expenditure, and

(*b*) another person (in this paragraph referred to as "the new owner") acquires the relevant interest in the whole or part of that land (whether by transfer, by operation of law or otherwise),

the former owner shall not be entitled to an allowance under this Schedule for any chargeable period of his after that related to the acquisition and the new owner shall be entitled to allowances under this Schedule for the chargeable period of his related to the acquisition and for subsequent chargeable periods falling within the writing-down period.

(2) If, in a case falling within sub-paragraph (1) above, the date of the acquisition occurs during a chargeable period of the former owner or its basis period, he shall be entitled only to an appropriate portion of an allowance for the chargeable period related to the acquisition and, similarly, if the date of the acquisition occurs during a chargeable period of the new owner or its basis period, he shall be entitled only to an appropriate portion of an allowance for the chargeable period (of his) related to the acquisition.

(3) Where the new owner acquires the relevant interest in part only of the land concerned, sub-paragraphs (1) and (2) above shall apply to so much only of the allowance as is properly referable to that part of the land as if it were a separate allowance.

(4) Where paragraph 3(3) above applies and the person who owns the interest into which the lease is merged is not the same as the person who owned the lease, the relevant interest shall be treated for the purposes of this Schedule as acquired by the owner of the interest into which the lease is merged.

(5) Where the relevant interest is a lease which comes to an end and paragraph 3(3) above does not apply, then, for the purposes of this Schedule—

(*a*) if a new lease is granted to a person who makes any payment to the outgoing lessee in respect of assets representing the expenditure in question, the new lease shall be treated as the same interest as the former lease and, accordingly, the relevant interest shall be treated as acquired by the incoming lessee; and

(*b*) if a new lease is granted to the person who was the lessee under the former lease, the new lease shall be treated as the same interest as the former lease; and

(*c*) in any other case, the former lease and the interest of the person who was the landlord under the former lease shall be treated as the same interest and, accordingly, the relevant interest shall be treated as acquired by that person.

(6) If, by virtue only of the operation of the preceding provisions of this paragraph and, where appropriate, section 75(2) of the Capital Allowances Act 1968, the total allowances which, apart from this sub-paragraph, would fall to be made under this Schedule in respect of any expenditure during the writing-down period appropriate to it would be less than the amount of that expenditure, then, for the chargeable period in which that writing-down

period ends, the allowance in respect of that expenditure shall be increased to such amount as will secure that the total of the allowances equals the amount of that expenditure.

(7) This paragraph has effect subject to the following provisions of this Schedule.

Buildings etc. bought unused

5.—(1) This paragraph applies where expenditure falling within paragraph 1(1) above is expenditure on the construction of a building, fence or other works and, before the building, fence or works comes to be used, the relevant interest is sold.

(2) Where this paragraph applies—

(*a*) the expenditure shall be left out of account for the purposes of this Schedule and, accordingly, any writing-down allowance made in respect of the expenditure shall be withdrawn and all such assessments and adjustments of assessments shall be made as may be necessary to give effect to that withdrawal;

(*b*) paragraph 4 above shall not apply; and

(*c*) the person who buys the relevant interest shall be treated for the purposes of this Schedule as having incurred, on the date when the purchase price becomes payable, expenditure falling within paragraph 1(1) above on the construction of the building, fence or other works.

(3) The expenditure referred to in sub-paragraph (2)(*c*) above is whichever is the lesser of—

(*a*) the net price paid by the person concerned for the purchase of the relevant interest; and

(*b*) the expenditure referred to in sub-paragraph (1) above.

(4) Where the relevant interest is sold more than once in circumstances falling within sub-paragraph (1) above, sub-paragraphs (2)(*c*) and (3) above shall have effect only in relation to the last of those sales.

Balancing allowances and charges

6.—(1) If, in respect of any expenditure falling within paragraph 1(1) above, a balancing event occurs in a chargeable period or its basis period and, apart from this paragraph, a person would be entitled to a writing-down allowance in respect of that expenditure for the chargeable period related to that event, no such allowance shall be made but an allowance or charge (in this paragraph referred to as a "balancing allowance" or a "balancing charge") shall, in the circumstances mentioned below, be made for that period to or, as the case may be, on the person entitled to the relevant interest immediately before that event occurs.

(2) In relation to any expenditure, the amount of any balancing allowance or charge shall be determined in accordance with the following provisions of this paragraph by reference to—

(*a*) the residue of that expenditure, that is to say, the amount of that expenditure falling to be taken into account for the purposes of this Schedule less the aggregate of any writing-down allowances made in respect of it (whether or not to the person to or on whom the allowance or charge is to be made); and

(*b*) subject to sub-paragraph (3) below, any sale, insurance, salvage or compensation moneys related to the event which gives rise to the balancing allowance or balancing charge.

(3) If, by virtue of sub-paragraph (2) or sub-paragraph (3) of paragraph 2 above only a portion of any expenditure falls to be taken into account for the purposes of this Schedule, any reference in the following provisions of this paragraph to sale, insurance, salvage or compensation moneys is a reference only to the like portion of those moneys.

(4) Where there are no sale, insurance, salvage or compensation moneys or where the residue of the expenditure immediately before the balancing event exceeds those moneys, a balancing allowance shall be made of an amount equal to that residue or, as the case may be, to the excess of it over those moneys.

(5) If the sale, insurance, salvage or compensation moneys exceed the residue of the expenditure immediately before the event, a balancing charge shall be made on an amount equal to that excess.

(6) Notwithstanding anything in sub-paragraph (5) above, in no case shall the amount on which a balancing charge is made on any person exceed the amount of the writing-down allowances made to him in respect of that expenditure before the balancing event.

(7) If a balancing event relates to—

(*a*) the acquisition of the relevant interest in part only of the land in which it subsisted at the time the expenditure was incurred, or (*b*) only part of the building, fence or other works on the construction of which the expenditure was incurred,

the preceding provisions of this paragraph shall apply to so much of the expenditure as is properly attributable to the part of the land, building, fence or other works concerned, as if it were an item of expenditure separate from the rest.

(8) This paragraph has effect subject to paragraph 9 below.

Balancing events

7.—(1) Subject to sub-paragraph (2) below, in relation to expenditure (in this paragraph referred to as "the original expenditure") for which, apart from paragraph 6 above, a person (in this paragraph referred to as "the former owner") would be entitled to a writing-down allowance, the following events are balancing events for the purposes of this Schedule—

(*a*) the acquisition of the relevant interest by another person (in this paragraph referred to as "the new owner") as mentioned in paragraph 4 above; and

(*b*) where any building, fence or other works on the construction of which the expenditure was incurred is demolished, destroyed or otherwise ceases to exist as such.

(2) An event falling within sub-paragraph (1) above is not a balancing event for the purposes of this Schedule unless an election is made with respect to that event by notice in writing given to the inspector not more than two years after the end of the chargeable period related to the occurrence of the event.

(3) Where, during the writing-down period applicable to the original expenditure, a balancing event falling within sub-paragraph (1)(*a*) above occurs, the amount of any writing-down allowances to which the new owner is entitled for chargeable periods which, or the basis periods for which, end after the balancing event shall be determined as if—

(*a*) that part of the writing-down period applicable to the original expenditure which falls after the balancing event were itself the writing-down period in which the allowances in respect of that expenditure were to be made; and

(*b*) subject to paragraph 9 below the allowances were in respect of expenditure equal to the residue of the original expenditure (determined under paragraph 6(2)(*a*) above) immediately before the balancing event less the amount of any balancing allowance made to the former owner or, as the case may be, plus the amount on which any balancing charge was made on him by reason of the balancing event.

(4) Subject to sub-paragraph (5) below, an election under this paragraph shall be made as follows—

(*a*) where the event falls within sub-paragraph (1)(*a*) above, jointly by the former owner and the new owner; and

(*b*) where the event falls within sub-paragraph (1)(*b*) above, by the former owner.

(5) No election may be made under this paragraph if any person by whom that election should be made is not within the charge to tax in the United Kingdom; and no election may be made in relation to an acquisition falling within sub-paragraph (1)(*a*) above if it appears with respect to that acquisition, or with respect to transactions of which that acquisition is one, that the sole or main benefit which (apart from Schedule 7 to the Capital Allowances Act 1968) might have been expected to accrue to the parties or any of them was the obtaining of an allowance, or a greater allowance, under this Schedule.

Exclusion of land values etc.

8.—(1) Any reference in this Schedule to expenditure incurred on the construction of a building does not include any expenditure incurred on the acquisition of, or of rights in or over, any land.

(2) Without prejudice to any provision of Part I of the Capital Allowances Act 1968 relating to the apportionment of sale, insurance, salvage or compensation moneys, the sum paid on the sale of the relevant interest in a building, fence or other works or any other sale, insurance, salvage or compensation moneys payable in respect of any building, fence or other works shall, for the purposes of this Schedule, be deemed to be reduced by an amount equal to so much thereof as, on a just apportionment, is attributable to assets representing expenditure other than expenditure in respect of which an allowance can be made under this Schedule.

Special provisions as to certain sales

9.—(1) In its application in relation to any sale which is material for the purposes of this Schedule, Schedule 7 to the Capital Allowances Act 1968 (transactions between connected persons etc.) shall have effect with the omission—

(*a*) of paragraph 4 (sales without change of control); and
(*b*) of any reference to paragraph 4 or any provision thereof in any other paragraph of that Schedule.

(2) For the purposes of this Schedule and the provisions of the Capital Allowances Act 1968 which are relevant to this Schedule, any transfer of the relevant interest (in relation to any expenditure falling within paragraph 1(1) above) otherwise than by way of sale shall be treated as a sale of the interest for a price other than that which it would have fetched if sold on the open market.

(3) If Schedule 7 to the Capital Allowances Act 1968 would not, apart from this sub-paragraph, have effect in relation to a transfer treated as a sale by virtue of sub-paragraph (2) above, that Schedule shall have effect in relation to it as if it were a sale falling within paragraph 1(1)(*a*) of that Schedule.

Restriction of balancing allowances on sale of buildings

10.—(1) This paragraph has effect where—
(*a*) the relevant interest in a building is sold subject to a subordinate interest; and
(*b*) a balancing allowance under paragraph 6 above would, apart from this paragraph, fall to be made to the person who is entitled to the relevant interest immediately before the sale (in this paragraph referred to as "the former owner") by virtue of the sale; and
(*c*) either—
(i) the former owner, the person to whom the relevant interest is sold and the grantee of the subordinate interest, or any two of them, are connected with each other within the terms of section 533 of the Taxes Act, or
(ii) it appears with respect to the sale or to the grant of the subordinate interest, or with respect to transactions including the sale or grant, that the sole or main benefit which, but for this paragraph, might have been expected to accrue to the parties or any of them was the obtaining of an allowance under this Schedule.

(2) For the purposes of paragraph 6 above the net proceeds to the former owner of the sale—
(*a*) shall be taken to be increased by an amount equal to any premium receivable by him for the grant of the subordinate interest; and
(*b*) where no rent, or no commercial rent, is payable in respect of the subordinate interest, shall be taken to be what those proceeds would have been if a commercial rent had been payable and the relevant interest had been sold in the open market (increased by any amount to be added under paragraph (*a*) of this sub-paragraph);

but the net proceeds of sale shall not by virtue of this sub-paragraph be taken to be greater than such amount as will secure that no balancing allowance falls to be made.

(3) Where sub-paragraph (2) above operates, in relation to a sale, to deny or reduce a balancing allowance in respect of any expenditure, paragraph 7(3) above shall have effect as if that balancing allowance had been made or, as the case may be, had not been reduced.

(4) In this paragraph—
"subordinate interest" means any interest in or right over the building in question (whether granted by the former owner or by somebody else);
"premium" includes any capital consideration except so much of any sum as corresponds to any amount of rent or profits falling to be computed by reference to that sum under section 80 of the Taxes Act (premium treated as rent or Schedule D profits);
"capital consideration" means consideration which consists of a capital sum or would be a capital sum if it had taken the form of a money payment;
"rent" includes any consideration which is not capital consideration;
"commercial rent" means such rent as may reasonably be expected to have been required in respect of the subordinate interest in question (having regard to any premium payable for the grant of the interest) if the transaction had been at arm's length.

(5) Where the terms on which a subordinate interest is granted are varied before the sale of the relevant interest, any capital consideration for the variation shall be treated for the purposes of this paragraph as a premium for the grant of the interest, and the question whether any and, if so, what rent is payable in respect of the interest shall be determined by reference to the terms as in force immediately before the sale.

Manner of making allowances and charges

11.—(1) Except as provided below, any allowance or charge made to or on any person under this Schedule shall be made to or on him in taxing his trade; and any reference in the following provisions of this paragraph to an allowance or charge of any description is a reference to an allowance or charge under this Schedule.

(2) Any allowance which falls to be made to a person for a chargeable period in which he is not carrying on a trade shall be made by way of discharge or repayment of tax.

(3) Any allowance which, under this paragraph, is to be made by way of discharge or repayment of tax shall be available primarily against agricultural income and forestry income and income which is the subject of a balancing charge.

(4) Effect shall be given to a balancing charge to be made on a person for a chargeable period in which he is not carrying on a trade,—

(*a*) if it is a charge to income tax, by making the charge under Case VI of Schedule D; and

(*b*) if it is a charge to corporation tax, by treating the amount on which the charge is to be made as agricultural income or forestry income.

General Note

This Schedule sets out the new code of capital allowances on agricultural land and buildings.

Para. 1 provides for the making of an annual writing-down allowance over a 25 year period up to an aggregate equal to capital expenditure incurred by a person having a major interest (defined in sub-para. 1(3)) in agricultural or forestry land. The expenditure must be incurred on the construction of farm-houses, farm or forestry buildings, cottages, fences or other works (sub-para. 1(1)).

If, when the building, fence or other works come to be used, it is used, for some purpose other than husbandry or forestry any allowance given will be withdrawn as provided under sub-para. 1(2).

Any conveyance or assignment of an interest in land by way of security is ignored for the purposes of this Schedule so long as a right of redemption subsists (sub-para. 1(4)).

The provisions of para. 2 as to qualifying expenditure are identical to those in C.A.A. 1968, s.68(3) thus:

(*a*) the expenditure must be incurred for the purposes of husbandry or forestry on the land referred to in para. 1;

(*b*) one-third only of the cost of a farm-house (or less, depending on the accommodation and amenities of the house in relation to the nature and extent of the farm) is qualifying expenditure; and

(*c*) an apportionment is made where the purpose of the asset (other than a farm-house) is, in part only, agriculture or husbandry.

"Relevant interest" is defined in para. 3 and follows the definition in C.A.A. 1968, s.11 in relation to the industrial buildings allowance. The writing-down allowance is made to the holder, for the time being, of that interest (sub-para. 4(1)). Para. 4 deals, generally, with the consequences which follow a transfer of the relevant interest. On a transfer during a chargeable period or of a part only of the land, an appropriate apportionment is made (sub-paras. 4(2)(3)).

Where the relevant interest is a lease which is extinguished by surrender or purchase of the reversion, the owner of the interest into which it merges is treated as acquiring the relevant interest (sub-para. 4(4)).

Where a lease which is the relevant interest terminates and the case does not fall within sub-para. 4(4) then; under sub-para. 4(5):

(*a*) if a new lease is granted to a lessee who makes a payment to the outgoing lessee in respect of assets representing qualifying expenditure, the new lessee is treated as owning the relevant interest;

(*b*) if a new lease is granted to the former lessee, that new lease becomes the relevant interest; and

(*c*) in any other case, the relevant interest is treated as acquired by the former landlord.

If, by reason only of the provisions of para. 4, the total allowances during the writing-down period would be less than the expenditure during that period then, for the chargeable period in which the writing-down period ends the allowance is increased to bring the total up to the amount of that expenditure (sub-para. 4(6)).

Under para. 5, if the relevant interest is sold before the asset is brought into use any allowances made to the vendor are withdrawn and the purchaser becomes entitled to allowances on the lesser of (*a*) the net price paid; and (*b*) the original expenditure. This has effect only to the last such sale if there have been more than one.

Paras. 6 and 7 govern balancing allowances and charges. Para. 7 defines "balancing events" on which a balancing adjustment is made, but only if an election is made under sub-para. 7(2). Such events are, under sub-para. 7(1), the transfer of the relevant interest or the demolition or destruction of any building, fence or other works. No such election may be made by a person not within the charge to tax in the United Kingdom nor where the sole or main benefit which might be expected to accrue is a capital allowance advantage.

Where such an election is made, the new owner, if any, becomes entitled to writing-down allowances over the remainder of the original 25 year period on the transferor's residue of expenditure increased or reduced by a balancing charge or allowance respectively (sub-para. 7(3)).

The election must be made by the transferor and transferee jointly or, as the case may be, by the former owner of the asset which has ceased to exist (sub-para. 7(4)).

Where para. 7 applies a balancing allowance or charge is made in place of writing-down allowance for the accounting period (or year of assessment) in which (or in the basis period for which) the balancing event occurs. The allowance or charge is made on the usual basis, the details being set out in para. 6.

Para. 8 provides that expenditure on land or any rights in or over land does not qualify for the allowance. On a sale or other receipt of moneys in respect of a building, fence or other works an apportionment is made to exclude assets on which no allowance may be claimed.

In relation to a sale "material for the purposes of this Schedule" (which appears to mean one between connected persons) para. 9 applies. The general effect is that a sale between parties which are connected or under common control, or where the main purpose is the obtaining of a capital allowance advantage or on a transfer other than a sale the Schedule applies as though there had been a sale at the open market value.

A balancing allowance is restricted under para. 10 where:

(*a*) the relevant interest is sold subject to a subordinate interest;

(*b*) an election for a balancing allowance under para. 6 is made under para. 7; and

(*c*) either:

(i) all or any two of the former owner, the purchaser of the relevant interest and the grantee of the subordinate interest are connected within I.C.T.A. 1970, s.533; or

(ii) the sole or main benefit which might be expected is the obtaining of an allowance under this Schedule.

In such a case the net proceeds of sale under para. 6 are increased by any premium obtained by the former owner for the grant of the subordinate interest and any actual proceeds are, where no, or no commercial, rent is payable for that subordinate interest, replaced by deemed proceeds computed on the basis that such rent is payable. Neither the addition of that premium nor the substitution of those deemed proceeds can, however, have the effect of converting a balancing allowance into a balancing charge (sub-para. 10(2)).

The allowances due to the new owner (under para. 7(3)) are unaffected by any reduction or elimination of the balancing allowance (sub-para. 10(3)).

Sub-para. 10(4) defines certain terms used in para. 10 and sub-para. 10(5) includes in the premium referred to above any capital consideration paid for a variation of the terms of the subordinate interest. Whether, and how much, rent is payable depends on the terms in force immediately before the sale.

The manner of making allowances and charges is set out in para. 11.

Section 57

SCHEDULE 16

New Expenditure on Leased Assets and on Certain Vehicles

Part I

Amendments of Finance Act 1980, Sections 64 to 68

1.—(1) In section 64, subsection (1) (exclusion of first-year allowances etc.) shall be omitted.

(2) In subsection (2)(*a*) of that section—

(*a*) the words "a first-year allowance could have been made to the lessee" shall be omitted; and

(*b*) after the words "in doing so" there shall be inserted "that expenditure would have fallen to be included, in whole or in part, in his qualifying expenditure for any chargeable period for the purposes of subsections (2), (2A) and (3) of section 44 of the Finance Act 1971 (writing-down allowances)".

(3) In subsection (6A) of that section for the words "first-year allowance" there shall be substituted "writing-down allowance of an amount determined without regard to section 70(2) of the Finance Act 1982".

(4) In subsection (8) of that section (the requisite period) at the beginning there shall be inserted "subject to subsection (8A) below" and for the word "four", in each place where it occurs, there shall be substituted "ten".

(5) After subsection (8) of that section there shall be inserted the following subsection—

"(8A) If the circumstances are such that machinery or plant is used for a qualifying purpose, subsection (8) above shall have effect as if each reference therein to ten years were a reference to four years."

(6) Subsection (10) of that section shall be omitted.

(7) In subsection (11) of that section—

(*a*) for the words from the beginning to "expenditure", in the first place where it occurs, there shall be substituted "Where expenditure is incurred";

(*b*) for the words "if it" there shall be substituted "which"; and

(*c*) for the words "plant; and so" there shall be substituted "plant, so".

2.—(1) In section 65 (writing-down allowances etc. in case of leased assets) in subsection (1) for the words from the beginning to "leasing" there shall be substituted "Where section 70 of the Finance Act 1982 applies to expenditure on the provision of machinery or plant for leasing".

(2) In subsection (6) of that section the words from the beginning to "1971; but" shall be omitted and for the words "that Schedule" there shall be substituted "Schedule 8 to the Finance Act 1971".

3. Sections 66 and 67 shall be omitted.

4.—(1) In section 68 (joint lessees), at the end of subsection (1) there shall be added "and—

(*a*) at least one of the joint lessees is a person falling within paragraphs (*a*) and (*b*) of subsection (1) of section 70 of the Finance Act 1982; and

(*b*) the leasing is not permitted leasing as defined in paragraph 7 of Schedule 16 to the Finance Act 1986".

(2) In subsection (2) of that section—

(*a*) for the words from the beginning to "shall not apply" there shall be substituted "If";

(*b*) the words "but if" shall be omitted; and

(*c*) for the words "it shall be regarded as used for a qualifying purpose" there shall be substituted "the expenditure on the provision of the machinery or plant shall be treated as not falling within subsection (1) of the said section 70".

(3) In subsection (3) of that section—

(*a*) the words from "a first-year" to "in respect of" shall be omitted;

(*b*) after the words "machinery or plant", where they first occur, there shall be inserted "is treated as not falling within subsection (1) of section 70 of the Finance Act 1982";

(*c*) for the words "and sections 65 and 66" there shall be substituted "the said section 70 and section 65 above"; and

(*d*) in paragraph (*b*) after the word "expenditure" there shall be inserted "(falling within subsection (1) of the said section 70)" and after the word "plant" there shall be inserted "used otherwise than for a qualifying purpose".

(4) Subsections (4) to (8) of that section shall be omitted.

Part II

Amendments of Finance Act 1982, Section 70 and Schedule 11

5.—(1) In section 70, in subsection (1) (application of section to foreign leasing which is not short-term leasing) for the words "not short-term leasing" there shall be substituted "neither short-term leasing nor the leasing of a ship, aircraft or transport container which is used for a qualifying purpose by virtue of subsections (5) to (7) of section 64 of the Finance Act 1980".

(2) In subsection (2)(*a*) of that section (reference to section 65 of the Finance Act 1980) for the words in parenthesis there shall be substituted "(as amended by Part I of Schedule 16 to the Finance Act 1986)".

(3) Subsection (3) of that section shall be omitted.

(4) In subsection (4) of that section,—

(*a*) the words "first-year allowances" shall be omitted; and

(*b*) for the words "as mentioned in subsection (3)(*b*) above" there shall be substituted "such that the machinery or plant in question is used otherwise than for a qualifying purpose, within the meaning of section 64 of the Finance Act 1980".

(5) In subsection (5) of that section—

(*a*) the words "a first-year allowance" shall be omitted; and

(*b*) for the words "section 66 of the Finance Act 1980" there shall be substituted "paragraph 8 of Schedule 16 to the Finance Act 1986".

(6) For subsection (6) of that section there shall be substituted the following subsection—

"(6) For the purposes of subsection (5) above, the allowances that have been made in respect of expenditure on any item of machinery or plant shall be determined as if that item were the only item of machinery or plant in respect of which section 44 of the Finance Act 1971 had effect."

(7) In subsection (7) of that section after the words "Finance Act 1980" there shall be inserted "(as amended by Part I of Schedule 16 to the Finance Act 1986)".

(8) In subsection (9) of that section,—

(*a*) for the words from "as, in a case" to "1980" there shall be substituted "as it has in section 64 of the Finance Act 1980 (as amended by Part I of Schedule 16 to the Finance Act 1986)";

(*b*) the words "and the provisions of Schedule 11 to this Act" shall be omitted; and

(*c*) at the end there shall be added "and

(*c*) as if the reference in subsection (5) of that section to a first-year allowance were a reference to a writing-down allowance".

6. In Schedule 11, paragraphs 3, 5 and 6 shall be omitted.

Part III

Supplementary Provisions as to Assets Leased Outside the United Kingdom

Interpretation

7.—(1) In this Part of this Schedule—

(*a*) "the principal section" means section 70 of the Finance Act 1982;

(*b*) a "non-resident" means such a person as is referred to in paragraphs (*a*) and (*b*) of subsection (1) of the principal section;

(*c*) "normal writing-down allowance" means a writing-down allowance of an amount determined without regard to subsection (2) of the principal section;

(*d*) "permitted leasing" means short-term leasing or the leasing of a ship, aircraft or transport container which is used for a qualifying purpose by virtue of subsections (5) to (7) of section 64 of the Finance Act 1980; and

(*e*) "short-term leasing" has the meaning assigned to it by section 64(3) of the Finance Act 1980;

and other expressions have the same meaning as in the principal section.

(2) Where new expenditure has been incurred by any person, any reference in this Part of this Schedule to the new expenditure having qualified for a normal writing-down allowance is a reference to the expenditure having fallen to be included, in whole or in part, in that person's qualifying expenditure for any chargeable period for the purposes of subsections (2), (2A) and (3) of section 44 of the Finance Act 1971, as that section has effect with respect to expenditure which does not fall within subsection (1) of the principal section.

Recovery of excess relief

8.—(1) Where new expenditure incurred by any person in providing machinery or plant has qualified for a normal writing-down allowance and the machinery or plant is at any time in the requisite period used for the purpose of being leased to a non-resident, otherwise than by permitted leasing,—

(*a*) an amount equal to the excess relief shall, in relation to the person to whom the machinery or plant then belongs, be treated as if it were a balancing charge to be made on him for the chargeable period for which, or in the basis period for which, the machinery or plant is first so used; and

(*b*) for the purposes of section 44 of the Finance Act 1971 (as it has effect with respect to expenditure which does not fall within subsection (1) of the principal section), an amount equal to the unused expenditure shall, in relation to that person, be treated as if it were a disposal value to be brought into account for the chargeable period referred to in paragraph (*a*) above; and

(*c*) section 44 of the Finance Act 1971 (as it has effect as mentioned in paragraphs (*a*) to (*e*) of subsection (2) of the principal section) shall apply as if a sum equal to the aggregate of the amounts in paragraphs (*a*) and (*b*) above were qualifying expenditure of that person for the next chargeable period and, for the purpose of subsequently bringing any disposal value into account, as if the machinery or plant had always been used for the purposes of the separate trade.

(2) The excess relief is the excess, if any, of—

(*a*) any normal writing-down allowances made in respect of the new expenditure for the chargeable period related to the incurring of the expenditure and any subsequent chargeable period up to and including that mentioned in sub-paragraph (1)(*a*) above, over

(*b*) the maximum writing-down allowance or allowances that could have been made in respect of the expenditure for those chargeable periods if no normal writing-down allowance had been or could have been made.

(3) The unused expenditure is the amount by which the new expenditure incurred in providing the machinery or plant exceeds the allowances referred to in sub-paragraph (2)(*a*) above.

(4) For the purposes of sub-paragraph (2) above, the normal writing-down allowances that were made in respect of new expenditure on any item of machinery or plant shall be determined as if that item were the only item of machinery or plant in relation to which the said section 44 had effect.

(5) Where the person to whom any machinery or plant belongs at a time when it is first used for the purpose of being leased to a non-resident, otherwise than by permitted leasing, has acquired it as a result of a transaction which was, or a series of transactions each of which was, between connected persons and a normal writing-down allowance in respect of expenditure on the provision of the machinery or plant has been made to any of those persons—

(*a*) sub-paragraph (2) above shall have effect as if it referred to that allowance and to the expenditure in respect of which it was made;

(*b*) for the purposes of that sub-paragraph any consideration paid or received on a disposal of the machinery or plant between connected persons shall be disregarded; and

(*c*) if a balancing allowance or balancing charge is made in respect of the machinery or plant there shall be made such adjustments of the total relief falling to be taken into account under paragraph (*a*) of that sub-paragraph as are just and reasonable in the circumstances;

but this sub-paragraph does not apply where section 154(2), section 155(1) or section 252(2) of the Taxes Act or sub-paragraphs (*a*) and (*b*) of paragraph 13 of Schedule 8 to the Finance Act 1971 (succession to trades), applied on the occasion of the transaction or transactions in question.

(6) Where the person to whom any machinery or plant belongs at such a time as is mentioned in sub-paragraph (5) above acquired it as there mentioned and—

(*a*) new expenditure incurred on the provision of the machinery or plant by any of the connected persons would have qualified for a normal writing-down allowance but such an allowance was not claimed or was disclaimed; and

(*b*) a balancing allowance is made to any of those persons in respect of that expenditure,

this paragraph shall with the necessary modifications apply as it applies where a normal writing-down allowance has been made.

(7) If at any time in the requisite period a ship is used for the purpose of being leased to a non-resident, otherwise than by permitted leasing, then, without prejudice to the other provisions of this paragraph,—

(*a*) no allowance shall be made in respect of it under sub-paragraph (5)(*c*) of paragraph 8A of Schedule 8 to the Finance Act 1971 for the chargeable period in which it is first so used or for any subsequent chargeable period;

(*b*) nothing in sub-paragraphs (8) and (9) of that paragraph shall affect the operation of sub-paragraph (1) above; and

(*c*) section 44 of that Act (as it has effect in accordance with section 65 of the Finance Act 1980) shall apply as if the amount of any allowance in respect of the ship which has been postponed under the said paragraph 8A and not made were qualifying expenditure for the next chargeable period after that in which the ship is first so used.

(8) Section 533 of the Taxes Act (connected persons) applies for the purposes of this paragraph.

Joint lessees

9.—(1) Without prejudice to the operation of paragraph 8 above, the provisions of this paragraph have effect where new expenditure is incurred on the provision of machinery or plant which is leased as mentioned in subsection (1) of section 68 of the Finance Act 1980, and any reference in the following provisions of this paragraph to section 68 is a reference to that section.

(2) Where, by virtue of subsection (2) of section 68, the whole or part of the new expenditure has qualified for a normal writing-down allowance and, at any time in the requisite period while it is leased as mentioned in that subsection—

(*a*) no lessee uses the machinery or plant for the purposes of a trade or trades the profits or gains of which are chargeable to income tax or corporation tax, and

(*b*) subsection (5) of the principal section does not apply at that time and has not applied at any earlier time,

paragraph 8 above and paragraph 10(2) below shall have effect as if the separate item of machinery or plant referred to in subsection (3)(*a*) of section 68 had at that time begun to be used for the purpose of being leased to a non-resident, otherwise than by permitted leasing.

(3) Where the whole or part of any new expenditure has qualified for a normal writing-down allowance and the machinery or plant is subsequently leased in the requisite period as mentioned in subsection (1) of section 68, sub-paragraph (2) above shall apply as if the whole of the expenditure had qualified for a normal writing-down allowance by virtue only of subsection (2) of that section.

(4) Where, by virtue of subsection (2) of section 68, the whole or part of the new expenditure has qualified for a normal writing-down allowance and, at the end of the requisite period, the machinery or plant in question is leased as mentioned in subsection (1) of that section but sub-paragraph (2) above has not had effect, then, if it appears that the extent to which the machinery or plant has been used for the purposes of such a trade or trades as are referred to in that sub-paragraph is less than that which was taken into account in determining the amount of the new expenditure which qualified for a normal writing-down allowance,—

(*a*) paragraph 8 above shall have effect as if a part of the expenditure corresponding to the reduction in the extent of such use were expenditure on the provision of a separate item of machinery or plant used for the purpose of leasing to a non-resident, otherwise than by permitted leasing, on the last day of the requisite period; and

(*b*) any disposal value subsequently brought into account in respect of the machinery or plant under section 44 of the Finance Act 1971 shall, instead of being apportioned in accordance with subsection (3) of section 68, be apportioned by reference to the extent of such use as determined at the end of that period.

Information

10.—(1) Where new expenditure is incurred on the provision of machinery or plant and, before the expenditure has qualified for a normal writing-down allowance, it is used for leasing to a non-resident and that leasing is permitted leasing, a claim by a person other than a company for a writing-down allowance which takes account of that expenditure and a return by a company of profits in the computation of which a deduction is made on account of such an allowance shall be accompanied by a certificate to that effect, setting out the description of permitted leasing.

(2) If, after any new expenditure has qualified for a normal writing-down allowance, the machinery or plant in question is at any time in the requisite period used for the purpose of being leased to a non-resident, otherwise than by permitted leasing, the person to whom it belongs at that time shall give written notice of that fact to the inspector.

(3) Subject to sub-paragraph (6) below, notice under sub-paragraph (2) above shall be given within three months after the end of the chargeable period or its basis period in which the machinery or plant is first used for leasing as mentioned in that sub-paragraph.

(4) A certificate or notice given by any person under sub-paragraph (1) or sub-paragraph (2) above by reference to any chargeable period or its basis period shall specify the non-resident to whom the machinery or plant has been leased and shall specify all the items of machinery or plant (if more than one) in respect of which the person in question is required to give a certificate or notice under this paragraph by reference to that period.

(5) Subject to sub-paragraph (6) below, where new expenditure is incurred on the provision of machinery or plant which is leased as mentioned in section 68(1) of the Finance Act 1980, the lessor shall, within three months after the end of the chargeable period or its basis period in which the machinery or plant is first so leased, give written notice to the inspector specifying—

(*a*) the names and addresses of the persons to whom the asset is jointly leased;

(*b*) the portion of the new expenditure which is properly attributable to each of those persons; and

(*c*) so far as it is within his knowledge, which of those persons is resident in the United Kingdom.

(6) If, at the end of the three months referred to in sub-paragraph (3) or sub-paragraph (5) above, the person required to give a notice under that sub-paragraph does not know and cannot reasonably be expected to know that any item of machinery or plant in respect of which he is required to give such a notice has been used or leased as mentioned in the sub-paragraph in question, he shall in respect of that item give the notice within thirty days of his coming to know that it has been so used or leased.

(7) In the Table in section 98 of the Taxes Management Act 1970 (penalties) at the end of the second column there shall be added—

"Paragraph 10 of Schedule 16 to the Finance Act 1986".

Part IV

Amendment of Finance Act 1980, Section 69

11. In section 69 (writing-down allowances etc. for cars) for the words from "any vehicle" onwards there shall be substituted "any mechanically propelled vehicle other than—

(*a*) a vehicle of a construction primarily suited for the conveyance of goods or burden of any description;

(*b*) a vehicle of a type not commonly used as a private vehicle and unsuitable to be so used;

(*c*) a vehicle to which paragraph 10 of Schedule 8 to the Finance Act 1971 applies (expensive motor cars); and

(*d*) subject to subsection (2) below, a vehicle provided wholly or mainly for hire to, or for the carriage of, members of the public in the ordinary course of a trade.

(2) Subsection (1)(*d*) above applies to a vehicle only if—

(*a*) the following conditions are satisfied—

(i) the number of consecutive days for which it is on hire to, or used for the carriage of, the same person will normally be less than 30; and

(ii) the total number of days for which it is on hire to, or used for the carriage of, the same person in any period of 12 months will normally be less than 90; or

(*b*) it is provided for hire to a person who will himself use it wholly or mainly for hire to, or the carriage of, members of the public in the ordinary course of a trade and in a manner complying with the conditions in paragraph (*a*) above.

(3) For the purposes of subsection (2) above, persons who are connected with each other shall be treated as the same person; and that subsection does not affect vehicles provided wholly or mainly as mentioned in section 64(12) above."

General Note

Part I of this Schedule amends the "leased asset" provisions of F.A. 1980, ss.64 to 68.

Para. 1 deletes subs. 64(1) excluding first-year allowances which is no longer required. Other references to first-year allowances are also omitted.

The "requisite period" remains four years where leased machinery or plant is used for a qualifying purpose (sub-para. 1(5)) but, in other cases, becomes ten years (sub-para. 1(4)).

The effect of F.A. 1980, s.65 ("writing-down allowance etc. in case of leased assets") is, by para. 2 of this Schedule, restricted to assets falling within F.A. 1982, s.70, *i.e.* assets leased outside the United Kingdom.

Para. 3 repeals F.A. 1980, ss.66 and 67 which applied only where a 100 per cent. first-year allowance had been made.

Para. 4 amends F.A. 1980, s.68 ("joint lessees") by restricting its application to cases where (*a*) at least one joint lessee is non-resident in the United Kingdom and uses the asset neither for the purposes of a trade carried on in the United Kingdom nor falling within F.A. 1973, s.38(4). ("territorial extension of charge to income tax, capital gains tax and corporation tax"); and (*b*) the leasing is not "permitted leasing" within para.7 of this Schedule. References to first-year allowances are omitted.

Part II of the Schedule amends F.A. 1982, s.70 ("allowances for assets leased outside the United Kingdom") and Part III imposes supplementary provisions in relation thereto.

Para. 5 excludes from the operation of the said s.70 the leasing of a ship, aircraft or transport container used for a qualifying purpose under F.A. 1980, s.64(5)–(7). By omitting subs. 70(3) the extension of the requisite period to ten years is repealed but it is reimposed in certain cases by para. 1(4) of this Schedule. References to first-year allowances are removed.

Para. 6 repeals paras. 3, 5 and 6 of Sched. 11 to F.A. 1982.

Paras. 7, 8, 9 and 10 provide new rules regarding assets leased outside the United Kingdom. These effectively replace the provisions of F.A. 1980, ss.66 and 67 (repealed by para. 3 of this Schedule). These rules do not apply to "permitted leasing", defined as short-term leasing or the leasing of a ship, aircraft or transport container used for a qualifying purpose under F.A. 1980, s.64(5) to (7). Where they apply, an amount equal to the "excess relief" (defined in sub-para. 8(2)) is treated as if it were a balancing charge to be made for the chargeable period or in the basis period for which the machinery or plant is first used for non-permitted leasing to a non-resident (sub-para. 8(1)(*a*)) and the "unused expenditure" (defined in sub-para. 8(3)) is treated as a disposal value to be brought into account for the same period (sub-para. 8(1)(*b*)). The aggregate of those two amounts is treated as qualifying expenditure for the next chargeable period and is brought into a separate pool (sub-para. 8(1)(*c*)).

Sub-paras. 8(5) and (6) provides that, in the case of transactions between connected persons, any consideration passing is ignored and allowances are made in relation to the original expenditure.

Provision is made in sub-para. 8(7) for adjusting allowances in respect of ships where writing-down allowances have been postponed.

Para. 9 preserves the provisions regarding joint lessees where the lease falls within F.A. 1980, s.68(1) as amended by para. 4 of this Schedule.

Para. 10 sets out the information which must be given to the Revenue and largely follows the lines of F.A. 1980, s.67 (repealed by para. 3 of this Schedule).

Part IV of this Schedule (*i.e.* para. 11) amends F.A. 1980, s.69 ("writing-down allowances etc. for cars"). This deletes the reference in s.69 to the definition in F.A. 1971, s.43. The separate pool for leased cars costing not more than £8,000 now applies to vehicles as defined in this para.

Section 62

SCHEDULE 17

Securities: Amendments of Finance Act 1985

1.—(1) The following shall be inserted at the end of paragraph 8 of Schedule 23 to the Finance Act 1985 (trustees)—

"(4) Sub-paragraph (1) above does not apply where the annual profits or gains are treated as received by the investment manager of a common investment fund for the time being designated as mentioned in section 413(1) of the Taxes Act (funds in court).

(5) Where the income or part of the income derived in a year of assessment from such a common investment fund or its investments consists of interest on securities, the income or part (as the case may be) shall for the purposes of section 413(1)(*a*) of the Taxes Act be calculated by treating it as the amount it would be apart from section 74(5) of this Act, but reduced by an amount (if any) equal to the excess of A over B.

(6) In sub-paragraph (5) above—

A is the total amount of allowances to which, by virtue of section 74(4) of this Act, the investment manager of the fund is entitled in the year of assessment in respect of all securities comprised in the fund, and

B is the total amount of annual profits or gains which, by virtue of section 74(2) of this Act, he is treated as receiving in the year of assessment in respect of those securities."

(2) Paragraph 8 shall be treated as having been enacted with sub-paragraphs (4) to (6).

2.—(1) Paragraph 15 of that Schedule (transfer of unrealised interest) shall be amended as follows.

(2) For sub-paragraph (5) there shall be substituted—

"(5) Section 75 of this Act applies for the purposes of this paragraph as if in subsection (1) the reference to section 73(2)(*a*) or (3)(*a*) were to sub-paragraph (2) or

(3) above and references to the year of assessment in which the interest period ends were to the year in which the settlement day falls, and as if in subsection (2) the reference to section 73(2)(*b*) or (3)(*b*) were to sub-paragraph (4) above."

(3) After sub-paragraph (7) there shall be inserted—

"(7A) Where sub-paragraph (4) above applies, section 33 of the Capital Gains Tax Act 1979 shall be disregarded in computing for capital gains tax purposes the gain accruing to the transferee if he disposes of the securities, but an amount equal to the amount of the unrealised interest shall be excluded from the sums mentioned in paragraph 33(5) below."

(4) This paragraph applies where securities are transferred after 18th March 1986.

3.—(1) The following shall be inserted after paragraph 15 of that Schedule—

"Variable interest rate

15A.—(1) This paragraph applies to securities other than securities falling within sub-parararagraph (2) or (4) below.

(2) Securities fall within this sub-paragraph if their terms of issue provide that throughout the period from issue to redemption (whenever redemption might occur) they are to carry interest at a rate which falls into one, and one only, of the following categories—

(*a*) a fixed rate which is the same throughout the period;

(*b*) a rate which bears to a standard published base rate the same fixed relationship throughout the period;

(*c*) a rate which bears to a published index of prices the same fixed relationship throughout the period.

(3) In sub-paragraph (2)(*c*) above "published index of prices" means the retail prices index (within the meaning of section 24 of the Finance Act 1980) or any similar general index of prices which is published by, or by an agent of, the government of any territory outside the United Kingdom.

(4) Securities fall within this sub-paragraph if they are deep discount securities and the rate of interest for each (or their only) interest period is equal to or less than the yield to maturity.

(5) In sub-paragraph (4) above "deep discount securities" and "yield to maturity" have the same meanings as in Schedule 9 to the Finance Act 1984; and for the purposes of that sub-paragraph the rate of interest for an interest period is, in relation to securities, the rate of return (expressed as a percentage) attributable to the interest applicable to them for the interest period.

(6) Sub-paragraphs (7) to (11) below apply if securities to which this paragraph applies are transferred at any time between the time they are issued and the time they are redeemed.

(7) If the securities are transferred without accrued interest they shall be treated for the purposes of this Chapter as transferred with accrued interest.

(8) The person entitled to the securities immediately before they are redeemed shall be treated for the purposes of this Chapter as transferring them with accrued interest on the day they are redeemed.

(9) Where there is a transfer as mentioned in sub-paragraph (6) above or by virtue of sub-paragraph (8) above, section 73 of this Act shall be construed as if the following were substituted for subsections (2)(*b*) and (3) to (8)—

"(3) In subsection (2)(*a*) above "the accrued amount" means such amount (if any) as an inspector decides is just and reasonable; and the jurisdiction of the General Commissioners or the Special Commissioners on any appeal shall include jurisdiction to review such a decision of the inspector."

(10) Sub-paragraph (11) below applies where there is a transfer by virtue of sub-paragraph (8) above and the settlement day in relation to the transfer falls after the end of a period which would (by virtue of paragraph 3(3) and (4) above and apart from this paragraph) be the only or last interest period in relation to the securities.

(11) For the purposes of this Chapter the period beginning with the day following that interest period and ending with the settlement day shall be treated as an interest period in relation to the securities; and paragraph 3(4) above shall not apply to it.

Interest in default

15B.—(1) This paragraph applies where, because of any failure to fulfil the obligation to pay interest on securities, the value (on a day mentioned in paragraph 3(6) or (7)(*a*) above, as the case may be) of the right to receive the interest payable on them on that day is less than the interest so payable.

(2) Paragraph 3(6) or (7)(*a*), as the case may be, shall be construed as if the reference to that interest were to an amount equal to that value.

15C.—(1) Where securities are transferred as mentioned in paragraph 15(1) above and, because of any failure to fulfil the obligation to pay interest on them, the value (on the day of the transfer) of the right to receive the unrealised interest is less than the amount of the unrealised interest, paragraph 15 above shall have effect as modified by sub-paragraphs (2) to (6) below.

(2) In sub-paragraphs (2) and (3) for "the unrealised interest" there shall be substituted "amount A".

(3) For sub-paragraph (4) there shall be substituted—

"(4) Where the transferee receives an amount by way of the unrealised interest (amount B) and that amount falls to be taken into account in computing tax charged for the chargeable period in which it is received, it shall for the purposes of the Tax Acts be treated as reduced by an amount (amount C) equal to—

(*a*) nil, if amounts have been previously received by the transferee by way of the unrealised interest and their aggregate is equal to or greater than the value (on the day of the transfer to the transferee) of the right to receive the unrealised interest,

(*b*) amount B, if that value is equal to or greater than amount B (aggregated with other amounts previously so received, if any),

(*c*) that value, if no amount has been previously so received and that value is less than amount B, or

(*d*) so much of that value as exceeds the aggregate of amounts previously so received, in any other case."

(4) In sub-paragraph (7) for "the amount of the unrealised interest" there shall be substituted "amount A".

(5) In sub-paragraph (7A) for "the amount of the unrealised interest" there shall be substituted "amount C".

(6) The following shall be substituted for sub-paragraph (8)—

"(8) In this paragraph 'amount A' means, in a case where the transferor acquired the securities by a transfer on or after 28th February 1986 with the right to receive unrealised interest,—

(*a*) an amount equal to amount D less amount E, or

(*b*) if amount D is equal to or less than amount E, nil.

(9) In this paragraph 'amount A' means, in a case not falling within sub-paragraph (8) above, an amount equal to amount D.

(10) In this paragraph 'amount D' is an amount equal to the value (on the day of the transfer by the transferor) of the right to receive the unrealised interest.

(11) In this paragraph 'amount E' means, in a case where the transferor (as transferee) has received in respect of these securities an amount or amounts falling within sub-paragraph (4) above,—

(*a*) an amount equal to amount F less the total received, or

(*b*) if amount F is equal to or less than the total received, nil.

(12) In this paragraph 'amount E' means, in any other case, an amount equal to amount F.

(13) In this paragraph 'amount F' means an amount equal to the value (on the day of the transfer to the transferor) of the right to receive the unrealised interest.

(14) In determining for the purposes of this paragraph which securities of a particular kind a person has transferred, he is to be taken to have transferred securities of that kind which he acquired later before securities of that kind which he acquired earlier.

(15) Where the unrealised interest is payable in a currency other than sterling—

(*a*) any amount received by way of the interest is for the purposes of this paragraph the sterling equivalent on the day it is received of the amount it would be apart from this sub-paragraph, and

(*b*) the value (on the day of a transfer) of the right to receive the interest is for the purposes of this paragraph the sterling equivalent (on that day) of the value it would be apart from this sub-paragraph;

and for this purpose the sterling equivalent is to be calculated by reference to the London closing rate of exchange for the day concerned."."

(2) In consequence of sub-paragraph (1) above, in paragraph 4(4) of that Schedule after "14" there shall be inserted ", 15A(8)".

(3) The reference in paragraph 15A(6) to a time of transfer is to a time falling after 18th March 1986; and sub-paragraph (2) above applies accordingly.

(4) Paragraphs 15B and 15C apply where securities are transferred after 18th March 1986.

4.—(1) The following shall be inserted after paragraph 32 of that Schedule—

"Building societies

32A.—(1) Sub-paragraphs (2) and (3) below apply where securities are transferred and the interest which falls due on them at the end of the interest period in which the settlement day falls is subject to arrangements under section 343 of the Taxes Act or to the provisions of regulations under subsection (1A) of that section; but those sub-paragraphs do not apply where the interest is subject to the provisions of those regulations and would on being paid (to whatever person) be a gross payment within the meaning of those regulations.

(2) Section 73(4) of this Act shall be construed as if the following were substituted for paragraphs (*a*) and (*b*)—

"(*a*) if the securities are transferred under an arrangement by virtue of which the transferee accounts to the transferor separately for the consideration for the securities and for an amount equal to the grossed up equivalent of the interest (if any) accruing to the settlement day, an amount equal to that amount, and

(*b*) in any other case, an amount equal to the accrued proportion of the grossed up equivalent of the interest applicable to the securities for the period."

(3) Section 73(5) of this Act shall be construed as if the following were substituted for paragraphs (*a*) and (*b*)—

"(*a*) if the securities are transferred under an arrangement by virtue of which the transferor accounts to the transferee for an amount equal to the grossed up equivalent of the interest (if any) accruing from the settlement day to the next interest payment day, an amount equal to that amount, and

(*b*) in any other case, an amount equal to the rebate proportion of the grossed up equivalent of the interest applicable to the securities for the period."

(4) Where the unrealised interest mentioned in paragraph 15 above is subject to arrangements under section 343 of the Taxes Act or to the provisions of regulations under subsection (1A) of that section, that paragraph shall be construed as if in sub-paragraphs (2), (3), (7) and (7A) "the unrealised interest" read "the grossed up equivalent of the unrealised interest"; but this does not apply where the unrealised interest is subject to the provisions of those regulations and would on being paid (to whatever person) be a gross payment within the meaning of those regulations.

(5) In calculating the grossed up equivalent of interest for the purposes of section 73(4)(*b*) and (5)(*b*) of this Act and paragraph 15(2), (3), (7) and (7A) above (as substituted or amended as mentioned in this paragraph) the interest shall, in a case where it is subject to the provisions of regulations under section 343(1A) of the Taxes Act, be treated as if it would, on being paid, not be a gross payment within the meaning of those regulations.

(6) For the purposes of the provisions of this Chapter mentioned in sub-paragraph (5) above the grossed up equivalent of interest is to be calculated by adding to the interest a sum found by applying the following formula—

$$\frac{S}{I + S} = R.$$

(7) In sub-paragraph (6) above—

S is the sum to be found,

I is the interest, and

R is the basic rate of income tax (expressed as a fraction) for the year of assessment in which the interest is payable.

32B.—(1) This paragraph applies where a sum is both interest mentioned in section 74(5) of this Act, paragraph 9(4) above or paragraph 39(4) below and dividends or interest in the case of which section 343(2)(*b*) or (3)(*c*) of the Taxes Act applies.

(2) In calculating the deduction of income tax as mentioned in section 343(2)(*b*) or (3)(*c*) any reduction mentioned in section 74(5), paragraph 9(4) or paragraph 39(4) shall be disregarded.

(3) The amount which is treated as reduced as mentioned in section 74(5), paragraph 9(4) or paragraph 39(4) shall be the amount the person concerned is treated as receiving by virtue of section 343(2)(*b*) or (3)(*c*) (rather than the interest which falls due).

Stock lending

32C.—(1) The effect of section 61(3) of the Finance Act 1986 (transfer for purposes of stock lending not taken into account in computing trade's profits or losses) shall be disregarded in construing section 75(1)(*a*) and (2)(*a*) of this Act.

(2) Where securities are transferred in circumstances such that by virtue of section 61(4) of the Finance Act 1986 any disposal and acquisition are disregarded for the purposes of capital gains tax, section 73(2) and (3) of this Act and paragraph 15 above do not apply."

(2) Paragraph 32A applies where securities are transferred after 18th March 1986.

(3) Paragraph 32B applies where interest falls due after 18th March 1986.

5.—(1) In paragraph 43 of that Schedule (manufactured dividends) for paragraph (*c*) of sub-paragraph (1) there shall be substituted—

"(*c*) any contract under which the securities are transferred to the seller, or the contract mentioned in paragraph (*b*) above, is one in the case of which section 477 of the Taxes Act (manufactured dividends) has effect and in relation to which the seller is the dividend manufacturer."

(2) In sub-paragraphs (2) and (3) of paragraph 43 after the word "contract" (in each place) there shall be inserted the words "mentioned in sub-paragraph (1)(*b*) above".

(3) This paragraph applies where the contract in relation to which the seller is the dividend manufacturer is made after 18th March 1986.

6.—(1) In paragraph 44 of that Schedule (information) in sub-paragraph (2) for the word "jobber" there shall be substituted the words "market maker".

(2) After sub-paragraph (5) of paragraph 44 there shall be inserted—

"(5A) In this paragraph "market maker", in relation to securities, means a person who—

(*a*) holds himself out at all normal times in compliance with the rules of The Stock Exchange as willing to buy and sell securities of the kind concerned at a price specified by him, and

(*b*) is recognised as doing so by the Council of The Stock Exchange."

(3) Sub-paragraphs (1) and (2) above apply in relation to transactions on or after the day of The Stock Exchange reforms.

(4) The Board may by regulations provide that—

(*a*) sub-paragraphs (2) and (3) of paragraph 44 and paragraph (*a*) of sub-paragraph (5A) (as inserted by sub-paragraph (2) above) shall have effect as if references to The Stock Exchange were to any recognised investment exchange or to any of those exchanges specified in the regulations, and

(*b*) paragraph (*b*) of sub-paragraph (5A) shall have effect as if the reference to the Council of The Stock Exchange were to the investment exchange concerned.

(5) In sub-paragraph (4) above "recognised investment exchange" means a recognised investment exchange within the meaning of the Financial Services Act 1986.

(6) Regulations under sub-paragraph (4) above shall apply in relation to transactions effected on or after such day, after the day of The Stock Exchange reforms as is specified in the regulations.

(7) The power to make regulations under sub-paragraph (4) above shall be exercisable by statutory instrument subject to annulment in pursuance of a resolution of the House of Commons.

(8) In this paragraph "the day of The Stock Exchange reforms" means the day on which the rule of The Stock Exchange that prohibits a person from carrying on business as both a broker and a jobber is abolished.

General Note

Para 1. The gross income fund administered for individuals with very small incomes under the terms of the Administration of Justice Act 1982, s.42, has two reliefs extended to it to maintain its existing benefits under I.C.T.A., s.413. The trustees of the fund will be liable to tax under the accrued income scheme only at the basic and not at the additional rate. Also, the accrued income scheme charge will not limit the trustees' exemption from income tax on distributed income.

Para. 2. F.A. 1985, Sched. 23, para. 15, catered for bearer bonds, transferred with unpresented coupons. The amendments in this paragraph are designed to prevent the buyer of such securities from obtaining a possible double relief from tax both on the acquisition of the bond and its subsequent disposal.

Para. 3 adds three new paragraphs to F.A. 1985, Sched. 23 to provide for other two circumstances not envisaged in the original legislation. Para. 15A is designed to prevent a recrudescence of bond washing through the issue of securities with artificially constructed variable interest rates. In such circumstances the accrued interest chargeable can be fixed by the Revenue at whatever amount they decide is just and reasonable, subject to appeal to the General or Special Commissioners. Paras. 15B and 15C allow relief where interest on bearer bonds is in default by charging the vendor only on the value rather than the nominal amount of the unpaid interest.

Para. 4 secures the smooth operation of the accrued income scheme in relation to building society bonds. Charges and reliefs under the scheme will be calculated by reference to the interest as grossed up under the arrangement for composite rate tax.

Para. 5 makes a minor technical adjustment to the provision relating to manufactured dividends. For further amendments with regard to I.C.T.A., s.477, see Sched. 18, paras. 5 and 6, *infra.*

Para. 6. The provisions regarding the obtaining of information by the Revenue are adjusted to reflect the effects of the "Big Bang." Powers are given to make regulations in relation to recognised investment exchanges covered by the forthcoming Financial Services Act.

Section 63

SCHEDULE 18

Securities: Other Provisions

Sale and re-purchase of securities

1.—(1) In section 469 of the Taxes Act (sale and re-purchase of securities) the following shall be inserted after subsection (6)—

"(6A) Subsections (1) and (2) above shall not apply where—

(*a*) the securities are Eurobonds or foreign government stock, and

(*b*) the owner of the securities carries on a trade which consists wholly or partly in dealing in securities and the person who agrees to buy or acquire the securities carries on such a trade.

(6B) Subsection (4) above shall not apply where—

(*a*) the securities are Eurobonds or foreign government stock, and

(*b*) the person from whom the person there mentioned agrees to buy or acquire the securities carries on a trade which consists wholly or partly in dealing in securities.

(6C) In subsections (6A) and (6B) above—

"Eurobond" has the same meaning as in section 472(5) below, and

"foreign government stock" means stock which is issued by a government other than that of the United Kingdom and is denominated in a currency other than sterling."

(2) Section 469 shall be treated as having been enacted with subsections (6A) to (6C).

(3) The reference in section 472(3) of the Taxes Act to a transaction which is to be left out of account by virtue of section 469(4) shall include a reference to a transaction which would fall to be so left out of account apart from section 469(6B).

(4) In section 469 the following shall be substituted for subsection (7)(*b*)—

"(*b*) 'securities' includes stocks and shares, except securities which are securities for the purposes of Chapter IV of Part II of the Finance Act 1985 (accrued income scheme etc.)."

(5) Sub-paragraph (4) above applies where the owner mentioned in section 469(1) agrees to sell or transfer, or (as the case may be) the person mentioned in section 469(4) agrees to buy or acquire, on or after such day as the Board may appoint for the purposes of this paragraph by order made by statutory instrument; and paragraph 41 of Schedule 23 to the Finance Act 1985 (section 469(1) and (2) not to apply in certain circumstances) shall cease to have effect where the owner agrees to sell or transfer on or after that day.

Purchase and sale of securities

2.—(1) In section 471 of the Taxes Act (purchase and sale of securities) the following shall be substituted for subsection (6)(*c*)—

"(*c*) 'securities' includes stocks and shares, except securities which are securities for the purposes of Chapter IV of Part II of the Finance Act 1985 (accrued income scheme etc.)."

(2) Sub-paragraph (1) above applies where the first buyer purchases after 18th March 1986; and section 475(6) of the Taxes Act and paragraph 42 of Schedule 23 to the Finance Act 1985 shall cease to have effect where the first buyer purchases after that date.

3.—(1) In section 472 of the Taxes Act (dealers in securities) the following shall be substituted for subsection (2)—

"(2) Subsection (1) of this section shall not apply if the subsequent sale is carried out by the first buyer in the ordinary course of his business as a market maker in securities of the kind concerned."

(2) At the end of that section there shall be inserted—

"(6) For the purposes of subsection (2) of this section a person is a market maker in securities of a particular kind if he—

(*a*) holds himself out at all normal times in compliance with the rules of The Stock Exchange as willing to buy and sell securities of that kind at a price specified by him, and

(*b*) is recognised as doing so by the Council of The Stock Exchange."

(3) This paragraph applies where the subsequent sale is carried out by the first buyer on or after the day of The Stock Exchange reforms.

4.—(1) The Board may by regulations provide for all or any of the following—

(*a*) that section 472(2) of the Taxes Act (as substituted by paragraph 3(1) above) shall not apply unless the subsequent sale is carried out in compliance with further conditions specified in the regulations;

(*b*) that section 472(6) of that Act (as inserted by paragraph 3(2) above) shall have effect as if the reference to The Stock Exchange in paragraph (*a*) were to any recognised investment exchange or to any of those exchanges specified in the regulations, and as if the reference to the Council of The Stock Exchange in paragraph (*b*) were to the investment exchange concerned;

(*c*) that for section 475(3) and (5) of that Act (which refer to The Stock Exchange Daily Official List) there shall be substituted such provisions as the Board think fit to take account of recognised investment exchanges.

(2) The regulations shall apply where the subsequent sale is carried out by the first buyer on or after such day, after the day of The Stock Exchange reforms, as is specified in the regulations.

Manufactured dividends

5.—(1) Section 477 of the Taxes Act (manufactured dividends) shall be amended as follows—

(*a*) in subsection (1), in paragraph (*a*), for the words "the seller is required to pay to the purchaser" there shall be substituted the words "one of the parties to the contract (the dividend manufacturer) is required to pay to the other";

(*b*) in that subsection, in paragraph (*b*) and the words following it, for the word "seller" (in each place) there shall be substituted the words "dividend manufacturer";

(*c*) in subsection (3) after the word "sold" there shall be inserted the words "or purchased";

(*d*) in subsection (4) for the word "seller" there shall be substituted the words "dividend manufacturer";

(*e*) in subsection (5) for the words "seller under" there shall be substituted the words "dividend manufacturer in relation to" and for the word "seller" (in the other two places) there shall be substituted the words "dividend manufacturer".

(2) Sub-paragraph (1) above applies where the contract for the sale of securities is made after 18th March 1986.

6.—(1) Section 477 of the Taxes Act shall also be amended as provided by this paragraph.

(2) In subsection (3) for the word "jobber" (in the first place where it occurs) there shall be substituted the words "market maker" and for the word "jobber" (in the second place where it occurs) there shall be substituted the words "market maker in securities of the kind concerned".

(3) In subsection (6) the following shall be substituted for the definitions of "broker" and "jobber"—

" "broker", in relation to securities, means a member of The Stock Exchange who carries on his business in the United Kingdom and is not, at the time the contract for the sale of the securities is made, a market maker in securities of the kind concerned,

"market maker", in relation to securities of a particular kind, means a person who—

(*a*) holds himself out at all normal times in compliance with the rules of The Stock Exchange as willing to buy and sell securities of that kind at a price specified by him and (*b*) is recognised as doing so by the Council of The Stock Exchange",

(4) Sub-paragraphs (2) and (3) above apply where the contract for the sale of securities is made on or after the day of The Stock Exchange reforms.

(5) The Board may by regulations provide that section 477(6) (as amended by sub-paragraph (3) above) shall have effect—

(*a*) as if references to The Stock Exchange in the definition of "broker" and in paragraph (*a*) of the definition of "market maker" were to any recognised investment exchange or to any of those exchanges specified in the regulations, and

(*b*) as if the reference to the Council of The Stock Exchange in paragraph (*b*) of the definition of "market maker" were to the investment exchange concerned.

(6) Regulations under sub-paragraph (5) above shall apply where the contract for the sale of securities is made on or after such day, after the day of The Stock Exchange reforms, as is specified in the regulations.

Information

7.—(1) In section 21 of the Taxes Management Act 1970 (stock jobbers' transactions) in subsections (1), (2) and (4) for the word "jobber" (in each place) there shall be substituted the words "market maker" and in subsection (5) for the word "jobbers" there shall be substituted the words "market makers".

(2) In subsection (7) of section 21 the following shall be substituted for the definitions of "broker" and "jobber"—

" "broker," in relation to securities, means a member of The Stock Exchange who carries on his business in the United Kingdom and is not a market maker in securities of the kind concerned;

"market maker", in relation to securities, means a person who—

(*a*) holds himself out at all normal times in compliance with the rules of The Stock Exchange as willing to buy and sell securities of the kind concerned at a price specified by him, and

(*b*) is recognised as doing so by the Council of The Stock Exchange";

(3) Sub-paragraphs (1) and (2) above apply in relation to transactions effected on or after the day of The Stock Exchange reforms.

(4) The Board may by regulations provide that section 21(7) (as amended by sub-paragraph (2) above) shall have effect—

(*a*) as if references to The Stock Exchange in the definition of "broker" and in paragraph (*a*) of the definition of "market maker" were to any recognised investment exchange or to any of those exchanges specified in the regulations, and

(*b*) as if the reference to the Council of The Stock Exchange in paragraph (*b*) of the definition of "market maker" were to the investment exchange concerned.

(5) Regulations under sub-paragraph (4) above shall apply in relation to transactions effected on or after such day, after the day of The Stock Exchange reforms, as is specified in the regulations.

8.—(1) In section 25 of the Taxes Management Act 1970 (information: chargeable gains) in subsection (4) for the word "jobber" there shall be substituted the words "market maker".

(2) At the end of section 25 there shall be inserted—

"(10) In this section "market maker", in relation to shares or securities, means a person who—

(*a*) holds himself out at all normal times in compliance with the rules of The Stock Exchange as willing to buy and sell shares or securities of the kind concerned at a price specified by him, and

(*b*) is recognised as doing so by the Council of The Stock Exchange."

(3) Sub-paragraphs (1) and (2) above apply in relation to transactions on or after the day of The Stock Exchange reforms.

(4) The Board may by regulations provide that—

(*a*) subsections (4) and (5) of section 25 and paragraph (*a*) of subsection (10) (as inserted by sub-paragraph (2) above) shall have effect as if references to The Stock Exchange were to any recognised investment exchange or to any of those exchanges specified in the regulations, and

(*b*) paragraph (*b*) of subsection (10) shall have effect as if the reference to the Council of The Stock Exchange were to the investment exchange concerned.

(5) Regulations under sub-paragraph (4) above shall apply in relation to transactions effected, on or after such day, after the day of The Stock Exchange reforms, as is specified in the regulations.

Miscellaneous

9.—(1) The Board may by regulations—

(*a*) substitute for section 477(3) of the Taxes Act a provision that section 477(1) shall not apply to such persons and in such circumstances as are specified in the substituted provision;

(*b*) substitute for section 21(1) of the Taxes Management Act 1970 a provision that the Board may exercise the powers conferred by section 21 in such circumstances as are specified in the substituted provision;

(*c*) make such incidental and consequential provisions (which may include the amendment of other provisions of section 477 or section 21) as appear to the Board to be appropriate.

(2) So far as they relate to section 477, the regulations shall apply where the contract for the sale of securities is made on or after such day, after the day of The Stock Exchange reforms, as is specified in the regulations.

(3) So far as they relate to section 21, the regulations shall apply in relation to transactions effected on or after such day, after the day of The Stock Exchange reforms, as is specified in the regulations.

General

10.—(1) In this Schedule "the day of The Stock Exchange reforms" means the day on which the rule of The Stock Exchange that prohibits a person from carrying on business as both a broker and a jobber is abolished.

(2) In this Schedule "recognised investment exchange" means a recognised investment exchange within the meaning of the Financial Services Act 1986.

(3) Any power to make regulations under this Schedule shall be exercisable by statutory instrument subject to annulment in pursuance of a resolution of the House of Commons.

General Note

Para. 1 takes sale and repurchase agreements for eurobonds and foreign government stock (in practice U.S. Treasury stocks), so-called "repos", outside the ambit of section 469. See further B.T.E. Bulletin, February 1986, p.12. For the future, section 469 will not apply to bonds within the accrued income scheme.

Para. 2 similarly takes bonds within the accrued income scheme outside the ambit of sections 471 to 475.

Para. 3 amends these sections to take account of the "Big Bang."

Para. 4 gives the Revenue power to make regulations in connection with these sections for other recognised investment exchanges and for other related purposes.

Paras. 5 and 6 amend and update section 477. See also Sched. 17, para. 5, *supra*.

Paras. 7 and 8 make amendments to the Taxes Management Act consequent on the "Big Bang" and confer power on the Revenue to extend by regulation the relevant provisions of the T.M.A. to recognised investment exchanges.

Para. 9 gives the Revenue further power to amend section 477 and T.M.A., s.21 by regulation.

Para. 10 contains definitions and provides for the regulations made under the Schedule to be by statutory instrument.

Section 101

SCHEDULE 19

Inheritance Tax

Part I

Amendments of 1984 Act

1. After section 3 there shall be inserted the following section—

"Potentially exempt transfers

3A.—(1) Any reference in this Act to a potentially exempt transfer is a reference to a transfer of value—

(*a*) which is made by an individual on or after 18th March 1986; and

(*b*) which, apart from this section, would be a chargeable transfer (or to the extent to which, apart from this section, it would be such a transfer); and (*c*) to the extent that it constitutes either a gift to another individual or a gift into an accumulation and maintenance trust or a disabled trust;

but this subsection has effect subject to any provision of this Act which provides that a disposition (or transfer of value) of a particular description is not a potentially exempt transfer.

(2) Subject to subsection (6) below, a transfer of value falls within subsection (1)(*c*) above, as a gift to another individual—

(*a*) to the extent that the value transferred is attributable to property which, by virtue of the transfer, becomes comprised in the estate of that other individual, otherwise than as settled property, or

(*b*) so far as that value is not attributable to property which becomes comprised in the estate of another person, to the extent that, by virtue of the transfer, the estate of that other individual is increased, otherwise than by an increase in the value of settled property comprised in his estate.

(3) Subject to subsection (6) below, a transfer of value falls within subsection (1)(*c*) above, as a gift into an accumulation and maintenance trust or a disabled trust, to the extent that the value transferred is attributable to property which, by virtue of the transfer, becomes settled property to which section 71 or 89 of this Act applies.

(4) A potentially exempt transfer which is made seven years or more before the death of the transferor is an exempt transfer and any other potentially exempt transfer is a chargeable transfer.

(5) During the period beginning on the date of a potentially exempt transfer and ending immediately before—

(*a*) the seventh anniversary of that date, or

(*b*) if it is earlier, the death of the transferor,

it shall be assumed for the purposes of this Act that the transfer will prove to be an exempt transfer.

(6) Where, under any provision of this Act, tax is in any circumstances to be charged as if a transfer of value had been made, that transfer shall be taken to be a transfer which is not a potentially exempt transfer."

2.—(1) In section 7 (rates of tax), in subsection (1)—

(*a*) at the beginning there shall be inserted the words "Subject to subsections (2), (4) and (5) below";

(*b*) for the words "ten years" there shall be substituted "seven years"; and

(*c*) the word "appropriate" shall be omitted.

(2) For subsection (2) of that section there shall be substituted the following subsection—

"(2) Except as provided by subsection (4) below, the tax charged on the value transferred by a chargeable transfer made before the death of the transferor shall be charged at one-half of the rate or rates referred to in subsection (1) above."

(3) In subsection (3) of that section for the words "each of the Tables" there shall be substituted "the Table".

(4) After subsection (3) of that section there shall be inserted the following subsections—

"(4) Subject to subsection (5) below, subsection (2) above does not apply in the case of a chargeable transfer made at any time within the period of seven years ending with the death of the transferor but, in the case of a chargeable transfer made within that period but more than three years before the death, the tax charged on the value transferred shall be charged at the following percentage of the rate or rates referred to in subsection (1) above—

(*a*) where the transfer is made more than three but not more than four years before the death, 80 per cent;

(*b*) where the transfer is made more than four but not more than five years before the death, 60 per cent;

(*c*) where the transfer is made more than five but not more than six years before the death, 40 per cent; and

(*d*) where the transfer is made more than six but not more than seven years before the death, 20 per cent.

(5) If, in the case of a chargeable transfer made before the death of the transferor, the tax which would fall to be charged in accordance with subsection (4) above is less than the tax which would have been chargeable (in accordance with subsection (2) above) if the transferor had not died within the period of seven years beginning with the date of the transfer, subsection (4) above shall not apply in the case of that transfer."

3.—(1) In section 8 (indexation) in subsection (1) for the words "new Tables for the Tables" there shall be substituted "a new Table for the Table".

(2) After subsection (1) of that section there shall be inserted the following subsection—

"(1A) For the purpose only of the application of Schedule 1 to this Act in accordance with subsection (1) above, a potentially exempt transfer which proves to be a chargeable transfer shall be assumed to be made on the date of the transferor's death."

(3) In subsection (2) of that section for the word "Tables", in each place where it occurs, there shall be substituted "Table" and for the words "they replace" there shall be substituted "it replaces".

(4) In subsection (4) of that section, for the word "Tables" there shall be substituted "Table".

4. In section 9 (transitional provisions on reduction of tax) for the words "new Tables" there shall be substituted "a new Table".

5. In section 19 (annual exemption), after subsection (3) there shall be inserted the following subsection—

"(3A) A transfer of value which is a potentially exempt transfer—

(*a*) shall in the first instance be left out of account for the purposes of subsections (1) to (3) above; and

(*b*) if it proves to be a chargeable transfer, shall for the purposes of those subsections be taken into account as if, in the year in which it was made, it was made later than any transfer of value which was not a potentially exempt transfer."

6. After section 26 there shall be inserted the following section—

"Potentially exempt transfer of property subsequently held for national purposes etc.

26A. A potentially exempt transfer which would (apart from this section) have proved to be a chargeable transfer shall be an exempt transfer to the extent that the value transferred by it is attributable to property which has been or could be designated under section 3(1) below and which, during the period beginning with the date of the transfer and ending with the death of the transferor,—

(*a*) has been disposed of by sale by private treaty to a body mentioned in Schedule 3 to this Act or has been disposed of to such a body otherwise than by sale, or

(*b*) has been disposed of in pursuance of section 230 below."

7. In section 30 (conditionally exempt transfers) after subsection (3) there shall be inserted the following subsections—

"(3A) The provisions of this section shall be disregarded in determining under section 3A above whether a transfer of value is a potentially exempt transfer.

(3B) No claim may be made under subsection (1) above with respect to a potentially exempt transfer until the transferor has died.

(3C) Subsection (1) above shall not apply to a potentially exempt transfer to the extent that the value transferred by it is attributable to property which has been disposed of by sale during the period beginning with the date of the transfer and ending with the death of the transferor."

8.—(1) In section 31 (designation and undertakings) after subsection (1) there shall be inserted the following subsection—

"(1A) Where the transfer of value in relation to which the claim for designation is made is a potentially exempt transfer which (apart from section 30 above) has proved to be a chargeable transfer, the question whether any property is appropriate for designation under this section shall be determined by reference to circumstances existing after the death of the transferor."

(2) After subsection (4F) of that section there shall be inserted the following subsection—

"(4G) In a case where—

(*a*) the transfer of value in question is a potentially exempt transfer which (apart from section 30 above) has proved to be a chargeable transfer, and

(*b*) at the time of the transferor's death an undertaking by such a person as is mentioned in section 30(1)(*b*) above given under paragraph 3(3) of Schedule 4 to this Act or under section 147 of the Capital Tax Act 1979 is in force with respect to any property to which the value transferred by the transfer is attributable,

that undertaking shall be treated for the purposes of this Chapter as an undertaking given under section 30 above."

9. In section 32 (chargeable events) in subsection (1) after the words "after the transfer" there shall be inserted "(or, if the transfer was a potentially exempt transfer, after the death of the transferor)".

10. In section 32A (associated properties) in subsection (2) after the words "after the transfer" there shall be inserted "(or, if the transfer was a potentially exempt transfer, after the death of the transferor)".

11.—(1) In section 33 (amount of charge in relation to conditionally exempt transfers), in subsection (1)(*b*)—

(*a*) in sub-paragraph (i) for the words "under the second Table in Schedule 1 to this Act" there shall be substituted "in accordance with section 7(2) above"; and

(*b*) in sub-paragraph (ii) for the words "under the appropriate Table" there shall be substituted "in accordance with the appropriate provision of section 7 above".

(2) For subsection (2) of that section there shall be substituted the following subsections—

"(2) For the purposes of subsection (1)(*b*)(ii) above the appropriate provision of section 7 above is—

(*a*) if the conditionally exempt transfer by the relevant person was made on death (but the property was not treated as forming part of his estate immediately before his death only by virtue of section 102(3) of the Finance Act 1986), subsection (1) of section 7; and

(*b*) in any other case, subsection (2) of section 7.

(2A) The rate or rates of tax determined under subsection (1)(*b*)(i) above in respect of any chargeable event shall not be affected by the death of the relevant person after that event.".

(3) In subsection (7) of that section at the beginning there shall be inserted the words "Subject to subsection (8) below".

(4) After that subsection there shall be added the following subsection—

"(8) Where after a conditionally exempt transfer of any property there is a potentially exempt transfer the value transferred by which is wholly or partly attributable to that property and either—

(*a*) the potentially exempt transfer is a chargeable event with respect to the property, or

(*b*) after the potentially exempt transfer, but before the death of the person who is the transferor in relation to the potentially exempt transfer, a chargeable event occurs with respect to the property,

the tax charged in accordance with this section by reference to that chargeable event shall be allowed as a credit against any tax which may become chargeable, by reason of the potentially exempt transfer proving to be a chargeable transfer, on so much of the value transferred by that transfer as is attributable to the property; and subsection (7) above shall not apply with respect to any tax so becoming chargeable."

12. In section 35 (conditional exemption on death before 7th April 1976) in subsection (3) for the words "section 33(7) above, the reference" there shall be substituted "section 33(7) and (8) above, references", and for the words "includes a reference" there shall be substituted "include references".

13. In section 38 (attribution of value to specific gifts) in subsection (6) after the words "section 5(5) above" there shall be inserted "or by virtue of section 103 of the Finance Act 1986" and at the end of that subsection there shall be added "and, to the extent that any liability of the transferor is abated under the said section 103, that liability shall be treated as a specific gift".

14. At the end of section 49 (treatment of interests in possession) there shall be added the following subsection—

"(3) Where a person becomes entitled to an interest in possession in settled property as a result of such a disposition as is mentioned in subsection (2) above, no transfer of value resulting from the giving of consideration as so mentioned shall be a potentially exempt transfer."

15. In section 55 (reversionary interest acquired by beneficiary) at the end of subsection (2) there shall be added "and such a disposition is not a potentially exempt transfer".

16.—(1) In section 66 (rate of ten-yearly charge) in subsection (3)(*b*) for the words "preceding ten years" there shall be substituted "preceding seven years".

(2) For paragraph (*c*) of subsection (3) of that section there shall be substituted—

"(*c*) on which tax is charged in accordance with section 7(2) of this Act".

(3) In subsection (5)(*a*) of that section for the word "ten" there shall be substituted "seven".

17. In section 67 (added property etc.) in subsections (3)(*b*) and (4) for the word "ten" there shall be substituted "seven".

18.—(1) In section 68 (rate before first ten-year anniversary) in subsection (4)(*b*) for the word "ten", in both places where it occurs, there shall be substituted "seven".

(2) For paragraph (*c*) of subsection (4) and for paragraph (*c*) of subsection (6) of that section there shall be substituted—

"(*c*) on which tax is charged in accordance with section 7(2) of this Act".

(3) In subsection (6)(*b*) of that section—

(*a*) for the word "ten", in the first place where it occurs, there shall be substituted "seven"; and

(*b*) in sub-paragraph (i) for the words "that period of ten years" there shall be substituted "the period of ten years ending with that day".

19.—(1) In section 78 (conditionally exempt occasions) in subsection (4) for the words from "and the appropriate Table" to the end there shall be substituted "and the appropriate provision of section 7 for the purposes of section 33(1)(*b*)(ii) is, if the settlement was created on his death, subsection (1) and, if not, subsection (2)."

(2) In subsection (5) of that section, in the substituted sub-paragraph (ii) for section 33(1)(*b*), for the words "under the appropriate Table" there shall be substituted "in accordance with the appropriate provision of section 7 above."

20. At the end of section 98 (effect of alteration of capital of close company etc.) there shall be added the following subsection—

"(3) The disposition referred to in subsection (1) above shall be taken to be one which is not a potentially exempt transfer."

21. After section 113 there shall be inserted the following sections—

"Transfers within seven years before death of transferor

113A.—(1) Where any part of the value transferred by a potentially exempt transfer which proves to be a chargeable transfer would (apart from this section) be reduced in accordance with the preceding provisions of this Chapter, it shall not be so reduced unless the conditions in subsection (3) below are satisfied.

(2) Where—

(*a*) any part of the value transferred by any chargeable transfer, other than a potentially exempt transfer, is reduced in accordance with the preceding provisions of this Chapter, and

(*b*) the transfer is made within seven years of the death of the transferor,

then, unless the conditions in subsection (3) below are satisfied, the additional tax chargeable by reason of the death shall be calculated as if the value transferred had not been so reduced.

(3) The conditions referred to in subsections (1) and (2) above are—

(*a*) that the original property was owned by the transferee throughout the period beginning with the date of the chargeable transfer and ending with the death of the transferor; and

(*b*) that, in relation to a notional transfer of value made by the transferee immediately before the death, the original property would (apart from section 106 above) be relevant business property.

(4) If the transferee has died before the transferor, the reference in subsection (3) above to the death of the transferor shall have effect as a reference to the death of the transferee.

(5) If the conditions in subsection (3) above are satisfied only with respect to part of the original property, then,—

(*a*) in a case falling within subsection (1) above, only a proportionate part of so much of the value transferred as is attributable to the original property shall be reduced in accordance with the preceding provisions of this Chapter, and

(*b*) in a case falling within subsection (2) above, the additional tax shall be calculated as if only a proportionate part of so much of the value transferred as was attributable to the original property had been so reduced.

(6) Where any shares owned by the transferee immediately before the death in question—

(*a*) would under any of the provisions of sections 77 to 86 of the Capital Gains Tax Act 1979 be identified with the original property (or part of it), or

(*b*) were issued to him in consideration of the transfer of a business or interest in a business consisting of the original property (or part of it),

they shall be treated for the purposes of this section as if they were the original property (or that part of it).

(7) This section has effect subject to section 113B below.

(8) In this section—

'the original property' means the property which was relevant business property in relation to the chargeable transfer referred to in subsection (1) or subsection (2) above; and 'the transferee' means the person whose property the original property became on that chargeable transfer or, where on the transfer the original property became or remained settled property in which no qualifying interest in possession (within the meaning of Chapter III of Part III of this Act) subsists, the trustees of the settlement.

Application of section 113A to replacement property

113B.—(1) Subject to subsection (2) below, this section applies where—

(*a*) the transferee has disposed of all or part of the original property before the death of the transferor; and

(*b*) the whole of the consideration received by him for the disposal has been applied by him in acquiring other property (in this section referred to as "the replacement property").

(2) This section does not apply unless—

(*a*) the replacement property is acquired, or a binding contract for its acquisition is entered into, within twelve months after the disposal of the original property (or, as the case may be, the part concerned); and

(*b*) the disposal and acquisition are both made in transactions at arm's length or on terms such as might be expected to be included in a transaction at arm's length.

(3) Where this section applies, the conditions in section 113A(3) above shall be taken to be satisfied in relation to the original property (or, as the case may be, the part concerned) if—

(*a*) the replacement property is owned by the transferee immediately before the death of the transferor; and

(*b*) throughout the period beginning with the date of the chargeable transfer and ending with the death (disregarding any period between the disposal and acquisition) either the original property or the replacement property was owned by the transferee; and

(*c*) in relation to a notional transfer of value made by the transferee immediately before the death, the replacement property would (apart from section 106 above) be relevant business property.

(4) If the transferee has died before the transferor, any reference in subsections (1) to (3) above to the death of the transferor shall have effect as a reference to the death of the transferee.

(5) In any case where—

(*a*) all or part of the original property has been disposed of before the death of the transferor or is excluded by section 113 above from being relevant business property in relation to the notional transfer of value referred to in section 113A(3)(*b*) above, and

(*b*) the replacement property is acquired, or a binding contract for its acquisition is entered into, after the death of the transferor but within twelve months after the disposal of the original property or part, and

(*c*) the transferor dies before the transferee,

subsection (3) above shall have effect with the omission of paragraph (*a*), and as if any reference to a time immediately before the death of the transferor or to the death were a reference to the time when the replacement property is acquired.

(6) Section 113A(6) above shall have effect in relation to the replacement property as it has effect in relation to the original property.

(7) Where a binding contract for the disposal of any property is entered into at any time before the disposal of the property, the disposal shall be regarded for the purposes of subsections (2)(*a*) and (5)(*b*) above as taking place at that time.

(8) In this section "the original property" and "the transferee" have the same meaning as in section 113A above."

22. After section 124 there shall be inserted the following sections—

"Transfers within seven years before death of transferor

124A.—(1) Where any part of the value transferred by a potentially exempt transfer which proves to be a chargeable transfer would (apart from this section) be reduced in accordance with the preceding provisions of this Chapter, it shall not be so reduced unless the conditions in subsection (3) below are satisfied.

(2) Where—

(*a*) any part of the value transferred by any chargeable transfer, other than a potentially exempt transfer, is reduced in accordance with the preceding provisions of this Chapter, and

(*b*) the transfer is made within seven years of the death of the transferor, then, unless the conditions in subsection (3) below are satisfied, the additional tax chargeable by reason of the death shall be calculated as if the value transferred had not been so reduced.

(3) The conditions referred to in subsections (1) and (2) above are—

(*a*) that the original property was owned by the transferee throughout the period beginning with the date of the chargeable transfer and ending with the death of the transferor (in this subsection referred to as "the relevant period") and it is not at the time of the death subject to a binding contract for sale; and

(*b*) except in a case falling within paragraph (*c*) below, that the original property is agricultural property immediately before the death and has been occupied (by the transferee or another) for the purposes of agriculture throughout the relevant period; and

(*c*) where the original property consists of shares in or securities of a company, that throughout the relevant period the agricultural property to which section 116 above applied by virtue of section 122(1) above on the chargeable transfer was owned by the company and occupied (by the company or another) for the purposes of agriculture.

(4) If the transferee has died before the transferor, the reference in subsection (3) above to the death of the transferor shall have effect as a reference to the death of the transferee.

(5) If the conditions in subsection (3) above are satisfied only with respect to part of the original property, then,—

(*a*) in a case falling within subsection (1) above, only a proportionate part of so much of the value transferred as is attributable to the original property shall be reduced in accordance with the preceding provisions of this Chapter, and

(*b*) in a case falling within subsection (2) above, the additional tax shall be calculated as if only a proportionate part of so much of the value transferred as was attributable to the original property had been so reduced.

(6) Where any shares owned by the transferee immediately before the death in question—

(*a*) would under any of the provisions of sections 77 to 86 of the Capital Gains Tax Act 1979 be identified with the original property (or part of it), or

(*b*) were issued to him in consideration of the transfer of agricultural property consisting of the original property (or part of it),

they shall be treated for the purposes of this section as if they were the original property (or that part of it).

(7) This section has effect subject to section 124B below.

(8) In this section—

'the original property' means the property which, in relation to the chargeable transfer referred to in subsection (1) or subsection (2) above, was either agricultural property to which section 116 above applied or shares or securities of a company owning agricultural property to which that section applied by virtue of section 122(1) above; and

'the transferee' means the person whose property the original property became on that chargeable transfer or, where on the transfer the original property became or remained settled property in which no qualifying interest in possession (within the meaning of Chapter III of Part III of this Act) subsists, the trustees of the settlement.

Application of section 124A to replacement property

124B.—(1) Subject to subsection (2) below, this section applies where—

(*a*) the transferee has disposed of all or part of the original property before the death of the transferor; and

(*b*) the whole of the consideration received by him for the disposal has been applied by him in acquiring other property (in this section referred to as "the replacement property").

(2) This section does not apply unless—

(*a*) the replacement property is acquired, or a binding contract for its acquisition is entered into, within twelve months after the disposal of the original property (or, as the case may be, the part concerned); and

(*b*) the disposal and acquisition are both made in transactions at arm's length or on terms such as might be expected to be included in a transaction at arm's length.

(3) Where this section applies, the conditions in section 124A(3) above shall be taken to be satisfied in relation to the original property (or, as the case may be, the part concerned) if—

(*a*) the replacement property is owned by the transferee immediately before the death of the transferor and is not at that time subject to a binding contract for sale; and

(*b*) throughout the period beginning with the date of the chargeable transfer and ending with the disposal, the original property was owned by the transferee and occupied (by the transferee or another) for the purposes of agriculture; and

(*c*) throughout the period beginning with the date when the transferee acquired the replacement property and ending with the death, the replacement property was owned by the transferee and occupied (by the transferee or another) for the purposes of agriculture; and

(*d*) the replacement property is agricultural property immediately before the death.

(4) If the transferee has died before the transferor, any reference in subsections (1) to (3) above to the death of the transferor shall have effect as a reference to the death of the transferee.

(5) In any case where—

(*a*) all or part of the original property has been disposed of before the death of the transferor or is subject to a binding contract for sale at the time of the death, and

(*b*) the replacement property is acquired, or a binding contract for its acquisition is entered into, after the death of the transferor but within twelve months after the disposal of the original property or part, and

(*c*) the transferor dies before the transferee,

subsection (3) above shall have effect with the omission of paragraphs (*a*) and (*c*), and as if any reference to a time immediately before the death of the transferor were a reference to the time when the replacement property is acquired.

(6) Section 124A(6) above shall have effect in relation to the replacement property as it has effect in relation to the original property.

(7) Where a binding contract for the disposal of any property is entered into at any time before the disposal of the property, the disposal shall be regarded for the purposes of subsections (2)(*a*) and (5)(*b*) above as taking place at that time.

(8) In this section "the original property" and "the transferee" have the same meaning as in section 124A above."

23.—(1) In section 131 (relief in respect of additional tax payable on transfers within three years of death), in subsection (1) for the words from "(by virtue" to "transfer and" there shall be substituted "because of the transferor's death within seven years of the transfer, tax becomes chargeable in respect of the value transferred by a potentially exempt transfer or (by virtue of section 7(4) above) additional tax becomes chargeable in respect of the value transferred by any other chargeable transfer and (in either case)".

(2) In subsection (2) of that section for the words "the additional tax", in each place where they occur, there shall be substituted "the tax or, as the case may be, additional tax".

(3) After that subsection there shall be inserted the following subsection—

"(2A) Where so much of the value transferred as is attributable to the value, or agricultural value, of the transferred property is reduced by any percentage (in this subsection referred to as "the appropriate percentage"), in accordance with Chapter I or Chapter II of this Part of this Act, references in subsection (2) above to the market value of the transferred property at any time shall have effect—

(*a*) in a case within Chapter I, as references to that market value reduced by the appropriate percentage; and

(*b*) in a case within Chapter II, as references to that market value less the appropriate percentage of the agricultural value of the transferred property at that time."

24. In section 142 (alteration of dispositions taking effect on death) at the end of subsection (5) there shall be added "or section 102 of the Finance Act 1986".

25. Sections 148 and 149 (exemptions for mutual transfers) shall not apply if the donee's transfer (as defined in section 148) is made on or after 18th March 1986.

26. In section 199 (liability for tax etc. on dispositions by transferor) for subsection (2) there shall be substituted the following subsection—

"(2) Subsection (1)(*a*) above shall apply in relation to—

(*a*) the tax on the value transferred by a potentially exempt transfer; and

(*b*) so much of the tax on the value transferred by any other chargeable transfer made within seven years of the transferor's death as exceeds what it would have been had the transferor died more than seven years after the transfer,

with the substitution for the reference to the transferor of a reference to his personal representatives."

27. In section 201 (liability for tax in respect of settled property), in subsection (2) for the words "three years", in each place where they occur, there shall be substituted "seven years".

28.—(1) In section 204 (limitation of liability), subsection (4) shall be omitted.

(2) In subsection (6)(*a*) of that section, after the word "transferor" there shall be inserted "or personal representative of the transferor".

(3) For subsection (7) of that section there shall be substituted the following subsections—

"(7) Where the tax exceeds what it would have been had the transferor died more than seven years after the transfer, subsection (6) above shall not apply in relation to the excess.

(8) A person liable by virtue of section 199(2) above for any tax as personal representative of the transferor shall be liable only to the extent that either—

(*a*) in consequence of subsections (2), (3) and (5) above, no person falling within paragraphs (*b*) to (*d*) of section 199(1) above is liable for the tax, or

(*b*) the tax remains unpaid twelve months after the end of the month in which the death of the transferor occurs,

and, subject to that, shall be liable only to the extent of the assets mentioned in subsection (1) above.

(9) Where by virtue of subsection (3) of section 102 of the Finance Act 1986 the estate of a deceased person is treated as including property which would not apart from that subsection form part of his estate, a person shall be liable under section 200(1)(*a*) above as personal representative for tax attributable to the value of that property only if the tax remains unpaid twelve months after the end of the month in which the death occurs and, subject to that, only to the extent of the assets mentioned in subsection (1) above."

29.—(1) In section 216 (delivery of accounts) in subsection (1) after paragraph (*b*) there shall be inserted the following paragraphs—

"(*bb*) is liable under section 199(1)(*b*) above for tax on the value transferred by a potentially exempt transfer which proves to be a chargeable transfer, or would be so liable if tax were chargeable on that value, or

(*bc*) is liable under section 200(1)(*c*) above for tax on the value transferred by a chargeable transfer made on death, so far as the tax is attributable to the value of property which, apart from section 102(3) of the Finance Act 1986, would not form part of the deceased's estate, or would be so liable if tax were chargeable on the value transferred on the death, or".

(2) In subsection (3) of that section after the words "his death" there shall be inserted "other than property which would not, apart from section 102(3) of the Finance Act 1986, form part of his estate".

(3) In subsection (6) of that section after paragraph (*a*) there shall be inserted the following paragraphs—

"(*aa*) in the case of an account to be delivered by a person within subsection (1)(*bb*) above, before the expiration of the period of twelve months from the end of the month in which the death of the transferor occurs;

(*ab*) in the case of an account to be delivered by a person within subsection (1)(*bc*) above, before the expiration of the period of twelve months from the end of the month in which the death occurs".

30.—(1) In section 226 (payment: general rules), in subsection (3) for the words "three years", in each place where they occur, there shall be substituted "seven years".

(2) After subsection (3) of that subsection there shall be inserted the following subsections—

"(3A) Without prejudice to subsection (3) above, the tax chargeable on the value transferred by a potentially exempt transfer which proves to be a chargeable transfer shall be due six months after the end of the month in which the transferor's death occurs.

(3B) So much (if any) of the tax chargeable on the value transferred by a chargeable transfer made under Chapter III of Part III of this Act within the period of seven years ending with the settlor's death as exceeds what it would have been had the settlor died more than seven years after the date of the transfer shall be due six months after the end of the month in which the death occurs."

31.—(1) In section 227 (payment by instalments) after subsection (1) there shall be inserted the following subsections—

"(1A) Subsection (1) above does not apply to tax payable on the value transferred by a potentially exempt transfer which proves to be a chargeable transfer, except to the extent that the tax is attributable to qualifying property which is owned by the transferee immediately before the death of the transferor (or, if earlier, his own death).

(1B) In subsection (1A) above "the transferee" means the person whose property the qualifying property became on the transfer or, where on the transfer the qualifying property became comprised in a settlement in which no qualifying interest in possession (within the meaning of Chapter III of Part III of this Act) subsists, the trustees of the settlement."

(2) In subsection (5) of that section after the words "subsection (1)(*b*) above" there shall be inserted "other than a case within subsection (1A) above where the transferee dies before the transferor".

32. In section 233 (interest on unpaid tax) in subsection (2) for paragraphs (*a*) and (*b*) there shall be substituted—

"(*a*) if the chargeable transfer was made on death or is a potentially exempt transfer, 9 per cent;

(*b*) in any other case, 11 per cent;"

33.—(1) In section 236 (application of section 233 in special cases etc.), in subsection (1)(*a*), for the words "three years" in each place where they occur, there shall be substituted "seven years".

(2) After subsection (1) of that section there shall be inserted the following subsection—

"(1A) Section 233 above shall apply in relation to the amount (if any) by which—

(*a*) the tax chargeable on the value transferred by a chargeable transfer made under Chapter III of Part III of this Act within the period of seven years ending with the settlor's death,

exceeds

(*b*) what that tax would have been had the settlor died more than seven years after the date of the transfer,

as if the chargeable transfer had been made on the death of the settlor."

34. In section 237 (imposition of charge) after subsection (3) there shall be inserted the following subsection—

"(3A) In the case of a potentially exempt transfer which proves to be a chargeable transfer—

(*a*) property concerned, or an interest in property concerned, which has been disposed of to a purchaser before the transferor's death is not subject to the Inland Revenue charge, but

(*b*) property concerned which has been otherwise disposed of before the death and property which at the death represents any property or interest falling within paragraph (*a*) above shall be subject to the charge;

and in this subsection "property concerned" means property to the value of which the value transferred by the transfer is wholly or partly attributable."

35. In section 239 (certificates of discharge) after subsection (2) there shall be inserted the following subsection—

"(2A) An application under subsection (1) or (2) above with respect to tax which is or may become chargeable on the value transferred by a potentially exempt transfer may not be made before the expiration of two years from the death of the transferor (except where the Board think fit to entertain the application at an earlier time after the death)."

36. For Schedule 1 (rates of tax), there shall be substituted—

"SCHEDULE 1

TABLE OF RATES OF TAX

Portion of value		*Rate of Tax*
Lower limit	*Upper limit*	*Per cent*
£	£	
0	71,000	Nil
71,000	95,000	30
95,000	129,000	35
129,000	164,000	40
164,000	206,000	45
206,000	257,000	50
257,000	317,000	55
317,000	—	60".

37.—(1) In Schedule 2 (provisions applying on reduction of tax),—

(*a*) for the word "new Tables", wherever occurring, there shall be substituted "a new Table"; and

(*b*) for the words "the Tables" wherever occurring, there shall be substituted "the Table".

(2) In paragraph (1)(*b*) of that Schedule for the word "come" there shall be substituted "comes".

(3) After paragraph 1 of that Schedule there shall be inserted the following paragraph—

"Death within seven years of potentially exempt transfer

1A. Where a person who has made a potentially exempt transfer before a reduction dies after that reduction (or after that and one or more subsequent reductions) and within the period of seven years beginning with the date of the transfer, tax shall be chargeable by reason of the transfer proving to be a chargeable transfer only if, and to the extent that, it would have been so chargeable if the Table in Schedule 1 as substituted by that reduction (or by the most recent of those reductions) had applied to that transfer."

(4) In paragraph 2 of that Schedule,—

(*a*) for the words "three years", wherever occurring, there shall be substituted "seven years"; and

(*b*) after the words "chargeable transfer" there shall be inserted "(other than a potentially exempt transfer)"; and

(*c*) the words "the first of" shall be omitted.

(5) In paragraph 3 of that Schedule, the words "the second of" shall be omitted.

(6) In paragraph 4 of that Schedule, the words "the first of" shall be omitted.

38.—(1) In Schedule 4 (maintenance funds for historic buildings etc.) in paragraph 14 (rate of charge) in sub-paragraphs (1) to (3), for the words "under the appropriate Table", wherever occurring, there shall be substituted "in accordance with the appropriate provision of section 7 of this Act".

(2) After sub-paragraph (1) of that paragraph there shall be inserted the following sub-paragraph—

"(1A) The rate or rates of tax determined under sub-paragraph (1) above in respect of any occasion shall not be affected by the death of the settlor after that occasion."

(3) In sub-paragraph (6) of that paragraph for the words "ten years there shall be substituted "seven years".

(4) For sub-paragraph (9) of that paragraph there shall be substituted the following sub-paragraph—

"(9) For the purposes of sub-paragraph (1) above the appropriate provision of section 7 of this Act is subsection (2), and for the purposes of sub-paragraphs (2) and (3) above it is (if the settlement was made on death) subsection (1) and (if not) subsection (2)."

39. In Schedule 6 (transition from estate duty) in paragraph 4(3) after the words "sections 33(7)" there shall be inserted the words "and (8)."

PART II

TRANSITIONAL PROVISIONS

40.—(1) Notwithstanding that Part I of this Schedule has effect with respect to events occurring on or after 18th March 1986, where a death or other event occurs on or after that date, nothing in that Part shall affect the tax chargeable on a transfer of value occurring before that date.

(2) Sub-paragraph (1) above does not authorise the making of a claim under section 149 of the 1984 Act where the donee's transfer, as defined in section 148 of that Act, occurs on or after 18th March 1986.

41. Where tax is chargeable under section 32 or section 32A of the 1984 Act by reason of a chargeable event occurring on or after 18th March 1986 and the rate or rates at which it is charged fall to be determined under the provisions of section 33(1)(*b*)(ii) of the 1984 Act by reference to a death which occurred before that date, those provisions shall apply (subject to paragraph 5 of Schedule 2 to that Act) as if the amendments of section 7 of, and Schedule 1 to, that Act contained in Part I of this Schedule had been in force at the time of the death.

42. Where tax is chargeable under paragraph 8 of Schedule 4 to the 1984 Act on any occasion on or after 18th March 1986 and the rate at which it is charged falls to be determined under paragraph 14 of that Schedule by reference to a death which occurred before that date, that paragraph shall apply (subject to paragraph 6 of Schedule 2 to the 1984 Act) as if the amendments of section 7 of, and Schedule 1 to, the 1984 Act contained in Part I of this Schedule had been in force at the time of the death.

43.—(1) This paragraph applies if, in the case of a settlement,—

(*a*) tax is charged under section 65 of the 1984 Act on an occasion falling on or after 18th March 1986; and

(*b*) the rate at which tax is so charged falls to be determined under section 69 of that Act (rate between ten-year anniversaries) by reference to the rate (in this paragraph referred to as "the last ten-year rate") at which tax was last charged under section 64 of that Act (or would have been charged apart from section 66(2) thereof); and

(*c*) the most recent ten-year anniversary fell before 18th March 1986.

(2) For the purpose of determining the rate at which tax is charged on the occasion referred to in sub-paragraph (1)(*a*) above, it shall be assumed that the last ten-year rate was what that rate would have been if, immediately before the ten-year anniversary referred to in sub-paragraph (1)(*c*) above, the amendments of sections 66 and 67 of the 1984 Act contained in Part I of this Schedule had been in force.

(3) Where this paragraph applies, paragraph 3 of Schedule 2 to the 1984 Act shall have effect as if—

(*a*) references to a reduction included references to a reduction by the substitution of a new Table in Schedule 1 to the 1984 Act; and

(*b*) in relation to a reduction resulting from the substitution of such a new Table, the reference to the second of the Tables in Schedule 1 to the 1984 Act were a reference to a Table in which the rates of tax were one-half of those specified in the new Table.

(4) In this paragraph "ten-year anniversary" has the same meaning as in Chapter III of Part III of the 1984 Act.

44. In relation to a death on or after 18th March 1986, paragraph 2 of Schedule 2 to the 1984 Act (provisions applying on reduction of tax) shall have effect, in a case where the chargeable transfer in question was made before 18th March 1986, as if—

(*a*) references to a reduction included references to a reduction by the substitution of a new Table in Schedule 1 to the 1984 Act; and

(*b*) the Table in Schedule 1 to the Act was the first Table in that Schedule.

45. In relation to a disposal of trees or underwood on or after 18th March 1986, paragraph 4 of Schedule 2 to the 1984 Act shall have effect, in a case where the death in question occurred before 18th March 1986, as mentioned in paragraphs (*a*) and (*b*) of paragraph 44 above.

46. Notwithstanding anything in section 3A of the 1984 Act, a transfer of value which is made on or after 1st July 1986 and which, by virtue of subsection (4) of section 49 of the Finance Act 1975 (transitional provision relating to estate duty deferment in respect of timber etc.), brings to an end the period during which estate duty is payable on the net moneys received from the sale of timber etc. is not a potentially exempt transfer.

General Note

Part I contains consequential amendments to the 1984 Act resulting from the restructuring of the tax. Some are of a fairly minor textual character. Paras. 4, 11 and 36 relate to the elimination of the Second Table; events other than death occasioning a charge will continue to attract half the rate on death. Paras. 16, 17 and 18 relate to the reduction in the cumulation period from 10 years to 7 years. Paras 23, 26 to 30 and 33 relate to the extension from 3 years to 7 years of the period during which an inter vivos gift may attract a charge on death (albeit now with taper relief). The main points of interest in the other paragraphs are noted below.

Para. 1 introduces the most important new definition for the purposes of I.H.T., that of the potentially exempt transfer ("PET"). The transfer in question must be by an individual either to another individual or into a trust for the disabled under section 89 of the 1984 Act or an accumulation and maintenance trust under section 71 of the Act. Where the individual making the gift survives for seven years, the transfer becomes exempt and in the interim it is assumed to be exempt.

It will therefore now be possible for an individual to pass on his assets to his descendants, whether of full age or minors, without charge to tax assuming he survives seven years.

Para. 2(4) introduces the tapering charge for gifts between three and seven years before death. The structure means that deaths between three and five years after a transfer could occasion a heavier charge than at present. At the lowest rate, the two taxes compare as follows:

Years before death	*C.T.T.*	*I.H.T.*
1–3	30	30
4	15	24 (30 × 80)
5	15	18 (30 × 60)
6	15	12 (30 × 40)
7	15	6 (30 × 20)
8 and earlier	15	Nil

Para. 3 applies the indexation provision to give inter vivos transfers which become chargeable the benefit of any higher thresholds applicable on death.

Para. 5. Unused annual exemptions may be utilised to frank potentially exempt transfers which become chargeable.

Paras. 6 to 10 amend the parts of the 1984 Act which deal with conditional exemption for heritage property and maintenance funds supporting such property. If a PET proves to be a chargeable transfer, it will be possible to make a conditional exemption claim at the time of death.

Para. 13. Debts and incumbrances caught under section 103 are to be treated as specific gifts for the purposes of section 38.

Para. 14 excludes from relief as a potentially exempt transfer the avoidance device whereby short term interests in settlements were created and sold for sums in excess of their real value.

Para. 15 similarly excludes such devices involving the acquisition of a reversionary interest by a beneficiary.

Para. 20 similarly excludes deemed transfers made by participators in close companies by way of alteration of share capital or the rights attaching to shares.

Para. 21 applies where a potentially exempt transfer is made which would be entitled to business property relief. The relief will be denied on the subsequent death of the donor within seven years unless the conditions for the relief have continued to be satisfied but will not be lost on disposal of the property provided similarly qualifying property is acquired within twelve months.

Para. 22 provides similarly in relation to agricultural property relief.

Para. 24. A gift with reservation is denied relief by way of deed of family arrangement.

Para. 25 abolishes the relief for mutual transfers.

Para. 31. The instalment option available in respect of land, shares in controlled companies and business assets is retained in respect of a potentially exempt transfer which becomes chargeable provided the property concerned has been retained by the transferee at the time of the death. Interest on such a transfer does not run until the relevant death.

Para. 32. Under section 233 of the 1984 Act, as amended by S.I. 1985/560, interest on unpaid tax arising from a chargeable transfer made on death was fixed at 9 per cent., and on other occasions at 11 per cent. This is continued for the I.H.T. regime, with PETs being given the benefit of the rate on death.

Para. 34. The Inland Revenue charge which attaches under section 237 of the 1984 Act to property which is the subject of a chargeable transfer is extended under the same conditions to a PET, unless it has been disposed of to a purchaser prior to the death of the transferor.

Para. 35. A certificate of discharge under section 239(2) of the 1984 Act may not be applied for in relation to a PET until two years after the death of the transferor.

Para. 37. Where a PET is made and there is a subsequent reduction in tax, the tax chargeable on a subsequent death will be relieved in accordance with that reduction.

Part II contains transitional provisions preserving charges which relate to events under the C.T.T. regime prior to the introduction of I.H.T.

Para. 40. A death after March 17, 1986 will still have any effect provided for under the previous legislation in relation to events before that date.

Para. 43. Similarly, the periodic charge on discretionary settlements is carried forward, mutatis mutandis, to the new regime.

Paras. 44 and 45 are drafting amendments consequential on the abolition of the Second Table in Schedule 1 of the 1984 Act.

Para. 46 extends for I.H.T. purposes a transitional provision applying for C.T.T. on disposals of timber where E.D. had been deferred.

Section 102

SCHEDULE 20

Gifts With Reservation

Interpretation and application

1.—(1) In this Schedule—

"the material date", in relation to any property means, in the case of property falling within subsection (3) of the principal section, the date of the donor's death and, in the case of property falling within subsection (4) of that section, the date on which the property ceases to be property subject to a reservation;

"the principal section" means section 102 of this Act; and

"property subject to a reservation" has the same meaning as in the principal section.

(2) Any reference in this Schedule to a disposal by way of gift is a reference to such a disposal which is made on or after 18th March 1986.

(3) This Schedule has effect for the purposes of the principal section and the 1984 Act.

Substitutions and accretions

2.—(1) Where there is a disposal by way of gift and, at any time before the material date, the donee ceases to have the possession and enjoyment of any of the property comprised in the gift, then on and after that time the principal section and the following provisions of this Schedule shall apply as if the property, if any, received by the donee in substitution for that property had been comprised in the gift instead of that property (but in addition to any other property comprised in the gift).

(2) This paragraph does not apply if the property disposed of by the gift—

(*a*) becomes settled property by virtue of the gift; or

(*b*) is a sum of money in sterling or any other currency.

(3) In sub-paragraph (1) above the reference to property received by the donee in substitution for property comprised in the gift includes in particular—

(*a*) in relation to property sold, exchanged or otherwise disposed of by the donee, any benefit received by him by way of consideration for the sale, exchange or other disposition; and

(*b*) in relation to a debt or security, any benefit received by the donee in or towards the satisfaction or redemption thereof; and

(*c*) in relation to any right to acquire property, any property acquired in pursuance of that right.

(4) Where, at a time before the material date, the donee makes a gift of property comprised in the gift to him, or otherwise voluntarily divests himself of any such property otherwise than for a consideration in money or money's worth not less than the value of the property at that time, then, unless he does so in favour of the donor, he shall be treated for the purposes of the principal section and sub-paragraph (1) above as continuing to have the possession and enjoyment of that property.

(5) For the purposes of sub-paragraph (4) above—

(*a*) a disposition made by the donee by agreement shall not be deemed to be made voluntarily if it is made to any authority who, when the agreement is made, is authorised by, or is or can be authorised under, any enactment to acquire the property compulsorily; and

(*b*) a donee shall be treated as divesting himself, voluntarily and without consideration, of any interest in property which merges or is extinguished in another interest held or acquired by him in the same property.

(6) Where any shares in or debentures of a body corporate are comprised in a gift and the donee is, as the holder of those shares or debentures, issued with shares in or debentures of the same or any other body corporate, or granted any right to acquire any such shares or debentures, then, unless the issue or grant is made by way of exchange for the first-mentioned shares or debentures, the shares or debentures so issued, or the right granted, shall be treated for the purposes of the principal section and this Schedule as having been comprised in the gift in addition to any other property so comprised.

(7) In sub-paragraph (6) above the reference to an issue being made or right being granted to the donee as the holder of shares or debentures shall be taken to include any case in which an issue or grant is made to him as having been the holder of those shares or debentures, or is made to him in pursuance of an offer or invitation made to him as being or having been the holder of those shares or debentures, or of an offer or invitation in connection with which any preference is given to him as being or having been the holder thereof.

3.—(1) Where either sub-paragraph (3)(*c*) or sub-paragraph (6) of paragraph 2 above applies to determine, for the purposes of the principal section, the property comprised in a gift made by a donor—

(*a*) the value of any consideration in money or money's worth given by the donee for the acquisition in pursuance of the right referred to in the said sub-paragraph (3)(*c*) or for the issue or grant referred to in the said sub-paragraph (6), as the case may be, shall be allowed as a deduction in valuing the property, comprised in the gift at any time after the consideration is given, but

(*b*) if any part (not being a sum of money) of that consideration consists of property comprised in the same or another gift from the donor and treated for the purposes of the 1984 Act as forming part of the donor's estate immediately before his death or as being attributable to the value transferred by a potentially exempt transfer made by him, no deduction shall be made in respect of it under this sub-paragraph.

(2) For the purposes of sub-paragraph (1) above, there shall be left out of account so much (if any) of the consideration for any shares in or debentures of a body corporate, or for the grant of any right to be issued with any such shares or debentures, as consists in the capitalisation of reserves of that body corporate, or in the retenion by that body corporate, by way of set-off or otherwise, of any property distributable by it, or is otherwise provided directly or indirectly out of the assets or at the expense of that or any associated body corporate.

(3) For the purposes of sub-paragraph (2) above, two bodies corporate shall be deemed to be associated if one has control of the other or if another person has control of both.

Donee predeceasing the material date

4. Where there is a disposal by way of gift and the donee dies before the date which is the material date in relation to any property comprised in the gift, paragraphs 2 and 3 above shall apply as if—

(*a*) he had not died and the acts of his personal representatives were his acts; and

(*b*) property taken by any person under his testamentary dispositions or his intestacy (or partial intestacy) were taken under a gift made by him at the time of his death.

Settled gifts

5.—(1) Where there is a disposal by way of gift and the property comprised in the gift becomes settled property by virtue of the gift, paragraphs 2 to 4 above shall not apply but, subject to the following provisions of this paragraph, the principal section and the following provisions of this Schedule shall apply as if the property comprised in the gift consisted of the property comprised in the settlement on the material date, except in so far as that property neither is, nor represents, nor is derived from, property originally comprised in the gift.

(2) If the settlement comes to an end at some time before the material date as respects all or any of the property which, if the donor had died immediately before that time, would be treated as comprised in the gift,—

(*a*) the property in question, other than property to which the donor then becomes absolutely and beneficially entitled in possession, and (*b*) any consideration (not consisting of rights under the settlement) given by the donor for any of the property to which he so becomes entitled,

shall be treated as comprised in the gift (in addition to any other property so comprised).

(3) Where property comprised in a gift does not become settled property by virtue of the gift, but is before the material date settled by the donee, sub-paragraphs (1) and (2) above shall apply in relation to property comprised in the settlement as if the settlement had been made by the gift; and for this purpose property which becomes settled property under any testamentary disposition of the donee or on his intestacy (or partial intestacy) shall be treated as settled by him.

(4) Where property comprised in a gift becomes settled property either by virtue of the gift or as mentioned in sub-paragraph (3) above, any property which—

(*a*) on the material date is comprised in the settlement, and

(*b*) is derived, directly or indirectly, from a loan made by the donor to the trustees of the settlement,

shall be treated for the purposes of sub-paragraph (1) above as derived from property originally comprised in the gift.

(5) Where, under any trust or power relating to settled property, income arising from that property after the material date is accumulated, the accumulations shall not be treated for the purposes of sub-paragraph (1) above as derived from that property.

Exclusion of benefit

6.—(1) In determining whether any property which is disposed of by way of gift is enjoyed to the entire exclusion, or virtually to the entire exclusion, of the donor and of any benefit to him by contract or otherwise—

(*a*) in the case of property which is an interest in land or a chattel, retention or assumption by the donor of actual occupation of the land or actual enjoyment of an incorporeal right over the land, or actual possession of the chattel shall be disregarded if it is for full consideration in money or money's worth;

(*b*) in the case of property which is an interest in land, any occupation by the donor of the whole or any part of the land shall be disregarded if—

(i) it results from a change in the circumstances of the donor since the time of the gift, being a change which was unforeseen at that time and was not brought about by the donor to receive the benefit of this provision; and

(ii) it occurs at a time when the donor has become unable to maintain himself through old age, infirmity or otherwise; and

(iii) it represents a reasonable provision by the donee for the care and maintenance of the donor; and

(iv) the donee is a relative of the donor or his spouse;

(*c*) a benefit which the donor obtained by virtue of any associated operations (as defined in section 268 of the 1984 Act) of which the disposal by way of gift is one shall be treated as a benefit to him by contract or otherwise.

(2) Any question whether any property comprised in a gift was at any time enjoyed to the entire exclusion, or virtually to the entire exclusion, of the donor and of any benefit to him shall (so far as that question depends upon the identity of the property) be determined by reference to the property which is at that time treated as property comprised in the gift.

(3) In the application of this paragraph to Scotland, references to a chattel shall be construed as references to a corporeal moveable.

7.—(1) Where arrangements are entered into under which—

(*a*) there is a disposal by way of gift which consists of or includes, or is made in connection with, a policy of insurance on the life of the donor or his spouse or on their joint lives, and

(*b*) the benefits which will or may accrue to the donee as a result of the gift vary by reference to benefits accruing to the donor or his spouse (or both of them) under that policy or under another policy (whether issued before, at the same time as or after that referred to in paragraph (*a*) above),

the property comprised in the gift shall be treated for the purposes of the principal section as not enjoyed to the entire exclusion, or virtually to the entire exclusion, of the donor.

(2) In sub-paragraph (1) above—

(*a*) the reference in paragraph (*a*) to a policy on the joint lives of the donor and his spouse includes a reference to a policy on their joint lives and on the life of the survivor; and

(*b*) the reference in paragraph (*b*) to benefits accruing to the donor or his spouse (or both of them) includes a reference to benefits which accrue by virtue of the exercise of rights conferred on either or both of them.

Agricultural property and business property

8.—(1) Where there is a disposal by way of gift of property which, in relation to the donor, is at that time—

(*a*) relevant business property within the meaning of Chapter I of Part V of the 1984 Act, or

(*b*) agricultural property, within the meaning of Chapter II of that Part, to which section 116 of that Act applies, or

(*c*) shares or securities to which section 122(1) of that Act applies (agricultural property of companies),

and that property is property subject to a reservation, then, subject to the following provisions of this paragraph, any question whether, on the material transfer of value, relief is available by virtue of Chapter I or Chapter II of Part V of the 1984 Act and, if so, what is the appropriate percentage for the relief shall be determined as if, so far as it is attributable to the property comprised in the gift, that transfer were a transfer of value by the donee.

(2) For the purpose only of determining whether, on the transfer of value which, by virtue of sub-paragraph (1) above, the donee is assumed to make, the requirement of section 106 or, as the case may be, section 117 of the 1984 Act (minimum period of ownership or occupation) is fulfilled,—

(*a*) ownership by the donor prior to the disposal by way of gift shall be treated as ownership by the donee; and

(*b*) occupation by the donor prior to the disposal and any occupation by him after that disposal shall be treated as occupation by the donee.

(3) Where the property disposed of by the gift consists of shares or securities falling within paragraph (*c*) of sub-paragraph (1) above, that sub-paragraph shall not apply unless—

(*a*) section 116 of the 1984 Act applied in relation to the value transferred by the disposal, and

(*b*) throughout the period beginning with the disposal and ending on the material date, the shares or securities are owned by the donee,

and for the purpose only of determining whether, on the transfer of value which, by virtue of sub-paragraph (1) above, the donee is assumed to make, the requirements of subsection (1) of section 123 of the 1984 Act are fulfilled, it shall be assumed that the requirement in paragraph (*b*) of that subsection (as to the ownership of the shares or securities) is fulfilled.

(4) In this paragraph, "the material transfer of value" means, as the case may require,—

(*a*) the transfer of value under section 4 of the 1984 Act on the death of the donor; or

(*b*) the transfer of value under subsection (4) of the principal section on the property concerned ceasing to be subject to a reservation.

(5) If the donee dies before the material transfer of value, then, as respects any time after his death, any reference in the preceding provisions of this paragraph to the donee shall be construed as a reference to his personal representatives or, as the case may require, the person (if any) by whom the property, shares or securities concerned were taken under a testamentary disposition made by the donee or under his intestacy (or partial intestacy).

General Note

The Schedule amplifies section 102, which treats a gift made with a reservation of interest for the donor as part of the donor's estate.

Para. 1 ties the Schedule in to section 102 and the 1984 Act.

Para. 2 traces the value of a gift made with reservation into property substituted for an original gift and into accretions to the gift *e.g.*, rights or bonus issues.

Para. 3 allows a deduction for any consideration given in respect of an accretion under para. 2 *e.g.*, payments for shares issued as rights.

Para. 4 substitutes where necessary a donee's personal representatives in the event of his death.

Para. 5 applies the foregoing provisions to property which becomes comprised in a settlement.

Para. 6 contains two useful reliefs from the application of section 102. Under sub-para. 1(*a*) retention by the donor of an interest in land or a chattel is disregarded if full consideration is given. Under sub-paragraph (1)(*b*) a donor may occupy land if this is the result of an unforeseen change in circumstances arising from the donor becoming unable to maintain himself and the occupation is a reasonable provision by a donee who is a relative for his care and maintenance.

Accordingly, a donor may reside in a house which he has given away without incurring the penalties of section 102 provided he pays a market rent or he becomes unable to maintain himself and the occupation is a reasonable provision for him by his family.

Para. 7 is designed to block a possible loophole through the use of insurance policies on the joint lives of the donor and his spouse.

Section 109

SCHEDULE 21

Modifications of Finance Act 1982, Schedule 18 in Relation to Elections Under Section 109 of this Act

General modifications

1.—(1) For any reference in the 1982 Schedule to ethane there shall be substituted a reference to light gases, as defined in section 109 of this Act.

(2) Except as provided below, any reference in the 1982 Schedule to section 134 of the Finance Act 1982 shall be construed as a reference to section 109 of this Act.

Specific modifications

2.—(1) In paragraph 1 (provisions as to the election), in sub-paragraph (2)(*b*) for the words "and not exceeding fifteen years" there shall be substituted "or in the case of an election made before 31st December 1986, beginning on 1st July 1986" and for sub-paragraph (2)(*d*) there shall be substituted—

"(*d*) specify the purposes for which the light gases to which the election applies will be applied or used,".

(2) At the end of that paragraph there shall be inserted the following sub-paragraph—

"(4) If an election relates to light gases, then, in addition to the matters referred to in sub-paragraph (2) above, the election shall contain—

(*a*) a description of the characteristics of the supply by which the disposal or appropriation is intended to be effected; and

(*b*) if that supply is of such a description that, if it were under a contract at arm's length, it is reasonable to expect that the price of the gas would vary with the level of the supply, a description of the pattern of supply which the party or parties to the election consider most probable."

3.—(1) In paragraph 2 (conditions for acceptance of an election) in sub-paragraph (1) after the words "and (3)" there shall be inserted "and paragraph 2A".

(2) In sub-paragraph (2) of that paragraph, after the words "such that" there shall be inserted "subject to paragraphs 2A and 3A below".

4. After paragraph 2 there shall be inserted the following paragraph—

"2A.—(1) The provisions of this paragraph apply if, having regard to the pattern of supply described in an election as mentioned in paragraph 1(4)(*b*) above, it is reasonable to assume that, under a contract for the sale at arm's length of the light gases to which the election applies, the consideration would include—

(*a*) any such payments as are referred to in subsection (2) of section 114 of the Finance Act 1984 ("take or pay" payments), or

(*b*) any capacity payments, as defined in subsection (5) of that section.

(2) The relevant contract—

(*a*) shall be assumed to be for the delivery of gas according to the pattern of supply described in the election; and

(*b*) shall be assumed to contain provision for such of the payments referred to in sub-paragraph (1) above as are appropriate to that pattern of supply.

(3) Sub-paragraph (1) of paragraph 2 above shall have effect as if for the words following "sale at arm's length" there were substituted "of the light gases to which the election applies, the total sums payable under the contract in respect of deliveries of gas in any chargeable period would not differ materially from the sums determined in accordance with the price formula specified in the election for gases disposed of or appropriated in that period; and if the Board are not so satisfied they shall reject the election".

(4) The price formula specifed in the election shall contain provisions for determining sums corresponding to such of the payments referred to in sub-paragraph (1) above as, by virtue of sub-paragraph (2) above, are assumed to be provided for by the relevant contract."

5.—(1) In paragraph 3 (definition of "the relevant contract") in paragraph (*a*) after the word "and", in the first place where it occurs, there shall be inserted the words "which, subject to sub-paragraph (3) below" and in the words following paragraph (*b*) for the words from "is not" onwards, there shall be substituted "which, subject to paragraph 2A(2) above, is not necessarily a contract for the sale of light gases for the purposes specified in the election".

(2) At the end of that paragraph there shall be added the following sub-paragraphs—

"(3) In the case of an election which relates to light gases which are "excluded oil", as defined in section 10(1) of the principal Act, sub-paragraph (1)(*a*) above shall have effect with the omission of the words from "and which" to "date of the election".

(4) Sub-paragraph (4) of paragraph 2A of Schedule 3 to the principal Act (assumptions as to consents in determining price under an arm's length contract) shall apply for the purposes of paragraphs 2 and 2A above as it applies for the purposes of paragraph 2 of that Schedule, substituting a reference to a relevant contract (as defined above) for any reference to the contract mentioned in paragraph 2(2) of that Schedule."

6.—After paragraph 3 there shall be inserted the following paragraph—

"Market value where paragraph 2A applies

3A.—(1) Where an election is accepted by the Board and the price formula contains provision for the determination of sums as mentioned in paragraph 2A(4) above, then, for the purpose of determining the market value of gas to which the election applies, section 114 of the Finance Act 1984 (which deals with the treatment of such payments as are referred to in paragraph 2A(1) above) shall have effect in relation to those sums and that gas as if—

(*a*) those sums were part of the consideration under a contract for the sale of gas to which the election applies, and

(*b*) that contract provided for delivery of the gas according to the pattern of supply described in the election,

and where the said section 114 has effect by virtue of this sub-paragraph, subsections (4), (6) and (7) of that section (which provide for and relate to the deemed delivery of one tonne of oil in certain periods) shall be treated for the purposes of the principal Act as providing for and relating to the deemed disposal or appropriation of one tonne of gas to which the election applies.

(2) Where sub-paragraph (1) above applies, the market value of the gas to which the election applies which is disposed of or appropriated in any chargeable period shall consist of—

(*a*) such amount (if any) as is determined in accordance with the price formula by reference to the quantity of gas disposed of or appropriated in that chargeable period; and

(*b*) any sums which, by virtue of sub-paragraph (1) above, either are treated as payments for gas supplied free of charge in that period or are treated as an additional element of the price received or receivable for gas disposed of or appropriated in that period.

(3) Where the market value of gas is determined as mentioned in sub-paragraph (2) above, any reference in the following provisions of this Schedule (however expressed) to the market value determined in accordance with the price formula is a reference to that value determined as mentioned in that sub-paragraph (that is to say, in accordance with the formula and section 114 of the Finance Act 1984 as applied by sub-paragraph (1) above).

(4) Where the market value of light gases to which an election applies is determined for a chargeable period as mentioned in sub-paragraph (2) above then, as respects a return for that period under paragraph 2 of Schedule 2 to the principal Act which is made by the participator who is the party or one of the parties to the election,—

(*a*) sub-paragraphs (2)(*a*)(iii) and (2)(*b*)(ii) of that paragraph (which require information with respect to each delivery or relevant appropriation of oil in the period) shall not apply in relation to the light gases to which the election applies; and

(*b*) there shall be included in his return a statement of the market value (determined as mentioned in sub-paragraph (2) above) of the light gases relevantly appropriated or disposed of by him in that period.

(5) Notwithstanding that, under sub-paragraph (2) above, a market value is determined for all the gas disposed of or appropriated in a particular chargeable period, for the purposes of determining—

(*a*) the market value referred to in section 2(5)(*d*) of the principal Act (stocks at the end of a period), and

(*b*) the market value referred to in subsection (1) or, as the case may be, subsection (2) of section 14 of that Act (valuation for corporation tax purposes of oil disposed of or appropriated),

then, except in a case where the only gas disposed of or appropriated in a particular chargeable period is a single tonne which, by virtue of sub-paragraph (1) above, is treated as being disposed of or appropriated, the market value determined as mentioned in sub-paragraph (2) above shall be apportioned rateably to each quantity of gas disposed of or appropriated in that period."

7. After paragraph 6 there shall be inserted the following paragraph—

"Price formula no longer appropriate for pattern of supply, etc.

6A.—(1) In any case where it appears to the Board—

(*a*) that light gases to which an election applies are being disposed of or appropriated in a manner, to an extent or by a pattern of supply which is different from that which was taken into consideration in the acceptance of the election, and

(*b*) that if, at the time the Board were considering whether the election should be accepted, they had taken into account as a probability the manner, extent or pattern of supply by which the gases are in fact being disposed of, they would have rejected the election,

then, subject to sub-paragraph (4) below, the election shall not have effect with respect to any chargeable period begining after the date on which the Board give notice under this paragraph to each of the parties to the election.

(2) Without prejudice to the generality of sub-paragraph (1) above, if at any time in a chargeable period the extent to which gases to which an election applies are disposed of or relevantly appropriated (including the case where none is so disposed of or appropriated) is such that, if the gas were being delivered under a contract at arm's length,—

(*a*) the seller would be likely to incur financial penalties by reason of a failure to meet requirements arising from the pattern of supply described in the election, and

(*b*) those penalties would not be insubstantial,

that shall be a ground for the Board to give notice under this paragraph.

(3) A notice under this paragraph shall state that, by reason of the matters referred to in sub-paragraph (1) above, the Board are no longer satisfied that the price formula specified in the election is appropriate to the disposals or appropriations actually being made of gases to which the election applies.

(4) If within the period of three months beginning on the date of a notice under this paragraph, the party or parties to the election give notice in writing to the Board—

(*a*) specifying a new price formula taking account of the manner, extent or pattern of supply by which the gases to which the election applies are being disposed of or appropriated, and

(*b*) containing, if appropriate, a description of the changed pattern of supply which, at the time of the notice, the party or parties to the election consider most probable,

then, if that new price formula is accepted by the Board in accordance with paragraph 7 below, so much of sub-paragraph (1) above as provides that the election shall not have effect with respect to certain periods shall not apply.

(5) If notice has been given under sub-paragraph (4) above and a new price formula has been accepted as mentioned in that sub-paragraph, then, for the purpose of determining, for any chargeable period beginning after the date on which the Board gave notice as mentioned in sub-paragraph (1) above, the market value of light gases to which the election applies, section 109 of the Finance Act 1986 shall have effect as if the new price formula were the forumula specified in the election."

8.—(1) In paragraph 7 (acceptance or rejection of new price formula) in sub-paragraph (2) after the words "paragraph 3" there shall be inserted "and, where appropriate, paragraphs 2A and 3A"; and at the end of paragraph (*b*) of that sub-paragraph there shall be inserted "or

(*c*) a new price formula specified in a notice under paragraph 6A(4) above";

and for the words from "were specified" onwards there shall be substituted "had been specified in, and at the time of, the election and as if the circumstances giving rise to the new price formula had been in contemplation at that time".

(2) In sub-paragraph (5) of that paragraph, after "6(5)(*b*)" there shall be inserted "or paragraph 6A(4)".

9.—(1) In paragraph 8 (appeals) in sub-paragraph (1) after paragraph (*d*) there shall be inserted the following paragraph—

"(*dd*) under paragraph 6A above, that a price formula is no longer appropriate".

(2) In sub-paragraph (4)(*b*) of that paragraph after "6(1)(*b*)" there shall be inserted "or paragraph 6A".

10. In paragraph 9 (returns)—

(*a*) after "6(1)(*b*)" there shall be inserted "or paragraph 6A"; and

(*b*) for the words "section 134(3) of this Act" there shall be substituted "section 109(4) of the Finance Act 1986"; and

(*c*) in paragraph (*b*) after "6" there shall be inserted "or paragraph 6A".

11.—(1) In paragraph 11 (interpretation) sub-paragraph (1) shall be omitted.

(2) In sub-paragraph (2) of that paragraph the words from "to an election" to "and any reference" shall be omitted.

(3) In sub-paragraph (4) of that paragraph for the words "section 134(2)(*a*) of this Act" there shall be substituted "section 109(3)(*a*) of the Finance Act 1986".

General Note

Sched. 18 to the Finance Act 1982, which contained administrative provisions in relation to the alternative valuation of ethane used for petrochemical purposes under s.134 of that Act, is applied to the similar system for light gases such as methane transferred between associated companies.

Section 111

SCHEDULE 22

Broadcasting: Additional Payments By Programme Contractors

Part I

Amendment of Broadcasting Act 1981

1.—(1) Section 32 of the Broadcasting Act 1981 (rental payments by programme contractors) shall be amended as follows.

(2) The following Table shall be substituted for the Table in subsection (4)—

"TABLE

RATES OF ADDITIONAL PAYMENTS

	Rate for determining amount of additional payments
First category profits	
For so much of the first category profits for the accounting period as does not exceed the free slice for those profits.	Nil.
For so much of the first category profits for the accounting period as exceeds the free slice for those profits.	The first category rate.
Second category profits	
For so much of the second category profits for the accounting period as does not exceed the free slice for those profits.	Nil.
For so much of the second category profits for the accounting period as exceeds the free slice for those profits.	The second category rate."

(3) After subsection (4) there shall be inserted the following subsection—

"(4A) For the purposes of this section—

"first category profits" and "second category profits" shall be determined in accordance with the provisions of Schedule 4 to this Act;

"first category rate" means—

(*a*) in relation to additional payments payable by virtue of subsection (1)(*b*)—

(i) nil, in the case of persons who are DBS programme contractors or DBS teletext contractors; and

(ii) 45 per cent, in any other case; and

(*b*) in relation to additional payments payable by virtue of subsection (2)(*b*), nil;

"free slice" means—

(*a*) in relation to first category profits, £800,000 or 2·8 per cent. of the advertising receipts for the accounting period (whichever is the greater); and

(*b*) in relation to second category profits, the amount (if any) by which the free slice in relation to first category profits exceeds the first category profits for the accounting perod; and

"second category rate" means—

(*a*) in relation to additional payments payable by virtue of subsection (1)(*b*)—

(i) nil, in the case of persons who are DBS programme contractors or DBS teletext contractors; and

(ii) 22·5 per cent. in any other case; and

(*b*) in relation to additional payments payable by virtue of subsection (2)(*b*), nil."

(4) In subsection (5) for the words from "sum", where it first occurs, to "above" there shall be substituted the words "relevant sum mentioned in subsection (4A)".

(5) In subsection (8) for the words "subsections (4)" there shall be substituted the words "any of the provisions of subsections (4), (4A)".

(6) In subsection (9)—

(*a*) the words "to amend subsections (4) and (5)" shall be omitted;

(*b*) for the words "those subsections", where they first occur, there shall be substituted the words "the provisions in question";

(*c*) for the words "those subsections", where they next occur, there shall be substituted the words "those provisions"; and

(*d*) for paragraph (c) there shall be substituted the following paragraphs—

"(*c*) only in their application in relation to first category profits of all, or specified, kinds;

(*d*) only in their application in relation to second category profits of all, or specified, kinds; or

(*e*) differently in their application as mentioned in paragraphs (*a*) to (*d*) respectively".

2.—(1) Section 34 of the Act of 1981 (instalments payable on account by programme contractors in respect of additional payments) shall be amended as follows.

(2) In subsection (2)(*b*) the words from "when the" to the end shall be omitted.

(3) For subsection (3) there shall be substituted the following subsection—

"(3) Where any amount falls to be paid to a programme contractor to adjust any overpayment made by him, that amount shall be paid to him—

(*a*) if the contract is for the supply of programmes to be broadcast for reception in areas or localities all of which are in Great Britain, out of the Consolidated Fund of the United Kingdom;

(*b*) if the contract is for the supply of programmes to be broadcast for reception in areas or localities all of which are in Northern Ireland, out of the Consolidated Fund of Northern Ireland; and

(*c*) if the contract is one which falls within subsection (2) of section 33, out of each of those Funds, apportioned in the same way as receipts are apportioned under subsection (3)(*c*) of that section."

3.—(1) Section 35 of the Act of 1981 (provision for supplementing additional payments) shall be amended as follows.

(2) In paragraph (*a*) of subsection (1) the words "or is" shall be inserted after the word "is", where it last occurs.

(3) For paragraph (*b*) of that subsection there shall be substituted the following paragraph—

"(*b*) the deficiency is, or would be, wholly or mainly attributable to either or both of the following—

(i) excessive expenditure forming part of the expenditure by reference to which those additional payments fall to be calculated;

(ii) in the case of second category profits, the receipt of consideration for the provision of any programme which is less than that which the contractor would have received had the transaction in question been in all repects at arm's length."

(4) In subsection (4), for the words "the accounting period to which it relates" there shall be substituted the words "the period of six months beginning with the date on which the programme contractor furnishes to the Authority, in accordance with the terms of his contract as a programme contractor, a copy of his audited accounts for the accounting period to which the order relates".

(5) After subsection (2) there shall be inserted the following subsection—

"(2A) In determining, for the purposes of subsection (1) of this section, whether in the case of a programme contractor any consideration received by him for the provision of any programme is less than that which the contractor would have received had the transaction in question been in all respects at arm's length, the Authority or the Secretary of State, as the case may be, shall have regard to such matters as they or he may consider relevant, and in particular to any available information as to—

(*a*) the consideration received for the provision by the contractor of the programme in other comparable markets;

(*b*) the consideration received by that or any other programme contractor for the provision of other comparable programmes in the same market."

4. For paragraph 2 of Schedule 4 to the Act of 1981 there shall be substituted the following paragraphs—

"2. A programme contractor's first category profits for an accounting period shall be ascertained in accordance with paragraph 2A and his second category profits for that accounting period shall be ascertained in accordance with paragraph 2B.

First category profits

2A.—(1) First category profits shall consist of the excess of relevant first category income over relevant first category expenditure.

(2) In this Schedule "relevant first category income" means—

(*a*) in relation to any programme contractor other than a DBS programme contractor or DBS teletext contractor, any income of his which is attributable to the provision by him of any programme for broadcasting on ITV, the Fourth Channel or a local sound broadcasting service (whether that programme is provided in the first place to the Authority or to any other person); and

(*b*) in relation to any DBS programme contractor or DBS teletext contractor, any income of his which is attributable to the provision by him to the Authority, in accordance with the terms of his contract as a DBS programme contractor or (as the case may be) DBS teletext contractor, of any programme for broadcasting in the Authority's DBS service to which his contract with the Authority relates.

(3) Without prejudice to the generality of sub-paragraph (2), "relevant first category income" includes—

(*a*) advertising receipts;

(*b*) income attributable directly or indirectly to any publication whose content (other than advertising) is wholly, or mainly, connected with programme schedules and scheduled programmes; and

(*c*) such part of any income which—

(i) accrues to any subsidiary of the programme contractor concerned; and

(ii) would be relevant first category income of that contractor if he and the subsidiary were a single programme contractor;

as, in the opinion of the Authority, should be attributed to the contractor as reflecting his financial interest in the subsidiary.

(4) In this Schedule "relevant first category expenditure" means any expenditure of the programme contractor concerned which is properly chargeable to revenue account and which is incurred in connection with the provision by him of—

(*a*) programmes of a kind mentioned in sub-paragraph (2)(*a*), in the case of a contractor who is not a DBS programme contractor or DBS teletext contractor; or (*b*) programmes of a kind mentioned in sub-paragraph (2)(*b*), in the case of a DBS programme contractor or DBS teletext contractor.

(5) Without prejudice to the generality of sub-paragraph (4), "relevant first category expenditure" includes—

(*a*) expenditure in connection with the sale or rights to insert advertisements in programmes;

(*b*) expenditure in connection with any publication whose content (other than advertising) is wholly, or mainly, connected with programme schedules and scheduled programmes;

(*c*) such part of any expenditure which—

(i) is incurred by any subsidiary of the programme contractor concerned; and

(ii) would be relevant first category expenditure of that contractor if he and the subsidiary were a single programme contractor;

as, in the opinion of the Authority, should be attributed to the contractor as reflecting his financial interest in the subsidiary; and

(*d*) in the case of a DBS programme contractor or DBS teletext contractor, any expenditure incurred by him in connection with the provision of the satellite transponder.

(6) In ascertaining relevant first category income or relevant first category expenditure no account shall be taken of interest on any loan.

(7) Where relevant first category income consists of advertising receipts, it shall be attributed to accounting periods in accordance with the foregoing provisions of this Schedule and the same principle shall be followed in relating other items of relevant first category income, and items of relevant first category expenditure, to accounting periods.

(8) In this paragraph "programme" means—

(*a*) in the application of this Schedule in relation to the additional payments mentioned in section 32(1)(*b*), a television programme; and

(*b*) in its application in relation to the additional payments mentioned in section 32(2)(*b*), a local sound broadcast.

Second category profits

2B.—(1) Second category profits shall consist of the excess of relevant second category income over relevant second category expenditure.

(2) In this Schedule "relevant second category income" means any income of the programme contractor concerned which is not relevant first category income but which accrues to him in connection (directly or indirectly) with the provision by him, for broadcasting, distribution or showing (whether or not within the United Kingdom)—

(*a*) in the case of a programme contractor other than a DBS programme contractor or DBS teletext contractor, of any programme provided by him for broadcasting on ITV, the Fourth Channel or a local sound broadcasting service, or intended by him to be so provided; or

(*b*) in the case of DBS programme contractor or DBS teletext contractor, of any programme broadcast in the Authority's DBS service to which his contract with the Authority relates, or intended to be so broadcast.

(3) Without prejudice to the generality of sub-paragraph (2), "relevant second category income" includes any income which—

(*a*) accrues to any person connected with the programme contractor concerned; and

(*b*) would be relevant second category income of that contractor if he and that person were a single programme contractor.

(4) In this Schedule "relevant second category expenditure" means any expenditure properly chargeable to revenue account which is not relevant first category expenditure but which is incurred by the programme contractor concerned in connection (directly or indirectly) with the provision by him of any programme of a kind mentioned in sub-paragraph (2)(*a*) or (as the case may be) (*b*) above.

(5) Without prejudice to the generality of sub-paragraph (4) above, "relevant second category expenditure" includes any expenditure which—

(*a*) is incurred by any person connected with the programme contractor concerned; and

(*b*) would be relevant second category expenditure of that contractor if he and that person were a single programme contractor.

(6) In ascertaining relevant second category income or relevant second category expenditure no account shall be taken of interest on any loan.

(7) Items of relevant second category income and items of relevant second category

expenditure shall be attributed to accounting periods in accordance with the foregoing provisions of this Schedule.

(8) In this paragraph "programme" means—

(*a*) in the application of this Schedule in relation to the additional payments mentioned in section 32(1)(*b*), a television programme; and

(*b*) in its application in relation to the additional payments mentioned in section 32(2)(*b*), a local sound broadcast.

Carry forward of certain losses

2C.—(1) Where, in any accounting period, the relevant first category expenditure of a programme contractor exceeds his relevant first category income sub-paragraph (3) shall apply.

(2) Where, in any accounting period, the relevant second category expenditure of a programme contractor exceeds his relevant second category income sub-paragraph (4) shall apply.

(3) Where this sub-paragraph applies—

(*a*) the excess shall, if the programme contractor has any relevant second category profits for the accounting period, be set against relevant second category income for that period as if the excess were relevant second category expenditure; and

(*b*) if any part of the excess then remains it shall be carried forward to the following accounting period and treated as relevant first category expenditure for that period.

(4) Where this sub-paragraph applies—

(*a*) the excess shall, if the programme contractor has any relevant first category profits for the accounting period, be set against relevant first category income for that period as if the excess were relevant first category expenditure; and

(*b*) if any part of the excess then remains it shall be carried forward to the following accounting period and treated as relevant second category expenditure for that period.

(5) When a programme contractor's contract with the Authority comes to an end, no losses incurred at any time during the currency of the contract may be carried forward under this paragraph and set against income attributable to any subsequent contract between him and the Authority."

5. In paragraph 3 of Schedule 4 to the Act of 1981—

(*a*) in sub-paragraph (1)(*a*), for the words "relevant income and relevant expenditure" there shall be substituted the words "income and expenditure of any category" and for the words "the profits" there shall be substituted the words "relevant category of profits"; and

(*b*) in sub-paragraph (1)(*b*), for the words "the profits" there shall be substituted the words "any category of profits".

6. In paragraph 4(1) of Schedule 4 to the Act of 1981, after the word "profits", in paragraph (*b*) there shall be inserted—

"or

(*bb*) the category in which any profits fall,".

7. In paragraph 7 of Schedule 4 to the Act of 1981, the following sub-paragraph shall be inserted after sub-paragraph (1)—

"(1A) Without prejudice to the generality of sub-paragraph (1) above, the duty imposed on the Authority by that sub-paragraph includes the duty to impose, so far as is reasonably practicable, such requirements as will enable the Authority to determine the amounts (if any) which, in relation to any programme contractor, are to be treated as relevant second category income and relevant secondary category expenditure by virtue, respectively, of sub-paragraphs (3) and (5) of paragraph 2B."

8.—(1) Paragraph 9 of Schedule 4 to the Act of 1981 shall be amended as follows.

(2) In sub-paragraph (1), the following shall be substituted for the definition of subsidiary—

"subsidiary", in relation to any person, means a company in which that person (whether alone or jointly with one or more persons and whether directly or through one or more nominees) holds, or is beneficially entitled to, 10 per cent. or more of the equity share capital, or possesses 10 per cent. or more of the voting power".

(3) The following sub-paragraphs shall be added at the end—

"(3) For the purposes of this Schedule a person shall be taken to be connected with a programme contractor—

(*a*) if he is a subsidiary of the contractor;

(*b*) where the contractor is a company, if he is a person who (whether alone or jointly with one or more persons and whether directly or through one or more nominees) holds, or is beneficially entitled to, 10 per cent. or more of the equity share capital, or possesses 10 per cent. or more of the voting power; or

(*c*) where any other person is connected with the contractor concerned by virtue of paragraph (*b*) above, if he is a company in which that other person (whether alone or jointly with one or more persons and whether directly or through one or more nominees) holds, or is beneficially entitled to, 10 per cent. or more of the equity share capital, or possesses 10 per cent. or more of the voting power;

but does not include any person whose trade consists wholly or mainly of the distribution of programmes by wireless telegraphy or cable.

(4) Where the same person falls within more than one category of programme contractor, the definitions of "first category rate" and "second category rate" in section 32(4A) shall not have the effect of applying the lower or lowest rate in respect of all of his first category profits or (as the case may be) all of his second category profits but, subject to section 32(6), those profits shall be apportioned, and the provisions of this Act applied, in such manner as the Authority consider appropriate with a view to securing that the overall amount payable by him by way of additional payments is, as near as may be, equal to the aggregate of the amounts which would be so payable if there were as many separate programme contractors as there are categories of programme contractor within which he falls."

Part II

Transitional Provisions

9.—(1) In this paragraph—

"new statutory provisions" means the provisions of the Broadcasting Act 1981 as amended by this Act; and

"existing statutory provisions" means the provisions of that Act as they had effect immediately before the passing of this Act.

(2) Any contract between the Authority and a programme contractor which is in force immediately before the passing of this Act shall, until it is varied or superseded by a further contract between them or expires or is otherwise terminated (whichever first occurs) be deemed to be modified by virtue of this Schedule so as—

(*a*) to substitute provisions in conformity with the new statutory provisions for so much of the contract as is in accordance with the existing statutory provisions and is not in conformity with the new statutory provisions, and

(*b*) to incorporate in the contract such additional provisions as a contract between the Authority and a programme contractor is required to include in accordance with the new statutory provisions;

and (subject to paragraph 4 of Schedule 4 to the Act of 1981) any provisions of the contract which provide for arbitration as to any matters contained in the contract in accordance with the existing statutory provisions shall be construed as making the like provision for arbitration in relation to matters deemed to be included in the contract by virtue of this sub-paragraph.

(3) Where it appears to the Authority that the new statutory provisions call for the inclusion of additional terms in any such contract, but do not afford sufficient particulars of what those terms should be, the Authority may, after consulting the programme contractor, decide what those terms are to be.

(4) This paragraph shall not be taken to have effect in relation to any contract entered into by a programme contractor and any person other than the Authority before the passing of this Act.

10.—(1) This paragraph applies in relation to any accounting period of a programme contractor which begins before 1st April 1986 and ends after 31st March 1986 ("the accounting period").

(2) The aditional payments payable by the programme contractor under section 32 of the Act of 1981 in relation to his profits for the accounting period shall be the aggregate of the following amounts—

(*a*) the amount payable by him on the assumption—

(i) that section 111 of this Act was not in force at any time during the accounting period; and

(ii) that his profits for the accounting period were reduced by multiplying them by $\frac{X}{X + Y}$; and

(*b*) the amount payable by him on the assumption that that section was in force throughout the accounting period and that both his first category profits for that period and his second category profits for that period were reduced by multiplying them

by $\frac{Y}{X + Y}$

where (taking any odd four days or more as a week)

X is the number of weeks in the accounting period falling before 1st April 1986; and

Y is the number of weeks in the accounting period falling after 31st March 1986.

(3) For the purposes of the application of paragraph 2C of Schedule 4 to the Act of 1981 in relation to losses incurred by the programme contractor during the accounting period, those losses shall be reduced by multiplying them

by $\frac{Y}{X + Y}$

where X and Y have the same meaning as in sub-paragraph (2) above.

General Note

This Schedule contains material not generally found in a Finance Act. It is designed to implement the recommendations of a working party studying the structure of the levy on Independent Television Contractors' profits. The purpose of the changes is to improve the incentive to cost efficiency by reducing the high marginal tax burden on profits from the provision of programmes in the U.K., while maintaining revenue by bringing overseas profits into charge to levy.

Para. 1 implements a reduction in the levy on first category profits, from the provision of programmes for ITV or Channel 4, from 66·7 per cent. to 45 per cent. and introduces a charge of 22·5 per cent. on second category profits, broadly from overseas business. The free slice of profits is increased from £650,000 to £800,000 in line with inflation since 1982.

Para. 2 enables refunds of overpayments of levy to be made during the accounting period in which the overpayment was made.

Para. 3 limits the Home Secretary's power to set a minimum levy liability by restricting it to a six-month period but extends it to cover cases where a contractor's overseas profits are deficient through transfer pricing.

Para. 4 contains definitions and also allows the carry forward of losses in either category after set off against losses in the other category but not into a new contract period.

Paras. 5 to 10 contain other mainly consequential amendments and transitional provisions.

Section 114

SCHEDULE 23

Repeals

Part I

Customs and Excise: Miscellaneous

Chapter	Short title	Extent of repeal
1979 c.4	The Alcoholic Liquor Duties Act 1979.	In section 15, subsections (6A) and (6B), in subsection (7) the words "restriction or requirement" and in subsection (8) the words "restriction or requirement". In section 46(2), the word "accidentally".
1981 c.35.	The Finance Act 1981.	In Schedule 8, paragraphs 2(*b*) and 14(*b*)
1985 c.54.	The Finance Act 1985.	Section 2.

Part II

Vehicles Excise Duty

Chapter	Short title	Extent of repeal
1971 c.10.	The Vehicles (Excise) Act 1971.	In section 23(*f*), the words from "and as" to "replacement". In paragraph 13 of Part I of Schedule 7, in the text of section 17(2) as modified, paragraph (*a*) and, in paragraph (*b*), the words from the beginning to "class". In paragraph 20 of Part I of Schedule 7, in the text of section 23 as modified, in subsection (1)(*e*) the words from "and for" to "book".
1972 c.10 (N.I.).	The Vehicles (Excise) Act (Northern Ireland) 1972.	In section 23(*f*) the words from "and as" to "replacement". In paragraph 13 of Part I of Schedule 9, in the text of section 17(2) as modified, paragraph (*a*) and, in paragraph (*b*), the words from the beginning to "class". In paragraph 20 of Part I of Schedule 9, in the text of section 23 as modified, in subsection (1)(*e*) the words from "and for" to "book".

The repeals in paragraph 13 of Part I of Schedule 7 to the Vehicles (Excise) Act 1971 and paragraph 13 of Part I of Schedule 9 to the Vehicles (Excise) Act (Northern Ireland) 1972 do not have effect with respect to the surrender of licences taken out before 1st January 1987.

Part III

Betting and Gaming Duties

Chapter or Number	Short title	Extent of repeal
1972 c.11 (N.I.)	The Miscellaneous Transferred Excise Duties Act (Northern Ireland) 1972.	Part III. In section 72(2), the words from the beginning to "Schedule 2". Schedules 1 and 2.
1974 c.30.	The Finance Act 1974.	Section 2(2) (as it remains in force in relation to Northern Ireland).
1981 c.63.	The Betting and Gaming Duties Act 1981.	In section 9(3)(*a*), the words "Northern Ireland or" and the words "of the Parliament of Northern Ireland or, as the case may be,". In section 12(4), the words from "and 'betting office licence'" to the end. In section 19(2) the words "Northern Ireland or" and the words "the Parliament of Northern Ireland or, as the case may be,". In section 20(2), the definition of "Great Britain". Section 35(4).
1985 c.54.	The Finance Act 1985.	In Schedule 5, paragraph 8.
S.I. 1985/1204 (N.I. 11).	The Betting, Gaming, Lotteries and Amusements (Northern Ireland) Order 1985.	In Schedule 19, paragraphs 11 to 15 and 17.

These repeals—

(*a*) so far as they relate to general betting duty or pool betting duty, come into force on the betting commencement date (as defined in section 6 of this Act), but do not affect duty in respect of bets made before that date; and

(*b*) so far as they relate to bingo duty, come into force on the bingo commencement date (as so defined).

Part IV

Licences Under the Customs and Excise Acts

Chapter	Short title	Extent of repeal
1979 c.4.	The Alcoholic Liquor Duties Act 1979.	In section 4(3), in the Table, the words "licence year". Section 12(2) and (3). Section 18(3) and (4). In section 25(1)(*b*), the words "has in his possession or". Section 47(3) and (4). Section 48(2) and (3). Section 54(3). Section 55(3). In section 56(1)(*a*), the word "renewal". Section 75(3) and (4). Section 81. Section 83.
1979 c.6.	The Matches and Mechanical Lighters Duties Act 1979.	Section 2(2) and (3).

Part V

Income Tax and Corporation Tax: General

Chapter	Short title	Extent of repeal
1970 c.10.	The Income and Corporation Taxes Act 1970.	In section 457(1A), the words from "and does not" to the end. In Schedule 8, paragraph 12.
1972 c.41.	The Finance Act 1972.	In section 100(6), the words from "if the limit" to "the relevant income and". Section 103(1) to (3). Section 107(3).
1974 c.30.	The Finance Act 1974.	Section 22(2). Section 37(2).
1977 c.36.	The Finance Act 1977.	In section 32(6), paragraph (*b*), and in paragraph (*c*) the words "or (*b*)".
1980 c.48.	The Finance Act 1980.	In Schedule 10, paragraphs 2 and 22.
1983 c.28.	The Finance Act 1983.	In Schedule 5, paragraph 5(8) to (11) and paragraph 7(3).
1984 c.43.	The Finance Act 1984.	Section 20(1) and (2).
1985 c.54.	The Finance Act 1985.	Section 49.

1. The repeal in section 457(1A) of the Income and Corporation Taxes Act 1970 and the repeal of section 49 of the Finance Act 1985 have effect for the year 1986–87 and subsequent years of assessment.

2. Subject to section 45(4) of this Act, the repeal in Schedule 8 to the Income and Corporation Taxes Act 1970 does not have effect with respect to any payment which, under section 187(4) of that Act, is treated as income received before 4th June 1986.

3. The repeal in section 100(6) of the Finance Act 1972 has effect with respect to accounting periods beginning on or after 3rd June 1986.

4. The repeal of section 107(3) of the Finance Act 1972 has effect where a company ceases to carry on a trade, or part of a trade, after 18th March 1986, subject to the application of section 42(3) of this Act with the words "the repeal does not" substituted for "those amendments do not".

5. The repeal of section 22(2) of the Finance Act 1974 has effect for the year 1986–87 and subsequent years of assessment.

6. The repeals in section 32(6) of the Finance Act 1977 have effect for the year 1984–85 and subsequent years of assessment.

7. The repeals in Schedule 5 to the Finance Act 1983 have effect in relation to shares issued at any time after 18th March 1986.

8. The repeals in section 20 of the Finance Act 1984 do not have effect with respect to any financial year ending before 1st April 1986.

Part VI

Income Tax and Corporation Tax: Capital Allowances

Chapter	Short title	Extent of repeal
1968 c.3	The Capital Allowances Act 1968.	Sections 51 to 66. Section 68. In section 70(3), the words from "and, in the case of" to "direct". Section 74(6). In section 75(1), the word "61,". Section 78(3). In section 79(4), the words "and section 65(1)". In section 83(1), the words "or section 56". In section 85(1)(*c*), the words "other than section 60". Schedules 5 and 6. In Schedule 7, paragraph 4(2)(*c*).
1971 c.68.	The Finance Act 1971.	Section 52.
1973 c.51.	The Finance Act 1973.	Section 31(6)(*c*).
1978 c.42.	The Finance Act 1978.	Section 39.
1985 c.54.	The Finance Act 1985.	Section 62.

1. The repeals of sections 68 and 74(6) of the Capital Allowances Act 1968 and section 39 of the Finance Act 1978 do not have effect with respect to expenditure incurred before 1st April 1986 nor with respect to expenditure under existing contracts, as defined in section 56(2) of this Act.

2. The remaining repeals, apart from the repeal of section 62 of the Finance Act 1985, have effect subject to the provisions of Schedule 14 to this Act.

Part VII

Capital Gains

Chapter	Short title	Extent of repeal
1984 c.43.	The Finance Act 1984.	In Schedule 13, paragraphs 2 and 3.
1985 c.54.	The Finance Act 1985.	Section 67(1).

These repeals have effect with respect to disposals on or after 2nd July 1986.

Part VIII

Securities

Chapter	Short title	Extent of repeal
1970 c.10.	The Income and Corporation Taxes Act 1970.	Section 475(6).
1985 c.54.	The Finance Act 1985.	In Schedule 23, paragraphs 41 and 42.

These repeals have effect in accordance with paragraphs 1(5) and 2(2) of Schedule 18 to this Act.

Part IX

Stamp Duty

(1) Reconstructions etc.

Chapter	Short title	Extent of repeal
1927 c.10.	The Finance Act 1927.	Section 55.
1928 c.17.	The Finance Act 1928.	Section 31.
1928 c.9 (N.I.).	The Finance Act (Northern Ireland) 1928.	Section 4.
1936 c.23 (N.I.).	The Finance (Companies' Stamp Duty) Act (Northern Ireland) 1936.	Section 1.
1980 c.48.	The Finance Act 1980.	In Schedule 18, paragraph 12(1) and (1A).
1985 c.54.	The Finance Act 1985.	Sections 78, 79 and 80.
1986 c.41.	The Finance Act 1986.	Section 73.

(2) Loan Capital

Chapter	Short title	Extent of repeal
1963 c.25.	The Finance Act 1963.	In section 62, subsections (2) and (6).
1963 c.22 (N.I.).	The Finance Act (Northern Ireland) 1963.	In section 11, subsections (2) and (5).
1967 c.54.	The Finance Act 1967.	Section 29.
1967 c.20 (N.I.).	The Finance Act (Northern Ireland) 1967.	Section 6.
1974 c.30.	The Finance Act 1974.	In Schedule 11, paragraphs 5 and 15. In Schedule 12, paragraphs 7 and 8.
1976 c.40.	The Finance Act 1976.	Section 126.
1980 c.48.	The Finance Act 1980.	Section 96.
1981 c.35.	The Finance Act 1981.	Section 109.

(3) Bearer Letters of Allotment etc.

Chapter	Short title	Extent of repeal
1891 c.39.	The Stamp Act 1891.	In Schedule 1, in the heading "Bearer Instrument", paragraph 2 of the exemptions.

(4) Changes in Financial Institutions

Chapter or Number	Short title	Extent of repeal
1920 c.18.	The Finance Act 1920.	Section 42.
1961 c.36.	The Finance Act 1961.	Section 34.
1961 c.10 (N.I.).	The Finance Act (Northern Ireland) 1961.	Section 4.
1973 c.51.	The Finance Act 1973.	In Schedule 21, paragraphs 1 and 3.
S.I. 1973/1323 (N.I. 18).	The Finance (Miscellaneous Provisions) (Northern Ireland) Order 1973.	In Schedule 3, paragraphs 1 and 3.
1976 c.40.	The Finance Act 1976.	In section 127, in subsection (1) the words "which is executed for the purposes of a stock exchange transaction", subsections (2) and (3), in subsection (5) the definitions of "jobber" and "stock exchange transaction", and in subsection (7) the words "and this section".
1980 c.48.	The Finance Act 1980.	Section 100.

1. The repeals under (1) above have effect in relation to any instrument executed in pursuance of a contract made on or after the day on which the rule of The Stock Exchange that prohibits a person from carrying on business as both a broker and a jobber is abolished.

2. The repeals under (2) above have effect in relation to any instrument to which section 79 of this Act applies.

3. The repeals under (4) above have effect as provided by the Treasury by order made by statutory instrument, and different provision may be made for different repeals.

Part X

Inheritance Tax

Chapter	Short title	Extent of repeal
1984 c.51.	The Capital Transfer Tax Act 1984.	In section 7(1)(*a*), the word "appropriate". Sections 148 and 149. In section 167(2), the words from "and shall not" to the end. Section 204(4). In section 236(3), the words "149". In Schedule 2, in paragraphs 2 and 4, the words "the first of", in paragraph 3 the words "the second of ", and paragraph 7.

1. The repeals of sections 148 and 149 of the Capital Transfer Tax Act 1984 and in sections 167 and 236 of, and Schedule 2 to, that Act have effect where the donee's transfer was made on or after 18th March 1986.

2. The remaining repeals have effect with respect to transfers of value made, and other events occurring, on or after 18th March 1986.

Part XI

Broadcasting: Additional Payments by Programme Contractors

Chapter	Short title	Extent of repeal
1981 c.68.	The Broadcasting Act 1981.	In section 32(9), the words "to amend subsections (4) and (5)". In section 34(2)(*b*), the words from "when the" to the end. In section 35(2)(*a*) and (*b*), the word "relevant".
1984 c.46.	The Cable and Broadcasting Act 1984.	Section 40(3).

These repeals shall be deemed to have come into force on 1st April 1986.

APPROPRIATION ACT 1986

(1986 c.42)

An Act to apply a sum out of the Consolidated Fund to the service of the year ending on 31st March 1987, to appropriate the supplies granted in this Session of Parliament, and to repeal certain Consolidated Fund and Appropriation Acts. [25th July 1986]

Grant out of the Consolidated Fund

Issue out of the Consolidated Fund for the year ending 31st March 1987

1. The Treasury may issue out of the Consolidated Fund of the United Kingdom and apply towards making good the supply granted to Her Majesty for the service of the year ending on 31st March 1987 the sum of £57,303,511,000.

Appropriation of Grants

Appropriation of sums voted for supply services

2. All sums granted by this Act and the other Acts mentioned in Schedule (A) annexed to this Act out of the said Consolidated Fund towards making good the supply granted to Her Majesty amounting, as appears by the said schedule, in the aggregate, to the sum of £103,250,242,146·89 are appropriated, and shall be deemed to have been appropriated as from the date of the passing of the Acts mentioned in the said Schedule (A), for the services and purposes expressed in Schedule (B) annexed hereto.

The abstract of schedules and schedules annexed hereto, with the notes (if any) to such schedules, shall be deemed to be part of this Act in the same manner as if they had been contained in the body thereof.

In addition to the said sums granted out of the Consolidated Fund, there may be applied out of any money directed, under section 2 of the Public Accounts and Charges Act 1891, to be applied as appropriations in aid of the grants for the services and purposes specified in Schedule (B) annexed hereto the sums respectively set forth in the last column of the said schedule.

Repeals

3. The enactments mentioned in Schedule (C) annexed to this Act are hereby repealed.

Short title

4. This Act may be cited as the Appropriation Act 1986.

ABSTRACT

OF

SCHEDULES (A) and (B) to which this Act refers

Section 2 SCHEDULE (A)

Grants out of the Consolidated Fund ... ... £103,250,242,146·89

Section 2 SCHEDULE (B).—Appropriation of Grants

	Supply Grants	Appropriations in Aid
1984–85 and 1985–86	£	£
Part 1. Defence and Civil (Excesses), 1984–85 -	155,484,146·89	25,311,454·23
Part 2. Supplementary, 1985–86 - - - - -	2,654,435,000·00	32,946,000·00
	£2,809,919,146·89	58,257,454·23

	Supply Grants	Appropriations in Aid
1986–87	£	£
Part 3. Class I - - - - - - - -	18,485,883,000·00	1,820,216,000·00
Part 4. Class II - - - - - - - -	1,856,167,000·00	148,557,000·00
Part 5. Class III - - - - - - -	930,000,000·00	—
Part 6. Class IV - - - - - - -	931,997,000·00	299,962,000·00
Part 7. Class V - - - - - - - -	1,996,668,000·00	978,189,000·00
Part 8. Class VI - - - - - - -	1,438,576,000·00	515,653,000·00
Part 9. Class VII - - - - - - -	3,274,504,000·00	576,408,000·00
Part 10. Class VIII - - - - - - -	2,674,621,000·00	148,902,000·00
Part 11. Class IX - - - - - - -	1,915,888,000·00	35,276,000·00
Part 12. Class X - - - - - - - -	10,124,895,000·00	19,862,000·00
Part 13. Class XI - - - - - - -	4,438,989,000·00	226,744,000·00
Part 14. Class XII - - - - - - -	3,299,216,000·00	1,119,427,000·00
Part 15. Class XIII - - - - - - -	283,427,000·00	356,000·00
Part 16. Class XIV - - - - - - -	13,158,493,000·00	3,049,465,000·00
Part 17. Class XV - - - - - - -	22,540,948,000·00	769,619,000·00
Part 18. Class XVI - - - - - - -	5,480,280,000·00	520,361,000·00
Part 19. Class XVII - - - - - - -	2,392,040,000·00	128,554,000·00
Part 20. Class XVIII - - - - - - -	1,449,366,000·00	3,921,000·00
Part 21. Class XIX - - - - - - -	1,991,844,000·00	320,975,000·00
Part 22. Class XX - - - - - - -	1,731,681,000·00	1,235,514,000·00
Part 23. Class XXA - - - - - - -	21,001,000·00	175,000·00
Part 24. Class XXB - - - - - - -	23,839,000·00	4,189,000·00
Total - - - - - - - - - £	100,440,323,000·00	11,922,325,000·00
Grand Total - - - - - - - £	103,250,242,146·89	11,980,582,454·23

SCHEDULE (A)

GRANTS OUT OF THE CONSOLIDATED FUND

	£
For the service of the year ended 31st March 1985—	
Under Act 1986 c.4	155,484,146·89
For the service of the year ended 31st March 1986—	
Under Act 1985 c.74	1,622,416,000·00
Under Act 1986 c.4	1,032,019,000·00
For the service of the year ending on 31st March 1987—	
Under Act 1985 c.74	43,136,812,000·00
Under this Act	57,303,511,000·00
TOTAL	£103,250,242,146·89

SCHEDULE (B)—PART 1

Defence and Civil (Excesses) 1984–85

DEFENCE AND CIVIL (EXCESSES), 1984–85

SUMS granted, and sums which may be applied as appropriations in aid in addition thereto, to make good excesses on certain grants for Defence and Civil Services for the year ended 31st March 1985, viz.:—

	Supply Grants	Surplus receipts available to be applied as Appropriations in Aid
	£	£
Vote		
CLASS I		
1. DEFENCE: PAY, ETC., OF THE ARMED FORCES AND CIVILIANS, STORES, SUPPLIES AND MISCELLANEOUS SERVICES - - - - - - - - -	30,150,968·73	—
CLASS IX		
10. LAW CHARGES, SCOTLAND (THE CROWN AGENT) -	106,600·67	17,979·91
CLASS XII		
2. SUPPLEMENTARY BENEFITS - - - - - -	102,034,083·44	25,228,022·74
CLASS XIII		
7. ECONOMIC AND FINANCIAL ADMINISTRATION: LIFE ASSURANCE PREMIUM RELIEF AND MORTGAGE INTEREST RELIEF (INLAND REVENUE) - - -	10,000,000·00	—
CLASS XIV		
1. CIVIL ACCOMMODATION SERVICES (PSA OF THE DEPARTMENT OF THE ENVIRONMENT) - - -	12,222,223·68	—
CLASS XVI		
3. SELECTIVE ASSISTANCE TO INDUSTRY IN WALES -	795,920·96	—
8. ENVIRONMENTAL SERVICES, ETC., AND OTHER HEALTH AND PERSONAL SOCIAL SERVICES, WALES - -	174,349·41	65,451·58
TOTAL, DEFENCE AND CIVIL (EXCESSES) 1984–85 £	155,484,146·89	25,311,454·23

Supplementary, 1985–86 SCHEDULE (B).—PART 9

SUPPLEMENTARY, 1985–86

SCHEDULE OF SUPPLEMENTARY SUMS granted, and of the sums which may be applied as appropriations in aid in addition thereto, to defray the charges for the Services herein particularly mentioned for the year ended 31st March 1986, viz.:—

	Supply Grants	Appropriations in Aid
	£	£
CLASS I		
Vote		
1. For expenditure by the Ministry of Defence on pay, allowances etc., of the Armed Forces and their Reserves and Cadet Forces etc., pay etc., of Defence Ministers and of certain civilian staff employed by the Ministry of Defence; on movements; certain stores; supplies and services; plant and machinery; charter and contract repair of ships; certain research; lands and buildings; sundry grants; payments abroad including contributions and subscriptions to international organisations; and grants in aid - - - -	75,000,000	23,464,000
2. For expenditure by the Procurement Executive of the Ministry of Defence in operating its Headquarters and Establishments and for its other common services; for research etc., by contract; lands and buildings; for development by contract, production, repair etc., and purchases for sale abroad of sea systems, land systems, air systems and associated equipment; for certain contingent liabilities, and for sundry other Procurement Executive services including those on repayment terms to non-exchequer customers - - -	131,937,000	18,735,000
6. For expenditure by the Ministry of Defence in connection with the sale of Government shares in Royal Ordnance plc - - - - - - -	100,000	—
CLASS II		
1. For expenditure by the Foreign and Commonwealth Office on the salaries, building and other accommodation services, and administration of H.M. Diplomatic Service, official information services, military aid, certain grants in aid and sundry other grants, services and loans - - - - - -	5,906,000	7,290,000
2. For expenditure by the Foreign and Commonwealth Office on grants and subscriptions, etc., to certain international organisations, special payments and assistance, and sundry other grants and services	301,000	—
3. For expenditure by the Foreign and Commonwealth Office on grants in aid of the British Broadcasting Corporation for external broadcasting and monitoring services - - - - - - - -	1,000,000	—
4. For expenditure by the Foreign and Commonwealth Office on a grant in aid of the British Council -	1,645,000	—

Vote	Supply Grants	Appropriations in Aid
Class II—*continued*	£	£
7. For expenditure by the Foreign and Commonwealth Office (Overseas Development Administration) on the official United Kingdom Aid Programme including capital subscriptions, other contributions and payments under guarantees to certain multilateral development banks and other bodies; subscriptions and grants in aid to certain international and regional organisations; bilateral capital aid and technical co-operation; refugee and other relief assistance; the cost of in-house Scientific Units; assistance, including grants in aid, to certain UK-based institutions and voluntary agencies; loans to the Commonwealth Development Corporation, and pensions and allowances in respect of overseas service	2,000	1,653,000
9. For payments to the Budget of the European Communities not covered by direct charges on the Consolidated Fund under section 2(3) of the European Communities Act 1972	135,917,000	—
CLASS III		
1. For expenditure by the Intervention Board for Agricultural Produce in giving effect in the United Kingdom to the agricultural support provisions of the Common Agricultural Policy of the European Community and to Community Food Aid measures and for certain other services	214,258,000	83,247,000
2. For expenditure by the Intervention Board for Agricultural Produce on central administration and miscellaneous services	1,468,000	*—*8,000*
3. For expenditure by the Ministry of Agriculture, Fisheries and Food on market regulation and production support, grants and loans for capital and other improvements, support for agriculture in special areas, animal health, land drainage, water supply, flood and coast protection, and certain other services	30,913,000	1,702,000
4. For expenditure by the Ministry of Agriculture, Fisheries and Food on commissioned research and development and advice, education and training services, botanical services, assistance to production, marketing and processing, support for the fishing industry, emergency and strategic food services, protective, agency and other services, including grants in aid and international subscriptions	560,000	66,000
CLASS IV		
1. For expenditure by the Department of Trade and Industry on regional development grants, selective assistance to industry, certain other services including UK contributions to the funding of buffer stock operations of international commodity agreements, a strategic mineral stockpile and the film industry	1,000	—

*Deficit.

Class IV—*continued*	Supply Grants	Appropriations in Aid
Vote	£	£
2. For expenditure by the Department of Trade and Industry on provision of land and buildings, inward investment promotion, other support services, promotion of tourism and standards including grants in aid	384,000	*—*24,000*
3. For expenditure by the Department of Energy on assistance to the coal industry including grants to the National Coal Board and payments to redundant workers - - - - - -	86,003,000	14,000,000
6. For expenditure by the Department of Trade and Industry on the Department's research establishments; industrial research and development and other support; general research and development on civil aeronautics and aeroengines and associated equipment; national and international space technology programmes; standards; loans, grants in aid, international subscriptions, certain other grants and protection of innovation - - -	416,000	—
7. For expenditure by the Department of Trade and Industry on support for the aerospace, shipbuilding and steel industries, including loans, grants and the purchase of assets, and assistance to redundant steel workers - - - - - -	40,810,000	*—*4,000,000*
9. For expenditure by the Export Credits Guarantee Department in connection with export credit guarantees, including an international subscription, special guarantees, refinancing and financing arrangements made for facilitating trade with other countries and assistance towards the cost of financing export credits, the purchase of securities, overseas investment insurance and cost escalation guarantees - - - - - -	61,468,000	*—*227,272,000*
11. For expenditure by the Office of Fair Trading -	800,000	—
12. For expenditure by the Department of Employment on general labour market services including a grant in aid, services for seriously disabled people, the promotion of tourism including grants in aid, and an international subscription - - - -	1,000	18,919,000
13. For expenditure by the Department of Employment on demand determined measures to promote and preserve employment opportunities, compensation for persons disabled by pneumoconiosis, byssinosis and diffuse mesothelioma, payments towards expenses of trade union ballots and compensation to persons for certain dismissals - -	1,000	14,318,000
15. For expenditure by the Department of Employment on a grant in aid to the Manpower Services Commission - - - - - - - -	19,994,000	—
16. For expenditure by the Department of Employment on the administration of benefit services and on central and miscellaneous services - - -	2,325,000	5,551,000

*Deficit.

Class IV—*continued* Vote	Supply Grants £	Appropriations in Aid £
17. For expenditure by the Department of Trade and Industry on central and miscellaneous services, on radio regulatory services, on services provided by the Ministry of Defence (Procurement Executive) Headquarters, on international subscriptions, on British Telecommunications Civil Defence, and on the fund for sub-postmasters	1,000	—
19. For refunds and repayments of petroleum licensing proceeds, and other payments in connection with such proceeds, to be made by the Department of Energy out of income received from application fees; from annual and other payments for exploration, production, mining and methane drainage licences; from royalty; and from the disposal of petroleum taken as royalty in kind	2,000	47,672,000
21. For Government investment in the British Steel Corporation and British Shipbuilders	176,000,000	—
22. For expenditure by the Department of Trade and Industry in connection with the sale of shares in British Telecommunications plc	1,000	6,766,000
25. For expenditure by the Department of Energy to meet preliminary expenses in connection with the sale of Government shares in the British Gas Corporation	850,000	—
26. For expenditure by Her Majesty's Treasury in connection with the sale of ordinary shares in Britoil plc	1,000	23,499,000
27. For expenditure by the Department of Trade and Industry in connection with the sale of Government shares in Rolls Royce plc	100,000	—
28. For expenditure by Her Majesty's Treasury in connection with the sale of Government shares in Cable and Wireless plc	1,000	22,999,000
Class V		
8. For the expenditure of the Victoria and Albert Museum including purchase grants in aid	100,000	—
10. For certain grants, indemnities and services for the benefit of the arts, for grants in aid to the Arts Council and certain other institutions and for a grant in aid to the National Heritage Memorial Fund and for payments to the Inland Revenue covering assets accepted in lieu of tax, and for expenditure on the Government Art Collection	420,000	—
Class VI		
1. For expenditure by the Department of Transport on roads and certain associated services including lighting and road safety, including a grant in aid, and certain grants	1,335,000	—
2. For expenditure by the Department of Transport on assistance to local transport; shipping; civil aviation; central administration; certain licensing and testing schemes; research and development; and certain other transport services including civil defence; a grant in aid and international subscriptions	1,000	—

Class VI—*continued*	Supply Grants	Appropriations in Aid
Vote	£	£
3. For expenditure by the Department of Transport on support to nationalised transport industries and assistance to local transport and ports	45,500,000	—
5. For expenditure by the Department of Transport in connection with the sale of shares in British Airways	749,000	*—*749,000*
Class VII		
1. For expenditure by the Department of the Environment on subsidies, the option mortgage scheme, improvements and investment, grants to housing associations and the Housing Corporation and sundry other housing services	19,681,000	—
Class VIII		
1. For expenditure by the Department of the Environment on other water supply, conservation and sewerage, certain local authority and local authority and other environmental services (including recreation), town and country planning (including compensation) and assistance to the construction industry	1,050,000	—
2. For expenditure by the Department of the Environment on other environmental services including grants in aid and international subscriptions, on grants in aid to the British Waterways Board and Development Commission, on bridgeworks, and on developing Civil Defence water services, and a contribution to the Lord Mayor of Bradford's Appeal Fund	4,450,000	—
3. For expenditure by the Department of Environment on derelict land reclamation, the urban programme and grants in aid for Urban Development Corporations	26,382,000	—
4. For expenditure by the Department of the Environment on royal palaces etc., royal parks etc., historic buildings, ancient monuments and certain public buildings, the national heritage, on grants in aid, other grants and on payments to the Inland Revenue covering assets accepted in lieu of tax and on the administration of those activities	10,430,000	—
Class IX		
1. For expenditure by the Lord Chancellor's Department on court services, the Law Commission, the Office of the Special Commissioners of Income Tax, the Office of the Social Security Commissioners, the Public Trustee Office and certain other legal services including grants in aid for the Council for Licensed Conveyancers and for administration of legal aid	2,000	2,049,000
2. For expenditure by the Northern Ireland Court Service on court services and certain other legal services including a grant in aid	355,000	100,000

*Deficit.

Class IX—*continued*	Supply Grants	Appropriations in Aid
Vote	£	£
3. For expenditure by the Departments of the Director of Public Prosecutions and the Procurator General and Treasury Solicitor on Crown Prosecutions and legal services	577,000	150,000
4. For grants to the Legal Aid Fund and for expenditure by the Lord Chancellor's Department on legal aid in criminal cases, court services, and costs paid from central funds	30,000,000	***—*900,000*
6. For expenditure by the Home Office on court services, compensation for criminal injuries, including a grant in aid, probation, police, community services, and superannuation payments for police and fire services	44,034,000	—
8. For expenditure by the Home Office on prisons (including central administrative staff) and associated stores in England and Wales and the Parole Board	24,137,000	***—*9,084,000*
10. For expenditure by the Lord Advocate's Departments on central and miscellaneous services including grants in aid	365,000	25,000
Class X		
1. For expenditure by the Department of Education and Science on schools, further education, teacher training, adult education, miscellaneous educational services and research, including grants in aid and international subscriptions	1,000	—
3. For expenditure by the Department of Education and Science on universities and certain other institutions, grants for higher and further education, grants in aid and a subscription to an international organisation	1,911,000	—
4. For expenditure by the Department of Education and Science and the University Grants Committee on administration	97,000	—
5. For a grant in aid of the Agricultural and Food Research Council	2,385,000	—
7. For a grant in aid of the Natural Environment Research Council	550,000	—
Class XI		
1. For expenditure by the Department of Health and Social Security on the provision of services under the national health service in England, on other health services including a grant in aid and on certain other services including research and services for the disabled	952,000	48,788,000
2. For expenditure by the Department of Health and Social Security on the provision of services under the national health service in England, on other health and personal social services, on welfare food and certain other services including grants under section 8 of the Industrial Development Act 1982	155,111,000	***—*51,648,000*

*Deficit.

Vote	Supply Grants	Appropriations in Aid
Class XI—*continued*	£	£
3. For expenditure by the Department of Health and Social Security on the provision of services under the national health service in England, on other health and personal social services including certain services in relation to the United Kingdom, and on research, exports, services for the disabled and certain other services including grants in aid and international subscriptions	1,307,000	***—*3,820,000*
Class XII		
1. For expenditure by the Department of Health and Social Security on non-contributory retirement pensions, Christmas bonus payments to pensioners, pensions etc., for disablement or death arising out of war or service in the armed forces after 2 September 1939 and on certain associated services, on attendance allowances, invalid care allowance, severe disablement allowance and mobility allowance	33,000,000	—
2. For expenditure by the Department of Health and Social Security on supplementary pensions and allowances	592,000,000	19,000,000
3. For expenditure by the Department of Health and Social Security on child benefit, one parent benefit, family income supplement and non-contributory maternity grant	25,000,000	—
4. For expenditure by the Department of Health and Social Security on rate rebate, rent allowance, and rate rebate subsidies, to housing, rating and local authorities, and on subsidies towards the administrative costs incurred by these authorities in operating the housing benefit scheme	307,700,000	—
5. For expenditure by the Department of Health and Social Security on administration and certain other services including an international subscription	9,756,000	5,711,000
Class XIII		
1. For the expenditure of the House of Lords	150,000	67,000
2. For expenditure of the House of Commons on members' salaries, allowances, pensions, etc., financial assistance to opposition parties and a grant in aid	196,000	—
5. For expenditure by the Customs and Excise Department including the expenses of value added tax tribunals and an international subscription	1,907,000	***—*500,000*
6. For the expenditure of the Inland Revenue Department	21,900,000	—
11. For expenditure by the Management and Personnel Office on the central management of the Civil Service, on the Office of the Chancellor of the Duchy of Lancaster, on the Office of the Parliamentary Counsel and certain other services including grants in aid	1,000	—
14. For the expenditure of the Office of Population Censuses and Surveys, including a grant in aid	1,000	140,000

*Deficit.

Class XIII—*continued*	Supply Grants	Appropriations in Aid
Vote	£	£
15. For the expenditure of the Land Registry - -	101,000	99,000
17. For the expenditure of the Cabinet Office, the expenses of the Chancellor of the Duchy of Lancaster, the Paymaster General and the Minister without Portfolio, their private offices and grants in aid to international organisations - - -	1,000	—
Class XIIIA		
1. For the expenditure of the House of Commons Commission - - - - - - - -	703,000	15,000
Class XIV		
5. For rates and contributions in lieu of rates paid by the Rating of Government Property Department in respect of property occupied by the Crown and premises occupied by representatives of commonwealth and foreign countries and international organisations - - - - - - - -	12,600,000	400,000
6. For the expenditure of the Department of the Government Actuary - - - - - -	1,000	49,000
Class XV		
1. For expenditure by the Department of Agriculture and Fisheries for Scotland on price guarantees, production grants and subsidies, grants and loans for capital and other improvements, support for agriculture in special areas and certain other services including services relating to livestock diseases - - - - - - - - -	21,421,000	312,000
5. For expenditure by the Industry Department for Scotland on selective assistance to industry, and on regional development grants - - - -	18,748,000	1,258,000
6. For expenditure by the Scottish Development Department in connection with acquisition of land and related services, on roads and certain associated services, including lighting and road safety, on assistance to local transport, on support for transport services in the Highlands and Islands, piers and harbours and on certain other transport services and grants, on housing subsidies, Royal Palaces and Royal Parks, historic buildings and ancient monuments, other central environmental services and grants in aid - - - - - -	4,648,000	—

Class XV—*continued*	Supply Grants	Appropriations in Aid
Vote	£	£
8. For expenditure by the Scottish Development Department on subsidies, the option mortgage scheme, improvements and investment, housing defects grants, certain rent registration expenses, capital grants to housing associations, loans and grants to first time purchasers and sundry other housing services	23,737,000	—
10. For expenditure by the Scottish Development Department in connection with water supply and sewerage, flood protection, town and country planning (including compensation), recreation, land reclamation, coast protection, urban programme and other local environment services	91,000	—
12. For expenditure by the Scottish Home and Health Department on legal aid and criminal injuries compensation (excluding administration), on police and fire services superannuation and police grant	6,005,000	281,000
13. For expenditure by the Scottish Courts Administration on costs and fees in connection with legal proceedings	426,000	—
14. For expenditure by the Scottish Home and Health Department on legal aid administration, certain services relating to crime, prisons, treatment of offenders, civil defence (including grants), and on fire and police services (excluding grants and superannuation), on the provision of services under the national health service, on other health services, on research, services for the disabled and certain other services including a grant in aid	6,961,000	—
15. For expenditure by the Scottish Education Department on schools, and certain grants to local authorities, higher and further education, libraries, miscellaneous educational services including compensation payments for redundant staff at colleges of education, research and administration, the Royal Scottish Museum and the National Museums of Scotland, certain grants for the arts, including purchase grants in aid, sport, social work and other grants in aid	1,054,000	—
16. For expenditure by the Scottish Education Department on awards to students receiving higher and further education	2,631,000	—
20. For expenditure by the Scottish Home and Health Department on the provision of services under the National Health Service in Scotland, on welfare food and certain other services	1,000	1,220,000
23. For the expenditure of the Department of the Registers of Scotland	1,000	899,000
24. For expenditure by the Scottish Office on Administration, Royal Commissions and certain other services	128,000	—

Vote	Supply Grants	Appropriations in Aid
	£	£
CLASS XVI		
2. For expenditure by the Welsh Office on market regulation and production support, grants and loans for capital and other improvements, support for agriculture in special areas, animal health and support services, land drainage, flood protection, water supply and certain other services - -	7,778,000	70,000
3. For expenditure by the Welsh Office on regional development grants, selective assistance to industry in assisted areas, and housing subsidy - -	18,021,000	*—*710,000*
5. For expenditure by the Welsh Office on assistance to agricultural production, food processing and marketing, certain other services including research, land management, assistance to the Welsh fishing industry including protective and other services, special assistance for rural and highland areas, on the Welsh Development Agency and some special and other services including grants in aid - - - - - -	1,000	—
6. For expenditure by the Welsh Office on subsidies, the option mortgage scheme, improvements, investment, grants to housing associations and sundry other housing services - - - - -	15,195,000	—
8. For expenditure by the Welsh Office in connection with water supply, sewerage, town and country planning (including compensation), recreation, other local services including clean air grants, coast protection, urban programme, family practitioner services under the National Health Service, welfare food, EC medical costs and grants to local authorities for secure accommodation -	28,168,000	*—*6,840,000*
9. For expenditure on Hospital and Community Health Services and supporting health services - -	3,000,000	—
CLASS XVII		
1. For expenditure by the Northern Ireland Office on central and miscellaneous services, services related to crime, police, prisons, training schools, probation and after-care etc., compensation schemes, Crown prosecutions and other legal services, grants in aid to Co-operation North and the Police Complaints Board, and certain other grants - - - - - - - - - - -	11,834,000	14,000
2. For expenditure by the Northern Ireland Office on a grant in aid of the Northern Ireland Consolidated Fund and other transfers - - - - -	85,000,000	—
CLASS XVIII		
4. For national parks supplementary grants to county councils in Wales - - - - - - -	29,000	—
6. For rate rebates and domestic rate relief grants to local authorities in England - - - - -	8,750,000	—
7. For rate rebate grants to local authorities in Wales	731,000	—
10. For supplementary grants for transport purposes to county councils in Wales - - - - - - -	9,000	—

*Deficit.

Class XVIII—*continued*	Supply Grants	Appropriations in Aid
Vote	£	£
11. For expenditure by the Department of Education and Science on superannuation, allowances and gratuities, etc., in respect of teachers, and the widows, children and dependants of deceased teachers - - - - - - - - -	25,000,000	*—*37,000,000*
14. For expenditure by the Scottish Home and Health Department on pensions, allowances, gratuities, etc., to or in respect of persons engaged in health services or in other approved employment - -	1,000	1,099,000
15. For payment of pensions, etc., to members of the United Kingdom Atomic Energy Authority's superannuation schemes and other related expenditure - - - - - - - -	1,000	4,574,000
Total Supplementary 1985–86 - - £	2,654,435,000	32,946,000

*Deficit.

Class I, 1986–87

SCHEDULE (B).—Part 3

Class I

Schedule of Sums granted, and of the sums which may be applied as appropriations in aid in addition thereto, to defray the charges of the several Services herein particularly mentioned, which will come in course of payment during the year ending on 31st March 1987, including provision for numbers of personnel as set out hereunder, viz.:—

	Sums not exceeding	
	Supply Grants	Appropriations in Aid
Vote	£	£
1. For expenditure by the Ministry of Defence on personnel costs etc., of the Armed Forces and their Reserves and Cadet Forces etc., (including provision for Naval Service to a number not exceeding 71,000, provision for Army Service to a number not exceeding 187,600, for the Individual Reserves to a number not exceeding 141,000, for the Territorial Army to a number not exceeding 86,000, for the Home Service Force to a number not exceeding 5,000, and for the Ulster Defence Regiment to a number not exceeding 7,780, and provision for Air Force Service to a number not exceeding 96,600, for RAF Reserves to a number not exceeding 6,900, and for the Royal Auxiliary Air Force to a number not exceeding 2,500); personnel costs etc. of Defence Ministers and of certain civilian staff employed by the Ministry of Defence; on movements; certain stores; supplies and services; plant and machinery; charter and contract repair of ships; certain research; lands and buildings; sundry grants; payments abroad including contributions and subscriptions to international organisations; and grants in aid - - - - - - - -	7,082,974,000	970,137,000

Class I—*continued*	Sums not exceeding	
	Supply Grants	Appropriations in Aid
Vote	£	£
2. For expenditure by the Procurement Executive of the Ministry of Defence in operating its Headquarters and Establishments and for its other common services; for research etc., by contract; lands and buildings; for development by contract, production, repair etc., and purchases for sale abroad of sea systems, land systems, air systems and associated equipment; for certain contingent liabilities, and for sundry other Procurement Executive services including those on repayment terms to non-exchequer customers (Revised sum) - - - - - - - - - -	8,520,180,000	585,851,000
3. For expenditure by the Ministry of Defence on retired pay, pensions etc. - - - - - -	978,552,000	1,156,000
4. For expenditure including loans by the Property Services Agency of the Department of the Environment on public building work and certain accommodation services etc., for defence purposes - - - - - - - - -	1,473,831,000	260,414,000
5. For operating the Royal Dockyards and for the repair of ships by contract including work undertaken on repayment terms for exchequer and non-exchequer customers - - - - - -	430,345,000	2,158,000
6. For expenditure by the Ministry of Defence in connection with the sale of Government shares in Royal Ordnance plc. - - - - - - -	1,000	500,000
TOTAL, CLASS I - - - - - - £	18,485,883,000	1,820,216,000

Class II, 1986–87 SCHEDULE (B).—PART 4

CLASS II

SCHEDULE OF SUMS granted, and of the sums which may be applied as appropriations in aid in addition thereto, to defray the charges of the several Services herein particularly mentioned, which will come in course of payment during the year ending on 31st March 1987, as set out hereunder, viz.:—

	Sums not exceeding	
	Supply Grants	Appropriations in Aid
	£	£
Vote		
1. For expenditure by the Foreign and Commonwealth Office on its salaries, building and other accommodation services, and administration, and those of HM Diplomatic Service official information services, sundry services and loans and a grant in aid for catering services	388,140,000	38,475,000
2. For expenditure by the Foreign and Commonwealth Office on grants and subscriptions, etc., to certain international organisations, certain grants in aid, special payments and assistance, military aid and sundry other grants and services (Revised sum)	99,557,000	24,754,000
3. For expenditure by the Foreign and Commonwealth Office on grants in aid of the British Broadcasting Corporation for external broadcasting and monitoring services	111,636,000	2,855,000
4. For expenditure by the Foreign and Commonwealth Office on a grant in aid of the British Council	50,694,000	—
5. For expenditure by the Foreign and Commonwealth Office (Overseas Development Administration) on the official United Kingdom Aid Programme including capital subscriptions and other contributions and payments under guarantees to certain multilateral development banks and other bodies; subscriptions and grants in aid to certain international and regional organisations; bilateral capital aid and technical co-operation; refugee and other relief assistance; the cost of in-house Scientific Units; assistance, including grants in aid, to certain UK-based institutions and voluntary agencies; loans to the Commonwealth Development Corporation; and pensions and allowances in respect of overseas service (Revised sum)	1,057,489,000	80,775,000
6. For expenditure by the Foreign and Commonwealth Office (Overseas Development Administration) on administration	27,262,000	151,000
7. For expenditure by the Foreign and Commonwealth Office (Overseas Development Administration) on pensions and superannuation payments etc., in respect of overseas service, pensions in respect of service with the Cotton Research Corporation and sundry other services and expenses	121,389,000	1,547,000
TOTAL, CLASS II £	1,856,167,000	148,557,000

SCHEDULE (B).—PART 5

CLASS III

SCHEDULE OF SUMS granted, and of the sums which may be applied as appropriations in aid in addition thereto, to defray the charges of the several Services herein particularly mentioned, which will come in course of payment during the year ending on 31st March 1987, including provision for numbers of personnel as set out hereunder, viz.:—

	Sums not exceeding	
	Supply Grants	Appropriations in Aid
	£	£
Vote 1. For payments to the Budget of the European Communities not covered by direct charges on the Consolidated Fund under section 2(3) of the European Communities Act 1972 - - -	930,000,000	—
TOTAL, CLASS III - - - - - - £	930,000,000	—

CLASS IV

SCHEDULE OF SUMS granted, and of the sums which may be applied as appropriations in aid in addition thereto, to defray the charges of the several Services herein particularly mentioned, which will come in course of payment during the year ending on 31st March 1987, viz.:—

	Sums not exceeding	
	Supply Grants	Appropriations in Aid
	£	£
Vote		
1. For expenditure by the Intervention Board for Agricultural Produce in giving effect in the United Kingdom to the agricultural support provisions of the Common Agricultural Policy of the European Community and to Community food aid measures and for certain other services	347,791,000	252,603,000
2. For expenditure by the Intervention Board for Agricultural Produce on central administration and miscellaneous services	27,376,000	517,000
3. For expenditure by the Ministry of Agriculture, Fisheries and Food on market support, grants and loans for capital and other improvements, support for agriculture in special areas, animal health, arterial drainage, flood and coast protection, and certain other services	153,063,000	18,499,000
4. For expenditure by the Ministry of Agriculture, Fisheries and Food on commissioned research and development and advice, education and training services, botanical services, assistance to production, marketing and processing, support for the fishing industry, emergency and strategic food services, protective, agency and other services, including grants in aid and international subscriptions (Revised sum)	139,393,000	17,297,000
5. For expenditure by the Ministry of Agriculture, Fisheries and Food on departmental research, advisory services and administration and certain other services	211,366,000	11,046,000
6. For a grant in aid of the Forestry Fund	53,008,000	—
TOTAL, CLASS IV £	931,997,000	299,962,000

Class V, 1986–87 SCHEDULE (B).—PART 7

CLASS V

SCHEDULE OF SUMS granted, and of the sums which may be applied as appropriations in aid in addition thereto, to defray the charges of the several Services herein particularly mentioned, which will come in course of payment during the year ending on 31st March 1987, viz.:—

	Sums not exceeding	
	Supply Grants	Appropriations in Aid
	£	£
Vote		
1. For expenditure by the Department of Trade and Industry on regional development grants, regional selective assistance, selective assistance to individual industries, certain other services including U.K. contributions to the funding of buffer stock operations of international commodity agreements, a strategic mineral stockpile and the film industry, and support for the aerospace, shipbuilding and steel industries, including loans, grants and the purchase of assets and assistance to redundant steel workers - - - -	456,058,000	108,431,000
2. For expenditure by the Department of Trade and Industry at its research establishments and on the running costs of its headquarters divisions, radio regulatory division and the Patent Office, support for innovation (including industrial research and development, aircraft and aeroengine research and development, and space technology programmes), promotion of standards, export promotion and trade co-operation, miscellaneous support services, grants in aid, international subscriptions, provision of land and buildings, loans, grants and other payments (Revised sum) - -	445,933,000	107,691,000
3. For expenditure by the Department of Trade and Industry on the regulation of trading practices, on consumer protection, and on central and miscellaneous services including grants in aid, international subscriptions, and grants to the fund for sub-postmasters - - - - - - - -	147,134,000	44,101,000
4. For Government investment in British Shipbuilders, grants from the shipbuilding intervention fund to assist public sector yards and assistance to redundant shipyard workers (including a Supplementary sum of £89,000,000) - - - - -	178,710,000	—
5. For expenditure by the Export Credits Guarantee Department on administration - - - -	43,154,000	1,300,000
6. For expenditure by the Export Credits Guarantee Department in connection with interest support to banks and other lenders providing fixed rate export finance, cost escalation protection and grants towards financing of exports to match foreign competition (Revised sum) - - -	286,394,000	12,707,000
7. For expenditure by the Export Credits Guarantee Department in connection with export credits guarantees including an international subscription, guarantees given in the national interest and overseas investment insurance (Revised sum) -	435,283,000	694,781,000

Class V—*continued*	Sums not exceeding	
	Supply Grants	Appropriations in Aid
Vote	£	£
8. For expenditure by the Department of Trade and Industry in connection with the sale of shares in British Telecommunications plc - - -	1,000	8,449,000
9. For expenditure by the Department of Trade and Industry in connection with the sale of Government shares in Rolls Royce plc - - -	4,000,000	—
10. For expenditure by the Department of Trade and Industry in connection with the sale of Government shares in British Aerospace plc - -	1,000	729,000
TOTAL, CLASS V - - - - - - £	1,996,668,000	978,189,000

Class VI, 1986–87

SCHEDULE (B).—PART 8

CLASS VI

SCHEDULE OF SUMS granted, and of the sums which may be applied as appropriations in aid in addition thereto, to defray the charges of the several Services herein particularly mentioned, which will come in course of payment during the year ending on 31st March 1987, viz.:—

	Sums not exceeding	
	Supply Grants	Appropriations in Aid
	£	£
Vote		
1. For expenditure by the Department of Energy on assistance to the coal industry including grants to the National Coal Board and payments to redundant workers - - - - - - - -	1,139,000,000	30,000,000
2. For expenditure by the Department of Energy in connection with the energy industries including related research and development, energy efficiency, oil storage, selective assistance to industry, promotion and security of oil and gas supplies, grants and certain other services, including subscriptions and contributions to international organisations - - - - - -	277,102,000	23,703,000
3. For expenditure by the Department of Energy on salaries and other services (Revised sum) - -	22,471,000	4,605,000
4. For refunds and repayments of petroleum licensing proceeds, and other payments in connection with such proceeds, to be made by the Department of Energy out of income received from application fees; from annual and other payments for exploration, production, mining and methane drainage licences; from royalty; and from the disposal of petroleum taken as royalty in kind - - -	1,000	394,446,000
5. For payment of pensions, etc., to members of the United Kingdom Atomic Energy Authority's superannuation schemes and other related expenditure - - - - - - - -	1,000	56,399,000
6. For expenditure by the Department of Energy in connection with the sale of Government shares in British Gas - - - - - - - -	1,000	6,500,000
TOTAL, CLASS VI - - - - - - £	1,438,576,000	515,653,000

Class VII, 1986–87 SCHEDULE (B).—PART 9

CLASS VII

SCHEDULE OF SUMS granted, and of the sums which may be applied as appropriations in aid in addition thereto, to defray the charges of the several Services herein particularly mentioned, which will come in course of payment during the year ending on 31st March 1987, including provision for numbers of personnel as set out hereunder, viz.:—

	Sums not exceeding	
	Supply Grants	Appropriations in Aid
	£	£
Vote		
1. For expenditure by the Department of Employment on the promotion of tourism including grants in aid, general labour market services including a grant in aid, services for seriously disabled people, and an international subscription (including a Supplementary sum of £82,400,000) - - -	1,309,406,000	327,000
2. For expenditure by the Department of Employment on demand determined measures to promote and preserve employment opportunities, compensation for persons disabled by pneumoconiosis, byssinosis and diffuse mesothelioma, payments towards expenses of trade union ballots and compensation to persons for certain dismissals (Revised sum) - - - - - - -	148,639,000	6,150,000
3. For expenditure by the Department of Employment on the administration of benefit services and on central and miscellaneous services (including a Supplementary sum of £1,500,000) - - -	62,005,000	301,963,000
4. For expenditure by the Department of Employment on a grant in aid to the Advisory, Conciliation and Arbitration Service - - - - - -	14,934,000	—
5. For expenditure by the Department of Employment on a grant in aid to the Health and Safety Commission - - - - - - - -	94,334,000	30,000
6. For expenditure by the Department of Employment on a grant in aid to the Manpower Services Commission (including a Supplementary sum of £78,354,000) - - - - - - - -	1,645,186,000	267,938,000
TOTAL, CLASS VII - - - - - - £	3,274,504,000	576,408,000

CLASS VIII

SCHEDULE OF SUMS granted, and of the sums which may be applied as appropriations in aid in addition thereto, to defray the charges of the several Services herein particularly mentioned, which will come in course of payment during the year ending on 31st March 1987, viz.:—

	Sums not exceeding	
	Supply Grants	Appropriations in Aid
	£	£
Vote		
1. For expenditure by the Department of Transport on the construction, improvement and maintenance of motorways and trunk roads, including the acquisition of land, scheme design and preparation, compensation, the purchase of maintenance vehicles and equipment and the maintenance and operation of Woolwich ferry	893,517,000	42,571,000
2. For expenditure by the Department of Transport on assistance to shipping; civil aviation; central administration; certain licensing and testing schemes; research and development; road safety; and certain other transport services including civil defence; and international subscriptions, including grants in aid	174,561,000	82,910,000
3. For expenditure by the Department of Transport on support to nationalised transport industries and to ports and rebate of fuel duty to bus operators	1,298,425,000	758,000
4. For expenditure by the Department of Transport in connection with driver and motor vehicle registration and licensing and the collection of revenue	113,105,000	7,489,000
5. For expenditure by the Department of Transport on transport supplementary grants to county councils and some district councils in England, and certain other grants and payments in support of local roads and transport expenditure (Revised sum)	194,011,000	13,485,000
6. For expenditure by the Department of Transport in connection with the sale of shares in British Airways	1,000	1,090,000
7. For expenditure by the Department of Transport in connection with the sale of shares in the British Airports Authority	1,000,000	—
8. For expenditure by the Department of Transport in connection with the sale of National Bus Company operations	1,000	599,000
TOTAL, CLASS VIII £	2,674,621,000	148,902,000

Class IX

Schedule of Sums granted, and of the sums which may be applied as appropriations in aid in addition thereto, to defray the charges of the several Services herein particularly mentioned, which will come in course of payment during the year ending on 31st March 1987, viz.:—

	Sums not exceeding	
	Supply Grants	Appropriations in Aid
	£	£
Vote		
1. For expenditure by the Department of the Environment on subsidies, improvements and investment, grants to housing associations and the Housing Corporation and sundry other services - -	1,874,635,000	35,201,000
2. For expenditure by the Department of the Environment on housing administration, including rent officers, rent assessment panels, and grant in aid to the Housing Corporation; housing research; housing management and mobility; grants to voluntary organisations concerned with homelessness; and contributions towards the work of the National Federation of Housing Associations -	41,253,000	75,000
Total, Class IX - - - - - - £	1,915,888,000	35,276,000

Class X, 1986–87 SCHEDULE (B).—PART 12

CLASS X

SCHEDULE OF SUMS granted, and of the sums which may be applied as appropriations in aid in addition thereto, to defray the charges of the several Services herein particularly mentioned, which will come in course of payment during the year ending on 31st March 1987, viz.:—

	Sums not exceeding	
	Supply Grants	Appropriations in Aid
Vote	£	£
1. For expenditure by the Department of the Environment on other water supply, conservation and sewerage, local authority and other environmental services (including recreation), town and country planning (including compensation) and assistance to the construction industry - -	27,371,000	120,000
2. For expenditure by the Department of the Environment on other environmental services including grants in aid and international subscriptions, on grants in aid to the Development Commission and British Waterways Board, on bridgeworks, and on developing Civil Defence water services and grants to New Towns - - - - - -	179,841,000	—
3. For expenditure by the Department of the Environment on derelict land reclamation, grants in aid for Urban Development Corporations, transitional grants for voluntary bodies, the Urban Programme and urban regeneration grant (including a Supplementary sum of £50,000) - -	350,639,000	—
4. For expenditure by the Department of the Environment on royal palaces, etc., royal parks, etc., historic buildings, ancient monuments and certain public buildings, the national heritage, on grants in aid, other grants and on payments to Inland Revenue covering assets accepted in lieu of tax, on an international subscription, and on the administration of those activities (Revised sum)	81,836,000	11,734,000
5. For expenditure by the Department of the Environment on central administration, including royal commissions, committees etc.; payments in connection with licence fees and environmental research and surveys including building and civil engineering research - - - - - - -	142,078,000	8,008,000
6. For expenditure by the Department of the Environment for rate support grants to local authorities in England - - - - - - - -	9,246,000,000	—
7. For expenditure by the Department of the Environment for national parks supplementary grants to local authorities in England - - - - -	6,430,000	—
8. For expenditure by the Department of the Environment for rate rebate grants to local authorities in England - - - - - - - - - - -	88,200,000	—
9. For expenditure by the Department of the Environment for the preliminary expenses incurred in connection with the sale of shares in the Water Services Public Limited Companies - - -	2,500,000	—
TOTAL, CLASS X - - - - - - £	10,124,895,000	19,862,000

Class XI, 1986–87 SCHEDULE (B).—PART 13

CLASS XI

SCHEDULE OF SUMS granted, and of the sums which may be applied as appropriations in aid in addition thereto, to defray the charges of the several Services herein particularly mentioned, which will come in course of payment during the year ending on 31st March 1987, viz.:—

	Sums not exceeding	
	Supply Grants	Appropriations in Aid
	£	£
Vote		
1. For expenditure by the Home Office on court services, compensation for criminal injuries, including a grant in aid, probation, police, community services, and superannuation payments for police and fire services - - - - - -	1,895,308,000	9,799,000
2. For expenditure by the Home Office on prisons (including central administrative staff) and associated stores in England and Wales, and the Parole Board - - - - - - - - -	639,111,000	34,074,000
3. For expenditure by the Home Office on court services, other services related to crime, probation and aftercare, police, fire, civil defence, control of immigration and nationality, issue of passports etc., other protective services and community services and other miscellaneous services including grants in aid and international subscriptions; and on administrative and operational staff (excluding prisons) and central services - -	363,237,000	45,733,000
4. For expenditure by the Home Office on grants to the British Broadcasting Corporation for home broadcasting and sundry other services - -	1,014,418,000	—
5. For expenditure by the Lord Chancellor's Department on the Court Service, the Law Commission, the Office of the Special Commissioners for Income Tax, the Office of the Social Security Commissioners, the VAT tribunals, the Public Trustee Office and certain other legal services, including grants in aid to the Council for Licensed Conveyancers and for administration of legal aid	89,211,000	136,288,000
6. For grants to the Legal Aid Fund and for expenditure by the Lord Chancellor's Department on legal aid in criminal cases, court services, and costs paid from central funds - - - -	437,704,000	850,000
TOTAL, CLASS XI - - - - - - £	4,438,989,000	226,744,000

SCHEDULE (B).—PART 14

CLASS XII

SCHEDULE OF SUMS granted, and of the sums which may be applied as appropriations in aid in addition thereto, to defray the charges of the several Services herein particularly mentioned, which will come in course of payment during the year ending on 31st March 1987, viz.:—

	Sums not exceeding	
	Supply Grants	Appropriations in Aid
	£	£
Vote		
1. For expenditure by the Department of Education and Science on schools, further education, teacher training, adult education, miscellaneous educational services and research, including grants in aid and international subscriptions	209,094,000	8,791,000
2. For expenditure by the Department of Education and Science on the assisted places scheme, student awards, education support grants and compensation payments to redundant teachers and staff of certain institutions	746,896,000	13,000
3. For expenditure by the Department of Education and Science on universities and certain other institutions, grants for higher and further education, grants in aid and a subscription to an international organisation (Revised sum)	1,562,274,000	1,528,000
4. For expenditure by the Department of Education and Science and the University Grants Committee on administration	53,604,000	1,823,000
5. For a grant in aid of the Agricultural and Food Research Council	52,679,000	—
6. For grants in aid of the Medical Research Council including subscriptions to certain international organisations	128,340,000	—
7. For a grant in aid of the Natural Environment Research Council	70,325,000	—
8. For grants in aid of the Science and Engineering Research Council including subscriptions to certain international organisations (including a Supplementary sum of £2,000,000)	315,529,000	—
9. For a grant in aid of the Economic and Social Research Council	23,634,000	—
10. For the expenditure of the British Museum (Natural History), including a purchase grant in aid	11,787,000	—
11. For grants in aid of the Royal Society and the Fellowship of Engineering, and the science policy studies programme of the Advisory Board for the Research Councils	6,953,000	—
12. For expenditure by the Department of Education and Science on superannuation allowances and gratuities, etc., in respect of teachers, and the widows, children and dependants of deceased teachers (Revised sum)	118,101,000	1,107,272,000
TOTAL, CLASS XII £	3,299,216,000	1,119,427,000

Class XIII, 1986–87 SCHEDULE (B).—PART 15

CLASS XIII

SCHEDULE OF SUMS granted, and of the sums which may be applied as appropriations in aid in addition thereto, to defray the charges of the several Services herein particularly mentioned, which will come in course of payment during the year ending on 31st March 1987, viz.:—

	Sums not exceeding	
	Supply Grants	Appropriations in Aid
Vote	£	£
1. For expenditure by the Office of Arts and Libraries on a grant in aid to the British Museum (Revised sum)	13,345,000	350,000
2. For expenditure by the Office of Arts and Libraries on a grant in aid to the Imperial War Museum (Revised sum)	4,497,000	—
3. For expenditure by the Office of Arts and Libraries on a grant in aid to the National Gallery (Revised sum)	6,771,000	—
4. For expenditure by the Office of Arts and Libraries on a grant in aid to the National Maritime Museum (Revised sum)	4,462,000	—
5. For expenditure by the Office of Arts and Libraries on a grant in aid to the National Portrait Gallery (Revised sum)	1,814,000	—
6. For expenditure by the Office of Arts and Libraries on a grant in aid to the Science Museum (Revised sum)	9,171,000	—
7. For expenditure by the Office of Arts and Libraries on a grant in aid to the Tate Gallery (Revised sum)	5,782,000	—
8. For expenditure by the Office of Arts and Libraries on a grant in aid to the Victoria and Albert Museum (Revised sum)	11,023,000	—
9. For expenditure by the Office of Arts and Libraries on a grant in aid to the Wallace Collection (Revised sum)	906,000	—
10. For certain grants for services for the benefit of the arts, for grants in aid to the Arts Council and certain other institutions, for a grant in aid to the National Heritage Memorial Fund and for payments to the Inland Revenue covering assets accepted in lieu of tax, for international subscriptions and for expenditure on the Government Art Collection (Revised sum)	171,312,000	5,000
11. For g ant in aid to the British Library and certain other institutions, payments in respect of Public Lending Right and for the expenses of the Royal Commission on Historical Manuscripts	53,144,000	—
12. For expenditure by the Office of Arts and Libraries on administration	1,200,000	1,000
TOTAL, CLASS XIII £	283,427,000	356,000

Class XIV, 1986–87 SCHEDULE (B).—PART 16

CLASS XIV

SCHEDULE OF SUMS granted, and of the sums which may be applied as appropriations in aid in addition thereto, to defray the charge of the several Services herein particularly mentioned, which will come in course of payment during the year ending on 31st March 1987, viz.:—

	Sums not exceeding	
	Supply Grants	Appropriations in Aid
Vote	£	£
1. For expenditure by the Department of Health and Social Security on the provision of services under the national health service in England, on other health services including a grant in aid and on certain other services including research (including a Supplementary Sum of £49,640,000) - -	9,670,212,000	1,615,171,000
2. For expenditure by the Department of Health and Social Security on the provision of services under the national health service in England, on other health and personal social services, on welfare food and certain other services including grants under section 8 of the Industrial Development Act 1982 - - - - - - - - -	3,098,859,000	476,164,000
3. For expenditure by the Department of Health and Social Security on the provision of services under the national health service in England, on other health and personal social services including certain services in relation to the United Kingdom, and on research, exports, services for the disabled and certain other services including grants in aid and international subscriptions (including a Supplementary sum of £360,000) - - - - -	389,421,000	28,208,000
4. For expenditure by the Department of Health and Social Security on pensions, allowances, gratuities, etc., to or in respect of persons engaged in health services or in other approved employment - - - - - - -	1,000	929,922,000
TOTAL, CLASS XIV - - - - - £	13,158,493,000	3,049,465,000

CLASS XV

SCHEDULE OF SUMS granted, and of the sums which may be applied as appropriations in aid in addition thereto, to defray the charges of the several Services herein particularly mentioned, which will come in course of payment during the year ending on 31st March 1987, viz.:—

	Sums not exceeding	
	Supply Grants	Appropriations in Aid
Vote	£	£
1. For expenditure by the Department of Health and Social Security on non-contributory retirement pensions, Christmas bonus payments to pensioners, pensions etc., for disablement or death arising out of war or service in the armed forces after 2 September 1939 and on sundry other services, on attendance allowances, invalid care allowance, severe disablement allowance, and mobility allowance	2,150,000,000	—
2. For expenditure by the Department of Health and Social Security on supplementary pensions and allowances	7,264,000,000	109,000,000
3. For expenditure by the Department of Health and Social Security on child benefit, one parent benefit, family benefit income supplements and non-contributory maternity grants	4,749,000,000	—
4. For expenditure by the Department of Health and Social Security on rent rebate, rent allowance and rate rebate subsidies, to housing, rating, and local authorities, and expenditure on subsidies towards the administrative costs incurred by these authorities in operating the housing benefit scheme (including a Supplementary sum of £229,000,000)	4,815,300,000	—
5. For expenditure by the Department of Health and Social Security on administration and certain other services including grants to voluntary organisations and an international subscription (including a Supplementary sum of £5,360,000)	1,168,648,000	660,619,000
6. For sums payable out of the Consolidated Fund to the National Insurance Fund	2,394,000,000	—
TOTAL, CLASS XV £	22,540,948,000	769,619,000

Class XVI

Schedule of Sums granted, and of the sums which may be applied as appropriations in aid in addition thereto, to defray the charges of the several Services herein particularly mentioned, which will come in course of payment during the year ending on 31st March 1987, viz.:—

	Sums not exceeding	
	Supply Grants	Appropriations in Aid
Vote	£	£
1. For expenditure by the Department of Agriculture and Fisheries for Scotland on price guarantees, production grants and subsidies, grants and loans for capital and other improvements, support for agriculture in special areas and certain other services including services relating to livestock diseases	54,795,000	15,186,000
2. For expenditure by the Department of Agriculture and Fisheries for Scotland on educational and advisory services, botanical services, assistance to marketing and processing, administration, land management and land settlement, livestock services, assistance to crofters, assistance to the Scottish fishing industry, protective and certain other services including research and development, special services and a grant in aid	75,166,000	4,757,000
3. For expenditure by the Industry Department for Scotland on grants in aid to the Scottish Development Agency and to the Highlands and Islands Development Board; on the promotion of tourism, including a grant in aid; on financial assistance to nationalised industries; on employment services in Scotland; on consumer protection, and on sundry other services in connection with trade and industry	128,268,000	3,330,000
4. For expenditure by the Industry Department for Scotland on a contribution to the Department of Employment towards the grant in aid to the Manpower Services Commission in relation to activities in Scotland (including a Supplementary sum of £9,008,000)	164,077,000	—
5. For expenditure by the Industry Department for Scotland on regional development grants and regional selective assistance	149,179,000	27,592,000
6. For expenditure by the Scottish Development Department in connection with acquisition of land and related services, on roads and certain associated services, including lighting and road safety, on assistance to local transport, on support for transport services in the Highlands and Islands, piers and harbours and on certain other transport services and grants, on housing subsidies, Royal Palaces and Royal Parks, historic buildings and ancient monuments, other central environmental services and grants in aid	148,874,000	4,833,000

Class XVI—*continued*	Sums not exceeding	
	Supply Grants	Appropriations in Aid
Vote	£	£
7. For expenditure by the Scottish Development Department on assistance to local transport, and on piers and harbours	25,920,000	—
8. For expenditure by the Scottish Development Department on subsidies, the option mortgage scheme, improvements and investment, housing defects grants, certain rent registration expenses, capital grants to housing associations, loans and grants to first time purchasers and sundry other housing services	253,305,000	513,000
9. For expenditure by the Industry Department for Scotland on grants to New Town Development Corporations in connection with housing and other services	44,895,000	—
10. For expenditure by the Scottish Development Department in connection with water supply and sewerage, flood prevention, town and country planning (including compensation), recreation, land reclamation, coast protection, urban programme and other local environmental services	25,176,000	—
11. For expenditure by the Scottish Courts Administration on court services, the Scottish Law Commission and certain other legal services, including a grant in aid	10,976,000	6,702,000
12. For expenditure by the Scottish Home and Health Department on legal aid and criminal injuries compensation (excluding administration), on police and fire services superannuation and police grant	202,926,000	112,000
13. For expenditure by the Scottish Courts Administration on costs and fees in connection with legal proceedings	2,678,000	—
14. For expenditure by the Scottish Home and Health Department on legal aid administration, certain services relating to crime, prisons, treatment of offenders, civil defence (including grants) and on fire and police services (excluding grants and superannuation), on the provision of services under the national health service, on other health services, on research, services for the disabled and certain other services including a grant in aid (including a Supplementary sum of £5,882,000)	1,604,152,000	172,454,000
15. For expenditure by the Scottish Education Department on schools and certain grants to local authorities, higher and further education, libraries, miscellaneous educational services including compensation payments for redundant staff at colleges of education, research and administration, grant in aid to the National Museums of Scotland, the National Galleries of Scotland and the National Library of Scotland including purchase grants in aid, certain grants for the arts, sport, social work, other grants in aid and certain payments on behalf of the European Community (Revised sum)	169,270,000	1,461,000

Class XVI—*continued*	Sums not exceeding	
	Supply Grants	Appropriations in Aid
Vote	£	£
16. For expenditure by the Scottish Education Department on awards to students receiving higher and further education - - - - - - -	104,281,000	10,000
17. For expenditure by the Scottish Home and Health Department on the provision of services under the National Health Service in Scotland, on welfare food and certain other services - - -	371,910,000	39,587,000
18. For the expenditure of the Scottish Record Office and on certain other services including a grant in aid - - - - - - - - - - -	1,782,000	385,000
19. For the expenditure of the General Register Office for Scotland - - - - - - - -	3,201,000	762,000
20. For the expenditure of the Department of the Registers of Scotland - - - - - - - -	1,000	10,793,000
21. For expenditure by the Scottish Office on administration, Royal Commissions and certain other services - - - - - - - - - -	106,492,000	2,874,000
22. For expenditure by the Scottish Office for rate support grants to local authorities in Scotland -	1,761,350,000	—
23. For expenditure by the Scottish Office for rate rebate grants to local authorities in Scotland - - -	36,000,000	—
24. For expenditure by the Scottish Home and Health Department on superannuation allowances and gratuities, etc., in respect of teachers, and the widows and dependants of deceased teachers -	35,605,000	102,617,000
25. For expenditure by the Scottish Home and Health Department on pensions, allowances, gratuities, etc., to or in respect of persons engaged in health service or in other approved employment - -	1,000	126,393,000
TOTAL, CLASS XVI - - - - - - - £	5,480,280,000	520,361,000

Class XVII, 1986–87 SCHEDULE (B).—PART 19

CLASS XVII

SCHEDULE OF SUMS granted, and of the sums which may be applied as appropriations in aid in addition thereto, to defray the charges of the several Services herein particularly mentioned, which will come in course of payment during the year ending on 31st March 1986, viz.:—

	Sums not exceeding	
	Supply Grants	Appropriations in Aid
Vote	£	£
1. For expenditure by the Welsh Office on market support, grants and loans for capital and other improvements, support for agriculture in special areas, animal health and support services, arterial drainage, flood and coast protection and certain other services	40,815,000	8,808,000
2. For expenditure by the Welsh Office on assistance to agricultural production, food processing and marketing, certain other services including research, land management, assistance to the Welsh fishing industry including protective and other services, special assistance for rural and highland areas, on the Welsh Development Agency and some special and other services including grants in aid	45,499,000	404,000
3. For expenditure by the Welsh Office on regional development grants, regional selective assistance and housing subsidy	97,637,000	7,011,000
4. For expenditure by the Welsh Office on a contribution to the Department of Employment towards the grant in aid to the Manpower Services Commission in relation to activities in Wales (including a supplementary sum of £5,712,000)	100,788,000	—
5. For expenditure by the Welsh Office on tourism, roads and certain associated services including road safety, housing administration, historic buildings and ancient monuments, other environmental services, civil defence (including grants), education, libraries and museums, centrally funded health services and personal social services, grants in aid, EC agency payments, other grants and certain other services, including research	186,260,000	4,753,000
6. For expenditure by the Welsh Office on housing subsidies, improvements and investment, the option mortgage scheme, grants to housing associations, water, sewerage, town and country planning (including compensation), recreation, other local services, including clean air grants, urban programme (including urban development grant), welfare food, EC medical costs, certain EC agency payments and other services	131,289,000	1,587,000
7. For expenditure by the Welsh Office on family practitioner services under the National Health Service	191,232,000	24,306,000

Class XVII—*continued*	Sums not exceeding	
	Supply Grants	Appropriations in Aid
Vote	£	£
8. For expenditure by the Welsh Office on Hospital and Community Health Services, supporting health services and family practitioner services administration and related services (including a Supplementary sum of £2,941,000)	657,687,000	80,484,000
9. For expenditure by the Welsh Office on central administration	36,951,000	1,201,000
10. For expenditure by the Welsh Office for rate support grants to local authorities in Wales	875,807,000	—
11. For expenditure by the Welsh Office for national parks supplementary grants to county councils in Wales	2,214,000	—
12. For expenditure by the Welsh Office for rate rebate grants to local authorities in Wales	6,265,000	—
13. For expenditure by the Welsh Office on supplementary grants for transport purposes to county councils in Wales	19,596,000	—
TOTAL, CLASS XVII £	2,392,040,000	128,554,000

Class XVIII, 1986–87

SCHEDULE (B).—PART 20

CLASS XVIII

SCHEDULE OF SUMS granted, and of the sums which may be applied as appropriations in aid in addition thereto, to defray the charges of the several Services herein particularly mentioned, which will come in course of payment during the year ending on 31st March 1987, viz.:—

	Sums not exceeding	
	Supply Grants	Appropriations in Aid
Vote	£	£
1. For expenditure by the Northern Ireland Office on central and miscellaneous services, services related to crime, police, prisons, training schools, probation and after-care etc., compensation schemes, crown prosecutions and other legal services, grants in aid to Co-operation North and the Police Complaints Board and certain other grants	474,366,000	3,921,000
2. For expenditure by the Northern Ireland Office on a grant in aid of the Northern Ireland Consolidated Fund and other transfers	975,000,000	—
TOTAL, CLASS XVIII £	1,449,366,000	3,921,000

Class XIX, 1986–87 SCHEDULE (B).—Part 21

Class XIX

Schedule of Sums granted, and of the sums which may be applied as appropriations in aid in addition thereto, to defray the charges of the several Services herein particularly mentioned, which will come in course of payment during the year ending on 31st March 1987, viz.:—

	Sums not exceeding	
	Supply Grants	Appropriations in Aid
Vote	£	£
1. For expenditure by the Central Office of Information on home and overseas publicity	70,977,000	—
2. For expenditure by the Customs and Excise Department including an international subscription	393,768,000	9,594,000
3. For expenditure by the Registry of Friendly Societies and the Building Societies Commission	2,368,000	1,247,000
4. For the expenditure of the Department of the Government Actuary	1,413,000	593,000
5. For expenditure by the Controller of Her Majesty's Stationery Office to compensate the HMSO Trading Fund for the provision of reports of parliamentary debates at less than full cost, and for the price concessions to public libraries	3,975,000	—
6. For expenditure by the Controller of Her Majesty's Stationery Office on the reimbursement of the HMSO Trading Fund in respect of goods and services supplied to the Houses of Parliament and to United Kingdom members of the European Assembly	13,483,000	130,000
7. For the expenditure of the Inland Revenue Department	960,417,000	45,900,000
8. For the expenditure of the Inland Revenue Department on life assurance premium relief and mortgage interest relief	138,000,000	—
9. For expenditure of the Inland Revenue Department for transitional relief, under the Finance Act 1965 and 1972, for companies with an overseas source of trading income	100,000	—
10. For the expenditure of the National Debt Office and Public Works Loan Commission	1,000	1,158,000
11. For the expenditure of the Department for National Savings	156,919,000	998,000
12. For expenditure by the Treasury on economic and financial administration, and for certain other services including grants in aid to certain parliamentary bodies and others	45,985,000	3,915,000
13. For expenditure by the Treasury in connection with the manufacture, storage and distribution of coinage for use in the United Kingdom	13,315,000	1,800,000
14. For expenditure by the Central Computer and Telecommunications Agency (Treasury) in connection with computers and general telecommunications including an international subscription	17,335,000	25,140,000

	Sums not exceeding	
	Supply Grants	Appropriations in Aid
Class XIX—*continued*		
Vote	£	£
15. For expenditure of the Civil Service Catering Organisation (Treasury) in connection with the provision of catering services - - - - - -	3,000	—
16. For rates and contributions in lieu of rates paid by the Rating of Government Property Department in respect of property occupied by the Crown and premises occupied by representatives of commonwealth and foreign countries and international organisations (including a Supplementary sum of £6,500,000) - - - - - - - - -	173,000,000	230,500,000
17. To repay to the Contingencies Fund certain miscellaneous advances - - - - - - -	785,000	—
Total, Class XIX - - - - - - £	1,991,844,000	320,975,000

Class XX, 1986–87 SCHEDULE (B).—PART 22

CLASS XX

SCHEDULE OF SUMS granted, and of the sums which may be applied as appropriations in aid in addition thereto, to defray the charges of the several Services herein particularly mentioned, which will come in course of payment during the year ending on 31st March 1987, viz.:—

	Sums not exceeding	
	Supply Grants	Appropriations in Aid
Vote	£	£
1. For the expenditure by the Management and Personnel Office on the central management of the civil service, on the Office of the Parliamentary Counsel and certain other services including grants in aid	32,160,000	1,566,000
2. For the expenditure by the Cabinet Office, including the Central Statistical Office and grants in aid to international organisations	14,767,000	4,365,000
3. For Her Majesty's foreign and other secret services	92,000,000	—
4. For the expenditure of the Charity Commission for England and Wales	5,124,000	1,000
5. For expenditure by the Paymaster General's Office on the superannuation of civil servants, pensions, etc., in respect of former members of the Royal Irish Constabulary and other pensions and non-recurrent payments; and for certain other services	1,161,565,000	234,880,000
6. For a grant in aid of the Commonwealth War Graves Commission	11,732,000	—
7. For the salaries of the Crown Estate Commissioners and the expenses of their office	642,000	—
8. For the expenditure of the House of Commons on members' salaries, allowances, pensions, etc., financial assistance to opposition parties and a grant in aid	35,666,000	—
9. For the expenditure of the House of Lords	10,633,000	260,000
10. For the expenditure of the Land Registry	1,000	89,818,000
11. For expenditure by the Ordnance Survey on the survey of Great Britain and other mapping services	18,709,000	34,427,000
12. For the expenditure of the Office of the Parliamentary Commissioner for Administration and the Health Service Commissioners for England, Scotland and Wales, including an international subscription	1,885,000	—
13. For expenditure by the Paymaster General's Office (Revised sum)	13,064,000	478,000
14. For the expenditure of the Department of Her Majesty's Most Honourable Privy Council	1,110,000	20,000
15. For the expenditure of the Public Record Office	10,171,000	927,000
16. For expenditure by the Office of Fair Trading	8,655,000	3,000
17. For expenditure by the Office of Telecommunications	1,000	3,858,000
18. For expenditure (partly recoverable), including loans, by the Property Services Agency of the Department of the Environment on acquisitions, public building work, accommodation services, administration and certain other services for civil purposes in the United Kingdom	147,503,000	846,411,000

Class XX—*continued*	Sums not exceeding	
	Supply Grants	Appropriations in Aid
Vote	£	£
19. For the expenditure of the Office of Population Censuses and Surveys, including a grant in aid	29,725,000	7,146,000
20. For expenditure by the Lord Advocate's Departments on central and miscellaneous services including grants in aid	15,799,000	55,000
21. For expenditure by the Crown Office on crown prosecutions and certain other legal services	3,106,000	3,000
22. For expenditure by the Northern Ireland Court Service on court services and certain other legal services including grants in aid	9,731,000	3,848,000
23. For expenditure by the Northern Ireland Court Service on legal aid and court services	7,659,000	—
24. For expenditure by the Departments of the Law Officers and the Procurator General and Treasury Solicitor on central and certain other services	8,947,000	1,029,000
25. For expenditure by the Department of the Procurator General and Treasury Solicitor on other legal services	2,511,000	725,000
26. For expenditure by the Crown Prosecution Service on central and miscellaneous services	64,714,000	29,000
27. For expenditure by the Director of Public Prosecutions on crown prosecutions	24,100,000	4,500,000
28. For expenditure by the Office of Gas Supply	1,000	1,165,000
TOTAL, CLASS XX £	1,731,681,000	1,235,514,000

Class XXA, 1986–87

SCHEDULE (B).—PART 23

CLASS XXA

SCHEDULE OF SUMS granted, and of the sums which may be applied as appropriations in aid in addition thereto, to defray the charges of the several Services herein particularly mentioned, which will come in course of payment during the year ending on 31st March 1987, viz.:—

	Sums not exceeding	
	Supply Grants	Appropriations in Aid
Vote	£	£
1. For expenditure by the House of Commons Commission	21,001,000	175,000
TOTAL, CLASS XXA £	21,001,000	175,000

Class XXB, 1986–87

SCHEDULE (B).—PART 24

CLASS XXB

SCHEDULE OF SUMS granted, and of the sums which may be applied as appropriations in aid in addition thereto, to defray the charges of the several Services herein particularly mentioned, which will come in course of payment during the year ending on 31st March 1987, viz.:—

	Sums not exceeding	
	Supply Grants	Appropriations in Aid
	£	£
Vote 1. For the expenditure of the National Audit Office including an international subscription - -	23,839,000	4,189,000
TOTAL, CLASS XXB - - - - - £	23,839,000	4,189,000

Section 3

SCHEDULE (C)

ENACTMENTS REPEALED

Chapter	Short title
1984 c.1 ...	Consolidated Fund Act 1984.
1984 c.44 ...	Appropriation Act 1984.
1984 c.61 ...	Consolidated Fund (No. 2) Act 1984.

CROWN AGENTS (AMENDMENT) ACT 1986

(1986 c. 43)

An Act to amend section 17 of the Crown Agents Act 1979.

[25th July 1986]

Parliamentary Debates

Hansard: H.C. Vol. 87, col. 138; H.C. Vol. 89, col. 1338; H.C. Vol. 99, col. 467; H.L. Vol. 476, col. 586; H.L. Vol. 477, col. 1089; H.L. Vol. 479, col. 9.

The Bill was considered by Standing Committee J on May 20, 1986.

Interest on Crown Agents' commencing capital debt: extension of "initial period"

1. In section 17 of the Crown Agents Act 1979 (interest on Crown Agents' commencing capital debt payable during initial period only if Secretary of State so determines)—

(*a*) in subsection (9), for the words from "five" to "seven" there shall be substituted the word "twelve"; and

(*b*) subsection (10) shall cease to have effect.

Short title

2. This Act may be cited as the Crown Agents (Amendment) Act 1986.

GAS ACT 1986

(1985 c. 44)

ARRANGEMENT OF SECTIONS

PART I

GAS SUPPLY

Introductory

Other functions of Director

An Act to provide for the appointment and functions of a Director General of Gas Supply and the establishment and functions of a Gas Consumers' Council; to abolish the privilege conferred on the British Gas Corporation by section 29 of the Gas Act 1972; to make new provision with respect to the supply of gas through pipes and certain related matters; to provide for the vesting of the property, rights and liabilities of the British Gas Corporation in a company nominated by the Secretary of State and the subsequent dissolution of that Corporation; to make provision with respect to, and to information furnished in connection with, agreements relating to the initial supply of gas won under the authority of a petroleum production licence; and for connected purposes. [25th July 1986]

Parliamentary Debates

Hansard: H.C. Vol. 87, col. 1045; H.C. Vol. 88, col. 767; H.C. Vol. 92, col. 42; H.C. Vol. 94, cols. 28, 29, 802; H.C. Vol. 102, cols. 77, 82; H.L. Vol. 472, col. 1350; H.L. Vol. 473, cols. 312, 1283; H.L. Vol. 474, cols. 140, 834; H.L. Vol. 475, cols. 80, 714, 1091; H.L. Vol. 476, col. 261; H.L. Vol. 477, col. 762; H.L. Vol. 478, cols. 97, 288, 1020.

The Bill was considered by Standing Committee F between December 17, 1985 and March 6, 1986.

Part I

Gas Supply

Introductory

The Director General of Gas Supply

1.—(1) The Secretary of State shall appoint an officer to be known as the Director General of Gas Supply (in this Act referred to as "the Director") for the purpose of performing the functions assigned to the Director by this Part.

(2) An appointment of a person to hold office as the Director shall not be for a term exceeding five years; but previous appointment to that office shall not affect eligibility for re-appointment.

(3) The Director may at any time resign his office as the Director by reasonable notice addressed to the Secretary of State; and the Secretary of State may remove any person from that office on the ground of incapacity or misbehaviour.

(4) Subject to subsections (2) and (3) above, the Director shall hold and vacate office as such in accordance with the terms of his appointment.

(5) The provisions of Schedule 1 to this Act shall have effect with respect to the Director.

The Gas Consumers' Council

2.—(1) There shall be a body corporate to be known as the Gas Consumers' Council (in this Part referred to as "the Council") for the purpose of performing the functions assigned to it by this Part.

(2) The Council shall consist of a chairman and such other members as the Secretary of State may from time to time appoint.

(3) In appointing members of the Council, the Secretary of State shall so far as practicable, ensure—

(*a*) that the members of the Council include members who, by reason of their familiarity with the special requirements and circumstances of the different areas of Great Britain or of small businesses, are able together to represent the interests of consumers of gas supplied through pipes in all those areas and of such businesses; and

(*b*) that the interests of consumers of gas supplied through pipes in different areas are represented by different members wherever that appears to the Secretary of State to be appropriate having regard to the manner in which the various parts of the gas supply industry in Great Britain organise themselves.

(4) A member of the Council shall hold and vacate office in accordance with the terms of the instrument appointing him and shall, on ceasing to hold office, be eligible for re-appointment.

(5) The provisions of Schedule 2 to this Act shall have effect with respect to the Council.

(6) In consequence of the provisions of this section, the National Gas Consumers' Council and the Regional Gas Consumers' Council shall cease to exist.

Abolition of Corporation's special privilege

3. As from such day as the Secretary of State may by order appoint for the purposes of this section and the following provisions of this Part (in this Act referred to as "the appointed day"), the privilege with respect to the supply of gas through pipes conferred on the British Gas Corporation (in this Act referred to as "the Corporation") by section 29 of the 1972 Act shall cease to exist.

General duties of Secretary of State and Director

4.—(1) The Secretary of State and the Director shall each have a duty to exercise the functions assigned to him by this Part in the manner which he considers is best calculated—

(*a*) to secure that persons authorised by or under this Part to supply gas through pipes so far as it is economical to do so, all reasonable demands for gas in Great Britain; and

(*b*) without prejudice to the generality of paragraph (*a*) above, to secure that such persons are able to finance the provision of gas supply services.

(2) Subject to subsection (1) above, the Secretary of State and the Director shall each have a duty to exercise the functions assigned to him by this Part in the manner which he considers is best calculated—

(*a*) to protect the interests of consumers of gas supplied through pipes in respect of the prices charged and the other terms of supply, the continuity of supply and the quality of the gas supply services provided;

(*b*) to promote efficiency and economy on the part of persons authorised by or under this Part to supply gas through pipes and the efficient use of gas supplied through pipes;

(*c*) to protect the public from dangers arising from the transmission or distribution of gas through pipes or from the use of gas supplied through pipes;

(*d*) to enable persons to compete effectively in the supply of gas through pipes at rates which, in relation to any premises, exceed 25,000 therms a year.

(3) In performing his duty under subsection (2) above to exercise functions assigned to him in the manner which he considers is best

calculated to protect the interests of consumers of gas supplied through pipes in respect of the quality of the gas supply services provided, the Secretary of State or, as the case may be, the Director shall take into account, in particular, the interests of those who are disabled or of pensionable age.

Authorisation of gas supply

Prohibition on unauthorised supply

5.—(1) Subject to subsection (2) and section 6 below, a person who supplies gas through pipes to any premises shall be guilty of an offence unless he is authorised to do so under section 7 or 8 below.

(2) Subsection (1) above is not contravened by a person supplying, for use in a building or part of a building in which he has an interest, gas supplied to the building by a person authorised to supply it by or under section 6, 7 or 8 below.

(3) A person guilty of an offence under this section shall be liable—

(*a*) on summary conviction, to a fine not exceeding the statutory maximum;

(*b*) on conviction on indictment, to a fine.

(4) No proceedings shall be instituted in England and Wales in respect of an offence under this section except by or on behalf of the Secretary of State or the Director.

Exception to section 5

6.—(1) Where a person (in this section referred to as a "gas supplier") notifies the Secretary of State that he proposes to undertake a supply of gas to any premises at a rate in excess of 2,000,000 therms a year (in this section referred to as "the required rate"), section 5(1) above is not contravened by that supply unless, within six weeks of receiving the notification, the Secretary of State notifies the supplier either—

(*a*) that he is of the opinion that the rate of supply to those premises would be unlikely to exceed the required rate; or

(*b*) that he is unable to form an opinion as to whether the rate of supply to those premises would or would not be likely to exceed the required rate.

(2) Where a gas supplier has given the Secretary of State a notification under section (1) above and—

(*a*) the rate of supply to the premises to which the notification relates fails to exceed the required rate for three successive periods of twelve months;

(*b*) the gas supplier fails to furnish the Secretary of State with such information as he may require for the purpose of determining whether the condition in paragraph (*a*) above is fulfilled; or

(*c*) the gas supplier fails to afford to the Secretary of State such facilities as he may require for the purpose of verifying any information furnished in pursuance of such a requirement as is mentioned in paragraph (*b*) above,

the Secretary of State may direct that the gas supplier's notification shall be treated as invalid for the purposes of that subsection except as regards gas previously supplied.

(3) As soon as practicable after receiving or giving a notification under subsection (1) above, or giving a direction under subsection (2) above, the Secretary of State shall send a copy of the notification or direction—

(*a*) to the Director;

(*b*) to the Health and Safety Executive; and

(*c*) to any public gas supplier whose authorised area includes the premises or any part of the premises to which the gas supplier's notification relates.

Authorisation of public gas suppliers

7.—(1) In this Part "public gas supplier" means any person who holds an authorisation under this section except where he is acting otherwise than for purposes connected with the supply of gas through pipes to premises in his authorised area.

(2) The Secretary of State after consultation with the Director may authorise any person to supply gas through pipes to any premises in that person's authorised area, that is to say, so much of the area designated in the authorisation as is not for the time being designated in a subsequent authorisation under this section.

(3) An application for an authorisation under this section shall be made in the prescribed manner; and within 14 days after the making of the application, the applicant shall—

(*a*) give notice of the application to any public gas supplier whose authorised area includes the whole or any part of the area to which the application relates; and

(*b*) publish a copy of the notice in the prescribed manner.

(4) Before granting an authorisation under this section, the Secretary of State shall give notice—

(*a*) stating that he proposes to grant the authorisation;

(*b*) stating the reasons why he proposes to grant the authorisation; and

(*c*) specifying the time (not being less than three months from the date of publication of the notice) within which representations or objections with respect to the proposed authorisation may be made,

and shall consider any representations or objections which are duly made and not withdrawn.

(5) A notice under subsection (4) above shall be given—

(*a*) by publishing the notice in such manner as the Secretary of State considers appropriate for bringing it to the attention of persons likely to be affected by the grant of the authorisation; and

(*b*) by sending a copy of the notice to the Health and Safety Executive and to any public gas supplier whose area includes the whole or any part of the area proposed to be designated in the authorisation.

(6) An authorisation under this section shall be in writing and, unless previously revoked in accordance with any term in that behalf contained in the authorisation, shall continue in force for such period as may be specified in or determined by or under the authorisation.

(7) An authorisation under this section may include—

(*a*) such conditions relating to the supply of gas, or requiring information to be furnished to the Director or published, as appear to the Secretary of State to be requisite or expedient having regard to the duties imposed by section 4 above;

(*b*) such conditions requiring arrangements to be made with respect to the provision of special services for meeting the needs of consumers of gas supplied through pipes who are disabled or pensionable age as appear to the Secretary of State to be requisite or expedient having regard to those duties;

(*c*) conditions requiring the rendering to the Secretary of State of a payment on the grant of the authorisation or payments during the currency of the authorisation or both of such amount or amounts as may be determined by or under the authorisation; and (*d*) conditions requiring the public gas supplier to furnish the Council in such manner and at such times with such information as appears to the Secretary of State to be requisite or expedient for the purpose of facilitating the exercise by the Council of the functions assigned to it by this Part or as may be reasonably required by the Council for that purpose;

and a condition included by virtue of this subsection in an authorisation under this section may contain provision for the condition to cease to have effect at such time before the end of the period referred to in subsection (6) above as may be determined by or under the authorisation.

(8) Without prejudice to the generality of paragraph (*a*) of subsection (7) above, conditions included by virtue of that paragraph in an authorisation under this section may require the public gas supplier—

(*a*) to comply with any direction given by the Director as to such matters as are specified in the authorisation or are of a description so specified;

(*b*) except in so far as the Director consents to his doing or not doing them, not to do or to do such things as are specified in the authorisation or are of a description so specified; and

(*c*) to refer for determination by the Director such questions arising under the authorisation as are specified in the authorisation or are of a description so specified.

(9) An authorisation under this section shall not include in the designation any area which is situated within 25 yards from a main of another public gas supplier unless—

(*a*) the Secretary of State is of the opinion that the main is not, and is not intended to be, a relevant main; or

(*b*) that other public gas supplier has consented in writing to the area being so included.

(10) As soon as practicable after granting an authorisation under this section, the Secretary of State shall send a copy of the authorisation—

(*a*) to the Director;

(*b*) to the Health and Safety Executive; and

(*c*) to any public gas supplier whose authorised area previously included the whole or any part of the area designated in the authorisation.

(11) Any sums received by the Secretary of State under this section shall be paid into the Consolidated Fund.

(12) In this section and section 8 below "relevant main", in relation to a public gas supplier, means any distribution main which is being used for the purpose of giving a supply of gas to any premises at a rate not exceeding 25,000 therms a year.

(13) Neither the requirement to consult with the Director imposed by subsection (2) above nor subsections (3) and (4) above shall apply to the granting of the authorisation under this section which, having regard to the provisions of this Part, needs to be granted to the Corporation before the appointed day.

Authorisation of other persons

8.—(1) The Secretary of State after consultation with the Director, or the Director with the consent of, or in accordance with a general authority given by, the Secretary of State, may authorise any person or persons of any class to supply gas through pipes to any premises specified or of a description specified in the authorisation.

(2) An application for an authorisation under this section to be granted to a particular person shall be made in the prescribed manner; and within 14 days after the making of the application, the applicant shall give notice

of the application to any public gas supplier whose authorised area includes the whole or any part of any premises to which the application relates.

(3) An authorisation under this section shall be in writing and, unless previously revoked in accordance with any term in that behalf contained in the authorisation, shall continue in force for such period as may be specified in or determined by or under the authorisation.

(4) An authorisation under this section may include—

(*a*) such conditions as appear to the grantor to be requisite or expedient having regard to the duties imposed by section 4(2)(*c*) above;

(*b*) such conditions as appear to the grantor to be requisite or expedient having regard to subsection (5) below; and

(*c*) conditions requiring the rendering to the grantor of a payment on the grant of the authorisation or payments during the currency of the authorisation or both of such amount or amounts as may be determined by or under the authorisation.

(5) An authorisation under this section shall not authorise the giving of a supply of gas to any premises situated within 25 yards from a main of a public gas supplier unless—

(*a*) the grantor is of the opinion that the main is not, and is not intended to be, a relevant main;

(*b*) the grantor has notified the public gas supplier that he is of the opinion that the rate of supply to those premises would be likely to exceed 25,000 therms a year; or

(*c*) the public gas supplier has consented in writing to the giving of the supply.

(6) As soon as practicable after granting an authorisation under this section, the grantor shall—

(*a*) send a copy of the authorisation to the Health and Safety Executive and to any public gas supplier whose authorised area includes the whole or any part of any premises to which the authorisation relates and, in the case of an authorisation granted by the Secretary of State, to the Director; and

(*b*) in the case of an authorisation granted to persons of any class, publish such a copy in such manner as he considers appropriate for bringing it to the attention of persons of that class.

(7) Any sums received by the Secretary of State or Director under this section shall be paid into the Consolidated Fund.

Supply of gas by public gas suppliers

General powers and duties

9.—(1) It shall be the duty of a public gas supplier—

(*a*) to develop and maintain an efficient, co-ordinated and economical system of gas supply; and

(*b*) subject to paragraph (*a*) above, to comply, so far as it is economical to do so, with any reasonable request for him to give a supply of gas to any premises.

(2) It shall also be the duty of a public gas supplier to avoid any undue preference in the supply of gas to persons entitled to a supply in pursuance of section 10(1) below.

(3) The following provisions shall have effect, namely—

(*a*) Schedule 3 to this Act (which provides for the acquisition of land by public gas suppliers); and

(*b*) Schedule 4 to this Act (which relates to the breaking up of streets and bridges by such suppliers).

Duty to supply certain premises

10.—(1) Subject to the following provisions of this Part and any regulations made under those provisions, a public gas supplier shall, upon being required to do so by the owner or occupier, give and continue to give a supply of gas to any premises which—

(*a*) are situated within 25 yards from a relevant main of the supplier; or

(*b*) are connected by a service pipe to any such main,

and in the case of premises falling within paragraph (*a*) above, shall also provide and lay any pipe that may be necessary for that purpose.

(2) Where any person requires a supply of gas in pursuance of subsection (1) above, he shall serve on the public gas supplier a notice specifying—

(*a*) the premises in respect of which the supply is required; and

(*b*) the day (not being earlier than a reasonable time after the service of the notice) upon which the supply is required to commence.

(3) Where any pipe is provided and laid by a public gas supplier in pursuance of subsection (1) above, the cost of providing and laying—

(*a*) so much of the pipe as is laid upon property owned or occupied by the person requiring the supply, not being property dedicated to public use; and

(*b*) so much of the pipe as is laid for a greater distance than 30 feet from any pipe of the supplier, although not on such property as is mentioned in paragraph (*a*) above,

shall, if the supplier so requires, be defrayed by that person.

(4) The Secretary of State may, after consultation with the Director, make provision by regulations for entitling a public gas supplier to require a person requiring a supply of gas in pursuance of subsection (1) above to pay to the supplier an amount in respect of the expenses of the laying of the main used for the purpose of giving that supply if—

(*a*) the supply is required within the prescribed period after the laying of the main;

(*b*) a person for the purpose of supplying whom the main was laid has made a payment to the supplier in respect of those expenses;

(*c*) the amount required does not exceed any amount paid in respect of those expenses by such a person or by any person previously required to make a payment under the regulations; and

(*d*) the supplier has not recovered those expenses in full.

(5) Nothing in subsection (1) above shall be taken as requiring a public gas supplier to supply gas to any premises in excess of 25,000 therms in any period of twelve months.

(6) Nothing in subsection (1) above shall be taken as requiring a public gas supplier to give or continue to give a supply of gas to any premises it—

(*a*) he is prevented from doing so by circumstances not within his control; or

(*b*) circumstances exist by reason of which his doing so would or might involve danger to the public, and he has taken all such steps as it was reasonable to take both to prevent the circumstances from occurring and to prevent them from having that effect.

(7) Where any person requires a new or increased supply of gas in pursuance of subsection (1) above for purposes other than domestic use, and the supply cannot be given without the laying of a new main, or the enlarging of an existing main, or the construction or enlarging of any other works required for the supply of gas by the public gas supplier, the supplier may, if he thinks fit, refuse to give the supply unless that person enters into a written contract with him—

(*a*) to continue to receive and pay for a supply of gas of such minimum quantity and for such minimum period as the supplier may reasonably require, having regard to the expense to be incurred by him in laying or enlarging the main or constructing or enlarging the other works; or

(*b*) to make such payment to the supplier (in addition to any payments to be made from time to time for gas supplied) as the supplier may reasonably require having regard to the matters aforesaid.

(8) Where any person requires a supply of gas in pursuance of subsection (1) above the purposes only of a stand-by supply for any premises having a separate supply of gas, or having a supply (in use or ready for use for the purpose for which the stand-by supply is required) of electricity, steam or other form of energy, the supplier may, if he thinks fit, refuse to give or discontinue the supply unless that person enters into a written contract with him to pay him such annual sum in addition to any charge for gas supplied as—

(*a*) will give him a reasonable return on the capital expenditure incurred by him in providing the stand-by supply; and

(*b*) will cover other expenditure incurred by him in order to meet the maximum possible demand for those premises.

(9) In this section "relevant main" has the same meaning as in section 7 above.

Power to require security

11.—(1) Where any person requires a supply of gas in pursuance of subsection (1) of section 10 above—

(*a*) the public gas supplier may require that person to give him reasonable security for the payment to him of all money which may become due to him in respect of the supply or, where any pipe falls to be provided and laid in pursuance of that subsection, the provision and laying of the pipe; and

(*b*) if that person fails to give such security, the supplier may if he thinks fit refuse to give the supply, or to provide and lay the pipe, for so long as the failure continues.

(2) Where any person who requires a supply of gas in pursuance of subsection (1) of section 10 above enters into such a contract as is mentioned in subsection (7) or (8) of that section—

(*a*) the public gas supplier may require that person to give him reasonable security for the payment to him of all money which may become due to him under the contract; and

(*b*) if that person fails to give such security, the supplier may if he thinks fit refuse to give the supply for so long as the failure continues.

(3) Where any person has not given such security as is mentioned in subsection (1) or (2) above, or the security given by any person has become invalid or insufficient—

(*a*) the public gas supplier may by notice require that person within seven days after the service of the notice, to give him reasonable security for the payment of all money which may become due to him in respect of the supply or, as the case may be, under the contract; and

(*b*) if that person fails to give such security, the supplier may if he thinks fit discontinue the supply for so long as the failure continues.

(4) Where any money is deposited with a public gas supplier by way of security in pursuance of this section, the supplier shall pay interest, at such rate as may from time to time be fixed by the supplier with the

approval of the Director, on every sum of 50p so deposited for every three months during which it remains in the hands of the supplier.

Standard method of charge

12.—(1) Subject to sections 13 and 14 below, a public gas supplier shall charge for gas supplied by him according to the number of therms supplied, that number being calculated in the prescribed manner on the basis of the declared calorific value of the gas.

(2) In this Part—

"calorific value", in relation to any gas, means the number of megajoules (gross) which would be produced by the combustion of one cubic metre of the gas measured at a temperature of 15°C and a pressure of 1013.25 millibars and, if the Secretary of State so determines, containing such an amount of water vapour as is specified in the determination;

"declared calorific value", in relation to any gas supplied by a public gas supplier, means calorific value declared by the supplier in accordance with regulations under subsection (3) below.

(3) Regulations shall make provision—

(*a*) as to the time when, and the manner in which, the calorific value of gas supplied by a public gas supplier is to be declared, and is to be brought to the notice of consumers;

(*b*) as to the time when any such declaration is to take effect; and

(*c*) for the adjustment of charges for gas in cases where an alteration of declared calorific value occurs in the course of a period for which such charges are made.

Alternative method of charge

13.—(1) If regulations under this section so provide, the number of therms supplied by a public gas supplier may, to such an extent as he think fit, be calculated in the prescribed manner on the basis of actual calorific values of the gas determined by the supplier in accordance with the regulations; and a public gas supplier is a relevant supplier for the purposes of this section in so far as the number of therms supplied by him is so calculated.

(2) Regulations may make provision—

(*a*) for requiring determinations of actual calorific values of gas supplied by relevant suppliers to be made at such places, at such times and in such manner as the Secretary of State may direct;

(*b*) for requiring such premises, apparatus and equipment as the Secretary of State may direct to be provided and maintained by relevant suppliers for the purpose of making such determinations;

(*c*) as to the manner in which calculations of the number of therms supplied by relevant suppliers are to be made; and

(*d*) as to the manner in which the results of such determinations are, and prescribed information with respect to the making of such calculations is, to be made available to the public.

(3) The Secretary of State shall appoint competent and impartial persons to carry out tests of apparatus and equipment provided and maintained by relevant suppliers in pursuance of regulations under this section for the purpose of ascertaining whether they comply with the regulations.

(4) Regulations may make provision—

(*a*) for persons representing the relevant supplier concerned to be present during the carrying out of such tests;

(*b*) for the manner in which the results of such tests are to be made available to the public; and

(*c*) for conferring powers of entry on property of relevant suppliers for the purpose of carrying out such tests and otherwise for the purposes of this section.

(5) There shall be paid out of money provided by Parliament to the persons appointed under subsection (3) above such remuneration and such allowances as may be determined by the Secretary of State with the approval of the Treasury, and such pensions as may be so determined may be paid out of money provided by Parliament to or in respect of those persons.

(6) Every person who is a relevant supplier during any period shall pay to the Secretary of State such proportion as the Secretary of State may determine of—

(*a*) any sums paid by him under subsection (5) above in respect of that period; and

(*b*) such part of his other expenses for that period as he may with the consent of the Treasury determine to be attributable to his functions in connection with the testing of apparatus and equipment for the purposes of this section;

and any liability under this subsection to pay to the Secretary of State sums on account of pensions (whether paid by him under subsection (5) above or otherwise) shall, if the Secretary of State so determines, be satisfied by way of contributions calculated, at such rate as may be determined by the Treasury, by reference to remuneration.

(7) The reference in subsection (6) above to expenses of the Secretary of State includes a reference to expenses incurred by any government department in connection with the Department of Energy, and to such sums as the Treasury may determine in respect of the use for the purposes of that Department of any premises belonging to the Crown.

(8) Any sums received by the Secretary of State under this section shall be paid into the Consolidated Fund.

Fixing of tariffs

14.—(1) Subject to the following provisions of this section, the prices to be charged by a public gas supplier for the supply of gas by him shall be in accordance with such tariffs as may be fixed from time to time by him, and those tariffs, which may relate to the supply of gas in different areas, cases and circumstances, shall be so framed as to show the methods by which and the principles on which the charges are to be made as well as the prices which are to be charged, and shall be published in such manner as in the opinion of the supplier will secure adequate publicity for them.

(2) A tariff fixed by a public gas supplier under subsection (1) above may include a standing charge in addition to the charge for the actual gas supplied, and may also include a rent or other charge in respect of any gas meter or other gas fittings provided by the supplier on the premises of the consumer.

(3) In fixing tariffs under subsection (1) above, a public gas supplier shall not show undue preference to any person or class of persons, and shall not exercise any undue discrimination against any person or class of persons; but this subsection shall not apply in relation to tariffs fixed under that subsection with respect to the prices to be charged for therms supplied to any premises in excess of 25,000 therms in any period of twelve months.

(4) Notwithstanding anything in section 12 or 13 above or the preceding provisions of this section, a public gas supplier may enter into a special

agreement with any consumer for the supply of gas to him on such terms as may be specified in the agreement if either—

(a) the tariffs in force are not appropriate owing to special circumstances; or

(b) the agreement provides for a minimum supply of gas to any premises in excess of 25,000 therms in any period of twelve months.

(5) In this Part "tariff customer" means a person who is supplied with gas by a public gas supplier otherwise than in pursuance of such an agreement as is mentioned in subsection (4) above.

Public gas supply code

15. The provisions of Schedule 5 to this Act (which relate to the supply of gas by public gas suppliers and connected matters) shall have effect.

Supply of gas by public gas suppliers and others

Standards of quality

16.—(1) The Secretary of State shall, after consultation with the Director and public gas suppliers, prescribe standards of pressure, purity and uniformity of calorific value to be complied with by the suppliers in supplying gas, and may after such consultation prescribe other standards with respect to the properties, condition and composition of gas so supplied.

(2) The Secretary of State shall, after consultation with the Director and such persons and organisations as the Secretary of State considers appropriate, prescribe standards of pressure and purity to be complied with by persons other than public gas suppliers in supplying gas through pipes, and may after such consultation prescribe standards of uniformity of calorific value and other standards with respect to the properties, condition and composition of gas so supplied.

(3) The Secretary of State shall appoint competent and impartial persons to carry out tests of gas supplied through pipes for the purpose of ascertaining whether it conforms with the standards prescribed under this section and (in the case of gas supplied by a public gas supplier) whether it is of or above the declared calorific value.

(4) Regulations may make provision—

(a) for requiring such tests to be carried out at such places as the Secretary of State may direct;

(b) for requiring such premises, apparatus and equipment as the Secretary of State may direct to be provided and maintained by persons supplying gas through pipes (in the following provisions of this section referred to as gas suppliers) for the purpose of carrying out such tests;

(c) for persons representing the gas supplier concerned to be present during the carrying out of such tests;

(d) for the manner in which the results of such tests are to be made available to the public; and

(e) for conferring powers of entry on property of gas suppliers for the purpose of deciding where tests are to be carried out and otherwise for the purposes of this section.

(5) There shall be paid out of money provided by Parliament to the persons appointed under subsection (3) above such remuneration and such allowances as may be determined by the Secretary of State with the approval of the Treasury, and such pensions as may be so determined may be paid out of money provided by Parliament to or in respect of those persons.

(6) Every person who is a gas supplier during any period shall pay to the Secretary of State such proportion as the Secretary of State may determine of—

(*a*) any sums paid by him under subsection (5) above in respect of that period; and

(*b*) such part of his other expenses for that period as he may with the consent of the Treasury determine to be attributable to his functions in connection with the testing of gas for the purposes of this section;

and any liability under this subsection to pay to the Secretary of State sums on account of pensions (whether paid by him under subsection (5) above or otherwise) shall, if the Secretary of State so determines, be satisfied by way of contributions calculated, at such rate as may be determined by the Treasury, by reference to remuneration.

(7) The reference in subsection (6) above to expenses of the Secretary of State includes a reference to expenses incurred by any government department in connection with the Department of Energy, and to such sums as the Treasury may determine in respect of the use for the purposes of that Department of any premises belonging to the Crown.

(8) Any sums received by the Secretary of State under this section shall be paid into the Consolidated Fund.

(9) Any reference in this section to a person supplying gas through pipes does not include a reference to a person supplying, for use in a building or part of a building in which he has an interest, gas supplied to the building by a person authorised to supply it by or under section 6, 7 or 8 above.

Meter testing and stamping

17.—(1) No meter shall be used for the purpose of ascertaining the quantity of gas supplied through pipes to any person unless it is stamped either by, or on the authority of, a meter examiner appointed under this section or in such other manner as may be authorised by regulations.

(2) Subject to subsections (3) and (4) below, it shall be the duty of a meter examiner, on being required to do so by any person and on payment of the prescribed fee, to examine any meter used or intended to be used for ascertaining the quantity of gas supplied to any person, and to stamp, or authorise the stamping of, that meter.

(3) A meter examiner shall not stamp, or authorise the stamping of, any meter unless he is satisfied that it is of such pattern and construction and is marked in such manner as is approved by the Secretary of State and that the meter conforms with such standards as may be prescribed.

(4) A meter examiner may stamp, or authorise the stamping of, a meter submitted to him, notwithstanding that he has not himself examined it, if—

(*a*) the meter was manufactured or repaired by the person submitting it;

(*b*) that person has obtained the consent of the Secretary of State to the submission; and

(*c*) any conditions subject to which the consent was given have been satisfied.

(5) The Secretary of State shall appoint competent and impartial persons as meter examiners for the purposes of this section.

(6) There shall be paid out of money provided by Parliament to meter examiners such remuneration and such allowances as may be determined by the Secretary of State with the approval of the Treasury, and such pensions as may be so determined may be paid out of money provided by Parliament to or in respect of such examiners.

(7) All fees payable in respect of the examination of meters by meter examiners shall be paid to the Secretary of State; and any sums received by him under this subsection shall be paid into the Consolidated Fund.

(8) Regulations may make provision—

(*a*) for re-examining meters already stamped, and for the cancellation of stamps in the case of meters which no longer conform with the prescribed standards and in such other circumstances as may be prescribed;

(*b*) for requiring meters to be periodically overhauled;

(*c*) for the revocation of any approval given by the Secretary of State to any particular pattern or construction of meter, and for requiring existing meters of that pattern or construction to be replaced within such period as may be prescribed; and

(*d*) for determining the fees to be paid for examining, stamping and re-examining meters, and the persons by whom they are to be paid.

(9) If any person supplies gas through a meter which has not been stamped under this section, he shall be guilty of an offence and liable on summary conviction to a fine not exceeding level 3 on the standard scale.

(10) Where the commission by any person of an offence under subsection (9) above is due to the act or default of some other person, that other person shall be guilty of the offence; and a person may be charged with and convicted of the offence by virtue of this subsection whether or not proceedings are taken against the first-mentioned person.

(11) In any proceedings for an offence under subsection (9) above it shall be a defence for the person charged to prove that he took all reasonable steps and exercised all due diligence to avoid committing the offence.

(12) The preceding provisions of this section shall not have effect in relation to the supply of gas to a person under any agreement providing for the quantity of gas supplied to him to be ascertained by a meter designed for rates of flow which, if measured at a temperature of 15°C and a pressure of 1013.25 millibars, would exceed 1600 cubic metres an hour.

Safety regulations

18.—(1) The general purposes of Part I of the Health and Safety at Work etc. Act 1974 (health, safety and welfare in connection with work, and control of dangerous substances etc.) shall include protecting the public from personal injury, fire, explosions and other dangers arising from the transmission or distribution of gas through pipes, or from the use of gas supplied through pipes.

(2) The Secretary of State may by regulations make provision for empowering any officer authorised by the relevant authority—

(*a*) to enter any premises in which there is a service pipe connected with a gas main, for the purpose of inspecting any gas fitting on the premises, any flue or means of ventilation used in connection with any such gas fitting, or any service pipe or other apparatus (not being a gas fitting) which is on the premises and is used for the supply of gas or is connected with a gas main;

(*b*) where he so enters any such premises, to examine or apply any test to any such object as is mentioned in paragraph (*a*) above and (where the object is a gas fitting) to verify what supply of air is available for it; and

(*c*) where in his opinion it is necessary to do so for the purpose of averting danger to life or property, and notwithstanding any contract previously existing, to disconnect and seal off any gas fitting or any part of the gas supply system on the premises, or cut off the supply of gas to the premises or, if no such supply is being given, to signify the refusal of the relevant authority to give or, as the case may be, allow such a supply.

(3) Where any regulations under subsection (2) above confer any power in accordance with paragraph (*c*) of that subsection, the regulations shall also include provision—

(*a*) for securing that, where any such power is exercised, the consumer will be notified as to the nature of the defect or other circumstances in consequence of which it has been exercised;

(*b*) for enabling any consumer so notified to appeal to the Secretary of State on the grounds that the defect or other circumstances in question did not constitute a danger such as to justify the action taken in the exercise of the power, or did not exist or have ceased to exist; and

(*c*) for enabling the Secretary of State to give such directions as may in accordance with the regulations be determined by him to be appropriate in consequence of any such appeal.

(4) Regulations made under subsection (2) above may make provision for prohibiting any person, except with the consent of the relevant authority or in pursuance of any directions given by the Secretary of State as mentioned in subsection (3)(*c*) above, from—

(*a*) reconnecting any gas fitting or part of any gas supply system which has been disconnected by or on behalf of the relevant authority in exercise of a power conferred by the regulations; or

(*b*) restoring the supply of gas to any premises where it has been cut off by or on behalf of the relevant authority in the exercise of any such power; or

(*c*) causing gas from a gas main to be supplied to any premises where in pursuance of the regulations the refusal of the relevant authority to give or, as the case may be, allow a supply to those premises has been signified and that refusal has not been withdrawn.

(5) Where in pursuance of any powers conferred by regulations made under subsection (2) above, entry is made on any premises by an officer authorised by the relevant authority—

(*a*) the officer shall ensure that the premises are left no less secure by reason of the entry; and

(*b*) the relevant authority shall make good, or pay compensation for, any damage caused by the officer, or by any person accompanying him in entering the premises, in taking any action therein authorised by the regulations, or in making the premises secure.

(6) Any officer exercising powers of entry conferred by regulations made under subsection (2) above may be accompanied by such persons as may be necessary or expedient for the purpose for which entry is made, or for the purposes of subsection (5) above.

(7) If any person intentionally obstructs any officer exercising powers of entry conferred by regulations made under subsection (2) above, he shall be guilty of an offence and liable on summary conviction to a fine not exceeding level 3 on the standard scale.

(8) The Rights of Entry (Gas and Electricity Boards) Act 1954 (entry under a justice's warrant) shall apply in relation to any powers of entry conferred by regulations made under subsection (2) above as if—

(*a*) any reference to a public gas supplier were a reference to the relevant authority; and

(*b*) any reference to an employee of a public gas supplier were a reference to an officer authorised by the relevant authority.

(9) In this section "the relevant authority"—

(*a*) in relation to dangers arising from the supply of gas by a public gas supplier, or from the use of gas supplied by such a supplier, means that supplier; and

(*b*) in relation to dangers arising from the supply of gas by a person other than a public gas supplier, or from the use of gas supplied by such a person, means the Secretary of State.

Use by other persons of pipe-lines belonging to public gas suppliers

Acquisition of rights to use pipe-lines

19.—(1) In the case of a pipe-line belonging to a public gas supplier, any person may, after giving the public gas supplier not less than 28 days' notice, apply to the Director for directions under this section which would secure to the applicant a right to have conveyed by the pipe-line, during a period specified in the application, quantities so specified of gas which—

(*a*) is of a kind so specified; and

(*b*) is of, or of a kind similar to, the kind which the pipe-line is designed to convey.

(2) Where an application is made under subsection (1) above, it shall be the duty of the Director—

(*a*) to decide whether the application is to be adjourned (so as to enable negotiations or further negotiations to take place), considered further or rejected;

(*b*) to give notice of his decision to the applicant; and

(*c*) in the case of a decision that the application is to be considered further, to give the supplier notice that it is to be so considered and an opportunity of being heard about the matter.

(3) Where, after further considering an application under subsection (1) above, the Director is satisfied that the giving of directions under this section would not prejudice the conveyance by the pipe-line of—

(*a*) the quantities of gas which the public gas supplier requires or may reasonably be expected to require to be conveyed by the pipe-line in order to secure the performance by the supplier of his duties under sections 9(1) and 10(1) above and his contractual obligations; and

(*b*) the quantities of gas which any person who has a right to have gas conveyed by the pipe-line is entitled to require to be so conveyed in the exercise of that right,

the Director may give such directions to the supplier.

(4) Directions under this section may—

(*a*) specify the terms on which the Director considers the public gas supplier should enter into an agreement with the applicant for all or any of the following purposes—

(i) for securing to the applicant the right to have conveyed by the pipe-line during the period specified in the directions the quantities so specified of gas which is of the kind so specified;

(ii) for securing that the exercise of that right is not prevented or impeded;

(iii) for regulating the charges which may be made for the conveyance of gas by virtue of that right;

(iv) for regulating the terms on which the supplier will supply gas to the applicant where the applicant's exercise of the right is temporarily interrupted by his inability to obtain gas from other sources;

(v) for securing to the applicant the right to have a pipe-line of his connected to the pipe-line by the supplier;

(*b*) specify the sums or the method of determining the sums which the Director considers should be paid by way of consideration for any such right; and

(*c*) require the supplier, if the applicant pays or agrees to pay those sums within a period specified in that behalf in the directions, to enter into an agreement with him on the terms so specified.

(5) In giving any directions under this section, the Director shall apply the principle that the public gas supplier should be entitled to receive by way of charges for the conveyance of gas by virtue of the right—

(*a*) the appropriate proportion of the costs incurred by the supplier in administering, maintaining and operating his pipe-line system; and

(*b*) a return equal to the appropriate proportion of the return received by the supplier (otherwise than by virtue of the right) on the capital value of that system (including so much of that return as is set aside to meet the need from time to time to renew that system).

(6) In subsection (5) above "the appropriate proportion" means such proportion as properly—

(*a*) reflects the use made of the public gas supplier's pipe-line system by virtue of the right as compared with the use made of that system for other purposes; and

(*b*) takes into account the sums paid by way of consideration for the right and any sums paid in respect of the pipe-line (whether by the applicant or by any other person) in pursuance of directions under section 20(4) or 21(1) below.

(7) Where directions under this section require the public gas supplier to accept an obligation to supply gas to any person, the obligation shall be to supply gas to that person only in circumstances where to do so would not prejudice the performance by the supplier of such of his duties under sections 9(1) and 10(1) above, and of his contractual obligations, as fall to be performed otherwise than on the temporary interruption of the exercise of a right conferred in pursuance of those directions or of any other directions under this section.

(8) An authorisation under section 7 above may include such conditions as appear to the Secretary of State requisite or expedient having regard to the provisions of this section and sections 20 and 21 below; and subsection (8) of section 7 above shall apply for the purposes of this subsection as it applies for the purposes of subsection (7)(*a*) of that section.

(9) Any reference in this section to a right to have a quantity of gas of any kind conveyed by a pipe-line is a reference to a right—

(*a*) to introduce that quantity of gas of that kind at one point in the pipe-line; and

(*b*) to take off such quantity as may be appropriate of gas of, or of a kind similar to, that kind at another point in the pipe-line.

(10) In this section and sections 20 and 21 below "pipe-line" has the same meaning as in the Pipe-lines Act 1962.

Construction of pipe-lines

20.—(1) A public gas supplier shall not at any time execute any works for the construction of a high pressure pipe-line which, when constructed, will exceed two miles in length unless, not less than two years (or such shorter period as the Director may allow) before that time, he has given notice to the Director stating that he intends to execute the works.

(2) A notice under subsection (1) above shall—

(*a*) specify the points between which the proposed pipe-line is to run and be accompanied by a map (drawn to a scale not less than 6 miles to the inch) on which is delineated the route which it is proposed to take;

(*b*) specify the length, diameter and capacity of the proposed pipe-line, the kind of gas which it is designed to convey and the quantities of gas which the public gas supplier requires or expects to require to be conveyed by the pipe-line in order to secure the performance by the supplier of his duties under sections 9(1) and 10(1) above and his contractual obligations; and

(*c*) contain such other particulars (if any) as may be prescribed.

(3) The Director shall publish in such manner as he considers appropriate notice of the receipt by him of any notice under subsection (1) above; and a notice so published shall—

(*a*) specify the points between which the proposed pipe-line is to run;

(*b*) name a place or places where a copy of the notice under subsection (1) above (and of the map accompanying it) may be inspected free of charge, and copies thereof may be obtained at a reasonable charge, at all reasonable hours; and

(*c*) specify the time within which, and the manner in which, representations may be made as to the matters mentioned in paragraphs (*a*) and (*b*) of subsection (4) below.

(4) Where in the light of any such representations duly made the Director is satisfied—

(*a*) that a demand exists or is likely to arise for the conveyance of gas of, or of a kind similar to, the kind specified in the notice under subsection (1) above; and

(*b*) that the routes along which the gas will require to be conveyed will severally be, as to the whole or any part thereof, the same or substantially the same as the route or any part of the route so specified,

then, subject to subsections (6) and (7) below, the Director may give directions to the public gas supplier in accordance with subsection (5) below.

(5) Directions under subsection (4) above may—

(*a*) require the public gas supplier to secure that the pipe-line, or any length of it specified in the directions, shall be so constructed as to be capable of conveying quantities so specified of gas of, or of a kind similar to, the kind specified in the notice under subsection (1) above;

(*b*) specify the sums or the method of determining the sums which the Director considers should be paid to the supplier by such of the persons who made representations to the Director as are specified in the directions for the purpose of defraying so much of the cost of constructing the pipe-line as is attributable to that requirement;

(*c*) specify the arrangements which the Director considers should be made by each of those persons, within a period specified in that behalf in the directions, for the purpose of securing that those sums will be paid to the supplier if he constructs the pipe-line in accordance with that requirement;

(*d*) provide that the supplier may, if such arrangements are not made by any of those persons within the period aforesaid, elect in the manner specified in the directions that the requirement shall have effect with such modifications as are so specified with a view to eliminating the consequences of the representations made by that person.

(6) The Director shall not give directions under subsection (4) above without first giving the public gas supplier particulars of the requirement

he proposes to specify in the directions and an opportunity of being heard about the matter; and the said particulars must be given to the supplier within six months of the Director receiving the notice under subsection (1) above.

(7) Where the Director proposes to give directions under subsection (4) above, it shall be his duty before doing so to give to any person whom he proposes to specify in the directions—

(*a*) particulars of the requirement which he proposes so to specify; and

(*b*) an opportunity of making an application under subsection (1) of section 19 above in respect of the proposed pipe-line;

and that section shall have effect in relation to such an application made by virtue of this subsection as if for references to a pipe-line there were substituted references to the proposed pipe-line and the reference in subsection (2) to the Director deciding whether the application is to be adjourned were omitted.

(8) If, after a notice under subsection (1) above has been given to the Director, the execution of the works to which the notice relates has not been substantially begun at the expiration of three years from the date on which it was given to him, or at the expiration of any extension of that period which he may allow, the notice shall be treated as invalid for the purposes of that subsection except as regards works previously executed.

(9) In this section and section 21 below "high pressure pipe-line" means any pipe-line which—

(*a*) has a design operating pressure exceeding 7 bars; or

(*b*) is of a class specified in an order made by the Secretary of State.

(10) In this section "construction", in relation to a pipe-line, includes placing, and "construct" and "constructed" shall, in relation to a pipe-line, be construed accordingly.

(11) For the purposes of this section the execution of works in land for the purpose of determining whether or not it is suitable for the placing in it of a pipe-line and the carrying out of surveying operations for the purpose of settling the route of a proposed pipe-line shall be deemed not to constitute the execution of works for the construction of a pipe-line.

(12) Any sums received by the Director under this section shall be paid into the Consolidated Fund.

Increase of capacity etc. of pipelines

21.—(1) If in the case of a pipe-line belonging to a public gas supplier it appears to the Director, on the application of a person other than the supplier—

(*a*) that the pipe-line can and should be modified by installing in it a junction through which another pipe-line may be connected to the pipe-line; or

(*b*) in the case of a high pressure pipe-line, that the capacity of the pipe-line can and should be increased by modifying apparatus and works associated with the pipe-line,

then, subject to subsection (3) below, the Director may, after giving to the supplier an opportunity of being heard about the matter, give directions to the supplier in accordance with subsection (2) below in consequence of the application.

(2) Directions under subsection (1) above may—

(*a*) specify the modifications which the Director considers should be made in consequence of the application;

(*b*) specify the sums or the method of determining the sums which the Director considers should be paid to the public gas supplier by the applicant for the purpose of defraying the cost of the modifications;

(*c*) specify the arrangements which the Director considers should be made by the applicant, within a period specified in that behalf in the directions, for the purpose of securing that those sums will be paid to the supplier if he carries out the modifications;

(*d*) require the supplier, if the applicant makes those arrangements within the period aforesaid, to carry out the modifications within a period specified in that behalf in the directions.

(3) Where the Director proposes to give directions under subsection (1) above, it shall be his duty before doing so to give to the applicant—

(*a*) particulars of the modifications which he proposes to specify in the directions; and

(*b*) an opportunity of making an application under subsection (1) of section 19 above in respect of the pipe-line;

and that section shall have effect in relation to such an application made by virtue of this subsection as if for references to a pipe-line there were substituted references to the pipe-line as it would be with those modifications and the reference in subsection (2) to the Director deciding whether the application is to be adjourned were omitted.

(4) References in this section to modifications include, in the case of modifications to any apparatus and works, references to changes in, substitutions for and additions to the apparatus and works; and the reference in subsection (1) above to apparatus and works associated with a pipe-line shall be construed in accordance with section 65(2) of the Pipe-lines Act 1962.

Effect of directions

22.—(1) The obligation to comply with any directions under section 19, 20(4) or 21(1) above (in this section referred to as "relevant directions") is a duty owed to any person who may be affected by a contravention of them.

(2) Where a duty is owed by virtue of subsection (1) above to any person any breach of the duty which causes that person to sustain loss or damage shall be actionable at the suit or instance of that person.

(3) In any proceedings brought against any person in pursuance of subsection (2) above, it shall be a defence for him to prove that he took all reasonable steps and exercised all due diligence to avoid contravening the relevant directions.

(4) Without prejudice to any right which any person may have by virtue of subsection (2) above to bring civil proceedings in respect of any contravention or apprehended contravention of any relevant directions, compliance with any such directions shall be enforceable by civil proceedings by the Director for an injunction or interdict or for any other appropriate relief.

Modification of public gas suppliers' authorisations

Modification by agreement

23.—(1) Subject to the following provisions of this section, the Director may modify the conditions of a public gas supplier's authorisation.

(2) Before making modifications under this section, the Director shall give notice—

(*a*) stating that he proposes to make the modifications and setting out their effect;

(*b*) stating the reasons why he proposes to make the modifications; and

(*c*) specifying the time (not being less than 28 days from the date of publication of the notice) within which representations or objections with respect to the proposed modifications may be made,

and shall consider any representations or objections which are duly made and not withdrawn.

(3) A notice under subsection (2) above shall be given—

(*a*) by publishing the notice in such manner as the Director considers appropriate for the purpose of bringing the notice to the attention of persons likely to be affected by the making of the modifications; and

(*b*) by sending a copy of the notice to the public gas supplier, to the Secretary of State and to the Council.

(4) The Director shall not make the modifications without the consent of the public gas supplier and if, within the time specified in the notice under subsection (2) above, the Secretary of State directs the Director not to make any modification, the Director shall comply with the direction.

(5) The Secretary of State shall not give a direction under subsection (4) above in respect of any modification affecting the supply of gas by the public gas supplier to tariff customers unless it appears to him that the modification should be made, if at all, under section 26 below.

Modification references to Monopolies Commission

24.—(1) The Director may make to the Monopolies and Mergers Commission (in this Part referred to as "the Monopolies Commission") a reference which is so framed as to require the Commission to investigate and report on the questions—

(*a*) whether any matters which relate to the supply of gas by a public gas supplier to tariff customers and which are specified in the reference operate, or may be expected to operate, against the public interest; and

(*b*) if so, whether the effects adverse to the public interest which those matters have or may be expected to have could be remedied or prevented by modifications of the conditions of the public gas supplier's authorisation.

(2) The Director may, at any time, by notice given to the Monopolies Commission vary a reference under this section by adding to the matters specified in the reference or by excluding from the reference some or all of the matters so specified; and on receipt of such notice the Commission shall give effect to the variation.

(3) The Director may specify in a reference under this section, or a variation of such a reference, for the purpose of assisting the Monopolies Commission in carrying out the investigation on the reference—

(*a*) any effects adverse to the public interest which, in his opinion, the matters specified in the reference or variation have or may be expected to have; and

(*b*) any modifications of the conditions of the authorisation by which, in his opinion, those effects could be remedied or prevented.

(4) As soon as practicable after making a reference under this section or a variation of such a reference, the Director—

(*a*) shall send a copy of the reference or variation to the public gas supplier and to the Council; and

(*b*) publish particulars of the reference or variation in such manner as he considers appropriate for the purpose of bringing the reference or variation to the attention of persons likely to be affected by it.

(5) It shall be the duty of the Director, for the purpose of assisting the Monopolies Commission in carrying out an investigation on a reference under this section, to give to the Commission—

(*a*) any information which is in his possession and which relates to matters falling within the scope of the investigation, and which is either requested by the Commission for that purpose or is information which in his opinion it would be appropriate for that purpose to give to the Commission without any such request; and

(*b*) any other assistance which the Commission may require, and which it is within his power to give, in relation to any such matters,

and the Commission, for the purpose of carrying out any such investigation, shall take account of any information given to them for that purpose under this subsection.

(6) In determining for the purposes of this section whether any particular matter operates, or may be expected to operate, against the public interest, the Monopolies Commission shall have regard to the matters as respects which duties are imposed on the Secretary of State and the Director by section 4 above.

(7) Sections 70 (time limit for report on merger reference), 81 (procedure in carrying out investigations) and 85 (attendance of witnesses and production of documents) of the Fair Trading Act 1973, Part II of Schedule 3 to that Act (performance of functions of the Monopolies Commission) and section 24 of the Competition Act 1980 (modifications of provisions about performance of such functions) shall apply in relation to references under this section as if—

(*a*) the functions of the Commission in relation to those references were functions under the said Act of 1973;

(*b*) the expression "merger reference" included a reference under this section;

(*c*) in the said section 70 references to the Secretary of State were references to the Director and the reference to three months were a reference to six months;

(*d*) in paragraph 11 of the said Schedule 3 the reference to section 71 of the said Act of 1973 were a reference to subsection (2) above; and

(*e*) paragraph 16(2) of that Schedule were omitted.

Reports on modification references

25.—(1) In making a report on a reference under section 24 above, the Monopolies Commission—

(*a*) shall include in the report definite conclusions on the questions comprised in the reference together with such an account of their reasons for those conclusions as in their opinion is expedient for facilitating proper understanding of those questions and of their conclusions;

(*b*) where they conclude that any of the matters specified in the reference operate, or may be expected to operate, against the public interest, shall specify in the report the effects adverse to the public interest which those matters have or may be expected to have; and

(*c*) where they conclude that any adverse effects so specified could be remedied or prevented by modifications of the conditions of the authorisation, shall specify in the report modifications by which those effects could be remedied or prevented.

(2) Where, on a reference under section 24 above, the Monopolies Commission conclude that the public gas supplier is a party to an agreement to which the Restrictive Trade Practices Act 1976 applies, the Commission, in making their report on that reference, shall exclude from their consideration the question whether the provisions of that agreement, in so far as they are provisions by virtue of which it is an agreement to which that Act applies, operate, or may be expected to operate, against

the public interest; and paragraph (*b*) of subsection (1) above shall have effect subject to the provisions of this subsection.

(3) Section 82 of the Fair Trading Act 1973 (general provisions as to reports) shall apply in relation to reports of the Monopolies Commission on references under section 24 above as it applies to reports of the Commission under that Act.

(4) A report of the Monopolies Commission on a reference under section 24 above shall be made to the Director.

(5) Subject to subsection (6) below, the Director shall—

(*a*) on receiving such a report, send a copy of it to the public gas supplier and to the Secretary of State; and

(*b*) not less than 14 days after that copy is received by the Secretary of State, send another copy to the Council and publish that other copy in such manner as he considers appropriate for bringing the report to the attention of persons likely to be affected by it.

(6) If it appears to the Secretary of State that the publication of any matter in such a report would be against the public interest or the commercial interests of any person, he may, before the end of the period of 14 days mentioned in subsection (5) above, direct the Director to exclude that matter from the copy of the report to be sent to the Council and published under that subsection.

Modification following report

26.—(1) Where a report of the Monopolies Commission on a reference under section 24 above—

(*a*) includes conclusions to the effect that any of the matters specified in the reference operate, or may be expected to operate, against the public interest;

(*b*) specifies effects adverse to the public interest which those matters have or may be expected to have;

(*c*) includes conclusions to the effect that those effects could be remedied or prevented by modifications of the conditions of the authorisation; and

(*d*) specifies modifications by which those effects could be remedied or prevented,

the Director shall, subject to the following provisions of this section, make such modifications of the conditions of the authorisation as appear to him requisite for the purpose of remedying or preventing the adverse effects specified in the report.

(2) Before making modifications under this section, the Director shall have regard to the modifications specified in the report.

(3) Before making modifications under this section, the Director shall give notice—

(*a*) stating that he proposes to make the modifications and setting out their effect;

(*b*) stating the reasons why he proposes to make the modifications; and

(*c*) specifying the time (not being less than 28 days from the date of publication of the notice) within which representations or objections with respect to the proposed modifications may be made,

and shall consider any representations or objections which are duly made and not withdrawn.

(4) A notice under subsection (3) above shall be given—

(*a*) by publishing the notice in such manner as the Director considers appropriate for the purpose of bringing the matters to which the notice relates to the attention of persons likely to be affected by the making of the modifications; and

(*b*) by sending a copy of the notice to the public gas supplier and to the Council.

Modification by order under other enactments

27.—(1) Where in the circumstances mentioned in subsection (2) below the Secretary of State by order exercises any of the powers specified in Parts I and II of Schedule 8 to the Fair Trading Act 1973 or section 10(2)(*a*) of the Competition Act 1980, the order may also provide for the modification of the conditions of a public gas supplier's authorisation to such extent as may appear to him to be requisite or expedient for the purpose of giving effect to or of taking account of any provision made by the order.

(2) Subsection (1) above shall have effect where—

(*a*) the circumstances are as mentioned in section 56(1) of the said Act of 1973 (order on report on monopoly reference) and the monopoly situation exists in relation to the supply of gas through pipes;

(*b*) the circumstances are as mentioned in section 73(1) of that Act (order on report on merger reference) and the two or more enterprises which ceased to be distinct enterprises were engaged in the supply of gas through pipes; or

(*c*) the circumstances are as mentioned in section 10(1) of the said Act of 1980 (order on report on competition reference) and the anti-competitive practice relates to the supply of gas through pipes.

(3) In this section expressions which are also used in the said Act of 1973 or the said Act of 1980 have the same meanings as in that Act.

Public gas suppliers: enforcement

Orders for securing compliance with certain provisions

28.—(1) Subject to subsections (2) and (5) and section 29 below, where the Director is satisfied that a public gas supplier is contravening, or has contravened and is likely again to contravene, any relevant condition or requirement, the Director shall by a final order make such provision as is requisite for the purpose of securing compliance with that condition or requirement.

(2) Subject to subsection (5) below, where it appears to the Director—

(*a*) that a public gas supplier is contravening, or has contravened and is likely again to contravene, any relevant condition or requirement; and

(*b*) that it is requisite that a provisional order be made,

the Director shall (instead of taking steps towards the making of a final order) by a provisional order make such provision as appears to him requisite for the purpose of securing compliance with that condition or requirement.

(3) In determining for the purposes of subsection (2)(*b*) above whether it is requisite that a provisional order be made, the Director shall have regard, in particular—

(*a*) to the extent to which any person is likely to sustain loss or damage in consequence of anything which, in contravention of the relevant condition or requirement, is likely to be done, or omitted to be done, before a final order may be made; and

(*b*) to the fact that the effect of the provisions of this section and section 30 below is to exclude the availability of any remedy (apart from under those provisions or for negligence) in respect of any contravention of a relevant condition or requirement.

(4) Subject to subsection (5) and section 29 below, the Director shall confirm a provisional order, with or without modifications, if—

(*a*) he is satisfied that the public gas supplier is contravening, or has contravened and is likely again to contravene, any relevant condition or requirement; and

(*b*) the provision made by the order (with any modifications) is requisite for the purpose of securing compliance with that condition or requirement.

(5) The Director shall not make a final order or make or confirm a provisional order if he is satisfied—

(*a*) that the duties imposed on him by section 4 above preclude the making or, as the case may be, the confirmation of the order; or

(*b*) that the contraventions were or the apprehended contraventions are of a trivial nature.

(6) Where the Director is satisfied as mentioned in subsection (5) above, he shall—

(*a*) give notice that he is so satisfied to the public gas supplier; and

(*b*) publish a copy of the notice in such manner as the Director considers appropriate for the purpose of bringing the matters to which the notice relates to the attention of persons likely to be affected by them.

(7) A final or provisional order—

(*a*) shall require the public gas supplier (according to the circumstances of the case) to do, or not to do, such things as are specified in the order or are of a description so specified;

(*b*) shall take effect at such time, being the earliest practicable time, as is determined by or under the order; and

(*c*) may be revoked at any time by the Director.

(8) In this section and sections 29 and 30 below—

"final order" means an order under this section other than a provisional order;

"provisional order" means an order under this section which, if not previously confirmed under subsection (4) above, will cease to have effect at the end of such period (not exceeding three months) as is determined by or under the order;

"relevant condition", in relation to a public gas supplier, means any condition of his authorisation;

"relevant requirement", in relation to a public gas supplier, means any requirement imposed on him by or under section 9(1) or (2), 10(1), 11(4), 12(1) or 14(1) or (3) above or any provision of paragraphs 1 to 4 and 14 of Schedule 5 to this Act.

Procedural requirements

29.—(1) Before making a final order or confirming a provisional order, the Director shall give notice—

(*a*) stating that he proposes to make or confirm the order and setting out its effect;

(*b*) stating the relevant condition or requirement, the acts or omissions which, in his opinion, constitute or would constitute contraventions of it and the other facts which, in his opinion, justify the making or confirmation of the order; and

(*c*) specifying the time (not being less than 28 days from the date of publication of the notice) within which representations or objections to the proposed order or confirmation of the order may be made,

and shall consider any representations or objections which are duly made and not withdrawn.

(2) A notice under subsection (1) above shall be given—

(*a*) by publishing the notice in such manner as the Director considers appropriate for the purpose of bringing the matters to which the notice relates to the attention of persons likely to be affected by them; and

(*b*) by sending a copy of the notice, and a copy of the proposed order or of the order proposed to be confirmed, to the public gas supplier.

(3) The Director shall not make a final order, or confirm a provisional order, with modifications except with the consent of the public gas supplier or after complying with the requirements of subsection (4) below.

(4) The said requirements are that the Director shall—

(*a*) give to the public gas supplier such notice as appears to him requisite of his proposal to make or confirm the order with modifications;

(*b*) specify the time (not being less than 28 days from the date of the service of the notice) within which representations or objections to the proposed modifications may be made; and

(*c*) consider any representations or objections which are duly made and not withdrawn.

(5) Before revoking a final order or a provisional order which has been confirmed, the Director shall give notice—

(*a*) stating that he proposes to revoke the order and setting out its effect; and

(*b*) specifying the time (not being less than 28 days) from the date of publication of the notice within which representations or objections to the proposed revocation may be made,

and shall consider any representations or objections which are duly made and not withdrawn.

(6) A notice under subsection (5) above shall be given—

(*a*) by publishing the notice in such manner as the Director considers appropriate for the purpose of bringing the matters to which the notice relates to the attention of persons likely to be affected by them; and

(*b*) by sending a copy of the notice to the public gas supplier.

(7) As soon as practicable after a final order is made or a provisional order is made or confirmed, the Director shall—

(*a*) serve a copy of the order on the public gas supplier; and

(*b*) publish such a copy in such manner as he considers appropriate for the purpose of bringing the order to the attention of persons likely to be affected by it.

Validity and effect of orders

30.—(1) If the public gas supplier is aggrieved by a final or provisional order and desires to question its validity on the ground that the making or confirmation of it was not within the powers of section 28 above or that any of the requirements of section 29 above have not been complied with in relation to it, he may within 42 days from the date of service on him of a copy of the order make an application to the court under this section.

(2) On any such application the court may, if satisfied that the making or confirmation of the order was not within those powers or that the interests of the public gas supplier have been substantially prejudiced by

a failure to comply with those requirements, quash the order or any provision of the order.

(3) Except as provided by this section, the validity of a final or provisional order shall not be questioned by any legal proceedings whatever.

(4) No criminal proceedings shall, by virtue of the making of a final order or the making or confirmation of a provisional order, lie against any person on the ground that he has committed, or aided, abetted, counselled or procured the commission of, or conspired or attempted to commit, or incited others to commit, any contravention of the order.

(5) The obligation to comply with a final or provisional order is a duty owed to any person who may be affected by a contravention of it.

(6) Where a duty is owed by virtue of subsection (5) above to any person any breach of the duty which causes that person to sustain loss or damage shall be actionable at the suit or instance of that person.

(7) In any proceedings brought against any person in pursuance of subsection (6) above, it shall be a defence for him to prove that he took all reasonable steps and exercised all due diligence to avoid contravening the order.

(8) Without prejudice to any right which any person may have by virtue of subsection (6) above to bring civil proceedings in respect of any contravention or apprehended contravention of a final or provisional order, compliance with any such order shall be enforceable by civil proceedings by the Director for an injunction or interdict or for any other appropriate relief.

(9) In this section "the court" means—

(*a*) in relation to England and Wales, the High Court;

(*b*) in relation to Scotland, the Court of Session.

Investigation of complaints etc.

Duty of Director to investigate certain matters

31.—(1) It shall be the duty of the Director to investigate any matter which appears to him to be an enforcement matter and which—

(*a*) is the subject of a representation (other than one appearing to the Director to be frivolous) made to the Director by or on behalf of a person appearing to the Director to have an interest in that matter; or

(*b*) is referred to him by the Council under subsection (2) below.

(2) It shall be the duty of the Council to refer to the Director any matter which appears to the Council to be an enforcement matter and which is the subject of a representation (other than one appearing to the Council to be frivolous) made to the Council by or on behalf of a person appearing to the Council to have an interest in that matter.

(3) In this section and section 32 below "enforcement matter" means any matter in respect of which any functions of the Director under section 28 above are or may be exercisable.

Duty of Council to investigate certain matters

32.—(1) It shall be the duty of the Council to investigate any matter which appears to it to be a matter to which subsection (2) below applies and which—

(*a*) is the subject of a representation (other than one appearing to the Council to be frivolous) made to the Council by or on behalf of a person appearing to the Council to have an interest in that matter; or

(*b*) is referred to it by the Director under subsection (3) below.

(2) This subsection applies to—

(*a*) any matter (not being an enforcement matter or a matter relating only to contract customers) in respect of which any functions of the Director under this Part are or may be exercisable; and

(*b*) any matter (not being an enforcement matter or a matter relating to tariff customers) which relates to the supply of gas through pipes and in respect of which any functions of the Director General of Fair Trading under the Fair Trading Act 1973 or the Competition Act 1980 are or may be exercisable.

(3) Subject to subsection (4) below, it shall be the duty of the Director to refer to the Council any matter which appears to the Director to be a matter falling within paragraph (*a*) of subsection (2) above and which is the subject of a representation (other than one appearing to the Director to be frivolous) made to the Director by or on behalf of a person appearing to the Director to have an interest in that matter.

(4) Nothing in subsection (3) above shall require the Director to refer to the Council any matter in respect of which he is already considering exercising functions under this Part.

(5) Where on an investigation under subsection (1) above any matter appears to the Council to be a matter falling within paragraph (*a*) of subsection (2) above in respect of which it would be appropriate for the Director to exercise any functions under this Part, the Council shall refer that matter to the Director with a view to his exercising those functions with respect to that matter.

(6) Where on an investigation under subsection (1) above any matter appears to the Council to be a matter falling within paragraph (*b*) of subsection (2) above in respect of which it would be appropriate for the Director General of Fair Trading to exercise any functions under the Fair Trading Act 1973 or the Competition Act 1980, the Council shall refer the matter to that Director with a view to his exercising those functions with respect to that matter.

(7) In this section "contract customer" means a person who is supplied with gas by a public gas supplier in pursuance of such an agreement as is mentioned in section 14(4) above.

Power of Council to investigate other matters

33.—(1) The Council shall have power to investigate any matter (not being a matter which it is its duty to investigate under section 32 above) which—

(*a*) appears to it to be a matter to which subsection (2) below applies and not to be an enforcement matter within the meaning of that section; and

(*b*) is the subject of a representation (other than one appearing to the Council to be frivolous) made to the Council by or on behalf of a person appearing to the Council to have an interest in that matter.

(2) This subsection applies to—

(*a*) any matter relating to the design, manufacture, importation or supply (whether by sale, hire or loan or otherwise) of gas fittings used or intended to be used by persons supplied with gas by public gas suppliers;

(*b*) any matter relating to the installation, maintenance or inspection of gas fittings used or intended to be used by such persons; and

(*c*) any other matter relating to, or to anything connected with, the use by such persons of gas supplied by such a supplier or the use of such fittings.

(3) Where the Council has investigated any matter under this section, it may prepare a report on that matter and (subject to section 42 below) shall send a copy of any such report to such (if any) of the following persons as it thinks appropriate, that is to say—

(*a*) any person to whom the report refers or who (whether or not he has made a representation to the Council) appears to the Council to have an interest in the matter to which the report relates;

(*b*) the Director General of Fair Trading or any person whose functions under any enactment appear to the Council to be exercisable in relation to that matter;

(*c*) any person who appears to the Council to be a person who ought to take account of the report in determining how to act in relation to that matter;

but nothing in this subsection shall require the Council to send any such copy to the Director.

Other functions of Director

General functions

34.—(1) It shall be the duty of the Director, so far as it appears to him practicable from time to time, to keep under review the carrying on both within and outside Great Britain of activities connected with the supply of gas through pipes.

(2) It shall also be the duty of the Director, so far as it appears to him practicable from time to time, to collect information with respect to the supply of gas through pipes, and the persons providing such supplies, with a view to his becoming aware of, and ascertaining the circumstances relating to, matters with respect to which his functions are exercisable.

(3) The Secretary of State may give general directions indicating—

(*a*) considerations to which the Director should have particular regard in determining the order of priority in which matters are to be brought under review in the performance of his duty under subsection (1) or (2) above; and

(*b*) considerations to which, in cases where it appears to the Director that any of his functions are exercisable, he should have particular regard in determining whether to exercise those functions.

(4) It shall be the duty of the Director, where either he considers it expedient or he is requested by the Secretary of State or the Director General of Fair Trading to do so, to give information, advice and assistance to the Secretary of State or that Director with respect to any matter in respect of which any function of the Director is exercisable.

Publication of information and advice

35.—(1) The Director may arrange for the publication, in such form and in such manner as he may consider appropriate, of such information and advice as it may appear to him to be expedient to give to tariff customers and potential tariff customers of public gas suppliers.

(2) In arranging for the publication of any such information or advice, the Director shall have regard to the need for excluding, so far as that is practicable—

(*a*) any matter which relates to the affairs of an individual, where the publication of that matter would or might, in the opinion of the Director, seriously and prejudicially affect the interests of that individual; and

(*b*) any matter which relates specifically to the affairs of a particular body of persons, whether corporate or un-incorporate, where publication of that matter would or might, in the opinion of the Director, seriously and prejudicially affect the interests of that body.

Keeping of register

36.—(1) The Director shall keep a register of notifications and directions under section 6 above, authorisations under section 7 or 8 above and final and provisional orders at such premises and in such form as he may determine.

(2) Subject to any direction given under subsection (3) below, the Director shall cause to be entered in the register the provisions of—

(*a*) every notification or direction under section 6 above;

(*b*) every authorisation under section 7 or 8 above and every modification or revocation of, and every direction or consent given or determination made under, such an authorisation; and

(*c*) every final or provisional order, every revocation of such an order and every notice under section 28(6) above.

(3) If it appears to the Secretary of State that the entry of any provision in the register would be against the public interest or the commercial interests of any person, he may direct the Director not to enter that provision in the register.

(4) The register shall be open to public inspection during such hours and subject to payment of such fee as may be prescribed by an order made by the Secretary of State.

(5) Any person may, on payment of such fee as may be prescribed by an order so made, require the Director to supply to him a copy of or extract from any part of the register, certified by the Director to be a true copy or extract.

(6) Any sums received by the Director under this section shall be paid into the Consolidated Fund.

(7) In this section "final order" and "provisional order" have the same meanings as in section 28 above.

Fixing of maximum charges for reselling gas

37.—(1) The Director shall from time to time fix maximum prices at which gas supplied by public gas suppliers may be resold, and shall publish the prices so fixed in such manner as in his opinion will secure adequate publicity therefor.

(2) Different prices may be fixed under this section in different classes of cases which may be defined by reference to areas, tariffs applicable to gas supplied by the suppliers or any other relevant circumstances.

(3) If any person resells any gas supplied by a public gas supplier at a price exceeding the maximum price fixed under this section and applicable thereto, the amount of the excess shall be recoverable by the person to whom the gas was resold.

Power to require information etc.

38.—(1) Where it appears to the Director that a public gas supplier may be contravening, or may have contravened, any relevant condition or requirement, the Director may, for any purpose connected with the exercise of his functions under section 28 or 31 above in relation to that matter, by notice signed by him—

(*a*) require any person to produce, at a time and place specified in the notice, to the Director or to any person appointed by him for the purpose, any documents which are specified or described in the notice and are in that person's custody or under his control; or (*b*) require any person carrying on any business to furnish to the Director such information as may be specified or described in the notice, and specify the time, the manner and the form in which any such information is to be furnished;

but no person shall be compelled for any such purpose to produce any documents which he could not be compelled to produce in civil proceedings before the court or, in complying with any requirement for the furnishing of information, to give any information which he could not be compelled to give in evidence in such proceedings.

(2) A person who without reasonable excuse fails to do anything duly required of him by a notice under subsection (1) above shall be guilty of an offence and liable on summary conviction to a fine not exceeding level 5 on the standard scale.

(3) A person who intentionally alters, suppresses or destroys any document which he has been required by any such notice to produce shall be guilty of an offence and liable—

(*a*) on summary conviction, to a fine not exceeding the statutory maximum;

(*b*) on conviction on indictment, to a fine.

(4) If a person makes default in complying with a notice under subsection (1) above, the court may, on the application of the Director, make such order as the court thinks fit for requiring the default to be made good; and any such order may provide that all the costs or expenses of and incidental to the application shall be borne by the person in default or by any officers of a company or other association who are responsible for its default.

(5) In this section—

"relevant condition" and "relevant requirement" have the same meanings as in section 28 above;

"the court" has the same meaning as in section 30 above.

Annual and other reports

39.—(1) The Director shall, as soon as practicable after the end of the year 1986 and of each subsequent calendar year, make to the Secretary of State a report on—

(*a*) his activities during that year; and

(*b*) the Monopolies Commission's activities during that year so far as relating to references made by him.

(2) Every such report shall include a general survey of developments, during the year to which it relates, in respect of matters falling within the scope of the Director's functions and shall set out any general directions given to the Director during that year under section 34(3) above.

(3) The Secretary of State shall lay a copy of every report made by the Director under subsection (1) above before each House of Parliament, shall send a copy of every such report to the Council and shall arrange for copies of every such report to be published in such manner as he may consider appropriate.

(4) The Director may also prepare such other reports as appear to him to be expedient with respect to such matters as are mentioned in subsection (2) above.

(5) The Director shall send a copy of any report prepared under subsection (4) above to the Council and may arrange for copies of any such report to be published in such manner as he may consider appropriate.

(6) In making or preparing any report under this section the Director shall have regard to the need for excluding, so far as that is practicable, the matters specified in section 35(2)(*a*) and (*b*) above.

Other functions of Council

General duty to advise Director

40. It shall be the duty of the Council to advise the Director on any matter which—

(*a*) appears to the Council to be a matter which relates to tariff customers and in respect of which any of the Director's functions are or may be exercisable; and

(*b*) is referred to it by the Director or is a matter on which it considers it should offer advice.

Annual reports

41.—(1) The Council shall, as soon as practicable after the end of the year 1986 and of each subsequent calendar year, make to the Director and to the Secretary of State a report on its activities during that year.

(2) Every such report shall include a statement of the matters on which, during the year to which it relates, the Council has advised the Director under section 40 above.

(3) The Council shall arrange for every such report to be published in such manner as it considers appropriate.

(4) In making any such report, the Council shall have regard to the need for excluding, so far as that is practicable—

(*a*) any matter which relates to the affairs of an individual, where the publication of that matter would or might, in the opinion of the Council, seriously and prejudicially affect the interests of that individual; and

(*b*) any matter which relates specifically to the affairs of a particular body of persons, whether corporate or un-incorporate, where publication of that matter would or might, in the opinion of the Council, seriously and prejudicially affect the interests of that body.

Miscellaneous

General restrictions on disclosure of information

42.—(1) Subject to the following provisions of this section, no information with respect to any particular business which—

(*a*) has been obtained under or by virtue of the provisions of this Part; and

(*b*) relates to the affairs of any individual or to any particular business,

shall, during the lifetime of that individual or so long as that business continues to be carried on, be disclosed without the consent of that individual or the person for the time being carrying on that business.

(2) Subsection (1) above does not apply to any disclosure of information which is made—

(*a*) for the purpose of facilitating the performance of any functions assigned to the Secretary of State, the Director or the Monopolies Commission by or under this Part;

(*b*) for the purpose of facilitating the performance of any functions of any Minister of the Crown, the Director General of Fair Trading or a local weights and measures authority in Great Britain under any of the enactments specified in subsection (3) below;

(*c*) for the purpose of facilitating the performance of any functions of the Health and Safety Executive under any enactment;

(*d*) in connection with the investigation of any criminal offence or for the purposes of any criminal proceedings;

(*e*) for the purposes of any civil proceedings brought under or by virtue of this Part or any of the enactments specified in subsection (3) below; or

(*f*) in pursuance of a Community obligation.

(3) The enactments referred to in subsection (2) above are—

(*a*) the Consumer Protection Act 1961;

(*b*) the Trade Descriptions Act 1968;

(*c*) the Fair Trading Act 1973;

(*d*) the Consumer Credit Act 1974;

(*e*) the Restrictive Trade Practices Act 1976;

(*f*) the Resale Prices Act 1976;

(*g*) the Consumer Safety Act 1978;

(*h*) the Estate Agents Act 1979; and

(*i*) the Competition Act 1980.

(4) Nothing in subsection (1) above shall be construed—

(*a*) as limiting the matters which may be published under section 35 above or may be included in, or made public as part of, a report of the Director, the Council or the Monopolies Commission under any provision of this Part other than section 33(3) above; or

(*b*) as applying to any information which has been so published or has been made public as part of such a report.

(5) Any person who discloses any information in contravention of this section shall be guilty of an offence and liable—

(*a*) on summary conviction, to a fine not exceeding the statutory maximum;

(*b*) on conviction on indictment, to imprisonment for a term not exceeding two years or to a fine or to both.

Making of false statements etc.

43.—(1) If any person, in giving any information or making any application for the purposes of any provision of this Part, or of any regulation made under any provision of this Part, makes any statement which he knows to be false in a material particular, or recklessly makes any statement which is false in a material particular, he shall be guilty of an offence and liable—

(*a*) on summary conviction, to a fine not exceeding the statutory maximum;

(*b*) on conviction on indictment, to a fine.

(2) Proceedings for an offence under subsection (1) above shall not in England and Wales be instituted except by or with the consent of the Secretary of State or the Director of Public Prosecutions.

Compensation to chairmen and officers of Consumers' Councils

44.—(1) The Secretary of State may pay—

(*a*) to the person who immediately before the appointed day is the chairman of the National Gas Consumers' Council; and

(*b*) to the persons who immediately before that day are the chairmen of the Regional Gas Consumers' Councils,

such sums by way of compensation for loss of office or loss or diminution of pension rights as the Secretary of State may with the approval of the Treasury determine.

(2) The Secretary of State may also pay to persons who immediately before the appointed day were officers of any of the Councils mentioned in subsection (1) above such sums by way of compensation for loss of employment, or loss or diminution of remuneration or pension rights, as the Secretary of State may with the approval of the Treasury determine.

(3) Any sums required by the Secretary of State for the purposes of this section shall be paid out of money provided by Parliament.

Supplemental

Offences by bodies corporate

45.—(1) Where a body corporate is guilty of an offence under this Part and that offence is proved to have been committed with the consent or connivance of, or to be attributable to any neglect on the part of, any director, manager, secretary or other similar officer of the body corporate or any person who was purporting to act in any such capacity he, as well as the body corporate, shall be guilty of that offence and shall be liable to be proceeded against and punished accordingly.

(2) Where the affairs of a body corporate are managed by its members, subsection (1) above shall apply in relation to the acts and defaults of a member in connection with his functions of management as if he were a director of the body corporate.

Service of notices etc.

46.—(1) Subject to subsection (2) below, any notice or other document required or authorised to be given, delivered or served under this Part or regulations made under this Part may be given, delivered or served either—

(*a*) by delivering it to the person to whom it is to be given or delivered or on whom it is to be served;

(*b*) by leaving it at the usual or last known place of abode of that person;

(*c*) by sending it in a prepaid letter addressed to that person at his usual or last known place of abode;

(*d*) in the case of a body corporate, by delivering it to the secretary or clerk of the body at their registered or principal office, or sending it in a prepaid letter addressed to the secretary or clerk of the body at that office; or

(*e*) if it is not practicable after reasonable inquiry to ascertain the name or address of a person to whom it should be given or delivered, or on whom it should be served, as being a person having any interest in premises, by addressing it to him by the description of the person having that interest in the premises (naming them) to which it relates and delivering it to some responsible person on the premises, or affixing it or a copy of it to some conspicuous part of the premises.

(2) Where this subsection applies in relation to a public gas supplier, subsection (1) above shall not apply to notices to be given to or served on the supplier under section 10 above or any provision of Schedule 5 to this Act but any such notice—

(*a*) may be given or served by delivering it at, or sending it in a prepaid letter to, an appropriate office of the supplier; and

(*b*) in the case of a notice under paragraph 7(2) or 12(1) of that Schedule, shall be treated as received by the supplier only if received by him at an appropriate office.

(3) Subsection (2) above applies in relation to a public gas supplier if he divides his authorised area into such areas as he thinks fit and—

(*a*) in the case of each area, fixes offices of his which are to be appropriate offices in relation to notices relating to matters arising in that area;

(*b*) publishes in each area, in such manner as he considers adequate, the addresses of the offices fixed by him for that area; and (*c*) endorses on every demand note for gas charges payable to him the addresses of the offices fixed for the area in question.

Provisions as to regulations

47.—(1) Regulations made under any provision of this Part may provide for the determination of questions of fact or of law which may arise in giving effect to the regulations and for regulating (otherwise than in relation to any court proceedings) any matters relating to the practice and procedure to be followed in connection with the determination of such questions, including provision—

(*a*) as to the mode of proof of any matter;

(*b*) as to parties and their representation;

(*c*) for the right to appear and be heard of the Secretary of State, the Director and other authorities; and

(*d*) as to awarding costs of proceedings for the determination of such questions, determining the amount thereof and the enforcement of awards thereof.

(2) Regulations made under any provision of this Part which prescribe a period within which things are to be done may provide for extending the period so prescribed.

(3) Regulations made under any provision of this Part may—

(*a*) make different provision for different areas or in relation to different cases or different circumstances; and

(*b*) provide for such exceptions, limitations and conditions, and make such supplementary, incidental or transitional provision, as the Secretary of State considers necessary or expedient.

(4) Regulations made under any provision of this Part may provide that any person contravening the regulations shall be guilty of an offence and liable on summary conviction to a fine not exceeding level 5 on the standard scale.

(5) Proceedings for an offence under any regulations made under any provision of this Part shall not in England and Wales be instituted except by or with the consent of the Secretary of State or the Director of Public Prosecutions.

(6) In any proceedings against any person for an offence under any regulations made under any provision of this Part, it shall be a defence for that person to show—

(*a*) that he was prevented from complying with the regulations by circumstances not within his control; or

(*b*) that circumstances existed by reason of which compliance with the regulations would or might have involved danger to the public and that he took all such steps as it was reasonable for him to take both to prevent the circumstances from occurring and to prevent them from having that effect.

(7) Any power conferred by this Part to make regulations shall be exercisable by statutory instrument which, except in the case of regulations under sections 7(3), 8(2) or 20(2) above, shall be subject to annulment in pursuance of a resolution of either House of Parliament.

Interpretation of Part I and savings

48.—(1) In this Part, unless the context otherwise requires—

"authorised area", in relation to a public gas supplier, has the meaning given by section 7(2) above;

"calorific value" has the meaning given by section 12(2) above;

"the Council" means the Gas Consumers' Council;

"declared calorific value" has the meaning given by section 12(2) above;

"distribution main", in relation to a public gas supplier, means any main of the supplier through which the supplier is for the time being distributing gas and which is not being used only for the purpose of conveying gas in bulk;

"gas" means—

(*a*) any substance in a gaseous state which consists wholly or mainly of—

(i) methane, ethane, propane, butane, hydrogen or carbon monoxide;

(ii) a mixture of two or more of those gases; or

(iii) a combustible mixture of one or more of those gases and air; and

(*b*) any other substance in a gaseous state which is gaseous at a temperature of 15°C and a pressure of 1013.25 millibars and is specified in an order made by the Secretary of State;

"gas fittings" means gas pipes and meters, and fittings, apparatus and appliances designed for use by consumers of gas for heating, lighting, motive power and other purposes for which gas can be used;

"holding company" has the same meaning as in the Companies Act 1985;

"information" includes accounts, estimates and returns;

"the Monopolies Commission" means the Monopolies and Mergers Commission;

"notice" means notice in writing;

"prescribed" means prescribed by regulations;

"public gas supplier" has the meaning given by section 7(1) above;

"regulations" means regulations made by the Secretary of State;

"subsidiary" has the same meaning as in the Companies Act 1985;

"tariff customer" has the meaning given by section 14(5) above;

"therm" means 105.506 megajoules.

(2) In this Part, except in section 18, references to the supply of gas do not include references—

(*a*) to the supply of gas (directly or indirectly) to a public gas supplier; or

(*b*) to the supply of gas by a company to any subsidiary or holding company of that company, or to any subsidiary of a holding company of that company.

(3) Nothing in this Part relating to the modification of a public gas supplier's authorisation shall authorise the inclusion in any such authorisation of any condition other than one such as is mentioned in section 7 above or, in the case of a modification under section 23 or 26 above, as would be so mentioned if the references to the Secretary of State in subsection (7)(*a*), (*b*) and (*d*) of the said section 7 were references to the Director.

(4) Nothing in this Part and nothing done under it shall prejudice or affect the operation of any of the relevant statutory provisions (whenever made) as defined in Part I of the Health and Safety at Work etc. Act 1974.

PART II

TRANSFER OF UNDERTAKING OF CORPORATION

Vesting of property etc. of Corporation in a company nominated by the Secretary of State

49.—(1) On such day as the Secretary of State may by order appoint for the purposes of this section (in this Act referred to as "the transfer date"), all the property, rights and liabilities to which the Corporation was entitled or subject immediately before that date shall (subject to section 50 below) become by virtue of this section property, rights and liabilities of a company nominated for the purposes of this section by the Secretary of State (in this Act referred to as "the successor company").

(2) The Secretary of State may, after consulting the Corporation, by order nominate for the purposes of this section any company formed and registered under the Companies Act 1985; but on the transfer date the company in question must be a company limited by shares which is wholly owned by the Crown.

(3) References in this Act to property, rights and liabilities of the Corporation are references to all such property, rights and liabilities, whether or not capable of being transferred or assigned by the Corporation.

(4) It is hereby declared for the avoidance of doubt that—

(*a*) any reference in this Act to property of the Corporation is a reference to property of the Corporation, whether situated in the United Kingdom or elsewhere; and

(*b*) any such reference to rights and liabilities of the Corporation is a reference to rights to which the Corporation is entitled, or (as the case may be) liabilities to which the Corporation is subject, whether under the law of the United Kingdom or of any part of the United Kingdom or under the law of any country or territory outside the United Kingdom.

(5) In the House of Commons Disqualification Act 1975 in Part III of Schedule 1 (other disqualifying offices) there shall be inserted (at the appropriate place) the following entry—

"Director of the successor company (within the meaning of the Gas Act 1986), being a director nominated or appointed by a Minister of the Crown or by a person acting on behalf of the Crown";

and the like insertion shall be made in Part III of Schedule 1 to the Northern Ireland Assembly Disqualification Act 1975.

British Gas Stock

50.—(1) On the transfer date all the rights and liabilities to which the Corporation was entitled or subject immediately before that date under the terms of issue of British Gas Stock shall become by virtue of this section rights and liabilities of the Treasury.

(2) As from the transfer date British Gas Stock shall be deemed for all purposes, but subject to the rights and liabilities mentioned in subsection (1) above, to have been created and issued under the National Loans Act 1968, and that Act and any other enactment, regulation or rule relating to securities issued under that Act shall apply accordingly to that Stock.

(3) As from the transfer date British Gas 3% Guaranteed Stock, 1990–95 shall be renamed "3% Exchequer Gas Stock, 1990–95".

(4) Before the transfer date the Corporation shall pay to the Treasury an amount equal to the interest (without any deduction for income tax) accruing on British Gas Stock in the period from the date when the last instalment of interest became payable on the Stock down to the transfer date.

(5) Any question arising between the Corporation and the Treasury as to the manner in which interest accrued on British Gas Stock is to be calculated for the purposes of subsection (4) above shall be determined by the Treasury; and the amount received by the Treasury under that subsection shall be paid into the National Loans Fund.

(6) Before the transfer date the Corporation shall pay to the Bank of England a sum equal to the amounts accruing in respect of unclaimed interest or redemption money on British Gas Stock before the transfer date (after deduction of income tax in the case of interest), but excluding any amounts represented by money in the hands of the Bank of England.

(7) The Bank of England shall deal with—

(*a*) the money paid to them under subsection (6) above; and

(*b*) the money already in their hands which represents such unclaimed interest or redemption money as is mentioned in that subsection,

as money entrusted to them for payment to holders of British Gas Stock and section 5 of the Miscellaneous Financial Provisions Act 1955 (which relates to unclaimed dividends etc. on Government Stock) shall apply accordingly.

(8) In this section "British Gas Stock" means any stock created and issued under section 21 of the 1972 Act or section 43 of the Gas Act 1948.

Initial Government holding in the successor company

51.—(1) As a consequence of the vesting in the successor company by virtue of section 49 above of property, rights and liabilities of the Corporation, the successor company shall issue such securities of the company as the Secretary of State may from time to time direct—

(*a*) to the Treasury or the Secretary of State; or

(*b*) to any person entitled to require the issue of the securities following their initial allotment to the Treasury or the Secretary of State.

(2) The Secretary of State shall not give a direction under subsection (1) above at a time when the successor company has ceased to be wholly owned by the Crown.

(3) Securities required to be issued in pursuance of this section shall be issued or allotted at such time or times and on such terms as the Secretary of State may direct.

(4) Shares issued in pursuance of this section—

(*a*) shall be of such nominal value as the Secretary of State may direct; and

(*b*) shall be issued as fully paid and treated for the purposes of the Companies Act 1985 as if they had been paid up by virtue of the payment to the successor company of their nominal value in cash.

(5) The Secretary of State shall not exercise any power conferred on him by this section, or dispose of any securities issued or of any rights to securities initially allotted to him in pursuance of this section, without the consent of the Treasury.

(6) Any dividends or other sums received by the Treasury or the Secretary of State in right of or on the disposal of any securities or rights acquired by virtue of this section shall be paid into the Consolidated Fund.

(7) Stamp duty shall not be chargeable under section 47 of the Finance Act 1973 in respect of any increase in the capital of the successor company which is effected by the issue of shares allotted at a time when the successor company was wholly owned by the Crown and is certified by the Treasury as having been—

(*a*) effected for the purpose of complying with the requirements of this section; or

(*b*) where any convertible securities were issued in pursuance of this section, effected in consequence of the exercise of the conversion rights attached to those securities.

Government investment in securities of the successor company

52.—(1) The Treasury or, with the consent of the Treasury, the Secretary of State may at any time acquire—

(*a*) securities of the successor company; or

(*b*) rights to subscribe for any such securities.

(2) The Secretary of State may not dispose of any securities or rights acquired under this section without the consent of the Treasury.

(3) Any expenses incurred by the Treasury or the Secretary of State in consequence of the provisions of this section shall be paid out of money provided by Parliament.

(4) Any dividends or other sums received by the Treasury or the Secretary of State in right of, or on the disposal of, any securities or rights acquired under this section shall be paid into the Consolidated Fund.

(5) Stamp duty shall not be chargeable under section 47 of the Finance Act 1973 in respect of any increase in the capital of the successor company which—

(*a*) is effected by the issue of shares allotted at a time when the company was wholly owned by the Crown; and

(*b*) is certified by the Treasury as having been effected by the issue of shares subscribed for by the Treasury or the Secretary of State under subsection (1)(*a*) above.

Exercise of functions through nominees

53.—(1) The Treasury or, with the consent of the Treasury, the Secretary of State may for the purposes of section 51 or 52 above appoint any person to act as the nominee, or one of the nominees, of the Treasury or the Secretary of State; and—

(*a*) securities of the successor company may be issued under section 51 above to any nominee of the Treasury or the Secretary of State appointed for the purposes of that section or to any person entitled to require the issue of the securities following their initial allotment to any such nominee; and

(*b*) any such nominee appointed for the purposes of section 52 above may acquire securities or rights under that section,

in accordance with directions given from time to time by the Treasury or, with the consent of the Treasury, by the Secretary of State.

(2) Any person holding any securities or rights as a nominee of the Treasury or the Secretary of State by virtue of subsection (1) above shall hold and deal with them (or any of them) on such terms and in such manner as the Treasury or, with the consent of the Treasury, the Secretary of State may direct.

Target investment limit for Government shareholding

54.—(1) As soon as he considers expedient and, in any case, not later than six months after the successor company ceases to be wholly owned by the Crown, the Secretary of State shall by order fix a target investment limit in relation to the shares for the time being held in that company by virtue of any provision of this Part by the Treasury and their nominees and by the Secretary of State and his nominees (in this section referred to as "the Government shareholding").

(2) The target investment limit shall be expressed as a proportion of the voting rights which are exercisable in all circumstances at general meetings of the successor company (in this section referred to as "the ordinary voting rights").

(3) The first target investment limit fixed under this section shall be equal to the proportion of the ordinary voting rights which is carried by the Government shareholding at the time when the order fixing the limit is made.

(4) The Secretary of State may from time to time by order fix a new target investment limit in place of the one previously in force under this section; but—

(*a*) any new limit must be lower than the one it replaces; and

(*b*) an order under this section may only be revoked by an order fixing a new limit.

(5) It shall be the duty of the Treasury and of the Secretary of State so to exercise—

(*a*) their powers under section 52 above and any power to dispose of any shares held by virtue of any provision of this Part; and

(*b*) their power to give directions to their respective nominees,

as to secure that the Government shareholding does not carry a proportion of the ordinary voting rights exceeding any target investment limit for the time being in force under this section.

(6) Notwithstanding subsection (5) above, the Treasury or the Secretary of State may take up, or direct any nominee of the Treasury or of the Secretary of State to take up, any rights for the time being available to them or him, or to that nominee, as an existing holder of shares or other securities of the successor company; but if, as a result, the proportion of the ordinary voting rights carried by the Government shareholding at any time exceeds the target investment limit, it shall be the duty of the Treasury or, as the case may be, the Secretary of State to comply with subsection (5) above as soon after that time as is reasonably practicable.

(7) For the purposes of this section the temporary suspension of any of the ordinary voting rights shall be disregarded.

Financial structure of the successor company

55.—(1) If the Secretary of State so directs at any time before the successor company ceases to be wholly owned by the Crown, such sum (not exceeding the accumulated realised profits of the Corporation) as may be specified in the direction shall be carried by the successor company to a reserve (in this section referred to as "the statutory reserve").

(2) The statutory reserve may only be applied by the successor company in paying up unissued shares of the company to be allotted to members of the company as fully paid bonus shares.

(3) Notwithstanding subsection (2) above, the statutory reserve shall not count as an undistributable reserve of the successor company for the purposes of section 264(3)(*d*) of the Companies Act 1985; but for the purpose of determining under that section whether the successor company may make a distribution at any time any amount for the time being standing to the credit of the statutory reserve shall be treated for the purposes of section 264(3)(*c*) as if it were unrealised profits of the company.

(4) For the purposes of any statutory accounts of the successor company—

(*a*) the vesting effected by virtue of section 49 above shall be taken to have been a vesting of all the property, rights and liabilities to which the Corporation was entitled or subject immediately before the end of the last complete financial year of the Corporation ending before the transfer date (other than any rights and liabilities which vest in the Treasury by virtue of section 50 above) and to have been effected immediately after the end of that year; and

(*b*) the value of any asset and the amount of any liability of the

Corporation taken to have been vested in the successor company by virtue of paragraph (*a*) above shall be taken to have been the value or (as the case may be) the amount assigned to that asset or liability for the purposes of the corresponding statement of accounts prepared by the Corporation in respect of that year.

(5) For the purposes of any statutory accounts of the successor company the amount to be included in respect of any item shall be determined as if anything done by the Corporation (whether by way of acquiring, revaluing or disposing of any asset or incurring, revaluing or discharging any liability, or by carrying any amount to any provision or reserve, or otherwise) had been done by the successor company.

Accordingly (but without prejudice to the generality of the preceding provision) the amount to be included from time to time in any reserves of the successor company as representing its accumulated realised profits shall be determined as if any profits realised and retained by the Corporation had been realised and retained by the successor company.

(6) References in this section to the statutory accounts of the successor company are references to any accounts prepared by the successor company for the purposes of any provision of the Companies Act 1985 (including group accounts); and in this section "complete financial year" means a financial year ending with 31st March.

Temporary restrictions on successor company's borrowings etc.

56.—(1) If articles of association of the successor company confer on the Secretary of State powers exercisable with the consent of the Treasury for, or in connection with, restricting the sums of money which may be borrowed or raised by the group during any period, those powers shall be exercisable in the national interest notwithstanding any rule of law and the provisions of any enactment.

(2) For the purposes of this section any alteration of the articles of association of the successor company which—

(*a*) has the effect of conferring or extending any such power as is mentioned in subsection (1) above; and

(*b*) is made at a time when that company has ceased to be wholly owned by the Crown,

shall be disregarded.

(3) In this section "group" means the successor company and all of its subsidiaries taken together.

Dissolution of the Corporation

57.—(1) The Corporation shall continue in existence after the transfer date until it is dissolved in accordance with subsection (2) below; and the period of its continued existence after the transfer date is in this Act referred to as "the transitional period".

(2) The Secretary of State may by order, after consulting the Corporation and the successor company, dissolve the Corporation on a day specified in the order, as soon as he is satisfied that nothing further remains to be done by the Corporation under Schedule 8 to this Act.

(3) During the transitional period section 1 of the 1972 Act shall have effect as if for subsection (2) (composition of Corporation) there were substituted the following subsection—

"(2) The Corporation shall consist of—

(*a*) a chairman appointed by the Secretary of State; and

(*b*) such one or more other persons as may be so appointed."

Statements in connection with flotation

58.—(1) This section shall apply where—

(*a*) an offer for sale to the public of any securities of the successor company is made by or on behalf of the Crown;

(*b*) any invitation or advertisement is issued (whether or not in documentary form) by or on behalf of the Crown in connection with the offer; and

(*c*) that invitation or advertisement does not contain all the listing particulars.

(2) None of the persons mentioned in subsection (3) below shall incur any civil liability by reason of the invitation or advertisement, or any omission from it, if—

(*a*) the contents of the invitation or advertisement were submitted to the Council of The Stock Exchange;

(*b*) that Council did not object to the contents of the invitation or advertisement; and

(*c*) the invitation or advertisement and the listing particulars, taken together, would not be likely to mislead persons of the kind likely to consider the offer.

(3) The persons referred to in subsection (2) above are—

(*a*) the Crown;

(*b*) any person acting on behalf of the Crown in connection with the offer;

(*c*) the maker of any statement contained in the invitation or advertisement;

(*d*) any person responsible for the preparation of, or of any part of, the listing particulars.

(4) The reference in subsection (2) above to a person mentioned in subsection (3) above incurring civil liability shall include a reference to any other person being entitled as against the person so mentioned to be granted any civil remedy or to rescind or repudiate any agreement.

(5) In this section "the listing particulars", in relation to the offer, means such particulars as, by virtue of any provision of any enactment other than this section or of any subordinate legislation, have been approved by the Council of The Stock Exchange for the purposes of the admission of the securities to which the offer relates to the Official List of The Stock Exchange.

Application of Trustee Investments Act 1961 in relation to investment in the successor company

59.—(1) For the purpose of applying paragraph 3(*b*) of Part IV of Schedule 1 to the Trustee Investments Act 1961 (which provides that shares and debentures of a company shall not count as wider-range and narrower-range investments respectively within the meaning of that Act unless the company has paid dividends in each of the five years immediately preceding that in which the investment is made) in relation to investment in shares or debentures of the successor company during the calendar year in which the transfer date falls ("the first investment year") or during any year following that year, the successor company shall be deemed to have paid a dividend as there mentioned—

(*a*) in every year preceding the first investment year which is included in the relevant five years; and

(*b*) in the first investment year, if that year is included in the relevant five years and the successor company does not in fact pay such a dividend in that year.

(2) In subsection (1) above "the relevant five years" means the five years immediately preceding the year in which the investment in question is made or proposed to be made.

Tax provisions

60.—(1) The successor company shall be treated—

(*a*) for all purposes of corporation tax and petroleum revenue tax; and

(*b*) for the purposes of the Gas Levy Act 1981,

as if it were the same person as the Corporation.

(2) The successor company shall not by virtue of subsection (1) above be regarded as a body falling within section 272(5) of the Income and Corporation Taxes Act 1970 (bodies established for carrying on industries or undertakings under national ownership or control).

(3) Where any debentures are issued in pursuance of section 51 above, any annual payment secured by those debentures shall be treated for all purposes of corporation tax as if it were a charge on income of the successor company.

(4) In consequence of the provisions of this Part, the said Act of 1981 shall have effect with the amendments specified in Schedule 6 to this Act.

Interpretation etc. of Part II

61.—(1) In this Part—

"debenture" includes debenture stock;

"securities", in relation to a company, includes shares, debentures, bonds and other securities of the company, whether or not constituting a charge on the assets of the company;

"shares" includes stock;

"subsidiary" has the same meaning as in the Companies Act 1985.

(2) An order under section 49 above nominating any company for the purposes of that section and an order under subsection (1) of that section appointing the transfer date may be varied or revoked by a subsequent order at any time before any property, rights or liabilities vest in any company by virtue of section 49 above.

(3) A company shall be regarded for the purposes of this Part as wholly owned by the Crown at any time when each of the issued shares in the company is held by, or by a nominee of, the Treasury or the Secretary of State.

PART III

MISCELLANEOUS AND GENERAL

Exclusion of certain agreements from Restrictive Trade Practices Act 1976

62.—(1) The Restrictive Trade Practices Act 1976 shall not apply, and that Act and the Restrictive Trade Practices Act 1956 shall be deemed never to have applied, to any agreement which—

(*a*) was made before 28th November 1985; and

(*b*) was an agreement containing provisions relating to, or to activities connected with, the supply at a relevant place or to the Corporation of gas won under the authority of a petroleum production licence.

(2) The said Act of 1976 shall not apply, and shall be deemed never to have applied, to any agreement which—

(*a*) is or was made on or after 28th November 1985;

(*b*) is or was an agreement containing provisions relating to, or to activities connected with, the supply otherwise than under an authorisation granted under section 7 above of gas won under the authority of a petroleum production licence; and

(c) satisfies such other conditions as may be specified in an order made by the Secretary of State.

(3) The conditions specified in an order under subsection (2) above may include—

(a) conditions which are to be satisfied in relation to a time before the coming into force of this section;

(b) conditions which refer any matter (which may be the general question whether the said Act of 1976 should apply to a particular agreement) to the Secretary of State for determination after such consultation as may be so specified.

(4) Any modification on or after 28th November 1985 of any agreement made before that date shall—

(a) if it relates exclusively to the identities of the parties to the agreement, be treated for the purposes of this section and the said Act of 1976 as a modification before that date; and

(b) in any other case, be treated for those purposes in relation to the original agreement as a separate agreement;

and, accordingly, in neither case shall the modification be capable of having the effect of requiring an agreement made before that date to be treated for those purposes as an agreement made on or after that date.

(5) For the purposes of this section, the following in particular, that is to say, exploration for gas and the production, transport and treatment of gas shall be regarded as activities connected with the supply of gas.

(6) In this section—

"gas" means any substance which is or (if it were in a gaseous state) would be gas within the meaning of Part I of this Act;

"petroleum production licence" means a licence granted under the Petroleum (Production) Act 1934 or the Petroleum (Production) Act (Northern Ireland) 1964 or any corresponding licence granted under the law of a country or territory outside the United Kingdom;

"relevant place", in relation to any gas won under the authority of a petroleum production licence, means—

(a) in the case of gas won at a place in the United Kingdom, that place or any place within one mile from that place;

(b) in the case of gas won at a place outside the United Kingdom and landed at a place in the United Kingdom, any place outside the United Kingdom, the place of landing or any place within one mile from the place of landing;

and expressions which are also used in the said Act of 1976 have the same meanings as in that Act.

(7) In relation to any supply before the appointed day, the reference in subsection (2) above to a supply of gas otherwise than under an authorisation granted under section 7 above shall have effect as a reference to a supply of gas otherwise than in performance of any duty imposed by the 1972 Act.

Restrictions on use of certain information

63.—(1) On granting an authorisation to any person under section 7 above the Secretary of State may give to that person such directions as appear to the Secretary of State to be requisite or expedient for the purpose of securing that, where any information is or has been furnished to that person or an associate of his by any other person in the course of any relevant negotiations, neither the person to whom the information is or has been furnished nor any associate of his obtains any unfair commercial advantage from his possession of the information.

(2) For the purposes of any directions given to any person under this section "relevant negotiations" means any negotiations for an agreement for the supply to that person of gas won under the authority of a petroleum production licence.

(3) As soon as practicable after giving any directions under this section, the Secretary of State shall publish a copy of the directions in such manner as he considers appropriate for the purpose of bringing the directions to the attention of persons likely to be affected by a contravention of them.

(4) The obligation to comply with any directions under this section is a duty owed to any person who may be affected by a contravention of them.

(5) Where a duty is owed by virtue of subsection (4) above to any person any breach of the duty which causes that person to sustain loss or damage shall be actionable at the suit or instance of that person.

(6) In any proceedings brought against any person in pursuance of subsection (5) above, it shall be a defence for him to prove that he took all reasonable steps and exercised all due diligence to avoid contravening the directions.

(7) Without prejudice to any right which any person may have by virtue of subsection (5) above to bring civil proceedings in respect of any contravention or apprehended contravention of any directions under this section, compliance with any such directions shall be enforceable by civil proceedings by the Secretary of State for an injunction or interdict or for any other appropriate relief.

(8) Directions given to any person under this section shall not be revoked or varied except with the consent of that person.

(9) For the purposes of this section a person is an associate of another if he and that other are connected with each other within the meaning of section 533 of the Income and Corporation Taxes Act 1970.

(10) In this section "gas" and "petroleum production licence" have the same meanings as in section 62 above.

Provisions as to orders

64.—(1) Any power conferred on the Secretary of State by this Act to make orders shall be exercisable by statutory instrument.

(2) Any statutory instrument containing an order under this Act, other than an order appointing a day or an order under section 20(9), 49(2) or 57(2) above, shall be subject to annulment in pursuance of a resolution of either House of Parliament.

Financial provisions

65. There shall be paid out of money provided by Parliament any administrative expenses incurred by the Secretary of State in consequence of the provisions of this Act and any increase attributable to this Act in the sums payable out of money so provided under any other Act.

General interpretation

66. In this Act, unless the context otherwise requires—

"the 1972 Act" means the Gas Act 1972;

"the appointed day" has the meaning given by section 3 above;

"contravention", in relation to any direction, condition, requirement, regulation or order, includes any failure to comply with it and cognate expressions shall be construed accordingly;

"the Corporation" means the British Gas Corporation;

"the Director" means the Director General of Gas Supply;
"modifications" includes additions, alterations and omissions and cognate expressions shall be construed accordingly;
"subordinate legislation" has the same meaning as in the Interpretation Act 1978;
"the successor company" has the meaning given by section 49(1) above;
"the transfer date" has the meaning given by section 49(1) above;
"the transitional period" has the meaning given by section 57(1) above.

Amendments, transitional provisions, savings and repeals

67.—(1) The enactments mentioned in Schedule 7 to this Act shall have effect subject to the amendments there specified (being minor amendments or amendments consequential on the preceding provisions of this Act).

(2) The Secretary of State may by order make such consequential modifications of any provision contained in any Act (whether public general or local) passed, or in subordinate legislation made, before the appointed day as appear to him necessary or expedient in respect of—

(*a*) any reference in that Act or subordinate legislation to the Corporation;
(*b*) any reference (in whatever terms) in that Act or subordinate legislation to a person carrying on a gas undertaking or to such an undertaking; or
(*c*) any reference in that Act or subordinate legislation to any enactment repealed by this Act.

(3) The transitional provisions and savings contained in Schedule 8 to this Act shall have effect; but those provisions and savings are without prejudice to sections 16 and 17 of the Interpretation Act 1978 (effect of repeals).

(4) The enactments mentioned in Schedule 9 to this Act (which include some which are spent or no longer of practical utility) are hereby repealed to the extent specified in the third column of that Schedule.

Short title, commencement and extent

68.—(1) This Act may be cited as the Gas Act 1986.

(2) The following provisions of this Act, namely—

Part I except sections 1 and 2;
section 66;
section 67(1) and Schedule 7;
section 67(2);
Part I of Schedule 8 and section 67(3) so far as relating to that Part; and
Part I of Schedule 9 and section 67(4) so far as relating to that Part,

shall come into force on the appointed day.

(3) The following provisions of this Act, namely—

Part II;
Part II of Schedule 8 and section 67(3) so far as relating to that Part; and
Part II of Schedule 9 and section 67(4) so far as relating to that Part,

shall come into force on the transfer date.

(4) Part III of Schedule 9 and section 67(4) so far as relating to that Part shall come into force on the dissolution of the Corporation.

(5) Subject to subsections (2) to (4) above, this Act shall come into force on such day as the Secretary of State may by order appoint; and different days may be so appointed for different provisions or for different purposes.

(6) This Act, except this section and the following provisions, namely—

sections 49 and 50;

section 58;

sections 62 and 63;

section 66;

paragraph 7 of Schedule 1 and section 1(5) so far as relating to that paragraph;

paragraph 8 of Schedule 2 and section 2(5) so far as relating to that paragraph;

paragraphs 15, 23 and 28 of Schedule 7 and section 67(1) so far as relating to those paragraphs; and

paragraphs 27 to 31 of Schedule 8 and section 67(3) so far as relating to those paragraphs; and

Schedule 9 and section 67(4) so far as relating to the repeal of section 33(2) of the 1972 Act and the repeals in the House of Commons Disqualification Act 1975,

does not extend to Northern Ireland.

SCHEDULES

Section 1(5)

SCHEDULE 1

Director General of Gas Supply

1. There shall be paid to the Director such remuneration, and such travelling and other allowances, as the Secretary of State with the approval of the Treasury may determine.

2. In the case of any such holder of the office of the Director as may be determined by the Secretary of State with the approval of the Treasury, there shall be paid such pension, allowance or gratuity to or in respect of him on his retirement or death, or such contributions or payments towards provision for such a pension, allowance or gratuity as may be so determined.

3. If, when any person ceases to hold office as the Director, the Secretary of State determines with the approval of the Treasury that there are special circumstances which make it right that he should receive compensation, there may be paid to him a sum by way of compensation of such amount as may be so determined.

4. The Director may, with the approval of the Treasury as to numbers and terms and conditions of service, appoint such staff as he may determine.

5. There shall be paid out of money provided by Parliament the remuneration of, and any travelling or other allowances payable under this Act to, the Director and any staff of the Director, any sums payable under this Act to or in respect of the Director and any expenses duly incurred by the Director or by any of his staff in consequence of the provisions of this Act.

6. In the Parliamentary Commissioner Act 1967 in Schedule 2 (departments and authorities subject to investigation) there shall be inserted (at the appropriate place) the following entry—

"Office of the Director General of Gas Supply".

7. In the House of Commons Disqualification Act 1975 in Part III of Schedule 1 (other disqualifying offices) there shall be inserted (at the appropriate place) the following entry—

"Director General of Gas Supply";

and the like insertion shall be made in Part III of Schedule 1 to the Northern Ireland Assembly Disqualification Act 1975.

8. The Director shall have an official seal for the authentication of documents required for the purposes of his functions.

9. The Documentary Evidence Act 1868 shall have effect as if the Director were included in the first column of the Schedule to that Act, as if the Director and any person authorised to act on behalf of the Director were mentioned in the second column of that Schedule, and as if the regulations referred to in that Act included any document issued by the Director or by any such person.

10. Anything authorised or required by or under this Act to be done by the Director may be done by any member of the staff of the Director who is authorised generally or specially in that behalf by the Director.

Section 2(5)

SCHEDULE 2

Gas Consumers' Council

1. The Council shall not be regarded as a servant or agent of the Crown or as enjoying any status, immunity or privilege of the Crown.

2. The Council may pay to any member such sums, whether by way of remuneration or allowances or otherwise, as the Secretary of State may with the approval of the Treasury determine.

3.—(1) Subject to sub-paragraph (2) below, the Council may, with the approval of the Secretary of State as to numbers and terms and conditions of service, appoint such staff as it may determine.

(2) The Council shall not appoint a person to act as principal officer of the Council except after consultation with the Secretary of State.

(3) For the purpose of ensuring that there are persons available in particular localities to assist the Council in the performance in those localities of its functions under this Act, the Council may, without any such approval as is required by sub-paragraph (1) above, appoint such persons to be so available as it may determine.

(4) Persons appointed under sub-paragraph (3) above shall not be paid any sums by the Council for or in respect of their services except sums reimbursing them for their travelling expenses and such of their other out-of-pocket expenses as do not relate to loss of remuneration.

(5) The consent of the Treasury shall be required for the giving by the Secretary of State of an approval for the purposes of sub-paragraph (1) above.

4. The Council shall have power to do anything which is calculated to facilitate, or is incidental or conducive to, the performance of any of its functions under this Act.

5. It shall be the duty of the Council to comply with any notice given by the Secretary of State with the approval of the Treasury requiring it to perform duties of a financial nature specified in the notice.

6. The Secretary of State or the Director may, to such extent as may be approved by the Treasury, defray or contribute towards the expenses of the Council.

7. Any sums required by the Secretary of State for the purposes of paragraph 6 above shall be paid out of money provided by Parliament.

8. In the House of Commons Disqualification Act 1975 in Part II of Schedule 1 (bodies of which all members are disqualified) there shall be inserted (at the appropriate place) the following entry—

"The Gas Consumers' Council";

and the like insertion shall be made in Part II of Schedule 1 to the Northern Ireland Assembly Disqualification Act 1975.

Section 9(3)

SCHEDULE 3

Acquisition of Land by Public Gas Suppliers

Part I

Powers of Acquisition Etc.

1.—(1) The Secretary of State, after consultation with the Director, may authorise a public gas supplier to purchase compulsorily any land.

(2) In sub-paragraph (1) above "land" includes any right over land; and the power of the Secretary of State under that sub-paragraph includes power to authorise the acquisition of rights over land by creating new rights as well as acquiring existing ones.

2.—(1) This paragraph applies to land which—

(*a*) for the purposes of the Acquisition of Land Act 1981, is or forms part of a common, open space or a fuel or field garden allotment; or

(*b*) for the purposes of the Acquisition of Land (Authorisation Procedure) (Scotland) Act 1947, is or forms part of a common or open space.

(2) Where for any purpose a public gas supplier has acquired, or proposes to acquire, any land to which this paragraph applies, or any right over any such land, and other land is

required for the purpose of being given in exchange for the land or right in question, the Secretary of State may authorise the supplier to purchase that other land compulsorily, or he may acquire it by agreement.

3. Where a public gas supplier has acquired any land by virtue of paragraph 1 above, he shall not dispose of that land or of any interest in or right over it except with the consent of the Director.

Part II

Procedure, Compensation Etc. (England and Wales)

Application of Acquisition of Land Act 1981 generally

4. The Acquisition of Land Act 1981 shall apply to a compulsory purchase by a public gas supplier of land or rights in England and Wales, subject, in the case of a compulsory acquisition of a right by the creation of a new right, to Schedule 3 to that Act.

New rights: general adaptation of Compulsory Purchase Act 1965

5. The Compulsory Purchase Act 1965 shall have effect with the modifications necessary to make it apply to a public gas supplier's compulsory acquisition of a right in England and Wales by the creation of a new right as it applies to the compulsory acquisition of land, so that, in appropriate contexts, references in that Act to land are to be read as referring, or as including references, to the right acquired or to be acquired, or to land over which the right is or is to be exercisable, according to the requirements of the particular context.

New rights: specific adaptations of Act of 1965

6. Without prejudice to the generality of paragraph 5 above, Part I of the said Act of 1965 shall apply in relation to a public gas supplier's compulsory acquisition of a right in England and Wales by the creation of a new right with the modifications specified in paragraphs 7 to 12 below.

7. For section 7 of that Act (measure of compensation) there shall be substituted the following section—

> "7. In assessing the compensation to be paid by the acquiring authority under this Act regard shall be had not only to the extent (if any) to which the value of the land over which the right is to be acquired is depreciated by the acquisition of the right but also to the damage (if any) to be sustained by the owner of the land by reason of its severance from other land of his, or injuriously affecting that other land by the exercise of the powers conferred by this or the special Act."

8. For subsection (1) of section 8 of that Act (protection for vendor against severance of house, garden, etc.) there shall be substituted the following subsections—

> "(1) No person shall be required to grant any right over part only—
>
> (*a*) of any house, building or manufactory; or
>
> (*b*) of a park or garden belonging to a house,
>
> if he is willing to sell the whole of the house, building, manufactory, park or garden, unless the Lands Tribunal determine that—
>
> (i) in the case of a house, building or manufactory, the part over which the right is proposed to be acquired can be made subject to that right without material detriment to the house, building or manufactory; or
>
> (ii) in the case of a park or garden, the part over which the right is proposed to be acquired can be made subject to that right without seriously affecting the amenity or convenience of the house;
>
> and if the Lands Tribunal so determine, the Tribunal shall award compensation in respect of any loss due to the acquisition of the right, in addition to its value; and thereupon the party interested shall be required to grant to the acquiring authority that right over the part of the house, building, manufactory, park or garden.
>
> (1A) In considering the extent of any material detriment to a house, building or manufactory, or any extent to which the amenity or convenience of a house is affected, the Lands Tribunal shall have regard not only to the right which is to be acquired over the land, but also to any adjoining or adjacent land belonging to the same owner and subject to compulsory purchase."

9. The following provisions of that Act (being provisions stating the effect of a deed poll executed in various circumstances where there is no conveyance by persons with interests in the land)—

section 9(4) (refusal by owners to convey);
Schedule 1, paragraph 10(3) (owners under incapacity);
Schedule 2, paragraph 2(3) (absent and untraced owners); and
Schedule 4, paragraphs 2(3) and 7(2) (common land),

shall be so modified as to secure that, as against persons with interests in the land which are expressed to be overridden by the deed, the right which is to be compulsorily acquired is vested absolutely in the acquiring authority.

10. Section 11 of that Act (powers of entry) shall be so modified as to secure that, as from the date on which the acquiring authority have served notice to treat in respect of any right, they have power, exercisable in the like circumstances and subject to the like conditions, to enter for the purpose of exercising that right (which shall be deemed for this purpose to have been created on the date of service of the notice); and sections 12 (penalty for unauthorised entry) and 13 (entry on sheriff's warrant in the event of obstruction) shall be modified correspondingly.

11. Section 20 of that Act (protection for interests of tenants at will etc.) shall apply with the modifications necessary to secure that persons with such interests as are mentioned in that section are compensated in a manner corresponding to that in which they would be compensated on a compulsory acquisition of that land, but taking into account only the extent (if any) of such interference with such an interest as is actually caused, or likely to be caused, by the exercise of the right in question.

12. Section 22 of that Act (protection of acquiring authority's possession where by inadvertence an estate, right or interest has not been got in) shall be so modified as to enable the acquiring authority, in circumstances corresponding to those referred to in that section, to continue entitled to exercise the right acquired, subject to compliance with that section as respects compensation.

New rights: compensation

13. The enactments in force in England and Wales with respect to compensation for the compulsory purchase of land shall apply with the necessary modifications as respects compensation in the case of a public gas supplier's compulsory acquisition of a right by the creation of a new right as they apply to compensation on the compulsory purchase of land and interests in land.

Part III

Procedure, Compensation Etc. (Scotland)

Application of Acquisition of Land (Authorisation Procedure) (Scotland) Act 1947 generally

14. The Acquisition of Land (Authorisation Procedure) (Scotland) Act 1947 shall apply to the compulsory purchase by a public gas supplier of land or rights in Scotland as if the supplier were a local authority within the meaning of that Act, and as if this Act had been in force immediately before the commencement of that Act.

New rights: general application of Act of 1947 and incorporated enactments

15. The enactments incorporated with this Act by virtue of Part I of Schedule 2 to the said Act of 1947 and that Act shall have effect with the modifications necessary to make them apply to a public gas supplier's compulsory acquisition of a right in Scotland by the creation of a new right as they apply to the compulsory acquisition of land, so that, in appropriate contexts, references in those enactments and that Act to land are to be read as referring, or as including references, to the right acquired or to be acquired, or to land over which the right is or is to be exercisable, according to the requirements of the particular context.

New rights: specific adaptations of Act of 1947

16. Without prejudice to the generality of paragraph 15 above, Part III of Schedule 1 to the said Act of 1947 (requirement of special parliamentary procedure, and other special provisions, in the case of acquisition of certain descriptions of land) shall apply in relation

to a public gas supplier's compulsory acquisition of a right in Scotland by the creation of a new right with the modifications specified in paragraphs 17 to 20 below.

17. In paragraph 9 of that Schedule (compulsory purchase affecting land of the National Trust for Scotland) for references to the compulsory purchase of land there shall be substituted references to the compulsory acquisition of rights over land.

18. In paragraph 10 of that Schedule (land of statutory undertakers)—

(*a*) for the words "land comprised in the order" there shall be substituted the words "land over which a right is to be acquired by virtue of the order";

(*b*) for the words "purchase of" there shall be substituted the words "acquisition of a right over";

(*c*) for the words "it can be purchased and not replaced" there shall be substituted the words "the right can be acquired"; and

(*d*) for sub-paragraph (ii) there shall be substituted the following sub-paragraph—

"(ii) that any detriment to the carrying on of the undertaking, in consequence of the acquisition of the right, can be made good by the undertakers by the use of other land belonging to, or available for acquisition by, them".

19. In paragraph 11 of that Schedule (common or open space), for sub-paragraph (1) there shall be substituted the following sub-paragraph—

"(1) In so far as a compulsory purchase order authorises the acquisition of a right over land forming part of a common or open space, it shall be subject to special parliamentary procedure unless the Secretary of State is satisfied—

(*a*) that the land, when burdened with that right, will be no less advantageous to those persons in whom it is vested and other persons, if any, entitled to rights of common or other rights, and to the public, than it was before; or

(*b*) that there has been or will be given in exchange for the right additional land which will as respects the persons in whom there is vested the land over which the right is to be acquired, the persons, if any, entitled to rights of common or other rights over that land, and the public, be adequate to compensate them for the disadvantages which result from the acquisition of the right, and that the additional land has been or will be vested in the persons in whom there is vested the land over which the right is to be acquired, and subject to the like rights, trusts and incidents as attach to that land apart from the compulsory purchase order; or

(*c*) that the land affected by the right to be acquired does not exceed 250 square yards in extent, and that the giving of other land in exchange for the right is unnecessary, whether in the interests of the persons, if any, entitled to rights of common or other rights or in the interests of the public,

and certifies accordingly."

20. In paragraph 12 of that Schedule, for the words "the purchase of" there shall be substituted the words "the acquisition of a right over".

21. Paragraph 10 above shall have effect in relation to the said Act of 1947 with the substitution of a reference to paragraph 3(1) of the Second Schedule to that Act for the reference to section 11 of the Compulsory Purchase Act 1965, and with the omission of the words from "and sections" to the end of the paragraph.

22. For paragraph 4 of the Second Schedule to the said Act of 1947 (protection for owner against severance of property) there shall be substituted the provisions substituted by paragraph 8 of this Schedule for section 8(1) of the said Act of 1965, and any reference in those provisions to the Lands Tribunal shall be construed as a reference to the Lands Tribunal for Scotland.

Restrictions on application of paragraphs 15 to 20 above

23. So much of paragraph 15 above as relates to the said Act of 1947, and paragraphs 16 to 20 above, shall not apply to any compulsory purchase to which, by virtue of section 12 or 13 of the Gas Act of 1965, Part I of Schedule 4 to that Act applies.

New Rights: specific adaptions of Lands Clauses Consolidation (Scotland) Act 1845

24. For section 61 of the Lands Clauses Consolidation (Scotland) Act 1845 (estimation of compensation) there shall be substituted the following section—

"61. In estimating the purchase money or compensation to be paid by the promoters of the undertaking in the Special Act, in any of the cases aforesaid, regard shall be had not only to the extent (if any) to which the value of the land over which the right is to be acquired is depreciated by the acquisition of the right, but also to the damage (if any) to be sustained by the owner of the land by reason of its severance from other land of his, or injuriously affecting that other land by the exercise of the powers conferred by this or the Special Act."

25. The following provisions of that Act (being provisions stating the effect of a notarial instrument or of a disposition executed in various circumstances where there is no conveyance by persons with interests in land)—

section 74 (failure by owner to convey);

section 76 (refusal to convey or show title or owner cannot be found);

section 98 (vesting of common land),

shall be so modified as to secure that, as against persons with interests in the land over which the right is to be compulsorily acquired such right is vested absolutely in the promoters of the undertaking.

26. Paragraph 11 above shall have effect in relation to that Act with the substitution of a reference to sections 114 and 115 thereof for the reference to section 20 of the Compulsory Purchase Act 1965.

27. Paragraph 12 above shall have effect in relation to that Act with the substitution of a reference to sections 117 and 118 thereof for any reference to section 22 of the said Act of 1965.

New rights: compensation

28. Paragraph 13 above shall have effect in relation to Scotland with the substitution of "Scotland" for "England and Wales".

29. This Part of this Schedule shall extend to Scotland only.

Section 9(3)

SCHEDULE 4

Power of Public Gas Suppliers to Break Up Streets, Bridges Etc.

1.—(1) Subject to the following provisions of this Schedule, a public gas supplier may execute the following kinds of works, that is to say, placing in or under any street or bridge and from time to time repairing, altering or removing—

(*a*) pipes, conduits, service pipes, cables, sewers and other works; and

(*b*) pressure governors, ventilators and other apparatus.

(2) Subject as aforesaid, a public gas supplier may execute any works requisite for or incidental to the purposes of any works falling within sub-paragraph (1) above, including for those purposes—

(*a*) opening or breaking up any street or bridge or any sewers, drains or tunnels within or under any street or bridge; and

(*b*) removing or using all earth and materials in or under any street or bridge.

(3) A public gas supplier shall do as little damage as possible in the exercise of the powers conferred by this paragraph and shall make compensation for any damage done in the exercise of those powers.

2.—(1) The powers of a public gas supplier under paragraph 1 above shall include power to erect in any street one or more structures for housing any apparatus, but only with the consent, which shall not be unreasonably withheld, of the highway authority.

(2) Any question whether or not consent to the erection of such a structure is unreasonably withheld shall be determined by a single arbitrator to be appointed by the parties or, in default of agreement, appointed by the Director.

(3) For the purposes of this paragraph the withholding of consent shall, to the extent that it is based on the ground that the structure ought to be erected elsewhere than in a street, be treated as unreasonable if the supplier shows either that there is no reasonably practicable alternative to erecting it in a street, or that all such alternatives would, on the balance of probabilities, involve greater danger to life or property.

3.—(1) Subject to sub-paragraph (2) below, nothing in paragraph 1 above shall empower a public gas supplier to lay down or place any pipe or other works into, through or against any building, or in any land not dedicated to the public use.

(2) A public gas supplier may exercise the powers conferred by paragraph 1 above in relation to any street which has been laid out but not dedicated to the public use for the purpose of giving a supply of gas to any premises which abut on the street.

4.—(1) Except in cases of emergency arising from defects in any pipes or other works, a street or bridge which—

(*a*) does not constitute for the purposes of the Highways Act 1980 a highway or part of a highway maintainable at the public expense; and

(*b*) is under the control or management of, or maintainable by, any railway authority or navigation authority,

shall not be opened or broken up under paragraph 1 above except with the consent, which shall not be unreasonably withheld, of that authority.

(2) Any question whether or not consent to the opening or breaking up of such a street or bridge is unreasonably withheld shall be determined by a single arbitrator to be appointed by the parties or, in default of agreement, appointed by the Director.

5.—(1) The powers conferred by paragraph 1 above shall be included among those to which section 20 of the Highways Act 1980 (restriction on laying of apparatus etc. in special roads) applies.

(2) Nothing in paragraph 1 above shall affect the application to any operation of sections 34 to 36 of the Coast Protection Act 1949.

6. In this Schedule—

"highway authority", in relation to a street, means the highway authority or other person having the control or management of the street;

"navigation authority" means any person or body of persons, whether incorporated or not, authorised by or under any enactment to work, maintain, conserve, improve or control any canal or other inland navigation, navigable river, estuary, harbour or dock;

"railway authority" means any person or body of persons, whether incorporated or not, authorised by any enactment to construct, work or carry on a railway; and

"street" includes any square, court, alley, highway, road, lane, thoroughfare, or public passage or place.

7. In its application to Scotland this Schedule shall have effect with the following modifications—

(*a*) in paragraphs 1 to 4, for the word "street", wherever it occurs, there shall be substituted the word "road";

(*b*) in paragraph 2(1), for the words "highway authority" there shall be substituted the words "roads authority or road managers";

(*c*) in paragraphs 2(2) and 4(2), for the word "arbitrator" there shall be substituted the word "arbiter";

(*d*) in paragraph 4(1), for the words "for the purposes of the Highways Act 1980 a highway or part of a highway maintainable at the public expense" there shall be substituted the words "a road within the meaning of the Roads (Scotland) Act 1984";

(*e*) in paragraph 5(1), for the words "section 20 of the Highways Act 1980" there shall be substituted the words "section 133 of the Roads (Scotland) Act 1984"; and

(*f*) in paragraph 6, the definition of "highway authority" shall be omitted and for the definition of "street" there shall be substituted the following definitions—

" 'road', 'roads authority' and 'road managers' have the same meanings as in the Public Utilities Street Works Act 1950."

Section 15

SCHEDULE 5

Public Gas Supply Code

Part I

Supply of Gas to Tariff Customers

Maintenance etc. of service pipes

1. A public gas supplier shall carry out any necessary work of maintenance, repair or renewal of any service pipe—

(*a*) by which a tariff customer is supplied with gas; and

(*b*) which was provided and laid otherwise than at the expense of the supplier or a predecessor of his,

and may recover the expenses reasonably incurred in so doing from the customer.

Alterations etc. of burners on change of calorific value

2. It shall be the duty of a public gas supplier, in the case of any alteration in the calorific value declared in respect of any gas supplied by him, to take at his own expense such steps as may be necessary to alter, adjust or replace the burners in the appliances of tariff customers who are supplied with that gas in such manner as to secure that the gas can be burned with safety and efficiency.

Consumption of gas to be ascertained by meter

3.—(1) Every tariff customer of a public gas supplier shall, if required to do so by the supplier, take his supply through a meter, and in default of his doing so the supplier may refuse to give or discontinue the supply of gas.

(2) A public gas supplier shall if so required by a tariff customer, supply to the customer, whether by way of sale, hire or loan, an appropriate meter (whether a prepayment meter or otherwise) for ascertaining the quantity of gas supplied by him; but in the case of a supply by way of hire or loan the customer shall, if so required by the supplier, before receiving the meter give to the supplier reasonable security for the due performance of his obligation to take proper care of it.

(3) Where any money is deposited with a public gas supplier by way of security in pursuance of this paragraph, the supplier shall pay interest, at such rate as may from time to time be fixed by the supplier with the approval of the Director, on every sum of 50p so deposited for every three months during which it remains in the hands of the supplier.

Meters to be kept in proper order

4.—(1) Every tariff customer shall at all times at his own expense, keep all meters belonging to him, whereby the quantity of gas supplied by the public gas supplier is registered, in proper order for correctly registering the quantity of gas, and in default of his doing so the supplier may discontinue the supply of gas through that meter.

(2) A public gas supplier shall at all times, at his own expense, keep all meters let for hire or lent by him to any tariff customer in proper order for correctly registering the quantity of gas supplied; but this sub-paragraph is without prejudice to any remedy the supplier may have against the customer for failure to take proper care of the meter.

(3) A public gas supplier shall have power to remove, inspect and re-install any meter by which the quantity of gas supplied by him to a tariff customer is registered, and shall, while any such meter is removed, fix a substituted meter on the premises; and, subject to sub-paragraph (4) below, the cost of removing, inspecting and re-installing a meter and of fixing a substituted meter shall be defrayed by the supplier.

(4) Where such a meter is removed for the purpose of being examined by a meter examiner in accordance with section 17 of this Act, the expenses incurred in removing, examining and re-installing the meter and fixing a substituted meter shall, if the meter is found in proper order, be defrayed by the person at whose request the examination is to be carried out but otherwise shall be defrayed by the owner of the meter.

(5) A meter is found in proper order for the purposes of sub-paragraph (4) above if it is found to register correctly or to register erroneously to a degree not exceeding the degree permitted by regulations under section 17 of this Act.

Meter as evidence of quantity of gas supplied

5.—(1) Subject to sub-paragraph (2) below, where gas is supplied to a tariff customer through a meter, the register of the meter shall be prima facie evidence of the quantity of gas supplied.

(2) Where a meter through which a tariff customer is supplied with gas is found, when examined by a meter examiner appointed under section 17 of this Act, to register erroneously to a degree exceeding the degree permitted by regulations under that section—

(*a*) the meter shall be deemed to have registered erroneously to the degree so found since the relevant date, except in a case where it is proved to have begun to register erroneously as aforesaid on some later date; and

(*b*) the amount of allowance to be made to, or the surcharge to be made on, the customer by the supplier in consequence of the erroneous registration shall be paid to or by the customer, as the case may be.

(3) In sub-paragraph (2) above "the relevant date" means the penultimate date on which, otherwise than in connection with the examination, the register of the meter was ascertained.

Installation of meters in new premises

6.—(1) This paragraph applies where a meter is to be used to register the quantity of gas supplied to a tariff customer and—

(*a*) the building has not previously been supplied with gas by the public gas supplier; or

(*b*) a new or substituted pipe is to be laid between the public gas supplier's main and the meter.

(2) Subject to sub-paragraph (3) below, the meter shall be installed as near as practicable to the main, but within the outside wall of the building.

(3) The meter may be installed otherwise than within the outside wall of the building if it is installed either—

(*a*) in accommodation of a type and construction approved by the public gas supplier by an approval given in relation to buildings generally, or to any class or description of buildings; or

(*b*) in a separate meter house or other accommodation outside the building approved by the supplier in the case of that particular building.

(4) If the requirements of this paragraph are not complied with, the public gas supplier may refuse to supply gas to the premises until those requirements have been complied with.

Recovery of gas charges etc.

7.—(1) A public gas supplier may recover from a tariff customer any charges due to him in respect of the supply of gas, or in respect of the supplying and fixing of any meter or fittings.

(2) If a tariff customer quits any premises at which gas has been supplied to him through a meter by a public gas supplier without giving notice thereof to the supplier so that it is received by the supplier at least twenty-four hours before he quits the premises, he shall be liable to pay the supplier all charges in respect of the supply of gas to the premises accruing due up to whichever of the following first occurs, namely—

(*a*) the twenty-eighth day after he gives such notice to the supplier;

(*b*) the next day on which the register of the meter falls to be ascertained; and

(*c*) the day from which any subsequent occupier of the premises requires the supplier to supply gas to the premises.

(3) Sub-paragraph (2) above, or a statement of the effect thereof, shall be endorsed upon every demand note for gas charges payable to a public gas supplier by a tariff customer.

(4) If a tariff customer quits any premises at which gas has been supplied to him by a public gas supplier without paying any amount due from him by way of charges in respect of the supply, the supplier—

(*a*) may refuse to furnish him with a supply of gas at any other premises until he pays the amount so due; but

(*b*) shall not be entitled to require payment of that amount from the next occupier of the premises.

(5) If a tariff customer has not, after the expiry of twenty-eight days from the making of a demand in writing by a public gas supplier for payment thereof, paid the charges due from him in respect of the supply of gas by the supplier to any premises, the supplier, after the expiration of not less than seven days' notice of his intention, may—

(*a*) cut off the supply to the premises by disconnecting the service pipe at the meter (whether the pipe belongs to the supplier or not) or by such other means as he thinks fit; and

(*b*) recover any expenses incurred in so doing from the customer.

(6) Where a public gas supplier has cut off the supply of gas to any premises in consequence of any default on the part of a tariff customer, the supplier shall not be under any obligation to resume the supply of gas to the customer so in default until he has made good the default and paid the reasonable expenses of re-connecting the supply.

PART II

SUPPLY OF GAS TO TARIFF CUSTOMERS AND OTHERS

Use of antifluctuators and valves

8.—(1) Where a person supplied with gas by a public gas supplier uses the gas for working or supplying an engine, gas compressor or other similar apparatus or any apparatus liable to produce in any main of the supplier a pressure less than atmospheric pressure (any such engine, compressor or apparatus being in this paragraph referred to as a "compressor"), he shall, if so required by the supplier by notice, fix in a suitable position and keep in use an appliance provided by him which will effectually prevent pressure fluctuation in the supply mains and any other inconvenience or danger being caused to other consumers of gas by reason that he and they are supplied with gas from the same source.

(2) Where a person supplied with gas by a public gas supplier uses for or in connection with the consumption of the gas so supplied any air at high pressure (in this paragraph referred to as "compressed air") or any gaseous substance not supplied by the supplier (in this paragraph referred to as "extraneous gas"), he shall, if so required by the supplier by notice, fix in a suitable position and keep in use an appliance provided by him which will effectually prevent the admission of the compressed air or extraneous gas into the service pipe or into any main through which gas is supplied by the supplier.

(3) Where a person is required by this paragraph to keep in use any appliance, he shall at his own expense keep it in proper order and repair, and repair, renew or replace it if it is not in proper order or repair.

(4) A person supplied with gas by a public gas supplier shall not be entitled to use a compressor, or any apparatus for using compressed air or extraneous gas, unless he has given to the supplier not less than fourteen days' notice of his intention to do so; but this sub-paragraph shall not apply to the use of any compressor or apparatus which was lawfully in use immediately before the appointed day.

(5) If any person makes default in complying with any provision of this paragraph, the public gas supplier may cut off the supply of gas to him and shall not be required to resume the supply until the default has been remedied to his reasonable satisfaction.

(6) A public gas supplier shall, as soon as is practicable after any person is first supplied with gas by him, give to that person notice of the effect of the preceding provisions of this paragraph; but this requirement shall not apply in the case of any person who is supplied with gas by the Corporation immediately before the appointed day, and to whom a notice has been given before that day pursuant to paragraph 18(6) of Schedule 4 to the 1972 Act (which imposes a similar requirement).

(7) A public gas supplier shall have power to disconnect, remove, test and replace any appliance which any person supplied with gas by him is required by this paragraph to keep in use, and any expenses incurred by the supplier under this sub-paragraph shall, if the appliance is found in proper order and repair, be paid by the supplier but otherwise shall be paid by that person.

Improper use of gas

9. If any person supplied with gas by a public gas supplier improperly uses or deals with the gas so as to interfere with the efficient supply of gas by the supplier (whether to that person or to any other person), the supplier may, if he thinks fit, discontinue the supply of gas to that person.

Injury to gas fittings and interference with meters

10.—(1) If any person intentionally or by culpable negligence—

(*a*) injures or allows to be injured any gas fitting belonging to a public gas supplier;

(*b*) alters the index to any meter used for measuring the quantity of gas supplied by such a supplier; or

(*c*) prevents any such meter from duly registering the quantity of gas supplied,

he shall be guilty of an offence and liable on summary conviction to a fine not exceeding level 3 on the standard scale.

(2) If an offence under sub-paragraph (1) above involves any injury to or interference with any gas fitting belonging to the public gas supplier, the supplier may also, until the matter has been remedied, but no longer, discontinue the supply of gas to the person so offending (notwithstanding any contract previously existing).

(3) Where any person is prosecuted for an offence under sub-paragraph (1)(*b*) or (*c*) above, the possession by him of artificial means for causing an alteration of the index of the meter or, as the case may be, the prevention of the meter from duly registering shall, if the meter was in his custody or under his control, be prima facie evidence that the alteration or prevention was intentionally caused by him.

Restoration of supply without consent

11.—(1) Where a supply of gas to any premises has been cut off by a public gas supplier otherwise than in the exercise of a power conferred by regulations under section 18(2) of this Act, no person shall, without the consent of the supplier, restore the supply.

(2) If any person acts in contravention of sub-paragraph (1) above, he shall be guilty of an offence and liable on summary conviction to a fine not exceeding level 3 on the standard scale and the supplier may again cut off the supply.

Failure to notify connection or disconnection of service pipe

12.—(1) No person shall connect any meter with a service pipe through which gas is supplied by a public gas supplier, or disconnect any meter from any such pipe, unless he has given to the supplier, so that it is received by the supplier at least twenty-four hours before he does so, notice of his intention to do so, specifying the time and place of the proposed connection or disconnection.

(2) If any person acts in contravention of sub-paragraph (1) above, he shall be guilty of an offence and liable on summary conviction to a fine not exceeding level 2 on the standard scale.

Prevention of escapes of gas

13.—(1) Where any gas escapes from any pipe of a public gas supplier, or from any pipe or other gas fitting used by a person supplied with gas by a public gas supplier, the supplier shall, immediately after being informed of the escape, prevent the gas from escaping (whether by cutting off the supply of gas to any premises or otherwise).

(2) If a public gas supplier fails within twelve hours from being so informed effectually to prevent the gas from escaping, he shall be guilty of an offence and liable on summary conviction to a fine not exceeding level 3 on the standard scale.

(3) In any proceedings for an offence under sub-paragraph (2) above it shall be a defence for the public gas supplier to prove that it was not reasonably practicable for him effectually to prevent the gas from escaping within the said period of twelve hours, and that he did effectually prevent the escape as soon as it was reasonably practicable for him to do so.

(4) Where a public gas supplier has reasonable cause to suspect that gas supplied by him is escaping, or may escape, in any premises, any officer authorised by the supplier may, on production of some duly authenticated document showing his authority, enter the premises, inspect the gas fittings, carry out any work necessary to prevent the escape and take any other steps necessary to avert danger to life or property.

(5) Where a public gas supplier has reasonable cause to suspect that gas supplied or conveyed by him which has escaped has entered, or may enter any premises, any officer authorised by the supplier may on production of some duly authenticated document showing his authority, enter the premises and take any steps necessary to avert danger to life or property.

Information as to escapes of gas

14. It shall be the duty of a public gas supplier to take such steps as are necessary to ensure that, if he is informed of an escape of gas that he is not required by paragraph 13 above to prevent, he passes the information on, as soon as reasonably practicable—

(*a*) to the person who appears to the public gas supplier to be responsible (whether under that paragraph or otherwise) for preventing the escape; or

(*b*) in the case of an escape occurring in the authorised area of another public gas supplier, to that other public gas supplier.

Entry during continuance of supply

15.—(1) Any officer authorised by a public gas supplier may at all reasonable times, on the production of some duly authenticated document showing his authority, enter any premises in which there is a service pipe connected with a gas main of the supplier for the purpose of—

(*a*) inspecting gas fittings;

(*b*) ascertaining the quantity of gas supplied;

(c) performing the duty imposed on the supplier by paragraph 1 or 2 above;
(d) exercising the power conferred on the supplier by paragraph 4(3) or 8(7) above; or
(e) in the case of premises where the supplier has reason to believe that a compressor or compressed air or extraneous gas is being used, inspecting the premises and ascertaining whether the provisions of paragraph 8 above are being complied with.

(2) Paragraphs (a) and (b) of sub-paragraph (1) above do not apply where the consumer has applied in writing to the supplier for the supplier to disconnect the service pipe and cease to supply gas to the premises and the supplier has failed to do so within a reasonable time.

(3) In this paragraph "compressor", "compressed air" and "extraneous gas" have the same meanings as in paragraph 8 above.

Entry on discontinuance of supply

16.—(1) Where—
(a) a public gas supplier is authorised by any provision of this Act (including any such provision as applied by such an agreement as is mentioned in section 14(4) of this Act) to cut off or discontinue the supply of gas to any premises;
(b) a person occupying premises supplied with gas by a public gas supplier ceases to require such a supply;
(c) a person entering into occupation of any premises previously supplied with gas by a public gas supplier does not take a supply of gas from the supplier; or
(d) a person entering into occupation of any premises previously supplied with gas through a meter belonging to a public gas supplier does not hire or borrow that meter,

any officer authorised by the supplier, after twenty-four hours' notice to the occupier, or to the owner or lessee of the premises if they are unoccupied, may at all reasonable times, on production of some duly authenticated document showing his authority, enter the premises for the purpose of removing any gas fitting.

(2) The notice required to be given by sub-paragraph (1) above may, in the case of unoccupied premises the owner or lessee of which is unknown to the supplier and cannot be ascertained after diligent inquiry, be given by affixing it upon a conspicuous part of the premises not less than forty-eight hours before the premises are entered.

Entry for replacing, repairing or altering pipes

17.—(1) Any officer authorised by a public gas supplier, after seven clear days' notice to the occupier of any premises, or to the owner or lessee of any premises which are unoccupied, may at all reasonable times, on production of some duly authenticated document showing his authority, enter the premises for the purpose of—
(a) placing a new pipe in the place of any existing pipe which has already been lawfully placed; or
(b) repairing or altering any such existing pipe.

(2) The notice required to be given by sub-paragraph (1) above may, in the case of unoccupied premises the owner or lessee of which is unknown to the supplier and cannot be ascertained after diligent inquiry, be given by affixing it upon a conspicuous part of the premises.

(3) In cases of emergency arising from defects in any pipes entry may be made under sub-paragraph (1) above without the notice required to be given by that sub-paragraph, but the notice shall then be given as soon as possible after the occurrence of the emergency.

Provisions as to powers of entry

18.—(1) Where in pursuance of any powers of entry conferred by this Part of this Schedule, entry is made on any premises by an officer authorised by a public gas supplier—
(a) the officer shall ensure that the premises are left no less secure by reason of the entry; and
(b) the supplier shall make good, or pay compensation for, any damage caused by the officer, or by any person accompanying him in entering the premises, in taking any action therein authorised by this Schedule, or in making the premises secure.

(2) Any officer exercising powers of entry conferred by this Part of this Schedule may be accompanied by such persons as may be necessary or expedient for the purpose for which the entry is made, or for the purposes of sub-paragraph (1) above.

(3) If any person intentionally obstructs any officer exercising powers of entry conferred by this Part of this Schedule, he shall be guilty of an offence and liable on summary conviction to a fine not exceeding level 3 on the standard scale.

(4) The Rights of Entry (Gas and Electricity Boards) Act 1954 (entry under a justice's warrant) shall apply in relation to any powers of entry conferred by this Part of this Schedule.

Gas fittings not to be subject to distress

19.—(1) Any gas fittings let for hire or lent to a consumer by a public gas supplier and marked or impressed with a sufficient mark or brand indicating the supplier as the owner thereof—

(*a*) shall not be subject to distress or be liable to be taken in execution under process of any court or any proceedings in bankruptcy against the person in whose possession they may be; and

(*b*) shall not be deemed to be landlord's fixtures, notwithstanding that they may be fixed or fastened to any part of the premises in which they may be situated.

(2) In the application of sub-paragraph (1)(*a*) above to Scotland, for the word "distress" and the words "in bankruptcy against" there shall be substituted respectively the word "poinding" and the words "for the sequestration of the estate of".

Section 60(4)

SCHEDULE 6

AMENDMENTS OF GAS LEVY ACT 1981

1.—(1) In subsection (1) of section 1 of the Gas Levy Act 1981—

(*a*) for the words "their revenues by the British Gas Corporation (in this Act referred to as 'the Corporation')" there shall be substituted the words "his revenues by any person"; and

(*b*) for the words "the Corporation", in the second place where they occur, there shall be substituted the words "that person".

(2) In subsection (2) of that section—

(*a*) for the words "the Corporation", in the first two places where they occur, there shall be substituted the words "any person";

(*b*) for the words "has agreed" there shall be substituted the words "had agreed"; and

(*c*) for the words "the Corporation", in the third place where they occur, there shall be substituted the words "the British Gas Corporation (in this section referred to as 'the Corporation')".

2. No order shall be made under section 2(3) of that Act specifying for the year 1991–92 or an earlier year a rate of levy higher than the rate for the preceding year.

3. For section 3 of that Act there shall be substituted the following section—

"Payment of levy

3.—(1) Gas levy shall be paid to the Secretary of State in respect of each period of three months ending on 30th June, 30th September, 31st December or 31st March in any year (in this section referred to as a "chargeable period").

(2) It shall be the duty of any person liable to pay gas levy to deliver to the Secretary of State—

(*a*) within four weeks after the end of each chargeable period, a return for that period which complies with subsection (3) below; and

(*b*) within three months after the end of each year, a return for that year which so complies.

(3) A return under subsection (2) above for any chargeable period or any year shall show the quantity, expressed both by volume and as a number of therms, of gas to which section 1 above applies which was supplied to or won by the person concerned in that period or that year.

(4) Not later than six weeks after the end of any chargeable period a person who is liable to pay gas levy in respect of that period shall pay to the Secretary of State an amount equal to the amount of gas levy which would be due from him for that period if the amount due were calculated exclusively by reference to the return for that period.

(5) If the amount which, otherwise than by way of interest, falls to be paid by any person under subsection (4) above in respect of the chargeable periods in any year differs from the actual amount of gas levy due from that person in respect of those

periods, then not later than four months after the end of that year the amount of the difference shall—

(*a*) where the former amount is greater, be repaid by the Secretary of State to that person; and

(*b*) where the latter amount is greater, be paid by that person to the Secretary of State.

(6) Where any amount falling to be paid under subsection (4) or (5) above is not paid within the period for payment specified in that subsection, that amount shall carry interest at the prescribed rate from the end of that period until payment; and in this subsection "paid" and "payment" include repaid and repayment, respectively.

(7) In this section 'the prescribed rate' means the rate prescribed for the purposes of section 86 of the Taxes Management Act 1970."

4.—(1) In subsection (1) of section 4 of that Act—

(*a*) for the words "the Corporation", in the first place where they occur, there shall be substituted the words "any person";

(*b*) for the words "for any year shall only be payable" there shall be substituted the words "shall be payable by that person for any year only"; and

(*c*) for the words "the Corporation", in the second place where they occur, there shall be substituted the words "that person".

(2) In subsection (2) of that section—

(*a*) for the words "the Corporation", in the first place where they occur, there shall be substituted the words "the person concerned"; and

(*b*) for the words "the Corporation", in the second place where they occur, there shall be substituted the words "that person".

5.—(1) In subsection (1) of section 5 of that Act—

(*a*) for the words "the Corporation", in the first place where they occur, there shall be substituted the words "any person liable to pay gas levy";

(*b*) for the word "them" there shall be substituted the word "him";

(*c*) for the words "the Corporation are using or propose" there shall be substituted the words "that person is using or proposes"; and

(*d*) for the words "the Corporation", in the third place where they occur, there shall be substituted the words "that person".

(2) For subsection (2) of that section there shall be substituted the following subsections—

"(2) The Secretary of State may, after consultation with any person liable to pay gas levy, give to that person directions specifying descriptions of measuring and testing equipment which he is to install, maintain and use for the purposes of this Act.

(3) It shall also be the duty of any person liable to pay gas levy to furnish the Secretary of State with such returns, accounts and other information as he from time to time requires for the purpose of verifying returns delivered to him under section 3(2) above, and to afford to the Secretary of State facilities for the verification of information so furnished."

6. After section 5 of that Act there shall be inserted the following section—

"Offences

5A.—(1) If any person without reasonable excuse—

(*a*) fails to deliver a return under section 3(2) above within the time allowed for doing so; or

(*b*) fails to comply with a requirement imposed by or under section 5 above,

that person shall be liable on summary conviction to a fine not exceeding level 5 on the standard scale.

(2) If any person, in making any return under section 3(2) above or in giving any information required under section 5(3) above, makes any statement which he knows to be false in a material particular, or recklessly makes any statement which is false in a material particular, that person shall be liable—

(*a*) on summary conviction, to a fine not exceeding the statutory maximum;

(*b*) on conviction on indictment, to a fine.

(3) Where a body corporate is guilty of an offence under this section and that offence is proved to have been committed with the consent or connivance of, or to be attributable to any neglect on the part of, any director, manager, secretary or other similar officer of the body corporate or any person who was purporting to act in any such capacity he, as well as the body corporate, shall be guilty of that offence, and shall be liable to be proceeded against and punished accordingly."

7.—(1) In subsection (2) of section 6 of that Act for the words "the Corporation by virtue of section 3(4)" there shall be substituted the words "any person by virtue of section 3(5)(*a*)".

(2) In subsection (3) of that section for the words "section 3(4)" there shall be substituted the words "section 3(5)(*a*)".

8. In section 7(2) of that Act for the definition of "year" there shall be substituted the following definition—

" 'year' means a period of twelve months ending with a 31st March."

Section 67(1)

SCHEDULE 7

Minor and Consequential Amendments

Interpretation

1. In this Schedule "public gas supplier" has the same meaning as in Part I of this Act.

Enactments relating to statutory undertakers etc.

2.—(1) A public gas supplier shall be deemed to be a statutory undertaker and his undertaking a statutory undertaking for the purposes of the following enactments, namely—

(i) the Public Health Act 1925;
(ii) the Public Health Act 1936;
(iii) Schedule 3 to the Water Act 1945;
(iv) the Acquisition of Land (Authorisation Procedure) (Scotland) Act 1947;
(v) section 4 of the Requisitioned Land and War Works Act 1948;
(vi) the Water Act 1948;
(vii) the National Parks and Access to the Countryside Act 1949;
(viii) the Reserve and Auxiliary Forces (Protection of Civil Interests) Act 1951;
(ix) the Landlord and Tenant Act 1954;
(x) the Opencast Coal Act 1958;
(xi) the Flood Prevention (Scotland) Act 1961;
(xii) section 17(10) of the Public Health Act 1961;
(xiii) the Pipe-lines Act 1962;
(xiv) Schedule 3 to the Harbours Act 1964;
(xv) Schedule 6 to the Gas Act 1965;
(xvi) section 10 of the Highlands and Islands Development (Scotland) Act 1965;
(xvii) section 56 of the Housing (Scotland) Act 1966;
(xviii) section 40 of the Forestry Act 1967;
(xix) section 50 of the Agriculture Act 1967;
(xx) sections 38 and 66 of the Countryside (Scotland) Act 1967;
(xxi) the New Towns (Scotland) Act 1968;
(xxii) section 11 of and paragraph 6 of Schedule 2 to the Countryside Act 1968;
(xxiii) section 22 of the Sewerage (Scotland) Act 1968;
(xxiv) sections 22, 40, 48, 49, 118(2), 127 to 129, 132, 149, 165(3), 181, 182, 183, 186, 192, 206(6), 209(3), 210(2), 216, 222, 223, 225 to 241, 245(7)(*a*), 255, 281(6)(*b*) and 290(2) of, and Schedule 10, paragraphs 1 to 3 of Schedule 19 and Schedule 20 to, the Town and Country Planning Act 1971;
(xxv) sections 19, 37, 45, 46, 108(2), 117 to 119, 121, 138, 154(3), 170 to 172, 175, 181, 195(6), 198(3), 199(2), 202(3), 205, 211, 212, 214, 216 to 230, 233(7), 242, 259, 266(6)(*b*) and 275(2) of, and Schedule 8, paragraphs 1 to 3 of Schedule 17 and Schedule 18 to, the Town and Country Planning (Scotland) Act 1972;
(xxvi) paragraph 36 of Schedule 16 to the Local Government Act 1972;
(xxvii) sections 51 and 71 of the Land Compensation Act 1973;
(xxviii) sections 47 and 67 of the Land Compensation (Scotland) Act 1973;
(xxix) section 73 of the Control of Pollution Act 1974;
(xxx) sections 33, 34 and 36A of the Housing (Scotland) Act 1974;
(xxxi) section 10(4) of the Scottish Development Agency Act 1975;
(xxxii) the Welsh Development Agency Act 1975;
(xxxiii) sections 15(3) and 26 of the Local Government (Miscellaneous Provisions) Act 1976;
(xxxiv) the Development of Rural Wales Act 1976;
(xxxv) section 9(3) of the Inner Urban Areas Act 1978;
(xxxvi) section 13 of the Electricity (Scotland) Act 1979;

(xxxvii) the Ancient Monuments and Archaeological Areas Act 1979;
(xxxviii) section 16 of and Schedule 4 to the Water (Scotland) Act 1980;
(xxxix) Parts XII and XVI and section 120 of the Local Government, Planning and Land Act 1980;
(xl) the Highways Act 1980;
(xli) the New Towns Act 1981;
(xlii) the Acquisition of Land Act 1981;
(xliii) the Civil Aviation Act 1982;
(xliv) section 30 of the Local Government (Miscellaneous Provisions) Act 1982;
(xlv) section 2(2)(*c*) of the Cycle Tracks Act 1984;
(xlvi) the Roads (Scotland) Act 1984;
(xlvii) the Building Act 1984;
(xlviii) sections 283(2) and 296 of the Housing Act 1985.

(2) References to gas undertakers in the following enactments shall have effect as references to a public gas supplier, namely—

(*a*) section 17(1)(*b*) of the Requisitioned Land and War Works Act 1945;
(*b*) the Local Government (Omnibus Shelters and Queue Barriers) (Scotland) Act 1958;
(*c*) section 215(2)(*a*) of the Town and Country Planning Act 1971;
(*d*) section 204(2)(*a*) of the Town and Country Planning (Scotland) Act 1972;
(*e*) sections 73(11)(*c*) and 74(11)(*b*) of the Highways Act 1980;
(*f*) section 48(6)(*c*) of the Civil Aviation Act 1982;
(*g*) paragraph 3 of Schedule 5 to the Road Traffic Regulation Act 1984.

(3) References in the Landlord and Tenant Act 1927 to a statutory company shall be deemed to include references to a public gas supplier.

(4) References to public utility undertakers in the Civil Defence Act 1939 shall be deemed to include references to a public gas supplier.

(5) A public gas supplier shall be deemed to be an undertaker for the purposes of sections 157 to 160 to the Highways Act 1980.

(6) A public gas supplier shall be deemed to be an excepted undertaker for the purposes of section 6 of the Water Act 1981.

(7) Paragraph 23 of Schedule 2 to the Telecommunications Act 1984 (undertakers' works) shall apply to a public gas supplier for the purposes of any works carried out by him.

(8) The reference in section 82(4) of the Building Act 1984 (provisions with respect to demolition orders) to a person authorised by an enactment to carry on an undertaking for the supply of gas shall have effect as a reference to a public gas supplier.

(9) In the following enactments, namely—

(*a*) the Water Act 1948;
(*b*) section 39 of the Opencast Coal Act 1958;
(*c*) paragraph 2 of Schedule 6 to the Gas Act 1965;
(*d*) the New Towns (Scotland) Act 1968;
(*e*) sections 206(6), 225 to 238, 281(6)(*b*) and 290(2) of, and Schedule 10 to, the Town and Country Planning Act 1971;
(*f*) sections 195(6), 214 to 227, 266(6)(*b*) and 275(2) of, and Schedule 8 to, the Town and Country Planning (Scotland) Act 1972;
(*g*) section 10(4) of the Scottish Development Agency Act 1975;
(*h*) the Welsh Development Agency Act 1975;
(*i*) the Development of Rural Wales Act 1976;
(*j*) the New Towns Act 1981,

"the appropriate Minister", in relation to a public gas supplier, shall mean the Secretary of State for Energy.

(10) In the following enactments, namely—

(*a*) the Pipe-lines Act 1962;
(*b*) Schedule 3 to the Harbours Act 1964;
(*c*) Section 121 of the Highways Act 1980; and
(*d*) the Acquisition of Land Act 1981,

"the appropriate Minister", in relation to a public gas supplier, shall mean the Secretary of State.

The Water Act 1945

3.—(1) Section 24(6) of the Water Act 1945 (power of statutory water undertaker to acquire land by agreement or compulsorily) shall have effect as if the reference to any persons authorised by any enactment to carry on any gas undertaking were a reference to a public gas supplier.

(2) In paragraph (*c*) of the proviso to section 70 of Schedule 3 to that Act (provisions to be incorporated in orders relating to water undertakings), for the words from "gas undertakers" to "them" there shall be substituted the words "public gas supplier (within the meaning of Part I of the Gas Act 1986), except under the supervision (if given) of an authorised officer of that supplier and in accordance with plans approved by that supplier".

The Rights of Entry (Gas and Electricity Boards) Act 1954

4.—(1) In section 1(2) of the Rights of Entry (Gas and Electricity Boards) Act 1954—

(*a*) for the words "the Gas Act 1972 or regulations made thereunder, by any other enactment relating to gas" there shall be substituted the words "the Gas Act 1986 or regulations made under it, by any other enactment relating to gas"; and

(*b*) for the words "the British Gas Corporation or an Electricity Board" there shall be substituted the words "a public gas supplier or an Electricity Board".

(2) In section 2(1)(*a*) of that Act—

(*a*) for the words "the Corporation or an" there shall be substituted the words "a public gas supplier or an"; and

(*b*) for the words "the Corporation or such" there shall be substituted the words "a public gas supplier or such".

(3) In the said section 2(1), for the words "the Corporation or Board or their employee", in both places where they occur, there shall be substituted the words "the supplier or Board or his or their employee".

(4) In section 2(3) of that Act, for the words "section 44 of the Gas Act 1972 (if entry is required for the purposes of the Corporation)" there shall be substituted the words "section 46 of the Gas Act 1986 (if entry is required for the purposes of a public gas supplier)".

(5) In section 3(1) of that Act—

(*a*) the definition of "the Corporation" shall be omitted;

(*b*) for the definition of "employee" there shall be substituted the following definition—

" 'employee', in relation to a public gas supplier or to an Electricity Board, means an officer, servant or agent of the supplier or of the Board;";

(*c*) after the definition of "premises" there shall be inserted the following definition—

" 'public gas supplier' has the same meaning as in Part I of the Gas Act 1986;".

The Pipe-lines Act 1962

5.—(1) In section 58(1) of the Pipe-lines Act 1962 (statutory bodies to whom, or in relation to whose pipe-lines, certain provisions of that Act do not apply), for paragraph (*a*) there shall be substituted the following paragraph —

"(*a*) a public gas supplier within the meaning of Part I of the Gas Act 1986;".

(2) Notwithstanding subsection (4) of the said section 58, but subject to sub-paragraph (3) below, the references to a pipe-line in sections 27(1) and 31(1) of the said Act of 1962 (protection of pipe-lines imperilled by buildings, structures or deposits) shall include references to any pipe-line vested in a public gas supplier other than one laid in a street or a service pipe.

(3) The application by virtue of sub-paragraph (2) above of the said section 27(1) and the said section 31(1) to a particular part of any pipe-line shall be dependent upon there having been previously deposited with every local authority in whose area the part lies by the public gas supplier a map, on a scale not less than 1 in 10,560, showing the route taken by the part.

(4) A local authority holding a map relating to a pipe-line vested in a public gas supplier shall keep the map at their offices, and shall secure that it is open to inspection by any person at all reasonable times free of charge.

(5) In this paragraph—

"local authority" means—

(*a*) in England and Wales, the council of a county, district or London borough, and the Common Council of the City of London; and

(*b*) in Scotland, an islands or district council;

"street" has the same meaning as in the Public Utilities Street Works Act 1950.

(6) In its application to Scotland this paragraph shall have effect as if for the word "street", in both places where it occurs, there were substituted the word "road".

The Gas Act 1965

6.—(1) The Gas Act 1965—

(*a*) shall have effect without the amendments made by paragraph 14 of Schedule 6 to the 1972 Act and the associated repeals made by Schedule 8 to that Act; and

(*b*) as so having effect, shall be amended as follows.

(2) In Part II, for the words "gas authority", wherever they occur, there shall be substituted the words "public gas supplier".

(3) In Part II, for the words "section 11 of the principal Act", wherever they occur, there shall be substituted the words "Schedule 3 to the principal Act".

(4) In section 4(2), the words from "shall relate only" to "statutory corporation and" shall be omitted.

(5) In section 5(5), for the words "inform the Minister that they object" there shall be substituted the words "informs the Minister that he objects".

(6) In section 6(1), for the word "apply" there shall be substituted the word "applies", for the word "satisfy" there shall be substituted the word "satisfies" and for the words "they think" there shall be substituted the words "he thinks".

(7) In section 6(2), for the words "have taken" there shall be substituted the words "has taken" and for the word "them" there shall be substituted the word "him".

(8) In section 6(3), for the word "them" there shall be substituted the word "him".

(9) In section 6(4), for the word "their" there shall be substituted the word "his" and for the word "cause" there shall be substituted the word "causes".

(10) In section 6(8), for the word "apply" there shall be substituted the word "applies" and for the word "they" there shall be substituted the word "he".

(11) In section 13(3), for the word "propose" there shall be substituted the word "proposes" and for the words "the said section 11" there shall be substituted the words "the said Schedule 3".

(12) In section 15(2), for the word "their" there shall be substituted the word "his".

(13) In section 16(1), for the words "develop or operate" there shall be substituted the words "develops or operates".

(14) In sections 16(5) and 18(9), for the word "fail" there shall be substituted the word "fails".

(15) In section 17(5), for the word "them" there shall be substituted the word "him".

(16) In section 19(3)—

(*a*) at the beginning there shall be inserted the words "Every public gas supplier to whom a storage authorisation order applies during any period shall pay to the Minister such proportion as the Minister may determine of"; and

(*b*) for the words "shall be repaid to him by the Gas Council and" there shall be substituted the words "and any sums received by the Minister under this subsection shall be".

(17) In section 19(4), for the words "the Gas Council in respect of sums payable by them" there shall be substituted the words "a public gas supplier in respect of sums payable by him".

(18) In section 21(1), for the words "Section 68(1)" there shall be substituted the words "Section 43(1)".

(19) In section 21(2), for the words "Section 69(1)" there shall be substituted the words "Section 43(2)" and for the words "section 68(1)" there shall be substituted the words "section 43(1)".

(20) In section 21(3), the words "any gas authority or" and the words "authority or", in the second place where they occur, shall be omitted.

(21) In section 22(1), for the words "Section 70" there shall be substituted the words "Section 46".

(22) In section 22(2), for the words '"Section 73 of the principal Act" there shall be substituted the words "Section 46 of the Gas Act 1972" and for the words "the principal Act", in the second place where they occur, there shall be substituted the words "that Act".

(23) In section 27(1), for the words "the Corporation" there shall be substituted the words "the public gas supplier concerned".

(24) In section 28(1)—

(*a*) the definition of "gas authority" shall be omitted; and

(*b*) for the definition of "large-scale map" there shall be substituted the following definition—

" 'large-scale map' means a map drawn on a scale not less than 1 in 10,560;"

(25) In section 32(2), for the words "the Gas Act 1948, 'Area Board' has the same meaning as in" there shall be substituted the words "the Gas Act 1986, 'public gas supplier' has the same meaning as in Part I of".

(26) In Schedule 2—
- (*a*) for the words "the applicants", wherever they occur, there shall be substituted the words "the applicant";
- (*b*) for the words "their proposals", wherever they occur, there shall be substituted the words "his proposals";
- (*c*) for the words "their application", wherever they occur, there shall be substituted the words "his application";
- (*d*) for the words "section 73 of the principal Act", wherever they occur, there shall be substituted the words "section 46 of the Gas Act 1972";
- (*e*) in paragraph 5(2), for the words "the applicants' " there shall be substituted the words "the applicant's";
- (*f*) in paragraph 9(1), for the words "they have been, or expect" there shall be substituted the words "he has been, or expects" and for the words "they must" there shall be substituted the words "he must";
- (*g*) in paragraph 9(2), for the word "have", in both places where it occurs, there shall be substituted the word "has"; and
- (*h*) in paragraph 14(1), for the words "gas authorities" there shall be substituted the words "public gas suppliers".

(27) In Schedule 6—
- (*a*) for the words "the applicants", wherever they occur, there shall be substituted the words "the applicant";
- (*b*) in paragraph 1(2), for the words "their application" there shall be substituted the words "his application";
- (*c*) in paragraph 1(4), for the words "their proposals" there shall be substituted the words "his proposals";
- (*d*) in paragraph 5, for the words "gas board" there shall be substituted the words "public gas supplier";
- (*e*) in paragraph 7(1), for the words "their powers" there shall be substituted the words "his powers"; and
- (*f*) in paragraph 7(2), for the words "their duty" there shall be substituted the words "his duty".

The Local Government (Scotland) Act 1966

7. In section 18(4) of the Local Government (Scotland) Act 1966, for the words "the British Gas Corporation" there shall be substituted the words "a public gas supplier within the meaning of Part I of the Gas Act 1986".

The General Rate Act 1967

8.—(1) In section 19(6) of the General Rate Act 1967 (definitions for purposes of the general rule for the ascertainment of rateable value), in paragraph (*b*) of the definition of "non-industrial building", after sub-paragraph (ii) there shall be inserted "; or
- (iii) any public gas supplier (within the meaning of Part I of the Gas Act 1986) or any private gas supplier (within the meaning of section 33A below)."

(2) For section 33 of that Act there shall be substituted the following section—

> **"Public gas suppliers**
>
> 33.—(1) Subject to subsection (2) and without prejudice to subsections (3) and (5) of this section, no premises occupied by a public gas supplier (within the meaning of Part I of the Gas Act 1986) to whom this section is applied by order of the Secretary of State shall be liable to be rated or to be included in any valuation list or in any rate; and in the following provisions of this section and in Schedule 6 to this Act 'relevant supplier' means any public gas supplier to whom this section is so applied.
>
> (2) The foregoing subsection shall not apply—
> - (*a*) to premises used as a dwelling; or
> - (*b*) to premises occupied by a relevant supplier wholly or mainly for the purposes of an undertaking for the supply of water; or
> - (*c*) to premises occupied and used by a relevant supplier wholly or mainly for the manufacture of plant or gas fittings; or

(*d*) to a shop, room or other place occupied and used by a relevant supplier wholly or mainly for the sale, display or demonstration of apparatus or accessories for use by consumers of gas (any use for the receipt of payments for gas supplied being disregarded); or

(*e*) subject and without prejudice to the provisions of paragraph 5 of Schedule 6 to this Act, to office premises occupied by a relevant supplier and not situated on operational land of his.

(3) For the purposes of the making and levying of a rate for any rating area for any rate period, if in the penultimate year—

(*a*) a relevant supplier—

(i) supplied gas to consumers in that area; or

(ii) manufactured gas in that area; or

(iii) produced gas in that area by the application to gas purchased by him of any process not consisting only of purification, or of blending with other gases, or of both purification and such blending; or

(*b*) private gas suppliers (within the meaning of section 33A of this Act) supplied to consumers in that area gas which had been conveyed (whether within or outside that area) by pipelines belonging to a relevant supplier,

the relevant supplier shall be treated as occupying in that area during that rate period a hereditament of a rateable value calculated in accordance with the provisions of an order under section 19 of, and paragraph 3 of Schedule 3 to, the Local Government Act 1974.

(4) The hereditament which a relevant supplier is to be treated as occupying in a rating area by virtue of subsection (3) of this section shall be taken not to be situated in any part of that area in which there are leviable, as an additional item of the rate, expenses which are not leviable in the area as a whole.

(5) If the Secretary of State is of opinion that payments by way of rates should be made by a relevant supplier by virtue of this subsection by reference to any premises occupied and used by him for the reception or liquefaction of gas or the evaporation of gas in a liquid state, being in any case gas purchased by him, the Secretary of State may, subject to paragraph 6 of Schedule 6 to this Act, make an order designating the premises for the purposes of this subsection and providing for the determination, by such method as may be specified by the order, of a value for the premises for those purposes.

(6) Where an order under subsection (5) of this section is in force, the relevant supplier shall be treated for rating purposes as occupying within the rating area in which the premises designated by the order are situated (and whether or not the relevant supplier occupies or is treated as occupying any other hereditament in that area) a hereditament of a rateable value equal to the value determined as mentioned in that subsection.

(7) Subject to paragraph 6 of Schedule 6 to this Act, the Secretary of State may by order provide that, in such of the provisions of this section, the said Schedule 6, or any other enactment relating to rating as may be specified in the order, any reference to the manufacture of gas shall include a reference to such dealings with gas as may be specified by the order.

(8) There shall have effect for the purposes of this section and an order under section 19 of, and paragraph 3 of Schedule 3 to, the Local Government Act 1974, the supplementary provisions contained in Schedule 6 to this Act; and for the purposes of this section, such an order and that Schedule—

(*a*) the expression 'gas' means any substance which is or (if it were in a gaseous state) would be gas within the meaning of Part I of the Gas Act 1986 and, without prejudice to the provisions of any order under subsection (7) of this section, the following operations—

(i) the liquefaction of gas, and

(ii) the evaporation of gas in a liquid state,

shall not of themselves be taken to constitute the manufacture of gas or the application of a process to gas;

(*b*) the expression 'penultimate year', in relation to a rate period or to a year, means the last but one year before that rate period or year;

(*c*) the expressions 'office premises' and 'operational land' have the meanings respectively assigned to them by section 32(8) of this Act." '

(3) After that section there shall be inserted the following section—

"Private gas suppliers

33A.—(1) The Secretary of State may by order provide that, in such cases and subject to such exceptions and modifications as may be prescribed by the order, section 33 of and Schedule 6 to this Act shall apply to premises occupied by private gas suppliers for or in connection with the supply of gas through pipes to consumers' premises.

(2) In this section—

'gas' has the same meaning as in Part I of the Gas Act 1986;

'private gas supplier' means a person who is authorised by section 6 of the said Act of 1986, or by an authorisation under section 8 of that Act, to supply gas through pipes to consumers' premises.

(3) Any statutory instrument containing an order under this section shall be subject to annulment in pursuance of a resolution of either House of Parliament."

(4) In paragraph 5(1)(*b*) of Schedule 3 to that Act (classes of machinery or plant deemed to be part of hereditament), for the words "the British Gas Corporation" there shall be substituted the words "a public gas supplier within the meaning of Part I of the Gas Act 1986".

(5) For Schedule 6 to that Act there shall be substituted the following Schedule—

"SCHEDULE 6

PUBLIC GAS SUPPLIERS

1. As respects each rating area in which a relevant supplier will fall to be treated as occupying during any rate period a hereditament of a rateable value calculated in accordance with an order under section 19 of, and paragraph 3 of Schedule 3 to, the Local Government Act 1974, it shall be the duty of the supplier, before the end of the month of October preceding the beginning of that period, to transmit to the rating authority and to the valuation officer a statement setting out particulars of all the matters referred to in such an order and relevant to the purpose of computing the rateable value of that hereditament.

2. On receipt of a statement under paragraph 1 above, the valuation officer shall calculate the rateable value of the hereditament which the relevant supplier is to be treated as occupying during the rate period in question, and shall notify the amount of that rateable value to the rating authority before the end of the month of December preceding the beginning of that rate period.

3. The duty imposed on a relevant supplier by paragraph 1 above shall be enforceable by civil proceedings by the rating authority or the valuation officer for an injunction or for any other appropriate relief; and the duty imposed on the valuation officer by paragraph 2 above shall be enforceable by mandamus at the instance of the rating authority.

4.—(1) Where the valuation officer notifies the amount of a rateable value to the rating authority in accordance with paragraph 2 above—

(*a*) the rating authority, in making and levying any rate for a rate period to which the notification relates, shall include the relevant supplier as the occupier of a hereditament of that rateable value; and

(*b*) the valuation officer, at or as soon as may be after the beginning of the year consisting of any such rate period, shall cause such alterations (if any) to be made in the valuation list as may be requisite for showing the relevant supplier in the list as the occupier of a hereditament of that rateable value, and if any such alteration is made after the beginning of the year, it shall be treated as having been made at the beginning of the year.

(2) If the year referred to in sub-paragraph (1)(*b*) above is a year beginning with the date on which a new valuation list comes into force, that sub-paragraph shall not apply, but the valuation officer shall include the relevant supplier in the list as the occupier of a hereditament of the said rateable value.

5. For the purposes of section 33(2)(*e*) of this Act, paragraph 8 of Schedule 5 to this Act shall have effect as if for any reference therein to section 32(2)(*b*) of this Act there were substituted a reference to the said section 33(2)(*e*), and as if it provided for the determination of any such question as is mentioned in sub-paragraph (3) or (4) thereof by the Secretary of State for Energy.

6. Before making any such order under section 33(5) or (7) of this Act, the Secretary of State shall consult with the relevant supplier, with such associations of local authorities as appear to him to be concerned, and with any local authority with whom consultation appears to him to be desirable; and any such order—

(*a*) may contain such incidental, supplemental and consequential provisions, including any provisions altering any enactment or instrument, as the Secretary of State considers expedient for the purposes of the order; and

(*b*) shall be subject to annulment in pursuance of a resolution of either House of Parliament."

The Transport Act 1968

9. In section 109(2) of the Transport Act 1968 (power of certain bodies to maintain or take over waterways and connected works), for paragraph (*d*) there shall be substituted the following paragraph—

"(*d*) a public gas supplier within the meaning of Part I of the Gas Act 1986;".

The Post Office Act 1969

10. In section 7(1A) of the Post Office Act 1969 (powers of the Post Office), after paragraph (*c*) there shall be inserted the following paragraph—

"(*ca*) a public gas supplier (within the meaning of Part I of the Gas Act 1986);".

The Chronically Sick and Disabled Persons Act 1970

11. In section 14(1) of the Chronically Sick and Disabled Persons Act 1970 (miscellaneous advisory committees), for the words "the National Gas Consumers' Council and the Regional Gas Consumers' Councils" there shall be substituted the words "the Gas Consumers' Council".

The Town and Country Planning Act 1971

12. In section 223(2) of the Town and Country Planning Act 1971 (cases in which land is to be treated as not being operational land of statutory undertakers), for the words "the Gas Act 1972 or" there shall be substituted the words "the Gas Act 1986 or".

The Town and Country Planning (Scotland) Act 1972

13. In section 212(2) of the Town and Country Planning (Scotland) Act 1972 (cases in which land is to be treated as not operational land of statutory undertakers), for the words "the Gas Act 1972" there shall be substituted the words "the Gas Act 1986".

The Land Compensation Act 1973

14.—(1) In section 44(2) of the Land Compensation Act 1973 (compensation for injurious affection), for the words "paragraph 13 of Schedule 2 to the Gas Act 1972" there shall be substituted the words "paragraph 7 of Schedule 3 to the Gas Act 1986".

(2) In section 58(2) of that Act (determination of material detriment where part of house etc. proposed for compulsory acquisition), for the words "paragraph 14 of Schedule 2 to the Gas Act 1972" there shall be substituted the words "paragraph 8 of Schedule 3 to the Gas Act 1986".

The Fair Trading Act 1973

15.—(1) The Director General of Fair Trading shall consult with the Director before publishing under section 124 of the Fair Trading Act 1973 (publication of information or advice) any information or advice which the Director has power to publish under section 35(1) of this Act.

(2) Section 125(1) of that Act (annual and other reports) shall not apply to activities of the Monopolies and Mergers Commission on which the Director is required to report by section 39(1) of this Act.

(3) In section 133(2) of that Act (exceptions to general restriction on disclosure of information), after the words "the Director General of Telecommunications," there shall be inserted the words "the Director General of Gas Supply," and after the words "the Telecommunications Act 1984," there shall be inserted the words "or the Gas Act 1986,".

(4) In Part I of Schedule 5 to that Act (goods and services referred to in section 16 of that Act), for paragraphs 1 and 2 there shall be substituted the following paragraph—

"1. Gas supplied through pipes to tariff customers (within the meaning of Part I of the Gas Act 1986)."

The Land Compensation (Scotland) Act 1973

16.—(1) In section 41(2) of the Land Compensation (Scotland) Act 1973 (compensation for injurious affection), for the words "paragraph 26 of Schedule 2 to the Gas Act 1972" there shall be substituted the words "paragraph 24 of Schedule 3 to the Gas Act 1986".

(2) In section 54(2) of that Act (determination of material detriment where part of house etc. proposed for compulsory acquisition), for the words "paragraph 24 of Schedule 2 to the Gas Act 1972" there shall be substituted the words "paragraph 22 of Schedule 3 to the Gas Act 1986".

The Local Government Act 1974

17. In Schedule 3 to the Local Government Act 1974 (hereditaments for determining the rateable value of which provision may be made under section 19(1) of that Act), for paragraph 3 there shall be substituted the following paragraphs—

"3. Any hereditament which a relevant supplier (within the meaning of section 33 of the principal Act) is to be treated as occupying in a rating area by virtue of that section.

3A. Any hereditament which a private gas supplier (within the meaning of section 33A of the principal Act) is to be treated as occupying in a rating area by virtue of section 33 of that Act as applied by order under the said section 33A.

3B.—(1) Any hereditament occupied for or in connection with the conveyance of gas through pipes other than one falling within paragraph 3 or 3A above.

(2) In this paragraph 'gas' has the same meaning as in Part I of the Gas Act 1986."

The Health and Safety at Work etc. Act 1974

18. At the end of section 34 of the Health and Safety at Work etc. Act 1974 (extension of time for bringing summary proceedings) there shall be inserted the following subsection—

"(6) In the application of subsection (4) above to Scotland, after the words 'applies to' there shall be inserted the words 'any offence under section 33(1)(*c*) above where the health and safety regulations concerned were made for the general purpose mentioned in section 18(1) of the Gas Act 1986 and '.

The Consumer Credit Act 1974

19. In section 174(3)(*a*) of the Consumer Credit Act 1974 (exceptions to general restriction on disclosure of information), after the words "the Telecommunications Act 1984" there shall be inserted the words "or the Gas Act 1986" and after the words "the Director General of Telecommunications," there shall be inserted the words "the Director General of Gas Supply,".

The Oil Taxation Act 1975

20. In paragraph 2A(4) of Schedule 3 to the Oil Taxation Act 1975 (petroleum revenue tax: miscellaneous provisions), for paragraphs (*a*) and (*b*) there shall be substituted the following paragraphs—

"(*a*) that any authorisation granted under section 7 or 8 of the Gas Act 1986 for the supply of the gas applies to the supply of the gas under the contract mentioned in sub-paragraph (2) of that paragraph; and

(*b*) that no authorisation is required under those sections for the supply of the gas under that contract if no such authorisation is required for the supply of the gas."

The Local Government (Scotland) Act 1975

21. In Schedule 1 to the Local Government (Scotland) Act 1975—

(*a*) in paragraphs 3 to 3B, for references to the Corporation there shall be substituted references to a public gas supplier;

(*b*) in paragraph 3, there shall be added at the end the following sub-paragraph—

"(3) In this paragraph and in paragraphs 3A and 3B below—

'gas' means any substance which is or (if it were in a gaseous state) would be gas within the meaning of Part I of the Gas Act 1986;

'public gas supplier' has the same meaning as in Part I of the Gas Act 1986;

'private gas supplier' means a person who is authorised by section 6 of the said Act of 1986, or by an authorisation under section 8 of that Act, to supply gas through pipes to consumers' premises."; and

(*c*) in paragraphs 3A and 3B, for references to a private supplier there shall be substituted references to a private gas supplier.

The Coal Industry Act 1975

22. Paragraph 5(3) of Schedule 1 to the Coal Industry Act 1975 (supplementary provisions relating to right to withdraw support) shall have effect as if the reference to a company or other body or person carrying on an undertaking primarily for the supply of gas for public purposes or to members of the public were a reference to a public gas supplier.

The Restrictive Trade Practices Act 1976

23. In section 41(1)(*a*) of the Restrictive Trade Practices Act 1976 (disclosure of information), after the words "the Director General of Telecommunications," there shall be inserted the words "the Director General of Gas Supply," and after the words "or the Telecommunications Act 1984" there shall be inserted the words "or the Gas Act 1986".

The Local Government (Miscellaneous Provisions) Act 1976

24. In section 33 of the Local Government (Miscellaneous Provisions) Act 1976 (restoration or continuation of supply of water, gas or electricity), for the word "undertakers", wherever it occurs, there shall be substituted the word "person".

The Land Drainage Act 1976

25. In section 112(2)(*a*) of the Land Drainage Act 1976 (protection of nationalised undertakings etc.), for the words "the British Gas Corporation" there shall be substituted the words "any public gas supplier within the meaning of Part I of the Gas Act 1986".

The Energy Act 1976

26.—(1) In section 9(1) of the Energy Act 1976 (liquefaction of off-shore natural gas), for the words from "with consent" to "such consent" there shall be substituted the words "authorised by an authorisation under section 7 or 8 of the Gas Act 1986 and in compliance with any conditions of that authorisation, or providing a supply for which such an authorisation".

(2) In section 12(2) of that Act (disposal of gas by flaring), for the words "the British Gas Corporation" there shall be substituted the words "a public gas supplier within the meaning of Part I of the Gas Act 1986".

The Estate Agents Act 1979

27. In section 10(3)(*a*) of the Estate Agents Act 1979 (exceptions to restrictions on disclosure of information), after the words "the Telecommunications Act 1984" there shall be inserted the words "or the Gas Act 1986" and after the words "the Director General of Telecommunications," there shall be inserted the words "the Director General of Gas Supply,".

The Competition Act 1980

28.—(1) In subsection (2)(*a*) of section 19 of the Competition Act 1980 (exceptions to restriction on disclosure of information), after the words "the Director General of Telecommunications," there shall be inserted the words "the Director General of Gas Supply,".

(2) In subsection (3) of that section, at the end there shall be inserted the following paragraph—

"(*h*) the Gas Act 1986."

The Acquisition of Land Act 1981

29. In section 28 of the Acquisition of Land Act 1981 (acquisition of rights over land by the creation of new rights), paragraph (*a*) shall be omitted and after paragraph (*f*) there shall be inserted the following paragraph—

"(*g*) paragraph 1 of Schedule 3 to the Gas Act 1986."

The Building Act 1984

30. In section 80(3) of the Building Act 1984 (notice to local authority of intended demolition), for paragraph (*b*) there shall be substituted the following paragraph—

"(*b*) any public gas supplier (as defined in Part I of the Gas Act 1986) in whose authorised area (as so defined) the building is situated,".

The Insolvency Act 1985

31. In sections 97(2)(*a*) and 200(4)(*a*) of the Insolvency Act 1985 (supplies by utilities to insolvency practitioners), for the words "the British Gas Corporation" there shall be substituted the words "a public gas supplier within the meaning of Part I of the Gas Act 1986".

The Bankruptcy (Scotland) Act 1985

32. In section 70(4)(*a*) of the Bankruptcy (Scotland) Act 1985 (supplies by utilities), for the words "the British Gas Corporation" there shall be substituted the words "a public gas supplier within the meaning of Part I of the Gas Act 1986".

Section 67(3)

SCHEDULE 8

Transitional Provisions and Savings

Part I

Provisions and Savings Coming into Force on Appointed Day

1.—(1) A notification received or given by the Secretary of State under subsection (1) of section 29A of the 1972 Act which is effective on the appointed day shall have effect as if received or given by the Secretary of State under subsection (1) of section 6 of this Act; and the provisions of this Act shall apply accordingly.

(2) A direction given by the Secretary of State under subsection (2) of the said section 29A which is effective on the appointed day shall have effect as if given by the Secretary of State under subsection (2) of the said section 6; and the provisions of this Act shall apply accordingly.

2. A consent given or having effect as if given under section 29 of the 1972 Act by the Secretary of State which is effective on the appointed day shall have effect as an authorisation granted by the Secretary of State under section 8 of this Act; and the provisions of this Act shall apply accordingly.

3. Any regulations made under section 25 of the 1972 Act which are effective on the appointed day shall have effect as if—

(*a*) they were made under section 12 of this Act; and

(*b*) references in those regulations to the Corporation were references to a public gas supplier within the meaning of Part I of this Act;

and the provisions of this Act shall apply accordingly.

4. Any regulations made or having effect as if made under section 29B of the 1972 Act which are effective on the appointed day shall have effect as if—

(*a*) they were made under section 16 of this Act; and

(*b*) references in those regulations to the Corporation were references to a public gas supplier within the meaning of Part I of this Act;

and the provisions of this Act shall apply accordingly.

5. Any meter which immediately before the appointed day is, or is treated as, stamped under section 30 of the 1972 Act shall be treated as stamped under section 17 of this Act.

6.—(1) This paragraph applies to any regulations made or having effect as if made under section 31 of the 1972 Act which—

(*a*) are effective on the appointed day; and

(*b*) do not make such provision as is mentioned in subsections (2) to (4) of that section or in section 42(2) of that Act.

(2) Any regulations to which this paragraph applies shall have effect as if made under section 15 of the Health and Safety at Work etc. Act 1974 for the general purpose mentioned in section 18(1) of this Act; and, subject to sub-paragraph (3) below, the provisions of Part I of that Act and the provisions of this Act shall apply accordingly.

(3) Section 1(2) of the said Act of 1974 shall have effect as if any regulations to which this paragraph applies were in force under an enactment specified in the third column of Schedule 1 to that Act.

(4) Section 20 of the said Act of 1974 shall have effect as if anything done before the appointed day in contravention of any regulations to which this paragraph applies had been done on or after that day.

7.—(1) A direction given by the Secretary of State under section 17 of the Oil and Gas (Enterprise) Act 1982 which is effective on the appointed day shall have effect as if given by the Director under section 19 of this Act; and the provisions of this Act shall apply accordingly.

(2) Any reference in a deed or other instrument to the functions of the Corporation shall be taken to include a reference to any obligations arising under an agreement entered into by the Corporation in pursuance of directions given or having effect as if given under section 19 of this Act.

8.—(1) A notice given to the Secretary of State under subsection (1) of section 15 of the Oil and Gas (Enterprise) Act 1982 which is effective on the appointed day shall have effect as if given to the Director under subsection (1) of section 20 of this Act and as if any map accompanying that notice and complying with the requirements of subsection (2) of the said section 15 complied with the requirements of subsection (2) of the said section 20; and the provisions of this Act shall apply accordingly.

(2) A notice published by the Secretary of State under section 15(3) of the said Act of 1982 which is effective on the appointed day shall have effect as if published by the Director under section 20(3) of this Act; and the provisions of this Act shall apply accordingly.

(3) A direction given by the Secretary of State under section 15(4) of the said Act of 1982 which is effective on the appointed day shall have effect as if given by the Director under section 20(4) of this Act; and the provisions of this Act shall apply accordingly.

9. A direction given by the Secretary of State under section 16(1) of the Oil and Gas (Enterprise) Act 1982 which is effective on the appointed day shall have effect as if given by the Director under section 21(1) of this Act; and the provisions of this Act shall apply accordingly.

10. Any maximum prices fixed by the Corporation under paragraph 12 of Schedule 4 to the 1972 Act which are effective on the appointed day shall have effect as if fixed by the Director under section 37 of this Act.

11. Any office fixed or address published before the appointed day for the purposes of section 44 of the 1972 Act shall be deemed on and after that day to have been fixed or published for the purposes of section 46(3) of this Act.

12.—(1) Where immediately before the appointed day there is in force an agreement which—

(*a*) confers or imposes on the Corporation any rights or liabilities; and

(*b*) refers (in whatever terms and whether expressly or by implication) to any provision of the 1972 Act, to the Corporation's statutory gas undertaking or to statutory purposes,

the agreement shall have effect, in relation to anything falling to be done on or after that day, as if for that reference there were substituted a reference to the corresponding provision of this Act, to the Corporation's undertaking as a public gas supplier or, as the case may require, to purposes connected with the supply of gas through pipes to premises in the Corporation's authorised area.

(2) In this paragraph "authorised area" and "public gas supplier" have the same meanings as in Part I of this Act.

(3) References in this paragraph to an agreement include references to a deed, bond or other instrument.

13. Where—

(*a*) any sum was deposited with the Corporation by way of security under any provision of the 1972 Act; and

(*b*) on and after the appointed day that sum is treated by the Corporation as deposited under any provision of this Act,

any period beginning three months or less before that day, being a period during which the sum was deposited with the Corporation, shall be treated for the purposes of the payment of interest on that sum as a period during which the sum was deposited under that provision of this Act.

14. The repeal by this Act of section 43 of the 1972 Act shall not affect the operation of that section in relation to offences committed before the appointed day.

15. The repeal by this Act of section 46 of the 1972 Act shall not affect the operation of that section as applied by section 22 of the Gas Act 1965.

16. The repeal by this Act of Schedule 4 to the 1972 Act shall not affect the operation on or after the appointed day of so much of that Schedule as relates to the determination by arbitration of any matter which immediately before that day falls to be determined by arbitration under that Schedule.

17. The repeal by this Act of any provision by virtue of which any enactment applies in relation to a person carrying on a gas undertaking shall not affect the continuing validity of anything done under that enactment before the appointed day; and that enactment shall continue for the purposes of anything so done to have effect on and after that day as if the enactment continued to apply in relation to the Corporation and, after the transfer date, to the successor company as it applied in relation to the Corporation before the appointed day.

Part II

Provisions and Savings Coming into Force on Transfer Date

18. An authorisation granted under section 7 of this Act to the Corporation which is effective on the transfer date shall have effect as if granted to the successor company.

19. A declaration made by the Corporation in accordance with regulations made, or having effect as if made, under section 12(3) of this Act which is effective on the transfer date shall have effect as if made by the successor company.

20. A tariff fixed, or having effect as fixed, under section 14(1) of this Act by the Corporation which is effective on the transfer date shall have effect as if fixed by the successor company.

21. A direction given, or having effect as if given, under section 19 of this Act to the Corporation which is effective on the transfer date shall have effect as if given to the successor company.

22.—(1) A notice given, or having effect as if given, under section 20(1) of this Act by the Corporation which is effective on the transfer date shall have effect as if given by the successor company.

(2) A direction given, or having effect as if given, under section 20(4) of this Act to the Corporation which is effective on the transfer date shall have effect as if given to the successor company.

23. A direction given, or having effect as if given, under section 21(1) of this Act to the Corporation which is effective on the transfer date shall have effect as if given to the successor company.

24. Any office fixed or address published by the Corporation for the purposes of section 46(3) of this Act, and any office or address having effect as if so fixed or published, shall be deemed on and after the transfer date to have been so fixed or published by the successor company.

25. A direction given under section 63 of this Act to the Corporation which is effective on the transfer date shall have effect as if given to the successor company.

26. A compulsory purchase order made by the Corporation which was made, or has effect as if made, by virtue of Schedule 3 to this Act and is effective on the transfer date shall have effect as if made by the successor company.

27.—(1) Where immediately before the transfer date there is in force an agreement which—

(a) confers or imposes on the Corporation any rights or liabilities which vest in the successor company by virtue of section 49 of this Act; and

(b) refers (in whatever terms and whether expressly or by implication) to a member or officer of the Corporation,

the agreement shall have effect, in relation to anything falling to be done on or after that date, as if for that reference there were substituted a reference to such person as that company may appoint or, in default of appointment, to the officer of that company who corresponds as nearly as may be to the member or officer of the Corporation in question.

(2) References in this paragraph to an agreement include references to a deed, bond or other instrument.

28.—(1) Any agreement made, transaction effected or other thing done by, to or in relation to the Corporation which is in force or effective immediately before the transfer date shall have effect as if made, effected or done by, to or in relation to the successor company, in all respects, as if the successor company were the same person, in law, as the Corporation, and accordingly references to the Corporation—

(a) in any agreement (whether or not in writing) and in any deed, bond or instrument;

(b) in any process or other document issued, prepared or employed for the purposes of any proceeding before any court or other tribunal or authority; and

(c) in any other document whatsoever (other than an enactment) relating to or affecting any property, right or liability of the Corporation which vests by virtue of section 49 of this Act in the successor company,

shall be taken as referring to the successor company.

(2) Nothing in sub-paragraph (1) above shall be taken as applying in relation to any agreement made, transaction effected or other thing done with respect to any right or liability of the Corporation which vests by virtue of section 50 of this Act in the Treasury.

29. It is hereby declared for the avoidance of doubt that—

(a) the effect of section 49 of this Act in relation to any contract of employment with the Corporation in force immediately before the transfer date is merely to modify the contract by substituting the successor company as the employer (and not to terminate the contract or vary it in any other way); and

(b) that section is effective to vest the rights and liabilities of the Corporation under any agreement or arrangement for the payment of pensions, allowances or gratuities in the successor company along with all other rights and liabilities of the Corporation;

and accordingly any period of employment with the Corporation or a wholly owned subsidiary of the Corporation shall count for all purposes as a period of employment with the successor company or (as the case may be) a wholly owned subsidiary of the successor company.

30.—(1) Any certificate issued or other thing done in pursuance of any regulation made or having effect as if made under section 21 of the 1972 Act which is in force as effective immediately before the transfer date shall have effect as if issued or done in pursuance of the corresponding enactment, regulation or rule relating to securities issued under the National Loans Act 1968.

(2) Any agreement made, transaction effected or other thing done in relation to any British Gas 3% Guaranteed Stock, 1990-95 which is in force or effective immediately before the transfer date shall have effect as if made, effected or done in relation to that Stock as renamed under subsection (3) of that section and, accordingly, references to that Stock in any agreement (whether or not in writing) or in any deed, bond, instrument or other document whatsoever shall be taken as referring to that Stock as so renamed.

(3) In this paragraph "British Gas Stock" has the same meaning as in section 50 of this Act.

31.—(1) It shall be the duty of the Corporation and of the successor company to take, as and when during the transitional period the successor company considers appropriate, all such steps as may be requisite to secure that the vesting in the successor company by virtue of section 49 of this Act or this paragraph of any foreign property, right or liability is effective under the relevant foreign law.

(2) During the transitional period, until the vesting in the successor company by virtue of section 49 of this Act or this paragraph of any foreign property, right or liability is effective under the relevant foreign law, it shall be the duty of the Corporation to hold that property or right for the benefit of, or to discharge that liability on behalf of, the successor company.

(3) Nothing in sub-paragraphs (1) and (2) above shall be taken as prejudicing the effect under the law of the United Kingdom or of any part of the United Kingdom of the vesting in the successor company by virtue of section 49 of this Act or this paragraph of any foreign property, right or liability.

(4) The Corporation shall have all such powers as may be requisite for the performance of its duty under this paragraph, but—

(*a*) it shall be the duty of the successor company during the transitional period to act on behalf of the Corporation (so far as possible) in performing the duty imposed on the Corporation by this paragraph; and

(*b*) any foreign property, rights and liabilities acquired or incurred by the Corporation during that period shall immediately become property, rights and liabilities of the successor company.

(5) References in this paragraph to any foreign property, right or liability are references to any property, right or liability as respects which any issue arising in any proceedings would have been determined (in accordance with the rules of private international law) by reference to the law of a country or territory outside the United Kingdom.

(6) Any expenses incurred by the Corporation under this paragraph shall be met by the successor company.

32.—(1) Notwithstanding the repeal by this Act of section 8 of the 1972 Act, it shall be the duty of the Corporation to make a report to the Secretary of State in accordance with that section in respect of each financial year of the Corporation ending before the transfer date.

(2) Notwithstanding the repeal by this Act of section 23 of that Act, it shall be the duty of the Corporation to prepare statements of accounts in accordance with subsection (1)(*b*) and (2) of that section in respect of each financial year of the Corporation ending before the transfer date, and that section shall continue to apply during the transitional period in relation to those statements and in relation also to the auditing of those statements and of accounts kept in accordance with subsection (1)(*a*) of that section in respect of that financial year.

(3) Any expenses incurred by the Corporation under this paragraph shall be met by the successor company.

33. Where by virtue of anything done before the transfer date, any enactment amended by Schedule 7 to the Act has effect in relation to the Corporation, that enactment shall have effect in relation to the successor company as if that company were the same person, in law, as the Corporation.

34. Every provision contained in a local Act, or in subordinate legislation, which is in force immediately before the transfer date and then applicable to the Corporation shall have effect as if—

(*a*) for references therein to the Corporation there were substituted references to the successor company; and

(*b*) for any reference (however worded and whether expressly or by implication) to the undertaking or business, or any part of the undertaking or business, of the Corporation there were substituted a reference to the undertaking or business, or the corresponding part of the undertaking or business, of the successor company.

35.—(1) Nothing in this Act shall affect the validity of anything done by, or in relation to, the Corporation before the transfer date under or by virtue of the Public Utilities Street Works Act 1950; and anything which, immediately before that date, is in process of being done under, or by virtue of, that Act by or in relation to it (including, in particular, any legal proceedings to which it is a party) may be continued by, or in relation to, the successor company.

(2) Any notice or direction given or other thing whatsoever done under the said Act of 1950 by the Corporation shall, if effective at the transfer date, continue in force and have effect as if similarly given or done by the successor company.

36.—(1) For the purposes of section 33 of the General Rate Act 1967 (public gas suppliers) the successor company shall be treated as if it were the same person as the Corporation.

(2) An order under subsection (1) of that section which applies that section to the Corporation and is effective on the transfer date shall have effect as if it applied that section to the successor company.

(3) An order under subsection (5) of that section which applies in relation to hereditaments occupied by the Corporation and is effective on the transfer date shall have effect as if it applied to the corresponding hereditaments occupied by the successor company.

37.—(1) Where an asset, or the right to receive an asset, vests in the successor company by virtue of section 49 of the Act, then for the purposes of Part I of the Industry Act 1972 and Part II of the Industrial Development Act 1982—

(*a*) so much of any expenditure incurred by the Corporation in providing that asset as is approved capital expenditure (of any description relevant for the purposes of regional development grant) in respect of which no payment of regional development grant has been made to the Corporation shall be treated as having been incurred by the successor company and not by the Corporation; and (*b*) where the asset itself vests in the successor company by virtue of section 49 of this Act, it shall be treated as a new asset if it would have fallen to be so treated if it had remained vested in the Corporation.

(2) In this paragraph "regional development grant" means a grant under Part I of the Industry Act 1972 or Part II of the Industrial Development Act 1982 and "approved capital expenditure" has the same meaning as it has for the purposes of the provisions relating to regional development grant.

38. An order under section 19 of the Local Government Act 1974 (rating of certain public utilities and other bodies) which applies in relation to hereditaments occupied by the Corporation and is effective on the transfer date shall have effect as if it applied to the corresponding hereditaments occupied by the successor company.

39. An order under section 6 of the Local Government (Scotland) Act 1975 (valuation by formula of certain lands and heritages) which applies in relation to lands and heritages occupied by the Corporation and is effective on the transfer date shall have effect as if it applied in relation to the corresponding lands and heritages occupied by the successor company.

40. The repeal by this Act of section 10 of and Schedule 1 to the Oil and Gas (Enterprise) Act 1982 shall not affect the operation of any scheme made under that section before the transfer date.

41.—(1) Where a distribution is proposed to be declared during the accounting reference period of the successor company which includes the transfer date or before any accounts are laid or filed in respect of that period, sections 270 to 276 of the Companies Act 1985 (accounts relevant for determining whether a distribution may be made by a company) shall have effect as if—

(*a*) references in section 270 to the company's accounts or to accounts relevant under that section; and

(*b*) references in section 273 to initial accounts,

included references to such accounts as, on the assumptions stated in sub-paragraph (2) below, would have been prepared under section 227 of that Act in respect of the relevant year.

(2) The said assumptions are—

(*a*) that the relevant year had been a financial year of the successor company;

(*b*) that the vesting effected by section 49 of this Act had been a vesting of all the property, rights and liabilities (other than any rights or liabilities which vest in the Treasury by virtue of section 50 of this Act) to which the Corporation was entitled or subject immediately before the beginning of the relevant year and had been effected immediately after the beginning of that year;

(*c*) that the value of any asset and the amount of any liability of the Corporation vested in the successor company by virtue of that section had been the value or (as the case may be) the amount assigned to that asset or liability for the purposes of the statement of accounts prepared by the Corporation in respect of the financial year immediately preceding the relevant year;

(*d*) that any securities of the successor company issued or allotted before the declaration of the distribution had been issued or allotted before the end of the relevant year; and

(*e*) such other assumptions (if any) as may appear to the directors of the successor company to be necessary or expedient for the purposes of this paragraph.

(3) For the purposes of the said accounts the amount to be included in respect of any item shall be determined as if anything done by the Corporation (whether by way of acquiring, revaluing or disposing of any asset or incurring, revaluing or discharging any liability, or by carrying any amount to any provision or reserve, or otherwise) had been done by the successor company.

Accordingly (but without prejudice to the generality of the preceding provision) the amount to be included in any reserves of the successor company as representing its accumulated realised profits shall be determined as if any profits realised and retained by the Corporation had been realised and retained by the successor company.

(4) The said accounts shall not be regarded as statutory accounts for the purposes of section 55 of this Act.

(5) In this paragraph—

"complete financial year" means a financial year ending with 31st March;

"the relevant year" means the last complete financial year of the Corporation ending before the transfer date;

"securities" has the same meaning as in Part II of this Act.

Section 67(4)

SCHEDULE 9

Repeals

Part I

Repeals Coming into Force on Appointed Day

Chapter	Short title	Extent of repeal
15 & 16 Geo. 5. c.71.	The Public Health Act 1925.	In section 7(3), the word "gas".
17 & 18 Geo. 5. c.36.	The Landlord and Tenant Act 1927.	In section 25(1) in the definition of "statutory company", the word "gas,".
23 & 24 Geo. 5. c.14.	The London Passenger Transport Act 1933.	In section 93(6), the words "gas or".
26 Geo. 5 & 1 Edw. 8. c.49.	The Public Health Act 1936.	In section 343 in the definition of "statutory undertakers", the word "gas,".
2 & 3 Geo. 6. c.31.	The Civil Defence Act 1939.	In section 90(1) in the definition of "Public utility undertakers", the word "gas," where it first occurs and the words "gas or" immediately after "supplying".
2 & 3 Geo. 6. c.xcix.	The London Gas Undertakings (Regulations) Act 1939.	The whole Act.
8 & 9 Geo. 6. c.42.	The Water Act 1945.	In section 1(1) of Schedule 3 in the definition of "statutory undertakers", the word "gas,".
10 & 11 Geo. 6. c.42.	The Acquisition of Land (Authorisation Procedure) (Scotland) Act 1947.	In section 7(1) in the definition of "statutory undertakers", the word "gas,".
11 & 12 Geo. 6. c.22.	The Water Act 1948.	In section 15(1) in the definition of "appropriate Minister" in paragraph (*b*), the word ", gas" and, in the definition of "statutory undertakers", the word "gas,".
2 & 3 Eliz. 2. c.21.	The Rights of Entry (Gas and Electricity Boards) Act 1954.	In section 3(1), the definition of "the Corporation".
6 & 7 Eliz. 2. c.69.	The Opencast Coal Act 1958.	In section 51(1) in the definition of "appropriate Minister", the word ", gas".
10 & 11 Eliz. 2. c.58.	The Pipe-lines Act 1962.	In section 66(1) in the definition of "statutory undertakers", the word "gas,".
1964 c.40.	The Harbours Act 1964.	In paragraph 6(2)(*c*) of Schedule 3, the word "gas,".
1965 c.36.	The Gas Act 1965.	In section 4(2), the words from "shall relate" to "statutory corporation and". In section 28(1), the definition of "the Corporation" and, in the definition of "statutory undertakers", the word "gas,".
1967 c.9.	The General Rate Act 1967.	In section 19(6) in the definition of "non-industrial building", the word "gas,".
1967 c.10.	The Forestry Act 1967.	In section 40(2)(*d*), the word "gas,".
1968 c.16.	The New Towns (Scotland) Act 1968.	In section 47(1) in the definition of "statutory undertakers", the word "gas,".

Chapter	Short title	Extent of repeal
1971 c.78.	The Town and Country Planning Act 1971.	In section 224(1)(*b*), the word ", gas". In section 290(1) in the definition of "statutory undertakers", the word ", gas".
1972 c.52.	The Town and Country Planning (Scotland) Act 1972.	In section 213(1)(*b*), the words "gas or". In section 275(1) in the definition of "statutory undertakers", the word "gas".
1972 c.60.	The Gas Act 1972.	Section 1(6). Section 2(1). Section 6(5). Sections 9 to 13. Part III. Section 34. Sections 37 to 47. In section 48(1), the definitions of "Area Board", "calorific value", "declared calorific value", "distribution main", "gas", "gas fittings", "the National Council", "Regional Council" and "therm". Section 49. Schedules 1 to 8.
1974 c.40.	The Control of Pollution Act 1974.	In section 73(1) in the definition of "statutory undertakers", the word "gas,".
1975 c.24.	The House of Commons Disqualification Act 1975.	In Schedule 1, in Part III, the entry relating to the Chairman in receipt of remuneration of the National Gas Consumers' Council or any Regional Gas Consumers' Council.
1975 c.30.	The Local Government (Scotland) Act 1975.	In Schedule 1, paragraph 3A(2).
1975 c.55.	The Statutory Corporations (Financial Provisions) Act 1975.	Section 6(2). In Schedule 3, Part II.
1975 c.70.	The Welsh Development Agency Act 1975.	In section 27(1) in the definition of "statutory undertakers", the word "gas,".
1976 c.75.	The Development of Rural Wales Act 1976.	In section 34(1) in the definition of "statutory undertakers.", the word "gas,". In column (1) of the table to paragraph 56(3) of Schedule 3, the word ", gas".
1976 c.76.	The Energy Act 1976.	In section 18(3), the words "or the British Gas Corporation".
1979 c.46.	The Ancient Monuments and Archaeological Areas Act 1979.	In section 61(2)(*a*), the word "gas,".
1980 c.37.	The Gas Act 1980.	The whole Act.
1980 c.65.	The Local Government, Planning and Land Act 1980.	In section 108(1)(*a*), the word "gas,". In section 120(3) in the definition of "statutory undertakers", the word "gas,". In section 170(1)(*a*), the word "gas,". In Schedule 16 in the definition of "statutory undertakers", the word "gas,". In paragraph 2 of Schedule 19, the word "gas,".

Chapter	Short title	Extent of repeal
1980 c.66.	The Highways Act 1980.	In section 121(6)(*a*), the word "gas,". In section 157(9), the word "gas,". In section 329(1), the definition of "gas undertakers". In section 329(1) in the definition of "statutory undertakers", the word "gas,".
1981 c.64.	The New Towns Act 1981.	In section 78(1)(*b*), the word ", gas". In section 79(1)(*a*)(iii), the word "gas,".
1981 c.67.	The Acquisition of Land Act 1981.	In section 8(1)(*a*)(iii), the word "gas,".
1982 c.16.	The Civil Aviation Act 1982.	In section 105(1) in the definition of "statutory undertakers", the word ", gas".
1982 c.23.	The Oil and Gas (Enterprise) Act 1982.	Sections 12 to 17. In section 32(1), the words "regulations or". In Schedule 3, paragraphs 5, 6 and 12 to 20.
1982 c.30.	The Local Government (Miscellaneous Provisions) Act 1982.	In section 30(1)(*b*), the words "gas or".
1984 c.12.	The Telecommunications Act 1984.	In paragraph 23(10)(*a*)(ii) of Schedule 2, the words "gas or".
1984 c.54.	The Roads (Scotland) Act 1984.	In Schedule 9, paragraph 71.
1984 c.55.	The Building Act 1984.	In section 126 in the definition of "statutory undertakers", the word "gas,".

Part II

Repeals Coming into Force on Transfer Date

Chapter	Short title	Extent of repeal
1970 c.10.	The Income and Corporation Taxes Act 1970.	In section 350, subsections (1) and (2).
1972 c.60.	The Gas Act 1972.	Section 1(3). In section 2, subsections (2) and (3). Sections 3 to 5. In section 6, subsections (1) to (4) and (6) to (8). Sections 7 and 8. Part II. Sections 32 and 33. Sections 35 and 36. Section 48 (so far as unrepealed). Section 50.
1979 c.14.	The Capital Gains Tax Act 1979.	In Schedule 2, in Part I, in paragraph 1(*b*), the words "and the Gas Act 1972".
1980 c.63.	The Overseas Development and Co-operation Act 1980.	In Schedule 1, in Part III, the entry relating to the British Gas Corporation.

Chapter	Short title	Extent of repeal
1982 c.23.	The Oil and Gas (Enterprise) Act 1982.	Sections 9 to 11. In section 32, in subsection (1), the words "and the power conferred by section 11(1) above to give directions", in subsection (2), the words from "an order" to "section 11(1) above", and subsection (3).
1982 c.23—*cont.*	The Oil and Gas (Enterprise) Act 1982—*cont.*	Sections 33 and 34. In section 36, the definitions of "the 1972 Act" and "the Gas Corporation". Schedule 1.
1982 c.39.	The Finance Act 1982.	Section 147.
1982 c.41.	The Stock Transfer Act 1982.	Section 1(3)(*d*).
1983 c.29.	The Miscellaneous Financial Provisions Act 1983.	In Schedule 2, the entry relating to the Gas Act 1972.
1985 c.62.	The Oil and Pipelines Act 1985.	Section 7(2).

Part III

Repeals Coming into Force on Dissolution of British Gas Corporation

Chapter	Short title	Extent of repeal
1972 c.60.	The Gas Act 1972.	In section 1, subsections (1), (2), (4) and (5).
1975 c.24.	The House of Commons Disqualification Act 1975.	In Schedule 1, in Part II, the entry relating to the British Gas Corporation.
1983 c.44.	The National Audit Act 1983.	In Schedule 4, the entry relating to the British Gas Corporation.

INSOLVENCY ACT 1986*

(1986 c. 45)

Tables of derivations and destinations will be found at the end of the Act. The Tables have no official status.

ARRANGEMENT OF SECTIONS

THE FIRST GROUP OF PARTS

COMPANY INSOLVENCY; COMPANIES WINDING UP

PART I

COMPANY VOLUNTARY ARRANGEMENTS

The proposal

* Annotations by Ian Fletcher, M.A., LL.M., M.C.L., Ph.D., Barrister, Professor of Law and Acting Head of Department of Law, University College of Wales, Aberystwyth; and Letitia Crabb, LL.B., LL.M., Solicitor, Lecturer in Law, University College of Wales, Aberystwyth. The annotators wish to acknowledge the assistance they derived from consultation of the Current Law annotations to those sections of the Companies Act 1985 which have been consolidated within the present Act. The annotations in question were the work of John Farrar, LL.B., LL.M., Ph.D., Professor of Law, University of Canterbury (N.Z.); and David Milman, LL.B., Ph.D., Lecturer in Law, University of Manchester.

Ascertainment and investigation of company's affairs

Administrator's proposals

Miscellaneous

PART III

RECEIVERSHIP

CHAPTER I

RECEIVERS AND MANAGERS (ENGLAND AND WALES)

Preliminary and general provisions

Receivers and managers appointed out of court

Provisions applicable to every receivership

Administrative receivers: general

Administrative receivers: ascertainment and investigation of company's affairs

Chapter II

Receivers (Scotland)

Chapter III

Receivers' Powers in Great Britain as a Whole

Part IV

Winding Up of Companies Registered under the Companies Acts

Chapter I

Preliminary

Modes of winding up

Contributories

Chapter II

Voluntary Winding Up (Introductory and General)

Resolutions for, and commencement of, voluntary winding up

Grounds and effect of winding-up petition

Commencement of winding up

Investigation procedures

Appointment of liquidator

Liquidation committees

The liquidator's functions

General powers of court

Enforcement of, and appeal from, orders

Chapter VII

Liquidators

Preliminary

Liquidator's powers and duties

Removal; vacation of office

Release of liquidator

Chapter VIII

Provisions of General Application in Winding Up

Preferential debts

Special managers

Disclaimer (England and Wales only)

Execution, attachment and the Scottish equivalents

Miscellaneous matters

Chapter IX

Dissolution of Companies After Winding Up

Chapter X

Malpractice before and during Liquidation;

Penalisation of Companies and Company Officers;

Investigations and Prosecutions

Offences of fraud, deception, etc.

Penalisation of directors and officers

Investigation and prosecution of malpractice

Part V

Winding up of Unregistered Companies

Part VI

Miscellaneous Provisions Applying to Companies which are Insolvent or in Liquidation

Office-holders

Management by administrators, liquidators, etc.

Adjustment of prior transactions (administration and liquidation)

Part VII

Interpretation for First Group of Parts

The Second Group of Parts

Insolvency of Individuals; Bankruptcy

Part VIII

Individual Voluntary Arrangements

Moratorium for insolvent debtor

Consideration and implementation of debtor's proposal

Part IX

Bankruptcy

Chapter I

Bankruptcy Petitions; Bankruptcy Orders

Preliminary

Creditor's petition

Debtor's petition

Other cases for special consideration

Commencement and duration of bankruptcy; discharge

Chapter II

Protection of Bankrupt's Estate and Investigation of His Affairs

Chapter III

Trustees in Bankruptcy

Tenure of office as trustee

297. Special cases.
298. Removal of trustee; vacation of office.
299. Release of trustee.
300. Vacancy in office of trustee.

Control of trustee

301. Creditors' committee.
302. Exercise by Secretary of State of functions of creditors' committee.
303. General control of trustee by the court.
304. Liability of trustee.

CHAPTER IV

ADMINISTRATION BY TRUSTEE

Preliminary

305. General functions of trustee.

Acquisition, control, and realisation of bankrupt's estate

306. Vesting of bankrupt's estate in trustee.
307. After-acquired property.
308. Vesting in trustee of certain items of excess value.
309. Time-limit for notice under s.307 or 308.
310. Income payments orders.
311. Acquisition by trustee of control.
312. Obligation to surrender control to trustee.
313. Charge on bankrupt's home.
314. Powers of trustee.

Disclaimer of onerous property

315. Disclaimer (general power).
316. Notice requiring trustee's decision.
317. Disclaimer of leaseholds.
318. Disclaimer of dwelling house.
319. Disclaimer of land subject to rentcharge.
320. Court order vesting disclaimed property.
321. Order under s.320 in respect of leaseholds.

Distribution of bankrupt's estate

322. Proof of debts.
323. Mutual credit and set-off.
324. Distribution by means of dividend.
325. Claims by unsatisfied creditors.
326. Distribution of property in specie.
327. Distribution in criminal bankruptcy.
328. Priority of debts.
329. Debts to spouse.
330. Final distribution.
331. Final meeting.
332. Saving for bankrupt's home.

Supplemental

333. Duties of bankrupt in relation to trustee.
334. Stay of distribution in case of second bankruptcy.
335. Adjustment between earlier and later bankruptcy estates.

PART XI

INTERPRETATION FOR SECOND GROUP OF PARTS

THE THIRD GROUP OF PARTS

MISCELLANEOUS MATTERS BEARING ON BOTH COMPANY AND INDIVIDUAL INSOLVENCY; GENERAL INTERPRETATION; FINAL PROVISIONS

PART XII

PREFERENTIAL DEBTS IN COMPANY AND INDIVIDUAL INSOLVENCY

PART XIII

INSOLVENCY PRACTITIONERS AND THEIR QUALIFICATION

Restrictions on unqualified persons acting as liquidator, trustee in bankruptcy, etc.

The requisite qualification, and the means of obtaining it

PART XIV

PUBLIC ADMINISTRATION (ENGLAND AND WALES)

Official receivers

The Official Petitioner

Insolvency Service finance, accounting and investment

Supplementary

PART XV

SUBORDINATE LEGISLATION

General insolvency rules

Fees orders

Specification, increase and reduction of money sums relevant in the operation of this Act

Insolvency practice

Other order-making powers

PART XVI

PROVISIONS AGAINST DEBT AVOIDANCE

(ENGLAND AND WALES ONLY)

PART XVII

MISCELLANEOUS AND GENERAL

PART XVIII

INTERPRETATION

PART XIX

FINAL PROVISIONS

An Act to consolidate the enactments relating to company insolvency and winding up (including the winding up of companies that are not insolvent, and of unregistered companies); enactments relating to the insolvency and bankruptcy of individuals; and other enactments bearing on those two subject matters, including the functions and qualification of insolvency practitioners, the public administration of insolvency, the penalisation and redress of malpractice and wrongdoing, and the avoidance of certain transactions at an undervalue.

[25th July 1986]

INTRODUCTION AND GENERAL NOTE

The Insolvency Act 1986, which received the Royal Assent on July 25, is a major landmark in the evolution of the insolvency law of England and Wales. When the Act comes into force on December 15, 1986, the principal statutory provisions relating to both corporate and individual insolvency will for the first time be contained within a single, well-structured statute. The only significant exception to that proposition concerns the provisions relating to the disqualification of directors, which have been separately consolidated in the Company Directors Disqualification Act 1986 (c.46). Thus, the process of extricating the statutory provisions governing corporate insolvency from their traditional location within the companies legislation (itself consolidated as recently as 1985), and of uniting them with the provisions governing the insolvency of individuals, has been carried to its logical conclusion by means of two successive statutes, each bearing the title "Insolvency Act", enacted in 1985 and 1986 respectively. The Insolvency Act 1985 (referred to hereafter as "the 1985 Act") was a necessary precursor to the consolidation of this area of the law, and effected numerous reforms to, as well as extensive repeals of, the wide variety of legislative provisions then in force relating to different aspects of personal and corporate insolvency. Although certain parts of the 1985 Act were brought into force during the course of 1986, the majority of the provisions of that Act will actually come into operation in their consolidated form within the Insolvency Act 1986. The commencement section of the 1986 Act, s.443, is so designed as to bring the whole of the Act into force immediately after the moment when Part III of the 1985 Act (dealing with individual insolvency and bankruptcy) comes into force for England and Wales. Thus, unusually, the commencement of the 1986 Act will be brought about through the making of a commencment order relating to a separate statute, namely the 1985 Act, the greater part of which will furthermore be repealed by virtue of Sched. 12 to the 1986 Act immediately after the moment of entering into force.

Although the 1986 Act effects a consolidation of the law of insolvency, it does not eliminate the historic distinction under English law whereby individual and corporate insolvency are respectively dealt with by means of separate codes of law. Thus, the First Group of Parts of the Act (Parts I–VII inclusive) governs the insolvency and winding-up of companies, while the Second Group of Parts (Parts VIII–XI inclusive) governs the insolvency of individuals and bankruptcy. Matters which bear upon both company and individual insolvency, and other general and final provisions, are gathered in the Third Group of Parts (Parts XII–XIX inclusive). However, one very notable aspect of the consolidation process is the achievement of an unprecedented unity and consistency in the statutory drafting of all provisions relating to insolvency. It is of course an established convention that a consolidation Act may effect drafting amendments to the law provided that these in no way alter its substance. The preparation of the Insolvency Bill 1986 was made the responsibility of a single, experienced, Parliamentary draftsman, Mr. Godfrey Carter, (also the principal draftsman of the Companies Act 1985) who has imposed a new, logical framework upon the form and sequence of the Act as a whole, while subjecting each individual section to a thorough process of recasting and redrafting with a view to enhancing the clarity of each provision while ensuring that stylistic unity is maintained throughout. The new style of drafting has the decided merits of being more straightforward, and far less ponderous, than that in which former insolvency legislation has been cast, and should prove somewhat less daunting to the non-specialist reader.

As a consolidation measure, the Insolvency Bill 1986 enjoyed an unremarkable and tranquil passage through all Parliamentary stages, commencing with its introduction in the House of Lords on May 13. There was minimal debate upon the floor of each House, and for its committee stage the Bill was referred to the Joint Committee on Consolidated Bills, and a mere handful of drafting corrections were made. The absence of controversy or contention which thus accompanied the enactment of the Insolvency Act 1986 was in marked contrast to the atmosphere attending every stage of the proceedings on the 1985 Act. The reforms first introduced by means of that earlier measure, and now serenely consolidated within the Act of 1986, were enacted under circumstances of exceptional drama and passion which were rendered all the more remarkable by reason of their association with an area of the law traditionally regarded as remote, obscure and technical, and essentially non-political in aspect. In view of the significance of the Parliamentary proceedings relating to the 1985 Act, as compared the the bland and uninformative nature of the reported proceedings on the Act of 1986, a full set of references to the Hansard reports relating to the 1985 Act is supplied at the end of this General Introduction, in addition to the references relating to the present Act itself. It is also worthwhile to recall that the reforms embodied in the 1985 Act were the product of an extended process of re-examination of the entire working of the insolvency law which began to gain in urgency in the period from 1975 onwards, as successive phases of economic recession brought about abnormally high levels of corporate and individual financial failures. At this time, the inadequacies of the legal provisions and the administrative machinery for dealing with insolvency became increasingly exposed, producing conditions conducive to the carrying out of the first thorough reform of either branch of insolvency law to have been undertaken since the second half of the 19th century, and indeed the first ever comprehensive restatement of the insolvency law in its entirety.

In 1975 a report by "Justice", the British section of the International Commission of Jurists, made numerous proposals for reform, some of which were soon afterwards adopted in the Insolvency Act 1976. The latter was, however, a short Act of limited scope, and was essentially an interim measure to alleviate some of the law's more serious shortcomings pending a wholesale review. Another line of investigation had been pursued since 1973 in consequence of the United Kingdom's accession to membership of the European Economic Community. Among the requirements of membership it became necessary to engage in negotiations with the other Member States in relation to a Draft EEC Bankruptcy Convention (concerning allocation of jurisdiction, choice of law, and international recognition in relation to all types of cross-border insolvency). To prepare for these negotiations an Advisory Committee was appointed in 1973 under the chairmanship of Mr. Kenneth Cork (as he then was). This Committee reported in August 1976 (Cmnd. 6602), at a time when Parliament was about to conclude the process of enactment of the Insolvency Act 1976, which received the Royal Assent on November 15 of that year. The Advisory Committee's Report demonstrated in a particularly cogent manner the desirability of undertaking a rigorous reform and modernisation of our domestic insolvency laws, the better to prepare our position for the conducting of serious negotiations with our EEC partners. In recognition of the fact that such a reform was already long overdue, the Secretary of State for Trade announced in October 1976 that he was to set up a Review Committee on Insolvency Law and Practice (Hansard, H.C. Vol. 918, October 1976, written answer No. 20). This Committee was established in January 1977, again under the chairmanship of Mr. (later Sir) Kenneth Cork, with the following terms of reference:

(i) to review the law and practice relating to insolvency, bankruptcy, liquidation and receiverships in England and Wales and to consider what reforms are necessary or desirable;
(ii) to examine the possibility of formulating a comprehensive insolvency system and the extent to which existing procedures might, with advantage, be harmonised and integrated;
(iii) to suggest possible less formal procedures as alternatives to bankruptcy and company winding up proceedings in appropriate circumstances.
(iv) to make recommendations.

The progress of the work of the Insolvency Law Review Committee was considerably affected by the change of Government after May 1979. As part of its general programme of scrutinising the cost-effectiveness of most aspects of public administration, the incoming Government made an approach to the Committee in August 1979 to elicit an early indication of their likely recommendations, viewed especially from the standpoint of achieving a reduction in the amount of time devoted by the personnel of the Insolvency Service to the fulfilment of their duties. In consequence, the Committee submitted an Interim Report to the Minister in October 1979, subsequently published in July 1980 (Cmnd. 7968) simultaneously with a Government Green Paper (Cmnd. 7967) purporting to respond to the intimations contained in the Interim Report. The Green Paper contained unsatisfactory and unconvincing proposals for the wholesale privatisation of insolvency procedures and was unfavourably received (see *e.g. Fletcher* (1981) 44 M.L.R. 77) and in their Final Report (see especially chap. 14) the Reivew Committee went to considerable lengths to refute the arguments previously put forward by Government for a radical re-shaping of the law in a way which would have resulted in the almost entire elimination of the active participation of the Insolvency Service. It is noteworthy that in their subsequent *White Paper, A Revised Framework for Insolvency Law* (Cmnd. 9175) of February 1984 the Government tacitly abandoned the drastic model for privatisation formulated in the *Green Paper* and indicated that other ways would be sought for achieving economies in the operation of the Insolvency Service (see especially chaps. 7 and 8, and also paras. 17–18, 71–74, 76–77, 82, 90–93, 96, 102, 105–107, 117–119, 120 and 124).

Regrettably, very little time was allowed following the publication of the *White Paper* for interested parties to submit comments before the process of drafting the Insolvency Bill was embarked upon. Neither the *Cork Report* nor the *White Paper* were the subject of any formal debate in either House of Parliament, and hence no official public proceedings took place in relation to the proposed re-shaping of the law prior to the introduction of the Insolvency Bill in the House of Lords on December 10, 1984. The deficiencies in the processes of consultation and public debate in preparation for a significant, if technical, piece of legislation to effect the first major overhaul of insolvency law for over a hundred years were undoubtedly responsible for the atmosphere of controversy and confusion which developed at successive stages over certain parts of what ought to have been a non-contentious, non-party Bill. The want of proper preparation for the introduction of the Bill furthermore resulted in the quite exceptionally high number of tabled amendments—estimated to have approached 1200 by the time of Royal Assent. A high proportion of these amendments were actually tabled by the government itself during successive stages in both Houses of Parliament. In the event, the Act did not receive Royal Assent until October 30, 1985, and was in the early stages of being brought into effect in a piecemeal fashion by means of Commencement orders made between January and May 1986 (S.I. 1986 Nos. 6, 185, 463, and 840), when the measure designed to supplant it as the Insolvency Act 1986 made its first public appearance on being presented and read for the first time in the House of Lords on May 13. The 1986 Act consists of 444 sections and 14 Schedules, and effects a consolidation (and consequential repeal) of almost the whole of the Act of 1985, together with those Parts of the Companies Act 1985 which relate to the insolvency and winding up of companies, chiefly Parts XIX, XX (apart from Chapter VI) and XXI. The Insolvency Services (Accounting and Investment) Act 1970 is also consolidated in the 1986 Act. The full list of enactments repealed is contained in Sched. 12, while Sched. 13 contains consequential amendments of the Companies Act 1985, and Sched. 14 contains consequential amendments of other enactments. Most of the statutory provisions previously in force in relation to insolvency were repealed either by the Insolvency Act 1985 (see Sched. 10 to that Act) or as a consequence of the consolidation of the Companies Acts of that same year (see Companies Consolidation (Consequential Provisions) Act 1985, Schedules 1 and 2).

The First Group of Parts

Part I. Contains the new type of company voluntary arrangement, first introduced in Chapter II of Part II of the Act of 1985, whereby a debtor company may conclude a composition of debts or scheme of arrangement of its affairs with its creditors.

Part II. Contains the new insolvency procedure known as the administration order procedure, first introduced in Chapter III of Part II of the 1985 Act, whereby the management of a failed or failing company may be placed under the control of an administrator for a period of time with a view to securing the survival of as much of the company as can be saved, or alternatively the most orderly and advantageous realisation of its assets as can be achieved.

Part III. Consolidates the law of receivership.

Chapter I. Is concerned with the law of receivers and managers in England and Wales.

Chapter II. Contains the law relating to Receivers in Scotland.

Chapter III. Deals with the cross-border operation of receivership provisions.

Part IV. Contains the law on the winding up of companies registered under the Companies Acts.

Chapter I. Specifies the different modes of winding up, and contains the statutory provisions applicable to contributories.

Chapter II. Contains the introductory and general provisions relating to voluntary winding up.

Chapter III. Contains the provisions applicable to members' voluntary winding up only.

Chapter IV. Contains the provisions applicable to creditors' voluntary winding up only.

Chapter V. Contains the provisions applying to both kinds of voluntary winding up.

Chapter VI. Contains the provisions applicable to winding up by the court (otherwise known as compulsory winding up).

Chapter VII. Deals with the appointment, removal and release of liquidators, and defines their powers and duties.

Chapter VIII. Contains provisions which are of general application to every mode of winding up.

Chapter IX. Deals with the dissolution of companies after winding up.

Chapter X. Contains provisions dealing with malpractice before and during liquidation, the penalisation of companies and company officers, and investigations and prosecutions. The respective malpractices of fraudulent trading and wrongful trading are governed by provisions within this Chapter.

Part V. Deals with the winding up of unregistered companies.

Part VI. Contains miscellaneous provisions applying to companies which are insolvent or in liquidation, and includes provisions governing entitlement of persons to hold any of the various types of office associated with company insolvency proceedings, particular powers and remedies available to office holders, and provisions regulating the adjustment of prior transactions entered into by companies which have subsequently gone into liquidation or administration.

Part VII. Is exclusively concerned with matters of interpretation relating to the First Group Of Parts.

The Second Group of Parts

Part VIII. Contains the provisions relating to the new form of voluntary arrangement, first introduced in Chapter I of Part III of the 1985 Act, whereby an individual debtor may conclude a composition of debts or scheme of arrangement of his affairs with his creditors.

Part IX. Contains the new, consolidated code of bankruptcy law, corresponding in substance to the enactments within Chapters II–VI inclusive of Part III of the 1985 Act. Among the most notable aspects of the law of bankruptcy in its newly recast state are the abolition of the concept of acts of bankruptcy and of the receiving order; new rules concerned with discharge from bankruptcy so that most first-time bankrupts will be automatically discharged after three years, or even after two in cases of summary administration; alterations in the provisions for public examination of bankrupts, so that this will only take place where the official receiver applies for one to be held; and an investigative process designed to help debtors who present their own bankruptcy petitions to explore the possibility of avoiding adjudication through some alternative procedure. There have also been important revisions to the rules defining the bankrupt's estate available for distribution to creditors, and in relation to the exemption of certain property from that category. There are special provisions regarding the position of the family home in the event of the bankruptcy of either spouse. The doctrine of reputed ownership has been abolished, as has the doctrine of relation-back of the trustees title to the bankrupt's property to a date anterior to that when the bankruptcy order is made. There is now a close parallel between the rules applicable in company insolvency and in bankruptcy whereby property which has been disposed of by the debtor at an undervalue or by way of a preference may be recovered for the benefit of the creditors. Similarly, parallel sets of rules are now applicable to enable the office holder in cases of individual or corporate insolvency to bring about the re-opening of any extortionate credit transactions into which the debtor may have entered.

Chapter I. Deals with bankruptcy petitions, bankruptcy orders and the commencement and duration of bankruptcy, including provisions concerning discharge from bankruptcy.

Chapter II. Defines the bankrupt's estate available for distribution to creditors, and also deals with the protection of the bankrupt's estate and investigation of his affairs.

Chapter III. Is concerned with the appointment, removal, replacement and release of trustees in bankruptcy, and with the control to be exercised over the trustee by a committee of creditors.

Chapter IV. Contains provisions relating to the administration of the bankruptcy by the trustee, including the acquisition, control and realisation of the bankrupt's estate, the disclaimer of onerous property and the distribution of the bankrupt's estate in accordance with the prescribed schedule of priorities.

Chapter V. Deals with the effect of bankruptcy on certain rights and transactions, including rights of occupation of the family home; the adjustment of prior transactions at an undervalue; and the avoidance of preferences.

Chapter VI. Contains the modernised code of criminal offences relating to bankruptcy.

Chapter VII. Deals with the powers of the court in bankruptcy.

Part IX. Contains general provisions relating to individual insolvency, and also includes a parallel section to that operating in company insolvency, whereby utility suppliers may be prevented from exploiting their position in such a way as to circumvent the principle of *pari passu* distribution in insolvency.

Part XI. Deals with matters of interpretation relating to the Second Group of Parts.

The Third Group of Parts

Part XII. Establishes, in conjunction with Sched. 6, the categories of preferential debts which are to apply in company and individual insolvency alike.

Part XIII. Contains the new provisions, originally introduced in Part I of the 1985 Act, regulating the provisions of the services of an insolvency practitioner, as defined in s.388, makes it a criminal offence to act as an insolvency practitioner when not qualified to do so, and prescribes the criteria to be satisfied for qualification to act as an insolvency practitioner, and the procedures whereby the necessary authorisation may be obtained.

Part XIV. Contains provisions dealing with the public administration of insolvency law in England and Wales, including provisions governing the appointment, functions and status of official receivers, and the financing of the Insolvency Service and the operation of the Insolvency Services Account.

Part XV. Contains enabling provisions under which the various forms of subordinate legislation relating to all aspects of insolvency law may be made, revised and periodically amended.

Part XVI. Contains the new provision of general law, replacing s.172 of the Law of Property Act 1925, whereby transactions defrauding creditors may be avoided and ancillary and restitutional remedies granted.

Part XVII. Contains miscellaneous and general provisions.

Part XVIII. Is concerned with matters of interpretation, in relation to expressions used generally throughtout the Act. In particular the meaning of the term "associate" is defined by s.435.

Part XIX. Contains the final provisions of the Act, including transitional provisions, savings, repeals, consequential amendments, extent, citation and commencement.

Schedule 1. Sets out the powers of an administrator or administrative receiver.

Schedule 2. Sets out the powers of a Scottish receiver.
Schedule 3. Relates to the making of orders in the course of winding up announced in vacation in Scotland.
Schedule 4. Sets out the powers of a liquidator in a winding up.
Schedule 5. Sets out the powers of a trustee in bankruptcy.
Schedule 6. Sets out the categories of preferential debts applicable in both company and individual insolvency.
Schedule 7. Is concerned with the Insolvency Practitioners Tribunal which determines cases on appeal where an authorisation to practice as an insolvency practitioner has been refused or revoked.
Schedule 8. Contains general enabling powers to authorise the making of detailed rules governing company insolvency.
Schedule 9. Contains general enabling powers to authorise the making of detailed rules governing individual insolvency.
Schedule 10. Sets out the table of punishments for all criminal offences under the Act.
Schedule 11. Contains transitional provisions and savings relating to various provisions of pre-existing legislation repealed or affected by the coming into force of this Act.
Schedule 12. Specifies the enactments repealed upon the coming into force of this Act.
Schedule 13. Sets out amendments to the Companies Act 1985 which are consequential upon this Act.
Schedule 14. Sets out consequential amendments to legislation apart from the Companies Act 1985.

PARLIAMENTARY DEBATES

Hansard: H.L. Vol. 474, col. 1038; Vol. 475, cols. 711–714; Vol. 477, cols. 420–422, 758, 1036; H.C. Vol. 120, cols. 152, 153.

PARLIAMENTARY DEBATES RELATING TO THE INSOLVENCY ACT 1985

Hansard: H.L. Vol. 458, cols. 875, 894; Vol. 459, cols. 565, 833, 835, 906, 1212, 1233; Vol. 461, col. 711; Vol. 462, cols. 11, 123, 606; Vol. 467, cols. 1093, 1188; H.C. Vol. 78, col. 141; Vol. 83. col. 526; Vol. 84, col. 677.

The Bill was considered in Committee by the House of Commons in Standing Committee E on May 14, 16, 21, 23 and 4, 6, 11, 13, 18 and 20 June, 1985.

ABBREVIATIONS

The 1985 Act: The Insolvency Act 1985. (c.65).
C.A. 1985 or *The Companies Act*: The Companies Act 1985. (c.6).
C.A. 1948: The Companies Act 1948. (c.38).
C.A. 1967: The Companies Act 1967. (c.81).
C.A. 1980: The Companies Act 1980. (c.22).
C. (F.C. & R.) (S) A. 1972: The Companies (Floating charges and Receivers) (Scotland) Act 1972. (c.76).
B.(Sc.): The Bankruptcy (Scotland) Act 1985. (c.66).
Cork Report: Final Report of the Review Committee on Insolvency Law and Practice (June 1982) Cmnd. 8558.
White Paper: A Revised Framework for Insolvency Law (February 1984) Cmnd. 9175.

THE FIRST GROUP OF PARTS

COMPANY INSOLVENCY; COMPANIES WINDING UP

PART I

COMPANY VOLUNTARY ARRANGEMENTS

The proposal

Those who may propose an arrangement

1.—(1) The directors of a company (other than one for which an administration order is in force, or which is being wound up) may make a proposal under this Part to the company and to its creditors for a composition in satisfaction of its debts or a scheme of arrangement of its affairs (from here on referred to, in either case, as a "voluntary arrangement").

(2) A proposal under this Part is one which provides for some person ("the nominee") to act in relation to the voluntary arrangement either as trustee or otherwise for the purpose of supervising its implementation; and the nominee must be a person who is qualified to act as an insolvency practitioner in relation to the company.

(3) Such a proposal may also be made—

(*a*) where an administration order is in force in relation to the company, by the administrator, and

(*b*) where the company is being wound up, by the liquidator.

DEFINITIONS

"administration order": s.8(2).
"director": s.251.
"person qualified to act as an insolvency practitioner": s.390.
"the administrator": s.8(2).
"the nominee": this section, subs. (2).
"to act as an insolvency practitioner": s.388.
"voluntary arrangement": this section, subs. (1).

GENERAL NOTE

The purpose underlying Part I (ss.1–7) is to make available a suitably simple procedure whereby a company may conclude a legally effective arrangement with its creditors. It was considered that the various procedures established under the provisions of the Companies Act 1985 (ss.425–427; 582, or 601) should be supplemented or replaced by a new procedure for voluntary arrangements, since the existing ones in practice proved cumbersome and unsuitable in the context of an attempt to rationalise the affairs of a company which is nearly or actually insolvent. The matter is discussed in section 2 of chap. 7 of the *Cork Report.* The provisions now contained in Part I broadly match the recommendations of the Cork Committee. The new procedure is so designed as to be available for use at any appropriate time, whether before or after the commencement of any proceedings whereby the company is to be wound up or an administration order employed. Ss.582 and 601 of the Companies Act 1985 are repealed by Sched. 12 to this Act. This section embodies the substance of s.20 of the 1985 Act.

Subs. (2)

Person who is qualified to act as an insolvency practitioner in relation to the company

In selecting a suitable person to occupy the position of "nominee," regard must be had both to the general requirements of s.390 with regard to qualification to act as an insolvency practitioner, and also to the possible existence of any ties or relationships between the nominee and the company which, if he were in due course to act as supervisor of the proposed arrangement, would give rise to a contravention of the rules of practice of the professional body to which he belongs, or of any regulations made under s.419 of this Act or rules made under s.10(2)(*b*) of the 1985 Act. An unqualified person who acts as supervisor of an arrangement under this Part of the Act commits a criminal offence under s.389, by virtue of the provision in s.388(1)(*b*).

Procedure where nominee is not the liquidator or administrator

2.—(1) This section applies where the nominee under section 1 is not the liquidator or administrator of the company.

(2) The nominee shall, within 28 days (or such longer period as the court may allow) after he is given notice of the proposal for a voluntary arrangement, submit a report to the court stating—

(*a*) whether, in his opinion, meetings of the company and of its creditors should be summoned to consider the proposal, and

(*b*) if in his opinion such meetings should be summoned, the date on which, and time and place at which, he proposes the meetings should be held.

(3) For the purposes of enabling the nominee to prepare his report, the person intending to make the proposal shall submit to the nominee—

(*a*) a document setting out the terms of the proposed voluntary arrangement, and

(*b*) a statement of the company's affairs containing—

(i) such particulars of its creditors and of its debts and other liabilities and of its assets as may be prescribed, and

(ii) such other information as may be prescribed.

(4) The court may, on an application made by the person intending to make the proposal, in a case where the nominee has failed to submit the report required by this section, direct that the nominee be replaced as such by another person qualified to act as an insolvency practitioner in relation to the company.

Definitions

"person qualified to act as an insolvency practitioner": s.390.
"prescribed": s.251.
"the administrator": s.8(2).
"the court": s.251; Companies Act 1985, s.744.
"the nominee": s.1(2).
"to act as an insolvency practitioner": s.388.

General Note

The purpose of this section, which is in substance identical to s.21 of the 1985 Act, is to ensure that any proposal for a voluntary arrangement is subjected to preliminary scrutiny by a qualified insolvency practitioner, who is required to form a professional judgment as to the soundness and feasibility of the proposal. If the company is in liquidation or is the subject of an administration order, the combined effect of subss. (1) and (3) of s.1 is that any proposal for an arrangement must be initiated by the liquidator or administrator, whose own professional judgment will inevitably have been brought to bear upon the proposal he has formulated. However if the liquidator or administrator does not intend personally to become the supervisor of the arrangement, and in all other cases where the proposal emanates from the directors pursuant to s.1(1), this section requires the nominee to pronounce his own judgment upon the proposal and report to the court, in effect, as to whether it is worthwhile taking the next immediate steps which would be required to bring the proposal into effect. The requirements of subs. (3) are designed to ensure that the nominee is able to form his judgment on the basis of sufficient information, and if in his opinion the proposal is unsound, or is unlikely to command the necessary support from the meetings of the company and of the creditors required to be convened under s.3, no further progress can be taken and the expense of holding abortive or futile meetings is thereby saved.

The terms of subs. (2) require the nominee to submit his report to the court within 28 days after receiving notice of the proposal, and in case he is unable or unwilling to do so within the time allowed, provision is made in subs. (4) for application to be made to the court for the replacement of the original nominee with some other, suitably qualified person. Such an application is to be made by the person intending to make the proposal for the voluntary arrangement.

Summoning of meetings

3.—(1) Where the nominee under section 1 is not the liquidator or administrator, and it has been reported to the court that such meetings as are mentioned in section 2(2) should be summoned, the person making the report shall (unless the court otherwise directs) summon those meetings for the time, date and place proposed in the report.

(2) Where the nominee is the liquidator or administrator, he shall summon meetings of the company and of its creditors to consider the proposal for such a time, date and place as he thinks fit.

(3) The persons to be summoned to a creditors' meeting under this section are every creditor of the company of whose claim and address the person summoning the meeting is aware.

DEFINITIONS
"the administrator": s.8(2).
"the nominee": s.1(2).

GENERAL NOTE
This makes it incumbent upon the person who has submitted a report under s.2 expressing the opinion that meetings of the company and of its creditors should be summoned, to assume responsibility for the summoning of those meetings at the time and place proposed, or otherwise according to the court's directions. The meeting of the company will be convened and conducted in accordance with the provisions contained in Chap. IV of Pt. XI of the Companies Act 1985; the convening of the creditors' meeting will take place subject to the requirement of subs. (3) indicating the persons to whom notice of the meeting must be sent. This section corresponds to s.22 of the 1985 Act.

Consideration and implementation of proposal

Decisions of meetings

4.—(1) The meetings summoned under section 3 shall decide whether to approve the proposed voluntary arrangement (with or without modifications).

(2) The modifications may include one conferring the functions proposed to be conferred on the nominee on another person qualified to act as an insolvency practitioner in relation to the company.

But they shall not include any modification by virtue of which the proposal ceases to be a proposal such as is mentioned in section 1.

(3) A meeting so summoned shall not approve any proposal or modification which affects the right of a secured creditor of the company to enforce his security, except with the concurrence of the creditor concerned.

(4) Subject as follows, a meeting so summoned shall not approve any proposal or modification under which—

(*a*) any preferential debt of the company is to be paid otherwise than in priority to such of its debts as are not preferential debts, or

(*b*) a preferential creditor of the company is to be paid an amount in respect of a preferential debt that bears to that debt a smaller proportion than is borne to another preferential debt by the amount that is to be paid in respect of that other debt.

However, the meeting may approve such a proposal or modification with the concurrence of the preferential creditor concerned.

(5) Subject as above, each of the meetings shall be conducted in accordance with the rules.

(6) After the conclusion of either meeting in accordance with the rules, the chairman of the meeting shall report the result of the meeting to the court, and, immediately after reporting to the court, shall give notice of the result of the meeting to such persons as may be prescribed.

(7) References in this section to preferential debts and preferential creditors are to be read in accordance with section 386 in Part XII of this Act.

DEFINITIONS
"administration order": s.8(2).
"modifications": s.436.
"person qualified to act as an insolvency practitioner": s.390.
"preferential creditor"; "preferential debt": s.386, Sched. 6.
"prescribed": s.251.
"secured creditor": s.248.
"the nominee": s.1(2).
"the rules": ss.251, 411.
"voluntary arrangement": s.1(1).

GENERAL NOTE

This section governs the conduct and procedure of meetings held for the purpose of deciding whether to approve the proposal for a voluntary arrangement made under s.1. There is provision in subs. (2) for the substitution of some other, qualified person to serve as the supervisor of the composition or scheme in place of the original nominee, and provision also for the effecting of modifications to the original proposal, subject to the limitation that the proposal as modified must remain compatible with the terms of s.1. The section corresponds to s.23 of the 1985 Act.

Subs. (3)

This preserves the position of any secured creditor of the company by providing that no arrangement which affects such a creditor's right to enforce his security can be approved without his consent.

Subs. (4)

This preserves the position of any preferential creditor of the company, by providing that no arrangement which affects such a creditor's right to receive payment in priority to any non-preferential debts, and in a proportion equal to that received by all other preferential creditors, can be approved without his consent.

Subs. (6)

The chairman of the meeting shall report the result . . . to the court

Note that the court itself has no further role to play in relation to the approval of the proposal, and that it does not rest with the court to decide whether the scheme shall become binding, unless some qualified party seeks to challenge the approved scheme under s.6 on either of the grounds specified in subs. (1) of that section.

Effect of approval

5.—(1) This section has effect where each of the meetings summoned under section 3 approves the proposed voluntary arrangement either with the same modifications or without modifications.

(2) The approved voluntary arrangement—

(*a*) takes effect as if made by the company at the creditors' meeting, and

(*b*) binds every person who in accordance with the rules had notice of, and was entitled to vote at, that meeting (whether or not he was present or represented at the meeting) as if he were a party to the voluntary arrangement.

(3) Subject as follows, if the company is being wound up or an administration order is in force, the court may do one or both of the following, namely—

(*a*) by order stay or sist all proceedings in the winding up or discharge the administration order;

(*b*) give such directions with respect to the conduct of the winding up or the administration as it thinks appropriate for facilitating the implementation of the approved voluntary arrangement.

(4) The court shall not make an order under subsection (3)(*a*)—

(*a*) at any time before the end of the period of 28 days beginning with the first day on which each of the reports required by section 4(6) has been made to the court, or

(*b*) at any time when an application under the next section or an appeal in respect of such an application is pending, or at any time in the period within which such an appeal may be brought.

DEFINITIONS

"administration order": s.8(2).
"modifications": s.436.
"the rules": ss.251, 411.
"voluntary arrangement": s.1(1).

General Note

This section, corresponding to s.24 of the 1985 Act, specifies the requirements for, and consequences of, the approval of a proposed voluntary arrangement. In addition to the matters mentioned in this section, by virtue of s.233(1)(*c*) the provisions of that section apply when a composition or scheme has taken effect through having been approved by the meetings convened under s.3.

Subs. (1)

This section has effect

This subsection introduces the crucial precondition that formal approval of a proposal put forward under this Part is dependent upon the proposal's being approved in identical terms by *both* of the meetings summoned under s.3. Only then do the effects specified in subs. (2) become operative.

Subs. (2)(b)

Binds every person who in accordance with the rules had notice of, and was entitled to vote at, that meeting

This operates in accordance with the requirement of natural justice that a person should not be bound by the outcome of a meeting of which he did not have notice, so that he lacked the opportunity to participate in its deliberations and voting. On the other hand, any person who was entitled to vote at either of the meetings convened under s.3 and who did receive notice, will be bound by the outcome regardless of whether or not he was present or represented.

Subs. (4)(a)

The delay of 28 days which must occur between the receipt by the court of the reports upon the outcome of the meetings summoned under s.3 and the making of any order under subs. (3)(*a*) corresponds to the interval of time allowed under s.6(3) for the bringing of any challenge under that section against the approved scheme.

Challenge of decisions

6.—(1) Subject to this section, an application to the court may be made, by any of the persons specified below, on one or both of the following grounds, namely—

(*a*) that a voluntary arrangement approved at the meetings summoned under section 3 unfairly prejudices the interests of a creditor, member or contributory of the company;

(*b*) that there has been some material irregularity at or in relation to either of the meetings.

(2) The persons who may apply under this section are—

(*a*) a person entitled, in accordance with the rules, to vote at either of the meetings;

(*b*) the nominee or any person who has replaced him under section 2(4) or 4(2); and

(*c*) if the company is being wound up or an administration order is in force, the liquidator or administrator.

(3) An application under this section shall not be made after the end of the period of 28 days beginning with the first day on which each of the reports required by section 4(6) has been made to the court.

(4) Where on such an application the court is satisfied as to either of the grounds mentioned in subsection (1), it may do one or both of the following, namely—

(*a*) revoke or suspend the approvals given by the meetings or, in a case falling within subsection (1)(*b*), any approval given by the meeting in question;

(*b*) give a direction to any person for the summoning of further meetings to consider any revised proposal the person who made the original proposal may make or, in a case falling within subsection (1)(*b*), a further company or (as the case may be) creditors' meeting to reconsider the original proposal.

(5) Where at any time after giving a direction under subsection (4)(*b*) for the summoning of meetings to consider a revised proposal the court is satisfied that the person who made the original proposal does not intend to submit a revised proposal, the court shall revoke the direction and revoke or suspend any approval given at the previous meetings.

(6) In a case where the court, on an application under this section with respect to any meeting—

(*a*) gives a direction under subsection (4)(*b*), or

(*b*) revokes or suspends an approval under subsection (4)(*a*) or (5),

the court may give such supplemental directions as it thinks fit and, in particular, directions with respect to things done since the meeting under any voluntary arrangement approved by the meeting.

(7) Except in pursuance of the preceding provisions of this section, an approval given at a meeting summoned under section 3 is not invalidated by any irregularity at or in relation to the meeting.

DEFINITIONS

"administration order": s.8(2).
"proposal": s.1(2).
"the administrator": s.8(2).
"the nominee": s.1(2).
"the rules": ss.251, 411.
"voluntary arrangement": s.1(1).

GENERAL NOTE

This section prescribes the steps which may be taken to challenge either the approved voluntary arrangement itself or the manner by which its approval was gained. The section also indicates which persons have standing to make application to the court by way of challenge, the grounds on which such challenge may be based, and the time limit within which the right of challenge is exercisable. Finally, the powers of the court on an application of this kind are laid down. The section corresponds to s.25 of the 1985 Act.

Subs. (1)(a)

Unfairly prejudices the interests of a creditor, member or contributory

No statutory test or guideline is laid down to indicate what degree of prejudice shall be regarded as unfair for the purposes of this subsection.

Subs. (3)

The period of 28 days

This period of time, running from the first day on which each of the reports submitted in accordance with the requirements of s.4(6) is made to the court, corresponds to the period of delay specified in s.5(4)(*a*), so that no order staying the winding up or discharging the administration order will be made by the court until the period has expired during which any qualified party could initiate a challenge to the arrangement whose approval has been reported to the court.

Subs. (7)

The wide effect of this provision ensures that, unless a challenge is mounted under the foregoing provisions of this section within the limited time allowed, an arrangement which has been ostensibly approved in the requisite manner cannot otherwise be invalidated despite the fact that at either of the meetings some irregularity may have occurred which could have formed the basis of a successful challenge, had the procedure been invoked in time.

Implementation of proposal

7.—(1) This section applies where a voluntary arrangement approved by the meetings summoned under section 3 has taken effect.

(2) The person who is for the time being carrying out in relation to the voluntary arrangement the functions conferred—

(*a*) by virtue of the approval on the nominee, or
(*b*) by virtue of section 2(4) or 4(2) on a person other than the nominee,

shall be known as the supervisor of the voluntary arrangement.

(3) If any of the company's creditors or any other person is dissatisfied by any act, omission or decision of the supervisor, he may apply to the court; and on the application the court may—

(*a*) confirm, reverse or modify any act or decision of the supervisor,
(*b*) give him directions, or
(*c*) make such other order as it thinks fit.

(4) The supervisor—

(*a*) may apply to the court for directions in relation to any particular matter arising under the voluntary arrangement, and
(*b*) is included among the persons who may apply to the court for the winding up of the company or for an administration order to be made in relation to it.

(5) The court may, whenever—

(*a*) it is expedient to appoint a person to carry out the functions of the supervisor, and
(*b*) it is inexpedient, difficult or impracticable for an appointment to be made without the assistance of the court,

make an order appointing a person who is qualified to act as an insolvency practitioner in relation to the company, either in substitution for the existing supervisor or to fill a vacancy.

(6) The power conferred by subsection (5) is exercisable so as to increase the number of persons exercising the functions of supervisor or, where there is more than one person exercising those functions, so as to replace one or more of those persons.

DEFINITIONS

"administration order": s.8(2).
"person qualified to act as an insolvency practitioner": s.390.
"the court": s.251; Companies Act 1985, s.744.
"the nominee": s.1(2).
"the supervisor of the voluntary arrangement": subs. (2).
"to act as an insolvency practitioner": s.388.
"voluntary arrangement": s.1(1).

GENERAL NOTE

This deals with the ensuing phases of implementation of an arrangement which has taken effect following approval under the foregoing sections of this Part. The formal title of "supervisor" attaches for the first time to the person who has hitherto carried out his functions in the capacity of "nominee" or as substitute for the nominee. Under ss.388(1)(*b*) and 389 it is a criminal offence for a person to act as supervisor of a composition or scheme at a time when he is not qualified to do so. Provision is made for any interested party to apply to the court in the event that the supervisor's conduct in office proves unsatisfactory, and the court enjoys overriding powers in relation to anything the supervisor may have done, and can issue directions to him as to his future conduct of his responsibilities. Correspondingly, the supervisor may take the initiative in seeking directions from the court by way of an application, and is clothed with the important right to apply for the company to be wound up or for an administration order to be made. Finally, the court enjoys the right to replace any person as supervisor, and to appoint further persons to act in that capacity either instead of or in addition to any person who may previously have exercised the functions of supervisor. This section corresponds to s.26 of the 1985 Act.

Part II

Administration Orders

Making etc. of administration order

Power of court to make order

8.—(1) Subject to this section, if the court—

(*a*) is satisfied that a company is or is likely to become unable to pay its debts (within the meaning given to that expression by section 123 of this Act), and

(*b*) considers that the making of an order under this section would be likely to achieve one or more of the purposes mentioned below,

the court may make an administration order in relation to the company.

(2) An administration order is an order directing that, during the period for which the order is in force, the affairs, business and property of the company shall be managed by a person ("the administrator") appointed for the purpose by the court.

(3) The purposes for whose achievement an administration order may be made are—

(*a*) the survival of the company, and the whole or any part of its undertaking, as a going concern;

(*b*) the approval of a voluntary arrangement under Part 1;

(*c*) the sanctioning under section 425 of the Companies Act of a compromise or arrangement between the company and any such persons as are mentioned in that section; and

(*d*) a more advantageous realisation of the company's assets than would be effected on a winding up;

and the order shall specify the purpose or purposes for which it is made.

(4) An administration order shall not be made in relation to a company after it has gone into liquidation, nor where it is—

(*a*) an insurance company within the meaning of the Insurance Companies Act 1982, or

(*b*) a recognised bank or licensed institution within the meaning of the Banking Act 1979, or an institution to which sections 16 and 18 of that Act apply as if it were a licensed institution.

Definitions

"administration order": subs. (2).
"administrator": subs. (2).
"goes into liquidation": s.247(2).
"insurance company": Insurance Companies Act 1982, ss.1, 96(1); Sched. 1, 2.
"recognised bank or licensed institution": Banking Act 1975, ss.48, 50.
"the court": s.251; Companies Act 1985, s.744.
"unable to pay its debts": subs. (1)(*a*); s.123.

Transitional Provision: Sched. 11, para. 1.

General Note

This section, together with the following provisions contained in ss.9–27 inclusive, comprising Pt. II of the Act, establishes a new, alternative procedure for dealing with the affairs of a potentially or actually insolvent company. The procedure, known as the administration order procedure, is aimed at procuring the rehabilitation and survival of the company as a going concern or, failing that, at securing a more advantageous realisation of the company's assets than would ensue from a winding up. The procedure can also be used in conjunction with an attempt to conclude an effective composition or arrangement between the company and its creditors. The proposal to establish such an institutionalised process of "company rescue" was one of the principal innovations of the *Cork Report,* chap. 9 of which bears the heading "the Administrator," after the title proposed for the insolvency practitioner whose appointment would arise from the making of an administration order but whose task it would become to carry out the order's objectives. The Government in their White Paper voiced agreement with this proposal for a new insolvency mechanism, and in two chapters (chaps. 6 and 14 respectively, headed "the Administrator" and "the Administrator Procedure") set out their own somewhat different vision of what the procedure would involve.

The inspirational model for the administrator was the receiver and manager (henceforth to be known as an administrative receiver) appointed under a floating charge: tribute was paid in para. 495 of the *Cork Report* to the successes in terms of the rescue and rehabilitation of ailing companies, which can be achieved by a combination of skill and imagination on the part of such a receiver and manager in the exercise of the powers conferred upon him by the terms of his appointment under a suitably-drafted floating charge. The powers conferred upon the administrator by virtue of the provisions within Pt. II of the Act are deliberately analogous to those of a receiver and manager which are to be found in Chap. I of Pt. III, although the basis of his appointment, and the formulation of the task with which he is entrusted, differ from those associated with the exercise of rights enjoyed by an individual creditor whose debt is secured by means of a floating charge. This section corresponds to s.27 of the 1985 Act.

Subs. (1)

This subsection indicates the circumstances in which the court is empowered to make an administration order in relation to a company.

The court may make an administration order

The terms of this subsection are permissive, not mandatory, and the court's powers in this respect are exercisable at its own discretion. The circumstances in which the court's discretion to make an administration order becomes exercisable are specified in paragraphs (*a*) and (*b*) of the subsection in the form of a compound requirement, each limb of which must be satisfied. The first precondition, expressed in para. (*a*), is that the court must be satisfied that the company is, or is likely to become, unable to pay its debts. The subsection incorporates by reference the definition of inability to pay debts which is embodied in s.123 of the Act. Thus any circumstances or facts which would render it possible for the company to be wound up by the court under s.122(1)(*f*) of the Act may in the alternative be utilised as the basis for making an administration order if application for this alternative species of order is duly made under s.9.

The second precondition to the court's being at liberty to make an administration order is contained in para. (*b*) which stipulates that the court must form the opinion that the making of such an order would be likely to promote one or more of the alternative purposes mentioned in paras. (*a*)–(*d*) inclusive of subs. (3). These grounds represent a relatively restricted approach to the operability of the administrator procedure as compared with the more open-ended vision of the authors of the *Cork Report* and are indeed more restrictively framed than the terms of the *White Paper* suggested they would be. Indeed, para. 506 of the *Cork Report* ventured the suggestion that it would be unwise to prescribe in legislative form the exact circumstances under which it would be expedient to appoint an administrator. Nevertheless, both the *Report* and the *White Paper* (para. 151) went on to declare, in almost identical terms, that a court should not consider appointing an administrator unless either of two alternative propositions was established. While the first alternative effectively corresponds to the "purpose" expressed in subs. (3)(*a*), there is no direct statutory equivalent of the second one, namely that "the interests of creditors, shareholders, employees or other interested parties would be better served by an administration order rather than some form of insolvency proceedings." The "purpose" currently expressed in subs. (3)(*d*) is at once more narrow and more specific than that.

Subs. (2)

This subsection supplies the statutory definition of the related terms "administrator" and "administration order." The subsection simply establishes an association between these two new terms of insolvency law and renders it necessary to infer that "the administrator" means "the person appointed by the court under an administration order for the purpose of managing the affairs, business and property of the company during the period for which the order is in force."

Subs. (4)

An administration order shall not be made . . .

In addition to the requirements imposed by way of precondition by the combined provisions of subs. (1) and subs. (3), the opening words of the former have the further effect that an administration order cannot be made in relation to a company if any of the three alternative propositions expressed in subs. (4) is true of it.

After the company has gone into liquidation

The unqualified terms of this proposition have the effect of precluding the making of an administration order after the company has already gone into any form of liquidation. The statutory meaning of the expression "goes into liquidation" is given in s.247(2).

(a) Where the company is an insurance company

The reason for this exclusion, given in para. 35 of the *White Paper,* is that such companies are the subject of special requirements in the Insurance Companies legislation, so that separate consideration will need to be given to the practicability of extending the administrator procedure to companies of this kind. Such a development, if it eventually takes place, will be effected by an amendment to the Insurance Companies legislation itself.

Finally, it may be noted that a further, mandatory ground on which the court's power to make an administration order is taken away arises from the provisions of s.9(3) which impose a mandatory obligation to dismiss the applications for an administration order in the circumstances there described.

Application for order

9.—(1) An application to the court for an administration order shall be by petition presented either by the company or the directors, or by a creditor or creditors (including any contingent or prospective creditor or creditors), or by all or any of those parties, together or separately.

(2) Where a petition is presented to the court—

(*a*) notice of the petition shall be given forthwith to any person who has appointed, or is or may be entitled to appoint, an administrative receiver of the company, and to such other persons as may be prescribed, and

(*b*) the petition shall not be withdrawn except with the leave of the court.

(3) Where the court is satisfied that there is an administrative receiver of the company, the court shall dismiss the petition unless it is also satisfied either—

(*a*) that the person by whom or on whose behalf the receiver was appointed has consented to the making of the order, or

(*b*) that, if an administration order were made, any security by virtue of which the receiver was appointed would—

(i) be liable to be released or discharged under sections 238 to 240 in Part VI (transactions at an undervalue and preferences),

(ii) be avoided under section 245 in that Part (avoidance of floating charges), or

(iii) be challengeable under section 242 (gratuitous alienations) or 243 (unfair preferences) in that Part, or under any rule of law in Scotland.

(4) Subject to subsection (3), on hearing a petition the court may dismiss it, or adjourn the hearing conditionally or unconditionally, or make an interim order or any other order that it thinks fit.

(5) Without prejudice to the generality of subsection (4), an interim order under that subsection may restrict the exercise of any powers of the directors or of the company (whether by reference to the consent of the court or of a person qualified to act as an insolvency practitioner in relation to the company, or otherwise).

DEFINITIONS

"administration order": s.8(2).

"administrative receiver": ss.29(2), 51, 251.

"person qualified to act as an insolvency practitioner": s.390.

"prescribed": s.251.

"the court": s.251; Companies Act 1985, s.744.
"to act as an insolvency practitioner": s.388.

General Note

This provision describes how an administration order may be obtained, the prescribed procedure being the presentation of a petition to the court by all or any of the parties referred to in subs. (1). There is also an important safeguard in subs. (3) to ensure that the position of a creditor who has appointed an administrative receiver of the company cannot be eroded against his will, unless that creditor's security is impeachable.

As was observed in the General Note to s.8 the inspiration of the development of the administrator procedure was derived in part from the appreciation of the constructive role capable of being played by a receiver and manager (henceforth to be known as an administrative receiver) where one can be appointed. The main purpose of the new procedure is therefore to ensure that such a rehabilitative programme can be undertaken in relation to any company able to benefit therefrom, regardless of whether there happens to exist a floating charge under whose terms an administrative receiver could be appointed by the creditor in whose favour the charge was created. It is not however part of the legislative intention to undercut the position of any creditor who takes a floating charge in this way, because the right to appoint a receiver is an integral aspect of the security device itself, and its erosion would have wide and serious implications for the whole realm of credit and security. Therefore, in line with the proposal in para. 153 of the *White Paper* (with which *cf.* the notably less absolute terms of paras. 503–504 of the *Cork Report*), subs. (3) protects the position of a debenture holder who has already appointed an administrative receiver by the time that an application for an administration order is heard by the court. In such circumstances the court is required to dismiss the application unless the debenture holder is prepared to consent in the making of an administration order. However, if it can be shown that the security on which the debenture holder's position is based is in reality capable of being overturned by virtue of either ss.238–240, 242, 243 or 245 of the Act, the court remains free to proceed at its discretion to make an administration order. Thereafter by virtue of s.11(3)(*b*) the right of any holder of a floating charge to appoint an administrative receiver becomes suspended for the period during which the order is in force. Bearing in mind that the provisions contained in Pt. III of the Act have in part the effect of ensuring that the duties of the administrative receiver will in future be owed on a more generally conceived basis than hitherto, the attempt has been made to strike a balance between the interests of the various parties involved, namely the debenture holder, the general body of creditors and the company itself, its members and its employees. This section corresponds to s.28 of the 1985 Act.

Subs. (1)

Application to the court

By virtue of s.251 any expression for whose interpretation provision is made in Pt. XXVI of the Companies Act and for which no definition is supplied by s.251 of this Act, is to be construed in accordance with the provision contained in the Companies Act. Hence the expression "court" should be understood in the sense laid down by s.744 of the Companies Act, namely "the court having jurisdiction to wind up the company."

The directors of the company are included among the various parties or combinations of parties on whom this subsection confers the right to make application for an administration order. There is no requirement that the directors need first obtain the endorsement of a general meeting of members before they present an application for an administration order. However, the drafting confines the right to make such application to the board of directors acting collectively and denies an individual director the standing to do so on his own. Nevertheless, if one or more individual directors vainly seek to persuade their colleagues that an administration order should be applied for, their actions may be of some significance from the aspect of their personal position and potential liability should the company subsequently pass into liquidation. This is because in determining a director's responsibility for a company's wrongful trading the court is required by s.214(3) to have regard to the steps taken by him with a view to minimising the potential loss to creditors. The fact that any of the directors is or are on record as having advocated recourse to the administration order procedure should help to ensure that the directors concerned are absolved from the sanctions and disabilities which are inflicted upon their colleagues on the board.

It may be noted that the suggestions in the *Cork Report* (para. 500) that a petition for an administration order should also be capable of being presented by the Secretary of State for Trade, or that the court should be empowered to make such an appointment *proprio motu* in lieu of an order for winding up (para. 510), were not adopted in the *White Paper* nor incorporated into the Act.

Subs. (2)

Notice of the petition

The requirement that notice of the presentation of a petition for an administration order must be given forthwith to any debenture holder (and to any other persons to be prescribed in the rules) is a necessary counterpart to the provisions in subs. (3)(*a*) whereby such persons are effectively enabled to prevent the court from making the order by the act of withholding their consent thereto. At the hearing of the petition it will be necessary to satisfy the court that the debenture holder has positively consented to the making of the order, otherwise the court is obliged to dismiss the petition. It is made a statutory duty that the requisite notice must be given "forthwith," but no indication is given as to who is required to give the notice although it is perhaps implicit that this duty is incumbent upon the party by whom the petition is presented. More detailed provision as to the manner in which such notice is to be given to debenture holders will be embodied in the company insolvency rules. The subsection is also silent as to whether, in the event that the petition for an administration order is presented by one or more creditors, there is any formal requirement that notice of the petition be sent to the company itself, in order that it may appear and be represented at the actual hearing by the court. This elementary requirement of justice, which was expressly proposed in para. 502 of the *Cork Report,* is a matter for which provision will be made in the insolvency rules and is presaged by the concluding reference to the giving of notice to "such other persons as may be prescribed."

Subs. (2)(b)

This provision enables the court to deal in an appropriate way with any petitions which prove to be vexatious or frivolous.

Subs. (3)(a)

The person . . . has consented to the making of the order

These words render it essential that the debenture holder by or on behalf of whom an administrative receiver was appointed must actually have given his positive consent to the making of an administration order. It would not be sufficient for the petitioner to show merely that the debenture holder has not expressed his dissent to the making of an administration order. However the position of a debenture holder who is merely entitled to appoint an administrative receiver but who has not yet done so by the time the petition for an administration order is heard, is not protected by this subsection. Earlier versions of the corresponding provision in the Insolvency Bill of 1984–85, which also gave such creditors a power of veto over the making of an administration order, were modified during the successive phases of transformation undergone by the 1985 Act during its passage through Parliament, with the result that a protected position is enjoyed only by a debenture holder who has actually appointed a receiver by the time of the hearing of the petition for an administration order.

Subss. (4), (5)

These provisions indicate that, apart from those cases where by virtue of subs. (3) the court is under a mandatory obligation to dismiss the petition, it enjoys a range of discretionary powers enabling it to respond to and deal with the instant case in the light of all the various interests involved.

Effect of application

10.—(1) During the period beginning with the presentation of a petition for an administration order and ending with the making of such an order or the dismissal of the petition—

(*a*) no resolution may be passed or order made for the winding up of the company;

(*b*) no steps may be taken to enforce any security over the company's property, or to repossess goods in the company's possession under any hire-purchase agreement, except with the leave of the court and subject to such terms as the court may impose; and

(*c*) no other proceedings and no execution or other legal process may be commenced or continued, and no distress may be levied, against the company or its property except with the leave of the court and subject to such terms as aforesaid.

(2) Nothing in subsection (1) requires the leave of the court—

(*a*) for the presentation of a petition for the winding up of the company,

(*b*) for the appointment of an administrative receiver of the company, or

(*c*) for the carrying out by such a receiver (whenever appointed) of any of his functions.

(3) Where—

(*a*) a petition for an administration order is presented at a time when there is an administrative receiver of the company, and

(*b*) the person by or on whose behalf the receiver was appointed has not consented to the making of the order,

the period mentioned in subsection (1) is deemed not to begin unless and until that person so consents.

(4) References in this section and the next to hire-purchase agreements include conditional sale agreements, chattel leasing agreements and retention of title agreements.

(5) In the application of this section and the next to Scotland, references to execution being commenced or continued include references to diligence being carried out or continued, and references to distress being levied shall be omitted.

Definitions

"administration order": s.8(2).
"administrative receiver": ss.29(2), 51, 251.
"chattel leasing agreement": s.251.
"conditional sale agreement": s.436; Consumer Credit Act 1974, s.198(1).
"hire purchase agreement": subs. (4); s.436; Consumer Credit Act 1974, s.189(1).
"property": s.436.
"retention of title agreement": s.251.

General Note

This section has the effect of imposing a moratorim over the company's affairs during the period between the date of presentation of a petition for an administration order and the date on which the court either makes the order sought or dismisses the petition. In particular no steps may be taken during that time to bring about the winding up of the company by means of a resolution for voluntary winding up, and no order for compulsory winding up may be made, although a winding up petition may be presented during this period. Simultaneously creditors' rights to enforce any security or charge, or to commence or continue other remedies or proceedings against the company or its property, can only be exercised with the leave of the court and subject to terms. This section corresponds to s.29 of the 1985 Act.

Subs. (1)

This provision defines the period of time during which a moratorium or "freeze" is imposed upon certain important aspects of the company's affairs, and also specifies the matters to which the "freezing" effect is applicable. As to the former, the period of time commences with the presentation (by a duly qualified party) of a petition for an administration order, and ends when the court disposes of the application by either making an administration order or dismissing the petition. As to the latter, the proceedings or steps which are forbidden to be taken during the aforesaid period are specified in paras. (*a*), (*b*) and (*c*) which are so drafted as to represent an exhaustive list of matters to which the "freeze" applies. Para. (*a*) prevents the company itself from passing a resolution for winding up (under s.84 of the Act), and also prevents any court before which proceedings for compulsory winding up of the company are already in progress from making an order for winding up. Since the paragraph contains no reference to the stage at which winding up proceedings may have arrived by the time the petition for an Administration Order is presented, it is accordingly possible for such a "stay of execution" to be attained through the taking of the requisite steps even at the very eleventh hour provided that the court before which winding up proceedings are in progress has not actually made an order for the winding up of the company. However as the petition for an Administration Order is presented to the court with jurisdiction to wind up the company it should be possible to dispose relatively speedily of any petition which is apparently presented (*e.g.* by the directors) for the purpose of delaying the making of an order for winding up.

Subs. (1)(b)

No steps may be taken

This subsubsection lists certain procedural steps which might otherwise be taken by creditors in relation to property belonging to or in the possession of the company, and which are forbidden to be taken without the leave of the court during the period for which the "freeze" is effective. These are, any steps to enforce any charge on or security over the company's property or steps to repossess any goods in the possession of the company under any retention of title agreement or under any hire purchase agreement, conditional sale agreement or chattel leasing agreement (the latter two types of agreement, and also the first type, being incorporated into the scope of this paragraph by virtue of subs. (4)).

Hire-purchase agreement

This is defined by s.189(1) of the Consumer Credit Act 1974 as "an agreement, other than a conditional sale agreement, under which (a) goods are bailed or (in Scotland), hired in return for periodical payments by the person to whom they are bailed or hired, and (b) the property in the goods will pass to the person if the terms of the agreement are complied with and one or more of the following occurs: (i) the exercise of an option to purchase by that person: (ii) the doing of any other specified act by any party to the agreement; (iii) the happening of any other specified event."

Conditional sale agreement

This is also defined by s.189(1) of the Consumer Credit Act 1984 and means "an agreement for the sale of goods or land under which the purchase price or part of it is payable by instalments, and the property in the goods or land is to remain in the seller (notwithstanding that the buyer is to be in possession of the goods or land) until such conditions as to the payment of instalments or otherwise as may be specified in the agreement are fulfilled."

Chattel leasing agreement

This is defined in s.251 as "an agreement for the bailment, or in Scotland, the hiring of goods, which is capable of subsisting for more than three months."

Retention of title agreement

This is defined in s.251 as "an agreement for the sale of goods to a company, being an agreement (*a*) which does not constitute a charge on the goods; but (*b*) under which, if the seller is not paid and the company is wound up, the seller will have priority over all other creditors of the company as respects the goods or any property representing the goods."

If the court grants the requisite leave to a creditor to whom the provisions of this paragraph apply, terms may be attached to the granting of leave, at the court's unfettered discretion.

Subs. (1)(c) No other proceedings . . .

This is so drafted as to give rise to a comprehensive prohibition against the commencement or continuation without the leave of the court of any other species of proceedings, or execution or other legal process, against the company apart from those already specifically covered by para. (*b*). However, the potential effects of this form of drafting are cut back by subs. (2), which excludes the three types of act therein described from being caught by the "freeze" imposed by subs. (1). Thus a petition for winding up the company may be presented (albeit the court may not make an order until the administration order application has been disposed of) and a debenture holder may appoint an administrative receiver of the company (by availing himself of the protection afforded by s.9(3)). It should be noted, however, that if a person entitled to appoint an administrative receiver does not avail himself of this final opportunity to do so following the presentation of a petition for an administration order, he will thereafter lose the right to resort to this remedy during the period for which the order is in force: s.11(3)(*b*).

Subs. (3)

The suspension introduced by this provision with regard to the commencement of the period of moratorium over the company's affairs is a logical counterpart to the provision in s.9(3) whereby the court is obliged to dismiss the petition at the eventual hearing if the consent of the debenture holder has not by then been obtained.

Effect of order

11.—(1) On the making of an administration order—

(*a*) any petition for the winding up of the company shall be dismissed, and

(*b*) any administrative receiver of the company shall vacate office.

(2) Where an administration order has been made, any receiver of part of the company's property shall vacate office on being required to do so by the administrator.

(3) During the period for which an administration order is in force—

(*a*) no resolution may be passed or order made for the winding up of the company;

(*b*) no administrative receiver of the company may be appointed;

(*c*) no other steps may be taken to enforce any security over the company's property, or to repossess goods in the company's possession under any hire-purchase agreement, except with the consent of the administrator or the leave of the court and subject (where the court gives leave) to such terms as the court may impose; and

(*d*) no other proceedings and no execution or other legal process may be commenced or continued, and no distress may be levied, against the company or its property except with the consent of the administrator or the leave of the court and subject (where the court gives leave) to such terms as aforesaid.

(4) Where at any time an administrative receiver of the company has vacated office under subsection (1)(*b*), or a receiver of part of the company's property has vacated office under subsection (2)—

(*a*) his remuneration and any expenses properly incurred by him, and

(*b*) any indemnity to which he is entitled out of the assets of the company,

shall be charged on and (subject to subsection (3) above) paid out of any property of the company which was in his custody or under his control at that time in priority to any security held by the person by or on whose behalf he was appointed.

(5) Neither an administrative receiver who vacates office under subsection (1)(*b*) nor a receiver who vacates office under subsection (2) is required on or after so vacating office to take any steps for the purpose of complying with any duty imposed on him by section 40 or 59 of this Act (duty to pay preferential creditors).

Definitions

"administration order": s.8(2).
"administrative receiver": ss.29(2), 51, 251.
"administrator": s.8(2).
"chattel leasing agreement": ss.10(4), 251.
"conditional sale agreement": ss.10(4), 436; Consumer Credit Act 1974, s.189(1).
"hire purchase agreement": ss.10(4), 436; Consumer Credit Act 1974, s.189(1).
"receiver": s.251.
"retention of title agreement": ss.10(4), 251.

General Note

The provisions of this section are applicable in most cases where the court makes an administration order in response to a petition presented under s.9. They have the effect in the first place of maintaining the general moratorium over the company's affairs which by virtue of s.10 commences with the presentation of the petition. To a certain extent therefore the provisions of s.11 simply complement those of s.10, but in certain other respects they go further. Thus under subss. (3)(*a*), (*c*) and (*d*), for the duration of the administration order remaining in force no steps may be taken to bring about the winding up of the company, and no steps to enforce any charge or security or to repossess goods may be taken, and no other proceedings or execution may be commenced or continued against the company or its property except with the consent of the administrator or the leave of the court, and subject to any terms which the court may impose. While these stipulations closely match those to be found in s.10, there is an additional stipulation in subs. (*b*) to forbid the appointment of an administrative receiver after an administration order has been made (in contrast to the position which obtains up until that moment by virtue of s.10(2)(*b*)). Moreover the sweeping provisions of subss. (1) and (2) have the effect that, once an administration order is made, other insolvency procedures are rendered inapplicable, any winding up petition must be dismissed and any administrative receiver must vacate the office, as must any receiver of part of the company's property if so required by the administrator, thus leaving the administrator himself free to embark upon his duties. This section corresponds to s.30 of the 1985 Act.

Subs. (1)(b)

Any administrative receiver of the company shall vacate office

A debenture holder who has appointed an administrative receiver before a petition for an administration order is presented, or who appoints one subsequently when still able to do so by virtue of s.10(2)(*b*), will not suffer any loss of protection because s.9(3) renders it obligatory for the court to dismiss the application for an administration order unless the consent of the debenture holder has been given to the making of the order. However, any debenture holder whose consent is sought should be aware of the consequences from his point of view, for not only must the administrative receiver whom he has appointed vacate office under this subsection, but by subs. (2)(*b*) no other appointment of an administrative receiver may be made for so long as the administration order is in force. This is the necessary corollary to the careful protection of the debenture holder's position and expectations maintained by the provisions of s.9(2)(*a*) and (3), and 10(2)(*b*): having been given due notice of the petition for an administration order, together with the opportunity to prevent the order from being made, a debenture holder who has elected instead to allow the administration order procedure to be embarked upon is not allowed to renege upon that decision until the administration order has run its course.

Subs. (3)(c)

Hire-purchase agreement

By virtue of s.10(4) this term is to be taken as referring also to conditional sale agreements, chattel leasing agreements and retention of title agreements. The statutory definitions of all four terms are reproduced above in the note to s.10(2)(*b*).

Subs. (3)(d)

No execution

By virtue of s.10(5), in relation to Scotland this term is to be construed as a reference to diligence.

Notification of order

12.—(1) Every invoice, order for goods or business letter which, at a time when an administration order is in force in relation to a company, is issued by or on behalf of the company or the administrator, being a document on or in which the company's name appears, shall also contain the administrator's name and a statement that the affairs, business and property of the company are being managed by the administrator.

(2) If default is made in complying with this section, the company and any of the following persons who without reasonable excuse authorises or permits the default, namely, the administrator and any officer of the company, is liable to a fine.

DEFINITIONS

"a fine": s.430; Sched. 10.

"administration order": s.8(2).

"administrator": s.8(2).
"business": s.436.
"officer of the company . . . in default": s.430(5).
"property": s.436.

General Note

This section is designed to ensure that persons dealing with the company during the period when an administration order is in force are furnished with proper notification of the fact that its affairs are being managed by an administrator, notice to that effect being required to be contained in every document bearing the company's name which is employed in business transactions. It is closely modelled upon the provision now contained in s.39 of the Act regarding notification of the appointment of a receiver and manager. The requirement of notice is especially important in that it enables any party dealing with the company to assess the implications of dealing with the company on credit terms, since it is necessary to contemplate the possibility that the administrator may not succeed in his basic objectives, and that the company may subsequently pass into an insolvent liquidation. The seriousness of the need to ensure that proper notification is given to parties dealing with the company is indicated by the fact that the sanction of criminality is employed as the means of seeking to ensure compliance with this requirement. Moreover the very fact that any default has been made constitutes an offence on the part of the company, irrespective of whether the person actually responsible for the act in question had a reasonable excuse or not. This section corresponds to s.31 of the 1985 Act.

Subs. (1)

Invoice, order for goods or business letter

The requirement concerning notification applies only in relation to three specified types of business document, and only where the company's name appears on or in the document in question. Thus a purely oral communication—or one conveyed by means of a telegram, telemessage or telex—would seem to be exempt from the requirements of this section whether the company's name is mentioned therein or not. So, too, would any business document which did not take the form of either an "invoice, order for goods or business letter", for example a receipt, a catalogue or brochure, or even a cheque. Moreover even a business document which did assume the form of an invoice, order for goods or business letter would be outside the ambit of the section, provided that the company's name itself did not appear. It will be a matter of integrity however for the person acting as administrator—mindful, naturally, of the criteria attaching to the obtaining and retention of a licence to act as an insolvency practitioner—to ensure that during the period in which the management of the company's affairs, business and property is his responsibility nothing is done which contravenes the spirit, as well as the letter, of this section of the Act. Contrast may be made, however, with the far wider terms of s.349 of the Companies Act in relation to the requirement that the company's name must appear in legible characters on all letters, notices and other official publications of the company.

At a time when an administration order is in force

This further delimits the requirement of notification in terms of the time during which any failure in respect of notification will give rise to the commission of a criminal offence. The section requires that the offending document must be "issued" at a time when an administration order is in force. Therefore if no such order was in force at the time when the document was "issued" (a term whose legal meaning is not defined in the Act), no offence will be committed even though, quite possibly, the order may have come into force by the time that the document is received or read by a party to whom notice of the administration order would be of relevance or interest.

Being a document on or in which the company's name appears

Any attempt to evade the operation of this subsection by omitting to mention the company's name on or in a document belonging to one of the three categories to which the requirement of notification attaches would at any rate give rise to the commission of an offence under s.349 of the Companies Act, which imposes the requirement that the company's name must appear in legible characters in a wide variety of documents including all business letters of the company, all orders for money or goods, and all bills of parcels, invoices, receipts and letters of credit of the company. The maximum fines which, by virtue of this provision of the Companies Act, may be imposed upon the company, or upon any officer of the company responsible for the contravention in question, are £400 in respect of each party liable, as specified by Sched. 24 to the Companies Act.

Subs. (2)

The company . . . is liable

It is apparently not open to the company to plead, in defence to a prosecution under this section, that the person by whom the default was authorised or permitted had a reasonable excuse for the action taken, even where that excuse results in the person in question escaping from conviction in the selfsame case.

Without reasonable excuse

These words relate solely to the persons subsequently referred to specifically as being liable to commit an offence under this section, namely the administrator and any officer of the company. These persons may therefore avoid criminal liability if they are able to furnish a reasonable excuse for their actions. It further follows from the wording of this subsection that if the default occurs through the action of some other person apart from the administrator or an officer of the company, and is done without the permission of any of the persons named in subs. (2), no criminal liability is incurred by any individual.

A fine

See Sched. 10 to the Act, and the General Note thereto, for information as to the maximum amount of the fine which may be imposed in respect of this offence.

Administrators

Appointment of administrator

13.—(1) The administrator of a company shall be appointed either by the administration order or by an order under the next subsection.

(2) If a vacancy occurs by death, resignation or otherwise in the office of the administrator, the court may by order fill the vacancy.

(3) An application for an order under subsection (2) may be made—

(*a*) by any continuing administrator of the company; or

(*b*) where there is no such administrator, by a creditors' committee established under section 26 below; or

(*c*) where there is no such administrator and no such committee, by the company or the directors or by any creditor or creditors of the company.

DEFINITIONS

"administration order": s.8(2).

"administrator": s.8(2).

"creditors' committee": s.26(1).

GENERAL NOTE

This provision governs the basis and mode of appointment of an administrator, and also empowers the court to fill a vacancy in the office of administrator arising after the making of the original administration order. The section corresponds to s.32 of the 1985 Act.

General powers

14.—(1) The administrator of a company—

(*a*) may do all such things as may be necessary for the management of the affairs, business and property of the company, and

(*b*) without prejudice to the generality of paragraph (*a*), has the powers specified in Schedule 1 to this Act;

and in the application of that Schedule to the administrator of a company the words "he" and "him" refer to the administrator.

(2) The administrator also has power—

(*a*) to remove any director of the company and to appoint any person to be a director of it, whether to fill a vacancy or otherwise, and (*b*) to call any meeting of the members or creditors of the company.

(3) The administrator may apply to the court for directions in relation to any particular matter arising in connection with the carrying out of his functions.

(4) Any power conferred on the company or its officers, whether by this Act or the Companies Act or by the memorandum or articles of association, which could be exercised in such a way as to interfere with the exercise by the administrator of his powers is not exercisable except with the consent of the administrator, which may be given either generally or in relation to particular cases.

(5) In exercising his powers the administrator is deemed to act as the company's agent.

(6) A person dealing with the administrator in good faith and for value is not concerned to inquire whether the administrator is acting within his powers.

DEFINITIONS

"administrator": s.8(2).
"business": s.436.
"property": s.436.

GENERAL NOTE

The purpose of this section is to establish the scope and extent of the powers enjoyed by an administrator upon appointment. Effectively, in conjunction with s.17, it provides for the powers and duties of the directors of the company to become exclusively exercisable by the administrator during the period for which the administration order is in force. The administrator thus occupies a position in relation to the company similar to that of an administrative receiver appointed under a floating charge. Although the directors are not automatically dismissed by virtue of the making of the order, their powers are suspended and the administrator has the power, under subs. (2)(*a*), to remove any director and to appoint any person to be a director either in place of or in addition to the members of the existing management team. The sweeping terms of the general powers described in subs. (1)(*a*) are supplemented by the specific provisions of Sched. 1 to the Act, which is made applicable to administrators by virtue of subs. (1)(*b*). An overriding statutory rule is embodied in subs. (4) to prevent any provision being inserted in the company's own memorandum or articles so as to create an impediment to an administrator's freedom of action. It may be noted besides that, although the directors are deprived of their powers of management during the period for which the administration order is in force, their statutory duties—such as the requirement to make annual returns—are not suspended, so that they remain responsible for the timely performance of these matters (*cf.* H.C. Standing Committee E, June 20, 1985, Col. 497). This section corresponds to s.33 of the 1985 Act.

Subs (2)(b)

Power . . . to call any meeting of the members or creditors of the company

The purpose of this power is to enable the administrator to consult creditors and members on matters of importance, and on which their assent is felt to be desirable. One such occasion would occur if, the rehabilitation of the company having been accomplished, the administrator were to prepare the way for his own discharge from office by seeking the confirmation by a meeting of the members of the company of the board of directors he had assembled to resume responsibility for the company's affairs following his departure. At the same time, a meeting of creditors could be convened so as to inform them of the impending development, and to ensure that the new board would command the confidence of the still-unpaid creditors.

Subs. (5)

This provision places the administrator in the same legal position as an administrative receiver in that all his actions in exercise of his official powers are deemed to be performed as agent on behalf of the company, which is thus bound by all that he does and which consequently incurs liability in respect of every action taken by the administrator. However, in contrast to the provisions of s.44 which apply to an administrative receiver, there is no statutory provision to the effect that an administrator contracts with personal liability. Such liability will therefore only arise if there is an express term to that effect in the contract entered into by the administrator as agent of the company.

Subs. (6)

A person dealing with the administrator in good faith and for value

This provision is designed to protect a third party dealing with the administrator in the manner specified, if it should transpire that the act or transaction was one which the administrator in reality had no power to perform. Thus neither the company nor the administrator are able to raise a defence that his act was *ultra vires*. No presumption is expressed to apply in relation to the aspect of good faith, nor as to the question whether value was given, and it will therefore be incumbent upon the third party claiming the protection of the subsection to establish that he did act in good faith, and that the transaction took place for value. The position can thus be contrasted with that arising under s.35 of the Companies Act (formerly s.9(1) of the European Communities Act 1972), which prevents the defence of *ultra vires* being raised against a person dealing with the company in good faith. Moreover a presumption is established by the terms of s.35(2) of the Companies Act to the effect that a person dealing with a company is to be deemed to have acted in good faith unless the contrary is proved, for the purpose of his being able to enjoy the benefit of the protection to which that section gives rise in cases where the transaction in question was one which it either lay outside the capacity of the company to enter into, or lay outside the power of the directors to bind the company thereto.

Power to deal with charged property, etc.

15.—(1) The administrator of a company may dispose of or otherwise exercise his powers in relation to any property of the company which is subject to a security to which this subsection applies as if the property were not subject to the security.

(2) Where, on an application by the administrator, the court is satisfied that the disposal (with or without other assets) of—

(*a*) any property of the company subject to a security to which this subsection applies, or

(*b*) any goods in the possession of the company under a hire-purchase agreement,

would be likely to promote the purpose or one or more of the purposes specified in the administration order, the court may by order authorise the administrator to dispose of the property as if it were not subject to the security or to dispose of the goods as if all rights of the owner under the hire-purchase agreement were vested in the company.

(3) Subsection (1) applies to any security which, as created, was a floating charge; and subsection (2) applies to any other security.

(4) Where property is disposed of under subsection (1), the holder of the security has the same priority in respect of any property of the company directly or indirectly representing the property disposed of as he would have had in respect of the property subject to the security.

(5) It shall be a condition of an order under subsection (2) that—

(*a*) the net proceeds of the disposal, and

(*b*) where those proceeds are less than such amount as may be determined by the court to be the net amount which would be realised on a sale of the property or goods in the open market by a willing vendor, such sums as may be required to make good the deficiency,

shall be applied towards discharging the sums secured by the security or payable under the hire-purchase agreement.

(6) Where a condition imposed in pursuance of subsection (5) relates to two or more securities, that condition requires the net proceeds of the disposal and, where paragraph (*b*) of that subsection applies, the sums mentioned in that paragraph to be applied towards discharging the sums secured by those securities in the order of their priorities.

(7) An office copy of an order under subsection (2) shall, within 14 days after the making of the order, be sent by the administrator to the registrar of companies.

(8) If the administrator without reasonable excuse fails to comply with subsection (7), he is liable to a fine and, for continued contravention, to a daily default fine.

(9) References in this section to hire-purchase agreements include conditional sale agreements, chattel leasing agreements and retention of title agreements.

DEFINITIONS

"administration order": s.8(2).
"administrative receiver": ss.29(2), 51, 251.
"administrator": s.8(2).
"a fine": s.430; Sched. 10.
"chattel leasing agreement": subs. (9), s.251.
"conditional sale agreement": subs. (9), s.436; Consumer Credit Act 1974, s.189(1).
"hire-purchase agreement": subs. (9); s.436; Consumer Credit Act 1974, s.189(1).
"property": s.436.
"retention of title agreement": subs. (9), s.251.

GENERAL NOTE

The function of this section, which corresponds to s.34 of the 1985 Act, is to empower the administrator to deal with and dispose of property of the company which is subject to a fixed or floating charge or to a combination of the two or of any goods in the possession of the company under a hire purchase agreement (as specially defined in subs. (9)). The advantage of such a provision is that by enabling the charged property to be disposed of as if it were not subject to any charge or security, the prospects for such a disposal are enhanced and the disposal value of the assets is maximised. The protection for the secured creditor of the company is that by virtue of subs. (5) the net proceeds of disposal, augmented out of other funds if necessary, must be applied towards discharging the debt whose security has been overreached by the application of this statutory power of disposal. During the process of enacting the 1985 Act, the technical difficulties of drafting a provision which would actually produce the desired legal effects proved to be formidable, and the counterpart of the present section was substituted for the original version as late as the Committee stage in the House of Commons (see H.C. Standing Committee E, June 20, 1985, cols. 483–4 and 537). The provision is intended to enable the administrator to deal with and dispose of property which is subject to a floating charge debenture, including the case where the debenture also contains one or more fixed charges. This purpose is achieved by means of the combined effects of subs. (1) together with subs. (3). Where the charge or security, as created, was a floating charge subss. (1) and (3) together have the effect of enabling the administrator to deal with the property without reference to the court. Where however the charge or security is of any other type, as where the property is covered by a fixed charge only or is subject to a hire-purchase or other agreement (as listed in subs. (9)), the administrator must obtain the authorisation of the court pursuant to subs. (2) before he is able to dispose of the property free from the relevant encumbrance. Since the property or goods which fall within the ambit of subs. (2) are also the subject of the moratorium arising under ss.10(1)(*b*) and 11(3)(*c*), the opportunity is established for the administrator and the owner of the property to negotiate satisfactory terms for the property's continued use or disposal. In the event however that no such agreement is forthcoming, the administrator may seek an order under subs. (2) of this section.

Subs. (5)(a)

The net proceeds of the disposal

This means net of the costs and expenses incurred in making the sale.

Subs. 5(b)

The net amount which would be realised on a sale . . . in the open market

This form of words establishes the maximum level of compensation which is payable to the person who holds a charge or security over property which is disposed of pursuant to a court order under subs. (2). The amount which is to be paid to that person towards the discharge of the debts owed to him by the company is the net amount equivalent to the open market value of the property disposed of. If the sale fails to yield net proceeds at least equal to this notional figure, the administrator must make up the deficiency out of other proceeds from realisations of company assets.

Operation of s.15 in Scotland

16.—(1) Where property is disposed of under section 15 in its application to Scotland, the administrator shall grant to the disponee an appropriate document of transfer or conveyance of the property, and—

(*a*) that document, or

(*b*) where any recording, intimation or registration of the document is a legal requirement for completion of title to the property, that recording, intimation or registration,

has the effect of disencumbering the property of or, as the case may be, freeing the property from the security.

(2) Where goods in the possession of the company under a hire-purchase agreement, conditional sale agreement, chattel leasing agreement or retention of title agreement are disposed of under section 15 in its application to Scotland, the disposal has the effect of extinguishing, as against the disponee, all rights of the owner of the goods under the agreement.

DEFINITIONS

"administrator": s.8(2).
"chattel leasing agreement": ss.15(9), 251.
"conditional sale agreement": ss.15(9), 436; Consumer Credit Act 1974, s.189(1).
"hire purchase agreement": ss.15(9), 436; Consumer Credit Act 1974, s.189(1).
"property": s.436.
"retention of title agreement": ss.15(9), 251.

GENERAL NOTE

This section embodies the provisions formerly contained in subss. (9) and (10) of s.34 of the 1985 Act. These provisions are exclusively applicable to Scotland, and thus a greater clarity is given to the special aspects of the operation of the administrator's powers of disposal under s.15 where these are exercised in Scotland.

General duties

17.—(1) The administrator of a company shall, on his appointment, take into his custody or under his control all the property to which the company is or appears to be entitled.

(2) The administrator shall manage the affairs, business and property of the company—

(*a*) at any time before proposals have been approved (with or without modifications) under section 24 below, in accordance with any directions given by the court, and

(*b*) at any time after proposals have been so approved, in accordance with those proposals as from time to time revised, whether by him or a predecessor of his.

(3) The administrator shall summon a meeting of the company's creditors if—

(*a*) he is requested, in accordance with the rules, to do so by one-tenth, in value, of the company's creditors, or

(*b*) he is directed to do so by the court.

DEFINITIONS

"business": s.436.
"modifications": s.436.
"property": s.436.
"the administrator": s.8(2).
"the rules": ss.251, 411.

General Note

This provision completes the conceptual framework within which the administration order is to operate, by requiring the administrator to take over control of the company's affairs, business and property. Thus he displaces the directors from their functions in relation to the company albeit they remain in office. While the directors' powers are suspended, the administrator is able to fulfil his duties imposed by this section, utilising the powers conferred on him by ss.14, 15 and 16 together with Sched. 1. The administrator's scope for acting is not an unfettered one, because of the requirements in subs. (2) that he act in accordance with any directions that the court may give prior to the approval of his proposals, and thereafter in accordance with the terms of those proposals themselves. A further check on the administrator's conduct will be introduced if the creditors at a meeting summoned under s.23 decide to establish a committee of creditors in accordance with the provisions of s.26. This section corresponds to s.35 of the 1985 Act.

Subs. (1)

The terms of this provision should be compared with those of s.144(1) of the Act with regard to the duties of a liquidator or provisional liquidator upon taking office.

Subs. (2)(b)

Proposals . . . as from time to time revised

See s.25 for the procedure whereby the administrator's proposals may be revised subsequently to their approval, and for the conditions under which this procedure is required to be initiated.

Subs. (3)

If (a) he is requested, in accordance with the rules

The insolvency rules will introduce a restriction upon the number of times such meetings can be convened by use of this coercive procedure, lest a group among the creditors, representing the necessary one-tenth in value, contrive to make a nuisance of themselves and thereby render the administrator's task unduly and unnecessarily onerous.

Discharge or variation of administration order

18.—(1) The administrator of a company may at any time apply to the court for the administration order to be discharged, or to be varied so as to specify an additional purpose.

(2) The administrator shall make an application under this section if—

(*a*) it appears to him that the purpose or each of the purposes specified in the order either has been achieved or is incapable of achievement, or

(*b*) he is required to do so by a meeting of the company's creditors summoned for the purpose in accordance with the rules.

(3) On the hearing of an application under this section, the court may by order discharge or vary the administration order and make such consequential provision as it thinks fit, or adjourn the hearing conditionally or unconditionally, or make an interim order or any other order it thinks fit.

(4) Where the administration order is discharged or varied the administrator shall, within 14 days after the making of the order effecting the discharge or variation, send an office copy of that order to the registrar of companies.

(5) If the administrator without reasonable excuse fails to comply with subsection (4), he is liable to a fine and, for continued contravention, to a daily default fine.

Definitions

"administration order": s.8(2).
"a fine": s.430, Sched. 10.
"the administrator": s.8(2).
"the rules": ss.251, 411.

General Note

This provision enables the administrator to apply to the court for the administration order to be varied or discharged. Such applications may be made at his discretion in the circumstances specified in subs. (1). In the circumstances described in subs. (2) the making of an application is obligatory. The further provisions of the section specify the powers of the court upon hearing any application under subs. (1) or (2), and lay down the steps to be taken by the administrator in the event that his application is successful. This section corresponds to s.36 of the 1985 Act.

Subs. (1)

An additional purpose

The purposes for which an administration order may be made are expressed in s.8(3). By the concluding words of that subsection, the court is required to specify which of the permitted purposes forms the basis of the order. The present subsection therefore caters for the possibility that the administrator's closer acquaintance with the company may persuade him that it would be expedient to include one or more additional purposes which were not specified in the original order. The precise determination of the purposes which are specified in the order is of particular importance, not least because the administrator's proposals, which are to be submitted for approval pursuant to s.23 must be framed with reference to the purpose or purposes specified in the administration order.

Subs. (5)

A fine

See Sched. 10 to the Act, and the General Note thereto.

Vacation of office

19.—(1) The administrator of a company may at any time be removed from office by order of the court and may, in the prescribed circumstances, resign his office by giving notice of his resignation to the court.

(2) The administrator shall vacate office if—

(*a*) he ceases to be qualified to act as an insolvency practitioner in relation to the company, or

(*b*) the administration order is discharged.

(3) Where at any time a person ceases to be administrator, the next two subsections apply.

(4) His remuneration and any expenses properly incurred by him shall be charged on and paid out of any property of the company which is in his custody or under his control at that time in priority to any security to which section 15(1) then applies.

(5) Any sums payable in respect of debts or liabilities incurred, while he was administrator, under contracts entered into or contracts of employment adopted by him or a predecessor of his in the carrying out of his or the predecessor's functions shall be charged on and paid out of any such property as is mentioned in subsection (4) in priority to any charge arising under that subsection.

For this purpose, the administrator is not to be taken to have adopted a contract of employment by reason of anything done or omitted to be done within 14 days after his appointment.

Definitions

"administration order": s.8(2).
"prescribed": s.251.
"property": s.436.
"qualified to act as an insolvency practitioner": s.390.
"to act as an insolvency practitioner in relation to a company": s.388(1).

General Note

This section makes provision for the voluntary or involuntary vacation of his office by the administrator. Provisions are included to safeguard the entitlement of a former administrator to receive his remuneration, and reimbursement of expenses, by means of a preferential charge over any property of the company which is in his custody or control at the time when he ceases to hold office. The terms of this section are similar in many respects to those of ss.171 and 172 (concerning removal of a liquidator in a voluntary and a compulsory winding up respectively) and to a lesser degree those of s.45 (concerning vacation of office by an administrative receiver), and s.62 (cessation of office by a receiver in Scotland). In particular the same approach is adopted with regard to the debts and liabilities of the administrator as that which applies in the case of a liquidator, namely that these form part of the costs of the administration and are payable first out of the assets (*cf.* s.156). This is in contrast with the position under a receivership, whereby the receiver incurs personal liability with a right of indemnity out of the assets (see ss.44(1), 45(3)). This section incorporates those provisions in s.37 of the 1985 Act which dealt with vacation of office by the administrator (subss. (1)–(3) inclusive).

Subs. (5)

The administrator is not to be taken to have adopted a contract of employment by reason of anything done or omitted to be done within 14 days after his appointment

This provision may be compared with that in s.44(2), which gives the same period of grace to an administrative receiver.

Release of administrator

20.—(1) A person who has ceased to be the administrator of a company has his release with effect from the following time, that is to say—

(*a*) in the case of a person who has died, the time at which notice is given to the court in accordance with the rules that he has ceased to hold office;

(*b*) in any other case, such time as the court may determine.

(2) Where a person has his release under this section, he is, with effect from the time specified above, discharged from all liability both in respect of acts or omissions of his in the administration and otherwise in relation to his conduct as administrator.

(3) However, nothing in this section prevents the exercise, in relation to a person who has had his release as above, of the court's powers under section 212 in Chapter X of Part IV (summary remedy against delinquent directors, liquidators, etc.).

DEFINITIONS

"the administrator": s.8(2).

"the rules": ss.251, 411.

GENERAL NOTE

This section incorporates those provisions in s.37 of the 1985 Act which dealt with release of the administrator following his vacation of office (subss. (4) and (5) of that section). The time when such release takes effect is indicated in subs. (1) and the legal significance of the concept of release is explained in subs. (2).

Subs. (3)

The court's powers under s.212

This saving provision in respect of the powers of the court under the section referred to ensures that, although the release of the administrator under this section has the effect of discharging him from liabilities of a contractual or tortious nature in respect of his conduct in office he shall remain amenable to the summary procedure established by s.212 which may be employed against a variety of persons who have been officers of, or who have acted as liquidator, administrator or administrative receiver of a company and in that capacity have misapplied or retained or otherwise dealt improperly with any money or other property of the company. Similar provisions to preserve the effects of s.212 are contained in ss.173(4) and 174(6) in relation to the release of the liquidator in a voluntary and in a compulsory winding up respectively.

Ascertainment and investigation of company's affairs

Information to be given by administrator

21.—(1) Where an administration order has been made, the administrator shall—

(*a*) forthwith send to the company and publish in the prescribed manner a notice of the order, and

(*b*) within 28 days after the making of the order, unless the court otherwise directs, send such a notice to all creditors of the company (so far as he is aware of their addresses).

(2) Where an administration order has been made, the administrator shall also, within 14 days after the making of the order, send an office copy of the order to the registrar of companies and to such other persons as may be prescribed.

(3) If the administrator without reasonable excuse fails to comply with this section, he is liable to a fine and, for continued contravention, to a daily default fine.

DEFINITIONS

"administration order": s.8(2).
"a fine": s.430; Sched. 10.
"prescribed": s.251.
"the administrator": s.8(2).

GENERAL NOTE

This section establishes a duty to be fulfilled by the administrator on appointment, whereby he is required to publish the order in the manner to be prescribed in the rules. He is also required to send notice of the administration order to the company itself, to all creditors of whose addresses he is aware, and finally (in the form of a sealed copy of the order of the court) to the registrar of companies. The period of time within which the administrator is required to perform each of these functions differs according to the identity of the party to whom notice is required to be given, and it is made a criminal offence for the administrator to contravene any requirement of the section without reasonable excuse. This section corresponds to s.38 of the 1985 Act.

Subs. (1)(b)

(so far as he is aware of their addresses)

It is apparently not incumbent upon the administrator to go to inordinate lengths in order to ascertain the addresses of the company's creditors: he must use his best endeavours and make reasonable enquiries and searches, but if he cannot thereby find a creditor's address he is under no obligation to search far and wide to discover it (*cf.* H.C. Standing Committee E, June 20, 1985, col. 492).

Subs. (3)

A fine

See the Note to Sched. 10 for explanation of the levels of fines which may be imposed by a court before which an administrator is convicted of a criminal offence under this section.

Statement of affairs to be submitted to administrator

22.—(1) Where an administration order has been made, the administrator shall forthwith require some or all of the persons mentioned below to make out and submit to him a statement in the prescribed form as to the affairs of the company.

(2) The statement shall be verified by affidavit by the persons required to submit it and shall show—

(*a*) particulars of the company's assets, debts and liabilities;

(*b*) the names and addresses of its creditors;

(*c*) the securities held by them respectively;

(*d*) the dates when the securities were respectively given; and (*e*) such further or other information as may be prescribed.

(3) The persons referred to in subsection (1) are—

(*a*) those who are or have been officers of the company;

(*b*) those who have taken part in the company's formation at any time within one year before the date of the administration order;

(*c*) those who are in the company's employment or have been in its employment within that year, and are in the administrator's opinion capable of giving the information required;

(*d*) those who are or have been within that year officers of or in the employment of a company which is, or within that year was, an officer of the company.

In this subsection "employment" includes employment under a contract for services.

(4) Where any persons are required under this section to submit a statement of affairs to the administrator, they shall do so (subject to the next subsection) before the end of the period of 21 days beginning with the day after that on which the prescribed notice of the requirement is given to them by the administrator.

(5) The administrator, if he thinks fit, may—

(*a*) at any time release a person from an obligation imposed on him under subsection (1) or (2), or

(*b*) either when giving notice under subsection (4) or subsequently, extend the period so mentioned;

and where the administrator has refused to exercise a power conferred by this subsection, the court, if it thinks fit, may exercise it.

(6) If a person without reasonable excuse fails to comply with any obligation imposed under this section, he is liable to a fine and, for continued contravention, to a daily default fine.

Definitions

"administration order": s.8(2).
"employment": subs. (3).
"fine": s.430; Sched. 10.
"officer of the company": s.251; Companies Act 1985, s.744.
"prescribed": s.251.
"the administrator": s.8(2).

General Note

This section governs the next step in the sequence of events which follow upon the making of an administration order. The requirement that a statement of the company's affairs be prepared in the prescribed form by one or more of the persons listed in subs. (3) is designed to harmonise as far as possible with the provisions contained in Parts III and IV of this Act, regarding the submission of a statement of the company's affairs in cases of receivership and compulsory winding up respectively (ss.47, 66 and 131). These standardised provisions obviate any question that the statement of affairs in the three kinds of insolvency procedure may somehow be on a different footing, taking one procedure as against another. The administrator—like an administrative receiver or the Official Receiver—enjoys a discretionary power to extend the period of 21 days specified in subs. (4) as the time limit for the submission of the statement of affairs, and the person involved has a right to appeal to the court if the administrator refuses to extend the time allowed. Similarly, the administrator is enabled to release someone from the obligation to supply him with information under this section, and there is again a right of appeal to the court if the administrator will not exercise his power of release. Subject to these possibilities of gaining an extended period of grace, or even a complete release from the obligation to supply information, failure to comply with the requirements of this section constitutes a criminal offence unless there is a reasonable excuse for non-compliance.

This section corresponds to s.39 of the 1985 Act.

Administrator's proposals

Statement of proposals

23.—(1) Where an administration order has been made, the administrator shall, within 3 months (or such longer period as the court may allow) after the making of the order—

(*a*) send to the registrar of companies and (so far as he is aware of their addresses) to all creditors a statement of his proposals for achieving the purpose or purposes specified in the order, and

(*b*) lay a copy of the statement before a meeting of the company's creditors summoned for the purpose on not less than 14 days' notice.

(2) The administrator shall also, within 3 months (or such longer period as the court may allow) after the making of the order, either—

(*a*) send a copy of the statement (so far as he is aware of their addresses) to all members of the company, or

(*b*) publish in the prescribed manner a notice stating an address to which members of the company should write for copies of the statement to be sent to them free of charge.

(3) If the administrator without reasonable excuse fails to comply with this section, he is liable to a fine and, for continued contravention, to a daily default fine.

DEFINITIONS

"administration order": s.8(2).
"a fine": s.430; Sched. 10.
"prescribed": s.251.
"the administrator": s.8(2).
"the purpose or purposes specified in the order": s.8(3).

GENERAL NOTE

The central element in the administration order procedure is the preparation by the administrator of a plan whereby the purposes specified in the administration order (if necessary augmented by means of the procedure established by s.18(1)) may be achieved. This will necessarily involve a considerable amount of preparation and consultation with all relevant parties, and thus a period of three months (capable of extension with the permission of the court) is allowed within which the administrator must prepare his proposals and send a statement of them to the parties indicated in subs. (1), and also publish them either in an individual manner to the members of the company, or by means of a notice as specified in subs. (2). A statement is also required to be laid before a meeting of the company's creditors convened for this purpose and conducted in accordance with the provisions of s.24. Only if approved in the manner there prescribed do the administrator's proposals become the basis on which, under s.17(2)(*b*), the administrator is subsequently required to exercise the powers which he enjoys by virtue of s.14 and Sched. 1.

This section corresponds to s.40 of the 1985 Act.

Consideration of proposals by creditors' meeting

24.—(1) A meeting of creditors summoned under section 23 shall decide whether to approve the administrator's proposals.

(2) The meeting may approve the proposals with modifications, but shall not do so unless the administrator consents to each modification.

(3) Subject as above, the meeting shall be conducted in accordance with the rules.

(4) After the conclusion of the meeting in accordance with the rules, the administrator shall report the result of the meeting to the court and shall give notice of that result to the registrar of companies and to such persons as may be prescribed.

(5) If a report is given to the court under subsection (4) that the meeting has declined to approve the administrator's proposals (with or without

modifications), the court may by order discharge the administration order and make such consequential provision as it thinks fit, or adjourn the hearing conditionally or unconditionally, or make an interim order or any other order that it thinks fit.

(6) Where the administration order is discharged, the administrator shall, within 14 days after the making of the order effecting the discharge, send an office copy of that order to the registrar of companies.

(7) If the administrator without reasonable excuse fails to comply with subsection (6), he is liable to a fine and, for continued contravention, to a daily default fine.

DEFINITIONS

"a fine": s.430; Sched. 10.
"modifications": s.436.
"prescribed": s.251.
"the administrator": s.8(2).
"the rules": ss.251, 411.

GENERAL NOTE

This section governs proceedings at the meeting of creditors convened by the administrator under s.23(1)(*b*) and also regulates the subsequent developments which must take place, depending upon the outcome of the meeting. If the creditors approve the administrator's proposals—with or without any modification effected in accordance with subs. (2)—the administrator is thereafter required to manage the affairs, business and property of the company in accordance with the approved proposals (s.17(2)(*b*)). No further authorisation is required in order to give the administrator's regime legal effect, and the requirement of subs. (4) with regard to the giving of notice to various parties, including the registrar of companies, and for the reporting of the outcome to the court, do not have the force of preconditions. Moreover, no criminal sanction is made applicable in any case of omission by the administrator to comply with the requirements of subs. (4).

If the creditors do not approve the proposals, and if no modified version can be agreed at the meeting under subs. (2), the provisions of subs. (5) become applicable following the administrator's giving his report to the court. The court enjoys a wide range of discretionary powers to enable it to make the most suitable arrangements in consequence of the collapse of the administrator's proposals. If the administration order is discharged the moratorium of the company's affairs is lifted and a winding-up petition may be presented, but the court may elect to adjourn the hearing to allow time for such a step to be prepared without any hiatus between the lifting of the moratorium imposed since the presentation of the petition for an administration order, and the reimposition of control over the company's affairs which will occur when a winding-up petition is presented.

As is also the case under ss.18(4) and 27(6), if the administration order is discharged in consequence of the non-approval of the proposals of the administrator, the latter is required to send the registrar of companies a sealed copy of the order of the court within 14 days after it is made. Non-compliance with this requirement constitutes a criminal offence under subs. (7). This section corresponds to s.41 of the 1985 Act.

Subs. (1)

Shall decide whether to approve

No indication is given within the Act of the manner in which voting is to be conducted when a meeting of creditors is taking its decision whether to approve an administrator's proposals. However, subs. (3) indicates that the meeting is to be conducted according to the rules, and it will be provided therein that decisions of the creditors' meetings shall be taken on the basis of a simple majority in value only. This accords with the main recommendation in the *Cork Report* regarding the matter of voting (paras. 920–925) that the power of a creditor's vote should be related to the value of his claim. The Government *White Paper* (para. 78) accepted this as the essential principle to be employed henceforth but rejected the collateral proposal in the *Cork Report* (para. 923) for a system of allotting each creditor one vote per £100 of debt or part thereof.

Any creditor who is dissatisfied with the majority decision at a meeting may utilise the procedure under s.27, provided the conditions specified in that section are satisfied, but he must do so within 28 days of the meeting.

Subs. (7)

A fine

See the Note to Sched. 10 for explanation of the levels of fines which may be imposed by a court before which an administrator is convicted of a criminal offence under this section.

Approval of substantial revisions

25.—(1) This section applies where—

(*a*) proposals have been approved (with or without modifications) under section 24, and

(*b*) the administrator proposes to make revisions of those proposals which appear to him substantial.

(2) The administrator shall—

(*a*) send to all creditors of the company (so far as he is aware of their addresses) a statement in the prescribed form of his proposed revisions, and

(*b*) lay a copy of the statement before a meeting of the company's creditors summoned for the purpose on not less than 14 days' notice;

and he shall not make the proposed revisions unless they are approved by the meeting.

(3) The administrator shall also either—

(*a*) send a copy of the statement (so far as he is aware of their addresses) to all members of the company, or

(*b*) publish in the prescribed manner a notice stating an address to which members of the company should write for copies of the statement to be sent to them free of charge.

(4) The meeting of creditors may approve the proposed revisions with modifications, but shall not do so unless the administrator consents to each modification.

(5) Subject as above, the meeting shall be conducted in accordance with the rules.

(6) After the conclusion of the meeting in accordance with the rules, the administrator shall give notice of the result of the meeting to the registrar of companies and to such persons as may be prescribed.

DEFINITIONS

"modifications": s.436.
"prescribed": s.251.
"the administrator": s.8(2).
"the rules": ss.251, 411.

GENERAL NOTE

This section operates in conjunction with s.17(2)(*b*), whereby the administrator is required to manage the company's affairs, business and property in accordance with the proposals which have been duly approved by the creditors at a meeting conducted under ss.23 and 24. S.17(2)(*b*) expressly contemplates the possibility of periodical revision of the proposals by means of the further process for seeking the approval of a meeting of creditors for which the present section makes provision. Subs. (1) defines the circumstances in which it becomes necessary for the administrator to obtain approval of a meeting of creditors to the revisions which he proposes to make. The provisions of subss. (2) and (3) regarding the giving of notice of the administrator's statement of his proposed revisions and for convening the meeting of creditors are essentially identical to those of s.23(1) and (2) which govern the sanctioning of the administrator's original proposals, save that there is no requirement that the registrar of companies shall receive a copy of the statement, although notice of the result of the meeting must be sent to him under subs. (6). The provisions of subss. (4) and (5) match those of s.24(2) and (3) with regard to the conduct of the meeting and the manner in which the creditors' approval is to be obtained. However, there is no requirement corresponding to that of s.24(4) whereby the result of the meeting must be reported to the court, although the drafting of subs. (6) leaves open the possibility that such a requirement could be included in the insolvency rules. This section corresponds to s.42 of the 1985 Act.

Subs. (1)(b)

Revisions . . . which appear to him substantial

This formulation is such as to make the necessity for the administrator to utilise the procedure under this section dependent upon his own subjective evaluation of the quality of the revisions he has in mind. If in his judgment any revisions which he contemplates making to the plan of action originally approved by the creditors are of a non-substantial nature, the obligation to seek fresh approval does not arise. The administrator is thus left free to make minor adjustments in his manner of going about the task entrusted to him, but his professional judgment and integrity must be brought to bear at all times with a view to respecting the requirements of the present section.

Subs. (2)

Approved by the meeting

As is the case under s.24(1) (*q.v.*) the method of voting on whether to approve the proposed revisions will be in accordance with the new principle that resolutions of creditors' meetings should be on the basis of a simple majority in value only. Any dissatisfied creditor may have recourse to the procedure under s.27, but must do so within 28 days after the meeting, in view of the provision of s.27(3)(*b*).

Miscellaneous

Creditors' committee

26.—(1) Where a meeting of creditors summoned under section 23 has approved the administrator's proposals (with or without modifications), the meeting may, if it thinks fit, establish a committee ("the creditors' committee") to exercise the functions conferred on it by or under this Act.

(2) If such a committee is established, the committee may, on giving not less than 7 days' notice, require the administrator to attend before it at any reasonable time and furnish it with such information relating to the carrying out of his functions as it may reasonably require.

DEFINITIONS

"the administrator": s.8(2).

"modifications": s.436.

GENERAL NOTE

Chap. 19 of the *Cork Report* contains numerous proposals for the law to be recast so as to give creditors a larger role in the conduct of insolvency proceedings, and also to provide them with a genuine incentive to take an active part. In particular, paras. 930–967 are devoted to a close examination of the way in which committees of creditors should function. The *White Paper* made only a lukewarm response to those proposals, devoting only two paragraphs (83–84) to the topic of creditors' committees. The present section (which is a parallel to ss.49 and 68 regarding creditors' committees in cases of receivership) leaves it to the creditors themselves to take the initiative in setting up a committee. They may do this at the meeting summoned by the administrator under s.23 to approve his proposals. The committee, if established, enjoys the right under subs. (2) to summon the administrator before it at seven days' notice and is entitled to obtain information from him regarding his performance in office. This section corresponds to s.43 of the 1985 Act.

Subs. (1)

The functions conferred on it by or on under this Act

Despite the insertion of this phrase in the subsection, there is no overt reference elsewhere in Pt. II of the Act to the functions of a creditors' committee under the administration order procedure. Apart from the specific powers conferred upon the committee by subs. (2), therefore, the committee's functions are left unspecified, although the way is left open for further provisions to be included in the rules, as provided for in para. 10 of Sched. 8. By contrast, the provisions of ss.141(1) and 142(1), and subsequent references in the Act to functions of a creditors' committee in a case of company liquidation, indicate that a more significant role is performed by a creditors' committee in that context.

Subs. (2)

At any reasonable time; . . . such information . . . as it may reasonably require

The purpose underlying the two references to reasonableness in relation to the committee's powers to summon the administrator to attend before them and to furnish them with information is to protect the administrator from unreasonable demands which might be made upon him, especially if the committee's view as to what ought to be done is at variance with his.

Protection of interests of creditors and members

27.—(1) At any time when an administration order is in force, a creditor or member of the company may apply to the court by petition for an order under this section on the ground—

(*a*) that the company's affairs, business and property are being or have been managed by the administrator in a manner which is unfairly prejudicial to the interests of its creditors or members generally, or of some part of its creditors or members (including at least himself), or

(*b*) that any actual or proposed act or omission of the administrator is or would be so prejudicial.

(2) On an application for an order under this section the court may, subject as follows, make such order as it thinks fit for giving relief in respect of the matters complained of, or adjourn the hearing conditionally or unconditionally, or make an interim order or any other order that it thinks fit.

(3) An order under this section shall not prejudice or prevent—

(*a*) the implementation of a voluntary arrangement approved under section 4 in Part I, or any compromise or arrangement sanctioned under section 425 of the Companies Act; or

(*b*) where the application for the order was made more than 28 days after the approval of any proposals or revised proposals under section 24 or 25, the implementation of those proposals or revised proposals.

(4) Subject as above, an order under this section may in particular—

(*a*) regulate the future management by the administrator of the company's affairs, business and property;

(*b*) require the administrator to refrain from doing or continuing an act complained of by the petitioner, or to do an act which the petitioner has complained he has omitted to do;

(*c*) require the summoning of a meeting of creditors or members for the purpose of considering such matters as the court may direct;

(*d*) discharge the administration order and make such consequential provision as the court thinks fit.

(5) Nothing in section 15 or 16 is to be taken as prejudicing applications to the court under this section.

(6) Where the administration order is discharged, the administration shall, within 14 days after the making of the order effecting the discharge, send an office copy of that order to the registrar of companies; and if without reasonable excuse he fails to comply with this subsection, he is liable to a fine and, for continued contravention, to a daily default fine.

DEFINITIONS

"administration order": s.8(2).
"a fine": s.430, Sched. 10.
"business": s.436.
"property": s.436.
"the administrator": s.8(2).

General Note

This section establishes a procedure, which may be invoked by any creditor or member of the company whose standing to complain about the administrator's conduct is founded upon actual or potential prejudice to his interest as a result of what has either been done or is proposed to be done. The court's powers are discretionary, and by virtue of subs. (3)(*a*) it is made impossible for the procedure under this section to be used to obstruct or overturn any voluntary arrangement approved under s.4 or any compromise or arrangement sanctioned under s.425 of the Companies Act 1985. Similarly, by subs. (3)(*b*) any complaint under this section concerning the effects of any of the administrator's proposals which have been approved or revised by means of the procedures laid down by ss.24 or 25 must be initiated within 28 days of the meeting by which the creditors' approval was given. This prevents any party from disrupting the administrator's work by petitioning for an order under this section when implementation of the proposals is well advanced. The expression "28 days" refers to business days, as defined in s.251. This section, apart from subs. (5) as noted below, corresponds to s.44 of the 1985 Act.

Subs. (5)

This provision is designed to ensure that the right of any interested party to make application to the court under this section is not impeded or cut down as a result of any possible construction which might be placed upon the provisions of ss.15 or 16, which enable the administrator to dispose of charged property free from encumbrance. Although this subsection has no counterpart in s.44 of the 1985 Act, its purpose and effect are clearly in accordance with the legislative intention underlying that provision, and its inclusion in the present section is seemingly *ex abundanti cautela*.

Subs. (6)

A fine

See Sched. 10 to the Act, and the General Note thereto.

Part III

Receivership

Chapter I

Receivers and Managers (England and Wales)

Preliminary and general provisions

Extent of this Chapter

28. This Chapter does not apply to receivers appointed under Chapter II of this Part (Scotland).

General Note

By way of introduction this provision emphasises that Chap. 1 of the Act does not apply to Scottish receivers.

Receivership in English law is a well-established equitable remedy. It is not the product of statutory intervention, unlike the position in Scotland. Consequently, much of the law is case-orientated, subject, of course, to some statutory modification. For a general review, see *Palmer* (23rd ed.), Chap. 46 and *Buckley* on the Companies Acts (14th ed.), p.276 *et seq*. It was for the first time put upon a proper statutory basis in Chap. IV, Pt. II, I.A. 1985. It was also amended at that time to bring it more into line with the Scottish Law (see Chap. 8, *Cork Report* and Chaps. 13 and 15 of the *White Paper*). Even after these changes it remained subject, in certain respects to Pt. XIX, C.A. 1985 and therefore the law had to be sought in two statutes. Both sets of provisions have now been consolidated in Chap. I of this Part.

Scottish Law had been governed by the Companies (Floating Charges and Receivers) (Scotland) Act 1972 and now, via Pt. XVIII, C.A. 1985, appears as Chap. II of this Part.

Thus, though differences survive, the same statute now governs, in neighbouring chapters, the law relating to both England and Wales and Scotland.

The degree of statutory regulation of the law of receivership in England and Wales was substantially increased by the provisions in the I.A. 1985. Besides amending several of the provisions of the C.A. 1985 noted below, completely new statutory provisions were introduced and find their place in the present consolidation. For instance, a statutory list of powers for a receiver is provided (s.42 and Sched. 1), as is a power to sell assets subject to a fixed charge (s.43). There is statutory confirmation of the receiver's status as the company's agent (s.44) and new rules on both the appointment of and vacation of office by a receiver (ss.33, 34, 45). The rules in Pt. XIII of the Act on the qualification of insolvency practitioners should also be noted. These provisions (except ss.33 and 34), will only apply to an administrative receiver—*i.e.* a receiver who takes control of the whole or the bulk of the company's assets to enforce a floating charge or a mixed security consisting of fixed and floating charges (s.29(2)).

Definitions

29.—(1) It is hereby declared that, except where the context otherwise requires—

(*a*) any reference in the Companies Act or this Act to a receiver or manager of the property of a company, or to a receiver of it, includes a receiver or manager, or (as the case may be) a receiver of part only of that property and a receiver only of the income arising from the property or from part of it; and

(*b*) any reference in the Companies Act or this Act to the appointment of a receiver or manager under powers contained in an instrument includes an appointment made under powers which, by virtue of any enactment, are implied in and have effect as if contained in an instrument.

(2) In this Chapter "administrative receiver" means—

(*a*) a receiver or manager of the whole (or substantially the whole) of a company's property appointed by or on behalf of the holders of any debentures of the company secured by a charge which, as created, was a floating charge, or by such a charge and one or more other securities; or

(*b*) a person who would be such a receiver or manager but for the appointment of some other person as the receiver of part of the company's property.

Definitions

"administrative receiver": subs. (2), s.251(*a*).
"floating charge": s.251.
"property": s.436.
"receiver": s.251.
"security": s.248(*b*).

General Note

This is an interpretation section which in subs. (1) makes it clear that references to receivers and managers of a company's property include (unless the contrary is intended) receivers and managers dealing with only part of a company's assets. References to receivers appointed under any instrument would include, for example, receivers appointed under s.101(i)(iii) of the Law of Property Act 1925. This interpretation provision is derived from 1948 Act, s.376 via s.500, C.A. 1985.

Subs. (2) supplies a statutory meaning for the expression "administrative receiver" for the purposes of Chap. I of Pt. III. The separate treatment of the law of receivership for England and Wales and for Scotland respectively is reflected in the further provisions of s.251, which indicates the statutory meaning of the terms "administrative receiver" and "receiver" for the purposes of Pts. I to VII the Act ("The First Group of Parts").

Disqualification of body corporate from acting as receiver

30. A body corporate is not qualified for appointment as receiver of the property of a company, and any body corporate which acts as such a receiver is liable to a fine.

DEFINITIONS

"body corporate": s.251; C.A. 1985, s.740.
"fine": s.430, Sched. 10.

GENERAL NOTE

This provision is derived from C.A. 1985, s.489.

English law (like the law of Scotland—s.51(3)(*a*) *supra*) still retains its largely irrational disqualification of corporations acting as receivers. For a criticism of the generality of this prohibition see Gower, *Principles of Modern Company Law* (4th ed., 1979), p.488. Surprisingly the Cork Committee (Cmnd. 8558, para. 744) supported the continuance of this prohibition. Where a corporation does assume such a position the appointment is void—*Portman Building Society* v. *Gallwey* [1955] 1 All E.R. 227—and a fine may be incurred.

Note

The ban on corporate receivers is reinforced by s.390(1) but this applies only to administrative receivers.

Disqualification of undischarged bankrupt

31. If a person being an undischarged bankrupt acts as receiver or manager of the property of a company on behalf of debenture holders, he is liable to imprisonment or a fine, or both.

This does not apply to a receiver or manager acting under an appointment made by the court.

DEFINITION

"fine or imprisonment": s.430, Sched. 10.

GENERAL NOTE

This is a much more justifiable ground for disqualification. For its origin see the Cohen Report (Cmnd. 6659, para. 69), 1948 Act, s.367 and 1985 Act, s.490. The comparable disqualification in Scotland is in s.51(3)(*b*). The prohibition does not apply to court-appointed receivers, but then the court is unlikely to appoint undischarged bankrupts as receivers. Before leaving the question of the disqualification of "undesirables" as receivers note s.295, C.A. 1985 and Ch. 1 of Pt. II, I.A. 1985, preventing certain company directors from acting as receivers. These two sets of provisions have been brought together in the Company Directors Disqualification Act 1986.

Power for court to appoint official receiver

32. Where application is made to the court to appoint a receiver on behalf of the debenture holders or other creditors of a company which is being wound up by the court, the official receiver may be appointed.

DEFINITION

"court": s.251; C.A. 1985, s.744.

GENERAL NOTE

Where the company is in liquidation this does not preclude the appointment of a receiver, but here the court can appoint the official receiver to act as receiver. For the role of the official receiver on liquidation see ss.399–401 *post.* This facility reproduces C.A. 1948, s.368 and C.A. 1985, s.491.

Receivers and managers appointed out of court

Time from which appointment is effective

33.—(1) The appointment of a person as a receiver or manager of a company's property under powers contained in an instrument—

(*a*) is of no effect unless it is accepted by that person before the end of the business day next following that on which the instrument of appointment is received by him or on his behalf, and

(*b*) subject to this, is deemed to be made at the time at which the instrument of appointment is so received.

(2) This section applies to the appointment of two or more persons as joint receivers or managers of a company's property under powers contained in an instrument, subject to such modifications as may be prescribed by the rules.

DEFINITIONS
"business day": s.251.
"prescribed": s.251.
"property": s.436.
"receiver": s.29(1)(*a*); s.251.
"the rules": ss.251, 411.

TRANSITIONAL PROVISION:
Sched. 11, para. 2.

GENERAL NOTE

This section is intended to give effect to the recommendations of the *Cork Report* (see paras. 470–474) to the effect that the appointment of a receiver should run from the time of receipt of the instrument of appointment by the receiver or his authorised representative, provided that he actually accepts the appointment. The rule which has been embodied in this section is to this extent a confirmation of the former case law expressed in *R. A. Cripps and Son Ltd.* v. *Wickenden* [1973] 1 W.L.R. 944; 2 All E.R. 606.

It was also recommended that the receiver's acceptance should be required to be in writing within 24-hours, and that his appointment should lapse if he has not accepted it within the 24 hour period. The adoption of this rule in subs. (1)(*a*) represents a considerable shortening, as against the previous period of seven days, of the time allowed for the receiver's acceptance.

Subs. (1)(a)

No indication is given in this section as to the mode in which acceptance must be made in order to be effective. It was indicated in para. 474 of the *Cork Report* that acceptance should be in writing, and provision will presumably be made for this matter in the rules, although the latter are not directly referred to in this part of the section.

Liability for invalid appointment

34. Where the appointment of a person as the receiver or manager of a company's property under powers contained in an instrument is discovered to be invalid (whether by virtue of the invalidity of the instrument or otherwise), the court may order the person by whom or on whose behalf the appointment was made to indemnify the person appointed against any liability which arises solely by reason of the invalidity of the appointment.

DEFINITION
"receiver": ss.29(1)(*a*), 251.

GENERAL NOTE

This section deals with liability in cases where, for any reason, the appointment of a person as receiver or manager is invalid. The Court enjoys a discretion to order those on whose behalf the appointment was made to indemnify the receiver against liability which arises solely by reason of the invalidity of the appointment. Therefore a receiver whose appointment is invalid is not entitled to any indemnity against any damages payable by him for personally mismanaging the conduct of his abortive receivership prior to the discovery of the invalidity of his appointment. In exercising its discretion under this section, the Court will seek to establish where the blame lies for the invalidity which has been discovered. For example, if a debenture comes to be held by an individual who has bought in the open market through a trustee, the Court might conclude that it would not be appropriate in the circumstances to impose liability upon the current holder in respect of a defect for which he was not personally responsible.

(Whether by virtue of the invalidity of the instrument or otherwise)

The parenthetical insertion is to allow for the fact that the invalidity of the receiver's appointment does not in all cases result from an invalidity of the instrument of appointment itself. One example of an alternative ground of invalidity would be where, in a subsequent winding up of the company, the charge on which the creditor's right to make the appointment was based is set aside under s.245 (*cf.* also *Rolled Steel Products (Holdings) Ltd.* v. *British Steel Corporation* [1982] Ch. 478, affd. [1984] B.C.L.C. 466; [1985] 3 All E.R. 52).

Application to court for directions

35.—(1) A receiver or manager of the property of a company appointed under powers contained in an instrument, or the persons by whom or on whose behalf a receiver or manager has been so appointed, may apply to the court for directions in relation to any particular matter arising in connection with the performance of the functions of the receiver or manager.

(2) On such an application, the court may give such directions, or may make such order declaring the rights of persons before the court or otherwise, as it thinks just.

Definition

"court": s.251; C.A. 1985, s.744.

General Note

This section was based on C.A. 1948, s.369(1) which enabled a receiver appointed out of court to apply to the court for guidance where difficulties arise. This facility was a result of the recommendations of the Cohen Committee (Cmnd. 6659, para. 67) and it has now, following proposals by the Cork Committee (Cmnd. 8558, para. 828), been extended to debenture holders. For the position in Scotland—see s.63(1) *infra*. On an application for directions the court enjoys general discretion.

Court's power to fix remuneration

36.—(1) The court may, on an application made by the liquidator of a company, by order fix the amount to be paid by way of remuneration to a person who, under powers contained in an instrument, has been appointed receiver or manager of the company's property.

(2) The court's power under subsection (1), where no previous order has been made with respect thereto under the subsection—

(*a*) extends to fixing the remuneration for any period before the making of the order or the application for it,

(*b*) is exercisable notwithstanding that the receiver or manager has died or ceased to act before the making of the order or the application, and

(*c*) where the receiver or manager has been paid or has retained for his remuneration for any period before the making of the order any amount in excess of that so fixed for that period, extends to requiring him or his personal representatives to account for the excess or such part of it as may be specified in the order.

But the power conferred by paragraph (*c*) shall not be exercised as respects any period before the making of the application for the order under this section, unless in the court's opinion there are special circumstances making it proper for the power to be exercised.

(3) The court may from time to time on an application made either by the liquidator or by the receiver or manager, vary or amend an order made under subsection (1).

DEFINITION

"court": s.251; C.A. 1985, s.744.

GENERAL NOTE

It is surprising that this little-used statutory provision has been retained. The receiver will normally ensure that the terms of his appointment will govern his appointment, and the chances of a particular liquidator challenging the remuneration of a fellow insolvency practitioner are remote. For the position in Scotland see s.58 *infra*.

Subs. (1)

This subsection allows a liquidator to apply to the court to have a receiver's remuneration fixed. It is based on C.A. 1985, s.494(1).

Subs. (2)

(Based on C.A. 1985, s.494(2). (Outlines the power of the court on such an application. Note that under subs. (2)(*c*) any excessive remuneration paid to a receiver can be clawed back by the court, though payments prior to the application should only be recovered in special circumstances.

Subs. (3)

Any order of the court fixing a receiver's remuneration can be varied. This reproduces C.A. 1985, s.494(3).

Liability for contracts, etc.

37.—(1) A receiver or manager appointed under powers contained in an instrument (other than an administrative receiver) is, to the same extent as if he had been appointed by order of the court—

(*a*) personally liable on any contract entered into by him in the performance of his functions (except in so far as the contract otherwise provides) and on any contract of employment adopted by him in the performance of those functions, and

(*b*) entitled in respect of that liability to indemnity out of the assets.

(2) For the purposes of subsection (1)(*a*), the receiver or manager is not to be taken to have adopted a contract of employment by reason of anything done or omitted to be done within 14 days after his appointment.

(3) Subsection (1) does not limit any right to indemnity which the receiver or manager would have apart from it, nor limit his liability on contracts entered into without authority, nor confer any right to indemnity in respect of that liability.

(4) Where at any time the receiver or manager so appointed vacates office—

(*a*) his remuneration and any expenses properly incurred by him, and

(*b*) any indemnity to which he is entitled out of the assets of the company,

shall be charged on and paid out of any property of the company which is in his custody or under his control at that time in priority to any charge or other security held by the person by or on whose behalf he was appointed.

GENERAL NOTE

This section renders a receiver appointed out of court personally liable for the contracts which he enters into though he will be protected by his indemnity. A receiver is not personally liable for pre-receivership contracts, see Buckley On the Companies Acts (14th ed.), p.283, though it is now debatable whether he can avoid a decree of specific performance—see *Freevale Ltd* v. *Metrostore Holdings Ltd* [1984] Ch. 199. Contractually a receiver appointed out of court is in the same position with regard to his own contracts as a court appointed receiver—*Burt, Boulton and Hayward* v. *Bull* [1895] 1 Q.B. 276. The Cork Committee (Cmnd. 8558, para. 463) refused calls to drop this personal liability but contracting out is possible. The section is derived in part from s.492(3), C.A. 1985 but the references to contracts of employment in subs. (1) and (2) are new. The effect is to give the receiver a period of grace during which he can decide whether to adopt any contracts of employment. Similar periods apply to administrative receivers (s.44) and administrators (s.19(5)). Subs. (4) is also new. In respect of his remuneration, expenses and indemnity, the receiver has the benefit of a charge which takes priority over any enjoyed by the person who appointed him. The personal liability of the receiver under this section may be contrasted with the provisions applicable to administrative receivers (s.44) and administrators (s.14(5)) both of whom are deemed additionally to act as agents of the company.

Receivership accounts to be delivered to registrar

38.—(1) Except in the case of an administrative receiver, every receiver or manager of a company's property who has been appointed under powers contained in an instrument shall deliver to the registrar of companies for registration the requisite accounts of his receipts and payments.

(2) The accounts shall be delivered within one month (or such longer period as the registrar may allow) after the expiration of 12 months from the date of his appointment and of every subsequent period of 6 months, and also within one month after he ceases to act as receiver or manager.

(3) The requisite accounts shall be an abstract in the prescribed form showing—

(*a*) receipts and payments during the relevant period of 12 or 6 months, or

(*b*) where the receiver or manager ceases to act, receipts and payments during the period from the end of the period of 12 or 6 months to which the last preceding abstract related (or, if no preceding abstract has been delivered under this section, from the date of his appointment) up to the date of his so ceasing, and the aggregate amount of receipts and payments during all preceding periods since his appointment.

(4) In this section "prescribed" means prescribed by regulations made by statutory instrument by the Secretary of State.

(5) A receiver or manager who makes default in complying with this section is liable to a fine and, for continued contravention, to a daily default fine.

Definitions

"fine", "default fine": s.430, Sched. 10.
"instrument": s.29(1)(*b*).
"receiver or manager": s.29(1)(*a*).
"registrar": s.744, C.A. 1985; s.251.
"registrar of companies": s.744, C.A. 1985; s.251.

General Note

The first accounts which the receiver must furnish are to be produced within 13 months of his appointment; subsequent accounts must be delivered at intervals of six months.

Provisions applicable to every receivership

Notification that receiver or manager appointed

39.—(1) When a receiver or manager of the property of a company has been appointed, every invoice, order for goods or business letter issued by or on behalf of the company or the receiver or manager or the liquidator of the company, being a document on or in which the company's name appears, shall contain a statement that a receiver or manager has been appointed.

(2) If default is made in complying with this section, the company and any of the following persons, who knowingly and wilfully authorises or permits the default, namely, any officer of the company, any liquidator of the company and any receiver or manager, is liable to a fine.

Definitions

"fine": s.430, Sched. 10.
"name": Pt. I, Chap. II, C.A. 1985.

General Note

Subs. (1)

(Derived from C.A. 1985, s.493). This subsection requires business communications to disclose that a receiver has been appointed. The Scottish counterpart is s.64 *infra*. This section must be linked to s.405(1), C.A. 1985 (entry of appointment in register of charges).

Subs. (2)

The sanction for non compliance is a fine, but note that contracts entered into in breach of the provision are not invalid.

Payment of debts out of assets subject to floating charge

40.—(1) The following applies, in the case of a company, where a receiver is appointed on behalf of the holders of any debentures of the company secured by a charge which, as created, was a floating charge.

(2) If the company is not at the time in course of being wound up, its preferential debts (within the meaning given to that expression by section 386 in Part XII) shall be paid out of the assets coming to the hands of the receiver in priority to any claims for principal or interest in respect of the debentures.

(3) Payments made under this section shall be recouped, as far as may be, out of the assets of the company available for payment of general creditors.

Definition

"preferential debts": s.386.

General Note

The preferential claims régime dates back to the end of the last century and, in spite of fierce criticism in the *Cork Report* (Cmnd. 8558, para. 1450), it will continue to apply in the foreseeable future though in watered down form—see Pt. XII; Sched. 6 and notes to ss.175 and 386.

Subss. (1), (2)

These state that a receiver acting to enforce a *floating* charge (not a *fixed* charge—*Re Lewis Merthyr Consolidated Collieries* [1929] 1 Ch. 498) is subject to the obligation to pay preferential claims. For derivation see C.A. 1985, s.196(2) (part).

Subs. (3)

Derivation C.A. 1985, s.196(5). This illustrates that although it is the holder of the floating charge who suffers initially as a result of the receiver's obligation to pay preferential claims it is ultimately the unsecured creditors who foot the bill.

Note

In the comparable provision in Scotland (s.59(2)) there is a useful machinery allowing the receiver to advertise for claims.

Enforcement of duty to make returns

41.—(1) If a receiver or manager of a company's property—

(*a*) having made default in filing, delivering or making any return, account or other document, or in giving any notice, which a receiver or manager is by law required to file, deliver, make or give, fails to make good the default within 14 days after the service on him of a notice requiring him to do so, or

(*b*) having been appointed under powers contained in an instrument, has, after being required at any time by the liquidator of the company to do so, failed to render proper accounts of his receipts and payments and to vouch them and pay over to the liquidator the amount properly payable to him,

the court may, on an application made for the purpose, make an order directing the receiver or manager (as the case may be) to make good the default within such time as may be specified in the order.

(2) In the case of the default mentioned in subsection (1)(*a*), application to the court may be made by any member or creditor of the company or by the registrar of companies; and in the case of the default mentioned in subsection (1)(*b*), the application shall be made by the liquidator.

In either case the court's order may provide that all costs of and incidental to the application shall be borne by the receiver or manager, as the case may be.

(3) Nothing in this section prejudices the operation of any enactment imposing penalties on receivers in respect of any such default as is mentioned in subsection (1).

Definitions

"court": s.744, C.A. 1985; s.251.
"receiver or manager": s.29(1)(*a*).
"registrar of companies": s.744, C.A. 1985; s.251.

General Note

Subs. (1)

This subsection which is derived from C.A. 1985, s.499(1), relates to the enforcement of a receiver's obligation to make returns, file accounts, etc. It establishes a machinery for enforcement of these obligations by a court order.

Subs. (2)

This subsection reproduces C.A. 1985, s.499(2) and indicates that the applications to the court will vary depending on whether the company is in liquidation or not. In any case the receiver can be ordered to pay the cost of the application.

Subs. (3)

This subsection emphasises that this enforcement procedure is in addition to the criminal penalties imposed on a receiver for failure to fulfil his obligations—see s.38(5) *supra.* This provision can be traced back to C.A. 1985, s.499(3).

Administrative receivers: general

General powers

42.—(1) The powers conferred on the administrative receiver of a company by the debentures by virtue of which he was appointed are deemed to include (except in so far as they are inconsistent with any of the provisions of those debentures) the powers specified in Schedule 1 to this Act.

(2) In the application of Schedule 1 to the administrative receiver of a company—

(*a*) the words "he" and "him" refer to the administrative receiver, and

(*b*) references to the property of the company are to the property of which he is or, but for the appointment of some other person as the receiver of part of the company's property, would be the receiver or manager.

(3) A person dealing with the administrative receiver in good faith and for value is not concerned to inquire whether the receiver is acting within his powers.

DEFINITIONS

"administrative receiver": s.251(*a*); s.29(2).
"property": s.436.
"receiver": s.251.

GENERAL NOTE

This section incorporates the provisions of Sched. 1 to the Act so that they apply to an administrative receiver appointed under this Chapter. Sched. 1 lists the powers with which an administrative receiver is invested but subs. (1) makes it clear that any express terms of the debenture itself may override any provisions of Sched. 1 insofar as they may be inconsistent with them.

Subs. (2)(b)

The restriction applied to the definition of "property of the company" in relation to the receiver's powers is intended to ensure that those powers are available only in respect of the property actually covered by the charge under which the administrative receiver was appointed, and not over the whole property of the company.

But for the appointment of some other person

This further clarifies the position of the administrative receiver by indicating what is the effect of the existence of any prior charges over parts of the Company's property which are also covered by a floating charge. Unless the prior charge holder has appointed a receiver, the administrative receiver has power to deal with those parts of the property, but once the prior charge holder appoints a receiver, the property in question ceases to be within the control of the administrative receiver or subject to his power. (The same position obtains in Scotland by virtue of s.55, which sets out the rules regarding precedence among receivers more clearly and in greater detail).

Subs. (3)

This provision, which is drafted in comparable terms to s.14(6) (*q.v.*) regarding dealings with an administrator, is designed to protect persons dealing with a receiver where they have dealt in good faith and for value.

Power to dispose of charged property, etc.

43.—(1) Where, on an application by the administrative receiver, the court is satisfied that the disposal (with or without other assets) of any relevant property which is subject to a security would be likely to promote a more advantageous realisation of the company's assets than would otherwise be effected, the court may by order authorise the administrative receiver to dispose of the property as if it were not subject to the security.

(2) Subsection (1) does not apply in the case of any security held by the person by or on whose behalf the administrative receiver was appointed, or of any security to which a security so held has priority.

(3) It shall be a condition of an order under this section that—

(*a*) the net proceeds of the disposal, and
(*b*) where those proceeds are less than such amount as may be determined by the court to be the net amount which would be realised on a sale of the property in the open market by a willing vendor, such sums as may be required to make good the deficiency,

shall be applied towards discharging the sums secured by the security.

(4) Where a condition imposed in pursuance of subsection (3) relates to two or more securities, that condition shall require the net proceeds of the disposal and, where paragraph (*b*) of that subsection applies, the sums mentioned in that paragraph to be applied towards discharging the sums secured by those securities in the order of their priorities.

(5) An office copy of an order under this section shall, within 14 days of the making of the order, be sent by the administrative receiver to the registrar of companies.

(6) If the administrative receiver without reasonable excuse fails to comply with subsection (5), he is liable to a fine and, for continued contravention, to a daily default fine.

(7) In this section "relevant property", in relation to the administrative receiver, means the property of which he is or, but for the appointment of some other person as the receiver of part of the company's property, would be the receiver or manager.

Definitions

"administrative receiver": ss.29(2); 251(*a*).
"fine", "daily default fine": s.430, Sched. 10.
"receiver": ss.251, 29(1)(*a*).
"relevant property": subs. (7).
"security": s.248(*b*).

Application

This section does not apply to Scotland (s.440(2)(*a*)).

General Note

This section is enacted in response to recommendations in the *Cork Report* paras. 1510–1513, and is designed to enable an administrative receiver to sell property free from a subsisting mortgage, charge, lien or other security if the Court is satisfied that such a sale is likely to promote a more advantageous realisation of the assets. The provision is considerably different from that contained in s.15 empowering an administrator to deal with charged property, and in particular it may be noted that an administrative receiver requires the authorisation of the Court in every instance where it is sought to dispose of property free from the effects of the charge or security. Moreover property which is subject to any charge falling within the terms of subs. (2) cannot be disposed of in this way. On the other hand, the same protection for the secured creditor's interest is achieved by subs. (3) as is accomplished in the case of the Administration Order procedure by s.15(5), and indeed the two provisions are here closely similar save that in s.49(3) there are no references to "goods" or "hire purchase agreement". The power of disposal under this section is partly designed to strengthen the receiver's position in any negotiations he may conduct with the charge holders in the hope of persuading them to sell a charged asset as part of a rescue scheme. If a secured creditor is unwilling to participate in such a scheme upon reasonable terms, and is thus threatening to frustrate the whole purpose of the receivership, the receiver can seek an order from the Court over-reaching the security in question. The section re-enacts s.49, I.A. 1985 with minor amendments.

Subs. (3)

(a) The net proceeds of the disposal; (b) the net amount which would be realised on a sale

See the Note to s.15(5).

Subs. (7)

This subsection is designed to prevent the power of sale from being exercisable in relation to properties over which there is a fixed charge but in respect of which the person who appointed the administrative receiver has no prior or subsequent floating charge.

Agency and liability for contracts

44.—(1) The administrative receiver of a company—

(*a*) is deemed to be the company's agent, unless and until the company goes into liquidation;

(*b*) is personally liable on any contract entered into by him in the carrying out of his functions (except in so far as the contract otherwise provides) and on any contract of employment adopted by him in the carrying out of those functions; and

(*c*) is entitled in respect of that liability to an indemnity out of the assets of the company.

(2) For the purposes of subsection (1)(*b*) the administrative receiver is not to be taken to have adopted a contract of employment by reason of anything done or omitted to be done within 14 days after his appointment.

(3) This section does not limit any right to indemnity which the administrative receiver would have apart from it, nor limit his liability on contracts entered into or adopted without authority, nor confer any right to indemnity in respect of that liability.

DEFINITIONS

"administrative receiver": ss.29(2), 251(*a*).
"company goes into liquidation": s.247(2).

GENERAL NOTE

This section reaffirms the principle that a receiver contracts with personal liability subject to a right to be indemnified out of the assets of the company in respect of his actions properly conducted within the terms of his authority. This liability may be avoided by means of an express provision in the contract, but is otherwise automatic. In addition the statutory rule is established that the receiver is to be deemed to be the agent of the company unless and until it goes into liquidation, and hence the company will be the contracting party in all cases regardless of whether the receiver is also personally liable on the contract. The provisions follow from the recommendations of paras. 455–469 of the *Cork Report,* and from para. 143 of the *White Paper.* The section re-enacts s.50, I.A. 1985 with minor amendments.

Subs. (2)

The administrative receiver is not to be taken as to have adopted a contract of employment by reason of anything done or omitted to be done within 14 days after his appointment

This provision, which is identically drafted to that of the rider to s.19(5), gives the administrative receiver a period of 14 days' grace from the time of his appointment, during which time he can assess the expediency of adopting any of the contracts of employment to which the company is a party, and if so can decide which of the contracts to adopt.

Subs. (3)

This subsection clarifies the position with respect to the indemnity to which a receiver is entitled under subs. (1)(*c*), and indicates that it only applies to liability incurred by the receiver in respect of contracts entered into or adopted by him in the carrying out of his functions. On the other hand the saving expression in respect of any other right of indemnity to which the receiver is entitled to is allow for the possibility that some express right of indemnity may be conferred by the instrument of appointment, and also takes account of the possibility that the court may exercise its discretion under s.34 where the receiver's appointment is invalid, to require the person who appointed the receiver to indemnify him against liability consequentially incurred.

Finally it is noteworthy that although all the provisions of this section are also included in the equivalent provision concerning the agency and liability of receivers in Scotland (s.57) the converse is not completely achieved because there are no counterparts in the statutory provisions for England and Wales of the provisions of s.57(4) and (7) which apply in Scotland only.

Vacation of office

45.—(1) An administrative receiver of a company may at any time be removed from office by order of the court (but not otherwise) and may resign his office by giving notice of his resignation in the prescribed manner to such persons as may be prescribed.

(2) An administrative receiver shall vacate office if he ceases to be qualified to act as an insolvency practitioner in relation to the company.

(3) Where at any time an administrative receiver vacates office—

(*a*) his remuneration and any expenses properly incurred by him, and
(*b*) any indemnity to which he is entitled out of the assets of the company,

shall be charged on and paid out of any property of the company which is in his custody or under his control at that time in priority to any security held by the person by or on whose behalf he was appointed.

(4) Where an administrative receiver vacates office otherwise than by death, he shall, within 14 days after his vacation of office, send a notice to that effect to the registrar of companies.

(5) If an administrative receiver without reasonable excuse fails to comply with subsection (4), he is liable to a fine and, for continued contravention, to a daily default fine.

Definitions

"administrative receiver": ss.29(2), 251(*a*).
"fine", "daily default fine": s.430, Sched. 10.
"prescribed": s.251.
"qualified to act as an insolvency practitioner in relation to company": s.390.
"security": s.248(*b*)

General Note

Subs. (1)

This subsection specifies the sole mode of removal from office of an administrative receiver, namely by order of the court. This corresponds to the recommendation of para. 492 of the *Cork Report* that the receiver's independence should be strengthened by abolishing the right of the holder of the charge to remove him without notice. No further provisions are supplied in the section to indicate by whom an application for a receiver's removal may be made, or upon what grounds and upon what basis (mandatory or discretionary) the court may remove him (*cf.* the different position regarding removal of a receiver in Scotland under s.62, *q.v.*). The section does however make provision for voluntary resignation by a receiver, subject to the requirement that he gives due notice of his resignation in a manner to be prescribed by the rules. This part of the subsection fulfils the recommendation of para. 491 of the *Cork Report,* where it was further suggested that the required period of notice should be one month, and that the receiver should be obliged to give this notice to the company or its liquidator, to the holder of the charge, to the holders of any fixed security over the property of the company, and to the receiver's committee (if any).

Subs. (2)

This maintains consistency with the provisions of Pt. XIII of the Act and in particular those of ss.388, 389, whereby it is a criminal offence for a person to act as an insolvency practitioner in relation to a company by acting as its administrative receiver at a time when he is not qualified to do so. The requirements for being qualified to act as an insolvency practitioner are contained in the provisions of s.390. Any administrative receiver who at any time ceases to satisfy any of those requirements is accordingly obliged by the present subsection to vacate office.

Subs. (3)

This provides protection for the receiver after the termination of his appointment, with regard to the payment of his remuneration and proper expenses, and also with regard to any indemnity to which he is entitled, by giving the receiver's entitlements priority as against any security held by the debenture holder.

Subss. (4), (5)

The requirement that the receiver must send notice of his vacation of office to the registrar of companies within 14 days, with the accompanying sanction of criminal penalties for non-compliance, is a counterpart to that attached to the discharge of an administration order by virtue of s.18(4) and (5) and s.24(6) and (7).

Administrative receivers: ascertainment and investigation of company's affairs

Information to be given by administrative receiver

46.—(1) Where an administrative receiver is appointed, he shall—

(*a*) forthwith send to the company and publish in the prescribed manner a notice of his appointment, and (*b*) within 28 days after his appointment, unless the court otherwise directs, send such a notice to all the creditors of the company (so far as he is aware of their addresses).

(2) This section and the next do not apply in relation to the appointment of an administrative receiver to act—

(*a*) with an existing administrative receiver, or

(*b*) in place of an administrative receiver dying or ceasing to act,

except that, where they apply to an administrative receiver who dies or ceases to act before they have been fully complied with, the references in this section and the next to the administrative receiver include (subject to the next subsection) his successor and any continuing administrative receiver.

(3) If the company is being wound up, this section and the next apply notwithstanding that the administrative receiver and the liquidator are the same person, but with any necessary modifications arising from that fact.

(4) If the administrative receiver without reasonable excuse fails to comply with this section, he is liable to a fine and, for continued contravention, to a daily default fine.

Definitions

"administrative receiver": ss.29(2), 251(*a*).
"prescribed": s.251.
"fine", "daily default fine": s.430, Sched. 10.

General Note

This section replaces s.52, I.A. 1985 and places the law of England and Wales on the same footing as that of Scotland with regard to the giving of notice of appointment by the person who becomes administrative receiver of a company (see s.65).

Subs. (1)

This provision is cast in terms identical to those of s.21 (regarding the giving of notice by an administrator) and thus creates a requirement in parallel to that imposed upon a liquidator with regard to the requirement that he should within 28 days advertise his appointment and advise all known creditors of the fact that it has taken place. This adopts the recommendation of para. 476 of the *Cork Report,* where it was also suggested that, in view of the cost involved, there should be no further requirement to send individual notice to shareholders, who would perforce need to rely on the general advertisement.

Subs. (2)

This is a sensible provision to make it clear that, when the requirements of subs. (1) have been complied with, there is no need to repeat the exercise of advertisement and giving of notice when any person is subsequently appointed as an additional administrative receiver or as a replacement to one who has died or ceased to act.

Statement of affairs to be submitted

47.—(1) Where an administrative receiver is appointed, he shall forthwith require some or all of the persons mentioned below to make out and submit to him a statement in the prescribed form as to the affairs of the company.

(2) A statement submitted under this section shall be verified by affidavit by the persons required to submit it and shall show—

(*a*) particulars of the company's assets, debts and liabilities;

(*b*) the names and addresses of its creditors;

(*c*) the securities held by them respectively;

(*d*) the dates when the securities were respectively given, and

(*e*) such further or other information as may be prescribed.

(3) The persons referred to in subsection (1) are—

(*a*) those who are or have been officers of the company;

(*b*) those who have taken part in the company's formation at any time within one year before the date of the appointment of the administrative receiver;

(*c*) those who are in the company's employment, or have been in its employment within that year, and are in the administrative receiver's opinion capable of giving the information required;

(*d*) those who are or have been within that year officers of or in the employment of a company which is, or within that year was, an officer of the company.

In this subsection "employment" includes employment under a contract for services.

(4) Where any persons are required under this section to submit a statement of affairs to the administrative receiver, they shall do so (subject to the next subsection) before the end of the period of 21 days beginning with the day after that on which the prescribed notice of the requirement is given to them by the administrative receiver.

(5) The administrative receiver, if he thinks fit, may—

(*a*) at any time release a person from an obligation imposed on him under subsection (1) or (2), or

(*b*) either when giving notice under subsection (4) or subsequently, extend the period so mentioned;

and where the administrative receiver has refused to exercise a power conferred by this subsection, the court, if it thinks fit, may exercise it.

(6) If a person without reasonable excuse fails to comply with any obligation imposed under this section, he is liable to a fine and, for continued contravention, to a daily default fine.

DEFINITIONS

"administrative receiver": s.29(2), 251(*a*).
"officers of the company": s.251; Companies Act 1985, s.744.
"prescribed": s.251.
"securities": s.248(*b*).

GENERAL NOTE

This section, which replaces s.53, I.A. 1985, is parallel to s.22 (*q.v.*), which relates to the obtaining of a statement of the company's affairs under the administration order procedure, and also to s.131, which applies where a company is wound up by the court. The three provisions are largely identical in substance, apart from the necessary differences in the relevant nomenclature employed, but the provisions of s.131 differ from those of both s.22 and the present section in that the Official Receiver enjoys a discretion to dispense with the requirement for a statement of affairs to be prepared, whereas both an administrator and an administrative receiver are under an obligation to require such a statement to be submitted. See also the General Note to s.22.

Report by administrative receiver

48.—(1) Where an administrative receiver is appointed, he shall, within 3 months (or such longer period as the court may allow) after his appointment, send to the registrar of companies, to any trustees for secured creditors of the company and (so far as he is aware of their addresses) to all such creditors a report as to the following matters, namely—

(*a*) the events leading up to his appointment, so far as he is aware of them;

(*b*) the disposal or proposed disposal by him of any property of the company and the carrying on or proposed carrying on by him of any business of the company;

(*c*) the amounts of principal and interest payable to the debenture holders by whom or on whose behalf he was appointed and the amounts payable to preferential creditors; and (*d*) the amount (if any) likely to be available for the payment of other creditors.

(2) The administrative receiver shall also, within 3 months (or such longer period as the court may allow) after his appointment, either—

(*a*) send a copy of the report (so far as he is aware of their addresses) to all unsecured creditors of the company; or

(*b*) publish in the prescribed manner a notice stating an address to which unsecured creditors of the company should write for copies of the report to be sent to them free of charge,

and (in either case), unless the court otherwise directs, lay a copy of the report before a meeting of the company's unsecured creditors summoned for the purpose on not less than 14 days' notice.

(3) The court shall not give a direction under subsection (2) unless—

(*a*) the report states the intention of the administrative receiver to apply for the direction, and

(*b*) a copy of the report is sent to the persons mentioned in paragraph (*a*) of that subsection, or a notice is published as mentioned in paragraph (*b*) of that subsection, not less than 14 days before the hearing of the application.

(4) Where the company has gone or goes into liquidation, the administrative receiver—

(*a*) shall, within 7 days after his compliance with subsection (1) or, if later, the nomination or appointment of the liquidator, send a copy of the report to the liquidator, and

(*b*) where he does so within the time limited for compliance with subsection (2), is not required to comply with that subsection.

(5) A report under this section shall include a summary of the statement of affairs made out and submitted to the administrative receiver under section 47 and of his comments (if any) upon it.

(6) Nothing in this section is to be taken as requiring any such report to include any information the disclosure of which would seriously prejudice the carrying out by the administrative receiver of his functions.

(7) Section 46(2) applies for the purposes of this section also.

(8) If the administrative receiver without reasonable excuse fails to comply with this section, he is liable to a fine and, for continued contravention, to a daily default fine.

DEFINITIONS

"administrative receiver": ss.29(2), 251(*a*).
"business": s.436.
"company goes into liquidation": s.247(2).
"fine", "daily default fine": s.430, Sched. 10.
"preferential creditor": s.386, Sched. 6.
"prescribed": s.251.
"property": s.436.
"secured creditor": s.248(*a*).

GENERAL NOTE

This provision adopts the recommendation made in para. 480 of the *Cork Report* and accepted with augmentation in paras. 147–148 of the *White Paper,* that a receiver should be required to furnish properly prepared information to the general body of creditors, so that they may be better informed and more directly involved. The section breaks new ground by requiring that the receiver's report must be sent to both secured and unsecured creditors and that the report is also to be laid before a meeting of the unsecured creditors unless the court accedes to an application for a dispensation from this requirement. If such a meeting is convened the creditors may exercise their right under s.49 to appoint a committee of creditors to maintain contact with the receiver and to obtain further information from him on a regular basis. The section is derived from s.54, I.A. 1985 with minor amendments.

Subs. (4)

This takes care of the possibility that the receivership may be overtaken by a winding up of the company. The requirement that the receiver's report must be sent also to the liquidator within the specified time is designed to ensure that the latter enjoys the benefit of immediate availability of the fruits of the receiver's earlier investigation and appraisal of the company's circumstances, while the provision in subs. 4(*b*) allows the receiver to be released from the obligation to notify the unsecured creditors, and to convene them in a meeting, pursuant to subs. (2), where the collective procedure of winding up has commenced, and the liquidator has been duly sent a copy of the report, before the expiry of the three month time limit contained in subs. (2).

Subs. (6)

This rather mysteriously worded provision is apparently designed to permit the administrative receiver to exclude from his report anything which might be considered commercially sensitive, such as sales transactions or other agreements in course of negotiation at the time when the report is issued (see H.C. Standing Committee E, June 20, 1985, col. 509). The subsection is drafted in terms which are both wide and vague, and open to a considerable amount of subjective interpretation by the administrative receiver. The fact that the receiver will henceforth in all cases be a qualified insolvency practitioner is presumably regarded as sufficient guarantee against abuse of the obvious scope in the section for substantial omissions to be made which would effectively render the report valueless.

Subs. (7)

This incorporates by reference the provisions of subs. (2) of s.46, so that a person who is appointed as a joint receiver in addition to one who is already serving, or a person appointed to replace a receiver who has died or ceased to act, shall not be placed in the absurd position of having to issue a report under this section when the task has already been performed by a person appointed previously.

Committee of creditors

49.—(1) Where a meeting of creditors is summoned under section 48, the meeting may, if it thinks fit, establish a committee ("the creditors' committee") to exercise the functions conferred on it by or under this Act.

(2) If such a committee is established, the committee may, on giving not less than 7 days' notice, require the administrative receiver to attend before it at any reasonable time and furnish it with such information relating to the carrying out by him of his functions as it may reasonably require.

Definition

"administrative receiver": ss.29(2), 251(*a*).

General Note

This section is a parallel to ss.26 (which applies with regard to an administration order) and 68 (which applies to Scotland). More elaborate provisions concerning the appointment and functions of a creditors' committee in a winding up by the court in England or in Scotland are contained in ss.141 and 142 respectively. See also the General Note to s.26, and the discussion in paras. 442–454 of the *Cork Report* regarding the need for greater accountability of receivers, and in paras. 477–479, 481 and 930–967 of the *Report* regarding meetings of creditors and committees of creditors.

Chapter II

Receivers (Scotland)

Extent of this Chapter

50. This Chapter extends to Scotland only.

General Note
See annotation to s.28.

Power to appoint receiver

51.—(1) It is competent under the law of Scotland for the holder of a floating charge over all or any part of the property (including uncalled capital), which may from time to time be comprised in the property and undertaking of an incorporated company (whether a company within the meaning of the Companies Act or not) which the Court of Session has jurisdiction to wind up, to appoint a receiver of such part of the property of the company as is subject to the charge.

(2) It is competent under the law of Scotland for the court, on the application of the holder of such a floating charge, to appoint a receiver of such part of the property of the company as is subject to the charge.

(3) The following are disqualified from being appointed as receiver—

(*a*) a body corporate;

(*b*) an undischarged bankrupt; and

(*c*) a firm according to the law of Scotland.

(4) A body corporate or a firm according to the law of Scotland which acts as a receiver is liable to a fine.

(5) An undischarged bankrupt who so acts is liable to imprisonment or a fine, or both.

(6) In this section, "receiver" includes joint receivers.

Definitions
"fine": s.430, Sched. 10.
"floating charge": s.462, C.A. 1985; s.251.
"holder of such a floating charge": s.70(1).

Transitional Provision: Sched. 11, para. 3.

General Note
The concept of a floating charge was transplanted into Scottish law by the Companies (Floating Charges) (Scotland) Act 1961. However it was soon recognised that this reform would not succeed unless the idea of a receiver, an ideal mechanism for enforcing such a security, was also transplanted—see Scottish Law Commission (1970) (Cmnd. 4336, para. 38): this was a dramatic reform in Scottish law which had no notion of a receiver. There was the possibility of a judicial factor to act as a caretaker during a debilitating internal dispute as in *Fraser, Petitioner* 1971 S.L.T. 146, but this was no true receiver. These provisions on receivers have posed major problems of interpretation for the courts. The response of the Scottish courts has been to view them as a sort of inviolate code which cannot be prejudiced by the common law of Scotland. For comments on the position in Scotland see *Palmer,* (23rd ed.), Ch. 47, *Reed* 1983 S.L.T. 229, 237, 261 and also the article by *Wilson* in 1984 S.L.T. 105. The section is derived from s.11, C. (F.C. & R.) (S.) A. 1972 and s.467, C.A. 1985. See generally note to s.28.

Subs. (1)
This subsection authorises the holder of a floating charge to appoint a receiver out of court in Scotland.

Subs. (2)
This subsection authorises the court to make such an appointment.

Subs. (3)
Neither a body corporate nor a firm under Scottish law can act as a receiver. Note that there is no provision in English law imposing a similar disqualification on a partnership—this is because the English partnership as opposed to the Scottish firm (Partnership Act 1890, s.4(2)) lacks legal personality. An undischarged bankrupt is also disqualified from acting as such by subs. (3). For disqualifications in England note ss.30–31 *supra.* Unqualified persons (see ss.388, 389) are banned from acting as "administrative receivers" (defined in s.251).

Subs. (4)

This subsection imposes the sanction of a fine where either a body corporate or firm acts as a receiver.

Subs. (5)

Where an undischarged bankrupt acts as a receiver, then on conviction, whether on indictment or after summary trial, he is liable to a fine *and/or* imprisonment.

Subs. (6)

All of the above provisions apply equally to joint receivers.

Circumstances justifying appointment

52.—(1) A receiver may be appointed under section 51(1) by the holder of the floating charge on the occurrence of any event which, by the provisions of the instrument creating the charge, entitles the holder of the charge to make that appointment and, in so far as not otherwise provided for by the instrument, on the occurrence of any of the following events, namely—

(*a*) the expiry of a period of 21 days after the making of a demand for payment of the whole or any part of the principal sum secured by the charge, without payment having been made;

(*b*) the expiry of a period of 2 months during the whole of which interest due and payable under the charge has been in arrears;

(*c*) the making of an order or the passing of a resolution to wind up the company;

(*d*) the appointment of a receiver by virtue of any other floating charge created by the company.

(2) A receiver may be appointed by the court under section 51(2) on the occurrence of any event which, by the provisions of the instrument creating the floating charge, entitles the holder of the charge to make that appointment and, in so far as not otherwise provided for by the instrument, on the occurrence of any of the following events, namely—

(*a*) where the court, on the application of the holder of the charge, pronounces itself satisfied that the position of the holder of the charge is likely to be prejudiced if no such appointment is made;

(*b*) any of the events referred to in paragraphs (*a*) to (*c*) of subsection (1).

DEFINITIONS

"floating charge": s.744, C.A. 1985; s.251; s.70(3), (4).
"receiver": s.70(1).
"holder of the floating charge": s.70(2).

GENERAL NOTE

This section is derived from s.12, C. (F. C. & R.) (S.) A. 1972 and s.468, C.A. 1985.

Subs. (1)

Specifies four grounds (*a*)–(*d*) upon which a holder of a floating charge may appoint a receiver out of court. These grounds may be varied by provisions in the instrument of charge itself. The reasons listed are commonly found in English debentures.

Subs. (2)

This subsection states that a court appointment may also be made where the instrument of charge permits it, on grounds (*a*)–(*c*) in subs. (1), and also where the court is "satisfied that the position of the holder of the charge is likely to be prejudiced if no such appointment is made" (subs. 2(*a*)). This is comparable to the English concept of "jeopardy" (see *Palmer*, (23rd ed.), para. 46–06), but it must be said that any sort of court appointment of a receiver these days is a rarity.

Mode of appointment by holder of charge

53.—(1) The appointment of a receiver by the holder of the floating charge under section 51(1) shall be by means of a validly executed instrument in writing ("the instrument of appointment"), a copy (certified in the prescribed manner to be a correct copy) whereof shall be delivered by or on behalf of the person making the appointment to the registrar of companies for registration within 7 days of its execution and shall be accompanied by a notice in the prescribed form.

(2) If any person without reasonable excuse makes default in complying with the requirements of subsection (1), he is liable to a fine and, for continued contravention, to a daily default fine.

(3) The instrument of appointment is validly executed—

- (*a*) by a company, if it is executed in accordance with the provisions of section 36 of the Companies Act as if it were a contract, and
- (*b*) by any other person, if it is executed in the manner required or permitted by the law of Scotland in the case of an attested deed.

(4) The instrument may be executed on behalf of the holder of the floating charge by virtue of which the receiver is to be appointed—

- (*a*) by any person duly authorised in writing by the holder to execute the instrument, and
- (*b*) in the case of an appointment of a receiver by the holders of a series of secured debentures, by any person authorised by resolution of the debenture-holders to execute the instrument.

(5) On receipt of the certified copy of the instrument of appointment in accordance with subsection (1), the registrar shall, on payment of the prescribed fee, enter the particulars of the appointment in the register of charges.

(6) The appointment of a person as a receiver by an instrument of appointment in accordance with subsection (1)—

- (*a*) is of no effect unless it is accepted by that person before the end of the business day next following that on which the instrument of appointment is received by him or on his behalf, and
- (*b*) subject to paragraph (*a*), is deemed to be made on the day on and at the time at which the instrument of appointment is so received, as evidenced by a written docquet by that person or on his behalf;

and this subsection applies to the appointment of joint receivers subject to such modifications as may be prescribed.

(7) On the appointment of a receiver under this section, the floating charge by virtue of which he was appointed attaches to the property then subject to the charge; and such attachment has effect as if the charge was a fixed security over the property to which it has attached.

Definitions

"fine", "daily default fine": s.430, Sched. 10.
"fixed security": s.70(1).
"holder of a floating charge": s.70(2).
"receiver": s.70(1).
"register of charges": s.70(1).
"registrar of companies": s.774, C.A. 1985.

General Note

This section specifies the procedure to be followed where a receiver is appointed out of court. Each subsection is based on the seven subsections in C. (F.C. and R.)(S.) A. 1972, s.13 and in s.469, C.A. 1985.

Subs. (1)

A formal instrument of appointment is required and the registrar must be notified within seven days.

Subs. (2)

Failure to comply with subs. (1) may result in a fine or daily default fine.

Subss. (3), (4)

These subsections state in detail how the instrument of appointment can be properly executed by the parties or their agents.

Subs. (5)

On notification the registrar must enter the fact of the appointment in his register of charges.

Subs. (6)

The appointment in Scottish law used to run from the date of the execution of the instrument of appointment. By way of contrast in English law the appointment only commenced when the receiver accepted it—Cork Committee (Cmnd. 8558, para. 473). Subs. (6) assimilates the law of England and Scotland. The appointment must be accepted within 24 hours and, subject to that, it will run from the date of the receipt of the letter of appointment.

Subs. (7)

The effect of the appointment is to crystallise the floating charge into a fixed security.

Appointment by court

54.—(1) Application for the appointment of a receiver by the court under section 51(2) shall be by petition to the court, which shall be served on the company.

(2) On such an application, the court shall, if it thinks fit, issue an interlocutor making the appointment of the receiver.

(3) A copy (certified by the clerk of the court to be a correct copy) of the court's interlocutor making the appointment shall be delivered by or on behalf of the petitioner to the registrar of companies for registration, accompanied by a notice in the prescribed form, within 7 days of the date of the interlocutor or such longer period as the court may allow.

If any person without reasonable excuse makes default in complying with the requirements of this subsection, he is liable to a fine and, for continued contravention, to a daily default fine.

(4) On receipt of the certified copy interlocutor in accordance with subsection (3), the registrar shall, on payment of the prescribed fee, enter the particulars of the appointment in the register of charges.

(5) The receiver is to be regarded as having been appointed on the date of his being appointed by the court.

(6) On the appointment of a receiver under this section, the floating charge by virtue of which he was appointed attaches to the property then subject to the charge; and such attachment has effect as if the charge were a fixed security over the property to which it has attached.

(7) In making rules of court for the purposes of this section, the Court of Session shall have regard to the need for special provision for cases which appear to the court to require to be dealt with as a matter of urgency.

Definitions

"fine", "daily default fine": s.430, Sched. 10.
"receiver": s.70(1).
"registrar": s.744, C.A. 1985.
"register of charges": s.70(1).
"registrar of companies": s.744, C.A. 1985.

General Note

This section describes the procedure to be followed where a receiver is appointed by the court. It is derived from s.14 C.(F.C. and R.)(S.)A. 1972 and s.470, C.A. 1985. It no longer refers to caution but an administrative receiver (s.251) to qualify as an insolvency practitioner would have to be covered by a caution (see ss.388–90 *infra*).

Subs. (1)
Application is to be by petition to the court.

Subs. (2)
The court enjoys general discretion as to whether to grant the interlocutor (order).

Subs. (3)
The petitioner must ensure that a copy of the interlocutor is sent to the registrar of companies within seven days, or longer if the court permits. Failure to do this may result in a fine, or daily default fine.

Subs. (4)
The registrar must enter the fact of the appointment in his register of charges.

Subss. (5), (6)
The appointment runs from the date of the court interlocutor and the effect of the appointment is to crystallise the floating charge.

Subs. (7)
The Court of Session is directed to make special rules enabling it to deal with urgent cases.

Powers of receiver

55.—(1) Subject to the next subsection, a receiver has in relation to such part of the property of the company as is attached by the floating charge by virtue of which he was appointed, the powers, if any, given to him by the instrument creating that charge.

(2) In addition, the receiver has under this Chapter the powers as respects that property (in so far as these are not inconsistent with any provision contained in that instrument) which are specified in Schedule 2 to this Act.

(3) Subsections (1) and (2) apply—

(*a*) subject to the rights of any person who has effectually executed diligence on all or any part of the property of the company prior to the appointment of the receiver, and

(*b*) subject to the rights of any person who holds over all or any part of the property of the company a fixed security or floating charge having priority over, or ranking pari passu with, the floating charge by virtue of which the receiver was appointed.

(4) A person dealing with a receiver in good faith and for value is not concerned to enquire whether the receiver is acting within his powers.

DEFINITIONS
"fixed security": s.70(1).
"floating charge": s.744, C.A. 1985; s.251; s.70(3), (4).
"receiver": s.70(1).

GENERAL NOTE
Subs. (1)
This subsection applies irrespective of whether the appointment was by the court or out of court.

Subs. (2)
The powers of a receiver in Scotland, previously listed in s.471(1), C.A. 1985, served as a model code for the powers of administrators and administrative receivers in England and Wales. The powers of the former having undergone drafting changes, are now listed in

Sched. 2, while those of the latter appear in Sched. 1. This list can of course be modified by the instrument under which the receiver was appointed.

Subs. (3)

The receiver's powers are subject to the rights of those persons who might have a prior claim on the company's assets—*e.g.* a prior chargee or a person who has prior to his appointment "effectually executed diligence" on the company's assets—on this phrase see the annotation to s.60 *infra*.

Subs. (4)

This protects a person dealing with the receiver in good faith and for value from the consequences of lack of authority.

Precedence among receivers

56.—(1) Where there are two or more floating charges subsisting over all or any part of the property of the company, a receiver may be appointed under this Chapter by virtue of each such charge; but a receiver appointed by, or on the application of, the holder of a floating charge having priority of ranking over any other floating charge by virtue of which a receiver has been appointed has the powers given to a receiver by section 55 and Schedule 2 to the exclusion of any other receiver.

(2) Where two or more floating charges rank with one another equally, and two or more receivers have been appointed by virtue of such charges, the receivers so appointed are deemed to have been appointed as joint receivers.

(3) Receivers appointed, or deemed to have been appointed, as joint receivers shall act jointly unless the instrument of appointment or respective instruments of appointment otherwise provide.

(4) Subject to subsection (5) below, the powers of a receiver appointed by, or on the application of, the holder of a floating charge are suspended by, and as from the date of, the appointment of a receiver by, or on the application of, the holder of a floating charge having priority of ranking over that charge to such extent as may be necessary to enable the receiver second mentioned to exercise his powers under section 55 and Schedule 2; and any powers so suspended take effect again when the floating charge having priority of ranking ceases to attach to the property then subject to the charge, whether such cessation is by virtue of section 62(6) or otherwise.

(5) The suspension of the powers of a receiver under subsection (4) does not have the effect of requiring him to release any part of the property (including any letters or documents) of the company from his control until he receives from the receiver superseding him a valid indemnity (subject to the limit of the value of such part of the property of the company as is subject to the charge by virtue of which he was appointed) in respect of any expenses, charges and liabilities he may have incurred in the performance of his functions as receiver.

(6) The suspension of the powers of a receiver under subsection (4) does not cause the floating charge by virtue of which he was appointed to cease to attach to the property to which it attached by virtue of section 53(7) or 54(6).

(7) Nothing in this section prevents the same receiver being appointed by virtue of two or more floating charges.

Definitions

"floating charge": s.744, C.A. 1985, s.251.
"holder of a floating charge": s.70(1).
"instrument of appointment": s.53(1), 70(1).
"receiver": s.70(1).

General Note

This section governs precedence amongst receivers where the company has created several floating charges over its assets. Its seven subsections mirror exactly the seven subsections of C.(F.C. and R.)(S.)A. 1972, s.16 and C.A. 1985, s.472.

Subs. (1)

This subsection anticipates the possibility of two or more receivers being appointed over the assets of the company but only the receiver acting for the floating charge enjoying priority has the powers specified under this Act.

Subss. (2), (3)

If floating charges rank equally then those receivers are deemed to be joint receivers and they must exercise their powers jointly.

Subs. (4)

A receiver's powers may be suspended where a receiver is subsequently appointed by a person with a prior floating charge.

Subs. (5)

The receiver, however, whose powers have been suspended must not hand over the assets gathered in by him until he receives an indemnity from the receiver who is supplanting him.

Subs. (6)

Where a receiver's powers are suspended this does not cause the floating charge under which he was appointed to refloat.

Subs. (7)

This subsection offers a way out of the problem of precedence among receivers. The holders of two or more floating charges can appoint the same person as receiver—but this of course can lead to conflicts of interest.

Agency and liability of receiver for contracts

57.—(1) A receiver is deemed to be the agent of the company in relation to such property of the company as is attached by the floating charge by virtue of which he was appointed.

(2) A receiver (including a receiver whose powers are subsequently suspended under section 56) is personally liable on any contract entered into by him in the performance of his functions, except in so far as the contract otherwise provides, and on any contract of employment adopted by him in the carrying out of those functions.

(3) A receiver who is personally liable by virtue of subsection (2) is entitled to be indemnified out of the property in respect of which he was appointed.

(4) Any contract entered into by or on behalf of the company prior to the appointment of a receiver continues in force (subject to its terms) notwithstanding that appointment, but the receiver does not by virtue only of his appointment incur any personal liability on any such contract.

(5) For the purposes of subsection (2), a receiver is not to be taken to have adopted a contract of employment by reason of anything done or omitted to be done within 14 days after his appointment.

(6) This section does not limit any right to indemnity which the receiver would have apart from it, nor limit his liability on contracts entered into or adopted without authority, nor confer any right to indemnity in respect of that liability.

(7) Any contract entered into by a receiver in the performance of his functions continues in force (subject to its terms) although the powers of the receiver are subsequently suspended under section 56.

Definitions

"floating charge": s.744, C.A. 1985; s.251.
"receiver": s.70(1).

General Note

This section is derived from s.473, C.A. 1985 as amended by s.58, I.A. 1985. The purpose of the amendment was to bring the Scottish provision into line with that applicable in England and Wales (now s.44 *supra*). The reference to contracts of employment in subs. (2) and the whole of subs. (5) and subs. (6) are new. See further the Note to s.44.

Remuneration of receiver

58.—(1) The remuneration to be paid to a receiver is to be determined by agreement between the receiver and the holder of the floating charge by virtue of which he was appointed.

(2) Where the remuneration to be paid to the receiver has not been determined under subsection (1), or where it has been so determined but is disputed by any of the persons mentioned in paragraphs (*a*) to (*d*) below, it may be fixed instead by the Auditor of the Court of Session on application made to him by—

(*a*) the receiver;
(*b*) the holder of any floating charge or fixed security over all or any part of the property of the company;
(*c*) the company; or
(*d*) the liquidator of the company.

(3) Where the receiver has been paid or has retained for his remuneration for any period before the remuneration has been fixed by the Auditor of the Court of Session under subsection (2) any amount in excess of the remuneration so fixed for that period, the receiver or his personal representatives shall account for the excess.

Definitions

"fixed security": s.70(1).
"holder of a floating charge": s.70(2).
"receiver": s.70(1).

General Note

This section regulates a receiver's remuneration. It is derived from s.474, C.A. 1985 (part).

Subs. (1)

As a general rule this will be fixed by agreement with the holder of the floating charge by virtue of which the receiver was appointed.

Subs. (2)

Where this has not been done, or where it is disputed, application to the Auditor of the Court of Session is possible for it to be determined.

Subs. (3)

If the receiver has received remuneration in excess of the figure fixed by the Auditor of the Court of Session he is liable to remit the excess.

Priority of debts

59.—(1) Where a receiver is appointed and the company is not at the time of the appointment in course of being wound up, the debts which fall under subsection (2) of this section shall be paid out of any assets coming to the hands of the receiver in priority to any claim for principal or interest by the holder of the floating charge by virtue of which the receiver was appointed.

(2) Debts falling under this subsection are preferential debts (within the meaning given by section 386 in Part XII) which, by the end of a period of 6 months after advertisement by the receiver for claims in the Edinburgh Gazette and in a newspaper circulating in the district where the company carries on business either—

(i) have been intimated to him, or

(ii) have become known to him.

(3) Any payments made under this section shall be recouped as far as may be out of the assets of the company available for payment of ordinary creditors.

DEFINITIONS

"holder of the floating charge": s.70(2).
"preferential debts": s.386.
"receiver": s.70(1).

GENERAL NOTE

This section, which is derived from s.475(1), (2) and (5), C.A. 1985 and I.A. 1985, Sched. 6, para. 20(2), deals with the repayment of preferential debts by the receiver out of the realised assets. The English counterpart is s.40 *supra*.

Subs. (1)

This subsection imposes the basic obligation to pay preferential debts on the receiver.

Subs. (2)

Preferential debts are those listed in Pt. XII of the Act *and* which have become known to the receiver within six months of him advertising for claims in the Edinburgh Gazette. This is a useful facility which is not to be found in English law. The Cork Committee (Cmnd. 8558, para. 490 has recommended its introduction.

Subs. (3)

Any payments made by the receiver out of the monies destined for the holder of the floating charge are to be recouped from the funds available for the general creditors.

Distribution of moneys

60.—(1) Subject to the next section, and to the rights of any of the following categories of persons (which rights shall, except to the extent otherwise provided in any instrument, have the following order of priority), namely—

(*a*) the holder of any fixed security which is over property subject to the floating charge and which ranks prior to, or pari passu with, the floating charge;

(*b*) all persons who have effectually executed diligence on any part of the property of the company which is subject to the charge by virtue of which the receiver was appointed;

(*c*) creditors in respect of all liabilities, charges and expenses incurred by or on behalf of the receiver;

(*d*) the receiver in respect of his liabilities, expenses and remuneration, and any indemnity to which he is entitled out of the property of the company; and

(*e*) the preferential creditors entitled to payment under section 59,

the receiver shall pay moneys received by him to the holder of the floating charge by virtue of which the receiver was appointed in or towards satisfaction of the debt secured by the floating charge.

(2) Any balance of moneys remaining after the provisions of subsection (1) and section 61 below have been satisfied shall be paid in accordance with their respective rights and interests to the following persons, as the case may require—

(*a*) any other receiver;

(*b*) the holder of a fixed security which is over property subject to the floating charge;

(*c*) the company or its liquidator, as the case may be.

(3) Where any question arises as to the person entitled to a payment under this section, or where a receipt or a discharge of a security cannot be obtained in respect of any such payment, the receiver shall consign the amount of such payment in any joint stock bank of issue in Scotland in name of the Accountant of Court for behoof of the person or persons entitled thereto.

DEFINITIONS

"fixed security": s.70(1).
"floating charge": s.744, C.A. 1985; s.251.
"receiver": s.70(1).

GENERAL NOTE

This section maps out the general order of repayment to be adopted by the receiver. It is derived from s.476, C.A. 1985 and I.A. 1985, Sched. 6, para. 21.

Subs. (1)

This subsection specifies, in order of priority, those claimants who take priority over the floating charge holder. As to those who have effectually executed diligence (para. (*b*)), see *Lord Advocate* v. *Royal Bank of Scotland,* 1977 S.C. 155; *Gordon Anderson Plant Ltd.* 1977 S.L.T. 7, *Cumbernauld Development Corp.* v. *Mustone Ltd.* 1983 S.L.T. (Sh.Ct.) 55 and *Forth and Clyde Construction* v. *Trinity Timber and Plywood Co.* 1984 S.L.T. 94.

Subs. (2)

After making all necessary payments the receiver must hand over the balance of any proceeds of realisation to either the company, its liquidator, any other receiver or chargee, whichever is the most appropriate.

Subs. (3)

Where disputes arise as to payment the disputed sum must be paid by the receiver into a recognised Scottish bank in the name of the Accountant of the Court pending settlement.

Disposal of interest in property

61.—(1) Where the receiver sells or disposes, or is desirous of selling or disposing, of any property or interest in property of the company which is subject to the floating charge by virtue of which the receiver was appointed and which is—

(*a*) subject to any security or interest of, or burden or encumbrance in favour of, a creditor the ranking of which is prior to, or pari passu with, or postponed to the floating charge, or

(*b*) property or an interest in property affected or attached by effectual diligence executed by any person,

and the receiver is unable to obtain the consent of such creditor or, as the case may be, such person to such a sale or disposal, the receiver may apply to the court for authority to sell or dispose of the property or interest in property free of such security, interest, burden, encumbrance or diligence.

(2) Subject to the next subsection, on such an application the court may, if it thinks fit, authorise the sale or disposal of the property or interest in question free of such security, interest, burden, encumbrance or diligence, and such authorisation may be on such terms or conditions as the court thinks fit.

(3) In the case of an application where a fixed security over the property or interest in question which ranks prior to the floating charge has not been met or provided for in full, the court shall not authorise the sale or disposal of the property or interest in question unless it is satisfied that

the sale or disposal would be likely to provide a more advantageous realisation of the company's assets than would otherwise be effected.

(4) It shall be a condition of an authorisation to which subsection (3) applies that—

(*a*) the net proceeds of the disposal, and

(*b*) where those proceeds are less than such amount as may be determined by the court to be the net amount which would be realised on a sale of the property or interest in the open market by a willing seller, such sums as may be required to make good the deficiency,

shall be applied towards discharging the sums secured by the fixed security.

(5) Where a condition imposed in pursuance of subsection (4) relates to two or more such fixed securities, that condition shall require the net proceeds of the disposal and, where paragraph (*b*) of that subsection applies, the sums mentioned in that paragraph to be applied towards discharging the sums secured by those fixed securities in the order of their priorities.

(6) A copy of an authorisation under subsection (2) certified by the clerk of court shall, within 14 days of the granting of the authorisation, be sent by the receiver to the registrar of companies.

(7) If the receiver without reasonable excuse fails to comply with subsection (6), he is liable to a fine and, for continued contravention, to a daily default fine.

(8) Where any sale or disposal is effected in accordance with the authorisation of the court under subsection (2), the receiver shall grant to the purchaser or disponee an appropriate document of transfer or conveyance of the property or interest in question, and that document has the effect, or, where recording, intimation or registration of that document is a legal requirement for completion of title to the property or interest, then that recording, intimation or registration (as the case may be) has the effect, of—

(*a*) disencumbering the property or interest of the security, interest, burden or encumbrance affecting it, and

(*b*) freeing the property or interest from the diligence executed upon it.

(9) Nothing in this section prejudices the right of any creditor of the company to rank for his debt in the winding up of the company.

DEFINITIONS

"fixed security": s.70(1).
"receiver": s.70(1).

GENERAL NOTE

This section is derived from s.477, C.A. 1985 as amended by s.59, I.A. 1985. In its amended form its provisions match s.43 of the present Act which relates to administrative receivers in England and Wales, subject to certain discrepancies attributable to the technical differences between English law and Scottish law. See Note to s.43 *supra*. The protection afforded to persons with a fixed security (s.477(2), C.A. 1985) has been diminished by the more liberal terms of subs. (3) and (4). "Effectual diligence"—see Note to s.60.

Cessation of appointment of receiver

62.—(1) A receiver may be removed from office by the court under subsection (3) below and may resign his office by giving notice of his resignation in the prescribed manner to such persons as may be prescribed.

(2) A receiver shall vacate office if he ceases to be qualified to act as an insolvency practitioner in relation to the company.

(3) Subject to the next subsection, a receiver may, on application to the court by the holder of the floating charge by virtue of which he was appointed, be removed by the court on cause shown.

(4) Where at any time a receiver vacates office—

(*a*) his remuneration and any expenses properly incurred by him, and

(*b*) any indemnity to which he is entitled out of the property of the company,

shall be paid out of the property of the company which is subject to the floating charge and shall have priority as provided for in section 60(1).

(5) When a receiver ceases to act as such otherwise than by death he shall, and, when a receiver is removed by the court, the holder of the floating charge by virtue of which he was appointed shall, within 14 days of the cessation or removal (as the case may be) give the registrar of companies notice to that effect, and the registrar shall enter the notice in the register of charges.

If the receiver or the holder of the floating charge (as the case may require) makes default in complying with the requirements of this subsection, he is liable to a fine and, for continued contravention, to a daily default fine.

(6) If by the expiry of a period of one month following upon the removal of the receiver or his ceasing to act as such no other receiver has been appointed, the floating charge by virtue of which the receiver was appointed—

(*a*) thereupon ceases to attach to the property then subject to the charge, and

(*b*) again subsists as a floating charge;

and for the purposes of calculating the period of one month under this subsection no account shall be taken of any period during which an administration order under Part II of this Act is in force.

Definitions

"floating charge": s.744, C.A. 1985; s.251.
"prescribed": s.70(1).
"property": s.436.
"qualified to act as an insolvency practitioner": s.390.
"receiver": s.70(1).

General Note

This section derives from s.478 of the Companies Act 1985 as amended by s.60, I.A. 1985. Its provisions now correspond closely in substance to those of s.45 of this Act, which are applicable in England and Wales. However, there is no counterpart in s.45 to the provision in subs. (3) which enables a receiver to be removed by the court on cause shown on an application by the holder of the floating charge by virtue of which the receiver was appointed. S.45 fails to indicate by whom an application may be made for the removal of an administrative receiver but the terms of subss. (1) and (3) of this section could perhaps serve as an analogy on which to base the proposition that the only party with standing to make application for the dismissal of an administrative receiver in England is the holder of the floating charge by virtue of which he was appointed.

Subs. (1)

See Note to s.45(1).

Subs. (2)

See Note to s.45(2).

Subs. (3)

Any dismissal of a receiver can only be by the court on cause shown.

Subs. (4)

See Note to s.45(3).

Subs. (5)

Notice of a receiver ceasing to act shall be given by the appropriate person to the registrar of companies within fourteen days of that happening, and the registrar must record the fact in his register of charges. Failure to do this can result in the receiver or the holder of the floating charge being fined.

Subs. (6)

If no replacement receiver is installed within one month then the floating charge will "refloat". The time limit is suspended while an administration order is in force because during that period any receiver will be supplanted by the administrator.

Powers of court

63.—(1) The court on the application of—

(*a*) the holder of a floating charge by virtue of which a receiver was appointed, or

(*b*) a receiver appointed under section 51,

may give directions to the receiver in respect of any matter arising in connection with the performance by him of his functions.

(2) Where the appointment of a person as a receiver by the holder of a floating charge is discovered to be invalid (whether by virtue of the invalidity of the instrument or otherwise), the court may order the holder of the floating charge to indemnify the person appointed against any liability which arises solely by reason of the invalidity of the appointment.

Definitions

"floating charge": s.744, C.A. 1985; s.251.
"holder of a floating charge": s.70(2).
"receiver": s.70(1).

General Note

This section re-enacts s.61, I.A. 1985, which completely replaced the provisions of s.479 of the Companies Act 1985 as originally enacted, and substituted new provisions which parallel in substance the position under the law applicable in England and Wales. Subs. (1) parallels for Scotland subs. (1) of s.35 (receivers and managers appointed out of court in England and Wales). Subs. (2) parallels for Scotland the provisions of s.34 of this Act (*q.v.*), which are applicable in England and Wales.

Notification that receiver appointed

64.—(1) Where a receiver has been appointed, every invoice, order for goods or business letter issued by or on behalf of the company or the receiver or the liquidator of the company, being a document on or in which the name of the company appears, shall contain a statement that a receiver has been appointed.

(2) If default is made in complying with the requirements of this section, the company and any of the following persons who knowingly and wilfully authorises or permits the default, namely any officer of the company, any liquidator of the company and any receiver, is liable to a fine.

Definitions

"fines": s.430, Sched. 10.
"receiver": s.70(1).

General Note

The parallel provision in English Law is s.39 *supra* (*q.v.*).

Subs. (1)

Where a receiver is appointed all invoices, business letters, etc., must disclose the fact of his appointment. For its predecessor see s.480(1), C.A. 1985.

Subs. (2)

Failure to comply with subs. (1) can result in fines for company officers, the receiver and liquidator where appropriate. For its derivation see s.480(2), C.A. 1985.

Information to be given by receiver

65.—(1) Where a receiver is appointed, he shall—
(*a*) forthwith send to the company and publish notice of his appointment, and
(*b*) within 28 days after his appointment, unless the court otherwise directs, send such notice to all the creditors of the company (so far as he is aware of their addresses).

(2) This section and the next do not apply in relation to the appointment of a receiver to act—
(*a*) with an existing receiver, or
(*b*) in place of a receiver who has died or ceased to act,
except that, where they apply to a receiver who dies or ceases to act before they have been fully complied with, the references in this section and the next to the receiver include (subject to subsection (3) of this section) his successor and any continuing receiver.

(3) If the company is being wound up, this section and the next apply notwithstanding that the receiver and the liquidator are the same person, but with any necessary modifications arising from that fact.

(4) If a person without reasonable excuse fails to comply with this section, he is liable to a fine and, for continued contravention, to a daily default fine.

DEFINITIONS
"fine", default fine": s.430, Sched. 10.
"modifications": s.436.
"receiver": s.70(1).

GENERAL NOTE
This section re-enacts s.62, I.A. 1985 which completely replaced the provisions of s.481 of the Companies Act 1985 as originally enacted, and substituted new provisions which match the substance of those contained in s.46 of this Act (*q.v.*) which applies to England and Wales.

Company's statement of affairs

66.—(1) Where a receiver of a company is appointed, the receiver shall forthwith require some or all of the persons mentioned in subsection (3) below to make out and submit to him a statement in the prescribed form as to the affairs of the company.

(2) A statement submitted under this section shall be verified by affidavit by the persons required to submit it and shall show—
(*a*) particulars of the company's assets, debts and liabilities;
(*b*) the names and addresses of its creditors;
(*c*) the securities held by them respectively;
(*d*) the dates when the securities were respectively given; and
(*e*) such further or other information as may be prescribed.

(3) The persons referred to in subsection (1) are—
(*a*) those who are or have been officers of the company;
(*b*) those who have taken part in the company's formation at any time within one year before the date of the appointment of the receiver;
(*c*) those who are in the company's employment or have been in its employment within that year, and are in the receiver's opinion capable of giving the information required;
(*d*) those who are or have been within that year officers of or in the employment of a company which is, or within that year was, an officer of the company.

In this subsection "employment" includes employment under a contract for services.

(4) Where any persons are required under this section to submit a statement of affairs to the receiver they shall do so (subject to the next subsection) before the end of the period of 21 days beginning with the day after that on which the prescribed notice of the requirement is given to them by the receiver.

(5) The receiver, if he thinks fit, may—

(*a*) at any time release a person from an obligation imposed on him under subsection (1) or (2), or

(*b*) either when giving the notice mentioned in subsection (4) or subsequently extend the period so mentioned,

and where the receiver has refused to exercise a power conferred by this subsection, the court, if it thinks fit, may exercise it.

(6) If a person without reasonable excuse fails to comply with any obligation imposed under this section, he is liable to a fine and, for continued contravention to a daily default fine.

Definitions

"fine", "default fine": s.430, Sched. 10.
"officers of the company": s.744, C.A. 1985; s.251.
"prescribed": s.70(1).
"receiver": s.70(1).

General Note

This section re-enacts s.63, I.A. 1985 which completely replaced the provisions of s.482 of the Companies Act 1985 as originally enacted, and substituted new provisions which match the substance of those contained in s.47 of this Act (*q.v.*), which applies to England and Wales.

Report by receiver

67.—(1) Where a receiver is appointed under section 51, he shall within 3 months (or such longer period as the court may allow) after his appointment, send to the registrar of companies, to the holder of the floating charge by virtue of which he was appointed and to any trustees for secured creditors of the company and (so far as he is aware of their addresses) to all such creditors a report as to the following matters, namely—

(*a*) the events leading up to his appointment, so far as he is aware of them;

(*b*) the disposal or proposed disposal by him of any property of the company and the carrying on or proposed carrying on by him of any business of the company;

(*c*) the amounts of principal and interest payable to the holder of the floating charge by virtue of which he was appointed and the amounts payable to preferential creditors; and

(*d*) the amount (if any) likely to be available for the payment of other creditors.

(2) The receiver shall also, within 3 months (or such longer period as the court may allow) after his appointment, either—

(*a*) send a copy of the report (so far as he is aware of their addresses) to all unsecured creditors of the company, or

(*b*) publish in the prescribed manner a notice stating an address to which unsecured creditors of the company should write for copies of the report to be sent to them free of charge,

and (in either case), unless the court otherwise directs, lay a copy of the report before a meeting of the company's unsecured creditors summoned for the purpose on not less than 14 days' notice.

(3) The court shall not give a direction under subsection (2) unless—

(*a*) the report states the intention of the receiver to apply for the direction, and

(*b*) a copy of the report is sent to the persons mentioned in paragraph *a* of that subsection, or a notice is published as mentioned in paragraph (*b*) of that subsection, not less than 14 days before the hearing of the application.

(4) Where the company has gone or goes into liquidation, the receiver—

(*a*) shall, within 7 days after his compliance with subsection (1) or, if later, the nomination or appointment of the liquidator, send a copy of the report to the liquidator, and

(*b*) where he does so within the time limited for compliance with subsection (2), is not required to comply with that subsection.

(5) A report under this section shall include a summary of the statement of affairs made out and submitted under section 66 and of his comments (if any) on it.

(6) Nothing in this section shall be taken as requiring any such report to include any information the disclosure of which would seriously prejudice the carrying out by the receiver of his functions.

(7) Section 65(2) applies for the purposes of this section also.

(8) If a person without reasonable excuse fails to comply with this section, he is liable to a fine and, for continued contravention, to a daily default fine.

(9) In this section "secured creditor", in relation to a company, means a creditor of the company who holds in respect of his debt a security over property of the company, and "unsecured creditor" shall be construed accordingly.

DEFINITIONS

"company goes into liquidation": s.247(2).
"fine", "default fine": s.430, Sched. 10.
"floating charge": s.744, C.A. 1985; s.251.
"holder of floating charge": s.70(2).
"preferential creditor": s.386.
"prescribed": s.70(1).
"receiver": s.70(1).
"security", "secured creditor", "unsecured creditor": subs. (9); s.248.

GENERAL NOTE

This new section is derived from s.64, I.A. 1985 and s.482A, C.A. 1985 and contains provisions which are nearly identical to those which apply in England and Wales by virtue of s.48 of this Act. However, it should be noted that under subs. (1) there is an additional requirement not included in s.48 of this Act, in that a Scottish receiver is required to send a copy of his report to the holder of the floating charge under which he was appointed. The additional subs. (9) in s.67 imports into that section a definition of "secured creditor" drafted in identical terms to the definition contained in the interpretation section for the First Group of Parts (s.248(*a*)). See further the General Note to s.48.

Committee of creditors

68.—(1) Where a meeting of creditors is summoned under section 67, the meeting may, if it thinks fit, establish a committee ("the creditors' committee") to exercise the functions conferred on it by or under this Act.

(2) If such a committee is established, the committee may on giving not less than 7 days' notice require the receiver to attend before it at any reasonable time and furnish it with such information relating to the carrying out by him of his functions as it may reasonably require.

DEFINITION

"the receiver": s.70(1).

General Note

This new section is derived from s.65, I.A. 1985 and s.482B, C.A. 1985 and contains provisions which are in substance the same as those of s.49 of this Act (*q.v.*) which applies to England and Wales. The meeting of creditors referred to in subs. (1) is that of the unsecured creditors, which the receiver must convene under s.67(2) *supra* within three months after his appointment, unless the court otherwise directs.

Enforcement of receiver's duty to make returns, etc.

69.—(1) If any receiver—

(*a*) having made default in filing, delivering or making any return, account or other document, or in giving any notice, which a receiver is by law required to file, deliver, make or give, fails to make good the default within 14 days after the service on him of a notice requiring him to do so; or

(*b*) has, after being required at any time by the liquidator of the company so to do, failed to render proper accounts of his receipts and payments and to vouch the same and to pay over to the liquidator the amount properly payable to him,

the court may, on an application made for the purpose, make an order directing the receiver to make good the default within such time as may be specified in the order.

(2) In the case of any such default as is mentioned in subsection (1)(*a*), an application for the purposes of this section may be made by any member or creditor of the company or by the registrar of companies; and, in the case of any such default as is mentioned in subsection (1)(*b*), the application shall be made by the liquidator; and, in either case, the order may provide that all expenses of and incidental to the application shall be borne by the receiver.

(3) Nothing in this section prejudices the operation of any enactments imposing penalties on receivers in respect of any such default as is mentioned in subsection (1).

Definitions

"court": s.744, C.A. 1985; s.251.
"receiver": s.70(1).
"registrar of companies": s.744, C.A. 1985.

General Note

This provision, which is mirrored in English Law by s.41 *supra*, deals with the enforcement of a receiver's duty to make returns.

Subs. (1)

Failure to perform this duty after notification that performance is required can be rectified by court order. For the relevant derivation see s.483, C.A. 1985 to which the present section exactly corresponds.

Subs. (2)

This subsection identifies those persons who may invoke this enforcement procedure and enables them to make the receiver pay their costs of application.

Subs. (3)

This subsection re-enacts subs. (3) of s.483, C.A. 1985 by providing that the above provisions do not supplant any criminal sanctions which the receiver may have incurred by his failure to submit returns.

Interpretation for Chapter II

70.—(1) In this Chapter, unless the contrary intention appears, the following expressions have the following meanings respectively assigned to them—

"company" means an incorporated company (whether or not a company within the meaning of the Companies Act) which the Court of Session has jurisdiction to wind up;

"fixed security", in relation to any property of a company, means any security, other than a floating charge or a charge having the nature of a floating charge, which on the winding up of the company in Scotland would be treated as an effective security over that property, and (without prejudice to that generality) includes a security over that property, being a heritable security within the meaning of the Conveyancing and Feudal Reform (Scotland) Act 1970;

"instrument of appointment" has the meaning given by section 53(1);

"prescribed" means prescribed by regulations made under this Chapter by the Secretary of State;

"receiver" means a receiver of such part of the property of the company as is subject to the floating charge by virtue of which he has been appointed under section 51;

"register of charges" means the register kept by the registrar of companies for the purposes of Chapter II of Part XII of the Companies Act;

"secured debenture" means a bond, debenture, debenture stock or other security which, either itself or by reference to any other instrument, creates a floating charge over all or any part of the property of the company, but does not include a security which creates no charge other than a fixed security; and

"series of secured debentures" means two or more secured debentures created as a series by the company in such a manner that the holders thereof are entitled pari passu to the benefit of the floating charge.

(2) Where a floating charge, secured debenture or series of secured debentures has been created by the company, then, except where the context otherwise requires, any reference in this Chapter to the holder of the floating charge shall—

(*a*) where the floating charge, secured debenture or series of secured debentures provides for a receiver to be appointed by any person or body, be construed as a reference to that person or body;

(*b*) where, in the case of a series of secured debentures, no such provision has been made therein but—

(i) there are trustees acting for the debenture-holders under and in accordance with a trust deed, be construed as a reference to those trustees, and

(ii) where no such trustees are acting, be construed as a reference to—

(*aa*) a majority in nominal value of those present or represented by proxy and voting at a meeting of debenture-holders at which the holders of at least one-third in nominal value of the outstanding debentures of the series are present or so represented, or

(*bb*) where no such meeting is held, the holders of at least one-half in nominal value of the outstanding debentures of the series.

(3) Any reference in this Chapter to a floating charge, secured debenture, series of secured debentures or instrument creating a charge includes, except where the context otherwise requires, a reference to that floating charge, debenture, series of debentures or instrument as varied by any instrument.

(4) References in this Chapter to the instrument by which a floating charge was created are, in the case of a floating charge created by words

in a bond or other written acknowledgement, references to the bond or, as the case may be, the other written acknowledgement.

General Note

This is an interpretation provision which is derived from ss.462(4), 484, 486 (part), C.A. 1985.

Subs. (1)

It is clear that the term "secured debenture" has a restricted meaning in Scottish Law—it does not include a debenture that confers only a *fixed* charge. It is important to note that the term "receiver" refers only to those receivers enforcing a floating charge.

Subs. (2)

By way of contrast a wide meaning is allocated to the phrase "the holder of a floating charge"—it includes trustees for debenture holders or the majority group of the holders of debentures in a series.

Subs. (3)

References to floating charges, secured debentures or instruments of charge include such items where they have been altered under s.466 of the C.A. 1985.

Subs. (4)

This subsection clarifies the phrase "an instrument by which a floating charge is created."

Prescription of forms, etc.; regulations

71.—(1) The notice referred to in section 62(5), and the notice referred to in section 65(1)(*a*) shall be in such form as may be prescribed.

(2) Any power conferred by this Chapter on the Secretary of State to make regulations is exercisable by statutory instrument; and a statutory instrument made in the exercise of the power so conferred to prescribe a fee is subject to annulment in pursuance of a resolution of either House of Parliament.

Definition

"prescribed": s.70(1).

General Note

This is an ancillary provision that reproduces in part the two subsections in s.485, C.A. 1985.

Subs. (1)

This subsection relates to the form of notices mentioned in ss.62(5) and 65(1) of this Act.

Subs. (2)

Regulations are to be made by the Secretary of State by statutory instrument and can be annulled by resolution of either House of Parliament.

Chapter III

Receivers' Powers in Great Britain as a Whole

Cross-border operation of receivership provisions

72.—(1) A receiver appointed under the law of either part of Great Britain in respect of the whole or any part of any property or undertaking of a company and in consequence of the company having created a charge which, as created, was a floating charge may exercise his powers in the other part of Great Britain so far as their exercise is not inconsistent with the law applicable there.

(2) In subsection (1) "receiver" includes a manager and a person who is appointed both receiver and manager.

DEFINITION

"floating charge": s.251; C.A. 1985, ss.462 and 744.

GENERAL NOTE

Subs. (1)

This subsection whose origin can be traced back to a proposal from the Scottish Law Commission in 1970 (Cmnd. 4336, para. 60), and which was formerly contained in the Administration of Justice Act 1977, s.7(1), enables a receiver appointed in one part of Great Britain to exercise his powers throughout Great Britain, in so far as this is not inconsistent with local law.

Subs. (2)

This subsection is an interpretation provision based on Administration of Justice Act 1977, s.7(2).

TRANSITIONAL PROVISION

Sched. 11, para. 4.

PART IV

WINDING UP OF COMPANIES REGISTERED UNDER THE COMPANIES ACTS

CHAPTER I

PRELIMINARY

Modes of winding up

Alternative modes of winding up

73.—(1) The winding up of a company, within the meaning given to that expression by section 735 of the Companies Act, may be either voluntary (Chapters II, III, IV and V in this Part) or by the court (Chapter VI).

(2) This Chapter, and Chapters VII to X, relate to winding up generally, except where otherwise stated.

DEFINITION

"company": s.735, C.A. 1985.

GENERAL NOTE

This section is derived from s.501 of the Companies Act 1985. A registered company can only be dissolved by winding up or striking off the register under s.652, C.A. 1985.

For voluntary winding-up, see Chaps. II, III, IV, and V *post.* Voluntary winding up under supervision has been abolished (s.438, Sched. 12) following the recommendation of the Cork Committee (Cmnd. 8558), paras. 182, 3. For winding up by the court see Chap. VI.

Contributories

Liability as contributories of present and past members

74.—(1) When a company is wound up, every present and past member is liable to contribute to its assets to any amount sufficient for payment of its debts and liabilities, and the expenses of the winding up, and for the adjustment of the rights of the contributories among themselves.

(2) This is subject as follows—

(*a*) a past member is not liable to contribute if he has ceased to be a member for one year or more before the commencement of the winding up;

(*b*) a past member is not liable to contribute in respect of any debt or liability of the company contracted after he ceased to be a member;

(*c*) a past member is not liable to contribute, unless it appears to the court that the existing members are unable to satisfy the contributions required to be made by them in pursuance of the Companies Act and this Act;

(*d*) in the case of a company limited by shares, no contribution is required from any member exceeding the amount (if any) unpaid on the shares in respect of which he is liable as a present or past member;

(*e*) nothing in the Companies Act or this Act invalidates any provision contained in a policy of insurance or other contract whereby the liability of individual members on the policy or contract is restricted, or whereby the funds of the company are alone made liable in respect of the policy or contract;

(*f*) a sum due to any member of the company (in his character of a member) by way of dividends, profits or otherwise is not deemed to be a debt of the company, payable to that member in a case of competition between himself and any other creditor not a member of the company, but any such sum may be taken into account for the purpose of the final adjustment of the rights of the contributories among themselves.

(3) In the case of a company limited by guarantee, no contribution is required from any member exceeding the amount undertaken to be contributed by him to the company's assets in the event of its being wound up; but if it is a company with a share capital, every member of it is liable (in addition to the amount so undertaken to be contributed to the assets), to contribute to the extent of any sums unpaid on shares held by him.

Definition

"contributory": s.79

General Note

This reproduces s.502, C.A. 1985.

In general every present member of the company is liable to contribute to the assets of the company on its winding up and in certain circumstances a past member is also liable. The maximum liability is limited in the case of a company limited by shares to the amount unpaid on the shares and in the case of a company limited by guarantee to the amount of the guarantee (s.74(2)(*d*) and (3)). The liability of a past member is governed by s.74(2)(*a*)–(*c*). For a discussion on contributories' petitions see *Palmer,* paras. 85–16 *et seq.*

Directors, etc., with unlimited liability

75.—(1) In the winding up of a limited company, any director or manager (whether past or present) whose liability is under the Companies Act unlimited is liable, in addition to his liability (if any) to contribute as an ordinary member, to make a further contribution as if he were at the commencement of the winding up a member of an unlimited company.

(2) However—

(*a*) a past director or manager is not liable to make such further contribution if he has ceased to hold office for a year or more before the commencement of the winding up;

(*b*) a past director or manager is not liable to make such further contribution in respect of any debt or liability of the company contracted after he ceased to hold office;

(*c*) subject to the company's articles, a director or manager is not liable to make such further contribution unless the court deems it necessary to require that contribution in order to satisfy the company's debts and liabilities, and the expense of the winding up.

General Note

This section which is based on s.503, C.A. 1985 deals with the effect in a winding up of the rare case where a past or present director or manager has unlimited personal liability. This applies where a special resolution has been passed to this effect and was dealt with by s.203 of the 1948 C.A. but is now dealt with in s.306, C.A. 1985. The alterations in the present section are merely minor drafting amendments.

See *Palmer,* para. 65–04 and footnote 16.

Liability of past directors and shareholders

76.—(1) This section applies where a company is being wound up and—

(*a*) it has under Chapter VII of Part V of the Companies Act (redeemable shares; purchase by a company of its own shares) made a payment out of capital in respect of the redemption or purchase of any of its own shares (the payment being referred to below as "the relevant payment"), and

(*b*) the aggregate amount of the company's assets and the amounts paid by way of contribution to its assets (apart from this section) is not sufficient for payment of its debts and liabilities, and the expenses of the winding up.

(2) If the winding up commenced within one year of the date on which the relevant payment was made, then—

(*a*) the person from whom the shares were redeemed or purchased, and

(*b*) the directors who signed the statutory declaration made in accordance with section 173(3) of the Companies Act for purposes of the redemption or purchase (except a director who shows that he had reasonable grounds for forming the opinion set out in the declaration),

are, so as to enable that insufficiency to be met, liable to contribute to the following extent to the company's assets.

(3) A person from whom any of the shares were redeemed or purchased is liable to contribute an amount not exceeding so much of the relevant payment as was made by the company in respect of his shares; and the directors are jointly and severally liable with that person to contribute that amount.

(4) A person who has contributed any amount to the assets in pursuance of this section may apply to the court for an order directing any other person jointly and severally liable in respect of that amount to pay him such amount as the court thinks just and equitable.

(5) Sections 74 and 75 do not apply in relation to liability accruing by virtue of this section.

(6) This section is deemed included in Chapter VII of Part V of the Companies Act for the purposes of the Secretary of State's power to make regulations under section 179 of that Act.

General Note

This section deals with the liability of past directors and shareholders for certain payments out of capital in connection with redemption or purchase by a private company of its own shares under s.171, C.A. 1985. It is based on ss.58(1)–(5) and 61, C.A. 1981 and s.504, C.A. 1985. See *Palmer,* paras. 33–23.

Limited company formerly unlimited

77.—(1) This section applies in the case of a company being wound up which was at some former time registered as unlimited but has re-registered—

(*a*) as a public company under section 43 of the Companies Act (or the former corresponding provision, section 5 of the Companies Act 1980), or

(*b*) as a limited company under section 51 of the Companies Act (or the former corresponding provision, section 44 of the Companies Act 1967).

(2) Notwithstanding section 74(2)(*a*), a past member of the company who was a member of it at the time of re-registration, if the winding up commences within the period of 3 years beginning with the day on which the company was re-registered, is liable to contribute to the assets of the company in respect of debts and liabilities contracted before that time.

(3) If no persons who were members of the company at that time are existing members of it, a person who at that time was a present or past member is liable to contribute as above notwithstanding that the existing members have satisfied the contributions, required to be made by them under the Companies Act and this Act.

This applies subject to section 74(2)(*a*) above and to subsection (2) of this section, but notwithstanding section 74(2)(*c*).

(4) Notwithstanding section 74(2)(*d*) and (3), there is no limit on the amount which a person who, at that time, was a past or present member of the company is liable to contribute as above.

General Note

This section which deals with the case of a limited liability company which was formerly unlimited is based on s.505, C.A. 1985.

See *Palmer*, paras. 85–47.

Unlimited company formerly limited

78.—(1) This section applies in the case of a company being wound up which was at some former time registered as limited but has been re-registered as unlimited under section 49 of the Companies Act (or the former corresponding provision, section 43 of the Companies Act 1967).

(2) A person who, at the time when the application for the company to be re-registered was lodged, was a past member of the company and did not after that again become a member of it is not liable to contribute to the assets of the company more than he would have been liable to contribute had the company not been re-registered.

General Note

This deals with the converse to s.77, namely an unlimited company which was formerly limited. It reproduces s.506, C.A. 1985.

Meaning of "contributory"

79.—(1) In this Act and the Companies Act the expression "contributory" means every person liable to contribute to the assets of a company in the event of its being wound up, and for the purposes of all proceedings for determining, and all proceedings prior to the final determination of, the persons who are to be deemed contributories, includes any person alleged to be a contributory.

(2) The reference in subsection (1) to persons liable to contribute to the assets does not include a person so liable by virtue of a declaration by the court under section 213 (imputed responsibility for company's fraudulent trading) or section 214 (wrongful trading) in Chapter X of this Part.

(3) A reference in a company's articles to a contributory does not (unless the context requires) include a person who is a contributory only by virtue of section 76.

This subsection is deemed included in Chapter VII of Part V of the Companies Act for the purposes of the Secretary of State's power to make regulations under section 179 of that Act.

GENERAL NOTE

This is based upon s.507, C.A. 1985. The generality of the definition in subs. (1) is limited by subs. (2) which originated in the I.A. 1985, Sched. 6, para. 5 and by subs. (3) which originated in the C.A. 1981, ss.58(6) and 61.

Nature of contributory's liability

80. The liability of a contributory creates a debt (in England and Wales in the nature of a specialty) accruing due from him at the time when his liability commenced, but payable at the time when calls are made for enforcing the liability.

GENERAL NOTE

This reproduces s.508, C.A. 1985 and makes the contributory's liability a specialty debt in England and Wales. The period of limitation is therefore 12 years. Wales was not expressly referred to in s.508 but was implied in the reference to England.

Contributories in case of death of a member

81.—(1) If a contributory dies either before or after he has been placed on the list of contributories, his personal representatives, and the heirs and legatees of heritage of his heritable estate in Scotland, are liable in a due course of administration to contribute to the assets of the company in discharge of his liability and are contributories accordingly.

(2) Where the personal representatives are placed on the list of contributories, the heirs or legatees of heritage need not be added, but they may be added as and when the court thinks fit.

(3) If in England and Wales the personal representatives make default in paying any money ordered to be paid by them, proceedings may be taken for administering the estate of the deceased contributory and for compelling payment out of it of the money due.

GENERAL NOTE

This reproduces s.509 C.A. 1985 and substitutes the personal representatives or heirs and legatees in Scotland for a deceased contributory.

Effect of contributory's bankruptcy

82.—(1) The following applies if a contributory becomes bankrupt, either before or after he has been placed on the list of contributories.

(2) His trustee in bankruptcy represents him for all purposes of the winding up, and is a contributory accordingly.

(3) The trustee may be called on to admit to proof against the bankrupt's estate, or otherwise allow to be paid out of the bankrupt's assets in due course of law, any money due from the bankrupt in respect of his liability to contribute to the company's assets.

(4) There may be proved against the bankrupt's estate the estimated value of his liability to future calls as well as calls already made.

GENERAL NOTE

This section which contains a similar provision to s.81 in respect of bankruptcy reproduces s.510, C.A. 1985. The trustee in bankruptcy represents the bankrupt contributory for all purposes of the winding up.

Companies registered under Companies Act, Part XXII, Chapter II

83.—(1) The following applies in the event of a company being wound up which has been registered under section 680 of the Companies Act (or previous corresponding provisions in the Companies Act 1948 or earlier Acts).

(2) Every person is a contributory, in respect of the company's debts and liabilities contracted before registration, who is liable—

(*a*) to pay, or contribute to the payment of, any debt or liability so contracted, or

(*b*) to pay, or contribute to the payment of, any sum for the adjustment of the rights of the members among themselves in respect of any such debt or liability, or

(*c*) to pay, or contribute to the amount of, the expenses of winding up the company, so far as relates to the debts or liabilities above-mentioned.

(3) Every contributory is liable to contribute to the assets of the company, in the course of the winding up, all sums due from him in respect of any such liability.

(4) In the event of the death, bankruptcy or insolvency of any contributory, provisions of this Act, with respect to the personal representatives, to the heirs and legatees of heritage of the heritable estate in Scotland of deceased contributories and to the trustees of bankrupt or insolvent contributories respectively, apply.

General Note

This section re-enacts s.511, C.A. 1985 and deals with contributories in the case of the winding up of the companies not formed under the Companies Acts but authorised to register under the Act.

Chapter II

Voluntary Winding Up (Introductory and General)

Resolutions for, and commencement of, voluntary winding up

Circumstances in which company may be wound up voluntarily

84.—(1) A company may be wound up voluntarily—

(*a*) when the period (if any) fixed for the duration of the company by the articles expires, or the event (if any) occurs, on the occurrence of which the articles provide that the company is to be dissolved, and the company in general meeting has passed a resolution requiring it to be wound up voluntarily;

(*b*) if the company resolves by special resolution that it be wound up voluntarily;

(*c*) if the company resolves by extraordinary resolution to the effect that it cannot by reason of its liabilities continue its business, and that it is advisable to wind up.

(2) In this Act the expression "a resolution for voluntary winding up" means a resolution passed under any of the paragraphs of subsection (1).

(3) A resolution passed under paragraph (*a*) of subsection (1), as well as a special resolution under paragraph (*b*) and an extraordinary resolution under paragraph (*c*), is subject to section 380 of the Companies Act (copy of resolution to be forwarded to registrar of companies within 15 days).

Definition

"special", "extraordinary" resolution: s.378, C.A. 1985.

General Note

This section re-enacts s.572, C.A. 1985 and deals with the circumstances in which a company may be wound up voluntarily. Although this section does not clearly say so there are two species of voluntary winding up—members' and creditors' voluntary winding up. Winding up subject to supervision by the court has been abolished. See General note to s.73.

The power to wind up voluntarily cannot be excluded by the articles although it is possible to restrict voting rights at meetings (*Re Peveril Gold Mines Ltd.* [1898] 1 Ch. 122 (C.A.)). See generally *Palmer,* Chap. 86.

Notice of resolution to wind up

85.—(1) When a company has passed a resolution for voluntary winding up, it shall, within 14 days after the passing of the resolution, give notice of the resolution by advertisement in the Gazette.

(2) If default is made in complying with this section, the company and every officer of it who is in default is liable to a fine and, for continued contravention, to a daily default fine.

For purposes of this subsection the liquidator is deemed an officer of the company.

Definition

"fine", "daily default fine": s.430, Sched. 10.

General Note

This section re-enacts s.573, C.A. 1985. It deals with the Gazetting of a notice of a resolution to wind up voluntarily. See *Palmer,* para. 86–02.

Commencement of winding up

86. A voluntary winding up is deemed to commence at the time of the passing of the resolution for voluntary winding up.

Transitional Provision

Sched. 11, para. 4.

General Note

This re-enacts s.574, C.A. 1985 and provides for commencement of the winding up at the date of the relevant resolution. See *Palmer,* para. 86–03.

Consequences of resolution to wind up

Effect on business and status of company

87.—(1) In case of a voluntary winding up, the company shall from the commencement of the winding up cease to carry on its business, except so far as may be required for its beneficial winding up.

(2) However, the corporate state and corporate powers of the company, notwithstanding anything to the contrary in its articles, continue until the company is dissolved.

General Note

This section re-enacts s.575, C.A. 1985. In essence it provides that although the company's status and powers subsist until dissolution, it shall cease to carry on business except so far as may be necessary for the purposes of winding up. The property remains in the company unless a vesting order is made under s.112.

As to the carrying on of the company's business it is sufficient that the liquidator bona fide and reasonably believes that the carrying on is necessary for the beneficial winding up of the company (*Re Great Eastern Electric Co. Ltd.* [1941] 1 Ch. 241). However, a liquidator must not carry on the business with a view to its financial reconstruction (*Re Wreck Recovery & Salvage Co.* (1880) 15 Ch.D. 353. The onus of proof that a matter is not necessary for the beneficial winding up is on the party objecting to it (*The Hire Purchase Furnishing Co. Ltd.* v. *Richens* (1887) 20 Q.B.D. 387 (C.A.)). See *Palmer,* para. 86–24.

Avoidance of share transfers, etc. after winding-up resolution

88. Any transfer of shares, not being a transfer made to or with the sanction of the liquidator, and any alteration in the status of the company's members, made after the commencement of a voluntary winding up, is void.

General Note

This re-enacts s.576, C.A. 1985 and avoids a transfer of shares after the commencement of the winding up unless it is made to or with the consent of the liquidator. The liquidator may give his consent without the necessity of getting the court's permission. A transfer without consent is void but not illegal (*Biederman* v. *Stone* (1867) L.R. 2 C.P. 504). The section only applies to transfers of shares, not transfers of debentures (*Re Goy & Co. Ltd., Farmer* v. *Goy & Co. Ltd.* [1900] 2 Ch. 149).

Declaration of solvency

Statutory declaration of solvency

89.—(1) Where it is proposed to wind up a company voluntarily, the directors (or, in the case of a company having more than two directors, the majority of them) may at a directors' meeting make a statutory declaration to the effect that they have made a full inquiry into the company's affairs and that, having done so, they have formed the opinion that the company will be able to pay its debts in full, together with interest at the official rate (as defined in section 251), within such period, not exceeding 12 months from the commencement of the winding up, as may be specified in the declaration.

(2) Such a declaration by the directors has no effect for purposes of this Act unless—

(*a*) it is made within the 5 weeks immediately preceding the date of the passing of the resolution for winding up, or on that date but before the passing of the resolution, and

(*b*) it embodies a statement of the company's assets and liabilities as at the latest practicable date before the making of the declaration.

(3) The declaration shall be delivered to the registrar of companies before the expiration of 15 days immediately following the date on which the resolution for winding up is passed.

(4) A director making a declaration under this section without having reasonable grounds for the opinion that the company will be able to pay its debts in full, together with interest at the official rate, within the period specified is liable to imprisonment or a fine, or both.

(5) If the company is wound up in pursuance of a resolution passed within 5 weeks after the making of the declaration, and its debts (together with interest at the official rate) are not paid or provided for in full within the period specified, it is to be presumed (unless the contrary is shown) that the director did not have reasonable grounds for his opinion.

(6) If a declaration required by subsection (3) to be delivered to the registrar is not so delivered within the time prescribed by that subsection, the company and every officer in default is liable to a fine and, for continued contravention, to a daily default fine.

See General Note to s.90 *infra*.

Distinction between "members' " and "creditors' " voluntary winding up

90. A winding up in the case of which a directors' statutory declaration under section 89 has been made is a "members' voluntary winding up"; and a winding up in the case of which such a declaration has not been made is a "creditors' voluntary winding up".

DEFINITION

"fine", "daily default fine": s.430, Sched. 10.

GENERAL NOTE

These sections re-enact ss.577 and 578, C.A. 1985 though the reference in subs. (1) and subs. (5) of s.89 to interest at the official rate is new. Only if a statutory declaration under s.577 is made can the voluntary winding up be a members' voluntary winding up. See generally *Palmer,* para. 86–05.

CHAPTER III

MEMBERS' VOLUNTARY WINDING UP

Appointment of liquidator

91.—(1) In a members' voluntary winding up, the company in general meeting shall appoint one or more liquidators for the purpose of winding up the company's affairs and distributing its assets.

(2) On the appointment of a liquidator all the powers of the directors cease, except so far as the company in general meeting or the liquidator sanctions their continuance.

GENERAL NOTE

This derives from s.580, C.A. 1985, but, unlike that section, refers only to the company's power to appoint a liquidator (and the effect of such appointment) and not to its power to fix the remuneration of a liquidator. The equivalent provisions in the case of a creditors' voluntary winding up are to be found in ss.100 and 103. The Cork Committee (para. 883) recommended changes in the manner in which the remuneration of the liquidator, *inter alia,* was fixed. The procedure is now contained in the Rules which provide that it be fixed, initially, by the liquidation committee, or if none, the meeting of creditors with final recourse to the court.

Power to fill vacancy in office of liquidator

92.—(1) If a vacancy occurs by death, resignation or otherwise in the office of liquidator appointed by the company, the company in general meeting may, subject to any arrangement with its creditors, fill the vacancy.

(2) For that purpose a general meeting may be convened by any contributory or, if there were more liquidators than one, by the continuing liquidators.

(3) The meeting shall be held in manner provided by this Act or by the articles, or in such manner as may, on application by any contributory or by the continuing liquidators, be determined by the court.

GENERAL NOTE

This re-enacts s.581, C.A. 1985, and deals with the power of the company to fill a vacancy in the office of liquidator. See s.104 for the power of the creditors in a creditors' voluntary winding up.

General company meeting at each year's end

93.—(1) Subject to sections 96 and 102, in the event of the winding up continuing for more than one year, the liquidator shall summon a general meeting of the company at the end of the first year from the commencement of the winding up, and of each succeeding year, or at the first convenient date within 3 months from the end of the year or such longer period as the Secretary of State may allow.

(2) The liquidator shall lay before the meeting an account of his acts and dealings, and of the conduct of the winding up, during the preceding year.

(3) If the liquidator fails to comply with this section, he is liable to a fine.

Definition
"fine": s.430, Sched. 10.

See General Note to s.94.

Final meeting prior to dissolution

94.—(1) As soon as the company's affairs are fully wound up, the liquidator shall make up an account of the winding up, showing how it has been conducted and the company's property has been disposed of, and thereupon shall call a general meeting of the company for the purpose of laying before it the account, and giving an explanation of it.

(2) The meeting shall be called by advertisement in the Gazette, specifying its time, place and object and published at least one month before the meeting.

(3) Within one week after the meeting, the liquidator shall send to the registrar of companies a copy of the account, and shall make a return to him of the holding of the meeting and of its date.

(4) If the copy is not sent or the return is not made in accordance with subsection (3), the liquidator is liable to a fine and, for continued contravention, to a daily default fine.

(5) If a quorum is not present at the meeting, the liquidator shall, in lieu of the return mentioned above, make a return that the meeting was duly summoned and that no quorum was present; and upon such a return being made, the provisions of subsection (3) as to the making of the return are deemed complied with.

(6) If the liquidator fails to call a general meeting of the company as required by subsection (1), he is liable to a fine.

Definition
"fine", "daily default fine": s.430, Sched. 10.

General Note
These sections re-enact ss.584 and 585 (part), C.A. 1985 with minor amendments and provide for a general meeting of the company at the end of each year or at the first convenient date within three months thereafter or such longer period as shall be allowed, and the final meeting and dissolution. The procedure for dissolution is much simpler than in the case of a compulsory winding up. No application to the Court is necessary. The company is automatically dissolved on the expiration of three months after registration of the return of the final meeting subject to an order by the court to defer dissolution (s.201). See *Palmer,* para. 86–62.

Effect of company's insolvency

95.—(1) This section applies where the liquidator is of the opinion that the company will be unable to pay its debts in full (together with interest at the official rate) within the period stated in the directors' declaration under section 89.

(2) The liquidator shall—

(*a*) summon a meeting of creditors for a day not later than the 28th day after the day on which he formed that opinion;

(*b*) send notices of the creditors' meeting to the creditors by post not less than 7 days before the day on which that meeting is to be held;

(*c*) cause notice of the creditors' meeting to be advertised once in the Gazette and once at least in 2 newspapers circulating in the relevant locality (that is to say the locality in which the company's principal place of business in Great Britain was situated during the relevant period); and

(*d*) during the period before the day on which the creditors' meeting is to be held, furnish creditors free of charge with such information concerning the affairs of the company as they may reasonably require;

and the notice of the creditors' meeting shall state the duty imposed by paragraph (*d*) above.

(3) The liquidator shall also—

(*a*) make out a statement in the prescribed form as to the affairs of the company;

(*b*) lay that statement before the creditors' meeting; and

(*c*) attend and preside at that meeting.

(4) The statement as to the affairs of the company shall be verified by affidavit by the liquidator and shall show—

(*a*) particulars of the company's assets, debts and liabilities;

(*b*) the names and addresses of the company's creditors;

(*c*) the securities held by them respectively;

(*d*) the dates when the securities were respectively given; and

(*e*) such further or other information as may be prescribed.

(5) Where the company's principal place of business in Great Britain was situated in different localities at different times during the relevant period, the duty imposed by subsection (2)(*c*) applies separately in relation to each of those localities.

(6) Where the company had no place of business in Great Britain during the relevant period, references in subsection (2)(*c*) and (5) to the company's principal place of business in Great Britain are replaced by references to its registered office.

(7) In this section "the relevant period" means the period of 6 months immediately preceding the day on which were sent the notices summoning the company meeting at which it was resolved that the company be wound up voluntarily.

(8) If the liquidator without reasonable excuse fails to comply with this section, he is liable to a fine.

DEFINITIONS

"fine": s.430, Sched. 10.
"interest at the official rate": s.251.
"members' voluntary winding up": s.90.
"prescribed": s.251.
"security": s.248(*b*).
"the Gazette": s.744, C.A. 1985; s.251.
"the relevant period": subs. (7).

GENERAL NOTE

This provision re-enacts (in part) s.83, I.A. 1985 and contains a series of provisions applicable in cases where a members' voluntary winding up has commenced in relation to a company which the liquidator subsequently finds or considers to be insolvent. The procedures which the liquidator is thereupon required to follow have the effect of transforming the winding up into a creditors' voluntary winding up whose commencement is deemed to have been effective since the commencement of the members' voluntary winding up.

Subs. (1)

The period stated in the directors' declaration under s.89

This refers to the statutory declaration of solvency which must be made by the directors of a company in order that it may be wound up by means of a members' voluntary winding up. Subs. (1) of that section requires the directors to declare that in their opinion the company will be able to pay its debts in full within a specified period, not exceeding 12 months from the commencement of winding up.

Subs. (2)(c)

Two newspapers circulating in the relevant locality

This can include "free" newspapers which are circulated on a local basis and posted through householders' letterboxes without charge to the recipients (H.C. Standing Committee E, June 11, 1985, cols. 277, 278).

Conversion to creditors' voluntary winding up

96. As from the day on which the creditors' meeting is held under section 95, this Act has effect as if—

(*a*) the directors' declaration under section 89 had not been made; and

(*b*) the creditors' meeting and the company meeting at which it was resolved that the company be wound up voluntarily were the meetings mentioned in section 98 in the next Chapter;

and accordingly the winding up becomes a creditors' voluntary winding up.

Definition

"creditors' voluntary winding up": s.90.

General Note

This re-enacts s.83(7), I.A. 1985. See General Note to s.95 *supra*.

Chapter IV

Creditors' Voluntary Winding Up

Application of this Chapter

97.—(1) Subject as follows, this Chapter applies in relation to a creditors' voluntary winding up.

(2) Sections 98 and 99 do not apply where, under section 96 in Chapter III, a members' voluntary winding up has become a creditors' voluntary winding up.

General Note

Subs. (1) limits the application of Ch. IV to a creditors' voluntary winding up while subs. (2) exempts such a winding-up resulting from a conversion from a members' voluntary winding up (see ss.95, 96) from the operation of ss.98 and 99 in view of the equivalent steps which will already have been taken under s.95.

Meeting of creditors

98.—(1) The company shall—

(*a*) cause a meeting of its creditors to be summoned for a day not later than the 14th day after the day on which there is to be held the company meeting at which the resolution for voluntary winding up is to be proposed;

(*b*) cause the notices of the creditors' meeting to be sent by post to the creditors not less than 7 days before the day on which that meeting is to be held; and

(*c*) cause notice of the creditors' meeting to be advertised once in the Gazette and once at least in two newspapers circulating in the relevant locality (that is to say the locality in which the company's principal place of business in Great Britain was situated during the relevant period).

(2) The notice of the creditors' meeting shall state either—

(*a*) the name and address of a person qualified to act as an insolvency practitioner in relation to the company who, during the period before the day on which that meeting is to be held, will furnish creditors free of charge with such information concerning the company's affairs as they may reasonably require; or

(*b*) a place in the relevant locality where, on the two business days falling next before the day on which that meeting is to be held, a list of the names and addresses of the company's creditors will be available for inspection free of charge.

(3) Where the company's principal place of business in Great Britain was situated in different localities at different times during the relevant period, the duties imposed by subsections (1)(*c*) and (2)(*b*) above apply separately in relation to each of those localities.

(4) Where the company had no place of business in Great Britain during the relevant period, references in subsections (1)(*c*) and (3) to the company's principal place of business in Great Britain are replaced by references to its registered office.

(5) In this section "the relevant period" means the period of 6 months immediately preceding the day on which were sent the notices summoning the company meeting at which it was resolved that the company be wound up voluntarily.

(6) If the company without reasonable excuse fails to comply with subsection (1) or (2), it is guilty of an offence and liable to a fine.

DEFINITIONS

"creditors' voluntary winding up": s.90.
"fine": s.430, Sched. 10.
"person qualified to act as an insolvency practitioner": s.390.
"prescribed": s.251.
"security": s.248(*b*).
"the Gazette": s.744, C.A. 1985; s.251.
"the relevant period": subs. (5).
"to act as an insolvency practitioner in relation to a company": s.388.

GENERAL NOTE

This section, which is designed to operate in close connection with s.166, replaces (in part) s.85, I.A. 1985. It governs the convening of a meeting of creditors following the passing by a company meeting of a resolution under s.84 for the winding up of the company, in circumstances where the winding up will be a creditors' voluntary winding up. At that meeting, the creditors may in turn exercise their right to nominate a person to be liquidator, in accordance with the provisions of s.100 which confers upon the creditors a pre-eminent right of appointment of the liquidator; the appointment as liquidator of the person, if any, who has been nominated by the company will only take place in default of any nomination by the creditors. As a further reform in the law aimed at improving the ability of creditors' meetings to act in a decisive way, the rules will provide for voting at creditors' meetings to to be on the basis of a majority in value only (see *Cork Report,* paras. 921–925; *White Paper,* para. 78).

Subs. (1)(c)

Two newspapers circulating in the relevant locality
Cf. General Note to s.95(2)(*c*).

Directors to lay statement of affairs before creditors

99.—(1) The directors of the company shall—

(*a*) make out a statement in the prescribed form as to the affairs of the company;

(*b*) cause that statement to be laid before the creditors' meeting under section 98; and

(*c*) appoint one of their number to preside at that meeting;

and it is the duty of the director so appointed to attend the meeting and preside over it.

(2) The statement as to the affairs of the company shall be verified by affidavit by some or all of the directors and shall show—

(*a*) particulars of the company's assets, debts and liabilities;
(*b*) the names and addresses of the company's creditors;
(*c*) the securities held by them respectively;
(*d*) the dates when the securities were respectively given; and
(*e*) such further or other information as may be prescribed.

(3) If—

(*a*) the directors without reasonable excuse fail to comply with subsection (1) or (2); or
(*b*) any director without reasonable excuse fails to comply with subsection (1), so far as requiring him to attend and preside at the creditors' meeting,

the directors are or (as the case may be) the director is guilty of an offence and liable to a fine.

GENERAL NOTE

This section replaces (in part) s.85, I.A. 1985.

Appointment of liquidator

100.—(1) The creditors and the company at their respective meetings mentioned in section 98 may nominate a person to be liquidator for the purpose of winding up the company's affairs and distributing its assets.

(2) The liquidator shall be the person nominated by the creditors or, where no person has been so nominated, the person (if any) nominated by the company.

(3) In the case of different persons being nominated, any director, member or creditor of the company may, within 7 days after the date on which the nomination was made by the creditors, apply to the court for an order either—

(*a*) directing that the person nominated as liquidator by the company shall be liquidator instead of or jointly with the person nominated by the creditors, or
(*b*) appointing some other person to be liquidator instead of the person nominated by the creditors.

GENERAL NOTE

This section is derived from s.589, C.A. 1985. See Note to s.98 and *Palmer,* paras. 86–11.

Appointment of liquidation committee

101.—(1) The creditors at the meeting to be held under section 98 or at any subsequent meeting may, if they think fit, appoint a committee ("the liquidation committee") of not more than 5 persons to exercise the functions conferred on it by or under this Act.

(2) If such a committee is appointed, the company may, either at the meeting at which the resolution for voluntary winding up is passed or at any time subsequently in general meeting, appoint such number of persons as they think fit to act as members of the committee, not exceeding 5.

(3) However, the creditors may, if they think fit, resolve that all or any of the persons so appointed by the company ought not to be members of the liquidation committee; and if the creditors so resolve—

(*a*) the persons mentioned in the resolution are not then, unless the court otherwise directs, qualified to act as members of the committee; and
(*b*) on any application to the court under this provision the court may, if it thinks fit, appoint other persons to act as such members in place of the persons mentioned in the resolution.

(4) In Scotland, the liquidation committee has, in addition to the powers and duties conferred and imposed on it by this Act, such of the powers and duties of commissioners on a bankrupt estate as may be conferred and imposed on liquidation committees by the rules.

General Note

This section replaces (in part) s.590, C.A. 1985, and the term "liquidation committee" replaces the term "committee of inspection". The procedure is now governed by the Rules.

Creditors' meeting where winding up converted under s.96

102. Where, in the case of a winding up which was, under section 96 in Chapter III, converted to a creditors' voluntary winding up, a creditors' meeting is held in accordance with section 95, any appointment made or committee established by that meeting is deemed to have been made or established by a meeting held in accordance with section 98 in this Chapter.

General Note

Where a winding up has been converted into a creditors' voluntary winding up under ss.95 and 96, no creditors' meeting under s.98 is necessary. S.102 deems the creditors' meeting which will have been held under s.95 to have been held under s.98 in order to render ss.100 and 101 applicable in such a case.

Cesser of directors' powers

103. On the appointment of a liquidator, all the powers of the directors cease, except so far as the liquidation committee (or, if there is no such committee, the creditors) sanction their continuance.

General Note

This replaces (in part) s.591, C.A. 1985. It is analogous to s.91(2) *supra,* which applies to a members' voluntary winding up.

Vacancy in office of liquidator

104. If a vacancy occurs, by death, resignation or otherwise, in the office of a liquidator (other than a liquidator appointed by, or by the direction of, the court) the creditors may fill the vacancy.

General Note

This re-enacts s.592, C.A. 1985 and deals with the creditors' power to fill a vacancy in the office of liquidator. For the procedure see the Rules.

Meetings of company and creditors at each year's end

105.—(1) If the winding up continues for more than one year, the liquidator shall summon a general meeting of the company and a meeting of the creditors at the end of the first year from the commencement of the winding up, and of each succeeding year, or at the first convenient date within 3 months from the end of the year or such longer period as the Secretary of State may allow.

(2) The liquidator shall lay before each of the meetings an account of his acts and dealings and of the conduct of the winding up during the preceding year.

(3) If the liquidator fails to comply with this section, he is liable to a fine.

(4) Where under section 96 a members' voluntary winding up has become a creditors' voluntary winding up, and the creditors' meeting under section 95 is held 3 months or less before the end of the first year

from the commencement of the winding up, the liquidator is not required by this section to summon a meeting of creditors at the end of that year.

GENERAL NOTE

This re-enacts s.594, C.A. 1985 with minor amendments and provides for general meetings of the company and meetings of the creditors at the end of each year. Subs. (4) is new and obviates the need for the first yearly meeting in the circumstances mentioned. See General Note to s.97.

Final meeting prior to dissolution

106.—(1) As soon as the company's affairs are fully wound up, the liquidator shall make up an account of the winding up, showing how it has been conducted and the company's property has been disposed of, and thereupon shall call a general meeting of the company and a meeting of the creditors for the purpose of laying the account before the meetings and giving an explanation of it.

(2) Each such meeting shall be called by advertisement in the Gazette specifying the time, place and object of the meeting, and published at least one month before it.

(3) Within one week after the date of the meetings (or, if they are not held on the same date, after the date of the later one) the liquidator shall send to the registrar of companies a copy of the account, and shall make a return to him of the holding of the meetings and of their dates.

(4) If the copy is not sent or the return is not made in accordance with subsection (3), the liquidator is liable to a fine and, for continued contravention, to a daily default fine.

(5) However, if a quorum is not present at either such meeting, the liquidator shall, in lieu of the return required by subsection (3), make a return that the meeting was duly summoned and that no quorum was present; and upon such return being made the provisions of that subsection as to the making of the return are, in respect of that meeting, deemed complied with.

(6) If the liquidator fails to call a general meeting of the company or a meeting of the creditors as required by this section, he is liable to a fine.

DEFINITION

"fine", "daily default fine": s.430, Sched. 10.

GENERAL NOTE

This re-enacts s.595(1)–(5), (8), C.A. 1985 and deals with the final meeting prior to dissolution. It is analogous to s.94 (*q.v.*). Dissolution is now dealt with in s.201.

CHAPTER V

PROVISIONS APPLYING TO BOTH KINDS OF VOLUNTARY WINDING UP

Distribution of company's property

107. Subject to the provisions of this Act as to preferential payments, the company's property in a voluntary winding up shall on the winding up be applied in satisfaction of the company's liabilities pari passu and, subject to that application, shall (unless the articles otherwise provide) be distributed among the members according to their rights and interests in the company.

GENERAL NOTE

This re-enacts s.597, C.A. 1985 and provides *inter alia* for payment of debts *pari passu.* This means of course *pari passu* within their particular class after allowing for secured creditors' rights. For preferential creditors see s.386 and Sched. 6 where the categories are now clearly stated.

For a discussion of the liquidator's duty to provide for all debts before distribution to the shareholders see *Pulsford* v. *Devenish* [1903] 2 Ch. 625.

Appointment or removal of liquidator by the court

108.—(1) If from any cause whatever there is no liquidator acting, the court may appoint a liquidator.

(2) The court may, on cause shown, remove a liquidator and appoint another.

General Note

This re-enacts s.599, C.A. 1985 and deals with the courts' power to appoint and remove a liquidator for cause shown. Some unfitness must be shown for removal (see *Re Sir John Moore Gold Mining Co.* (1879) 12 Ch. D. 325 (C.A.)). A liquidator may appeal against removal (*Re Adam Eyton Ltd.* (1887) 36 Ch. D. 299 (C.A.)). See *Palmer,* paras. 86–48.

Notice by liquidator of his appointment

109.—(1) The liquidator shall, within 14 days after his appointment, publish in the Gazette and deliver to the registrar of companies for registration a notice of his appointment in the form prescribed by statutory instrument made by the Secretary of State.

(2) If the liquidator fails to comply with this section, he is liable to a fine and, for continued contravention, to a daily default fine.

Definition

"fine", "daily default fine": s.430, Sched. 10.

General Note

This re-enacts s.600, C.A. 1985 and deals with gazetting and registration of the liquidator's appointment.

Acceptance of shares, etc., as consideration for sale of company property

110.—(1) This section applies, in the case of a company proposed to be, or being, wound up voluntarily, where the whole or part of the company's business or property is proposed to be transferred or sold to another company ("the transferee company"), whether or not the latter is a company within the meaning of the Companies Act.

(2) With the requisite sanction, the liquidator of the company being, or proposed to be, wound up ("the transferor company") may receive, in compensation or part compensation for the transfer or sale, shares, policies or other like interests in the transferee company for distribution among the members of the transferor company.

(3) The sanction requisite under subsection (2) is—

(*a*) in the case of a members' voluntary winding up, that of a special resolution of the company, conferring either a general authority on the liquidator or an authority in respect of any particular arrangement, and

(*b*) in the case of a creditors' voluntary winding up, that of either the court or the liquidation committee.

(4) Alternatively to subsection (2), the liquidator may (with that sanction) enter into any other arrangement whereby the members of the transferor company may, in lieu of receiving cash, shares, policies or other like interests (or in addition thereto), participate in the profits of, or receive any other benefit from, the transferee company.

(5) A sale or arrangement in pursuance of this section is binding on members of the transferor company.

(6) A special resolution is not invalid for purposes of this section by reason that it is passed before or concurrently with a resolution for voluntary winding up or for appointing liquidators; but, if an order is made within a year for winding up the company by the court, the special resolution is not valid unless sanctioned by the court.

General Note

This re-enacts and re-drafts ss.582(1)–(4), (7) and 593, C.A. 1985. Subss. (5), (6) and (8) of s.582 can now be found in s.111 *infra*. S.110 deals with a reconstruction where a liquidator of a company in voluntary winding up sells its business or property and in consideration of the transfer receives shares or other choses in action for distribution among the members in the transferor company. For a discussion of this see Weinberg and Blank, *Takeovers and Mergers* (4th ed.) Chaps. 6 and 7 and Buckley, *Companies Acts* (14th ed.) Vol. 1, pp.676–684. The section applies to a members' and a creditors' voluntary winding up with the difference referred to in subs. (3). Where there is a compulsory winding up it is arguable that a sale of this kind can be effected under s.167(1)(*b*). However in *Re London and Exchange Bank* (1867) 16 L.T. 340 Lord Romilly took a contrary view. *Cf. Re Agra and Masterman's Bank* (1866) L.R. 12 Eq. 509n and see Buckley, *Companies Acts, op. cit.* p.676.

Dissent from arrangement under s.110

111.—(1) This section applies in the case of a voluntary winding up where, for the purposes of section 110(2) or (4), there has been passed a special resolution of the transferor company providing the sanction requisite for the liquidator under that section.

(2) If a member of the transferor company who did not vote in favour of the special resolution expresses his dissent from it in writing, addressed to the liquidator and left at the company's registered office within 7 days after the passing of the resolution, he may require the liquidator either to abstain from carrying the resolution into effect or to purchase his interest at a price to be determined by agreement or by arbitration under this section.

(3) If the liquidator elects to purchase the member's interest, the purchase money must be paid before the company is dissolved and be raised by the liquidator in such manner as may be determined by special resolution.

(4) For purposes of an arbitration under this section, the provisions of the Companies Clauses Consolidation Act 1845 or, in the case of a winding up in Scotland, the Companies Clauses Consolidation (Scotland) Act 1845 with respect to the settlement of disputes by arbitration are incorporated with this Act, and—

(*a*) in the construction of those provisions this Act is deemed the special Act and "the company" means the transferor company, and

(*b*) any appointment by the incorporated provisions directed to be made under the hand of the secretary or any two of the directors may be made in writing by the liquidator (or, if there is more than one liquidator, then any two or more of them).

General Note

This deals with the rights of dissenting members where a special resolution has been passed providing the sanction for the liquidator to effect a reconstruction under either subs. (2) or subs. (4) of s.110. Subject to subs. (2), they consist of a right to block the reconstruction or be bought out.

Reference of questions to court

112.—(1) The liquidator or any contributory or creditor may apply to the court to determine any question arising in the winding up of a company, or to exercise, as respects the enforcing of calls or any other matter, all or any of the powers which the court might exercise if the company were being wound up by the court.

(2) The court, if satisfied that the determination of the question or the required exercise of power will be just and beneficial, may accede wholly or partially to the application on such terms and conditions as it thinks fit, or may make such other order on the application as it thinks just.

(3) A copy of an order made by virtue of this section staying the proceedings in the winding up shall forthwith be forwarded by the company, or otherwise as may be prescribed, to the registrar of companies, who shall enter it in his records relating to the company.

General Note

This re-enacts s.602, C.A. 1985 and is a wide and useful power to apply to the court on matters arising in the course of a voluntary winding up. See *Palmer,* paras. 86–19 for a discussion of the extent of this jurisdiction.

Court's power to control proceedings (Scotland)

113. If the court, on the application of the liquidator in the winding up of a company registered in Scotland, so directs, no action or proceeding shall be proceeded with or commenced against the company except by leave of the court and subject to such terms as the court may impose.

General Note

This re-enacts s.603, C.A. 1985 and gives the court in Scotland power to control proceedings.

No liquidator appointed or nominated by company

114.—(1) This section applies where, in the case of a voluntary winding up, no liquidator has been appointed or nominated by the company.

(2) The powers of the directors shall not be exercised, except with the sanction of the court or (in the case of a creditors' voluntary winding up) so far as may be necessary to secure compliance with sections 98 (creditors' meeting) and 99 (statement of affairs), during the period before the appointment or nomination of a liquidator of the company.

(3) Subsection (2) does not apply in relation to the powers of the directors—

(*a*) to dispose of perishable goods and other goods the value of which is likely to diminish if they are not immediately disposed of, and

(*b*) to do all such other things as may be necessary for the protection of the company's assets.

(4) If the directors of the company without reasonable excuse fail to comply with this section, they are liable to a fine.

Definitions

"creditors' voluntary winding up": s.90.
"fine": s.430, Sched. 10.

General Note

The purpose of this section is to strengthen the protection of the company's assets, and of the creditors' interests therein, during the critical period between the passing of a resolution for voluntary winding up under s.84, and the appointment of a liquidator under either s.91 or s.100 of that Act, depending on whether the winding up is a members' or a creditors' voluntary winding up. Paras. 667–673 of the *Cork Report* called attention to the need for such better protection, and the validity of the case for reform was conceded in paras. 128–133 of the *White Paper.* The provisions of this section, together with those of ss.98 and 99, form a carefully-planned response to the problem. This section covers the position up to the time of appointment of a liquidator, and effectively deprives the directors of their freedom to exercise their powers without the sanction of the court, except for the purposes specified in subss. (2) and (3).

Expenses of voluntary winding up

115. All expenses properly incurred in the winding up, including the remuneration of the liquidator, are payable out of the company's assets in priority to all other claims.

General Note

This re-enacts s.604, C.A. 1985 and gives the liquidator's costs priority over all other claims. See *Palmer,* paras. 86–28.

Saving for certain rights

116. The voluntary winding up of a company does not bar the right of any creditor or contributory to have it wound up by the court; but in the case of an application by a contributory the court must be satisfied that the rights of the contributories will be prejudiced by a voluntary winding up.

General Note

This re-enacts s.605, C.A. 1985 and allows an application for a compulsory winding up order. In the case of a contributory it must be shown that the rights of the contributory will be prejudiced by a voluntary winding up. Normally in the case of a creditor's petition the court has regard to the wishes of the majority of creditors but this is not an inflexible rule (*Re Southard & Co. Ltd.* [1979] 1 W.L.R. 1198 (C.A.)). See *Palmer,* paras. 85–06—85–07.

Chapter VI

Winding Up by the Court

Jurisdiction (England and Wales)

High Court and county court jurisdiction

117.—(1) The High Court has jurisdiction to wind up any company registered in England and Wales.

(2) Where the amount of a company's share capital paid up or credited as paid up does not exceed £120,000, then (subject to this section) the county court of the district in which the company's registered office is situated has concurrent jurisdiction with the High Court to wind up the company.

(3) The money sum for the time being specified in subsection (2) is subject to increase or reduction by order under section 416 in Part XV.

(4) The Lord Chancellor may by order in a statutory instrument exclude a county court from having winding-up jurisdiction, and for the purposes of that jurisdiction may attach its district, or any part thereof, to any other county court, and may by statutory instrument revoke or vary any such order.

In exercising the powers of this section, the Lord Chancellor shall provide that a county court is not to have winding-up jurisdiction unless it has for the time being jurisdiction for the purposes of Parts VIII to XI of this Act (individual insolvency).

(5) Every court in England and Wales having winding-up jurisdiction has for the purposes of that jurisdiction all the powers of the High Court; and every prescribed officer of the court shall perform any duties which an officer of the High Court may discharge by order of a judge of that court or otherwise in relation to winding up.

(6) For the purposes of this section, a company's "registered office" is the place which has longest been its registered office during the 6 months immediately preceding the presentation of the petition for winding up.

General Note

This reproduces s.512, C.A. 1985 with minor amendments.

Proceedings taken in wrong court

118.—(1) Nothing in section 117 invalidates a proceeding by reason of its being taken in the wrong court.

(2) The winding up of a company by the court in England and Wales, or any proceedings in the winding up, may be retained in the court in which the proceedings were commenced, although it may not be the court in which they ought to have been commenced.

General Note

This reproduces s.513, C.A. 1985 and deals with proceedings taken in the wrong court. Transfer is dealt with in s.75A, B and C of the County Courts Act 1959. These provisions were added by Sched. 3 to the Supreme Court Act 1981.

Proceedings in county court; case stated for High Court

119.—(1) If any question arises in any winding-up proceedings in a county court which all the parties to the proceedings, or which one of them and the judge of the court, desire to have determined in the first instance in the High Court, the judge shall state the facts in the form of a special case for the opinion of the High Court.

(2) Thereupon the special case and the proceedings (or such of them as may be required) shall be transmitted to the High Court for the purposes of the determination.

General Note

This section, which provides for a case stated procedure from the County Court to the High Court, re-enacts s.514, C.A. 1985. For an example of such a reference see *Re Mawcon Ltd.* [1969] 1 W.L.R. 78. Pennycuick J. said that that was the first case which had been stated pursuant to that provision.

Jurisdiction (Scotland)

Court of Session and sheriff court jurisdiction

120.—(1) The Court of Session has jurisdiction to wind up any company registered in Scotland.

(2) When the Court of Session is in vacation, the jurisdiction conferred on that court by this section may (subject to the provisions of this Part) be exercised by the judge acting as vacation judge in pursuance of section 4 of the Administration of Justice (Scotland) Act 1933.

(3) Where the amount of a company's share capital paid up or credited as paid up does not exceed £120,000, the sheriff court of the sheriffdom in which the company's registered office is situated has concurrent jurisdiction with the Court of Session to wind up the company; but—

(*a*) the Court of Session may, if it thinks expedient having regard to the amount of the company's assets to do so—
  (i) remit to a sheriff court any petition presented to the Court of Session for winding up such a company, or
  (ii) require such a petition presented to a sheriff court to be remitted to the Court of Session; and

(*b*) the Court of Session may require any such petition as abovementioned presented to one sheriff court to be remitted to another sheriff court; and

(*c*) in a winding up in the sheriff court the sheriff may submit a stated case for the opinion of the Court of Session on any question of law arising in that winding up.

(4) For purposes of this section, the expression "registered office" means the place which has longest been the company's registered office during the 6 months immediately preceding the presentation of the petition for winding up.

(5) The money sum for the time being specified in subsection (3) is subject to increase or reduction by order under section 416 in Part XV.

GENERAL NOTE

This reproduces with minor amendments s.515, C.A. 1985. It deals with the winding-up jurisdiction of the Court of Session and Sheriff's Court in Scotland.

See *Palmer,* para. 87–03.

Power to remit winding up to Lord Ordinary

121.—(1) The Court of Session may, by Act of Sederunt, make provision for the taking of proceedings in a winding up before one of the Lords Ordinary; and, where provision is so made, the Lord Ordinary has, for the purposes of the winding up, all the powers and jurisdiction of the court.

(2) However, the Lord Ordinary may report to the Inner House any matter which may arise in the course of a winding up.

GENERAL NOTE

This reproduces s.516, C.A. 1985. It provides for the making of rules by the Court of Session for remission of winding up to the Lord Ordinary.

Grounds and effect of winding-up petition

Circumstances in which company may be wound up by the court

122.—(1) A company may be wound up by the court if—

(*a*) the company has by special resolution resolved that the company be wound up by the court,

(*b*) being, a public company which was registered as such on its original incorporation, the company has not been issued with a certificate under section 117 of the Companies Act (public company share capital requirements) and more than a year has expired since it was so registered,

(*c*) it is an old public company, within the meaning of the Consequential Provisions Act,

(*d*) the company does not commence its business within a year from its incorporation or suspends its business for a whole year,

(*e*) the number of members is reduced below 2,

(*f*) the company is unable to pay its debts,

(*g*) the court is of the opinion that it is just and equitable that the company should be wound up.

(2) In Scotland, a company which the Court of Session has jurisdiction to wind up may be wound up by the Court if there is subsisting a floating charge over property comprised in the company's property and undertaking, and the court is satisfied that the security of the creditor entitled to the benefit of the floating charge is in jeopardy.

For this purpose a creditor's security is deemed to be in jeopardy if the Court is satisfied that events have occurred or are about to occur which render it unreasonable in the creditor's interests that the company should retain power to dispose of the property which is subject to the floating charge.

DEFINITIONS

"public company": s.1(3), C.A. 1985.

"special resolution": s.378, C.A. 1985.

"unable to pay its debts": s.123.

GENERAL NOTE

This originated as s.222, C.A. 1948 (as amended by Sched. 3 para. 27, C.A. 1980 and s.4 C. (F. C. and 12) (S.) Act 1972) and for a brief period became s.517, C.A. 1985. S.122(1) deals with the grounds for a compulsory winding up and s.122(2) with the winding up of a company in Scotland which has granted a floating charge which is in jeopardy. In Scotland the floating charge is a statutory creation, hence the need for this express provision. The grounds specified in s.122(1) represent the original grounds specified in the C.A. 1948 as amended by the C.A. 1980. Examples of (*a*) are rare in practice; (*b*) and (*c*) are a result of the minimum capital requirements introduced in the C.A. 1980; (*d*), like the whole of s.122, is descretionary. The court may refuse to make an order where there are good reasons for the delay and bona fides will be considered—*Re Capital Fire Insurance Association* (1882) 21 Ch.D. 209, 222. The figure in (*e*) was seven for public companies before 1980. (*f*) is the most common in practice, and the following are the general principles which emerge from the cases. An unsatisfied creditor has a prima facie right to an order but there are exceptions which arise out of the opening words of s.122. These are (1) where the petitioner's debt does not exceed £750 (originally £50) (2) where the debt is bona fide disputed by the company (3) where the company has paid or tendered payment of the petitioner's debt (4) where the winding up is opposed by other creditors and (5) where the company is in the process of being wound up voluntarily. For a full discussion of these principles see *Palmer,* paras. 85–06—85–07.

(*g*) has been the subject of considerable flux in the caselaw culminating in the House of Lord's decision in *Ebrahimi* v. *Westbourne Galleries Ltd.* [1973] A.C. 360 which established that the court's discretion under this head is not limited to circumstances *ejusdem generis* to (*a*)–(*f*) and, in particular, existed where an equitable relationship of confidence between the members had been violated. See *Palmer,* para. 85–08; D. D. Prentice (1973) 89 L.Q.R. 107; M. R. Chesterman (1973) 36 M.L.R. 129.

Definition of inability to pay debts

123.—(1) A company is deemed unable to pay its debts—

(*a*) if a creditor (by assignment or otherwise) to whom the company is indebted in a sum exceeding £750 then due has served on the company, by leaving it at the company's registered office, a written demand (in the prescribed form) requiring the company to pay the sum so due and the company has for 3 weeks thereafter neglected to pay the sum or to secure or compound for it to the reasonable satisfaction of the creditor, or

(*b*) if, in England and Wales, execution or other process issued on a judgment, decree or order of any court in favour of a creditor of the company is returned unsatisfied in whole or in part, or

(*c*) if, in Scotland, the inducíae of a charge for payment on an extract decree, or an extract registered bond, or an extract registered protest, have expired without payment being made, or

(*d*) if, in Northern Ireland, a certificate of unenforceability has been granted in respect of a judgment against the company, or

(*e*) if it is proved to the satisfaction of the court that the company is unable to pay its debts as they fall due.

(2) A company is also deemed unable to pay its debts if it is proved to the satisfaction of the court that the value of the company's assets is less than the amount of its liabilities, taking into account its contingent and prospective liabilities.

(3) The money sum for the time being specified in subsection (1)(*a*) is subject to increase or reduction by order under section 416 in Part XV.

GENERAL NOTE

This section is derived from s.518, C.A. 1985 and contains the statutory definition of inability to pay debts in relation to companies. The analogous provision in relation to individuals is s.268. See *Buckley,* Vol. 1, pp.534–5; *Palmer,* paras. 85–06—85–07.

Application for winding up

124.—(1) Subject to the provisions of this section, an application to the court for the winding up of a company shall be by petition presented either by the company, or the directors, or by any creditor or creditors (including any contingent or prospective creditor or creditors), contributory or contributories, or by all or any of those parties, together or separately.

(2) Except as mentioned below, a contributory is not entitled to present a winding-up petition unless either—

(*a*) the number of members is reduced below 2, or

(*b*) the shares in respect of which he is a contributory, or some of them, either were originally allotted to him, or have been held by him, and registered in his name, for at least 6 months during the 18 months before the commencement of the winding up, or have devolved on him through the death of a former holder.

(3) A person who is liable under section 76 to contribute to a company's assets in the event of its being wound up may petition on either of the grounds set out in section 122(1)(*f*) and (*g*), and subsection (2) above does not then apply; but unless the person is a contributory otherwise than under section 76, he may not in his character as contributory petition on any other ground.

This subsection is deemed included in Chapter VII of Part V of the Companies Act (redeemable shares; purchase by a company of its own shares) for the purposes of the Secretary of State's power to make regulations under section 179 of that Act.

(4) A winding-up petition may be presented by the Secretary of State—

(*a*) if the ground of the petition is that in section 122(1)(*b*) or (*c*), or

(*b*) in a case falling within section 440 of the Companies Act (expedient in the public interest, following report of inspectors, etc.).

(5) Where a company is being wound up voluntarily in England and Wales, a winding-up petition may be presented by the official receiver attached to the court as well as by any other person authorised in that behalf under the other provisions of this section; but the court shall not make a winding-up order on the petition unless it is satisfied that the voluntary winding up cannot be continued with due regard to the interests of the creditors or contributories.

DEFINITION

"contributory": s.79.

GENERAL NOTE

This section is derived from s.519, C.A. 1985. Though re-modelled, its substance remains the same except that the requirement, previously embodied in s.519(5), that a contingent or prospective creditor had to provide security for costs (or caution, in Scotland) has been dropped. In practice most petitions are creditors' petitions within subs. (1). See *Palmer,* paras. 85–06; 85–12.

Subs. (3)

Where a person claims the status of contributory *solely* under s.76 *supra* (which relates to liability resulting from the redemption or purchase by a private company, out of capital, of its own shares: see s.171, C.A. 1985) he may petition only on grounds (*f*) and (*g*) of s.122. In such a case he does not have to comply with subs. (2). If he can claim the status of contributory under some other section (see *supra* ss.74, 75, 77, 78) all of the grounds are available subject to subs. (2).

Powers of court on hearing of petition

125.—(1) On hearing a winding-up petition the court may dismiss it, or adjourn the hearing conditionally or unconditionally, or make an interim order, or any other order that it thinks fit; but the court shall not refuse to make a winding-up order on the ground only that the company's assets have been mortgaged to an amount equal to or in excess of those assets, or that the company has no assets.

(2) If the petition is presented by members of the company as contributories on the ground that it is just and equitable that the company should be wound up, the court, if it is of opinion—

(*a*) that the petitioners are entitled to relief either by winding up the company or by some other means, and

(*b*) that in the absence of any other remedy it would be just and equitable that the company should be wound up,

shall make a winding-up order; but this does not apply if the court is also of the opinion both that some other remedy is available to the petitioners and that they are acting unreasonably in seeking to have the company wound up instead of pursuing that other remedy.

Definition
"contributories": s.79

General Note
This section which deals with the court's powers on the hearing of a petition re-enacts s.520, C.A. 1985.

The court has a broad discretion and wide powers to dismiss, adjourn or make an order but it may not refuse to make an order only on the ground of insufficiency of assets. Formerly it was possible to do this. The English courts are nevertheless reluctant to allow the winding-up proceedings to be used as a collector of small claims. See, *e.g. Re Standring & Co. Ltd.* (1895) 39 S.J. 603; *Re Fancy Dress Balls Co. Ltd.* (1899) 43 S.J. 657. In Scotland the courts adopt a different attitude. See further *Palmer,* para. 85–06.

Subs. (2)
The court will only make an order that the company shall be wound up under s.122(*g*) as a last resort. It will, therefore, decline to do so where some other, less drastic remedy is available and the petitioner is being unreasonable in not pursuing it.

Power to stay or restrain proceedings against company

126.—(1) At any time after the presentation of a winding-up petition, and before a winding-up order has been made, the company, or any creditor or contributory, may—

(*a*) where any action or proceeding against the company is pending in the High Court or Court of Appeal in England and Wales or Northern Ireland, apply to the court in which the action or proceeding is pending for a stay of proceedings therein, and

(*b*) where any other action or proceeding is pending against the company, apply to the court having jurisdiction to wind up the company to restrain further proceedings in the action or proceeding;

and the court to which application is so made may (as the case may be) stay, sist or restrain the proceedings accordingly on such terms as it thinks fit.

(2) In the case of a company registered under section 680 of the Companies Act (pre-1862 companies; companies formed under legislation other than the Companies Acts) or the previous corresponding legislation, where the application to stay, sist or restrain is by a creditor, this section extends to actions and proceedings against any contributory of the company.

Definition
"contributory": s.79

General Note

This section which gives the court power to stay proceedings against the company after a petition and before an order to wind up has been made is a re-enactment with minor amendments of s.521, C.A. 1985. Subs. (2) relates to companies not formed under the Companies Act but authorised to register. S.126 should also be read with s.128 which deals with the avoiding of attachments and s.130(2) which prohibits proceedings after an order has been made unless leave of the court is obtained. See also the wide powers of the court in the case of a voluntary winding up in s.112.

See *Palmer,* para. 85–29.

Avoidance of property dispositions, etc.

127. In a winding up by the court, any disposition of the company's property, and any transfer of shares, or alteration in the status of the company's members, made after the commencement of the winding up is, unless the court otherwise orders, void.

Definitions

"commencement of the winding up": s.129.
"property": s.436.

General Note

This re-enacts s.522, C.A. 1985. The section avoids dispositions, etc., of property of the company made after the commencement of winding up unless the court otherwise orders. For a recent consideration of the section by the Court of Appeal see *Re Gray's Inn Construction Co. Ltd.* [1980] 1 All E.R. 814. This case deals with the operation of a company's bank account. See also the useful discussion by Oliver J. in *Re Leslie Engineers Co. Ltd.* [1976] 2 All E.R. 85, 90–96.

Avoidance of attachments, etc.

128.—(1) Where a company registered in England and Wales is being wound up by the court, any attachment, sequestration, distress or execution put in force against the estate or effects of the company after the commencement of the winding up is void.

(2) This section, so far as relates to any estate or effects of the company situated in England and Wales, applies in the case of a company registered in Scotland as it applies in the case of a company registered in England and Wales.

Definition

"commencement of the winding up": s.129.

General Note

This re-enacts s.523, C.A. 1985 and avoids execution, etc., put in force after the commencement of the winding up.

Note that there is no reference to Northern Ireland in the old s.523 or this section (and see s.441) and also that the court is not given a discretion under this particular section. However it has been held since 1864 that the section is to be read with and is controlled by ss.126 and 130(2): *Re Exhall Coal Mining Co.* (1864) 4 De G.J. & Sm. 377. Thus a creditor can apply for leave to proceed under s.130(2). It is difficult to see why s.128 should be read in this way. See further Buckley, *Companies Acts (*14th ed.), Vol. 1, p.558.

Commencement of winding up

Commencement of winding up by the court

129.—(1) If, before the presentation of a petition for the winding up of a company by the court, a resolution has been passed by the company for voluntary winding up, the winding up of the company is deemed to have commenced at the time of the passing of the resolution; and unless the court, on proof of fraud or mistake, directs otherwise, all proceedings taken in the voluntary winding up are deemed to have been validly taken.

(2) In any other case, the winding up of a company by the court is deemed to commence at the time of the presentation of the petition for winding up.

TRANSITIONAL PROVISION

Sched. 11, para. 4.

GENERAL NOTE

This re-enacts s.524, C.A. 1985 and subs. (1) dates back to the 1929 Act. The section backdates the commencement of the winding up to the presentation of the petition or an earlier resolution to wind up voluntarily. Compare s.86 which relates to voluntary winding up.

Consequences of winding-up order

130.—(1) On the making of a winding-up order, a copy of the order must forthwith be forwarded by the company (or otherwise as may be prescribed) to the registrar of companies, who shall enter it in his records relating to the company.

(2) When a winding-up order has been made or a provisional liquidator has been appointed, no action or proceeding shall be proceeded with or commenced against the company or its property, except by leave of the court and subject to such terms as the court may impose.

(3) When an order has been made for winding up a company registered under section 680 of the Companies Act, no action or proceeding shall be commenced or proceeded with against the company or its property or any contributory of the company, in respect of any debt of the company, except by leave of the court, and subject to such terms as the court may impose.

(4) An order for winding up a company operates in favour of all the creditors and of all contributories of the company as if made on the joint petition of a creditor and of a contributory.

GENERAL NOTE

This re-enacts with minor amendment s.525, C.A. 1985 and deals with some of the consequences of a winding up order. Subs. (1) provides for a copy of the order to be filed with the registrar of companies. Subs. (2) has been referred to above in connection with s.126.

This section is not exhaustive as to the effects of a winding up order. It does not for instance deal with the effect of winding up on contracts, especially contracts of employment. See *Palmer,* paras. 85–28.

Investigation procedures

Company's statement of affairs

131.—(1) Where the court has made a winding-up order or appointed a provisional liquidator, the official receiver may require some or all of the persons mentioned in subsection (3) below to make out and submit to him a statement in the prescribed form as to the affairs of the company.

(2) The statement shall be verified by affidavit by the persons required to submit it and shall show—

(*a*) particulars of the company's assets, debts and liabilities;
(*b*) the names and addresses of the company's creditors;
(*c*) the securities held by them respectively;
(*d*) the dates when the securities were respectively given; and
(*e*) such further or other information as may be prescribed or as the official receiver may require.

(3) The persons referred to in subsection (1) are—

(*a*) those who are or have been officers of the company;

(*b*) those who have taken part in the formation of the company at any time within one year before the relevant date;

(*c*) those who are in the company's employment, or have been in its employment within that year, and are in the official receiver's opinion capable of giving the information required;

(*d*) those who are or have been within that year officers of, or in the employment of, a company which is, or within that year was, an officer of the company.

(4) Where any persons are required under this section to submit a statement of affairs to the official receiver, they shall do so (subject to the next subsection) before the end of the period of 21 days beginning with the day after that on which the prescribed notice of the requirement is given to them by the official receiver.

(5) The official receiver, if he thinks fit, may—

(*a*) at any time release a person from an obligation imposed on him under subsection (1) or (2) above; or

(*b*) either when giving the notice mentioned in subsection (4) or subsequently, extend the period so mentioned;

and where the official receiver has refused to exercise a power conferred by this subsection, the court, if it thinks fit, may exercise it.

(6) In this section—

"employment" includes employment under a contract for services; and

"the relevant date" means—

(*a*) in a case where a provisional liquidator is appointed, the date of his appointment; and

(*b*) in a case where no such appointment is made, the date of the winding-up order.

(7) If a person without reasonable excuse fails to comply with any obligation imposed under this section, he is liable to a fine and, for continued contravention, to a daily default fine.

(8) In the application of this section to Scotland references to the official receiver are to the liquidator or, in a case where a provisional liquidator is appointed, the provisional liquidator.

TRANSITIONAL PROVISION

Sched. 11, para. 5.

DEFINITIONS

"employment": subs. (6).
"fine"; "daily default fine": s.430, Sched. 10.
"officers of the company": s.251, C.A. 1985, s.744.
"prescribed": s.251.
"security": s.248(*b*).
"the official receiver": s.399.
"the relevant date": subs. (6).

GENERAL NOTE

This section replaces s.66, I.A. 1985. Apart from necessary differences of nomenclature employed with regard to the office holder concerned, the provisions of subss. (2)–(5) inclusive are in substance identical to those in ss.22, 47 and 66 of this Act which are respectively concerned with the statement of affairs to be submitted to an administrator, to an administrative receiver, and to a Scottish receiver. The forms of statement will be prescribed in the rules, and will be closely similar for all types of insolvency proceedings. See also the General Note to s.22.

Subs. (1)

The making of a winding up order by a court takes place under ss.117 and 120, which apply to courts in England and Wales and in Scotland respectively. The appointment of a provisional liquidator in either England or Scotland may take place under the provisions of s.135. One important distinction is to be noted in the drafting of this subsection, as against the drafting of ss.22(1), 47(1) and 66(1), in that the use of the word "may" has the effect of making it a matter for the discretion of the official receiver (or in Scotland, the liquidator or the provisional liquidator) whether to require a statement of affairs to be prepared, whereas in the case of the other insolvency proceedings the requirement is a compulsory one. The purpose underlying this variation in the case of a winding up is to maintain the previous facility for the official receiver to dispense with a statement of affairs in certain cases, such as where the directors cannot be found or where there is insufficient information to enable a statement to be prepared, or where the director concerned is incapable of performing the task because of illness.

Subs. (4)

For the purpose of calculating the period of 21 days, the effective date on which notice will be deemed to have been given by the official receiver will be the date on which the documents are dispatched.

Subs. (8)

This additional provision is necessitated by the fact that there is no office of official receiver under Scottish law. In Scotland therefore the role allocated to the official receiver in England and Wales for the purpose of this section must perforce be played by the liquidator. However, if a provisional liquidator has been appointed in Scottish winding up proceedings his position under this section is identical to that of a provisional liquidator appointed in England and Wales.

Investigation by official receiver

132.—(1) Where a winding-up order is made by the court in England and Wales, it is the duty of the official receiver to investigate—

(*a*) if the company has failed, the causes of the failure; and

(*b*) generally, the promotion, formation, business, dealings and affairs of the company,

and to make such report (if any) to the court as he thinks fit.

(2) The report is, in any proceedings, prima facie evidence of the facts stated in it.

Definitions

"business": s.436.

"the official receiver": s.399.

General Note

This section replaces s.67, I.A. 1985.

Subs. (1)(a)

If the company has failed

This takes account of the possibility that a winding up order may be made by the court in circumstances where the company is not insolvent, in which case an investigation into "the causes of the company's failure" will be patently unnecessary. It may be noted however that, although the obligation to investigate is compulsory where the company is insolvent, the making of a report to the court remains a matter for the official receiver's discretion by virtue of the concluding words of this subsection.

Subs. (1)(b)

Generally . . .

This paragraph is drafted without regard to the possibility that a winding up order may be made by the court in respect of a company which is not insolvent. Hence, in all cases where a winding up order is made, and regardless of which of the grounds mentioned in s.122 has furnished the basis for the order, the official receiver must carry out an investigation into the promotion, formation, business, dealing and affairs of the company. However, as mentioned above in relation to para. (*a*) the duty to report to the court is in each case a matter for the official receiver's discretion and it is therefore to be expected that in cases where the company is not insolvent the Official Receiver will elect to report only if serious irregularities come to light.

Public examination of officers

133.—(1) Where a company is being wound up by the court, the official receiver or, in Scotland, the liquidator may at any time before the dissolution of the company apply to the court for the public examination of any person who—

(*a*) is or has been an officer of the company; or

(*b*) has acted as liquidator or administrator of the company or as receiver or manager or, in Scotland, receiver of its property; or

(*c*) not being a person falling within paragraph (*a*) or (*b*), is or has been concerned, or has taken part, in the promotion, formation or management of the company.

(2) Unless the court otherwise orders, the official receiver or, in Scotland, the liquidator shall make an application under subsection (1) if he is requested in accordance with the rules to do so by—

(*a*) one-half, in value, of the company's creditors; or

(*b*) three-quarters, in value, of the company's contributories.

(3) On an application under subsection (1), the court shall direct that a public examination of the person to whom the application relates shall be held on a day appointed by the court; and that person shall attend on that day and be publicly examined as to the promotion, formation or management of the company or as to the conduct of its business and affairs, or his conduct or dealings in relation to the company.

(4) The following may take part in the public examination of a person under this section and may question that person concerning the matters mentioned in subsection (3), namely—

(*a*) the official receiver;

(*b*) the liquidator of the company;

(*c*) any person who has been appointed as special manager of the company's property or business;

(*d*) any creditor of the company who has tendered a proof or, in Scotland, submitted a claim in the winding up;

(*e*) any contributory of the company.

DEFINITIONS

"administrator": s.8(2).
"business": s.436.
"contributory": s.79.
"officer of the company": s.251; C.A. 1985, s.744.
"prescribed": s.251.
"property": s.436.
"receiver in Scotland": s.70(1).
"receiver or manager": s.29(1)(*a*).
"the official receiver": s.399.
"the rules": s.251.

GENERAL NOTE

This section replaces subs. (1)–(4) of s.68, I.A. 1985 which are repealed. In Chap. 12 of the *Cork Report* a strong case was made out for a revival of the use of the public examination in cases of company insolvency, so that it should function in the same way as the public examination of individuals in cases of bankruptcy (see paras. 653–657). This proposal was accepted in the *White Paper* (paras. 91–94), and the present section duly carries it into effect. It provides for the holding of a public examination whenever a company is being wound up by the court, irrespective of whether the company is insolvent or not. Most importantly, it is no longer a pre-condition to the holding of a public examination that the official receiver should first make a report alleging fraud, as was formerly required under s.563(1) of the Companies Act 1985.

Subs. (1)(b)

Has acted as liquidator or . . .

This power to examine a former liquidator of a company may be of particular significance in cases where a voluntary liquidation is converted into a compulsory winding up under s.124(5). The official receiver, or the liquidator appointed under the compulsory winding up proceedings, may find it expedient to cause the former liquidator to undergo public examination, for example where it appears that the conduct of the voluntary liquidation was coloured by some irregularity. The power made available by this subsection is thus a component in the overall strategy aimed at eradicating the excesses and malpractices to which the decision in *Re Centrebind Ltd.* [1967] 1 W.L.R. 377; [1966] 3 All E.R. 889 subsequently gave rise. Other elements in this same strategy include the new provisions of Pt. XIII of this Act regulating the ability of persons to act as insolvency practitioners within the law, and the special provision in ss.98 and 99 (*q.v.*).

Subs. (4)(c)

Special manager of the company's property or business

Such appointments may be made under the provisions of s.177 which replaces s.90, I.A. 1985.

Enforcement of s.133

134.—(1) If a person without reasonable excuse fails at any time to attend his public examination under section 133, he is guilty of a contempt of court and liable to be punished accordingly.

(2) In a case where a person without reasonable excuse fails at any time to attend his examination under section 133 or there are reasonable grounds for believing that a person has absconded, or is about to abscond, with a view to avoiding or delaying his examination under that section, the court may cause a warrant to be issued to a constable or prescribed officer of the court—

(*a*) for the arrest of that person; and

(*b*) for the seizure of any books, papers, records, money or goods in that person's possession.

(3) In such a case the court may authorise the person arrested under the warrant to be kept in custody, and anything seized under such a warrant to be held, in accordance with the rules, until such time as the court may order.

DEFINITIONS

"prescribed": s.251.

"the rules": s.251.

GENERAL NOTE

This re-enacts subs. (5) and (6) of s.68, I.A. 1985 and deals with the enforcement of the provisions relating to public examination of officers (see Note to s.133).

Appointment of liquidator

Appointment and powers of provisional liquidator

135.—(1) Subject to the provisions of this section, the court may, at any time after the presentation of a winding-up petition, appoint a liquidator provisionally.

(2) In England and Wales, the appointment of a provisional liquidator may be made at any time before the making of a winding-up order; and either the official receiver or any other fit person may be appointed.

(3) In Scotland, such an appointment may be made at any time before the first appointment of liquidators.

(4) The provisional liquidator shall carry out such functions as the court may confer on him.

(5) When a liquidator is provisionally appointed by the court, his powers may be limited by the order appointing him.

GENERAL NOTE

This section re-enacts s.532, C.A. 1985 and s.69(3), I.A. 1985. It deals with the appointment of a provisional liquidator.

Subs. (5)

As appearing in the C.A. 1948 (s.238(4)) this enabled the order to limit or *restrict* the powers of the provisional liquidator. The present subs. simply refers to limit.

If the court imposed conditions this would arguably not limit the scope of the power itself but simply restrict the manner of its exercise *cf.* Lord Oaksey in *Tool Metal Manufacturing Co. Ltd.* v. *Tungsten Electric Co. Ltd.* [1955] 2 All E.R. 657, 671, in the context of "restrict" in the Patents and Designs Act 1907, s.28(1).

See generally *Palmer,* paras. 85–32.

Functions of official receiver in relation to office of liquidator

136.—(1) The following provisions of this section have effect, subject to section 140 below, on a winding-up order being made by the court in England and Wales.

(2) The official receiver, by virtue of his office, becomes the liquidator of the company and continues in office until another person becomes liquidator under the provisions of this Part.

(3) The official receiver is, by virtue of his office, the liquidator during any vacancy.

(4) At any time when he is the liquidator of the company, the official receiver may summon separate meetings of the company's creditors and contributories for the purpose of choosing a person to be liquidator of the company in place of the official receiver.

(5) It is the duty of the official receiver—

(*a*) as soon as practicable in the period of 12 weeks beginning with the day on which the winding-up order was made, to decide whether to exercise his power under subsection (4) to summon meetings, and

(*b*) if in pursuance of paragraph (*a*) he decides not to exercise that power, to give notice of his decision, before the end of that period, to the court and to the company's creditors and contributories, and

(*c*) (whether or not he has decided to exercise that power) to exercise his power to summon meetings under subsection (4) if he is at any time requested, in accordance with the rules, to do so by one-quarter, in value, of the company's creditors;

and accordingly, where the duty imposed by paragraph (*c*) arises before the official receiver has performed a duty imposed by paragraph (*a*) or (*b*), he is not required to perform the latter duty.

(6) A notice given under subsection (5)(*b*) to the company's creditors shall contain an explanation of the creditors' power under subsection (5)(*c*) to require the official receiver to summon meetings of the company's creditors and contributories.

DEFINITIONS

"contributory": s.79.
"the official receiver": s.399.
"the rules": s.251.

GENERAL NOTE

This section partly replaces the provisions of s.70, I.A. 1985, which are repealed. It also incorporates the provisions announced in paras. 75–77 of the *White Paper* (see also the general discussion in Chap. 19 of the *Cork Report*), that it should become a matter for the judgment of the official receiver to determine whether any useful purpose will be served by the convening of meetings of the company's creditors and contributories for the purpose of choosing a private-sector liquidator to replace the official receiver. Under the terms of subs. (4) the convening of these meetings is now a discretionary matter for the official receiver, and subs. (5) allows the official receiver a period of up to 12 weeks from the date of the winding up order within which to decide whether to summon them. However, subs. (5)(*c*) enables one or more creditors, if representing at least one quarter in value of the company's creditors, by means of a formal request to render it obligatory for the official receiver to convene the meetings.

Subs. (1)

Subject to s.140 below

This proviso allows for the possibility that, in the case where a winding up order is made immediately upon the discharge of an administration order, the court is empowered by s.140(1) to appoint as liquidator the person who has been acting as the administrator of the company. In such a case, the official receiver does not become liquidator by virtue of subs. (2) of this section, nor does he incur the duties imposed by subs. (5)(*a*) and (*b*), but he will nevertheless become liquidator by virtue of his office during any vacancy, as provided by subs. (3) of this section.

Subs. (6)

An explanation of the creditors' power

This is to ensure that in cases where the official receiver decides not to convene meetings under subs. (4) of this section the creditors have notification of their power to compel him to call such meetings, using the procedure specified in subs. (5)(*c*).

Appointment by Secretary of State

137.—(1) In a winding up by the court in England and Wales the official receiver may, at any time when he is the liquidator of the company, apply to the Secretary of State for the appointment of a person as liquidator in his place.

(2) If meetings are held in pursuance of a decision under section 136(5)(*a*), but no person is chosen to be liquidator as a result of those meetings, it is the duty of the official receiver to decide whether to refer the need for an appointment to the Secretary of State.

(3) On an application under subsection (1), or a reference made in pursuance of a decision under subsection (2), the Secretary of State shall either make an appointment or decline to make one.

(4) Where a liquidator has been appointed by the Secretary of State under subsection (3), the liquidator shall give notice of his appointment to the company's creditors or, if the court so allows, shall advertise his appointment in accordance with the directions of the court.

(5) In that notice or advertisement the liquidator shall—

(*a*) state whether he proposes to summon a general meeting of the company's creditors under section 141 below for the purpose of determining (together with any meeting of contributories) whether a liquidation committee should be established under that section, and

(*b*) if he does not propose to summon such a meeting, set out the power of the company's creditors under that section to require him to summon one.

Transitional Provision

Sched. 11, para. 6.

General Note

As an alternative to the mode of appointment of a liquidator by means of specially convened meetings under s.136(4) *supra,* s.137 enables the official receiver to apply to the Secretary of State to appoint a liquidator in his place. The same possibility arises by virtue of subs. (2) of s.137 if meetings are convened that do not result in the choice of a person as liquidator, for example because of deadlock among the persons attending the respective meetings, so that no choice in accordance with the provisions of s.136 can be made. In either circumstance, the Secretary of State is left free to decline to make an appointment, in which case the official receiver continues to be the liquidator of the company *ex officio* in accordance with subs. (2) of s.136.

Appointment of liquidator in Scotland

138.—(1) Where a winding-up order is made by the court in Scotland, a liquidator shall be appointed by the court at the time when the order is made.

(2) The liquidator so appointed (here referred to as "the interim liquidator") continues in office until another person becomes liquidator in his place under this section or the next.

(3) The interim liquidator shall (subject to the next subsection) as soon as practicable in the period of 28 days beginning with the day on which the winding-up order was made or such longer period as the court may allow, summon separate meetings of the company's creditors and contributories for the purpose of choosing a person (who may be the person who is the interim liquidator) to be liquidator of the company in place of the interim liquidator.

(4) If it appears to the interim liquidator, in any case where a company is being wound up on grounds including its inability to pay its debts, that it would be inappropriate to summon under subsection (3) a meeting of the company's contributories, he may summon only a meeting of the company's creditors for the purpose mentioned in that subsection.

(5) If one or more meetings are held in pursuance of this section but no person is appointed or nominated by the meeting or meetings, the interim liquidator shall make a report to the court which shall appoint either the interim liquidator or some other person to be liquidator of the company.

(6) A person who becomes liquidator of the company in place of the interim liquidator shall, unless he is appointed by the court, forthwith notify the court of that fact.

DEFINITIONS

"contributory": s.79.

"the interim liquidator": subs. (2).

GENERAL NOTE

The need for this section results from the separate arrangements for winding up in Scotland, where there is no office of official receiver. Accordingly the provisions made in s.136 with regard to England and Wales are inappropriate in Scotland, where it is the practice, following the presentation of a winding up petition, to appoint a provisional liquidator under s.135. In most cases the provisional liquidator will subsequently be appointed as liquidator in accordance with subs. (1) of the present section and become the "interim liquidator" by virtue of subs. (2). *Cf.* s.136, *supra,* which applies to England and Wales.

One notable difference between the drafting of this section and that of s.136 is with regard to the duty to summon meetings of the company's creditors and contributories. Whereas s.136(4) allows the official receiver a discretion whether or not to summon meetings of either kind, subss. (3) and (4) of this section render it obligatory for an interim liquidator to convene a meeting of the company's creditors, albeit he is accorded a discretion whether to convene a meeting of contributories. A further difference between English law and Scots law arises if no choice of a person as liquidator results from any meetings which are held. Whereas s.137(2) allows the official receiver a discretion whether to apply to the Secretary of State for the appointment of a liquidator, subs. (5) of this section renders it obligatory for the interim liquidator to report the matter to the court, and further obliges the court to make an appointment of some person or other as liquidator of the company.

Choice of liquidator at meetings of creditors and contributories

139.—(1) This section applies where a company is being wound up by the court and separate meetings of the company's creditors and contributories are summoned for the purpose of choosing a person to be liquidator of the company.

(2) The creditors and the contributories at their respective meetings may nominate a person to be liquidator.

(3) The liquidator shall be the person nominated by the creditors or, where no person has been so nominated, the person (if any) nominated by the contributories.

(4) In the case of different persons being nominated, any contributory or creditor may, within 7 days after the date on which the nomination was made by the creditors, apply to the court for an order either—

(*a*) appointing the person nominated as liquidator by the contributories to be a liquidator instead of, or jointly with, the person nominated by the creditors; or

(*b*) appointing some other person to be liquidator instead of the person nominated by the creditors.

Definition

"contributory": s.79.

General Note

This section is designed to lay down a clearer indication of the manner in which a liquidator is to be chosen. It is designed as an analogue to s.100, which deals with the same situation in a creditor's voluntary winding up. However, the present section differs in particular from s.100(3), since the latter section includes a right for a director to make application to the court to settle any dispute over the appointment of the liquidator, whereas subs. (4) of this section accords no such right to a director in the case of a compulsory winding up. This is a consequence of the fact that the making of an order for compulsory winding up terminates the directors' authority to act in relation to the company, and they are accordingly excluded from the category of interested persons with standing to apply to the court on the question of who is to be liquidator.

Appointment by the court following administration or voluntary arrangement

140.—(1) Where a winding-up order is made immediately upon the discharge of an administration order, the court may appoint as liquidator of the company the person who has ceased on the discharge of the administration order to be the administrator of the company.

(2) Where a winding-up order is made at a time when there is a supervisor of a voluntary arrangement approved in relation to the company under Part I, the court may appoint as liquidator of the company the person who is the supervisor at the time when the winding-up order is made.

(3) Where the court makes an appointment under this section, the official receiver does not become the liquidator as otherwise provided by section 136(2), and he has no duty under section 136(5) (*a*) or (*b*) in respect of the summoning of creditors' or contributories' meetings.

Definitions

"administration order": s.8(2).

"administrator of the company": s.8(2).

"supervisor of a composition or scheme": s.7(2).

General Note

This section makes provision for the expeditious transformation of an administration order procedure under Pt. II or a composition or scheme under Pt. I into a compulsory winding up in appropriate cases. It does so by enabling the court when making the winding up order to appoint as liquidator the person who has lately ceased to be administrator in consequence of the discharge of the administration order, or who is acting as supervisor of the voluntary arrangement, as the case may be. There are consequential provisions in subs. (3) to modify the application of s.136 in view of the fact that in such cases the official receiver will not be liquidator in the first instance. Discharge of an administration order is governed by ss.18, 24(5) and 27(4)(*d*).

Liquidation committees

Liquidation committee (England and Wales)

141.—(1) Where a winding-up order has been made by the court in England and Wales and separate meetings of creditors and contributories have been summoned for the purpose of choosing a person to be liquidator, those meetings may establish a committee ("the liquidation committee") to exercise the functions conferred on it by or under this Act.

(2) The liquidator (not being the official receiver) may at any time, if he thinks fit, summon separate general meetings of the company's creditors and contributories for the purpose of determining whether such a committee should be established and, if it is so determined, of establishing it.

The liquidator (not being the official receiver) shall summon such a meeting if he is requested, in accordance with the rules, to do so by one-tenth, in value, of the company's creditors.

(3) Where meetings are summoned under this section, or for the purpose of choosing a person to be liquidator, and either the meeting of creditors or the meeting of contributories decides that a liquidation committee should be established, but the other meeting does not so decide or decides that a committee should not be established, the committee shall be established in accordance with the rules, unless the court otherwise orders.

(4) The liquidation committee is not to be able or required to carry out its functions at any time when the official receiver is liquidator; but at any such time its functions are vested in the Secretary of State except to the extent that the rules otherwise provide.

(5) Where there is for the time being no liquidation committee, and the liquidator is a person other than the official receiver, the functions of such a committee are vested in the Secretary of State except to the extent that the rules otherwise provide.

DEFINITIONS
"contributory": s.79.
"the official receiver": s.399.
"the rules": s.251.

GENERAL NOTE

This section re-enacts s.74, I.A. 1985. The committee is by implication to be composed of both creditors and contributories, although this is nowhere indicated in the drafting of the section itself. The possibility of establishing a committee consisting of creditors is also provided for elsewhere in the Act in relation to other types of company insolvency proceedings, namely the administration order procedure, administrative receivership, and receivership in Scotland. The relevant provisions of the Act are ss.26, 49 and 68 (*q.v.*). It is in relation to winding up however that the role of the committee of creditors and contributories is most fully elaborated, building as it does on the law and practice developed in relation to what were previously termed "committees of inspection."

Subs. (1)

The functions conferred on it by or under this Act

In keeping with the recommendations in Chapter 19 of the *Cork Report* the discredited concept of "creditor control," which was largely mythical, has been relinquished in favour of a policy of encouraging "creditor participation." Accordingly the title "committee of inspection" has been abandoned, and the committee, if any, which is formed by the creditors is simply charged with the task of exercising "the functions conferred on it by or under this Act." In addition to the functions arising directly under those statutory enactments, the possibility is provided that further functions may be conferred in the rules, as authorised by para. 10 of Sched. 8 to the Act.

Subs. (2)

The liquidator (not being the official receiver) may at any time . . . summon separate general meetings

This caters for the possibility that a private sector liquidator may take up office, pursuant to ss.136, 139 or 140, without it having been resolved whether a committee of creditors is to be appointed. The liquidator is given a discretion to convene meetings of the creditors and contributories at any time for the purpose of deciding whether such a committee shall be established, and it can be rendered obligatory for him to convene such meetings if a formal request to this effect is made by one tenth in value of its creditors. This process may also be invoked following the direct appointment of a liquidator under s.137(4), since subs. (5) of that section obliges the liquidator to notify all creditors whether he intends to summon a meeting of creditors, and further obliges him to inform creditors of their power to compel him to summon such a meeting if he is not otherwise intending to do so.

Subs. (4)

Except to the extent that the rules otherwise provide

This allows the functions which are by this subsection expressed to be vested in the Secretary of State to be delegated to the official receiver himself as a matter of course, by means of a provision to that effect inserted in the rules. *Cf.* Companies (Winding Up) Rules 1949 (S.I. 1949 No. 330) Rule 214.

Liquidation committee (Scotland)

142.—(1) Where a winding-up order has been made by the court in Scotland and separate meetings of creditors and contributories have been summoned for the purpose of choosing a person to be liquidator or, under section 138(4), only a meeting of creditors has been summoned for that purpose, those meetings or (as the case may be) that meeting may establish a committee ("the liquidation committee") to exercise the functions conferred on it by or under this Act.

(2) The liquidator may at any time, if he thinks fit, summon separate general meetings of the company's creditors and contributories for the purpose of determining whether such a committee should be established and, if it is so determined, of establishing it.

(3) The liquidator, if appointed by the court otherwise than under section 139(4)(*a*), is required to summon meetings under subsection (2) if he is requested, in accordance with the rules, to do so by one-tenth, in value, of the company's creditors.

(4) Where meetings are summoned under this section, or for the purpose of choosing a person to be liquidator, and either the meeting of creditors or the meeting of contributories decides that a liquidation committee should be established, but the other meeting does not so decide or decides that a committee should not be established, the committee shall be established in accordance with the rules, unless the court otherwise orders.

(5) Where in the case of any winding up there is for the time being no liquidation committee, the functions of such a committee are vested in the court except to the extent that the rules otherwise provide.

(6) In addition to the powers and duties conferred and imposed on it by this Act, a liquidation committee has such of the powers and duties of commissioners in a sequestration as may be conferred and imposed on such committees by the rules.

DEFINITIONS

"contributory": s.79.

"the rules": s.251.

General Note

This section replaces s.75, I.A. 1985. The first subsection is applicable where meetings of the company's creditors and contributories, or of the creditors only, are convened by the interim liquidator under s.138(2) or (3) respectively for the purpose of choosing a liquidator. Such meetings are empowered to resolve also to appoint a committee to exercise the functions conferred on it by or under this Act and may proceed to do so. If no such course is adopted at that stage, subs. (2) confers a discretionary power on the liquidator to summon such meetings at any subsequent time, subject to the possibility that this can be rendered obligatory where one-tenth in value of the creditors formally request that meetings be summoned.

The liquidator's functions

General functions in winding up by the court

143.—(1) The functions of the liquidator of a company which is being wound up by the court are to secure that the assets of the company are got in, realised and distributed to the company's creditors and, if there is a surplus, to the persons entitled to it.

(2) It is the duty of the liquidator of a company which is being wound up by the court in England and Wales, if he is not the official receiver—

(*a*) to furnish the official receiver with such information,

(*b*) to produce to the official receiver, and permit inspection by the official receiver of, such books, papers and other records, and

(*c*) to give the official receiver such other assistance,

as the official receiver may reasonably require for the purposes of carrying out his functions in relation to the winding up.

Definition

"official receiver": s.399.

General Note

This re-enacts s.69(1) and (2), I.A. 1985.

Custody of company's property

144.—(1) When a winding-up order has been made, or where a provisional liquidator has been appointed, the liquidator or the provisional liquidator (as the case may be) shall take into his custody or under his control all the property and things in action to which the company is or appears to be entitled.

(2) In a winding up by the court in Scotland, if and so long as there is no liquidator, all the property of the company is deemed to be in the custody of the court.

General Note

This re-enacts s.537, C.A. 1985 and deals with the liquidator taking control of the company's property. Unlike bankruptcy there is no automatic *cessio bonorum* to the liquidator, but see s.145 *post.* See *Palmer,* para. 85–38.

Vesting of company property in liquidator

145.—(1) When a company is being wound up by the court, the court may on the application of the liquidator by order direct that all or any part of the property of whatsoever description belonging to the company or held by trustees on its behalf shall vest in the liquidator by his official name; and thereupon the property to which the order relates vests accordingly.

(2) The liquidator may, after giving such indemnity (if any) as the court may direct, bring or defend in his official name any action or other legal proceeding which relates to that property or which it is necessary to bring

or defend for the purpose of effectually winding up the company and recovering its property.

GENERAL NOTE

This re-enacts s.538, C.A. 1985 and deals with a vesting order to vest the company's property in the liquidator. Originally this occurred by operation of law in the case of an official manager, the predecessor of the modern liquidator, but today an order is necessary. Such applications are not, however, common. See *Palmer,* para. 85–38.

Duty to summon final meeting

146.—(1) Subject to the next subsection, if it appears to the liquidator of a company which is being wound up by the court that the winding up of the company is for practical purposes complete and the liquidator is not the official receiver, the liquidator shall summon a final general meeting of the company's creditors which—

(*a*) shall receive the liquidator's report of the winding up, and

(*b*) shall determine whether the liquidator should have his release under section 174 in Chapter VII of this Part.

(2) The liquidator may, if he thinks fit, give the notice summoning the final general meeting at the same time as giving notice of any final distribution of the company's property but, if summoned for an earlier date, that meeting shall be adjourned (and, if necessary, further adjourned) until a date on which the liquidator is able to report to the meeting that the winding up of the company is for practical purposes complete.

(3) In the carrying out of his functions in the winding up it is the duty of the liquidator to retain sufficient sums from the company's property to cover the expenses of summoning and holding the meeting required by this section.

DEFINITIONS

"official receiver": s.399.
"property": s.436.

TRANSITIONAL PROVISION

Sched. 11, para. 6(3).

GENERAL NOTE

This section replaces s.78, I.A. 1985 and concerns the conclusion of the liquidator's performance of his functions. The procedure for bringing a compulsory winding up to its conclusion has undergone a considerable modification, in accordance with the proposals in paras. 102–104 of the *White Paper.* The liquidator's duty to summon a final meeting of the company's creditors as a preliminary to the gaining of his release under s.174 gives rise to a parallel procedure to those prescribed for each kind of voluntary winding up by ss.94 and 106 respectively. The provisions of this section are applicable to England and Scotland alike, and are to be followed in all cases except those where use is made of the procedure for bringing about the early dissolution of the company under s.202 or s.204, as appropriate (*q.v.*). In view of the inevitable cost of convening a final meeting of creditors, subs. (3) requires the liquidator to retain sufficient sums from the company's property to cover this expense. S.172(8) provides for the liquidator to vacate office as soon as he has given notice to the court and the registrar of companies of the holding and outcome of a meeting under this section.

General powers of court

Power to stay or sist winding up

147.—(1) The court may at any time after an order for winding up, on the application either of the liquidator or the official receiver or any creditor or contributory, and on proof to the satisfaction of the court that all proceedings in the winding up ought to be stayed or sisted, make an order staying or sisting the proceedings, either altogether or for a limited time, on such terms and conditions as the court thinks fit.

(2) The court may, before making an order, require the official receiver to furnish to it a report with respect to any facts or matters which are in his opinion relevant to the application.

(3) A copy of every order made under this section shall forthwith be forwarded by the company, or otherwise as may be prescribed, to the registrar of companies, who shall enter it in his records relating to the company.

General Note

This re-enacts s.549, C.A. 1985. It expressly refers to the Scots procedure of sist.

The section gives the court a general power to stay any proceedings in a winding up. An application to stay or an appeal are the only ways in which a winding up can be halted after the order has been entered—*Re Lyric Syndicate* (1900) 17 T.L.R. 162. Before then it may be rescinded in an appropriate case—see generally *Palmer,* para. 85–299.

Settlement of list of contributories and application of assets

148.—(1) As soon as may be after making a winding-up order, the court shall settle a list of contributories, with power to rectify the register of members in all cases where rectification is required in pursuance of the Companies Act or this Act, and shall cause the company's assets to be collected, and applied in discharge of its liabilities.

(2) If it appears to the court that it will not be necessary to make calls on or adjust the rights of contributories, the court may dispense with the settlement of a list of contributories.

(3) In settling the list, the court shall distinguish between persons who are contributories in their own right and persons who are contributories as being representatives of or liable for the debts of others.

General Note

This re-enacts s.550, C.A. 1985 with a minor amendment and deals with settlement of a list of contributories. See *Palmer,* para. 85–46.

Debts due from contributory to company

149.—(1) The court may, at any time after making a winding-up order, make an order on any contributory for the time being on the list of contributories to pay, in manner directed by the order, any money due from him (or from the estate of the person whom he represents) to the company, exclusive of any money payable by him or the estate by virtue of any call in pursuance of the Companies Act or this Act.

(2) The court in making such an order may—

(*a*) in the case of an unlimited company, allow to the contributory by way of set-off any money due to him or the estate which he represents from the company on any independent dealing or contract with the company, but not any money due to him as a member of the company in respect of any dividend or profit, and

(*b*) in the case of a limited company, make to any director or manager whose liability is unlimited or to his estate the like allowance.

(3) In the case of any company, whether limited or unlimited, when all the creditors are paid in full (together with interest at the official rate), any money due on any account whatever to a contributory from the company may be allowed to him by way of set-off against any subsequent call.

Definition

"contributory": s.79.

"interest at the official rate": s.251.

General Note

This re-enacts s.552, C.A. 1985. The reference in subs. (3) to "interest at the official rate" is new. The liability of a contributory referred to in subs. (2)(*a*) derives from s.74(1). The liability of a director or manager referred to in subs. (2)(*b*) derives from s.75. By subs. (2) both categories of contributory are permitted to set-off any amount due to them "on any independent dealing or contract with the company." See *Palmer,* para. 85–59.

Power to make calls

150.—(1) The court may, at any time after making a winding-up order, and either before or after it has ascertained the sufficiency of the company's assets, make calls on all or any of the contributories for the time being settled on the list of the contributories to the extent of their liability, for payment of any money which the court considers necessary to satisfy the company's debts and liabilities, and the expenses of winding up, and for the adjustment of the rights of the contributories among themselves, and make an order for payment of any calls so made.

(2) In making a call the court may take into consideration the probability that some of the contributories may partly or wholly fail to pay it.

Definition

"contributory": s.79.

General Note

This re-enacts s.553, C.A. 1985. The power to make calls exists to satisfy the company's debts and liabilities, the expenses of winding up, and in order to adjust the rights of the contributories amongst themselves. See *Palmer,* para. 85–48.

Payment into bank of money due to company

151.—(1) The court may order any contributory, purchaser or other person from whom money is due to the company to pay the amount due into the Bank of England (or any branch of it) to the account of the liquidator instead of to the liquidator, and such an order may be enforced in the same manner as if it had directed payment to the liquidator.

(2) All money and securities paid or delivered into the Bank of England (or branch) in the event of a winding up by the court are subject in all respects to the orders of the court.

General Note

This re-enacts s.554, C.A. 1985 and deals with an order for payment of money owed to the company directly into the Bank of England.

Order on contributory to be conclusive evidence

152.—(1) An order made by the court on a contributory is conclusive evidence that the money (if any) thereby appearing to be due or ordered to be paid is due, but subject to any right of appeal.

(2) All other pertinent matters stated in the order are to be taken as truly stated as against all persons and in all proceedings except proceedings in Scotland against the heritable estate of a deceased contributory; and in that case the order is only prima facie evidence for the purpose of charging his heritable estate, unless his heirs or legatees of heritage were on the list of contributories at the time of the order being made.

General Note

This re-enacts s.555, C.A. 1985 and deals with the conclusiveness of orders against contributories.

Power to exclude creditors not proving in time

153. The court may fix a time or times within which creditors are to prove their debts or claims or to be excluded from the benefit of any distribution made before those debts are proved.

General Note

This re-enacts s.557, C.A. 1985 and allows the court to fix time for proof of debts and to exclude creditors who fail to prove in time from distributions made before proof of their debts.

A creditor can prove at any time before dissolution but will be excluded from the benefit of distributions made before proof.

See generally *Re Kit Hill Tunnel, ex p. Williams* (1881) 16 Ch.D. 590; *Harrison* v. *Kirk* [1904] A.C. 1. See *Palmer,* paras. 85–57.

Adjustment of rights of contributories

154. The court shall adjust the rights of the contributories among themselves and distribute any surplus among the persons entitled to it.

General Note

This re-enacts s.558 and deals with the adjustment of the rights of contributories *inter se.* The provision is mandatory. It is also the only provision about distribution which applies to a compulsory winding up. See *Palmer,* paras. 85–49.

Inspection of books by creditors, etc.

155.—(1) The court may, at any time after making a winding-up order, make such order for inspection of the company's books and papers by creditors and contributories as the court thinks just; and any books and papers in the company's possession may be inspected by creditors and contributories accordingly, but not further or otherwise.

(2) Nothing in this section excludes or restricts any statutory rights of a government department or person acting under the authority of a government department.

General Note

This re-enacts s.559, C.A. 1985 and deals with the court's power to regulate access to the books and papers of the company by creditors and contributories. Normally a special case must be made out for inspection of the books (*Re Joint Stock Discount Co., ex p. Buchan* (1866) 36 L.J.Ch. 150).

Payment of expenses of winding up

156. The court may, in the event of the assets being insufficient to satisfy the liabilities, make an order as to the payment out of the assets of the expenses incurred in the winding up in such order of priority as the court thinks just.

General Note

This re-enacts s.560, C.A. 1985. It deals with the power of the court to make an order for payment of the expenses of winding-up out of the assets (s.560 referred to "costs, charges and expenses). Collection and distribution of the companies assets is also dealt with in the Rules.

Attendance at company meetings (Scotland)

157. In the winding up by the court of a company registered in Scotland, the court has power to require the attendance of any officer of the company at any meeting of creditors or of contributories, or of a liquidation committee, for the purpose of giving information as to the trade, dealings, affairs or property of the company.

General Note

This re-enacts s.562, C.A. 1985 with a minor amendment by the substitution of "liquidation committee" for "committee of inspection."

Power to arrest absconding contributory

158. The court, at any time either before or after making a winding-up order, on proof of probable cause for believing that a contributory is about to quit the United Kingdom or otherwise to abscond or to remove or conceal any of his property for the purpose of evading payment of calls, may cause the contributory to be arrested and his books and papers and moveable personal property to be seized and him and them to be kept safely until such time as the court may order.

Definition

"contributory": s.79.

General Note

This section re-enacts s.565, C.A. 1985. It deals with the power of the court to arrest an absconding contributory about to quit the United Kingdom.

Powers of court to be cumulative

159. Powers conferred by this Act and the Companies Act on the court are in addition to, and not in restriction of, any existing powers of instituting proceedings against a contributory or debtor of the company, or the estate of any contributory or debtor, for the recovery of any call or other sums.

General Note

This re-enacts s.566, C.A. 1985.

Delegation of powers to liquidator (England and Wales)

160.—(1) Provision may be made by rules for enabling or requiring all or any of the powers and duties conferred and imposed on the court in England and Wales by the Companies Act and this Act in respect of the following matters—

(*a*) the holding and conducting of meetings to ascertain the wishes of creditors and contributories,

(*b*) the settling of lists of contributories and the rectifying of the register of members where required, and the collection and application of the assets,

(*c*) the payment, delivery, conveyance, surrender or transfer of money, property, books or papers to the liquidator,

(*d*) the making of calls,

(*e*) the fixing of a time within which debts and claims must be proved,

to be exercised or performed by the liquidator as an officer of the court, and subject to the court's control.

(2) But the liquidator shall not, without the special leave of the court, rectify the register of members, and shall not make any call without either that special leave or the sanction of the liquidation committee.

General Note

This re-enacts s.567, C.A. 1985 and deals with the power to make rules concerning the delegation by the court to the liquidator of the matters listed in subs. (1)(*a*)–(*e*). All these matters are, in fact, covered by the Rules (promulgated under s.411 *infra*).

Enforcement of, and appeal from, orders

Orders for calls on contributories (Scotland)

161.—(1) In Scotland, where an order, interlocutor or decree has been made for winding up a company by the court, it is competent to the court, on production by the liquidators of a list certified by them of the names of the contributories liable in payment of any calls, and of the amount due by each contributory, and of the date when that amount became due, to pronounce forthwith a decree against those contributories for payment of the sums so certified to be due, with interest from that date until payment (at 5 per cent. per annum) in the same way and to the same effect as if they had severally consented to registration for execution, on a charge of 6 days, of a legal obligation to pay those calls and interest.

(2) The decree may be extracted immediately, and no suspension of it is competent, except on caution or consignation, unless with special leave of the court.

General Note

This re-enacts s.569, C.A. 1985 and deals with the power of Scots courts to make orders for calls on contributories. See *Palmer,* paras. 87–40.

Appeals from orders in Scotland

162.—(1) Subject to the provisions of this section and to rules of court, an appeal from any order or decision made or given in the winding up of a company by the court in Scotland under this Act lies in the same manner and subject to the same conditions as an appeal from an order or decision of the court in cases within its ordinary jurisdiction.

(2) In regard to orders or judgments pronounced by the judge acting as vacation judge in pursuance of section 4 of the Administration of Justice (Scotland) Act 1933—

(*a*) none of the orders specified in Part I of Schedule 3 to this Act are subject to review, reduction, suspension or stay of execution, and

(*b*) every other order or judgment (except as mentioned below) may be submitted to review by the Inner House by reclaiming motion enrolled within 14 days from the date of the order or judgment.

(3) However, an order being one of those specified in Part II of that Schedule shall, from the date of the order and notwithstanding that it has been submitted to review as above, be carried out and receive effect until the Inner House have disposed of the matter.

(4) In regard to orders or judgments pronounced in Scotland by a Lord Ordinary before whom proceedings in a winding up are being taken, any such order or judgment may be submitted to review by the Inner House by reclaiming motion enrolled within 14 days from its date; but should it not be so submitted to review during session, the provisions of this section in regard to orders or judgments pronounced by the judge acting as vacation judge apply.

(5) Nothing in this section affects provisions of the Companies Act or this Act in reference to decrees in Scotland for payment of calls in the winding up of companies, whether voluntary or by the court.

General Note

This re-enacts s.571, C.A. 1985 and deals with the system of appeals from orders in Scotland. See *Palmer,* paras. 87–04.

Chapter VII

Liquidators

Preliminary

Style and title of liquidators

163. The liquidator of a company shall be described—

(*a*) where a person other than the official receiver is liquidator, by the style of "the liquidator" of the particular company, or

(*b*) where the official receiver is liquidator, by the style of "the official receiver and liquidator" of the particular company;

and in neither case shall he be described by an individual name.

Definition

"the official receiver": s.399.

General Note

This replaces and reproduces in substance the provisions of s.533(7), C.A. 1985. The provisions are now relocated so as to make them applicable to every mode of winding up.

Corrupt inducement affecting appointment

164. A person who gives, or agrees or offers to give, to any member or creditor of a company any valuable consideration with a view to securing his own appointment or nomination, or to securing or preventing the appointment or nomination of some person other than himself, as the company's liquidator is liable to a fine.

Definition

"fine": s.430, Sched. 10.

General Note

This re-enacts s.635, C.A. 1985 and makes it an offence to give or offer a corrupt inducement in connection with the appointment of a liquidator.

Liquidator's powers and duties

Voluntary winding up

165.—(1) This section has effect where a company is being wound up voluntarily, but subject to section 166 below in the case of a creditors' voluntary winding up.

(2) The liquidator may—

(*a*) in the case of a members' voluntary winding up, with the sanction of an extraordinary resolution of the company, and

(*b*) in the case of a creditors' voluntary winding up, with the sanction of the court or the liquidation committee (or, if there is no such committee, a meeting of the company's creditors),

exercise any of the powers specified in Part I of Schedule 4 to this Act (payment of debts, compromise of claims, etc.).

(3) The liquidator may, without sanction, exercise either of the powers specified in Part II of that Schedule (institution and defence of proceedings; carrying on the business of the company) and any of the general powers specified in Part III of that Schedule.

(4) The liquidator may—

(*a*) exercise the court's power of settling a list of contributories (which list is prima facie evidence of the liability of the persons named in it to be contributories),

(*b*) exercise the court's power of making calls,
(*c*) summon general meetings of the company for the purpose of obtaining its sanction by special or extraordinary resolution or for any other purpose he may think fit.

(5) The liquidator shall pay the company's debts and adjust the rights of the contributories among themselves.

(6) Where the liquidator in exercise of the powers conferred on him by this Act disposes of any property of the company to a person who is connected with the company (within the meaning of section 249 in Part VII), he shall, if there is for the time being a liquidation committee, give notice to the committee of that exercise of his powers.

Definitions

"connected with the company": s.249.
"creditors' voluntary winding up": s.90.
"extraordinary resolution": s.378, C.A. 1985.
"members' voluntary winding up": s.90.
"special resolution": s.378, C.A. 1985.

General Note

The layout of this section follows that in s.598, C.A. 1985 which defined the powers and duties of a liquidator in a voluntary winding up by means of a cross reference to s.539 C.A. 1985. The present section is the same in substance (save for the addition of subs. (6)) as s.598 but defines the powers and duties by means of references to relevant parts of Sched. 4. Where sanction is required (see subs. (2)) it can be furnished by an extraordinary resolution of the company in the case of a members' voluntary winding up and by the court or liquidation committee or, in the absence of the latter, a meeting of the creditors' in the case of a creditors' voluntary winding up. S.166 *infra* contains further provisions governing the liquidator's powers and duties in the case of a creditors' voluntary winding up.

Subs. (6)

This was introduced in Sched. 6, para. 41, I.A. 1985. Its purpose is to enable the liquidation committee to challenge such a disposition. See the General Note to s.314(6) *infra* which is the equivalent provision relating to individual insolvency.

Creditors' voluntary winding up

166.—(1) This section applies where, in the case of a creditors' voluntary winding up, a liquidator has been nominated by the company.

(2) The powers conferred on the liquidator by section 165 shall not be exercised, except with the sanction of the court, during the period before the holding of the creditors' meeting under section 98 in Chapter IV.

(3) Subsection (2) does not apply in relation to the power of the liquidator—
(*a*) to take into his custody or under his control all the property to which the company is or appears to be entitled;
(*b*) to dispose of perishable goods and other goods the value of which is likely to diminish if they are not immediately disposed of; and
(*c*) to do all such other things as may be necessary for the protection of the company's assets.

(4) The liquidator shall attend the creditors' meeting held under section 98 and shall report to the meeting on any exercise by him of his powers (whether or not under this section or under section 112 or 165).

(5) If default is made—
(*a*) by the company in complying with subsection (1) or (2) of section 98, or
(*b*) by the directors in complying with subsection (1) or (2) of section 99,

the liquidator shall, within 7 days of the relevant day, apply to the court for directions as to the manner in which that default is to be remedied.

(6) "The relevant day" means the day on which the liquidator was nominated by the company or the day on which he first became aware of the default, whichever is the later.

(7) If the liquidator without reasonable excuse fails to comply with this section, he is liable to a fine.

DEFINITIONS

"creditors' voluntary winding up": s.90.
"fine": s.430, Sched. 10.
"property": s.436.
"the relevant day": subs. (6).

GENERAL NOTE

This section, in conjunction with s.98 and also s.114 is aimed at eradicating certain abusive practices associated with the voluntary winding up of companies, and in particular those practices whereby the shareholders have acted at short notice to place the company in liquidation and to appoint a liquidator, whereupon a delay of several weeks may ensue before the convening of a creditors' meeting to confirm the appointment. This practice has become known as "centrebinding" after the name of the case in which it was decided that the technical offence committed by the company in failing to convene the creditors' meeting within 24 hours of the members' meeting did not have the further consequence that the liquidator's appointment, or any exercise of his powers, were rendered retrospectively invalid (*Re Centrebind Ltd.* [1967] 1 W.L.R. 377; [1966] 3 All E.R. 889). The dangerous loss of protection for the company's assets, and for the creditors' interest, attendant upon such practices was the subject of vigorous proposals in paras. 667–673 of the *Cork Report,* accepted with reservations in paras. 128–133 of the *White Paper.* This section does not have the effect of preventing the shareholders from passing an immediate resolution for winding up, and then proceeding to nominate a liquidator. But the basis upon which this is to be done is solely now for the purpose of preserving and safeguarding the assets, rather than the converse. Until a creditors' meeting is convened under s.89, therefore, subs. (2) of this section deprives the liquidator of the power to exercise the majority of the powers conferred by s.165 except with the sanction of the court. In effect the liquidator is limited to acting as a provisional liquidator for the time being, since subs. (3) allows him to take steps which ensure the preservation and protection of durable assets, and the expeditious disposal of perishable or wasting ones. In other respects however it is made the professional duty of the liquidator to prepare for the convening of the creditors' meeting under s.98, and he is charged with the duty under subs. (5) of making application to the court within seven days if the company or the directors fail to comply with the requirements of s.98. The decision in *Re Centrebind Ltd. (supra)* itself is thus overruled by this statutory provision, because any exercise of his ostensible powers by a liquidator in contravention of this section will be *ultra vires* and invalid. Moreover, any liquidator so acting will not only commit a criminal offence under subs. (7) of this section, but will be liable to civil remedy under s.212 and to further sanctions under Part XIII of the Act with regard to his authorisation to act as an insolvency practitioner.

Winding up by the court

167.—(1) Where a company is being wound up by the court, the liquidator may—

(*a*) with the sanction of the court or the liquidation committee, exercise any of the powers specified in Parts I and II of Schedule 4 to this Act (payment of debts; compromise of claims, etc.; institution and defence of proceedings; carrying on of the business of the company), and

(*b*) with or without that sanction, exercise any of the general powers specified in Part III of that Schedule.

(2) Where the liquidator (not being the official receiver), in exercise of the powers conferred on him by this Act—

(*a*) disposes of any property of the company to a person who is connected with the company (within the meaning of section 249 in Part VII), or

(*b*) employs a solicitor to assist him in the carrying out of his functions, he shall, if there is for the time being a liquidation committee, give notice to the committee of that exercise of his powers.

(3) The exercise by the liquidator in a winding up by the court of the powers conferred by this section is subject to the control of the court, and any creditor or contributory may apply to the court with respect to any exercise or proposed exercise of any of those powers.

DEFINITION

"connected with the company": s.249.

GENERAL NOTE

This reproduces and re-drafts parts of s.539 (subss. (1), (2), (2A), and (3)). The powers of the liquidator are no longer expressed in the section but are to be found in Schedule 4.

Subs. (2)

This was introduced in Sched. 6, para. 31(3), I.A. 1985. See Notes to ss.165 and 314(6).

Supplementary powers (England and Wales)

168.—(1) This section applies in the case of a company which is being wound up by the court in England and Wales.

(2) The liquidator may summon general meetings of the creditors or contributories for the purpose of ascertaining their wishes; and it is his duty to summon meetings at such times as the creditors or contributories by resolution (either at the meeting appointing the liquidator or otherwise) may direct, or whenever requested in writing to do so by one-tenth in value of the creditors or contributories (as the case may be).

(3) The liquidator may apply to the court (in the prescribed manner) for directions in relation to any particular matter arising in the winding up.

(4) Subject to the provisions of this Act, the liquidator shall use his own discretion in the management of the assets and their distribution among the creditors.

(5) If any person is aggrieved by an act or decision of the liquidator, that person may apply to the court; and the court may confirm, reverse or modify the act or decision complained of, and make such order in the case as it thinks just.

GENERAL NOTE

This re-enacts s.540(3)–(6), C.A. 1985. The section deals with the exercise and control of the liquidator's powers and supplements s.167. The liquidator is instructed to have regard to the directions of the creditors and contributories and if he fails to do so an aggrieved person may apply to the court under s.168(5). The provision is similar to s.314(7) and the same principles apply—see *Leon* v. *York-O-Matic Ltd.* [1966] 3 All E.R. 277. The liquidator himself may use these provisions where he considers that the directions of the committee of inspection are unwise—see *Re Consolidated Diesel Engine Manufacturers Ltd.* [1915] 1 Ch. 192. See *Palmer,* paras. 85–39.

Supplementary powers (Scotland)

169.—(1) In the case of a winding up in Scotland, the court may provide by order that the liquidator may, where there is no liquidation committee, exercise any of the following powers, namely—

(*a*) to bring or defend any action or other legal proceeding in the name and on behalf of the company, or

(*b*) to carry on the business of the company so far as may be necessary for its beneficial winding up,

without the sanction or intervention of the court.

(2) In a winding up by the court in Scotland, the liquidator has (subject to the rules) the same powers as a trustee on a bankrupt estate.

General Note

This re-enacts s.539(4), (5), C.A. 1985.

Enforcement of liquidator's duty to make returns, etc.

170.—(1) If a liquidator who has made any default—

(*a*) in filing, delivering or making any return, account or other document, or

(*b*) in giving any notice which he is by law required to file, deliver, make or give,

fails to make good the default within 14 days after the service on him of a notice requiring him to do so, the court has the following powers.

(2) On an application made by any creditor or contributory of the company, or by the registrar of companies, the court may make an order directing the liquidator to make good the default within such time as may be specified in the order.

(3) The court's order may provide that all costs of and incidental to the application shall be borne by the liquidator.

(4) Nothing in this section prejudices the operation of any enactment imposing penalties on a liquidator in respect of any such default as is mentioned above.

General Note

This re-enacts s.636, C.A. 1985 and deals with the enforcement of the liquidator's obligation to make returns etc.

Removal; vacation of office

Removal, etc. (voluntary winding up)

171.—(1) This section applies with respect to the removal from office and vacation of office of the liquidator of a company which is being wound up voluntarily.

(2) Subject to the next subsection, the liquidator may be removed from office only by an order of the court or—

(*a*) in the case of a members' voluntary winding up, by a general meeting of the company summoned specially for that purpose, or

(*b*) in the case of a creditors' voluntary winding up, by a general meeting of the company's creditors summoned specially for that purpose in accordance with the rules.

(3) Where the liquidator was appointed by the court under section 108 in Chapter V, a meeting such as is mentioned in subsection (2) above shall be summoned for the purpose of replacing him only if he thinks fit or the court so directs or the meeting is requested, in accordance with the rules—

(*a*) in the case of a members' voluntary winding up, by members representing not less than one-half of the total voting rights of all the members having at the date of the request a right to vote at the meeting, or

(*b*) in the case of a creditors' voluntary winding up, by not less than one-half, in value, of the company's creditors.

(4) A liquidator shall vacate office if he ceases to be a person who is qualified to act as an insolvency practitioner in relation to the company.

(5) A liquidator may, in the prescribed circumstances, resign his office by giving notice of his resignation to the registrar of companies.

(6) Where—

(*a*) in the case of a members' voluntary winding up, a final meeting of the company has been held under section 94 in Chapter III, or

(*b*) in the case of a creditors' voluntary winding up, final meetings of the company and of the creditors have been held under section 106 in Chapter IV,

the liquidator whose report was considered at the meeting or meetings shall vacate office as soon as he has complied with subsection (3) of that section and has given notice to the registrar of companies that the meeting or meetings have been held and of the decisions (if any) of the meeting or meetings.

Definitions

"creditors' voluntary winding up": s.90.
"members' voluntary winding up": s.90.
"person qualified to act as an insolvency practitioner": s.390.
"the rules": s.251.
"to act as an insolvency practitioner in relation to a company": s.388(1).

General Note

This section contains a series of provisions under which a liquidator may be removed from office, or may resign or be required to vacate his office, in either a creditors' or a members' voluntary winding up, and is thus the counterpart of s.172, which applies in cases of winding up by the court. Where in a creditors' voluntary winding up a vacancy occurs in the office of liquidator, whether by death, resignation or otherwise, the creditors have the right to fill the vacancy under s.104. Alternatively, in a voluntary winding up of either type, the court may appoint a liquidator under s.108(1) if from any cause there is no liquidator acting.

Subs. (2)

The liquidator may be removed from office only by an order of the court

Such an order may be sought under s.108(2), which empowers the court at its discretion to remove a liquidator "on cause shown", and to appoint another.

Subs. (3)

This restriction upon the convening of a meeting under subs. (2) is applicable where the court has exercised its discretionary powers under s.108 to appoint a liquidator where there is none acting, or to remove a liquidator for cause shown and to appoint another. The fact that such a liquidator's appointment has been made by the court, and not by either the creditors or the members acting under s.100 is made the basis for imposing restrictions upon the circumstances in which the members or the creditors may procure the convening of a meeting at which the liquidator's removal may be resolved upon.

Subs. (4)

If he ceases to be a person who is qualified to act as an insolvency practitioner

See s.390 for the requirements for being qualified to act as an insolvency practitioner, and ss.391–393 inclusive (and relevant General Notes) for authorisation to act, and withdrawal of authorisation to act, as an insolvency practitioner.

Removal, etc. (winding up by the court)

172.—(1) This section applies with respect to the removal from office and vacation of office of the liquidator of a company which is being wound up by the court, or of a provisional liquidator.

(2) Subject as follows, the liquidator may be removed from office only by an order of the court or by a general meeting of the company's creditors summoned specially for that purpose in accordance with the rules; and a provisional liquidator may be removed from office only by an order of the court.

(3) Where—

(*a*) the official receiver is liquidator otherwise than in succession under section 136(3) to a person who held office as a result of a nomination by a meeting of the company's creditors or contributories, or

(*b*) the liquidator was appointed by the court otherwise than under section 139(4)(*a*) or 140(1), or was appointed by the Secretary of State,

a general meeting of the company's creditors shall be summoned for the purpose of replacing him only if he thinks fit, or the court so directs, or the meeting is requested, in accordance with the rules, by not less than one-quarter, in value, of the creditors.

(4) If appointed by the Secretary of State, the liquidator may be removed from office by a direction of the Secretary of State.

(5) A liquidator or provisional liquidator, not being the official receiver, shall vacate office if he ceases to be a person who is qualified to act as an insolvency practitioner in relation to the company.

(6) A liquidator may, in the prescribed circumstances, resign his office by giving notice of his resignation to the court.

(7) Where an order is made under section 204 (early dissolution in Scotland) for the dissolution of the company, the liquidator shall vacate office when the dissolution of the company takes effect in accordance with that section.

(8) Where a final meeting has been held under section 146 (liquidator's report on completion of winding up), the liquidator whose report was considered at the meeting shall vacate office as soon as he has given notice to the court and the registrar of companies that the meeting has been held and of the decisions (if any) of the meeting.

DEFINITIONS

"person qualified to act as an insolvency practitioner in relation to the company": s.390.
"the official receiver": s.399.
"the rules": s.251.

TRANSITIONAL PROVISION

Sched. 11, para. 6(3).

GENERAL NOTE

This section re-enacts s.79, I.A. 1985. Appointments of provisional liquidators may take place under s.135.

Subs. (2)

One consequence of this provision is that it is rendered impossible in a compulsory winding up for the contributories of the Company to procure the removal of the liquidator merely by means of a meeting of their own number. (*cf.* s.171(2)(*a*), (3) in relation to a members' voluntary winding up). Therefore, although it is possible under s.139(3) or (4)(*a*) for the contributories" nominee to become the liquidator of the Company, those same persons cannot remove him at will: an Order of the Court, or a resolution carried by a general meeting of the Company's creditors, are the only ways of bringing about the removal of a liquidator from office, except in the special cases falling under subss. (3), (4) and (5).

Subs. (4)

If appointed by the Secretary of State

Such appointments may take place under s.137, in the circumstances specified in subss. (1) and (2) of that section.

Subs. (5)

. . . If he ceases to be a person who is qualified to act as an insolvency practitioner in relation to the company.

See s.390 and General Note thereto, for the requirements for being qualified to act as an insolvency practitioner, and ss.391–393 inclusive (and relevant General Notes) for authorisation to act, and withdrawal of authorisation to act, as an insolvency practitioner.

Release of liquidator

Release (voluntary winding up)

173.—(1) This section applies with respect to the release of the liquidator of a company which is being wound up voluntarily.

(2) A person who has ceased to be a liquidator shall have his release with effect from the following time, that is to say—

(*a*) in the case of a person who has been removed from office by a general meeting of the company or by a general meeting of the company's creditors that has not resolved against his release or who has died, the time at which notice is given to the registrar of companies in accordance with the rules that that person has ceased to hold office;

(*b*) in the case of a person who has been removed from office by a general meeting of the company's creditors that has resolved against his release, or by the court, or who has vacated office under section 171(4) above, such time as the Secretary of State may, on the application of that person, determine;

(*c*) in the case of a person who has resigned, such time as may be prescribed;

(*d*) in the case of a person who has vacated office under subsection (6)(*a*) of section 171, the time at which he vacated office;

(*e*) in the case of a person who has vacated office under subsection (6)(*b*) of that section—

(i) if the final meeting of the creditors referred to in that subsection has resolved against that person's release, such time as the Secretary of State may, on an application by that person, determine, and

(ii) if that meeting has not resolved against that person's release, the time at which he vacated office.

(3) In the application of subsection (2) to the winding up of a company registered in Scotland, the references to a determination by the Secretary of State as to the time from which a person who has ceased to be liquidator shall have his release are to be read as references to such a determination by the Accountant of Court.

(4) Where a liquidator has his release under subsection (2), he is, with effect from the time specified in that subsection, discharged from all liability both in respect of acts or omissions of his in the winding up and otherwise in relation to his conduct as liquidator.

But nothing in this section prevents the exercise, in relation to a person who has had his release under subsection (2), of the court's powers under section 212 of the Act (summary remedy against delinquent directors, liquidators, etc.).

DEFINITION

"prescribed": s.251.

GENERAL NOTE

This section is concerned with the release of a liquidator of a company in a voluntary winding up, and is therefore the counterpart of s.174 which applies in cases of winding up by the court. Specific provision is made for each of the ways in which the functions of the liquidator may come to an end in relation to a company. A time specified in each instance as that at which his release takes effect constitutes the moment from which the liquidator is discharged from all liability in respect of his conduct in office. Despite this the possibility is retained by means of the concluding *proviso* in subs. (4), of a subsequent application being made under s.212 in respect of any misconduct rendering the former liquidator liable to make restitution for any money or property, or to make payment by way of compensation.

Subs. (2)(c)

Such time as may be prescribed

The resignation of a liquidator in a voluntary liquidation may be effected under s.171(5). The provision that the release of a liquidator who has resigned shall take effect from a time to be prescribed in the rules permits a reconciliation of the need for a speedy vacation of office by the liquidator under some circumstances, such as illness, with the need to ensure that a release from liability is not accorded before there has been proper time to assess the liquidator's conduct. The provision should also be helpful in ensuring that a liquidator will not be able, through the expedient of resigning, to avoid complying with the requirements of s.94 or s.106 with regard to the summoning of final meetings when the company's affairs are fully wound up.

Release (winding up by the court)

174.—(1) This section applies with respect to the release of the liquidator of a company which is being wound up by the court, or of a provisional liquidator.

(2) Where the official receiver has ceased to be liquidator and a person becomes liquidator in his stead, the official receiver has his release with effect from the following time, that is to say—

(*a*) in a case where that person was nominated by a general meeting of creditors or contributories, or was appointed by the Secretary of State, the time at which the official receiver gives notice to the court that he has been replaced;

(*b*) in a case where that person is appointed by the court, such time as the court may determine.

(3) If the official receiver while he is a liquidator gives notice to the Secretary of State that the winding up is for practical purposes complete, he has his release with effect from such time as the Secretary of State may determine.

(4) A person other than the official receiver who has ceased to be a liquidator has his release with effect from the following time, that is to say—

(*a*) in the case of a person who has been removed from office by a general meeting of creditors that has not resolved against his release or who has died, the time at which notice is given to the court in accordance with the rules that that person has ceased to hold office;

(*b*) in the case of a person who has been removed from office by a general meeting of creditors that has resolved against his release, or by the court or the Secretary of State, or who has vacated office under section 172(5) or (7), such time as the Secretary of State may, on an application by that person, determine;

(*c*) in the case of a person who has resigned, such time as may be prescribed;

(*d*) in the case of a person who has vacated office under section 172(8)—

(i) if the final meeting referred to in that subsection has resolved against that person's release, such time as the Secretary of State may, on an application by that person, determine, and

(ii) if that meeting has not so resolved, the time at which that person vacated office.

(5) A person who has ceased to hold office as a provisional liquidator has his release with effect from such time as the court may, on an application by him, determine.

(6) Where the official receiver or a liquidator or provisional liquidator has his release under this section, he is, with effect from the time specified in the preceding provisions of this section, discharged from all liability

both in respect of acts or omissions of his in the winding up and otherwise in relation to his conduct as liquidator or provisional liquidator.

But nothing in this section prevents the exercise, in relation to a person who has had his release under this section, of the court's powers under section 212 (summary remedy against delinquent directors, liquidators, etc.).

(7) In the application of this section to a case where the order for winding up has been made by the court in Scotland, the references to a determination by the Secretary of State as to the time from which a person who has ceased to be liquidator has his release are to such a determination by the Accountant of Court.

DEFINITIONS

"contributory": s.79.
"prescribed": s.251.
"the official receiver": s.399.
"the rules": s.251.

TRANSITIONAL PROVISION

Sched. 11, para. 6(4).

GENERAL NOTE

This section replaces s.80, I.A. 1985 which is repealed. It makes specific provisions for the release of the liquidator in relation to each of the ways in which the functions of the official receiver or liquidator may come to an end in relation to a Company. The time specified in each instance as that at which his release takes effect constitutes the moment from which the liquidator is discharged from all liability in respect of his conduct in office, although it is nevertheless possible for a subsequent application to be made under s.212 in respect of any misconduct rendering him liable to make restitution of any money or property, or to make payment by way of compensation.

Subs. (4)(c)

Such time as may be prescribed

A person may resign as liquidator by virtue of s.172(6), in accordance with the procedure thereunder prescribed. The resignation procedure in the new insolvency rules will be based upon that previously contained in rule 167 of the Companies (Winding Up) Rules 1949 (S.I. 1949 No. 330) whereby the liquidator must obtain permission from the creditors or the court before he is able to resign.

In some cases, such as where the liquidator is in ill health, it may be necessary for the liquidator to be allowed to resign without delay, but on the other hand it is equally desirable that some time should be allowed for proper consideration of all the circumstances concerning his conduct in office. The facilities in this para. whereby provision may be made in the rules for the liquidator's release to be postponed for a period after he has been permitted to resign is therefore a useful safeguard. It should also ensure that a liquidator will not be able, by the expedient of resigning, to avoid complying with the requirements of s.146 with regard to the summoning of a final meeting of creditors. In ordinary cases therefore the liquidator will be obliged to make a formal request for his release on the basis of his final report presented to the final meeting of creditors.

Subs. (6)

The court's powers under s.212

The proviso in this subsection ensures that the summary remedy provided by s.212 for use against delinquent liquidators, among others, continues to be available even after the liquidator's release has become effective.

CHAPTER VIII

PROVISIONS OF GENERAL APPLICATION IN WINDING UP

Preferential debts

Preferential debts (general provision)

175.—(1) In a winding up the company's preferential debts (within the meaning given by section 386 in Part XII) shall be paid in priority to all other debts.

(2) Preferential debts—

(*a*) rank equally among themselves after the expenses of the winding up and shall be paid in full, unless the assets are insufficient to meet them, in which case they abate in equal proportions; and

(*b*) so far as the assets of the company available for payment of general creditors are insufficient to meet them, have priority over the claims of holders of debentures secured by, or holders of, any floating charge created by the company, and shall be paid accordingly out of any property comprised in or subject to that charge.

DEFINITIONS

"floating charge": s.251.
"holder of a floating charge": s.70(1).
"preferential debt": s.386, Sched. 6.
"property": s.436.

GENERAL NOTE

This section re-enacts subs. (1) and (2) of s.89, I.A. 1985 and reflects some of the arguments and recommendations in chap. 32 of the *Cork Report,* although the Government strove to resist the efforts made at successive Parliamentary stages to cut down the Crown's privileged position as a preferential creditor for unpaid tax, as advocated in paras. 1409–1444 and 1450 of the *Cork Report.* Victories over the Government were gained in divisions in both Houses (*Hansard,* H.L. Vol. 462, cols. 628–640, H.C. Standing Committee E, June 11, 1985, cols. 304–324; see also H.L., Vol. 462, cols. 172–180) whereby Sched. 6 was amended so as to eliminate Crown preference in respect of taxes assessed upon the company directly as taxpayer to the Inland Revenue, and also to eliminate the preferential status formerly accorded to local rates. A further amendment was carried which had the effect of restricting Crown preference in respect of outstanding payments of value added tax to a period of six months, as against the period of twelve months which is applicable for other debts due to Customs and Excise. These victories were not only significant in themselves, but also symbolise an important change of attitude towards the traditional categories of preferential debt, whose status can no longer be regarded as sacrosanct. A further matter of importance is that the law regarding preferential debts has been completely unified for cases of company and individual insolvency alike, since the same Sched. 6 also applies in relation to individual insolvency by virtue of s.386(1).

Subs. (2)

This provision maintains the previous legal position with regard to the application of the *pari passu* principle to the preferential debts. Para. (*b*) also maintains the existing rule that preferential debts enjoy priority over the claims of holders of a floating charge, although this is not the case with regard to any fixed charge created by the company over any of its property (*Re Lewis Merthyr Consolidated Collieries* [1929] 1 Ch. 498; *cf. Christonette International Ltd., Re* [1982] 3 All E.R. 225).

Preferential charge on goods distrained

176.—(1) This section applies where a company is being wound up by the court in England and Wales, and is without prejudice to section 128 (avoidance of attachments, etc.).

(2) Where any person (whether or not a landlord or person entitled to rent) has distrained upon the goods or effects of the company in the

period of 3 months ending with the date of the winding-up order, those goods or effects, or the proceeds of their sale, shall be charged for the benefit of the company with the preferential debts of the company to the extent that the company's property is for the time being insufficient for meeting them.

(3) Where by virtue of a charge under subsection (2) any person surrenders any goods or effects to a company or makes a payment to a company, that person ranks, in respect of the amount of the proceeds of sale of those goods or effects by the liquidator or (as the case may be) the amount of the payment, as a preferential creditor of the company, except as against so much of the company's property as is available for the payment of preferential creditors by virtue of the surrender or payment.

General Note

This provision re-enacts subs. (3) and (4) of s.89 of the I.A. 1985 and has the effect of rendering void any attachment, sequestration, distress or execution put into force against the estate or effects of a company after the commencement of a winding up by the court in England and Wales or in Scotland.

Special managers

Power to appoint special manager

177.—(1) Where a company has gone into liquidation or a provisional liquidator has been appointed, the court may, on an application under this section, appoint any person to be the special manager of the business or property of the company.

(2) The application may be made by the liquidator or provisional liquidator in any case where it appears to him that the nature of the business or property of the company, or the interests of the company's creditors or contributories or members generally, require the appointment of another person to manage the company's business or property.

(3) The special manager has such powers as may be entrusted to him by the court.

(4) The court's power to entrust powers to the special manager includes power to direct that any provision of this Act that has effect in relation to the provisional liquidator or liquidator of a company shall have the like effect in relation to the special manager for the purposes of the carrying out by him of any of the functions of the provisional liquidator or liquidator.

(5) The special manager shall—

(*a*) give such security or, in Scotland, caution as may be prescribed;
(*b*) prepare and keep such accounts as may be prescribed; and
(*c*) produce those accounts in accordance with the rules to the Secretary of State or to such other persons as may be prescribed.

Definitions

"business": s.436.
"company goes into liquidation": s.247(2).
"contributory": s.79.
"prescribed": s.251.
"property": s.436.
"security": s.248(*b*).
"the rules": s.251.

General Note

This re-enacts s.90, I.A. 1985 which allowed a considerably widened scope for the making of application to the court of a special manager to be appointed. Formerly, such applications could only be made by the Official Receiver as liquidator of the company, but there is no such restriction in the present section and application may be made by the liquidator or provisional liquidator of the company at the time in question.

Subs. (1)

Provisional liquidator . . . appointed

The appointment of a provisional liquidator in a winding up by the court may take place under s.135.

The court may . . . appoint any person

The functions of a special manager are not among the matters mentioned in s.388(1), which lists the ways in which a person acts as an insolvency practitioner in relation to a company for the purposes of that section. Hence it is not legally required that the person appointed as special manager should be a qualified insolvency practitioner, nor will an unqualified person commit a criminal offence under s.389 by accepting such an appointment and performing the role assigned to him.

This section is drafted in parallel to s.370, which applies in relation to bankruptcy.

Disclaimer (England and Wales only)

Power to disclaim onerous property

178.—(1) This and the next two sections apply to a company that is being wound up in England and Wales.

(2) Subject as follows, the liquidator may, by the giving of the prescribed notice, disclaim any onerous property and may do so notwithstanding that he has taken possession of it, endeavoured to sell it, or otherwise exercised rights of ownership in relation to it.

(3) The following is onerous property for the purposes of this section—

(*a*) any unprofitable contract, and

(*b*) any other property of the company which is unsaleable or not readily saleable or is such that it may give rise to a liability to pay money or perform any other onerous act.

(4) A disclaimer under this section—

(*a*) operates so as to determine, as from the date of the disclaimer, the rights, interests and liabilities of the company in or in respect of the property disclaimed; but

(*b*) does not, except so far as is necessary for the purpose of releasing the company from any liability, affect the rights or liabilities of any other person.

(5) A notice of disclaimer shall not be given under this section in respect of any property if—

(*a*) a person interested in the property has applied in writing to the liquidator or one of his predecessors as liquidator requiring the liquidator or that predecessor to decide whether he will disclaim or not, and

(*b*) the period of 28 days beginning with the day on which that application was made, or such longer period as the court may allow, has expired without a notice of disclaimer having been given under this section in respect of that property.

(6) Any person sustaining loss or damage in consequence of the operation of a disclaimer under this section is deemed a creditor of the company to the extent of the loss or damage and accordingly may prove for the loss or damage in the winding up.

Definitions

"onerous property": subs. (3).
"prescribed": s.251.
"property": s.436.

General Note

This section, in conjunction with ss.179–182 re-enacts ss.91 and 92, I.A. 1985 which changed the law in several important ways. The opportunity was taken to harmonise the provisions on disclaimer in winding up with those applicable in bankruptcy, now contained in ss.315–321 of this Act. The topic of disclaimer is considered in Chap. 27 of the *Cork Report.*

The most important change in the law of disclaimer in winding up was that leave of the court is no longer required when the liquidator is someone other than the official receiver. The powers of a private sector liquidator were thus enhanced to match those traditionally enjoyed in such matters by the official receiver, and also by a trustee in bankruptcy (in most cases). Secondly, the types of property which can be disclaimed were widened. Formerly the power of disclaimer was exercisable in relation to land bound by onerous covenants; to shares in companies; to unprofitable contracts; and to any other property that was unsaleable, or not readily saleable by reason of its binding its possessor to the performance of any onerous act or to the payment of any sum of money. Now the power of disclaimer is expressed to be exercisable in relation to "onerous property" as defined in subs. (3), so that it suffices if property is simply unsaleable, without any necessity that it be also subject to any onerous requirement. Conversely, it now suffices if property is subject to an onerous requirement albeit this does not have the effect of rendering the property unsaleable or not readily saleable. Thirdly, there is now no time limit within which the power of disclaimer must be exercised. The twelve-month limit formerly imposed by s.618(3) of the Companies Act 1985 was excluded contrary to the recommendation in para. 1195 of the *Cork Report.*

It is hoped that these more liberally drafted powers of disclaimer will bring about a revival in their use, and consequently bring about a simplification of the liquidator's overall task. The shortcomings of the disclaimer provisions formerly in force as s.323 of the Companies Act 1948 (latterly ss.618, 619 of the Companies Act 1985), were demonstrated in *Re Potters Oil Ltd. (in liquidation)* [1985] P.C.C. 148.

Subs. (6)

Note that s.181(5) requires that the effect of any order made under s.181 shall be taken into account in assessing the extent of a person's claim for the purposes of this subsection.

Disclaimer of leaseholds

179.—(1) The disclaimer under section 178 of any property of a leasehold nature does not take effect unless a copy of the disclaimer has been served (so far as the liquidator is aware of their addresses) on every person claiming under the company as underlessee or mortgagee and either—

(*a*) no application under section 181 below is made with respect to that property before the end of the period of 14 days beginning with the day on which the last notice served under this subsection was served; or

(*b*) where such an application has been made, the court directs that the disclaimer shall take effect.

(2) Where the court gives a direction under subsection (1)(*b*) it may also, instead of or in addition to any order it makes under section 181, make such orders with respect to fixtures, tenant's improvements and other matters arising out of the lease as it thinks fit.

General Note

This re-enacts subs. (5) and (6) of s.91, I.A. 1985 and provides that a disclaimer of leasehold property shall not take effect unless a copy of the disclaimer has been served upon any underlessee or mortgagee and they have made either no application or no successful application to the court under s.181. The terms upon which the court can make an order under s.181 are governed by s.182. See generally Note to s.178. The equivalent provision in relation to individual insolvency is s.317.

Land subject to rentcharge

180.—(1) The following applies where, in consequence of the disclaimer under section 178 of any land subject to a rentcharge, that land vests by operation of law in the Crown or any other person (referred to in the next subsection as "the proprietor").

(2) The proprietor and the successors in title of the proprietor are not subject to any personal liability in respect of any sums becoming due under the rentcharge except sums becoming due after the proprietor, or some person claiming under or through the proprietor, has taken possession or control of the land or has entered into occupation of it.

General Note

This re-enacts subs. (7) of s.91, I.A. 1985. Disclaimer does not impose upon the Crown or other person benefited an obligation under the rentcharge. The equivalent provision in relation to individual insolvency is s.319. See generally Note to s.178.

Powers of court (general)

181.—(1) This section and the next apply where the liquidator has disclaimed property under section 178.

(2) An application under this section may be made to the court by—

(*a*) any person who claims an interest in the disclaimed property, or

(*b*) any person who is under any liability in respect of the disclaimed property, not being a liability discharged by the disclaimer.

(3) Subject as follows, the court may on the application make an order, on such terms as it thinks fit, for the vesting of the disclaimed property in, or for its delivery to—

(*a*) a person entitled to it or a trustee for such a person, or

(*b*) a person subject to such a liability as is mentioned in subsection (2)(*b*) or a trustee for such a person.

(4) The court shall not make an order under subsection (3)(*b*) except where it appears to the court that it would be just to do so for the purpose of compensating the person subject to the liability in respect of the disclaimer.

(5) The effect of any order under this section shall be taken into account in assessing for the purpose of section 178(6) the extent of any loss or damage sustained by any person in consequence of the disclaimer.

(6) An order under this section vesting property in any person need not be completed by conveyance, assignment or transfer.

Definition

"property": s.436.

General Note

This section operates in conjunction with ss.178 and 179 and empowers the court to vest the disclaimed property in the categories of person mentioned in subs. (3). The effect of such an order has to be taken into account in assessing the extent of any loss in respect of which a person is allowed to prove under s.178(6) (see subs. (5)).

Powers of court (leaseholds)

182.—(1) The court shall not make an order under section 181 vesting property of a leasehold nature in any person claiming under the company as underlessee or mortgagee except on terms making that person—

(*a*) subject to the same liabilities and obligations as the company was subject to under the lease at the commencement of the winding up, or

(*b*) if the court thinks fit, subject to the same liabilities and obligations as that person would be subject to if the lease had been assigned to him at the commencement of the winding up.

(2) For the purposes of an order under section 181 relating to only part of any property comprised in a lease, the requirements of subsection (1) apply as if the lease comprised only the property to which the order relates.

(3) Where subsection (1) applies and no person claiming under the company as underlessee or mortgagee is willing to accept an order under section 181 on the terms required by virtue of that subsection, the court may, by order under that section, vest the company's estate or interest in the property in any person who is liable (whether personally or in a representative capacity, and whether alone or jointly with the company) to perform the lessee's covenants in the lease.

The court may vest that estate and interest in such a person freed and discharged from all estates, incumbrances and interests created by the company.

(4) Where subsection (1) applies and a person claiming under the company as underlessee or mortgagee declines to accept an order under section 181, that person is excluded from all interest in the property.

General Note

This section re-enacts subss. (5)–(8) of s.92, I.A. 1985.

Execution, attachment and the Scottish equivalents

Effect of execution or attachment (England and Wales)

183.—(1) Where a creditor has issued execution against the goods or land of a company or has attached any debt due to it, and the company is subsequently wound up, he is not entitled to retain the benefit of the execution or attachment against the liquidator unless he has completed the execution or attachment before the commencement of the winding up.

(2) However—

(*a*) if a creditor has had notice of a meeting having been called at which a resolution for voluntary winding up is to be proposed, the date on which he had notice is substituted, for the purpose of subsection (1), for the date of commencement of the winding up;

(*b*) a person who purchases in good faith under a sale by the sheriff any goods of a company on which execution has been levied in all cases acquires a good title to them against the liquidator; and

(*c*) the rights conferred by subsection (1) on the liquidator may be set aside by the court in favour of the creditor to such extent and subject to such terms as the court thinks fit.

(3) For the purposes of this Act—

(*a*) an execution against goods is completed by seizure and sale, or by the making of a charging order under section 1 of the Charging Orders Act 1979;

(*b*) an attachment of a debt is completed by receipt of the debt; and

(*c*) an execution against land is completed by seizure, by the appointment of a receiver, or by the making of a charging order under section 1 of the Act above-mentioned.

(4) In this section, "goods" includes all chattels personal; and "the sheriff" includes any officer charged with the execution of a writ or other process.

(5) This section does not apply in the case of a winding up in Scotland.

Definition

"commencement of winding up": ss.86, 129.

General Note

This re-enacts s.621, C.A. 1985. The section corresponds to s.346 which applies to insolvency of individuals and prevents a creditor who has issued execution or attachment from enjoying the fruits thereof unless he has completed the execution or attachment before the commencement of the winding up. S.183(2)(*b*) protects a bona fide purchaser of goods from the sheriff and s.183(2)(*c*) gives the court a general discretion to set aside the rights of the liquidator under the section. As to the court's exercise of its discretion see *Re Grosvenor Metal Co. Ltd.* [1950] Ch. 63; *Re Suidair International Airways Ltd.* [1951] Ch. 165 and *Re Redman (Builders) Ltd.* [1964] 1 All E.R. 851. See *Palmer,* paras. 85–72.

Duties of sheriff (England and Wales)

184.—(1) The following applies where a company's goods are taken in execution and, before their sale or the completion of the execution (by the receipt or recovery of the full amount of the levy), notice is served on the sheriff that a provisional liquidator has been appointed or that a winding-up order has been made, or that a resolution for voluntary winding up has been passed.

(2) The sheriff shall, on being so required, deliver the goods and any money seized or received in part satisfaction of the execution to the liquidator; but the costs of execution are a first charge on the goods or money so delivered, and the liquidator may sell the goods, or a sufficient part of them, for the purpose of satisfying the charge.

(3) If under an execution in respect of a judgment for a sum exceeding £250 a company's goods are sold or money is paid in order to avoid sale, the sheriff shall deduct the costs of the execution from the proceeds of sale or the money paid and retain the balance for 14 days.

(4) If within that time notice is served on the sheriff of a petition for the winding up of the company having been presented, or of a meeting having been called at which there is to be proposed a resolution for voluntary winding up, and an order is made or a resolution passed (as the case may be), the sheriff shall pay the balance to the liquidator, who is entitled to retain it as against the execution creditor.

(5) The rights conferred by this section on the liquidator may be set aside by the court in favour of the creditor to such extent and subject to such terms as the court thinks fit.

(6) In this section, "goods" includes all chattels personal; and "the sheriff" includes any officer charged with the execution of a writ or other process.

(7) The money sum for the time being specified in subsection (3) is subject to increase or reduction by order under section 416 in Part XV.

(8) This section does not apply in the case of a winding up in Scotland.

General Note

This re-enacts s.622, C.A. 1985. It deals with the duties of a sheriff where goods are seized in execution in England and Wales and before their sale or completion of the execution notice is served of winding up. The sheriff must if required deliver up the goods, etc., but the costs of execution are a first charge thereon. S.184(3) deals with goods seized in execution for a judgment for a sum exceeding £250. Here the sheriff must deduct the cost of execution and retain the balance for 14 days.

Effect of diligence (Scotland)

185.—(1) In the winding up of a company registered in Scotland, the following provisions of the Bankruptcy (Scotland) Act 1985—

(*a*) subsections (1) to (6) of section 37 (effect of sequestration on diligence); and

(*b*) subsections (3), (4), (7) and (8) of section 39 (realisation of estate),

apply, so far as consistent with this Act, in like manner as they apply in the sequestration of a debtor's estate, with the substitutions specified below and with any other necessary modifications.

(2) The substitutions to be made in those sections of the Act of 1985 are as follows—

(*a*) for references to the debtor, substitute references to the company;

(*b*) for references to the sequestration, substitute references to the winding up;

(*c*) for references to the date of sequestration, substitute references to the commencement of the winding up of the company; and

(*d*) for references to the permanent trustee, substitute references to the liquidator.

(3) In this section, "the commencement of the winding up of the company" means, where it is being wound up by the court, the day on which the winding-up order is made.

(4) This section, so far as relating to any estate or effects of the company situated in Scotland, applies in the case of a company registered in England and Wales as in the case of one registered in Scotland.

General Note

This section is derived from s.623, C.A. 1985 and Sched. 7, para. 21 of the Bankruptcy (Scotland) Act 1985. It deals with the effect of diligence (see further Note to s.60) in the case of a company registered in Scotland. It incorporates by reference the provisions (of the Bankruptcy (Scotland) Act 1985) mentioned in subs. (1) subject to the substitutions (which are necessary to render the provisions appropriate to a company) which are set out in subs. (2)

Miscellaneous matters

Rescission of contracts by the court

186.—(1) The court may, on the application of a person who is, as against the liquidator, entitled to the benefit or subject to the burden of a contract made with the company, make an order rescinding the contract on such terms as to payment by or to either party of damages for the non-performance of the contract, or otherwise as the court thinks just.

(2) Any damages payable under the order to such a person may be proved by him as a debt in the winding up.

General Note

This re-enacts s.619(4), C.A. 1985. Rescission of contracts by the court has been severed from the disclaimer provisions which now appear in ss.178–82 *supra*.

Power to make over assets to employees

187.—(1) On the winding up of a company (whether by the court or voluntarily), the liquidator may, subject to the following provisions of this section, make any payment which the company has, before the commencement of the winding up, decided to make under section 719 of the Companies Act (power to provide for employees or former employees on cessation or transfer of business).

(2) The power which a company may exercise by virtue only of that section may be exercised by the liquidator after the winding up has commenced if, after the company's liabilities have been fully satisfied and provision has been made for the expenses of the winding up, the exercise of that power has been sanctioned by such a resolution of the company as would be required of the company itself by section 719(3) before that commencement, if paragraph (*b*) of that subsection were omitted and any other requirement applicable to its exercise by the company had been met.

(3) Any payment which may be made by a company under this section (that is, a payment after the commencement of its winding up) may be made out of the company's assets which are available to the members on the winding up.

(4) On a winding up by the court, the exercise by the liquidator of his powers under this section is subject to the court's control, and any creditor

or contributory may apply to the court with respect to any exercise or proposed exercise of the power.

(5) Subsections (1) and (2) above have effect notwithstanding anything in any rule of law or in section 107 of this Act (property of company after satisfaction of liabilities to be distributed among members).

General Note

This re-enacts s.659, C.A. 1985 and deals with the liquidator's power to make over assets to employees in satisfaction of the amount decided to be provided under s.719, C.A. 1985 on cessation or transfer of business. This overrides s.107 *supra*.

Notification that company is in liquidation

188.—(1) When a company is being wound up, whether by the court or voluntarily, every invoice, order for goods or business letter issued by or on behalf of the company, or a liquidator of the company, or a receiver or manager of the company's property, being a document on or in which the name of the company appears, shall contain a statement that the company is being wound up.

(2) If default is made in complying with this section, the company and any of the following persons who knowingly and wilfully authorises or permits the default, namely, any officer of the company, any liquidator of the company and any receiver or manager, is liable to a fine.

Definitions

"fine": s.430, Sched. 10.
"officer of the company": s.251; C.A. 1985, s.740.
"receiver or manager": s.29(1)(*a*).

General Note

This re-enacts s.637, C.A. 1985 and deals with the publicity to be given to the winding up on commercial documents. Compare s.12 (administration orders) and s.39 (appointment of receiver or manager).

Interest on debts

189.—(1) In a winding up interest is payable in accordance with this section on any debt proved in the winding up, including so much of any such debt as represents interest on the remainder.

(2) Any surplus remaining after the payment of the debts proved in a winding up shall, before being applied for any other purpose, be applied in paying interest on those debts in respect of the periods during which they have been outstanding since the company went into liquidation.

(3) All interest under this section ranks equally, whether or not the debts on which it is payable rank equally.

(4) The rate of interest payable under this section in respect of any debt ("the official rate" for the purposes of any provision of this Act in which that expression is used) is whichever is the greater of—

(*a*) the rate specified in section 17 of the Judgments Act 1838 on the day on which the company went into liquidation, and
(*b*) the rate applicable to that debt apart from the winding up.

(5) In the application of this section to Scotland—

(*a*) references to a debt proved in a winding up have effect as references to a claim accepted in a winding up, and
(*b*) the reference to section 17 of the Judgments Act 1838 has effect as a reference to the rules.

Definitions

"company goes into liquidation": s.247(2).
"the rules": s.251.

General Note

This prescribes the circumstances under which interest is payable on any debt proved in a winding up. Subs. (4) also establishes the formula by which the rate of interest payable is to be determined. The provision completely changes the former law, which was rigorously criticised in chapter 31 of the *Cork Report* in terms which were accepted in paras. 85–89 of the *White Paper*. Payment of interest in a winding up was formerly held (*Re Theo Garvin Ltd.* [1969] 1 Ch. 624) to be governed by the restrictive and anachronistic provisions of s.66 of the Bankruptcy Act 1914, made applicable in winding up by virtue of s.612 of the Companies Act 1985 (the respective sections of both Acts were repealed by I.A. 1985). This section, which re-enacts s.93, I.A. 1985, provides for payment of interest, at the rate prescribed in subs. (4), in respect of the period since the company went into liquidation. Interest up to the date of insolvency, calculated at the appropriate contract rate, is included in the creditors' claim for which proof is lodged. Payment of post-insolvency interest can only occur if there is a surplus after all creditor's claims have been met in full (including claims for pre-insolvency interest). Under s.244, the liquidator can reopen a contract which constitutes an extortionate credit transaction, and the contractual rate of interest may be adjusted by the court.

Subs. (3)

All interest . . . ranks equally

This applies the *pari passu* rule to all the company's debts for the purposes of payment of interest under this section. There is no differentiation between preferential and non-preferential debts for this purpose.

Subs. (4)

The rate specified in section 17 of the Judgments Act 1838

This provision ensures that a certain statutory minimum level is payable under this section, in respect of every one of the company's debts, regardless of whether a right to interest was reserved under the contract. If, on the other hand, the contract did specify a rate of interest, that rate would be payable in respect of the post-insolvency period, provided that the rate is greater than the statutory rate applicable to judgment debts at the relevant date, and provided that the terms of the contract are not revised under s.244.

Documents exempt from stamp duty

190.—(1) In the case of a winding up by the court, or of a creditors' voluntary winding up, the following has effect as regards exemption from duties chargeable under the enactments relating to stamp duties.

(2) If the company is registered in England and Wales, the following documents are exempt from stamp duty—

(*a*) every assurance relating solely to freehold or leasehold property, or to any estate, right or interest in, any real or personal property, which forms part of the company's assets and which, after the execution of the assurance, either at law or in equity, is or remains part of those assets, and

(*b*) every writ, order, certificate, or other instrument or writing relating solely to the property of any company which is being wound up as mentioned in subsection (1), or to any proceeding under such a winding up.

"Assurance" here includes deed, conveyance, assignment and surrender.

(3) If the company is registered in Scotland, the following documents are exempt from stamp duty—

(*a*) every conveyance relating solely to property which forms part of the company's assets and which, after the execution of the conveyance, is or remains the company's property for the benefit of its creditors,

(*b*) any articles of roup or sale, submission and every other instrument and writing whatsoever relating solely to the company's property, and (*c*) every deed or writing forming part of the proceedings in the winding up.

"Conveyance" here includes assignation, instrument, discharge, writing and deed.

GENERAL NOTE

This re-enacts s.638, C.A. 1985 and exempts the specified documents from stamp duty in an insolvent winding up.

Company's books to be evidence

191. Where a company is being wound up, all books and papers of the company and of the liquidators are, as between the contributories of the company, prima facie evidence of the truth of all matters purporting to be recorded in them.

GENERAL NOTE

This re-enacts s.639, C.A. 1985 and makes the company's books and papers prima facie evidence as between contributories of the company. The truth of the evidence can be rebutted (*Re Great Northern Salt and Chemical Works, ex parte Kennedy* (1890) 44 Ch.D. 472). See *Palmer,* paras. 86–16.

Information as to pending liquidations

192.—(1) If the winding up of a company is not concluded within one year after its commencement, the liquidator shall, at such intervals as may be prescribed, until the winding up is concluded, send to the registrar of companies a statement in the prescribed form and containing the prescribed particulars with respect to the proceedings in, and position of, the liquidation.

(2) If a liquidator fails to comply with this section, he is liable to a fine and, for continued contravention, to a daily default fine.

DEFINITIONS

"fine"; "daily default fine": s.430, Sched. 10.

GENERAL NOTE

This re-enacts s.641, C.A. 1985 and deals with the obligation of the liquidator to file statements about the progress of the liquidation. See Winding Up Rules.

Unclaimed dividends (Scotland)

193.—(1) The following applies where a company registered in Scotland has been wound up, and is about to be dissolved.

(2) The liquidator shall lodge in an appropriate bank or institution as defined in section 73(1) of the Bankruptcy (Scotland) Act 1985 (not being a bank or institution in or of which the liquidator is acting partner, manager, agent or cashier) in the name of the Accountant of Court the whole unclaimed dividends and unapplied or undistributable balances, and the deposit receipts shall be transmitted to the Accountant of Court.

(3) The provisions of section 58 of the Bankruptcy (Scotland) Act 1985 (so far as consistent with this Act and the Companies Act) apply with any necessary modifications to sums lodged in a bank or institution under this section as they apply to sums deposited under section 57 of the Act first mentioned.

GENERAL NOTE

This re-enacts s.643, C.A. 1985 with minor amendments and deals with unclaimed dividends and balances in Scotland. See *Palmer,* paras. 87–80.

Resolutions passed at adjourned meetings

194. Where a resolution is passed at an adjourned meeting of a company's creditors or contributories, the resolution is treated for all purposes as having been passed on the date on which it was in fact passed, and not as having been passed on any earlier date.

DEFINITION

"contributory": s.74.

GENERAL NOTE

This re-enacts s.644, C.A. 1985 and deals with resolutions passed at adjourned meetings of creditors or contributories.

Meetings to ascertain wishes of creditors or contributories

195.—(1) The court may—

(*a*) as to all matters relating to the winding up of a company, have regard to the wishes of the creditors or contributories (as proved to it by any sufficient evidence), and

(*b*) if it thinks fit, for the purpose of ascertaining those wishes, direct meetings of the creditors or contributories to be called, held and conducted in such manner as the court directs, and appoint a person to act as chairman of any such meeting and report the result of it to the court.

(2) In the case of creditors, regard shall be had to the value of each creditor's debt.

(3) In the case of contributories, regard shall be had to the number of votes conferred on each contributory by the Companies Act or the articles.

GENERAL NOTE

This re-enacts s.645, C.A. 1985 and contains the useful general power of the court to convene meetings of creditors or contributories to ascertain their wishes. As to the weight given to the creditors' wishes on the making of a winding-up order see *Palmer,* paras. 85–06—85–07.

Judicial notice of court documents

196. In all proceedings under this Part, all courts, judges and persons judicially acting, and all officers, judicial or ministerial, of any court, or employed in enforcing the process of any court shall take judicial notice—

(*a*) of the signature of any officer of the High Court or of a county court in England and Wales, or of the Court of Session or a sheriff court in Scotland, or of the High Court in Northern Ireland, and also

(*b*) of the official seal or stamp of the several offices of the High Court in England and Wales or Northern Ireland, or of the Court of Session, appended to or impressed on any document made, issued or signed under the provisions of this Act or the Companies Act, or any official copy of such a document.

GENERAL NOTE

This re-enacts s.646, C.A. 1985 and provides for judicial notice to be taken of signature of court officers in different parts of the United Kingdom.

Commission for receiving evidence

197.—(1) When a company is wound up in England and Wales or in Scotland, the court may refer the whole or any part of the examination of witnesses—

(*a*) to a specified county court in England and Wales, or
(*b*) to the sheriff principal for a specified sheriffdom in Scotland, or
(*c*) to the High Court in Northern Ireland or a specified Northern Ireland County Court,

("specified" meaning specified in the order of the winding-up court).

(2) Any person exercising jurisdiction as a judge of the court to which the reference is made (or, in Scotland, the sheriff principal to whom it is made) shall then, by virtue of this section, be a commissioner for the purpose of taking the evidence of those witnesses.

(3) The judge or sheriff principal has in the matter referred the same power of summoning and examining witnesses, of requiring the production and delivery of documents, of punishing defaults by witnesses, and of allowing costs and expenses to witnesses, as the court which made the winding-up order.

These powers are in addition to any which the judge or sheriff principal might lawfully exercise apart from this section.

(4) The examination so taken shall be returned or reported to the court which made the order in such manner as that court requests.

(5) This section extends to Northern Ireland.

General Note

This re-enacts s.647, C.A. 1985 and deals with special commissions for receiving evidence in a winding up in England, Wales or Scotland. Northern Ireland is not mentioned in the opening words of s.197(1) but s.197(5) provides that the section extends to Northern Ireland and Northern Ireland is referred to in s.197(1)(*c*). For a full discussion of these changes see the Report by the Law Commission and Scottish Law Commission—Amendment to the Companies Acts 1948 to 1981, p.16 *et seq.*

Court order for examination of persons in Scotland

198.—(1) The court may direct the examination in Scotland of any person for the time being in Scotland (whether a contributory of the company or not), in regard to the trade, dealings, affairs or property of any company in course of being wound up, or of any person being a contributory of the company, so far as the company may be interested by reason of his being a contributory.

(2) The order or commission to take the examination shall be directed to the sheriff principal of the sheriffdom in which the person to be examined is residing or happens to be for the time; and the sheriff principal shall summon the person to appear before him at a time and place to be specified in the summons for examination on oath as a witness or as a haver, and to produce any books or papers called for which are in his possession or power.

(3) The sheriff principal may take the examination either orally or on written interrogatories, and shall report the same in writing in the usual form to the court, and shall transmit with the report the books and papers produced, if the originals are required and specified by the order or commission, or otherwise copies or extracts authenticated by the sheriff.

(4) If a person so summoned fails to appear at the time and place specified, or refuses to be examined or to make the production required, the sheriff principal shall proceed against him as a witness or haver duly cited; and failing to appear or refusing to give evidence or make production may be proceeded against by the law of Scotland.

(5) The sheriff principal is entitled to such fees, and the witness is entitled to such allowances, as sheriffs principal when acting as commissioners under appointment from the Court of Session and as witnesses and havers are entitled to in the like cases according to the law and practice of Scotland.

(6) If any objection is stated to the sheriff principal by the witness, either on the ground of his incompetency as a witness, or as to the production required, or on any other ground, the sheriff principal may, if he thinks fit, report the objection to the court, and suspend the examination of the witness until it has been disposed of by the court.

General Note

This re-enacts s.648, C.A. 1985 and allows the court to direct the examination in Scotland of any person for the time being in Scotland.

Costs of application for leave to proceed (Scottish companies)

199. Where a petition or application for leave to proceed with an action or proceeding against a company which is being wound up in Scotland is unopposed and is granted by the court, the costs of the petition or application shall, unless the court otherwise directs, be added to the amount of the petitioner's or applicant's claim against the company.

General Note

This re-enacts s.649, C.A. 1985. The section deals with costs in connection with an application for leave to proceed with an action against a company being wound up in Scotland, which is unopposed.

Affidavits etc. in United Kingdom and overseas

200.—(1) An affidavit required to be sworn under or for the purposes of this Part may be sworn in the United Kingdom, or elsewhere in Her Majesty's dominions, before any court, judge or person lawfully authorised to take and receive affidavits, or before any of Her Majesty's consuls or vice-consuls in any place outside Her dominions.

(2) All courts, judges, justices, commissioners and persons acting judicially shall take judicial notice of the seal or stamp or signature (as the case may be) of any such court, judge, person, consul or vice-consul attached, appended or subscribed to any such affidavit, or to any other document to be used for the purposes of this Part.

General Note

This re-enacts s.650, C.A. 1985. The section deals with the formalities for swearing affidavits.

Chapter IX

Dissolution of Companies After Winding Up

Dissolution (voluntary winding up)

201.—(1) This section applies, in the case of a company wound up voluntarily, where the liquidator has sent to the registrar of companies his final account and return under section 94 (members' voluntary) or section 106 (creditors' voluntary).

(2) The registrar on receiving the account and return shall forthwith register them; and on the expiration of 3 months from the registration of the return the company is deemed to be dissolved.

(3) However, the court may, on the application of the liquidator or any other person who appears to the court to be interested, make an order deferring the date at which the dissolution of the company is to take effect for such time as the court thinks fit.

(4) It is the duty of the person on whose application an order of the court under this section is made within 7 days after the making of the

order to deliver to the registrar an office copy of the order for registration; and if that person fails to do so he is liable to a fine and, for continued contravention, to a daily default fine.

Definitions

"members' voluntary winding up": s.90.
"creditors' voluntary winding up": s.90.
"fine", "daily default fine": s.430, Sched. 10.

General Note

This is derived from ss.585(5), (6), and 595(6), (7), C.A. 1985. It applies to both members' and creditors' voluntary winding up where the liquidator has complied with s.94 or s.106 respectively and the registrar has registered the account and return. It is now located with other provisions relating to dissolution (of companies wound up by the court) derived from the I.A. 1985. See General Note to s.202.

Early dissolution (England and Wales)

202.—(1) This section applies where an order for the winding up of a company has been made by the court in England and Wales.

(2) The official receiver, if—

(*a*) he is the liquidator of the company, and

(*b*) it appears to him—

(i) that the realisable assets of the company are insufficient to cover the expenses of the winding up, and

(ii) that the affairs of the company do not require any further investigation,

may at any time apply to the registrar of companies for the early dissolution of the company.

(3) Before making that application, the official receiver shall give not less than 28 days' notice of his intention to do so to the company's creditors and contributories and, if there is an administrative receiver of the company, to that receiver.

(4) With the giving of that notice the official receiver ceases (subject to any directions under the next section) to be required to perform any duties imposed on him in relation to the company, its creditors or contributories by virtue of any provision of this Act, apart from a duty to make an application under subsection (2) of this section.

(5) On the receipt of the official receiver's application under subsection (2) the registrar shall forthwith register it and, at the end of the period of 3 months beginning with the day of the registration of the application, the company shall be dissolved.

However, the Secretary of State may, on the application of the official receiver or any other person who appears to the Secretary of State to be interested, give directions under section 203 at any time before the end of that period.

Definitions

"contributory": s.79.
"the official receiver": s.399.

General Note

This section is designed to enable the official receiver to bring his responsibilities to an early end in cases where he, as the liquidator, discovers that the realisable assets of the company are insufficient to cover the expenses of the winding up. The further precondition to the official receiver's ability to apply to the registrar of companies for an early dissolution of the company is that the offical receiver considers that the affairs of the company do not require further investigation. Should it subsequently transpire that either of the official receiver's conclusions as to the assets of the company and as to the impeccable character of the company's affairs was incorrect, or if there is any other reason to suggest that an early dissolution is inappropriate, the official receiver himself or other interested parties have a limited time in which to apply for directions to the Secretary of State under s.203. The effective period within which such an application may be made consists of the 28 days' period of notice specified in subs. (3), together with the period of three months specified in subs. (5).

The section which re-enacts subs. (1)–(3), (6) of s.76, I.A. 1985, reflects the recommendations in paras. 649–651 of the *Cork Report,* accepted in modified form in paras. 105–107 of the *White Paper.* Since up to a third of companies which enter compulsory liquidation have either no assets or so few as to be practically worthless, the accelerated procedure under this section should save the time of the official receiver as well as the expense of, *inter alia,* the sending out of final notice of the official receiver's intention to apply for his release. By virtue of subs. (4), the sending of notice of intention to apply for early dissolution of the company simultaneously releases the official receiver from his duties in relation to the company in question, subject to any directions which may later be issued by the Secretary of State pursuant to s.203.

Consequence of notice under s.202

203.—(1) Where a notice has been given under section 202(3), the official receiver or any creditor or contributory of the company, or the administrative receiver of the company (if there is one) may apply to the Secretary of State for directions under this section.

(2) The grounds on which that application may be made are—

(*a*) that the realisable assets of the company are sufficient to cover the expenses of the winding up;

(*b*) that the affairs of the company do require further investigation; or

(*c*) that for any other reason the early dissolution of the company is inappropriate.

(3) Directions under this section—

(*a*) are directions making such provision as the Secretary of State thinks fit for enabling the winding up of the company to proceed as if no notice had been given under section 202(3), and

(*b*) may, in the case of an application under section 202(5), include a direction deferring the date at which the dissolution of the company is to take effect for such period as the Secretary of State thinks fit.

(4) An appeal to the court lies from any decision of the Secretary of State on an application for directions under this section.

(5) It is the duty of the person on whose application any directions are given under this section, or in whose favour an appeal with respect to an application for such directions is determined, within 7 days after the giving of the directions or the determination of the appeal, to deliver to the registrar of companies for registration such a copy of the directions or determination as is prescribed.

(6) If a person without reasonable excuse fails to deliver a copy as required by subsection (5), he is liable to a fine and, for continued contravention, to a daily default fine.

DEFINITIONS

"contributory": s.79.
"administrative receiver": ss.251, 29(2).
"fine", "daily default fine": s.430, Sched. 10.

GENERAL NOTE

This re-enacts subss. (4), (5), (7)–(10) of s.76 I.A. 1985 and allows the categories of person mentioned in subs. (1) to challenge an early dissolution of the company under s.202, by applying to the Secretary of State for directions. See also Note to s.202.

Early dissolution (Scotland)

204.—(1) This section applies where a winding-up order has been made by the court in Scotland.

(2) If after a meeting or meetings under section 138 (appointment of liquidator in Scotland) it appears to the liquidator that the realisable assets of the company are insufficient to cover the expenses of the winding up, he may apply to the court for an order that the company be dissolved.

(3) Where the liquidator makes that application, if the court is satisfied that the realisable assets of the company are insufficient to cover the expenses of the winding up and it appears to the court appropriate to do so, the court shall make an order that the company be dissolved in accordance with this section.

(4) A copy of the order shall within 14 days from its date be forwarded by the liquidator to the registrar of companies, who shall forthwith register it; and, at the end of the period of 3 months beginning with the day of the registration of the order, the company shall be dissolved.

(5) The court may, on an application by any person who appears to the court to have an interest, order that the date at which the dissolution of the company is to take effect shall be deferred for such period as the court thinks fit.

(6) It is the duty of the person on whose application an order is made under subsection (5), within 7 days after the making of the order, to deliver to the registrar of companies such a copy of the order as is prescribed.

(7) If the liquidator without reasonable excuse fails to comply with the requirements of subsection (4), he is liable to a fine and, for continued contravention, to a daily default fine.

(8) If a person without reasonable excuse fails to deliver a copy as required by subsection (6), he is liable to a fine and, for continued contravention, to a daily default fine.

DEFINITIONS

"fine", "daily default fine": s.430, Sched. 10.
"prescribed": s.251.

GENERAL NOTE

This section creates a counterpart procedure for Scotland to that established under ss.202 and 203 for England and Wales. Some of the differences between the two procedures are attributable to the fact that there is no office of Official Receiver in Scotland, so that the office holder in a winding up is invariably the liquidator. However, a liquidator may make application under this section merely upon discovering that the realisable assets of the company are insufficient to cover the expenses of the winding up. There is no further necessity for the liquidator to be satisfied as to the additional condition which applies in England and Wales under s.202(2)(*b*)(ii). Moreoever, in contrast to the procedure under s.202, a liquidator in Scotland makes application to the court for an order of dissolution and is not required by the provisions of this section to give prior notice to the company's creditors and contributories of his intention to do so. Although the court in Scotland has jurisdiction under subs. (5) to entertain applications from interested parties seeking deferral of the taking effect of the court's order for dissolution of the company, there is no counterpart to the provisions of s.203 for the issue of directions, either by the court or by any other authority. S.172(8) provides for the liquidator to vacate office when the dissolution of the company takes effect in accordance with subs. (4) of this section. See also the General Note to s.202.

Dissolution otherwise than under ss.202–204

205.—(1) This section applies where the registrar of companies receives—

(*a*) a notice served for the purposes of section 172(8) (final meeting of creditors and vacation of office by liquidator), or
(*b*) a notice from the official receiver that the winding up of a company by the court is complete.

(2) The registrar shall, on receipt of the notice, forthwith register it; and, subject as follows, at the end of the period of 3 months beginning with the day of the registration of the notice, the company shall be dissolved.

(3) The Secretary of State may, on the application of the official receiver or any other person who appears to the Secretary of State to be interested, give a direction deferring the date at which the dissolution of the company is to take effect for such period as the Secretary of State thinks fit.

(4) An appeal to the court lies from any decision of the Secretary of State on an application for a direction under subsection (3).

(5) Subsection (3) does not apply in a case where the winding-up order was made by the court in Scotland, but in such a case the court may, on an application by any person appearing to the court to have an interest, order that the date at which the dissolution of the company is to take effect shall be deferred for such period as the court thinks fit.

(6) It is the duty of the person—

(*a*) on whose application a direction is given under subsection (3);

(*b*) in whose favour an appeal with respect to an application for such a direction is determined; or

(*c*) on whose application an order is made under subsection (5),

within 7 days after the giving of the direction, the determination of the appeal or the making of the order, to deliver to the registrar for registration such a copy of the direction, determination or order as is prescribed.

(7) If a person without reasonable excuse fails to deliver a copy as required by subsection (6), he is liable to a fine and, for continued contravention, to a daily default fine.

Definitions

"prescribed": s.251.
"the official receiver": s.399.
"fine", "daily default fine": s.430, Sched. 10.

General Note

This provision re-enacts s.81, I.A. 1985 with minor amendments. Unlike the provisions for early dissolution, which are contained in ss.202–204, the distinctive procedures for England and for Scotland are here contained in different parts of the same section. Two alternative sequences of events are envisaged under subs. (1). The first begins with the liquidator's convening of a final meeting of creditors under s.172, followed by his giving of notice of the conclusion of the meeting to the Registrar of Companies, pursuant to s.172(8). The second begins with the Official Receiver, as liquidator of the company, giving notice to the registrar that the winding up by the court is complete. In either event, the registration of the notice by the Registrar marks the commencement of the period of three months at the end of which the company will be dissolved, unless in the meantime, an interested party has succeeded in obtaining a deferral of the dissolution by means of the procedure laid down by subs. (3) for England and Wales and by subs. (5) for Scotland.

Chapter X

Malpractice before and during Liquidation; Penalisation of Companies and Company Officers; Investigations and Prosecutions

Offences of fraud, deception, etc.

Fraud, etc. in anticipation of winding up

206.—(1) When a company is ordered to be wound up by the court, or passes a resolution for voluntary winding up, any person, being a past or present officer of the company, is deemed to have committed an offence if, within the 12 months immediately preceding the commencement of the winding up, he has—

(*a*) concealed any part of the company's property to the value of £120 or more, or concealed any debt due to or from the company, or

(*b*) fraudulently removed any part of the company's property to the value of £120 or more, or

(*c*) concealed, destroyed, mutilated or falsified any book or paper affecting or relating to the company's property or affairs, or

(*d*) made any false entry in any book or paper affecting or relating to the company's property or affairs, or

(*e*) fraudulently parted with, altered or made any omission in any document affecting or relating to the company's property or affairs, or

(*f*) pawned, pledged or disposed of any property of the company which has been obtained on credit and has not been paid for (unless the pawning, pledging or disposal was in the ordinary way of the company's business).

(2) Such a person is deemed to have committed an offence if within the period above mentioned he has been privy to the doing by others of any of the things mentioned in paragraphs (*c*), (*d*) and (*e*) of subsection (1); and he commits an offence if, at any time after the commencement of the winding up, he does any of the things mentioned in paragraphs (*a*) to (*f*) of that subsection, or is privy to the doing by others of any of the things mentioned in paragraphs (*c*) to (*e*) of it.

(3) For purposes of this section, "officer" includes a shadow director.

(4) It is a defence—

(*a*) for a person charged under paragraph (*a*) or (*f*) of subsection (1) (or under subsection (2) in respect of the things mentioned in either of those two paragraphs) to prove that he had no intent to defraud, and

(*b*) for a person charged under paragraph (*c*) or (*d*) of subsection (1) (or under subsection (2) in respect of the things mentioned in either of those two paragraphs) to prove that he had no intent to conceal the state of affairs of the company or to defeat the law.

(5) Where a person pawns, pledges or disposes of any property in circumstances which amount to an offence under subsection (1)(*f*), every person who takes in pawn or pledge, or otherwise receives, the property knowing it to be pawned, pledged or disposed of in such circumstances, is guilty of an offence.

(6) A person guilty of an offence under this section is liable to imprisonment or a fine, or both.

(7) The money sums specified in paragraphs (*a*) and (*b*) of subsection (1) are subject to increase or reduction by order under section 416 in Part XV.

DEFINITIONS

"officer": s.251; s.744, C.A. 1985; subs. (3).
"commencement of winding up": ss.86, 129.
"shadow director": s.251; s.741, C.A. 1985.
"imprisonment or fine": s.430, Sched. 10.

GENERAL NOTE

This re-enacts s.624, C.A. 1985 with minor amendment and deals with fraud and other malpractices perpetrated by past or present officers of the company in the twelve months immediately preceding the commencement of the winding up or at any time after the commencement of winding up. An offence is committed if the officer does any of the things mentioned in subs. (1)(*a*)–(*f*) or is privy to the doing by others of any of the things mentioned in subs. (1)(*c*)–(*e*). In the circumstances set out subs. (1)(*f*) an offence may also be committed by third parties who knowingly take an interest in the property (see subs. (5)).

Transactions in fraud of creditors

207.—(1) When a company is ordered to be wound up by the court or passes a resolution for voluntary winding up, a person is deemed to have committed an offence if he, being at the time an officer of the company—

(*a*) has made or caused to be made any gift or transfer of, or charge on, or has caused or connived at the levying of any execution against, the company's property, or

(*b*) has concealed or removed any part of the company's property since, or within 2 months before, the date of any unsatisfied judgment or order for the payment of money obtained against the company.

(2) A person is not guilty of an offence under this section—

(*a*) by reason of conduct constituting an offence under subsection (1)(*a*) which occurred more than 5 years before the commencement of the winding up, or

(*b*) if he proves that, at the time of the conduct constituting the offence, he had no intent to defraud the company's creditors.

(3) A person guilty of an offence under this section is liable to imprisonment or a fine, or both.

Definitions

"commencement of the winding up": ss.86, 129.
"imprisonment or a fine": s.430, Sched. 10.
"officer": s.251; s.744, C.A. 1985.

General Note

This is derived from s.625, C.A. 1985 but it has been re-drafted and another defence (subs. (2)(*a*)) has been added. It creates a general offence in relation to transactions in fraud of creditors prior to the winding up.

Misconduct in course of winding up

208.—(1) When a company is being wound up, whether by the court or voluntarily, any person, being a past or present officer of the company, commits an offence if he—

(*a*) does not to the best of his knowledge and belief fully and truly discover to the liquidator all the company's property, and how and to whom and for what consideration and when the company disposed of any part of that property (except such part as has been disposed of in the ordinary way of the company's business), or

(*b*) does not deliver up to the liquidator (or as he directs) all such part of the company's property as is in his custody or under his control, and which he is required by law to deliver up, or

(*c*) does not deliver up to the liquidator (or as he directs) all books and papers in his custody or under his control belonging to the company and which he is required by law to deliver up, or

(*d*) knowing or believing that a false debt has been proved by any person in the winding up, fails to inform the liquidator as soon as practicable, or

(*e*) after the commencement of the winding up, prevents the production of any book or paper affecting or relating to the company's property or affairs.

(2) Such a person commits an offence if after the commencement of the winding up he attempts to account for any part of the company's property by fictitious losses or expenses; and he is deemed to have committed that

offence if he has so attempted at any meeting of the company's creditors within the 12 months immediately preceding the commencement of the winding up.

(3) For purposes of this section, "officer" includes a shadow director.

(4) It is a defence—

(*a*) for a person charged under paragraph (*a*), (*b*) or (*c*) of subsection (1) to prove that he had no intent to defraud, and

(*b*) for a person charged under paragraph (*e*) of that subsection to prove that he had no intent to conceal the state of affairs of the company or to defeat the law.

(5) A person guilty of an offence under this section is liable to imprisonment or a fine, or both.

DEFINITIONS

"commencement of the winding up": ss.86, 129.
"imprisonment or a fine": s.430, Sched. 10.
"officer": subs. (3), s.251; s.744, C.A. 1985.
"shadow director": s.251; s.741, C.A. 1985.

GENERAL NOTE

This re-enacts s.626, C.A. 1985 with minor amendments. It deals with misconduct in the course of winding up. In subs. (1)(*a*) the liquidator must now be informed "as soon as practicable" rather than, as previously, within one month (I.A. 1985, Sched. 6, para. 43).

Falsification of company's books

209.—(1) When a company is being wound up, an officer or contributory of the company commits an offence if he destroys, mutilates, alters or falsifies any books, papers or securities, or makes or is privy to the making of any false or fraudulent entry in any register, book of account or document belonging to the company with intent to defraud or deceive any person.

(2) A person guilty of an offence under this section is liable to imprisonment or a fine, or both.

DEFINITIONS

"contributory": s.79.
"imprisonment or a fine": s.430, Sched. 10.
"officer": s.251; s.744, C.A. 1985.

GENERAL NOTE

This re-enacts s.627, C.A. 1985 and deals with falsification of a company's books.

Material omissions from statement relating to company's affairs

210.—(1) When a company is being wound up, whether by the court or voluntarily, any person, being a past or present officer of the company, commits an offence if he makes any material omission in any statement relating to the company's affairs.

(2) When a company has been ordered to be wound up by the court, or has passed a resolution for voluntary winding up, any such person is deemed to have committed that offence if, prior to the winding up, he has made any material omission in any such statement.

(3) For purposes of this section, "officer" includes a shadow director.

(4) It is a defence for a person charged under this section to prove that he had no intent to defraud.

(5) A person guilty of an offence under this section is liable to imprisonment or a fine, or both.

DEFINITIONS
"imprisonment or a fine": s.430, Sched. 10.
"officer": subs. (3), s.251; s.744. C.A. 1985.
"shadow director": s.251; s.741, C.A. 1985.

GENERAL NOTE
This re-enacts s.628, C.A. 1985 and deals with material omissions from statements relating to the company's affairs made either while the company is being wound up (subs. (1)) or prior to the winding up (subs. (2)).

False representations to creditors

211.—(1) When a company is being wound up, whether by the court or voluntarily, any person, being a past or present officer of the company—

(*a*) commits an offence if he makes any false representation or commits any other fraud for the purpose of obtaining the consent of the company's creditors or any of them to an agreement with reference to the company's affairs or to the winding up, and

(*b*) is deemed to have committed that offence if, prior to the winding up, he has made any false representation, or committed any other fraud, for that purpose.

(2) For purposes of this section, "officer" includes a shadow director.

(3) A person guilty of an offence under this section is liable to imprisonment or a fine, or both.

DEFINITIONS
"imprisonment or a fine": s.430, Sched. 10.
"officer": subs. (2), s.251; s.744, C.A. 1985.
"shadow director": s.251; s.741, C.A. 1985.

GENERAL NOTE
This re-enacts s.629, C.A. 1985 with minor amendment and deals with false representations to creditors made either while the company is being wound up (subs. (1)(*a*)) or prior to the winding up (subs. (1)(*b*)).

Penalisation of directors and officers

Summary remedy against delinquent directors, liquidators, etc.

212.—(1) This section applies if in the course of the winding up of a company it appears that a person who—

(*a*) is or has been an officer of the company,

(*b*) has acted as liquidator, administrator or administrative receiver of the company, or

(*c*) not being a person falling within paragraph (*a*) or (*b*), is or has been concerned, or has taken part, in the promotion, formation or management of the company,

has misapplied or retained, or become accountable for, any money or other property of the company, or been guilty of any misfeasance or breach of any fiduciary or other duty in relation to the company.

(2) The reference in subsection (1) to any misfeasance or breach of any fiduciary or other duty in relation to the company includes, in the case of a person who has acted as liquidator or administrator of the company, any misfeasance or breach of any fiduciary or other duty in connection with the carrying out of his functions as liquidator or administrator of the company.

(3) The court may, on the application of the official receiver or the liquidator, or of any creditor or contributory, examine into the conduct of the person falling within subsection (1) and compel him—

(*a*) to repay, restore or account for the money or property or any part of it, with interest at such rate as the court thinks just, or

(*b*) to contribute such sum to the company's assets by way of compensation in respect of the misfeasance or breach of fiduciary or other duty as the court thinks just.

(4) The power to make an application under subsection (3) in relation to a person who has acted as liquidator or administrator of the company is not exercisable, except with the leave of the court, after that person has had his release.

(5) The power of a contributory to make an application under subsection (3) is not exercisable except with the leave of the court, but is exercisable notwithstanding that he will not benefit from any order the court may make on the application.

Definitions

"administrative receiver": s.251.
"administrator": s.8.
"contributory": s.79.

General Note

The purpose of this section which re-enacts s.19, I.A. 1985 is to provide a summary procedure whereby any person who has at any time mishandled or appropriated property belonging to an insolvent company may be swiftly brought to account and ordered to make restitution in whatever way is appropriate. This replaces the procedure established under s.561 of the Companies Act 1985. The range of persons who may be proceeded against under this section is a wide one, and extends to those who have acted as insolvency practitioners in relation to the company, as well as to those who are or have been its officers, or who have in any way been concerned in its promotion, formation or management. Thus the so-called "cowboy-liquidator" may be brought to book under this section just as readily as may the "delinquent director".

Subs. (1)

A person who . . . (b) has acted as liquidator, administrator . . . of the company

Note the effect of subs. (4) on the power to make applications under subs. (3) in relation to such persons.

Subs. (3)

The court

In the absence of any special definition or designation regarding jurisdiction to entertain an application under this section, it is appropriate to conclude that application should be made to the court by which the company is being wound up.

On the application . . . of any . . . contributory

Such applications are subject to the qualification imposed by subs. (5) with regard to the obtaining of leave of the court, but it is notable that a contributory is not debarred from making application on the ground that he will not personally benefit from any order to which the proceedings may give rise.

Fraudulent trading

213.—(1) If in the course of the winding up of a company it appears that any business of the company has been carried on with intent to defraud creditors of the company or creditors of any other person, or for any fraudulent purpose, the following has effect.

(2) The court, on the application of the liquidator may declare that any persons who were knowingly parties to the carrying on of the business in the manner above-mentioned are to be liable to make such contributions (if any) to the company's assets as the court thinks proper.

General Note

This is derived from s.630(1), (2) C.A. 1985 as amended by Sched. 6, para. 6(1), I.A. 1985. Subs. (1) is unchanged but subs. (2) has been amended so as to permit only the liquidator to make the application (previously the subs. referred also to the official receiver or any creditor or contributory) and to bring the form of declaration into line with that applicable in s.214(1) *infra.* Under the new form of declaration the person is merely "liable to make such contributions (if any) to the company's assets as the court thinks proper" and is not made directly liable for any of the company's debts (compare previous wording: "personally responsible, without any limitation of liability, for all or any of the debts or other liabilities of the company".).

Because of the difficulty of establishing intent to defraud (see Maugham J. in *Re William C. Leitch Brothers Ltd.* [1932] 2 Ch. 71, 77; *Re Patrick Lyon Ltd.* [1933] 2 Ch. 786, 790; *Palmer,* para. 85–84) a similar, but new, remedy encompassing, broadly, negligent trading appears in the next section ("wrongful trading"). Though broader in this respect, the new remedy is narrower in two other respects: it applies only to directors (compare "any persons who were knowingly parties") and to *insolvent* liquidations (compare "in the course of winding up".). The concept of fraudulent trading may therefore still be useful in the context of civil liability and it remains the sole basis of criminal liability (see s.458, C.A. 1985).

As to carrying on business see *Re Gerald Cooper Chemicals Ltd.* [1978] 2 All E.R. 49 and *Re Sarflax Ltd.* [1979] 1 All E.R. 529.

For the persons covered see *Re Maidstone Building Provisions Ltd.* [1971] 3 All E.R. 363 (company secretary and financial adviser not party to carrying on business by reason of omission to advise) but compare *Panorama Developments (Guildford) Ltd.* v. *Fidelis Furnishing Fabrics Ltd.* [1971] 2 All E.R. 1028. See J. H. Farrar [1980] J.B.L. 336. See also *Re Maney & Sons de Luxe Service Station Ltd.* [1968] N.Z.L.R. 624 (N.Z.C.A.).

Wrongful trading

214.—(1) Subject to subsection (3) below, if in the course of the winding up of a company it appears that subsection (2) of this section applies in relation to a person who is or has been a director of the company, the court, on the application of the liquidator, may declare that that person is to be liable to make such contribution (if any) to the company's assets as the court thinks proper.

(2) This subsection applies in relation to a person if—

(*a*) the company has gone into insolvent liquidation.

(*b*) at some time before the commencement of the winding up of the company, that person knew or ought to have concluded that there was no reasonable prospect that the company would avoid going into insolvent liquidation, and

(*c*) that person was a director of the company at that time;

but the court shall not make a declaration under this section in any case where the time mentioned in paragraph (*b*) above was before 28th April 1986.

(3) The court shall not make a declaration under this section with respect to any person if it is satisfied that after the condition specified in subsection (2)(*b*) was first satisfied in relation to him that person took every step with a view to minimising the potential loss to the company's creditors as (assuming him to have known that there was no reasonable prospect that the company would avoid going into insolvent liquidation) he ought to have taken.

(4) For the purposes of subsections (2) and (3), the facts which a director of a company ought to know or ascertain, the conclusions which he ought to reach and the steps which he ought to take are those which would be known or ascertained, or reached or taken, by a reasonably diligent person having both—

(*a*) the general knowledge, skill and experience that may reasonably be expected of a person carrying out the same functions as are carried out by that director in relation to the company, and

(*b*) the general knowledge, skill and experience that that director has.

(5) The reference in subsection (4) to the functions carried out in relation to a company by a director of the company includes any functions which he does not carry out but which have been entrusted to him.

(6) For the purposes of this section a company goes into insolvent liquidation if it goes into liquidation at a time when its assets are insufficient for the payment of its debts and other liabilities and the expenses of the winding up.

(7) In this section "director" includes a shadow director.

(8) This section is without prejudice to section 213.

DEFINITIONS

"commencement of winding up": ss.86, 129.
"director": subs. (7); s.741, C.A. 1985.
"goes into insolvent liquidation": subs. (6).
"shadow director": s.251, s.741, C.A. 1985.

GENERAL NOTE

The provisions of this section which re-enact s.15, I.A. 1985 generated much controversy and discussion both inside and outside Parliament. However, in this instance the enacted section corresponds reasonably closely to the clause first published in the Bill. The origins of the section lie in the Cork Committee's analysis, in chap. 44 of their report, of the shortcomings of the law imposing criminal and civil responsibility for fraudulent trading, formerly embodied in s.332 of the Companies Act 1948 and latterly in ss.458 and 630 of the Companies Act 1985. The Committee proposed a severing of the criminal and civil provisions (duly accomplished in the Act of 1985) and the introduction on the civil side of a new and broader concept of "wrongful trading" to overcome misconceptions as to the degree of culpability necessary to cause a director to incur the partial or total loss of the immunity resulting from limited liability. Although the Cork Committee went to the length (unusual in their Report) of including a draft statutory clause containing a proposed definition of wrongful trading (para. 1806) the Government consistently resisted and overcame all attempts to incorporate such a provision in the Act (see *Hansard* H.L. Vol. 461, cols. 742–753; Vol. 462, cols. 37–48; H.C. Standing Committee E, June 6, 1985, cols. 218–233; H.C. Vol. 83, cols. 559–570). The result has been to leave the courts with a wide discretionary power by which directors may be made liable to contribute to the assets of an insolvent company.

The circumstances in which the court may make a declaration under this section are stated in subs. (2), while the exculpatory formula whereby a director may endeavour to persuade the court not to impose such liability, is expressed in subs. (3). It is also notable that the right to apply to the court for a declaration under this section is confined to the liquidator by whom the company is being wound up.

Subs. (1)

If in the course of the winding up of a company

This condition is an important one since it restricts the availability of the remedy to be sought under this section to cases where the company is being wound up. Subs. (2)(*a*) imposes the further refinement that the company must have gone into insolvent liquidation. Therefore an application can only be made in the case of a creditors' voluntary winding up or of a compulsory winding up of an insolvent company. See Note to s.213.

Person who is or has been a director of the company

This expression is qualified by the provision in subs. (2)(*c*) which imposes the requirement that the person against whom a declaration is sought must have been a director of the company at a time when, prior to the commencement of its winding up, he knew or ought to have concluded that an insolvent liquidation was practically inevitable. Therefore no liability under this section will fall upon a person who ceases to be a director at a time when he has no knowledge that the company has no reasonable prospect of averting insolvent liquidation, provided it is also the case that there were at the time no facts which he ought to have known or ascertained and from which the company's subsequent fate might reasonably have been deduced (see subss. (2)(*b*) and (4)).

The court

No special indication is given as to which court or courts have jurisdiction to hear an application under this section. It may be assumed however that the application should be made to the court by which the company is being wound up or, if the liquidation is a voluntary one, to any court which would have had jurisdiction to wind up the company (*cf.* s.744, C.A. 1985).

On the application of the liquidator

The liquidator is the only person by whom an application may be made under this section. In a compulsory winding up the official receiver acts as liquidator by virtue of s.136(2) of this Act, unless a different person is appointed by virtue of ss.139 or 140. In most cases the necessary evidence will be difficult to assemble, and the liquidator is likely to be in the best position to decide whether the requirements of this section could be established to the satisfaction of the court. All persons who have relevant knowledge or evidence should therefore transmit that information to the liquidator. No procedure is laid down whereby interested parties can take steps to compel the liquidator to apply to the court for a declaration under this section, and hence the proper recourse for those who consider that the liquidator is unreasonably declining to make such an application is to write to the Secretary of State complaining about the liquidator's conduct in office.

Such contribution (if any) to the company's assets as the court thinks proper

This indicates that the court enjoys a complete discretion as to the extent to which, if at all, it will order any director to forfeit the immunities of limited liability and make a contribution to the company's assets, thereby augmenting the amount available to be distributed in the liquidation. Individual cases will therefore be decided on their merits, and it may be some time before any clear set of principles becomes established to determine what levels of acumen and conduct will be required of directors henceforth, and with what degree of severity they will be penalised for failure to attain those levels. See also note to s.213.

Subs. (2)

(a) The company has gone into insolvent liquidation

This expression is defined by subs. (6) as meaning that the company has gone into liquidation at a time when its assets were insufficient for the payment of its debts and other liabilities and the expenses of the winding up. Since the final outcome of a liquidation may be affected by developments which take place after the technical commencement of the winding up, it will be necessary to determine the state of the company's affairs at the time when it went into liquidation within the meaning of this Part of the Act. This is fixed by s.247(2) as the date on which the company passes a resolution for voluntary winding up or, if no such resolution is passed, the date on which an order for winding up is made by the court. If at that date the company was not insolvent within the meaning of subs. (6) the provisions of this section cannot be utilised at all.

(b) At some time before the commencement of the winding up of the company

The statutory definition of the commencement of winding up is contained in s.86 (voluntary winding up) and s.129 (winding up by the court).

That person knew or ought to have concluded

The actual state of a person's knowledge at the relevant date will be a matter to be established on the basis of the evidence. However, the provisions of subs. (4) indicate that a director cannot escape from responsibility by somehow maintaining himself in a state of ignorance of the company's true situation: the facts which he ought to know or ascertain, and the conclusions which he ought to reach, must be considered by the court in relation to the hypothetical standard of conduct of the "reasonably diligent person". Therefore the court may impose responsibility if it is satisfied that a director either was unaware of facts which he ought to have known or ascertained, or did not arrive at appropriate conclusions on the basis of the facts which he did know. In effect, such a determination involves the court in the fixing of a particular date which constitutes the "moment of truth" for each individual director, utilising the test contained in subs. (4).

No reasonable prospect that the company would avoid going into insolvent liquidation

The inclusion of the notion of reasonableness in relation to the judgment to be formed as to the company's prospect of survival is designed to eliminate any scope for a director to escape responsibility on the basis of a *bona fide* belief, however misguided or unreasonable, that the company would somehow avoid insolvency. The provisions formerly contained in s.332 of the Companies Act 1984 regarding fraudulent trading (now s.213 of this Act) enable a director to escape liability if he has behaved honestly, albeit his conduct may have been reckless or unreasonable. Such a defence will not be available where responsibility for wrongful trading under the present section is concerned. See note to s.213.

Subs. (3)

The court shall not made a declaration

This mandatory form of words has the effect that if the defence established by this subsection is made out the court is completely deprived of all discretion in the determination of the case, and can make no declaration of responsibility against the director concerned.

After the condition specified in subsection (2)(b) was first satisfied

This again invokes the concept of the "moment of truth" as discussed above in the comment upon subs. (2)(*b*), and makes this the pivotal event for the purpose of evaluating the subsequent conduct of the individual director. Since, as has been explained, responsibility may in appropriate cases be imposed upon a director in respect of his failure to ascertain facts of which he ought to have known, the probability exists that such a director will also fail to satisfy the requirements of the statutory defence, which are that from that first moment onwards he must have done all that could reasonably be expected of him with a view to minimising the potential loss to the company's creditors. It is clearly intended that a director should lose the protection of this subsection if any significant interval of time has elapsed between his personal "moment of truth" and the time when he began to take the requisite action to protect creditors' interests, no matter how energetic those belated steps may have been.

Every step . . . as . . . he ought to have taken

The evaluation of a director's conduct is to be made in accordance with the test prescribed in subs. (4), which applies the criterion of the hypothetical, reasonably diligent person to determine what steps ought to be taken with a view to minimising the potential loss to the company's creditors.

Subs. (4)

A reasonably diligent person

This hypothetical figure serves as a basis for assessing the conduct of directors for the purposes of subs. (2) and (3). The court is required to arrive at a conclusion as to the appropriate conduct of such an hypothetical person assuming him to have possessed in combination the levels of general knowledge, skill and experience specified in paras. (*a*) and (*b*). It will be noticed that these two paragraphs respectively refer to objective and subjective levels of knowledge, skill and experience. Therefore a director cannot derive any advantage from the fact that his personal qualities are lower than those which may reasonably be expected of a director entrusted with the functions which actually repose in him, while at the same time a director who subjectively possesses unusually high levels of knowledge, skill or experience will fall to be judged according to a commensurately higher standard.

Proceedings under ss.213, 214

215.—(1) On the hearing of an application under section 213 or 214, the liquidator may himself give evidence or call witnesses.

(2) Where under either section the court makes a declaration, it may give such further directions as it thinks proper for giving effect to the declaration; and in particular, the court may—

(*a*) provide for the liability of any person under the declaration to be a charge on any debt or obligation due from the company to him, or on any mortgage or charge or any interest in a mortgage or charge on assets of the company held by or vested in him, or any person on his behalf, or any person claiming as assignee from or through the person liable or any person acting on his behalf, and

(*b*) from time to time make such further order as may be necessary for enforcing any charge imposed under this subsection.

(3) For the purposes of subsection (2), "assignee"—

(*a*) includes a person to whom or in whose favour, by the directions of the person made liable, the debt, obligation, mortgage or charge was created, issued or transferred or the interest created, but

(*b*) does not include an assignee for valuable consideration (not including consideration by way of marriage) given in good faith and without notice of any of the matters on the ground of which the declaration is made.

(4) Where the court makes a declaration under either section in relation to a person who is a creditor of the company, it may direct that the whole or any part of any debt owed by the company to that person and any interest thereon shall rank in priority after all other debts owed by the company and after any interest on those debts.

(5) Sections 213 and 214 have effect notwithstanding that the person concerned may be criminally liable in respect of matters on the ground of which the declaration under the section is to be made.

GENERAL NOTE

This governs proceedings under ss.213 and 214 *supra* and is derived from s.630(3)–(6), C.A. 1985 and Sched. 6, paras. 6(2), (3), I.A. 1985 respectively and permits the court to make further directions to give effect to any declaration under s.213(2) or s.214(1).

Restriction on re-use of company names

216.—(1) This section applies to a person where a company ("the liquidating company") has gone into insolvent liquidation on or after the appointed day and he was a director or shadow director of the company at any time in the period of 12 months ending with the day before it went into liquidation.

(2) For the purposes of this section, a name is a prohibited name in relation to such a person if—

(*a*) it is a name by which the liquidating company was known at any time in that period of 12 months, or

(*b*) it is a name which is so similar to a name falling within paragraph (*a*) as to suggest an association with that company.

(3) Except with leave of the court or in such circumstances as may be prescribed, a person to whom this section applies shall not at any time in the period of 5 years beginning with the day on which the liquidating company went into liquidation—

(*a*) be a director of any other company that is known by a prohibited name, or

(*b*) in any way, whether directly or indirectly, be concerned or take part in the promotion, formation or management of any such company, or

(*c*) in any way, whether directly or indirectly, be concerned or take part in the carrying on of a business carried on (otherwise than by a company) under a prohibited name.

(4) If a person acts in contravention of this section, he is liable to imprisonment or a fine, or both.

(5) In subsection (3) "the court" means any court having jurisdiction to wind up companies; and on an application for leave under that subsection, the Secretary of State or the official receiver may appear and call the attention of the court to any matters which seem to him to be relevant.

(6) References in this section, in relation to any time, to a name by which a company is known are to the name of the company at that time or to any name under which the company carries on business at that time.

(7) For the purposes of this section a company goes into insolvent liquidation if it goes into liquidation at a time when its assets are insufficient for the payment of its debts and other liabilities and the expenses of the winding up.

(8) In this section "company" includes a company which may be wound up under Part V of this Act.

DEFINITIONS

"a prohibited name": subs. (2)(*a*), (*b*).
"company": subs. (8).
"goes into insolvent liquidation": subs. (7).
"goes into liquidation": s.247(2).
"imprisonment or a fine": s.430, Sched. 10.
"prescribed": s.251.
"shadow director": C.A. 1985, s.741(2); s.251.
"the court": subs. (5).
"the liquidating company": subs. (1).

GENERAL NOTE

The purpose of this clause is to provide a means of combating the so-called "Phoenix syndrome", whereby company directors may contrive to mislead the public by utilising a company name closely similar to that of a failed company in order to conduct a business virtually identical to that formerly carried on by the latter. Rather than prohibit altogether the future use of a company name which may in itself be a disposable asset from which creditors in the winding up may derive some benefit, the section seeks to curb any abusive use of the company name by those who have been directors or shadow directors of the company within the twelve months prior to the commencement of its insolvent liquidation. During the next five years after the date of commencement of liquidation such persons must not be involved in any other company which uses the same, or a very similar, name including the trading style used by the liquidated company, unless they have first obtained the leave of the court to do so. Contravention of this prohibition is made a criminal offence for the person concerned, and by virtue of s.217(1)(*a*) also leads to personal liability for any debts incurred by the new company when that director is involved in its management.

It thus remains possible for a director of a failed company to buy out the company's name and business and to re-establish the venture in a genuine way, but in order to do this it will be necessary to obtain the approval of the court; otherwise not only will the director commit a criminal offence, but he will also forfeit the protection of limited liability.

Subs. (3)(c)

A business carried on (otherwise than by a company)

This has the effect of preventing a former director of a failed company from evading the provisions of this section through the utilisation of an alternative basis, such as a partnership, under which to carry on a business under a prohibited name.

Subs. (5)

Any court having jurisdiction to wind up companies

The wide terms of the jurisdiction conferred by means of the definition ascribed to the word "court" in this context leave it open to a director who wishes to be involved with a business which uses a prohibited name to seek the leave of that court which is most conveniently situated for the purpose in hand. There is no necessity for the application to be made to the court by which the failed company was wound up, or by which that company could have been wound up, at the time it became insolvent.

Personal liability for debts, following contravention of s.216

217.—(1) A person is personally responsible for all the relevant debts of a company if at any time—

(*a*) in contravention of section 216, he is involved in the management of the company, or

(*b*) as a person who is involved in the management of the company, he acts or is willing to act on instructions given (without the leave of the court) by a person whom he knows at that time to be in contravention in relation to the company of section 216.

(2) Where a person is personally responsible under this section for the relevant debts of a company, he is jointly and severally liable in respect

of those debts with the company and any other person who, whether under this section or otherwise, is so liable.

(3) For the purposes of this section the relevant debts of a company are—

(*a*) in relation to a person who is personally responsible under paragraph (*a*) of subsection (1), such debts and other liabilities of the company as are incurred at a time when that person was involved in the management of the company, and

(*b*) in relation to a person who is personally responsible under paragraph (*b*) of that subsection, such debts and other liabilities of the company as are incurred at a time when that person was acting or was willing to act on instructions given as mentioned in that paragraph.

(4) For the purposes of this section, a person is involved in the management of a company if he is a director of the company or if he is concerned, whether directly or indirectly, or takes part, in the management of the company.

(5) For the purposes of this section a person who, as a person involved in the management of a company, has at any time acted on instructions given (without the leave of the court) by a person whom he knew at that time to be in contravention in relation to the company of section 216 is presumed, unless the contrary is shown, to have been willing at any time thereafter to act on any instructions given by that person.

(6) In this section "company" includes a company which may be wound up under Part V.

DEFINITIONS

"company": subs. (6).
"involved in the management of a company": subs. (4).
"the relevant debts": subs. (3).

GENERAL NOTE

This section creates a potent sanction against various kinds of misconduct by persons in relation to company management. It does so by providing that certain individuals shall be denied the privileges normally associated with limited liability, and shall be personally liable for the relevant debts of any company in relation to which they act in a prohibited manner. The prohibited manner of acting is cast in two modes. The first mode (expressed in subs. (1)(*a*)) consists of being personally involved in the management of a company in contravention of s.216 by virtue of the fact that the name of the company constitutes a "prohibited name" with respect to the individual in question. The second mode (expressed in subs. (1)(*b*)) consist of knowingly acting or being willing to act on the instructions given (without leave of the court) by a person in contravention of s.216, thereby becoming the medium through which that person is able to assert an influence on the affairs of the company. Thus personal liability will be incurred not only by any person who, while subject to the prohibition, acts as a director or as a shadow director within the meaning of s.741(2) of the Companies Act 1985, but also by any person who, though not personally the subject of any such legal prohibition, consciously lends himself to the arrangement whereby the prohibited party contrives to circumvent the law's intentions.

Subs. (2)

Jointly and severally liable

This provision ensures that whenever two or more persons incur personal responsibility for the same debts of a company by virtue of this section, liability shall be shared on an equal basis as between those persons themselves. But by providing that their liability shall be several as well as joint, the process of recovery is greatly facilitated since proceedings can be directed against any one of them who is both traceable and solvent. The full amount of the sum which constitutes the "relevant debts" of a company (as defined in subs. (3)) may be recovered from any such person, leaving him in his turn to seek contribution from any other persons who may have incurred joint liability with him.

Subs. (5)

This subsection establishes a significant presumption with regard to the concept of a person's willingness to act on the instructions of another for the purposes of this section (see subss. (1)(*b*) and (3)(*b*)). Effectively, once it is established that a person involved in the management of a company has at any time acted on such instructions in a manner which contravenes subs. (1)(*b*), he is presumed to have been willing to act on any instructions of a similar character given by that other person at any time thereafter. Thus, having once compromised himself, anyone to whom this subsection applies will continue to incur personal liability for the company's debts unless he can prove to the court that his subsequent actions in relation to the company were not accompanied by a willingness on his part to act on the instructions given by the person who was barred from involvement in company management for the time being.

Investigation and prosecution of malpractice

Prosecution of delinquent officers and members of company

218.—(1) If it appears to the court in the course of a winding up by the court that any past or present officer, or any member, of the company has been guilty of any offence in relation to the company for which he is criminally liable, the court may (either on the application of a person interested in the winding up or of its own motion) direct the liquidator to refer the matter to the prosecuting authority.

(2) "The prosecuting authority" means—

(*a*) in the case of a winding up in England and Wales, the Director of Public Prosecutions, and

(*b*) in the case of a winding up in Scotland, the Lord Advocate.

(3) If in the case of a winding up by the court in England and Wales it appears to the liquidator, not being the official receiver, that any past or present officer of the company, or any member of it, has been guilty of an offence in relation to the company for which he is criminally liable, the liquidator shall report the matter to the official receiver.

(4) If it appears to the liquidator in the course of a voluntary winding up that any past or present officer of the company, or any member of it, has been guilty of an offence in relation to the company for which he is criminally liable, he shall—

(*a*) forthwith report the matter to the prosecuting authority, and

(*b*) furnish to that authority such information and give to him such access to and facilities for inspecting and taking copies of documents (being information or documents in the possession or under the control of the liquidator and relating to the matter in question) as the authority requires.

(5) Where a report is made to him under subsection (4), the prosecuting authority may, if he thinks fit, refer the matter to the Secretary of State for further enquiry; and the Secretary of State—

(*a*) shall thereupon investigate the matter, and

(*b*) for the purpose of his investigation may exercise any of the powers which are exercisable by inspectors appointed under section 431 or 432 of the Companies Act to investigate a company's affairs.

(6) If it appears to the court in the course of a voluntary winding up that—

(*a*) any past or present officer of the company, or any member of it, has been guilty as above-mentioned, and

(*b*) no report with respect to the matter has been made by the liquidator to the prosecuting authority under subsection (4),

the court may (on the application of any person interested in the winding up or of its own motion) direct the liquidator to make such a report.

On a report being made accordingly, this section has effect as though the report had been made in pursuance of subsection (4).

Definition
"officer": s.251; s.744, C.A. 1985.

General Note
This re-enacts s.632, C.A. 1985 with the addition of a subsection (subs. (3), see Sched. 6, para. 44, I.A. 1985). It deals with the procedure for prosecuting delinquent officers and members of companies being wound up in England and Wales and Scotland. In England and Wales it deals with the liaison between the liquidator, the Director of Public Prosecutions, the Official Receiver and the Department of Trade and Industry. In Scotland there is no D.P.P. and the relevant officer is the Lord Advocate. In the past not many prosecutions have been brought.

Obligations arising under s.218

219.—(1) For the purpose of an investigation by the Secretary of State under section 218(5), any obligation imposed on a person by any provision of the Companies Act to produce documents or give information to, or otherwise to assist, inspectors appointed as mentioned in that subsection is to be regarded as an obligation similarly to assist the Secretary of State in his investigation.

(2) An answer given by a person to a question put to him in exercise of the powers conferred by section 218(5) may be used in evidence against him.

(3) Where criminal proceedings are instituted by the prosecuting authority or the Secretary of State following any report or reference under section 218, it is the duty of the liquidator and every officer and agent of the company past and present (other than the defendant or defender) to give to that authority or the Secretary of State (as the case may be) all assistance in connection with the prosecution which he is reasonably able to give.

For this purpose "agent" includes any banker or solicitor of the company and any person employed by the company as auditor, whether that person is or is not an officer of the company.

(4) If a person fails or neglects to give assistance in the manner required by subsection (3), the court may, on the application of the prosecuting authority or the Secretary of State (as the case may be) direct the person to comply with that subsection; and if the application is made with respect to a liquidator, the court may (unless it appears that the failure or neglect to comply was due to the liquidator not having in his hands sufficient assets of the company to enable him to do so) direct that the costs shall be borne by the liquidator personally.

Definition
"officer": s.251; s.744, C.A. 1985.

General Note
This re-enacts s.633, C.A. 1985.

Part V

Winding Up of Unregistered Companies

Meaning of "unregistered company"

220.—(1) For the purposes of this Part, the expression "unregistered company" includes any trustee savings bank certified under the enactments relating to such banks, any association and any company, with the following exceptions—

(*a*) a railway company incorporated by Act of Parliament,

(*b*) a company registered in any part of the United Kingdom under the Joint Stock Companies Acts or under the legislation (past or present) relating to companies in Great Britain.

(2) On such day as the Treasury appoints by order under section 4(3) of the Trustee Savings Banks Act 1985, the words in subsection (1) from "any trustee" to "banks" cease to have effect and are hereby repealed.

General Note

This is derived from s.665, C.A. 1985 and defines the meaning of unregistered company. Previously the definition expressly included "any partnership (whether limited or not)" and expressly excluded specified types of partnerships. Neither the words of inclusion nor the words of exclusion are present in the section now. One can speculate that partnerships are still included by virtue of the general phrase "any association and any company" in subs. (1). The inclusion of trustee savings banks would appear to be temporary (subs. (2)).

Winding up of unregistered companies

221.—(1) Subject to the provisions of this Part, any unregistered company may be wound up under this Act; and all the provisions of this Act and the Companies Act about winding up apply to an unregistered company with the exceptions and additions mentioned in the following subsections.

(2) If an unregistered company has a principal place of business situated in Northern Ireland, it shall not be wound up under this Part unless it has a principal place of business situated in England and Wales or Scotland, or in both England and Wales and Scotland.

(3) For the purpose of determining a court's winding-up jurisdiction, an unregistered company is deemed—

(*a*) to be registered in England and Wales or Scotland, according as its principal place of business is situated in England and Wales or Scotland, or

(*b*) if it has a principal place of business situated in both countries, to be registered in both countries;

and the principal place of business situated in that part of Great Britain in which proceedings are being instituted is, for all purposes of the winding up, deemed to be the registered office of the company.

(4) No unregistered company shall be wound up under this Act voluntarily.

(5) The circumstances in which an unregistered company may be wound up are as follows—

(*a*) if the company is dissolved, or has ceased to carry on business, or is carrying on business only for the purpose of winding up its affairs;

(*b*) if the company is unable to pay its debts;

(*c*) if the court is of opinion that it is just and equitable that the company should be wound up.

(6) A petition for winding up a trustee savings bank may be presented by the Trustee Savings Banks Central Board or by a commissioner appointed under section 35 of the Trustee Savings Banks Act 1981 as well as by any person authorised under Part IV of this Act to present a petition for the winding up of a company.

On such day as the Treasury appoints by order under section 4(3) of the Trustee Savings Bank Act 1985, this subsection ceases to have effect and is hereby repealed.

(7) In Scotland, an unregistered company which the Court of Session has jurisdiction to wind up may be wound up by the court if there is subsisting a floating charge over property comprised in the company's property and undertaking, and the court is satisfied that the security of the creditor entitled to the benefit of the floating charge is in jeopardy.

For this purpose a creditor's security is deemed to be in jeopardy if the court is satisfied that events have occurred or are about to occur which render it unreasonable in the creditor's interests that the company should retain power to dispose of the property which is subject to the floating charge.

DEFINITION
"unregistered company": s.220.

GENERAL NOTE
This re-enacts s.666, C.A. 1985 (in part). It deals with the winding up of unregistered companies under the Act. Subss. (2) and (3) deal with companies with principal places of business in different parts of the United Kingdom. Unregistered companies can only be wound up compulsorily. They cannot be wound up voluntarily (subs. (4)). (Note *Palmer,* para. 86–01 to the effect that they can register under Chap. II of Part XXII, C.A. 1985 and then wind up voluntarily). Subs. (5) specifies the grounds—(*a*) dissolution or cesser of business (*b*) inability to pay debts (*c*) it is just and equitable to wind the company up. In Scotland such a company can be wound up if a floating charge is in jeopardy (subs. (7)). The reference, previously in subs. (7) of s.666, to limited partnerships has been dropped. See also note to s.220.

An illegal association cannot be wound up under the Act (*Re Padstow Total Loss and Collision Assurance Association* (1882) 20 Ch.D. 137); see further Buckley, *The Companies Acts, op. cit.* Vol. 1, pp.845–846.

Inability to pay debts: unpaid creditor for £750 or more

222.—(1) An unregistered company is deemed (for the purposes of section 221) unable to pay its debts if there is a creditor, by assignment or otherwise, to whom the company is indebted in a sum exceeding £750 then due and—

(*a*) the creditor has served on the company, by leaving at its principal place of business, or by delivering to the secretary or some director, manager or principal officer of the company, or by otherwise serving in such manner as the court may approve or direct, a written demand in the prescribed form requiring the company to pay the sum due, and

(*b*) the company has for 3 weeks after the service of the demand neglected to pay the sum or to secure or compound for it to the creditor's satisfaction.

(2) The money sum for the time being specified in subsection (1) is subject to increase or reduction by regulations under section 417 in Part XV; but no increase in the sum so specified affects any case in which the winding-up petition was presented before the coming into force of the increase.

DEFINITION
"unregistered company": s.220.

GENERAL NOTE
This re-enacts s.667, C.A. 1985 as slightly amended by Sched. 6, para. 50, I.A. 1985. The statutory demand referred to in subs. (1)(*a*) must be "in prescribed form". See rules. See also note to s.224.

Inability to pay debts: debt remaining unsatisfied after action brought

223. An unregistered company is deemed (for the purposes of section 221) unable to pay its debts if an action or other proceeding has been instituted against any member for any debt or demand due, or claimed to be due, from the company, or from him in his character of member, and—

(*a*) notice in writing of the institution of the action or proceeding has been served on the company by leaving it at the company's principal place of business (or by delivering it to the secretary, or some director, manager or principal officer of the company, or by otherwise serving it in such manner as the court may approve or direct), and

(*b*) the company has not within 3 weeks after service of the notice paid, secured or compounded for the debt or demand, or procured the action or proceeding to be stayed or sisted, or indemnified the defendant or defender to his reasonable satisfaction against the action or proceeding, and against all costs, damages and expenses to be incurred by him because of it.

DEFINITION

"unregistered company": s.220.

GENERAL NOTE

This re-enacts s.668, C.A. 1985 as slightly amended by Sched. 6, para. 51, I.A. 1985. In subs. (*b*) the company now has three weeks (*cf.* 19 days) to pay, etc. See also note to s.224, and s.417.

Inability to pay debts: other cases

224.—(1) An unregistered company is deemed (for purposes of section 221) unable to pay its debts—

(*a*) if in England and Wales execution or other process issued on a judgment, decree or order obtained in any court in favour of a creditor against the company, or any member of it as such, or any person authorised to be sued as nominal defendant on behalf of the company, is returned unsatisfied;

(*b*) if in Scotland the inducíae of a charge for payment on an extract decree, or an extract registered bond, or an extract registered protest, have expired without payment being made;

(*c*) if in Northern Ireland a certificate of unenforceability has been granted in respect of any judgment, decree or order obtained as mentioned in paragraph (*a*);

(*d*) if it is otherwise proved to the satisfaction of the court that the company is unable to pay its debts as they fall due.

(2) An unregistered company is also deemed unable to pay its debts if it is proved to the satisfaction of the court that the value of the company's assets is less than the amount of its liabilities, taking into account its contingent and prospective liabilities.

DEFINITION

"unregistered company": s.220.

GENERAL NOTE

This re-enacts s.669, C.A. 1985 as amended by Sched. 6, para. 52, I.A. 1985. Subs. (1)(*d*) has been clarified by the addition of the words "as they fall due" and subs. (2) sets out new circumstances in which an unregistered company is deemed unable to pay its debts (presumably, for the purposes of s.221, although this is not stated) namely, where, for the moment, the company is able to meet its debts as they fall due but, in the long term, taking into account its contingent and prospective liabilities, the value of its assets will be less than the amount of its liabilities. It is in these circumstances that an administration order (see s.8) may be appropriate in the case of a registered company but is apparently unavailable to an unregistered company (see 229(2)).

Ss. 222, 223, and 224 all deal with the inability of the company to pay its debts. Ss. 222 and 224 are the equivalents to s.123(*a*), (*b*), (*c*), (*d*) and (*e*) which apply to registered companies. S.223 has no such equivalent, being partly based upon the supposition that a member may be liable for the company's debts, which supposition is generally inapplicable to registered companies.

Oversea company may be wound up though dissolved

225. Where a company incorporated outside Great Britain which has been carrying on business in Great Britain ceases to carry on business in Great Britain, it may be wound up as an unregistered company under this Act, notwithstanding that it has been dissolved or otherwise ceased to exist as a company under or by virtue of the laws of the country under which it was incorporated.

General Note

This re-enacts s.670, C.A. 1985 and provides for the winding up of an oversea company even though it has been dissolved under the law of its incorporation. This was the section used in the famous Russian Bank cases after they were dissolved by Bolshevik decrees in the Russian Revolution. See the learned articles by K. Lipstein (1952) C.L.J. 198 and M. A. Mann (1955) 18 M.L.R. 8. See also B. Mcpherson, Q.C., *The Law of Company Liquidation* (2nd ed.), p.410 *et seq.*

S.225 is expository only and does not limit the jurisdiction conferred by s.221—see the Russian bank cases cited by Buckley *op. cit.*, Vol. 1, p.852 footnote 3.

Contributories in winding up of unregistered company

226.—(1) In the event of an unregistered company being wound up, every person is deemed a contributory who is liable to pay or contribute to the payment of any debt or liability of the company, or to pay or contribute to the payment of any sum for the adjustment of the rights of members among themselves, or to pay or contribute to the payment of the expenses of winding up the company.

(2) Every contributory is liable to contribute to the company's assets all sums due from him in respect of any such liability as is mentioned above.

(3) In the case of an unregistered company engaged in or formed for working mines within the stannaries, a past member is not liable to contribute to the assets if he has ceased to be a member for 2 years or more either before the mine ceased to be worked or before the date of the winding-up order.

(4) In the event of the death, bankruptcy or insolvency of any contributory, the provisions of this Act with respect to the personal representatives, to the heirs and legatees of heritage of the heritable estate in Scotland of deceased contributories, and to the trustees of bankrupt or insolvent contributories, respectively apply.

Definition

"unregistered company": s.220.

General Note

This re-enacts s.671, C.A. 1985 and deals with contributories in the case of a winding up of an unregistered company. The liability is as a member or partner not a mere debtor (*Re Shields Marine Insurance Association, Lee and Moor's Case* (1868) L.R. 5 Eq. 368).

Power of court to stay, sist or restrain proceedings

227. The provisions of this Part with respect to staying, sisting or restraining actions and proceedings against a company at any time after the presentation of a petition for winding up and before the making of a winding-up order extend, in the case of an unregistered company, where the application to stay, sist or restrain is presented by a creditor, to actions and proceedings against any contributory of the company.

See note to s.228.

Actions stayed on winding-up order

228. Where an order has been made for winding up an unregistered company, no action or proceeding shall be proceeded with or commenced against any contributory of the company in respect of any debt of the company, except by leave of the court, and subject to such terms as the court may impose.

DEFINITIONS

"contributory": s.226..
"unregistered company": s.220.

GENERAL NOTE

Ss.227 and 228 re-enact ss.672 and 673, C.A. 1985. These sections deal with the power of the Court to stay proceedings after a petition and before an order to wind up, and the automatic stay of proceedings on the making of a winding-up order unless leave of the Court is obtained. These are the equivalents of ss.126 and 130(2).

Provisions of this Part to be cumulative

229.—(1) The provisions of this Part with respect to unregistered companies are in addition to and not in restriction of any provisions in Part IV with respect to winding up companies by the court; and the court or liquidator may exercise any powers or do any act in the case of unregistered companies which might be exercised or done by it or him in winding up companies formed and registered under the Companies Act.

(2) However, an unregistered company is not, except in the event of its being wound up, deemed to be a company under the Companies Act, and then only to the extent provided by this Part of this Act.

GENERAL NOTE

This re-enacts s.674, C.A. 1985 and provides that these provisions are in addition to those in Pt. IV. This is except as expressly provided to the contrary (*Rudlow* v. *Great Britain Mutual Life Assurance Society* (1881) 17 Ch.D. 600, 612 (C.A.)).

PART VI

MISCELLANEOUS PROVISIONS APPLYING TO COMPANIES WHICH ARE INSOLVENT OR IN LIQUIDATION

Office-holders

Holders of office to be qualified insolvency practitioners

230.—(1) Where an administration order is made in relation to a company, the administrator must be a person who is qualified to act as an insolvency practitioner in relation to the company.

(2) Where an administrative receiver of a company is appointed, he must be a person who is so qualified.

(3) Where a company goes into liquidation, the liquidator must be a person who is so qualified.

(4) Where a provisional liquidator is appointed, he must be a person who is so qualified.

(5) Subsections (3) and (4) are without prejudice to any enactment under which the official receiver is to be, or may be, liquidator or provisional liquidator.

DEFINITIONS

"administration order", "administrator": s.8(2).
"administrative receiver": s.251(*a*), (*b*).
"company goes into liquidation": s.247(2).
"person qualified to act as an insolvency practitioner": s.390.
"provisional liquidator": s.135.
"the official receiver": s.399(1).

"to act as an insolvency practitioner in relation to a company": s.388(1).

General Note

This section corresponds to ss.95(1), (2) and 96(1) of the 1985 Act. It imposes the requirement that in each of the four types of insolvency proceeding mentioned in subss. (1)–(4) respectively, the person appointed as office-holder must in each case be a qualified insolvency practitioner, within the meaning of ss.388 and 390. Therefore every administrator, administrative receiver, liquidator or provisional liquidator must, by virtue of this section, be a person qualified to act as an insolvency practitioner in relation to the company in question. If the person appointed lacks such qualification, his appointment will be invalid, albeit s.232 will apply to render valid any acts done by the office holder before either his want of qualification is cured, or he formally relinquishes office or is removed therefrom. Under s.389, (*q.v.*) any person who acts as an insolvency practitioner in relation to a company at a time when he is not qualified to do so commits a criminal offence of strict liability. The provisions of s.388(1)(*a*) indicate that a person acts as an insolvency practitioner in relation to a company by acting as any of the four types of office holder listed above. However, s.388(1)(*b*) also provides that a person acts as an insolvency practitioner in relation to a company by acting as supervisor of a voluntary arrangement approved under Pt. I of the Act, and s.389 accordingly makes it a criminal offence for an unqualified person to act in this capacity also. By an apparent oversight, no requirement to the effect that a supervisor of a voluntary arrangement must be a qualified insolvency practitioner was included in ss.95(1), (2) or 96(1) of the 1985 Act, and hence the process of consolidation in the present Act could not alter that want of provision. However, the same net effect is accomplished by the inclusion in s.1(2) of the requirement that the nominee in a proposal for a voluntary arrangement must be a person who is qualified to act as an insolvency practitioner in relation to the company, a requirement reinforced by the further provisions in ss.2(4), 4(2) and 7(5). Nevertheless, the consequence of the present statutory provisions is that, with the exception of s.233, a supervisor of a company voluntary arrangement concluded under Pt. I is unable to avail himself of the various powers and remedies enjoyed by the other types of office-holder by virtue of Pt. VI. Moreover, the supervisor of a voluntary arrangement is excluded from the list of office-holders whose acts are validated by virtue of s.232 in cases where their appointment is defective for any of the stated reasons.

Appointment to office of two or more persons

231.—(1) This section applies if an appointment or nomination of any person to the office of administrator, administrative receiver, liquidator or provisional liquidator—

(*a*) relates to more than one person, or

(*b*) has the effect that the office is to be held by more than one person.

(2) The appointment or nomination shall declare whether any act required or authorised under any enactment to be done by the administrator, administrative receiver, liquidator or provisional liquidator is to be done by all or any one or more of the persons for the time being holding the office in question.

Definitions

"administrative receiver": s.251.
"administrator": s.8(2).
"provisional liquidator": s.135.

General Note

This section, whose provisions correspond to ss.95(1), (2) and 96(2) of the 1985 Act, replaces s.589(5) of the Companies Act 1985, which is repealed. The drafting of the new version is a considerable improvement over the old one in terms of clarity, and has the merit of making it a positive requirement that the terms of appointment are to contain a specific indication whether the joint office holders are required to act together, or whether any one or more of them may validly perform any act which falls to be performed.

Validity of office-holder's acts

232. The acts of an individual as administrator, administrative receiver, liquidator or provisional liquidator of a company are valid notwithstanding any defect in his appointment, nomination or qualifications.

DEFINITIONS
"administrative receiver": s.251.
"administrator": s.8(2).
"provisional liquidator": s.135.

GENERAL NOTE
This provision preserves the validity of the acts of any of the four types of office holder described in s.230(1)–(4), whose appointment, nomination or qualifications turn out to be defective. Thus if it transpires that an office holder was not qualified to act as an insolvency practitioner in relation to the company, any acts performed by him in his capacity as office holder, prior to that discovery, will be valid by virtue of this provision although the office holder will have committed a criminal offence under s.389 and will also be obliged to vacate his office forthwith (under s.19(2)(*a*); s.45(2) or s.172(5), as the case may be). As mentioned in the Note to s.230, through an apparent legislative oversight the position of supervisor of a voluntary arrangement was omitted from the definition of "office holder" contained in s.95(1) of the 1985 Act, although it was included within the definition of "acting as an insolvency practitioner in relation to a company" by means of an amendment which now constitutes s.388(1)(*b*) (see H.C. Vol. 83, col. 580). S.1(2) imposes the requirement that the nominee (potentially the supervisor) in relation to a proposed voluntary arrangement must be a person who is qualified to act as an insolvency practitioner in relation to the company, and hence the appointment of any unqualified person to the position of supervisor will be defective, while if the person appointed purports to act in that capacity he will commit a criminal offence under s.389. However, no clear indication is given within the Act with regard to the validity or otherwise of any acts which may be performed by such a person prior to the time when the defective nature of his appointment as supervisor is discovered and his removal from office takes effect. This section corresponds to ss.95(1), (2) and 96(3) of the 1985 Act.

Management by administrators, liquidators, etc.

Supplies of gas, water, electricity, etc.

233.—(1) This section applies in the case of a company where—
(*a*) an administration order is made in relation to the company, or
(*b*) an administrative receiver is appointed, or
(*c*) a voluntary arrangement under Part I, approved by meetings summoned under section 3, has taken effect, or
(*d*) the company goes into liquidation, or
(*e*) a provisional liquidator is appointed;

and "the office-holder" means the administrator, the administrative receiver, the supervisor of the voluntary arrangement, the liquidator or the provisional liquidator, as the case may be.

(2) If a request is made by or with the concurrence of the office-holder for the giving, after the effective date, of any of the supplies mentioned in the next subsection, the supplier—
(*a*) may make it a condition of the giving of the supply that the office-holder personally guarantees the payment of any charges in respect of the supply, but
(*b*) shall not make it a condition of the giving of the supply, or do anything which has the effect of making it a condition of the giving of the supply, that any outstanding charges in respect of a supply given to the company before the effective date are paid.

(3) The supplies referred to in subsection (2) are—
(*a*) a public supply of gas,
(*b*) a supply of electricity by an Electricity Board,

(*c*) a supply of water by statutory water undertakers or, in Scotland, a water authority,

(*d*) a supply of telecommunication services by a public telecommunications operator.

(4) "The effective date" for the purposes of this section is whichever is applicable of the following dates—

(*a*) the date on which the administration order was made,

(*b*) the date on which the administrative receiver was appointed (or, if he was appointed in succession to another administrative receiver, the date on which the first of his predecessors was appointed),

(*c*) the date on which the voluntary arrangement was approved by the meetings summoned under section 3,

(*d*) the date on which the company went into liquidation,

(*e*) the date on which the provisional liquidator was appointed.

(5) The following applies to expressions used in subsection (3)—

(*a*) "public supply of gas" means a supply of gas by the British Gas Corporation or a public gas supplier within the meaning of Part I of the Gas Act 1986,

(*b*) "Electricity Board" means the same as in the Energy Act 1983,

(*c*) "water authority" means the same as in the Water (Scotland) Act 1980, and

(*d*) "telecommunication services" and "public telecommunications operator" mean the same as in the Telecommunications Act 1984, except that the former does not include services consisting in the conveyance of programmes included in cable programme services (within the meaning of the Cable and Broadcasting Act 1984).

Definitions

"a Water Authority": subs. (5)(*c*); Water (Scotland) Act 1980, ss.3, 109(1).
"administration order": s.8(2).
"administrative receiver": s.251.
"an Electricity Board": subs. (5)(*b*); Energy Act 1983, s.26.
"cable programme services": Cable & Broadcasting Act 1984, ss.2(1), 56(1).
"company goes into liquidation": s.247(2).
"provisional liquidator": s.135.
"public supply of gas": subs. (5)(*a*); Gas Act 1986, ss.7(1), 48(1), (2).
"public telecommunications operator": subs. (5)(*d*); Telecommunications Act 1984, ss.9(3), 106(1).
"supplies": subs. (3).
"telecommunication services": subs. (5)(*d*); Telecommunications Act 1984, ss.4(3), 106(1).
"the office holder": subs. (1).
"the effective date": subs. (4).
"voluntary arrangement": s.1(1).

General Note

In Chap. 33 of the *Cork Report* the position of public utilities is discussed in the context of creditors with special rights, with emphasis upon the use which may be made of their monopoly position by the suppliers of such commercially essential services as electricity, gas, water and the telephone. In paras. 1451–1462 of the *Report* it is made clear that public utilities as creditors have the capability, although technically they are unsecured and non-preferential, to compel the office holder in insolvency proceedings to settle the company's outstanding account in full against the threat that otherwise supplies will be discontinued. This section is enacted in response to the recommendation in para. 1462 that the public utilities should be required to treat the office holder as a new customer with statutory right to receive supplies separate and distinct from the company whose account is in arrear. Hence, the supplier may make it a condition of the giving of the supply that the office holder personally guarantees the payment of any charges in respect of subsequent supplies, but may not make it a condition that any outstanding charges in respect of previous supplies are paid. This section corresponds to ss.95 and 97 of the 1985 Act.

Subs. (2)(b)

Or do anything which has the effect of making it a condition of the giving of the supply . . .

This is designed to meet the possibility that a monopoly supplier may use indirect means to ensure full payment of charges outstanding in respect of past supplies. One example has been the imposition of a requirement that subsequent supplies are obtained via a coin-in-the-slot meter which is so calibrated that the rate at which the service is being charged for is at a premium, thereby enabling the utility effectively to recoup the arrears while ostensibly supplying the service without imposing a condition that outstanding charges in respect of a supply given before the relevant date are paid.

This section forms a parallel to s.372, which applies in relation to the insolvency of an individual.

Getting in the company's property

234.—(1) This section applies in the case of a company where—

(*a*) an administration order is made in relation to the company, or

(*b*) an administrative receiver is appointed, or

(*c*) the company goes into liquidation, or

(*d*) a provisional liquidator is appointed;

and "the office-holder" means the administrator, the administrative receiver, the liquidator or the provisional liquidator, as the case may be.

(2) Where any person has in his possession or control any property, books, papers or records to which the company appears to be entitled, the court may require that person forthwith (or within such period as the court may direct) to pay, deliver, convey, surrender or transfer the property, books, papers or records to the office-holder.

(3) Where the office-holder—

(*a*) seizes or disposes of any property which is not property of the company, and

(*b*) at the time of seizure or disposal believes, and has reasonable grounds for believing, that he is entitled (whether in pursuance of an order of the court or otherwise) to seize or dispose of that property,

the next subsection has effect.

(4) In that case the office-holder—

(*a*) is not liable to any person in respect of any loss or damage resulting from the seizure or disposal except in so far as that loss or damage is caused by the office-holder's own negligence, and

(*b*) has a lien on the property, or the proceeds of its sale, for such expenses as were incurred in connection with the seizure or disposal.

DEFINITIONS

"administration order": s.8(2).
"administrative receiver": s.251.
"company goes into liquidation": s.247(2).
"property": s.436.
"provisional liquidator": s.135.
"records": s.436.
"the court": s.251, C.A. 1985, s.744.
"the office holder": subs. (1).

GENERAL NOTE

This replaces in part the former provisions of s.551 of the Companies Act 1985, which is repealed. The new provision is more widely applicable than that which it replaces, and is drafted so as to operate in administration and receivership proceedings as well as in winding up. Also the court's order may now be made against "any person" who satisfies the criteria laid down in subs. (2). Subs. (2) has also been approximated as closely as possible to the provisions in s.312 relating to surrender of property to a trustee in bankruptcy. In addition, subss. (3) and (4) together confer immunity upon the office holder, provided he has acted bona fide and without negligence, in respect of the wrongful seizure or disposal of property which did not belong to the company at the relevant time. This section corresponds to ss.95(1), (2) and 98 of the 1985 Act.

Duty to co-operate with office-holder

235.—(1) This section applies as does section 234; and it also applies, in the case of a company in respect of which a winding-up order has been made by the court in England and Wales, as if references to the office-holder included the official receiver, whether or not he is the liquidator.

(2) Each of the persons mentioned in the next subsection shall—

(*a*) give to the office-holder such information concerning the company and its promotion, formation, business, dealings, affairs or property as the office-holder may at any time after the effective date reasonably require, and

(*b*) attend on the office-holder at such times as the latter may reasonably require.

(3) The persons referred to above are—

(*a*) those who are or have at any time been officers of the company,

(*b*) those who have taken part in the formation of the company at any time within one year before the effective date,

(*c*) those who are in the employment of the company, or have been in its employment (including employment under a contract for services) within that year, and are in the office-holder's opinion capable of giving information which he requires,

(*d*) those who are, or have within that year been, officers of, or in the employment (including employment under a contract for services) of, another company which is, or within that year was, an officer of the company in question, and

(*e*) in the case of a company being wound up by the court, any person who has acted as administrator, administrative receiver or liquidator of the company.

(4) For the purposes of subsections (2) and (3), "the effective date" is whichever is applicable of the following dates—

(*a*) the date on which the administration order was made,

(*b*) the date on which the administrative receiver was appointed or, if he was appointed in succession to another administrative receiver, the date on which the first of his predecessors was appointed,

(*c*) the date on which the provisional liquidator was appointed, and

(*d*) the date on which the company went into liquidation.

(5) If a person without reasonable excuse fails to comply with any obligation imposed by this section, he is liable to a fine and, for continued contravention, to a daily default fine.

DEFINITIONS

"administration order": s.8(2).
"administrative receiver": s.251.
"administrator": s.8(2).
"business": s.436.
"date company goes into liquidation": s.247(2).
"officer of the company": s.251; C.A. 1985, s.744.
"property": s.436.
"the effective date": subs. (4).
"the office holder": s.234(1).
"the official receiver": s.399(1).
"provisional liquidator": s.135.

GENERAL NOTE

The investigative powers conferred by this section are designed to assist a liquidator to carry out his task quickly and effectively. In particular, private examinations for the office holder conducted under this section will facilitate the investigation of the company's affairs and dealings, the tracing of assets whose existence and whereabouts may be difficult to discover, and also the gaining of information about any transactions whereby the company's assets may have been disposed of in circumstances that may render them recoverable. This section corresponds to ss.95(1), (2) and 99 of the 1985 Act.

Subs. (1)

It is noteworthy that no reference is made to a supervisor of a voluntary arrangement in the list of persons who are included among those within the definition of "office-holder" for the purposes of this section, by virtue of s.234(1). Similarly, subs. (3)(*e*) omits to provide that the supervisor of a voluntary arrangement shall be one of the persons who are liable to be made to supply the liquidator with such information as he may reasonably require.

Subs. (5)

A fine

See Sched. 10 for the table of punishments which may be imposed for this offence.

Inquiry into company's dealings, etc.

236.—(1) This section applies as does section 234; and it also applies in the case of a company in respect of which a winding-up order has been made by the court in England and Wales as if references to the office-holder included the official receiver, whether or not he is the liquidator.

(2) The court may, on the application of the office-holder, summon to appear before it—

(*a*) any officer of the company,

(*b*) any person known or suspected to have in his possession any property of the company or supposed to be indebted to the company, or

(*c*) any person whom the court thinks capable of giving information concerning the promotion, formation, business, dealings, affairs or property of the company.

(3) The court may require any such person as is mentioned in subsection (2)(*a*) to (*c*) to submit an affidavit to the court containing an account of his dealings with the company or to produce any books, papers or other records in his possession or under his control relating to the company or the matters mentioned in paragraph (*c*) of the subsection.

(4) The following applies in a case where—

(*a*) a person without reasonable excuse fails to appear before the court when he is summoned to do so under this section, or

(*b*) there are reasonable grounds for believing that a person has absconded, or is about to abscond, with a view to avoiding his appearance before the court under this section.

(5) The court may, for the purpose of bringing that person and anything in his possession before the court, cause a warrant to be issued to a constable or prescribed officer of the court—

(*a*) for the arrest of that person, and

(*b*) for the seizure of any books, papers, records, money or goods in that person's possession.

(6) The court may authorise a person arrested under such a warrant to be kept in custody, and anything seized under such a warrant to be held, in accordance with the rules, until that person is brought before the court under the warrant or until such other time as the court may order.

DEFINITIONS

"business": s.436.

"officer of the company": s.251; C.A. 1985, s.744.

"property": s.436.

"records": s.436.

"the court": s.251; C.A. 1985, s.744.

"the office holder": s.234(1).

"the official receiver": s.399(1).

General Note

This section, together with s.237, replaces the former provisions of s.561 of the Companies Act 1985, which is repealed. The drafting of the new provisions is considerably modified and clarified, and they are relocated among the provisions applying generally in company insolvency proceedings. The court's power to summon persons belonging to any of the categories mentioned in subs. (2) is thus exercisable in administration or receivership proceedings, as well as in liquidations. It is made clear that the power of summons is activated by an application made by the office holder, a matter which was not stated in s.561 of the Companies Act.

Private examinations before the court under this section will assist the office holder in his duties to recover and realise assets of the company for the benefit of creditors. The procedure will be especially helpful where the person summoned has failed to co-operate fully with the office holder in the manner required by s.235. This section corresponds to ss.95(1), (2) and 100(1), (2) and (6) of the 1985 Act.

Subs. (1)

In addition to the reference to s.234, whereby the expression "the office-holder" is declared to apply to an administrator, an administrative receiver, a liquidator or a provisional liquidator, this subsection also contains an express provision to the effect that, in the case of a compulsory winding up, references to the office-holder include the official receiver, whether or not he is the liquidator.

This complements the independent investigative role of the official receiver by enabling him to invoke the powers established by this section even though he may not be the liquidator of the company for the time being. However, the subsection confers these powers on the official receiver only in the case of a company which has gone into compulsory liquidation in England and Wales. It does not therefore apply in the case of other insolvency procedures, including a voluntary winding-up, nor does it apply where the company is being wound up by the court in Scotland.

Court's enforcement powers under s.236

237.—(1) If it appears to the court, on consideration of any evidence obtained under section 236 or this section, that any person has in his possession any property of the company, the court may, on the application of the office-holder, order that person to deliver the whole or any part of the property to the office-holder at such time, in such manner and on such terms as the court thinks fit.

(2) If it appears to the court, on consideration of any evidence so obtained, that any person is indebted to the company, the court may, on the application of the office-holder, order that person to pay to the office-holder, at such time and in such manner as the court may direct, the whole or any part of the amount due, whether in full discharge of the debt or otherwise, as the court thinks fit.

(3) The court may, if it thinks fit, order that any person who if within the jurisdiction of the court would be liable to be summoned to appear before it under section 236 or this section shall be examined in any part of the United Kingdom where he may for the time being be, or in a place outside the United Kingdom.

(4) Any person who appears or is brought before the court under section 236 or this section may be examined on oath, either orally or (except in Scotland) by interrogatories, concerning the company or the matters mentioned in section 236(2)(*c*).

Definitions

"property": s.436.
"the court": s.251; C.A. 1985, s.744.
"the office holder": ss.236(1), 234(1).

General Note

This section, which corresponds to subss. (3)–(5) and (7) of s.100 of the 1985 Act, confers a variety of powers upon the court which it may exercise, as appropriate, when acting in response to an application by the office-holder to summon before it any of the persons mentioned in s.236(2). The powers are widely drawn, and enable the court to make orders against other persons besides those who have been summoned under s.236 to appear and give evidence or to produce books, papers or other records. Thus, in the light of information gained by the investigative procedures established by s.236, the court may proceed under s.237 to enforce the delivery up of company property to the office holder by those persons found to be in possession of it, and likewise to order persons found to be indebted to the company to make full or partial payment to the office holder.

Adjustment of prior transactions (administration and liquidation)

Transactions at an undervalue (England and Wales)

238.—(1) This section applies in the case of a company where—

(*a*) an administration order is made in relation to the company, or

(*b*) the company goes into liquidation;

and "the office-holder" means the administrator or the liquidator, as the case may be.

(2) Where the company has at a relevant time (defined in section 240) entered into a transaction with any person at an undervalue, the office-holder may apply to the court for an order under this section.

(3) Subject as follows, the court shall, on such an application, make such order as it thinks fit for restoring the position to what it would have been if the company had not entered into that transaction.

(4) For the purposes of this section and section 241, a company enters into a transaction with a person at an undervalue if—

(*a*) the company makes a gift to that person or otherwise enters into a transaction with that person on terms that provide for the company to receive no consideration, or

(*b*) the company enters into a transaction with that person for a consideration the value of which, in money or money's worth, is significantly less than the value, in money or money's worth, of the consideration provided by the company.

(5) The court shall not make an order under this section in respect of a transaction at an undervalue if it is satisfied—

(*a*) that the company which entered into the transaction did so in good faith and for the purpose of carrying on its business, and

(*b*) that at the time it did so there were reasonable grounds for believing that the transaction would benefit the company.

DEFINITIONS

"a relevant time": s.240.
"administration order": s.8(2).
"company goes into liquidation": s.247(2).
"the administrator": s.8(2).
"the court": s.251; C.A. 1985, s.744.
"the office holder": subs. (1).
"transaction": s.436.
"transaction at an undervalue": subs. (4).

TRANSITIONAL PROVISION

Sched. 11, para. 9.

APPLICATION

This section does not apply to Scotland (s.440(2)(*a*)).

GENERAL NOTE

This section, together with ss.239–243, was enacted in response to the carefully argued recommendations in Chap. 28 of the *Cork Report,* discussed in paras. 61–69 of the *White Paper.* The new provisions replace ss.614–616 of the Companies Act 1985 and s.44 of the Bankruptcy Act 1914, which are all repealed. S.172 of the Law of Property Act 1925, which is also repealed, is replaced by s.423 of this Act. In addition to the improved clarity of the drafting of the new provisions to enable various kinds of transactions to be set aside, important changes are made in the law. The law relating to transactions at an undervalue and preferences in company insolvency is now self-contained within this Part of the Act, although the provisions are closely parallel to those applicable in bankruptcy, now to be found in Pt. IX of the Act as ss.339–342. The provisions of s.423 (*q.v.*) are applicable both to corporate and to individual insolvency.

Instead of the former terms, "fraudulent conveyance" and "fraudulent preference", with their open connotations of fraud and moral turpitude, the new provisions employ the more neutral terminology of "transactions at an undervalue" and "(voidable) preference". The two concepts are distinct, although both may well be found to apply to one and the same transaction. On the other hand, a transaction may in some circumstances be voidable as a transaction at an undervalue albeit it did not amount to a voidable preference. This section corresponds to ss.95(1)(*a*), (b) and 101(1) (part)–(3) of the 1985 Act.

Subs. (1)

Office holder

In contrast to the position under ss.230–237, the definition of the term for the purposes of ss.238–246 inclusive is cut down, so as to exclude an administrative receiver. This is further emphasised by the internal subheading standing before ss.238–246 as printed, which indicates that these provisions apply only to administration and liquidation. The remedy established in this section is therefore not available in cases of receivership. On the other hand, it is readily conceivable that in some situations an administrative receiver would find it advantageous to be able to invoke it, but in such cases it would appear that the only way in which to set about the process of recovering assets which have been disposed of at an undervalue, or by way of a preference, is for a company which is in receivership to be put into compulsory liquidation, or for an administration order to be obtained, so that a new office holder can be appointed with standing to apply to the court for an order under this section.

Subs. (2)

This has the effect of restricting the power to make an application under this section to the person who qualifies as "the office holder" in the instant case.

Subs. (3)

This indicates in a general way the court's wide discretionary powers upon an application under this section. Further, specific powers are conferred upon the court by s.241.

Subs. (4)

This supplies the statutory test for "a transaction at an undervalue" for the purposes of this section and s.239 together. However, subs. (5) deprives the court of any discretion to make an order under this section if the two conditions therein specified are met. These effectively require the court to be convinced that the undervalue transaction was a genuine business transaction carried out in good faith in the reasonable belief that it would benefit the company. Moreover, as required by subs. (2), one of the conditions contained in s.240(2) must be met in order that the time when the transaction was entered into shall count as a "relevant time" for the purposes of this section. In consequence, for a transaction to be voidable under this section it must take place at a time when the company is already insolvent, or when the company's circumstances are such that the very transaction itself has the effect of causing the company to become insolvent in the sense employed in s.123 of the Act.

Preferences (England and Wales)

239.—(1) This section applies as does section 238.

(2) Where the company has at a relevant time (defined in the next section) given a preference to any person, the office-holder may apply to the court for an order under this section.

(3) Subject as follows, the court shall, on such an application, make such order as it thinks fit for restoring the position to what it would have been if the company had not given that preference.

(4) For the purposes of this section and section 241, a company gives a preference to a person if—

(*a*) that person is one of the company's creditors or a surety or guarantor for any of the company's debts or other liabilities, and

(*b*) the company does anything or suffers anything to be done which (in either case) has the effect of putting that person into a position which, in the event of the company going into insolvent liquidation, will be better than the position he would have been in if that thing had not been done.

(5) The court shall not make an order under this section in respect of a preference given to any person unless the company which gave the preference was influenced in deciding to give it by a desire to produce in relation to that person the effect mentioned in subsection (4)(*b*).

(6) A company which has given a preference to a person connected with the company (otherwise than by reason only of being its employee) at the time the preference was given is presumed, unless the contrary is shown, to have been influenced in deciding to give it by such a desire as is mentioned in subsection (5).

(7) The fact that something has been done in pursuance of the order of a court does not, without more, prevent the doing or suffering of that thing from constituting the giving of a preference.

Definitions

"company gives a preference": subs. (4).
"person connected with the company": ss.249, 435.
"the court": s.251; C.A. 1985, s.744.
"the office holder": subs. (1), s.238(1).

Transitional Provision

Sched. 11, para. 9.

Application

This section does not apply to Scotland (s.440(2)(*a*)).

General Note

This section forms part of the group of provisions under which prior transactions entered into by a company may be adjusted or avoided upon application by the office holder (as defined in s.238(1)). A liquidator or administrator may therefore apply to the court under this section for an order under subs. (3) relating to any preference given to a person by the company at "a relevant time", as defined for this purpose by s.240. This section corresponds to ss.95(1)(*a*), (*b*) and 101(1) (part), (4)–(7) and (11) of the 1985 Act.

Subs. (4)

This supplies the statutory test for the giving of a preference to any person by the company. The drafting implements the recommendation in paras. 1270–1276 of the *Cork Report* where it was argued that in the case of a voidable preference the burden of repayment should be borne by the party intended to be preferred. In the case where the party who has been preferred is the surety or guarantor of a debt owed to some other creditor, it is now possible to proceed directly against the surety or guarantor quite independently of any proceedings which may be taken against the creditor.

Subs. (5)

This modifies the pre-existing law which required that, to be voidable, a payment should have been made with a dominant intention of preferring the creditor. What is henceforth required is that the intention to prefer should have "influenced" the company in deciding to give the preference. In accordance with the recommendations of the *Cork Report,* the task of a liquidator or administrator seeking to have a preference declared voidable is made easier in cases where the recipient of the preference is connected with the company. This is accomplished by two provisions within this section and s.240. First, a special presumption is introduced in subs. (6), whose effect is to shift the burden of proof to the receipient of the preference, who must effectively show that in giving it the company was *not* influenced by the desire to prefer that person within the terms of subs. (4)(*b*); and secondly s.240(1)(*a*) prescribes the more extended period of two years prior to the commencement date which is to be applicable in cases where the recipient is a connected person, so that any transaction taking place within this period takes place at a "relevant time" for the purposes of this section. The meaning of "connected person" is a compound one, provided partly by s.249 and partly by s.435. The former provision indicates that "connected person" means a director or shadow director of the company or an associate of a person who is either of those things, or a person who is an associate of the company. The latter provision supplies an elaborately drafted definition of the pivotal term "associate". Thus the range of persons onto whom a burden of proof may be placed by the combined effects of subss. (5) and (6) is potentially very large. However, the statutory meaning of "connected person" is especially modified for the purposes of the present section by the words in parentheses in subs. (6), which preclude a person from being treated as a "connected person" for this purpose if the sole ground of his or her connection consists in the fact of being an employee of the company.

The majority opinion in the *Cork Report* (para. 1256) was in favour or a retention of the existing rule whereby a payment by a debtor in response to pressure from the creditor should not be treated as a voidable preference, and that a creditor who has taken active steps to obtain payment of his own debt ought in principle to be allowed to retain the fruits of his diligence. Subject to what has been said above regarding the altered burden of proof in cases of payments to connected persons, it would appear that this section has left it open to argument that a payment made by a company in response to pressure from its creditor, although amounting to a preference, is not rendered voidable under this section because the company was not influenced in deciding to give the preference by a *desire* to produce in relation to the creditor the effect mentioned in subs. (4)(*b*).

"Relevant time" under ss.238, 239

240.—(1) Subject to the next subsection, the time at which a company enters into a transaction at an undervalue or gives a preference is a relevant time if the transaction is entered into, or the preference given—

(*a*) in the case of a transaction at an undervalue or of a preference which is given to a person who is connected with the company (otherwise than by reason only of being its employee), at a time in the period of 2 years ending with the onset of insolvency (which expression is defined below),

(*b*) in the case of a preference which is not such a transaction and is not so given, at a time in the period of 6 months ending with the onset of insolvency, and

(*c*) in either case, at a time between the presentation of a petition for the making of an administration order in relation to the company and the making of such an order on that petition.

(2) Where a company enters into a transaction at an undervalue or gives a preference at a time mentioned in subsection (1)(*a*) or (*b*), that time is not a relevant time for the purposes of section 238 or 239 unless the company—

(*a*) is at that time unable to pay its debts within the meaning of section 123 in Chapter VI of Part IV, or

(*b*) becomes unable to pay its debts within the meaning of that section in consequence of the transaction or preference;

but the requirements of this subsection are presumed to be satisfied, unless the contrary is shown, in relation to any transaction at an undervalue which is entered into by a company with a person who is connected with the company.

(3) For the purposes of subsection (1), the onset of insolvency is—

(*a*) in a case where section 238 or 239 applies by reason of the making of an administration order or of a company going into liquidation immediately upon the discharge of an administration order, the date of the presentation of the petition on which the administration order was made, and

(*b*) in a case where the section applies by reason of a company going into liquidation at any other time, the date of the commencement of the winding up.

DEFINITIONS

"a relevant time": this section.
"administration order": s.8(2).
"commencement of winding up": ss.86, 129.
"company gives a preference": s.239(4).
"company goes into liquidation": s.247(2).
"company unable to pay its debts": s.123.
"person connected with the company": ss.249, 435.
"the onset of insolvency": subs. (3).
"transaction": s.436.
"transaction at an undervalue": s.238(4).

TRANSITIONAL PROVISION

Sched. 11, para. 9.

APPLICATION

This section does not apply to Scotland (s.440(2)(*a*)).

GENERAL NOTE

This section, which corresponds to subss. (8)–(11) of s.101 of the 1985 Act, establishes the meaning of the expression "relevant time" for the purposes of ss.238 and 239. This expression bears a variable meaning, according to the context in which it is used. Both s.238(2) and s.239(2) contain the requirement that a transaction must take place, or preference be given, at "a relevant time" in order that its validity may be called into question under either of those two sections. Thus, the present section has the effect of setting the outer boundaries of the period of time within which a particular act or transaction will take place at "a relevant time".

Subs. (1)(a)

This establishes the period of two years ending with the onset of insolvency (as defined in subs. (3)) as the period within which an act will take place at "a relevant time" whenever the party in whose favour a transaction at an undervalue is entered into, or a preference is given, by the company is a person who is connected with that company. The meaning of "connected person" is supplied by the combined provisions of ss.249 and 435 (*q.v.*) and, as was explained in the General Note to s.239(5), the recommendation of the *Cork Report,* duly adopted in these provisions of the Act, was that it should be made easier for a liquidator or administrator to obtain the avoidance of prior transactions operating in favour of persons connected with the company.

Subs. (1)(b)

This establishes the period of six months ending with the onset of insolvency (again, defined in subs. (3)), as the period within which an act will take place at "a relevant time" where the provisions of subs. (1)(*a*) do not apply.

Subs. (2)

This establishes a further precondition to any moment of time counting as a "relevant time" for the purposes of this section and those to which it is linked. It is necessary that it be established that, at the time when the company entered into the transaction, or gave the preference, in question the company was at that time unable to pay its debts (within the meaning of s.123) or, alternatively, that the company became unable to pay its debts (in the same, technical sense) in consequence of the transaction or preference itself. In normal cases, the burden of proving the company's inability to pay its debts will be cast upon the party seeking to avoid the transaction—namely the office holder. However, the proviso to this subsection reverses that burden of proof whenever the party in whose favour a transaction at an undervalue was entered into was a person connected with company (in the sense explained in relation to subs. (1)(*a*) *supra*). This reversal of the burden of proof in such cases is again in accordance with the recommendation of the *Cork Report,* as explained in the General Note to s.239.

Subs. (3)

This supplies the meaning of the expression "the onset of insolvency" for the purposes of subs. (1)

Orders under ss.238, 239

241.—(1) Without prejudice to the generality of sections 238(3) and 239(3), an order under either of those sections with respect to a transaction or preference entered into or given by a company may (subject to the next subsection)—

(*a*) require any property transferred as part of the transaction, or in connection with the giving of the preference, to be vested in the company,

(*b*) require any property to be so vested if it represents in any person's hands the application either of the proceeds of sale of property so transferred or of money so transferred,

(*c*) release or discharge (in whole or in part) any security given by the company,

(*d*) require any person to pay, in respect of benefits received by him from the company, such sums to the office-holder as the court may direct,

(*e*) provide for any surety or guarantor whose obligations to any person were released or discharged (in whole or in part) under the transaction, or by the giving of the preference, to be under such new or revived obligations to that person as the court thinks appropriate,

(*f*) provide for security to be provided for the discharge of any obligation imposed by or arising under the order, for such an obligation to be charged on any property and for the security or charge to have the same priority as a security or charge released or discharged (in whole or in part) under the transaction or by the giving of the preference, and

(*g*) provide for the extent to which any person whose property is vested by the order in the company, or on whom obligations are imposed by the order, is to be able to prove in the winding up of the company for debts or other liabilities which arose from, or were released or discharged (in whole or in part) under or by, the transaction or the giving of the preference.

(2) An order under section 238 or 239 may affect the property of, or impose any obligation on, any person whether or not he is the person with whom the company in question entered into the transaction or (as the case may be) the person to whom the preference was given; but such an order—

(*a*) shall not prejudice any interest in property which was acquired from a person other than the company and was acquired in good faith, for value and without notice of the relevant circumstances, or prejudice any interest deriving from such an interest, and

(*b*) shall not require a person who received a benefit from the transaction or preference in good faith, for value and without notice of the relevant circumstances to pay a sum to the office-holder, except where that person was a party to the transaction or the payment is to be in respect of a preference given to that person at a time when he was a creditor of the company.

(3) For the purposes of this section the relevant circumstances, in relation to a transaction or preference, are—

(*a*) the circumstances by virtue of which an order under section 238 or (as the case may be) 239 could be made in respect of the transaction or preference if the company were to go into liquidation, or an administration order were made in relation to the company, within a particular period after the transaction is entered into or the preference given, and

(*b*) if that period has expired, the fact that the company has gone into liquidation or that such an order has been made.

(4) The provisions of sections 238 to 241 apply without prejudice to the availability of any other remedy, even in relation to a transaction or preference which the company had no power to enter into or give.

DEFINITIONS

"administration order": s.8(2).
"company goes into liquidation": s.247(2).
"preference given by a company": s.239(4).
"property": s.436.
"security": s.248(*b*).
"the officer holder": s.238(1).
"the relevant circumstances": subs. (3).
"transaction": ss.238(4), 436.

TRANSITIONAL PROVISION

Sched. 11, para. 9.

APPLICATION

This section does not apply to Scotland (s.440(2)(*a*)).

GENERAL NOTE

This section indicates the various types of order which may be made by a court in the exercise of its powers under s.238 or s.239. The opening words of subs. (1) are designed to ensure that the court's powers with regard to the type of order it may make are not restricted to those described in this section. The court could therefore devise some other form of order which in the court's estimation would be more apt to attain the purposes at which ss.238(3) and 239(3) are aimed.

This section corresponds to ss.95(1) and 102 of the 1985 Act.

Gratuitous alienations (Scotland)

242.—(1) Where this subsection applies and—

(*a*) the winding up of a company has commenced, an alienation by the company is challengeable by—

(i) any creditor who is a creditor by virtue of a debt incurred on or before the date of such commencement, or

(ii) the liquidator;

(*b*) an administration order is in force in relation to a company, an alienation by the company is challengeable by the administrator.

(2) Subsection (1) applies where—

(*a*) by the alienation, whether before or after 1st April 1986 (the coming into force of section 75 of the Bankruptcy (Scotland) Act 1985), any part of the company's property is transferred or any claim or right of the company is discharged or renounced, and

(*b*) the alienation takes place on a relevant day.

(3) For the purposes of subsection (2)(*b*), the day on which an alienation takes place is the day on which it becomes completely effectual; and in that subsection "relevant day" means, if the alienation has the effect of favouring—

(*a*) a person who is an associate (within the meaning of the Bankruptcy (Scotland) Act 1985) of the company, a day not earlier than 5 years before the date on which—

(i) the winding up of the company commences, or

(ii) as the case may be, the administration order is made; or

(*b*) any other person, a day not earlier than 2 years before that date.

(4) On a challenge being brought under subsection (1), the court shall grant decree of reduction or for such restoration of property to the company's assets or other redress as may be appropriate; but the court shall not grant such a decree if the person seeking to uphold the alienation establishes—

(*a*) that immediately, or at any other time, after the alienation the company's assets were greater than its liabilities, or

(*b*) that the alienation was made for adequate consideration, or

(*c*) that the alienation—

(i) was a birthday, Christmas or other conventional gift, or

(ii) was a gift made, for a charitable purpose, to a person who is not an associate of the company,

which, having regard to all the circumstances, it was reasonable for the company to make:

Provided that this subsection is without prejudice to any right or interest acquired in good faith and for value from or through the transferee in the alienation.

(5) In subsection (4) above, "charitable purpose" means any charitable, benevolent or philanthropic purpose, whether or not it is charitable within the meaning of any rule of law.

(6) For the purposes of the foregoing provisions of this section, an alienation in implementation of a prior obligation is deemed to be one for which there was no consideration or no adequate consideration to the extent that the prior obligation was undertaken for no consideration or no adequate consideration.

(7) A liquidator and an administrator have the same right as a creditor has under any rule of law to challenge an alienation of a company made for no consideration or no adequate consideration.

(8) This section applies to Scotland only.

Definitions

"administration order": s.8(2).
"associate": Bankruptcy (Scotland) Act 1985, s.74.
"charitable purpose": subs. (5).
"commencement of winding up": ss.86, 129.
"property": s.436.
"relevant day": subs. (3).
"the administrator": s.8(2).

Transitional Provision

Sched. 11, para. 9.

Application

This section applies to Scotland only (subs. (8)).

General Note

This section corresponds to s.615A of the Companies Act, as inserted by para. 20 of Sched. 7 to the Bankruptcy (Scotland) Act 1985 and now repealed. It provides for the reduction of gratuitous alienations in Scotland, and is the counterpart of s.238, under which transactions at an undervalue may be avoided in England and Wales. It is notable that the respective periods within which such transactions may be avoided are considerably longer in cases falling under the law of Scotland. Subs. (3) prescribes a period extending back five years from the date of commencement of winding up, or the making of the administration order, (as the case may be) in the case of any transaction favouring a person who is an associate of the company (as defined in s.74 of the Bankruptcy (Scotland) Act 1985), while the relevant period in the case of alienations favouring persons who are not associates of the company is two years before the commencement date. This contrasts with the period of two years specified in s.240(1) (*q.v.*) in relation to transactions at an undervalue entered into with any person, whether or not that person is connected with the company (within the combined meaning derived from ss.249 and 435).

Unfair preferences (Scotland)

243.—(1) Subject to subsection (2) below, subsection (4) below applies to a transaction entered into by a company, whether before or after 1st April 1986, which has the effect of creating a preference in favour of a creditor to the prejudice of the general body of creditors, being a preference created not earlier than 6 months before the commencement of the winding up of the company or the making of an administration order in relation to the company.

(2) Subsection (4) below does not apply to any of the following transactions—

(*a*) a transaction in the ordinary course of trade or business;

(*b*) a payment in cash for a debt which when it was paid had become payable, unless the transaction was collusive with the purpose of prejudicing the general body of creditors;

(*c*) a transaction whereby the parties to it undertake reciprocal obligations (whether the performance by the parties of their respective obligations occurs at the same time or at different times) unless the transaction was collusive as aforesaid;

(*d*) the granting of a mandate by a company authorising an arrestee to pay over the arrested funds or part thereof to the arrester where—

(i) there has been a decree for payment or a warrant for summary diligence, and

(ii) the decree or warrant has been preceded by an arrestment on the dependence of the action or followed by an arrestment in execution.

(3) For the purposes of subsection (1) above, the day on which a preference was created is the day on which the preference became completely effectual.

(4) A transaction to which this subsection applies is challengeable by—

(*a*) in the case of a winding up—

(i) any creditor who is a creditor by virtue of a debt incurred on or before the date of commencement of the winding up, or

(ii) the liquidator; and

(*b*) in the case of an administration order, the administrator.

(5) On a challenge being brought under subsection (4) above, the court, if satisfied that the transaction challenged is a transaction to which this section applies, shall grant decree of reduction or for such restoration of property to the company's assets or other redress as may be appropriate;

Provided that this subsection is without prejudice to any right or interest acquired in good faith and for value from or through the creditor in whose favour the preference was created.

(6) A liquidator and an administrator have the same right as a creditor has under any rule of law to challenge a preference created by a debtor.

(7) This section applies to Scotland only.

DEFINITIONS

"administration order": s.8(2).
"commencement of winding up": ss.86, 129.
"day on which a preference was created": subs. (3).
"property": s.436.
"the administrator": s.8(2).

TRANSITIONAL PROVISION

Sched. 11, para. 9.

APPLICATION

This section applies to Scotland only (subs. (7)).

General Note

This section corresponds to s.615B of the Companies Act as inserted by para. 20 of Sched. 7 to the Bankruptcy (Scotland) Act 1985 and now repealed. It provides for the reduction of unfair preferences, and for other appropriate redress including the restoration of property to the company's assets. The section applies only to Scotland, and is the counterpart under the law of that jurisdiction to the provision in s.239 for the avoidance of preferences under the law of England and Wales. It is notable that under the law of Scotland the period within which a preference is reducible is in all cases the six months prior to the commencement of winding up or the making of an administration order: any preference created within that period is reducible if it satisfies the other requirements of this section, irrespective of whether the person favoured thereby is or is not an associate of the company. By contrast, under s.240(1)(*a*) a preference given by a company to a person who is connected with it is voidable at English law if the onset of insolvency occurs at any time up to two years thereafter.

Another point of contrast between the English and Scottish provisions concerning preferences is that, under subs. (4)(*a*) of this section, an unfair preference is in a Scottish winding up challengeable by either the liquidator or by any creditor coming within the terms of sub-para. (i), whereas in an English winding up only the liquidator, as office holder, is entitled to make application under s.239(2).

Extortionate credit transactions

244.—(1) This section applies as does section 238, and where the company is, or has been, a party to a transaction for, or involving, the provision of credit to the company.

(2) The court may, on the application of the office-holder, make an order with respect to the transaction if the transaction is or was extortionate and was entered into in the period of 3 years ending with the day on which the administration order was made or (as the case may be) the company went into liquidation.

(3) For the purposes of this section a transaction is extortionate if, having regard to the risk accepted by the person providing the credit—

(*a*) the terms of it are or were such as to require grossly exorbitant payments to be made (whether unconditionally or in certain contingencies) in respect of the provision of the credit, or

(*b*) it otherwise grossly contravened ordinary principles of fair dealing;

and it shall be presumed, unless the contrary is proved, that a transaction with respect to which an application is made under this section is or, as the case may be, was extortionate.

(4) An order under this section with respect to any transaction may contain such one or more of the following as the court thinks fit, that is to say—

(*a*) provision setting aside the whole or part of any obligation created by the transaction,

(*b*) provision otherwise varying the terms of the transaction or varying the terms on which any security for the purposes of the transaction is held,

(*c*) provision requiring any person who is or was a party to the transaction to pay to the office-holder any sums paid to that person, by virtue of the transaction, by the company,

(*d*) provision requiring any person to surrender to the office-holder any property held by him as security for the purposes of the transaction,

(*e*) provision directing accounts to be taken between any persons.

(5) The powers conferred by this section are exercisable in relation to any transaction concurrently with any powers exercisable in relation to that transaction as a transaction at an undervalue or under section 242 (gratuitous alienations in Scotland).

Definitions

"administration order": s.8(2).

"company goes into liquidation": s.247(2).

"extortionate transaction": subs. (3).
"security": s.248(*b*).
"the office holder": s.238(1).
"transaction": s.436.
"transaction at an undervalue": s.238(4).

Transitional Provision
Sched. 11, para. 9.

General Note
The purpose of this section, which is parallel to s.343 applicable in cases of individual insolvency, is to provide a procedure whereby a liquidator or administrator may apply to the court to reopen a credit bargain which has been entered into by the company as debtor on terms which are extortionate. The overall scheme of the section, and in particular the definition of "extortionate transaction" supplied in subs. (3), is modelled on the provisions in ss.137–139 inclusive of the Consumer Credit Act 1974, which allow the reopening of extortionate credit bargains in cases falling within the ambit of that Act. The present section, which pre-supposes that the company is either in liquidation or is subject to an administration order, permits the reopening of any kind of transaction involving the provision of credit to the company. The court's powers under subs. (4) are exercisable upon a finding that the transaction was extortionate within the meaning of subs. (3). This section corresponds to ss.95(1)(*a*), (*b*) together with 103 of the 1985 Act.

Subs. (3)

It shall be presumed, unless the contrary is proved . . .
These words give rise to a rebuttable presumption that the transaction in question was extortionate. They therefore have the effect of imposing a burden of proof upon the party who occupies the role of creditor in the transaction to which the company was a party. That party must prove to the Court that the transaction was *not* extortionate within the meaning of this subsection. Although this involves the proving of a negative, it accords with the precedent set in s.171(7) of the Consumer Credit Act 1974. The latter provision also furnishes a precedent for the additional feature in the drafting of the present subsection whereby, in order to avail himself of the presumption that a bargain is extortionate, the party seeking to have the transaction re-opened is not even required to make out a prima facie case that it is or was of dubious commercial fairness. All that is required is that the office holder make application under subs. (2) in respect of a credit transaction entered by the company as debtor within three years prior to the commencement of the insolvency proceedings. Thereupon, the transaction must be presumed by the Court to be extortionate unless the contrary is proved by the creditor.

Avoidance of certain floating charges

245.—(1) This section applies as does section 238, but applies to Scotland as well as to England and Wales.

(2) Subject as follows, a floating charge on the company's undertaking or property created at a relevant time is invalid except to the extent of the aggregate of—

(*a*) the value of so much of the consideration for the creation of the charge as consists of money paid, or goods or services supplied, to the company at the same time as, or after, the creation of the charge,

(*b*) the value of so much of that consideration as consists of the discharge or reduction, at the same time as, or after, the creation of the charge, of any debt of the company, and

(*c*) the amount of such interest (if any) as is payable on the amount falling within paragraph (*a*) or (*b*) in pursuance of any agreement under which the money was so paid, the goods or services were so supplied or the debt was so discharged or reduced.

(3) Subject to the next subsection, the time at which a floating charge is created by a company is a relevant time for the purposes of this section if the charge is created—

(*a*) in the case of a charge which is created in favour of a person who is connected with the company, at a time in the period of 2 years ending with the onset of insolvency,

(*b*) in the case of a charge which is created in favour of any other person, at a time in the period of 12 months ending with the onset of insolvency, or

(*c*) in either case, at a time between the presentation of a petition for the making of an administration order in relation to the company and the making of such an order on that petition.

(4) Where a company creates a floating charge at a time mentioned in subsection (3)(*b*) and the person in favour of whom the charge is created is not connected with the company, that time is not a relevant time for the purposes of this section unless the company—

(*a*) is at that time unable to pay its debts within the meaning of section 123 in Chapter VI of Part IV, or

(*b*) becomes unable to pay its debts within the meaning of that section in consequence of the transaction under which the charge is created.

(5) For the purposes of subsection (3), the onset of insolvency is—

(*a*) in a case where this section applies by reason of the making of an administration order, the date of the presentation of the petition on which the order was made, and

(*b*) in a case where this section applies by reason of a company going into liquidation, the date of the commencement of the winding up.

(6) For the purposes of subsection (2)(*a*) the value of any goods or services supplied by way of consideration for a floating charge is the amount in money which at the time they were supplied could reasonably have been expected to be obtained for supplying the goods or services in the ordinary course of business and on the same terms (apart from the consideration) as those on which they were supplied to the company.

DEFINITIONS

"a relevant time": subs. (3).
"administration order": s.8(2).
"commencement of winding up": ss.86, 129.
"company goes into liquidation": s.247(2).
"company unable to pay its debts": s.123.
"floating charge": s.251; C.A. 1985, s.462.
"person connected with the company": ss.249, 435.
"property": s.436.
"the onset of insolvency": subs. (5).
"value of goods or services provided by way of consideration for a floating charge": subs. (6).

TRANSITIONAL PROVISION

Sched. 11, para. 9.

GENERAL NOTE

This section reforms and replaces s.617 of the Companies Act 1985, which is repealed. Reform was recommended in paras. 1551–1556 of the *Cork Report.* The new provisions strengthen the rules under which a floating charge created within twelve months prior to the commencement of the insolvency proceedings, (or, in the case of such a charge created in favour of a connected person, within two years of that date) is rendered invalid by the fact of the company's going into liquidation or becoming the subject of an administration order. Such invalidity is effective except to the extent of money paid or goods supplied to the company at the time when the charge is created or subsequently. By subs. (4) it is made a precondition to the operation of the invalidating rule that the company was either insolvent at the time of the creation of the floating charge or was rendered insolvent in consequence of the very transaction under which the floating charge was created. However, in the case where the person in whose favour the charge was created was connected with the company (as defined in s.249) together with s.435 the precondition as to the company's state of insolvency is not applicable, and hence all such charges are rendered invalid if the company goes into liquidation or an administration order procedure within two years of the date of their creation. This is particularly aimed at preventing those who are directors or shadow directors of the company, and other persons closely involved with its management, from conferring upon themselves an enhanced priority over the unsecured creditors by means of a floating charge security in return for any finance which they may provide to the company. The invalidation of a floating charge under this section does not affect the existence of the actual debt which was previously secured thereby: the debt remains, but becomes an unsecured debt in consequence of the application of this section. This section corresponds to ss.95(1)(*a*), (*b*) together with 104 of the 1985 Act.

Subs. (2)(a)

Money paid, or goods or services supplied

These words replace the more restrictive phrase "any cash paid" which formerly were contained in s.617 of the Companies Act 1985. Although these words were held to be applicable to a case where payment was made by cheque (*Re Matthew Ellis Ltd.* [1933] Ch. 458), there was doubt as to their applicability in a case where goods or services are supplied against the giving of a floating charge security.

Subs. (2)(b)

This is intended to provide for cases such as where a company grants a floating charge in favour of a bank to secure further advances. Payments, subsequently made by the bank to creditors of the company in whose favour cheques have been drawn, will qualify for exemption from the consequences of the invalidation of the floating charge. This confirms the case-law ruling based on the previously applicable statutory provision, as applied in *Re Yeovil Glove Co. Ltd.* [1965] Ch. 148.

Unenforceability of liens on books, etc.

246.—(1) This section applies in the case of a company where—

(*a*) an administration order is made in relation to the company, or

(*b*) the company goes into liquidation, or

(*c*) a provisional liquidator is appointed;

and "the office-holder" means the administrator, the liquidator or the provisional liquidator, as the case may be.

(2) Subject as follows, a lien or other right to retain possession of any of the books, papers or other records of the company is unenforceable to the extent that its enforcement would deny possession of any books, papers or other records to the office-holder.

(3) This does not apply to a lien on documents which give a title to property and are held as such.

Definitions

"administration order": s.8(2).
"company goes into liquidation": s.247(2).
"property": s.436.
"provisional liquidator": s.135.
"records": s.436.
"the office holder": subs. (1).

Application

This section does not apply to Scotland (s.440(2)(*a*)).

General Note

This section gives the office holder an overriding right to gain possession of any of the company's books, papers or records which may be subject to a lien or other right of retention existing in favour of some other party. This is subject to the exception in favour of the holder of a lien on documents which give a title to property and which are held as such. The provision establishes a parallel provision for company insolvency to that applicable in bankruptcy by virtue of s.349. Provision will be made in the rules for the provisions of s.38(4) of the Bankruptcy (Scotland) Act 1985 to apply to winding up in Scotland, with the consequence that a consistent set of provisions will in fact apply in England and Wales and in Scotland with regard to liens in the event of insolvency. This section corresponds to ss.95(1)(*a*), (*b*), and (2), together with 105 of the 1985 Act.

Part VII

Interpretation for First Group of Parts

"Insolvency" and "go into liquidation"

247.—(1) In this Group of Parts, except in so far as the context otherwise requires, "insolvency", in relation to a company, includes the approval of a voluntary arrangement under Part I, the making of an administration order or the appointment of an administrative receiver.

(2) For the purposes of any provision in this Group of Parts, a company goes into liquidation if it passes a resolution for voluntary winding up or an order for its winding up is made by the court at a time when it has not already gone into liquidation by passing such a resolution.

Definitions

"administration order": s.8.
"administrative receiver": s.251.
"voluntary winding up": s.84(1), 90.

General Note

Subs. (2) defines the time at which a company "goes into liquidation" as the moment when it passes a resolution for voluntary winding up, if it has done so. This is not affected by the fact that, at a later stage, the court may have made an order for winding up under s.124(5). The company goes into liquidation at the date of the winding up order where there has been no previous resolution for voluntary winding up. (Compare the definition of "commencement of winding-up" in ss.86, 129). See generally Note to s.251.

"Secured creditor", etc.

248. In this Group of Parts, except in so far as the context otherwise requires—

(*a*) "secured creditor", in relation to a company, means a creditor of the company who holds in respect of his debt a security over property of the company, and "unsecured creditor" is to be read accordingly; and

(*b*) "security" means—

(i) in relation to England and Wales, any mortgage, charge, lien or other security, and

(ii) in relation to Scotland, any security (whether heritable or moveable), any floating charge and any right of lien or preference and any right of retention (other than a right of compensation or set off).

General Note

See Note to s.251.

"Connected" with a company

249. For the purposes of any provision in this Group of Parts, a person is connected with a company if—

(*a*) he is a director or shadow director of the company or an associate of such a director or shadow director, or

(*b*) he is an associate of the company;

and "associate" has the meaning given by section 435 in Part XVIII of this Act.

DEFINITION
"director", "shadow director": s.741, C.A. 1985, s.251.

GENERAL NOTE
See Note to s.251.

"Member" of a company

250. For the purposes of any provision in this Group of Parts, a person who is not a member of a company but to whom shares in the company have been transferred, or transmitted by operation of law, is to be regarded as a member of the company, and references to a member or members are to be read accordingly.

GENERAL NOTE
This section gives an extended meaning to "member" of a company. For the purposes of the First Group of Parts, transferees and persons taking by operation of law are members although their names may not have been entered on the Register of Members. See Note to s.251.

Expressions used generally

251. In this Group of Parts, except in so far as the context otherwise requires—

"administrative receiver" means—

(*a*) an administrative receiver as defined by section 29(2) in Chapter I of Part III, or

(*b*) a receiver appointed under section 51 in Chapter II of that Part in a case where the whole (or substantially the whole) of the company's property is attached by the floating charge;

"business day" means any day other than a Saturday, a Sunday, Christmas Day, Good Friday or a day which is a bank holiday in any part of Great Britain;

"chattel leasing agreement" means an agreement for the bailment or, in Scotland, the hiring of goods which is capable of subsisting for more than 3 months;

"contributory" has the meaning given by section 79;

"director" includes any person occupying the position of director, by whatever name called;

"floating charge" means a charge which, as created, was a floating charge and includes a floating charge within section 462 of the Companies Act (Scottish floating charges);

"office copy", in relation to Scotland, means a copy certified by the clerk of court;

"the official rate", in relation to interest, means the rate payable under section 189(4);

"prescribed" means prescribed by the rules;

"receiver", in the expression "receiver or manager", does not include a receiver appointed under section 51 in Chapter II of Part III;

"retention of title agreement" means an agreement for the sale of goods to a company, being an agreement—

(*a*) which does not constitute a charge on the goods, but

(*b*) under which, if the seller is not paid and the company is wound up, the seller will have priority over all other creditors of the company as respects the goods or any property representing the goods;

"the rules" means rules under section 411 in Part XV; and

"shadow director", in relation to a company, means a person in accordance with whose directions or instructions the directors of the company are accustomed to act (but so that a person is not deemed a shadow director by reason only that the directors act on advice given by him in a professional capacity);

and any expression for whose interpretation provision is made by Part XXVI of the Companies Act, other than an expression defined above in this section, is to be construed in accordance with that provision.

GENERAL NOTE

Ss.247–251 define the meaning of terms and expressions for the purposes of the First Group of Parts. Ss.247, 248 and 251 apply "except in so far as the context otherwise provides". In relation to Chapter II (Receivers (Scotland)) further definitions are contained in s.70. Construction of terms in the First Group of Parts may also be affected by ss.435 (associate) and 436 (which applies to expressions used generally in the Act). The scope of s.251 as a definition provision is enlarged by the incorporation into it of most of the definitions contained in Pt. XXVI, C.A. 1985.

Other definition sections which do not however relate to the First Group of Parts are ss.381–385 (Second Group of Parts: Individual Insolvency, Bankruptcy).

THE SECOND GROUP OF PARTS

INSOLVENCY OF INDIVIDUALS; BANKRUPTCY

GENERAL NOTE

None of the provisions of this group of Parts apply in relation to Scotland: s.440(2)(*d*). For individual insolvency in Scotland see the Bankruptcy (Scotland) Act 1985.

TRANSITIONAL PROVISIONS

Sched. 11, paras. 10–19.

PART VIII

INDIVIDUAL VOLUNTARY ARRANGEMENTS

Moratorium for insolvent debtor

Interim order of court

252.—(1) In the circumstances specified below, the court may in the case of a debtor (being an individual) make an interim order under this section.

(2) An interim order has the effect that, during the period for which it is in force—

(*a*) no bankruptcy petition relating to the debtor may be presented or proceeded with, and

(*b*) no other proceedings, and no execution or other legal process, may be commenced or continued against the debtor or his property except with the leave of the court.

DEFINITIONS

"bankruptcy petition": s.381(3).
"property": s.436.
"the debtor": s.385(1).

GENERAL NOTE

This section, which is derived from s.112(1) and (3) of the 1985 Act, makes provision for an interim order to be made where an individual intends to make a voluntary arrangement with his creditors. The purpose of the interim order is to allow time for the formulation of proposals, and hence the main effects of the order, as expressed in subs. (2), are that during the period for which the order is in force no bankruptcy petition relating to the debtor may be presented or proceeded with, and no other proceedings or execution or other legal process may be commenced or continued against the debtor's person or property except with the leave of the court. The moratorium thus imposed is of very considerable significance, and it has been necessary to provide safeguards against the possible misuse of the facility for making an application for an interim order as a means of delaying creditors' pursuit of their legitimate remedies, including bankruptcy proceedings. The court is therefore clothed by s.255(2) with discretionary powers as to the granting of an interim order in response to an application, while s.255(1) establishes several preconditions to the court's being at liberty to exercise the discretion in a positive way through the making of the order sought. Under s.255(1) the court cannot make an interim order unless satisfied as to the debtor's *bona fides* in making the application; that he has not given previous indication of a propensity to utilise the procedure as a delaying tactic through the making of a similar application within the previous twelve months; and that independent professional endorsement of the application is evidenced by the fact that a duly qualified insolvency practitioner has signified his willingness to act in relation to the debtor's proposal.

Application for interim order

253.—(1) Application to the court for an interim order may be made where the debtor intends to make a proposal to his creditors for a composition in satisfaction of his debts or a scheme of arrangement of his affairs (from here on referred to, in either case, as a "voluntary arrangement").

(2) The proposal must provide for some person ("the nominee") to act in relation to the voluntary arrangement either as trustee or otherwise for the purpose of supervising its implementation.

(3) Subject as follows, the application may be made—

(*a*) if the debtor is an undischarged bankrupt, by the debtor, the trustee of his estate, or the official receiver, and

(*b*) in any other case, by the debtor.

(4) An application shall not be made under subsection (3)(*a*) unless the debtor has given notice of his proposal (that is, the proposal to his creditors for a voluntary arrangement) to the official receiver and, if there is one, the trustee of his estate.

(5) An application shall not be made while a bankruptcy petition presented by the debtor is pending, if the court has, under section 273 below, appointed an insolvency practitioner to inquire into the debtor's affairs and report.

Definitions

"bankrupt": s.381(1).
"bankruptcy petition": s.381(3).
"estate": ss.283, 385(1).
"interim order": s.252.
"property": s.436.
"proposal for a composition or scheme of arrangement": subss. (1), (2).
"the court": ss.373, 385(1).
"the debtor": s.385(1).
"the nominee": subs. (2).
"the official receiver": s.399(1).
"voluntary arrangement": subs. (1).

General Note

This section is derived from s.110 of the 1985 Act, together with subss. (1)–(3), inclusive of s.111 of that Act. Subss. (1) and (2) indicate the scope of application of the provisions contained in Pt. VIII, concerning voluntary arrangements between a debtor and his creditors. The meanings borne by the terms "proposals" and "nominee" within this Chapter are also explained. The new procedure for voluntary arrangements, for which this Part makes provision, is additional to that for which provision is made by the Deeds of Arrangement Act 1914. Some sections of that Act are repealed by Pt. III of Sched. 10 to the 1985 Act, but most parts have been left unrepealed, contrary to the recommendations of the *Cork Report* (para. 366), Chaps. 5–7 of which contain extensive proposals for a new range of procedures and remedies as alternatives to bankruptcy or winding up. The Government consistently gave utterance to their belief that the Deeds of Arrangement Act, which has virtually ceased to be used in recent years, could undergo a revival in use as a consequence of the other changes in personal insolvency law contained in the Act (*cf.* H.C. Standing Committee E, June 13, 1985, col. 339).

The new procedure for voluntary arrangements replaces the two types of procedure formerly available under the now-repealed provisions of ss.16 and 21 of the Bankruptcy Act 1914. The new voluntary arrangement procedure is available to any debtor, whether or not he is a bankrupt, provided that he can satisfy the criteria contained in s.255(1). Where the debtor is an undischarged bankrupt subs. (3)(*a*) authorises the making of an application for an interim order, pending consideration of the proposal, to be made by the bankrupt himself or by the trustee of his estate or by the official receiver. To ensure that proper notice is given to those responsible for the administration of a bankrupt's estate, subs. (4) prohibits the making of an application for an interim order until notice thereof has been given to the Official Receiver and to the trustee in bankruptcy, if any. The latter officials are then able to report to the court any relevant facts or circumstances which should be taken into consideration in deciding whether to approve the debtor's application.

Subs. (5)

This ensures a proper interaction between the provisions concerned with the making of an application under this Part with a view to concluding a voluntary arrangement, and those governing the determination of a bankruptcy petition already presented by the debtor himself under s.272. Under the circumstances specified in s.27(1), the court at the hearing of a debtor's petition must postpone a final determination until it has obtained a report based on an inquiry into the debtor's affairs, including investigation as to whether the debtor is willing to make a proposal for a composition or scheme under Part VIII. Where a person has been appointed under s.273(2) to inquire into the debtor's affairs and to report, the court may make an interim order under s.252 by virtue of the authorisation conferred by s.274(3)(*a*). Therefore, the fact that an application for an interim order under the present section cannot be made by a debtor whose own bankruptcy petition is for the time being pending before the court does not prevent the making of such an interim order by the court itself, acting upon its own initiative in the exercise of the power conferred by ss.252 and 274(3).

Effect of application

254.—(1) At any time when an application under section 253 for an interim order is pending, the court may stay any action, execution or other legal process against the property or person of the debtor.

(2) Any court in which proceedings are pending against an individual may, on proof that an application under that section has been made in respect of that individual, either stay the proceedings or allow them to continue on such terms as it thinks fit.

Definitions

"bankruptcy petition": s.381(3).
"interim order": s.252.
"property": s.436.
"the court": ss.373, 385(1).
"the debtor": s.385(1).

General Note

This section corresponds to subss. (4) and (5) of s.111 of the 1985 Act.

Subs. (1)

This introduces a discretionary power for the court to effect a moratorium with respect to legal proceedings and enforcement processes in favour of a debtor on whose behalf an application under this section is pending.

Subs. (2)

This is a complementary power to that contained in subs. (4), and enables the court before which proceedings are pending against a debtor to adopt whatever course of action it thinks fit, pending the conclusion of the procedure for effecting a voluntary arrangement.

Thus, regardless of whether a stay of action or other process is imposed by the court to which application has been made for an interim order, any other court in which proceedings are pending against the debtor may take an independent initiative under this subsection with regard to the matters over which it is exercising jurisdiction.

Cases in which interim order can be made

255.—(1) The court shall not make an interim order on an application under section 253 unless it is satisfied—

(*a*) that the debtor intends to make such a proposal as is mentioned in that section;

(*b*) that on the day of the making of the application the debtor was an undischarged bankrupt or was able to petition for his own bankruptcy;

(*c*) that no previous application has been made by the debtor for an interim order in the period of 12 months ending with that day; and

(*d*) that the nominee under the debtor's proposal to his creditors is a person who is for the time being qualified to act as an insolvency practitioner in relation to the debtor, and is willing to act in relation to the proposal.

(2) The court may make an order if it thinks that it would be appropriate to do so for the purpose of facilitating the consideration and implementation of the debtor's proposal.

(3) Where the debtor is an undischarged bankrupt, the interim order may contain provision as to the conduct of the bankruptcy, and the administration of the bankrupt's estate, during the period for which the order is in force.

(4) Subject as follows, the provision contained in an interim order by virtue of subsection (3) may include provision staying proceedings in the bankruptcy or modifying any provision in this Group of Parts, and any provision of the rules in their application to the debtor's bankruptcy.

(5) An interim order shall not, in relation to a bankrupt, make provision relaxing or removing any of the requirements of provisions in this Group of Parts, or of the rules, unless the court is satisfied that that provision is unlikely to result in any significant diminution in, or in the value of, the debtor's estate for the purposes of the bankruptcy.

(6) Subject to the following provisions of this Part, an interim order made on an application under section 253 ceases to have effect at the end of the period of 14 days beginning with the day after the making of the order.

DEFINITIONS

"bankrupt": s.381(1).
"bankruptcy petition": s.381(3).
"estate": s.385(1).
"interim order": s.252.
"person qualified to act as an insolvency practitioner": s.390.
"property": s.436.
"proposal": s.253(1), (2).
"the court": ss.373, 385(1).
"the debtor": s.385(1).
"the nominee": s.253(2).
"the rules": ss.384, 412.
"to act as an insolvency practitioner in relation to an individual": s.388(2), (3).

GENERAL NOTE

This section comprises the provisions formerly contained in subss. (1), (2), and (4)–(7) inclusive, of s.112 of the 1985 Act.

Subs. (1)(b)

This requirement in relation to a debtor's eligibility to apply for an interim order has the effect of restricting the availability of this form of voluntary arrangement to those cases where the debtor is already either an undischarged bankrupt or in a state of insolvency. S.272(1) provides that a debtor's petition may be presented to the court only on the ground that the debtor is unable to pay his debts. Therefore if it can be shown that a debtor is able to pay his debts which are currently due, he will be unable to obtain an interim order under this section, and hence will be deprived of the possibility of thereby postponing the need to meet his obligations.

Subss. (4) and (5)

These provisions further ensure that the staying of bankruptcy proceedings in appropriate cases during the currency of an interim order does not operate at the expense of the preservation of the bankrupt's estate for the benefit of his creditors collectively. The court's power to include a staying provision in its interim order is a discretionary one, and the discretion is controlled by the terms of subs. (5) which have regard to the need to ensure that the creditor's ultimate expectations under the bankruptcy administration are not significantly jeopardised.

Subs. (6)

The period of 14 days may be extended by the court on the application of the nominee, pursuant to s.256(4).

Nominee's report on debtor's proposal

256.—(1) Where an interim order has been made on an application under section 253, the nominee shall, before the order ceases to have effect, submit a report to the court stating—

(*a*) whether, in his opinion, a meeting of the debtor's creditors should be summoned to consider the debtor's proposal, and

(*b*) if in his opinion such a meeting should be summoned, the date on which, and time and place at which, he proposes the meeting should be held.

(2) For the purpose of enabling the nominee to prepare his report the debtor shall submit to the nominee—

(*a*) a document setting out the terms of the voluntary arrangement which the debtor is proposing, and

(*b*) a statement of his affairs containing—

(i) such particulars of his creditors and of his debts and other liabilities and of his assets as may be prescribed, and

(ii) such other information as may be prescribed.

(3) The court may, on an application made by the debtor in a case where the nominee has failed to submit the report required by this section, do one or both of the following, namely—

(*a*) direct that the nominee shall be replaced as such by another person qualified to act as an insolvency practitioner in relation to the debtor;

(*b*) direct that the interim order shall continue, or (if it has ceased to have effect) be renewed, for such further period as the court may specify in the direction.

(4) The court may, on the application of the nominee, extend the period for which the interim order has effect so as to enable the nominee to have more time to prepare his report.

(5) If the court is satisfied on receiving the nominee's report that a meeting of the debtor's creditors should be summoned to consider the debtor's proposal, the court shall direct that the period for which the interim order has effect shall be extended, for such further period as it may specify in the direction, for the purpose of enabling the debtor's proposal to be considered by his creditors in accordance with the following provisions of this Part.

(6) The court may discharge the interim order if it is satisfied, on the application of the nominee—

(*a*) that the debtor has failed to comply with his obligations under subsection (2), or

(*b*) that for any other reason it would be inappropriate for a meeting of the debtor's creditors to be summoned to consider the debtor's proposal.

DEFINITIONS

"affairs": s.385(2).
"creditor": s.383(1).
"debt": ss.382(3), 385(1).
"interim order": s.252.
"liability": s.382(4).
"person qualified to act as an insolvency practitioner": s.390.
"prescribed": s.384(1).
"proposal": s.353(1), (2).
"the court": ss.373, 385(1).
"the debtor": s.385(1).
"the nominee": s.253(2).
"to act as an insolvency practitioner in relation to an individual": s.388(2), (3).

GENERAL NOTE

This section specifies what steps are to be taken by a person as the nominee under a proposal which is intended to be made by a debtor by whom, or on behalf of whom, an application has been made under s.253 resulting in the making of an interim order under s.252. Unless the nominee successfully applies to the court under subs. (4) for an extension of the period for which the interim order has effect, the consequence of s.255(6) is that the order will lapse at the end of 14 days from the date on which it was made. This section corresponds to s.113 of the 1985 Act.

Subs. (1)

This provision, which is analogous to that of s.2(2) relating to voluntary arrangements made by companies, requires the nominee to form a professional judgment of the terms of the proposal which the debtor is intending to put to his creditors. This opinion must be based upon an appraisal of the debtor's affairs and circumstances derived from information which the debtor himself must supply. This information is supplied in the form of a statement of affairs which the debtor is obliged to furnish pursuant to the provisions of subs. (2)(*b*). Only if the nominee concludes that it would be worthwhile to put the debtor's proposals to a meeting of creditors, and if he duly reports to the court in those terms, will the court give the necessary direction under subs. (5), which has the effect of prolonging the duration of the interim order pending the convening of a creditors' meeting under s.257.

Subs. (3)

This provides for the possibility that the nominee may fail to submit his report under subs. (1) within the limited time allowed. The debtor may take the initiative of applying to the court under this subsection with a view to having the original nominee replaced by some other, and to obtain an extension or renewal of the interim order to allow the nominee more time in which to prepare and submit his report.

Subs. (4)

This allows the nominee himself to apply for an extension of the interim order to allow him more time in which to prepare and submit his report.

Subs. (6)

This enables the court to discharge the interim order ahead of the time at which it would otherwise cease to have effect by virtue of s.255(6). The reference to the debtor's obligation under subs. (2) lends emphasis to the debtor's duty to co-operate readily and willingly with the nominee, while the alternative ground offered by para. (*b*) indicates that the nominee must act with professional integrity and independence of judgment in deciding whether or not it would be appropriate for a meeting of creditors to be summoned.

Summoning of creditors' meeting

257.—(1) Where it has been reported to the court under section 256 that a meeting of the debtor's creditors should be summoned, the nominee (or his replacement under section 256(3)(*a*)) shall, unless the court otherwise directs, summon that meeting for the time, date and place proposed in his report.

(2) The persons to be summoned to the meeting are every creditor of the debtor of whose claim and address the person summoning the meeting is aware.

(3) For this purpose the creditors of a debtor who is an undischarged bankrupt include—

(*a*) every person who is a creditor of the bankrupt in respect of a bankruptcy debt, and

(*b*) every person who would be such a creditor if the bankruptcy had commenced on the day on which notice of the meeting is given.

Definitions

"bankrupt": s.381(1).
"bankruptcy debt": s.382.
"creditor": s.383.
"debt": ss.382(3), 385(1).
"interim order": s.252.
"the court": ss.373, 385(1).
"the debtor": s.385(1).

General Note

This section governs the next stage following the making of a report to the court by a person responsible for doing so under s.256 or s.274, advocating the summoning of a meeting of creditors under this section. Normally the person who has submitted the report is also responsible for summoning the meeting, but the court has the power to direct otherwise. This section corresponds to s.114 of the 1985 Act.

Subs. (2)

This indicates that the summoning of creditors to the meeting is to be by personal communication to each creditor of whose claim and address the convenor of the meeting is aware. This information should be established from the debtor's statement of affairs submitted under s.256(2)(*b*). The section itself imposes no requirement that the summoning of the meeting is to be publicly advertised (see also H.C. Standing Committee E, June 13, 1985, col. 344).

Subs. (3)

Every person who would be such a creditor if the bankruptcy had commenced on the day on which notice of the meeting is given

This subsection indicates which persons qualify as "creditors" for the purpose of being entitled to be summoned to a meeting under this section. In the case of a debtor who is an undischarged bankrupt, the eligible creditors include not only those who are creditors in the existing bankruptcy but also those who have become creditors of the bankrupt since the commencement of his existing bankruptcy, and who therefore would not be qualified to lodge proof in that administration. These post-adjudication creditors are brought into the fold for the purposes of an arrangement under this Part by having regard to the position they would have occupied if the commencement of the bankruptcy had been on the date when notice of the meeting is given, rather than at the date on which the bankruptcy order was made.

Consideration and implementation of debtor's proposal

Decisions of creditors' meeting

258.—(1) A creditors' meeting summoned under section 257 shall decide whether to approve the proposed voluntary arrangement.

(2) The meeting may approve the proposed voluntary arrangement with modifications, but shall not do so unless the debtor consents to each modification.

(3) The modifications subject to which the proposed voluntary arrangement may be approved may include one conferring the functions proposed to be conferred on the nominee on another person qualified to act as an insolvency practitioner in relation to the debtor.

But they shall not include any modification by virtue of which the proposal ceases to be a proposal such as is mentioned in section 253.

(4) The meeting shall not approve any proposal or modification which affects the right of a secured creditor of the debtor to enforce his security, except with the concurrence of the creditor concerned.

(5) Subject as follows, the meeting shall not approve any proposal or modification under which—

(*a*) any preferential debt of the debtor is to be paid otherwise than in priority to such of his debts as are not preferential debts, or

(*b*) a preferential creditor of the debtor is to be paid an amount in respect of a preferential debt that bears to that debt a smaller proportion than is borne to another preferential debt by the amount that is to be paid in respect of that other debt.

However, the meeting may approve such a proposal or modification with the concurrence of the preferential creditor concerned.

(6) Subject as above, the meeting shall be conducted in accordance with the rules.

(7) In this section "preferential debt" has the meaning given by section 386 in Part XII; and "preferential creditor" is to be construed accordingly.

DEFINITIONS

"bankrupt": s.381(1).
"creditor": s.383(1).
"interim order": s.252.
"modifications": s.436.
"person qualified to act as an insolvency practitioner": s.390.
"preferential debt", "preferential creditor": subs. (7), s.386; Sched. 6.
"prescribed": s.384(1).
"proposal": s.253(1), (2).
"secured creditor", "security": s.383.
"the court": ss.373, 385(1).
"the debtor": s.385(1).
"the nominee": s.253(2).
"the rules": ss.384, 412.
"to act as an insolvency practitioner in relation to an individual": s.388(2), (3).
"voluntary arrangement": s.253(1).

GENERAL NOTE

This section contains the main provisions which are applicable where a creditors' meeting is convened under s.257 for the purpose of considering a proposal for a composition or scheme of arrangement made by a debtor. The section corresponds to subss. (1) to (6) inclusive, and subs. (9), of s.115 of the 1985 Act.

Subs. (1)

Provision will be made in the rules, which are referred to in subs. (6), to deal with the conduct of the meeting and with matters of procedure. The rules will specify that the creditors' decision whether to approve the debtor's proposals shall be taken on the basis of a majority in value only of the creditors voting in person or by proxy at the meeting.

Subs. (2)

This provision allowing the meeting to approve the debtor's proposal in modified form, provided that the debtor assents to every modification so made, is a counterpart to the provisions in ss.4(1), (2) and 24(1), (2) which respectively apply to voluntary arrangements by companies and to an administrator's proposals for achieving the purposes of an administration order.

Subs. (3)

This enables the creditors at their meeting to approve the substitution of some other, suitably qualified, person in place of the original nominee. If such a substitution is effected the person so appointed will in due course become supervisor of the composition or scheme, within the meaning of s.263(2), and from then onwards will displace the original nominee with regard to the ensuing responsibilities imposed by this Part.

The proviso to this subsection imposes a necessary limitation upon the competence of the creditors' meeting to approve modifications to the debtor's original proposals, even with the concurrence of the debtor himself. Any modification whose effect is such that the proposal overall is no longer compatible with the basic concept laid down by s.253 is invalid and ineffectual. It would be open to any person from among those listed in s.262(2) to apply to the court under that section, challenging the validity of what has taken place.

Subss. (4), (5)

These provisions safeguard the positions of secured and preferential creditors respectively, so that it is not possible for a composition or scheme to be validly approved which adversely affects their rights and interest, for example by depriving any debt of the priority which it would enjoy in bankruptcy, unless this happens with the concurrence of the creditor affected (*cf.* also s.4(3), (4)). Any secured or preferential creditor whose rights under either of these subsections are improperly infringed may utilise the procedure for challenging the meeting's decision under s.262.

Report of decisions to court

259.—(1) After the conclusion in accordance with the rules of the meeting summoned under section 257, the chairman of the meeting shall report the result of it to the court and, immediately after so reporting, shall give notice of the result of the meeting to such persons as may be prescribed.

(2) If the report is that the meeting has declined (with or without modifications) to approve the debtor's proposal, the court may discharge any interim order which is in force in relation to the debtor.

DEFINITIONS

"interim order": s.252.
"modifications": s.436.
"prescribed": s.384(1).
"proposal": s.253(1), (2).
"the court": ss.373, 385(1).
"the debtor": s.385(1).
"the rules": ss.384, 412.

GENERAL NOTE

This section comprises subss. (7) and (8) of s.115 of the 1985 Act.

Subs. (1)

The rules for the conduct of creditors' meetings convened under s.257 and this section will provide for the appointment of a person to be Chairman of the meeting. In most cases it is likely that a nominee, or anyone whom the court may have appointed in place of the nominee pursuant to s.256(3)(*a*), will act as Chairman of the meeting. The purport of this subsection is that the duty to report the result of the meeting to the court, and to give notice of the result in the prescribed manner, is cast upon whoever served as Chairman at the meeting. If that person was the nominee, and if also the creditors have decided in accordance with s.258(3) to substitute some other person in his place, the immediate functions which are required to be performed under this subsection must nevertheless be performed by the person who served as Chairman of the meeting. The court has no further function to perform in response to the report, unless any qualified person raises a challenge to the decision of the meeting under s.262.

Subs. (2)

This provides for the possibility that the creditors may fail to approve the debtor's proposal, and authorises the court to discharge any interim order which is in force with regard to the debtor, thereby ending the moratorium enjoyed since the order was originally made under s.252.

Effect of approval

260.—(1) This section has effect where the meeting summoned under section 257 approves the proposed voluntary arrangement (with or without modifications).

(2) The approved arrangement—

(*a*) takes effect as if made by the debtor at the meeting, and

(*b*) binds every person who in accordance with the rules had notice of, and was entitled to vote at, the meeting (whether or not he was present or represented at it) as if he were a party to the arrangement.

(3) The Deeds of Arrangement Act 1914 does not apply to the approved voluntary arrangement.

(4) Any interim order in force in relation to the debtor immediately before the end of the period of 28 days beginning with the day on which the report with respect to the creditors' meeting was made to the court under section 259 ceases to have effect at the end of that period.

This subsection applies except to such extent as the court may direct for the purposes of any application under section 262 below.

(5) Where proceedings on a bankruptcy petition have been stayed by an interim order which ceases to have effect under subsection (4), that petition is deemed, unless the court otherwise orders, to have been dismissed.

DEFINITIONS

"bankrupt": s.381(1).
"bankruptcy order": s.381(2).
"bankruptcy petition": s.381(3).
"estate": ss.283, 385(1).
"interim order": s.252.
"modifications": s.436.
"the court": ss.373, 385(1).
"the debtor": s.385(1).
"the rules": ss.384, 412.
"voluntary arrangement": s.253(1).

GENERAL NOTE

This section specifies what are the legal consequences of the approval of a proposed voluntary arrangement by a meeting of creditors summoned under s.257. The principal event is that the approved composition or scheme binds every person who had notice of and was entitled to vote at the meeting, regardless of whether he in fact attended or was represented at it, and regardless of whether he voted for or against the proposal. The only courses of action open to any creditor who is dissatisfied by the terms of the arrangement as approved, or by the manner in which the meeting was conducted, are either to raise a challenge against the meeting's decision under s.262 within the time allowed by subs. (3) of that section, or to present a petition for a bankruptcy order against the debtor under s.264(1)(*c*), subject to the requirements of s.276 being met. This section comprises subss. (1)–(3), (6) and (7) of s.116 of the 1985 Act.

Subs. (3)

The exclusionary words regarding the Deeds of Arrangement Act 1914 ensure that there is no question of any right or duty to register an arrangement which has been approved under s.258 in order for it to become legally effective and binding.

Subs. (4)

This preserves the effects of the moratorium brought about by the making of an interim order under s.252, up until the end of the period of time allowed for bringing a challenge under s.262 to the decision of the creditors' meeting. The court is nevertheless empowered by s.262(6) to prolong the effects of the interim order for a further period of time in the case where a challenge is brought under s.262.

Effect where debtor an undischarged bankrupt

261.—(1) Subject as follows, where the creditors' meeting summoned under section 257 approves the proposed voluntary arrangement (with or without modifications) and the debtor is an undischarged bankrupt, the court may do one or both of the following, namely—

(*a*) annul the bankruptcy order by which he was adjudged bankrupt;

(*b*) give such directions with respect to the conduct of the bankruptcy and the administration of the bankrupt's estate as it thinks appropriate for facilitating the implementation of the approved voluntary arrangement.

(2) The court shall not annul a bankruptcy order under subsection (1)—

(*a*) at any time before the end of the period of 28 days beginning with the day on which the report of the creditors' meeting was made to the court under section 259, or

(*b*) at any time when an application under section 262 below, or an appeal in respect of such an application, is pending or at any time in the period within which such an appeal may be brought.

DEFINITIONS

"bankrupt": s.381(1).
"bankruptcy order": s.381(2).
"creditor": s.383(1).
"modifications": s.436.
"the court": ss.373, 385(1).
"voluntary arrangement": s.253(1).

GENERAL NOTE

This section comprises subss. (4) and (5) of s.116 of the 1985 Act. It makes provision for the case where approval is given by the creditors to a proposal for a voluntary arrangement made by a debtor who has already undergone adjudication.

Subs. (1)

This enables the court at its discretion to deal with any bankruptcy order which may be in force in relation to the debtor in either or both of the ways specified. However, subs. (2) prevents the court from annulling the bankruptcy order until after the elapse of the period of time within which any challenge to the meeting's decision may be brought under s.262 by a party eligible to do so, and until after the final determination of any such challenge as may be brought under that section.

Challenge of meeting's decision

262.—(1) Subject to this section, an application to the court may be made, by any of the persons specified below, on one or both of the following grounds, namely—

(*a*) that a voluntary arrangement approved by a creditors' meeting summoned under section 257 unfairly prejudices the interests of a creditor of the debtor;

(*b*) that there has been some material irregularity at or in relation to such a meeting.

(2) The persons who may apply under this section are—

(*a*) the debtor;

(*b*) a person entitled, in accordance with the rules, to vote at the creditors' meeting;

(*c*) the nominee (or his replacement under section 256(3)(*a*) or 258(3)); and (*d*) if the debtor is an undischarged bankrupt, the trustee of his estate or the official receiver.

(3) An application under this section shall not be made after the end of the period of 28 days beginning with the day on which the report of the creditors' meeting was made to the court under section 259.

(4) Where on an application under this section the court is satisfied as to either of the grounds mentioned in subsection (1), it may do one or both of the following, namely—

(*a*) revoke or suspend any approval given by the meeting;

(*b*) give a direction to any person for the summoning of a further meeting of the debtor's creditors to consider any revised proposal he may make or, in a case falling within subsection (1)(*b*), to reconsider his original proposal.

(5) Where at any time after giving a direction under subsection (4)(*b*) for the summoning of a meeting to consider a revised proposal the court is satisfied that the debtor does not intend to submit such a proposal, the court shall revoke the direction and revoke or suspend any approval given at the previous meeting.

(6) Where the court gives a direction under subsection (4)(*b*), it may also give a direction continuing or, as the case may require, renewing, for such period as may be specified in the direction, the effect in relation to the debtor of any interim order.

(7) In any case where the court, on an application made under this section with respect to a creditors' meeting, gives a direction under subsection (4)(*b*) or revokes or suspends an approval under subsection (4)(*a*) or (5), the court may give such supplemental directions as it thinks fit and, in particular, directions with respect to—

(*a*) things done since the meeting under any voluntary arrangement approved by the meeting, and

(*b*) such things done since the meeting as could not have been done if an interim order had been in force in relation to the debtor when they were done.

(8) Except in pursuance of the preceding provisions of this section, an approval given at a creditors' meeting summoned under section 257 is not invalidated by any irregularity at or in relation to the meeting.

Definitions

"a creditor": s.383(1).
"bankrupt": s.381(1).
"estate": ss.283, 385(1).
"interim order": s.252.
"proposal": s.253(1), (2).
"the court": ss.373, 385(1).
"the debtor": s.385(1).
"the nominee": s.253(2).
"the official receiver": s.399(1).
"the rules": ss.384, 412.
"voluntary arrangement": s.253(1), (2).

General Note

The procedure established under this section represents the sole means of bringing about a judicial scrutiny of either the terms of an approved arrangement, or of the manner in which approval was obtained at the meeting of creditors. Even if there has been irregularity at or in relation to the meeting, subs. (8) makes it clear that this does not *per se* render the creditors' approval invalid. Only if a successful application is made under this section may the result of the meeting be undone, and it is to be noted that subs. (1)(*b*) introduces the requirement that the court be satisfied that the irregularity was a material one. This section corresponds to s.117 of the 1985 Act.

Subs. (1)

Only the grounds specified in this subsection may, jointly or individually, serve as a basis for the exercise of the court's powers under subs. (4).

Subs. (2)

This indicates which persons have standing to invoke the procedure for challenge under this section.

Subs. (3)

This imposes a time limit of 28 days for the bringing of an application under this section. Time begins to run from the day on which the Chairman of the creditors' meeting reports to the court upon the result thereof, as required by s.259(1).

Subs. (4)

This sets out the powers of the court where it is satisfied that the applicant's case has been made out as required by subs. (1). The powers are discretionary, and include the possibility, where a material irregularity has taken place at or in relation to the meeting, that the meeting may be reconvened at the court's discretion by the same or by some other person as convenor to reconsider the original proposal afresh.

Subs. (6)

This enables the court to extend the moratorium consequential upon the making of an interim order under s.252, to allow the extra time required for reconvening the meeting of creditors pursuant to directions given by the court under subs. (4)(*b*).

Subs. (7)

This enables the court to give consequential or supplemental directions upon the principal order or direction which it makes in the exercise of the powers conferred by subss. (4) or (5).

Implementation and supervision of approved voluntary arrangement

263.—(1) This section applies where a voluntary arrangement approved by a creditors' meeting summoned under section 257 has taken effect.

(2) The person who is for the time being carrying out, in relation to the voluntary arrangement, the functions conferred by virtue of the approval on the nominee (or his replacement under section 256(3)(*a*) or 258(3)) shall be known as the supervisor of the voluntary arrangement.

(3) If the debtor, any of his creditors or any other person is dissatisfied by any act, omission or decision of the supervisor, he may apply to the court; and on such an application the court may—

(*a*) confirm, reverse or modify any act or decision of the supervisor,
(*b*) give him directions, or
(*c*) make such other order as it thinks fit.

(4) The supervisor may apply to the court for directions in relation to any particular matter arising under the voluntary arrangement.

(5) The court may, whenever—

(*a*) it is expedient to appoint a person to carry out the functions of the supervisor, and
(*b*) it is inexpedient, difficult or impracticable for an appointment to be made without the assistance of the court,

make an order appointing a person who is qualified to act as an insolvency practitioner in relation to the debtor, either in substitution for the existing supervisor or to fill a vacancy.

This is without prejudice to section 41(2) of the Trustee Act 1925 (power of court to appoint trustees of deeds of arrangement).

(6) The power conferred by subsection (5) is exercisable so as to increase the number of persons exercising the functions of the supervisor or, where there is more than one person exercising those functions, so as to replace one or more of those persons.

DEFINITIONS

"a creditor": s.383(1).
"person qualified to act as an insolvency practitioner": s.390.
"the court": ss.373, 385(1).
"the debtor": s.385(1).
"the nominee": s.253(2).
"the supervisor of the composition or scheme": subs. (2).
"to act as an insolvency practitioner in relation to an individual": s.388(2), (3).
"voluntary arrangement": s.253(1), (2).

GENERAL NOTE

This section governs the implementation of an approved composition or scheme which has taken effect under s.260. The person responsible for carrying out this task is known as the supervisor, and will be either the original nominee, if he is still acting, or any person who may have been substituted in place of the original nominee, either by the court under s.256(3)(*a*) or by the meeting of creditors under s.258(3). Under subs. (3) the court has both jurisdiction to entertain an application from the debtor, or any of the creditors, or any other person who is dissatisfied by the supervisor's performance of his functions, and overriding powers in relation to the implementation of the arrangement. The supervisor may also seek directions from the court under subs. (4) if need arises. Provision is also made under subss. (5) and (6) for replacement of the supervisor by some other duly qualified person. This power may be utilised to fill any vacancy which may arise, and also to increase the number of persons exercising the functions of the supervisor. This section corresponds to s.118 of the 1985 Act.

PART IX

BANKRUPTCY

CHAPTER I

BANKRUPTCY PETITIONS; BANKRUPTCY ORDERS

Preliminary

Who may present a bankruptcy petition

264.—(1) A petition for a bankruptcy order to be made against an individual may be presented to the court in accordance with the following provisions of this Part—

(*a*) by one of the individual's creditors or jointly by more than one of them,
(*b*) by the individual himself,
(*c*) by the supervisor of, or any person (other than the individual) who is for the time being bound by, a voluntary arrangement proposed by the individual and approved under Part VIII, or
(*d*) where a criminal bankruptcy order has been made against the individual, by the Official Petitioner or by any person specified in the order in pursuance of section 39(3)(*b*) of the Powers of Criminal Courts Act 1973.

(2) Subject to those provisions, the court may make a bankruptcy order on any such petition.

DEFINITIONS

"bankruptcy order": s.381(2).
"creditor": s.383(1).
"criminal bankruptcy order": s.385(1); Powers of Criminal Courts Act 1973, s.39(1).
"person bound by a composition or scheme": s.260(1)(*b*).
"the court": ss.373, 385(1).

"the Official Petitioner": s.402; Powers of Criminal Courts Act 1973, s.41(1).
"the supervisor of a voluntary arrangement": s.263(2).

GENERAL NOTE

This provision is of great importance. It specifies the persons who may, singly or jointly, present a petition for a bankruptcy order to be made against an individual. The section corresponds to s.119(1) of the 1985 Act.

Subs. (1)(a)

Creditors' petitions are governed by the provisions of ss.267–271 inclusive.

Subs. (1)(b)

Debtors' petitions are governed by the provisions of ss.272–275 inclusive.

Subs. (1)(c)

The court cannot make a bankruptcy order on a petition under this heading unless at least one of the conditions specified in s.276(1) is met.

Subs. (1)(d)

This maintains the operation of the criminal bankruptcy procedure at present established under ss.39–41 of the Powers of Criminal Courts Act 1973, together with Sched. 2 to that Act. However, it is possible that the procedure will be superseded by new legislation aimed at giving courts more effective powers to deprive convicted offenders of the proceeds of their crimes. Further provisions applicable in cases where a petition is based on a criminal bankruptcy order are contained in s.277. See also s.266(4).

Subs. (2)

The court may make a bankruptcy order on any such petition

This indicates the discretionary nature of the court's power to make a bankruptcy order, even where the prescribed legal requirements for the making of an order are fully met. Additional, broad discretionary powers to dismiss a petition under certain circumstances are conferred by s.266(3) and by s.271(3).

Conditions to be satisfied in respect of debtor

265.—(1) A bankruptcy petition shall not be presented to the court under section 264(1)(*a*) or (*b*) unless the debtor—

(*a*) is domiciled in England and Wales,

(*b*) is personally present in England and Wales on the day on which the petition is presented, or

(*c*) at any time in the period of 3 years ending with that day—

(i) has been ordinarily resident, or has had a place of residence, in England and Wales, or

(ii) has carried on business in England and Wales.

(2) The reference in subsection (1)(*c*) to an individual carrying on business includes—

(*a*) the carrying on of business by a firm or partnership of which the individual is a member, and

(*b*) the carrying on of business by an agent or manager for the individual or for such a firm or partnership.

DEFINITIONS

"bankruptcy petition": s.381(3).
"business": s.436.
"the court": ss.373, 385(1).
"the debtor": s.385(1).

GENERAL NOTE

This section, comprising subss. (2) and (3) of s.119 of the 1985 Act, specifies five alternative requirements with regard to the debtor's forensic connections with the territory of England and Wales, one of which at least must be satisfied if the court in England and Wales is to be capable of exercising jurisdiction in bankruptcy with respect of that individual.

The section contains vestigial remains of the former provisions of s.4 of the Bankruptcy Act 1914, now repealed. However, many aspects of the previous law and procedure regarding the commencement of bankruptcy proceedings have been completely eliminated, in fulfilment of many of the recommendations contained in Chaps. 10 and 11 of the *Cork Report.* In particular the whole concept of the act of bankruptcy has been abolished (*cf. Cork Report,* paras. 529, 530; *White Paper* para. 18(iv)), as has the preliminary species of order formerly known as a receiving order. However, as Chap. 12 of the *White Paper* indicated, the Government did not accept the entirely new framework of insolvency proceedings for which the *Cork Report* made elaborate proposals, and which would have reserved bankruptcy proper for use only in the more serious cases where the stigma and notoriety attaching to bankruptcy could be said to be appropriate. Under Pt. IX of the Act, the bankruptcy order remains the principal species of insolvency proceeding, although the new voluntary procedure under Pt. VIII is intended to provide an acceptable alternative to bankruptcy for all the parties concerned.

Subs. (1)

This somewhat resembles the former s.4(1)(*d*) of the Bankruptcy Act 1914, but there are significant changes in the jurisdictional criteria which have been embodied in the new law. The much-criticised domiciliary connecting factor has been retained as a useful basis on which to ensure that an absconding debtor may remain amenable to the bankruptcy jurisdiction of our courts for a considerable time after leaving these shores. The grounds stated in paras. (*a*)–(*c*) represent alternative tests, and it is enough to satisfy any one of them. The ground stated in para. (*b*), whereby the court's jurisdiction is established if the debtor was personally present in England and Wales on the day on which the petition is presented, is potentially capable of being used by a foreign creditor against a foreign debtor who merely happens to be in this country temporarily. It was assumed, perhaps too readily, on behalf of the Government that English courts would not entertain a petition in such cases (H.C. Standing Committee E, June 13, 1985, col. 351), but although the court could dismiss a petition under such circumstances at its discretion, it is under no obligation to do so: *cf. Re Pascal* (1876) 1 Ch.D. 509. On the other hand, this ground of jurisdiction could readily be used to enable a domestic creditor to present a petition against a foreign debtor who makes successive visits to this country and incurs credit without paying his debts.

The three grounds contained in para. (*c*), which utilise a residential or "doing of business" basis of jurisdiction, read in conjunction with subs. (2), are comparable to the grounds included in s.4(1)(*d*) of the Bankruptcy Act 1914, but with the important difference that the specified period, within which any such contact suffices to ground the jurisdiction of the court, is now any time within three years ending with the day a petition is presented. This is a considerable enlargement over the former period of one year, and is designed to prevent persons from too easily escaping from the jurisdiction of the courts by departing abroad before effective action can be taken against them. One example would be directors who have been implicated in wrongful trading by a company some considerable time before the eventual liquidation of the company and before their transgressions come to light.

Has carried on business

This ground can operate in association with the rule, established in *Theophile* v. *Solicitor General* [1950] A.C. 186, that a person who has once carried on business here does not cease to do so until he has discharged all trading debts and liabilities, including taxes, relating to that activity. By means of this useful decision of the House of Lords, a debtor who apparently ceased to trade more than three years before the date of presentation of the petition may yet be brought within the ambit of para. (*c*)(ii).

Other preliminary conditions

266.—(1) Where a bankruptcy petition relating to an individual is presented by a person who is entitled to present a petition under two or more paragraphs of section 264(1), the petition is to be treated for the purposes of this Part as a petition under such one of those paragraphs as may be specified in the petition.

(2) A bankruptcy petition shall not be withdrawn without the leave of the court.

(3) The court has a general power, if it appears to it appropriate to do so on the grounds that there has been a contravention of the rules or for any other reason, to dismiss a bankruptcy petition or to stay proceedings on such a petition; and, where it stays proceedings on a petition, it may do so on such terms and conditions as it thinks fit.

(4) Without prejudice to subsection (3), where a petition under section 264(1)(*a*), (*b*) or (*c*) in respect of an individual is pending at a time when a criminal bankruptcy order is made against him, or is presented after such an order has been so made, the court may on the application of the Official Petitioner dismiss the petition if it appears to it appropriate to do so.

DEFINITIONS

"bankruptcy petition": s.381(3).
"criminal bankruptcy order": s.385(1); Powers of Criminal Courts Act 1973, s.39(1).
"the court": ss.373, 385(1).
"the Official Petitioner": s.402; Powers of Criminal Courts Act 1973, s.41(1).
"the rules": ss.384, 412.

GENERAL NOTE

This section comprises subss. (4)–(7) of s.119 of the 1985 Act.

Subs. (2)

This restates the rule formerly contained in s.5(7) of the Bankruptcy Act 1914 (repealed) and is a safeguard against misuse of the legal machinery of bankruptcy. This provision applies to petitions presented by a creditor or by a debtor, and hence a provision specifically concerned with the withdrawal of a debtor's petition, which was originally included in the Bill within the clause now embodied as s.272 of this Act, was deleted in Committee (H.C. Standing Committee E, June 13, 1985, col. 360).

Creditor's petition

Grounds of creditor's petition

267.—(1) A creditor's petition must be in respect of one or more debts owed by the debtor, and the petitioning creditor or each of the petitioning creditors must be a person to whom the debt or (as the case may be) at least one of the debts is owed.

(2) Subject to the next three sections, a creditor's petition may be presented to the court in respect of a debt or debts only if, at the time the petition is presented—

(*a*) the amount of the debt, or the aggregate amount of the debts, is equal to or exceeds the bankruptcy level,
(*b*) the debt, or each of the debts, is for a liquidated sum payable to the petitioning creditor, or one or more of the petitioning creditors, either immediately or at some certain, future time, and is unsecured,
(*c*) the debt, or each of the debts, is a debt which the debtor appears either to be unable to pay or to have no reasonable prospect of being able to pay, and
(*d*) there is no outstanding application to set aside a statutory demand served (under section 268 below) in respect of the debt or any of the debts.

(3) A debt is not to be regarded for the purposes of subsection (2) as a debt for a liquidated sum by reason only that the amount of the debt is specified in a criminal bankruptcy order.

(4) "The bankruptcy level" is £750; but the Secretary of State may by order in a statutory instrument substitute any amount specified in the order for that amount or (as the case may be) for the amount which by

virtue of such an order is for the time being the amount of the bankruptcy level.

(5) An order shall not be made under subsection (4) unless a draft of it has been laid before, and approved by a resolution of, each House of Parliament.

DEFINITIONS

"a creditor", "creditor's petition": ss.264(1)(*a*), 385(1).
"criminal bankruptcy order": s.385(1); Powers of Criminal Courts Act 1973, s.39(1).
"debt": ss.382(3), 385(1).
"secured", "unsecured": ss.383, 385(1).
"statutory demand": s.268(1)(*a*).
"the bankruptcy level": subs. (4).
"the court": ss.373, 385(1).
"the debtor": s.385(1).

TRANSITIONAL PROVISIONS

Sched. 11, paras. 10–12.

GENERAL NOTE

This section, to be read in conjunction with ss.268–270, sets out the conditions which must be satisfied before a creditor or creditors can present a bankruptcy petition against a debtor. In many respects the section restates the existing law formerly contained in parts of ss.4 and 5 of the Bankruptcy Act 1914 (repealed), but the drafting is considerably modified and many purely procedural matters are removed to the rules.

The main innovation in this section is to be found in subs. (2)(*c*) and (*d*), and in the subsequent provisions of this and the next following section dependent thereto. This introduces, in place of the former requirements of the Bankruptcy Act relating to acts of bankruptcy, the new single concept of the debtor's apparent inability to pay the debt on which the petition is founded (or, in the case of a petition founded on a debt which is not immediately payable, if the debtor appears to have no reasonable prospect of being able to pay the debt). This accords with the recommendation in para. 535 of the *Cork Report*. The provisions of s.268 enable the petitioning creditor to establish the debtor's present or prospective inability to pay, for the purposes of subs. (2)(*c*), by serving on the debtor the appropriate form of statutory demand, which thus becomes the counterpart to the procedure which has long been applicable in relation to company winding up, and is now embodied in s.123(1)(*a*) of the Act. The debtor's failure to comply with the terms of a statutory demand served in accordance with subss. (1)(*a*) or (2)(*a*) of s.268 has the consequence that the requirement imposed by subs. (2)(*c*) is duly met. Alternatively, under s.268(1)(*b*), in the case of a debt which is presently due an unsatisfied execution in respect of a judgment debt due to the petitioning creditor will similarly fulfil the requirement imposed by subs. (2)(*c*) (*cf.* s.123(1)(*b*)). S.271(1)(*b*) and (4) contains further provisions applicable to the court's hearing of the creditor's petition, regarding the reasonable prospect of the debtor's being able to pay his debt.

This section comprises subss. (1), (2) and (7)–(9) of s.120 of the 1985 Act.

Subs. (1)

This is so drafted as to make it a legal requirement that the debt in respect of which a creditor presents a bankruptcy petition is a debt which is actually owed to the petitioning creditor himself. This restates the existing law under s.4(1)(*a*) of the Bankruptcy Act 1914 (repealed).

Subs. (2)(a)

The bankruptcy level

This is specified in subs. (4) as £750, but that provision, together with subs. (5), also enables the Secretary of State to vary the level by statutory instrument at any time, subject to the obtaining of Parliamentary approval for the draft instrument by means of the "positive" procedure.

Subs. (2(b)

This largely follows the substance of s.4(1)(*b*) of the Bankruptcy Act 1914 (repealed) but with the important addition of the words "and is unsecured". This establishes the main principle that a petitioning creditor's right to resort to bankruptcy proceedings arises from the fact that his debtor appears unable to pay a debt which is unsecured. However, this is subject to the exception created by s.269 which specifies the circumstances in which the petitioning creditor's debt need not be unsecured.

Subs. (2)(d)

Application to set aside a statutory demand

This form of application is alluded to in subss. (1)(*a*) and (2)(*c*) of s.268, where it is also indicated that the relevant procedural provisions for such applications will be contained in the rules.

Definition of "inability to pay", etc.; the statutory demand

268.—(1) For the purposes of section 267(2) (*c*), the debtor appears to be unable to pay a debt if, but only if, the debt is payable immediately and either—

(*a*) the petitioning creditor to whom the debt is owed has served on the debtor a demand (known as "the statutory demand") in the prescribed form requiring him to pay the debt or to secure or compound for it to the satisfaction of the creditor, at least 3 weeks have elapsed since the demand was served and the demand has been neither complied with nor set aside in accordance with the rules, or

(*b*) execution or other process issued in respect of the debt on a judgment or order of any court in favour of the petitioning creditor, or one or more of the petitioning creditors to whom the debt is owed, has been returned unsatisfied in whole or in part.

(2) For the purposes of section 267(2)(*c*) the debtor appears to have no reasonable prospect of being able to pay a debt if, but only if, the debt is not immediately payable and—

(*a*) the petitioning creditor to whom it is owed has served on the debtor a demand (also known as "the statutory demand") in the prescribed form requiring him to establish to the satisfaction of the creditor that there is a reasonable prospect that the debtor will be able to pay the debt when it falls due,

(*b*) at least 3 weeks have elapsed since the demand was served, and

(*c*) the demand has been neither complied with nor set aside in accordance with the rules.

DEFINITIONS

"creditor": s.383.
"debt": ss.382(3), 385(1).
"the debtor": s.385(1).
"the rules": ss.384, 412.
"the statutory demand": subss. (1)(*a*), (2)(*a*).

GENERAL NOTE

This section operates in relation to the provision in s.267(2)(*c*), whereby a creditor is enabled to present a bankruptcy petition against a debtor if the debt in respect of which the petition is presented is one which the debtor appears either to be unable to pay or to have no reasonable prospect of being able to pay. By means of the service of a statutory demand for payment in accordance with the terms of this section, or alternatively on the basis of an unsatisfied execution as provided for in subs. (1)(*a*), the petitioning creditor is provided with the means of fulfilling the condition imposed by s.267(2)(*c*).

This section comprises subss. (3) and (4) of s.120 of the 1985 Act.

Subs. (1)

If, but only if

These words are important, because they carry the effect that the provisions within s.268 itself constitute the sole means of fulfilling the condition imposed by s.267(2)(*c*).

Creditor with security

269.—(1) A debt which is the debt, or one of the debts, in respect of which a creditor's petition is presented need not be unsecured if either—

(*a*) the petition contains a statement by the person having the right to enforce the security that he is willing, in the event of a bankruptcy order being made, to give up his security for the benefit of all the bankrupt's creditors, or

(*b*) the petition is expressed not to be made in respect of the secured part of the debt and contains a statement by that person of the estimated value at the date of the petition of the security for the secured part of the debt.

(2) In a case falling within subsection (1)(*b*) the secured and unsecured parts of the debt are to be treated for the purposes of sections 267 to 270 as separate debts.

DEFINITIONS

"creditor": s.383.
"creditor's petition": ss.264(1)(*a*), 385(1).
"debt": ss.382(3), 385(1).
"security", "secured", "unsecured": ss.383, 385(1).
"the bankrupt": s.381(1).

GENERAL NOTE

This section, which corresponds to subs. (5) of s.120 of the 1985 Act, specifies the circumstances under which a creditor may present a bankruptcy petition in respect of a debt which is secured. This provision therefore qualifies the concluding three words of s.267(2)(*b*), which are to the general effect that the petitioning creditor's debt must be unsecured.

Expedited petition

270. In the case of a creditor's petition presented wholly or partly in respect of a debt which is the subject of a statutory demand under section 268, the petition may be presented before the end of the 3-week period there mentioned if there is a serious possibility that the debtor's property or the value of any of his property will be significantly diminished during that period and the petition contains a statement to that effect.

DEFINITIONS

"creditor's petition": ss.264(1)(*a*), 385(1).
"debt": ss.382(3), 385(1).
"property": s.436.
"statutory demand": ss.268(1)(*a*), (2)(*a*).
"the debtor": s.385(1).

GENERAL NOTE

This section corresponds to subs. (6) of s.120 of the 1985 Act. It establishes an exception to the normal rule in ss.268(1)(*a*) and (2)(*b*) whereby the debtor on whom a statutory demand is served is allowed a minimum period of three weeks within which to comply with the demand. If it can be shown that a delay of even this period of time before a creditor's petition can be presented would carry the risk of significant impairment to the creditors' interests, in the manner specified in the section, the creditor's petition may be presented before the end of three weeks from the date of service of the statutory demand. However, s.271(2) precludes the court from making a bankruptcy order in such cases until the three-week period has duly expired.

Proceedings on creditor's petition

271.—(1) The court shall not make a bankruptcy order on a creditor's petition unless it is satisfied that the debt, or one of the debts, in respect of which the petition was presented is either—

(*a*) a debt which, having been payable at the date of the petition or having since become payable, has been neither paid nor secured or compounded for, or

(*b*) a debt which the debtor has no reasonable prospect of being able to pay when it falls due.

(2) In a case in which the petition contains such a statement as is required by section 270, the court shall not make a bankruptcy order until at least 3 weeks have elapsed since the service of any statutory demand under section 268.

(3) The court may dismiss the petition if it is satisfied that the debtor is able to pay all his debts or is satisfied—

(*a*) that the debtor has made an offer to secure or compound for a debt in respect of which the petition is presented,

(*b*) that the acceptance of that offer would have required the dismissal of the petition, and

(*c*) that the offer has been unreasonably refused;

and, in determining for the purposes of this subsection whether the debtor is able to pay all his debts, the court shall take into account his contingent and prospective liabilities.

(4) In determining for the purposes of this section what constitutes a reasonable prospect that a debtor will be able to pay a debt when it falls due, it is to be assumed that the prospect given by the facts and other matters known to the creditor at the time he entered into the transaction resulting in the debt was a reasonable prospect.

(5) Nothing in sections 267 to 271 prejudices the power of the court, in accordance with the rules, to authorise a creditor's petition to be amended by the omission of any creditor or debt and to be proceeded with as if things done for the purposes of those sections had been done only by or in relation to the remaining creditors or debts.

DEFINITIONS

"bankruptcy order": s.381(2).
"creditor", "creditor's petition": ss.264(1)(*a*), 383, 385(1).
"debt": ss.382(3), 385(1).
"liability": s.382(4).
"petition", "bankruptcy petition": s.381(3).
"secured", "unsecured": ss.383, 385(1).
"statutory demand": ss.268(1)(*a*), (2)(*a*).
"the court": ss.373, 385(1).
"the rules": ss.384, 412.
"transaction": s.436.

GENERAL NOTE

This governs the actual hearing of the creditor's petition for a bankruptcy order against the debtor, and requires the court to adopt a certain course of action in relation to a series of specified matters. The section corresponds to s.121 of the 1985 Act.

Subs. (1)

This contains important requirements as to the court's duty to satisfy itself that the petitioning creditor's debt is either one which has become due and has in no sense been satisfied, or one which though not presently due for payment is a debt which the debtor has no reasonable prospect of being able to pay when it does so fall due. This provision must be read in conjunction with subs. (4), which effectively requires the creditor whose petition is based upon a debt payable at a future time to show that circumstances have materially altered since he allowed the debtor to incur the liability, and that there was at that time a reasonable prospect, which has subsequently ceased to be operative, that the debt would be paid on time. Subs. (4) thus prevents a creditor from taking a calculated risk concerning the debtor's continuing solvency, in the anticipation that it will be possible for him to resort to bankruptcy proceedings ahead of the repayment date if that assumption proves ill founded: there is an irrebuttable presumption that the prospect of repayment given by the facts and other matters known to the creditor at the time he entered into the transaction with the debtor was a reasonable one.

Subs. (2)

Such a statement as is required by s.270

This refers to the special provision in s.270 whereby a creditor may be allowed to present a petition before the expiry of the three week period allowed for the debtor to comply with a statutory demand for payment. This rule applies where the petition contains a statement that there is a serious possibility that the debtor's estate will be significantly diminished before the expiry of the three week period, thereby reducing the prospect for creditors to receive any return by way of dividend out of the available assets.

Subs. (3)

This in an elaboration upon the previous law contained in s.5(3) of the Bankruptcy Act 1914 (repealed). The essential principle is retained that the debtor ought not to be adjudicated bankrupt if he is able to pay all his debts. The novel requirement is that the debtor must also have made an offer to secure or compound for the petitioning creditor's debt under circumstances where acceptance of that offer would have required the dismissal of the petition, and that offer has been unreasonably refused. No guidance is supplied in the Act concerning what would constitute an unreasonable refusal of an offer by a creditor, and it will therefore be for the court to determine this question in individual cases.

Debtor's petition

Grounds of debtor's petition

272.—(1) A debtor's petition may be presented to the court only on the grounds that the debtor is unable to pay his debts.

(2) The petition shall be accompanied by a statement of the debtor's affairs containing—

(*a*) such particulars of the debtor's creditors and of his debts and other liabilities and of his assets as may be prescribed, and

(*b*) such other information as may be prescribed.

DEFINITIONS

"affairs": s.385(2).
"creditor": s.383.
"debt", "liability": ss.382(4), 383, 385(1).
"debtor's petition": ss.264(1)(*b*), 385(1).
"prescribed": s.384(1).
"the court": ss.373, 385(1).
"the debtor": s.385(1).

GENERAL NOTE

This retains the right of a debtor to petition for his own adjudication as a bankrupt, as formerly provided by s.6 of the Bankruptcy Act 1914 (repealed). The law is unchanged in requiring that the debtor must demonstrate an inability to pay his debts, which is declared to be the sole ground on which the court may make a bankruptcy order under this section. The section creates new law in requiring the debtor's statement of affairs to be filed simultaneously with the presentation of his petition. A further, apparent change from past law has been effected by the omission of any provision that a debtor's petition cannot be withdrawn after presentment without leave of the court (formerly provided by s.6(2) of the Bankruptcy Act 1914). This is now covered by the provision to that effect in s.266(2), which applies in relation to all bankruptcy petitions, whether presented by the debtor himself or by a creditor. This section corresponds to s.122 of the 1985 Act.

Appointment of insolvency practitioner by the court

273.—(1) Subject to the next section, on the hearing of a debtor's petition the court shall not make a bankruptcy order if it appears to the court—

(*a*) that if a bankruptcy order were made the aggregate amount of the bankruptcy debts, so far as unsecured, would be less than the small bankruptcies level, (*b*) that if a bankruptcy order were made, the value of the bankrupt's estate would be equal to or more than the minimum amount,

(*c*) that within the period of 5 years ending with the presentation of the petition the debtor has neither been adjudged bankrupt nor made a composition with his creditors in satisfaction of his debts or a scheme of arrangement of his affairs, and

(*d*) that it would be appropriate to appoint a person to prepare a report under section 274.

"The minimum amount" and "the small bankruptcies level" mean such amounts as may for the time being be prescribed for the purposes of this section.

(2) Where on the hearing of the petition, it appears to the court as mentioned in subsection (1), the court shall appoint a person who is qualified to act as an insolvency practitioner in relation to the debtor—

(*a*) to prepare a report under the next section, and

(*b*) subject to section 258(3) in Part VIII, to act in relation to any voluntary arrangement to which the report relates either as trustee or otherwise for the purpose of supervising its implementation.

DEFINITIONS

"affairs": s.385(2).
"bankrupt": s.381(1).
"bankruptcy debt": s.382.
"bankruptcy order": s.381(2).
"debtor's petition": ss.264(1)(*b*), 385(1).
"estate": ss. 283, 385(1).
"person qualified to act as an insolvency practitioner": s.390.
"prescribed": s.384(1).
"report": s.274.
"secured", "unsecured": ss.383, 385(1).
"the court": ss.373, 385(1).
"the minimum amount": subs. (1).
"the small bankruptcies level": subs. (1).
"to act as an insolvency practitioner in relation to an individual": s.388(2), (3).
"voluntary arrangement": s.253(1)

GENERAL NOTE

This section is actually concerned with one particular line of development which is to be explored by the court at the hearing of a debtor's petition presented under s.272. Although the Act does not follow all the recommendations in Chap. 11 of the *Cork Report* to the effect that a range of some four different insolvency procedures should be available in relation to individuals, the court is now required to give active consideration to the circumstances of each debtor presenting his own petition, in order to establish whether the possibility exists for the conclusion of a voluntary arrangement between the debtor and his creditors under Part VIII. Even if this alternative process to the making of a bankruptcy order is not undertaken, the court must still have regard to the appropriateness of invoking the summary administration procedure through the issue of a summary administration certificate under s.275.

This section corresponds to subss. (1), (2) and (8) of s.123 of the 1985 Act.

Subs. (1)

The court shall not make a bankruptcy order

Despite the mandatory terms of this provision, it may be noted that para. (*d*) of this subsection involves the court in an exercise of appraisal as to the appropriateness of embarking upon the procedure specified in subs. (2) in conjunction with s.274. Therefore, even if the factual elements contained in paras. (*a*)–(*c*) are established before the court, the final decision whether to set in motion the procedure for seeking a voluntary arrangement rests with the court itself on the basis of its own assessment of the prospects for success of such an initiative.

Para. (a): The small bankruptcies level . . .; (b) the minimum amount

The concluding words of the subsection indicate that these amounts will be prescribed in the rules.

Para. (c): The period of five years

Cf. the period of twelve months specified in s.255(1)(*c*) in cases where a voluntary arrangement is being sought by application made under s.253.

Subs. (2)

The court shall appoint a person

The expenses of the person appointed to prepare a report under the terms of this and the next section are to be met out of the deposit lodged by the debtor when his bankruptcy petition is presented.

Action on report of insolvency practitioner

274.—(1) A person appointed under section 273 shall inquire into the debtor's affairs and, within such period as the court may direct, shall submit a report to the court stating whether the debtor is willing, for the purposes of Part VIII, to make a proposal for a voluntary arrangement.

(2) A report which states that the debtor is willing as above mentioned shall also state—

(*a*) whether, in the opinion of the person making the report, a meeting of the debtor's creditors should be summoned to consider the proposal, and

(*b*) if in that person's opinion such a meeting should be summoned, the date on which, and time and place at which, he proposes the meeting should be held.

(3) On considering a report under this section the court may—

(*a*) without any application, make an interim order under section 252, if it thinks that it is appropriate to do so for the purpose of facilitating the consideration and implementation of the debtor's proposal, or

(*b*) if it thinks it would be inappropriate to make such an order, make a bankruptcy order.

(4) An interim order made by virtue of this section ceases to have effect at the end of such period as the court may specify for the purpose of enabling the debtor's proposal to be considered by his creditors in accordance with the applicable provisions of Part VIII.

(5) Where it has been reported to the court under this section that a meeting of the debtor's creditors should be summoned, the person making the report shall, unless the court otherwise directs, summon that meeting for the time, date and place proposed in his report.

The meeting is then deemed to have been summoned under section 257 in Part VIII, and subsections (2) and (3) of that section, and sections 258 to 263 apply accordingly.

Definitions

"bankruptcy order": s.381(2).
"creditor": s.383.
"debtor": s.385(1).
"proposal": s.253(1), (2).
"the court": ss.373, 385(1).
"voluntary arrangement": s.253(1).

General Note

This section, which combines together provisions formerly contained within ss.111(3), 112(1), (7)(*b*), 114(1) and 123(3)–(5) of the 1985 Act, is applicable where the court appoints an insolvency practitioner under s.273(2) to undertake the tasks specified in that subsection. As indicated in the General Note to s.273, the purpose of this prescribed procedure, which the court must observe in every case where a debtor's petition is presented, is to ensure that proper consideration is given to the possibility of utilising the new procedure for effecting a voluntary arrangement between the debtor and his creditors, as an alternative to the debtor undergoing adjudication as a bankrupt.

Subs. (3)

An interim order under s.252

The making of an interim order introduces a moratorium in respect of the debtor's person and property pending the determination of the process of seeking to conclude a voluntary arrangement between the debtor and his creditors. The ensuing stages of the procedure take place in accordance with the provisions contained in ss.256–263.

Summary administration

275.—(1) Where on the hearing of a debtor's petition the court makes a bankruptcy order and the case is as specified in the next subsection, the court shall, if it appears to it appropriate to do so, issue a certificate for the summary administration of the bankrupt's estate.

(2) That case is where it appears to the court—

(*a*) that if a bankruptcy order were made the aggregate amount of the bankruptcy debts so far as unsecured would be less than the small bankruptcies level (within the meaning given by section 273), and

(*b*) that within the period of 5 years ending with the presentation of the petition the debtor has neither been adjudged bankrupt nor made a composition with his creditors in satisfaction of his debts or a scheme of arrangement of his affairs,

whether the bankruptcy order is made because it does not appear to the court as mentioned in section 273(1)(*b*) or (*d*), or it is made because the court thinks it would be inappropriate to make an interim order under section 252.

(3) The court may at any time revoke a certificate issued under this section if it appears to it that, on any grounds existing at the time the certificate was issued, the certificate ought not to have been issued.

Definitions

"bankrupt": s.381(1).
"bankruptcy debt": s.382.
"bankruptcy order": s.381(2).
"debtor's petition": ss.264(1)(*b*), 285(1).
"interim order": s.252(2).
"secured", "unsecured": ss.383, 385(1).
"the court": ss.373, 385(1).
"the small bankruptcies level": s.273(1).

General Note

This section corresponds to subs. (6) and (7) of s.126 of the 1985 Act. It provides for the summary administration of a bankrupt's estate to take place pursuant to a certificate issued by the court in the exercise of its discretion upon being satisfied that the requirements of subs. (2) are fulfilled. Summary administration is a long established procedure for use in cases where the aggregate amount of a bankrupt's unsecured debts is relatively small. The monetary figure which represents the upper limit for the use of this procedure is the amount known as the "small bankruptcies level" which, as provided in s.273(1), is an amount to be prescribed in an order made with reference to that subsection under s.418(1) of the Act.

Other cases for special consideration

Default in connection with voluntary arrangement

276.—(1) The court shall not make a bankruptcy order on a petition under section 264(1)(*c*) (supervisor of, or person bound by, voluntary arrangement proposed and approved) unless it is satisfied—

(*a*) that the debtor has failed to comply with his obligations under the voluntary arrangement, or

(*b*) that information which was false or misleading in any material particular or which contained material omissions—

(i) was contained in any statement of affairs or other document supplied by the debtor under Part VIII to any person, or

(ii) was otherwise made available by the debtor to his creditors at or in connection with a meeting summoned under that Part, or

(*c*) that the debtor has failed to do all such things as may for the purposes of the voluntary arrangement have been reasonably required of him by the supervisor of the arrangement.

(2) Where a bankruptcy order is made on a petition under section 264(1)(*c*), any expenses properly incurred as expenses of the administration of the voluntary arrangement in question shall be a first charge on the bankrupt's estate.

Definitions

"affairs": s.385(2).
"bankruptcy order": s.381(2).
"creditor": s.383.
"estate": ss.283, 385(1).
"supervisor of a voluntary arrangement": s.263(2).
"the bankrupt": s.381(1).
"the court": ss.373, 385(1).
"the debtor": s.385(1).
"voluntary arrangement": s.253(1)

General Note

This section controls the operation of s.264(1)(*c*), under which a petition for a bankruptcy order to be made against an individual may be presented by the supervisor of, or any person (other than the individual himself) who is for the time being bound by a composition or scheme which has taken effect under Part VIII. S.260(2) indicates which persons are bound by such an arrangement. Paras. (*a*), (*b*), and (*c*) of subs. (1) of the present section restrict the scope for any of the persons mentioned in s.264(1)(*c*) to procure the arranging debtor's adjudication, by imposing alternative requirements, one of which at least must be established to the satisfaction of the court before it is empowered to make a bankruptcy order on such a petition. This section corresponds to s.124 of the 1985 Act.

Subs. (2)

This safeguards the claims for expenses of the supervisor and other persons who have been responsible for the administration of the voluntary arrangement up to the time of its discontinuation consequential upon the debtor's adjudication. These expenses become pre-preferential debts in the bankruptcy.

Petition based on criminal bankruptcy order

277.—(1) Subject to section 266(3), the court shall make a bankruptcy order on a petition under section 264(1)(*d*) on production of a copy of the criminal bankruptcy order on which the petition is based.

This does not apply if it appears to the court that the criminal bankruptcy order has been rescinded on appeal.

(2) Subject to the provisions of this Part, the fact that an appeal is pending against any conviction by virtue of which a criminal bankruptcy order was made does not affect any proceedings on a petition under section 264(1)(*d*) based on that order.

(3) For the purposes of this section, an appeal against a conviction is pending—

(*a*) in any case, until the expiration of the period of 28 days beginning with the date of conviction;

(*b*) if notice of appeal to the Court of Appeal is given during that period and during that period the appellant notifies the official receiver of it, until the determination of the appeal and thereafter for so long as an appeal to the House of Lords is pending within the meaning of section 40(5) of the Powers of Criminal Courts Act 1973.

Definitions

"appeal to the House of Lords": Powers of Criminal Courts Act 1973, s.40(5).
"bankruptcy order": s.381(2).
"criminal bankruptcy order": s.385(1); Powers of Criminal Courts Act 1973, s.39(1).
"the court": ss.373, 385(1).
"the official receiver": s.399(1).

General Note

This makes provision for an adjudication of bankruptcy to take place on a petition presented under s.264(1)(*d*) by the Official Petitioner or any person specified in the criminal bankruptcy order on which the petition is based. A criminal bankruptcy order may be made under the provisions contained in ss.39–41 inclusive of the Powers of Criminal Courts Act 1973, together with Sched. 2 to that Act. The procedure is designed to facilitate the recovery of the proceeds of criminal activity, or of compensation for the victims of such activities, by making it possible for a criminal convicted before the Crown Court to undergo subsequent adjudication by the Bankruptcy Court, upon a petition presented on the basis of a criminal bankruptcy order, made at its discretion by the court of criminal jurisdiction. However, the procedure is not considered to be a satisfactory or effective way of depriving convicted offenders of the proceeds of their crimes, and may in due course be replaced under fresh legislation.

Commencement and duration of bankruptcy; discharge

Commencement and continuance

278. The bankruptcy of an individual against whom a bankruptcy order has been made—

(*a*) commences with the day on which the order is made, and
(*b*) continues until the individual is discharged under the following provisions of this Chapter.

Definition

"bankruptcy order": s.381(2).

Transitional Provisions

Sched. 11, paras. 10–12.

General Note

This section, which comprises subs. (1) of s.126 of the 1985 Act, supplies the basic statutory authority for determining the technical dates of commencement of bankruptcy and the termination thereof. With the abolition of the former concept of the "act of bankruptcy," the doctrine of "relation back" of the commencement of bankruptcy has likewise disappeared, so that the commencement date is the day on which the bankruptcy order itself is made. The duration of bankruptcy, until either the debtor is discharged or the bankruptcy order is annulled, is controlled by the further provisions in ss.279–282.

Duration

279.—(1) Subject as follows, a bankrupt is discharged from bankruptcy—

(*a*) in the case of an individual who was adjudged bankrupt on a petition under section 264(1)(*d*) or who had been an undischarged bankrupt at any time in the period of 15 years ending with the commencement of the bankruptcy, by an order of the court under the section next following, and (*b*) in any other case, by the expiration of the relevant period under this section.

(2) That period is as follows—

(*a*) where a certificate for the summary administration of the bankrupt's estate has been issued and is not revoked before the bankrupt's discharge, the period of 2 years beginning with the commencement of the bankruptcy, and

(*b*) in any other case, the period of 3 years beginning with the commencement of the bankruptcy.

(3) Where the court is satisfied on the application of the official receiver that an undischarged bankrupt in relation to whom subsection (1)(*b*) applies has failed or is failing to comply with any of his obligations under this Part, the court may order that the relevant period under this section shall cease to run for such period, or until the fulfilment of such conditions (including a condition requiring the court to be satisfied as to any matter), as may be specified in the order.

(4) This section is without prejudice to any power of the court to annul a bankruptcy order.

DEFINITIONS

"bankrupt": s.381(1).
"bankruptcy order": s.381(2).
"date of commencement of bankruptcy": s.278(*a*).
"the official receiver": s.399(1).
"the relevant period": subss. (2), (3).

TRANSITIONAL PROVISION:

Sched. 11, para. 13.

GENERAL NOTE

This provides the framework of rules under which a bankruptcy shall come to an end by discharge, apart from cases where discharge is granted by order of the court under s.280, or where a bankruptcy is annulled under s.261(1)(*a*) or s.282.

The provisions for discharge from bankruptcy formerly contained in s.26 of the Bankruptcy Act 1914 and ss.7 and 8 of the Insolvency Act 1976 are repealed, and those provisions are replaced with a less complex scheme of approach, as follows. Persons who are adjudicated bankrupt for the first time will obtain an automatic discharge after the elapse of three years from the commencement of bankruptcy, and in the case where the summary administration procedure is employed that period is shortened to two years. In the case where a person has previously been adjudicated bankrupt, and had the status of undischarged bankrupt at any time in the period of fifteen years prior to the date of commencement of his subsequent bankruptcy, it will be necessary for him to apply for discharge under s.280. So, too, where a person is adjudicated bankrupt on a petition under s.264(1)(*d*) based upon a criminal bankruptcy order made against the person in question. No applications for discharge by bankrupts falling into either of these categories may be entertained until after the elapse of at least five years from the commencement of bankruptcy (s.280(1)). Finally, where an undischarged bankrupt who is eligible for automatic discharge after three or two years, as the case may be, is reported to the Official Receiver as failing or as having failed to comply with the obligations to which, as an undischarged bankrupt, he is subject for the time being the court may make an order which suspends the running of time up to automatic discharge. Such an order may operate for a specified period, or until such time as the court is satisfied that the bankrupt is properly fulfilling his legal obligations and duties. The provisions for discharge under this section bear no correspondence to the relevant recommendations of the *Cork Report* (paras. 605–615), but are broadly in line with the proposals in paras. 117–119 of the *White Paper.*

Discharge by order of the court

280.—(1) An application for an order of the court discharging an individual from bankruptcy in a case falling within section 279(1)(*a*) may be made by the bankrupt at any time after the end of the period of 5 years beginning with the commencement of the bankruptcy.

(2) On an application under this section the court may—

(*a*) refuse to discharge the bankrupt from bankruptcy,

(*b*) make an order discharging him absolutely, or

(*c*) make an order discharging him subject to such conditions with respect to any income which may subsequently become due to him, or with respect to property devolving upon him, or acquired by him, after his discharge, as may be specified in the order.

(3) The court may provide for an order falling within subsection (2)(*b*) or (*c*) to have immediate effect or to have its effect suspended for such period, or until the fulfilment of such conditions (including a condition requiring the court to be satisfied as to any matter), as may be specified in the order.

Definitions

"commencement of bankruptcy": s.278(*a*).
"property": s.436.
"the bankrupt": s.381(1).
"the court": ss.373, 385(1).

General Note

This section becomes applicable under the circumstances stated in s.279(1)(*a*). The procedure for seeking discharge from bankruptcy through application to the court is now reserved for cases where a person undergoes adjudication within fifteen years of any time at which he was previously an undischarged bankrupt, or where a person is adjudicated as a result of the making of a criminal bankruptcy order against him. In neither case may an application be made by the bankrupt sooner than five years from the date of the making of the bankruptcy order.

The new provision effects a drastic simplification of the law previously contained in s.26 of the Bankruptcy Act 1914 (repealed). There is no longer any requirement that the court have regard to the bankrupt's conduct prior to and during bankruptcy, and the subsidiary code of so-called "bankruptcy offences" has completely disappeared. Of the former facility, which was seldom used in practice, for the court to grant the bankrupt a certificate of misfortune in conjunction with the order of discharge, there is no trace within the new provisions.

The court's powers in relation to an application for discharge are set out in subs. (2), and are fully discretionary. The court thus enjoys the option of refusing to make an order of discharge, or of granting one either on absolute or on conditional terms, and in either of those cases the court may provide for the order to have immediate effect or to be suspended for a specified or an indefinite period. The provisions of this and the previous section are aimed at striking a balance between rehabilitation and deterrence, and to provide encouragement to the bankrupt to contribute further towards the payment to creditors after his discharge (*cf.* H.L. Vol. 459, col. 1257; H.C. Standing Committee E, June 18, 1985, col. 370). The range of powers available to the court under this section, although shorn of the former accompanying detailed provisions as to their exercise, should be sufficiently familiar to enable the courts to perform their task in a manner which may prove to be not too dissimilar to their accustomed practice.

This section corresponds to s.127 of the 1985 Act.

Subs. (2)

On an application under this section

Where such an application is made, the official receiver is required by s.289(2) to make a report to the court with regard to the debtor's conduct and affairs, and the court must consider that report before determining what order, if any, to make.

Effect of discharge

281.—(1) Subject as follows, where a bankrupt is discharged, the discharge releases him from all the bankruptcy debts, but has no effect—

(*a*) on the functions (so far as they remain to be carried out) of the trustee of his estate, or (*b*) on the operation, for the purposes of the carrying out of those functions, of the provisions of this Part;

and, in particular, discharge does not affect the right of any creditor of the bankrupt to prove in the bankruptcy for any debt from which the bankrupt is released.

(2) Discharge does not affect the right of any secured creditor of the bankrupt to enforce his security for the payment of a debt from which the bankrupt is released.

(3) Discharge does not release the bankrupt from any bankruptcy debt which he incurred in respect of, or forbearance in respect of which was secured by means of, any fraud or fraudulent breach of trust to which he was a party.

(4) Discharge does not release the bankrupt from any liability in respect of a fine imposed for an offence or from any liability under a recognisance except, in the case of a penalty imposed for an offence under an enactment relating to the public revenue or of a recognisance, with the consent of the Treasury.

(5) Discharge does not, except to such extent and on such conditions as the court may direct, release the bankrupt from any bankruptcy debt which—

(*a*) consists in a liability to pay damages for negligence, nuisance or breach of a statutory, contractual or other duty, being damages in respect of personal injuries to any person, or

(*b*) arises under any order made in family proceedings or in domestic proceedings.

(6) Discharge does not release the bankrupt from such other bankruptcy debts, not being debts provable in his bankruptcy, as are prescribed.

(7) Discharge does not release any person other than the bankrupt from any liability (whether as partner or co-trustee of the bankrupt or otherwise) from which the bankrupt is released by the discharge, or from any liability as surety for the bankrupt or as a person in the nature of such a surety.

(8) In this section—

"domestic proceedings" means domestic proceedings within the meaning of the Magistrates' Courts Act 1980 and any proceedings which would be such proceedings but for section 65(1)(ii) of that Act (proceedings for variation of order for periodical payments);

"family proceedings" means the same as in Part V of the Matrimonial and Family Proceedings Act 1984;

"fine" means the same as in the Magistrates' Courts Act 1980; and

"personal injuries" includes death and any disease or other impairment of a person's physical or mental condition.

DEFINITIONS

"bankrupt": s.381(1).
"bankruptcy debt": s.382.
"creditor": s.383.
"debt": ss.382(3), 385(1).
"domestic proceedings": subs. (8).
"family": s.385(1).
"family proceedings": subs. (8).
"fine": subs. (8).
"liability": s.382(4).
"personal injuries": subs. (8).
"prescribed": s.384(1).
"secured", "unsecured creditor": ss.383, 385(1).

General Note

This section defines the effects of an order of discharge from bankruptcy and also indicates the exact limits of those effects. The section also indicates clearly which kinds of debt or liability are not released as a consequence of discharge from bankruptcy. The essential principle is that discharge releases the bankrupt from all those debts known as "the bankruptcy debts." These are defined in s.382(1) and (2) as any debt or liability to which the bankrupt is subject at the commencement of bankruptcy or which, though the bankrupt did not become subject to them until after the commencement of the bankruptcy (or even until after his discharge therefrom), arise from an obligation incurred before the commencement of bankruptcy. The term "bankruptcy debt" also includes any amount specified in a criminal bankruptcy order made against the debtor before the commencement of bankruptcy, and any interest provable in accordance with s.322(2).

As a general rule, all claims which are provable in bankruptcy are also released by discharge. There are long-standing exceptions to this rule, which are re-enacted in subss. (3), (4) and (5). Certain kinds of debt or liability are not admissible to proof in the bankruptcy of the person who has incurred them. On principle, any debt or liability which is excluded from the category of provable debts is correspondingly excluded from the category of debts from which the bankrupt is released by his discharge. This effect is preserved by subs. (6). Formerly, s.30(1) of the Bankruptcy Act 1914 (repealed) expressly excluded from proof in bankruptcy any claims for damages in tort which were unliquidated at the commencement of bankruptcy. This provision was criticised and its abolition recommended in paras. 1310–1318 of the *Cork Report.* Subs. (6) of this section indicates that the category of non-provable debts will be delineated in the rules, so it remains to be seen to what extent unliquidated claims in tort will henceforth be admissible to proof. However, it is significant that subs. (5)(*a*) now provides that certain debts resulting from liability in tort or contract shall not be released by discharge from bankruptcy except to such extent and on such conditions as the court may direct. The debts in question are those which arise in respect of personal injuries to any person resulting from negligence, nuisance or breach of a statutory, contractual or other duty. A non-exhaustive meaning of the term "personal injuries" is supplied in subs. (8).

This section corresponds to s.128 of the 1985 Act.

Court's power to annul bankruptcy order

282.—(1) The court may annul a bankruptcy order if it at any time appears to the court—

(*a*) that, on any grounds existing at the time the order was made, the order ought not to have been made, or

(*b*) that, to the extent required by the rules, the bankruptcy debts and the expenses of the bankruptcy have all, since the making of the order, been either paid or secured for to the satisfaction of the court.

(2) The court may annul a bankruptcy order made against an individual on a petition under paragraph (*a*), (*b*) or (*c*) of section 264(1) if it at any time appears to the court, on an application by the Official Petitioner—

(*a*) that the petition was pending at a time when a criminal bankruptcy order was made against the individual or was presented after such an order was so made, and

(*b*) no appeal is pending (within the meaning of section 277) against the individual's conviction of any offence by virtue of which the criminal bankruptcy order was made;

and the court shall annul a bankruptcy order made on a petition under section 264(1)(*d*) if it at any time appears to the court that the criminal bankruptcy order on which the petition was based has been rescinded in consequence of an appeal.

(3) The court may annul a bankruptcy order whether or not the bankrupt has been discharged from the bankruptcy.

(4) Where the court annuls a bankruptcy order (whether under this section or under section 261 in Part VIII)—

(*a*) any sale or other disposition of property, payment made or other thing duly done, under any provision in this Group of Parts, by or under the authority of the official receiver or a trustee of the bankrupt's estate or by the court is valid, but

(*b*) if any of the bankrupt's estate is then vested, under any such provision, in such a trustee, it shall vest in such person as the court may appoint or, in default of any such appointment, revert to the bankrupt on such terms (if any) as the court may direct;

and the court may include in its order such supplemental provisions as may be authorised by the rules.

(5) In determining for the purposes of section 279 whether a person was an undischarged bankrupt at any time, any time when he was a bankrupt by virtue of an order that was subsequently annulled is to be disregarded.

DEFINITIONS

"bankrupt": s.381(1).
"bankruptcy debt": s.382.
"bankruptcy order": s.381(2).
"criminal bankruptcy order": s.385(1); Powers of Criminal Courts Act 1973, s.39(1).
"estate": ss.283, 385(1).
"property": s.436.
"secured": ss.383, 385(1).
"the court": ss.373, 385(1).
"the Official Petitioner": s.402; Powers of Criminal Courts Act 1973, s.41(1).
"the official receiver": s.399(1).
"the rules": ss.384, 412.

GENERAL NOTE

This section gathers together the various circumstances in which, and the grounds upon which, the court may annul a bankruptcy order.

The section corresponds to s.129 of the 1985 Act.

Subs. (1)

This reproduces the substance of s.29(1) of the Bankruptcy Act 1914 (repealed), but with the addition of the qualifying proviso that the court's discretionary power of annulment under para. (*a*) must be exercised on the basis of grounds existing at the time the bankruptcy order was made. On the other hand, the ground for annulment contained in para. (*b*) is more liberally conceived than the former provision in that it does not require that all the debts should have actually been paid before the annulment of the bankruptcy order can take place, provided that all the debts and expenses of the bankruptcy are at least adequately secured for.

Subs. (2)

See also s.266(4), which allows the court to dismiss a petition which is pending at a time when a criminal bankruptcy order is made against the debtor, or which is presented after the making of such an order. The intention underlying that provision, as also the present subsection, is to allow the criminal bankruptcy order to furnish the basis for the petition and adjudication in order that the amount mentioned in that order may count as a bankruptcy debt within the definition of that term contained in s.382(1).

CHAPTER II

PROTECTION OF BANKRUPT'S ESTATE AND INVESTIGATION OF HIS AFFAIRS

Definition of bankrupt's estate

283.—(1) Subject as follows, a bankrupt's estate for the purposes of any of this Group of Parts comprises—

(*a*) all property belonging to or vested in the bankrupt at the commencement of the bankruptcy, and

(*b*) any property which by virtue of any of the following provisions of this Part is comprised in that estate or is treated as falling within the preceding paragraph.

(2) Subsection (1) does not apply to—

(*a*) such tools, books, vehicles and other items of equipment as are necessary to the bankrupt for use personally by him in his employment, business or vocation;

(*b*) such clothing, bedding, furniture, household equipment and provisions as are necessary for satisfying the basic domestic needs of the bankrupt and his family.

This subsection is subject to section 308 in Chapter IV (certain excluded property reclaimable by trustee).

(3) Subsection (1) does not apply to—

(*a*) property held by the bankrupt on trust for any other person, or

(*b*) the right of nomination to a vacant ecclesiastical benefice.

(4) References in any of this Group of Parts to property, in relation to a bankrupt, include references to any power exercisable by him over or in respect of property except in so far as the power is exercisable over or in respect of property not for the time being comprised in the bankrupt's estate and—

(*a*) is so exercisable at a time after either the official receiver has had his release in respect of that estate under section 299(2) in Chapter III or a meeting summoned by the trustee of that estate under section 331 in Chapter IV has been held, or

(*b*) cannot be so exercised for the benefit of the bankrupt;

and a power exercisable over or in respect of property is deemed for the purposes of any of this Group of Parts to vest in the person entitled to exercise it at the time of the transaction or event by virtue of which it is exercisable by that person (whether or not it becomes so exercisable at that time).

(5) For the purposes of any such provision in this Group of Parts, property comprised in a bankrupt's estate is so comprised subject to the rights of any person other than the bankrupt (whether as a secured creditor of the bankrupt or otherwise) in relation thereto, but disregarding—

(*a*) any rights in relation to which a statement such as is required by section 269(1)(*a*) was made in the petition on which the bankrupt was adjudged bankrupt, and

(*b*) any rights which have been otherwise given up in accordance with the rules.

(6) This section has effect subject to the provisions of any enactment not contained in this Act under which any property is to be excluded from a bankrupt's estate.

DEFINITIONS

"bankrupt": s.381(1).
"business": s.436.
"commencement of bankruptcy": s.278(*a*).
"estate": s.385(1) and this section.
"family": s.385(1).
"property": subs. (4), s.436.
"the official receiver": s.399(1).
"the rules": ss.384, 412.
"transaction": s.436.

GENERAL NOTE

This section replaces, and considerably modifies, the former provisions concerning the bankrupt's available property which were contained in s.38 of the Bankruptcy Act 1914 (repealed). The pre-existing law was described, and in many respects criticised, in Chaps. 22–24 inclusive of the *Cork Report*.

This section corresponds to s.130 of the 1985 Act.

Subs. (1)

All property belonging to or vested in the bankrupt at the commencement of the bankruptcy

This fixes the point in time at which the "stock taking," so to speak, is to be carried out in relation to the bankrupt's estate. The property thereby discovered to belong to or be vested in the bankrupt is capable of augmentation according to the further provisions of this Part of the Act, but is diminished, on the other hand, in consequence of the exemptions contained in subss. (2)–(6) inclusive. A notable change in the rule regarding the vesting of the bankrupt's available estate in his trustee in bankruptcy (pursuant to s.306 *et seq.*) is the abolition of the doctrine of "relation back" of the trustee's title, formerly contained in s.37 of the Bankruptcy Act 1914. This doctrine in its existing form was rendered anomalous by the abolition of the concept of acts of bankruptcy. However, important provisions imposing restrictions on a debtor's powers of disposal of property in the period following the presentation of a bankruptcy petition relating to the debtor are contained in s.284. The powers of the trustee in bankruptcy to recover property disposed of by the bankrupt at any time prior to the commencement of bankruptcy, together with other provisions for the protection and enhancement of the bankrupt's available estate, are now contained in ss.339–344 inclusive. Another notable change in the law is the abolition of the "reputed ownership" doctrine, formerly enacted in s.38(*c*) of the Bankruptcy Act 1914 (repealed), and the subject of a separate chapter in the *Cork Report* (Chap. 23) in which its repeal was forcefully recommended.

The relevant provisions with regard to the effects of bankruptcy upon the bankrupt's interest in any matrimonial home are contained in ss.336–338. The trustee's rights in relation to the bankrupt's after-acquired property are contained in s.307.

Subs. (2)

This exempting provision replaces that formerly enacted as s.38(2) of the Bankruptcy Act 1914 (repealed), and is not only more reasonable and flexible than its predecessor, in accordance with the more enlightened policy by which the law is now meant to be infused, but is also drafted in language more suitable to the present day. The recommendations of Chap. 24 of the *Cork Report* have been closely followed, including the notable inclusion of "vehicles" and other items of equipment falling within the terms of the broad, but practical, formula which governs all cases of exemption under para. (*a*), namely that the exempted item should be *necessary* to the bankrupt for *personal* use in the context of his employment, business or vocation. Section 436 defines the term "business" as including a trade or profession. Most notably, there is no longer any arbitrary monetary limit imposed upon the total value of property to which this statutory exemption may attach.

The provisions of s.308 sensibly enable the trustee in bankruptcy to reclaim any item of exempted property which proves to be of intrinsically greater value than the cost of a reasonable substitute capable of performing the same functions.

Subs. (3)(a)

This restates the existing law formerly expressed in s.38(1) of the Bankruptcy Act 1914 (repealed).

Subs. (3)(b)

This restates the existing law, which was previously contained in the infelicitiously drafted s.38(*b*) of the Bankruptcy Act 1914. Other components of that repealed provision are now subsumed under subs. (4).

Restrictions on dispositions of property

284.—(1) Where a person is adjudged bankrupt, any disposition of property made by that person in the period to which this section applies is void except to the extent that it is or was made with the consent of the court, or is or was subsequently ratified by the court.

(2) Subsection (1) applies to a payment (whether in cash or otherwise) as it applies to a disposition of property and, accordingly, where any payment is void by virtue of that subsection, the person paid shall hold the sum paid for the bankrupt as part of his estate.

(3) This section applies to the period beginning with the day of the presentation of the petition for the bankruptcy order and ending with the vesting, under Chapter IV of this Part, of the bankrupt's estate in a trustee.

(4) The preceding provisions of this section do not give a remedy against any person—

(*a*) in respect of any property or payment which he received before the commencement of the bankruptcy in good faith, for value and without notice that the petition had been presented, or

(*b*) in respect of any interest in property which derives from an interest in respect of which there is, by virtue of this subsection, no remedy.

(5) Where after the commencement of his bankruptcy the bankrupt has incurred a debt to a banker or other person by reason of the making of a payment which is void under this section, that debt is deemed for the purposes of any of this Group of Parts to have been incurred before the commencement of the bankruptcy unless—

(*a*) that banker or person had notice of the bankruptcy before the debt was incurred, or

(*b*) it is not reasonably practicable for the amount of the payment to be recovered from the person to whom it was made.

(6) A disposition of property is void under this section notwithstanding that the property is not or, as the case may be, would not be comprised in the bankrupt's estate; but nothing in this section affects any disposition made by a person of property held by him on trust for any other person.

DEFINITIONS

"bankrupt": s.381(1).
"bankruptcy petition": s.381(3).
"commencement of bankruptcy": s.278(*a*).
"debt": ss.382(3), 385(1).
"estate": ss.283, 385(1).
"property": s.436.

GENERAL NOTE

This section applies restrictions on dispositions of property made by a bankrupt between the time of the presentation of the petition for the bankruptcy order which is subsequently made against him and the time when his estate vests in his trustee in bankruptcy under Chap. IV of Part IX. The making of a bankruptcy order has the effect of rendering void any disposition of property made by the bankrupt during the period since the presentation of the bankruptcy petition, except to the extent that the disposition was made with the consent of the court or is or has been subsequently ratified by the court.

This section corresponds to s.131 of the 1985 Act.

Subs. (2)

This extends the meaning of "disposition of property" in subs. (1) so that it applies to any payment in cash or in kind which is made by a debtor during the "suspect period" following the presentation of a bankruptcy petition against him.

Subs. (4)

This creates a protected position in favour of certain persons who are to enjoy immunity against any remedy which might otherwise result from the fact that a payment or disposition is rendered void by this section. This protection arises in favour of a person who either has received the property or payment before the day on which the bankruptcy order was made; has dealt in good faith; for value; and without notice that the bankruptcy petition had been presented, or has derived his interest in the property from an interest which is already protected on that basis.

Subs. (5)

This provides a specially enhanced degree of protection for bankers and others, and is designed as a replacement for the former protective provision contained in s.4 of the Bankruptcy (Amendment) Act 1926 (repealed). It will give protection to bankers, among others, who, after the commencement of bankruptcy, honour a cheque drawn by the bankrupt before the commencement date in effecting a payment which in the event is rendered void by this section. The debt thus incurred by the bankrupt would, but for this subsection, not be provable in the bankruptcy because it was incurred after the commencement of bankruptcy. However, provided that the banker did not have notice of the bankruptcy before the debt was incurred by, in the example chosen, the banker's honouring the cheque, and provided also that it is not reasonably practicable for the amount of the payment to be recovered from the party by whom or on whose behalf payment was collected, the payment is by virtue of this subsection deemed to have been made before the commencement of bankruptcy, with the consequence that it will count as a provable debt in the bankruptcy.

Restriction on proceedings and remedies

285.—(1) At any time when proceedings on a bankruptcy petition are pending or an individual has been adjudged bankrupt the court may stay any action, execution or other legal process against the property or person of the debtor or, as the case may be, of the bankrupt.

(2) Any court in which proceedings are pending against any individual may, on proof that a bankruptcy petition has been presented in respect of that individual or that he is an undischarged bankrupt, either stay the proceedings or allow them to continue on such terms as it thinks fit.

(3) After the making of a bankruptcy order no person who is a creditor of the bankrupt in respect of a debt provable in the bankruptcy shall—

(*a*) have any remedy against the property or person of the bankrupt in respect of that debt, or

(*b*) before the discharge of the bankrupt, commence any action or other legal proceedings against the bankrupt except with the leave of the court and on such terms as the court may impose.

This is subject to sections 346 (enforcement procedures) and 347 (limited right to distress).

(4) Subject as follows, subsection (3) does not affect the right of a secured creditor of the bankrupt to enforce his security.

(5) Where any goods of an undischarged bankrupt are held by any person by way of pledge, pawn or other security, the official receiver may, after giving notice in writing of his intention to do so, inspect the goods.

Where such a notice has been given to any person, that person is not entitled, without leave of the court, to realise his security unless he has given the trustee of the bankrupt's estate a reasonable opportunity of inspecting the goods and of exercising the bankrupt's right of redemption.

(6) References in this section to the property or goods of the bankrupt are to any of his property or goods, whether or not comprised in his estate.

Definitions

"bankrupt": s.381(1).
"bankruptcy order": s.381(2).
"bankruptcy petition": s.381(3).
"creditor": s.383.
"debt": ss.382(3), 385(1).
"goods": subs. (6).
"property": subs. (6), s.436.
"security", "unsecured creditor": ss.383, 385(1).
"the court": ss.373, 385(1).
"the debtor": s.385(1).
"the Official Receiver": s.399(1).

General Note

This provides for a moratorium under the control of the court in respect of all kinds of action and legal process against the person or property of a debtor or bankrupt, with effect from the moment of the presentation of a bankruptcy petition respecting him or her. The provision essentially re-enacts the existing law under ss.7 and 9 of the Bankruptcy Act 1914 (repealed). The new provision also maintains the existing exemption from the moratorium in respect of any creditors whose debts would not be provable in the bankruptcy: such creditors remain free to commence or continue any legal proceedings against the debtor pertaining to claims of that character.

This section corresponds to s.132 of the 1985 Act.

Subs. (4)

This is the customary saving in respect of the right of a secured creditor to enforce his security notwithstanding the bankruptcy and notwithstanding the general terms of the moratorium imposed by this section.

Subs. (5)

This re-enacts, with only minor amendments of drafting, s.59 of the Bankruptcy Act 1914 (repealed).

Power to appoint interim receiver

286.—(1) The court may, if it is shown to be necessary for the protection of the debtor's property, at any time after the presentation of a bankruptcy petition and before making a bankruptcy order, appoint the official receiver to be interim receiver of the debtor's property.

(2) Where the court has, on a debtor's petition, appointed an insolvency practitioner under section 273 and it is shown to the court as mentioned in subsection (1) of this section, the court may, without making a bankruptcy order, appoint that practitioner, instead of the official receiver, to be interim receiver of the debtor's property.

(3) The court may by an order appointing any person to be an interim receiver direct that his powers shall be limited or restricted in any respect; but, save as so directed, an interim receiver has, in relation to the debtor's property, all the rights, powers, duties and immunities of a receiver and manager under the next section.

(4) An order of the court appointing any person to be an interim receiver shall require that person to take immediate possession of the debtor's property or, as the case may be, the part of it to which his powers as interim receiver are limited.

(5) Where an interim receiver has been appointed, the debtor shall give him such inventory of his property and such other information, and shall attend on the interim receiver at such times, as the latter may for the purpose of carrying out his functions under this section reasonably require.

(6) Where an interim receiver is appointed, section 285(3) applies for the period between the appointment and the making of a bankruptcy order on the petition, or the dismissal of the petition, as if the appointment were the making of such an order.

(7) A person ceases to be interim receiver of a debtor's property if the bankruptcy petition relating to the debtor is dismissed, if a bankruptcy order is made on the petition or if the court by order otherwise terminates the appointment.

(8) References in this section to the debtor's property are to all his property, whether or not it would be comprised in his estate if he were adjudged bankrupt.

DEFINITIONS

"bankruptcy order": s.381(2).
"bankruptcy petition": s.381(3).
"debtor": s.385(1).
"debtor's petition": ss.264(1)(*b*), 385(1).
"property": subs. (8), s.436.
"the court": ss.373, 385(1).
"the official receiver": s.399(1).

General Note

This section empowers the court after presentation of a bankruptcy petition and before a bankruptcy order is made to appoint the official receiver to be interim receiver of the debtor's estate where this is shown to be necessary for the protection of the debtor's property. This procedure replaces the stage in the former bankruptcy procedure established under the provisions of ss.3 and 6(1) of the Bankruptcy Act 1914 (repealed), whereby a receiving order was made in all cases as the court's initial order upon the hearing of a bankruptcy petition, with the official receiver being constituted as receiver for that purpose. The elimination of the receiving order from the new bankruptcy procedure has left a necessity for provision to be made for protective arrangements of the kind embodied in the present section. Usually, the official receiver will assume responsibility for the task of interim receiver unless the court utilises its power under subs. (2) to appoint some other person than the official receiver to this position. This power is exercisable where a debtor's petition is presented in circumstances where the court is required by s.273(2) to appoint a qualified insolvency practitioner to prepare a report as to the debtor's willingness to make a proposal for a voluntary arrangement. Subs. (2) authorises the court to appoint that person as interim receiver with, usually, the rights, powers and duties of a receiver and manager under s.287.

This section corresponds to s.133 of the 1985 Act.

Receivership pending appointment of trustee

287.—(1) Between the making of a bankruptcy order and the time at which the bankrupt's estate vests in a trustee under Chapter IV of this Part, the official receiver is the receiver and (subject to section 370 (special manager)) the manager of the bankrupt's estate and is under a duty to act as such.

(2) The function of the official receiver while acting as receiver or manager of the bankrupt's estate under this section is to protect the estate; and for this purpose—

(*a*) he has the same powers as if he were a receiver or manager appointed by the High Court, and

(*b*) he is entitled to sell or otherwise dispose of any perishable goods comprised in the estate and any other goods so comprised the value of which is likely to diminish if they are not disposed of.

(3) The official receiver while acting as receiver or manager of the estate under this section—

(*a*) shall take all such steps as he thinks fit for protecting any property which may be claimed for the estate by the trustee of that estate,

(*b*) is not, except in pursuance of directions given by the Secretary of State, required to do anything that involves his incurring expenditure,

(*c*) may, if he thinks fit (and shall, if so directed by the court) at any time summon a general meeting of the bankrupt's creditors.

(4) Where—

(*a*) the official receiver acting as receiver or manager of the estate under this section seizes or disposes of any property which is not comprised in the estate, and

(*b*) at the time of the seizure or disposal the official receiver believes, and has reasonable grounds for believing, that he is entitled (whether in pursuance of an order of the court or otherwise) to seize or dispose of that property,

the official receiver is not to be liable to any person in respect of any loss or damage resulting from the seizure or disposal except in so far as that loss or damage is caused by his negligence; and he has a lien on the property, or the proceeds of its sale, for such of the expenses of the bankruptcy as were incurred in connection with the seizure or disposal.

(5) This section does not apply where by virtue of section 297 (appointment of trustee; special cases) the bankrupt's estate vests in a trustee immediately on the making of the bankruptcy order.

Definitions
"bankrupt": s.381(1).
"bankruptcy order": s.381(2).
"creditor": s.383.
"estate": ss.283, 385(1).
"property": s.436.
"the official receiver": s.399(1).

General Note
The streamlining of bankruptcy procedure under this Act has led to the discontinuation of the use of receiving orders. However, in most cases (apart from those governed by s.297) an interval of time will elapse between the making of the bankruptcy order and the formal appointment of a trustee in bankruptcy in whom the bankrupt's estate will then automatically vest by virtue of s.306. To safeguard and maintain the bankrupt's property during that interval of time, this section provides for the official receiver to be receiver and manager of the bankrupt's estate with the same powers as a receiver or manager appointed by the High Court. The duties of the official receiver in this capacity are defined, and provision made for the summoning of a meeting of creditors either on the initiative of the official receiver or at the court's direction. Subs. (4) provides the customary immunity for the official receiver when acting in the bona fide and reasonable belief that property which he is seizing or of which he is disposing is part of that which he is entitled to seize or dispose of in pursuance of his functions under this section. Where the circumstances are such as to render it expedient that a special manager be appointed, an application may be made to the court by the Official Receiver under s.370. If a special manager is appointed the official receiver's functions and status in relation to the bankrupt's estate, pending the appointment of a trustee in bankruptcy, are reduced to those of a receiver only.
This section corresponds to s.134 of the 1985 Act.

Statement of affairs

288.—(1) Where a bankruptcy order has been made otherwise than on a debtor's petition, the bankrupt shall submit a statement of his affairs to the official receiver before the end of the period of 21 days beginning with the commencement of the bankruptcy.

(2) The statement of affairs shall contain—
(*a*) such particulars of the bankrupt's creditors and of his debts and other liabilities and of his assets as may be prescribed, and
(*b*) such other information as may be prescribed.

(3) The official receiver may, if he thinks fit—
(*a*) release the bankrupt from his duty under subsection (1), or
(*b*) extend the period specified in that subsection;
and where the official receiver has refused to exercise a power conferred by this section, the court, if it thinks fit, may exercise it.

(4) A bankrupt who—
(*a*) without reasonable excuse fails to comply with the obligation imposed by this section, or
(*b*) without reasonable excuse submits a statement of affairs that does not comply with the prescribed requirements,
is guilty of a contempt of court and liable to be punished accordingly (in addition to any other punishment to which he may be subject).

Definitions
"bankruptcy order": s.381(2).
"commencement of bankruptcy": s.278(*a*).
"creditor": s.383.
"debt", "liability": ss.382(3), (4), 385(1).
"debtor's petition": ss.264(1)(*b*), 385(1).
"prescribed": s.384(1).
"the bankrupt": s.381(1).
"the official receiver": s.399(1).

General Note

This provision replaces the former s.14 of the Bankruptcy Act 1914 (repealed), and modifies considerably the requirements attached to the bankrupt's traditional duty to supply a statement of affairs to the official receiver. The period of time allowed for the preparation and submission of the statement is set at 21 days from the date of the bankruptcy order, and can be extended by the official receiver at his discretion. This is a far more realistic time limit than the seven days which were formerly allowed, and which moreover could only be extended by order of the court. The official receiver is also clothed with a discretion to release the bankrupt from the duty to submit a statement of affairs. This is designed to a certain extent as a parallel to the provision in s.131(1) relating to the preparation of a statement of affairs of a company in a winding up by the court, whereby the requirement is invocable at the official receiver's discretion. It is intended that the official receiver should exercise his discretion under this section to release a bankrupt who is too ill to lodge a statement of affairs, but in such cases the rules will provide that the official receiver will be subject to a duty to send out a report to all creditors explaining why no statement has been obtained.

This section corresponds to s.135 of the 1985 Act.

Subs. (1)

Bankruptcy order has been made otherwise than on a debtor's petition

This exception arises because, under s.272(2), where a debtor's petition is presented to the court it must be accompanied by a statement of the debtor's affairs in the prescribed form.

Investigatory duties of official receiver

289.—(1) Subject to subsection (5) below, it is the duty of the official receiver to investigate the conduct and affairs of every bankrupt and to make such report (if any) to the court as he thinks fit.

(2) Where an application is made by the bankrupt under section 280 for his discharge from bankruptcy, it is the duty of the official receiver to make a report to the court with respect to the prescribed matters; and the court shall consider that report before determining what order (if any) to make under that section.

(3) A report by the official receiver under this section shall, in any proceedings, be prima facie evidence of the facts stated in it.

(4) In subsection (1) the reference to the conduct and affairs of a bankrupt includes his conduct and affairs before the making of the order by which he was adjudged bankrupt.

(5) Where a certificate for the summary administration of the bankrupt's estate is for the time being in force, the official receiver shall carry out an investigation under subsection (1) only if he thinks fit.

Definitions

"bankrupt": s.381(1).
"estate": ss.283, 385(1).
"prescribed": s.384(1).
"the court": ss.373, 385(1).
"the official receiver": s.399(1).

General Note

This section is of considerable importance in that it imposes a statutory duty upon the official receiver to investigate the conduct and affairs of every bankrupt, and to report to the court if he deems it appropriate to do so. The further duty established by subs. (2) in relation to an application for discharge is a restatement of the former requirement under s.26(2) of the Bankruptcy Act 1914 (repealed), and is relocated here as a logical part of the recitation of the official receiver's investigatory duties. The Act thus commits the official receiver to an active involvement in all cases of bankruptcy, even where a privately appointed trustee in bankruptcy assumes responsibility for the administration of the bankruptcy. The Government have thus conceded the validity and importance of the vigorously-argued case made out in Chap. 14 of the *Cork Report* (esp. paras. 714–731), and have relented from their previously announced intention to withdraw the official receiver completely from all responsibility in personal bankruptcy (see the Government's Green Paper of July 1980, Cmnd. 7967; *Fletcher* (1981) 44 M.L.R. 77). The statements contained in paras. 36 and 37 of the *White Paper* indicate that the Cork Committee's arguments subsequently prevailed, and this was acknowledged during Committee proceedings in the House of Commons (see H.C. Standing Committee E, June 18, 1985, cols. 379–380).

This section corresponds to s.136 of the 1985 Act.

Public examination of bankrupt

290.—(1) Where a bankruptcy order has been made, the official receiver may at any time before the discharge of the bankrupt apply to the court for the public examination of the bankrupt.

(2) Unless the court otherwise orders, the official receiver shall make an application under subsection (1) if notice requiring him to do so is given to him, in accordance with the rules, by one of the bankrupt's creditors with the concurrence of not less than one-half, in value, of those creditors (including the creditor giving notice).

(3) On an application under subsection (1), the court shall direct that a public examination of the bankrupt shall be held on a day appointed by the court; and the bankrupt shall attend on that day and be publicly examined as to his affairs, dealings and property.

(4) The following may take part in the public examination of the bankrupt and may question him concerning his affairs, dealings and property and the causes of his failure, namely—

(*a*) the official receiver and, in the case of an individual adjudged bankrupt on a petition under section 264(1)(*d*), the Official Petitioner,

(*b*) the trustee of the bankrupt's estate, if his appointment has taken effect,

(*c*) any person who has been appointed as special manager of the bankrupt's estate or business,

(*d*) any creditor of the bankrupt who has tendered a proof in the bankruptcy.

(5) If a bankrupt without reasonable excuse fails at any time to attend his public examination under this section he is guilty of a contempt of court and liable to be punished accordingly (in addition to any other punishment to which he may be subject).

Definitions

"affairs": s.385(2).
"bankrupt": s.381(1).
"bankruptcy order": s.381(2).
"business": s.436.
"creditor": s.383(1).
"estate": ss.283, 385(1).
"property": s.436.
"the court": ss.373, 385(1).
"the Official Petitioner": s.402(1); Powers of Criminal Courts Act 1973, s.41(1).
"the official receiver": s.399(1).
"the rules": ss.384, 412.

General Note

This replaces the previous provisions regarding public examination of bankrupts contained in s.15 of the Bankruptcy Act 1914 as modified by s.6 of the Insolvency Act 1976 (both repealed). Under those provisions, the holding of a public examination was obligatory in all cases unless the court by order dispensed with the requirement on specified grounds in response to an application by the official receiver. The new provisions of this section reverse the position so that the holding of a public examination will only take place if the official receiver makes application to the court for this to be done, and the court accedes to his request. The initiative will come from the official receiver in most cases as a consequence of his conclusions drawn after performing his investigative functions under s.289, but subs. (2)

also enables the creditors, or at least so many of them as represent one-half in value of the bankrupt's debts, to serve notice on the official receiver requiring him to apply to the court for a direction that a public examination be held. However, in such cases the court can override the creditors' wishes and order the official receiver not to make the application. Where however the official receiver makes application upon his own initiative under subs. (1), subs. (3) leaves the court with no discretion in the matter, and a direction must be issued for a public examination to be held.

Where a public examination is held, the form and procedure to be followed are basically unchanged, save that subs. (4)(*a*) includes the right of the Official Petitioner (that is, the Director of Public Prosecutions) to participate in the public examination of a bankrupt adjudicated on a criminal bankruptcy order. Although the participation of the official receiver is no longer expressed in mandatory terms, in practice it may be taken for granted that this will occur.

This section corresponds to s.137 of the 1985 Act.

Duties of bankrupt in relation to official receiver

291.—(1) Where a bankruptcy order has been made, the bankrupt is under a duty—

(*a*) to deliver possession of his estate to the official receiver, and

(*b*) to deliver up to the official receiver all books, papers and other records of which he has possession or control and which relate to his estate and affairs (including any which would be privileged from disclosure in any proceedings).

(2) In the case of any part of the bankrupt's estate which consists of things possession of which cannot be delivered to the official receiver, and in the case of any property that may be claimed for the bankrupt's estate by the trustee, it is the bankrupt's duty to do all such things as may reasonably be required by the official receiver for the protection of those things or that property.

(3) Subsections (1) and (2) do not apply where by virtue of section 297 below the bankrupt's estate vests in a trustee immediately on the making of the bankruptcy order.

(4) The bankrupt shall give the official receiver such inventory of his estate and such other information, and shall attend on the official receiver at such times, as the official receiver may for any of the purposes of this Chapter reasonably require.

(5) Subsection (4) applies to a bankrupt after his discharge.

(6) If the bankrupt without reasonable excuse fails to comply with any obligation imposed by this section, he is guilty of a contempt of court and liable to be punished accordingly (in addition to any other punishment to which he may be subject).

Definitions

"affairs": s.385(2).
"bankruptcy order": s.381(2).
"estate": ss.283, 385(1).
"property": s.436.
"records": s.436.
"the bankrupt": s.381(1).
"the official receiver": s.399(1).

General Note

This section conveniently gathers together in one discrete provision a statement of the various duties under which a person is placed as a consequence of undergoing bankruptcy adjudication, and to which, with respect to the matters specified in subs. (4), he remains subject even after discharge from bankruptcy. The latter provision restates the law previously contained in s.26(9) of the Bankruptcy Act 1914 (repealed). Other parts of the section restate the law previously contained in s.22 of the Act of 1914. The duty to deliver up to the official receiver all books, papers and other records relating to the bankrupt's own estate and affairs admits of no exception, even in the case of items which would ordinarily be protected by legal professional privilege.

This section corresponds to s.138 of the 1985 Act.

Chapter III

Trustees in Bankruptcy

Tenure of office as trustee

Power to make appointments

292.—(1) The power to appoint a person as trustee of a bankrupt's estate (whether the first such trustee or a trustee appointed to fill any vacancy) is exercisable—

(*a*) except at a time when a certificate for the summary administration of the bankrupt's estate is in force, by a general meeting of the bankrupt's creditors;

(*b*) under section 295(2), 296(2) or 300(6) below in this Chapter, by the Secretary of State; or

(*c*) under section 297, by the court.

(2) No person may be appointed as trustee of a bankrupt's estate unless he is, at the time of the appointment, qualified to act as an insolvency practitioner in relation to the bankrupt.

(3) Any power to appoint a person as trustee of a bankrupt's estate includes power to appoint two or more persons as joint trustees; but such an appointment must make provision as to the circumstances in which the trustees must act together and the circumstances in which one or more of them may act for the others.

(4) The appointment of any person as trustee takes effect only if that person accepts the appointment in accordance with the rules. Subject to this, the appointment of any person as trustee takes effect at the time specified in his certificate of appointment.

(5) This section is without prejudice to the provisions of this Chapter under which the official receiver is, in certain circumstances, to be trustee of the estate.

Definitions

"bankrupt": s.381(1).
"creditor": s.383(1).
"estate": ss.283, 385(1).
"person qualified to act as an insolvency practitioner": s.390.
"the court": ss.373, 385(1).
"the official receiver": s.399(1).
"the rules": ss.384, 412.
"to act as an insolvency practitioner in relation to an individual": s.388(2), (3).

General Note

This section specifies when the power to appoint a trustee in bankruptcy is exercisable, and makes provision with respect to the persons who may be appointed. In conformity with the general policy underlying the Act as manifested in the provisions of Pt. XIII, the person appointed to the position of trustee in bankruptcy must in all cases be a duly qualified insolvency practitioner within the meaning of that Part of the Act.

This section corresponds to s.139 of the 1985 Act.

Subs. (4)

Certificate of appointment

Provisions governing the form and contents of the certificate of appointment will be contained in the rules, in accordance with powers contained in para. 11 of Sched. 9.

Summoning of meeting to appoint first trustee

293.—(1) Where a bankruptcy order has been made and no certificate for the summary administration of the bankrupt's estate has been issued, it is the duty of the official receiver, as soon as practicable in the period of 12 weeks beginning with the day on which the order was made, to decide whether to summon a general meeting of the bankrupt's creditors for the purpose of appointing a trustee of the bankrupt's estate.

This section does not apply where the bankruptcy order was made on a petition under section 264(1)(*d*) (criminal bankruptcy); and it is subject to the provision made in sections 294(3) and 297(6) below.

(2) Subject to the next section, if the official receiver decides not to summon such a meeting, he shall, before the end of the period of 12 weeks above mentioned, give notice of his decision to the court and to every creditor of the bankrupt who is known to the official receiver or is identified in the bankrupt's statement of affairs.

(3) As from the giving to the court of a notice under subsection (2), the official receiver is the trustee of the bankrupt's estate.

DEFINITIONS

"bankrupt": s.381(1).
"bankruptcy order": s.381(2).
"bankruptcy petition": s.381(3).
"creditor": s.383(1).
"estate": ss.383, 385(1).
"the court": ss.373, 385(1).
"the official receiver": s.399(1).

GENERAL NOTE

This section imposes a duty on the official receiver to decide within twelve weeks of the day on which the bankruptcy order is made whether to call a meeting of creditors for the purpose of appointing a trustee in bankruptcy. If the official receiver decides not to convene such a meeting he is required to notify the court and every known creditor of the bankrupt, and will be required at the same time to send the creditors a summary of the statement of affairs and a report thereon. The combined despatch of the notice together with supporting information will save duplication of costs and expenses. Where no meeting of creditors has been summoned, or where the official receiver has decided not to summon a meeting, s.294 empowers one-quarter or more in value of the creditors to require the official receiver to call a meeting. Where the available assets are so small as to render the administration of the estate an uneconomic proposition for a privately-appointed trustee, this provision to enable the formality of the creditors' meeting to be omitted is a sensible measure to avoid needless wastage of costs. The provision accords with the proposals in paras. 75–79 of the *White Paper,* and is a parallel to that in s.136 relating to the role of the official receiver in the winding up of a company by the court.

This section corresponds to s.140 of the 1985 Act.

Subs. (1)

No certificate for the summary administration of the bankrupt's estate has been issued

The procedure which may result in the making of a summary administration order is prescribed in s.275. S.297(2) provides that where such a certificate is issued, the official receiver shall be trustee of the bankrupt's estate, which thus obviates the need for the summoning of a meeting of creditors. However, s.297(3) empowers the court at its discretion to appoint some other person than the official receiver as trustee of the bankrupt's estate.

Where the bankruptcy order was made on a petition under s.264(1)(d)

This refers to the making of a bankruptcy order under the provision specified, consequential upon a criminal bankruptcy order. S.297(1) provides that in such cases the official receiver shall be trustee of the bankrupt's estate, which thus obviates the need for the summoning of a meeting of creditors at this stage of the bankruptcy administration.

Subs. (3)

This provides that where the official receiver gives the required notice to the effect that no meeting of creditors is to be held, the official receiver himself shall become trustee in bankruptcy with effect from the date of the giving of notice.

Power of creditors to requisition meeting

294.—(1) Where in the case of any bankruptcy—

(*a*) the official receiver has not yet summoned, or has decided not to summon, a general meeting of the bankrupt's creditors for the purpose of appointing the trustee, and

(*b*) a certificate for the summary administration of the estate is not for the time being in force,

any creditor of the bankrupt may request the official receiver to summon such a meeting for that purpose.

(2) If such a request appears to the official receiver to be made with the concurrence of not less than one-quarter, in value, of the bankrupt's creditors (including the creditor making the request), it is the duty of the official receiver to summon the requested meeting.

(3) Accordingly, where the duty imposed by subsection (2) has arisen, the official receiver is required neither to reach a decision for the purposes of section 293(1) nor (if he has reached one) to serve any notice under section 293(2).

DEFINITIONS

"creditor": s.383(1).
"estate": ss.283, 385(1).
"the bankrupt": s.381(1).
"the official receiver": s.399(1).

GENERAL NOTE

This section makes provision for the creditors to compel the official receiver to convene a creditors' meeting for the purpose of appointing a trustee in bankruptcy, provided that at least one-quarter in value of the creditors are in favour of such a proceeding. But no such requirement can be imposed by the creditors where a certificate for the summary administration of the bankrupt's estate has been made under the procedure established in s.275.

This section corresponds to s.141 of the 1985 Act.

Failure of meeting to appoint trustee

295.—(1) If a meeting summoned under section 293 or 294 is held but no appointment of a person as trustee is made, it is the duty of the official receiver to decide whether to refer the need for an appointment to the Secretary of State.

(2) On a reference made in pursuance of that decision, the Secretary of State shall either make an appointment or decline to make one.

(3) If—

(*a*) the official receiver decides not to refer the need for an appointment to the Secretary of State, or

(*b*) on such a reference the Secretary of State declines to make an appointment,

the official receiver shall give notice of his decision or, as the case may be, of the Secretary of State's decision to the court.

(4) As from the giving of notice under subsection (3) in a case in which no notice has been given under section 293(2), the official receiver shall be trustee of the bankrupt's estate.

DEFINITIONS

"estate": ss.283, 385(1).
"the bankrupt": s.381(1).
"the court": ss.373, 385(1).
"the official receiver": s.399(1).

General Note

This provides for the case where a general meeting of creditors is convened under either s.293 or s.294, but no appointment of a trustee in bankruptcy results therefrom. The official receiver must thereupon decide whether or not to refer the matter to the Secretary of State. If this is done, the Secretary of State may at his discretion appoint a qualified person to be the trustee in bankruptcy, but it is not obligatory that he should do so. If the official receiver decides not to refer the matter to the Secretary of State, or if the latter, upon such a reference, declines to make an appointment, subs. (4) provides that the official receiver shall be the trustee in bankruptcy with effect from the date of his giving the requisite notice to the court as required by subs. (3).

This section corresponds to s.142 of the 1985 Act.

Appointment of trustee by Secretary of State

296.—(1) At any time when the official receiver is the trustee of a bankrupt's estate by virtue of any provision of this Chapter (other than section 297(1) below) he may apply to the Secretary of State for the appointment of a person as trustee instead of the official receiver.

(2) On an application under subsection (1) the Secretary of State shall either make an appointment or decline to make one.

(3) Such an application may be made notwithstanding that the Secretary of State has declined to make an appointment either on a previous application under subsection (1) or on a reference under section 295 or under section 300(4) below.

(4) Where the trustee of a bankrupt's estate has been appointed by the Secretary of State (whether under this section or otherwise), the trustee shall give notice to the bankrupt's creditors of his appointment or, if the court so allows, shall advertise his appointment in accordance with the court's directions.

(5) In that notice or advertisement the trustee shall—

(*a*) state whether he proposes to summon a general meeting of the bankrupt's creditors for the purpose of establishing a creditors' committee under section 301, and

(*b*) if he does not propose to summon such a meeting, set out the power of the creditors under this Part to require him to summon one.

Definitions

"creditor": s.383(1).
"estate": ss.283, 385(1).
"the bankrupt": s.381(1).
"the court": ss.373, 385(1).
"the official receiver": s.399(1).

Transitional Provision

Sched. 11, para. 14.

General Note

This provides a general permission for the official receiver to apply to the Secretary of State for the appointment of a person as trustee in bankruptcy in place of the official receiver himself. Such an application may be made at any time when the official receiver is the trustee in bankruptcy, and is exercisable regardless of whether previous applications for such an appointment have been made under this section itself, or under s.295 or s.300(4). However it is not made obligatory for the Secretary of State to make an appointment in response to such an application, and in default of any such appointment the official receiver will continue to be trustee in bankruptcy, either by virtue of the general provision contained in s.300(2), or by virtue of any other particular provision under which he came to hold that office (see ss.293(3), 295(4), 297(1), (2)).

This section corresponds to s.143 of the 1985 Act.

Subs. (4)

This provides for the case where a trustee in bankruptcy is appointed by the Secretary of State in response to an application made under subs. (1), or in response to a reference made under s.295(2). The requirement is imposed that the trustee thus appointed shall notify the creditors of his appointment, or advertise the fact if the court so allows, and give indication whether he proposes to summon a general meeting for the purpose of establishing a creditors' committee under s.301. This subsection is a parallel to the provision of s.297(7) which applies where the trustee is appointed by the court.

Special cases

297.—(1) Where a bankruptcy order is made on a petition under section 264(1)(*d*) (criminal bankruptcy), the official receiver shall be trustee of the bankrupt's estate.

(2) Subject to the next subsection, where the court issues a certificate for the summary administration of a bankrupt's estate, the official receiver shall, as from the issue of that certificate, be the trustee.

(3) Where such a certificate is issued or is in force, the court may, if it thinks fit, appoint a person other than the official receiver as trustee.

(4) Where a bankruptcy order is made in a case in which an insolvency practitioner's report has been submitted to the court under section 274 but no certificate for the summary administration of the estate is issued, the court, if it thinks fit, may on making the order appoint the person who made the report as trustee.

(5) Where a bankruptcy order is made (whether or not on a petition under section 264(1)(*c*)) at a time when there is a supervisor of a voluntary arrangement approved in relation to the bankrupt under Part VIII, the court, if it thinks fit, may on making the order appoint the supervisor of the arrangement as trustee.

(6) Where an appointment is made under subsection (4) or (5) of this section, the official receiver is not under the duty imposed by section 293(1) (to decide whether or not to summon a meeting of creditors).

(7) Where the trustee of a bankrupt's estate has been appointed by the court, the trustee shall give notice to the bankrupt's creditors of his appointment or, if the court so allows, shall advertise his appointment in accordance with the directions of the court.

(8) In that notice or advertisement he shall—

(*a*) state whether he proposes to summon a general meeting of the bankrupt's creditors for the purpose of establishing a creditors' committee under section 301 below, and

(*b*) if he does not propose to summon such a meeting, set out the power of the creditors under this Part to require him to summon one.

DEFINITIONS

"bankruptcy order": s.381(2).
"creditor": s.383(1).
"estate": ss.283, 385(1).
"the court": ss.373, 385(1).
"the official receiver": s.399(1).
"supervisor of a voluntary arrangement": s.263(2).
"voluntary arrangement": s.253(1).

GENERAL NOTE

This section determines how the appointment of the trustee in bankruptcy shall take place in certain specially defined cases. Where the operation of any of the provisions contained in subss. (3), (4) or (5) results in the appointment of a trustee in bankruptcy being made by the court, subs. (7) applies with the effect that the trustee must give notice to the creditors of his appointment, or alternatively advertise the fact if the court so allows, and also give indication whether he proposes to summon a general meeting for the purpose of establishing a creditors' committee under s.301. This provision is a parallel to that of s.296(4).

This section corresponds to s.144 of the 1985 Act.

Removal of trustee; vacation of office

298.—(1) Subject as follows, the trustee of a bankrupt's estate may be removed from office only by an order of the court or by a general meeting of the bankrupt's creditors summoned specially for that purpose in accordance with the rules.

(2) Where the official receiver is trustee by virtue of section 297(1), he shall not be removed from office under this section.

(3) A general meeting of the bankrupt's creditors shall not be held for the purpose of removing the trustee at any time when a certificate for the summary administration of the estate is in force.

(4) Where the official receiver is trustee by virtue of section 293(3) or 295(4) or a trustee is appointed by the Secretary of State or (otherwise than under section 297(5)) by the court, a general meeting of the bankrupt's creditors shall be summoned for the purpose of replacing the trustee only if—

(*a*) the trustee thinks fit, or
(*b*) the court so directs, or
(*c*) the meeting is requested by one of the bankrupt's creditors with the concurrence of not less than one-quarter, in value, of the creditors (including the creditor making the request).

(5) If the trustee was appointed by the Secretary of State, he may be removed by a direction of the Secretary of State.

(6) The trustee (not being the official receiver) shall vacate office if he ceases to be a person who is for the time being qualified to act as an insolvency practitioner in relation to the bankrupt.

(7) The trustee may, in the prescribed circumstances, resign his office by giving notice of his resignation to the court.

(8) The trustee shall vacate office on giving notice to the court that a final meeting has been held under section 331 in Chapter IV and of the decision (if any) of that meeting.

(9) The trustee shall vacate office if the bankruptcy order is annulled.

Definitions

"creditor": s.383(1).
"estate": ss.283, 385(1).
"person qualified to act as an insolvency practitioner": s.390.
"prescribed": s.384(1).
"the bankrupt": s.381(1).
"the court": ss.373, 385(1).
"the official receiver": s.399(1).
"the rules": ss.384, 412.
"to act as an insolvency practitioner in relation to an individual": s.388(2), (3).

General Note

This section contains provisions regulating the circumstances in which, and the procedure by which, a trustee in bankruptcy may be removed from office. The provisions of subss. (6)–(9) inclusive specify in which circumstances a trustee in bankruptcy must vacate his office, and by what means he may resign it.

The section corresponds to s.145 of the 1985 Act.

Subs. (1)

This provides that the only two ways in which a trustee may be removed from office are either by an order of the court or alternatively by a specially convened meeting of the bankrupt's creditors. This is subject to the provision in subs. (2) whereby neither of these possible methods of removal is applicable in the case where the official receiver is serving as the trustee in bankruptcy by virtue of s.297(1), which requires the official receiver to be trustee where the bankruptcy order is made in consequence of a criminal bankruptcy order.

Further restrictions on the scope for removal of a trustee by means of a general meeting of creditors are imposed by subss. (3), (4) and (5).

Subs. (6)

This follows the general policy of the act as a whole, whereby any person who acts as an insolvency practitioner within the meaning of s.388 must be qualified to do so at all relevant times. Under most circumstances a person occupying the office of trustee in bankruptcy who ceases to be qualified to act as an insolvency practitioner in relation to the bankrupt will commit a criminal offence under s.389(1) if he does not immediately vacate office. However, s.391(5) enables transitional arrangements to be included in any order made under subs. (4) of that section whereby the Secretary of State revokes an authorisation previously granted to a professional body conferring upon the members of that body the status of qualified insolvency practitioners for the purposes of this Act. Such arrangements, if made, may enable those affected by the order to conclude their involvement in any existing bankruptcies in an orderly manner, without thereby committing a criminal offence.

Subs. (9)

Annulment of a bankruptcy order may take place in accordance with the provisions of s.282.

Release of trustee

299.—(1) Where the official receiver has ceased to be the trustee of a bankrupt's estate and a person is appointed in his stead, the official receiver shall have his release with effect from the following time, that is to say—

(*a*) where that person is appointed by a general meeting of the bankrupt's creditors or by the Secretary of State, the time at which the official receiver gives notice to the court that he has been replaced, and

(*b*) where that person is appointed by the court, such time as the court may determine.

(2) If the official receiver while he is the trustee gives notice to the Secretary of State that the administration of the bankrupt's estate in accordance with Chapter IV of this Part is for practical purposes complete, he shall have his release with effect from such time as the Secretary of State may determine.

(3) A person other than the official receiver who has ceased to be the trustee shall have his release with effect from the following time, that is to say—

(*a*) in the case of a person who has been removed from office by a general meeting of the bankrupt's creditors that has not resolved against his release or who has died, the time at which notice is given to the court in accordance with the rules that that person has ceased to hold office;

(*b*) in the case of a person who has been removed from office by a general meeting of the bankrupt's creditors that has resolved against his release, or by the court, or by the Secretary of State, or who has vacated office under section 298(6), such time as the Secretary of State may, on an application by that person, determine;

(*c*) in the case of a person who has resigned, such time as may be prescribed;

(*d*) in the case of a person who has vacated office under section 298(8)—

(i) if the final meeting referred to in that subsection has resolved against that person's release, such time as the Secretary of State may, on an application by that person, determine; and

(ii) if that meeting has not so resolved, the time at which the person vacated office.

(4) Where a bankruptcy order is annulled, the trustee at the time of the annulment has his release with effect from such time as the court may determine.

(5) Where the official receiver or the trustee has his release under this section, he shall, with effect from the time specified in the preceding provisions of this section, be discharged from all liability both in respect of acts or omissions of his in the administration of the estate and otherwise in relation to his conduct as trustee.

But nothing in this section prevents the exercise, in relation to a person who has had his release under this section, of the court's powers under section 304.

DEFINITIONS

"a bankrupt": s.381(1).
"creditor": s.383(1).
"estate": ss.283, 385(1).
"prescribed": s.384(1).
"the court": ss.373, 385(1).
"the official receiver": s.399(1).
"the rules": ss.384, 412.

TRANSITIONAL PROVISION

Sched. 11, para. 14.

GENERAL NOTE

This section provides how, and to what extent, a trustee in bankruptcy is released from liability for his acts or omissions upon his ceasing to hold office. The provisions are so designed as to form a parallel to those of ss.173 and 174, regarding the release of the liquidator in voluntary and in compulsory winding up respectively. Separate provisions are made concerning the manner and timing of the release of a trustee in bankruptcy, depending upon the circumstances in which the termination of his office comes about. Subss. (1) and (2) are concerned with the release of the official receiver when acting as trustee in bankruptcy.

This section corresponds to s.146 of the 1985 Act.

Subs. (3)

This concerns the release of the trustee when some person other than the official receiver is the holder of that office. Provision is made to ensure that, where the trustee is removed from office in circumstances where his conduct has been less than satisfactory, adequate time for investigation is allowed before the trustee's release takes effect. However, provision is inserted in subs. (5) to preserve the application of s.304 even in cases where the person concerned has had his release under this section.

Subs. (5)

This specifies the extent of the release from liability accorded to the trustee with effect from the relevant date determined according to the preceding provisions of this section, with a proviso, as mentioned above, whereby the provisions of s.304 remain applicable even after that moment.

Vacancy in office of trustee

300.—(1) This section applies where the appointment of any person as trustee of a bankrupt's estate fails to take effect or, such an appointment having taken effect, there is otherwise a vacancy in the office of trustee.

(2) The official receiver shall be trustee until the vacancy is filled.

(3) The official receiver may summon a general meeting of the bankrupt's creditors for the purpose of filling the vacancy and shall summon such a meeting if required to do so in pursuance of section 314(7) (creditors' requisition).

(4) If at the end of the period of 28 days beginning with the day on which the vacancy first came to the official receiver's attention he has not

summoned, and is not proposing to summon, a general meeting of creditors for the purpose of filling the vacancy, he shall refer the need for an appointment to the Secretary of State.

(5) Where a certificate for the summary administration of the estate is for the time being in force—

(*a*) the official receiver may refer the need to fill any vacancy to the court or, if the vacancy arises because a person appointed by the Secretary of State has ceased to hold office, to the court or the Secretary of State, and

(*b*) subsections (3) and (4) of this section do not apply.

(6) On a reference to the Secretary of State under subsection (4) or (5) the Secretary of State shall either make an appointment or decline to make one.

(7) If on a reference under subsection (4) or (5) no appointment is made, the official receiver shall continue to be trustee of the bankrupt's estate, but without prejudice to his power to make a further reference.

(8) References in this section to a vacancy include a case where it is necessary, in relation to any property which is or may be comprised in a bankrupt's estate, to revive the trusteeship of that estate after the holding of a final meeting summoned under section 331 or the giving by the official receiver of notice under section 299(2).

Definitions

"a bankrupt": s.381(1).
"creditor": s.383(1).
"estate": ss.283, 385(1).
"property": s.436.
"the court": ss.373, 385(1).
"the official receiver": s.399(1).

General Note

This section makes provision to enable a vacancy in the office of trustee in bankruptcy to be filled, according to the circumstances in which the vacancy has arisen. However, the appointment of a replacement in office is not made mandatory, and it is possible for the vacancy to be left unfilled. In such cases, the residual provision in subs. (2) (and in subs. (5)), whereby the official receiver is statutory trustee during any vacancy, ensures that the conduct of the bankruptcy continues to its proper conclusion. When so acting as trustee during any period of vacancy, as is indicated by subs. (3), the official receiver is subject to the effects of s.314(7) whereby at least one-tenth in value of the creditors may compel the trustee to summon a general meeting of creditors. Subs. (4) also renders it obligatory for the official receiver to refer the matter to the Secretary of State within 28 days of becoming aware of the vacancy if he himself has taken no steps to convene a meeting of creditors for the purpose of filling the vacancy. However, the Secretary of State is not obliged to respond by making any appointment (subs. (6)).

This section corresponds to s.147 of the 1985 Act.

Control of trustee

Creditors' committee

301.—(1) Subject as follows, a general meeting of a bankrupt's creditors (whether summoned under the preceding provisions of this Chapter or otherwise) may, in accordance with the rules, establish a committee (known as "the creditors' committee") to exercise the functions conferred on it by or under this Act.

(2) A general meeting of the bankrupt's creditors shall not establish such a committee, or confer any functions on such a committee, at any time when the official receiver is the trustee of the bankrupt's estate, except in connection with an appointment made by that meeting of a person to be trustee instead of the official receiver.

DEFINITIONS
"creditor": s.383(1).
"estate": ss.283, 385(1).
"the bankrupt": s.381(1).
"the official receiver": s.399(1).
"the rules": ss.384, 412.

GENERAL NOTE

In Chap. 19 of the *Cork Report* there is extended discussion of the role of creditors, and of creditors' committees, in controlling and supervising the trustee's conduct of the administration of a bankrupt's estate. Paras. 83 and 84 of the *White Paper* indicated a general acceptance of the basic thrust of these recommendations, but in the course of the gestation of the 1985 Act there was a considerable re-appraisal of the relationship to be struck between the committee of creditors and the trustee in bankruptcy, having regard to the fact that the latter will in all cases henceforth be a qualified insolvency practitioner. In view of that, it was thought inappropriate to apply the nomenclature of "supervisory committee", as originally intended. The expression "creditors' committee" has been adopted by the draftsman of the present Act.

The present section completely replaces the provision under s.20 of the Bankruptcy Act 1914 (repealed) under which creditors could formerly appoint a committee of inspection. It empowers the creditors at a general meeting to appoint a committee in accordance with the rules to function for the purposes of the Act. A general meeting for this purpose may be convened by the trustee of his own initiative in accordance with the general authorisation contained is s.314(7). Ss.296(5)(*a*) and 297(8)(*a*) direct the trustee to have regard to the practicability of establishing a creditors' committee. If however the trustee elects not to convene the meeting for this purpose he can be compelled to do so under the further provisions in s.314(7) if at least one-tenth in value of the creditors concur in formally requesting him to summon one.

This section corresponds to s.148 of the 1985 Act.

Subs. (2)

This lays down a rule to the effect that no meeting of creditors may establish a committee under this section at any time when the official receiver is trustee, except where this happens in conjunction with the appointment by such a meeting of a person to replace the official receiver as trustee. This provision complements s.302(1).

Exercise by Secretary of State of functions of creditors' committee

302.—(1) The creditors' committee is not to be able or required to carry out its functions at any time when the official receiver is trustee of the bankrupt's estate; but at any such time the functions of the committee under this Act shall be vested in the Secretary of State, except to the extent that the rules otherwise provide.

(2) Where in the case of any bankruptcy there is for the time being no creditors' committee and the trustee of the bankrupt's estate is a person other than the official receiver, the functions of such a committee shall be vested in the Secretary of State, except to the extent that the rules otherwise provide.

DEFINITIONS
"creditor": s.383(1).
"estate": ss.283, 385(1).
"the bankrupt": s.381(1).
"the official receiver": s.399(1).
"the rules": ss.384, 412.

GENERAL NOTE

This provides for the functions which would otherwise be vested by the Act in a committee of creditors to be vested in the Secretary of State during any period when the official receiver is the trustee in bankruptcy, and to be likewise vested in the Secretary of State at any time when a person other than the official receiver is the trustee in bankruptcy but no committee has been established under s.301.

This section corresponds to s.149 of the 1985 Act.

General control of trustee by the court

303.—(1) If a bankrupt or any of his creditors or any other person is dissatisfied by any act, omission or decision of a trustee of the bankrupt's estate, he may apply to the court; and on such an application the court may confirm, reverse or modify any act or decision of the trustee, may give him directions or may make such other order as it thinks fit.

(2) The trustee of a bankrupt's estate may apply to the court for directions in relation to any particular matter arising under the bankruptcy.

Definitions
"a bankrupt": s.381(1).
"creditor": s.383(1).
"estate": ss.283, 385(1).
"modify", "modifications": s.436.
"the court": ss.373, 385(1).

General Note
Subs. (1) restates the former provisions of s.80 of the Bankruptcy Act 1914 (repealed) in establishing a general principle that the trustee's actions are ultimately subject to control by the court at the instance of any properly interested party. Subs. (2) restates the former provisions of s.79(3) of the Act of 1914 in enabling the trustee to seek directions from the court at any time.

This section corresponds to s.150 of the 1985 Act.

Liability of trustee

304.—(1) Where on an application under this section the court is satisfied—

(*a*) that the trustee of a bankrupt's estate has misapplied or retained, or become accountable for, any money or other property comprised in the bankrupt's estate, or

(*b*) that a bankrupt's estate has suffered any loss in consequence of any misfeasance or breach of fiduciary or other duty by a trustee of the estate in the carrying out of his functions,

the court may order the trustee, for the benefit of the estate, to repay, restore or account for money or other property (together with interest at such rate as the court thinks just) or, as the case may require, to pay such sum by way of compensation in respect of the misfeasance or breach of fiduciary or other duty as the court thinks just.

This is without prejudice to any liability arising apart from this section.

(2) An application under this section may be made by the official receiver, the Secretary of State, a creditor of the bankrupt or (whether or not there is, or is likely to be, a surplus for the purposes of section 330(5) (final distribution)) the bankrupt himself.

But the leave of the court is required for the making of an application if it is to be made by the bankrupt or if it is to be made after the trustee has had his release under section 299.

(3) Where—

(*a*) the trustee seizes or disposes of any property which is not comprised in the bankrupt's estate, and

(*b*) at the time of the seizure or disposal the trustee believes, and has reasonable grounds for believing, that he is entitled (whether in pursuance of an order of the court or otherwise) to seize or dispose of that property,

the trustee is not liable to any person (whether under this section or otherwise) in respect of any loss or damage resulting from the seizure or disposal except in so far as that loss or damage is caused by the negligence of the trustee; and he has a lien on the property, or the proceeds of its sale, for such of the expenses of the bankruptcy as were incurred in connection with the seizure or disposal.

DEFINITIONS

"a bankrupt": s.381(1).
"creditor": s.383(1).
"estate": ss.283, 385(1).
"property": s.436.
"the court": ss.373, 385(1).
"the official receiver": s.399(1).

GENERAL NOTE

This section establishes a summary procedure against the trustee in respect of loss to the estate caused by his misapplication or retention of property, or by his misfeasance or breach of duty. It provides a parallel procedure for bankruptcy to that established by s.212 in relation to corporate insolvency. By virtue of s.299(5) a person who has ceased to be trustee remains subject to the provisions of this section despite the fact that he may have gained his release from liability under s.299, but in such cases subs. (2) of this section requires the leave of the court before an application can be made.

This section corresponds to s.151 of the 1985 Act.

Subs. (2)

This states what persons are qualified to make application under this section for an order to be made against a trustee or former trustee in bankruptcy within the terms of subs. (1). A bankrupt is allowed to make application irrespective of whether there is or is not likely to be a surplus at the conclusion of the bankruptcy which would be returnable to him under s.330(5), but in order to prevent vexatious or obstructive applications by a bankrupt against his own trustee, the leave of the court is required for the bringing of all such applications.

Subs. (3)

This provides the trustee with a statutory defence in respect of certain kinds of liability incurred when he seizes or disposes of property not comprised in the bankrupt's estate, in the bona fide and reasonable exercise of his functions in office, unless the trustee has acted with negligence.

CHAPTER IV

ADMINISTRATION BY TRUSTEE

Preliminary

General functions of trustee

305.—(1) This Chapter applies in relation to any bankruptcy where either—

(*a*) the appointment of a person as trustee of a bankrupt's estate takes effect, or

(*b*) the official receiver becomes trustee of a bankrupt's estate.

(2) The function of the trustee is to get in, realise and distribute the bankrupt's estate in accordance with the following provisions of this Chapter; and in the carrying out of that function and in the management of the bankrupt's estate the trustee is entitled, subject to those provisions, to use his own discretion.

(3) It is the duty of the trustee, if he is not the official receiver—

(*a*) to furnish the official receiver with such information,

(*b*) to produce to the official receiver, and permit inspection by the official receiver of, such books, papers and other records, and

(*c*) to give the official receiver such other assistance,

as the official receiver may reasonably require for the purpose of enabling him to carry out his functions in relation to the bankruptcy.

(4) The official name of the trustee shall be "the trustee of the estate of . . . , a bankrupt" (inserting the name of the bankrupt); but he may be referred to as "the trustee in bankruptcy" of the particular bankrupt.

DEFINITIONS
"a bankrupt": s.381(1).
"estate": ss.283, 385(1).
"the official receiver": s.399(1).
"records": s.436.

GENERAL NOTE
Chap. IV contains provisions governing the powers and functions of the trustee, the vesting of the bankrupt's estate in the trustee, and the realisation and distribution of the estate to those entitled. This section states the scope of application of the provisions of Chap. IV, and describes the functions of the trustee in bankruptcy with regard to the estate, and his duty with respect to the official receiver, in broad and general terms.
This section corresponds to s.152 of the 1985 Act.

Subs. (1)

The appointment of a person as trustee . . . takes effect
See s.292(4).

The official receiver becomes trustee of the bankrupt's estate
See ss.295(4), 297(1), (2), 300(1), (2), (7).

Subs. (2)

The trustee is entitled . . . to use his own discretion
This restates the provision as to the discretionary powers of the trustee in bankruptcy which was formerly contained in s.79(4) of the Bankruptcy Act 1914 (repealed).

Subs. (3)
This provision is a parallel to s.143(2) which applies in respect of the liquidator of a company in a compulsory winding up.

Acquisition, control and realisation of bankrupt's estate

Vesting of bankrupt's estate in trustee

306.—(1) The bankrupt's estate shall vest in the trustee immediately on his appointment taking effect or, in the case of the official receiver, on his becoming trustee.

(2) Where any property which is, or is to be, comprised in the bankrupt's estate vests in the trustee (whether under this section or under any other provision of this Part), it shall so vest without any conveyance, assignment or transfer.

DEFINITIONS
"estate": ss.283, 385(1).
"property": s.436.
"the bankrupt": s.381(1).
"the official receiver": s.399(1).
"the trustee": s.385(1).

GENERAL NOTE
This section provides for the vesting of the bankrupt's estate in the trustee in bankruptcy immediately upon the latter's appointment taking effect. In the case where the official receiver becomes trustee under any of the provisions of the Act, the vesting occurs simultaneously with his becoming trustee. All vesting of property by virtue of this section occurs automatically by operation of law, without the need for any conveyance, assignment or transfer. This restates with greater clarity and precision the law formerly contained in s.18(1) of the Bankruptcy Act 1914 (repealed).
This section corresponds to s.153 of the 1985 Act.

After-acquired property

307.—(1) Subject to this section and section 309, the trustee may by notice in writing claim for the bankrupt's estate any property which has been acquired by, or has devolved upon, the bankrupt since the commencement of the bankruptcy.

(2) A notice under this section shall not be served in respect of—

(*a*) any property falling within subsection (2) or (3) of section 283 in Chapter II,

(*b*) any property which by virtue of any other enactment is excluded from the bankrupt's estate, or

(*c*) without prejudice to section 280(2)(*c*) (order of court on application for discharge), any property which is acquired by, or devolves upon, the bankrupt after his discharge.

(3) Subject to the next subsection, upon the service on the bankrupt of a notice under this section the property to which the notice relates shall vest in the trustee as part of the bankrupt's estate; and the trustee's title to that property has relation back to the time at which the property was acquired by, or devolved upon, the bankrupt.

(4) Where, whether before or after service of a notice under this section—

(*a*) a person acquires property in good faith, for value and without notice of the bankruptcy, or

(*b*) a banker enters into a transaction in good faith and without such notice,

the trustee is not in respect of that property or transaction entitled by virtue of this section to any remedy against that person or banker, or any person whose title to any property derives from that person or banker.

(5) References in this section to property do not include any property which, as part of the bankrupt's income, may be the subject of an income payments order under section 310.

Definitions

"bankrupt": s.381(1).
"commencement of the bankruptcy": s.278(*a*).
"estate": ss.283, 385(1).
"property": subs. (5), s.436.
"transaction": s.436.
"the official receiver": s.399(1).
"the trustee": s.385(1).

General Note

This section establishes a procedure whereby any property acquired by the bankrupt after the date of the bankruptcy order may be vested in the trustee upon the latter's intervention to claim it. In Chap. 26 of the *Cork Report* the case was argued for the retention of the basic principle, formerly expressed in s.38(*a*) of the Bankruptcy Act 1914 (repealed) that a bankrupt's available property includes such property as may be acquired by or devolve upon him before his discharge—usually referred to as "after-acquired" property. However, it was recommended at paras. 1151–1157 and 1181 that the statutory rule should be modified so that after-acquired property should not vest automatically in the trustee until he intervenes to claim it. This would entail the reversal of the decision of the Court of Appeal in *Re Pascoe* [1944] Ch. 219, and a restoration of the rule formerly regarded as expressing the law on this matter, as indicated by *dicta* in *Cohen* v. *Mitchell* (1890) 25 Q.B.D. 262. Governmental acceptance of these proposals was indicated in paras. 111–114 of the *White Paper*. The present section implements these recommendations. The trustee in bankruptcy may claim the bankrupt's available, after-acquired property by means of a notice served pursuant to subs. (1), provided that notice is served within the time limit established by the provisions of s.309.

This section corresponds to subs. (1)–(4) and (7) of s.154 of the 1985 Act.

Subss. (3) and (4)

These are important provisions which together establish a rule that where the trustee duly serves notice under subs. (1), any property thereby claimed for the bankrupt's estate shall vest in the trustee with effect from the time at which the property was first acquired by, or devolved upon, the bankrupt himself. The doctrine of relation back in this context is subject to the operation of the provisions in subs. (4) which confer protection, in the cases therein mentioned in paras. (*a*) and (*b*), upon persons dealing with the bankrupt in relation to any after-acquired property which the trustee claims, or has claimed, for the estate. As recommended in para. 1145–1150 of the *Cork Report,* this maintains the position formerly established in s.47 of the Bankruptcy Act 1914 (repealed) but is drafted with greater clarity so as to leave it beyond doubt that a third party (including a banker) can only enjoy the protection of subs. (4) if he has acted without notice of the bankruptcy.

Vesting in trustee of certain items of excess value

308.—(1) Subject to the next section, where—

(*a*) property is excluded by virtue of section 283(2) (tools of trade, household effects, etc.) from the bankrupt's estate, and

(*b*) it appears to the trustee that the realisable value of the whole or any part of that property exceeds the cost of a reasonable replacement for that property or that part of it,

the trustee may by notice in writing claim that property or, as the case may be, that part of it for the bankrupt's estate.

(2) Upon the service on the bankrupt of a notice under this section, the property to which the notice relates vests in the trustee as part of the bankrupt's estate; and, except against a purchaser in good faith, for value and without notice of the bankruptcy, the trustee's title to that property has relation back to the commencement of the bankruptcy.

(3) The trustee shall apply funds comprised in the estate to the purchase by or on behalf of the bankrupt of a reasonable replacement for any property vested in the trustee under this section; and the duty imposed by this subsection has priority over the obligation of the trustee to distribute the estate.

(4) For the purposes of this section property is a reasonable replacement for other property if it is reasonably adequate for meeting the needs met by the other property.

Definitions

"bankrupt": s.381(1).
"estate": ss.283, 385(1).
"property": s.436.
"reasonable replacement": subs. (4).
"the trustee": s.385(1).

General Note

This section operates in conjunction with s.283, subs. (2) of which indicates what property is excluded from the bankrupt's available estate. Under the procedure established by this section, the trustee may claim by means of a notice in writing any item of the bankrupt's exempted property which appears to have a higher intrinsic value than the cost of providing a reasonable replacement for the bankrupt or his family to use. The cost of providing such a replacement is by subs. (3) made a first charge on the funds comprised in the bankrupt's estate. Such a procedure for substitution of items of exempt property was recommended in para. 1109 of the *Cork Report.*

Subs. (4)

This endeavours to provide a definition of the term "reasonable replacement" for the purposes of this section, but is somewhat tautologous in that the notion of reasonableness occurs both in the definition and in the term defined. Essentially, it will be a matter of judgment for the trustee in bankruptcy in the first instance to determine whether a proposed substitute is a "reasonable replacement", subject to the bankrupt's right to refer the matter to the court under s.303(1) if he is dissatisfied with the trustee's decision. In a case where the trustee is personally uncertain of his own assessment, he may seek directions from the court under s.303(2).

Time-limit for notice under s.307 or 308

309.—(1) Except with the leave of the court, a notice shall not be served—

(*a*) under section 307, after the end of the period of 42 days beginning with the day on which it first came to the knowledge of the trustee that the property in question had been acquired by, or had devolved upon, the bankrupt;

(*b*) under section 308, after the end of the period of 42 days beginning with the day on which the property in question first came to the knowledge of the trustee.

(2) For the purposes of this section—

(*a*) anything which comes to the knowledge of the trustee is deemed in relation to any successor of his as trustee to have come to the knowledge of the successor at the same time; and

(*b*) anything which comes (otherwise than under paragraph (*a*)) to the knowledge of a person before he is the trustee is deemed to come to his knowledge on his appointment taking effect or, in the case of the official receiver, on his becoming trustee.

DEFINITIONS

"property": ss.307(5), 436.
"the bankrupt": s.381(1).
"the court": ss.373, 385(1).
"the official receiver": s.399(1).
"the trustee": s.385(1).

GENERAL NOTE

This section prescribes the time limits for the service of notice by the trustee in the exercise of his powers under ss.307 and 308. It also provides rules for determining the moment at which a matter is deemed to come to the knowledge of the trustee for the time being, for the purpose of establishing the date from which time commences to run. The section is a combination of the provisions formerly contained in ss.154(5), (6) and 155(3) of the 1985 Act.

Income payments orders

310.—(1) The court may, on the application of the trustee, make an order ("an income payments order") claiming for the bankrupt's estate so much of the income of the bankrupt during the period for which the order is in force as may be specified in the order.

(2) The court shall not make an income payments order the effect of which would be to reduce the income of the bankrupt below what appears to the court to be necessary for meeting the reasonable domestic needs of the bankrupt and his family.

(3) An income payments order shall, in respect of any payment of income to which it is to apply, either—

(*a*) require the bankrupt to pay the trustee an amount equal to so much of that payment as is claimed by the order, or

(*b*) require the person making the payment to pay so much of it as is so claimed to the trustee, instead of to the bankrupt.

(4) Where the court makes an income payments order it may, if it thinks fit, discharge or vary any attachment of earnings order that is for the time being in force to secure payments by the bankrupt.

(5) Sums received by the trustee under an income payments order form part of the bankrupt's estate.

(6) An income payments order shall not be made after the discharge of the bankrupt, and if made before, shall not have effect after his discharge except—

(*a*) in the case of a discharge under section 279(1)(*a*) (order of court), by virtue of a condition imposed by the court under section 280(2)(*c*) (income, etc. after discharge), or

(*b*) in the case of a discharge under section 279(1)(*b*) (expiration of relevant period), by virtue of a provision of the order requiring it to continue in force for a period ending after the discharge but no later than 3 years after the making of the order.

(7) For the purposes of this section the income of the bankrupt comprises every payment in the nature of income which is from time to time made to him or to which he from time to time becomes entitled, including any payment in respect of the carrying on of any business or in respect of any office or employment.

Definitions

"bankrupt": s.381(1).
"business": s.436.
"court": ss.373, 385(1).
"estate": ss.283, 385(1).
"family": s.385(1).
"income of the bankrupt": subs. (7).
"income payments order": subs. (1).
"the trustee": s.385(1).

General Note

This enables the court on the application of the trustee to make an income payments order whereby a proportion of the income of the bankrupt is claimed for his estate and made available for distribution to creditors. It represents a completely fresh approach in place of the former provisions of s.51 of the Bankruptcy Act 1914 (repealed). Paras. 1158–1163 of the *Cork Report,* while accepting the principle that a proportion of the bankrupt's earnings (net of tax) should be retainable for the maintenance of himself and his family, advocated a more emphatic policy of seeking to maximise the contribution towards the payment of debts by contributions from the bankrupt's surplus income. The principle is re-affirmed that any income of an undischarged bankrupt constitutes after-acquired property, so that the proper approach should be to ascertain by investigation what proportion of income can be regarded as "necessary" for meeting the reasonable domestic needs of the bankrupt and his family (meaning, in this context, the persons who are living with him *and* are dependent upon him: s.385(1)). This approach was accepted in para. 114 of the *White Paper* and forms the basis of this section.

Subs. (4)

Attachment of earnings order

Such orders may be made under the provisions of the Attachment of Earnings Act 1971, ss.1(2)(*c*) and (5).

Subs. (6)

This establishes the general rule that an income payments order may not be made after the discharge of the bankrupt, nor be made so as to remain in effect after that date, subject to the saving, in paras. (*a*) and (*b*), in respect of the exercise of powers vested in the court, firstly under s.280(2)(*c*) whereby the court may make an order for discharge subject to any conditions with respect to any subsequent income or subsequently acquired property, and secondly under s.279(3) whereby the court may make an order, subject to specified conditions, suspending the running of time towards the automatic discharge of the bankrupt under subs. 1(*b*) of that section.

Acquisition by trustee of control

311.—(1) The trustee shall take possession of all books, papers and other records which relate to the bankrupt's estate or affairs and which belong to him or are in his possession or under his control (including any which would be privileged from disclosure in any proceedings).

(2) In relation to, and for the purpose of acquiring or retaining possession of, the bankrupt's estate, the trustee is in the same position as if he were a receiver of property appointed by the High Court; and the court may, on his application, enforce such acquisition or retention accordingly.

(3) Where any part of the bankrupt's estate consists of stock or shares in a company, shares in a ship or any other property transferable in the books of a company, office or person, the trustee may exercise the right to transfer the property to the same extent as the bankrupt might have exercised it if he had not become bankrupt.

(4) Where any part of the estate consists of things in action, they are deemed to have been assigned to the trustee; but notice of the deemed assignment need not be given except in so far as it is necessary, in a case where the deemed assignment is from the bankrupt himself, for protecting the priority of the trustee.

(5) Where any goods comprised in the estate are held by any person by way of pledge, pawn or other security and no notice has been served in respect of those goods by the official receiver under subsection (5) of section 285 (restriction on realising security), the trustee may serve such a notice in respect of the goods; and whether or not a notice has been served under this subsection or that subsection, the trustee may, if he thinks fit, exercise the bankrupt's right of redemption in respect of any such goods.

(6) A notice served by the trustee under subsection (5) has the same effect as a notice served by the official receiver under section 285(5).

Definitions

"affairs": s.385(2).
"bankrupt": s.381(1).
"estate": ss.283, 385(1).
"property": s.436.
"records": s.436.
"security", "secured creditor": ss.383, 385(1).
"the official receiver": s.399(1).
"the trustee": s.385(1).

General Note

This section requires the trustee to take control of the bankrupt's estate and of all his papers and records relating thereto. For this purpose the trustee is clothed with the powers and right enjoyed by a receiver of property appointed by the High Court, and may invoke any appropriate remedies for the purpose of enforcing his rights of acquisition and retention. The force of this provision is augmented by those of s.333 whereby the duties of the bankrupt in relation to his trustee are laid down.

The consequential provisions contained in subss. (3)–(6) inclusive of this section facilitate the acquisition by the trustee of such parts of the bankrupt's property as are of an incorporeal nature—choses in action—or such as are transferable only through the instrumentality of some third party, or such as are held by any person who has a security interest or right of retention over them. The section largely restates, with suitable updating in the drafting, the provisions formerly contained in s.48 of the Bankruptcy Act 1914 (repealed).

This section corresponds to s.157 of the 1985 Act.

Subs. (1)

(including any which would be privileged from disclosure in any proceedings)

These words in parentheses serve to eliminate all scope for argument to the effect that any document may be exempted from the trustee's power of acquisition under this section by virtue of the fact that it is covered by professional legal privilege.

Obligation to surrender control to trustee

312.—(1) The bankrupt shall deliver up to the trustee possession of any property, books, papers or other records of which he has possession or control and of which the trustee is required to take possession.

This is without prejudice to the general duties of the bankrupt under section 333 in this Chapter.

(2) If any of the following is in possession of any property, books, papers or other records of which the trustee is required to take possession, namely—

(*a*) the official receiver,

(*b*) a person who has ceased to be trustee of the bankrupt's estate, or

(*c*) a person who has been the supervisor of a voluntary arrangement approved in relation to the bankrupt under Part VIII,

the official receiver or, as the case may be, that person shall deliver up possession of the property, books, papers or records to the trustee.

(3) Any banker or agent of the bankrupt or any other person who holds any property to the account of, or for, the bankrupt shall pay or deliver to the trustee all property in his possession or under his control which forms part of the bankrupt's estate and which he is not by law entitled to retain as against the bankrupt or trustee.

(4) If any person without reasonable excuse fails to comply with any obligation imposed by this section, he is guilty of a contempt of court and liable to be punished accordingly (in addition to any other punishment to which he may be subject).

DEFINITIONS

"bankrupt": s.381(1).
"estate": ss.283, 385(1).
"property": s.436.
"records": s.436.
"supervisor of a voluntary arrangement": s.263(2).
"the official receiver": s.399(1).
"the trustee": s.385(1).

GENERAL NOTE

The provisions of this section are largely complementary to those of s.311, and impose a duty upon the bankrupt, and also upon the persons referred to in subs. (2), to surrender control of the bankrupt's property, papers and records to the trustee. By subs. (4), failure on the part of any person to comply with any obligation imposed by this section is punishable *per se* as a contempt of court. S.349 makes general provision regarding the unenforceability of any liens or other rights of retention of the books, papers or records of the bankrupt, in face of the right of the trustee in bankruptcy to acquire possession thereof.

This section corresponds to s.158 of the 1985 Act.

Charge on bankrupt's home

313.—(1) Where any property consisting of an interest in a dwelling house which is occupied by the bankrupt or by his spouse or former spouse is comprised in the bankrupt's estate and the trustee is, for any reason, unable for the time being to realise that property, the trustee may apply to the court for an order imposing a charge on the property for the benefit of the bankrupt's estate.

(2) If on an application under this section the court imposes a charge on any property, the benefit of that charge shall be comprised in the bankrupt's estate and is enforceable, up to the value from time to time of the property secured, for the payment of any amount which is payable otherwise than to the bankrupt out of the estate and of interest on that amount at the prescribed rate.

(3) An order under this section made in respect of property vested in the trustee shall provide, in accordance with the rules, for the property to cease to be comprised in the bankrupt's estate and, subject to the charge (and any prior charge), to vest in the bankrupt.

(4) Subsections (1) and (2) and (4) to (6) of section 3 of the Charging Orders Act 1979 (supplemental provisions with respect to charging orders) have effect in relation to orders under this section as in relation to charging orders under that Act.

DEFINITIONS

"bankrupt": s.381(1).
"dwelling-house": s.385(1).
"estate": ss.283, 385(1).
"property": s.436.
"prescribed": s.384.
"the court": ss.373, 385(1).
"the rules": ss.384, 412.
"the trustee": s.385(1).

GENERAL NOTE

This section makes special provision with respect to the bankrupt's interest in a dwelling-house occupied by the bankrupt or by his spouse or former spouse, in cases where the trustee is unable for the time being to realise that property. The section enables the trustee to apply to the court for a charging order to be made in respect of the property for the benefit of the bankrupt's estate. Subs. (4) incorporates by reference certain supplemental provisions of the Charging Orders Act 1979 in relation to an order made under this section.

The procedure established by this section is of particular relevance in view of the provisions of ss.336 and 337 which give rise to the possibility that the rights of occupation of the bankrupt personally, or of the bankrupt's spouse, or former spouse, may under certain circumstances be held to outweigh for a time the interests of the bankrupt's creditors in relation to the property in question. By s.332(2), the fact that an order has been made, or has been applied for, under this section is a condition which, if fulfilled, enables the trustee in bankruptcy to summon a final meeting of creditors under s.331 despite the fact that he has been unable to realise property in the estate consisting of an interest in a dwelling-house which is occupied by the bankrupt or by his or her past or present spouse.

This section corresponds to s.159 of the 1985 Act.

Powers of trustee

314.—(1) The trustee may—

(*a*) with the permission of the creditors' committee or the court, exercise any of the powers specified in Part I of Schedule 5 to this Act, and

(*b*) without that permission, exercise any of the general powers specified in Part II of that Schedule.

(2) With the permission of the creditors' committee or the court, the trustee may appoint the bankrupt—

(*a*) to superintend the management of his estate or any part of it,

(*b*) to carry on his business (if any) for the benefit of his creditors, or

(*c*) in any other respect to assist in administering the estate in such manner and on such terms as the trustee may direct.

(3) A permission given for the purposes of subsection (1)(*a*) or (2) shall not be a general permission but shall relate to a particular proposed exercise of the power in question; and a person dealing with the trustee in good faith and for value is not to be concerned to enquire whether any permission required in either case has been given.

(4) Where the trustee has done anything without the permission required by subsection (1)(*a*) or (2), the court or the creditors' committee may, for the purpose of enabling him to meet his expenses out of the bankrupt's estate, ratify what the trustee has done.

But the committee shall not do so unless it is satisfied that the trustee has acted in a case of urgency and has sought its ratification without undue delay.

(5) Part III of Schedule 5 to this Act has effect with respect to the things which the trustee is able to do for the purposes of, or in connection with, the exercise of any of his powers under any of this Group of Parts.

(6) Where the trustee (not being the official receiver) in exercise of the powers conferred on him by any provision in this Group of Parts—

(*a*) disposes of any property comprised in the bankrupt's estate to an associate of the bankrupt, or

(*b*) employs a solicitor,

he shall, if there is for the time being a creditors' committee, give notice to the committee of that exercise of his powers.

(7) Without prejudice to the generality of subsection (5) and Part III of Schedule 5, the trustee may, if he thinks fit, at any time summon a general meeting of the bankrupt's creditors.

Subject to the preceding provisions in this Group of Parts, he shall summon such a meeting if he is requested to do so by a creditor of the bankrupt and the request is made with the concurrence of not less than one-tenth, in value, of the bankrupt's creditors (including the creditor making the request).

(8) Nothing in this Act is to be construed as restricting the capacity of the trustee to exercise any of his powers outside England and Wales.

DEFINITIONS

"associate": ss.435, 436.
"bankrupt": s.381(1).
"bankruptcy debt": s.382.
"business": s.436.
"creditor": s.383(1).
"debt", "liability": ss.382(3), (4), 385(1).
"estate": ss.283, 385(1).
"property": s.436.
"security", "secured": ss.383, 385(1).
"the court": ss.373, 385(1).
"the official receiver": s.399(1).
"the trustee": s.385(1).

TRANSITIONAL PROVISION

Sched. 11, para. 14(6).

GENERAL NOTE

This section, which operates in conjunction with Sched. 5 to the Act, specifies the general powers of the trustee in bankruptcy, and indicates which of them are exercisable on his own initiative without permission (subs. (1)(*b*)), and which are exercisable with the permission of the creditors' committee (if there is one) or otherwise of the court (subss. (1)(*a*), (2)). The provisions of the first two subsections, together with Sched. 5, largely restate the provisions formerly contained in ss.55, 56 and 57 of the Bankruptcy Act 1914 (repealed). However, in accordance with the recommendation in paras. 795–6 of the *Cork Report* the former requirement that the trustee must obtain the permission of the creditors' committee before employing a solicitor has been replaced by the requirement in subs. (6) that, where a trustee other than the official receiver employs a solicitor in the exercise of his powers under this Part, he must give notice of that fact to the creditors' committee if there is one in being at the time.

This section corresponds to s.160 of the 1985 Act, save that the provisions contained in subss. (1) and (2) of that section are now contained in Sched. 5 to the present Act.

Subs. (6)(a)

Disposes of any property . . . to an associate of the bankrupt

It has been assumed that the requirements under Pt. XIII of this Act, whereby all privately appointed trustees in bankruptcy are henceforth required to be qualified insolvency practitioners within the meaning of s.390, will largely ensure the discontinuation of certain notorious malpractices whereby trustees in bankruptcy have collusively disposed of assets at a low price to persons connected with the bankrupt. This subsection therefore does not deprive the trustee of the power to dispose of any property belonging to the bankrupt's estate to a person who is an associate of the bankrupt (within the meaning of s.435), but it does impose the requirement that the trustee must inform the creditors' committee (if there is one) of any transaction falling into this category. The onus then rests with the committee to determine whether the transaction was abusive or not, and if necessary to challenge the trustee's act under s.303. Furthermore the trustee remains amenable to the procedure for imposing summary liability under s.304 even after he has obtained his release under s.299. He could therefore be challenged retrospectively on account of any transaction not initially perceived to be abusive and detrimental to the creditors' interests.

Subs. (7)

This confers a wide power upon the trustee to summon a general meeting of creditors at any time at his own discretion. It also establishes a procedure whereby one or more creditors, representing at least one-tenth in value of the bankrupt's creditors, may formally compel the trustee to convene a general meeting.

Disclaimer of onerous property

Disclaimer (general power)

315.—(1) Subject as follows, the trustee may, by the giving of the prescribed notice, disclaim any onerous property and may do so notwithstanding that he has taken possession of it, endeavoured to sell it or otherwise exercised rights of ownership in relation to it.

(2) The following is onerous property for the purposes of this section, that is to say—

(*a*) any unprofitable contract, and

(*b*) any other property comprised in the bankrupt's estate which is unsaleable or not readily saleable, or is such that it may give rise to a liability to pay money or perform any other onerous act.

(3) A disclaimer under this section—

(*a*) operates so as to determine, as from the date of the disclaimer, the rights, interests and liabilities of the bankrupt and his estate in or in respect of the property disclaimed, and

(*b*) discharges the trustee from all personal liability in respect of that property as from the commencement of his trusteeship,

but does not, except so far as is necessary for the purpose of releasing the bankrupt, the bankrupt's estate and the trustee from any liability, affect the rights or liabilities of any other person.

(4) A notice of disclaimer shall not be given under this section in respect of any property that has been claimed for the estate under section 307 (after-acquired property) or 308 (personal property of bankrupt exceeding reasonable replacement value), except with the leave of the court.

(5) Any person sustaining loss or damage in consequence of the operation of a disclaimer under this section is deemed to be a creditor of the bankrupt to the extent of the loss or damage and accordingly may prove for the loss or damage as a bankruptcy debt.

Definitions

"bankrupt": s.381(1).
"bankruptcy debt": s.382.
"commencement of trusteeship": s.292(4).
"creditor": s.383(1).
"estate": ss.283, 385(1).
"liability": s.283(4).
"onerous property": subs. (2).
"prescribed": s.384.

"property": s.436.
"the court": ss.201, 211(1).
"the trustee": s.385(1).

General Note

This section empowers the trustee to disclaim onerous property (as defined in subs. (2)) which is comprised in the bankrupt's estate. Chap. 27 of the *Cork Report* was devoted to a consideration of the disclaimer codes formerly applicable in winding-up and in bankruptcy respectively. The former, which were embodied in ss.618 and 619 of the Companies Act 1985 together with Pt. I of Sched. 20 to that Act (repealed) are now replaced by ss.178–182 of this Act, while the latter, formerly contained in s.54 of the Bankruptcy Act 1914 (repealed) are replaced by this section. The provisions concerning disclaimer in bankruptcy are now largely harmonised with those applicable in a winding-up: see General Note to ss.178–182.

This section corresponds to subss. (1)–(4) and (10) of s.161 of the 1985 Act.

Subs. (3)(b)

As from the commencement of his trusteeship

This phrase is intended to emphasise that a disclaimer is only effective to discharge the disclaiming trustee from liability in respect of the disclaimed property from the date specified. No predecessor in the office of trustee will obtain any discharge from liability by virtue of a disclaimer effected by the incumbent office holder.

Subs. (4)

Where the trustee in bankruptcy has previously exercised his powers under s.307 to claim an item of after-acquired property, or under s.308 to claim an item of property originally exempted from passing into the bankrupt's estate, he is not allowed to disclaim any property so claimed except with the leave of the court. This provision corresponds to the recommendation in para. 1199 of the *Cork Report.*

Subs. (5)

Note that s.320(5) requires the effect of any order made under that section to be taken into account in assessing for the purposes of this subsection the extent of any loss or damage sustained in consequence of the disclaimer.

Notice requiring trustee's decision

316.—(1) Notice of disclaimer shall not be given under section 315 in respect of any property if—

(*a*) a person interested in the property has applied in writing to the trustee or one of his predecessors as trustee requiring the trustee or that predecessor to decide whether he will disclaim or not, and

(*b*) the period of 28 days beginning with the day on which that application was made has expired without a notice of disclaimer having been given under section 315 in respect of that property.

(2) The trustee is deemed to have adopted any contract which by virtue of this section he is not entitled to disclaim.

Definitions

"property": s.436.
"the trustee": s.385(1).

General Note

This section, which corresponds to s.161(5) of the 1985 Act, establishes a procedure whereby a person interested in property comprised in the bankrupt's estate may put an end to any uncertainty regarding the possibility of the trustee's exercising the power of disclaimer under s.315 with regard to the property in question. By making the written application referred to in subs. (1)(*a*), the person interested sets in motion a process by which the trustee must either exercise the power of disclaimer within 28 days, or lose altogether the right to disclaim the property affected.

Disclaimer of leaseholds

317.—(1) The disclaimer of any property of a leasehold nature does not take effect unless a copy of the disclaimer has been served (so far as the trustee is aware of their addresses) on every person claiming under the bankrupt as underlessee or mortgagee and either—

(*a*) no application under section 320 below is made with respect to the property before the end of the period of 14 days beginning with the day on which the last notice served under this subsection was served, or

(*b*) where such an application has been made, the court directs that the disclaimer is to take effect.

(2) Where the court gives a direction under subsection (1)(*b*) it may also, instead of or in addition to any order it makes under section 320, make such orders with respect to fixtures, tenant's improvements and other matters arising out of the lease as it thinks fit.

Definitions

"property": s.436.
"the bankrupt": s.381(1).
"the court": ss.373, 385(1).
"the trustee": s.385(1).

General Note

This section, which comprises the provisions formerly contained in subss. (6) and (7) of s.161 of the 1985 Act, contains particular rules applicable in the case where the trustee exercises the power of disclaimer under s.315 in relation to property of a leasehold nature.

Disclaimer of dwelling house

318. Without prejudice to section 317, the disclaimer of any property in a dwelling house does not take effect unless a copy of the disclaimer has been served (so far as the trustee is aware of their addresses) on every person in occupation of or claiming a right to occupy the dwelling house and either—

(*a*) no application under section 320 is made with respect to the property before the end of the period of 14 days beginning with the day on which the last notice served under this section was served, or

(*b*) where such an application has been made, the court directs that the disclaimer is to take effect.

Definitions

"dwelling house": s.385(1).
"property": s.436.
"the court": ss.373, 385(1).

General Note

This section, which comprises the provision formerly contained in s.161(8) of the 1985 Act, has application in the case where the trustee exercises the power of disclaimer under s.315 in relation to a dwelling house.

Disclaimer of land subject to rentcharge

319.—(1) The following applies where, in consequence of the disclaimer under section 315 of any land subject to a rentcharge, that land vests by operation of law in the Crown or any other person (referred to in the next subsection as "the proprietor").

(2) The proprietor, and the successors in title of the proprietor, are not subject to any personal liability in respect of any sums becoming due under the rentcharge, except sums becoming due after the proprietor, or

some person claiming under or through the proprietor, has taken possession or control of the land or has entered into occupation of it.

DEFINITION

"the proprietor": subs. (2).

GENERAL NOTE

This section, which comprises the provision formerly contained in s.161(9) of the 1985 Act, has application in the case where the trustee exercises the power of disclaimer under s.315 in relation to any land subject to a rentcharge. The section confers protection upon the Crown or any other person (here referred to as "the proprietor") in whom the land consequently vests by operation of law, and ensures that those parties are not liable for any sums becoming due under the rentcharge prior to the date when the proprietor first takes possession or control of the land, or enters into occupation of it.

Court order vesting disclaimed property

320.—(1) This section and the next apply where the trustee has disclaimed property under section 315.

(2) An application may be made to the court under this section by—

(*a*) any person who claims an interest in the disclaimed property,

(*b*) any person who is under any liability in respect of the disclaimed property, not being a liability discharged by the disclaimer, or

(*c*) where the disclaimed property is property in a dwelling house, any person who at the time when the bankruptcy petition was presented was in occupation of or entitled to occupy the dwelling house.

(3) Subject as follows in this section and the next, the court may, on an application under this section, make an order on such terms as it thinks fit for the vesting of the disclaimed property in, or for its delivery to—

(*a*) a person entitled to it or a trustee for such a person,

(*b*) a person subject to such a liability as is mentioned in subsection (2)(*b*) or a trustee for such a person, or

(*c*) where the disclaimed property is property in a dwelling house, any person who at the time when the bankruptcy petition was presented was in occupation of or entitled to occupy the dwelling house.

(4) The court shall not make an order by virtue of subsection (3)(*b*) except where it appears to the court that it would be just to do so for the purpose of compensating the person subject to the liability in respect of the disclaimer.

(5) The effect of any order under this section shall be taken into account in assessing for the purposes of section 315(5) the extent of any loss or damage sustained by any person in consequence of the disclaimer.

(6) An order under this section vesting property in any person need not be completed by any conveyance, assignment or transfer.

DEFINITIONS

"dwelling-house": s.385(1).
"liability": s.382(4).
"property": s.436.
"the court": ss.373, 385(1).
"the trustee": s.385(1).

GENERAL NOTE

The provisions of this section are complementary to those of ss.315–319, and provide for the court to make a vesting order upon the application of any of the persons mentioned in subs. (2), being a person who either has an interest in, or is subject to, a continuing liability in respect of any property disclaimed by the trustee under s.315. This section bears a general similarity to s.181, which makes comparable provisions for the court to make vesting orders in respect of property disclaimed by a liquidator under ss.178–180. The overall clarity of drafting in this new section is a considerable improvement over that of the former provisions of s.54(6) of the Bankruptcy Act 1914 (repealed).

This section corresponds to subss. (1)–(4), (9) and (10) of s.162 of the 1985 Act.

Order under s.320 in respect of leaseholds

321.—(1) The court shall not make an order under section 320 vesting property of a leasehold nature in any person, except on terms making that person—

(*a*) subject to the same liabilities and obligations as the bankrupt was subject to under the lease on the day the bankruptcy petition was presented, or

(*b*) if the court thinks fit, subject to the same liabilities and obligations as that person would be subject to if the lease had been assigned to him on that day.

(2) For the purposes of an order under section 320 relating to only part of any property comprised in a lease, the requirements of subsection (1) apply as if the lease comprised only the property to which the order relates.

(3) Where subsection (1) applies and no person is willing to accept an order under section 320 on the terms required by that subsection, the court may (by order under section 320) vest the estate or interest of the bankrupt in the property in any person who is liable (whether personally or in a representative capacity and whether alone or jointly with the bankrupt) to perform the lessee's covenants in the lease.

The court may by virtue of this subsection vest that estate and interest in such a person freed and discharged from all estates, incumbrances and interests created by the bankrupt.

(4) Where subsection (1) applies and a person declines to accept any order under section 320, that person shall be excluded from all interest in the property.

Definitions
"property": s.436.
"the bankrupt": s.381(1).
"the court": ss.373, 385(1).

General Note
This section, which comprises subss. (5)–(8) of s.162 of the 1985 Act, contains provisions which apply in the case where a vesting order is made under s.320 in respect of property of a leasehold nature which has been disclaimed by the trustee under s.315.

Subs. (3)
It is to be noted that the word "estate" is twice used in this subsection, but in a sense different from that which is ascribed to the term by the combined provisions of ss.283 and 385(1), which apply in the context of any reference to the *corpus* of property of which the bankrupt is divested in consequence of his adjudication. In this subsection, the term "estate" is employed in its alternative sense, referring to "an estate or interest in property."

Distribution of bankrupt's estate

Proof of debts

322.—(1) Subject to this section and the next, the proof of any bankruptcy debt by a secured or unsecured creditor of the bankrupt and the admission or rejection of any proof shall take place in accordance with the rules.

(2) Where a bankruptcy debt bears interest, that interest is provable as part of the debt except in so far as it is payable in respect of any period after the commencement of the bankruptcy.

(3) The trustee shall estimate the value of any bankruptcy debt which, by reason of its being subject to any contingency or contingencies or for any other reason, does not bear a certain value.

(4) Where the value of a bankruptcy debt is estimated by the trustee under subsection (3) or, by virtue of section 303 in Chapter III, by the court, the amount provable in the bankruptcy in respect of the debt is the amount of the estimate.

DEFINITIONS

"bankrupt": s.381(1).
"bankruptcy debt": s.382.
"commencement of the bankruptcy": s.278(*a*).
"debt": ss.382(3), 385(1).
"secured creditor", unsecured creditor": ss.383, 385(1).
"the court": ss.373, 385(1).
"the rules": ss.384, 412.
"the trustee": s.385(1).

GENERAL NOTE

This section provides that the proof of bankruptcy debts by all categories of creditor shall take place in accordance with provisions to be contained in the rules. These provisions replace those formerly contained in s.32 of, and the Second Sched. to, the Bankruptcy Act 1914 (repealed).

This section corresponds to s.163 of the 1985 Act.

Subs. (2)

This specifies that interest is provable as part of a debt for any period up to the date of the making of the bankruptcy order. Payments in respect of any interest due for the period since the commencement of bankruptcy will only be made, pursuant to s.328(4), if any surplus remains after the payment in full of the preferential and ordinary debts.

Subss. (3), (4)

These provisions establish the principle that proof may be lodged in respect of debts whose value is uncertain by virtue of the fact that they are subject to one or more contingencies. The amount for which such a debt is admitted to proof will be the value estimated by the trustee, subject to the right of the proving creditor, or any other person who is dissatisfied by the trustee's decision, to apply to the court under s.303(1). Alternatively, under s.303(2) the trustee himself may apply to the court for directions in case of uncertainty. In either type of case, the court's estimate is then substituted for that of the trustee.

Mutual credit and set-off

323.—(1) This section applies where before the commencement of the bankruptcy there have been mutual credits, mutual debts or other mutual dealings between the bankrupt and any creditor of the bankrupt proving or claiming to prove for a bankruptcy debt.

(2) An account shall be taken of what is due from each party to the other in respect of the mutual dealings and the sums due from one party shall be set off against the sums due from the other.

(3) Sums due from the bankrupt to another party shall not be included in the account taken under subsection (2) if that other party had notice at the time they became due that a bankruptcy petition relating to the bankrupt was pending.

(4) Only the balance (if any) of the account taken under subsection (2) is provable as a bankruptcy debt or, as the case may be, to be paid to the trustee as part of the bankrupt's estate.

DEFINITIONS

"bankruptcy debt": s.382.
"bankruptcy petition": s.381(3).

"commencement of the bankruptcy": s.278(*a*).
"creditor": s.383(1).
"debt": ss.382(3), 385(1).
"estate": ss.283, 385(1).
"the bankrupt": s.381(1).

General Note

This section re-enacts the provisions formerly contained in s.31 of the Bankruptcy Act 1914 (repealed), with the drafting suitably clarified and amended to take account of the abolition of acts of bankruptcy and receiving orders. The substance of the law is unchanged, and thus the new section fails to respond to the recommendations in Chap. 30 of the *Cork Report* that amendments should be made so as to permit parties to contract out of the provisions regarding set-off, and so as to preclude, in particular, the operation of set-off where liabilities exist in favour of and against different Departments of State operating under the Crown (see paras. 1343–1348 and 1362). Consequently, cases decided under s.31 of the Bankruptcy Act 1914 remain good law, including those which held that it was not possible for parties to contract out of the statutory requirement of set-off (see *National Westminster Bank Ltd.* v. *Halesowen Presswork and Assemblies Ltd.* [1972] A.C. 785), nor to contract for the set-off of any claims which could not be set off under the statutory provision where to do so would violate the principle of *pari passu* distribution in an insolvency (see *British Eagle Airlines Ltd.* v. *Compagnie Nationale Air France* [1975] 1 W.L.R. 758, H.L.). The settled law on the requirement of mutuality is confirmed by the reiteration of the word "mutual" in subs. (1) but, through the application of the doctrine that the Crown is one and indivisible, this will continue to operate in relation to the Crown in a way which is one-sided and arguably unfair to the general body of creditors. Amendments to the Involvency Bill 1985 which would have deprived the Crown of this privileged position were unsuccessfully moved at various stages before both Houses of Parliament (H.L. Vol. 459, cols. 1268–1270; H.C. Standing Committee E, June 18, 1985, cols. 397–404; *ibid.* June 20, 1985, col. 545).

This section corresponds to s.164 of the 1985 Act.

Subs. (3)

This restates the substance of the *proviso* to s.31 of the Bankruptcy Act 1914 (repealed), and is an important safeguard against abusive arrangements, working against the concept of equality of treatment of creditors, which may be concluded between a debtor and his creditor at a time when bankruptcy proceedings are pending.

Distribution by means of dividend

324.—(1) Whenever the trustee has sufficient funds in hand for the purpose he shall, subject to the retention of such sums as may be necessary for the expenses of the bankruptcy, declare and distribute dividends among the creditors in respect of the bankruptcy debts which they have respectively proved.

(2) The trustee shall give notice of his intention to declare and distribute a dividend.

(3) Where the trustee has declared a dividend, he shall give notice of the dividend and of how it is proposed to distribute it; and a notice given under this subsection shall contain the prescribed particulars of the bankrupt's estate.

(4) In the calculation and distribution of a dividend the trustee shall make provision—

(*a*) for any bankruptcy debts which appear to him to be due to persons who, by reason of the distance of their place of residence, may not have had sufficient time to tender and establish their proofs,

(*b*) for any bankruptcy debts which are the subject of claims which have not yet been determined, and

(*c*) for disputed proofs and claims.

Definitions

"bankrupt": s.381(1).
"bankruptcy debt": s.382.

"creditor": s.383(1).
"estate": ss.283, 385(1).
"prescribed": s.384.
"the trustee": s.385(1).

General Note

This section, in conjunction with ss.325–327, essentially re-enacts, the law as previously stated in ss.56(9), 62–65 and 68 of the Bankruptcy Act 1914 (repealed). However, there is no longer any provision requiring the trustee to distribute dividends at specified intervals of time.

This section corresponds to subss. (1)–(4) of s.165 of the 1985 Act.

Claims by unsatisfied creditors

325.—(1) A creditor who has not proved his debt before the declaration of any dividend is not entitled to disturb, by reason that he has not participated in it, the distribution of that dividend or any other dividend declared before his debt was proved, but—

(*a*) when he has proved that debt he is entitled to be paid, out of any money for the time being available for the payment of any further dividend, any dividend or dividends which he has failed to receive; and

(*b*) any dividend or dividends payable under paragraph (*a*) shall be paid before that money is applied to the payment of any such further dividend.

(2) No action lies against the trustee for a dividend, but if the trustee refuses to pay a dividend the court may, if it thinks fit, order him to pay it and also to pay, out of his own money—

(*a*) interest on the dividend, at the rate for the time being specified in section 17 of the Judgments Act 1838, from the time it was withheld, and

(*b*) the costs of the proceedings in which the order to pay is made.

Definitions

"creditor": s.383(1).
"debt": ss.382(3), 385(1).
"the court": ss.373, 385(1).
"the trustee": s.385(1).

General Note

This section comprises the provisions formerly contained in subss. (5) and (6) of s.165 of the 1985 Act. It specifies the conditions under which creditors who come in late to proof are eligible to receive dividends, and also prescribes the extent to which the trustee is subject to challenge or control with regard to his decision whether or not to pay a dividend at any particular time. See also the General Note to s.324.

Distribution of property in specie

326.—(1) Without prejudice to sections 315 to 319 (disclaimer), the trustee may, with the permission of the creditors' committee, divide in its existing form amongst the bankrupt's creditors, according to its estimated value, any property which from its peculiar nature or other special circumstances cannot be readily or advantageously sold.

(2) A permission given for the purposes of subsection (1) shall not be a general permission but shall relate to a particular proposed exercise of the power in question; and a person dealing with the trustee in good faith and for value is not to be concerned to enquire whether any permission required by subsection (1) has been given.

(3) Where the trustee has done anything without the permission required by subsection (1), the court or the creditors' committee may, for

the purpose of enabling him to meet his expenses out of the bankrupt's estate, ratify what the trustee has done.

But the committee shall not do so unless it is satisfied that the trustee acted in a case of urgency and has sought its ratification without undue delay.

DEFINITIONS

"creditor": s.383(1).
"creditors' committee": s.301(1).
"estate": ss.283, 385(1).
"property": s.436.
"the bankrupt": s.381(1).
"the court": ss.373, 385(1).
"the trustee": s.385(1).

GENERAL NOTE

This section, which corresponds to subss. (7) and (8) of s.165 of the 1985 Act, makes provision for the division amongst the creditors in its existing form of any of the bankrupt's property which cannot be readily or advantageously sold.

Distribution in criminal bankruptcy

327. Where the bankruptcy order was made on a petition under section 264(1)(*d*) (criminal bankruptcy), no distribution shall be made under sections 324 to 326 so long as an appeal is pending (within the meaning of section 277) against the bankrupt's conviction of any offence by virtue of which the criminal bankruptcy order on which the petition was based was made.

DEFINITIONS

"appeal pending": s.277(3); Powers of Criminal Courts Act 1973, s.40(5).
"bankruptcy order": s.381(2).
"criminal bankruptcy order": s.385(1); Powers of Criminal Courts Act 1973, s.39(1).
"the bankrupt": s.381(1).

GENERAL NOTE

This section, which corresponds to s.165(9) of the 1985 Act, embodies a special rule for the case where a bankruptcy order is made on a petition based upon a criminal bankruptcy order, as provided for by s.264(1)(*d*). Where an appeal is pending against the bankrupt's conviction of any offence by virtue of which the criminal bankruptcy order came to be made, there can be no distribution of dividend in the bankruptcy, albeit the trustee may proceed with the other stages of his administration and realisation of the bankrupt's estate, in preparation for the eventual distribution of dividends.

Priority of debts

328.—(1) In the distribution of the bankrupt's estate, his preferential debts (within the meaning given by section 386 in Part XII) shall be paid in priority to other debts.

(2) Preferential debts rank equally between themselves after the expenses of the bankruptcy and shall be paid in full unless the bankrupt's estate is insufficient for meeting them, in which case they abate in equal proportions between themselves.

(3) Debts which are neither preferential debts nor debts to which the next section applies also rank equally between themselves and, after the preferential debts, shall be paid in full unless the bankrupt's estate is insufficient for meeting them, in which case they abate in equal proportions between themselves.

(4) Any surplus remaining after the payment of the debts that are preferential or rank equally under subsection (3) shall be applied in paying interest on those debts in respect of the periods during which they have

been outstanding since the commencement of the bankruptcy; and interest on preferential debts ranks equally with interest on debts other than preferential debts.

(5) The rate of interest payable under subsection (4) in respect of any debt is whichever is the greater of the following—

(*a*) the rate specified in section 17 of the Judgments Act 1838 at the commencement of the bankruptcy, and

(*b*) the rate applicable to that debt apart from the bankruptcy.

(6) This section and the next are without prejudice to any provision of this Act or any other Act under which the payment of any debt or the making of any other payment is, in the event of bankruptcy, to have a particular priority or to be postponed.

Definitions

"bankrupt": s.381(1).
"debt": ss.382(3), 385(1).
"estate": ss.283, 385(1).
"preferential debt": s.386; Sched. 6.

General Note

This section, together with s.386 and Sched. 6, provides for the order of priority in which proved debts are to be paid. These provisions replace the heavily-amended provisions of s.33 and also s.36 of the Bankruptcy Act 1914 (repealed). The provisions of Sched. 6 are common to both bankruptcy and winding up, and apply in relation to the latter pursuant to the provisions of s.175. As explained in the General Note to that section, the new common code of preferential debts represents a qualified victory for those who sought to reform this aspect of insolvency law in accordance with the recommendations of the *Cork Report* (see esp. paras. 1409–1444 and 1450). The main debates and divisions on matters of principle and substance occurred in relation to the earlier section of the Act, as mentioned in the General Note to s.175. For priority of debts in a former bankruptcy in the event of a second, or subsequent, bankruptcy, see s.335(*b*).

This section corresponds to subss. (1)–(5) and (7) of s.166 of the 1985 Act.

Subss. (4), (5)

These provisions replace the former s.66 of the Bankruptcy Act 1914 (repealed). In view of the fact that s.322(2) now makes provable any claim for interest accrued due up to the commencement of bankruptcy, the present subsections are concerned exclusively with payment of dividend in respect of interest for the period during which the debts have been outstanding since the date of the bankruptcy order. This provision forms a parallel to s.189 which applies in winding up.

Debts to spouse

329.—(1) This section applies to bankruptcy debts owed in respect of credit provided by a person who (whether or not the bankrupt's spouse at the time the credit was provided) was the bankrupt's spouse at the commencement of the bankruptcy.

(2) Such debts—

(*a*) rank in priority after the debts and interest required to be paid in pursuance of section 328(3) and (4), and

(*b*) are payable with interest at the rate specified in section 328(5) in respect of the period during which they have been outstanding since the commencement of the bankruptcy;

and the interest payable under paragraph (*b*) has the same priority as the debts on which it is payable.

Definitions

"bankruptcy debt": s.382.
"commencement of the bankruptcy": s.278(*a*).
"the bankrupt": s.381(1).

General Note

This section, which corresponds to s.166(6) of the 1985 Act, has the effect of relegating the entitlement of the bankrupt's spouse to receive dividends in respect of credit which he or she has provided to the bankrupt. Such debts are made payable only after the preferential and the ordinary creditors have received payment in full in accordance with the provisions of subss. (2) and (3) of s.328, together with interest payable in accordance with subs. (4) of that section. The position of the bankrupt's spouse as a postponed creditor was formerly governed by the provisions of s.36 of the Bankruptcy Act 1914 (repealed). The drafting of the present section is a considerable improvement over the former provision, and its scope has been widened so as to apply in an identical manner, regardless of whether it is the husband or the wife who is the bankrupt party in any given case.

Final distribution

330.—(1) When the trustee has realised all the bankrupt's estate or so much of it as can, in the trustee's opinion, be realised without needlessly protracting the trusteeship, he shall give notice in the prescribed manner either—

(*a*) of his intention to declare a final dividend, or

(*b*) that no dividend, or further dividend, will be declared.

(2) The notice under subsection (1) shall contain the prescribed particulars and shall require claims against the bankrupt's estate to be established by a date ("the final date") specified in the notice.

(3) The court may, on the application of any person, postpone the final date.

(4) After the final date, the trustee shall—

(*a*) defray any outstanding expenses of the bankruptcy out of the bankrupt's estate, and

(*b*) if he intends to declare a final dividend, declare and distribute that dividend without regard to the claim of any person in respect of a debt not already proved in the bankruptcy.

(5) If a surplus remains after payment in full and with interest of all the bankrupt's creditors and the payment of the expenses of the bankruptcy, the bankrupt is entitled to the surplus.

Definitions

"bankrupt": s.381(1).
"creditor": s.383(1).
"debt": ss.382(3), 385(1).
"estate": ss.283, 385(1).
"the final date": subs. (2).
"prescribed": s.384.
"the court": ss.373, 385(1).
"the trustee": s.385(1).

General Note

This section provides for the final distribution of dividend, or alternatively for the giving of notification by the trustee that no dividend, or no further dividend, will be declared. It marks the beginning of the concluding phase of the trustee's responsibilities. S.331(3) authorises the trustee to adopt the cost-saving procedure of sending out the notice of the final meeting to be convened under that section at the same time as he sends out the notice required to be sent under this section.

Subss. (1)–(4) inclusive reproduce the former s.67 of the Bankruptcy Act 1914 (repealed) in restructured form, and subs. (5) restates the law formerly contained in s.69 of that Act.

This section corresponds to s.167 of the 1985 Act.

Final meeting

331.—(1) Subject as follows in this section and the next, this section applies where—

(*a*) it appears to the trustee that the administration of the bankrupt's estate in accordance with this Chapter is for practical purposes complete, and

(*b*) the trustee is not the official receiver.

(2) The trustee shall summon a final general meeting of the bankrupt's creditors which—

(*a*) shall receive the trustee's report of his administration of the bankrupt's estate, and

(*b*) shall determine whether the trustee should have his release under section 299 in Chapter III.

(3) The trustee may, if he thinks fit, give the notice summoning the final general meeting at the same time as giving notice under section 330(1); but, if summoned for an earlier date, that meeting shall be adjourned (and, if necessary, further adjourned) until a date on which the trustee is able to report to the meeting that the administration of the bankrupt's estate is for practical purposes complete.

(4) In the administration of the estate it is the trustee's duty to retain sufficient sums from the estate to cover the expenses of summoning and holding the meeting required by this section.

Definition

"bankrupt": s.381(1).
"court": ss.373, 385(1).
"creditor": s.383(1).
"estate": ss.283, 385(1).
"release": s.299(5).
"the official receiver": s.399(1).
"the trustee": s.385(1).

General Note

This section provides for the convening of a final meeting of creditors when the administration of the bankrupt's estate is complete. No such requirement is imposed in cases where the official receiver is acting as trustee, which is likely to be the case whenever the assets available for distribution are small. The twin purposes of the meeting are that the trustee should deliver a report upon his administration of the bankrupt's estate, and that the creditors should determine whether the trustee is to have his release under s.299. If the meeting resolves against release of the trustee, the provisions of s.299(3)(*d*)(i) become applicable with effect that the trustee must apply to the Secretary of State to determine at what date his release shall become effective. If the final meeting does not resolve against his release, the trustee's release is effective, in accordance with s.299(3)(*d*)(ii) from the time at which he vacates office. There is no provision in s.331 itself requiring the trustee to report to the court upon the outcome of the final meeting, but s.298(8) provides that on his giving notice to the court that such a final meeting has been held, together with a report of any decisions there taken, the trustee shall vacate office. In view of the fact that final meetings of creditors are frequently ill attended, provision will be made in the rules to enable the creditors to vote by proxy.

This section corresponds to subss. (1), (2) and (4) of s.168 of the 1985 Act.

Saving for bankrupt's home

332.—(1) This section applies where—

(*a*) there is comprised in the bankrupt's estate property consisting of an interest in a dwelling house which is occupied by the bankrupt or by his spouse or former spouse, and

(*b*) the trustee has been unable for any reason to realise that property.

(2) The trustee shall not summon a meeting under section 331 unless either—

(*a*) the court has made an order under section 313 imposing a charge on that property for the benefit of the bankrupt's estate, or

(*b*) the court has declined, on an application under that section, to make such an order, or

(*c*) the Secretary of State has issued a certificate to the trustee stating that it would be inappropriate or inexpedient for such an application to be made in the case in question.

DEFINITIONS

"dwelling house": s.385(1).
"estate": ss.283, 385(1).
"property": s.436.
"the bankrupt": s.381(1).
"the court": ss.373, 385(1).
"the trustee": s.385(1).

GENERAL NOTE

This section provides for the possibility that the trustee may have been unable to realise property consisting of an interest in a dwelling-house because of a right of occupation by the bankrupt or his present or former spouse. Under s.336 or s.337, such rights may be held to outweigh for a time the interests of creditors in the bankruptcy, and in such circumstances it is the purpose of this subsection to prevent the bankruptcy administration being brought to its conclusion through the holding of a final meeting of creditors, unless one of the alternative conditions mentioned in paras. (*a*)–(*c*) inclusive has been fulfilled. These include the possibility that a charging order has been made by the court under s.313, or that an application for such an order has been made without success.

This section corresponds to s.168(3) of the 1985 Act.

Supplemental

Duties of bankrupt in relation to trustee

333.—(1) The bankrupt shall—

(*a*) give to the trustee such information as to his affairs,
(*b*) attend on the trustee at such times, and
(*c*) do all such other things,

as the trustee may for the purposes of carrying out his functions under any of this Group of Parts reasonably require.

(2) Where at any time after the commencement of the bankruptcy any property is acquired by, or devolves upon, the bankrupt or there is an increase of the bankrupt's income, the bankrupt shall, within the prescribed period, give the trustee notice of the property or, as the case may be, of the increase.

(3) Subsection (1) applies to a bankrupt after his discharge.

(4) If the bankrupt without reasonable excuse fails to comply with any obligation imposed by this section, he is guilty of a contempt of court and liable to be punished accordingly (in addition to any other punishment to which he may be subject).

DEFINITIONS

"affairs": s.385(2).
"bankrupt": s.381(1).
"commencement of the bankruptcy": s.278(*a*).
"court": ss.373, 385(1).
"property": s.436.
"prescribed": s.384.
"the trustee": s.385(1).

GENERAL NOTE

This section provides for a duty of co-operation with the trustee, to which the bankrupt is subject throughout the duration of the bankruptcy and also, in the case of the matters mentioned in subs. (1), after his discharge. The section re-enacts in considerably revised form the duties formerly imposed upon the debtor by s.22 of the Bankruptcy Act 1914 (repealed). A new provision is that contained in subs. (2), whereby the bankrupt must notify his trustee of any after-acquired property or increase of income which accrues to him after the commencement of bankruptcy. This is to enable the trustee to take appropriate action to claim the property, or a proportion of the income, for the estate under s.307.

This section corresponds to s.169 of the 1985 Act.

Stay of distribution in case of second bankruptcy

334.—(1) This section and the next apply where a bankruptcy order is made against an undischarged bankrupt; and in both sections—

(*a*) "the later bankruptcy" means the bankruptcy arising from that order,

(*b*) "the earlier bankruptcy" means the bankruptcy (or, as the case may be, most recent bankruptcy) from which the bankrupt has not been discharged at the commencement of the later bankruptcy, and

(*c*) "the existing trustee" means the trustee (if any) of the bankrupt's estate for the purposes of the earlier bankruptcy.

(2) Where the existing trustee has been given the prescribed notice of the presentation of the petition for the later bankruptcy, any distribution or other disposition by him of anything to which the next subsection applies, if made after the giving of the notice, is void except to the extent that it was made with the consent of the court or is or was subsequently ratified by the court.

This is without prejudice to section 284 (restrictions on dispositions of property following bankruptcy order).

(3) This subsection applies to—

(*a*) any property which is vested in the existing trustee under section 307(3) (after-acquired property);

(*b*) any money paid to the existing trustee in pursuance of an income payments order under section 310; and

(*c*) any property or money which is, or in the hands of the existing trustee represents, the proceeds of sale or application of property or money falling within paragraph (*a*) or (*b*) of this subsection.

Definitions

"bankrupt": s.381(1).
"bankruptcy order": s.381(2).
"bankruptcy petition": s.381(3).
"commencement of the bankruptcy": s.278(*a*).
"discharged": s.279.
"estate": ss.283, 385(1).
"prescribed": s.384.
"property": s.436.
"the court": ss.373, 385(1).
"the earlier bankruptcy": subs. (1)(*b*).
"the existing trustee": subs. (1)(*c*).
"the later bankruptcy": subs. (1)(*a*).
"the rules": ss.207, 211(1).
"the trustee": s.385(1).

Transitional Provision

Sched. 11, para. 16.

General Note

This section and s.335 together make special provision for cases where a bankruptcy order is made against a person who, at the time in question, is undischarged from a previous bankruptcy adjudication which he has undergone. Such situations were formerly provided for by s.39 of the Bankruptcy Act 1914, as substituted by s.3 of the Bankruptcy (Amendment) Act 1926 (repealed). Paras. 1164–1168 of the *Cork Report* endorsed the earlier proposals of the Blagden Committee (Cmnd. 221, para. 114) in advocating a change in the law, so that while the trustee of a former bankruptcy should continue to be admitted as a creditor in any subsequent bankruptcy in respect of any unsatisfied balance of debts provable in the former bankruptcy, he should not, as hitherto, be entitled to any dividend as such creditor until the other creditors in the later bankruptcy have been paid in full, including the payment of interest on those other debts. These recommendations are adopted in ss.334 and 335 and are enacted by subss. (5) and (6) of s.335 in particular.

This section corresponds to subss. (1)–(3) of s.170 of the 1985 Act.

Adjustment between earlier and later bankruptcy estates

335.—(1) With effect from the commencement of the later bankruptcy anything to which section 334(3) applies which, immediately before the commencement of that bankruptcy, is comprised in the bankrupt's estate for the purposes of the earlier bankruptcy is to be treated as comprised in the bankrupt's estate for the purposes of the later bankruptcy and, until there is a trustee of that estate, is to be dealt with by the existing trustee in accordance with the rules.

(2) Any sums which in pursuance of an income payments order under section 310 are payable after the commencement of the later bankruptcy to the existing trustee shall form part of the bankrupt's estate for the purposes of the later bankruptcy; and the court may give such consequential directions for the modification of the order as it thinks fit.

(3) Anything comprised in a bankrupt's estate by virtue of subsection (1) or (2) is so comprised subject to a first charge in favour of the existing trustee for any bankruptcy expenses incurred by him in relation thereto.

(4) Except as provided above and in section 334, property which is, or by virtue of section 308 (personal property of bankrupt exceeding reasonable replacement value) is capable of being, comprised in the bankrupt's estate for the purposes of the earlier bankruptcy, or of any bankruptcy prior to it, shall not be comprised in his estate for the purposes of the later bankruptcy.

(5) The creditors of the bankrupt in the earlier bankruptcy and the creditors of the bankrupt in any bankruptcy prior to the earlier one, are not to be creditors of his in the later bankruptcy in respect of the same debts; but the existing trustee may prove in the later bankruptcy for—

(*a*) the unsatisfied balance of the debts (including any debt under this subsection) provable against the bankrupt's estate in the earlier bankruptcy;

(*b*) any interest payable on that balance; and

(*c*) any unpaid expenses of the earlier bankruptcy.

(6) Any amount provable under subsection (5) ranks in priority after all the other debts provable in the later bankruptcy and after interest on those debts and, accordingly, shall not be paid unless those debts and that interest have first been paid in full.

Definitions

"commencement of the bankruptcy": s.278(*a*).
"creditor": s.383(1).
"debt": ss.382(3), 385(1).
"estate": ss.283, 385(1).
"modification": s.436.
"property": s.436.
"the bankrupt": s.381(1).
"the court": ss.373, 385(1).
"the earlier bankruptcy": s.334(1)(*b*).
"the existing trustee": s.334(1)(*c*).
"the later bankruptcy": s.334(1)(*a*).
"trustee": s.385(1).

General Note

This section corresponds to subss. (4)–(9) of s.170 of the 1985 Act. The section operates in conjunction with s.334, and applies in the case where an undischarged bankrupt undergoes a second or subsequent adjudication. See also the General Note to s.334.

Subs. (4)

Property which is, . . . or by virtue of s.308 . . . is capable of being, comprised in the bankrupt's estate

These words have the effect of excluding from the bankrupt's estate for the purpose of the later bankruptcy property which the bankrupt actually owned at the date of commencement of the earlier bankruptcy, but which was at that time exempted from his estate by virtue of s.283(2). Such property, however, remains subject to the right of the trustee under s.308 to claim the exempted item for the estate in exchange for the provision of a less expensive replacement.

Chapter V

Effect of Bankruptcy on Certain Rights, Transactions, Etc.

Rights of occupation

Rights of occupation etc. of bankrupt's spouse

336.—(1) Nothing occurring in the initial period of the bankruptcy (that is to say, the period beginning with the day of the presentation of the petition for the bankruptcy order and ending with the vesting of the bankrupt's estate in a trustee) is to be taken as having given rise to any rights of occupation under the Matrimonial Homes Act 1983 in relation to a dwelling house comprised in the bankrupt's estate.

(2) Where a spouse's rights of occupation under the Act of 1983 are a charge on the estate or interest of the other spouse, or of trustees for the other spouse, and the other spouse is adjudged bankrupt—

(*a*) the charge continues to subsist notwithstanding the bankruptcy and, subject to the provisions of that Act, binds the trustee of the bankrupt's estate and persons deriving title under that trustee, and

(*b*) any application for an order under section 1 of that Act shall be made to the court having jurisdiction in relation to the bankruptcy.

(3) Where a person and his spouse or former spouse are trustees for sale of a dwelling house and that person is adjudged bankrupt, any application by the trustee of the bankrupt's estate for any order under section 30 of the Law of Property Act 1925 (powers of court where trustees for sale refuse to act) shall be made to the court having jurisdiction in relation to the bankruptcy.

(4) On such an application as is mentioned in subsection (2) or (3) the court shall make such order under section 1 of the Act of 1983 or section 30 of the Act of 1925 as it thinks just and reasonable having regard to—

(*a*) the interests of the bankrupt's creditors,

(*b*) the conduct of the spouse or former spouse, so far as contributing to the bankruptcy,

(*c*) the needs and financial resources of the spouse or former spouse,

(*d*) the needs of any children, and

(*e*) all the circumstances of the case other than the needs of the bankrupt.

(5) Where such an application is made after the end of the period of one year beginning with the first vesting under Chapter IV of this Part of the bankrupt's estate in a trustee, the court shall assume, unless the circumstances of the case are exceptional, that the interests of the bankrupt's creditors outweigh all other considerations.

Definitions

"bankrupt": s.381(1).
"creditor": s.383(1).
"dwelling house": s.385(1).
"estate": ss.283, 385(1).
"the court": ss.373, 385(1).

General Note

The provisions of this section, and those of s.337, represent a compromise position reached at a late stage in the process of enactment. During the enactment of the Insolvency Bill 1985, a series of vigorous debates took place in both Houses regarding the issues of principle and policy associated with the treatment of the matrimonial home in the case of bankruptcy of either spouse (see esp. *Hansard,* H.L. Vol. 459, cols. 1262–1267; H.L. Vol. 462, cols. 160–171; H.L. Vol. 467, cols 1265–1270; H.C. Standing Committee E, June 18, 1985, cols. 372–376 and 394–395; H.C. Vol. 83, cols. 545–549 and 601–602). These debates took as their starting point the arguments and recommendations contained in paras. 1114–1131 of the *Cork Report* with regard to the family home. The use of the term "family home" is appropriate, since it serves to indicate the principal argument for the making of some provision for postponement of the ability of the trustee in bankruptcy to realise the bankrupt's interest in this particular item of property, namely the claims of the bankrupt's spouse, children and other dependents to a roof over their heads. In very few cases decided under the law prior to the enactment of this Act have the competing claims of the bankrupt's spouse and children been accorded sufficient significance so as to outweigh those of the creditors. The *Cork Report* therefore proposed a new approach which would delay, but not cancel, enforcement of the creditors' rights. The liberal terms in which the Report's recommendations were cast, although enthusiastically supported in some speeches delivered in both Houses, have not been completely embodied in the provisions ultimately enacted in this and the following section, but they at least afford the possibility for the court to strike an appropriate balance in any given case. Much will also depend upon the attitude adopted by trustees in bankruptcy in selecting the point in time at which to press for a realisation of the bankrupt's interest in the family home (*cf. Cork Report,* para. 1119).

One important innovation which is included in the section is the facilitation of a consolidation of the hearing of applications relating to the family home before the court having jurisdiction in bankruptcy. Provision is thus made in subs. (2)(*b*) for any application for an order under s.1 of the Matrimonial Homes Act 1983 to be heard by the bankruptcy court, and the same court likewise enjoys, by virtue of subs. (3), an exclusive jurisdiction to entertain an application by the trustee in bankruptcy for an order under s.30 of the Law of Property Act 1925. The same consolidation is effected in subs. (4) of s.337.

This section corresponds to s.171 of the 1985 Act.

Subs. (2)

Subs. 1 of the Matrimonial Homes Act 1983 confers on a spouse without any beneficial interest in the matrimonial home, rights of occupation as against the other spouse. Hitherto, where the spouse with a beneficial estate became bankrupt the spouse without any such interest lost his or her rights of occupation as against the trustee in bankruptcy. This subsection reverses that former position so that the spouse who has no beneficial interest in the property is placed in a similar position to a spouse with a beneficial interest.

Subs. (3)

This provides for the case where the spouse of the bankrupt already has a beneficial interest in the matrimonial home. No change is effected to the pre-existing law, whereby the trustee in bankruptcy must obtain an order of the court under s.30 of the Law of Property Act 1925 before being able to sell the property concerned.

Subs. (4)

This sets out the powers of the court in relation to any application made under subss. (2) of (3). The court's discretion to make "such order as it thinks just and reasonable" must be exercised with regard to the various interests therein listed, which are based on those already contained in s.1(3) of the Matrimonial Homes Act 1983. Notably, the personal needs of the bankrupt are expressly excluded from consideration. Only the spouse and children of the bankrupt are expressly mentioned as persons whose needs the court is required to consider, and it is debatable whether the court may properly have regard, under the general heading of "all the circumstances of the case" to the needs of any other dependents, including any "ailing or elderly or adult members of the family" as mentioned in paras. 1120–1121 of the *Cork Report.*

Subs. (5)

Unless the circumstances of the case are exceptional

This provision redresses the balance between the competing interests of the creditors and the bankrupt's spouse and children in favour of the former, in any case where application is not brought until a year has elapsed since the bankrupt's property first vested in a trustee under the provisions of Chap. IV of this Part (see s.303 and also ss.295(4) and 297). However, the way has been left open for argument on behalf of the spouse and children to be advanced on a basis such as exceptional hardship or inconvenience which would be occasioned by the sale of the family home at the time the application is made. In such instances the cases decided under the law prior to the coming into force of this Act are likely to be of at least a persuasive authority in the judicial determination of the expression italicised above (see *e.g. Re Turner* [1975] 1 All E.R. 5; *Re Bailey* [1977] 2 All E.R. 26; *Re Holliday* [1981] 1 Ch. 405; *Re Lowrie* [1981] 3 All E.R. 353).

Rights of occupation of bankrupt

337.—(1) This section applies where—

(*a*) a person who is entitled to occupy a dwelling house by virtue of a beneficial estate or interest is adjudged bankrupt, and

(*b*) any persons under the age of 18 with whom that person had at some time occupied that dwelling house had their home with that person at the time when the bankruptcy petition was presented and at the commencement of the bankruptcy.

(2) Whether or not the bankrupt's spouse (if any) has rights of occupation under the Matrimonial Homes Act 1983—

(*a*) the bankrupt has the following rights as against the trustee of his estate—

(i) if in occupation, a right not to be evicted or excluded from the dwelling house or any part of it, except with the leave of the court,

(ii) if not in occupation, a right with the leave of the court to enter into and occupy the dwelling house, and

(*b*) the bankrupt's rights are a charge, having the like priority as an equitable interest created immediately before the commencement of the bankruptcy, on so much of his estate or interest in the dwelling house as vests in the trustee.

(3) The Act of 1983 has effect, with the necessary modifications, as if—

(*a*) the rights conferred by paragraph (*a*) of subsection (2) were rights of occupation under that Act,

(*b*) any application for leave such as is mentioned in that paragraph were an application for an order under section 1 of that Act, and

(*c*) any charge under paragraph (*b*) of that subsection on the estate or interest of the trustee were a charge under that Act on the estate or interest of a spouse.

(4) Any application for leave such as is mentioned in subsection (2) (*a*) or otherwise by virtue of this section for an order under section 1 of the Act of 1983 shall be made to the court having jurisdiction in relation to the bankruptcy.

(5) On such an application the court shall make such order under section 1 of the Act of 1983 as it thinks just and reasonable having regard to the interests of the creditors, to the bankrupt's financial resources, to the needs of the children and to all the circumstances of the case other than the needs of the bankrupt.

(6) Where such an application is made after the end of the period of one year beginning with the first vesting (under Chapter IV of this Part)

of the bankrupt's estate in a trustee, the court shall assume, unless the circumstances of the case are exceptional, that the interests of the bankrupt's creditors outweigh all other considerations.

DEFINITIONS
"bankrupt": s.381(1).
"bankruptcy petition": s.381(3).
"commencement of the bankruptcy": s.278(*a*).
"creditor": s.383(1).
"dwelling house": s.385(1).
"estate": ss.283, 385(1).
"modifications": s.436.
"the court": ss.373, 385(1).
"the trustee": s.385(1).

GENERAL NOTE
This section applies the principles of s.336, in a more limited manner, to the case where a bankrupt has actual custody of children. This provides for cases where the bankrupt has no spouse with occupational rights or, because of divorce, no spouse at all, but nevertheless has children to bring up. Subs. (1)(*b*) expressly provides that only persons under the age of 18 are to be taken into account by the court. Subs. (5) further provides that the needs of such children are to be taken into account by the court, but not the needs of the bankrupt himself. As is the case under s.336(5), the court is required to assume, unless the circumstances are exceptional, that in a case where application is made by the trustee for an order under s.1 of the Matrimonial Homes Act 1983 more than one year after the date when the bankrupt's estate first vested in a trustee, the interests of the creditors are of paramount consideration.
This section corresponds to s.172 of the 1985 Act.

Payments in respect of premises occupied by bankrupt

338. Where any premises comprised in a bankrupt's estate are occupied by him (whether by virtue of the preceding section or otherwise) on condition that he makes payments towards satisfying any liability arising under a mortgage of the premises or otherwise towards the outgoings of the premises, the bankrupt does not, by virtue of those payments, acquire any interest in the premises.

DEFINITIONS
"bankrupt": s.381(1).
"estate": ss.283, 385(1).
"liability": s.382(4).

GENERAL NOTE
This section preserves the pre-existing legal position where a bankrupt is able, for whatever reason, to continue to occupy premises comprised in his estate and makes mortgage payments or pays other outgoings in relation to the property. If such payments give rise to the acquisition by the bankrupt, after the commencement of his bankruptcy, of an interest in the property, the former prohibitions of s.38 of the Bankruptcy Act 1914 (repealed) had the effect of causing that interest to vest automatically in his trustee as after-acquired property. The present section perpetuates the rule whereby the bankrupt does not personally acquire an interest in the premises despite the fact that he may have made the payments required of him.
This section corresponds to s.173 of the 1985 Act.

Adjustment of prior transactions, etc.

Transactions at an undervalue

339.—(1) Subject as follows in this section and sections 341 and 342, where an individual is adjudged bankrupt and he has at a relevant time (defined in section 341) entered into a transaction with any person at an undervalue, the trustee of the bankrupt's estate may apply to the court for an order under this section.

(2) The court shall, on such an application, make such order as it thinks fit for restoring the position to what it would have been if that individual had not entered into that transaction.

(3) For the purposes of this section and sections 341 and 342, an individual enters into a transaction with a person at an undervalue if—

(*a*) he makes a gift to that person or he otherwise enters into a transaction with that person on terms that provide for him to receive no consideration,

(*b*) he enters into a transaction with that person in consideration of marriage, or

(*c*) he enters into a transaction with that person for a consideration the value of which, in money or money's worth, is significantly less than the value, in money or money's worth, of the consideration provided by the individual.

DEFINITIONS

"a relevant time": s.341.
"bankrupt": s.381(1).
"bankruptcy petition": s.381(3).
"estate": ss.283, 385(1).
"the court": ss.373, 385(1).
"transaction": s.436.
"transaction at an undervalue": subs. (3).
"trustee": s.385(1).

TRANSITIONAL PROVISION

Sched. 11, para. 17.

GENERAL NOTE

This section, together with ss.340–342, forms a parallel set of provisions to those of ss.238–241 which apply in cases of company insolvency. The two sets of provisions are in most respects identical in substance, but differ in matters of detail and terminology reflecting the differences between the respective legal frameworks within which the two branches of insolvency law traditionally operate. For comment upon the general operation of the section, and of the underlying policy thereto, see the General Note to s.238. The following comments indicate the principal respects in which ss.238–241 and ss.339–342 differ from each other in substance.

(i) There is no equivalent provision in s.238 to that contained in subs. (3)(*b*) of s.339, which refers to transactions entered into in consideration of marriage. In consequence the counterpart of s.339(3)(*c*) is s.238(4)(*b*).

(ii) There is no counterpart in s.339 to s.238(5).

(iii) S.340(5) speaks of the giving of a preference by an individual to a person who at the time was an "associate" of his; s.239(6) on the other hand speaks of the giving of a preference by a company to a person who at the time was "connected with" the company. However, the latter expression is defined by s.249 as comprising those persons who are "associates" of the company, and also those who are directors or shadow directors of the company, or associates of such persons. Thus the concept of the "associated person", as defined in s.435, comes to be applicable in both situations albeit in the case of company insolvency it does so alongside other forms of involvement with the company.

(iv) There are important differences of detail as between s.341(1) and s.240(1), both of which contain rules for fixing the periods within which the act of giving a preference or entering into a transaction at an undervalue will take place "at a relevant time" for the purposes of the respective groups of sections. The cumulative effect of the differences between these two key subsections is to create a major distinction between preferences or transactions at an undervalue which are given or entered into by a company on the one hand, and those which are given or entered into by an individual on the other.

(v) The statutory definition of "insolvency" for the purposes of s.240(2) is supplied by reference to the concept of "inability to pay debts" within the meaning of s.123 of the Act, where six alternative criteria are stated; the definition of "insolvency" for the purposes of the equivalent subsection of s.341 (subs. (2)), is supplied by s.341(3) which states only two alternative criteria for establishing individual insolvency.

(vi) There is no equivalent in s.341 to s.240(3).

(vii) There are no equivalents in ss.238–241 to the provisions of subss. (4) and (5) of s.341, which are concerned with cases where a bankruptcy order is made upon a petition based on a criminal bankruptcy order against an individual who has been convicted of a criminal offence.

Ss.339–342 replace the provisions formerly contained in ss.42 and 44 of the Bankruptcy Act 1914 (repealed), and do so in a manner broadly in line with the proposals contained in Chap. 28 of the *Cork Report.*

S.339 corresponds to subss. (1) and (2) of s.173 of the 1985 Act.

Preferences

340.—(1) Subject as follows in this and the next two sections, where an individual is adjudged bankrupt and he has at a relevant time (defined in section 341) given a preference to any person, the trustee of the bankrupt's estate may apply to the court for an order under this section.

(2) The court shall, on such an application, make such order as it thinks fit for restoring the position to what it would have been if that individual had not given that preference.

(3) For the purposes of this and the next two sections, an individual gives a preference to a person if—

(*a*) that person is one of the individual's creditors or a surety or guarantor for any of his debts or other liabilities, and

(*b*) the individual does anything or suffers anything to be done which (in either case) has the effect of putting that person into a position which, in the event of the individual's bankruptcy, will be better than the position he would have been in if that thing had not been done.

(4) The court shall not make an order under this section in respect of a preference given to any person unless the individual who gave the preference was influenced in deciding to give it by a desire to produce in relation to that person the effect mentioned in subsection (3)(*b*) above.

(5) An individual who has given a preference to a person who, at the time the preference was given, was an associate of his (otherwise than by reason only of being his employee) is presumed, unless the contrary is shown, to have been influenced in deciding to give it by such a desire as is mentioned in subsection (4).

(6) The fact that something has been done in pursuance of the order of a court does not, without more, prevent the doing or suffering of that thing from constituting the giving of a preference.

Definitions

"a relevant time": s.341(1), (2).
"associate": s.435.
"bankrupt": s.381(1).
"creditor": s.383(1).
"debt": ss.382(3), 385(1).
"estate": ss.283, 385(1).
"gives a preference": subs. (3).
"the court": s.373, 385(1).
"the trustee": s.385(1).

General Note

This section forms part of the group of sections (ss.339–342) concerned with the adjustment of antecedent transactions which were either concluded at an undervalue or constituted preferences within the meaning of this section.

This section corresponds to subss. (1) (part), (3)–(6) and (12) (part) of s.174 of the 1985 Act. For further information, see the General Note to s.339.

"Relevant time" under ss. 339, 340

341.—(1) Subject as follows, the time at which an individual enters into a transaction at an undervalue or gives a preference is a relevant time if the transaction is entered into or the preference given—

(*a*) in the case of a transaction at an undervalue, at a time in the period of 5 years ending with the day of the presentation of the bankruptcy petition on which the individual is adjudged bankrupt,

(*b*) in the case of a preference which is not a transaction at an undervalue and is given to a person who is an associate of the individual (otherwise than by reason only of being his employee), at a time in the period of 2 years ending with that day, and

(*c*) in any other case of a preference which is not a transaction at an undervalue, at a time in the period of 6 months ending with that day.

(2) Where an individual enters into a transaction at an undervalue or gives a preference at a time mentioned in paragraph (*a*), (*b*) or (*c*) of subsection (1) (not being, in the case of a transaction at an undervalue, a time less than 2 years before the end of the period mentioned in paragraph (*a*)), that time is not a relevant time for the purposes of sections 339 and 340 unless the individual—

(*a*) is insolvent at that time, or

(*b*) becomes insolvent in consequence of the transaction or preference;

but the requirements of this subsection are presumed to be satisfied, unless the contrary is shown, in relation to any transaction at an undervalue which is entered into by an individual with a person who is an associate of his (otherwise than by reason only of being his employee).

(3) For the purposes of subsection (2), an individual is insolvent if—

(*a*) he is unable to pay his debts as they fall due, or

(*b*) the value of his assets is less than the amount of his liabilities, taking into account his contingent and prospective liabilities.

(4) A transaction entered into or preference given by a person who is subsequently adjudged bankrupt on a petition under section 264(1)(*d*) (criminal bankruptcy) is to be treated as having been entered into or given at a relevant time for the purposes of sections 339 and 340 if it was entered into or given at any time on or after the date specified for the purposes of this subsection in the criminal bankruptcy order on which the petition was based.

(5) No order shall be made under section 339 or 340 by virtue of subsection (4) of this section where an appeal is pending (within the meaning of section 277) against the individual's conviction of any offence by virtue of which the criminal bankruptcy order was made.

Definitions

"appeal pending": s.277(3); Powers of Criminal Courts Act 1973, s.40(5).
"a relevant time": subss. (1), (2).
"associate": s.435.
"bankrupt": s.381(1).
"bankruptcy petition": s.381(3).
"criminal bankruptcy order": s.385(1); Powers of Criminal Courts Act 1973, s.39(1).
"debt": ss.382(3), 385(1).
"gives a preference": s.340(3).
"insolvent": subs. (3).
"transaction": s.436.
"transaction at an undervalue": s.339(3).

General Note

This section forms part of the group of sections (ss.339–342) concerned with the adjustment of antecedent transactions. This section supplies the meaning of the expression "a relevant time", where it appears in ss.339 and 340. The section corresponds to subss. (7)–(11) and (12) (part) of s.174 of the 1985 Act. See also the General Note to s.339.

Orders under ss.339, 340

342.—(1) Without prejudice to the generality of section 339(2) or 340(2), an order under either of those sections with respect to a transaction or preference entered into or given by an individual who is subsequently adjudged bankrupt may (subject as follows)—

(*a*) require any property transferred as part of the transaction, or in connection with the giving of the preference, to be vested in the trustee of the bankrupt's estate as part of that estate;

(*b*) require any property to be so vested if it represents in any person's hands the application either of the proceeds of sale of property so transferred or of money so transferred;

(*c*) release or discharge (in whole or in part) any security given by the individual;

(*d*) require any person to pay, in respect of benefits received by him from the individual, such sums to the trustee of his estate as the court may direct;

(*e*) provide for any surety or guarantor whose obligations to any person were released or discharged (in whole or in part) under the transaction or by the giving of the preference to be under such new or revived obligations to that person as the court thinks appropriate;

(*f*) provide for security to be provided for the discharge of any obligation imposed by or arising under the order, for such an obligation to be charged on any property and for the security or charge to have the same priority as a security or charge released or discharged (in whole or in part) under the transaction or by the giving of the preference; and

(*g*) provide for the extent to which any person whose property is vested by the order in the trustee of the bankrupt's estate, or on whom obligations are imposed by the order, is to be able to prove in the bankruptcy for debts or other liabilities which arose from, or were released or discharged (in whole or in part) under or by, the transaction or the giving of the preference.

(2) An order under section 339 or 340 may affect the property of, or impose any obligation on, any person whether or not he is the person with whom the individual in question entered into the transaction or, as the case may be, the person to whom the preference was given; but such an order—

(*a*) shall not prejudice any interest in property which was acquired from a person other than that individual and was acquired in good faith, for value and without notice of the relevant circumstances, or prejudice any interest deriving from such an interest, and

(*b*) shall not require a person who received a benefit from the transaction or preference in good faith, for value and without notice of the relevant circumstances to pay a sum to the trustee of the bankrupt's estate, except where he was a party to the transaction or the payment is to be in respect of a preference given to that person at a time when he was a creditor of that individual.

(3) Any sums required to be paid to the trustee in accordance with an order under section 339 or 340 shall be comprised in the bankrupt's estate.

(4) For the purposes of this section the relevant circumstances, in relation to a transaction or preference, are—

(*a*) the circumstances by virtue of which an order under section 339 or 340 could be made in respect of the transaction or preference if the individual in question were adjudged bankrupt within a particular period after the transaction is entered into or the preference given, and

(*b*) if that period has expired, the fact that that individual has been adjudged bankrupt within that period.

Definitions
"bankrupt": s.381(1).
"creditor": s.383(1).
"debt": ss.382(3), 385(1).
"estate": ss.283, 385(1).
"preference": s.340(3).
"property": s.436.
"security": ss.383, 385(1).
"the court": ss.373, 385(1).
"the relevant circumstances": subs. (4).
"the trustee": s.385(1).
"transaction": s.436.

Transitional Provision
Sched. 11, para. 17.

General Note
This section forms part of the group of sections (ss.339–342) concerned with the adjustment of antecedent transactions. This section prescribes the powers of the court with regard to the making of orders in response to applications made under s.339 or s.340. The section is an almost exact parallel to s.241, which is applicable in cases of company insolvency. The divergences in matters of substance between the two sections are that there is no counterpart in s.241 to subs. (3) of this section, while there is no counterpart in this section to s.241(4). This section corresponds to s.175 of the 1985 Act. See also General Note to s.241.

Extortionate credit transactions

343.—(1) This section applies where a person is adjudged bankrupt who is or has been a party to a transaction for, or involving, the provision to him of credit.

(2) The court may, on the application of the trustee of the bankrupt's estate, make an order with respect to the transaction if the transaction is or was extortionate and was not entered into more than 3 years before the commencement of the bankruptcy.

(3) For the purposes of this section a transaction is extortionate if, having regard to the risk accepted by the person providing the credit—

(*a*) the terms of it are or were such as to require grossly exorbitant payments to be made (whether unconditionally or in certain contingencies) in respect of the provision of the credit, or

(*b*) it otherwise grossly contravened ordinary principles of fair dealing;

and it shall be presumed, unless the contrary is proved, that a transaction with respect to which an application is made under this section is or, as the case may be, was extortionate.

(4) An order under this section with respect to any transaction may contain such one or more of the following as the court thinks fit, that is to say—

(*a*) provision setting aside the whole or part of any obligation created by the transaction;

(*b*) provision otherwise varying the terms of the transaction or varying the terms on which any security for the purposes of the transaction is held;

(*c*) provision requiring any person who is or was party to the transaction to pay to the trustee any sums paid to that person, by virtue of the transaction, by the bankrupt;

(*d*) provision requiring any person to surrender to the trustee any property held by him as security for the purposes of the transaction;

(*e*) provision directing accounts to be taken between any persons.

(5) Any sums or property required to be paid or surrendered to the trustee in accordance with an order under this section shall be comprised in the bankrupt's estate.

(6) Neither the trustee of a bankrupt's estate nor an undischarged bankrupt is entitled to make an application under section 139(1)(*a*) of the Consumer Credit Act 1974 (re-opening of extortionate credit agreements) for any agreement by which credit is or has been provided to the bankrupt to be re-opened.

But the powers conferred by this section are exercisable in relation to any transaction concurrently with any powers exercisable under this Act in relation to that transaction as a transaction at an undervalue.

DEFINITIONS

"bankrupt": s.381(1).
"estate": ss.283, 385(1).
"extortionate": subs. (3).
"property": s.436.
"security": ss.383, 385(1).
"the court": ss.373, 385(1).
"the trustee": s.385(1).
"transaction": s.436.
"transaction at an undervalue": s.339(3).

TRANSITIONAL PROVISION

Sched. 11, para. 17.

GENERAL NOTE

This section enables the court, on the application of the trustee in bankruptcy, to vary or set aside any extortionate credit transaction between the bankrupt and a creditor. The section is a parallel to s.244, which applies in relation to companies in liquidation or subject to an administration order. In almost every respect the two sections are identical in substance, with differences in drafting attributable to the different legal frameworks within which company insolvency and individual bankruptcy respectively operate. Thus, subs. (2) of s.244 provides that an application to the court may be made by the office holder, whereas subs. (2) of this section provides that the right of application is exercisable by the trustee in bankruptcy. The two points of difference in matters of substance between the two sections are found, first in subs. (5) of this section, which has no counterpart in s.244, and secondly in the opening part of subs. (6) of this section, which precludes the making of any application under s.139(1)(*a*) of the Consumer Credit Act 1984 by the trustee in bankruptcy or the bankrupt, to which there is necessarily no counterpart in subs. (5) of s.244. See also General Note to s.244.

This section corresponds to s.176 of the 1985 Act.

Avoidance of general assignment of book debts

344.—(1) The following applies where a person engaged in any business makes a general assignment to another person of his existing or future book debts, or any class of them, and is subsequently adjudged bankrupt.

(2) The assignment is void against the trustee of the bankrupt's estate as regards book debts which were not paid before the presentation of the bankruptcy petition, unless the assignment has been registered under the Bills of Sale Act 1878.

(3) For the purposes of subsections (1) and (2)—

(*a*) "assignment" includes an assignment by way of security or charge on book debts, and

(*b*) "general assignment" does not include—

(i) an assignment of book debts due at the date of the assignment from specified debtors or of debts becoming due under specified contracts, or

(ii) an assignment of book debts included either in a transfer of a business made in good faith and for value or in an assignment of assets for the benefit of creditors generally.

(4) For the purposes of registration under the Act of 1878 an assignment of book debts is to be treated as if it were a bill of sale given otherwise than by way of security for the payment of a sum of money; and the provisions of that Act with respect to the registration of bills of sale apply accordingly with such necessary modifications as may be made by rules under that Act.

DEFINITIONS

"assignment", "general assignment": subs. (3).
"bankrupt": s.381(1).
"bankruptcy petition": s.381(3).
"business": s.436.
"creditor": s.383(1).
"debt": ss.382(3), 385(1).
"estate": ss.283, 385(1).
"modification": s.436.
"security": ss.383, 385(1).

TRANSITIONAL PROVISION

Sched. 11, para. 17.

GENERAL NOTE

This section makes void as against the trustee in bankruptcy certain assignments of book debts not registered under the Bills of Sale Act 1878. It re-enacts the substance of s.43 of the Bankruptcy Act 1914 (repealed), with suitably modernised drafting.

The section corresponds to s.177 of the 1985 Act.

Contracts to which bankrupt is a party

345.—(1) The following applies where a contract has been made with a person who is subsequently adjudged bankrupt.

(2) The court may, on the application of any other party to the contract, make an order discharging obligations under the contract on such terms as to payment by the applicant or the bankrupt of damages for non-performance or otherwise as appear to the court to be equitable.

(3) Any damages payable by the bankrupt by virtue of an order of the court under this section are provable as a bankruptcy debt.

(4) Where an undischarged bankrupt is a contractor in respect of any contract jointly with any person, that person may sue or be sued in respect of the contract without the joinder of the bankrupt.

DEFINITIONS

"bankrupt": s.381(1).
"bankruptcy debt": s.382.
"the court": ss.373, 385(1).

GENERAL NOTE

This section enables the court to discharge a contract between the bankrupt and another person, on the latter's application, upon such terms as the court thinks equitable.

This section corresponds to s.178 of the 1985 Act.

Enforcement procedures

346.—(1) Subject to section 285 in Chapter II (restrictions on proceedings and remedies) and to the following provisions of this section, where the creditor of any person who is adjudged bankrupt has, before the commencement of the bankruptcy—

(*a*) issued execution against the goods or land of that person, or

(*b*) attached a debt due to that person from another person,

that creditor is not entitled, as against the official receiver or trustee of the bankrupt's estate, to retain the benefit of the execution or attachment, or any sums paid to avoid it, unless the execution or attachment was completed, or the sums were paid, before the commencement of the bankruptcy.

(2) Subject as follows, where any goods of a person have been taken in execution, then, if before the completion of the execution notice is given to the sheriff or other officer charged with the execution that that person has been adjudged bankrupt—

(*a*) the sheriff or other officer shall on request deliver to the official receiver or trustee of the bankrupt's estate the goods and any money seized or recovered in part satisfaction of the execution, but

(*b*) the costs of the execution are a first charge on the goods or money so delivered and the official receiver or trustee may sell the goods or a sufficient part of them for the purpose of satisfying the charge.

(3) Subject to subsection (6) below, where—

(*a*) under an execution in respect of a judgment for a sum exceeding such sum as may be prescribed for the purposes of this subsection, the goods of any person are sold or money is paid in order to avoid a sale, and

(*b*) before the end of the period of 14 days beginning with the day of the sale or payment the sheriff or other officer charged with the execution is given notice that a bankruptcy petition has been presented in relation to that person, and

(*c*) a bankruptcy order is or has been made on that petition,

the balance of the proceeds of sale or money paid, after deducting the costs of execution, shall (in priority to the claim of the execution creditor) be comprised in the bankrupt's estate.

(4) Accordingly, in the case of an execution in respect of a judgment for a sum exceeding the sum prescribed for the purposes of subsection (3), the sheriff or other officer charged with the execution—

(*a*) shall not dispose of the balance mentioned in subsection (3) at any time within the period of 14 days so mentioned or while there is pending a bankruptcy petition of which he has been given notice under that subsection, and

(*b*) shall pay that balance, where by virtue of that subsection it is comprised in the bankrupt's estate, to the official receiver or (if there is one) to the trustee of that estate.

(5) For the purposes of this section—

(*a*) an execution against goods is completed by seizure and sale or by the making of a charging order under section 1 of the Charging Orders Act 1979;

(*b*) an execution against land is completed by seizure, by the appointment of a receiver or by the making of a charging order under that section;

(*c*) an attachment of a debt is completed by the receipt of the debt.

(6) The rights conferred by subsections (1) to (3) on the official receiver or the trustee may, to such extent and on such terms as it thinks fit, be set aside by the court in favour of the creditor who has issued the execution or attached the debt.

(7) Nothing in this section entitles the trustee of a bankrupt's estate to claim goods from a person who has acquired them in good faith under a sale by a sheriff or other officer charged with an execution.

(8) Neither subsection (2) nor subsection (3) applies in relation to any execution against property which has been acquired by or has devolved upon the bankrupt since the commencement of the bankruptcy, unless, at the time the execution is issued or before it is completed—

(*a*) the property has been or is claimed for the bankrupt's estate under section 307 (after-acquired property), and

(*b*) a copy of the notice given under that section has been or is served on the sheriff or other officer charged with the execution.

Definitions

"bankrupt": s.381(1).
"bankruptcy order": s.381(2).
"bankruptcy petition": s.381(3).
"commencement of the bankruptcy": s.278(*a*).
"creditor": s.383(1).
"debt": ss.382(3), 385(1).
"estate": ss.283, 385(1).
"execution or attachment completed": subs. (5).
"prescribed": s.384.
"the court": ss.373, 385(1).
"the official receiver": s.399(1).
"the trustee": s.385(1).

General Note

This section regulates the effects of bankruptcy upon procedures for executing judgment against the property of the bankrupt. The provisions of the section restate, in an expanded and generally clearer form, the provisions formerly contained in ss.40 and 41 of the Bankruptcy Act 1914 (repealed).

This section corresponds to s.179 of the 1985 Act.

Subs. (1)

Subject to section 285

The saving for the effects of s.285 allows for the possibility that the court may exercise its powers under that section to stay any action, execution or other legal process at any time when proceedings on a bankruptcy petition are pending, or after an adjudication of bankruptcy has taken place.

Distress, etc.

347.—(1) The right of any landlord or other person to whom rent is payable to distrain upon the goods and effects of an undischarged bankrupt for rent due to him from the bankrupt is available (subject to subsection (5) below) against goods and effects comprised in the bankrupt's estate, but only for 6 months' rent accrued due before the commencement of the bankruptcy.

(2) Where a landlord or other person to whom rent is payable has distrained for rent upon the goods and effects of an individual to whom a bankruptcy petition relates and a bankruptcy order is subsequently made on that petition, any amount recovered by way of that distress which—

(*a*) is in excess of the amount which by virtue of subsection (1) would have been recoverable after the commencement of the bankruptcy, or

(*b*) is in respect of rent for a period or part of a period after the distress was levied,

shall be held for the bankrupt as part of his estate.

(3) Where any person (whether or not a landlord or person entitled to rent) has distrained upon the goods or effects of an individual who is adjudged bankrupt before the end of the period of 3 months beginning with the distraint, so much of those goods or effects, or of the proceeds of their sale, as is not held for the bankrupt under subsection (2) shall be

charged for the benefit of the bankrupt's estate with the preferential debts of the bankrupt to the extent that the bankrupt's estate is for the time being insufficient for meeting those debts.

(4) Where by virtue of any charge under subsection (3) any person surrenders any goods or effects to the trustee of a bankrupt's estate or makes a payment to such a trustee, that person ranks, in respect of the amount of the proceeds of the sale of those goods or effects by the trustee or, as the case may be, the amount of the payment, as a preferential creditor of the bankrupt, except as against so much of the bankrupt's estate as is available for the payment of preferential creditors by virtue of the surrender or payment.

(5) A landlord or other person to whom rent is payable is not at any time after the discharge of a bankrupt entitled to distrain upon any goods or effects comprised in the bankrupt's estate.

(6) Where in the case of any execution—

(*a*) a landlord is (apart from this section) entitled under section 1 of the Landlord and Tenant Act 1709 or section 102 of the County Courts Act 1984 (claims for rent where goods seized in execution) to claim for an amount not exceeding one year's rent, and

(*b*) the person against whom the execution is levied is adjudged bankrupt before the notice of claim is served on the sheriff or other officer charged with the execution,

the right of the landlord to claim under that section is restricted to a right to claim for an amount not exceeding 6 months' rent and does not extend to any rent payable in respect of a period after the notice of claim is so served.

(7) Nothing in subsection (6) imposes any liability on a sheriff or other officer charged with an execution to account to the official receiver or the trustee of a bankrupt's estate for any sums paid by him to a landlord at any time before the sheriff or other officer was served with notice of the bankruptcy order in question.

But this subsection is without prejudice to the liability of the landlord.

(8) Nothing in this Group of Parts affects any right to distrain otherwise than for rent; and any such right is at any time exercisable without restriction against property comprised in a bankrupt's estate, even if that right is expressed by any enactment to be exercisable in like manner as a right to distrain for rent.

(9) Any right to distrain against property comprised in a bankrupt's estate is exercisable notwithstanding that the property has vested in the trustee.

(10) The provisions of this section are without prejudice to a landlord's right in a bankruptcy to prove for any bankruptcy debt in respect of rent.

DEFINITIONS

"bankrupt": s.381(1).
"bankruptcy order": s.381(2).
"bankruptcy petition": s.381(3).
"commencement of the bankruptcy": s.278(*a*).
"creditor": s.383(1).
"estate": ss.283, 385(1).
"preferential debt": s.386; Sched. 6.
"property": s.436.
"the official receiver": s.399(1).
"the trustee": s.385(1).

GENERAL NOTE

This section regulates the levying of distress by a landlord and by other persons on the property of the bankrupt. It restates the law formerly contained in s.35 of the Bankruptcy Act 1914 (repealed), with suitable improvements to, and modernisation of, the drafting.

This section corresponds to s.180 of the 1985 Act.

Apprenticeships, etc.

348.—(1) This section applies where—

(*a*) a bankruptcy order is made in respect of an individual to whom another individual was an apprentice or articled clerk at the time when the petition on which the order was made was presented, and

(*b*) the bankrupt or the apprentice or clerk gives notice to the trustee terminating the apprenticeship or articles.

(2) Subject to subsection (6) below, the indenture of apprenticeship or, as the case may be, the articles of agreement shall be discharged with effect from the commencement of the bankruptcy.

(3) If any money has been paid by or on behalf of the apprentice or clerk to the bankrupt as a fee, the trustee may, on an application made by or on behalf of the apprentice or clerk, pay such sum to the apprentice or clerk as the trustee thinks reasonable, having regard to—

(*a*) the amount of the fee,

(*b*) the proportion of the period in respect of which the fee was paid that has been served by the apprentice or clerk before the commencement of the bankruptcy, and

(*c*) the other circumstances of the case.

(4) The power of the trustee to make a payment under subsection (3) has priority over his obligation to distribute the bankrupt's estate.

(5) Instead of making a payment under subsection (3), the trustee may, if it appears to him expedient to do so on an application made by or on behalf of the apprentice or clerk, transfer the indenture or articles to a person other than the bankrupt.

(6) Where a transfer is made under subsection (5), subsection (2) has effect only as between the apprentice or clerk and the bankrupt.

DEFINITIONS

"bankrupt": s.381(1).
"bankruptcy order": s.381(2).
"bankruptcy petition": s.381(3).
"commencement of the bankruptcy": s.278(*a*).
"estate": ss.283, 385(1).
"trustee": s.385(1).

GENERAL NOTE

This restates, with necessary modifications in the drafting, the law previously contained in s.34 of the Bankruptcy Act 1914 (repealed), whereby special provisions regulate the effect of the bankruptcy on the apprentices or articled clerks of the bankrupt.

This section corresponds to s.181 of the 1985 Act.

Unenforceability of liens on books, etc.

349.—(1) Subject as follows, a lien or other right to retain possession of any of the books, papers or other records of a bankrupt is unenforceable to the extent that its enforcement would deny possession of any books, papers or other records to the official receiver or the trustee of the bankrupt's estate.

(2) Subsection (1) does not apply to a lien on documents which give a title to property and are held as such.

DEFINITIONS

"bankrupt": s.381(1).
"estate": ss.283, 385(1).
"property": s.436.
"records": s.436.
"the official receiver": s.399(1).

General Note

This section renders certain liens on the books, papers and records of the bankrupt unenforceable against the trustee. The extent of the unenforceability of such liens is limited to the matter of the right of the official receiver or the trustee to gain possession of the items of property to which any lien is applicable. Moreover, subs. (2) expressly preserves the right of any lienholder to retain possession of documents which give title to property and which are held as such, as where a mortgage is effected by a deposit of title deeds. However, the section does effectively modify the principle long established in the case law whereby the trustee in bankruptcy was held to take "subject to equities", and hence to be affected by any pre-existing lien or other possessory right existing in favour of a third party before the commencement of bankruptcy.

This section corresponds to s.182 of the 1985 Act.

Chapter VI

Bankruptcy Offences

Preliminary

General Note

This chapter restates in modern terms the offences contained in Pt. VII of the Bankruptcy Act 1914 (repealed), and revises the penalties for those offences. The offences are grouped in a more logical way than under the provisions of the former legislation. Offences associated with insolvency are discussed in Chap. 48 of the *Cork Report.*

Transitional Provision

Sched 11, para. 18.

Scheme of this Chapter

350.—(1) Subject to section 360(3) below, this Chapter applies where the court has made a bankruptcy order on a bankruptcy petition.

(2) This Chapter applies whether or not the bankruptcy order is annulled, but proceedings for an offence under this Chapter shall not be instituted after the annulment.

(3) Without prejudice to his liability in respect of a subsequent bankruptcy, the bankrupt is not guilty of an offence under this Chapter in respect of anything done after his discharge; but nothing in this Group of Parts prevents the institution of proceedings against a discharged bankrupt for an offence committed before his discharge.

(4) It is not a defence in proceedings for an offence under this Chapter that anything relied on, in whole or in part, as constituting that offence was done outside England and Wales.

(5) Proceedings for an offence under this Chapter or under the rules shall not be instituted except by the Secretary of State or by or with the consent of the Director of Public Prosecutions.

(6) A person guilty of any offence under this Chapter is liable to imprisonment or a fine, or both.

Definitions

"affairs": s.385(2).
"annulment": s.282.
"bankrupt": s.381(1).
"bankruptcy order": s.381(2).
"bankruptcy petition": s.381(3).
"discharge": ss.279, 280, 281.
"the court": ss.373, 385(1).

General Note

This section corresponds to subss. (1)–(3), (5) and (6), together with s.192, of the 1985 Act.

Subs. (5)

This imposes a general rule that no prosecution may be brought for an offence under this Chapter or under the rules except by the Secretary of State or by or with the consent of the Director of Public Prosecutions. This accords with the reommendation made in paras. 1892–1894 of the *Cork Report.*

Subs. (6)

Sched. 10 contains the list of punishments which may be imposed for offences under this Chapter.

Definitions

351. In the following provisions of this Chapter—

(*a*) references to property comprised in the bankrupt's estate or to property possession of which is required to be delivered up to the official receiver or the trustee of the bankrupt's estate include any property which would be such property if a notice in respect of it were given under section 307 (after-acquired property) or 308 (personal property and effects of bankrupt having more than replacement value);

(*b*) "the initial period" means the period between the presentation of the bankruptcy petition and the commencement of the bankruptcy; and

(*c*) a reference to a number of months or years before petition is to that period ending with the presentation of the bankruptcy petition.

Definitions

"bankrupt": s.381(1).
"bankruptcy petition": s.381(3).
"commencement of the bankruptcy": s.278(*a*).
"estate": ss.283, 385(1).
"months before petition": para. (*c*).
"property": para. (*a*); s.436.
"the initial period": para. (*b*).
"the official receiver": s.399(1).
"the trustee": s.385(1).
"years before petition": para. (*c*).

General Note

This section contains special definitions of terms in relation to their use within Chapter VI of Part IX.

This section corresponds to ss.184(5) and 187(3)(*a*) of the 1985 Act.

Defence of innocent intention

352. Where in the case of an offence under any provision of this Chapter it is stated that this section applies, a person is not guilty of the offence if he proves that, at the time of the conduct constituting the offence, he had no intent to defraud or to conceal the state of his affairs.

General Note

This provision has the effect that a burden of proof is cast upon the bankrupt in respect of any charges brought against him under the provisions to which this section applies. Thus, although the offences in question are cast as offences of strict liability, the bankrupt can escape conviction if he effectively proves that he lacked the relevant *mens rea,* namely an intention to defraud or to conceal the state of his affairs. The presence of this section also serves as a general aid to judicial construction of the subsequent sections in which the specific criminal offences are prescribed, since it is evidence of a legislative intention to create offences of strict liability in respect of all those provisions which contain no internal reference to the intention or state of mind of the accused person (*cf. Sweet* v. *Parsley* [1969] 1 All E.R. 347; [1970] A.C. 132).

This section corresponds to s.183(4) of the 1985 Act.

Wrongdoing by the bankrupt before and after bankruptcy

Non-disclosure

353.—(1) The bankrupt is guilty of an offence if—

(*a*) he does not to the best of his knowledge and belief disclose all the property comprised in his estate to the official receiver or the trustee, or

(*b*) he does not inform the official receiver or the trustee of any disposal of any property which but for the disposal would be so comprised, stating how, when, to whom and for what consideration the property was disposed of.

(2) Subsection (1)(*b*) does not apply to any disposal in the ordinary course of a business carried on by the bankrupt or to any payment of the ordinary expenses of the bankrupt or his family.

(3) Section 352 applies to this offence.

DEFINITIONS

"business": s.436.
"estate": ss.283, 385(1).
"family": s.385(1).
"property": ss.351(*a*), 436.
"the bankrupt": s.381(1).
"the official receiver": s.399(1).
"trustee": s.385(1).

GENERAL NOTE

This section deals with offences relating to the failure by the bankrupt to disclose property to the official receiver or trustee in bankruptcy as required by law, and to supply other relevant information regarding dealings with his available property.

This section corresponds to ss.183(4) and 184(1) of the 1985 Act.

Subs. (3)

See s.352 and General Note thereto.

Concealment of property

354.—(1) The bankrupt is guilty of an offence if—

(*a*) he does not deliver up possession to the official receiver or trustee, or as the official receiver or trustee may direct, of such part of the property comprised in his estate as is in his possession or under his control and possession of which he is required by law so to deliver up,

(*b*) he conceals any debt due to or from him or conceals any property the value of which is not less than the prescribed amount and possession of which he is required to deliver up to the official receiver or trustee, or

(*c*) in the 12 months before petition, or in the initial period, he did anything which would have been an offence under paragraph (*b*) above if the bankruptcy order had been made immediately before he did it.

Section 352 applies to this offence.

(2) The bankrupt is guilty of an offence if he removes, or in the initial period removed, any property the value of which was not less than the

prescribed amount and possession of which he has or would have been required to deliver up to the official receiver or the trustee.

Section 352 applies to this offence.

(3) The bankrupt is guilty of an offence if he without reasonable excuse fails, on being required to do so by the official receiver or the court—

(*a*) to account for the loss of any substantial part of his property incurred in the 12 months before petition or in the initial period, or

(*b*) to give a satisfactory explanation of the manner in which such a loss was incurred.

DEFINITIONS

"bankrupt": s.381(1).
"bankruptcy order": s.381(2).
"debt": ss.382(3), 385(1).
"estate": ss.283, 385(1).
"months before petition": s.351(*c*).
"prescribed": s.384.
"property": ss.351(*a*), 436.
"the initial period": s.351(*b*).
"the official receiver": s.399(1).
"the trustee": s.385(1).

GENERAL NOTE

This section establishes criminal offences in relation to various acts of concealment of property, or of failure to deliver up possession of property as required by law.

This section corresponds to ss.183(4) and 184(2)–(4) of the 1985 Act.

Subss. (1) and (2)

See General Note to s.352.

Subs. (1)(c)

This provision is so worded as to give rise to criminal liability if a person is subsequently adjudicated on a bankruptcy petition presented within twelve months after he does any of the acts referred to.

Concealment of books and papers; falsification

355.—(1) The bankrupt is guilty of an offence if he does not deliver up possession to the official receiver or the trustee, or as the official receiver or trustee may direct, of all books, papers and other records of which he has possession or control and which relate to his estate or his affairs.

Section 352 applies to this offence.

(2) The bankrupt is guilty of an offence if—

(*a*) he prevents, or in the initial period prevented, the production of any books, papers or records relating to his estate or affairs;

(*b*) he conceals, destroys, mutilates or falsifies, or causes or permits the concealment, destruction, mutilation or falsification of, any books, papers or other records relating to his estate or affairs;

(*c*) he makes, or causes or permits the making of, any false entries in any book, document or record relating to his estate or affairs; or

(*d*) in the 12 months before petition, or in the initial period, he did anything which would have been an offence, under paragraph (*b*) or (*c*) above if the bankruptcy order had been made before he did it.

Section 352 applies to this offence.

(3) The bankrupt is guilty of an offence if—

(*a*) he disposes of, or alters or makes any omission in, or causes or permits the disposal, altering or making of any omission in, any book, document or record relating to his estate or affairs, or (*b*) in the 12 months before petition, or in the initial period, he did anything which would have been an offence under paragraph (*a*) if the bankruptcy order had been made before he did it.

Section 352 applies to this offence.

DEFINITIONS

"affairs": s.385(2).
"bankrupt": s.381(1).
"bankruptcy order": s.381(2).
"commencement of the bankruptcy": s.278(*a*).
"estate": ss.283, 385(1).
"months before petition": s.351(*c*).
"petition", "bankruptcy petition": s.381(3).
"records": s.436.
"the initial period": s.351(*b*).
"the official receiver": s.399(1).
"the trustee": s.385(1).

GENERAL NOTE

This section sets out the offences which may be committed by a bankrupt in relation to his books, papers and other records. The prohibited acts include concealment, non-delivery, falsification, mutilation or destruction of any of the items in question.

This section corresponds to ss.183(4) and 185 of the 1985 Act.

Subss. (1), (2) and (3)

See General Note to s.352.

Subss. (2)(d) , (3)(b)

These provisions are so worded as to give rise to criminal liability if a person is subsequently adjudicated on a bankruptcy petition presented within twelve months after he does any of the acts referred to. Where the bankrupt has been engaged in business, references to certain types of "records" within this section apply with the substitution of two years for 12 months: s.361(4).

False statements

356.—(1) The bankrupt is guilty of an offence if he makes or has made any material omission in any statement made under any provision in this Group of Parts and relating to his affairs.

Section 352 applies to this offence.

(2) The bankrupt is guilty of an offence if—

(*a*) knowing or believing that a false debt has been proved by any person under the bankruptcy, he fails to inform the trustee as soon as practicable; or

(*b*) he attempts to account for any part of his property by fictitious losses or expenses; or

(*c*) at any meeting of his creditors in the 12 months before petition or (whether or not at such a meeting) at any time in the initial period, he did anything which would have been an offence under paragraph (*b*) if the bankruptcy order had been made before he did it; or

(*d*) he is, or at any time has been, guilty of any false representation or other fraud for the purpose of obtaining the consent of his creditors, or any of them, to an agreement with reference to his affairs or to his bankruptcy.

DEFINITIONS

"affairs": s.385(2).
"bankrupt": s.381(1).
"commencement of the bankruptcy": s.278(*a*).
"creditor": s.383(1).
"debt": ss.382(3), 385(1).

"estate": ss.283, 385(1).
"months before petition": s.351(*c*).
"petition", "bankruptcy petition": s.381(3).
"property": s.436.
"the initial period": s.351(*b*).
"trustee": s.385(1).

General Note

This section establishes criminal offences committed through the making of false statements by the bankrupt.

This section corresponds to ss.183(4) and 186 of the 1985 Act.

Subs. (1)

See General Note to s.352.

Subs. (2)(c)

This provision is so worded as to give rise to criminal liability if a person is subsequently adjudicated bankrupt on a petition presented within 12 months after the creditors' meeting at which the act referred to was done.

Fraudulent disposal of property

357.—(1) The bankrupt is guilty of an offence if he makes or causes to be made, or has in the period of 5 years ending with the commencement of the bankruptcy made or caused to be made, any gift or transfer of, or any charge on, his property.

Section 352 applies to this offence.

(2) The reference to making a transfer of or charge on any property includes causing or conniving at the levying of any execution against that property.

(3) The bankrupt is guilty of an offence if he conceals or removes, or has at any time before the commencement of the bankruptcy concealed or removed, any part of his property after, or within 2 months before, the date on which a judgment or order for the payment of money has been obtained against him, being a judgment or order which was not satisfied before the commencement of the bankruptcy.

Section 352 applies to this offence.

Definitions

"bankrupt": s.381(1).
"commencement of the bankruptcy": s.278(*a*).
"estate": ss.283, 385(1).
"property": ss.351(*a*), 436.
"the official receiver": s.399(1).

General Note

This section establishes criminal offences committed through the fraudulent disposal of property by the bankrupt. There is one change of a substantive nature regarding the offence created by subs. (1), as against that previously created by s.156(*b*) of the Bankruptcy Act 1914 (repealed). In the former provision, the offence of fraudulent disposal of property could be committed through any act of disposal at any time before the commencement of bankruptcy, without limitation as to the period of time involved. The period of five years before the commencement of bankruptcy has now been introduced in subs. (1) as enacted, and is commensurate with the period of time allowed under s.339 whereby gifts and undervalued transactions can be challenged if the bankrupt was insolvent at the time of the transaction (see s.341(1)(*a*)).

This section corresponds to ss.183(4) and 187(1) and (3)(*b*) of the 1985 Act.

Subss. (1) and (3)

See General Note to s.352.

Absconding

358. The bankrupt is guilty of an offence if—

(*a*) he leaves, or attempts or makes preparations to leave, England and Wales with any property the value of which is not less than the prescribed amount and possession of which he is required to deliver up to the official receiver or the trustee, or

(*b*) in the 6 months before petition, or in the initial period, he did anything which would have been an offence under paragraph (*a*) if the bankruptcy order had been made immediately before he did it.

Section 352 applies to this offence.

DEFINITIONS

"bankrupt": s.381(1).
"months before petition": s.351(*c*).
"prescribed": s.384.
"property": ss.351(*a*), 436.
"the initial period": s.351(*b*).
"the official receiver": s.399(1).
"trustee": s.385(1).

GENERAL NOTE

This offence was formerly contained in s.159 of the Bankruptcy Act 1914 (repealed). In para. 1889 of the *Cork Report* there was criticism of the inclusion of a prescribed monetary figure (latterly £250) employed in conjunction with the commission of this offence, and it was recommended that there should be no financial limit as to amount or value of property, the proposed test being simply whether the property with which the bankrupt absconds belongs to that part of his estate which is divisible among his creditors. The inclusion in the present subsection of a reference to "prescribed amount" of value therefore constitutes a rejection of the Cork Committee's recommendation and a retention of the former rule, with the facility for effecting its upward revision periodically by means of a statutory instrument.

This section corresponds to ss.183(4) and 187(2) of the 1985 Act. See also the General Note to s.352.

Fraudulent dealing with property obtained on credit

359.—(1) The bankrupt is guilty of an offence if, in the 12 months before petition, or in the initial period, he disposed of any property which he had obtained on credit and, at the time he disposed of it, had not paid for.

Section 352 applies to this offence.

(2) A person is guilty of an offence if, in the 12 months before petition or in the initial period, he acquired or received property from the bankrupt knowing or believing—

(*a*) that the bankrupt owed money in respect of the property, and

(*b*) that the bankrupt did not intend, or was unlikely to be able, to pay the money he so owed.

(3) A person is not guilty of an offence under subsection (1) or (2) if the disposal, acquisition or receipt of the property was in the ordinary course of a business carried on by the bankrupt at the time of the disposal, acquisition or receipt.

(4) In determining for the purposes of this section whether any property is disposed of, acquired or received in the ordinary course of a business carried on by the bankrupt, regard may be had, in particular, to the price paid for the property.

(5) In this section references to disposing of property include pawning or pledging it; and references to acquiring or receiving property shall be read accordingly.

DEFINITIONS

"bankrupt": s.381(1).
"business": s.436.

"dispose of property": subs. (5).
"months before petition": s.351(*c*).
"petition", "bankruptcy petition": s.381(3).
"property": ss.351(*a*), 436.
"the initial period": s.351(*b*).

General Note

This section establishes criminal offences which may be committed by the bankrupt or by other persons fraudulently dealing with property obtained on credit.

This section corresponds to ss.183(4) and 188 of the 1985 Act.

Subs. (1)

See General Note to s.352.

Obtaining credit; engaging in business

360.—(1) The bankrupt is guilty of an offence if—

(*a*) either alone or jointly with any other person, he obtains credit to the extent of the prescribed amount or more without giving the person from whom he obtains it the relevant information about his status; or

(*b*) he engages (whether directly or indirectly) in any business under a name other than that in which he was adjudged bankrupt without disclosing to all persons with whom he enters into any business transaction the name in which he was so adjudged.

(2) The reference to the bankrupt obtaining credit includes the following cases—

(*a*) where goods are bailed to him under a hire-purchase agreement, or agreed to be sold to him under a conditional sale agreement, and

(*b*) where he is paid in advance (whether in money or otherwise) for the supply of goods or services.

(3) A person whose estate has been sequestrated in Scotland, or who has been adjudged bankrupt in Northern Ireland, is guilty of an offence if, before his discharge, he does anything in England and Wales which would be an offence under subsection (1) if he were an undischarged bankrupt and the sequestration of his estate or the adjudication in Northern Ireland were an adjudication under this Part.

(4) For the purposes of subsection (1)(*a*), the relevant information about the status of the person in question is the information that he is an undischarged bankrupt or, as the case may be, that his estate has been sequestrated in Scotland and that he has not been discharged.

Definitions

"bankrupt": s.381(1).
"business": s.436.
"estate": ss.283, 385(1).
"obtaining credit": subs. (2).
"prescribed": s.384.
"the relevant information": subs. (4).
"transaction": s.436.

General Note

This section deals with offences committed by an undischarged bankrupt through the obtaining of credit without revealing his status or through his engaging in business under a name other than that in which he was adjudged bankrupt, without disclosing his other identity in any business transaction entered into. This section re-enacts, with some modifications and with up-to-date drafting, the provisions formerly contained in s.155 of the Bankruptcy Act 1914 (repealed).

This section corresponds to s.189 of the 1985 Act.

Subss. (1)(a), (3), (4)

These subsections together establish an improved provision by comparison to that of the former s.155(*a*) of the Bankruptcy Act 1914 (repealed), since they create throughout the whole of the United Kingdom an integrated regime to control one of the most important, and best known, disabilities attaching to the status of an undischarged bankrupt. A person who has incurred equivalent personal disabilities under the laws of either of the other two parts of the United Kingdom will commit a criminal offence if he fails to make the requisite disclosure when obtaining credit from any person in England and Wales. *Cf.* Bankruptcy (Scotland) Act 1985, s.67(9), (10).

The use of the drafting device of referring to the "prescribed amount" has the effect of ensuring that the monetary amount applicable to the commission of an offence under this section can be revised periodically by statutory instrument. This offence has traditionally been one of strict liability, its purpose being to protect members of the public from risk of loss by dealing with a person presumed to be creditworthy. The maintenance of this characteristic of strict liability under the present section accords with the recommendation of the *Cork Report* (paras. 132, 1840–1845; and 1882).

Subss. (1)(b), (3)

These subsections also effect a sensible integration of the provisions regarding the offence formerly specified in s.155(*b*) of the Bankruptcy Act 1914 (repealed), so that a sequestration in Scotland or an adjudication in Northern Ireland are equated with adjudication in England and Wales for the purposes of rendering the person concerned subject to criminal liability for engaging in business transactions in England and Wales under an *alias*. A further refinement in the drafting consists in the insertion of the words "(whether directly or indirectly)" in relation to engagement in business, so that an undischarged bankrupt who utilises an agent to perform business on his behalf, or who otherwise contrives to control a business from behind the scenes, can also be convicted if the other ingredients of this offence are made out. (*Cf.* The drafting of the parallel provision in s.302(1) of the Companies Act 1985 whereby an undischarged bankrupt is prohibited from acting in the management of companies either directly or indirectly.)

Subs. (2)(b)

The purpose of this provision, which is an alteration to the former law, is to reverse the anomaly resulting from the decision of the House of Lords in *Fisher* v. *Raven* [1964] A.C. 210, in which an undischarged bankrupt who obtained payment in advance to carry out work which he then failed to perform was held not to have committed an offence under s.155(*a*) of the Bankruptcy Act 1914 because he did not obtain "credit" within the meaning of that section. A strict interpretation of the term "credit" was adopted by the House of Lords whereby the offence could only be committed if a bankrupt obtained "credit in respect of the payment or repayment of money." That ruling is now reversed by the present provision, which expressly renders it an offence for an undischarged bankrupt to receive advanced payments—whether in money or in another form—for the supply of goods or services without informing those concerned of his current status.

Failure to keep proper accounts of business

361.—(1) Where the bankrupt has been engaged in any business for any of the period of 2 years before petition, he is guilty of an offence if he—

(*a*) has not kept proper accounting records throughout that period and throughout any part of the initial period in which he was so engaged, or

(*b*) has not preserved all the accounting records which he has kept.

(2) The bankrupt is not guilty of an offence under subsection (1)—

(*a*) if his unsecured liabilities at the commencement of the bankruptcy did not exceed the prescribed amount, or

(*b*) if he proves that in the circumstances in which he carried on business the omission was honest and excusable.

(3) For the purposes of this section a person is deemed not to have kept proper accounting records if he has not kept such records as are necessary to show or explain his transactions and financial position in his business, including—

(*a*) records containing entries from day to day, in sufficient detail, of all cash paid and received,

(*b*) where the business involved dealings in goods, statements of annual stock-takings, and

(*c*) except in the case of goods sold by way of retail trade to the actual customer, records of all goods sold and purchased showing the buyers and sellers in sufficient detail to enable the goods and the buyers and sellers to be identified.

(4) In relation to any such records as are mentioned in subsection (3), subsections (2)(*d*) and (3)(*b*) of section 355 apply with the substitution of 2 years for 12 months.

DEFINITIONS

"bankrupt": s.381(1).
"business": s.436.
"commencement of the bankruptcy": s.278(*a*).
"petition", "bankruptcy petition": s.381(3).
"prescribed": s.384.
"proper accounting records": subs. (3).
"records": s.436.
"transaction": s.436.
"unsecured", "secured": ss.383, 385(1).

GENERAL NOTE

This section deals with the failure of the bankrupt to keep proper accounts. The section restates the former provisions of s.158 of the Bankruptcy Act 1914 (repealed), by comparison to which the drafting of the present section is improved and modernised. As recommended in para. 1887 of the *Cork Report* there is no longer any requirement that a special order of the bankruptcy court must be made as a precondition for the bringing of a prosecution under this section.

This section corresponds to s.190 of the 1985 Act.

Gambling

362.—(1) The bankrupt is guilty of an offence if he has—

(*a*) in the 2 years before petition, materially contributed to, or increased the extent of, his insolvency by gambling or by rash and hazardous speculations, or

(*b*) in the initial period, lost any part of his property by gambling or by rash and hazardous speculations.

(2) In determining for the purposes of this section whether any speculations were rash and hazardous, the financial position of the bankrupt at the time when he entered into them shall be taken into consideration.

DEFINITIONS

"bankrupt": s.381(1).
"petition", "bankruptcy petition": s.381(3).
"property": ss.351(*a*), 436.
"rash and hazardous speculations": see subs. (2).
"the initial period": s.251(*b*).
"years before petition": s.251(*c*).

GENERAL NOTE

This section creates two related offences which may be committed by a person who has contributed to his bankruptcy by gambling or by rash and hazardous speculations. This largely restates the law formerly contained in s.157(1)(*a*), (*b*) of the Bankruptcy Act 1914 (repealed), but in addition to the appropriate modernisation of drafting the present section broadens the scope of the offence through the omission of any references to the bankrupt's having been engaged in any trade or business, and to the existence of outstanding trade or business debts. Any bankrupt can now be convicted of these offences if the necessary ingredients are proved, regardless of whether he is or has been engaged in any trade or business. It was at one stage (H.C. Standing Committee E, June 18, 1985, cols. 414–415) declared to be intended that this section would reverse the decision in *R.* v. *Vaccari* [1958] 1 All E.R. 468 in which it was held that income or profits tax was not a debt "contracted in the course and for the purposes of" a trade or business for the purposes of the commission of an offence under s.157(1) of the Bankruptcy Act 1914. The elimination of all reference to a trading context for the commission of an offence under the present action has had the consequence of rendering this former nice distinction irrelevant.

As recommended in para. 1887 of the *Cork Report* there is no longer any requirement that a special order be made by the bankruptcy court in order that a prosecution may be brought under this section.

This section corresponds to s.191 of the 1985 Act.

Chapter VII

Powers of Court In Bankruptcy

General control of court

363.—(1) Every bankruptcy is under the general control of the court and, subject to the provisions in this Group of Parts, the court has full power to decide all questions of priorities and all other questions, whether of law or fact, arising in any bankruptcy.

(2) Without prejudice to any other provision in this Group of Parts, an undischarged bankrupt or a discharged bankrupt whose estate is still being administered under Chapter IV of this Part shall do all such things as he may be directed to do by the court for the purposes of his bankruptcy or, as the case may be, the administration of that estate.

(3) The official receiver or the trustee of a bankrupt's estate may at any time apply to the court for a direction under subsection (2).

(4) If any person without reasonable excuse fails to comply with any obligation imposed on him by subsection (2), he is guilty of a contempt of court and liable to be punished accordingly (in addition to any other punishment to which he may be subject).

Definitions

"bankrupt": s.381(1).
"estate": ss.283, 385(1).
"the court": ss.373, 385(1).
"the official receiver": s.399(1).
"trustee": s.385(1).

General Note

This section places every bankruptcy under the general control of the relevant court, empowers the court to direct the bankrupt to do things for the purposes of the bankruptcy and for the realisation of the estate both before and, in certain cases, after he obtains his discharge, and provides for the official receiver and the trustee in bankruptcy to apply at any time to the court for the issue of such a direction in relation to the bankrupt.

This section corresponds to s.193 of the 1985 Act.

Power of arrest

364.—(1) In the cases specified in the next subsection the court may cause a warrant to be issued to a constable or prescribed officer of the court—

(*a*) for the arrest of a debtor to whom a bankruptcy petition relates or of an undischarged bankrupt, or of a discharged bankrupt whose estate is still being administered under Chapter IV of this Part, and

(*b*) for the seizure of any books, papers, records, money or goods in the possession of a person arrested under the warrant, and may authorise a person arrested under such a warrant to be kept in custody, and anything seized under such a warrant to be held, in accordance with the rules, until such time as the court may order.

(2) The powers conferred by subsection (1) are exercisable in relation to a debtor or undischarged or discharged bankrupt if, at any time after the presentation of the bankruptcy petition relating to him or the making of the bankruptcy order against him, it appears to the court—

(*a*) that there are reasonable grounds for believing that he has absconded, or is about to abscond, with a view to avoiding or delaying the payment of any of his debts or his appearance to a bankruptcy petition or to avoiding, delaying or disrupting any proceedings in bankruptcy against him or any examination of his affairs, or

(*b*) that he is about to remove his goods with a view to preventing or delaying possession being taken of them by the official receiver or the trustee of his estate, or

(*c*) that there are reasonable grounds for believing that he has concealed or destroyed, or is about to conceal or destroy, any of his goods or any books, papers or records which might be of use to his creditors in the course of his bankruptcy or in connection with the administration of his estate, or

(*d*) that he has, without the leave of the official receiver or the trustee of his estate, removed any goods in his possession which exceed in value such sum as may be prescribed for the purposes of this paragraph, or

(*e*) that he has failed, without reasonable excuse, to attend any examination ordered by the court.

DEFINITIONS

"affairs": s.385(2).
"bankrupt": s.381(1).
"bankruptcy order": s.381(2).
"bankruptcy petition": s.381(3).
"creditor": s.383(1).
"debt": ss.382(3), 385(1).
"debtor": s.385(1).
"estate": ss.283, 385(1).
"prescribed": s.384.
"records": s.436.
"the court": ss.373, 385(1).
"the official receiver": s.399(1).
"the rules": ss.384, 412.

GENERAL NOTE

This section sets out the circumstances in which the court may authorise the arrest of a debtor or bankrupt, and the seizure of documents, money or goods in his possession. This section restates, with suitable modifications and modernisation in the drafting, the former provisions of s.23 of the Bankruptcy Act 1914 (repealed).

This section corresponds to s.194 of the 1985 Act.

Subs. (2)

It may be noted that the wide terms of application of the powers of arrest and seizure under this section apply against a debtor even after he has obtained his discharge from bankruptcy under the provisions of ss.279–281 of the Act.

Seizure of bankrupt's property

365.—(1) At any time after a bankruptcy order has been made, the court may, on the application of the official receiver or the trustee of the bankrupt's estate, issue a warrant authorising the person to whom it is directed to seize any property comprised in the bankrupt's estate which is, or any books, papers or records relating to the bankrupt's estate or affairs which are, in the possession or under the control of the bankrupt or any other person who is required to deliver the property, books, papers or records to the official receiver or trustee.

(2) Any person executing a warrant under this section may, for the purpose of seizing any property comprised in the bankrupt's estate or any books, papers or records relating to the bankrupt's estate or affairs, break open any premises where the bankrupt or anything that may be seized under the warrant is or is believed to be and any receptacle of the bankrupt which contains or is believed to contain anything that may be so seized.

(3) If, after a bankruptcy order has been made, the court is satisfied that any property comprised in the bankrupt's estate is, or any books, papers or records relating to the bankrupt's estate or affairs are, concealed in any premises not belonging to him, it may issue a warrant authorising any constable or prescribed officer of the court to search those premises for the property, books, papers or records.

(4) A warrant under subsection (3) shall not be executed except in the prescribed manner and in accordance with its terms.

Definitions

"affairs": s.385(2).
"bankrupt": s.381(1).
"bankruptcy order": s.381(2).
"estate": ss.283, 385(1).
"prescribed": s.384.
"property": s.436.
"records": s.436.
"the court": ss.373, 385(1).
"the official receiver": s.399(1).
"trustee": s.385(1).

General Note

This section empowers the court to authorise the seizure of property comprised in the bankrupt's estate, and to issue warrants for the purpose of enabling authorised persons to enter premises belonging to the bankrupt or to others, and to search for and seize any relevant property or documents to be found there. The section restates in updated form the provisions formerly contained in s.49 of the Bankruptcy Act 1914 (repealed).

This section corresponds to s.195 of the 1985 Act.

Inquiry into bankrupt's dealings and property

366.—(1) At any time after a bankruptcy order has been made the court may, on the application of the official receiver or the trustee of the bankrupt's estate, summon to appear before it—

(*a*) the bankrupt or the bankrupt's spouse or former spouse,

(*b*) any person known or believed to have any property comprised in the bankrupt's estate in his possession or to be indebted to the bankrupt,

(*c*) any person appearing to the court to be able to give information concerning the bankrupt or the bankrupt's dealings, affairs or property.

The court may require any such person as is mentioned in paragraph (*b*) or (*c*) to submit an affidavit to the court containing an account of his dealings with the bankrupt or to produce any documents in his possession or under his control relating to the bankrupt or the bankrupt's dealings, affairs or property.

(2) Without prejudice to section 364, the following applies in a case where—

(*a*) a person without reasonable excuse fails to appear before the court when he is summoned to do so under this section, or

(*b*) there are reasonable grounds for believing that a person has absconded, or is about to abscond, with a view to avoiding his appearance before the court under this section.

(3) The court may, for the purpose of bringing that person and anything in his possession before the court, cause a warrant to be issued to a constable or prescribed officer of the court—

(*a*) for the arrest of that person, and

(*b*) for the seizure of any books, papers, records, money or goods in that person's possession.

(4) The court may authorise a person arrested under such a warrant to be kept in custody, and anything seized under such a warrant to be held, in accordance with the rules, until that person is brought before the court under the warrant or until such other time as the court may order.

Definitions

"bankrupt": s.381(1).
"bankruptcy order": s.381(2).
"estate": ss.283, 385(1).
"prescribed": s.384.
"property": s.436.
"records": s.436.
"the court": ss.373, 385(1).
"the official receiver": s.399(1).
"the rules": ss.384, 412.
"trustee": s.385(1).

General Note

This section empowers the court to examine the bankrupt and other persons as to his affairs, dealings or property. The law is restated, with suitable modifications and modernisation in drafting, from the provision formerly contained in s.25 of the Bankruptcy Act 1914 (repealed). The provisions of s.369 apply for the purposes of any examination under this section.

This section corresponds to subss. (1) and (2) of s.196 of the 1985 Act.

Court's enforcement powers under s.366

367.—(1) If it appears to the court, on consideration of any evidence obtained under section 366 or this section, that any person has in his possession any property comprised in the bankrupt's estate, the court may, on the application of the official receiver or the trustee of the bankrupt's estate, order that person to deliver the whole or any part of the property to the official receiver or the trustee at such time, in such manner and on such terms as the court thinks fit.

(2) If it appears to the court, on consideration of any evidence obtained under section 366 or this section, that any person is indebted to the bankrupt, the court may, on the application of the official receiver or the trustee of the bankrupt's estate, order that person to pay to the official receiver or trustee, at such time and in such manner as the court may direct, the whole or part of the amount due, whether in full discharge of the debt or otherwise as the court thinks fit.

(3) The court may, if it thinks fit, order that any person who if within the jurisdiction of the court would be liable to be summoned to appear before it under section 366 shall be examined in any part of the United Kingdom where he may be for the time being, or in any place outside the United Kingdom.

(4) Any person who appears or is brought before the court under section 366 or this section may be examined on oath, either orally or by

interrogatories, concerning the bankrupt or the bankrupt's dealings, affairs and property.

Definitions
"affairs": s.385(2).
"bankrupt": s.381(1).
"debt": ss.382(3), 385(1).
"estate": ss.283, 385(1).
"property": s.436.
"the court": ss.373, 385(1).
"the official receiver": s.399(1).
"trustee": s.385(1).

General Note
This section operates in conjunction with s.366, and empowers the court to make orders, consequential upon the examination of a person under s.366, to require the delivery up of property or the making of any payment to the official receiver or trustee, as appropriate.
This section corresponds to subss. (3)–(6) of s.196 of the 1985 Act.

Provision corresponding to s.366, where interim receiver appointed

368. Sections 366 and 367 apply where an interim receiver has been appointed under section 286 as they apply where a bankruptcy order has been made, as if—
(*a*) references to the official receiver or the trustee were to the interim receiver, and
(*b*) references to the bankrupt and to his estate were (respectively) to the debtor and his property.

Definitions
"bankrupt": s.381(1).
"bankruptcy order": s.381(2).
"debtor": s.385(1).
"estate": ss.283, 385(1).
"property": s.436.
"the official receiver": s.399(1).
"trustee": s.385(1).

General Note
This section, which corresponds to s.196(7) of the 1985 Act, embodies the modifications which are necessarily applicable to the operation of s.366 during any period when an interim receiver of a debtor's property has been appointed under s.286. The adjustments in terminology arise from the fact that no bankruptcy order will at that stage have been made, so that references to "the bankrupt" and to his "estate" are inappropriate, and technically incorrect. By virtue of s.369(7), the provisions of that section do not apply for the purposes of an examination which takes place under ss.366 and 367 during the period when an interim receiver has been appointed.

Order for production of documents by inland revenue

369.—(1) For the purposes of an examination under section 290 (public examination of bankrupt) or proceedings under sections 366 to 368, the court may, on the application of the official receiver or the trustee of the bankrupt's estate, order an inland revenue official to produce to the court—
(*a*) any return, account or accounts submitted (whether before or after the commencement of the bankruptcy) by the bankrupt to any inland revenue official,
(*b*) any assessment or determination made (whether before or after the commencement of the bankruptcy) in relation to the bankrupt by any inland revenue official, or
(*c*) any correspondence (whether before or after the commencement

of the bankruptcy) between the bankrupt and any inland revenue official.

(2) Where the court has made an order under subsection (1) for the purposes of any examination or proceedings, the court may, at any time after the document to which the order relates is produced to it, by order authorise the disclosure of the document, or of any part of its contents, to the official receiver, the trustee of the bankrupt's estate or the bankrupt's creditors.

(3) The court shall not address an order under subsection (1) to an inland revenue official unless it is satisfied that that official is dealing, or has dealt, with the affairs of the bankrupt.

(4) Where any document to which an order under subsection (1) relates is not in the possession of the official to whom the order is addressed, it is the duty of that official to take all reasonable steps to secure possession of it and, if he fails to do so, to report the reasons for his failure to the court.

(5) Where any document to which an order under subsection (1) relates is in the possession of an inland revenue official other than the one to whom the order is addressed, it is the duty of the official in possession of the document, at the request of the official to whom the order is addressed, to deliver it to the official making the request.

(6) In this section "inland revenue official" means any inspector or collector of taxes appointed by the Commissioners of Inland Revenue or any person appointed by the Commissioners to serve in any other capacity.

(7) This section does not apply for the purposes of an examination under sections 366 and 367 which takes place by virtue of section 368 (interim receiver).

Definitions

"affairs": s.385(2).
"bankrupt": s.381(1).
"commencement of the bankruptcy": s.278(*a*).
"creditor": s.383(1).
"estate": ss.283, 385(1).
"Inland Revenue official": subs. (6).
"the official receiver": s.399(1).
"the court": ss.373, 385(1).
"trustee": s.385(1).

General Note

This section empowers the court to order the Inland Revenue to produce tax records relating to the bankrupt for the purpose of a public examination under s.290 or an examination under ss.366–368.

This section corresponds to s.197 of the 1985 Act.

Power to appoint special manager

370.—(1) The court may, on an application under this section, appoint any person to be the special manager—

(*a*) of a bankrupt's estate, or
(*b*) of the business of an undischarged bankrupt, or
(*c*) of the property or business of a debtor in whose case the official receiver has been appointed interim receiver under section 286.

(2) An application under this section may be made by the official receiver or the trustee of the bankrupt's estate in any case where it appears to the official receiver or trustee that the nature of the estate, property or business, or the interests of the creditors generally, require the appointment of another person to manage the estate, property or business.

(3) A special manager appointed under this section has such powers as may be entrusted to him by the court.

(4) The power of the court under subsection (3) to entrust powers to a special manager includes power to direct that any provision in this Group of Parts that has effect in relation to the official receiver, interim receiver or trustee shall have the like effect in relation to the special manager for the purposes of the carrying out by the special manager of any of the functions of the official receiver, interim receiver or trustee.

(5) A special manager appointed under this section shall—

(*a*) give such security as may be prescribed,

(*b*) prepare and keep such accounts as may be prescribed, and

(*c*) produce those accounts in accordance with the rules to the Secretary of State or to such other persons as may be prescribed.

Definitions

"bankrupt": s.381(1).
"business": s.436.
"creditor": s.383(1).
"debtor": s.385(1).
"estate": ss.283, 385(1).
"interim receiver": s.286.
"prescribed": s.384.
"property": s.436.
"the court": ss.373, 385(1).
"the official receiver": s.399(1).
"the rules": ss.384, 412.
"trustee": s.385(1).

General Note

This section enables the court to appoint a special manager of the bankrupt's estate or business, or of the estate or business of a debtor in respect of whom an interim receiver has been appointed under s.286. An appointment under this section may also be made if expedient between the date of the bankruptcy order and the time at which the bankrupt's estate vests in a trustee in bankruptcy. In such cases it is indicated in s.287(1) that the appointment of a special manager has the effect of reducing the role of the official receiver in relation to the estate to that of a receiver only.

This section effects a considerable change in the law compared with the provisions formerly embodied in s.10 of the Bankruptcy Act 1914 (repealed). The official receiver no longer has the authority personally to appoint a special manager, but must apply to the court for such an appointment. On the other hand it is also competent now for the trustee in bankruptcy to apply to the court. There is no longer any requirement that one or more of the creditors should initiate the process whereby the appointment of a special manager is sought: the official receiver or trustee, as the case may be, can act on his own initiative.

The equivalent provision to this section in the winding up of companies is s.177 and the two sections are drafted in parallel.

This section corresponds to s.198 of the 1985 Act.

Re-direction of bankrupt's letters, etc.

371.—(1) Where a bankruptcy order has been made, the court may from time to time, on the application of the official receiver or the trustee of the bankrupt's estate, order the Post Office to re-direct and send or deliver to the official receiver or trustee or otherwise any postal packet (within the meaning of the Post Office Act 1953) which would otherwise be sent or delivered by them to the bankrupt at such place or places as may be specified in the order.

(2) An order under this section has effect for such period, not exceeding 3 months, as may be specified in the order.

Definitions

"bankrupt": s.381(1).
"bankruptcy order": s.381(2).

"postal packet": Post Office Act 1953, s.87(1).
"the court": ss.373, 385(1).
"the official receiver": s.399(1).
"trustee": s.385(1).

General Note

This section, which restates in substance the provisions formerly contained in s.24 of the Bankruptcy Act 1914 (repealed), permits the court to order the redirection of the bankrupt's post. The definition of "postal packet" contained in s.87(1) of the Post Office Act 1953 makes the term applicable to letters, postcards, parcels and telegrams. This section corresponds to s.199 of the 1985 Act.

Part X

Individual Insolvency: General Provisions

Supplies of gas, water, electricity, etc.

372.—(1) This section applies where on any day ("the relevant day")—

(*a*) a bankruptcy order is made against an individual or an interim receiver of an individual's property is appointed, or

(*b*) a voluntary arrangement proposed by an individual is approved under Part VIII, or

(*c*) a deed of arrangement is made for the benefit of an individual's creditors;

and in this section "the office-holder" means the official receiver, the trustee in bankruptcy, the interim receiver, the supervisor of the voluntary arrangement or the trustee under the deed of arrangement, as the case may be.

(2) If a request falling within the next subsection is made for the giving after the relevant day of any of the supplies mentioned in subsection (4), the supplier—

(*a*) may make it a condition of the giving of the supply that the office-holder personally guarantees the payment of any charges in respect of the supply, but

(*b*) shall not make it a condition of the giving of the supply, or do anything which has the effect of making it a condition of the giving of the supply, that any outstanding charges in respect of a supply given to the individual before the relevant day are paid.

(3) A request falls within this subsection if it is made—

(*a*) by or with the concurrence of the office-holder, and

(*b*) for the purposes of any business which is or has been carried on by the individual, by a firm or partnership of which the individual is or was a member, or by an agent or manager for the individual or for such a firm or partnership.

(4) The supplies referred to in subsection (2) are—

(*a*) a public supply of gas,

(*b*) a supply of electricity by an Electricity Board,

(*c*) a supply of water by statutory water undertakers,

(*d*) a supply of telecommunication services by a public telecommunications operator.

(5) The following applies to expressions used in subsection (4)—

(*a*) "public supply of gas" means a supply of gas by the British Gas Corporation or a public gas supplier within the meaning of Part I of the Gas Act 1986;

(*b*) "Electricity Board" means the same as in the Energy Act 1983; and (*c*) "telecommunication services" and "public telecommunications operator" mean the same as in the Telecommunications Act 1984, except that the former does not include services consisting in the conveyance of programmes included in cable programme services (within the meaning of the Cable and Broadcasting Act 1984).

DEFINITIONS

"bankruptcy order": s.381(1).
"business": s.436.
"cable programme services": Cable and Broadcasting Act 1984, ss.2(1), 56(1).
"trustee": s.385(1).
"creditor": s.383(1).
"deed of arrangement": Deeds of Arrangement Act 1914, s.1.
"Electricity Board": Energy Act 1983, s.26.
"interim receiver": s.286.
"property": s.436.
"public supply of gas": subs. (5)(*a*); Gas Act 1986, ss.7(1), 48(1), (2).
"public telecommunications operator": subs. (5)(*c*); Telecommunications Act 1984, ss.9(3), 106(1).
"supervisor": s.263(2).
"telecommunication services": subs. (5)(*c*); Telecommunications Act 1984, ss.4(3), 106(1).
"the office holder": subs. (1).
"the official receiver": s.399(1).
"the relevant day": subs. (1).
"voluntary arrangement": s.253(1).

GENERAL NOTE

This section forms a parallel to s.233, which applies in relation to companies. Although the drafting and structure of the two sections differ in places, the substantial content is the same. The effects of the provisions, and the purposes underlying their enactment, are discussed in the General Note to s.233 (*q.v.*).

This section corresponds to s.200 of the 1985 Act.

Jurisdiction in relation to insolvent individuals

373.—(1) The High Court and the county courts have jurisdiction throughout England and Wales for the purposes of the Parts in this Group.

(2) For the purposes of those Parts, a county court has, in addition to its ordinary jurisdiction, all the powers and jurisdiction of the High Court; and the orders of the court may be enforced accordingly in the prescribed manner.

(3) Jurisdiction for the purposes of those Parts is exercised—

(*a*) by the High Court in relation to the proceedings which, in accordance with the rules, are allocated to the London insolvency district, and

(*b*) by each county court in relation to the proceedings which are so allocated to the insolvency district of that court.

(4) Subsection (3) is without prejudice to the transfer of proceedings from one court to another in the manner prescribed by the rules; and nothing in that subsection invalidates any proceedings on the grounds that they were initiated or continued in the wrong court.

DEFINITIONS

"insolvency district of a county court": s.374(4)(*b*).
"London insolvency district": s.374(4)(*a*).
"prescribed": s.384.
"the court": s.385(1) and this section.
"the rules": ss.384, 412.

GENERAL NOTE

This section makes provision for the exercise of individual insolvency jurisdiction to be performed by the High Court and by those county courts upon which jurisdiction in insolvency matters is conferred under s.374(1) and (4). The division of jurisdiction as between the High Court and the county court respectively is indicated by subs. (3). The provisions of subs. (2) are of considerable significance in that they confer upon a county court, when exercising insolvency jurisdiction under this Part of the Act, all the powers and jurisdiction of the High Court, and further provide that the orders of the county court in such cases are to be enforceable like orders of the High Court. This restates the former provisions of s.103 of the Bankruptcy Act 1914 (repealed). Other matters pertaining to jurisdiction, and to transfers of proceedings, will be contained in the insolvency rules.

The jurisdictional arrangements for individual insolvency enacted by this section are thus substantially the same as those formerly contained in s.96 of the Bankruptcy Act 1914 (repealed). The arguments in Chap. 20 of the *Cork Report* in favour of the creation of a new and separate system of specialised insolvency courts to exercise jurisdiction over all insolvency matters relating to companies and individuals alike have thus been rejected, despite an attempt to introduce amendments to the 1985 Insolvency Bill which would have provided for an Insolvency Court to be established (see H.C. Standing Committee E, June 18, 1985, cols. 418–423). This is one of the most prominent examples of the non-adoption of one of the principal recommendations of the *Cork Report.*

This section corresponds to s.201 of the 1985 Act.

Insolvency districts

374.—(1) The Lord Chancellor may by order designate the areas which are for the time being to be comprised, for the purposes of the Parts in this Group, in the London insolvency district and the insolvency district of each county court; and an order under this section may—

(*a*) exclude any county court from having jurisdiction for the purposes of those Parts, or

(*b*) confer jurisdiction for those purposes on any county court which has not previously had that jurisdiction.

(2) An order under this section may contain such incidental, supplemental and transitional provisions as may appear to the Lord Chancellor necessary or expedient.

(3) An order under this section shall be made by statutory instrument and, after being made, shall be laid before each House of Parliament.

(4) Subject to any order under this section—

(*a*) the district which, immediately before the appointed day, is the London bankruptcy district becomes, on that day, the London insolvency district;

(*b*) any district which immediately before that day is the bankruptcy district of a county court becomes, on that day, the insolvency district of that court, and

(*c*) any county court which immediately before that day is excluded from having jurisdiction in bankruptcy is excluded, on and after that day, from having jurisdiction for the purposes of the Parts in this Group.

Definitions

"court": ss.373, 385(1).

"insolvency district of a county court": subs. (4)(*b*).

"London insolvency district": subs. (4)(*a*).

General Note

This section provides for the Lord Chancellor to designate by order the areas that are to be comprised within the London bankruptcy district and within the insolvency district of each county court having individual insolvency jurisdiction. The Lord Chancellor is also empowered to exclude any county court from having jurisdiction under this Part, and to make alterations in the jurisdictional allocations from time to time. Such arrangements, and changes, may be effected by statutory instrument subject only to the "notice" requirement in relation to Parliament.

This section corresponds to s.202 of the 1985 Act.

Subs. (4)

The London bankruptcy district

The district comprising the London bankruptcy district immediately prior to the coming into force of this Act, and which thereby becomes the London insolvency district, is the district defined in s.99 of the Bankruptcy Act 1914 together with Sched. 3 thereto, as amended subsequently by statutory instrument. See Sched. 3 to the Civil Courts Order 1983, S.I. 1983 No. 713, amended by S.I. 1984 No. 1075; S.I. 1984 No. 297; S.I. 1985 No. 511. The list of metropolitan county courts whose county court districts together comprised the London bankruptcy district was latterly as follows: Barnet; Bloomsbury; Bow; Brentford; Brompton (now known as the West London County Court); Clerkenwell; Edmonton; Ilford; Lambeth; Marylebone; Shoreditch (amalgamated with the Whitechapel County Court); Southwark; Wandsworth; Westminster; Willesden; and the Mayor's and City of London Court.

Subs. (4)(b)

District which . . . is the bankruptcy district of a county court

Prior to the enactment of this Act the arrangements for allocation of bankruptcy jurisdiction to county courts were contained in Sched. 3 to the Civil Courts Order 1983, S.I. 1983 No. 713, amended by the subsequently made statutory instruments which are listed above.

Appeals etc. from courts exercising insolvency jurisdiction

375.—(1) Every court having jurisdiction for the purposes of the Parts in this Group may review, rescind or vary any order made by it in the exercise of that jurisdiction.

(2) An appeal from a decision made in the exercise of jurisdiction for the purposes of those Parts by a county court or by a registrar in bankruptcy of the High Court lies to a single judge of the High Court; and an appeal from a decision of that judge on such an appeal lies, with the leave of the judge or of the Court of Appeal, to the Court of Appeal.

(3) A county court is not, in the exercise of its jurisdiction for the purposes of those Parts, to be subject to be restrained by the order of any other court, and no appeal lies from its decision in the exercise of that jurisdiction except as provided by this section.

Definition

"court": ss.373, 385(1).

General Note

This section provides for courts exercising individual insolvency jurisdiction to have powers to review, rescind or vary orders made by them, and further provides for the manner in which appeals are to be made. While the provisions of subs. (1) restate those formerly embodied in s.108(1) of the Bankruptcy Act 1914 (repealed), the provisions in subs. (2) effect a considerable alteration to the arrangement for repeals in bankruptcy matters. All appeals from a first instance decision, whether made by a county court or by a Registrar of the High Court, now lie to a single judge of the High Court and any appeal from the decision of that judge lies with leave in the final instance to the Court of Appeal. There is no longer any provision for a final appeal, subject to the granting of leave, to be made to the House of Lords as was formerly possible under s.108(2)(*b*) of the Bankruptcy Act 1914 (repealed) in cases where proceedings originated in the High Court.

This section corresponds to s.203 of the 1985 Act.

Time-limits

376. Where by any provision in this Group of Parts or by the rules the time for doing anything is limited, the court may extend the time, either before or after it has expired, on such terms, if any, as it thinks fit.

Definitions

"the court": ss.373, 385(1).

"the rules": ss.384, 412.

GENERAL NOTE

This confers upon courts which exercise jurisdiction under this Group of Parts of the Act a discretionary power to extend time limits in insolvency proceedings, either prospectively or retrospectively, in particular cases.

This section corresponds to s.204 of the 1985 Act.

Formal defects

377. The acts of a person as the trustee of a bankrupt's estate or as a special manager, and the acts of the creditors' committee established for any bankruptcy, are valid notwithstanding any defect in the appointment, election or qualifications of the trustee or manager or, as the case may be, of any member of the committee.

DEFINITIONS

"creditors' committee": s.301(1).
"estate": ss.283, 385(1).
"special manager": s.198.
"trustee": s.385(1).

GENERAL NOTE

This section validates the acts of persons who have been purportedly appointed to any of the positions mentioned, despite the fact that their appointment, election or qualifications may be defective. There appears to be a *casus omissus* within the section with respect to persons who have been appointed to the position of supervisor of a voluntary arrangement under Part VIII, and whose appointments are defective. The provisions of this section as enacted make no reference to the validation of the acts of such persons, the defective nature of whose appointments may not come to light until some time has elapsed. The present section differs considerably from the former s.147 of the Bankruptcy Act 1914 (repealed), under which the validity of any act done by a person whose appointment was defective or irregular was made dependent upon whether that person had done the act in good faith.

This section corresponds to s.205 of the 1985 Act.

Exemption from stamp duty

378. Stamp duty shall not be charged on—

(*a*) any document, being a deed, conveyance, assignment, surrender, admission or other assurance relating solely to property which is comprised in a bankrupt's estate and which, after the execution of that document, is or remains at law or in equity the property of the bankrupt or of the trustee of that estate,

(*b*) any writ, order, certificate or other instrument relating solely to the property of a bankrupt or to any bankruptcy proceedings.

DEFINITIONS

"bankrupt": s.381(1).
"estate": ss.283, 385(1).
"property": s.436.

GENERAL NOTE

This provides for exemption from stamp duty for certain documents involved in bankruptcy proceedings. The section restates the former provisions of s.148 of the Bankruptcy Act 1914 (repealed).

This section corresponds to s.206 of the 1985 Act.

Annual report

379. As soon as practicable after the end of 1986 and each subsequent calendar year, the Secretary of State shall prepare and lay before each House of Parliament a report about the operation during that year of so much of this Act as is comprised in this Group of Parts, and about proceedings in the course of that year under the Deeds of Arrangement Act 1914.

General Note

This section, which corresponds to s.210 of the 1985 Act, requires the Secretary of State for Trade to lay an annual report before Parliament on individual insolvency and about proceedings under the Deeds of Arrangement Act 1914.

Part XI

Interpretation for Second Group of Parts

Introductory

380. The next five sections have effect for the interpretation of the provisions of this Act which are comprised in this Group of Parts; and where a definition is provided for a particular expression, it applies except so far as the context otherwise requires.

General Note

This section, which has no counterpart in the 1985 Act, has the function of introducing the group of five sections, namely ss.381–385, which supply the definitions of various terms used within Parts VIII–XI of the Act. Although these definitions are to apply wherever the expression to which they relate is used within the second Group of Parts, this is subject to the proviso that an expression may have a divergent meaning where this is required by the particular context in which the expression is used. See also Part XVIII, which supplies the interpretation of expressions used in a particular sense throughout the Act as a whole.

"Bankrupt" and associated terminology

381.—(1) "Bankrupt" means an individual who has been adjudged bankrupt and, in relation to a bankruptcy order, it means the individual adjudged bankrupt by that order.

(2) "Bankruptcy order" means an order adjudging an individual bankrupt.

(3) "Bankruptcy petition" means a petition to the court for a bankruptcy order.

Definitions

"bankrupt": subs. (1).
"bankruptcy order": subs. (2).
"bankruptcy petition": subs. (3).
"the court": ss.373, 385(1).

General Note

This definition section supplies the meaning of the expressions "bankrupt", "bankruptcy order" and "bankruptcy petition" for the purposes of Parts VIII–XI.

"Bankruptcy debt", etc.

382.—(1) "Bankruptcy debt", in relation to a bankrupt, means (subject to the next subsection) any of the following—

(*a*) any debt or liability to which he is subject at the commencement of the bankruptcy,

(*b*) any debt or liability to which he may become subject after the commencement of the bankruptcy (including after his discharge from bankruptcy) by reason of any obligation incurred before the commencement of the bankruptcy,

(*c*) any amount specified in pursuance of section 39(3)(*c*) of the Powers of Criminal Courts Act 1973 in any criminal bankruptcy order made against him before the commencement of the bankruptcy, and

(*d*) any interest provable as mentioned in section 322(2) in Chapter IV of Part IX.

(2) In determining for the purposes of any provision in this Group of Parts whether any liability in tort is a bankruptcy debt, the bankrupt is deemed to become subject to that liability by reason of an obligation incurred at the time when the cause of action accrued.

(3) For the purposes of references in this Group of Parts to a debt or liability, it is immaterial whether the debt or liability is present or future, whether it is certain or contingent or whether its amount is fixed or liquidated, or is capable of being ascertained by fixed rules or as a matter of opinion; and references in this Group of Parts to owing a debt are to be read accordingly.

(4) In this Group of Parts, except in so far as the context otherwise requires, "liability" means (subject to subsection (3) above) a liability to pay money or money's worth, including any liability under an enactment, any liability for breach of trust, any liability in contract, tort or bailment and any liability arising out of an obligation to make restitution.

DEFINITIONS

"bankrupt": s.381(1).
"bankruptcy debt": subs. (1).
"commencement of the bankruptcy": s.278(*a*).
"criminal bankruptcy order": s.385(1); Powers of Criminal Courts Act 1973, s.39(1).
"debt": subs. (3), s.385(1).
"discharge": s.281.
"liability": subs. (4).

GENERAL NOTE

This section supplies the meaning of the expression "bankruptcy debt," and of the related expressions "debt" and "liability" for the purposes of Parts VIII–XI. This section corresponds to subss. (1) (part), (2) and (3) of s.211 of the 1985 Act.

"Creditor", "security", etc.

383.—(1) "Creditor"—

(*a*) in relation to a bankrupt, means a person to whom any of the bankruptcy debts is owed (being, in the case of an amount falling within paragraph (*c*) of the definition in section 382(1) of "bankruptcy debt", the person in respect of whom that amount is specified in the criminal bankruptcy order in question), and

(*b*) in relation to an individual to whom a bankruptcy petition relates, means a person who would be a creditor in the bankruptcy if a bankruptcy order were made on that petition.

(2) Subject to the next two subsections and any provision of the rules requiring a creditor to give up his security for the purposes of proving a debt, a debt is secured for the purposes of this Group of Parts to the extent that the person to whom the debt is owed holds any security for the debt (whether a mortgage, charge, lien or other security) over any property of the person by whom the debt is owed.

(3) Where a statement such as is mentioned in section 269(1)(*a*) in Chapter I of Part IX has been made by a secured creditor for the purposes of any bankruptcy petition and a bankruptcy order is subsequently made on that petition, the creditor is deemed for the purposes of the Parts in this Group to have given up the security specified in the statement.

(4) In subsection (2) the reference to a security does not include a lien on books, papers or other records, except to the extent that they consist of documents which give a title to property and are held as such.

Definitions

"bankrupt": s.381(1).
"bankruptcy debt": s.382.
"bankruptcy order": s.381(2).
"bankruptcy petition": s.381(3).
"creditor": subs. (1).
"criminal bankruptcy order": s.385(1); Powers of Criminal Courts Act 1973, s.39(1).
"property": s.436.
"records": s.436.
"security": subss. (2), (3), (4).

General Note

This section supplies the meaning of the expressions "creditor" and "security," and hence of related expressions such as "secured" and "secured creditor." This section corresponds to subss. (1) (part), and (5)–(7) of s.211 of the 1985 Act.

"Prescribed" and "the rules"

384.—(1) Subject to the next subsection, "prescribed" means prescribed by the rules; and "the rules" means rules made under section 412 in Part XV.

(2) References in this Group of Parts to the amount prescribed for the purposes of any of the following provisions—

section 273;
section 346(3);
section 354(1) and (2);
section 358;
section 360(1);
section 361(2); and
section 364(2)(*d*),

and references in those provisions to the prescribed amount are to be read in accordance with section 418 in Part XV and orders made under that section.

General Note

This section supplies the meaning of the expressions "prescribed" and "the rules" where used throughout Parts VIII–XI. This section corresponds to parts of ss.209(1) and 211(1) of the 1985 Act.

Miscellaneous definitions

385.—(1) The following definitions have effect—

"the court", in relation to any matter, means the court to which, in accordance with section 373 in Part X and the rules, proceedings with respect to that matter are allocated or transferred;

"creditor's petition" means a bankruptcy petition under section 264(1)(*a*);

"criminal bankruptcy order" means an order under section 39(1) of the Powers of Criminal Courts Act 1973;

"debt" is to be construed in accordance with section 382(3);

"the debtor"—

(*a*) in relation to a proposal for the purposes of Part VIII, means the individual making or intending to make that proposal, and
(*b*) in relation to a bankruptcy petition, means the individual to whom the petition relates;

"debtor's petition" means a bankruptcy petition presented by the debtor himself under section 264(1)(*b*);

"dwelling house" includes any building or part of a building which is occupied as a dwelling and any yard, garden, garage or outhouse belonging to the dwelling house and occupied with it;

"estate", in relation to a bankrupt is to be construed in accordance with section 283 in Chapter II of Part IX;
"family", in relation to a bankrupt, means the persons (if any) who are living with him and are dependent on him;
"secured" and related expressions are to be construed in accordance with section 383; and
"the trustee", in relation to a bankruptcy and the bankrupt, means the trustee of the bankrupt's estate.

(2) References in this Group of Parts to a person's affairs include his business, if any.

GENERAL NOTE

This is the miscellaneous definition section covering a variety of expressions which are used in a particular sense throughout Parts VIII–XI. The section corresponds to subss. (1) (part) and (4) of s.211 of the 1985 Act.

THE THIRD GROUP OF PARTS

MISCELLANEOUS MATTERS BEARING ON BOTH COMPANY AND INDIVIDUAL INSOLVENCY; GENERAL INTERPRETATION; FINAL PROVISIONS

PART XII

PREFERENTIAL DEBTS IN COMPANY AND INDIVIDUAL INSOLVENCY

Categories of preferential debts

386.—(1) A reference in this Act to the preferential debts of a company or an individual is to the debts listed in Schedule 6 to this Act (money owed to the Inland Revenue for income tax deducted at source; VAT, car tax, betting and gaming duties; social security and pension scheme contributions; remuneration etc. of employees); and references to preferential creditors are to be read accordingly.

(2) In that Schedule "the debtor" means the company or the individual concerned.

(3) Schedule 6 is to be read with Schedule 3 to the Social Security Pensions Act 1975 (occupational pension scheme contributions).

DEFINITIONS

"preferential creditors": subs. (1); Sched. 6.
"preferential debts": subs. (1); Sched. 6.
"the debtor": subs. (2); Sched. 6.

GENERAL NOTE

This section completes the process of establishing a single set of provisions regarding the categories of preferential debts applicable to both company and individual insolvency. This process was begun in the 1985 Act, Sched. 4 to which furnished a common set of provisions regarding preferential debts applicable to the two types of insolvency by virtue of the provisions of ss.89 and 166 of that Act. The present section is a single provision whose own terms cause it to be applicable to both types of insolvency, and provide a common point of reference—namely to the provisions of Sched. 6—for all occasions when the expressions "preferential debts" or "preferential creditors" are used anywhere in the Act. Consequently, subs. (2) provides for the expression "the debtor" to bear a flexible meaning where it appears in Sched. 6, so that it can denote a company or an individual, according to the context of any particular case to which the provisions fall to be applied.

"The relevant date"

387.—(1) This section explains references in Schedule 6 to the relevant date (being the date which determines the existence and amount of a preferential debt).

(2) For the purposes of section 4 in Part I (meetings to consider company voluntary arrangement), the relevant date in relation to a company which is not being wound up is—

(*a*) where an administration order is in force in relation to the company, the date of the making of that order, and

(*b*) where no such order has been made, the date of the approval of the voluntary arrangement.

(3) In relation to a company which is being wound up, the following applies—

(*a*) if the winding up is by the court, and the winding-up order was made immediately upon the discharge of an administration order, the relevant date is the date of the making of the administration order;

(*b*) if the case does not fall within paragraph (*a*) and the company—

(i) is being wound up by the court, and

(ii) had not commenced to be wound up voluntarily before the date of the making of the winding-up order,

the relevant date is the date of the appointment (or first appointment) of a provisional liquidator or, if no such appointment has been made, the date of the winding-up order;

(*c*) if the case does not fall within either paragraph (*a*) or (*b*), the relevant date is the date of the passing of the resolution for the winding up of the company.

(4) In relation to a company in receivership (where section 40 or, as the case may be, section 59 applies), the relevant date is—

(*a*) in England and Wales, the date of the appointment of the receiver by debenture-holders, and

(*b*) in Scotland, the date of the appointment of the receiver under section 53(6) or (as the case may be) 54(5).

(5) For the purposes of section 258 in Part VIII (individual voluntary arrangements), the relevant date is, in relation to a debtor who is not an undischarged bankrupt, the date of the interim order made under section 252 with respect to his proposal.

(6) In relation to a bankrupt, the following applies—

(*a*) where at the time the bankruptcy order was made there was an interim receiver appointed under section 286, the relevant date is the date on which the interim receiver was first appointed after the presentation of the bankruptcy petition;

(*b*) otherwise, the relevant date is the date of the making of the bankruptcy order.

DEFINITIONS

"administration order": s.8(2).
"bankrupt": s.281(1).
"bankruptcy order": s.281(2).
"bankruptcy petition": s.281(3).
"commencement of winding up by the court": s.129.
"company voluntary arrangement": s.1(1).
"date of appointment of receiver": s.33 (England and Wales); ss.53(6), 54(5) (Scotland).
"date of approval of voluntary arrangement": s.5(2)(*a*).
"discharged"; "undischarged": ss.278(*b*), 279–281.
"individual voluntary arrangement": s.253(1).
"interim order": s.252(2).
"interim receiver": s.286.
"preferential debt": s.386(1); Sched. 6.

"proposal": s.253(1), (2).
"the relevant date": subs. (1) and remainder of this section.

General Note

The purpose of this section is to make comprehensive provision with regard to the meaning to be ascribed to the expression "the relevant date" in the various contexts in which it is used throughout Sched. 6 and in different sections within the main body of the Act. The provisions collected within this section originate from ss.196(2)–(4) and 475(3), (4) of the Companies Act, and from ss.23(8), 115(10), Sched. 4, Pt. II para. 1(2), (3) and Sched. 6 paras. 15(4) and 20(3) of the 1985 Act.

Part XIII

Insolvency Practitioners and their Qualification

Restrictions on unqualified persons acting as liquidator, trustee in bankruptcy, etc.

Meaning of "act as insolvency practitioner"

388.—(1) A person acts as an insolvency practitioner in relation to a company by acting—

(*a*) as its liquidator, provisional liquidator, administrator or administrative receiver, or

(*b*) as supervisor of a voluntary arrangement approved by it under Part I.

(2) A person acts as an insolvency practitioner in relation to an individual by acting—

(*a*) as his trustee in bankruptcy or interim receiver of his property or as permanent or interim trustee in the sequestration of his estate; or

(*b*) as trustee under a deed which is a deed of arrangement made for the benefit of his creditors or, in Scotland, a trust deed for his creditors; or

(*c*) as supervisor of a voluntary arrangement proposed by him and approved under Part VIII; or

(*d*) in the case of a deceased individual to the administration of whose estate this section applies by virtue of an order under section 421 (application of provisions of this Act to insolvent estates of deceased persons), as administrator of that estate.

(3) References in this section to an individual include, except in so far as the context otherwise requires, references to a partnership and to any debtor within the meaning of the Bankruptcy (Scotland) Act 1985.

(4) In this section—

"administrative receiver" has the meaning given by section 251 in Part VII;

"company" means a company within the meaning given by section 735(1) of the Companies Act or a company which may be wound up under Part V of this Act (unregistered companies); and

"interim trustee" and "permanent trustee" mean the same as in the Bankruptcy (Scotland) Act 1985.

(5) Nothing in this section applies to anything done by the official receiver.

Definitions

"acts as an insolvency practitioner": subss. (1), (2), (3).
"administrative receiver": subs. (4); s.251.

"administrator": s.8(2).
"company": subs. (4), ss.220, 221; Companies Act 1985, s.735(1).
"individual": subs. (3).
"interim receiver": s.286.
"interim trustee": subs. (4); Bankruptcy (Scotland) Act 1985, s.2.
"partnership": subs. (3).
"permanent trustee": subs. (4); Bankruptcy (Scotland) Act 1985, s.3.
"property": s.436.
"provisional liquidator": s.135.
"supervisor of a voluntary arrangement": ss.7(2) (companies), 263(2) (individuals).
"the official receiver": s.399(1).
"voluntary arrangement": ss.1(1) (companies), 253(1) (individuals).

Transitional Provision

Sched. 11, para. 21.

General Note

This section defines the various ways in which a person may act as an insolvency practitioner for the purposes of Part XIII. The *Cork Report* made cogent recommendations for the introduction of legal regulations applicable to insolvency practitioners (see Chaps. 15, 16 and 17), partly aimed at ensuring a generally high level of competence and skill on the part of those so acting, but partly also to combat certain abusive practices, particularly in relation to voluntary liquidations, by ensuring that all those who serve in any capacity such as liquidator, trustee in bankruptcy, administrator, or administrative receiver are personally subject to the disciplinary control of a recognised professional organisation. The *White Paper* (Chapter 1) duly endorsed the proposal that exacting professional standards should be made applicable to insolvency practitioners, and the provisions of Pt. XIII, together with Sched. 7 and further rules and regulations to be made pursuant to the powers conferred by s.419, are designed to bring this about.

This section corresponds to subss. (2)–(6) of s.1 of the 1985 Act.

Subs. (1)

This subsection defines the concept of acting as an insolvency practitioner in relation to a company. The four ways in which a person may so act in relation to a company are by acting as its liquidator, administrator, or administrative receiver, or as the supervisor of a voluntary arrangement concluded under Part I.

Para. (a)

Liquidator: under Part IV of the Act, a person other than the official receiver may be appointed as liquidator of a company in the course of a compulsory winding up, while in the case of either of the forms of voluntary winding up (members' or creditors' voluntary winding up) a private liquidator is always appointed. The respective modes of appointment of a private liquidator in the three different types of winding up are specified in ss.135–140, 91–92 and 100 of the Act. The powers, duties and responsibilities of a liquidator are defined in ss.165–170 of the Act. The extensiveness and complexity of the liquidator's powers in themselves make it desirable that the person undertaking to serve in this capacity possesses a degree of professional competence and experience as well as being of unquestioned integrity. In recent years it had become a matter of considerable notoriety that, while the majority of those accustomed to function as liquidators of companies undoubtedly satisfied all three of the foregoing criteria, there were others who did not. Greatest concern centred around those instances where the initiative in nominating and appointing the liquidator rests with members of the company themselves, particularly where these are virtually synonymous with the active members of the board of directors (see *Cork Report,* paras. 772–774). The wording of subs. (1) ensures that in every type of winding up the only person lawfully eligible to serve as liquidator (apart from the Official Receiver himself where this is possible) is one who at the time of acting possesses the requisite qualification, according to s.390, authorising him so to act. An amendment to the Insolvency Bill 1985, tabled before the House of Lords in Committee, which was designed to limit the application of what is now subs. (1) to those cases where the company is insolvent, was withdrawn (*Hansard* H.L. Vol. 459, cols. 565–568). The provision therefore applies to every type of winding up in which a liquidator is appointed, and regardless of whether the company is actually insolvent at the time. The deletion from the terms of the 1985 Bill as originally published of any additional ground of disqualification based upon any personal association between an insolvency practitioner and the company in relation to which he acts means that the delicate and complicated matter of potential conflict of interest or want of impartiality on the part of the liquidator will be regulated by the ethical code and practical guidelines subscribed to by the professional body to which the liquidator will in most instances belong. For the purposes of criminal liability under s.389, only the grounds of non-qualification specified in s.390 are relevant.

Administrator: The new procedure for making an administration order in respect of a company which is actually or nearly insolvent is created by Part II of the Act (ss.8–27 inclusive). The term "administrator" is defined in s.8(2), which makes it apparent that the administrator is a person appointed under the terms of an administration order made by the court, whereby for the duration of the period for which the order is in force the affairs, business and property of the company are to be managed by the person appointed. Further provisions concerning the powers and duties of an administrator, and the mode of his appointment to and vacation of office, are contained in ss.13–25 inclusive. As envisaged in Chap. 9 of the *Cork Report,* and subsequently affirmed by Chap. 14 of the *White Paper,* the administrator will need to possess special skills and aptitudes in order to be capable of fulfilling his responsibilities, and this office is accordingly included among the list of those which can only be undertaken by a person who is duly qualified to act as an insolvency practitioner in accordance with the provisions of s.390.

Administrative receiver: This new term is given statutory meaning by s.251 and means, in relation to a company registered in England and Wales, either (i) a receiver or manager of the whole (or substantially the whole) of the company's property appointed by or on behalf of the holders of any debentures of the company secured by a charge which, as created, was a floating charge, or by a floating charge and one or more fixed charges; or (ii) a person who would be such a receiver or manager but for the appointment of some other person as a receiver of part of the company's property. In relation to a company registered in Scotland, the use of the established term "receiver" has been retained. However, by virtue of s.251 the expression "administrative receiver," whenever it is used in the Second Group Parts, includes a receiver appointed under s.51 of the Act. Moreover, subs. (4), below, confers upon the expression "administrative receiver" the same meaning as it bears in Part II of the Act, and hence the provisions of Part XIII are equally applicable to a person appointed as a receiver of a company in Scotland as they are to a person appointed as administrative receiver of a company in England and Wales.

It is a part of the policy of the Act to place the law of receivers and managers of companies upon a clear, statutory basis and thereby to define their powers and duties, and to impose an appropriate degree of control and accountability which has hitherto been wanting under the law of England and Wales at least. Clear and comprehensive recommendations to this effect were contained in Chap. 8 of the *Cork Report,* and accepted (with certain reservations) in Chap. 5 of the *White Paper.* The provisions which accomplished this purpose are contained in Chapter I of Part III (ss.28–49) in relation to England and Wales, and by Chapter II of Part III (ss.50–71) in relation to Scotland. All the arguments concerning the attributes of skill, experience and integrity which have been deployed with regard to liquidators and administrators of companies are equally applicable in the case of administrative receivers, and hence all persons acting in this latter capacity henceforth will be required to be qualified insolvency practitioners within the meaning of this Part of the Act.

Para. (b)

Supervisor of a voluntary arrangement: Pt. I of the Act (ss.1–7) contains provisions regulating voluntary arrangements between a company and its creditors. Such arrangements, which may take the form of either a composition or a scheme of arrangement, must be administered by a person who is qualified to act as an insolvency practitioner in relation to the company. The person nominated for the purpose, who may be the liquidator or administrator of the company or some other person, will in due course become the supervisor of the composition or scheme if it is duly approved in accordance with the relevant provisions of that Part of the Act. In accordance with the overall policy of the Act, a person occupying the position of supervisor must be a qualified insolvency practitioner, and hence it is made a criminal offence for an unqualified person to serve in this capacity in relation to a company.

Subs. (2)

This subsection defines the concept of acting as an insolvency practitioner in relation to an individual. In England and Wales a person can so act in any of the following five ways, namely by acting as the individual's trustee in bankruptcy; as interim receiver of his property; as administrator of his estate; as trustee under a deed of arrangement made for the benefit of his creditors; or as supervisor of a voluntary arrangement proposed by the individual and approved under Pt. VIII of the Act. In Scotland, a person can act as an insolvency practitioner in relation to an individual in any of the following three ways, namely by acting as permanent or interim trustee in the sequestration of his estate, or as trustee under a trust deed for his creditors.

Para. (a)

Trustee in bankruptcy: This is the title conferred upon the person in whom, by virtue of s.306, the bankrupt's estate vests and by whom the property thus made available is administered and distributed among the creditors in accordance with the provisions of Chapter IV of Part IX of the Act (ss.305–335). Depending upon the circumstances the power to appoint a person as trustee of a bankrupt's estate is exercisable by a general meeting of the bankrupt's creditors, by the Secretary of State, or by the court: s.292.

Interim receiver: In certain cases, following the presentation of a bankruptcy petition but before the making of any bankruptcy order it may be necessary for the protection of the debtor's property that it be placed in the hands of a person clothed with the powers of a receiver and manager. S.286 duly empowers the court to make the necessary appointment upon cause shown, and to appoint either the official receiver or some other person to be interim receiver. A particularly apt occasion for the appointment of some person other than the Official Receiver to serve in this capacity will arise when, pursuant to s.273(2), the court has had occasion on the hearing of a debtor's petition to appoint a qualified insolvency practitioner to prepare a report based upon an enquiry into the debtor's affairs and to investigate whether the debtor is able and willing to make a proposal for a composition or scheme of arrangement. S.286(2) specifically contemplates the possibility that the person so appointed may at the court's discretion be subsequently appointed to be interim receiver of the debtor's property where the need for such an appointment is established.

Permanent trustee: In Scots law, the sequestration of the estate of a living or deceased debtor is conducted, as required by the Bankruptcy (Scotland) Act 1985, by a permanent trustee elected in accordance with s.24 of that Act. Since there is no office in Scotland equivalent to that of official receiver under the law of England and Wales, the permanent trustee in a Scottish sequestration will inevitably be a private individual. In view of this, Scottish law has traditionally taken care to specify those categories of person who are ineligible for election as permanent trustee, either on general grounds or on grounds referable to the circumstances of the instant case. S.24(2) of the Bankruptcy (Scotland) Act 1985 is the current enactment embodying the grounds of ineligibility, and it is noteworthy that para. (*b*) of that subs. refers to "a person who is not qualified to act as an insolvency practitioner or who, though qualified to act as an insolvency practitioner, is not qualified to act as such in relation to the debtor." The provisions of ss.388(2)(*a*) and 389 of the Insolvency Act therefore complement those of the Scottish legislation by rendering it a criminal offence for a person who is unqualified in the meaning of Part XIII of the Insolvency Act to act as a permanent trustee in a Scottish sequestration.

Interim trustee: S.2 of the Bankruptcy (Scotland) Act 1985 requires that in every sequestration there is to be appointed an interim trustee whose functions, as prescribed in that section, are to safeguard the debtor's estate pending the appointment of a permanent trustee, and to conduct the preliminary stages of the sequestration prior to, and indeed preparatory to, the election of a permanent trustee. The provisions of s.1(1)(*b*) of the same Act require the Accountant of Court (to be known for this purpose as "the Accountant in Bankruptcy") to maintain a list of persons from which interim trustees are to be appointed, and it will become part of the responsibilities of the Accountant in Bankruptcy to ensure that all persons whose names appear on his list are properly qualified in terms of Part XIII of the Insolvency Act 1986, with particular reference to the provisions of s.390 thereof. Nevertheless, the offence of acting as an insolvency practitioner when unqualified to do so is so formulated as to make it evident that a person may commit the offence, under certain circumstances, despite the fact that his name may for the time being be included upon the list maintained by the Accountant in Bankruptcy. If the person in question is in reality unqualified to act as an insolvency practitioner an offence will be committed by virtue of his commencing to act pursuant to his appointment as interim trustee. It is to be noted that s.2(3)(*a*) of the Bankruptcy (Scotland) Act makes provision for a person's name to be removed from the list of potential interim trustees at his own request, and it is thus incumbent upon a person who lacks, or who loses, the requisite qualification to take the necessary steps to procure the removal of his name from the list, or at the very least to decline to accept or to act upon any appointment resulting from the fact that his name still appears on the list.

Para. (b)

Trustee under a deed of arrangment: Contrary to the recommendation contained in Chap. 7 of the *Cork Report* whereby its repeal and replacement were advocated, the majority of the provisions of the Deeds of Arrangement Act 1914 remain in force (see *White Paper,* paras. 22–23). Pt. III of Sched. 10 to the Insolvency Act 1985 effects the repeal only of ss.19(2) and 27, together with parts of s.24 of the Act of 1914. It will therefore continue to be possible for a debtor to utilise the procedure established by the Deeds of Arrangement Act although in practice it is unlikely that many will choose to do so. In such cases, however, it will be necessary for a person to serve as trustee of the Deed of Arrangement in accordance with the requirements of the extant provisions of the Act of 1914. Henceforth it will be incumbent upon any person who is invited to serve as trustee of a Deed of Arrangement to ensure that he fulfils the requirements for being a qualified insolvency practitioner for the purpose in contemplation.

Trustee under a trust deed for creditors: In Scotland the statutory provisions governing voluntary trust deeds for creditors are, by virtue of s.59 of the Bankruptcy (Scotland) Act 1985, contained in Sched. 5 to that Act. The voluntary trust deed for creditors constitutes an alternative to sequestration, and is allowed to operate with minimal formal regulation (see Scottish Law Commission Report on Bankruptcy, Chap. 24). As in the case of deeds of arrangement under the law of England and Wales, the making of a voluntary trust deed usually takes the form of a conveyance by the debtor of his whole property to a trustee for the benefit of the debtor's creditors generally. The same considerations as are stated above in relation to prospective trustees under a deed of arrangement will henceforth attach also to any person who is invited to serve as trustee under a voluntary trust deed, and it will thus be incumbent upon that person to consider whether he fulfils the requirements for being a qualified insolvency practitioner for this purpose.

Para. (c)

Supervisor of a voluntary arrangement: The provisions of Pt. VIII of the Act (ss.252–263) introduce a new procedure for the conclusion of voluntary arrangements between a debtor and his creditors within the overall framework of the Insolvency Act itself. This procedure, which may be utilised either before or after the making of a bankruptcy order against the debtor, is devised in accordance with the strategy disclosed in the *White Paper* (paras. 21–23, 135–139) whereby the increased use of voluntary procedures is to be encouraged. The procedure involves the making of an application to the court for an interim order whose effect is to suspend all other proceedings against the debtor or his property. This moratorium will normally operate for a period of fourteen days, during which time the feasibility of the making of a voluntary arrangement is to be explored and reported upon by a person named in the application (and hence known as "the nominee") who is for the time being qualified to act as an insolvency practitioner in relation to the debtor (ss.253–256). If the nominee's report indicates that further progress is practicable and worthwhile, the proposal may subsequently be submitted to a creditor's meeting summoned for this purpose, and if there approved, the arrangement becomes effective and binding upon all creditors to whom notice of the meeting had been given (ss.257–261). In that event the implementation and supervision of the arrangement are functions which are automatically conferred upon the person who is known as "the supervisor of the voluntary arrangement" (s.263(2)). The supervisor will either be the person originally identified as the nominee in the initial application to the court, or some other person qualified to act as an insolvency practitioner in relation to the debtor, who has been substituted for the nominee in accordance with the provisions of s.256(3) or s.258(3). In every instance therefore the supervisor of a composition or scheme governed by the provisions of Pt. VIII must fulfil the requirements for qualification described in Pt. XIII of the Act, and any person who acts as supervisor of an arrangement when he is unqualified to do so will thereby commit a criminal offence under s.390.

Para. (d)

Administrator of that estate: Where a deceased individual's estate is insolvent, the estate may be administered under the law of bankruptcy in a specially modified form. The modifications in question will be specified in an Order made pursuant to s.421. The term "administrator" means in this context the person by whom that estate is administered in accordance with the modified procedure. The person appointed to be administrator of such an estate therefore assumes the equivalent functions, powers and duties in relation to the estate of the deceased insolvent as are assumed by the trustee in bankruptcy in normal cases where the bankrupt is alive.

Subs. (3)

This subsection extends the application of the provisions of subs. (2) in two ways, first by specifying that any reference to an individual in the earlier subs. shall include a reference to a partnership, and secondly by providing that in Scotland the reference to an individual shall include a reference to any debtor within the meaning of the Bankruptcy (Scotland) Act 1985. S.420 of the Act empowers the Lord Chancellor to make an order specially modifying the statutory regime to be applicable in relation to insolvent partnerships. Since a partnership in England and Wales is an unincorporated association with no separate legal personality of its own, proceedings resulting from insolvency of a partnership necessarily involve all those persons who are partners in the firm. The established approach is that while bankruptcy proceedings may commence and take place in the name of the firm, the making of a bankruptcy order against the firm takes effect in law as an order made against each person who is a partner of the firm at the date of the order (see the former provisions of the Bankruptcy Act 1914, s.119, Bankruptcy Rules 1952, S.I. 1952, No. 2113 (L.14), r.285), so that each partner becomes individually bankrupt. At the point of adjudication therefore the apparent entity of the firm effectively disappears, although special rules must be applied in the administration of the bankruptcy of each partner so as to distinguish between his separate affairs and his partnership affairs. Accordingly, in various situations the firm or partnership may constitute the entity in relation to which insolvency procedures, or a certain stage of them, are taking place and it follows that a person may be called upon to act as an insolvency practitioner in relation to the partnership. By virtue of subs. (3) such a person will need to fulfil all the requirements of Pt. XIII with regard to qualification as an insolvency practitioner when acting in relation to a partnership, just as when acting in relation to any individual.

In relation to Scottish law, s.73(1) of the Bankruptcy (Scotland) Act 1985 indicates that the term "debtor" includes a deceased debtor or, as the context requires, an executor or person entitled to be appointed as executor. Moreover under Scots law the process of sequestration is applicable to a variety of other entities besides living and deceased individuals, since it may take place in relation to trust estates, partnerships, limited partnerships, un-incorporated bodies and bodies corporate other than those which, being incorporated under the Companies Act, are consequently required to be wound up under the provisions of this Act (see Bankruptcy (Scotland) Act 1985, s.6). The extension of meaning thus conferred by subs. (3) upon the word "debtor" as arising within the context of Scots law ensures that in any insolvency proceedings in Scotland relating to an entity for which sequestration is a competent proceeding, the requirements of Pt. XIII with regard to qualification to act as an insolvency practitioner must be fulfilled by any person who acts in any of the capacities referred to in subs. (2)

Subs. (4)

Administrative receiver: This term is discussed in the note to subs. (1) above.

Company: Section 735 of the Companies Act 1985 defines this term as meaning a company formed and registered under that Act, or an existing company, which is further defined as a company formed and registered under the former Companies Acts of 1856–1983 (with the exception of companies registered under former companies legislation in what was then Ireland prior to the creation of the Republic of Ireland).

Interim trustee; Permanent trustee: The meanings of these terms, as defined in the Bankruptcy (Scotland) Act 1985, are discussed in the note to subs. (2) above.

Subs. (5)

This subsection ensures that no action undertaken by the official receiver shall give rise to criminal liability on his part, even though it might transpire that for some reason he did not at the relevant time fulfil the requirements of being a "qualified person" within the meaning of Pt. XIII. Hence, whenever it occurs that the official receiver, in performance of the duties of his office and in particular of those which arise by virtue of the provisions of the Insolvency Act itself, acts as an insolvency practitioner in relation to either a company or an individual within the meaning of this section, he enjoys immunity from criminal liability which he might otherwise incur by virtue of this Part of the Act. In Chap. 7 of their *White Paper,* the Government effectively conceded the validity of the case made out in Chap. 14 of the *Cork Report* in favour of maintaining the active involvement of the Insolvency Service in all aspects of corporate and individual insolvency. The statutory provisions pertaining to the appointment, status and functions of official receivers are contained in ss.399–401, and will be further augmented by rules to be made subsequently in accordance with the provisions of ss.411, 412 and 413.

Acting without qualification an offence

389.—(1) A person who acts as an insolvency practitioner in relation to a company or an individual at a time when he is not qualified to do so is liable to imprisonment or a fine, or to both.

(2) This section does not apply to the official receiver.

DEFINITIONS

"acts as an insolvency practitioner": s.388.
"fine": s.430, Sched. 10.
"imprisonment": s.430, Sched. 10.
"qualified to act as an insolvency practitioner": s.390.
"the official receiver": s.399(1).

Transitional Provision

Sched. 11, para. 21.

GENERAL NOTE

This section introduces a new criminal offence into the law, whereby a person may be criminally liable if he acts as an insolvency practitioner when he is not qualified to do so. The offence is one of strict liability, and it will afford no defence to any person charged therewith that he either was without all knowledge of his lack of qualification, or reasonably believed himself to be qualified to act. The purpose underlying Pt. XIII of the Act (ss.388–397 inclusive) is to bring about the proper regulation of all those aspects of insolvency proceedings whose administration is capable of being conducted wholly or partly by someone other than the official receiver. The various capacities in which a person may act as an insolvency practitioner for the purposes of Pt. XIII of the Act are specified in subss. (1), (2) and (3) of s.388.

This section corresponds to s.1(1) of the 1985 Act.

Subs. (1)

Acts as an insolvency practitioner . . . when he is not qualified: The ingredients of this new criminal offence are indicated, and the possible penalties are prescribed. The offence is committed by any person who acts as an insolvency practitioner (as defined in subss. (1), (2) and (3) of s.388) at a time when he is not qualified to do so. The offence was converted into one of strict liability by means of a government amendment made in Committee of the House of Commons, which removed from the 1985 Insolvency Bill all reference to the state of knowledge of the accused person at the time of committing the offence. The requirements which are to be met in order for an individual to be qualified to act as an insolvency practitioner are laid down in s.390, and the procedure relating to the issue and revocation of certificates of authorisation is specified in and controlled by ss.391–398 inclusive.

Imprisonment or a fine: See s.430 and Sched. 10 with regard to the levels of punishment which may be imposed for offences committed under this section.

The requisite qualification, and the means of obtaining it

Persons not qualified to act as insolvency practitioners

390.—(1) A person who is not an individual is not qualified to act as an insolvency practitioner.

(2) A person is not qualified to act as an insolvency practitioner at any time unless at that time—

(*a*) he is authorised so to act by virtue of membership of a professional body recognised under section 391 below, being permitted so to act by or under the rules of that body, or

(*b*) he holds an authorisation granted by a competent authority under section 393.

(3) A person is not qualified to act as an insolvency practitioner in relation to another person at any time unless—

(*a*) there is in force at that time security or, in Scotland, caution for the proper performance of his functions, and (*b*) that security or caution meets the prescribed requirements with respect to his so acting in relation to that other person.

(4) A person is not qualified to act as an insolvency practitioner at any time if at that time—

(*a*) he has been adjudged bankrupt or sequestration of his estate has been awarded and (in either case) he has not been discharged,

(*b*) he is subject to a disqualification order made under the Company Directors Disqualification Act 1986, or

(*c*) he is a patient within the meaning of Part VII of the Mental Health Act 1983 or section 125(1) of the Mental Health (Scotland) Act 1984.

DEFINITIONS

"a competent authority": s.392(2).
"bankrupt": s.381(1).
"discharged": ss.279–281.
"patient": Mental Health Act 1983, ss.94, 112; Mental Health (Scotland) Act 1984, s.125(1).
"to act as an insolvency practitioner": s.388.

TRANSITIONAL PROVISION

Sched. 11, para. 21.

GENERAL NOTE

This section establishes the meaning of the expression "qualified insolvency practitioner" for the purposes of the Act. It does so by prescribing a series of requirements which must be met in relation to a person in order that he or she may lawfully act as an insolvency practitioner in relation to a company or an individual. The section is drafted in negative terms throughout; that is to say the various propositions of which it is composed are so formulated as to specify in what circumstances, or upon what ground, a person is *not* qualified to act as an insolvency practitioner. Converting these propositions into positive terms, it transpires that in order to be a qualified insolvency practitioner a person (i) must be an individual; (ii) must be currently authorised to act as an insolvency practitioner by virtue of the provisions of either para. (*a*) or (*b*) of subs. (2); and (iii) must have furnished the requisite security or caution for the proper performance of his functions (subs. (3)). Furthermore, paras. (*a*), (*b*) and (*c*) of subs. (4) specify three separate grounds, each of which in itself is sufficient to disqualify a person from acting as an insolvency practitioner during any period for which he or she is subject to the disqualifying ground in question. As mentioned above in the notes to s.388(1) the original provisions of the Bill were modified during the course of its progress through Parliament so as to remove any grounds of disqualification of an *ad hoc* character based upon personal links between the insolvency practitioner and the party in relation to which he acts. Such matters, which raise intricate problems of actual or potential conflict of interest or want of impartiality, have been left to be regulated by the ethical and disciplinary codes established by the professional bodies to which insolvency practitioners are expected to belong, and should be covered in practical guidelines issued by those bodies to their members.

This section corresponds to ss.2 and 3(1) of the 1985 Act.

Subs. (1)

The effect of this provision is to allow only natural persons (*i.e.* individuals) to act as insolvency practitioners within the meaning of the Act. Accordingly no corporate or quasi-corporate entity may act as an insolvency practitioner within the meaning of s.388, irrespective of whether the entity in question enjoys fully or partially the attributes of legal personality which enable it to undertake other kinds of activity. On the other hand, provisions elsewhere in the Act indicate that it is possible for more than one person to act jointly as insolvency practitioners in the same case (see ss.13(3), 139(4)(*a*), 231(1)). Such an arrangement is clearly not precluded by the terms of s.390(1), which merely impose the requirement that each of the persons who are the subject of such a joint appointment must be an individual, and must be fully qualified in his own right to act in the instant case.

Subs. (2)

This subsection establishes the main basis of eligibility to act as an insolvency practitioner. It is made a *sine qua non* that a person must be duly authorised to act in this capacity. Such authorisation may be gained either as a consequence of membership of a recognised professional body, whose rules permit the individual in question to act as an insolvency practitioner (s.391), or as a consequence of the grant of such authorisation in response to an application submitted to the relevant authority created for this purpose (ss.392–398 inclusive).

Subs. (3)

This lays down the second main condition of eligibility to act as an insolvency practitioner. The individual in question must maintain in force at all relevant times such security (or, in Scotland, caution) for the proper performance of his functions as may be prescribed. Moreover, the security must satisfy the prescribed requirements with regard to the actual person in relation to whom the insolvency practitioner acts. The determination of the appropriate nature and extent of the security or bonding to be furnished will be administered by the Department of Trade in accordance with already established practice. An important new feature is that the requirement of furnishing security will be applicable to all cases where a person is to act as an insolvency practitioner and not merely, as formerly, to those cases where a receiver or liquidator is appointed by the court, or where a trustee in bankruptcy is appointed. This standardised requirement of compulsory bonding is in accordance with the recommendations of the *Cork Report* (paras. 763–767). In Chap. 9 of the *White Paper* it is indicated that intending insolvency practitioners will be able to provide either special or general security, the latter form being especially suitable in cases where the individual wishes to be at liberty to act in numerous cases, often at short notice (see para. 44).

Subs. (4)

The three paras. of this subsection establish three alternative grounds, any of which will furnish the basis of disqualification from acting as an insolvency practitioner during any period for which it is applicable to the individual in question. The status of "undischarged bankrupt" (para. (*a*)) attaches to a person with effect from the day on which a bankruptcy order is made against him (s.278(*a*)) and continues until such time as his discharge from bankruptcy becomes effective by virtue of the provisions of either s.279 or 280, or until the bankruptcy order is annulled pursuant to s.282. In Scotland, the sequestration of a debtor's estate is effective from the date of the making of the order of sequestration (see Bankruptcy (Scotland) Act 1985, ss.12, 31).

An order disqualifying a person from company management may be made under the Company Directors Disqualification Act 1986. The maximum and minimum duration of such orders, and the date of their commencement in force, varies depending upon the circumstances in which they are made and upon the statutory provision upon which they are based. However, the maximum periods which may be specified in the order of the court which makes it are fixed by ss.2(3), 3(5), 4(3), 5(5), 6(4), 8(4) or 10(2) of the Disqualification Act, and are five years in the case of an order made under s. 3 or s.5 of that Act, or made by a court of summary jurisdiction, and 15 years in any other case. The only statutory provision which imposes a minimum period which may be specified as the period of disqualification is s.6(4) of the Disqualification Act, which applies exclusively to orders made under that section and imposes a minimum period of disqualification of two years, and a maximum of 15 years.

A person who has been judicially assessed to be incapable, by reason of mental disorder, of managing and administering his affairs is classified as a "patient" for the purposes of Pt. VII of the Mental Health Act 1983. While such a person remains subject to the jurisdiction of the Court of Protection, he will incur the disqualification from acting as an insolvency practitioner established by para. (*c*). A similar definition of "patient" is employed in the Mental Health (Scotland) Act 1984 (s.125(1)), and an identical disqualification, from the aspect of acting as an insolvency practitioner, arises out of para. (*c*) with respect to any person who is a patient within the meaning of either the English or the Scottish Mental Health legislation.

Recognised professional bodies

391.—(1) The Secretary of State may by order declare a body which appears to him to fall within subsection (2) below to be a recognised professional body for the purposes of this section.

(2) A body may be recognised if it regulates the practice of a profession and maintains and enforces rules for securing that such of its members as are permitted by or under the rules to act as insolvency practitioners—

(*a*) are fit and proper persons so to act, and
(*b*) meet acceptable requirements as to education and practical training and experience.

(3) References to members of a recognised professional body are to persons who, whether members of that body or not, are subject to its rules in the practice of the profession in question.

The reference in section 390(2) above to membership of a professional body recognised under this section is to be read accordingly.

(4) An order made under subsection (1) in relation to a professional body may be revoked by a further order if it appears to the Secretary of State that the body no longer falls within subsection (2).

(5) An order of the Secretary of State under this section has effect from such date as is specified in the order; and any such order revoking a previous order may make provision whereby members of the body in question continue to be treated as authorised to act as insolvency practitioners for a specified period after the revocation takes effect.

Definitions

"member of recognised professional body": subs. (3).
"recognised professional body": subss. (1), (2).
"to act as an insolvency practitioner": s.388(1), (2), (3).

General Note

This section provides the basis upon which most persons will acquire an authorisation to act as an insolvency practitioner, as required by s.390(2), whereby it is provided that a member of a recognised professional body is authorised to act as an insolvency practitioner if he is permitted so to act by the rules of that body. The function of determining who, in the main, are to be authorised to act as insolvency practitioners has been delegated to a number of accounting and legal bodies whose precise identity will be revealed when the Secretary of State exercises the power conferred by subs. (1) to make one or more orders declaring which are to be the recognised professional bodies for the purposes of this section. The provision as enacted represents a radical recasting of the provisions of the 1985 Insolvency Bill as originally published, whereby entitlement to practice as an insolvency practitioner would have been in all cases based upon the possession of a certificate obtainable only by individual application to the Secretary of State. For those persons who are not members of recognised bodies, a modified form of the latter mode of application still furnishes the means by which the requisite authorisation to practice may be sought (see ss.392–398 inclusive). The enacted provisions represent an abandonment of one of the principal recommendations of the *Cork Report* (see Chaps. 15, 16 and 17) that all insolvency practitioners should not only be required to be members of a recognised professional body but should also be required to hold a practising certificate issued by the Secretary of State on an individual basis. It may be questioned whether the sanction of withdrawal of recognition from a professional body will prove to be as potent an incentive to the maintenance of high standards in practice, as would have been the case under the original terms of the Bill whereby the Secretary of State would have been empowered directly to withhold or revoke the licence of any person whose conduct showed him or her to be unfit to act as an insolvency practitioner.

This section corresponds to subss. (2)–(5) of s.3 of the 1985 Act.

Subs. (1)

This provision has the effect of enabling the Secretary of State in effect to delegate to those professional bodies recognised for this purpose, by means of the procedure laid down in subss. (2)–(5) inclusive, the function of determining which of their members shall be authorised to act as insolvency practitioners. It will be ultimately left for each of the bodies in question to determine what rules and procedures to adopt for this purpose, but the provisions of subss. (2) and (4) clearly indicate that these matters will be appraised by the Secretary of State in the course of deciding whether to recognise any given professional body for the purposes of this section. Moreover, efforts will be made to try to achieve the maximum amount of equivalence of treatment between the individual bodies with regard to the standards to be applied, and with regard to the qualifications, education, training and experience to be required of those acting as insolvency practitioners (H.C. Vol. 83, cols. 527–528).

Subs. (2)

This prescribes the criteria which must be satisfied in order for the discretionary power contained in subs. (1) to become exerciseable. While the actual application of their own rules is quite naturally left to the professional bodies themselves, the Secretary of State must first be satisfied that the rules in question are adequate to ensure that those who thereby gain authorisation to practice as insolvency practitioners are both "fit and proper persons so to act" and also "meet acceptable requirements as to education, practical training and experience". While the latter requirement may be capable of quite exact and objective definition, the former one will inevitably entail a degree of subjectivity of judgment on the part of those ultimately responsible for assessing whether a person is "fit and proper". In neither case however does the subsection make provision for these matters to be regulated by means of a uniform set of rules ministerially prescribed.

Subs. (3)

The second part of this subsection is designed to ensure that the provisions of s.390(2) are applicable to all persons who are subject to the rules of a particular body in the practice of their profession, whether or not those persons are actually members of that body.

Subs. (5)

This provision controls the timing and duration of the effectiveness of any recognition conferred upon a professional body under subs. (1). It also enables transitional provisions to be included in any order revoking such recognition, thereby ensuring that the members of any professional body whose recognition is revoked may, if appropriate, be authorised to complete any items of regulated insolvency business upon which they are already engaged at the date on which their professional body ceases to be recognised for the purposes of s.390(2)(*a*).

Authorisation by competent authority

392.—(1) Application may be made to a competent authority for authorisation to act as an insolvency practitioner.

(2) The competent authorities for this purpose are—

(*a*) in relation to a case of any description specified in directions given by the Secretary of State, the body or person so specified in relation to cases of that description, and

(*b*) in relation to a case not falling within paragraph (*a*), the Secretary of State.

(3) The application—

(*a*) shall be made in such manner as the competent authority may direct,

(*b*) shall contain or be accompanied by such information as that authority may reasonably require for the purpose of determining the application, and

(*c*) shall be accompanied by the prescribed fee;

and the authority may direct that notice of the making of the application shall be published in such manner as may be specified in the direction.

(4) At any time after receiving the application and before determining it the authority may require the applicant to furnish additional information.

(5) Directions and requirements given or imposed under subsection (3) or (4) may differ as between different applications.

(6) Any information to be furnished to the competent authority under this section shall, if it so requires, be in such form or verified in such manner as it may specify.

(7) An application may be withdrawn before it is granted or refused.

(8) Any sums received under this section by a competent authority other than the Secretary of State may be retained by the authority; and any sums so received by the Secretary of State shall be paid into the Consolidated Fund.

DEFINITIONS

"prescribed": s.384.
"the competent authority": subs. (2).
"to act as an insolvency practitioner": s.388(1), (2), (3).

GENERAL NOTE

This section, which operates in conjunction with ss.393–398 inclusive, is applicable in those cases where a person who wishes to obtain authorisation to act as an insolvency practitioner is not a member of any professional body which has been recognised by the Secretary of State for the purposes of s.390(2)(*a*). Such persons may seek authorisation to practice as insolvency practitioners by making an application under this section to the body or person to be specified in directions given by the Secretary of State and referred to hereafter as "the competent body". Similar applications may also be made by any persons who, despite being members of a recognised professional body, have for some reason failed to obtain, or have been deprived of, authorisation to practise conferred by the body in question. Application under s.392 could thus constitute a species of appeal from a decision of a professional body acting under s.390(2), but it is clear that both the competent body and the Insolvency Practitioners Tribunal will take into account the reasons why the applicant has been excluded from practice by the decision of his own professional body. Moreover, it is declared ministerial policy to achieve as close an equivalence of treatment as possible between the professional bodies on the one hand and the way authorisation is carried out by the Department of Trade on the other (H.C. Vol. 83, cols. 527, 528).

This section corresponds to ss.4 and 11 (part) of the 1985 Act.

Subss. (1), (3)

These control the manner in which applications for authorisation under s.393 are to be made, and includes powers enabling the competent authority to issue directions as to the form and contents of the application. The fees to be charged to applicants will be separately prescribed by regulations made by the Secretary of State. The nature and amount of the information which an applicant may lawfully be required to supply is limited only by the qualification, in para. (*b*) of subs. (3), that it must be such as the authority may reasonably require for the purpose in hand. In practice this is likely to prove to be a very broad power of inquiry, especially in cases where it transpires that the applicant might be expected to have obtained authorisation under s.390(2)(*a*) by virtue of his past or present membership of a recognised professional body.

The further power enabling the authority to arrange for the publication of notice of the making of any application under s.392 provides additional and important possibilities for information to be supplied by third parties.

Subss. (2)–(8)

The provisions are concerned with ordinary matters of detail associated with subs. (1) and are self explanatory.

Grant, refusal and withdrawal of authorisation

393.—(1) The competent authority may, on an application duly made in accordance with section 392 and after being furnished with all such information as it may require under that section, grant or refuse the application.

(2) The authority shall grant the application if it appears to it from the information furnished by the applicant and having regard to such other information, if any, as it may have—

(*a*) that the applicant is a fit and proper person to act as an insolvency practitioner, and

(*b*) that the applicant meets the prescribed requirements with respect to education and practical training and experience.

(3) An authorisation granted under this section, if not previously withdrawn, continues in force for such period not exceeding the prescribed maximum as may be specified in the authorisation.

(4) An authorisation so granted may be withdrawn by the competent authority if it appears to it—

(*a*) that the holder of the authorisation is no longer a fit and proper person to act as an insolvency practitioner, or

(*b*) without prejudice to paragraph (a), that the holder—

(i) has failed to comply with any provision of this Part or of any regulations made under this Part or Part XV, or

(ii) in purported compliance with any such provision, has furnished the competent authority with false, inaccurate or misleading information.

(5) An authorisation granted under this section may be withdrawn by the competent authority at the request or with the consent of the holder of the authorisation.

Definitions

"prescribed": s.384.
"the competent authority": s.392(2).
"to act as an insolvency practitioner": s.388(1), (2), (3).

General Note

This section makes provision for the granting of authorisation to act as insolvency practitioners to those applicants who are unable to gain an authorisation by virtue of s.390(2)(*a*). The power to grant such authorisation is expressed to be conferred upon "the competent authority", which will be a body of person specified in directions given by the Secretary of State. In the absence of such directions, the Secretary of State himself constitutes "the relevant authority" for this purpose (s.392(2)(*b*)). The section also prescribes the criteria to be applied in deciding whether to grant or refuse an authorisation. These are nearly identical to those required by s.391(2) to be applied by professional bodies in granting authorisations under that section, save that in the case of authorisations sought under s.393 the requirements with respect to education and practical training and experience will be prescribed by regulations.

This section corresponds to s.5 of the 1985 Act.

Subs. (1)

This expresses the power to grant or refuse authorisation in response to an application made under s.392.

Subs. (2)

This subsection provides that if the criteria specified in paras. (*a*) and (*b*) are satisfied, the relevant authority must grant the application. However, as is also true with regard to applications falling under s.391(2), the requirement in para. (*a*) that the applicant must be considered to be a fit and proper person to act as an insolvency practitioner involves the exercise of a subjective judgment on the part of the authority which is deciding the case. On the other hand it is a purely objective question whether the applicant also meets the prescribed requirements referred to in para. (*b*). The subsection also expressly sanctions the consideration of other information besides that supplied by the applicant personally. Thus, for example, the authority may have regard to any information supplied by third parties who receive notice of the application as a result of directions for publication made under s.392(3).

Subs. (3)

This provision indicates that a maximum duration for each grant of authorisation will be prescribed in regulations. It was originally proposed that all insolvency practitioners would be required to apply annually for the renewal of their authorisation to practise, but the administrative burden which would result from such a short-term validity of authorisation has clearly militated in favour of a more extended period, yet to be specified. However, the authority is empowered to specify a lesser period than the prescribed maximum, and it is furthermore possible for an authorisation to be withdrawn pursuant to subs. (4) or (5).

Subs. (4)

This important provision empowers the relevant authority to withdraw an authorisation which it has previously granted, if either of the grounds specified in para. (*a*) or para. (*b*) is found to be met. In view of the declared ministerial intention to procure a co-ordination of the standards of treatment in cases falling under ss.391 and 395 respectively, it may be anticipated that, in order to gain the necessary recognition for the purposes of s.391, professional bodies will need to show that their own disciplinary procedures include provisions comparable to those in s.393(4).

Notices

394.—(1) Where a competent authority grants an authorisation under section 393, it shall give written notice of that fact to the applicant, specifying the date on which the authorisation takes effect.

(2) Where the authority proposes to refuse an application, or to withdraw an authorisation under section 393(4), it shall give the applicant or holder of the authorisation written notice of its intention to do so, setting out particulars of the grounds on which it proposes to act.

(3) In the case of a proposed withdrawal the notice shall state the date on which it is proposed that the withdrawal should take effect.

(4) A notice under subsection (2) shall give particulars of the rights exercisable under the next two sections by a person on whom the notice is served.

Definition

"the competent authority": s.392(2).

General Note

This section ensures fulfilment of the essential requirements, including those of natural justice, that a person be informed in writing of decisions affecting his or her legal rights and interests. In cases where the relevant authority is proposing to refuse or to withdraw an authorisation it is especially important that the person affected should be given adequate notice of what is impending, and of the grounds upon which the authority is proposing to act, in order that the rights of appeal under ss.395 and 396 may be exercised in a timely and effective manner.

This section corresponds to s.6 of the 1985 Act.

Subs. (1)

This provision applies to cases where an authorisation is to be granted, and is virtually self explanatory. The requirement that written notice must be given to the applicant, including a specification of the date on which the authorisation takes effect, is important especially in view of the criminal consequences ensuing from any infraction of the provisions of s.389. Since that section creates an offence of strict liability, it would be particularly unfortunate if a person to whom an authorisation had actually been granted were to incur criminal liability (with the possible result that authorisation would on that account be subsequently withdrawn), merely by virtue of the fact that he undertook some action as an insolvency practitioner before the date on which the authorisation came into effect, thus infringing s.389 in conjunction with s.390(2).

Subs. (2)

The important aspect of this provision is that in addition to the requirement that an applicant or holder must be informed in writing of any proposed refusal or withdrawal of authorisation, it is made obligatory for the relevant authority to state in writing the grounds on which the decision would be taken. By virtue of subs. (4) the notice must also inform the person to whom it is addressed of the rights exerciseable under ss.395 and 396.

Subs. (3)

This provision is essentially complementary to that contained in subs. (1), being designed to ensure that in cases where an authorisation is withdrawn the person who is thereby to be deprived of his qualification to act as an insolvency practitioner is given written notification of the date upon which the withdrawal is to take effect. This is particularly important in view of the criminal consequences which will ensue if the person in question thereafter performs any of the acts mentioned in s.388(1), (2) and (3).

Right to make representations

395.—(1) A person on whom a notice is served under section 394(2) may within 14 days after the date of service make written representations to the competent authority.

(2) The competent authority shall have regard to any representations so made in determining whether to refuse the application or withdraw the authorisation, as the case may be.

DEFINITION

"the competent authority": s.392(2).

GENERAL NOTE

This provision creates the first mode of recourse which is available to a person on whom a notice of a proposed refusal or withdrawal of authorisation is served pursuant to s.394(2). In the first instance the person affected has the right to make written representations to the authority within 14 days after the date of service of the notice, and the authority is required to have regard to any such representations in reaching its final decision.

This section corresponds to s.7 of the 1985 Act.

Reference to Tribunal

396.—(1) The Insolvency Practitioners Tribunal ("the Tribunal") continues in being; and the provisions of Schedule 7 apply to it.

(2) Where a person is served with a notice under section 394(2), he may—

(*a*) at any time within 28 days after the date of service of the notice, or

(*b*) at any time after the making by him of representations under section 395 and before the end of the period of 28 days after the date of the service on him of a notice by the competent authority that the authority does not propose to alter its decision in consequence of the representations,

give written notice to the authority requiring the case to be referred to the Tribunal.

(3) Where a requirement is made under subsection (2), then, unless the competent authority—

(*a*) has decided or decides to grant the application or, as the case may be, not to withdraw the authorisation, and

(*b*) within 7 days after the date of the making of the requirement, gives written notice of that decision to the person by whom the requirement was made,

it shall refer the case to the Tribunal.

DEFINITIONS

"the competent authority": s.392(2).

"the Tribunal": subs. (1), Sched. 7.

GENERAL NOTE

This provision in conjunction with s.397 lays down the main procedure for appeal in cases where the relevant authority proposes not to grant, or proposes to withdraw, an authorisation to act as an insolvency practitioner. Following the service on him of the notice required by s.394(2), the person concerned may in the first instance elect to make representations to the competent authority under s.395. Alternatively (or subsequently, if any representations made under s.395 are ineffectual) the person on whom service of notice has originally taken place under s.394(2) may within 28 days thereof give written notice to the authority in question, invoking his right to have the matter determined by the Insolvency Practitioners Tribunal, which is maintained in existence by subs. (1) of this section together with the provisions of Sched. 7. Thereupon, unless before the expiry of the same 28 day period the authority relents from its former proposal and duly notifies the person concerned to that effect, a reference to the Tribunal becomes mandatory. The latter body is required by s.397 to formulate a reasoned opinion which essentially determines the way in which the case will be finally decided by the relevant authority, with whom the final duty of decision nevertheless reposes. Appeal from the Tribunal's decision lies, either directly or by way of case stated, to the High Court or the Court of Session, pursuant to s.13 of the Tribunals and Inquiries Act 1971, as amended by Sched. 14 to this Act and by para. 5 of Sched. 1 to the 1985 Act.

This section corresponds to ss.8(1), (2) and (6) and 11 (part) of the 1985 Act.

Action of Tribunal on reference

397.—(1) On a reference under section 396 the Tribunal shall—

(*a*) investigate the case, and

(*b*) make a report to the competent authority stating what would in their opinion be the appropriate decision in the matter and the reasons for that opinion,

and it is the duty of the competent authority to decide the matter accordingly.

(2) The Tribunal shall send a copy of the report to the applicant or, as the case may be, the holder of the authorisation; and the competent authority shall serve him with a written notice of the decision made by it in accordance with the report.

(3) The competent authority may, if he thinks fit, publish the report of the Tribunal.

Definitions

"the competent authority": s.392(2).
"the Tribunal": s.396(1).

General Note

This section prescribes the procedure to be followed by the Insolvency Practitioners Tribunal when a case is referred to it under s.396.

This section corresponds to subss. (3)–(5) of s.8 of the 1985 Act.

Subs. (1)

This specifies the twofold duties of the Insolvency Practitioners Tribunal in every case referred to it under s.396(3). In its investigation the Tribunal must comply with the requirements of Sched. 7 to the Act, notably those of para. 4 thereof, which make it obligatory that a reasonable opportunity be afforded for representations to be made by or on behalf of the person whose case is the subject of the investigation. In other respects the Tribunal is left with considerable latitude as to the approach to be adopted in conducting its investigation of the case, as required by para. (a) of this subsection, but is required in its subsequent report to the competent authority to state not only its opinion as to the appropriate decision in the matter but also the reasons for that opinion. The purport of that opinion is effectively determinative of the matter, since it is stated to be the duty of the competent authority to "decide the matter accordingly".

Subs. (2)

This provision gives rise to a requirement that the person whose case has been referred to the Insolvency Practitioners Tribunal must receive both a copy of the Tribunal's report and, in due course, a written notice from the authority of its decision made in accordance with that report. Although no further right of appeal against this final decision is embodied in the Act, the information thus required to be furnished to the person concerned should serve to indicate whether any possible grounds exist for seeking to challenge the Tribunal's opinion, and the decision based thereon, by way of an application for judicial review.

Subs. (3)

The power to bring about publication of the Tribunal's report in any given case is a discretionary one, vested in the competent authority.

Refusal or withdrawal without reference to Tribunal

398. Where in the case of any proposed refusal or withdrawal of an authorisation either—

(*a*) the period mentioned in section 396(2)(*a*) has expired without the making of any requirement under that subsection or of any representations under section 395, or

(*b*) the competent authority has given a notice such as is mentioned in section 396(2)(*b*) and the period so mentioned has expired without the making of any such requirement, the competent authority may give written notice of the refusal or withdrawal to the person concerned in accordance with the proposal in the notice given under section 394(2).

DEFINITION

"the competent authority": s.392(2).

GENERAL NOTE

This section completes the sequence of procedures consequential upon the formation by the competent authority, acting under s.393(1) or (4), of a proposal to refuse or to withdraw an authorisation to act as an insolvency practitioner. If, following the service of notice of that proposal under s.394(2), the person concerned does not within the 28 days allowed avail himself of the right to require that his case be referred to the Insolvency Practitioners Tribunal, the competent authority is empowered to render its own decision final by serving written notice upon him of the refusal or withdrawal of his authorisation. This provision does not however oblige the authority to decide the matter in the manner initially indicated by the terms of the earlier notice.

This section corresponds to s.9 of the 1985 Act.

PART XIV

PUBLIC ADMINISTRATION (ENGLAND AND WALES)

Official Receivers

Appointment, etc. of official receivers

399.—(1) For the purposes of this Act the official receiver, in relation to any bankruptcy or winding up, is any person who by virtue of the following provisions of this section or section 401 below is authorised to act as the official receiver in relation to that bankruptcy or winding up.

(2) The Secretary of State may (subject to the approval of the Treasury as to numbers) appoint persons to the office of official receiver, and a person appointed to that office (whether under this section or section 70 of the Bankruptcy Act 1914)—

(*a*) shall be paid out of money provided by Parliament such salary as the Secretary of State may with the concurrence of the Treasury direct,

(*b*) shall hold office on such other terms and conditions as the Secretary of State may with the concurrence of the Treasury direct, and

(*c*) may be removed from office by a direction of the Secretary of State.

(3) Where a person holds the office of official receiver, the Secretary of State shall from time to time attach him either to the High Court or to a county court having jurisdiction for the purposes of the second Group of Parts of this Act.

(4) Subject to any directions under subsection (6) below, an official receiver attached to a particular court is the person authorised to act as the official receiver in relation to every bankruptcy or winding up falling within the jurisdiction of that court.

(5) The Secretary of State shall ensure that there is, at all times, at least one official receiver attached to the High Court and at least one attached to each county court having jurisdiction for the purposes of the second Group of Parts; but he may attach the same official receiver to two or more different courts.

(6) The Secretary of State may give directions with respect to the disposal of the business of official receivers, and such directions may, in particular—

(*a*) authorise an official receiver attached to one court to act as the official receiver in relation to any case or description of cases falling within the jurisdiction of another court;

(*b*) provide, where there is more than one official receiver authorised to act as the official receiver in relation to cases falling within the jurisdiction of any court, for the distribution of their business between or among themselves.

(7) A person who at the coming into force of section 222 of the Insolvency Act 1985 (replaced by this section) is an official receiver attached to a court shall continue in office after the coming into force of that section as an official receiver attached to that court under this section.

Definition

"the official receiver": subs. (1).

Application

This section does not apply to Scotland (ss.410, 440(2)(*c*).

General Note

This section provides for the office of the official receiver to be constituted and organised under the direction of the Secretary of State for Trade. The manner of appointing persons to the office, and the allocation of official receivers to the insolvency courts, are also specified. The provisions replace, and greatly expand upon, part of the former provisions of s.70 of the Bankruptcy Act 1914 (repealed). The principle of the continued involvement of the official receiver in all types of individual and incorporate insolvency proceedings, as powerfully advocated in Chap. 14 of the *Cork Report,* was accepted in Chap. 7 of the *White Paper,* and duly embodied throughout the provisions of this Act (see H.C. Standing Committee E, June 18, 1984, cols. 379–382).

This section corresponds to s.222 of the 1985 Act.

Functions and status of official receivers

400.—(1) In addition to any functions conferred on him by this Act, a person holding the office of official receiver shall carry out such other functions as may from time to time be conferred on him by the Secretary of State.

(2) In the exercise of the functions of his office a person holding the office of official receiver shall act under the general directions of the Secretary of State and shall also be an officer of the court in relation to which he exercises those functions.

(3) Any property vested in his official capacity in a person holding the office of official receiver shall, on his dying, ceasing to hold office or being otherwise succeeded in relation to the bankruptcy or winding up in question by another official receiver, vest in his successor without any conveyance, assignment or transfer.

Definitions

"the official receiver": s.399(1).

"property": s.436.

Application

This section does not apply to Scotland or to Northern Ireland (ss.410, 440(2)(*c*), 441).

General Note

This section makes further provision with regard to the official receiver and indicates the status and functions which attach to that office. This section, which replaces in part the former provisions of ss.70 and 72 of the Bankruptcy Act 1914 (repealed), corresponds to s.223 of the 1985 Act.

Subs. (3)

This makes provision of the transfer of property vested in an official receiver in his official capacity, upon his dying or ceasing to hold office.

Deputy official receivers and staff

401.—(1) The Secretary of State may, if he thinks it expedient to do so in order to facilitate the disposal of the business of the official receiver attached to any court, appoint an officer of his department to act as deputy to that official receiver.

(2) Subject to any directions given by the Secretary of State under section 399 or 400, a person appointed to act as deputy to an official receiver has, on such conditions and for such period as may be specified in the terms of his appointment, the same status and functions as the official receiver to whom he is appointed deputy.

Accordingly, references in this Act (except section 399(1) to (5)) to an official receiver include a person appointed to act as his deputy.

(3) An appointment made under subsection (1) may be terminated at any time by the Secretary of State.

(4) The Secretary of State may, subject to the approval of the Treasury as to numbers and remuneration and as to the other terms and conditions of the appointments, appoint officers of his department to assist official receivers in the carrying out of their functions.

DEFINITION

"the official receiver": s.399(1).

APPLICATION

This section does not apply to Scotland (s.440(2)(*c*)).

GENERAL NOTE

This section authorises the Secretary of State to appoint deputy official receivers and other supporting staff, as circumstances require, to assist official receivers in the carrying out of their functions. This section, which replaces the former provisions of ss.71 and 75 of the Bankruptcy Act 1914 (repealed), corresponds to s.224 of the 1985 Act.

The Official Petitioner

Official Petitioner

402.—(1) There continues to be an officer known as the Official Petitioner for the purpose of discharging, in relation to cases in which a criminal bankruptcy order is made, the functions assigned to him by or under this Act; and the Director of Public Prosecutions continues, by virtue of his office, to be the Official Petitioner.

(2) The functions of the Official Petitioner include the following—

(*a*) to consider whether, in a case in which a criminal bankruptcy order is made, it is in the public interest that he should himself present a petition under section 264(1)(*d*) of this Act;

(*b*) to present such a petition in any case where he determines that it is in the public interest for him to do so;

(*c*) to make payments, in such cases as he may determine, towards expenses incurred by other persons in connection with proceedings in pursuance of such a petition; and

(*d*) to exercise, so far as he considers it in the public interest to do so, any of the powers conferred on him by or under this Act.

(3) Any functions of the Official Petitioner may be discharged on his behalf by any person acting with his authority.

(4) Neither the Official Petitioner nor any person acting with his authority is liable to any action or proceeding in respect of anything done

or omitted to be done in the discharge, or purported discharge, of the functions of the Official Petitioner.

(5) In this section "criminal bankruptcy order" means an order under section 39(1) of the Powers of Criminal Courts Act 1973.

Definitions

"criminal bankruptcy order": subs. (5); Powers of Criminal Courts Act 1973, s.39(1).
"the Official Petitioner": subs. (1); Powers of Criminal Courts Act 1973, s.41(1).

Application

This section does not apply to Scotland (ss.410, 440(2)(*c*)).

General Note

This section makes provision for the continued existence of the office of Official Petitioner, which is a position occupied by the Director of Public Prosecutions *ex officio*. This office exists in relation to the procedure for making an order or adjudication against an individual following the making of a criminal bankruptcy order against him. A petition based upon such an order may be presented under s.264(1)(*d*); related provisions are contained in ss.266(4), 277, 282(2), 290(4)(*a*), 297(1), 327, and 341(4): see the General Notes to the respective provisions.

Insolvency Service finance, accounting and investment

Insolvency Services Account

403.—(1) All money received by the Secretary of State in respect of proceedings under this Act as it applies to England and Wales shall be paid into the Insolvency Services Account kept by the Secretary of State with the Bank of England; and all payments out of money standing to the credit of the Secretary of State in that account shall be made by the Bank of England in such manner as he may direct.

(2) Whenever the cash balance standing to the credit of the Insolvency Services Account is in excess of the amount which in the opinion of the Secretary of State is required for the time being to answer demands in respect of bankrupts' estates or companies' estates, the Secretary of State shall—

(*a*) notify the excess to the National Debt Commissioners, and
(*b*) pay into the Insolvency Services Investment Account ("the Investment Account") kept by the Commissioners with the Bank of England the whole or any part of the excess as the Commissioners may require for investment in accordance with the following provisions of this Part.

(3) Whenever any part of the money so invested is, in the opinion of the Secretary of State, required to answer any demand in respect of bankrupts' estates or companies' estates, he shall notify to the National Debt Commissioners the amount so required and the Commissioners—

(*a*) shall thereupon repay to the Secretary of State such sum as may be required to the credit of the Insolvency Services Account, and
(*b*) for that purpose may direct the sale of such part of the securities in which the money has been invested as may be necessary.

Definitions

"bankrupt": s.381(1).
"bankrupts' estates": ss.283, 385(1).
"the Investment Account": subs. (2)(*b*).

Application

This section does not apply to Scotland (s.410).

GENERAL NOTE

In Chap. 17 of the *Cork Report* a number of criticisms were expressed of the established rules under which liquidators and trustees in bankruptcy are severely restricted in their handling and investment of funds received by them in the course of acting in office. In particular, the obligation to pay money immediately into the Insolvency Services Account at the Bank of England, instead of into a local account specially opened for the purpose, was seen as both cumbersome and costly, in that the return of interest paid on moneys initially deposited in the Insolvency Services Account is well below currently obtainable commercial rates. It was thus observed (*C.R.* paras. 847–854) that this shortfall in receipts of interest has a direct and adverse effect upon the creditors' eventual returns in respect of the amounts owed to them. The *Cork Committee* recommendations for a change in the rules, so that trustees and liquidators would have greater control over the placement of funds on deposit pending their distribution to creditors, were not accepted in Chap. 8 of the *White Paper* and have not been carried into the new insolvency legislation. Ss.403–409 accordingly consolidate the existing law formerly contained in the Insolvency Services (Accounting and Investment) Act 1970 (hereafter referred to as "INS 1970") as amended by the provisions of the Insolvency Act 1976 (hereafter referred to as "INS 1976").

This section corresponds to s.1 of INS 1970 and s.3 of INS 1976, as amended by para. 28 of Sched. 8 to the 1985 Act.

Investment Account

404. Any money standing to the credit of the Investment Account (including any money received by the National Debt Commissioners by way of interest on or proceeds of any investment under this section) may be invested by the Commissioners, in accordance with such directions as may be given by the Treasury, in any manner for the time being specified in Part II of Schedule 1 to the Trustee Investments Act 1961.

DEFINITION

"the Investment Account": s.403(2)(*b*).

APPLICATION

This section does not apply to Scotland (s.410).

GENERAL NOTE

This section corresponds to s.2 of INS 1970.

Application of income in Investment Account; adjustment of balances

405.—(1) Where the annual account to be kept by the National Debt Commissioners under section 409 below shows that in the year for which it is made up the gross amount of the interest accrued from the securities standing to the credit of the Investment Account exceeded the aggregate of—

(*a*) a sum, to be determined by the Treasury, to provide against the depreciation in the value of the securities, and

(*b*) the sums paid into the Insolvency Services Account in pursuance of the next section together with the sums paid in pursuance of that section to the Commissioners of Inland Revenue,

the National Debt Commissioners shall, within 3 months after the account is laid before Parliament, cause the amount of the excess to be paid out of the Investment Account into the Consolidated Fund in such manner as may from time to time be agreed between the Treasury and the Commissioners.

(2) Where the said annual account shows that in the year for which it is made up the gross amount of interest accrued from the securities standing to the credit of the Investment Account was less than the aggregate mentioned in subsection (1), an amount equal to the deficiency shall, at such times as the Treasury direct, be paid out of the Consolidated Fund into the Investment Account.

(3) If the Investment Account is insufficient to meet its liabilities the Treasury may, on being informed of the insufficiency by the National Debt Commissioners, issue the amount of the deficiency out of the Consolidated Fund and the Treasury shall certify the deficiency to Parliament.

DEFINITIONS
"the Insolvency Services Account": s.403(1).
"the Investment Account": s.403(2)(*b*).

APPLICATION
This section does not apply to Scotland (s.410).

GENERAL NOTE
This section corresponds to s.3 of INS 1970 as amended by para. 5 of Sched. 2 to INS 1976.

Interest on money received by liquidators and invested

406. Where under rules made by virtue of paragraph 16 of Schedule 8 to this Act (investment of money received by company liquidators) a company has become entitled to any sum by way of interest, the Secretary of State shall certify that sum and the amount of tax payable on it to the National Debt Commissioners; and the Commissioners shall pay, out of the Investment Account—

(*a*) into the Insolvency Services Account, the sum so certified less the amount of tax so certified, and
(*b*) to the Commissioners of Inland Revenue, the amount of tax so certified.

DEFINITIONS
"the Insolvency Services Account": s.403(1).
"the Investment Account": s.403(2)(*b*).

APPLICATION
This section does not apply to Scotland (s.410).

GENERAL NOTE
This section corresponds to s.4 of INS 1970, as amended by para. 6 of Sched. 2 to INS 1976 and by para. 17 of Sched. 8 to the 1985 Act.

Unclaimed dividends and undistributed balances

407.—(1) The Secretary of State shall from time to time pay into the Consolidated Fund out of the Insolvency Services Account so much of the sums standing to the credit of that Account as represents—

(*a*) dividends which were declared before such date as the Treasury may from time to time determine and have not been claimed, and
(*b*) balances ascertained before that date which are too small to be divided among the persons entitled to them.

(2) For the purposes of this section the sums standing to the credit of the Insolvency Services Account are deemed to include any sums paid out of that Account and represented by any sums or securities standing to the credit of the Investment Account.

(3) The Secretary of State may require the National Debt Commissioners to pay out of the Investment Account into the Insolvency Services Account the whole or part of any sum which he is required to pay out of that account under subsection (1); and the Commissioners may direct the sale of such securities standing to the credit of the Investment Account as may be necessary for that purpose.

DEFINITIONS
"the Insolvency Services Account": s.403(1).
"the Investment Account": s.403(2)(*b*).

APPLICATION
This section does not apply to Scotland (s.410).

GENERAL NOTE
This section corresponds to s.5 of INS 1970, as amended by para. 7 of Sched. 2 to INS 1976.

Recourse to Consolidated Fund

408. If, after any repayment due to it from the Investment Account, the Insolvency Services Account is insufficient to meet its liabilities, the Treasury may, on being informed of it by the Secretary of State, issue the amount of the deficiency out of the Consolidated Fund, and the Treasury shall certify the deficiency to Parliament.

DEFINITIONS
"the Insolvency Services Account": s.403(1).
"the Investment Account": s.403(2)(*b*).

APPLICATION
This section does not apply to Scotland (s.410).

GENERAL NOTE
This section corresponds to s.6 of INS 1970, as amended by para. 8 of Sched. 2 to INS 1976.

Annual financial statement and audit

409.—(1) The National Debt Commissioners shall for each year ending on 31st March prepare a statement of the sums credited and debited to the Investment Account in such form and manner as the Treasury may direct and shall transmit it to the Comptroller and Auditor General before the end of November next following the year.

(2) The Secretary of State shall for each year ending 31st March prepare a statement of the sums received or paid by him under section 403 above in such form and manner as the Treasury may direct and shall transmit each statement to the Comptroller and Auditor General before the end of November next following the year.

(3) Every such statement shall include such additional information as the Treasury may direct.

(4) The Comptroller and Auditor General shall examine, certify and report on every such statement and shall lay copies of it, and of his report, before Parliament.

DEFINITION
"the Investment Account": s.403(2)(*b*).

APPLICATION
This section does not apply to Scotland (s.410).

GENERAL NOTE
This section corresponds to s.7 of INS 1970, as amended by para. 9 of Sched. 2 to INS 1976.

Supplementary

Extent of this Part

410. This Part of this Act extends to England and Wales only.

General Note

This section has the effect of limiting the application of all the provisions in Part XIV to England and Wales only. There is a partial overlap between the effect of this section, which applies to ss.399–410 as a block, and the effect of s.440(2)(*c*), which specifically excludes ss.399–402 from extending to Scotland. Moreover, s.441 is so drafted that only the provisions of the Act which are therein mentioned extend to Northern Ireland: none of the sections within Part XIV is mentioned in s.441 at all.

This section corresponds to s.9(3) of INS 1970 in conjunction with s.14(6) of INS 1976. The effect of s.236(3)(i) of the 1985 Act is also maintained in relation to provisions now contained in Part XIV of this Act which correspond to ss.222–225 of the 1985 Act, so that the extent of those provisions continues to be confined to England and Wales only.

Part XV

Subordinate Legislation

General insolvency rules

Company insolvency rules

411.—(1) Rules may be made—

(*a*) in relation to England and Wales, by the Lord Chancellor with the concurrence of the Secretary of State, or

(*b*) in relation to Scotland, by the Secretary of State,

for the purpose of giving effect to Parts I to VII of this Act.

(2) Without prejudice to the generality of subsection (1), or to any provision of those Parts by virtue of which rules under this section may be made with respect to any matter, rules under this section may contain—

(*a*) any such provision as is specified in Schedule 8 to this Act or corresponds to provision contained immediately before the coming into force of section 106 of the Insolvency Act 1985 in rules made, or having effect as if made, under section 663(1) or (2) of the Companies Act (old winding-up rules), and

(*b*) such incidental, supplemental and transitional provisions as may appear to the Lord Chancellor or, as the case may be, the Secretary of State necessary or expedient.

(3) In Schedule 8 to this Act "liquidator" includes a provisional liquidator; and references above in this section to Parts I to VII of this Act are to be read as including the Companies Act so far as relating to, and to matters connected with or arising out of, the insolvency or winding up of companies.

(4) Rules under this section shall be made by statutory instrument subject to annulment in pursuance of a resolution of either House of Parliament.

(5) Regulations made by the Secretary of State under a power conferred by rules under this section shall be made by statutory instrument and, after being made, shall be laid before each House of Parliament.

(6) Nothing in this section prejudices any power to make rules of court.

Definitions

"liquidator": subs. (3), Sched. 8.

"rules": s.251 and this section.

Transitional Provision
Sched. 11, para. 8.

General Note
This is an enabling section which confers a rule-making power upon the persons designated in subs. (1). The matters mentioned in Sched. 8 are expressly incorporated into the rule-making authority conferred by this section, but subs. (2) is so drafted as to avoid cutting down the more general language of subs. (1), which effectively confers an unfettered discretion with regard to the rules which may be made, provided these are ultimately reconcilable with the authorised purpose of giving effect to Pts. I–VII of the Act.
This section corresponds to s.106 of the 1985 Act.

Subs. (4)
This provides for the "negative" procedure to be applicable in relation to any statutory instrument whereby rules are made under this section. The rules will therefore come into force unless a resolution of either House is passed in opposition.

Individual insolvency rules (England and Wales)

412.—(1) The Lord Chancellor may, with the concurrence of the Secretary of State, make rules for the purpose of giving effect to Parts VIII to XI of this Act.

(2) Without prejudice to the generality of subsection (1), or to any provision of those Parts by virtue of which rules under this section may be made with respect to any matter, rules under this section may contain—

(*a*) any such provision as is specified in Schedule 9 to this Act or corresponds to provision contained immediately before the appointed day in rules made under section 132 of the Bankruptcy Act 1914; and

(*b*) such incidental, supplemental and transitional provisions as may appear to the Lord Chancellor necessary or expedient.

(3) Rules under this section shall be made by statutory instrument subject to annulment in pursuance of a resolution of either House of Parliament.

(4) Regulations made by the Secretary of State under a power conferred by rules under this section shall be made by statutory instrument and, after being made, shall be laid before each House of Parliament.

(5) Nothing in this section prejudices any power to make rules of court.

Definition
"rules": s.384 and this section.

Application
This section does not apply to Scotland (s.440(2)(*c*)).

Transitional Provision
Sched. 11, para. 19.

General Note
This section, together with Sched. 9, defines the scope and extent of the power to make subordinate legislation in respect of individual insolvency. Subs. (1) provides that this power is exercisable by the Lord Chancellor with the concurrence of the Secretary of State for Trade, while subs. (3) indicates that rules made under this section are to be made by statutory instrument, subject to the "negative" procedure for annulment by resolution of either House of Parliament. Subs. (4) indicates that regulations made by the Secretary of State pursuant to any power conferred by the rules is simply subject to the "notice" requirement in relation to Parliament.
This section corresponds to s.207 of the 1985 Act.

Insolvency Rules Committee

413.—(1) The committee established under section 10 of the Insolvency Act 1976 (advisory committee on bankruptcy and winding-up rules) continues to exist for the purpose of being consulted under this section.

(2) The Lord Chancellor shall consult the committee before making any rules under section 411 or 412.

(3) Subject to the next subsection, the committee shall consist of—

(*a*) a judge of the High Court attached to the Chancery Division;
(*b*) a circuit judge;
(*c*) a registrar in bankruptcy of the High Court;
(*d*) the registrar of a county court;
(*e*) a practising barrister;
(*f*) a practising solicitor; and
(*g*) a practising accountant;

and the appointment of any person as a member of the committee shall be made by the Lord Chancellor.

(4) The Lord Chancellor may appoint as additional members of the committee any persons appearing to him to have qualifications or experience that would be of value to the committee in considering any matter with which it is concerned.

Definition

"the committee," "the insolvency rules committee"; "advisory committee on bankruptcy and winding up rules": subs. (1).

Application

This section does not apply to Scotland (s.440(2)(*c*)).

General Note

This section perpetuates the existence of the Committee, formerly known as the Advisory Committee on Bankruptcy and Winding Up Rules, which was established by s.10 of the Insolvency Act 1976 (repealed) and is henceforth known as the Insolvency Rules Committee. The section specifies the composition of the Committee and the mode of appointment of those who are to be its members. The Lord Chancellor is required to consult the Committee before making any rules under s.411 or s.412 of this Act (subs. (2)).

This section corresponds to s.226 of the 1985 Act.

Fees orders

Fees orders (company insolvency proceedings)

414.—(1) There shall be paid in respect of—

(*a*) proceedings under any of Parts I to VII of this Act, and
(*b*) the performance by the official receiver or the Secretary of State of functions under those Parts,

such fees as the competent authority may with the sanction of the Treasury by order direct.

(2) That authority is—

(*a*) in relation to England and Wales, the Lord Chancellor, and
(*b*) in relation to Scotland, the Secretary of State.

(3) The Treasury may by order direct by whom and in what manner the fees are to be collected and accounted for.

(4) The Lord Chancellor may, with the sanction of the Treasury, by order provide for sums to be deposited, by such persons, in such manner and in such circumstances as may be specified in the order, by way of security for fees payable by virtue of this section.

(5) An order under this section may contain such incidental, supplemental and transitional provisions as may appear to the Lord Chancellor,

the Secretary of State or (as the case may be) the Treasury necessary or expedient.

(6) An order under this section shall be made by statutory instrument and, after being made, shall be laid before each House of Parliament.

(7) Fees payable by virtue of this section shall be paid into the Consolidated Fund.

(8) References in subsection (1) to Parts I to VII of this Act are to be read as including the Companies Act so far as relating to, and to matters connected with or arising out of, the insolvency or winding up of companies.

(9) Nothing in this section prejudices any power to make rules of court; and the application of this section to Scotland is without prejudice to section 2 of the Courts of Law Fees (Scotland) Act 1895.

DEFINITION

"the official receiver": s.399(1).

GENERAL NOTE

Subss. (1), (2)

This section, which corresponds to ss.106(5) and 107 of the 1985 Act, makes provision for the levying of fees in respect of proceedings relating to company insolvency falling within this Part of the Act or under the Companies Act 1985. The power of determination regarding the levels of fees in England and Wales is vested exclusively in the Lord Chancellor in England and Wales, whereas the rule-making powers under s.411 are exercisable by the Lord Chancellor with the concurrence of the Secretary of State for Trade. In the case of Scotland, the relevant powers under both this section and s.411 are vested in the Secretary of State for Scotland.

Subs. (4)

This provides for the levying of deposits as security for fees payable under this section.

Subs. (6)

This prescribes the mode of enactment, with a requirement merely that any order made under this section be laid before each House of Parliament. No procedure is prescribed for opposing or modifying any Order so laid before Parliament.

Fees orders (individual insolvency proceedings in England and Wales)

415.—(1) There shall be paid in respect of—

(*a*) proceedings under Parts VIII to XI of this Act, and

(*b*) the performance by the official receiver or the Secretary of State of functions under those Parts,

such fees as the Lord Chancellor may with the sanction of the Treasury by order direct.

(2) The Treasury may by order direct by whom and in what manner the fees are to be collected and accounted for.

(3) The Lord Chancellor may, with the sanction of the Treasury, by order provide for sums to be deposited, by such persons, in such manner and in such circumstances as may be specified in the order, by way of security for—

(*a*) fees payable by virtue of this section, and

(*b*) fees payable to any person who has prepared an insolvency practitioner's report under section 274 in Chapter I of Part IX.

(4) An order under this section may contain such incidental, supplemental and transitional provisions as may appear to the Lord Chancellor or, as the case may be, the Treasury, necessary or expedient.

(5) An order under this section shall be made by statutory instrument and, after being made, shall be laid before each House of Parliament.

(6) Fees payable by virtue of this section shall be paid into the Consolidated Fund.

(7) Nothing in this section prejudices any power to make rules of court.

Definitions

"insolvency practitioner": ss.388, 390.
"the official receiver": s.399(1).

Application

This section does not apply to Scotland (s.440(2)(*c*)).

General Note

This section confers powers to require the payment of fees in individual insolvency proceedings. These powers are exercisable by the Lord Chancellor with the sanction of the Treasury. Subs. (5) indicates that fees orders made pursuant to this enabling provision are to be made by statutory instrument, subject to the "notice" requirement in relation to Parliament.

This section corresponds to ss.207(5) and 208(1)–(3) and (5) of the 1985 Act.

Subs. (3)(b)

Person who has prepared an insolvency practitioner's report under section 274

This provision enables the deposit made by a debtor when presenting his own petition for a bankruptcy order under s.272 to be used to meet the fees of any insolvency practitioner whom the court may appoint under s.273(2) to give advice and assistance to the debtor, and to prepare a report under s.274, with a view to the debtor's avoiding bankruptcy if possible and proposing instead a scheme or composition under Part VIII of the Act. This is intended to enable as many small debtors as possible to avoid bankruptcy altogether and to opt instead for the new voluntary procedure established by the Act.

Specification, increase and reduction of money sums relevant in the operation of this Act

Monetary limits (companies winding up)

416.—(1) The Secretary of State may by order in a statutory instrument increase or reduce any of the money sums for the time being specified in the following provisions in the first Group of Parts—

section 117(2) (amount of company's share capital determining whether county court has jurisdiction to wind it up);

section 120(3) (the equivalent as respects sheriff court jurisdiction in Scotland);

section 123(1)(*a*) (minimum debt for service of demand on company by unpaid creditor);

section 184(3) (minimum value of judgment, affecting sheriff's duties on levying execution);

section 206(1)(*a*) and (*b*) (minimum value of company property concealed or fraudulently removed, affecting criminal liability of company's officer).

(2) An order under this section may contain such transitional provisions as may appear to the Secretary of State necessary or expedient.

(3) No order under this section increasing or reducing any of the money sums for the time being specified in section 117(2), 120(3) or 123(1)(*a*) shall be made unless a draft of the order has been laid before and approved by a resolution of each House of Parliament.

(4) A statutory instrument containing an order under this section, other than an order to which subsection (3) applies, is subject to annulment in pursuance of a resolution of either House of Parliament.

Definition

"property": s.346.

GENERAL NOTE

This section corresponds to s.664 of the Companies Act, as amended by para. 49 of Sched. 6 to the 1985 Act. The section empowers the Secretary of State to amend the monetary limits applicable under the sections specified in subs. (1). Two different procedures are specified for the adoption of orders made under this section. Any order made in relation to the sums specified in ss.117(2), 120(3) or 123(1)(*a*) is by subs. (3) required to undergo the "positive" procedure for adoption by each House of Parliament. Orders other than those to which subs. (3) applies are by subs. (4) made subject to the "negative" procedure only.

Money sum in s.222

417. The Secretary of State may by regulations in a statutory instrument increase or reduce the money sum for the time being specified in section 222(1) (minimum debt for service of demand on unregistered company by unpaid creditor); but such regulations shall not be made unless a draft of the statutory instrument containing them has been approved by resolution of each House of Parliament.

DEFINITION

"unregistered company": s.220(1).

GENERAL NOTE

This section corresponds to part of s.667(2) of the Companies Act, and enables the Secretary of State to amend the monetary limit applicable under s.222(1) for service of a statutory demand by an unpaid creditor in relation to an unregistered company. The adjustment of the equivalent limit, specified in s.123(1)(*a*), in relation to companies which qualify as registered companies for the purposes of the Act will take place under the provisions of s.416. In each case, the making of the relevant order requires a "positive" resolution by each House of Parliament (see General Note to s.416).

Monetary limits (bankruptcy)

418.—(1) The Secretary of State may by order prescribe amounts for the purposes of the following provisions in the second Group of Parts—

section 273 (minimum value of debtor's estate determining whether immediate bankruptcy order should be made; small bankruptcies level);

section 346(3) (minimum amount of judgment, determining whether amount recovered on sale of debtor's goods is to be treated as part of his estate in bankruptcy);

section 354(1) and (2) (minimum amount of concealed debt, or value of property concealed or removed, determining criminal liability under the section);

section 358 (minimum value of property taken by a bankrupt out of England and Wales, determining his criminal liability);

section 360(1) (maximum amount of credit which bankrupt may obtain without disclosure of his status);

section 361(2) (exemption of bankrupt from criminal liability for failure to keep proper accounts, if unsecured debts not more than the prescribed minimum);

section 364(2)(*d*) (minimum value of goods removed by the bankrupt, determining his liability to arrest);

and references in the second Group of Parts to the amount prescribed for the purposes of any of those provisions, and references in those provisions to the prescribed amount, are to be construed accordingly.

(2) An order under this section may contain such transitional provisions as may appear to the Secretary of State necessary or expedient.

(3) An order under this section shall be made by statutory instrument subject to annulment in pursuance of a resolution of either House of Parliament.

DEFINITION

"prescribed": s.384 and this section.

APPLICATION

This section does not apply to Scotland (s.440(2)(*c*)).

GENERAL NOTE

This section confers power upon the Secretary of State to prescribe monetary limits for the purposes of the specified sections of the Act. Any order made under this section is by subs. (3) made subject to the "negative" procedure for annulment by either House of Parliament.

This section corresponds to subss. (1) (part), (2) and (3) of s.209 of the 1985 Act.

Insolvency practice

Regulations for purposes of Part XIII

419.—(1) The Secretary of State may make regulations for the purpose of giving effect to Part XIII of this Act; and "prescribed" in that Part means prescribed by regulations made by the Secretary of State.

(2) Without prejudice to the generality of subsection (1) or to any provision of that Part by virtue of which regulations may be made with respect to any matter, regulations under this section may contain—

(*a*) provision as to the matters to be taken into account in determining whether a person is a fit and proper person to act as an insolvency practitioner;

(*b*) provision prohibiting a person from so acting in prescribed cases, being cases in which a conflict of interest will or may arise;

(*c*) provision imposing requirements with respect to—

(i) the preparation and keeping by a person who acts as an insolvency practitioner of prescribed books, accounts and other records, and

(ii) the production of those books, accounts and records to prescribed persons;

(*d*) provision conferring power on prescribed persons—

(i) to require any person who acts or has acted as an insolvency practitioner to answer any inquiry in relation to a case in which he is so acting or has so acted, and

(ii) to apply to a court to examine such a person or any other person on oath concerning such a case;

(*e*) provision making non-compliance with any of the regulations a criminal offence; and

(*f*) such incidental, supplemental and transitional provisions as may appear to the Secretary of State necessary or expedient.

(3) Any power conferred by Part XIII or this Part to make regulations, rules or orders is exercisable by statutory instrument subject to annulment by resolution of either House of Parliament.

(4) Any rule or regulation under Part XIII or this Part may make different provision with respect to different cases or descriptions of cases, including different provision for different areas.

DEFINITIONS

"prescribed": subs. (1).

"records": s.436.

"to act as an insolvency practitioner": s.488.

GENERAL NOTE

This section authorises the making of rules and regulations for the purposes of any of the matters falling within Pt. XIII. It thus governs all references concerning the making of regulations and "prescribed" matters contained in ss.390(3)(*b*), 392(3)(*c*), 393(2)(*b*) and (3), and 5(3), and also any rules made under para. 4(4) of Sched. 7. Subs. (2)(*e*) confers an important power on the Secretary of State to create further criminal offences for non-compliance with any of the regulations to be made in the exercise of his powers under Pt. XIII.

This section corresponds to ss.10, and 11 (part) of the 1985 Act.

Subs. (2)

This subsection indicates a number of particular matters in relation to which the Secretary of State is empowered to make regulations in addition to the more general power conferred on him by the terms of subs. (1). Some of these matters, such as that referred to in para. (*b*) concerning cases of conflict of interest, were originally intended to be governed by provisions of the Act itself. However the complexity of the issues raised by the originally published draft of these provisions was demonstrated on several occasions during the debates to the 1985 Bill on both Houses of Parliament, and it was subsequently decided to leave these matters to be regulated by statutory instrument. Where an insolvency practitioner is a member of a recognised professional body the rules and practices of that body will be directly applicable to determine, for example, whether he or she is a "fit and proper person" as required by s.391(2)(*a*). Similarly, professional bodies generally issue their own guidelines to their members regarding matters where a conflict of interest may arise. However, since it is intended that as far as possible uniform standards should be applicable to all insolvency practitioners, the regulations to be made under paras. (*a*) and (*b*) could become norms in relation to which the rules and practices of each separate professional body will have to be aligned. Alternatively any professional body whose rules and practices fail to match the norms established by the regulations could be denied, or be deprived of, recognition under s.391(1).

Subs. (3)

This prescribes the manner in which regulations, rules or orders are to be made by the Secretary of State in the exercise of the power conferred by Pt. XIII of the Act. The mode of enactment is to be by statutory instrument which is subject to annulment on the adoption of a resolution to that effect by either House of Parliament. This "negative" procedure for enactment of rules and regulations has the effect of requiring a positive, and successful, Parliamentary initiative to be undertaken in order to prevent the instrument from becoming legally effective.

Subs. (4)

This provision effectively widens the scope of the rule making power conferred by subs. (1), so as to authorise the Secretary of State to make separate and different provisions for cases described or classified in different ways. It also confers an authority to treat different areas of the country in accordance with different provisions. The most prominent occasions for the use of this latter power of differentiation will arise in relation to the need to make distinctive provisions with regard to Scotland on the one hand and England and Wales on the other, but the subsection contains no specific limitation in this respect and hence it would be permissible to establish further categories of distinction with reference to area or location, for example as between the London metropolitan area and the rest of the country.

Other order-making powers

Insolvent partnerships

420.—(1) The Lord Chancellor may, by order made with the concurrence of the Secretary of State, provide that such provisions of this Act as may be specified in the order shall apply in relation to insolvent partnerships with such modifications as may be so specified.

(2) An order under this section may make different provision for different cases and may contain such incidental, supplemental and transitional provisions as may appear to the Lord Chancellor necessary or expedient.

(3) An order under this section shall be made by statutory instrument subject to annulment in pursuance of a resolution of either House of Parliament.

Definition
"modifications": s.436.

Application
This section does not apply to Scotland (s.440(2)(*c*)).

General Note
This section confers power upon the Lord Chancellor to apply the provisions of the Act with modifications to the winding up of insolvent partnerships. This power is exercisable by means of statutory instrument subject to the "negative" procedure for annulment by either House of Parliament. This provision removes to the realm of delegated legislation a specialised topic formerly covered by the provisions of ss.33(6), 63(1), 114, 116, 117, 119 and 127 of the Bankruptcy Act 1914 (repealed). The problems associated with this subject are discussed in Chap. 39 of the *Cork Report.*

This section corresponds to s.227 of the 1985 Act.

Insolvent estates of deceased persons

421.—(1) The Lord Chancellor may, by order made with the concurrence of the Secretary of State, provide that such provisions of this Act as may be specified in the order shall apply to the administration of the insolvent estates of deceased persons with such modifications as may be so specified.

(2) An order under this section may make different provision for different cases and may contain such incidental, supplemental and transitional provisions as may appear to the Lord Chancellor necessary or expedient.

(3) An order under this section shall be made by statutory instrument subject to annulment in pursuance of a resolution of either House of Parliament.

(4) For the purposes of this section the estate of a deceased person is insolvent if, when realised, it will be insufficient to meet in full all the debts and other liabilities to which it is subject.

Definitions
"insolvent estate of deceased person": subs. (4).
"modifications": s.436.

Application
This section does not apply to Scotland (s.440(2)(*c*)).

General Note
This section confers power upon the Lord Chancellor to apply the provisions of the Act with modifications to the insolvent estates of deceased persons. This power is exercisable by means of statutory instrument subject to the "negative" procedure for annulment by either House of Parliament. This provision removes to the realm of delegated legislation the provisions with regard to the administration of the estates of deceased insolvents which were formerly contained in s.130 of the Bankruptcy Act 1914 (repealed). Recommendations for improving the legal provisions applicable to such cases were made in Chap. 40 of the *Cork Report.*

This section corresponds to s.228 of the 1985 Act.

Recognised banks, etc.

422.—(1) The Secretary of State may, by order made with the concurrence of the Treasury and after consultation with the Bank of England, provide that such provisions in the first Group of Parts as may be specified in the order shall apply in relation to—

(*a*) recognised banks and licensed institutions within the meaning of the Banking Act 1979, and

(*b*) institutions to which sections 16 and 18 of that Act apply as if they were licensed institutions, with such modifications as may be so specified.

(2) An order under this section may make different provision for different cases and may contain such incidental, supplemental and transitional provisions as may appear to the Secretary of State necessary or expedient.

(3) An order under this section shall be made by statutory instrument subject to annulment in pursuance of a resolution of either House of Parliament.

DEFINITIONS

"modifications": s.436.

"recognised bank or licensed institution": Banking Act 1979, ss.48, 50.

GENERAL NOTE

This section confers power upon the Secretary of State to apply any provisions of the first Group of Parts of the Act to recognised banks and licensed institutions within the meaning of the Banking Act 1979, and to other institutions to which the provisions of that Act apply. This power is exercisable by means of statutory instrument subject to the "negative" procedure for annulment by either House of Parliament. The provision paves the way, following consultation with the Bank of England, for provisions to be made to enable banks and other lending institutions to be wound up, and to become subject to other insolvency procedures, including the Administration Order procedure, using a modified form of the procedures established under this Act. Pending the making of any order under this section, s.8(4)(*b*) prevents the Administration Order procedure from applying to recognised banks and licensed institutions.

This section corresponds to s.229 of the 1985 Act.

PART XVI

PROVISIONS AGAINST DEBT AVOIDANCE (ENGLAND AND WALES ONLY)

Transactions defrauding creditors

423.—(1) This section relates to transactions entered into at an undervalue; and a person enters into such a transaction with another person if—

(*a*) he makes a gift to the other person or he otherwise enters into a transaction with the other on terms that provide for him to receive no consideration;

(*b*) he enters into a transaction with the other in consideration of marriage; or

(*c*) he enters into a transaction with the other for a consideration the value of which, in money or money's worth, is significantly less than the value, in money or money's worth, of the consideration provided by himself.

(2) Where a person has entered into such a transaction, the court may, if satisfied under the next subsection, make such order as it thinks fit for—

(*a*) restoring the position to what it would have been if the transaction had not been entered into, and

(*b*) protecting the interests of persons who are victims of the transaction.

(3) In the case of a person entering into such a transaction, an order shall only be made if the court is satisfied that it was entered into by him for the purpose—

(*a*) of putting assets beyond the reach of a person who is making, or may at some time make, a claim against him, or

(*b*) of otherwise prejudicing the interests of such a person in relation to the claim which he is making or may make.

(4) In this section "the court" means the High Court or—

(*a*) if the person entering into the transaction is an individual, any other court which would have jurisdiction in relation to a bankruptcy petition relating to him;

(*b*) if that person is a body capable of being wound up under Part IV or V of this Act, any other court having jurisdiction to wind it up.

(5) In relation to a transaction at an undervalue, references here and below to a victim of the transaction are to a person who is, or is capable of being, prejudiced by it; and in the following two sections the person entering into the transaction is referred to as "the debtor".

Definitions

"bankruptcy petition": s.381(3).
"the court": subs. (4).
"the debtor": subs. (5).
"transaction": s.436.
"transaction entered into at an undervalue": subs. (1).
"victim of a transaction at an undervalue": subs. (5).

Application

This section does not apply to Scotland (s.440(2)(*c*)).

Transitional Provision

Sched. 11, para. 20.

General Note

This section, together with ss.424 and 425, replaces s.172 of the Law of Property Act 1925, which is repealed. The new provisions enable the court, where a person has entered into a transaction at an undervalue with the purpose of defeating the claims of creditors, to make orders restoring the *status quo ante* and protecting the position of persons prejudiced. The case for the repeal and replacement of s.172 of the Law of Property Act 1925 was convincingly argued in Chap. 28 of the *Cork Report* (see paras. 1210–1220, and 1283–1284). The sections now enacted are designed to operate in harmony with the provisions regarding transactions at an undervalue and preferences contained in ss.238–241 and 339–342, which apply in cases of corporate and of individual insolvency respectively. The definition supplied in each group of sections for the key expression "transaction at an undervalue" is identical for all three, save that, for obvious and logical reasons, there is no counterpart in s.238(4) to the references in ss.339(3)(*b*) and 423(1)(*b*) to entering into a transaction with another person in consideration of marriage.

Ss.423–425 correspond to s.212 of the 1985 Act.

Those who may apply for an order under s.423

424.—(1) An application for an order under section 423 shall not be made in relation to a transaction except—

(*a*) in a case where the debtor has been adjudged bankrupt or is a body corporate which is being wound up or in relation to which an administration order is in force, by the official receiver, by the trustee of the bankrupt's estate or the liquidator or administrator of the body corporate or (with the leave of the court) by a victim of the transaction;

(*b*) in a case where a victim of the transaction is bound by a voluntary arrangement approved under Part I or Part VIII of this Act, by the supervisor of the voluntary arrangement or by any person who (whether or not so bound) is such a victim; or

(*c*) in any other case, by a victim of the transaction.

(2) An application made under any of the paragraphs of subsection (1) is to be treated as made on behalf of every victim of the transaction.

Definitions

"administration order": s.8(2).
"bankrupt": s.381(1).

"estate": ss.283, 385(1).
"supervisor of the voluntary arrangement": ss.7(2) (companies); 263(2) (individuals).
"the administrator": s.8(2).
"the debtor": s.433(5).
"the official receiver": s.399(1).
"transaction": ss.423(1), 436.
"victim of the transaction": s.423(5).
"voluntary arrangement": ss.1(2) (companies); 253(1) (individuals).

APPLICATION

This section does not apply to Scotland (s.440(2)(*c*)).

TRANSITIONAL PROVISION

Sched. 11, para. 20.

GENERAL NOTE

This section, which operates in conjunction with ss.423 and 425, prescribes which persons are allowed to apply for an order under s.423 in respect of a transaction in fraud of creditors, within the meaning of that section. See the General Note to s.423.

Provision which may be made by order under s.423

425.—(1) Without prejudice to the generality of section 423, an order made under that section with respect to a transaction may (subject as follows)—

(*a*) require any property transferred as part of the transaction to be vested in any person, either absolutely or for the benefit of all the persons on whose behalf the application for the order is treated as made;

(*b*) require any property to be so vested if it represents, in any person's hands, the application either of the proceeds of sale of property so transferred or of money so transferred;

(*c*) release or discharge (in whole or in part) any security given by the debtor;

(*d*) require any person to pay to any other person in respect of benefits received from the debtor such sums as the court may direct;

(*e*) provide for any surety or guarantor whose obligations to any person were released or discharged (in whole or in part) under the transaction to be under such new and revived obligations as the court thinks appropriate;

(*f*) provide for security to be provided for the discharge of any obligation imposed by or arising under the order, for such an obligation to be charged on any property and for such security or charge to have the same priority as a security or charge released or discharged (in whole or in part) under the transaction.

(2) An order under section 423 may affect the property of, or impose any obligation on, any person whether or not he is the person with whom the debtor entered into the transaction; but such an order—

(*a*) shall not prejudice any interest in property which was acquired from a person other than the debtor and was acquired in good faith, for value and without notice of the relevant circumstances, or prejudice any interest deriving from such an interest, and

(*b*) shall not require a person who received a benefit from the transaction in good faith, for value and without notice of the relevant circumstances to pay any sum unless he was a party to the transaction.

(3) For the purposes of this section the relevant circumstances in relation to a transaction are the circumstances by virtue of which an order under section 423 may be made in respect of the transaction.

(4) In this section "security" means any mortgage, charge, lien or other security.

DEFINITIONS
"property": s.436.
"security": subs. (4).
"the court": s.423(4).
"the debtor": s.423(5).
"the relevant circumstances": subs. (3).
"transaction": ss.423(1), 436.

APPLICATION
This section does not apply to Scotland (s.440(2)(*c*)).

TRANSITIONAL PROVISION
Sched. 11, para. 20.

GENERAL NOTE
This section, which operates in conjunction with ss.423 and 424, prescribes what matters may be included in an order made by the court in the exercise of its jurisdiction under s.423. See the General Note to s.423.

PART XVII

MISCELLANEOUS AND GENERAL

Co-operation between courts exercising jurisdiction in relation to insolvency

426.—(1) An order made by a court in any part of the United Kingdom in the exercise of jurisdiction in relation to insolvency law shall be enforced in any other part of the United Kingdom as if it were made by a court exercising the corresponding jurisdiction in that other part.

(2) However, without prejudice to the following provisions of this section, nothing in subsection (1) requires a court in any part of the United Kingdom to enforce, in relation to property situated in that part, any order made by a court in any other part of the United Kingdom.

(3) The Secretary of State, with the concurrence in relation to property situated in England and Wales of the Lord Chancellor, may by order make provision for securing that a trustee or assignee under the insolvency law of any part of the United Kingdom has, with such modifications as may be specified in the order, the same rights in relation to any property situated in another part of the United Kingdom as he would have in the corresponding circumstances if he were a trustee or assignee under the insolvency law of that other part.

(4) The courts having jurisdiction in relation to insolvency law in any part of the United Kingdom shall assist the courts having the corresponding jurisdiction in any other part of the United Kingdom or any relevant country or territory.

(5) For the purposes of subsection (4) a request made to a court in any part of the United Kingdom by a court in any other part of the United Kingdom or in a relevant country or territory is authority for the court to which the request is made to apply, in relation to any matters specified in the request, the insolvency law which is applicable by either court in relation to comparable matters falling within its jurisdiction.

In exercising its discretion under this subsection, a court shall have regard in particular to the rules of private international law.

(6) Where a person who is a trustee or assignee under the insolvency law of any part of the United Kingdom claims property situated in any other part of the United Kingdom (whether by virtue of an order under

subsection (3) or otherwise), the submission of that claim to the court exercising jurisdiction in relation to insolvency law in that other part shall be treated in the same manner as a request made by a court for the purpose of subsection (4).

(7) Section 38 of the Criminal Law Act 1977 (execution of warrant of arrest throughout the United Kingdom) applies to a warrant which, in exercise of any jurisdiction in relation to insolvency law, is issued in any part of the United Kingdom for the arrest of a person as it applies to a warrant issued in that part of the United Kingdom for the arrest of a person charged with an offence.

(8) Without prejudice to any power to make rules of court, any power to make provision by subordinate legislation for the purpose of giving effect in relation to companies or individuals to the insolvency law of any part of the United Kingdom includes power to make provision for the purpose of giving effect in that part to any provision made by or under the preceding provisions of this section.

(9) An order under subsection (3) shall be made by statutory instrument subject to annulment in pursuance of a resolution of either House of Parliament.

(10) In this section "insolvency law" means—

(*a*) in relation to England and Wales, provision made by or under this Act or sections 6 to 10, 12, 15, 19(*c*) and 20 (with Schedule 1) of the Company Directors Disqualification Act 1986 and extending to England and Wales;

(*b*) in relation to Scotland, provision extending to Scotland and made by or under this Act, sections 6 to 10, 12, 15, 19(*c*) and 20 (with Schedule 1) of the Company Directors Disqualification Act 1986, Part XVIII of the Companies Act or the Bankruptcy (Scotland) Act 1985;

(*c*) in relation to Northern Ireland, provision made by or under the Bankruptcy Acts (Northern Ireland) 1857 to 1980, Part V, VI or IX of the Companies Act (Northern Ireland) 1960 or Part IV of the Companies (Northern Ireland) Order 1978;

(*d*) in relation to any relevant country or territory, so much of the law of that country or territory as corresponds to provisions falling within any of the foregoing paragraphs;

and references in this subsection to any enactment include, in relation to any time before the coming into force of that enactment the corresponding enactment in force at that time.

(11) In this section "relevant country or territory" means—

(*a*) any of the Channel Islands or the Isle of Man, or

(*b*) any country or territory designated for the purposes of this section by the Secretary of State by order made by statutory instrument.

DEFINITIONS

"insolvency law": subs. (10).
"property": s.436.
"relevant country or territory": subs. (11).

APPLICATION

This section applies to Northern Ireland (s.441(1)(*a*)).

GENERAL NOTE

This section was introduced into the 1985 Insolvency Bill as late as the Report Stage in the House of Commons (H.C. Vol. 83, col. 550), in place of the original, far less extensive clause. It has the effect of replacing the former provisions of ss.121–123 inclusive of the Bankruptcy Act 1914 (repealed) with an extensive and potentially far-reaching provision for inter-jurisdictional co-operation and enforcement of insolvency orders of all kinds, relating to both individual and corporate insolvency. The enactment of such a provision was advocated in Chap. 49 of the *Cork Report* (see esp. paras. 1909–1913).

In the first instance, the effect of the provisions contained in subss. (1)–(10) inclusive is that courts in the United Kingdom are required to enforce orders made by the courts of other United Kingdom jurisdictions in the exercise of jurisdiction in relation to insolvency law. Thus a complete intra-United Kingdom system of reciprocal enforcement is established in respect of bankruptcy, winding up, receivership and the administration order and voluntary arrangement procedures. Similarly, extended effect is given to orders made under the Company Directors Disqualification Act 1986. The provisions ensure that, where property exists in one jurisdiction of the United Kingdom but the insolvency proceedings are taking place in another, all such property can be protected and claimed for the benefit of the insolvent estate's creditors. Care has been taken in the drafting of the provisions however to avoid the anomalous and inelegant provision for automatic vesting of property in another jurisdiction, which was latterly a much-criticised aspect of the terms in which the Bankruptcy Act 1914 was drafted.

This section corresponds to s.213 of the 1985 Act.

Relevant country or territory

A further aspect of the provisions within this section is that they are so designed as to lend themselves to the creation of a framework for international legal co-operation in insolvency matters. This extension results from the inclusion in subs. (5) of reference to a request made to a court in any part of the United Kingdom by a court in "a relevant country or territory" as being a basis of authority for the requested court to provide the assistance referred to in subs. (4), and to apply, in relation to any matters specified in the request, the insolvency law which is applicable by *either* the requested court *or* the requesting court in relation to comparable matters falling within its jurisdiction. Express direction is also given to the requested court to have regard in particular to the rules of private international law. In the definition of "relevant country or territory" supplied by subs. (11) the possibility is established for the Secretary of State by statutory instrument to designate for the purposes of this section any country or territory with which satisfactory arrangements either already exist, or may be concluded in the future, for trans-jurisdictional co-operation in insolvency matters. Thus, not only should it be possible for designations to be accorded to those Commonwealth countries, and remaining colonial territories, with which arrangements have hitherto existed under s.122 of the Bankruptcy Act 1914 (repealed), but in due course an arrangement could be put into effect among the member states of the EEC, and with other states with which the United Kingdom has an established tradition of legal co-operation.

Parliamentary disqualification

427.—(1) Where a court in England and Wales or Northern Ireland adjudges an individual bankrupt or a court in Scotland awards sequestration of an individual's estate, the individual is disqualified—

(*a*) for sitting or voting in the House of Lords,

(*b*) for being elected to, or sitting or voting in, the House of Commons, and

(*c*) for sitting or voting in a committee of either House.

(2) Where an individual is disqualified under this section, the disqualification ceases—

(*a*) except where the adjudication is annulled or the award recalled or reduced without the individual having been first discharged, on the discharge of the individual, and

(*b*) in the excepted case, on the annulment, recall or reduction, as the case may be.

(3) No writ of summons shall be issued to any lord of Parliament who is for the time being disqualified under this section for sitting and voting in the House of Lords.

(4) Where a member of the House of Commons who is disqualified under this section continues to be so disqualified until the end of the period of 6 months beginning with the day of the adjudication or award, his seat shall be vacated at the end of that period.

(5) A court which makes an adjudication or award such as is mentioned in subsection (1) in relation to any lord of Parliament or member of the

House of Commons shall forthwith certify the adjudication or award to the Speaker of the House of Lords or, as the case may be, to the Speaker of the House of Commons.

(6) Where a court has certified an adjudication or award to the Speaker of the House of Commons under subsection (5), then immediately after it becomes apparent which of the following certificates is applicable, the court shall certify to the Speaker of the House of Commons—

(*a*) that the period of 6 months beginning with the day of the adjudication or award has expired without the adjudication or award having been annulled, recalled or reduced, or

(*b*) that the adjudication or award has been annulled, recalled or reduced before the end of that period.

(7) Subject to the preceding provisions of this section, so much of this Act and any other enactment (whenever passed) and of any subordinate legislation (whenever made) as—

(*a*) makes provision for or in connection with bankruptcy in one or more parts of the United Kingdom, or

(*b*) makes provision conferring a power of arrest in connection with the winding up or insolvency of companies in one or more parts of the United Kingdom,

applies in relation to persons having privilege of Parliament or peerage as it applies in relation to persons not having such privilege.

DEFINITIONS

"annulled": s.282.
"bankrupt": s.381(1).
"discharge": ss.279–281 inclusive.

APPLICATION

This section applies to Northern Ireland (s.441(1)(*a*)).

GENERAL NOTE

This section provides for the disqualification of individuals made bankrupt in any part of the United Kingdom for sitting or voting in either House of Parliament and for being elected to the House of Commons; the disqualification continues until the bankruptcy is discharged or annulled. The section further provides for the notification of the bankruptcy of any Member of the House of Commons or Lord of Parliament to the Speaker of the relevant House, and also provides that parliamentary privilege shall not be invokable anywhere in the United Kingdom against the inception of personal insolvency proceedings or against the exercise of any powers of arrest conferred by the Act.

One notable alteration to the law effected by this provision is the removal of the long-standing discrepancy between Scots law and that of England and Wales with regard to the disqualification periods imposed where a Member of Parliament or Peer undergoes sequestration of his estate or is adjudicated bankrupt, as the case may be. In the case of bankruptcy declared in Scotland, a Peer or Member has long been eligible to be elected to, or to sit and vote in the House immediately upon discharge from bankruptcy. In England and Wales and in Northern Ireland a further period of five years' disqualification after the discharge from bankruptcy was formerly imposed upon all Members of either House, and also upon holders of other public offices, by virtue of the extant provisions of bankruptcy statutes of 1871, 1883 and 1890, all of which are repealed by Pt. IV of Sched. 10 to the 1985 Act. This accords with the recommendations in paras. 1849 and 1850 of the *Cork Report* where it is argued that civil rehabilitation of a bankrupt should be made fully effective from the date when his discharge from bankruptcy becomes effective.

This section corresponds to s.214 of the 1985 Act.

Exemptions from Restrictive Trade Practices Act

428.—(1) No restriction in respect of any of the matters specified in the next subsection shall, on or after the appointed day, be regarded as a restriction by virtue of which the Restrictive Trade Practices Act 1976 applies to any agreement (whenever made).

(2) Those matters are—

(*a*) the charges to be made, quoted or paid for insolvency services supplied, offered or obtained;

(*b*) the terms or conditions on or subject to which insolvency services are to be supplied or obtained;

(*c*) the extent (if any) to which, or the scale (if any) on which, insolvency services are to be made available, supplied or obtained;

(*d*) the form or manner in which insolvency services are to be made available, supplied or obtained;

(*e*) the persons or classes of persons for whom or from whom, or the areas or places in or from which, insolvency services are to be made available or supplied or are to be obtained.

(3) In this section "insolvency services" means the services of persons acting as insolvency practitioners or carrying out under the law of Northern Ireland functions corresponding to those mentioned in section 388(1) or (2) in Part XIII, in their capacity as such; and expressions which are also used in the Act of 1976 have the same meaning here as in that Act.

DEFINITIONS

"insolvency services": subs. (3).

"person acting as an insolvency practitioner": s.388.

APPLICATION

This section applies to Northern Ireland (s.441(1)(*a*)).

GENERAL NOTE

This section operates in relation to an amendment inserted in Sched. 1 to the Restrictive Trade Practices Act 1976 by s.217(4) of the 1985 Act, so that the provisions of the Restrictive Trade Practices Act do not apply to the provision of insolvency services under this Act.

This section corresponds to subss. (1)–(3) of s.217 of the 1985 Act.

Disabilities on revocation of administration order against an individual

429.—(1) The following applies where a person fails to make any payment which he is required to make by virtue of an administration order under Part VI of the County Courts Act 1984.

(2) The court which is administering that person's estate under the order may, if it thinks fit—

(*a*) revoke the administration order, and

(*b*) make an order directing that this section and section 12 of the Company Directors Disqualification Act 1986 shall apply to the person for such period, not exceeding 2 years, as may be specified in the order.

(3) A person to whom this section so applies shall not—

(*a*) either alone or jointly with another person, obtain credit to the extent of the amount prescribed for the purposes of section 360(1)(*a*) or more, or

(*b*) enter into any transaction in the course of or for the purposes of any business in which he is directly or indirectly engaged.

without disclosing to the person from whom he obtains the credit, or (as the case may be) with whom the transaction is entered into, the fact that this section applies to him.

(4) The reference in subsection (3) to a person obtaining credit includes—

(*a*) a case where goods are bailed or hired to him under a hire-purchase agreement or agreed to be sold to him under a conditional sale agreement, and

(*b*) a case where he is paid in advance (whether in money or otherwise) for the supply of goods or services.

(5) A person who contravenes this section is guilty of an offence and liable to imprisonment or a fine, or both.

DEFINITIONS

"administration order": County Courts Act 1984, s.112(2).
"business": s.436.
"obtaining credit": subs. (4).
"transaction": s.436.

APPLICATION

Subss. (1) and (2) of this section do not apply to Scotland (s.440(2)(*c*)).

GENERAL NOTE

This section makes provision for the imposition of several of the principal disabilities and disqualifications which apply to an undischarged bankrupt to be made applicable by order to a person who has been the subject of an administration order under the County Courts Act 1984 (Pt. VI). The order whereby these consequences are imposed upon an individual may be made by the court which has been administering the administration order if the court at its discretion decides to revoke that order. The provision is designed to counteract any attempt by a debtor to use the administration order procedure as a delaying tactic against creditors. This section replaces the provisions formerly contained in s.11 of the Insolvency Act 1976 (repealed).

This section corresponds to subss. (1) and (3)–(5) of s.221 of the 1985 Act.

Subss. (3), (4)

These provisions are drafted in terms substantially identical to those of s.360(1), (2) (*q.v.*).

Subs. (5)

Imprisonment or a fine

See Sched. 10 for the levels of punishment which may be imposed in respect of any offences committed under this section.

Provision introducing Schedule of punishments

430.—(1) Schedule 10 to this Act has effect with respect to the way in which offences under this Act are punishable on conviction.

(2) In relation to an offence under a provision of this Act specified in the first column of the Schedule (the general nature of the offence being described in the second column), the third column shows whether the offence is punishable on conviction on indictment, or on summary conviction, or either in the one way or the other.

(3) The fourth column of the Schedule shows, in relation to an offence, the maximum punishment by way of fine or imprisonment under this Act which may be imposed on a person convicted of the offence in the way specified in relation to it in the third column (that is to say, on indictment or summarily), a reference to a period of years or months being to a term of imprisonment of that duration.

(4) The fifth column shows (in relation to an offence for which there is an entry in that column) that a person convicted of the offence after continued contravention is liable to a daily default fine; that is to say, he is liable on a second or subsequent conviction of the offence to the fine specified in that column for each day on which the contravention is continued (instead of the penalty specified for the offence in the fourth column of the Schedule).

(5) For the purpose of any enactment in this Act whereby an officer of a company who is in default is liable to a fine or penalty, the expression "officer who is in default" means any officer of the company who knowingly and wilfully authorises or permits the default, refusal or contravention mentioned in the enactment.

DEFINITIONS

"daily default fine": subs. (4).
"officer of a company": s.251; Companies Act 1985, s.744.
"officer who is in default": subs. (5).

GENERAL NOTE

This section has the effect of causing the Schedule of punishments contained in Sched. 10 to be applicable to offences made punishable by the other provisions of the Act. The section further supplies guidance as to the manner in which the information contained in Sched. 10 is to be interpreted and applied.

This section corresponds to s.730 of the Companies Act and to the general purport of provisions throughout the Act of 1985 relating to offences and punishments.

Subs. (1)

This subsection states that the penalties for the various offences under this Act now are set out in table form in Sched. 10.

Subss. (2)–(4)

These subsections instruct the reader in the use of the table in Sched. 10. Basically it contains five columns which in order across the page state: (1) the section number creating the offence; (2) the general nature of the offence so created; (3) the mode of prosecution; (4) the maximum punishment corresponding with each mode of prosecution; and (5) the daily default fine (where it is applicable). The latter is explained further in subs. (4).

Subs. (4)

This subsection re-enacts what was s.730(4) of the Companies Act. It explains the term "default fine" wherever it appears throughout the Act and particularly in the fifth column of the table in Sched. 10. It is important because it establishes that for continuing offences under the Act a second or subsequent conviction makes the company (and officers when specified—see in particular s.432) liable to the default fine specified in the fifth column of Sched. 10 for each day the contravention continues and *not* for the penalty specified for the offence in column 4. The company and officers in default are not liable to both fines in those instances.

Subs. (5)

This subsection re-enacts what was s.440(2) of the Companies Act 1948. It defines the term "officer in default" wherever that appears in the Companies Acts as any officer who "knowingly and wilfully" authorises or permits what is prohibited by those provisions of the Acts. In criminal law terms the highest form of *mens rea* or guilty mind must be proved (*i.e.* intention as to consequence and knowledge as to circumstances) if a conviction is to be obtained. Proof of any lesser "state of mind" such as recklessness or negligence or inadvertence should not be sufficient.

See *Palmer,* para. 4–21.

Summary proceedings

431.—(1) Summary proceedings for any offence under any of Parts I to VII of this Act may (without prejudice to any jurisdiction exercisable apart from this subsection) be taken against a body corporate at any place at which the body has a place of business, and against any other person at any place at which he is for the time being.

(2) Notwithstanding anything in section 127(1) of the Magistrates' Courts Act 1980, an information relating to such an offence which is triable by a magistrates' court in England and Wales may be so tried if it is laid at any time within 3 years after the commission of the offence and within 12 months after the date on which evidence sufficient in the opinion of the Director of Public Prosecutions or the Secretary of State (as the case may be) to justify the proceedings comes to his knowledge.

(3) Summary proceedings in Scotland for such an offence shall not be commenced after the expiration of 3 years from the commission of the offence.

Subject to this (and notwithstanding anything in section 331 of the Criminal Procedure (Scotland) Act 1975), such proceedings may (in Scotland) be commenced at any time within 12 months after the date on which evidence sufficient in the Lord Advocate's opinion to justify the proceedings came to his knowledge or, where such evidence was reported to him by the Secretary of State, within 12 months after the date on which it came to the knowledge of the latter; and subsection (3) of that section applies for the purpose of this subsection as it applies for the purpose of that section.

(4) For purposes of this section, a certificate of the Director of Public Prosecutions, the Lord Advocate or the Secretary of State (as the case may be) as to the date on which such evidence as is referred to above came to his knowledge is conclusive evidence.

Definitions

"body corporate": s.251; Companies Act 1985, s.740.
"other person": s.432(2), (3).
"place of business": s.251; Companies Act 1985, s.744.

General Note

This section makes provision for the taking of summary proceedings for any offence committed under the provisions of Parts I–VII of the Act, and also prescribes how and where such proceedings are to take place.

This section corresponds to s.731 of the Companies Act and s.108(1) of the 1985 Act.

Subs. (1)

This subsection was s.49(2) of the Companies Act 1967. It states where summary proceedings may be taken against companies and other persons.

Subs. (2)

This subsection was s.49(3) of the 1967 Act. It states the time within which such proceedings must be commenced.

Subs. (3)

This subsection was s.49(4) of the 1967 Act. It states the position relating to the time for commencing such proceedings in Scotland.

Subs. (4)

This subsection was s.49(4) (1967) with the substitution therein of the Secretary of State in place of the Board of Trade as one of the certifying authorities. Note, from an administrative law point of view this subsection is of interest in that it purports to oust the jurisdiction of the court by declaring that the certificate of any of those three authorities is conclusive for purposes of ascertaining when the limitation period commenced to run.

Offences by bodies corporate

432.—(1) This section applies to offences under this Act other than those excepted by subsection (4).

(2) Where a body corporate is guilty of an offence to which this section applies and the offence is proved to have been committed with the consent or connivance of, or to be attributable to any neglect on the part of, any director, manager, secretary or other similar officer of the body corporate or any person who was purporting to act in any such capacity he, as well as the body corporate, is guilty of the offence and liable to be proceeded against and punished accordingly.

(3) Where the affairs of a body corporate are managed by its members, subsection (2) applies in relation to the acts and defaults of a member in connection with his functions of management as if he were a director of the body corporate.

(4) The offences excepted from this section are those under sections 30, 39, 51, 53, 54, 62, 64, 66, 85, 89, 164, 188, 201, 206, 207, 208, 209, 210 and 211.

Definitions

"body corporate": s.251; Companies Act 1985, s.740.
"director": s.251; Companies Act 1985, s.741.

General Note

This section makes provision for certain persons to be guilty of an offence under this Act, with the exception of offences under the sections listed in subs. (4), where a body corporate commits the offence with their consent or connivance or through their neglect.

This section corresponds to s.230 of the 1985 Act.

Admissibility in evidence of statements of affairs, etc.

433. In any proceedings (whether or not under this Act)—

(*a*) a statement of affairs prepared for the purposes of any provision of this Act which is derived from the Insolvency Act 1985, and

(*b*) any other statement made in pursuance of a requirement imposed by or under any such provision or by or under rules made under this Act,

may be used in evidence against any person making or concurring in making the statement.

General Note

This section makes provision for the admissibility in evidence of statements of affairs prepared for the purpose of any provision of the Act which is derived from the 1985 Act, and of any other statement made under a requirement imposed by the Act or by any subsidiary rules. This section largely re-enacts the provisions of s.663(3) of the Companies Act 1985 (repealed) and of the decision in *R.* v. *Pike* [1902] 1 K.B. 552, decided under the Bankruptcy Acts 1883–1890. The making of a statement of affairs may take place under the provisions of ss.22, 47, 66, 131 or 288.

This section corresponds to s.231 of the 1985 Act.

Crown application

434. For the avoidance of doubt it is hereby declared that provisions of this Act which derive from the Insolvency Act 1985 bind the Crown so far as affecting or relating to the following matters, namely—

(*a*) remedies against, or against the property of, companies or individuals;

(*b*) priorities of debts;

(*c*) transactions at an undervalue or preferences;

(*d*) voluntary arrangements approved under Part I or Part VIII, and

(*e*) discharge from bankruptcy.

Definitions

"discharge from bankruptcy": ss.279–281.
"preference": ss.239(4) and 340(3).
"property": s.436.
"transaction at an undervalue": ss.238(4), 339(3), 423(1).
"voluntary arrangement": ss.1(2) (companies); 253(1) (individuals).

General Note

This contains the customary declaration, for the avoidance of doubt, that certain provisions of the Act bind the Crown. The provisions in question are those which derive from the Insolvency Act 1985. Provisions which derive from other legislation consolidated into the present Act will have been previously subject to the Crown application provisions of the statutes from which they are respectively derived.

This section corresponds to s.234 of the 1985 Act.

Part XVIII

Interpretation

Meaning of "associate"

435.—(1) For the purposes of this Act any question whether a person is an associate of another person is to be determined in accordance with the following provisions of this section (any provision that a person is an associate of another person being taken to mean that they are associates of each other).

(2) A person is an associate of an individual if that person is the individual's husband or wife, or is a relative, or the husband or wife of a relative, of the individual or of the individual's husband or wife.

(3) A person is an associate of any person with whom he is in partnership, and of the husband or wife or a relative of any individual with whom he is in partnership; and a Scottish firm is an associate of any person who is a member of the firm.

(4) A person is an associate of any person whom he employs or by whom he is employed.

(5) A person in his capacity as trustee of a trust other than—

(*a*) a trust arising under any of the second Group of Parts or the Bankruptcy (Scotland) Act 1985, or

(*b*) a pension scheme or an employees' share scheme (within the meaning of the Companies Act),

is an associate of another person if the beneficiaries of the trust include, or the terms of the trust confer a power that may be exercised for the benefit of, that other person or an associate of that other person.

(6) A company is an associate of another company—

(*a*) if the same person has control of both, or a person has control of one and persons who are his associates, or he and persons who are his associates, have control of the other, or

(*b*) if a group of two or more persons has control of each company, and the groups either consist of the same persons or could be regarded as consisting of the same persons by treating (in one or more cases) a member of either group as replaced by a person of whom he is an associate.

(7) A company is an associate of another person if that person has control of it or if that person and persons who are his associates together have control of it.

(8) For the purposes of this section a person is a relative of an individual if he is that individual's brother, sister, uncle, aunt, nephew, niece, lineal ancestor or lineal descendant, treating—

(*a*) any relationship of the half blood as a relationship of the whole blood and the stepchild or adopted child of any person as his child, and

(*b*) an illegitimate child as the legitimate child of his mother and reputed father;

and references in this section to a husband or wife include a former husband or wife and a reputed husband or wife.

(9) For the purposes of this section any director or other officer of a company is to be treated as employed by that company.

(10) For the purposes of this section a person is to be taken as having control of a company if—

(*a*) the directors of the company or of another company which has control of it (or any of them) are accustomed to act in accordance with his directions or instructions, or

(*b*) he is entitled to exercise, or control the exercise of, one third or more of the voting power at any general meeting of the company or of another company which has control of it;

and where two or more persons together satisfy either of the above conditions, they are to be taken as having control of the company.

(11) In this section "company" includes any body corporate (whether incorporated in Great Britain or elsewhere); and references to directors and other officers of a company and to voting power at any general meeting of a company have effect with any necessary modifications.

Definitions

"associate": this section.
"body corporate": s.251; Companies Act 1985, s.740.
"company": subs. (11).
"director": s.251; Companies Act 1985, s.741.
"modifications": s.436.
"officer": s.251; Companies Act 1985, s.744.

General Note

This elaborately drafted section supplies the statutory meaning of the word "associate" where used in this Act. The section applies to Scotland, but doubts were expressed during debate to the Insolvency Bill 1985 in the House of Lords whether the concept of "associate" now embodied in this Act would cover all the cases formerly caught under Scots law by the expression "conjunct or confident person" (*Hansard,* H.L. Vol. 459, cols. 1271–1272). *Cf.* Chap. 21 of the *Cork Report,* entitled "Connected Persons."

This section corresponds to s.233 of the 1985 Act.

Expressions used generally

436. In this Act, except in so far as the context otherwise requires (and subject to Parts VII and XI)—

"the appointed day" means the day on which this Act comes into force under section 443;
"associate" has the meaning given by section 435;
"business" includes a trade or profession;
"the Companies Act" means the Companies Act 1985;
"conditional sale agreement" and "hire-purchase agreement" have the same meanings as in the Consumer Credit Act 1974;
"modifications" includes additions, alterations and omissions and cognate expressions shall be construed accordingly;
"property" includes money, goods, things in action, land and every description of property wherever situated and also obligations and every description of interest whether present or future or vested or contingent, arising out of, or incidental to, property;
"records" includes computer records and other non-documentary records;
"subordinate legislation" has the same meaning as in the Interpretation Act 1978; and
"transaction" includes a gift, agreement or arrangement, and references to entering into a transaction shall be construed accordingly.

General Note

This is the definition section with respect to the entire Act, and supplies the statutory meaning of terms and expressions which are used in a consistent sense throughout the Act. Other definition sections, whose provisions are applicable only to a specific part of the Act, are found at ss.247–251 and 380–385.

This section corresponds in part to s.232 of the 1985 Act.

Part XIX

Final Provisions

Transitional provisions and savings

437. The transitional provisions and savings set out in Schedule 11 to this Act shall have effect, the Schedule comprising the following Parts—

Part I: company insolvency and winding up (matters arising before appointed day, and continuance of proceedings in certain cases as before that day);

Part II: individual insolvency (matters so arising, and continuance of bankruptcy proceedings in certain cases as before that day);

Part III: transactions entered into before the appointed day and capable of being affected by orders of the court under Part XVI of this Act;

Part IV: insolvency practitioners acting as such before the appointed day; and

Part V: general transitional provisions and savings required consequentially on, and in connection with, the repeal and replacement by this Act and the Company Directors Disqualification Act 1986 of provisions of the Companies Act, the greater part of the Insolvency Act 1985 and other enactments.

Definitions

"appointed day": s.443.

"insolvency practitioners": s.288.

General Note

This section, which has no identical counterpart in either the 1985 Act or the Companies Act, gives effect to the transitional provisions and savings set out in Sched. 11. It also explains the general structure of that Schedule, which is subdivided into five parts.

Repeals

438. The enactments specified in the second column of Schedule 12 to this Act are repealed to the extent specified in the third column of that Schedule.

General Note

This section, which has no idential counterpart in either the 1985 Act or the Companies Act, gives effect to the repeals listed in Sched. 12. In addition to effecting the repeal of most of the provisions of the 1985 Act (apart from those provisions which are to be repealed by the separate provisions of the Company Directors Disqualification Act 1986), this section together with Sched. 12 effects the repeal of s.235(3) of, and Sched. 10 to, the 1985 Act. However, before the present Act, and its repealing provisions, enter into force by virtue of s.443, the repeals of other legislation which take place under Sched. 10 to the 1985 Act will already have been accomplished through the bringing into force of that Schedule by means of commencement orders made under s.236(2) of the 1985 Act.

Amendments of enactments

439.—(1) The Companies Act is amended as shown in Parts I and II of Schedule 13 to this Act, being amendments consequential on this Act and the Company Directors Disqualification Act 1986.

(2) The enactments specified in the first column of Schedule 14 to this Act (being enactments which refer, or otherwise relate, to those which are repealed and replaced by this Act or the Company Directors Disqualification Act 1986) are amended as shown in the second column of that Schedule.

(3) The Lord Chancellor may by order make such consequential modifications of any provision contained in any subordinate legislation made before the appointed day and such transitional provisions in connection with those modifications as appear to him necessary or expedient in respect of—

(*a*) any reference in that subordinate legislation to the Bankruptcy Act 1914;

(*b*) any reference in that subordinate legislation to any enactment repealed by Part III or IV of Schedule 10 to the Insolvency Act 1985; or

(*c*) any reference in that subordinate legislation to any matter provided for under the Act of 1914 or under any enactment so repealed.

(4) An order under this section shall be made by statutory instrument subject to annulment in pursuance of a resolution of either House of Parliament.

Definitions

"appointed day": s.443.
"modification": s.436.

General Note

This section, which has no identical counterpart in either the 1985 Act or the Companies Act, gives effect to the amendments to the Companies Act which are contained in Sched. 13. These amendments are consequential on the provisions of this Act and those of the Company Directors Disqualification Act 1986. Power is also conferred upon the Lord Chancellor, under subs. (3), to make consequential modifications of any subordinate legislation made before the day on which this Act enters into force. Any order so made by the Lord Chancellor is, by virtue of subs. (4), subject to the "negative" procedure for annulment by resolution of either House of Parliament.

Extent (Scotland)

440.—(1) Subject to the next subsection, provisions of this Act contained in the first Group of Parts extend to Scotland except where otherwise stated.

(2) The following provisions of this Act do not extend to Scotland—

(*a*) in the first Group of Parts—
section 43;
sections 238 to 241; and
section 246;

(*b*) the second Group of Parts;

(*c*) in the third Group of Parts—
sections 399 to 402,
sections 412, 413, 415, 418, 420 and 421,
sections 423 to 425, and
section 429(1) and (2); and

(*d*) in the Schedules—
Parts II and III of Schedule 11; and
Schedules 12 and 14 so far as they repeal or amend enactments which extend to England and Wales only.

General Note

This section indicates which sections or Parts of this Act do, and which do not, extend to Scotland. The section corresponds to s.236(3) of the 1985 Act.

Subss. (1), (2)(a)

These provide that all provisions in Parts I–VII apply to Scotland, with the exception of the provisions contained in ss.43, 238–241 and 246. However, in s.28 it is provided that Chap. I of Pt. III does not apply to receivers appointed under Chap. II of the same Part.

Subs. (2)(b)

This provides that none of the provisions in Parts VIII–XI extend to Scotland.

Subs. (2)(c), (d)

These provide that the specified sections within Parts XII–XIX and the specified Parts or provisions of Scheds. 11 and 12 do not extend to Scotland.

Extent (Northern Ireland)

441.—(1) The following provisions of this Act extend to Northern Ireland—

(*a*) sections 197, 426, 427 and 428; and

(*b*) so much of section 439 and Schedule 14 as relates to enactments which extend to Northern Ireland.

(2) Subject as above, and to any provision expressly relating to companies incorporated elsewhere than in Great Britain, nothing in this Act extends to Northern Ireland or applies to or in relation to companies registered or incorporated in Northern Ireland.

General Note

This section has the effect that nothing in the Act, with the exception of the provisions mentioned in subs. (1), extends to Northern Ireland or applies to or in relation to companies registered or incorporated there. The section corresponds to s.236(4) of the 1985 Act and s.745 of the Companies Act.

Extent (other territories)

442. Her Majesty may, by Order in Council, direct that such of the provisions of this Act as are specified in the Order, being provisions formerly contained in the Insolvency Act 1985, shall extend to any of the Channel Islands or any colony with such modifications as may be so specified.

Definition

"modifications": s.436.

General Note

This section makes provision for the extended application of certain provisions of this Act to any of the Channel Islands or any colony. This power is exercisable by the Queen by means of an Order in Council, and may be made in respect of any provisions now contained in this Act which were formerly contained in the 1985 Act.

Commencement

443. This Act comes into force on the day appointed under section 236(2) of the Insolvency Act 1985 for the coming into force of Part III of that Act (individual insolvency and bankruptcy), immediately after that Part of that Act comes into force for England and Wales.

General Note

This section, which has no exact counterpart in the 1985 Act, provides for the commencement of the Act. The provision is somewhat unusual in that it provides for the Act as a whole to come into force on a day to be appointed in relation to the commencement of a specified Part of another Act, namely Part III of the 1985 Act. The technique thus employed will ensure that this Act enters into force at the earliest practicable date, which is a matter essentially dependent upon the completion of the entire range of subordinate legislation which will operate in conjunction with the new insolvency law provisions contained in this Act. The 1985 Act has served as an indispensable adjunct to the process of preparation of the various new Rules, Orders and Regulations, but for the most part their actual operation will take place under the aegis of the Insolvency Act 1986. Accordingly, the setting of an appointed day under s.236(2) of the 1985 Act with regard to Part III of that Act will enable the 1985 Act itself to come fully into force, albeit briefly, whereupon the 1986 Act will displace it by virtue of the provisions in this section, in conjunction with the repealing provisions within s.438 and Sched. 12 (*q.v.*).

Citation

444. This Act may be cited as the Insolvency Act 1986.

General Note

This section provides for the citation of the Act.

SCHEDULES

Sections 14, 42

SCHEDULE 1

Powers of Administrator or Administrative Receiver

1. Power to take possession of, collect and get in the property of the company and, for that purpose, to take such proceedings as may seem to him expedient.
2. Power to sell or otherwise dispose of the property of the company by public auction or private contract or, in Scotland, to sell, feu, hire out or otherwise dispose of the property of the company by public roup or private bargain.
3. Power to raise or borrow money and grant security therefor over the property of the company.
4. Power to appoint a solicitor or accountant or other professionally qualified person to assist him in the performance of his functions.
5. Power to bring or defend any action or other legal proceedings in the name and on behalf of the company.
6. Power to refer to arbitration any question affecting the company.
7. Power to effect and maintain insurances in respect of the business and property of the company.
8. Power to use the company's seal.
9. Power to do all acts and to execute in the name and on behalf of the company any deed, receipt or other document.
10. Power to draw, accept, make and endorse any bill of exchange or promissory note in the name and on behalf of the company.
11. Power to appoint any agent to do any business which he is unable to do himself or which can more conveniently be done by an agent and power to employ and dismiss employees.
12. Power to do all such things (including the carrying out of works) as may be necessary for the realisation of the property of the company.
13. Power to make any payment which is necessary or incidental to the performance of his functions.
14. Power to carry on the business of the company.
15. Power to establish subsidiaries of the company.
16. Power to transfer to subsidiaries of the company the whole or any part of the business and property of the company.
17. Power to grant or accept a surrender of a lease or tenancy of any of the property of the company, and to take a lease or tenancy of any property required or convenient for the business of the company.
18. Power to make any arrangement or compromise on behalf of the company.
19. Power to call up any uncalled capital of the company.
20. Power to rank and claim in the bankruptcy, insolvency, sequestration or liquidation of any person indebted to the company and to receive dividends, and to accede to trust deeds for the creditors of any such person.
21. Power to present or defend a petition for the winding up of the company.
22. Power to change the situation of the company's registered office.
23. Power to do all other things incidental to the exercise of the foregoing powers.

General Note

This Schedule is linked to ss.14 and 42, which are respectively concerned with the powers of administrators and administrative receivers. A common table of provisions is thus enacted to define the powers which are conferred upon persons holding either of these offices under this Act. This is an appropriate, and a somewhat symbolic, way of acknowledging the fact that the office of administrator has been inspired by, and created as an analogy to, that of the administrative receiver when operated in an enlightened and even an altruistic manner.

This Schedule corresponds to Sched 3 to the 1985 Act.

Section 55

SCHEDULE 2

Powers of a Scottish Receiver (Additional to Those Conferred on him by the Instrument of Charge)

1. Power to take possession of, collect and get in the property from the company or a liquidator thereof or any other person, and for that purpose, to take such proceedings as may seem to him expedient.
2. Power to sell, feu, hire out or otherwise dispose of the property by public roup or private bargain and with or without advertisement.
3. Power to raise or borrow money and grant security therefor over the property.
4. Power to appoint a solicitor or accountant or other professionally qualified person to assist him in the performance of his functions.
5. Power to bring or defend any action or other legal proceedings in the name and on behalf of the company.
6. Power to refer to arbitration all questions affecting the company.
7. Power to effect and maintain insurances in respect of the business and property of the company.
8. Power to use the company's seal.
9. Power to do all acts and to execute in the name and on behalf of the company any deed, receipt or other document.
10. Power to draw, accept, make and endorse any bill of exchange or promissory note in the name and on behalf of the company.
11. Power to appoint any agent to do any business which he is unable to do himself or which can more conveniently be done by an agent, and power to employ and dismiss employees.
12. Power to do all such things (including the carrying out of works), as may be necessary for the realisation of the property.
13. Power to make any payment which is necessary or incidental to the performance of his functions.
14. Power to carry on the business of the company or any part of it.
15. Power to grant or accept a surrender of a lease or tenancy of any of the property, and to take a lease or tenancy of any property required or convenient for the business of the company.
16. Power to make any arrangement or compromise on behalf of the company.
17. Power to call up any uncalled capital of the company.
18. Power to establish subsidiaries of the company.
19. Power to transfer to subsidiaries of the company the business of the company or any part of it and any of the property.
20. Power to rank and claim in the bankruptcy, insolvency, sequestration or liquidation of any person or company indebted to the company and to receive dividends, and to accede to trust deeds for creditors of any such person.
21. Power to present or defend a petition for the winding up of the company.
22. Power to change the situation of the company's registered office.
23. Power to do all other things incidental to the exercise of the powers mentioned in section 55(1) of this Act or above in this Schedule.

General Note

This Schedule is linked to s.55, which is concerned with the powers of a receiver appointed under a floating charge in Scotland. The list of powers corresponds to that formerly contained in s.471(1) of the Companies Act, as amended by s.57 of the 1985 Act.

Section 162

SCHEDULE 3

Orders in Course of Winding Up Pronounced in Vacation (Scotland)

Part I

Orders Which are to be Final

Orders under section 153, as to the time for proving debts and claims.

Orders under section 195 as to meetings for ascertaining wishes of creditors or contributories.

Orders under section 198, as to the examination of witnesses in regard to the property or affairs of a company.

Part II

Orders Which are to take Effect Until Matter Disposed of by Inner House

Orders under section 126(1), 130(2) or (3) 147, 227 or 228, restraining or permitting the commencement or the continuance of legal proceedings.

Orders under section 135(5), limiting the powers of provisional liquidators.

Orders under section 108, appointing a liquidator to fill a vacancy.

Orders under section 167 or 169, sanctioning the exercise of any powers by a liquidator, other than the powers specified in paragraphs 1, 2 and 3 of Schedule 4 to this Act.

Orders under section 158, as to the arrest and detention of an absconding contributory and his property.

General Note

This Schedule corresponds to Sched. 16 to the Companies Act. It operates in conjunction with s.162, which governs appeals from orders in Scotland, and has the effect of indicating which orders of the vacation judge are to be final, and which are to take effect until the matter has been submitted to review by the Inner House and the matter there disposed of.

Sections 165, 167

SCHEDULE 4

Powers of Liquidator in a Winding Up

Part I

Powers Exercisable with Sanction

1. Power to pay any class of creditors in full.

2. Power to make any compromise or arrangement with creditors or persons claiming to be creditors, or having or alleging themselves to have any claim (present or future, certain or contingent, ascertained or sounding only in damages) against the company, or whereby the company may be rendered liable.

3. Power to compromise, on such terms as may be agreed—

(*a*) all calls and liabilities to calls, all debts and liabilities capable of resulting in debts, and all claims (present or future, certain or contingent, ascertained or sounding only in damages) subsisting or supposed to subsist between the company and a contributory or alleged contributory or other debtor or person apprehending liability to the company, and

(*b*) all questions in any way relating to or affecting the assets or the winding up of the company,

and take any security for the discharge of any such call, debt, liability or claim and give a complete discharge in respect of it.

Part II

Powers Exercisable Without Sanction in Voluntary Winding Up, with Sanction in Winding Up by the Court

4. Power to bring or defend any action or other legal proceeding in the name and on behalf of the company.

5. Power to carry on the business of the company so far as may be necessary for its beneficial winding up.

Part III

Powers Exercisable Without Sanction in any Winding Up

6. Power to sell any of the company's property by public auction or private contract, with power to transfer the whole of it to any person or to sell the same in parcels.

7. Power to do all acts and execute, in the name and on behalf of the company, all deeds, receipts and other documents and for that purpose to use, when necessary, the company's seal.

8. Power to prove, rank and claim in the bankruptcy, insolvency or sequestration of any contributory for any balance against his estate, and to receive dividends in the bankruptcy, insolvency or sequestration in respect of that balance, as a separate debt due from the bankrupt or insolvent, and rateably with the other separate creditors.

9. Power to draw, accept, make and indorse any bill of exchange or promissory note in the name and on behalf of the company, with the same effect with respect to the company's liability as if the bill or note had been drawn, accepted, made or indorsed by or on behalf of the company in the course of its business.

10. Power to raise on the security of the assets of the company any money requisite.

11. Power to take out in his official name letters of administration to any deceased contributory, and to do in his official name any other act necessary for obtaining payment of any money due from a contributory or his estate which cannot conveniently be done in the name of the company.

In all such cases the money due is deemed, for the purpose of enabling the liquidator to take out the letters of administration or recover the money, to be due to the liquidator himself.

12. Power to appoint an agent to do any business which the liquidator is unable to do himself.

13. Power to do all such other things as may be necessary for winding up the company's affairs and distributing its assets.

General Note

This Schedule operates in conjunction with ss.165 and 167, which refer to the powers of a liquidator in a voluntary and in a compulsory winding up respectively. Pt. I of the Schedule assimilates the provisions formerly contained in ss.539(*d*)–(*f*) and 598(1); Pt. II those formerly contained in ss.539(1)(*a*),(*b*) and 598(2); and Pt. III those formerly contained in ss.539(2) and 598(2) of the Companies Act. The three Parts of the Schedule now set out in a convenient form, and with greatly improved clarity, the powers exercisable by a liquidator with or without sanction (as defined in ss.165, 166 and 167 respectively) under the different forms of winding up.

Section 314

SCHEDULE 5

Powers of Trustee in Bankruptcy

Part I

Powers Exercisable with Sanction

1. Power to carry on any business of the bankrupt so far as may be necessary for winding it up beneficially and so far as the trustee is able to do so without contravening any requirement imposed by or under any enactment.

2. Power to bring, institute or defend any action or legal proceedings relating to the property comprised in the bankrupt's estate.

3. Power to accept as the consideration for the sale of any property comprised in the bankrupt's estate a sum of money payable at a future time subject to such stipulations as to security or otherwise as the creditors' committee or the court thinks fit.

4. Power to mortgage or pledge any part of the property comprised in the bankrupt's estate for the purpose of raising money for the payment of his debts.

5. Power, where any right, option or other power forms part of the bankrupt's estate, to make payments or incur liabilities with a view to obtaining, for the benefit of the creditors, any property which is the subject of the right, option or power.

6. Power to refer to arbitration, or compromise on such terms as may be agreed on, any debts, claims or liabilities subsisting or supposed to subsist between the bankrupt and any person who may have incurred any liability to the bankrupt.

7. Power to make such compromise or other arrangement as may be thought expedient with creditors, or persons claiming to be creditors, in respect of bankruptcy debts.

8. Power to make such compromise or other arrangement as may be thought expedient with respect to any claim arising out of or incidental to the bankrupt's estate made or capable of being made on the trustee by any person or by the trustee on any person.

Part II

General Powers

9. Power to sell any part of the property for the time being comprised in the bankrupt's estate, including the goodwill and book debts of any business.

10. Power to give receipts for any money received by him, being receipts which effectually discharge the person paying the money from all responsibility in respect of its application.

11. Power to prove, rank, claim and draw a dividend in respect of such debts due to the bankrupt as are comprised in his estate.

12. Power to exercise in relation to any property comprised in the bankrupt's estate any powers the capacity to exercise which is vested in him under Parts VIII to XI of this Act.

13. Power to deal with any property comprised in the estate to which the bankrupt is beneficially entitled as tenant in tail in the same manner as the bankrupt might have dealt with it.

Part III

Ancillary Powers

14. For the purposes of, or in connection with, the exercise of any of his powers under Parts VIII to XI of this Act, the trustee may, by his official name—

(*a*) hold property of every description,
(*b*) make contracts,
(*c*) sue and be sued,
(*d*) enter into engagements binding on himself and, in respect of the bankrupt's estate, on his successors in office,
(*e*) employ an agent,
(*f*) execute any power of attorney, deed or other instrument;

and he may do any other act which is necessary or expedient for the purposes of or in connection with the exercise of those powers.

General Note

This Schedule operates in conjunction with s.314, which refers to the powers of a trustee in bankruptcy. Pt. I of the Schedule assimilates the provisions of s.160(2), Pt. II those of s.160(1), and Pt. III those of s.160(6) of the 1985 Act. The three Parts together indicate which powers are exercisable by the trustee with sanction (*i.e.* with the permission of the creditors' committee if there is one, or otherwise with the permission of the court: s.314(1)(*a*)) and which are exercisable on the trustee's own initiative without that permission (s.314(1)(*b*)).

Section 386

SCHEDULE 6

The Categories of Preferential Debts

Category 1: Debts due to Inland Revenue

1. Sums due at the relevant date from the debtor on account of deductions of income tax from emoluments paid during the period of 12 months next before that date.

The deductions here referred to are those which the debtor was liable to make under section 204 of the Income and Corporation Taxes Act 1970 (pay as you earn), less the amount of the repayments of income tax which the debtor was liable to make during that period.

2. Sums due at the relevant date from the debtor in respect of such deductions as are required to be made by the debtor for that period under section 69 of the Finance (No. 2) Act 1975 (sub-contractors in the construction industry).

Category 2: Debts due to Customs and Excise

3. Any value added tax which is referable to the period of 6 months next before the relevant date (which period is referred to below as "the 6-month period").

For the purposes of this paragraph—

(*a*) where the whole of the prescribed accounting period to which any value added tax is attributable falls within the 6-month period, the whole amount of that tax is referable to that period; and

(*b*) in any other case the amount of any value added tax which is referable to the 6-month period is the proportion of the tax which is equal to such proportion (if any) of the accounting reference period in question as falls within the 6-month period;

and in sub-paragraph (*a*) "prescribed" means prescribed by regulations under the Value Added Tax Act 1983.

4. The amount of any car tax which is due at the relevant date from the debtor and which became due within a period of 12 months next before that date.

5. Any amount which is due—

(*a*) by way of general betting duty or bingo duty, or

(*b*) under section 12(1) of the Betting and Gaming Duties Act 1981 (general betting duty and pool betting duty recoverable from agent collecting stakes), or

(*c*) under section 14 of, or Schedule 2 to, that Act (gaming licence duty),

from the debtor at the relevant date and which became due within the period of 12 months next before that date.

Category 3: Social security contributions

6. All sums which on the relevant date are due from the debtor on account of Class 1 or Class 2 contributions under the Social Security Act 1975 or the Social Security (Northern Ireland) Act 1975 and which became due from the debtor in the 12 months next before the relevant date.

7. All sums which on the relevant date have been assessed on and are due from the debtor on account of Class 4 contributions under either of those Acts of 1975, being sums which—

(*a*) are due to the Commissioners of Inland Revenue (rather than to the Secretary of State or a Northern Ireland department), and

(*b*) are assessed on the debtor up to 5th April next before the relevant date,

but not exceeding, in the whole, any one year's assessment.

Category 4: Contributions to occupational pension schemes, etc.

8. Any sum which is owed by the debtor and is a sum to which Schedule 3 to the Social Security Pensions Act 1975 applies (contributions to occupational pension schemes and state scheme premiums).

Category 5: Remuneration, etc., of employees

9. So much of any amount which—

(*a*) is owed by the debtor to a person who is or has been an employee of the debtor, and

(*b*) is payable by way of remuneration in respect of the whole or any part of the period of 4 months next before the relevant date,

as does not exceed so much as may be prescribed by order made by the Secretary of State.

10. An amount owed by way of accrued holiday remuneration, in respect of any period of employment before the relevant date, to a person whose employment by the debtor has been terminated, whether before, on or after that date.

11. So much of any sum owed in respect of money advanced for the purpose as has been applied for the payment of a debt which, if it had not been paid, would have been a debt falling within paragraph 9 or 10.

12. So much of any amount which—

(*a*) is ordered (whether before or after the relevant date) to be paid by the debtor under the Reserve Forces (Safeguard of Employment) Act 1985, and

(*b*) is so ordered in respect of a default made by the debtor before that date in the discharge of his obligations under that Act,

as does not exceed such amount as may be prescribed by order made by the Secretary of State.

Interpretation for Category 5

13.—(1) For the purposes of paragraphs 9 to 12, a sum is payable by the debtor to a person by way of remuneration in respect of any period if—

(*a*) it is paid as wages or salary (whether payable for time or for piece work or earned wholly or partly by way of commission) in respect of services rendered to the debtor in that period, or

(*b*) it is an amount falling within the following sub-paragraph and is payable by the debtor in respect of that period.

(2) An amount falls within this sub-paragraph if it is—

(*a*) a guarantee payment under section 12(1) of the Employment Protection (Consolidation) Act 1978 (employee without work to do for a day or part of a day);

(*b*) remuneration on suspension on medical grounds under section 19 of that Act;

(*c*) any payment for time off under section 27(3) (trade union duties), 31(3) (looking for work, etc.) or 31A(4) (ante-natal care) of that Act; or

(*d*) remuneration under a protective award made by an industrial tribunal under section 101 of the Employment Protection Act 1975 (redundancy dismissal with compensation).

14.—(1) This paragraph relates to a case in which a person's employment has been terminated by or in consequence of his employer going into liquidation or being adjudged bankrupt or (his employer being a company not in liquidation) by or in consequence of—

(*a*) a receiver being appointed as mentioned in section 40 of this Act (debenture-holders secured by floating charge), or

(*b*) the appointment of a receiver under section 53(6) or 54(5) of this Act (Scottish company with property subject to floating charge), or

(*c*) the taking of possession by debenture-holders (so secured), as mentioned in section 196 of the Companies Act.

(2) For the purposes of paragraphs 9 to 12, holiday remuneration is deemed to have accrued to that person in respect of any period of employment if, by virtue of his contract of employment or of any enactment that remuneration would have accrued in respect of that period if his employment had continued until he became entitled to be allowed the holiday.

(3) The reference in sub-paragraph (2) to any enactment includes an order or direction made under an enactment.

15. Without prejudice to paragraphs 13 and 14—

(*a*) any remuneration payable by the debtor to a person in respect of a period of holiday or of absence from work through sickness or other good cause is deemed to be wages or (as the case may be) salary in respect of services rendered to the debtor in that period, and

(*b*) references here and in those paragraphs to remuneration in respect of a period of holiday include any sums which, if they had been paid, would have been treated for the purposes of the enactments relating to social security as earnings in respect of that period.

Orders

16. An order under paragraph 9 or 12—
(*a*) may contain such transitional provisions as may appear to the Secretary of State necessary or expedient;
(*b*) shall be made by statutory instrument subject to annulment in pursuance of a resolution of either House of Parliament.

Definitions
"accrued holiday remuneration": para. 14.
"preferential debt","preferential creditor": s.386(1).
"prescribed": paras. 3, 9, 12.
"remuneration in respect of a period of holiday": para. 15.
"the debtor": s.386(2).
"the relevant date": s.387.
"sum payable by way of remuneration in respect of a period": para. 13.

General Note
This Schedule, which operates in conjunction with s.386, provides a list of preferential debts applicable on a common basis in winding up and in bankruptcy, and incorporated into the workings of Pts. IV and IX of the Act respectively by means of the provisions of ss.175 and 328. For details of the significant changes in the categories of debts which now are accorded preferential status in insolvency proceedings, see the General Notes to the two sections referred to, especially the former. Paras. 13–15 supply the definitions of various words or expressions for the purposes of the Schedule.
This Schedule corresponds to Pt. I, and paras. 2–4 of Pt. II, of Sched. 4 to the 1985 Act.

Section 396

SCHEDULE 7

Insolvency Practitioners Tribunal

Panels of members

1.—(1) The Secretary of State shall draw up and from time to time revise—
(*a*) a panel of persons who are barristers, advocates or solicitors, in each case of not less than 7 years' standing, and are nominated for the purpose by the Lord Chancellor or the Lord President of the Court of Session, and
(*b*) a panel of persons who are experienced in insolvency matters;
and the members of the Tribunal shall be selected from those panels in accordance with this Schedule.
(2) The power to revise the panels includes power to terminate a person's membership of either of them, and is accordingly to that extent subject to section 8 of the Tribunals and Inquiries Act 1971 (which makes it necessary to obtain the concurrence of the Lord Chancellor and the Lord President of the Court of Session to dismissals in certain cases).

Remuneration of members

2. The Secretary of State may out of money provided by Parliament pay to members of the Tribunal such remuneration as he may with the approval of the Treasury determine; and such expenses of the Tribunal as the Secretary of State and the Treasury may approve shall be defrayed by the Secretary of State out of money so provided.

Sittings of Tribunal

3.—(1) For the purposes of carrying out their functions in relation to any cases referred to them, the Tribunal may sit either as a single tribunal or in two or more divisions.
(2) The functions of the Tribunal in relation to any case referred to them shall be exercised by three members consisting of—

(*a*) a chairman selected by the Secretary of State from the panel drawn up under paragraph 1(1)(*a*) above, and
(*b*) two other members selected by the Secretary of State from the panel drawn up under paragraph 1(1)(*b*).

Procedure of Tribunal

4.—(1) Any investigation by the Tribunal shall be so conducted as to afford a reasonable opportunity for representations to be made to the Tribunal by or on behalf of the person whose case is the subject of the investigation.

(2) For the purposes of any such investigation, the Tribunal—

(*a*) may by summons require any person to attend, at such time and place as is specified in the summons, to give evidence or to produce any books, papers and other records in his possession or under his control which the Tribunal consider it necessary for the purposes of the investigation to examine, and
(*b*) may take evidence on oath, and for the purpose administer oaths, or may, instead of administering an oath, require the person examined to make and subscribe a declaration of the truth of the matter respecting which he is examined;

but no person shall be required, in obedience to such a summons, to go more than ten miles from his place of residence, unless the necessary expenses of his attendance are paid or tendered to him.

(3) Every person who—

(*a*) without reasonable excuse fails to attend in obedience to a summons issued under this paragraph, or refuses to give evidence, or
(*b*) intentionally alters, suppresses, conceals or destroys or refuses to produce any document which he may be required to produce for the purpose of an investigation by the Tribunal,

is liable to a fine.

(4) Subject to the provisions of this paragraph, the Secretary of State may make rules for regulating the procedure on any investigation by the Tribunal.

(5) In their application to Scotland, sub-paragraphs (2) and (3) above have effect as if for any reference to a summons there were substituted a reference to a notice in writing.

General Note

This Schedule, which operates in conjunction with s.396, deals with the composition, functions and procedures of the Insolvency Practitioners Tribunal, whose purpose is to consider and determine appeals which are referred to it under s.396 in cases where an applicant for, or holder of, an authorisation to practice as an insolvency practitioner has been notified that the relevant authority proposes to refuse the application, or to withdraw the authorisation, as the case may be.

Although the Schedule contains rules which govern the procedure of the Tribunal in performing its investigative function, provision is made in para. 4(4) for the Secretary of State to make additional rules for regulating this procedure.

This Schedule corresponds to paras. 1–4 of Sched. 1 to the 1985 Act.

Section 411

SCHEDULE 8

Provisions Capable of Inclusion in Company Insolvency Rules

Courts

1. Provision for supplementing, in relation to the insolvency or winding up of companies, any provision made by or under section 117 of this Act (jurisdiction in relation to winding up).

2. Provision for regulating the practice and procedure of any court exercising jurisdiction for the purposes of Parts I to VII of this Act or the Companies Act so far as relating to, and to matters connected with or arising out of, the insolvency or winding up of companies, being any provision that could be made by rules of court.

Notices, etc.

3. Provision requiring notice of any proceedings in connection with or arising out of the insolvency or winding up of a company to be given or published in the manner prescribed by the rules.

4. Provision with respect to the form, manner of serving, contents and proof of any petition, application, order, notice, statement or other document required to be presented, made, given, published or prepared under any enactment or subordinate legislation relating to, or to matters connected with or arising out of, the insolvency or winding up of companies.

5. Provision specifying the persons to whom any notice is to be given.

Registration of voluntary arrangements

6. Provision for the registration of voluntary arrangements approved under Part I of this Act, including provision for the keeping and inspection of a register.

Provisional liquidator

7. Provision as to the manner in which a provisional liquidator appointed under section 135 is to carry out his functions.

Conduct of insolvency

8. Provision with respect to the certification of any person as, and as to the proof that a person is, the liquidator, administrator or administrative receiver of a company.

9. The following provisions with respect to meetings of a company's creditors, contributories or members—

(*a*) provision as to the manner of summoning a meeting (including provision as to how any power to require a meeting is to be exercised, provision as to the manner of determining the value of any debt or contribution for the purposes of any such power and provision making the exercise of any such power subject to the deposit of a sum sufficient to cover the expenses likely to be incurred in summoning and holding a meeting);

(*b*) provision specifying the time and place at which a meeting may be held and the period of notice required for a meeting;

(*c*) provision as to the procedure to be followed at a meeting (including the manner in which decisions may be reached by a meeting and the manner in which the value of any vote at a meeting is to be determined);

(*d*) provision for requiring a person who is or has been an officer of the company to attend a meeting;

(*e*) provision creating, in the prescribed circumstances, a presumption that a meeting has been duly summoned and held;

(*f*) provision as to the manner of proving the decisions of a meeting.

10.—(1) Provision as to the functions, membership and proceedings of a committee established under section 26, 49, 68, 101, 141 or 142 of this Act.

(2) The following provisions with respect to the establishment of a committee under section 101, 141 or 142 of this Act, that is to say—

(*a*) provision for resolving differences between a meeting of the company's creditors and a meeting of its contributories or members;

(*b*) provision authorising the establishment of the committee without a meeting of contributories in a case where a company is being wound up on grounds including its inability to pay its debts; and

(*c*) provision modifying the requirements of this Act with respect to the establishment of the committee in a case where a winding-up order has been made immediately upon the discharge of an administration order.

11. Provision as to the manner in which any requirement that may be imposed on a person under any of Parts I to VII of this Act by the official receiver, the liquidator, administrator or administrative receiver of a company or a special manager appointed under section 177 is to be so imposed.

12. Provision as to the debts that may be proved in a winding up, as to the manner and conditions of proving a debt and as to the manner and expenses of establishing the value of any debt or security.

13. Provision with respect to the manner of the distribution of the property of a company that is being wound up, including provision with respect to unclaimed funds and dividends.

14. Provision which, with or without modifications, applies in relation to the winding up of companies any enactment contained in Parts VIII to XI of this Act or in the Bankruptcy (Scotland) Act 1985.

Financial provisions

15. Provision as to the amount, or manner of determining the amount, payable to the liquidator, administrator or administrative receiver of a company or a special manager appointed under section 177, by way of remuneration for the carrying out of functions in connection with or arising out of the insolvency or winding up of a company.

16. Provision with respect to the manner in which moneys received by the liquidator of a company in the course of carrying out his functions as such are to be invested or otherwise handled and with respect to the payment of interest on sums which, in pursuance of rules made by virtue of this paragraph, have been paid into the Insolvency Services Account.

17. Provision as to the fees, costs, charges and other expenses that may be treated as the expenses of a winding up.

18. Provision as to the fees, costs, charges and other expenses that may be treated as properly incurred by the administrator or administrative receiver of a company.

19. Provision as to the fees, costs, charges and other expenses that may be incurred for any of the purposes of Part I of this Act or in the administration of any voluntary arrangement approved under that Part.

Information and records

20. Provision requiring registrars and other officers of courts having jurisdiction in England and Wales in relation to, or to matters connected with or arising out of, the insolvency or winding up of companies—

(*a*) to keep books and other records with respect to the exercise of that jurisdiction, and

(*b*) to make returns to the Secretary of State of the business of those courts.

21. Provision requiring a creditor, member or contributory, or such a committee as is mentioned in paragraph 10 above, to be supplied (on payment in prescribed cases of the prescribed fee) with such information and with copies of such documents as may be prescribed.

22. Provision as to the manner in which public examinations under sections 133 and 134 of this Act and proceedings under sections 236 and 237 are to be conducted, as to the circumstances in which records of such examinations or proceedings are to be made available to prescribed persons and as to the costs of such examinations and proceedings.

23. Provision imposing requirements with respect to—

(*a*) the preparation and keeping by the liquidator, administrator or administrative receiver of a company, or by the supervisor of a voluntary arrangement approved under Part I of this Act, of prescribed books, accounts and other records;

(*b*) the production of those books, accounts and records for inspection by prescribed persons;

(*c*) the auditing of accounts kept by the liquidator, administrator or administrative receiver of a company, or the supervisor of such a voluntary arrangement; and

(*d*) the issue by the administrator or administrative receiver of a company of such a certificate as is mentioned in section 22(3)(*b*) of the Value Added Tax Act 1983 (refund of tax in cases of bad debts) and the supply of copies of the certificate to creditors of the company.

24. Provision requiring the person who is the supervisor of a voluntary arrangement approved under Part I, when it appears to him that the voluntary arrangement has been fully implemented and that nothing remains to be done by him under the arrangement—

(*a*) to give notice of that fact to persons bound by the voluntary arrangement, and

(*b*) to report to those persons on the carrying out of the functions conferred on the supervisor of the arrangement.

25. Provision as to the manner in which the liquidator of a company is to act in relation to the books, papers and other records of the company, including provision authorising their disposal.

26. Provision imposing requirements in connection with the carrying out of functions under section 7(3) of the Company Directors Disqualification Act 1986 (including, in particular, requirements with respect to the making of periodic returns).

General

27. Provision conferring power on the Secretary of State to make regulations with respect to so much of any matter that may be provided for in the rules as relates to the carrying out of the functions of the liquidator, administrator or administrative receiver of a company.

28. Provision conferring a discretion on the court.

29. Provision conferring power on the court to make orders for the purpose of securing compliance with obligations imposed by or under section 22, 47, 66, 131, 143(2) or 235 of this Act or section 7(4) of the Company Directors Disqualification Act 1986.

30. Provision making non-compliance with any of the rules a criminal offence.

31. Provision making different provision for different cases or descriptions of cases, including different provisions for different areas.

Definition

"liquidator": s.411(3).

General Note

This is a general enabling Schedule to authorise the making of secondary legislation in the form of company insolvency rules, to be made by statutory instrument under s.411(4). The various matters in respect of which such rules may make provision are indicated in the various paragraphs. Para. 27 authorises the inclusion within the Rules of subsidiary enabling provisions to authorise the Secretary of State to make regulations with respect to further matters to be specified. Such regulations will also be made by statutory instrument, pursuant to the authority conferred by s.411(5).

This Schedule corresponds to Sched. 5 to the 1985 Act.

Section 412

SCHEDULE 9

Provisions Capable of Inclusion in Individual Insolvency Rules

Courts

1. Provision with respect to the arrangement and disposition of the business under Parts VIII to XI of this Act of courts having jurisdiction for the purpose of those Parts, including provision for the allocation of proceedings under those Parts to particular courts and for the transfer of such proceedings from one court to another.

2. Provision for enabling a registrar in bankruptcy of the High Court or a registrar of a county court having jurisdiction for the purposes of those Parts to exercise such of the jurisdiction conferred for those purposes on the High Court or, as the case may be, that county court as may be prescribed.

3. Provision for regulating the practice and procedure of any court exercising jurisdiction for the purposes of those Parts, being any provision that could be made by rules of court.

4. Provision conferring rights of audience, in courts exercising jurisdiction for the purposes of those Parts, on the official receiver and on solicitors.

Notices, etc.

5. Provision requiring notice of any proceedings under Parts VIII to XI of this Act or of any matter relating to or arising out of a proposal under Part VIII or a bankruptcy to be given or published in the prescribed manner.

6. Provision with respect to the form, manner of serving, contents and proof of any petition, application, order, notice, statement or other document required to be presented, made, given, published or prepared under any enactment contained in Parts VIII to XI or subordinate legislation under those Parts or Part XV (including provision requiring prescribed matters to be verified by affidavit).

7. Provision specifying the persons to whom any notice under Parts VIII to XI is to be given.

Registration of voluntary arrangements

8. Provision for the registration of voluntary arrangements approved under Part VIII of this Act, including provision for the keeping and inspection of a register.

Interim receiver

9. Provision as to the manner in which an interim receiver appointed under section 286 is to carry out his functions, including any such provision as is specified in relation to the trustee of a bankrupt's estate in paragraph 21 or 27 below.

Receiver or manager

10. Provision as to the manner in which the official receiver is to carry out his functions as receiver or manager of a bankrupt's estate under section 287, including any such provision as is specified in relation to the trustee of a bankrupt's estate in paragraph 21 or 27 below.

Administration of individual insolvency

11. Provision with respect to the certification of the appointment of any person as trustee of a bankrupt's estate and as to the proof of that appointment.

12. The following provision with respect to meetings of creditors—

(*a*) provision as to the manner of summoning a meeting (including provision as to how any power to require a meeting is to be exercised, provision as to the manner of determining the value of any debt for the purposes of any such power and provision making the exercise of any such power subject to the deposit of a sum sufficient to cover the expenses likely to be incurred in summoning and holding a meeting);

(*b*) provision specifying the time and place at which a meeting may be held and the period of notice required for a meeting;

(*c*) provision as to the procedure to be followed at such a meeting (including the manner in which decisions may be reached by a meeting and the manner in which the value of any vote at a meeting is to be determined);

(*d*) provision for requiring a bankrupt or debtor to attend a meeting;

(*e*) provision creating, in the prescribed circumstances, a presumption that a meeting has been duly summoned and held; and

(*f*) provision as to the manner of proving the decisions of a meeting.

13. Provision as to the functions, membership and proceedings of a creditors' committee established under section 301.

14. Provision as to the manner in which any requirement that may be imposed on a person under Parts VIII to XI of this Act by the official receiver, the trustee of a bankrupt's estate or a special manager appointed under section 370 is to be so imposed and, in the case of any requirement imposed under section 305(3) (information etc. to be given by the trustee to the official receiver), provision conferring power on the court to make orders for the purpose of securing compliance with that requirement.

15. Provision as to the manner in which any requirement imposed by virtue of section 310(3) (compliance with income payments order) is to take effect.

16. Provision as to the terms and conditions that may be included in a charge under section 313 (dwelling house forming part of bankrupt's estate).

17. Provision as to the debts that may be proved in any bankruptcy, as to the manner and conditions of proving a debt and as to the manner and expenses of establishing the value of any debt or security.

18. Provision with respect to the manner of the distribution of a bankrupt's estate, including provision with respect to unclaimed funds and dividends.

19. Provision modifying the application of Parts VIII to XI of this Act in relation to a debtor or bankrupt who has died.

Financial provisions

20. Provision as to the amount, or manner of determining the amount, payable to an interim receiver, the trustee of a bankrupt's estate or a special manager appointed under section 370 by way of remuneration for the performance of functions in connection with or arising out of the bankruptcy of any person.

21. Provision with respect to the manner in which moneys received by the trustee of a bankrupt's estate in the course of carrying out his functions as such are to be handled.

22. Provision as to the fees, costs, charges and other expenses that may be treated as the expenses of a bankruptcy.

23. Provision as to the fees, costs, charges and other expenses that may be incurred for any of the purposes of Part VIII of this Act or in the administration of any voluntary arrangement approved under that Part.

Information and records

24. Provision requiring registrars and other officers of courts having jurisdiction for the purposes of Parts VIII to XI—

(*a*) to keep books and other records with respect to the exercise of that jurisdiction and of jurisdiction under the Deeds of Arrangement Act 1914, and

(*b*) to make returns to the Secretary of State of the business of those courts.

25. Provision requiring a creditor or a committee established under section 301 to be supplied (on payment in prescribed cases of the prescribed fee) with such information and with copies of such documents as may be prescribed.

26. Provision as to the manner in which public examinations under section 290 and proceedings under sections 366 to 368 are to be conducted, as to the circumstances in which records of such examinations and proceedings are to be made available to prescribed persons and as to the costs of such examinations and proceedings.

27. Provision imposing requirements with respect to—

(*a*) the preparation and keeping by the trustee of a bankrupt's estate, or the supervisor of a voluntary arrangement approved under Part VIII, of prescribed books, accounts and other records;

(*b*) the production of those books, accounts and records for inspection by prescribed persons; and

(*c*) the auditing of accounts kept by the trustee of a bankrupt's estate or the supervisor of such a voluntary arrangement.

28. Provision requiring the person who is the supervisor of a voluntary arrangement approved under Part VIII, when it appears to him that the voluntary arrangement has been fully implemented and that nothing remains to be done by him under it—

(*a*) to give notice of that fact to persons bound by the voluntary arrangement, and

(*b*) to report to those persons on the carrying out of the functions conferred on the supervisor of it.

29. Provision as to the manner in which the trustee of a bankrupt's estate is to act in relation to the books, papers and other records of the bankrupt, including provision authorising their disposal.

General

30. Provision conferring power on the Secretary of State to make regulations with respect to so much of any matter that may be provided for in the rules as relates to the carrying out of the functions of an interim receiver appointed under section 286, of the official receiver while acting as a receiver or manager under section 287 or of a trustee of a bankrupt's estate.

31. Provision conferring a discretion on the court.

32. Provision making non-compliance with any of the rules a criminal offence.

33. Provision making different provision for different cases, including different provision for different areas.

General Note

This is a general enabling Schedule to authorise the making of secondary legislation in the form of individual insolvency rules, to be made by statutory instrument under s.412. The various matters in respect of which such rules may make provision are indicated in the various paragraphs. Para. 30 authorises the inclusion within the Rules of subsidiary enabling provisions to authorise the Secretary of State to make regulations with respect to further matters to be specified. Such regulations will also be made by statutory instrument pursuant to the authority conferred by s.412(4).

This Schedule corresponds to Sched. 7 to the 1985 Act.

Section 430

SCHEDULE 10

Punishment of Offences under this Act

Note: In the fourth and fifth columns of this Schedule, "the statutory maximum" means—
(a) in England and Wales, the prescribed sum under section 32 of the Magistrates' Courts Act 1980 (c. 43), and
(b) in Scotland, the prescribed sum under section 289B of the Criminal Procedure (Scotland) Act 1975 (c. 21).

Section of Act creating offence	General nature of offence	Mode of prosecution	Punishment	Daily default fine (where applicable)
12(2)	Company and others failing to state in correspondence etc. that administrator appointed.	Summary.	One-fifth of the statutory maximum.	
15(8)	Failure of administrator to register office copy of court order permitting disposal of charged property.	Summary.	One-fifth of the statutory maximum.	One-fiftieth of the statutory maximum.
18(5)	Failure of administrator to register office copy of court order varying or discharging administration order.	Summary.	One-fifth of the statutory maximum.	One-fiftieth of the statutory maximum.
21(3)	Administrator failing to register administration order and give notice of appointment.	Summary.	One-fifth of the statutory maximum.	One-fiftieth of the statutory maximum.
22(6)	Failure to comply with provisions relating to statement of affairs, where administrator appointed.	1. On indictment. 2. Summary.	A fine. The statutory maximum	 One-tenth of the statutory maximum.
23(3)	Administrator failing to send out, register and lay before creditors statement of his proposals.	Summary.	One-fifth of the statutory maximum.	One-fiftieth of the statutory maximum.
24(7)	Administrator failing to file court order discharging administration order under s.24.	Summary.	One-fifth of the statutory maximum.	One-fiftieth of the statutory maximum.
27(6)	Administrator failing to file court order discharging administration order under s.27.	Summary.	One-fifth of the statutory maximum.	One-fiftieth of the statutory maximum.
30	Body corporate acting as receiver.	1. On indictment. 2. Summary.	A fine. The statutory maximum.	

Section of Act creating offence	General nature of offence	Mode of prosecution	Punishment	Daily default fine (where applicable)
31	Undischarged bankrupt acting as receiver or manager.	1. On indictment. 2. Summary.	2 years or a fine, or both. 6 months or the statutory maximum, or both.	
38(5)	Receiver failing to deliver accounts to registrar.	Summary.	One-fifth of the statutory maximum.	One-fiftieth of the statutory maximum.
39(2)	Company and others failing to state in correspondence that receiver appointed.	Summary.	One-fifth of the statutory maximum.	
43(6)	Administrative receiver failing to file office copy of order permitting disposal of charged property.	Summary.	One-fifth of the statutory maximum.	One-fiftieth of the statutory maximum.
45(5)	Administrative receiver failing to file notice of vacation of office.	Summary.	One-fifth of the statutory maximum.	One-fiftieth of the statutory maximum.
46(4)	Administrative receiver failing to give notice of his appointment.	Summary.	One-fifth of the statutory maximum.	One-fiftieth of the statutory maximum.
47(6)	Failure to comply with provisions relating to statement of affairs where administrative receiver appointed.	1. On indictment. 2. Summary.	A fine. The statutory maximum.	 One-tenth of the statutory maximum.
48(8)	Administrative receiver failing to comply with requirements as to his report.	Summary.	One-fifth of the statutory maximum.	One-fiftieth of the statutory maximum.
51(4)	Body corporate or Scottish firm acting as receiver.	1. On indictment. 2. Summary.	A fine. The statutory maximum.	
51(5)	Undischarged bankrupt acting as receiver (Scotland).	1. On indictment. 2. Summary.	2 years or a fine, or both. 6 months or the statutory maximum, or both.	
53(2)	Failing to deliver to registrar copy of instrument of appointment of receiver.	Summary.	One-fifth of the statutory maximum.	One-fiftieth of the statutory maximum.
54(3)	Failing to deliver to registrar the court's interlocutor appointing receiver.	Summary.	One-fifth of the statutory maximum.	One-fiftieth of the statutory maximum.

Section of Act creating offence	General nature of offence	Mode of prosecution	Punishment	Daily default fine (where applicable)
61(7)	Receiver failing to send to registrar certified copy of court order authorising disposal of charged property.	Summary.	One-fifth of the statutory maximum.	One-fiftieth of the statutory maximum.
62(5)	Failing to give notice to registrar of cessation or removal of receiver.	Summary.	One-fifth of the statutory maximum.	One-fiftieth of the statutory maximum.
64(2)	Company and others failing to state on correspondence etc. that receiver appointed.	Summary.	One-fifth of the statutory maximum.	
65(4)	Receiver failing to send or publish notice of his appointment.	Summary.	One-fifth of the statutory maximum.	One-fiftieth of the statutory maximum.
66(6)	Failing to comply with provisions concerning statement of affairs, where receiver appointed.	1. On indictment. 2. Summary.	A fine. The statutory maximum.	 One-tenth of the statutory maximum.
67(8)	Receiver failing to comply with requirements as to his report.	Summary.	One-fifth of the statutory maximum.	One-fiftieth of the statutory maximum.
85(2)	Company failing to give notice in Gazette of resolution for voluntary winding up.	Summary.	One-fifth of the statutory maximum.	One-fiftieth of the statutory maximum.
89(4)	Director making statutory declaration of company's solvency without reasonable grounds for his opinion.	1. On indictment. 2. Summary.	2 years or a fine, or both. 6 months or the statutory maximum, or both.	
89(6)	Declaration under section 89 not delivered to registrar within prescribed time.	Summary.	One-fifth of the statutory maximum.	One-fiftieth of the statutory maximum.
93(3)	Liquidator failing to summon general meeting of company at each year's end.	Summary.	One-fifth of the statutory maximum.	
94(4)	Liquidator failing to send to registrar a copy of account of winding up and return of final meeting.	Summary.	One-fifth of the statutory maximum.	One-fiftieth of the statutory maximum.
94(6)	Liquidator failing to call final meeting.	Summary.	One-fifth of the statutory maximum.	
95(8)	Liquidator failing to comply with s.95, where company insolvent.	Summary.	The statutory maximum.	

Section of Act creating offence	General nature of offence	Mode of prosecution	Punishment	Daily default fine (where applicable)
98(6)	Company failing to comply with s.98 in respect of summoning and giving notice of creditors' meeting.	1. On indictment. 2. Summary.	A fine. The statutory maximum.	
99(3)	Directors failing to attend and lay statement in prescribed form before creditors' meeting.	1. On indictment. 2. Summary.	A fine. The statutory maximum.	
105(3)	Liquidator failing to summon company general meeting and creditors' meeting at each year's end.	Summary.	One-fifth of the statutory maximum.	
106(4)	Liquidator failing to send to registrar account of winding up and return of final meetings.	Summary.	One-fifth of the statutory maximum.	One-fiftieth of the statutory maximum.
106(6)	Liquidator failing to call final meeting of company or creditors.	Summary.	One-fifth of the statutory maximum.	
109(2)	Liquidator failing to publish notice of his appointment.	Summary.	One-fifth of the statutory maximum.	One-fiftieth of the statutory maximum.
114(4)	Directors exercising powers in breach of s.114, where no liquidator.	Summary.	The statutory maximum.	
131(7)	Failing to comply with requirements as to statement of affairs, where liquidator appointed.	1. On indictment. 2. Summary.	A fine. The statutory maximum.	One-tenth of the statutory maximum.
164	Giving, offering etc. corrupt inducement affecting appointment of liquidator.	1. On indictment. 2. Summary.	A fine. The statutory maximum.	
166(7)	Liquidator failing to comply with requirements of s.166 in creditors' voluntary winding up.	Summary.	The statutory maximum.	
188(2)	Default in compliance with s.188 as to notification that company being wound up.	Summary.	One-fifth of the statutory maximum.	
192(2)	Liquidator failing to notify registrar as to progress of winding up.	Summary.	One-fifth of the statutory maximum.	One-fiftieth of the statutory maximum.
201(4)	Failing to deliver to registrar office copy of court order deferring dissolution.	Summary.	One-fifth of the statutory maximum.	One-fiftieth of the statutory maximum.
203(6)	Failing to deliver to registrar copy of directions or result of appeal under s.203.	Summary.	One-fifth of the statutory maximum.	One-fiftieth of the statutory maximum.

Section of Act creating offence	General nature of offence	Mode of prosecution	Punishment	Daily default fine (where applicable)
204(7)	Liquidator failing to deliver to registrar copy of court order for early dissolution.	Summary.	One-fifth of the statutory maximum.	One-fiftieth of the statutory maximum.
204(8)	Failing to deliver to registrar copy of court order deferring early dissolution.	Summary.	One-fifth of the statutory maximum.	One-fiftieth of the statutory maximum.
205(7)	Failing to deliver to registrar copy of Secretary of State's directions or court order deferring dissolution.	Summary.	One-fifth of the statutory maximum.	One-fiftieth of the statutory maximum.
206(1)	Fraud etc. in anticipation of winding up.	1. On indictment. 2. Summary.	7 years or a fine, or both. 6 months or the statutory maximum, or both.	
206(2)	Privity to fraud in anticipation of winding up; fraud, or privity to fraud, after commencement of winding up.	1. On indictment. 2. Summary.	7 years or a fine, or both. 6 months or the statutory maximum, or both.	
206(5)	Knowingly taking in pawn or pledge, or otherwise receiving, company property.	1. On indictment. 2. Summary.	7 years or a fine, or both. 6 months or the statutory maximum, or both.	
207	Officer of company entering into transaction in fraud of company's creditors.	1. On indictment. 2. Summary.	2 years or a fine, or both. 6 months or the statutory maximum, or both.	
208	Officer of company misconducting himself in course of winding up.	1. On indictment. 2. Summary.	7 years or a fine, or both. 6 months or the statutory maximum, or both.	
209	Officer or contributory destroying, falsifying, etc. company's books.	1. On indictment. 2. Summary.	7 years or a fine, or both. 6 months or the statutory maximum, or both.	
210	Officer of company making material omission from statement relating to company's affairs.	1. On indictment. 2. Summary.	7 years or a fine, or both. 6 months or the statutory maximum, or both.	
211	False representation or fraud for purpose of obtaining creditors' consent to an agreement in connecton with winding up.	1. On indictment. 2. Summary.	7 years or a fine, or both. 6 months or the statutory maximum, or both.	

Section of Act creating offence	General nature of offence	Mode of prosecution	Punishment	Daily default fine (where applicable)
216(4)	Contravening restrictions on re-use of name of company in insolvent liquidation.	1. On indictment. 2. Summary.	2 years or a fine, or both. 6 months or the statutory maximum, or both.	
235(5)	Failing to co-operate with office-holder.	1. On indictment. 2. Summary.	A fine. The statutory maximum.	One-tenth of the statutory maximum.
353(1)	Bankrupt failing to disclose property or disposals to official receiver or trustee.	1. On indictment. 2. Summary.	7 years or a fine, or both. 6 months or the statutory maximum, or both.	
354(1)	Bankrupt failing to deliver property to, or concealing property from, official receiver or trustee.	1. On indictment. 2. Summary.	7 years or a fine, or both. 6 months or the statutory maximum, or both.	
354(2)	Bankrupt removing property which he is required to deliver to official receiver or trustee.	1. On indictment. 2. Summary.	7 years or a fine, or both. 6 months or the statutory maximum, or both.	
354(3)	Bankrupt failing to account for loss of substantial part of property.	1. On indictment. 2. Summary.	2 years or a fine, or both. 6 months or the statutory maximum, or both.	
355(1)	Bankrupt failing to deliver books, papers and records to official receiver or trustee.	1. On indictment. 2. Summary.	7 years or a fine, or both. 6 months or the statutory maximum, or both.	
355(2)	Bankrupt concealing, destroying etc. books, papers or records, or making false entries in them.	1. On indictment. 2. Summary.	7 years or a fine, or both. 6 months or the statutory maximum, or both.	
355(3)	Bankrupt disposing of, or altering, books, papers or records relating to his estate or affairs.	1. On indictment. 2. Summary.	7 years or a fine, or both. 6 months or the statutory maximum, or both.	
356(1)	Bankrupt making material omission in statement relating to his affairs.	1. On indictment. 2. Summary.	7 years or a fine, or both. 6 months or the statutory maximum, or both.	

Section of Act creating offence	General nature of offence	Mode of prosecution	Punishment	Daily default fine (where applicable)
356(2)	Bankrupt making false statement, or failing to inform trustee, where false debt proved.	1. On indictment. 2. Summary.	7 years or a fine, or both. 6 months or the statutory maximum, or both.	
357	Bankrupt fraudulently disposing of property.	1. On indictment. 2. Summary.	2 years or a fine, or both. 6 months or the statutory maximum, or both.	
358	Bankrupt absconding with property he is required to deliver to official receiver or trustee.	1. On indictment. 2. Summary.	2 years or a fine, or both. 6 months or the statutory maximum, or both.	
359(1)	Bankrupt disposing of property obtained on credit and not paid for.	1. On indictment. 2. Summary.	7 years or a fine, or both. 6 months or the statutory maximum, or both.	
359(2)	Obtaining property in respect of which money is owed by a bankrupt.	1. On indictment. 2. Summary.	7 years or a fine, or both. 6 months or the statutory maximum, or both.	
360(1)	Bankrupt obtaining credit or engaging in business without disclosing his status or name in which he was made bankrupt.	1. On indictment. 2. Summary.	2 years or a fine, or both. 6 months or the statutory maximum, or both.	
360(3)	Person made bankrupt in Scotland or Northern Ireland obtaining credit, etc. in England and Wales.	1. On indictment. 2. Summary.	2 years or a fine, or both. 6 months or the statutory maximum, or both.	
361(1)	Bankrupt failing to keep proper accounting records.	1. On indictment. 2. Summary.	2 years or a fine, or both. 6 months or the statutory maximum, or both.	
362	Bankrupt increasing extent of insolvency by gambling.	1. On indictment. 2. Summary.	2 years or a fine, or both. 6 months or the statutory maximum, or both.	
389	Acting as insolvency practitioner when not qualified.	1. On indictment. 2. Summary.	2 years or a fine, or both. 6 months or the statutory maximum, or both.	

Section of Act creating offence	General nature of offence	Mode of prosecution	Punishment	Daily default fine (where applicable)
429(5)	Contravening s.429 in respect of disabilities imposed by county court on revocation of administration order.	1. On indictment. 2. Summary.	2 years or a fine, or both. 6 months or the statutory maximum, or both.	
Sch. 7, para. 4(3)	Failure to attend and give evidence to Insolvency Practitioners Tribunal; suppressing, concealing, etc. relevant documents.	Summary.	Level 3 on the standard scale within the meaning given by section 75 of the Criminal Justice Act 1982.	

DEFINITIONS

"officer who is in default": s.430(5).
"period of months": s.430(3).
"period of years": s.430(3).
"the statutory maximum": *Note* at head of this Schedule.

GENERAL NOTE

This Schedule, which operates in conjunction with s.430, constitutes a complete table of the punishments which may be imposed for conviction of any offence under any provision of this Act. The Schedule collects together provisions regarding levels of punishment which were previously dispersed throughout the provisions of the 1985 Act and the Companies Act, and in Part of Sched. 24 to the latter.

It is indicated in s.430 that the first column of this Schedule specifies the respective sections of the Act, totalling 78 in all, under which criminal offences are created. The general nature of each offence is described, alongside the section number, in the second column. The third column shows whether the offence is triable by either or both of the two modes of trial (summary or on indictment), while the fourth column shows the maximum punishment by way of a fine or imprisonment which may be imposed upon conviction, according to the mode of trial employed. The fifth column shows (where relevant) the level of the daily default fine which may be imposed upon a person convicted of the offence after continued contravention. (See also the General Note to s.430, esp. to subs. (4) thereof.)

Where the prescribed penalty consists of, or may include, a fine, the amount of the fine is expressed in columns four and five in terms of a specified percentage of "the statutory maximum." As is explained in the *Note* placed at the beginning of the Schedule, this expression means, in England and Wales, the prescribed sum under s.32 of the Magistrates' Courts Act 1980 (c.43), and in Scotland, the prescribed sum under s.289B of the Criminal Procedure (Scotland) Act 1975 (c.21). These two sections authorise the Secretary of State at his discretion to substitute by order such other sum as appears to him to be justified by the change in the value of money since the last occasion when the prescribed sum was fixed. Currently, the prescribed statutory maximum in each jurisdiction is £2,000: see Criminal Penalties, etc. (Increase) Order 1984 (S.I. 1984 No. 447) and Increase of Criminal Penalties etc. (Scotland) Order 1984 (S.I. 1984 No. 526).

Section 437

SCHEDULE 11

TRANSITIONAL PROVISIONS AND SAVINGS

PART I

COMPANY INSOLVENCY AND WINDING UP

Administration orders

1.—(1) Where any right to appoint an administrative receiver of a company is conferred by any debentures or floating charge created before the appointed day, the conditions precedent to the exercise of that right are deemed to include the presentation of a petition applying for an administration order to be made in relation to the company.

(2) "Administrative receiver" here has the meaning assigned by section 251.

Receivers and managers (England and Wales)

2.—(1) In relation to any receiver or manager of a company's property who was appointed before the appointed day, the new law does not apply; and the relevant provisions of the former law continue to have effect.

(2) "The new law" here means Chapter I of Part III, and Part VI, of this Act; and "the former law" means the Companies Act and so much of this Act as replaces provisions of that Act (without the amendments in paragraphs 15 to 17 of Schedule 6 to the Insolvency Act 1985, or the associated repeals made by that Act), and any provision of the Insolvency Act 1985 which was in force before the appointed day.

(3) This paragraph is without prejudice to the power conferred by this Act under which rules under section 411 may make transitional provision in connection with the coming into

force of those rules; and such provision may apply those rules in relation to the receiver or manager of a company's property notwithstanding that he was appointed before the coming into force of the rules or section 411.

Receivers (Scotland)

3.—(1) In relation to any receiver appointed under section 467 of the Companies Act before the appointed day, the new law does not apply and the relevant provisions of the former law continue to have effect.

(2) "The new law" here means Chapter II of Part III, and Part VI, of this Act; and "the former law" means the Companies Act and so much of this Act as replaces provisions of that Act (without the amendments in paragraphs 18 to 22 of Schedule 6 to the Insolvency Act 1985 or the associated repeals made by that Act), and any provision of the Insolvency Act 1985 which was in force before the appointed day.

(3) This paragraph is without prejudice to the power conferred by this Act under which rules under section 411 may make transitional provision in connection with the coming into force of those rules; and such provision may apply those rules in relation to a receiver appointed under section 467 notwithstanding that he was appointed before the coming into force of the rules or section 411.

Winding up already in progress

4.—(1) In relation to any winding up which has commenced, or is treated as having commenced, before the appointed day, the new law does not apply, and the former law continues to have effect, subject to the following paragraphs.

(2) "The new law" here means any provisions in the first Group of Parts of this Act which replace sections 66 to 87 and 89 to 105 of the Insolvency Act 1985; and "the former law" means Parts XX and XXI of the Companies Act (without the amendments in paragraphs 23 to 52 of Schedule 6 to the Insolvency Act 1985, or the associated repeals made by that Act).

Statement of affairs

5.—(1) Where a winding up by the court in England and Wales has commenced, or is treated as having commenced, before the appointed day, the official receiver or (on appeal from a refusal by him) the court may, at any time on or after that day—

(*a*) release a person from an obligation imposed on him by or under section 528 of the Companies Act (statement of affairs), or

(*b*) extend the period specified in subsection (6) of that section.

(2) Accordingly, on and after the appointed day, section 528(6) has effect in relation to a winding up to which this paragraph applies with the omission of the words from "or within" onwards.

Provisions relating to liquidator

6.—(1) This paragraph applies as regards the liquidator in the case of a winding up by the court in England and Wales commenced, or treated as having commenced, before the appointed day.

(2) The official receiver may, at any time when he is liquidator of the company, apply to the Secretary of State for the appointment of a liquidator in his (the official receiver's) place; and on any such application the Secretary of State shall either make an appointment or decline to make one.

(3) Where immediately before the appointed day the liquidator of the company has not made an application under section 545 of the Companies Act (release of liquidators), then—

(*a*) except where the Secretary of State otherwise directs, sections 146(1) and (2) and 172(8) of this Act apply, and section 545 does not apply, in relation to any liquidator of that company who holds office on or at any time after the appointed day and is not the official receiver;

(*b*) section 146(3) applies in relation to the carrying out at any time after that day by any liquidator of the company of any of his functions; and (*c*) a liquidator in relation to whom section 172(8) has effect by virtue of this paragraph has his release with effect from the time specified in section 174(4)(*d*) of this Act.

(4) Subsection (6) of section 174 of this Act has effect for the purposes of sub-paragraph (3)(*c*) above as it has for the purposes of that section, but as if the reference to section 212 were to section 631 of the Companies Act.

(5) The liquidator may employ a solicitor to assist him in the carrying out of his functions without the permission of the committee of inspection; but if he does so employ a solicitor he shall inform the committee of inspection that he has done so.

Winding up under supervision of the court

7. The repeals in Part II of Schedule 10 to the Insolvency Act 1985 of references (in the Companies Act and elsewhere) to a winding up under the supervision of the court do not affect the operation of the enactments in which the references are contained in relation to any case in which an order under section 606 of the Companies Act (power to order winding up under supervision) was made before the appointed day.

Saving for power to make rules

8.—(1) Paragraphs 4 to 7 are without prejudice to the power conferred by this Act under which rules made under section 411 may make transitional provision in connection with the coming into force of those rules.

(2) Such provision may apply those rules in relation to a winding up notwithstanding that the winding up commenced, or is treated as having commenced, before the coming into force of the rules or section 411.

Setting aside of preferences and other transactions

9.—(1) Where a provision in Part VI of this Act applies in relation to a winding up or in relation to a case in which an administration order has been made, a preference given, floating charge created or other transaction entered into before the appointed day shall not be set aside under that provision except to the extent that it could have been set aside under the law in force immediately before that day, assuming for this purpose that any relevant administration order had been a winding-up order.

(2) The references above to setting aside a preference, floating charge or other transaction include the making of an order which varies or reverses any effect of a preference, floating charge or other transaction.

Part II

Individual Insolvency

Bankruptcy (general)

10.—(1) Subject to the following provisions of this Part of this Schedule, so much of this Act as replaces Part III of the Insolvency Act 1985 does not apply in relation to any case in which a petition in bankruptcy was presented, or a receiving order or adjudication in bankruptcy was made, before the appointed day.

(2) In relation to any such case as is mentioned above, the enactments specified in Schedule 8 to that Act, so far as they relate to bankruptcy, and those specified in Parts III and IV of Schedule 10 to that Act, so far as they so relate, have effect without the amendments and repeals specified in those Schedules.

(3) Where any subordinate legislation made under an enactment referred to in sub-paragraph (2) is in force immediately before the appointed day, that subordinate legislation continues to have effect on and after that day in relation to any such case as is mentioned in sub-paragraph (1).

11.—(1) In relation to any such case as is mentioned in paragraph 10(1) the references in any enactment or subordinate legislation to a petition, order or other matter which is provided for under the Bankruptcy Act 1914 and corresponds to a petition, order or other matter provided for under provisions of this Act replacing Part III of the Insolvency Act 1985 continue on and after the appointed day to have effect as references to the petition, order or matter provided for by the Act of 1914; but otherwise those references have effect on and after that day as references to the petition, order or matter provided for by those provisions of this Act.

(2) Without prejudice to sub-paragraph (1), in determining for the purposes of section 279 of this Act (period of bankruptcy) or paragraph 13 below whether any person was an undischarged bankrupt at a time before the appointed day, an adjudication in bankruptcy and an annulment of a bankruptcy under the Act of 1914 are to be taken into account in the same way, respectively, as a bankruptcy order under the provisions of this Act replacing Part III of the Insolvency Act 1985 and the annulment under section 282 of this Act of such an order.

12. Transactions entered into before the appointed day have effect on and after that day as if references to acts of bankruptcy in the provisions for giving effect to those transactions continued to be references to acts of bankruptcy within the meaning of the Bankruptcy Act 1914, but as if such acts included failure to comply with a statutory demand served under section 268 of this Act.

Discharge from old bankruptcy

13.—(1) Where a person—

(*a*) was adjudged bankrupt before the appointed day or is adjudged bankrupt on or after that day on a petition presented before that day, and

(*b*) that person was not an undischarged bankrupt at any time in the period of 15 years ending with the adjudication,

that person is deemed (if not previously discharged) to be discharged from his bankruptcy for the purposes of the Bankruptcy Act 1914 at the end of the discharge period.

(2) Subject to sub-paragraph (3) below, the discharge period for the purposes of this paragraph is—

(*a*) in the case of a person adjudged bankrupt before the appointed day, the period of 3 years beginning with that day, and

(*b*) in the case of a person who is adjudged bankrupt on or after that day on a petition presented before that day, the period of 3 years beginning with the date of the adjudication.

(3) Where the court exercising jurisdiction in relation to a bankruptcy to which this paragraph applies is satisfied, on the application of the official receiver, that the bankrupt has failed, or is failing, to comply with any of his obligations under the Bankruptcy Act 1914, any rules made under that Act or any such rules as are mentioned in paragraph 19(1) below, the court may order that the discharge period shall cease to run for such period, or until the fulfilment of such conditions (including a condition requiring the court to be satisfied as to any matter) as may be specified in the order.

Provisions relating to trustee

14.—(1) This paragraph applies as regards the trustee in the case of a person adjudged bankrupt before the appointed day, or adjudged bankrupt on or after that day on a petition presented before that day.

(2) The official receiver may at any time when he is the trustee of the bankrupt's estate apply to the Secretary of State for the appointment of a person as trustee instead of the official receiver; and on any such application the Secretary of State shall either make an appointment or decline to make one.

(3) Where on the appointed day the trustee of a bankrupt's estate has not made an application under section 93 of the Bankruptcy Act 1914 (release of trustee), then—

(*a*) except where the Secretary of State otherwise directs, sections 298(8), 304 and 331(1) to (3) of this Act apply, and section 93 of the Act of 1914 does not apply, in relation to any trustee of the bankrupt's estate who holds office on or at any time after the appointed day and is not the official receiver;

(*b*) section 331(4) of this Act applies in relation to the carrying out at any time on or after the appointed day by the trustee of the bankrupt's estate of any of his functions; and

(*c*) a trustee in relation to whom section 298(8) of this Act has effect by virtue of this paragraph has his release with effect from the time specified in section 299(3)(*d*).

(4) Subsection (5) of section 299 has effect for the purposes of sub-paragraph (3)(*c*) as it has for the purposes of that section.

(5) In the application of subsection (3) of section 331 in relation to a case by virtue of this paragraph, the reference in that subsection to section 330(1) has effect as a reference to section 67 of the Bankruptcy Act 1914.

(6) The trustee of the bankrupt's estate may employ a solicitor to assist him in the carrying out of his functions without the permission of the committee of inspection; but if he does so employ a solicitor, he shall inform the committee of inspection that he has done so.

Copyright

15. Where a person who is adjudged bankrupt on a petition presented on or after the appointed day is liable, by virtue of a transaction entered into before that day, to pay royalties or a share of the profits to any person in respect of any copyright or interest in copyright comprised in the bankrupt's estate, section 60 of the Bankruptcy Act 1914 (limitation on trustee's powers in relation to copyright) applies in relation to the trustee of that estate as it applies in relation to a trustee in bankruptcy under the Act of 1914.

Second bankruptcy

16.—(1) Sections 334 and 335 of this Act apply with the following modifications where the earlier bankruptcy (within the meaning of section 334) is a bankruptcy in relation to which the Act of 1914 applies instead of the second Group of Parts in this Act, that is to say—

(*a*) references to property vested in the existing trustee under section 307(3) of this Act have effect as references to such property vested in that trustee as was acquired by or devolved on the bankrupt after the commencement (within the meaning of the Act of 1914) of the earlier bankruptcy; and

(*b*) references to an order under section 310 of this Act have effect as references to an order under section 51 of the Act of 1914.

(2) Section 39 of the Act of 1914 (second bankruptcy) does not apply where a person who is an undischarged bankrupt under that Act is adjudged bankrupt under this Act.

Setting aside of preferences and other transactions

17.—(1) A preference given, assignment made or other transaction entered into before the appointed day shall not be set aside under any of sections 339 to 344 of this Act except to the extent that it could have been set aside under the law in force immediately before that day.

(2) References in sub-paragraph (1) to setting aside a preference, assignment or other transaction include the making of any order which varies or reverses any effect of a preference, assignment or other transaction.

Bankruptcy offences

18.—(1) Where a bankruptcy order is made under this Act on or after the appointed day, a person is not guilty of an offence under Chapter VI of Part IX in respect of anything done before that day; but, notwithstanding the repeal by the Insolvency Act 1985 of the Bankruptcy Act 1914, is guilty of an offence under the Act of 1914 in respect of anything done before the appointed day which would have been an offence under that Act if the making of the bankruptcy order had been the making of a receiving order under that Act.

(2) Subsection (5) of section 350 of this Act applies (instead of sections 157(2), 158(2), 161 and 165 of the Act of 1914) in relation to proceedings for an offence under that Act which are instituted (whether by virtue of sub-paragraph (1) or otherwise) after the appointed day.

Power to make rules

19.—(1) The preceding provisions of this Part of this Schedule are without prejudice to the power conferred by this Act under which rules under section 412 may make transitional provision in connection with the coming into force of those rules; and such provision may apply those rules in relation to a bankruptcy notwithstanding that it arose from a petition presented before either the coming into force of the rules or the appointed day.

(2) Rules under section 412 may provide for such notices served before the appointed day as may be prescribed to be treated for the purposes of this Act as statutory demands served under section 268.

Part III

Transitional Effect of Part XVI

20.—(1) A transaction entered into before the appointed day shall not be set aside under Part XVI of this Act except to the extent that it could have been set aside under the law in force immediately before that day.

(2) References above to setting aside a transaction include the making of any order which varies or reverses any effect of a transaction.

Part IV

Insolvency Practitioners

21. Where an individual began to act as an insolvency practitioner in relation to any person before the appointed day, nothing in section 390(2) or (3) prevents that individual from being qualified to act as an insolvency practitioner in relation to that person.

Part V

General Transitional Provisions and Savings

Interpretation for this Part

22. In this Part of this Schedule, "the former enactments" means so much of the Companies Act as is repealed and replaced by this Act, the Insolvency Act 1985 and the other enactments repealed by this Act.

General saving for past acts and events

23. So far as anything done or treated as done under or for the purposes of any provision of the former enactments could have been done under or for the purposes of the corresponding provision of this Act, it is not invalidated by the repeal of that provision but has effect as if done under or for the purposes of the corresponding provision; and any order, regulation, rule or other instrument made or having effect under any provision of the former enactments shall, insofar as its effect is preserved by this paragraph, be treated for all purposes as made and having effect under the corresponding provision.

Periods of time

24. Where any period of time specified in a provision of the former enactments is current immediately before the appointed day, this Act has effect as if the corresponding provision had been in force when the period began to run; and (without prejudice to the foregoing) any period of time so specified and current is deemed for the purposes of this Act—

(*a*) to run from the date or event from which it was running immediately before the appointed day, and

(*b*) to expire (subject to any provision of this Act for its extension) whenever it would have expired if this Act had not been passed;

and any rights, priorities, liabilities, reliefs, obligations, requirements, powers, duties or exemptions dependent on the beginning, duration or end of such a period as above mentioned shall be under this Act as they were or would have been under the former enactments.

Internal cross-references in this Act

25. Where in any provision of this Act there is a reference to another such provision, and the first-mentioned provision operates, or is capable of operating, in relation to things done or omitted, or events occurring or not occurring, in the past (including in particular past acts of compliance with any enactment, failures of compliance, contraventions, offences and convictions of offences), the reference to the other provision is to be read as including a reference to the corresponding provision of the former enactments.

Punishment of offences

26.—(1) Offences committed before the appointed day under any provision of the former enactments may, notwithstanding any repeal by this Act, be prosecuted and punished after that day as if this Act had not passed.

(2) A contravention of any provision of the former enactments committed before the appointed day shall not be visited with any severer punishment under or by virtue of this Act than would have been applicable under that provision at the time of the contravention; but where an offence for the continuance of which a penalty was provided has been committed under any provision of the former enactments, proceedings may be taken under this Act in respect of the continuance of the offence on and after the appointed day in the like manner as if the offence had been committed under the corresponding provision of this Act.

References elsewhere to the former enactments

27.—(1) A reference in any enactment, instrument or document (whether express or implied, and in whatever phraseology) to a provision of the former enactments (including the corresponding provision of any yet earlier enactment) is to be read, where necessary to retain for the enactment, instrument or document the same force and effect as it would have had but for the passing of this Act, as, or as including, a reference to the corresponding provision by which it is replaced in this Act.

(2) The generality of the preceding sub-paragraph is not affected by any specific conversion of references made by this Act, nor by the inclusion in any provision of this Act of a reference (whether express or implied, and in whatever phraseology) to the provision of the former enactments corresponding to that provision, or to a provision of the former enactments which is replaced by a corresponding provision of this Act.

Saving for power to repeal provisions in section 51

28. The Secretary of State may by order in a statutory instrument repeal subsections (3) to (5) of section 51 of this Act and the entries in Schedule 10 relating to subsections (4) and (5) of that section.

Saving for Interpretation Act 1978 ss.16, 17

29. Nothing in this Schedule is to be taken as prejudicing sections 16 and 17 of the Interpretation Act 1978 (savings from, and effect of, repeals); and for the purposes of section 17(2) of that Act (construction of references to enactments repealed and replaced, etc.), so much of section 18 of the Insolvency Act 1985 as is replaced by a provision of this Act is deemed to have been repealed by this Act and not by the Company Directors Disqualification Act 1986.

DEFINITIONS

"the former enactments": para. 22.
"the former law": paras. 2(2), 3(2), 4(2).
"the new law": para. 2(2), 3(2), 4(2).

GENERAL NOTE

This Schedule contains transitional provisions and savings in respect of the bringing into force of this Act. The various paragraphs indicate what particular transitional arrangement is to apply to the specified sections of the Act as they come into force. Throughout the foregoing annotations, references to the relevant paragraph of this Schedule are included alongside the General Note for every section of the Act to which transitional provisions apply. The first 21 paras. of this Schedule correspond to various paras. in Sched. 9 to the 1985 Act (for the full list of correspondences, see the Tables of Derivations and of Destinations). Paras. 22–29 are without any counterparts in the 1985 Act.

Section 438

SCHEDULE 12

Enactments Repealed

Chapter	Short title	Extent of repeal
1970 c.8.	The Insolvency Services (Accounting and Investment) Act 1970.	The whole Act.
1976 c.60.	The Insolvency Act 1976.	Section 3.
1985 c.6.	The Companies Act 1985.	In section 463(4), the words "Subject to section 617". Sections 467 to 485. In section 486, in the definition of "company" the words "other than in Chapter II of this Part"; and the definitions of "instrument of appointment", "prescribed", "receiver" and "register of charges". Sections 488 to 650. Sections 659 to 664. Sections 665 to 674. Section 709(4). Section 710(4). Section 724. Schedule 16. In Schedule 24, the entries relating to section 467; all entries thereafter up to and including section 641(2); and the entry relating to section 710(4).
1985 c.65.	The Insolvency Act 1985.	Sections 1 to 11. Section 15. Section 17. Section 19. Sections 20 to 107. Section 108(1) and (3) to (7). Sections 109 to 211. Sections 212 to 214. Section 216. Section 217(1) to (3). Sections 221 to 234. In section 235, subsections (2) to (5). In section 236, subsections (3) to (5). In Schedule 1, paragraphs 1 to 4, and sub-paragraph (4) of paragraph 5. Schedules 3 to 5. In Schedule 6, paragraphs 5, 6, 9, 15 to 17, 20 to 22, 25 to 44 and 48 to 52. Schedule 7. In Schedule 9, paragraphs 1 and 4 to 24. Schedule 10.
1985 c.66.	The Bankruptcy (Scotland) Act 1985.	In Schedule 7, paragraphs 19 to 22.
1986 c.44.	The Gas Act 1986.	In Schedule 7, paragraph 31.

General Note

This Schedule, in conjunction with s.438, effects the repeal, in whole or in part, of the various enactments listed within columns one and two, to the extent specified in column three. The enactments thereby repealed are those whose provisions are consolidated in the present Act.

Section 439(1)

SCHEDULE 13

Consequential Amendments of Companies Act 1985

Part I

Internal and Other Section References Amended or Re-amended

Section of Act	Consequential amendment or re-amendment
Section 13(4)	After "this Act", add "and the Insolvency Act".
Section 44(7)	In paragraph (*a*), for "section 582" substitute "section 110 of the Insolvency Act".
Section 103(7)	In paragraph (*a*), the same amendment.
Section 131(7)	The same amendment.
Section 140(2)	In paragraph (*b*), for "section 518" substitute "section 123 of the Insolvency Act".
Section 153(3)	In paragraph (*f*), for "section 582" substitute "section 110 of the Insolvency Act". In paragraph (*g*), for "Chapter II of Part II of the Insolvency Act 1985" substitute "Part I of the Insolvency Act".
Section 156(3)	For "section 517" substitute "section 122 of the Insolvency Act".
Section 173(4)	The same amendment.
Section 196	For this section substitute— "196.—(1) The following applies in the case of a company registered in England and Wales, where debentures of the company are secured by a charge which, as created, was a floating charge. (2) If possession is taken, by or on behalf of the holders of any of the debentures, of any property comprised in or subject to the charge, and the company is not at that time in course of being wound up, the company's preferential debts shall be paid out of assets coming into the hands of the person taking possession in priority to any claims for principal or interest in respect of the debentures. (3) "Preferential debts" means the categories of debts listed in Schedule 6 to the Insolvency Act; and for the purposes of that Schedule "the relevant date" is the date of possession being taken as above mentioned. (4) Payments made under this section shall be recouped, as far as may be, out of the assets of the company available for payment of general creditors."
Section 222(4)	For "section 106 of the Insolvency Act 1985" substitute "section 411 of the Insolvency Act".
Section 225	At the end of the section add— "(8) At any time when an administration order under Part II of the Insolvency Act is in force, this section has effect as if subsections (3) and (5) to (7) were omitted".
Section 380(4)	In paragraph (*j*), for "section 572(1)(*a*)" substitute "section 84(1)(*a*) of the Insolvency Act".
Section 441(1)	For "section 13 of the Insolvency Act 1985" substitute "section 8 of the Company Directors Disqualification Act 1986".
Section 449(1)	In paragraph (*ba*), for "section 12 or 13 of the Insolvency Act 1985" substitute "section 6, 7 or 8 of the Company Directors Disqualification Act 1986".
Section 461(6)	For "section 106 of the Insolvency Act 1985" substitute "section 411 of the Insolvency Act".
Section 462(5)	After "this Part" insert "and Part III of the Insolvency Act 1986".
Section 463(2)	For "Part XX (except section 623(4))" substitute "Part IV of the Insolvency Act (except section 185)".

Section of Act	Consequential amendment or re-amendment
Section 463(3)	For this subsection substitute— "(3) Nothing in this section derogates from the provisions of sections 53(7) and 54(6) of the Insolvency Act (attachment of floating charge on appointment of receiver), or prejudices the operation of sections 175 and 176 of that Act (payment of preferential debts in winding up)".
Section 464(6)	For "section 89 of the Insolvency Act 1985" substitute "sections 175 and 176 of the Insolvency Act".
Section 657(2)	For "subsections (3) and (5) to (7) of section 91 of the Insolvency Act 1985 and section 92 of that Act" substitute "section 178(4) and sections 179 to 182 of the Insolvency Act".
Section 658(1)	For "Subsection (7) of section 91 of the Insolvency Act 1985" substitute "Section 180 of the Insolvency Act".
Section 711(2)	In paragraph (*b*), for "section 600" substitute "section 109 of the Insolvency Act".
Section 733	In subsection (1), omit "295(7)". In subsection (3), for "216(3) or 295(7)" substitute "or 216(3)".

Part II

Amendment of Part XXVI (Interpretation)

In Part XXVI of the Companies Act, after section 735, insert the following section—

"Relationship of this Act to Insolvency Act

735A.—(1) In this Act "the Insolvency Act" means the Insolvency Act 1986; and in the following provisions of this Act, namely, sections 375(1)(*b*), 425(6)(*a*), 440, 449(1)(*a*) and (*d*), 460(2), 675, 676, 677, 699(1), 728 and Schedule 21, paragraph 6(1), the words "this Act" are to be read as including Parts I to VII of that Act, sections 411, 413, 414, 416 and 417 in Part XV of that Act, and also the Company Directors Disqualification Act 1986.

(2) In sections 704(5), 706(1), 707(1), 708(1)(*a*) and (4), 710(5), 713(1), 729 and 732(3) references to the Companies Acts include Parts I to VII of the Insolvency Act, sections 411, 413, 414, 416 and 417 in Part XV of that Act, and also the Company Directors Disqualification Act 1986.

(3) Subsections (1) and (2) apply unless the contrary intention appears."

General Note

This Schedule, in conjunction with s.439(1), effects consequential amendments to the Companies Act. These are all drafting amendments consequential on this Act and the Company Directors Disqualification Act 1986. Pt. II of the Schedule makes an important addition to Pt. XXVI of the Companies Act, concerned with interpretation of that Act: a new s.735A is added to supply a definition of the expression "The Insolvency Act" for the purposes of the Companies Act.

Section 439(2)

SCHEDULE 14

CONSEQUENTIAL AMENDMENTS OF OTHER ENACTMENTS

Enactment	Amendment
Deeds of Arrangement Act 1914 (c.47):	
Section 3(1)	For "Part III of the Insolvency Act 1985" substitute "Parts VIII to XI of the Insolvency Act 1986".
Section 3(4)	The same amendment.
Section 11(1) and (2)	In each subsection, the same amendment.
Section 15(1)	For "section 207 of the Insolvency Act 1985" substitute "section 412 of the Insolvency Act 1986".
Section 16	The same amendment as of section 3(1).
Section 23	The same amendment.
Section 30(1)	For the definition of "property" substitute— " 'property' has the meaning given by section 436 of the Insolvency Act 1986".
Law of Property Act 1925 (c.20):	
Section 52(2)(*b*)	For "section 91 or 161 of the Insolvency Act 1985" substitute "sections 178 to 180 or sections 315 to 319 of the Insolvency Act 1986".
Land Registration Act 1925 (c.21):	
Section 42(2)	For "section 161 of the Insolvency Act 1985" substitute "sections 315 to 319 of the Insolvency Act 1986".
Section 112AA(3)(*a*)	For "the Insolvency Act 1985 or the Companies Act 1985" substitute "the Insolvency Act 1986".
Third Parties (Rights against Insurers) Act 1930 (c.25):	
Section 1	In subsection (1)(*b*), for the words from "a composition" to "that Chapter" substitute "a voluntary arrangement proposed for the purposes of Part I of the Insolvency Act 1986 being approved under that Part". In subsection (2), for "228 of the Insolvency Act 1985" substitute "421 of the Insolvency Act 1986". In subsection (3), the same amendment.
Section 2	In subsection (1), the same amendment as of section 1(2). In subsection (1A), for the words from "composition or scheme" to the end of the subsection substitute "voluntary arrangement proposed for the purposes of, and approved under, Part I or Part VIII of the Insolvency Act 1986".
Section 4	In paragraph (*b*), the same amendment as of section 1(2).
Exchange Control Act 1947 (c.14):	
Schedule 4	In paragraphs 6 and 8(4), for "section 120 of the Insolvency Act 1985" substitute "sections 267 to 270 of the Insolvency Act 1986".
Arbitration Act 1950 (c.27):	
Section 3(2)	For "committee established under section 148 of the Insolvency Act 1985" substitute "creditors' committee established under section 301 of the Insolvency Act 1986".

Enactment	Amendment
Agricultural Marketing Act 1958 (c.47):	
Schedule 2	For paragraph 4 substitute— "4.—(1) A scheme shall provide for the winding up of the board, and for that purpose may apply Part V of the Insolvency Act 1986 (winding up of unregistered companies), subject to the following modifications. (2) For the purposes of sections 221, 222 and 224 of the Act of 1986, the principal place of business of the board is deemed to be the office of the board the address of which is registered by the Minister under paragraph 3 above. (3) Section 223 does not apply. (4) Section 224 applies as if the words "or any member of it as such" were omitted. (5) A petition for winding up the board may be presented by the Minister as well as by any person authorised under Part IV of the Insolvency Act 1986 to present a petition for winding up a company".
Charities Act 1960 (c.58):	
Section 30(1)	For "Companies Act 1985" substitute "Insolvency Act 1986".
Licensing Act 1964 (c.26):	
Section 8(1)	In paragraph (*c*), for the words from "composition or scheme" to "Act 1985" substitute "voluntary arrangement proposed by the holder of the licence has been approved under Part VIII of the Insolvency Act 1986"; and for "composition or scheme" substitute "voluntary arrangement".
Section 10(5)	For the words from "composition or scheme" to "Act 1985" substitute "voluntary arrangement proposed by the holder of a justices' licence has been approved under Part VIII of the Insolvency Act 1986"; and for "composition or scheme" substitute "voluntary arrangement".
Industrial and Provident Societies Act 1965 (c.12):	
Section 55	For "Companies Act 1985" substitute "Insolvency Act 1986".
Medicines Act 1968 (c.67):	
Section 72(4)	For the words from "composition or scheme" to the end of the subsection substitute "voluntary arrangement proposed for the purposes of, and approved under, Part VIII of the Insolvency Act 1986".
Income and Corporation Taxes Act 1970 (c.10):	
Section 247(7)	For "Companies Act 1985" substitute "Insolvency Act 1986".
Section 265(5)	For "538 of the Companies Act 1985" substitute "145 of the Insolvency Act 1986".
Conveyancing and Feudal Reform (Scotland) Act 1970 (c.35):	
Schedule 3	In Standard Condition 9(2)(*b*), for "228 of the Insolvency Act 1985" substitute "421 of the Insolvency Act 1986".

Enactment	Amendment
Tribunals and Inquiries Act 1971 (c.62):	
Schedule 1	For paragraph 10A substitute— "10A. The Insolvency Practitioners Tribunal referred to in section 396 of the Insolvency Act 1986".
Superannuation Act 1972 (c.11):	
Section 5(2)	For "156 of the Insolvency Act 1985" substitute "310 of the Insolvency Act 1986"; and for "the said section 156" substitute "the said section 310".
Road Traffic Act 1972 (c.20):	
Section 150	In subsection (1)(*b*), for "228 of the Insolvency Act 1985" substitute "421 of the Insolvency Act 1986". In subsection (2), the same amendment.
Finance Act 1972 (c.41):	
Schedule 16	In paragraph 13(5), for "Companies Act 1985" substitute "Insolvency Act 1986".
Land Charges Act 1972 (c.61):	
Section 16(2)	For "207 of the Insolvency Act 1985" substitute "412 of the Insolvency Act 1986"; and for "Part III" substitute "Parts VIII to XI".
Matrimonial Causes Act 1973 (c.18):	
Section 39	For "section 174 of the Insolvency Act 1985" substitute "section 339 or 340 of the Insolvency Act 1986".
Powers of Criminal Courts Act 1973 (c.62):	
Section 39(3)	In paragraph (*d*), for "174(10) of the Insolvency Act 1985" substitute "341(4) of the Insolvency Act 1986".
Friendly Societies Act 1974 (c.46):	
Section 87(2)	For "Companies Act 1985" substitute "Insolvency Act 1986".
Social Security Pensions Act 1975 (c.60):	
Section 58	The section is to have effect as orginally enacted, and without the amendment made by paragraph 26(1) of Schedule 8 to the Insolvency Act 1985.
Schedule 3	At the end of paragraph 3(1) add— "or (in the case of a company not in liquidation)— (*a*) the appointment of a receiver as mentioned in section 40 of the Insolvency Act 1986 (debenture-holders secured by floating charge), or (*b*) the appointment of a receiver under section 53(6) or 54(5) of that Act (Scottish company with property subject to floating charge), or (*c*) the taking of possession by debenture-holders (so secured) as mentioned in section 196 of the Companies Act 1985". In paragraph 4, for the words from the beginning to "Act 1985" substitute "Section 196(3) of the Companies Act 1985 and section 387 of the Insolvency Act 1986 apply as regards the meaning in this Schedule of the expression 'the relevant date'.".

Enactment	Amendment
Recess Elections Act 1975 (c.66):	
Section 1(2)	In the definition of "certificate of vacancy", for "214(6)(*a*) of the Insolvency Act 1985" substitute "427(6)(*a*) of the Insolvency Act 1986".
Policyholders Protection Act 1975 (c.75):	
Section 5(1)(*a*)	For "Companies Act 1985" substitute "Insolvency Act 1986".
Section 15(1)	For "532 of the Companies Act 1985" substitute "135 of the Insolvency Act 1986".
Section 16(1)(*b*)	The same amendment as of section 5(1)(*a*).
Development Land Tax Act 1976 (c.24):	
Section 33(1)	For "538 of the Companies Act 1985" substitute "145 of the Insolvency Act 1986".
Restrictive Trade Practices Act 1976 (c.34):	
Schedule 1	For paragraph 9A (inserted by Insolvency Act 1985, section 217(4)) substitute— "9A. Insolvency services within the meaning of section 428 of the Insolvency Act 1986".
Employment Protection (Consolidation) Act 1978 (c.44):	
Section 106(5)	In paragraph (*b*), for "228 of the Insolvency Act 1985" substitute "421 of the Insolvency Act 1986". In paragraph (*c*), for the words from "a composition or" to the end of the paragraph substitute "a voluntary arrangement proposed for the purposes of Part I of the Insolvency Act 1986 is approved under that Part".
Section 106(6)	The same amendment as of section 106(5)(*c*).
Section 122	In subsection (7), for "181 of the Insolvency Act 1985" substitute "348 of the Insolvency Act 1986"; and for "section 106" substitute "section 411". In subsection (9), for the words from "composition or scheme" to "Act 1985" substitute "voluntary arrangement proposed for the purposes of, and approved under, Part I or VIII of the Insolvency Act 1986".
Section 123(6)	For the words from "composition or scheme" to "Act 1985" substitute "voluntary arrangement proposed for the purposes of, and approved under, Part I or VIII of the Insolvency Act 1986".
Section 125(2)	For paragraph (*a*) substitute— "(*a*) the following provisions of the Insolvency Act 1986— (i) sections 175 and 176, 328 and 329, 348 and Schedule 6, and (ii) any rules under that Act applying section 348 of it to the winding up of a company; and"
Section 127(1)	In paragraph (*b*), for "228 of the Insolvency Act 1985" substitute "421 of the Insolvency Act 1986". In paragraph (*c*), for the words from "composition or" to the end of the paragraph substitute "voluntary arrangement proposed for the purposes of Part I of the Insolvency Act 1986 is approved under that Part".
Section 127(2)	In paragraph (*c*), the same amendment as of section 127(1)(*c*).

Enactment	Amendment
Credit Unions Act 1979 (c.34):	
Section 6(1)	For "517(1)(*e*) of the Companies Act 1985" substitute "122(1)(*e*) of the Insolvency Act 1986"; and for "517(1)(*e*) of the Act of 1985" substitute "122(1)(*e*) of the Act of 1986".
Banking Act 1979 (c.37):	
Section 6(3)	In paragraph (*b*), for "Part XXI of the Companies Act 1985" substitute "Part V of the Insolvency Act 1986".
Section 18	In subsection (1), for "Companies Act 1985" substitute "Insolvency Act 1986"; and in paragraph (*a*) of the subsection for "518" substitute "123". In subsection (2), for "Companies Act 1985" substitute "Insolvency Act 1986"; and for "Part XXI" substitute "Part V". In subsection (4)— in paragraph (*a*), for "Companies Act 1985" substitute "Insolvency Act 1986"; in paragraph (*b*), for "518 of the said Act of 1985" substitute "123 of the said Act of 1986"; and in paragraph (*c*), for "Part XXI of the said Act of 1985" substitute "Part V of the said Act of 1986".
Section 19	In subsection (2), for paragraph (*ba*) substitute— "(*ba*) in connection with any proceedings under any provision of— (i) Part XVIII or XX of the Companies Act 1985, or (ii) Parts I to VII of the Insolvency Act 1986 (other than sections 236 and 237)". In subsection (8), for paragraphs (*a*) and (*aa*) substitute— "(*a*) for the references in subsection (2) to Part XVIII or XX of the Companies Act 1985 and Parts I to VII of the Insolvency Act 1986, there shall be substituted references to Parts V, VI and IX of the Companies Act (Northern Ireland) 1960 (the reference to sections 236 and 237 of the Act of 1986 being disregarded)".
Section 28	In subsection (3), in paragraph (*c*), for "83 of the Insolvency Act 1985" substitute "95 of the Insolvency Act 1986". In subsection (4), in paragraph (*a*), for "Part XXI of the Companies Act 1985" substitute "Part V of the Insolvency Act 1986". In subsection (6)(*b*), for sub-paragraphs (ii) to (iv) substitute— "(ii) to be a member of a liquidation committee established under Part IV or V of the Insolvency Act 1986; (iii) to be a member of a creditors committee appointed under section 301 of that Act; and (iv) to be a commissioner under section 30 of the Bankruptcy (Scotland) Act 1985"; (v) to be a member of a committee of inspection appointed for the purposes of Part V or Part IX of the Companies Act (Northern Ireland)1960; and (in the passage following sub-paragraph (iv)) for "such a committee as is mentioned in paragraph (*b*)(ii) or (iv) above" substitute "a liquidation committee, creditors' committee or committee of inspection".

Enactment	Amendment
Section 28—*cont.*	In subsection (7), in paragraph (*b*), for the words from "section 116(4)" to the end of the paragraph substitute "section 261(1) of the Insolvency Act 1986 to any person in whom the property of the firm is vested under section 282(4) of that Act"
Section 31(7)	For paragraph (*a*) substitute— "(*a*) for England and Wales, under sections 411 and 412 of the Insolvency Act 1986"; and in paragraph (*b*) for "the said section 106" substitute "section 411 of that Act".
British Aerospace Act 1980 (c.26):	
Section 9(1)	In paragraph (*a*), for "Companies Act 1985" substitute "Insolvency Act 1986".
Public Passenger Vehicles Act 1981 (c.14):	
Section 19(3)	In paragraph (*a*), for "Chapter III of Part II of the Insolvency Act 1985" substitute "Part II of the Insolvency Act 1986".
Finance Act 1981 (c. 35):	
Section 55(4)	For "Companies Act 1985" substitute "Insolvency Act 1986".
Supreme Court Act 1981 (c.54):	
Section 40A(2)	For "section 179 of the Insolvency Act 1985" substitute "section 346 of the Insolvency Act 1986"; and for "621 of the Companies Act 1985" substitute "183 of the Insolvency Act 1986".
Trustee Savings Banks Act 1981(c.65):	
Section 31	In paragraph (*b*), for "666 to 669 of the Companies Act 1985" substitute "221 to 224 of the Insolvency Act 1986".
Section 54(2)	For "666(6) of the Companies Act 1985" substitute "221(6) of the Insolvency Act 1986".
Iron and Steel Act 1982 (c.25):	
Schedule 4	In paragraph 3(3) after "Companies Act 1985" insert "or the Insolvency Act 1986".
Civil Jurisdiction and Judgments Act 1982 (c.27):	
Section 18(3)	In paragraph (*ba*), for "213 of the Insolvency Act 1985" substitute "426 of the Insolvency Act 1986".
Schedule 5	In paragraph (1), for "Companies Act 1985" substitute "Insolvency Act 1986".

Enactment	Amendment
Insurance Companies Act 1982 (c.50):	
Section 53	For "Companies Act" (the first time) substitute "Insolvency Act 1986"; and for "Companies Act" (the second time) substitute "that Act of 1986".
Section 54	In subsection (1), for "the Companies Act" (the first time) substitute "Part IV or V of the Insolvency Act 1986"; and in paragraph (*a*), for "518 or sections 667 to 669" substitute "123 or sections 222 to 224". In subsection (4) for "Companies Act" (the first time) substitute "Insolvency Act 1986".
Section 55	In subsection (5), for "subsection (3) of section 540 of the Companies Act" substitute "section 168(2) of the Insolvency Act 1986". In subsection (6), for "631 of the Companies Act" substitute "212 of the Insolvency Act 1986".
Section 56	In subsection (4), for "Section 90(5) of the Insolvency Act 1985" substitute "Section 177(5) of the Insolvency Act 1986"; and for "section 90 of the said Act of 1985" substitute "section 177 of the said Act of 1986". In subsection (7), for "section 539(1) of the Companies Act" substitute "section 167 of, and Schedule 4 to, the Insolvency Act 1986".
Section 59	In subsection (1), for "106 of the Insolvency Act 1985" substitute "411 of the Insolvency Act 1986". In subsection (2), for "106 of the Insolvency Act 1985" substitute "411 of the Insolvency Act 1986"; and for "section 89 of, and Schedule 4 to, the Insolvency Act 1985" substitute "sections 175 and 176 of, and Schedule 6 to, the Insolvency Act 1986".
Section 96(1)	In the definition of "insolvent", for "517 and 518 or section 666 of the Companies Act" substitute "122 and 123 or section 221 of the Insolvency Act 1986".
Finance Act 1983 (c.28):	
Schedule 5	In paragraph 5(4), for "Companies Act 1985" substitute "Insolvency Act 1986".
Telecommunications Act 1984 (c.12):	
Section 68(1)	In paragraph (*a*), for "Companies Act 1985" substitute "Insolvency Act 1986".
County Courts Act 1984 (c.28):	
Section 98	For subsection (3) substitute— "(3) The provisions of this section have effect subject to those of sections 183, 184 and 346 of the Insolvency Act 1986".
Section 102	For subsection (8) substitute— "(8) Nothing in this section affects section 346 of the Insolvency Act 1986".
Section 109(2)	For "179 of the Insolvency Act 1985" substitute "346 of the Insolvency Act 1986".

Enactment	Amendment
Finance Act 1985 (c.54): Section 79	Omit the word "altogether"; and after "Companies Act 1985" insert "sections 110 and 111 of the Insolvency Act 1986".
Housing Act 1985 (c.68): Schedule 18	In paragraphs 3(4) and 5(3), for "228 of the Insolvency Act 1985" substitute "421 of the Insolvency Act 1986".

General Note

This Schedule in conjunction with s.439(2), effects consequential amendments to the enactments listed in column one, which are enactments which refer, or otherwise relate to those which are repealed and replaced by this Act or the Company Directors Disqualification Act 1986. The extent of each amendment is shown in column two.

TABLE OF DERIVATIONS

Note: The following abbreviations are used in this Table:—

"INS 1970"	=	The Insolvency Services (Accounting and Investment) Act 1970 (c.8).
"INS 1976"	=	The Insolvency Act 1976 (c.60)
"CA"	=	The Companies Act 1985 (c.6)
"IA"	=	The Insolvency Act 1985 (c.65).
"B(Sc)"	=	The Bankruptcy (Scotland) Act 1985 (c.66)

Provision	Derivation
1	IA s.20.
2	IA s.21.
3	IA s.22.
4	IA s.23(1)–(6), (7) (part).
5	IA s.24.
6	IA s.25.
7	IA s.26.
8	IA s.27.
9	IA s.28.
10	IA s.29.
11	IA s.30.
12	IA s.31.
13	IA s.32.
14	IA s.33.
15	IA s.34(1)–(8), (12).
16	IA s.34(9), (10).
17	IA s.35.
18	IA s.36.
19	IA s.37(1)–(3).
20	IA s.37(4), (5).
21	IA s.38.
22	IA s.39.
23	IA s.40.
24	IA s.41.
25	IA s.42.
26	IA s.43.
27	IA ss.34(11), 44.
28	CA s.488; IA s.45(1)
29	CA s.500; IA s.45(2).
30	CA s.489.
31	CA s.490.
32	CA s.491.
33	IA s.46.
34	IA s.47.
35	CA s.492(1), (2); IA Sch. 6 para. 16(2).
36	CA s.494.
37	CA s.492(3); IA Sch. 6 para. 16(3), (4).
38	CA s.498; IA Sch. 6 para. 17.
39	CA s.493.
40	CA s.196 (part); IA Sch. 6 para. 15(2), (3).
41	CA s.499.
42	IA s.48.
43	IA s.49.
44	IA s.50.
45	IA s.51.
46	IA s.52.
47	IA s.53.
48	IA s.54.
49	IA s.55.
50	CA s.487.
51	CA s.467.

Provision	Derivation
52	CA s.468.
53	CA s.469; IA s.56 (part).
54	CA s.470.
55	CA s.471; IA s.57.
56	CA s.472.
57	CA s.473; IA s.58.
58	CA s.474.
59	CA s.475; IA Sch. 6 para. 20(2).
60	CA s.476; IA Sch. 6 para. 21.
61	CA s.477; IA s.59.
62	CA s.478; IA s.60, Sch. 6 para. 13.
63	CA s.479; IA s.61.
64	CA s.480.
65	CA s.481; IA s.62.
66	CA s.482; IA s.63.
67	CA s.482A; IA s.64.
68	CA s.482B; IA s.65.
69	CA s.483.
70	CA ss.462(4), 484, 486 (part).
71	CA s.485.
72	CA s.724.
73	CA s.501.
74	CA s.502.
75	CA s.503.
76	CA s.504.
77	CA s.505.
78	CA s.506.
79	CA s.507; IA Sch. 6 para. 5.
80	CA s.508.
81	CA s.509.
82	CA s.510.
83	CA s.511.
84	CA s.572.
85	CA s.573.
86	CA s.574.
87	CA s.575.
88	CA s.576.
89	CA s.577; IA Sch. 6 para. 35.
90	CA s.578.
91	CA s.580.
92	CA s.581.
93	CA s.584; IA Sch. 6 para. 36.
94	CA s.585(1)–(4), (7).
95	IA s.83(1)–(6), (9), (10).
96	IA s.83(7) (part).
97	CA s.587; IA s.85(1).
98	IA s.85(2), (3), (6)–(8), (9)(*a*), (10).
99	IA s.85(4), (5), (9)(*b*), (*c*), (10).
100	CA s.589; IA Sch. 6 para. 37(1), (2).
101	CA s.590; IA Sch. 6 para. 38(2)–(4).
102	IA s.83(7) (part).
103	CA s.591; IA Sch. 6 para. 39.
104	CA s.592.
105	CA s.594; IA s.83(8).
106	CA s.595(1)–(5), (8).
107	CA s.597.
108	CA s.599.
109	CA s.600.
110	CA ss.582(1)–(4), (7), 593; IA Sch. 6 para. 40.
111	CA s.582(5), (6), (8).

Provision	Derivation
112	CA s.602.
113	CA s.603.
114	IA s.82.
115	CA s.604.
116	CA s.605.
117	CA s.512; IA Sch. 6 paras. 25, 26.
118	CA s.513.
119	CA s.514.
120	CA s.515; IA Sch. 6 para. 25.
121	CA s.516.
122	CA s.517.
123	CA s.518; IA Sch. 6 paras. 25, 27.
124	CA s.519; IA Sch. 6 para. 28.
125	CA s.520.
126	CA s.521.
127	CA s.522.
128	CA s.523.
129	CA s.574.
130	CA s.525; IA Sch. 6 para. 29.
131	IA s.66.
132	IA s.67.
133	IA s.68(1)–(4).
134	IA s.68(5), (6).
135	CA s.532; IA s.69(3).
136	IA s.70(1)–(3), (4)(*a*), (5), (6).
137	IA s.70(4)(*b*), (7)–(9).
138	CA s.535; IA s.71, Sch. 6 para. 30.
139	IA s.72.
140	IA s.73.
141	IA s.74.
142	IA s.75.
143	IA s.69(1), (2).
144	CA s.537.
145	CA s.538.
146	IA s.78.
147	CA s.549.
148	CA s.550.
149	CA s.552; IA Sch. 6 para. 32.
150	CA s.553.
151	CA s.554.
152	CA s.555.
153	CA s.557.
154	CA s.558.
155	CA s.559.
156	CA s.560.
157	CA s.562; IA Sch. 6 para. 33.
158	CA s.565.
159	CA s.566.
160	CA s.567; IA Sch. 6 para. 34.
161	CA s.569.
162	CA s.571.
163	IA s.94.
164	CA s.635.
165	CA ss.539(1)(*d*), (*e*), (*f*), 598; IA s.84(1), Sch. 6 para. 41.
166	IA s.84.
167	CA ss.539(1), (2), (2A), (3); IA Sch. 6 para. 31(2), (3).
168	CA s.540(3)–(6).
169	CA s.539(4), (5); IA Sch. 6 para. 31(4).
170	CA s.636.
171	IA s.86.

Provision	Derivation
172	IA s.79.
173	IA s.87.
174	IA s.80.
175	IA s.89(1), (2).
176	IA s.89(3), (4).
177	IA s.90.
178	IA s.91(1)–(4), (8).
179	IA s.91(5), (6).
180	IA s.91(7).
181	IA s.92(1)–(4), (9), (10).
182	IA s.92(5)–(8).
183	CA s.621.
184	CA s.622; IA Sch. 6 para. 25.
185	CA s.623; B(Sc) Sch. 7 para. 21.
186	CA s.619(4).
187	CA s.659; IA Sch. 6 para. 48.
188	CA s.637.
189	IA s.93.
190	CA s.638.
191	CA s.639.
192	CA s.641.
193	CA s.643; B(Sc) Sch. 7 para. 22.
194	CA s.644.
195	CA s.645.
196	CA s.646.
197	CA s.647.
198	CA s.648.
199	CA s.649.
200	CA s.650.
201	CA ss.585(5), (6), 595(6), (7).
202	IA s.76(1)–(3), (6).
203	IA s.76(4), (5), (7)–(10).
204	IA s.77.
205	IA s.81.
206	CA s.624; IA Sch. 6 para. 25.
207	CA s.625; IA Sch. 6 para. 42.
208	CA s.626; IA Sch. 6 para. 43.
209	CA s.627.
210	CA s.628.
211	CA s.629.
212	IA s.19.
213	CA s.630(1), (2); IA Sch. 6 para. 6(1).
214	IA ss.12(9), 15(1)–(5), (7), Sch. 9 para. 4.
215	CA s.630(3)–(6); IA s.15(6), Sch. 6 para. 6(2), (3).
216	IA s.17, Sch. 9 para. 5.
217	IA s.18(1) (part), (2)–(6).
218	CA s.632; IA Sch. 6 para. 44.
219	CA s.633.
220	CA s.665.
221	CA s.666.
222	CA s.667; IA Sch. 6 para. 50.
223	CA s.668; IA Sch. 6 para. 51.
224	CA s.669; IA Sch. 6 para. 52.
225	CA s.670.
226	CA s.671.
227	CA s.672.
228	CA s.673.
229	CA s.674.
230	IA ss.95(1), (2), 96(1).
231	IA ss.95(1), (2), 96(2).

Provision	Derivation
232	IA ss.95(1), (2), 96(3).
233	IA ss.95, 97.
234	IA ss.95(1), (2), 98.
235	IA ss.95(1), (2), 99.
236	IA ss.95(1), (2), 100(1), (2), (6).
237	IA s.100(3)–(5), (7).
238	IA ss.95(1)(*a*), (*b*), 101(1) (part)–(3).
239	IA ss.95(1)(*a*), (*b*), 101(1) (part), (4)–(7), (11).
240	IA s.101(8)–(11).
241	IA ss.95(1), 102.
242	CA s.615A; B(Sc) Sch. 7 para. 20.
243	CA s.615B; B(Sc) Sch. 7 para. 20.
244	IA ss.95(1)(*a*), (*b*), 103.
245	IA ss.95(1)(*a*), (*b*), 104.
246	IA ss.95(1)(*a*), (*b*), (2), 105.
247	IA s.108(3) (part), (4).
248	IA s.108(3) (part).
249	IA s.108(5).
250	IA s.108(6).
251	IA s.108(3) (part).
252	IA s.112(1) (part), (3).
253	IA ss.110, 111(1), (2), (3) (part).
254	IA s.111(4), (5).
255	IA s.112(1) (part), (2), (4)–(7)(*a*).
256	IA s.113.
257	IA s.114(1) (part), (2), (3).
258	IA s.115(1)–(6), (9), (10).
259	IA s.115(7), (8).
260	IA s.116(1)–(3), (6), (7).
261	IA s.116(4), (5).
262	IA s.117.
263	IA s.118.
264	IA s.119(1).
265	IA s.119(2), (3).
266	IA s.119(4)–(7).
267	IA s.120(1), (2), (7)–(9).
268	IA s.120(3), (4).
269	IA s.120(5).
270	IA s.120(6).
271	IA s.121.
272	IA s.122.
273	IA s.123(1), (2), (8).
274	IA ss.111(3) (part), 112(1) (part), (7)(*b*), 114(1) (part), 123(3)–(5).
275	IA s.123(6), (7).
276	IA s.124.
277	IA s.125.
278	IA s.126(1).
279	IA s.126(2)–(5).
280	IA s.127.
281	IA s.128.
282	IA s.129.
283	IA s.130.
284	IA s.131.
285	IA s.132.
286	IA s.133.
287	IA s.134.
288	IA s.135.
289	IA s.136.
290	IA s.137.
291	IA s.138.

Provision	Derivation
292	IA s.139.
293	IA s.140.
294	IA s.141.
295	IA s.142.
296	IA s.143.
297	IA s.144.
298	IA s.145.
299	IA s.146.
300	IA s.147.
301	IA s.148.
302	IA s.149.
303	IA s.150.
304	IA s.151.
305	IA s.152.
306	IA s.153.
307	IA s.154(1)–(4), (7).
308	IA s.155(1), (2), (4), (5).
309	IA ss.154(5), (6), 155(3).
310	IA s.156.
311	IA s.157.
312	IA s.158.
313	IA s.159.
314	IA s.160.
315	IA s.161(1)–(4), (10).
316	IA s.161(5).
317	IA s.161(6), (7).
318	IA s.161(8).
319	IA s.161(9).
320	IA s.162(1)–(4), (9), (10).
321	IA s.162(5)–(8).
322	IA s.163.
323	IA s.164.
324	IA s.165(1)–(4).
325	IA s.165(5), (6).
326	IA s.165(7), (8).
327	IA s.165(9).
328	IA s.166(1)–(5), (7).
329	IA s.166(6).
330	IA s.167.
331	IA s.168(1), (2), (4).
332	IA s.168(3).
333	IA s.169.
334	IA s.170(1)–(3).
335	IA s.170(4)–(9).
336	IA s.171.
337	IA s.172.
338	IA s.173.
339	IA s.174(1) (part), (2).
340	IA s.174(1) (part), (3)–(6), (12) (part).
341	IA s.174(7)–(11), (12) (part).
342	IA s.175.
343	IA s.176.
344	IA s.177.
345	IA s.178.
346	IA s.179.
347	IA s.180.
348	IA s.181.
349	IA s.182.
350	IA ss.183(1)–(3), (5), (6), 192.

Provision	Derivation
351	IA ss.184(5), 187(3)(*a*).
352	IA s.183(4).
353	IA ss.183(4), 184(1).
354	IA ss.183(4), 184(2)–(4).
355	IA ss.183(4), 185.
356	IA ss.183(4), 186.
357	IA ss.183(4), 187(1)(3)(*b*).
358	IA ss.183(4), 187(2).
359	IA ss.183(4), 188.
360	IA s.189.
361	IA s.190.
362	IA s.191.
363	IA s.193.
364	IA s.194.
365	IA s.195.
366	IA s.196(1), (2).
367	IA s.196(3)–(6).
368	IA s.196(7).
369	IA s.197.
370	IA s.198.
371	IA s.199.
372	IA s.200.
373	IA s.201.
374	IA s.202.
375	IA s.203.
376	IA s.204.
377	IA s.205.
378	IA s.206.
379	IA s.210.
380	—
381	IA s.211(1) (part).
382	IA s.211(1) (part), (2), (3).
383	IA s.211(1) (part), (5)–(7).
384	IA ss.209(1) (part), 211(1) (part).
385	IA s.211(1) (part), (4).
386	CA ss.196(2), 475(1); IA ss.23(7), 89(1), 108(3), 115(9), 166(1), Sch. 4 para. 1(1), Sch. 6 para. 15(3).
387	CA ss.196(2)–(4), 475(3), (4); IA ss.23(8), 115(10), Sch. 4 Pt. II para.1(2), (3), Sch. 6 paras. 15(4), 20(3).
388	IA s.1(2)–(6).
389	IA s.1(1).
390	IA ss.2, 3(1).
391	IA s.3(2)–(5).
392	IA ss.4, 11 (part).
393	IA s.5.
394	IA s.6.
395	IA s.7.
396	IA ss.8(1), (2), (6), 11 (part).
397	IA s.8(3)–(5).
398	IA s.9.
399	IA s.222.
400	IA s.223.
401	IA s.224.
402	IA s.225.
403	INS 1970 s.1; INS 1976 s.3; IA Sch. 8 para. 28.
404	INS 1970 s.2.
405	INS 1970 s.3; INS 1976 Sch. 2 para. 5.
406	INS 1970 s.4; INS 1976 Sch. 2 para. 6; IA Sch. 8 para. 17.
407	INS 1970 s.5; INS 1976 Sch. 2 para. 7.
408	INS 1970 s.6; INS 1976 Sch. 2 para. 8.

Provision	Derivation
409	INS 1970 s.7; INS 1976 Sch. 2 para. 9.
410	INS 1970 s.9(3); INS 1976 s.14(6); IA s.236(3)(i).
411	IA s.106.
412	IA s.207.
413	IA s.226.
414	IA ss.106(5), 107.
415	IA ss.207(5), 208(1)–(3), (5).
416	CA s.664; IA Sch. 6 para. 49.
417	CA s.667(2) (part).
418	IA s.209(1) (part), (2), (3).
419	IA ss.10, 11 (part).
420	IA s.227.
421	IA s.228.
422	IA s.229.
423	IA s.212(1), (3), (7) (part).
424	IA s.212(2).
425	IA s.212(4)–(6), (7) (part).
426	IA s.213.
427	IA s.214.
428	IA s.217(1)–(3).
429	IA s.221(1), (3)–(5).
430	CA s.730; IA passim.
431	CA s.731; IA s.108(1).
432	IA s.230.
433	IA s.231.
434	IA s.234.
435	IA s.233.
436	IA s.232 (part).
437	—
438	—
439	—
440	IA s.236(3).
441	CA s.745; IA s.236(4).
442	IA s.236(5).
443	—
444	—
Sch. 1	IA Sch. 3.
Sch. 2	CA s.471(1); IA s.57.
Sch. 3	CA Sch. 16.
Sch. 4	
Pt. I	CA ss.539(1)(*d*)–(*f*), 598(1).
Pt. II	CA ss.539(1)(*a*), (*b*), 598(2).
Pt. III	CA ss.539(2), 598(2).
Sch. 5	
Pt. I	IA s.160(2).
Pt. II	IA s.160(1).
Pt. III	IA s.160(6).
Sch. 6	IA Sch. 4 Pt. I, Pt. II paras. 2–4.
Sch. 7	IA Sch. 1.
Sch. 8	IA Sch. 5.
Sch. 9	IA Sch. 7.
Sch. 10	CA and IA passim.
Sch. 11	
para. 1	IA Sch. 9 para. 6.
2	IA Sch. 9 para. 7.
3	IA Sch. 9 para. 8.
4	IA Sch. 9 para. 9(1).
5	IA Sch. 9 para. 9(2).
6	IA Sch. 9 para. 9(3)–(5), (8).

Provision	Derivation
Sch. 11	
para. 7	IA Sch. 9 para. 9(6).
8	IA Sch. 9 para. 9(7).
9	IA Sch. 9 para. 10.
10	IA Sch. 9 para. 11.
11	IA Sch. 9 para. 12.
12	IA Sch. 9 para. 13.
13	IA Sch. 9 para. 14.
14	IA Sch. 9 paras. 15, 16, 17.
15	IA Sch. 9 para. 18.
16	IA Sch. 9 para. 19.
17	IA Sch. 9 para. 20.
18	IA Sch. 9 para. 21.
19	IA Sch. 9 para. 22.
20	IA Sch. 9 para. 24.
21	IA Sch. 9 para. 1.
22–28	—
Schs. 12–14	—

TABLE OF DESTINATIONS

Insolvency Services (Accounting and Investment) Act 1970 (c.8)

1970	1986
s.1	s.403
2	404
3	405
4	406
5	407
6	408
7	409
9(3)	410

Insolvency Act 1976 (c.60)

1976	1986
s.3	s.403
14(6)	410
Sch. 2,	
para. 5	405
para. 6	406
para. 7	407
para. 8	408
para. 9	409

Companies Act 1985 (c.6)

1985	1986
s.196 (part)	s.40
(2)	386, 387
(3), (4)	387
462(4)	70
467	51
468	52
469	53
470	54
471	55
(1)	Sch. 2
472	s.56
473	57
474	58
475	59
(1)	386
(3), (4)	387
476	60
477	61
478	62
479	63
480	64
481	65
482	66
482A	67
482B	68
483	69
484	70
485	71
486 (part)	70
487	50
488	28
489	30
490	31
491	32
492(1), (2)	35
(3)	37
493	39
494	36
498	38
499	41
500	29

1985	1986
s.501	s.73
502	74
503	75
504	76
505	77
506	78
507	79
508	80
509	81
510	82
511	83
512	117
513	118
514	119
515	120
516	121
517	122
518	123
519	124
520	125
521	126
522	127
523	128
524	129
525	130
532	135
535	138
537	144
538	145
539(1)	167
(*a*), (*b*)	Sch. 4, Pt. II
(*d*)–(*f*)	s.165, Sch. 4, Pt. I
(2)	s.167, Sch. 4, Pt. III
(2A), (3)	s.167
(4), (5)	169
540(3)–(6)	168
549	147
550	148
552	149

1985	1986
s.553	s.150
554	151
555	152
557	153
558	154
559	155
560	156
562	157
565	158
566	159
567	160
569	161
571	162
572	84
573	85
574	86
575	87
576	88
577	89
578	90
580	91
581	92
582(1)–(4)	110
(5), (6)	111
(7)	110
(8)	111
584	93
585(1)–(4)	94
(5), (6)	201
(7)	94
587	97
589	100
590	101
591	103
592	104
593	110
594	105
595(1)–(5)	106
(6), (7)	201
(8)	106
597	107

COMPANIES ACT 1985 (c.6)—*continued*

1985	1986
s.598	s.165
(1)	Sch. 4, Pt. I
(2)	Sch. 4, Pts. II, III
599	s.108
600	109
602	112
603	113
604	115
605	116
615A	242
615B	243
619(4)	186
621	183
622	184
623	185
624	206
625	207
626	208
627	209

1985	1986
s.628	s.210
629	211
630(1), (2)	213
(3)–(6)	215
632	218
633	219
635	164
636	170
637	188
638	190
639	191
641	192
643	193
644	194
645	195
646	196
647	197
648	198
649	199
650	200

1985	1986
s.659	s.187
664	416
665	220
666	221
667	222
(2) (part)	417
668	223
669	224
670	225
671	226
672	227
673	228
674	229
724	72
730	430
731	431
745	441
Sch. 16	Sch. 3

INSOLVENCY ACT 1985 (c.65)

1985	1986
s.1(1)	s.389
(2)–(6)	388
2	390
3(1)	390
(2)–(5)	391
4	392
5	393
6	394
7	395
8(1), (2)	396
(3)–(5)	397
(6)	396
9	398
10	419
11 (part)	ss.392, 396, 419
12(9)	s.214
15(1)–(5)	214
(6)	215
(7)	214
17	216
18(1) (part), (2)–(6)	217
19	212
20	1
21	2
22	3
23(1)–(6)	4
(7)	386
(7) (part)	4
(8)	387
24	5
25	6
26	7
27	8
28	9
29	10
30	11
31	12
32	13
33	14
34(1)–(8)	15
(9), (10)	16
(11)	27
(12)	15

1985	1986
s.35	s.17
36	18
37(1)–(3)	19
(4), (5)	20
38	21
39	22
40	23
41	24
42	25
43	26
44	27
45(1)	28
(2)	29
46	33
47	34
48	42
49	43
50	44
51	45
52	46
53	47
54	48
55	49
56 (part)	53
57	55, Sch. 2
58	57
59	61
60	62
61	63
62	65
63	66
64	67
65	68
66	131
67	132
68(1)–(4)	133
(5), (6)	134
69(1), (2)	143
(3)	135
70(1)–(3)	136
(4)(*a*)	136
(*b*)	137
(5), (6)	136
(7)–(9)	137
71	138

1985	1986
s.72	s.139
73	140
74	141
75	142
76(1)–(3)	202
(4), (5)	203
(6)	202
(7)–(10)	203
77	204
78	146
79	172
80	174
81	205
82	114
83(1)–(6)	95
(7) (part)	ss.96, 102
(8)	s.105
(9), (10)	95
84	166
(1)	165
85(1)	97
(2), (3)	98
(4), (5)	99
(6)–(8)	98
(9)(*a*)	98
(*b*), (*c*)	99
(10)	ss.98, 99
86	s.171
87	173
89(1)	ss.175, 386
(2)	175
(3), (4)	176
90	177
91(1)–(4)	178
(5), (6)	179
(7)	180
(8)	178
92(1)–(4)	181
(5)–(8)	182
(9), (10)	181
93	189
94	163

INSOLVENCY ACT 1985 (c.65)—*continued*

1985	1986
s.95	s.233
(1)	ss.230–232, 234–236, 241
(*a*), (*b*)	238, 239, 244–246
(2)	230–232, 234–236, 246
96(1)	s.230
(2)	231
96(3)	232
97	233
98	234
99	235
100(1), (2)	236
(3)–(5)	237
(6)	236
(7)	237
101(1) (part)	ss.238, 239
(2), (3)	238
(4)–(7)	239
(8)–(10)	240
(11)	ss.239, 240
102	s.241
103	244
104	245
105	246
106	411
(5)	414
107	414
108(1)	431
(3)	386
(3) (part)	ss.247, 248, 251
(4)	s.247
(5)	249
(6)	250
110	253
111(1), (2)	253
(3) (part)	ss.253, 274
(4), (5)	s.254
112(1) (part)	ss.252, 255, 274
(2)	s.255
(3)	252
(4)–(6)	255
(7)(*a*)	255
(*b*)	274
113	256
114(1) (part)	ss.257, 274
(2), (3)	257
115(1)–(6)	258
(7), (8)	259
(9)	ss.258, 386
(10)	258, 387
116(1)–(3)	260
(4), (5)	261
(6), (7)	260
117	262
118	263
119(1)	264
(2), (3)	265
(4)–(7)	266
120(1), (2)	267
120(3), (4)	268
(5)	269
(6)	270
(7)–(9)	267
121	271
122	272

1985	1986
s.123(1), (2)	s.273
(3)–(5)	274
(6), (7)	275
(8)	273
124	276
125	277
126(1)	278
(2)–(5)	279
127	280
128	281
129	282
130	283
131	284
132	285
133	286
134	287
135	288
136	289
137	290
138	291
139	292
140	293
141	294
142	295
143	296
144	297
145	298
146	299
147	300
148	301
149	302
150	303
151	304
152	305
153	306
154(1)–(4)	307
(5), (6)	309
(7)	307
155(1), (2)	308
(3)	309
(4), (5)	308
156	310
157	311
158	312
159	313
160	314
(1)	Sch. 5, Pt. II
(2)	Pt. I
(6)	Pt. III
161(1)–(4)	315
(5)	316
(6), (7)	317
(8)	318
(9)	319
(10)	315
162(1)–(4)	320
(5)–(8)	321
(9), (10)	320
163	322
164	323
165(1)–(4)	324
(5), (6)	325
(7), (8)	326
(9)	327
166(1)	ss.328, 386
(2)–(5)	s.328
(6)	329
(7)	328
167	330

1985	1986
s.168(1), (2)	s.331
(3)	332
(4)	331
169	333
170(1)–(3)	334
(4)–(9)	335
171	336
172	337
173	338
174(1) (part)	ss.339, 340
(2)	s.339
(3)–(6)	340
(7)–(11)	341
(12) (part)	ss.340, 341
175	s.342
176	343
177	344
178	345
179	346
180	347
181	348
182	349
183(1)–(3)	350
(4)	ss.352–359
(5), (6)	350
184(1)	353
(2)–(4)	354
(5)	351
185	355
186	356
187(1)	357
(2)	358
(3)(*a*)	351
(*b*)	357
188	359
189	360
190	361
191	362
192	350
193	363
194	364
195	365
196(1), (2)	366
196(3)–(6)	367
(7)	368
197	369
198	370
199	371
200	372
201	373
202	374
203	375
204	376
205	377
206	378
207	412
(5)	415
208(1)–(3), (5)	415
209(1) (part)	ss.384, 418
209(2), (3)	s.418
210	379
211(1) (part)	ss.381–385
(2), (3)	s.382
(4)	385
(5)–(7)	383

1985	1986
s.212(1)	s.423
(2)	424
(3)	423
(4)–(6)	425
(7) (part)	ss.423, 425
213	426
214	427
217(1)–(3)	428
221(1), (3)–(5)	429
222	399
223	400
224	401
225	402
226	413
227	420
228	421
229	422
230	432
231	433
232 (part)	436
233	435
234	434
236(3)	440
(*i*)	410
(4)	441
236(5)	442
Sch. 1	Sch. 7
Sch. 3	Sch. 1
Sch. 4, Pt. I	Sch. 6
para. 1(1)	s.386
Pt. II, para. 1(2), (3)	387
paras. 2–4	Sch. 6
Sch. 5	Sch. 8
Sch. 6, para. 5	s.79
6(1)	213

1985	1986
Sch. 6, para. 6(2), (3)	215
13	62
15(2)	40
(3)	ss.40, 386
(4)	s.387
16(2)	35
(3), (4)	37
17	38
20(2)	59
(3)	387
21	60
25	ss.117, 120, 123, 184, 206
26	s.117
27	123
28	124
29	130
30	138
31(2), (3)	167
(4)	169
32	149
33	157
34	160
35	89
36	93
37(1), (2)	100
38(2)–(4)	101
39	103
40	110
41	165
42	207
43	208
44	218
48	187

1985	1986
Sch. 6, para. 49	s.416
50	222
51	223
52	224
Sch. 7	Sch. 9
Sch. 8, para. 17	s.400
28	403
Sch. 9, para. 1	Sch. 11, para. 21
4	s.214
5	216
6	Sch. 11, para. 1
7	2
8	3
9(1)	4
(2)	5
(3)–(5)	6
(6)	7
(7)	8
(8)	6
10	9
11	10
12	11
13	12
14	13
paras. 15–17	14
para. 18	15
19	16
20	17
21	18
22	19
24	20

BANKRUPTCY (SCOTLAND) ACT 1985 (c.66)

1985	1986
Sched. 7, para. 20	ss.242, 243
21	s.185
22	193